GIACOMO CASANOVA

CHEVALIER DE SEINGALT

HISTORY OF MY LIFE

FIRST TRANSLATED INTO ENGLISH
IN ACCORDANCE WITH THE
ORIGINAL FRENCH MANUSCRIPT
BY WILLIAM R. TRASK

ABRIDGED BY PETER WASHINGTON

WITH AN INTRODUCTION
BY JOHN JULIUS NORWICH

EVERYMAN'S LIBRARY
Alfred A. Knopf New York London Toronto

290

THIS IS A BORZOI BOOK
PUBLISHED BY ALFRED A. KNOPF

First included in Everyman's Library, 2006 (UK), 2007 (US)
Volumes 1 & 2, English translation copyright © 1966 and renewed 1994
by Harcourt, Inc.
Volumes 3 & 4, English translation copyright © 1967 and renewed 1995
by Harcourt, Inc.
Volumes 5 & 6, English translation copyright © 1968 and renewed 1996
by Harcourt, Inc.
Volumes 7 & 8, English translation copyright © 1969 by Harcourt, Inc.
Volumes 9 & 10, English translation copyright © 1970 and renewed
1998 by Harcourt, Inc.
Volumes 11 & 12, English translation copyright © 1971 by
Harcourt, Inc.
Published by arrangement with Harcourt, Inc.

Originally published as *Histoire de ma vie*, Edition intégrale, by Jacques
Casanova de Seingalt, Vénitien, by F. A. Brockhaus, Wiesbaden,
Librairie Plon, Paris, 1960. © F. A. Brockhaus, Wiesbaden, 1960.

Introduction Copyright © 2006 by John Julius Norwich
Bibliography and Chronology Copyright © 2006 by Everyman's Library
Typography by Peter B. Willberg

US website: www.randomhouse.com/everymans

ISBN: 0-307-26557-9 (US)
1-85715-290-5 (UK)

A CIP catalogue reference for this book is available from the
British Library

Book design by Barbara de Wilde and Carol Devine Carson

Printed and bound in Germany by GGP Media GmbH, Pössneck

GENERAL CONTENTS

———

INTRODUCTION

Many years ago when I was writing a history of Venice, I remember pointing out that one of the chief difficulties of my task was the deep Venetian mistrust of what we would now call the Cult of Personality. The great cities of the Italian mainland had no such inhibitions: one has only to think of the Medici in Florence, the della Scala in Verona, the Gonzaga in Mantua, the Este in Ferrara, the Sforza and the Visconti in Milan. Some were enlightened rulers, some were monstrous despots; all, for better or for worse, dominated their fellow-citizens and turned nominal republics into autocracies, if not dictatorships.

From anything of this kind the Venetians turned away with a shudder. The Most Serene Republic might not have been totally democratic – political power rested, after all, only with those adult males whose families were listed in the Golden Book – but it was certainly more so (with the arguable exception of Switzerland) than any other country in Europe, and they were determined to keep it that way. The basic principle of their constitution was accordingly to ensure that no one family or individual could ever wax too great. The Doge was a figurehead, able to act at all only when he was surrounded by his six *Savii* or wise men; even then he probably wielded less effective power than the Queen of England today. The real government of the country was in the hands of black-robed and faceless committees, their composition constantly changing. How the historian longs for some tremendous, larger-than-life character to sink his teeth into; alas, again and again he is doomed to disappointment.

Who, then, is the most famous Venetian in history? Not Doge Enrico Dandolo who, when already in his eighties and almost stone-blind, led his countrymen against Constantinople in what was ridiculously known as the Fourth Crusade; not Daniele Manin, who in 1848 headed the Venetian revolution against the occupying Habsburgs and briefly resuscitated the Republic; not even Titian and Tintoretto – whose achievements and reputations, immortal as they are, are familiar only to a cultivated minority. There can, I submit, be but one answer. The single Venetian name which is not only universally known but has even entered legend is that of a reprobate, adventurer, gambler, libertine and rakehell: Giovanni Giacomo Casanova.

Now this says a lot about Casanova; but it says even more about Venice. By the time he was born in 1725, what had once been the greatest commercial empire in the world had changed beyond recognition. The Turks had mopped up the entire Eastern Mediterranean, and the discovery of the Cape Route to the Indies had done the rest. Venice, her former occupation gone, had looked elsewhere for a *raison d'être.* She had consequently made herself the pleasure capital of Europe, a Las Vegas before her time – but, being Venice, a Las Vegas with style. The timely institution of the Grand Tour ensured her a constant flow of visitors, of rich young milords from across the Alps – and above all from England – travelling probably with their tutors and valets, heading first for Rome to put the finishing touches to their classical education but always taking care to return through Venice where, quite apart from the art, the architecture and the glorious music, Carnival went on for half the year, the gambling was for higher stakes and the courtesans more beautiful, obliging and technically skilled than anywhere else. Thus it was that his native city fitted Casanova like a glove; he could only have been a Venetian.

He was, however, a Venetian of a rare – perhaps a unique – breed. We can hardly call him a great man, but he possessed in full measure two of the most important ingredients of greatness: total self-confidence and superabundant energy. He feared nobody. He was equally at home in a palace or a tavern, a church or a brothel. Since his principal income came from gambling – he claimed to hate spending money that derived from any other source – his fortunes rose and fell. When he was in funds he lived like a grand seigneur, dispensing largesse not only to beautiful women but to servants and beggars and indeed to anyone who needed it. There was of course the occasional spell of bad luck, but it never seems to have lasted; fate – assisted by nerves of steel – was always with him in the long run, and when it failed he had his magic to fall back on.

He fancied himself as a sorcerer and necromancer, and though his success in these fields was based entirely on an excellent memory, a gift of the gab and quite extraordinary powers of persuasion and deceit, so brilliantly did he get away with it time after time that he sometimes even found himself wondering whether there wasn't something in the hocus-pocus after all.

And he had a third great strength – a negative strength perhaps, but every bit as important as the other two. He was totally devoid of a sense of morality. He describes his deceptions, his scams and his confidence tricks with pride; and his occasionally hair-raising sexual exploits are recounted without a glimmer of shame or regret. Baudelaire once remarked that the single and supreme delight of love lies in the certainty that one is doing evil; to Casanova such an idea would have been incomprehensible. Love for him had no connection with evil; it meant pleasure, pure and simple. It was also ephemeral; even his affair with Henriette – the mysterious French adventuress whom he met in Cesena in 1749 and who was probably the love of his life – lasted only seven months. The moment that a love affair ceased to be pleasurable it was time to stop – and to look elsewhere.

Many readers of these outrageous memoirs have found themselves mystified by the author's frequent protestations of his profound Christian faith; in fact, the vast majority of his Venetian contemporaries probably felt much as he did. This was, after all, the Age of Reason. You went to mass, you observed the outward formalities; insofar as you ever thought about it much, you even believed – up to a point. You believed in God, you believed in Jesus Christ, you believed in confession and absolution. You did not, on the other hand, believe in hell. And – least of all in Venice – you never let belief cramp your style.

This book is fundamentally an autobiography; and it is not normally necessary, when introducing autobiographies, to do more than summarize, very briefly, the events that are to be described in greater detail in the work itself. But there is nothing normal about the *Histoire de ma vie*. First of all, it is enormously long: uncut, it runs to no less than twelve volumes – this abridgement amounts to just under half of it – and it is often difficult to see the wood for the trees. Secondly, the author's tendency to embroider and exaggerate – even when he is not shamelessly inventing – means that if we are to get at the truth we must often rely on sources other than his own testimony. It may be worthwhile, therefore, to give here a brief account of the main facts of his life.

It is typical of Casanova to trace his descent, as he does in this book, from some obscure Spanish hidalgo of Saragossa. The truth, a good deal less romantic, is that he was the illegitimate son of a shoemaker's beautiful daughter, an actress named Zanetta Farussi. Some thirteen months before his birth on 2 April 1725, Zanetta had married a young dancer by the name of Gaetano Casanova; but it seems virtually certain that Giacomo was in fact the son of one Michele Grimani, who owned the theatre at S. Samuele where Gaetano and Zanetta were both employed. Even by the standards of eighteenth-century Venice, Zanetta seems to have been a girl who made friends easily; in 1727, while she was on tour in London, she was to give birth to her second son, Francesco, whose father was said to be the Prince of Wales – destined in that same year to succeed to the throne as King George II.

His parents' long absences from Venice meant that the baby was effectively brought up by his maternal grandmother. From the beginning he seems to have been a sickly child, subject to violent nosebleeds which, he tells us, were finally cured by witchcraft. By the age of nine, however, he was strong enough to be sent to Dr Gozzi's school in Padua. We can take with a pinch of salt his statement that he learnt to read in a month, but he certainly showed unusual intelligence. He seems to have been precocious in other ways too: he almost immediately fell in love with Gozzi's teenaged sister Bettina, who gave him his first lessons in sex. After four years with Dr Gozzi and Bettina, he enrolled at the legal faculty of the University of Padua, where he took his degree in 1742. Law, however, had little attraction and for him and he decided instead to enter the priesthood. With half a dozen love affairs already behind him and well over a hundred still to come, he should have known better: his short stay in the seminary of S. Cipriano on Murano ended in his expulsion for suspected homosexuality.

To many readers this may come as something of a surprise; and Casanova himself provides a perfectly innocent if slightly improbable explanation. But he has no hesitation in admitting to other homosexual adventures in the course of his life, so we must accept that he was at least to some degree attracted to men – though never remotely as much as to women. At an early age, too, he seems to have discovered an interest in transvestism; but this too was indulged only on rare occasions.

At this point we encounter the first of several mysteries in Casanova's life: why, in the spring of 1743, was he imprisoned in the fortress of S. Andrea where some two thousand Albanians – soldiers and their families – were temporarily stationed? The *Histoire* is far from clear. There is evidence elsewhere to show that in the previous year he may have gone to Corfu as secretary to some Venetian official, and the nationality of the garrison suggests that he got into some sort of trouble there. In any event, he protests that he was treated during his captivity with every consideration – which seems to have been true, since it was there that he contracted his first (though by no means his last) bout of venereal disease.

It says a good deal for Casanova's powers of persuasion that after this experience he was taken on as secretary by two prominent churchmen, first by the Bishop of Martorano in Calabria and soon afterwards by Cardinal Acquaviva, Spanish Ambassador to the Holy See, on whose behalf he wrote a number of love poems for His Eminence to send to his inamorata. But scandal followed wherever he went and, after further affairs in Rome and Naples, Corfu and Constantinople, by the end of 1745 he was back in Venice, virtually penniless and playing the violin (only, we are told, moderately well) in his parents' old theatre of S. Samuele. At the ripe old age of twenty his luck, it seemed, had deserted him.

Not, however, for long. In April 1746 he was leaving a ball for which he had been playing, when a senator to whom he had done some small service offered him a lift in his gondola, and during the short journey suffered a sudden stroke. Casanova jumped ashore, found a doctor, brought him to the senator's palazzo and remained at his bedside for several days, during which he completely won the patient's confidence, both by his apparently profound knowledge of medicine and by his professed mastery of cabbalistic healing. Thanks at least partially to his ministrations, the senator – he was in fact a distinguished patrician named Matteo Giovanni Bragadin – made a remarkably rapid recovery and before long decided to adopt him as a son. Casanova moved into the palazzo, where he was given his own apartment with a servant, a personal gondola and a generous allowance. For the next three years everything went his way: the girls were amenable, the cards were on his side. But, as so often in his life, it was too good to last. Two unpleasant scandals followed in quick succession – from neither of which he emerged with much credit – and Bragadin, putting away all thoughts of adoption, had to advise him to leave Venice while he was still free to do so.

He did – this was the time of the passionate but short-lived affair with Henriette – but the charges were dropped, and by the spring of 1750 he was back in Venice for a few weeks before leaving on what for him was the beginning of his own Grand Tour. He first travelled – via Lyon, where he became a Free-mason – to Paris, of which he gives a fascinating account of the social, theatrical and what one might call the prostitutional scene. There he remained two years before going on to Dresden, whence – having successfully dealt with his seventh bout of the clap – he continued to Prague and Vienna. By the summer of 1753 he was back in Venice, carrying on a simultaneous affair – engineered and excitedly witnessed by the French Ambassador, the Abbé de Bernis – with a nun and one of the girls from her convent: an episode thanks to which he became for the second time a person of interest to the Venetian authorities.

Once they had decided to take action against him, there was no lack of evidence. His contempt for Christianity, his constant debauching of young girls and married women, his cheating at cards, his false claims to nobility, his pretended magic, even – Venice being Venice – his intimate relations with foreigners in the city, any of these alone was enough to condemn him. On 26 July 1755 over thirty men burst into his rooms, confiscated all his books on magic and astrology and informed him that he was under arrest. He was given no opportunity of defending himself, nor even notified of his trial. On 12 September he was found guilty of 'public outrages against the holy religion' and sentenced to five years' imprisonment.

Every visitor to Venice knows the *prigioni*, which are linked by the celebrated Bridge of Sighs to the Doge's Palace. Their inmates would be relegated either to the *pozzi* (literally, the wells) or to the *piombi* (the leads). The *pozzi* were hideously damp and in winter frequently flooded; the *piombi* were small and completely unfurnished. Being immediately under the roof, they were also, in the summer months, murderously hot, their ceilings so low that even a moderately tall man could barely stand upright. Five years in such conditions would probably have been more than even Casanova – who was five foot nine – could have endured; even the fifteen months of his actual imprisonment must have seemed an eternity.

The story of his eventual escape has become a classic in the genre, and is remarkably well told in the *Histoire*. It brought him fame and, up to a point, fortune and he was to dine out on it for the rest of his life. One question, however, refuses to go away: could anyone – least of all Giacomo Casanova – tell a story hundreds of times without elaboration and exaggeration? Surely not: allowances have to be made. Of the essential features in his account, on the other hand, the Venetian State Archives provide ample confirmation. They also strongly suggest that no similar escape had ever been achieved before. Casanova's tale may have lost nothing in the telling, but he certainly had plenty to boast about.

He fled to Paris where, with the help of his old friend de Bernis, now Foreign Minister, he launched the first French state lottery. This made him rich; and his friendship with the Marquise d'Urfé, whose almost unbelievable credulity he ruthlessly exploited over the next seven years, made him richer still. Meanwhile his success with women and at the gaming tables continued undiminished, and all might have been well had he not decided to invest his growing wealth in the painted silk industry. It proved a disaster. Before long one of his employees had absconded with the funds and all the materials from the warehouse. Fraud was suspected, and Casanova found himself once again under arrest; but there was no proof against him – for once he seems to have been perfectly innocent – and after four days he regained his liberty.

For the next quarter of a century he was almost constantly on the move, with characteristically fluctuating fortunes. In Stuttgart he was imprisoned for debt; in Florence he was asked to leave; in Rome, on the other hand, he was received by Pope Clement XIII, who invested him with a high papal order. In Naples he fell in love with the sixteen-year-old Leonilda, to whom he proposed marriage only to discover that she was his own daughter. (This did not stop him going to bed with her – and again, after seventeen years, with her mother.) In Paris and Marseilles, he continued his exploitation of the luckless if gullible Marquise d'Urfé throughout 1762; only towards the end of 1763 did the scales finally fall from her eyes. It was in London, with a prostitute of Denmark Street known as La Charpillon, that Casanova finally met his match. She robbed him, deceived him and humiliated him at every turn. From this time on, he confessed, his life went downhill all the way.

By 1764 England too had become too hot for him. He fled to Berlin, where Frederick the Great offered him the post of tutor to a group of aristocratic cadets. He turned it down – the money wasn't good enough – and went on to Moscow, where he had an audience with Catherine the Great, and thence to Poland. In Warsaw he fought a duel (over an actress) with a Polish nobleman, on whom he inflicted a serious wound. The nobleman almost died; to Casanova's own reputation, on the other hand, the encounter did nothing but good. Reports of the duel spread across Europe: if Count Franciszek Branicki had condescended to fight a duel with the Chevalier de Seingalt – a name which he had adopted a few years before without a trace of justification – the said Chevalier must be a figure to be reckoned with.

And yet, as we read of his constant peregrinations, the impression becomes ever stronger that Casanova is no longer a wandering adventurer; he is a hunted man. In 1767 he was expelled from Vienna and returned to Paris; then, in November, Louis XV issued a *lettre de cachet* which obliged him to leave France. No longer welcome in most of central Europe, he hoped for better luck in Spain – only to spend six weeks in

a Barcelona gaol. On his way back to Italy he fell seriously
ill at Aix-en-Provence, and was nursed back to health by a
mysterious woman who proved to be the servant of his old love
Henriette. Only in 1774, after the usual succession of fortunes
won and lost, of women seduced and tumbled, was he allowed
to return to Venice, where he settled down to make his living
as a writer.

He was not altogether a novice. As early as 1752 he had produced an Italian translation of the libretto of Jean-Philippe
Rameau's opera *Zoroastre*, which had subsequently been
performed at Dresden. Seventeen years later, in 1769, he had
composed a bitter attack on Amelot de la Houssaye's *Histoire du
gouvernement de Venise*, a recent work which had severely criticized the Serenissima. His purpose in coming to the Republic's
defence had been simply to work his passage back into Venetian
favour, in the hopes that he might at last be permitted to return
after his thirteen-year exile. The ban was in fact to remain in
force for another five years; but the book certainly caused a
considerable stir and sold like hot cakes – the only real literary
success that Casanova was to enjoy in his lifetime. His third
work, published in 1772, was a good deal less successful. He
called it *Lana caprina* – 'goat's wool', an Italian expression meaning 'utter nonsense'; it is in essence a somewhat heavy-handed
satire, describing a debate between two university professors
on the question of whether or not a woman's reasoning power
is controlled by her womb. There have been several recent
editions – none, so far as I am aware, in English – but by all but
serious Casanova buffs the work may safely be forgotten.

His most important serious enterprise – though unfinished
– was his *Istoria delle turbolenze della Polonia*, 'History of the Polish
Upheavals', published in 1774. Casanova had done much of
the preliminary research during his stay in Poland in 1765–6,
and his original intention (concision, alas, was never his forte)
had been for a work of no less than seven volumes; but owing
to a dispute with the printer – and, probably, an insufficient
number of subscribers – only three of these volumes were ever
written. The same fate, alas, befell his next project, undertaken
after his return to Venice: a translation of Homer's *Iliad* into
Italian *ottava rima* (a verse form in which each stanza consists

of eight iambic pentameters, rhyming abababcc. The best-known example in English is Byron's *Don Juan*.) After three instalments this too was discontinued. There followed various other attempts to make ends meet, including translations of two novels and the publishing of two magazines, the literary monthly *Opuscoli miscellanei* and a theatrical weekly – which for some reason he wrote in French – called *Le Messager de Thalie*. The former ran to seven numbers (one of which included his account of his duel with Branicki), the latter to eleven.

Then, in 1782, there came another catastrophe. The details are complicated and unnecessary to go into here; suffice it to say that Casanova was acting as a middleman between a debtor and his creditor and that, having as he thought successfully negotiated the business, he accused the creditor of having reneged on the pre-arranged fee. A violent quarrel ensued during which blows were struck, and a patrician named Carlo Grimani in whose palazzo it occurred took the creditor's side and asked Casanova to leave. Furious, Casanova refused to do so, and when he finally returned home wrote in revenge a thinly-disguised allegory, *Né amori né donne; ovvero la stalla ripulita*, 'Neither Loves nor Ladies, or The Cleaned-up Stable', in which he claimed not only that he was the illegitimate son of Grimani's father Michele, but that Grimani was himself the illegitimate son of someone else. On 17 January 1783 he was obliged for the third time to leave Venice in a hurry.

Casanova was now fifty-seven. He was once again down on his luck, money was running short, the girls were showing less interest than before. He also had to face up to the fact that he would never be able to support himself as an author. There followed another *Wanderjahr*: Vienna, Innsbruck, Augsburg, Frankfurt, Aachen, Paris – where he met Benjamin Franklin and nearly joined an expedition to Madagascar – Dresden, Berlin, Prague. Few men of his day can have known the roads and cities of Europe as well as he. Returning to Vienna in February 1784 he renewed his old acquaintance with Mozart's librettist Lorenzo da Ponte, and served briefly as secretary to the Venetian Ambassador Sebastiano Foscarini. Then, at last, he found his salvation: Count Josef Karl Emmanuel von Waldstein, who offered him a permanent position as librarian

in his castle at Dux in Bohemia. Casanova was initially un-
enthusiastic, but after the sudden death of Foscarini he had
little choice.

It was at Dux that he lived for the last fourteen years of his
life, and at Dux that he was to die. There were occasional
short journeys away – notably to Prague in 1787, where he met
Mozart and – on the evidence of two pages in his handwriting – may even have collaborated with da Ponte on the
last act of *Don Giovanni*; for the rest, he sat in the library at Dux,
writing and writing. In 1788 he produced a long, sprawling
novel – science fiction before its time – which he called *Icosameron, or the History of Edward and Elizabeth, who Spent Eighty-one
Years among the Megamicros, Aboriginal Inhabitants of the Protocosmos
in the Interior of the Earth*. More surprising still, perhaps, was
the publication in 1790 of three mathematical studies on the
Duplication of the Cube. None of these had much success; but
that same year of 1790 also saw the beginning of the work on
his *Histoire de ma vie*, which was to make his name immortal.

And it did more: it made his life worth living. At Dux he
was cut off from his friends and, since Waldstein was frequently
abroad, for much of the time desperately lonely. To make
matters worse, he was cordially detested by the major-domo of
the castle, a certain Georg Feldkirchner, who was irritated
by his pretensions to gentility and took a sadistic delight in
humiliating him in every way he could. As he grew more and
more depressed, Casanova's only hope was to lose himself in
the past – to *jouir par réminiscence*, as he not very delicately put it.
He wrote compulsively, perhaps even maniacally: the first
draft of what must be one of the longest autobiographies ever
written – even though it ends with his return to Venice in 1774
when he was still a mere forty-nine – was completed after only
two years, although he was revising it until within a few days of
his death as more and more little vignettes and episodes flooded
back into his memory. (The 122 women with whom he claims
to have had adventures certainly constitute a respectable total;
but how many more, one wonders, may he have forgotten?)

'I have often observed,' he wrote somewhat ruefully, 'that
for the greater part of my life I have been trying to make
myself ill, and then, when I had achieved this, trying to get

GIACOMO CASANOVA

well again. I have been equally successful in both; and now that I enjoy perfect health I regret being unable to make myself ill; but old age, an illness as cruel as it is inevitable, forces me to be well in spite of myself.' So for some years it did; but at last the inevitable occurred, and on 4 June 1798, two months after his seventy-third birthday, Giacomo Casanova died – of a urinary infection – at Dux. Just a year before, there had been another death, far more momentous: that of the Most Serene Republic of Venice, which on Friday 12 May 1797, after well over a thousand years, had voted itself out of existence. Theoretically the way was now clear for the old man to return home, but he made no attempt to do so. Age and sickness may have played their part in his decision; but what would he have done in a Venice overrun by Napoleon's troops, with the Lions of St Mark hacked from their niches and the Golden Book publicly burnt in the Piazza? The Venice that he had known and loved was gone, never to return; he preferred to remain in Bohemia with his memories.

Astonishingly enough, it was not until the early 1960s that the *Histoire de ma vie* first saw the light of day in its original form, unexpurgated and unabridged. Casanova had given the manuscript on his deathbed to his sister's son-in-law Carlo Angioloni, whose son had sold it in 1820 to the Leipzig publishing firm of Brockhaus. It was then rather loosely adapted and translated into German, and soon afterwards this German translation was pirated and translated back into French – by which time it bore little resemblance to the original. All this was bad enough; but now Brockhaus compounded the confusion by commissioning a local professor named Laforgue to edit the manuscript and produce a definitive French edition.

What followed was a disgrace. Casanova's Italianate French was part of the book's charm; Laforgue – having unaccountably lost four chapters – now corrected what was left, polished it and bowdlerized it, occasionally, however, introducing additional pieces of explicit smut of his own invention. A typical French anti-clerical republican of his time, he also cut most of the author's solemn professions of Christian faith and toned down his vitriolic remarks about the Revolution of 1789. This travesty of the original not only claimed to be authoritative; it

CHRONOLOGY

HISTORICAL EVENTS

First of three rebellions in Corsica against Genoese control. J. S. Bach's *St Matthew Passion* first performed in Leipzig.
Canaletto enters into a working arrangement with Joseph Smith. Resident in Venice since 1700 (and British consul after 1744), Smith is a bibliophile and art collector whose other protégés include the brothers Marco and Sebastiano Ricci, Zuccarelli and Rosalba Carriera. He acts as agent and go-between with their patrons among the English nobility. Studio of Gianantonio Guardi (1699–1760) active in Venice, specializing in religious painting. (According to Casanova his brother Francesco studied with Guardi *c.*1739–49). *Experimenta* of Marco Ricci (1676–1729) published (Ricci was one of the first Venetian etchers of the 18th century).

Second Treaty of Vienna between Austria, Great Britain, Spain, Russia and the United Provinces. Independent principality of Monaco comes under French protection (to 1814).

Canaletto: *A Regatta on the Grand Canal*; *The Bucintoro at the Molo on Ascension Day*: the artist's work becoming increasingly popular.

First Family Compact signed by Bourbon France and Spain. War of Polish Succession (to 1735), France and Spain supporting Stanislas Leszczynski; Austria, Russia and Prussia the Elector Friedrich August II of Saxony. The latter is successful, and reigns as Augustus III of Poland (to 1763).
Pergolesi's comic intermezzo *La serva padrona* ('The maid as mistress') first performed in Naples.
Austrian army defeated by French and Spanish in Italy. As a result the peace treaty of 1735 awards former Habsburg lands – Naples and Sicily – to Bourbon Spain which rules them for more than a century. (The Habsburgs receive Parma and Piacenza in exchange).
The composer J. A. Hasse becomes Kappellmeister at the Saxon court in Dresden (to 1764).

xxvii

DATE	AUTHOR'S LIFE	LITERARY CONTEXT
1734–7	Giacomo is sent to Padua to be tutored by Dr Antonio Gozzi in preparation for a career in the church. Falls in love with Dr Gozzi's younger sister, Bettina, who gives him his first lessons in sex.	
1735		Metastasio: 'La Libertà' (canzonetta). Lesage completes *Gil Blas*. Horace Walpole's correspondence begins (to 1797; first published in part 1798).
1736		Goldoni: *Don Giovanni Tenorio*. Metastasio: *Temistocle*. Radicati: *Discours moraux, historiques et politiques*. Crébillon *fils*: *Les Egarements du coeur et de l'esprit* (to 1738).
1737	Giacomo is enrolled at Padua University, where he studies civil and canon law.	Algarotti: *Newtonianismo per le dame* ('Newtonianism for ladies'). Marivaux: *Les Fausses confidences*.
1738		Goldoni: *L'uomo di mondo* ('The man of the world'). *Antiquitates italicae medii aevi* (to 1743): 75 essays on medieval history published by historiographer L. A. Muratori, court librarian at Modena.
1739	Leaves Padua and lives largely in Venice.	Conti: *Poesie e prose*. Hume: *Treatise of Human Nature*.
1740	Attracts the patronage of Senator Malipiero. Simultaneous seduction of two sisters, Nanetta and Marta Savorgnan.	Marivaux: *L'Epreuve*. Prévost: *L'Histoire d'une grecque moderne*. Cibber: *An Apology for the Life of Colley Cibber*. Richardson: *Pamela* (to 1741).

CHRONOLOGY

Alvise Pisani, member of Venice's richest family, becomes Doge (to 1741).
He succeeds in preserving Venetian neutrality in spite of European wars and
diplomatic crises. *Prospectus Magni Canalis Venetiarum*: 14 prints of Venetian
views engraved by Visentini after Canaletto.
Russo-Turkish War (Austria joining on the Russian side in 1737).

Reform of Venetian shipping laws leads to a boom in shipbuilding. Venice
also abandons her protectionist policies, resulting in an increase in the
transit trade.
Linnaeus: *Sysema Naturae* (introducing system of plant classification).
Pergolesi's *Stabat Mater* (1736): the composer dies the following year.

Death of Gian-Gastone, last Medici ruler of Tuscany; Tuscany comes under
Habsburg dominion for more than a century. Karl Eugen becomes Duke of
Württemberg (to 1793) at the age of 9.
Niccolò Jommelli makes his debut as an opera composer in Naples with
L'errore amoroso; by the time of his death in 1774 he had composed more than
60 operas.
By the Third Treaty of Vienna Stanislas Leszczynski is compensated for loss
of Poland with the Duchy of Lorraine (to pass to France on his death).
In Eminenti: first of a series of papal bulls condemning Freemasonry.

Russia, Austria and the Ottoman Empire sign the Treaty of Belgrade.
Outbreak of Anglo-Spanish War (War of Captain Jenkin's Ear).
Death of Emperor Charles VI; accession of Maria Theresa. Death of
Frederick William I of Prussia; accession of Frederick II ('the Great'). War of
Austrian Succession (to 1748) begins with Frederick's attack on Silesia.
Britain supports Austria (as do, intermittently, Sardinia and Savoy); France,
Spain and Bavaria support Prussia. Italy once more becomes a field of
conflict and the major belligerents except Prussia are keen to extend power
and influence there. Benedict XIV becomes Pope.
Tiepolo: *Road to Calvary*. Piazzetta: *The Soothsayer*; *Beach Idyll*. By the 1740s
Piazzetta has a flourishing studio in Venice producing religious and genre
paintings. (According to Casanova, his brother Giovanni Battista studied
with Piazzetta 1749–52).

DATE	AUTHOR'S LIFE	LITERARY CONTEXT
1741	Casanova takes minor orders, becoming an *abate*. Graduates from Padua University.	Duclos: *Les Confessions du comte de ****.
1742	Abandons the idea of a career in the church. Possible service in Corfu as secretary to Giacomo da Riva, Governor of the Galleys, though Casanova himself puts this in 1744.	Fielding: *Shamela*; *Joseph Andrews*.
1743	Death of his grandmother, Marzia Farussi (March). Falls foul of Senator Malipiero for showing too much interest in his actress protégée, Teresa Imer. The Grimanis send him to the monastery of San Cipriano on Murano to continue his studies; he is soon expelled for suspected homosexuality (July). He is later imprisoned in the fortress of Sant'Andrea. Through Zanetta's influence, he is appointed secretary to Bernardo de Bernardis, the new bishop of Martorano. Misadventures with Frate Stefano on the journey south. Appalled by the harsh landscape and cultural poverty of Calabria, he resigns his position on arrival. Travels to Rome, via Naples. Enlivens the journey by embarking on an affair with Donna Lucrezia, wife of a lawyer with whom he shared a carriage. Enters the service of Cardinal Acquaviva, the Spanish ambassador to the Holy See. Enjoys consorting with the elite of Roman society.	Goldoni: *La donna di garbo* ('The woman of Garbo'): by 1743 Goldoni had perfected his new style of comedy, combining elements of Molière with *commedia dell'arte*. Death of John, Lord Hervey, author of the *Memoirs of the Reign of George II* (published 1848).
1744	A career in the church is ruled out when Casanova is dismissed by the Cardinal for helping his French teacher's daughter to elope. He is sent, at his own request, to Constantinople. Stopping over at Ancona he falls	G. Pivati: *Dizionario universale*. Muratori: *Annali d'Italia* (to 1749). Marivaux: *La Dispute*. Johnson: *Life of Mr Richard Savage*.

CHRONOLOGY

Pietro Grimani (a Fellow of the Royal Society) becomes Doge (to 1752).
Death of Vivaldi.

Charles Albrecht of Bavaria is crowned Holy Roman Emperor but almost
immediately is driven from Munich by Austrian troops.
Karl Theodor becomes Elector of the Palatinate (from 1777 also Elector of
Bavaria). Mannheim school of composers flourishes at his court.
Fall of Walpole in England. Handel's *Messiah* first performed in Dublin.
Celsius devises centigrade scale.
Death of the last Medici, the widowed Electress Palatine, Anna Maria Luisa,
leaving all the Medici art collections to the state of Tuscany, together with
the Laurentian Library, Michelangelo's Medici Chapel and numerous
Renaissance villas. On the whole, 18th-century travellers remained
unimpressed, preferring the architecture of Naples and Rome.
Battle of Dettingen: George II leads the Pragmatic army to victory against
the French.

Thirty-one drawings and etchings of Canaletto published (to 1746).
Henry Pelham chief minister in Britain (to 1754).

DATE	AUTHOR'S LIFE	LITERARY CONTEXT
1744 *cont.*	in love with 'Bellino', a girl singer posing as a *castrato*, to whom he proposes, later changing his mind because marriage to an actress would not be respectable. Joins the Venetian army and is posted to Corfu.	
1745	Acquires a taste for gambling and loses all his money. Pursuit of Signora Foscari. Visits Constantinople. Returns with his regiment to Venice and resigns from the army. Down on his luck, he becomes second violinist in the orchestra at the San Samuele theatre (December).	Goldoni: *Il servitore di due padroni* ('The servant of two masters'). Crébillon *fils*: *Le Sopha*.
1746	Casanova helps Matteo Giovanni Bragadin when he suffers a stroke (April) and afterwards uses his knowledge of cabbalistic healing to gain ascendancy over him. The grateful patrician unofficially adopts him as his son, enabling Casanova to live a life of pleasure for three years. Bragadin's friends Marco Barbaro and Marco Dandolo also become his lifelong patrons.	Condillac: *Essai sur l'origine des connaissances humaines.*
1747		Maffei: *Il Raguet.* Voltaire: *Zadig.* Mme de Graffigny: *Lettres péruviennes* (after Montesquieu's *Lettres persanes*, 1721).
1748	Casanova's wild behaviour draws unwanted attention from the church authorities, obliging him to leave Venice (December).	Goldoni: *La vedova scaltra* ('The artful widow'). La Mettrie: *L'Homme machine.* Montesquieu: *L'Esprit des lois.* Crébillon *père*: *Catilina.* Diderot: *Les Bijoux indiscrets.* Hume: *An Enquiry Concerning Human Understanding.*

CHRONOLOGY

Death of Charles Albrecht of Bavaria; Maximilian III Joseph becomes Elector (to 1777), making peace with the Habsburgs. A man of the Enlightenment, he fosters agriculture and industry, reforms the law codes, abolishes press censorship and founds an Academy of Sciences (1759). Maria Theresa secures the election of her husband, Francis Stephen of Lorraine, as Holy Roman Emperor (Francis I). Jacobite rising in Britain under 'The Young Pretender' ('Bonnie Prince Charlie'), Stuart claimant to the throne.
Battle of Fontenoy: French victory under Marshal de Saxe. Madame de Pompadour becomes titular mistress of Louis XV.
Palace of Sans Souci built at Potsdam for Frederick the Great to his own plans (to 1747).
Death of Philip V; Ferdinand VI becomes King of Spain (to 1759). Spain during the 18th century is fast losing its former political and economic standing in Europe.
Battle of Culloden in Scotland; defeat of Jacobites and suppression of the rebellion; Prince Charles Edward spends the rest of his life in exile.
Tiepolo's frescoes in the Palazzo Labia, Venice (to 1747).

Orangist revolution in the United Provinces with the accession of William IV as Stadtholder of all seven provinces, thus terminating the republic which had existed since the death of Stadtholder William III (William III of England) in 1702
Venetian artist Bellotto employed by Elector Friedrich August II of Saxony, painting a remarkable series of views of Dresden (to 1757).
War of Austrian Succession ends in stalemate. By the Treaty of Aix-la-Chapelle Maria Theresa, confirmed as Empress, keeps all her lands except Silesia, which is ceded to Prussia. In Italy, changes are few: Spain is awarded Parma and Piacenza and Sardinia gains part of the Milanese. This balance of forces obtains until the Napoleonic Wars.
Excavation of Pompeii begins.
Euler, mathematical wizard of his age, publishes *Introductio in Analysis Infinitorum*, employing symbols which became the basis for standard

DATE	AUTHOR'S LIFE	LITERARY CONTEXT

1748 *cont.*

Richardson: *Clarissa* (to 1749).
Smollett: *Roderick Random*.
Cleland: *Memoirs of a Woman of Pleasure* (to 1749).
Teresia Constantia Phillips's *An Apology for the Conduct of Teresia Constantia Phillips* scandalizes the British public.
Laetitia Pilkington: *Memoirs* (vols 1 and 2).

1749 In Mantua he meets Antonio Stefano Balletti, a dancer, who becomes a lifelong friend.
At Cesena he encounters a Frenchwoman, Henriette, disguised as a soldier, and accompanies her to Parma and Geneva. She is arguably the love of his life.

Arcadia in Brenta first performed in Venice, beginning a highly successful collaboration in *opera buffa* between Goldoni and the composer Galuppi (also known as 'Il Buranello').
Muratori: *Della pubblica felicità oggetto de' buoni principi* ('On the welfare of the people which is the aim of good princes').
Diderot: *Lettre sur les aveugles*.
Buffon: *Histoire naturelle* (to 1788).
Fielding: *Tom Jones*.

1750 Henriette reluctantly goes back to her family. Casanova returns to Venice. In May he embarks on a Grand Tour of Europe with Balletti. In Lyons he becomes a Freemason.

Metastasio: *Attilio Regolo* (1st perf.).
Goldoni: *La bottega del caffè* ('The coffee-shop'); *Il bugiardo* ('The liar'); *Il vero amico*; *Il teatro comico*.
Gasparo Gozzi: *Lettere diverse* (and 1752).
Turgot: *Tableaux philosophiques des progrès successifs de l'esprit humain*.
Mme de Graffigny: *Cénie*.

1750–52 First sojourn in Paris where he frequents both court and brothel. Learns the language from Crébillon *père*. Passes much of his time with the Balletti family.

CHRONOLOGY

HISTORICAL EVENTS

mathematical notation. Euler enjoyed enormous prestige and was
headhunted by both Catherine the Great and Frederick the Great.
Completion of the Bayreuth opera house, commissioned by the Margravine
Wilhelmine of Bayreuth, sister of Frederick the Great, and designed by
G. G. Bibiena and Joseph Saint-Pierre.

The new Duke and Duchess of Parma are Philip, son of Philip V of Spain,
and Louise-Elisabeth, eldest daughter of Louis XV; French influences are
dominant. A Frenchman, Guillaume du Tillot, becomes chief minister
(to 1771); he imports French intellectuals (e.g. Condillac) to Parma, artists,
such as Petitot and the sculptor Boudard, along with many skilled workers.
A champion of the Enlightenment, he exiles the Jesuits and fosters culture
and science.
Creation of a centralized *Directorium in Publicis et Cameralibus* (union of the
separate chanceries of Austria and Bohemia under Count Haugwitz), a key
step in Maria Theresa's administrative and financial reforms in the
Habsburg dominions.
New tax, the *vingtième*, introduced by Machault in France: his attempts to
improve the government's financial position end in failure in 1751.
The Fortune-Teller, earliest surviving work of Francesco Casanova, painted
around this time.

Accademia Veneziana di Pittura e Scultura founded. Guardi brothers work
on the scenes from the story of Tobias in the church of the Archangel
Raphael in Venice – one of the finest examples of 18th-century Venetian
decorative art.
Death of J. S. Bach in Leipzig.

GIACOMO CASANOVA

DATE	AUTHOR'S LIFE	LITERARY CONTEXT
1751		*Encyclopédie* published (to 1772). Last vol. (of 25) of historiographer Muratori's *Rerum italicarum scripturas*, in its time the greatest collection of national history in Europe. Galiani: *Della moneta* ('On Money'). Voltaire: *Le Siècle de Louis XIV.* Smollett: *Peregrine Pickle.* Cleland: *Memoirs of a Coxcomb.*
1752	Departs with his brother Francesco for Dresden, where his actress mother is in the service of the Elector of Saxony. At the Elector's request, he supplies an Italian translation of the libretto to Rameau's opera *Zoroastre*, which is performed in Dresden in February.	Voltaire: *Micromégas.* Martinelli: *Istoria critica della vita civile.* Migliavacca (pupil of Metastasio) becomes court poet to the King of Poland at Dresden. Hume: *Political Discourses.* First odes of Giuseppe Parini published.
1753	His first play, *La Moluccheide*, a parody of Racine, is performed at the Dresden State Theatre on 22 February, and well received. Visits Prague and Vienna, arriving back in Venice in May. Falls in love with Caterina Capretti (C.C.) whose father puts her in a convent. *Ménage a quatre* with C.C. and M.M., a nun, and M.M.'s lover the Abbé de Bernis, French ambassador to Venice.	Goldoni: *La locandiera* ('The landlady'). Tabarrani: *Observationes Anatomicae.* Rolli: *Poetici componimenti.* Melchior Grimm chief editor of *Correspondance littéraire*, the m/s journal of the Philosophes (to 1773). Buffon: *Discours sur le style.*
1754		Goldoni: *Il filosofo di campagna* (set by Galuppi); *Le masssere* ('The cook-maids'); *Le donne de casa soa* ('The good housewives'); *Il campiello* ('The public square'). Condillac: *Traité des sensations.* Crébillon *père*: *Le Triumvirat.* Crébillon *fils*: *Ah! quel conte*; *Les Heureux Orphelins.* Richardson: *Sir Charles Grandison.* Lord Waldegrave: *Memoirs* (covering years 1754–8, published 1821).

CHRONOLOGY

Tiepolo works on the new Residenz of the Prince-Bishop of Würzburg in collaboration with the artist Balthazar Neumann – one of his major projects abroad. Completion of the court church at Dresden (begun in 1739), designed by the Italian architect Chiavari in the Roman Baroque style (the rulers of Saxony were Catholic though their subjects were Lutheran).
Pietro Longhi: 'True likeness of a rhinoceros brought to Venice in 1751'. Longhi was famous for his pictures of Venetian life and manners.
A renewed dispute between Venice and Austria leads to the historic Patriarchate of Aquilea being abolished and divided into two bishoprics.

Giovanni Battista Casanova in Rome where he becomes well-known for his drawings after the Antique, many of which are later engraved as illustrations for Winckelmann's *History of the Art of Antiquity* (including two drawings of fictitious wall-paintings, forgeries only discovered after the book's publication – much to the author's fury).
Franklin devises lightning conductor.

Count (later Prince) Kaunitz becomes Austrian Chancellor. He assumes overall direction of Maria Theresa's government in 1760, when he replaces Count Haugwitz.
Jommelli serves as Kapellmeister to the Duke of Württemberg at Stuttgart (to 1769), where he produces one or two operas a year to libretti by Metastasio.
The British Museum founded in London.

Doge Francesco Loredan insists on government endorsement of papal dispensations and privileges granted to Venetian citizens. This proves unacceptable to Pope Benedict XIV and the dispute escalates when Maria Theresa and Louis XV take his side against Venice.
Maria Theresa appoints Gluck Kapellmeister to the court theatre in Vienna (to 1770).

GIACOMO CASANOVA

ATE	AUTHOR'S LIFE	LITERARY CONTEXT
1755	A succession of scandals and scams draws Casanova unfavourably to the attention of both church and state, and culminates in his arrest and imprisonment in the Leads (July).	Morellet: *Code de la nature.* Rousseau: *Discours sur l'origine de l'inégalité.* Crébillon *fils*: *La Nuit et le moment.* Lessing: *Miss Sara Sampson.* Winckelmann: *Thoughts on the Imitation of Greek Works in Painting and Sculpture.*
1756	Escapes on the night of 31 October/1 November and flees Venice. Dines out on the story for years.	Voltaire: *Essai sur les moeurs.* Mirabeau: *L'Ami des hommes.* Zimmermann: *On Loneliness.*
1757	Arrives in Paris. Supported by De Bernis, he establishes a state lottery and makes his fortune. Manon Balletti falls in love with him and they become engaged, though as usual he does not let this cramp his style. Ministry of Foreign Affairs sends him to Dunkirk as a spy. Financially rewarding friendship with the Marquise d'Urfé whose credulity he exploits for the next seven years.	Dispute in Venice between playwrights Goldoni and Carlo Gozzi, the latter despising the foreign influences in the work of the former. Gozzi publishes his satire *La tartana degl'influssi per l'anno 1756.* Haller: *Elementa Physiologiae Corporis Humani* (to 1766). Hume: *The Natural History of Religion.* Bettinelli: *Lettere virgiliane.*
1758	Secret mission to Holland where he successfully sells French government bonds and makes some fruitful business deals of his own. Affair with Esther. Meets Teresa Imer again, who seeks his assistance but will not agree to hand over to him 6-year-old Sophie, probably his daughter, offering instead her 12-year-old son Giuseppe.	G. Gozzi: *Difesa di Dante* (reply to Bettinelli, above). Martinelli: *Lettere familiari e critiche.* Helvétius: *De l'Esprit* Mme d'Epinay: *Lettres à mon fils.*
1759	Back in Paris, meets and is unimpressed by Rousseau. Infatuation with Giustiniana Wynne, pregnant by his friend Andrea Memmo, for whom he is accused of procuring an abortion. Sells his lottery offices and invests unwisely in a silk-printing factory. Creditors have him imprisoned in the Fort-l'Evêque. Leaves Paris for Amsterdam. Manon Balletti breaks off their engagement.	Voltaire: *Candide.* Quesnay: *Tableau economique* (founding document of the Physiocratic doctrine). Mme d'Epinay: *Mes Moments heureux.* Maffei: *Dell'arte magica* ('On witchcraft'). Sterne: *Tristram Shandy* (to 1767). Johnson: *Rasselas.*

CHRONOLOGY

Lisbon earthquake (1 Nov). Paoli leads Corsican revolt against the Genoese.
Karl Eugen, Duke of Württemburg (1737–93) assumes full control of
government. His ambitious building programme in and around Stuttgart –
the New Palace and the Palace of Solitude; modifications to Ludwigsburg –
is only one of his extravagances, to finance which he raises illegal taxes and
collects them by force.
University of Moscow founded.

Renversements des alliances: Austria, France and Russia sign First Treaty of
Versailles; Great Britain and Prussia sign the Convention of Westminster.
Outbreak of Seven Years' War (Britain and France fighting in the colonies;
Britain subsidizing Frederick the Great's army on the Continent).
Formation of Pitt/Newcastle ministry in Britain – an effective wartime
coalition.
Empress Elizabeth of Russia founds School of Fine Arts in St Petersburg,
staffed mainly by French painters and sculptors. Death of composer
Domenico Scarlatti.

The death of Pope Benedict XIV and fortuitous succession of Clement XIII
– Carlo Rezzonico, a Venetian – restores cordial relations between Venice
and the Vatican. Cardinal de Bernis falls into disgrace with Louis XV and
retires to his château of Vic-sur-Aisne. Choiseul chief minister in France
(to 1770).
Tiepolo's *Marriage of Ludovico Rezzonico and Faustina Savorgnan* (ceiling of the
Ca'Rezzonico in Venice). By this time Tiepolo's work as a decorator in the
Rococo style has become well-known throughout Europe. Gian Domenico
Tiepolo (his son) paints *Il Riposo di Pulcinella*.
Haydn's first 5 symphonies (to 1760).

On the death of Ferdinand VI of Spain, his half-brother Charles VII of the
Two Sicilies abdicates in order to succeed to the Spanish throne as Charles
III (to 1788). Spain begins to regain some of her lost prestige during his
reign. Legal and administrative reforms are introduced and measures taken
to improve the economy. In Naples he is succeeded by his son, aged 8, as
Ferdinand IV (deposed 1799 though later restored).
Tanucci chief minister in Naples till 1776. He successfully attacks the
privileges of the church and abolishes the Inquisition.
Count Firmian appointed Maria Theresa's plenipotentiary in Lombardy.
He initiates a period of collaboration with Milanese intellectuals in bringing
about administrative reform (Pietro Verri, for example, is employed by the
government from 1766).

DATE	AUTHOR'S LIFE	LITERARY CONTEXT
1759 *cont.*		
1760	Wanders through Europe – Cologne, Stuttgart, Zurich, Berne (in Switzerland he briefly toys with becoming a monk) and Geneva (he lays claim to several meetings with Voltaire at Ferney); Grenoble, Aix-en-Bains, Avignon, Marseilles, Genoa, Florence, Rome – indulging in his usual intrigues, financial and sexual. In Rome he spends time with his brother Giovanni and his friends, the painter Raphael Mengs and the art historian Johann Winckelmann.	Goldoni: *I rusteghi* ('The country-folk'). Baretti's highly successful *Dictionary of the English and Italian Languages.* Algarotti: *Viaggi di Russia.* Diderot: *La Réligieuse.* Voltaire: *Tancrède.* Mirabeau: *Théorie des impôt.* Macpherson: *Fragments of Ancient Poetry* (first Ossian collection).
1761	Visits Naples where he proposes marriage to 16-year-old Leonilda, whose mother turns out to be Lucrezia, with whom he had had a torrid affair 17 years before, and who claims that Leonilda is his daughter. Casanova sleeps with them both before returning to Rome, where Pope Clement XIII makes him a knight in the Papal Order of the Holy Spur. Travels to Florence, Bologna, Modena, Parma, Turin and Chambéry, ending up in Paris. When things get too hot for him there, he decamps to Munich and Augsburg – where he gambles and loses heavily – on business for the Marquise d'Urfé. He is robbed by his servants and mistress, a dancer called La Renaud, and suffers a severe (though not his first) case of venereal disease, undergoing an operation which nearly kills him.	C. Gozzi: *L'amore delle tre melarancei* ('The love of three oranges'). Goldoni: The *Villeggiature* (countryside) trilogy. Launch of *Osservatore Veneto*, in the style of *The Spectator*, one of three periodicals founded by Gasparo Gozzi in Venice in the early 1760s. Rousseau: *La Nouvelle Héloïse.* Diderot: *Le Neveu de Rameau.*

CHRONOLOGY

Etienne de Silhouette Comptroller-General of Finances in France
(March–Nov). Britain's *annus mirabilis*: year of victories.

Ippolita ed Aricia performed in Parma, first of a brilliant series of operas by
the composer Tommaso Traetta, an appointee of Du Tillot. His work effects
a compromise between the French and Italian styles.

Amsterdam strengthening her position as Europe's premier financial centre:
huge sums of Dutch money are invested abroad, especially in England but
also in France and Sweden, and later in the century, Russia.

Death of George II and accession of George III in Britain. George III
appoints his favourite, Lord Bute, Secretary of State; within a year he is
chief minister. The new administration favours a speedy ending to the war.

Zurich flourishing as centre of German Swiss literature and culture, with
author and critic J. J. Bodmer and J. J. Breitinger at the forefront.

The city-state of Genoa expanding rapidly as a financial centre second only
to Amsterdam, lending money to both France and the Habsburgs in the
second half of the century.

Emergence of Francesco Guardi (1712–93) as an important painter of
Venetian *vedute* (views). Francesco Casanova: *Surprise Attack on a Wagon and
Camp*. Francesco by now established in Paris as a successful court and salon
painter of battle, hunting and equestrian scenes. Rameau's last *comédie-ballet*,
Les Paladins. Piccinni's *La buona figliuola*, a setting of Goldoni's operatic
version of Richardson's *Pamela*, is a tremendous success in Rome.

Angelo Querini's unsuccesssful attack on Venice's traditional government:
the Council of Ten and the three Inquisitors of State.

Completion of Mengs' fresco 'Parnassus' at Villa Albani, Rome, in the
Neoclassical style. Mengs arrives in Spain as court painter (to 1769, and
again 1773–7).

In Modena Duke Francesco III opens the Galleria Estense to the public
(though in 1746 he had sold one hundred of his most valuable paintings to
the Elector of Saxony). He is also a generous patron of building work and
the city of Modena is transformed during his reign (1737–80).

Cesare Beccaria and the Verri brothers form the Società dei Pugni, a
discussion group for Milanese intellectuals. Helvetic Society formed by Swiss
intellectuals in Zurich to discuss political reform.

Morgagni's *De Sedibus et Causis Morborum per Anatomen Indagatis*, one of the
first books on pathological anatomy.

Haydn enters the service of Prince Esterházy in Hungary.

Marriage of George III and Princess Charlotte of Mecklenburg-Strelitz.

GIACOMO CASANOVA

DATE	AUTHOR'S LIFE	LITERARY CONTEXT
1762	Further developments in Casanova's mission to turn the Marquise d'Urfé – at her own request – into a man ...The operation is postponed. In Geneva, he indulges in his speciality – the twin seduction – this time involving Hedwig, the bluestocking daughter of a Protestant minister, and her cousin Helena. Next stop Turin.	Goldoni: *Le baruffe chiozzotte* ('Squabbles in Chioggia'). Goldoni leaves Venice to take up a court appointment in Paris, and is also put in charge of the Théâtre Italien. He never returns to Italy. C. Gozzi: *Turandot; Il re cervo* ('The king stag'); *La donna serpente* ('The snake woman'). Baretti: *Lettere familiari a' suoi tre fratelli* ... (to 1763). Rousseau: *Emile*; *Le Contrat social*. Alessandro Longhi's *Compendio delle vite de' pittori Veneziani*, an account of the lives of contemporary Venetian painters.
1763	Milan. More gambling, more women. In Marseilles attempts another 'regeneration' of the Marquise, who is finally disabused as to his magical powers. After a short visit to Paris, removes to London (June) where he thankfully returns Giuseppe to his mother, now Teresa Cornelys. Probably hoping to set up another state lottery, he attends court and makes many aristocratic acquaintances. Affair with Pauline. Meets his nemesis in the form of 'La Charpillon', a prostitute who leads him on, fleeces and humiliates him. Casanova marks his decline – he was never rich again – from this period.	Parini: first two parts of *Il Giorno* (to 1765). G. Gozzi: *Sermoni* (vol. 1). Cesarotti: *Poemi de Ossian* (Italian translation of Macpherson's Ossian poems). Barretti edits *Frusta letteraria* ('The literary scourge'), a Venetian journal on English lines, prohibited by the authorities in 1766. Crébillon *fils*: *Le Hasard du coin du feu*. Frederick the Great: *Histoire de la Guerre de Sept Ans*. First edition of the letters of Lady Mary Wortley Montagu (1689–1762).

CHRONOLOGY

Marco Foscarini becomes Doge. A scholarly man, he leaves a history of Venetian literature unfinished when he dies after only ten months in office. Consul Joseph Smith sells his complete collections to George III for £20,000. Three years later he sells his entire library for £10,000. It forms the nucleus of the King's Library, now in the British Museum.

Charles-Emmanuel, Duke of Savoy and King of Sardinia, frees serfs on royal estates and encourages those of the nobility to negotiate their own freedom – part of a programme of modernization that runs throughout his reign (1730–73).

Accession of Catherine II ('the Great') in Russia.

Collapse of Anglo-Prussian alliance. Loss of her ally leaves Britain diplomatically isolated in Europe.

Gluck's *Orfeo ed Euridice* produced in Vienna. The 6-year-old Mozart plays for the Empress Maria Theresa in Vienna. Galuppi appointed *Maestro di cappella* at St Mark's, the highest musical appointment in Venice.

The new Doge, another Alvise Mocenigo, negotiates treaties with Algiers, Tunis, Tripoli and Morocco, agreeing to pay them an annual fee for Venetian shipping to sail through their waters unmolested by pirates. Humiliating for Venice, which had formerly commanded the Mediterranean, these treaties are largely disregarded.

Peace of Paris redefines colonial interests of Britain and France to Britain's advantage; Peace of Hurbertusburg more or less reinstates *status quo ante bellum* in Europe, though it also confirms Prussia's new status as a Great Power.

Death of Friedrich August II, Elector of Saxony (also King Augustus III of Poland) ends union of Saxony and Poland. Death of his son Friedrich Christian two months later; regency of Electress Maria Antonia on behalf of the infant Friedrich August III, who rules until 1827. No longer a major player in Europe, Saxony enjoys a reasonably tolerant and enlightened administration; economic prosperity helps it to continue its rich cultural tradition.

Resignation of the increasingly unpopular Lord Bute in Britain, and his replacement by Lord Grenville. Issue 45 of the *North Briton* denounced by the government as a Seditious Libel; arrest of John Wilkes under a contentious general warrant, launching him on his career as a popular defender of 'Liberty' against the tyranny of the administration.

Johann Winckelmann becomes president of the Collection of Antiquities in the Vatican and Vatican librarian. Catherine II founds Russia's first College of Medicine.

DATE	AUTHOR'S LIFE	LITERARY CONTEXT
1764	Destitute, he leaves England for ever (March). Spends the next three-and-a-half years travelling almost continuously. In Prussia, declines Frederick the Great's offer of an appointment as tutor to a new corps of cadets (not enough money in it); moves on to St Petersburg.	Beccaria: *Dei delitti e delle pene* ('Of crime and punishment'), the most important Italian contribution to European Enlightenment. Launch of Pietro Verri's periodical *Il Caffè*, organ of the Milanese Enlightenment (to 1766). Voltaire: *Dictionnaire philosophique*. Goudar: *L'Espion chinois* (letters from an imaginary Chinese visitor to Europe.) Poinsinet: *La Cercle ou la soirée à la mode*. Winckelmann: *History of the Art of Antiquity*. Cleland: *The Surprises of Love*. Walpole: *The Castle of Otranto*.
1765	Two audiences with Catherine the Great whom he urges to reform the Russian calendar, and to set up a state lottery. She declines. Departs for Warsaw where he attracts the interest of King Stanislas II but is not offered the employment he seeks.	Genovese: *Lezioni di commercio o sia di economici civile* ('Lectures on commerce or civil economics'). Goldoni: *Il ventaglio* ('The fan'). C. Gozzi: *L'augellin belverde* ('The pretty little green bird'). The Venetian Ferdinando Facchinei publishes his refutation of Beccaria. Mme Riccoboni: *Ernestine*. *Ephémérides du citoyen* (journal of the Physiocrats: to 1772).
1766	Fights a duel over an actress with Count Franciszek Branicki, wounding him severely. Though obliged to leave Poland, he does so with a reputation considerably enhanced. To Dresden, where he sees his mother and sister but again fails to obtain a lottery licence.	Bettinelli: *Lettere inglesi*. Turgot: *Réflexions sur la formation et la distribution des richesses*. Lessing: *Laocöon, or the Boundaries between Painting and Poetry*. Smollett: *Travels through France and Italy*.

CHRONOLOGY

Frederick the Great engages in a decade of reconstruction following the Seven Years' War. He reforms the currency, abolishes internal tariffs, takes measures to improve industry, transport and agriculture and to introduce compulsory education. Far from demobilizing, he also greatly expands his army (in 1765 he opens the new War Academy Casanova was uninterested in, staffed by famous savants).

Russo-Prussian alliance to control Poland; Count Stanislas Poniatowski is elected, becoming Stanislas II Augustus, the last King of Poland. He instigates some short-lived reforms, attempting to curb the power of the Polish magnates; further reforms blocked by Russia and Prussia.

Jesuits expelled from France. Death of Madame de Pompadour.

Sir William Hamilton, diplomat, antiquarian and art collector, appointed British Envoy Extraordinary (Ambassador 1767) in Naples (to 1800).

Giovanni Paisiello's first comic opera (he would write over 100) – *Il ciarlone*.

Founding of the Amigos del País in Spain to encourage agriculture, industry, arts and sciences.

Catherine II engaged in overhaul of Russia's administrative structure. Showing great interest in the ideas of the Enlightenment she maintains a correspondence with French *Encylopédistes*, including Voltaire, Diderot and d'Alembert.

On the death of his father Francis I, Joseph II becomes Holy Roman Emperor and co-ruler with his mother Maria Theresa of the Habsburg territories. Grand Duke Leopold becomes ruler of Tuscany (to 1790). Grenville's Stamp Act antagonizes American colonists.

Many of Giovanni Battista Casanova's best drawings published as illustrations in *Antichità di Ercolano* ('Antiquities of Herculaneum'), commissioned by Charles VII, Bourbon King of Naples and continued by his son Ferdinand IV.

Boucher becomes court painter to Louis XV.

Death of James Edward Stuart ('The Old Pretender') in Rome; his son Charles Edward takes up residence in Rome (to 1774) but unlike his father is not recognized as King of Great Britain by the Pope.

Lorraine formally incorporated in France on the death of Stanislas Leszczynski.

Esquilache riots in Spain; the Count de Aranda leads the government after Charles III, having conceded to the rioters' demands, flees the city, and helps to negotiate a peaceful solution; 6-year programme of reform begins.

Salieri leaves school in Venice to continue his musical studies in Vienna where he spends most of his life, composing more than 40 operas and becoming Kapellmeister in 1788. Venetian artist Bellotti employed in Warsaw by Stanislas II of Poland (to 1780). Cavendish isolates hydrogen.

DATE	AUTHOR'S LIFE	LITERARY CONTEXT
1767	To Vienna where he breaks the gambling laws and is expelled from the city. To Paris, where Louis XV issues a *lettre de cachet*, ordering him out of France – probably at the request of the d'Urfé family. Heads for Spain. Death in Venice of his faithful friend and patron Matteo Bragadin.	Holbach: *Le Christianisme dévoilé*. Voltaire: *L'Ingénu*. Catherine the Great's *Instruction to the Commission for the Compilation of a New Code of Laws*.
1768	To Madrid. He quickly manages to be arrested, imprisoned and excommunicated. Affair with Ignacia. Gains friendship of King Charles III's chief minister, the Count de Aranda, a Freemason. Seeks involvement in project to establish a Swiss-German colony in the Sierra Morena but falls foul of the Venetian ambassador and is advised to leave. To Barcelona, where he is seduced by Nina Bergonzi, mistress of Count Ricla, Captain General of Catalonia. The Count sends two assassins to dispatch him in a dark alley. Casanova runs his sword through one of them. Arrested at the instigation of an old enemy, Giacomo Passano, he spends six weeks in prison while his papers are checked, filling the hours with writing his refutation of de la Houssaye's derogatory *Histoire du gouvernement de Venise*.	Baretti: *An Account of the Manners and Customs of Italy*. Crébillon *fils*: *Lettres de la duchesse de ****. Frederick the Great: *Political Testament*. Fanny Burney begins her Diary (to 1840; published 1842–6 and 1889). Sterne: *A Sentimental Journey through France and Italy*.
1769	To France again. Falls seriously ill at Aix-en-Provence and is nursed by a mysterious old woman who turns out to have been sent to him by Henriette, whom he had loved twenty years previously. She forbids him to visit her but the two begin a correspondence which lasts many years. Meets Giuseppe Balsamo, the future Count	Rousseau: *Considérations sur le gouvernement de Pologne*. Correspondence between Mme de l'Epinay and Fernando Galiani begins (to 1782; first published 1818).

CHRONOLOGY

The Venetian government suppresses 127 monasteries and convents, almost halving the monastic population, and raising three million ducats by the sale of their lands.

Catherine II's Legislative Committee meets. Expulsion of Jesuits from Spain. Gluck's preface to *Alceste* sets out the aims of his 'reform' of opera. Paisiello's first big success, *L'Idola cinese* (Naples). Fragonard paints *The Swing*. Priestley: *History and Present State of Electricity*.

Russo-Turkish war (to 1774), resulting in considerable territorial gains for Russia. French purchase of Corsica from the Genoese.

Bar Confederation formed in Poland: Polish magnates rebel against Stanislas II's reforms and against Russian interference. Armed struggle continues until 1772.

Angelo Emo put in command of the Venetian navy with instructions to take action against pirates – which he does with some success.

Outbreaks of violence in the city-state of Geneva, following demands that power should be shared more widely amongst its citizens (and again in 1782). First census in Spain, instigated by the Count de Aranda.

Sopra la riproduzioni animali: Spallanzani's first important work on animal reproduction (Spallanzani would in 1780 perform the first artificial insemination, using a dog).

Death of Canaletto.

The young Joseph II visits Venice incognito; the extravagance of the festivities planned in his honour provokes anti-government feeling. Opposition to the established order increases as young intellectuals and nobles excluded from the governing class question the indebtedness of the Republic, and the concentration of power in the hands of a declining number of very rich families; they find a spokesman in Giorgio Pisani.

Death of Pope Clement XIII, succeeded by Clement XIV (to 1774).

Maria Theresa and Count Firmian engaged in reforming education in Lombardy, developing both the University of Pavia (where the biologist Spallanzani becomes Professor of Natural History this year) and the Palatine Schools (where the poet Parini is appointed to a newly-created Chair of Belles-Lettres).

DATE	AUTHOR'S LIFE	LITERARY CONTEXT
1769 *cont.*	Cagliostro, like Casanova one of the 18th century's great charlatans. To Lugano, Italy, where he publishes his *Confutazione*, hoping to mollify the Venetian authorities.	
1770	Turin, Parma, Bologna, Pisa, the baths of S. Giuliano (where he meets Bonnie Prince Charlie, now fat and 51), Leghorn, Pisa again, Siena, Rome, Naples, womanizing and gambling all the way, now losing more than he wins. In Naples his chief cronies are Tommaso Medini and Ange Goudar, adventurers-cum-writers like himself. Also becomes friendly with the British consul Sir William Hamilton. In Salerno he visits Donna Lucrezia and their daughter Leonilda, now married to a 71-year-old marquis whose dearest wish is for a son and heir. Casanova, as a fellow Mason, obliges, and Leonilda's son is born the following year. In Rome he joins the circle of his old friend Cardinal de Bernis, French ambassador. Enjoys initiating the inmates of a convent to the ways of high society.	Baretti: *A Journey from London to Genoa, through England, Portugal, Spain and France.* Martinelli: *Istoria d'Inghilterra* (to 1773; first history of England to be written in Italian). Galiani: *Dialogue sur le commerce des blés* (attacks Physiocrat doctrines). Holbach: *Système de la nature.* Chamfort: *Le Marchand de Smyrne.*
1771	Becomes a member of two famous literary Academies, the *L'Accademia degli Arcadi* and *L'Accademia degli Infecondi di Roma.* Leaves for Florence in June, resolving to change his mode of life but before long is lured back into the old habits and accordingly expelled from the city in December.	P. Verri: *Meditazioni sull'economia politica.* Goldoni: *Le Bourru bienfaisant.* Crébillon *fils*: *Lettres athéniennes.* Mackenzie: *The Man of Feeling.* Smollett: *Humphrey Clinker.* Catherine the Great embarks on her memoirs.
1772	In Bologna works on his translation of the *Iliad* into modern Tuscan and publishes *Lana caprina*, a satire on the	Tiraboschi: *Storia della letteratura italiani* (to 1782). Galiani: *Dialogue sur les femmes.* Lessing: *Emilia Galotti.*

CHRONOLOGY

Mengs decorating the Camera di Papiri in the Vatican (to 1772).
Improved steam engine using condenser designed by James Watt.
Volta's first study in electricity, *De vi attractiva ignis electrici.*

Death of G. B. Tiepolo. His last commission had been to decorate the throne rooms in the Royal Palace at Madrid.
In desperation the Estates of Württemberg call for imperial and foreign (Prussian, British and Danish) intervention to control the despotic government of Karl Eugen: a formal compromise (*Erbvergleich*) is reached.
Famine in Bohemia and Saxony.
Marriage of the Dauphin and Marie-Antoinette, daughter of Empress Maria Theresa.

Parlement of Paris exiled by Maupeou.
Du Tillot is dismissed by Ferdinand, Duke of Parma, who had succeeded his father in 1765. The period of reform comes to an end, and the Jesuits are allowed to return.
Duke Francesco III of Modena promulgates the Este Code, a new law code influenced by Enlightenment principles of equality and reason. He also transfers his court to Varese – territory granted him for life by the Habsburg Empire.
Mozart (aged 15) visits Venice during a 2-year sojourn in Italy with his father. Grétry: *Zémire et Azor.*
First partition of Poland, which loses nearly a third of her territory to Russia, Austria and Prussia.

DATE	AUTHOR'S LIFE	LITERARY CONTEXT
1772 *cont.*	condition of women. His quest to return to Venice is advanced by correspondence with Pietro Zaguri, a young Venetian nobleman who undertakes to plead his cause, and on whose advice he transfers, via Ancona (enlivened by an affair with Leah) to Trieste, where the Venetian State Inquisitors can more easily keep an eye on his mode of life.	
1773	In Trieste and Görz, works on his *Istoria delle turbolenze della Polonia* ('History of the Polish upheavals'). Performs various services for the Republic in order to ingratiate himself with the Venetian authorities.	Diderot: *Jacques le fataliste.* Diderot in Russia (to 1774). Herder edits *Of German Character and Art* ('Storm and Stress' manifesto).
1774	Affair with actress Irene Rinaldi – the last to be described in his memoirs. His political manoeuverings finally pay off and he is granted permission to return to Venice. His 18-year exile at an end, he enters the city on 11 September. Living with Marco Dandolo (friend of his late protector, Bragadin), he hopes to support himself by his pen. First volume of his Polish history published.	First edition of Lord Chesterfield's letters to his son. Goethe: *The Sorrows of Young Werther.* De Ligne: *Lettres à Eugénie sur les spectacles.*
1775	First volume of his *Iliad* published. His literary projects proving insufficiently lucrative, Casanova supplements his income by turning government informant, taking up a position as part-time secretary to Carlo Spinoza, a Genoese diplomat (and an old gambling acquaintance) in whose activities the Inquisitors are interested.	Alfieri's first tragedy, *Cleopatra*, performed in Turin. Galiani/Lorenzi: *Socrate immaginario* set by Paisiello. Beaumarchais: *Le Barbier de Séville.* Sheridan: *The Rivals.* Johnson: *A Journey to the Western Islands of Scotland.* Charke: *A Narrative of the Life of Mrs Charlotte Charke.*
1776	Under the alias of Antonio Pratolini, he is hired on a casual basis as a spy, submitting reports on many matters adversely	Arcadian poetess Maria Morelli ('Corilla Olimpica') crowned as Poet Laureate on the Capitoline Hill in Rome.

CHRONOLOGY

Pope Clement XIV suppresses the Jesuit order. Peasant revolt in Russia led by Pugachev (to 1775). Boston Tea Party.

Death of Louis XV of France; succeeded by his grandson, Louis XVI. Fall of Maupeou and recall of the *parlements*. Turgot Comptroller-General of Finances (to 1776).
In Venice the Great Council decrees that the principal casino – the Ridotto at S. Moisè – be closed and that all 'games of hazard' be prohibited. However, gambling continues unabated.
With the *Allgemeine Schulordnung* the Habsburgs begin to create the first truly universal sysem of education in Europe.
Gluck's *Iphigénie en Aulide* produced in Paris. Goya enters royal service in Spain, becoming principal court painter in 1789. Priestley discovers oxygen.

In Venice a proposal to offer seats on the Great Council for sale to a further forty families is adopted after fierce debate; in the event, only ten families avail themselves of the opportunity. Pius VI becomes Pope. Catherine II's reform of provincial government in Russia. Peasant revolt in Bohemia.

American Declaration of Independence. War until 1783, with France (1778) and Spain (1779) also fighting against Britain.

DATE	AUTHOR'S LIFE	LITERARY CONTEXT
1776 *cont.*	affecting religion, morals, public security, commerce and manufacture. Death of Manon Blondel (*née* Balletti). Death of his mother in Dresden.	Martinelli: *Storia del Governo d'Inghilterra e delle sue colonie in India e nell'America settentrionale.* Mably: *De la Législation.* Haller: *Bibliotecae Practicae* (medical bibliography) (to 1788). Klinger: *Storm and Stress.* Gibbon: *The Decline and Fall of the Roman Empire* (to 1788). Smith: *The Wealth of Nations.*
1777	Second volume of Casanova's *Iliad* published. Death of Bettina Gozzi, his very first love, in Casanova's arms, and of La Charpillon.	P. Verri: *Osservazioni sulla tortura; Riccordi a mia figlia.* Baretti: *Discours sur Shakespeare et sur Monsieur Voltaire.* De Ligne: *Céphalide* (libretto). Sheridan: *The School for Scandal.*
1778	Publication of the third volume of his history of Poland, and the third volume of the *Iliad*. The printer refuses to print any more without payment, and both projects come to a final halt.	Death of Voltaire (whose library is purchased by Catherine the Great) and Rousseau. Casti writing his *Novelle galanti* (to 1802). Burney: *Evelina.*
1779	Publishes a bitterly critical response to a volume of eulogies of Voltaire. Moves out of Dandolo's house to set up home with Francesca Buschini, a seamstress, who is devoted to him. He remains with her until he leaves Venice and corresponds with her for some years after his departure. Spends two months in Ancona on government business (and renewing his affair with Leah).	Galanti: *Elogio de Niccolò Machiavelli.* Mme de Genlis: *Théâtre d'Education* (4 vols, to 1780). Lessing: *Nathan the Wise.* Ignacy Krasicki: *Fables and Parables; Satires.* Johnson: *Lives of the English Poets* (to 1781).
1780	He is transferred to the civil service, receiving a regular monthly salary.	Filangieri: *La scienza della legislazione.* Alessandro Verri: *Le avventure di Saffo poetessa di mitilene.* Wieland: *Oberon.*

CHRONOLOGY

Andrea Tron – dominant political figure in Venice – introduces severe anti-Jewish legislation, effectively debarring Jews from playing a role in Venetian commerce. Death without heirs of Maximilian III Joseph of Bavaria; succeeded by Karl Theodor, Elector Palatine, reuniting the two states and provoking the War of Bavarian Succession (1778–9).
Gluck's *Armide* (Paris).

Death of Doge Mocenigo. Death of 'Bonnie Prince Charlie' in Rome. Mozart's 'Paris' Symphony. Cimarosa's first big success, *L'Italiana in Londra* (Rome). Salieri visits Italy (to 1780): his opera *Europa riconosciuta* premiered at at the newly built opera house of La Scala, Milan.

Election of Paolo Renier – well-known for his veniality – as Doge. By the Treaty of Teschen Karl Theodor is confirmed as Elector of Bavaria (to 1799), losing some territory to Austria. In Bavaria (in contrast to the Palatinate) his rule is characterized by narrow clericalism, and he is deeply unpopular. Unsuccessful siege of Gibraltar (to 1782) by Spanish and French troops. Triumph of Gluck's *Iphigénie en Tauride* in Paris ends the squabble between his partisans and those of Piccinni.

Death of Maria Theresa. Joseph II in sole control of the Habsburg territories.
The radical Giorgio Pisani is elected Procurator of St Mark, and, together with Carlo Contarino, embarks on a vociferous campaign against government corruption and inefficiency. Both are arrested and imprisoned. Spallanzani interprets the process of digestion: *Dissertazioni di fisica animale e vegetabile.*

DATE	AUTHOR'S LIFE	LITERARY CONTEXT
1780–81	Arranges for a company of French actors to visit Venice and starts a weekly magazine to publicize performances. Written entirely in French – by Casanova himself – it fails to find a market. Brings out seven issues of another magazine, *Opuscoli miscellanei*, which folds due to the usual lack of funds.	
1781	Turns in information against his former guardian, the Abbé Grimani (May) – possibly the reason why he is dismissed from his salaried employment at the end of the year.	Alfieri: *America libera* (5 odes). Schiller: *The Robbers*. Kant: *Critique of Pure Reason*. De Ligne: *Coup d'oeil sur Beloeil et les principaux jardins de l'Europe*.
1782	Publication of his *Venetian Anecdotes*. Hired to secure payment of a debt of honour from Carlo Spinoza to one Signor Carletti, Casanova becomes involved in an ugly brawl at the palace of Carlo Grimani. Accused of cowardice, in revenge he writes *Né amori né donne*, a scandalous attack on the patrician society of Venice, in which he reveals publicly for the first time that he is the illegitimate son of Michele Grimani. He also claims that Carlo Grimani is a bastard. He is ordered by the State Procurator to leave Venice for ever.	Casti becomes court poet in Vienna (to 1796) on the death of Metastasio. Alfieri: *Saul*. A. Verri: *Le notti romane* (to 1790). Rousseau: *Les Confessions* (and 1789); *Les Rêveries du promeneur solitaire*. Laclos: *Les Liaisons dangereuses*.
1783	Casanova departs on 17 January. Wanders throughout the cities of Europe seeking employment. In September reaches Paris where he stays with his brother Francesco, meets Benjamin Franklin, and considers joining an expedition to Madagascar. Death of his brother Gaetano.	Alfieri's first ten tragedies published in Siena (includes *Antigone*, *Filippo* and *Timoleone*).

CHRONOLOGY

HISTORICAL EVENTS

Planet Uranus discovered by Herschel.

Numerous reforms introduced by Joseph II (to 1785), amongst them the partial abolition of serfdom; introduction of religious toleration; abolition of the Inquisititon and confiscation of monastic lands; judicial reform including abolition of the death penalty; relaxation of state censorship; a protectionist policy to promote industry.

Last man to be burnt alive for a religious offence executed in Seville – even in Spain, where Catholicism is stronger than any other major state, the power of the Inquisition is rapidly declining.

Mozart's *Idomeneo* performed in Munich.

Pope Pius VI visits Venice – the first visit by a reigning Pope since 1177. Completion of the *murazzi* – gigantic sea walls, some 4 kilometres long, begun in 1744.

Grand Duke Leopold of Tuscany presents his subjects with a constitution – while it remains a paper scheme only, it is the climax of a highly successful programme of reform of his dominions inspired by theories of the Enlightenment.

Paisiello's setting of *Il barbiere di Siviglia* premiered in St Petersburg, where he is serving as court composer to Catherine the Great; this becomes very popular throughout Italy. Mozart's first concert in Vienna. *The Abduction from the Seraglio* performed by command of Joseph II; 'Haffner' Symphony composed. Fuseli: *The Nightmare.*

Princess Dashkova appointed President of the Russian Academy of Sciences.

The Venetian Senate rejects proposals for a treaty of trade and friendship with the United States of America. Treaty of Versailles ends the American War of Independence. William Pitt the Younger becomes chief minister in Britain.

Lo sposo di tre (Goldoni/Cherubini) premiered in Venice. Haydn: *Armida* (last opera for the Eszerháza). Piccinni: *Didon* (Paris). First manned flight in a hot air balloon (France).

Fashionable portrait painter (and later memoirist) Elisabeth Vigée-Lebrun (1755–1842) appointed to the Paris's Royal Academy by Marie-Antoinette.

GIACOMO CASANOVA

DATE	AUTHOR'S LIFE	LITERARY CONTEXT
1784	In Vienna (February) Casanova is employed by Sebastiano Foscarini, Venetian ambassador to the Empire. He prepares papers for the negotiations between the Dutch and the Venetians and composes his *Lettre historico-critique sur un fait connu, dépendant d'une cause peu connue,* a presentation of the Venetian cause in the dispute. Falls in love with a young woman, Caton, and considers marriage. Introduced to Count Josef Karl Emmanuel von Waldstein, a fellow Freemason with an interest in magic, whose offer of employment at his castle in Dux, Bohemia, Casanova has no alternative but to take up after Foscarini's death in April.	Alfieri: *Mirra* (to 1786). Da Ponte appointed poet to the Court Opera in Vienna (to 1792). Beaumarchais: *Le Mariage de Figaro.* Sade writes *Les 120 Journées de Sodome* (to 1785). Necker: *Traité de l'administration des finances de France.* Herder: *Outline of a Philosophical History of Humanity* (to 1791). Schiller: *Intrigue and Love.*
1784–98	For the cosmopolitan Casanova, Dux feels like a prison. The Count is often absent and he does not get on with the other inmates of the castle. However, he is not completely isolated, receiving and paying visits, particularly to his old friend the Prince de Ligne at Teplitz. Casanova's post of librarian also affords him ample time for writing.	Pindemonte: *Prose e poesie campestri* ('Prose and poetry of the countryside') (1784–8).
1785		Cesarotti: *Saggio sulla filosofia delle lingue.* Schiller: 'Ode to Joy'. Boswell: *The Journal of a Tour to the Hebrides.*
1786	Publishes *Soliloque d'un penseur* in a vain attempt to attract the patronage of Emperor Joseph II and thus escape from Dux. Dallies briefly with Anna Kleer, daughter of the castle porter. Last letter from Francesca Buschini, still devoted, now reduced to penury.	Goethe: *Iphigenia in Tauris.* Bürger: *Wonderful Travels on Water and Land ... Adventures of Baron Münchhausen.* Hester Thrale Piozzi: *Anecdotes of the Late Samuel Johnson.*

CHRONOLOGY

Holland declares war on Venice (9 January) after the Venetian government refuses to compensate Dutch merchants defrauded by Venetian citizens with the connivance of the Venetian envoy to Holland. Joseph II offers to mediate.

Paisiello: *Il rè Teodoro in Venezia* (text by Casti) first performed in Vienna.

Grètry: *Richard Coeur-de-Lion* (Paris).

Catherine the Great's Charter to the Nobility.

Casanova's fellow charlatan Count Cagliostro at the height of his career as a magician, healer, soothsayer and alchemist; his séances are all the rage amongst fashionable Parisian society. By the end of the year, however, he is implicated in the Affair of the Diamond Necklace and imprisoned in the Bastille for six months.

Death of Frederick the Great. He had turned Prussia into an economically strong, politically reformed state, as well as a great military power. Accession of Frederick William II.

After a two-year naval war, Angelo Emo and a tiny Venetian fleet force the Bey of Tunis into submission on favourable terms, and the Mediterranean is finally made safe for European shipping.

Statute of State Education in Russia.

Mozart's 'Prague' Symphony. Mozart/Da Ponte (after Beaumarchais): *Le nozze di Figaro.*

GIACOMO CASANOVA

DATE	AUTHOR'S LIFE	LITERARY CONTEXT
1787	Visits Prague where there is evidence that he met Mozart. He renews acqaintance with Mozart's librettist da Ponte and may have been associated in some way with the libretto of *Don Giovanni*, which opens in Prague on 29 October.	Goldoni: *Mémoires de M. Goldoni*. Da Ponte produces librettos (to 1788) for Mozart (*Don Giovanni*), Salieri (*Axur, re d'Ormus*) and Martín y Soler (*L'Arbore di Diana*). Alfieri publishes his 'four tragedies of liberty' (to 1789) including *Bruto Primo*, dedicated to George Washington. Louvet: *Les Amours du chevalier de Faublas* (to 1789). Touring her southern territories with Catherine the Great, the Prince de Ligne writes his picturesque *Lettres à la marquise de Coigny*. Schiller: *Don Carlos*.
1788	Visits Dresden and Leipzig. Publishes an account of his escape from the Leads, and a 5-volume proto science-fiction novel, *Icosameron* – a financial disaster.	Goldoni: Collected edition of his works published in Venice (to 1789). Alfieri publishes his five political treatises, including *Della tirannide*, in one volume. La Bretonne: *Les Nuits de Paris* (to 1794). First publication of the memoirs of the duc de Saint-Simon (1675–1755). Schiller: *The Gods of Greece*. Kant: *Critique of Practical Reason*.
1789	Casanova becomes increasingly depressed and considers suicide. The French Revolution shocks him deeply, the girls have run out, his vendettas against the castle staff intensify.	Baffo: Complete Works (poems) (posthumous publication). Alfieri: *Rime* (sonnets). Bernadin de St Pierre: *Paul et Virginie*. Mme de Staël: *Lettres sur Rousseau*. Equiano: *The Interesting Narrative of the Life of Olaudah Equiano*.

CHRONOLOGY

Russo-Turkish War (to 1792) in which the Russians make further territorial gains. Washington chosen as first President of the United States of Amercia (inaugurated in 1789).
Gazzaniga: *Don Giovanni Tenorio* (Venice).

Joseph II enters Russo-Turkish war as Russia's ally. Casanova's friend the Prince de Ligne, appointed a field-marshal by Catherine II, is present at the siege of Belgrade. Revolt of Hungarian nobles against Joseph II's extension of his administrative reforms, and particularly against his rigorous policy of Germanization. The 'Great Sejm' meets in Poland (to 1792) – intended to raise money to support Russia's war against Turkey it is dominated by politicians intent upon internal reform and independence from Russia. Stanislas II lends his support to the Patriotic Party from 1790 and a constitution is adopted in 1791.
Death of Charles III of Spain; accession of Charles IV.

Death of Paolo Renier and election of Lodovico Manin as 118th – and last – Doge of Venice.
Joseph II attempts to impose a new constitution on the Belgian Estates: when it is rejected, an Austrian army invades Brussels. A patriotic army is raised and by the end of the year, independence has been declared.
(Prominent among the rebels were relatives of the Prince de Ligne, himself from Hainault but also a friend of the Emperor; asked to lead them he politely declined, saying he 'never revolted in the winter').
French Revolution. Meeting of the States General; Third Estate adopt title of National Assembly. Storming of the Bastille; abolition of feudal privileges; secularization of church lands.
Joseph II attempts to alleviate the condition of the peasantry by abolishing the *corvée* and setting a maximum tax rate of 30 per cent on produce in the Habsburg dominions.
Lavoisier: *Elementary Treatise on Chemistry*.

GIACOMO CASANOVA

DATE	AUTHOR'S LIFE	LITERARY CONTEXT
1790	Begins work on his *Histoire de ma vie*. Publishes three mathematical studies on the problem of the duplication of the cube.	Galanti: *Nova descrizione storica e geografica delle Sicilie.* Rousseau: *Considérations sur le gouvernement de Pologne* (written 1771). Maffei: Collected Works. Radischev: *Journey from St Petersburg to Moscow.*
1791	Visits Prague for the coronation of Leopold II. Meets and is much impressed by a young Italian marquis, his son by his own daughter Leonilda. Turns down Leonilda's offer of a home with her in Salerno.	Sade: *Justine.* Louvet: *Emilie de Varmont.* Boswell: *Life of Samuel Johnson* Paine: *Rights of Man.*
1792	The feud at the castle having turned extremely nasty, the Count dismisses Casanova's principal antagonists, the major-domo 'Faulkircher' and his henchman 'Viderol' (Casanova's nicknames for them). Ennui sets in after the departure of his adversaries. Finishes the first draft of his memoirs about this time.	Alfieri: *Vita* (first draft of his memoirs, published posthumously in 1804). C. Gozzi: Collected Works (10 vols) published in Venice. Florian: *Fables.* Franklin: *Autobiography* (published in French in Paris). Chénier: *Hymnes sur les Suisses.* Young: *Travels in France.* Wollstonecraft: *A Vindication of the Rights of Woman.*
1793		Death of Goldoni.

CHRONOLOGY

French agents seeking to spread revolutionary ideas throughout Italy; the Venetian government tightens its grip against radicalism in the Republic. Beginning of revolution in Switzerland; numerous petitions from the peasants presented throughout the 1790s. Joseph revokes most of his reforms in Hungary (January). After his death (February) armed rebellion is only narrowly averted. Joseph's brother Leopold, Grand Duke of Tuscany, succeeds him as Emperor.

Mozart/Da Ponte: *Così fan tutte* first performed at the Burgtheater, Vienna. Louis XVI accepts new constitution; attempts flight but is arrested. Re-entry of Austrian forces into Brussels and end of the Belgian revolt.

Victor Emmanuel of Sardinia invites Venice to join a league of Italian Princes to resist the Jacobin threat; Venice, still hoping to remain neutral, declines.

Leopold II is crowned King of Bohemia – the last monarch to hold that title. Mozart: *La clemenza di Tito* (a commission from the Bohemian government to celebrate Leopold II's coronation in Prague); *The Magic Flute*; Requiem. Death of Mozart. In a move to conciliate Czech nationalists Leopold founds a Chair in the Czech language at the Charles University of Prague. The Prince de Ligne is made Captain-General of Hainault.

Cagliostro arrested and later sentenced to death by the Inquisition for attempting to set up a Masonic Lodge in Rome. The sentence is commuted to life imprisonment and he dies six years later in the castle of San Leo, near Montefeltro.

France declared a Republic. Paris mob invades the Tuileries (10 August). September massacre of Royalists. Outbreak of French Revolutionary Wars. French military successes in the Rhineland. Dumouriez overruns the Austrian Netherlands. French occupation of Nice and Savoy. Venice refuses to join Sardinia and Naples in a neutral defensive league.

In Poland Confederation of Targowica enlists Russian and Prussian aid against the Patriotic Party; capitulation of Stanislas II.

Death of Emperor Leopold II. He is succeeded by his son as Francis II, the last Holy Roman Emperor.

Revolution in Geneva brings down the ruling oligarchy.

Cimarosa: *Il matrimonio segreto* (Vienna). Completion of the Fenice theatre in Venice.

Louis XVI and later Queen Marie-Antoinette guillotined. Austria retakes the Netherlands. French Constitution of 1793 voted. Committee of Public Safety. Reign of Terror. Assassination of Marat. Royalist risings in the Vendée (to 1796). Approached once more by Great Britain, Austria, Prussia, Spain and Sardinia to join their coalition for the defence of Europe, Venice refuses. The Senate even votes against breaking off diplomatic relations with France. Only Francesco Pessaro argues that – given Venice's position in the centre of the war zone – neutrality would only work if backed by strength, and calls upon the Republic to re-arm.

Second partition of Poland: Russia and Prussia make vast gains.

David: *Death of Marat.*

GIACOMO CASANOVA

DATE	AUTHOR'S LIFE	LITERARY CONTEXT
1794		Louvet: *Monsieur Nicolas.* Chénier: *Le Jeune Captive.* Fichte: *Doctrine of Knowledge.* Godwin: *Caleb Williams.*
1795	In a last attempt to escape from the isolation of Dux, Casanova visits Weimar, Dresden and Berlin in a futile quest for employment as a librarian or writer. Death of his brother Giovanni.	Bertola: *Viaggio sul Reno e ne' suoi contorni* ('Travels on the Rhine and its banks').
1796	Reworks the manuscript of his memoirs.	Laplace: *Système du monde.* Goethe: *Hermann and Dorothea.* Gibbon: *Memoirs of My Life and Writing.* Wollstonecraft: *Letters Written During a Short Residence in Sweden, Norway and Denmark.* Mary Hays: *Memoirs of Emma Courtney.* Charles Burney: *Memoirs and Letters of Metastasio.*
1797	Publishes *A Léonard Snetlage*, a criticism of Snetlage's new French dictionary. Writes the Preface to his memoirs.	C. Gozzi: *Memorie inutili* (memoirs). Casti: *Poem tartaro* ('Tartar poem'). De Bernis: *Oeuvres melées en prose et en vers* (posthumous publication). De Bernis's memoirs and correspondence are published in 1878. Chateaubriand: *Essai sur les révolutions.* De Ligne: *Mélanges militaires, littéraires et sentimentaires* (34 vols to 1811). Hölderlin: *Hyperion.* Schlegel: *Ideas towards a Philosophy of Nature.*

CHRONOLOGY

HISTORICAL EVENTS

French victory at Fleurus and reconquest of the Netherlands. Execution of Dantonists. Execution of the poet Chénier and the scientist Lavoisier. Fall of Robespierre. Jacobin Club closed. New law code passed in Prussia. Volta begins the experiments which in 1800 end with his demonstration of the first electric battery.

French armies subdue Holland; the Batavian Republic set up as a satellite state. Prussia and Spain make peace with France. Death of Louis XVII. Revolt of 13 vendémiaire; dissolution of the Convention; rule of the Directory begins.

French forces win their first victory against the Austrians at Loano, on Italian soil. Venice antagonizes France by allowing Austrian troops to cross her territory.

Third partition of Poland dismembers the country completely; abdication of Stanislas II Augustus.

France strikes at Austria through Italy, Bonaparte leading the successful campaign. In April Sardinia surrenders, losing Savoy and Nice to France. Bonaparte defeats the Austrians at the Bridge of Lodi and takes Milan in May. Routs Austrian forces at Castiglione in August. Niccolò Foscarini appointed *Proveditor-Generale in Terra Firma*, proving no match for Bonaparte who by threat of force and skilful diplomacy gains from Venice control of Verona. Half-hearted attempts made by the Senate to mobilize the remains of the navy and to strengthen the army; these are swiftly abandoned. Bonaparte repeatedly offers Venice an alliance (August to October) but is refused.

Death of Catherine the Great. Jenner creates successful smallpox vaccine. Bonaparte wins Battle of Rivoli. Fall of Mantua to French (February) leaves Italy free from Austrian control. Bonaparte marches on Vienna. Radicals in Bergamo, Brescia and Crema, incited by French officers, rebel against Venetian rule. Venice raises a militia to quell the revolt; instead peasant soldiers attack the French, to avenge their depredations in the countryside. Venice is forced to make a humiliating apology. French troops suppress a rising against them in Verona at Easter. Bonaparte makes a provisional peace with the Austrians at Leoben (18 April); secretly he offers them some Venetian territory, in spite of Venice's neutrality. Rashly, Venetians fire on a French ship attempting to enter their harbour, killing five (20 April). Bonaparte formally declares war. The Great Council votes to accept his ultimatum (abandonment of their constitution; acceptance of democracy) before most of the terrified patricians flee. The city is occupied by the French whose Democratic Republic (May) is far from democratic. Lombardy, Bologna and Modena become the Cisalpine Republic; Genoa becomes the Ligurian Republic. In October, by the Treaty of Campo Formio, Bonaparte hands Venice over to the Austrians. The Emperor recognizes French annexations of the Austrian Netherlands, the left bank of the Rhine and Northern Italy. Britain the only member of the First Coalition still in arms against France. Coup d'état of 18 fructidor in France: moderates purged from councils.

DATE	AUTHOR'S LIFE	LITERARY CONTEXT
1798	Develops a septic infection of the genito-urinary tract (weakened by at least 11 bouts of venereal disease and the mercury used in their treatment). Dies on 4 June, his last words allegedly 'I have lived as a philosopher and die as a Christian'.	Schiller: *Wallenstein*. Godwin: *Memoirs of the Author of a Vindication of the Rights of Woman*. Wordsworth and Coleridge: *Lyrical Ballads*. Dorothy Wordsworth: *Visit to Hamburgh and a Journey ... to Goslar 1798–9*.
1809		*Lettres et pensées du field-maréchal prince de Ligne* with a preface by Mme de Staël.
1812–14		Publication of the correspondence of Baron von Grimm (1723–1807).
1814		Death of the Prince de Ligne. His memoirs, *Fragments de l'histoire de ma vie*, remain unpublished until 1927.
1818		Publication of letters and correspondence of Mme d'Epinay (1726–83 as *Histoire de Madame de Monbrillant*; also of Abbé Galiani (1728–87).
1822	A German version of the memoirs published (to 1828) in an adapted version by the Leipzig publisher F. A. Brockhaus.	Memoirs of André Morellet (1727–1819) published. First volume of Horace Walpole's memoirs published.
1823		Memoirs of Lorenzo da Ponte (1749–1838) published.
1825		Memoirs of Mme de Genlis (1746–1830) published.
1826	Publication of *L'Histoire de ma vie*, heavily edited, by the same publisher (to 1838).	

HISTORICAL EVENTS

France annexes Geneva. Revolution in Vaud gives the French the
opportunity to invade Switzerland, establishing the Helvetic Republic;
the Papal States are also overrun and a Roman Republic set up.
Napoleon's Egyptian campaign. Nelson's naval victory at Aboukir.

F O R E W O R D

———

Reducing Casanova's memoirs to just under half their original length has not been easy. Although there are times when the author rambles, his rambling usually turns out to have a purpose. Then there are the amours for which the book is notorious. Surely, one seduction differs little from another? But, despite a reputation in which he connived, Casanova was no mere serial seducer: conquest mattered to him less than love. Unlike many a celebrated amorist, he treated women as equals and delighted in distinguishing each of his mistresses as an individual. What appears to be repetition is often fond discrimination.

Furthermore, his erotic adventures, elaborate and varied though they were, form only part of the memoirs. Equally important are the author's travels throughout Europe and the Mediterranean; his detailed accounts of contemporary manners; his activities as con-artist and genuine businessman (often hard to distinguish); his gambling; his dabblings in magic and alternative healing; various literary and theatrical enterprises; and set-piece encounters with the great. Then there are the comic episodes of everyday life in which this narrative abounds: parties, meetings at inns, weddings, the miseries of eighteenth-century travel, medical problems, arguments and rapprochements, money troubles, descriptions of meals and clothes, misunderstandings, fights, flights, expulsions and embarrassments of every kind. These are described in terms which are always piquant and often wonderfully farcical. Without sacrificing his love affairs, I have tried to preserve such aspects of Casanova's life in proportion to their importance in his story.

The author's literary gifts also make the book difficult to abridge. In addition to a genius for page-turning anecdotes, he has what we now think of as the novelist's feeling for large-scale literary architecture. This is apparent in the book's over-all scheme, but also in the shaping of individual interludes (such as his masterly account of how he escaped from the

Doge's prison). Although Casanova left his book unfinished – and heaven knows how long it would have been otherwise – what he completed amounts to far more than a series of random episodes. The memoirs have been compared to a picaresque novel but an analogy with Proust also suggests itself. Characters recur, experiences are repeated in new circumstances, places revisited, philosophies assessed, adventures pondered, all with cumulative force. (For more on Casanova's method of composition, see the translator's textual note on page 1178). As the author ages, shadows fall across the brilliant surface of his story. A Proustian sense of the passage of time appears, compounded by an equally Proustian need to understand the relationship between outward events and personal evolution.

Such features make it essential that any abridgement of the memoirs retains their scope and scale while making them accessible to readers who have other calls on their attention. I have tried to do this by maintaining the major narrative threads throughout, sometimes at the expense of intriguing detours. Where necessary, short linking passages have been included to cover omissions. If such omissions send readers back to the full text of Willard Trask's superb translation, so much the better.

Peter Washington

HISTORY OF MY LIFE

Volume One

CONTENTS

3

8

History of my life to the year 1797*

Nequicquam sapit qui sibi non sapit. Cic. ad Treb.

("He knows nothing who does not draw
profit from what he knows.")[1]

*Casanova was prevented by death from fulfilling this
promise. His memoirs end with the summer of 1774.

PREFACE

I begin by declaring to my reader that, by everything good or bad that I have done throughout my life, I am sure that I have earned merit or incurred guilt, and that hence I must consider myself a free agent. The doctrine of the Stoics,[2] and of any other sect, on the power of Destiny is a figment of the imagination which smacks of atheism. I am not only a monotheist but a Christian whose faith is strengthened by philosophy, which has never injured anything.

I believe in the existence of an immaterial God, creator and lord of all forms; and what proves to me that I have never doubted it is that I have always counted upon his providence, turning to him through prayer in all my tribulations and always finding my prayer granted. Despair kills; prayer dissipates it; and after praying man trusts and acts. What means the Being of Beings employs to avert the evils which hang over those who implore his aid is a question above the power of human intelligence, which, even as it contemplates the incomprehensibility of Divine Providence, cannot but adore it. Our ignorance becomes our only resource; and the truly happy are they who cherish it. So we must pray to God and believe that we have obtained grace even when appearances tell us that we have not. As for the bodily position we should assume when we address our requests to the Creator, a line of Petrarch's[3] instructs us:

Con le ginocchia della mente inchine.

("With the knees of the mind bent.")[4]

Man is a free agent; but he is not free if he does not believe it, for the more power he attributes to Destiny, the more he deprives himself of the power which God granted him when he gave him *reason*.

Reason is a particle of the Creator's divinity. If we use it to make ourselves humble and just, we cannot but please him who gave it to us. God does not cease to be God except for those who consider his nonexistence possible. They cannot suffer a greater punishment.

Though man is free, he must not believe that he is free to do whatever he pleases. He becomes a slave as soon as he decides to act when he is moved by some passion. *Nisi paret imperat* ("Unless it obeys, it commands").[5] He who has the strength to defer acting until he is calm again is the wise man. Such a being is rare.

The reader who likes to think will see in these memoirs that, since I never aimed at a set goal, the only system I followed, if system it may be called, was to let myself go wherever the wind which was blowing drove me. What vicissitudes in this independence from method and system! My ill fortune no less than my good proved to me that both in this physical world and in the moral world good comes from evil as evil comes from good. My errors will show thoughtful readers these opposite roads or will teach them the great art of straddling the ditch. The one thing necessary is courage, for strength without confidence is useless. I have often seen good fortune fall in my lap as the result of some incautious step which should have cast me into the abyss; and, though I blamed myself, I thanked God. On the other hand, I have also seen an overwhelming misfortune follow upon a course of conduct duly weighed by prudence; I was humiliated; but, sure that I had been right, I soon consoled myself.

Despite an excellent moral foundation, the inevitable fruit of the divine principles which were rooted in my heart, I was all my life the victim of my senses; I have delighted in going astray and I have constantly lived in error, with no other consolation than that of knowing I had erred. For this reason I hope, dear reader, that, far from finding my history mere impudent boasting, you will find that it has the tone suited to a general confession, though in the style of my narratives you will find neither a show of repentance nor the constraint of one who blushes to confess his escapades. My follies are the follies of youth. You will see that I laugh at them, and if you are kind you will laugh at them with me.

You will laugh when you discover that I often had no scruples about deceiving nitwits and scoundrels and fools when I found it necessary. As for women, this sort of reciprocal deceit cancels itself out, for when love enters in, both parties are usually dupes. But fools are a very different matter. I always congratulate myself when I remember catching them in my snares, for they are insolent and presumptuous to the point of challenging intelligence. We avenge intelligence when we deceive a fool, and the victory is worth the effort, for a fool is encased in armor and we do not know where to attack him. In short, deceiving a fool is an exploit worthy of an intelligent man. What has infused my very blood with an unconquerable hatred of the whole tribe of fools from the day of my birth is that I become a fool myself whenever I am in their company. They are, however, to be distinguished from the class of men whom we term stupid, for since the stupidity of the latter is due only to their lack of education, I rather like them. I have found some of them who were very decent and whose stupidity was almost a kind of wit. They are like eyes which, but for a cataract, would be extremely beautiful.

If you, my dear reader, will consider the nature of this preface, you will find it easy to see my purpose in it. I have written it because I want you to know me before you read me. It is only at coffee-houses and inns that we converse with strangers.

I have written my story, and no one can object to that. But am I wise to give it to a public of which I know nothing but what is to its discredit? No! I know that I am being unwise. But I need something to occupy me, something to make me laugh; so why should I deny myself?

Expulit elleboro morbum, bilemque meraco.

("He drove out the disease and the bile with pure hellebore.")[6]

An ancient author tells me, in lecture-hall tones: "If thou hast not done things worthy to be written, at least write things worthy to be read."[7] It is a precept as brilliant as a diamond of the first water cut in England,[8] but it does not apply to me, for I am writing neither the biography of a famous man nor a romance. Worthy or unworthy, my life is my subject, my subject is my life. Having lived it without ever thinking that I should take a fancy to write it, it may have an interest which it might not have if I had lived it intending to write it in my old age and, what is more, to publish it.

In this year 1797, at the age of seventy-two, when, though I am still breathing, I can say *vixi* ("I have lived"), I can find no pleasanter pastime than to converse with myself about my own affairs and to provide a most worthy subject for laughter to my well-bred audience, for such is the society which has always shown its friendship for me and which I have always frequented. To write well, I have but to imagine that my readers will belong to it: *Quaecumque dixi, si placuerint, dictavit auditor* ("If what I have said has been pleasing, it is the reader who will have dictated it").[9] As for the uninitiated whom I cannot prevent from reading me, it will be enough for me to know that it was not for them that I wrote.

Remembering the pleasures I enjoyed, I renew them, and I laugh at the pains which I have endured and which I no longer feel. A member of the universe, I speak to the air and I imagine I am rendering an account of my stewardship as the majordomo does to his master, before vanishing. So far as my future is concerned, as a philosopher I have never thought it worth worrying over since I know nothing about it, and as a Christian, I know that faith must believe without arguing and that the purest faith keeps the deepest silence. I know that I have existed, and since I am sure of that because I have felt, I also know that I shall no longer exist when I have ceased to feel. If by any chance I continue to feel after my death, I shall have no more doubts; but I will give the lie to anyone who comes to tell me that I am dead.

Since my history should begin with the earliest fact which my memory can recall to me, it will begin when I had reached the age of eight years and four months. Before then, if it is true that *vivere cogitare est* ("to live is to think"),[10] I did not live, I vegetated. Since human thought consists only in comparisons drawn in order to examine relationships, it cannot precede the existence of memory. The organ of memory did not develop in my head until eight years and four months after my birth; it was only then that my soul began to be capable of receiving impressions. How an immaterial substance which can *nec tangere nec tangi* ("neither touch nor be touched")[11] can receive impressions no man on earth can explain.

A consoling philosophy maintains, in harmony with religion, that the dependence of the soul upon the senses and organs is only fortuitous and temporary and that the soul will be free and happy when the death of the body liberates it from their tyranny. This is all very fine but, religion apart, it is not certain. So, since I cannot be perfectly sure that I am immortal until after I have ceased to live, I may be forgiven if I am in no hurry to learn this truth. A knowledge purchased at the price of life is bought too dearly. Meanwhile, I worship God, I refrain from committing any injustice and shun those who are unjust, though I do nothing to harm them. I am content to abstain from doing them good. Snakes are not to be cherished.

I must also say something about my temperament and my char-acter. Here the most indulgent among my readers will not be those who are least endowed with honesty and intelligence.

I have been of all the four temperaments: the phlegmatic in my childhood, the sanguine in my youth, then the bilious, and

PREFACE

finally the melancholic, which would seem to be with me to
remain. By adapting my diet to my constitution, I have always
enjoyed good health, and having once learned that what impairs it
is always excess, either in eating or in abstaining, I have never had
any physician but myself. But I have found that abstinence is the
more dangerous by far. Too much brings on indigestion, *too little*
kills. At my present advanced age I find that, despite an excellent
stomach, I should eat but once a day, but what makes up to me
for this privation is sweet sleep and the ease with which I set
down my thoughts on paper without any need to indulge in
paradoxes or to weave a tissue of sophisms more apt to deceive
me than my readers, for I could never bring myself to give them
counterfeit coin if I knew it was counterfeit.

The sanguine temperament made me extremely susceptible to
the seduction of any pleasurable sensation, always cheerful, eager to
pass from one enjoyment to another and ingenious in inventing
them. From it came my inclination to make new acquaintances as
well as my readiness to break them off, though always for some good
reason and never from mere fickleness. Defects arising from a
temperament cannot be corrected, because our temperament is
independent of our powers; but character is another matter. It is
constituted by heart and mind and, since temperament has very little
influence here, it follows that character depends on upbringing and
that it can be altered and reformed.

I leave it to others to decide if my character is good or bad, but
such as it is, anyone versed in physiognomy can easily read it in my
face. It is only there that a man's character becomes visible, for
the physiognomy is its seat. It is worth noting that men who
have no physiognomy, and there are a great many such, are equally
lacking in what is called a character. Hence the diversity of physi-
ognomies will be equal to the diversity of characters.

Having observed that I have all my life acted more from the
force of feeling than from my reflections, I have concluded that
my conduct has depended more on my character than on my
mind, after a long struggle between them in which I have alternately found myself with too little intelligence for my character
and too little character for my intelligence. But enough of this, for
it is a matter on which *si brevis esse volo obscurus fio* ("when I try to
be brief, I become obscure").[12] I believe that, without offending
against modesty, I can apply to myself these words from my
beloved Vergil:

19

Nec sum adeo informis: nuper me in litore vidi
Cum placidum ventis staret mare.[13]

("I am not such a monster; lately I saw my reflection by the shore when the sea was calm.")

Cultivating whatever gave pleasure to my senses was always the chief business of my life; I have never found any occupation more important. Feeling that I was born for the sex opposite to mine, I have always loved it and done all that I could to make myself loved by it. I have also been extravagantly fond of good food and irresistibly drawn by anything which could excite curiosity.

I had friends who did me good turns, and I was so fortunate on all such occasions as to have it in my power to show them my gratitude; and I had execrable enemies who persecuted me and whom I did not destroy only because I could not. I would never have forgiven them if I had not forgotten the wrongs they did me. The man who forgets a wrong has not forgiven it, he has simply forgotten it; for forgiveness comes from a heroic sentiment in a noble heart and a magnanimous mind, whereas forgetting comes from weakness of memory or from an easy apathy natural to a pacific soul, and often from a need for peace and quiet; for hatred, in the end, kills the unfortunate man who fosters it.

If anyone calls me a sensualist he will be wrong, for the power of my senses never drew me from my duty when I had one. For the same reason Homer should never have been taxed with drunkenness: *Laudibus arguitur vini vinosus Homerus* ("Homer's praise of wine convicts him of having been given to wine").[14]

I have always liked highly seasoned dishes: macaroni prepared by a good Neapolitan cook, *olla podrida*,[15] good sticky salt cod from Newfoundland, high game on the very edge, and cheeses whose perfection is reached when the little creatures which inhabit them become visible. As for women, I have always found that the one I was in love with smelled good, and the more copious her sweat the sweeter I found it.

What a depraved taste! How disgraceful to admit it and not blush for it! This sort of criticism makes me laugh. It is precisely by virtue of my coarse tastes, I have the temerity to believe, that I am happier than other men, since I am convinced that my tastes make me capable of more pleasure. Happy they who know how to obtain pleasure without harming anyone; they are madmen who imagine

that the Great Being can enjoy the griefs, the sufferings, the absti-
nences which they offer him in sacrifice, and that he loves none but
fanatics who inflict them on themselves. God can demand of his
creatures only that they practice the virtues whose seed he has sown
in their souls, and he has given us nothing which is not meant to
make us happy: self-esteem, desire for praise, emulation, vigor,
courage, and a power which no tyranny can take from us: the
power to kill ourselves if, after calculating, be it rightly or wrongly,
we are unfortunate enough to find it our best recourse. It is the
strongest proof of that moral freedom in us which sophism has so
often argued against. Yet nature rightly holds it in abhorrence; and
all religions cannot but forbid it.

A would-be freethinker told me one day that I could not call
myself a philosopher and at the same time accept revelation.

If we do not doubt it in the physical world, why should we not
accept it in religion? It is only a question of the form which it takes.
Spirit speaks to spirit, not to the ears. The principles of all that we
know must have been revealed to those who handed them down to
us by the great and supreme principle which contains all principles.
The bee making its hive, the swallow building its nest, the ant
digging its hole, the spider weaving its web would never have
done anything without a previous eternal revelation. We must either
believe that this is so, or admit that matter thinks. Why not, Locke[16]
would say, if God so willed? But we dare not do such honor to
matter. So let us hold to revelation.

The great philosopher who, after studying nature, thought he
could cry "Victory!" when he concluded that nature was God, died
too soon. If he had lived a few more years he would have gone
much further and his journey would not have been a long one.
Finding himself in his author, he could no longer have denied him:
in eo movemur, et sumus ("in him we move and have our being").[17]
He would have found him inconceivable; and it would not have
troubled him. Could God, the great principle of principles, and who
never had a principle—could even he conceive himself if to conceive himself he had to know his own principle? O happy ignorance! Spinoza, the virtuous Spinoza, died without having attained to
it. He would have died a wise man, with the right to expect the
reward of his virtues, if he had supposed that his soul was immortal.

It is not true that an expectation of reward is unworthy of
true virtue and impairs its purity, for, on the contrary, it helps to
sustain virtue, since man is too weak to wish to be virtuous only for

his own satisfaction. I believe that Amphiaraus,[18] who *vir bonus esse quam videri malebat* ("chose to be good rather than to seem good"),[19] is sheer fable. In short, I believe that there is not an honest man in the world without some sort of expectation. And now I will set forth mine.

I expect the friendship, the esteem, and the gratitude of my readers. Their gratitude, if reading my memoirs will have given them instruction and pleasure. Their esteem if, doing me justice, they will have found that I have more virtues than faults; and their friendship as soon as they come to find me deserving of it by the frankness and good faith with which I submit myself to their judgment without in any way disguising what I am.

They will find that I have always loved truth so passionately that I have often resorted to lying as a way of first introducing it into minds which were ignorant of its charms. They will not condemn me when they see me emptying my friends' purses to satisfy my whims. They were possessed by chimerical projects, and by making them hope for their success I at the same time hoped to cure them of their folly by opening their eyes. I deceived them to make them wise; and I did not consider myself guilty, because what I did was not prompted by avarice. I was simply paying for my pleasures with money allotted to acquiring possessions which nature makes it impossible to obtain. I should consider myself guilty if I were a rich man today. I have nothing; whatever I had, I have squandered; and this consoles and justifies me. It was money which was to be spent on follies; I merely changed its application by making it pay for mine.

If I am deceived in my hope of pleasing, I admit that I should be sorry, but not sorry enough to make me repent of having written, for nothing can change the fact that I have found it a pastime. The cruelty of boredom! It can only be because they had forgotten it that the inventors of the pains of hell did not include it among them.

Yet I will confess that I cannot rid myself of the fear of being hissed. It is too natural a fear for me to dare boast that I am above it; and I am far from consoling myself by hoping that when my memoirs are published I shall be no more. It horrifies me even to imagine myself contracting the slightest obligation to death, which I loathe. Happy or unhappy, life is the only treasure which man possesses, and they who do not love it do not deserve it. Honor is set above it only because dishonor blasts it. If a man faced with this choice kills himself, philosophy can have nothing to say. O death!

cruel law of nature which reason cannot but condemn, for it operates only to destroy reason. Cicero[20] says that it frees us from our ills. That great philosopher records the expenditure, but does not include the receipts in his accounting. I do not remember if, when he wrote his Tusculans, his Tulliola was dead. Death is a monster which drives an attentive spectator from the great theater before the play in which he is infinitely interested is over. This alone is reason enough to hate it.

In these memoirs the reader will not find all my adventures. I have left out those which would have offended the people who played a part in them, for they would cut a sorry figure in them. Even so, there are those who will sometimes think me only too indiscreet; I am sorry for it. If I become wise before I die, and if I have time, I will burn my whole manuscript. At the moment I have not the strength of mind for that.

Those who think that I lay on too much color when I describe certain amorous adventures in detail will be wrong, unless, that is, they consider me a bad painter altogether. I beg them to forgive me if, in my old age, my soul is reduced to feeling no joys but those of memory. Virtue will skip all the pictures which may affright it; and I am glad to give it this warning in my preface. So much the worse for those who do not read it. The preface stands to the work as the bill does to the play. It is to be read. I have not written these memoirs for those young people who can only save themselves from falling by spending their youth in ignorance, but for those whom experience of life has rendered proof against being seduced, whom living in the fire has transformed into salamanders. Since true virtues are only habits, I can say that the truly virtuous are those happy people who practice them without any effort. Such people have no notion of intolerance. It is for them that I have written. I have written in French instead of in Italian because the French language is more widely known than mine. The purists who, finding turns of expression proper to my native country in my style, will criticize me on that score will be right if they are prevented from understanding me. The Greeks relished Theophrastus[21] despite his Eresian expressions, as the Romans did their Livy[22] despite his "Patavinity." If I succeed in interesting, I hope I may benefit by the same indulgence. All Italy relishes Algarotti[23] although his style is full of Gallicisms.

Yet it is worth observing that among all the living languages in the republic of letters,[24] French is the only one which its presiding judges[25] have sentenced not to enrich itself at the expense of the other languages, whereas these, though all richer than French, pillaged it not only of its words but also of its mannerisms as soon as they realized that these little thefts beautified them. Yet those who subjected it to this law at the same time admitted its poverty. They said that since it had reached the point of possessing all the beauties of which it was capable, the slightest foreign admixture would disfigure it. This judgment may have been handed down by prejudice. In Lully's[26] day the whole nation thought the same of its music, until Rameau[27] came to teach it better. Today, under the Republican government, eloquent orators and learned writers have already convinced all Europe that they will raise French to a pitch of beauty and power which the world has not yet seen in any other language. In the short space of five years it has already acquired some hundred words which are amazing either for their sweetness or their majesty or their noble harmony. Is it possible, for example, to invent anything more beautiful in the realm of language than *ambulance, Franciade,*[28] *monarchien, sansculottisme*? Long live the Republic! A body without a head cannot possibly commit follies.

The motto which I have flaunted justifies my digressions and the commentaries in which I indulge, perhaps too often, on my exploits of various kinds: *nequicquam sapit qui sibi non sapit.*[29] For the same reason I always felt a need to hear myself praised in good company:

Excitat auditor studium, laudataque virtus
crescit, et immensum gloria calcar habet.

("Having an audience makes one try harder, virtue grows by praise, and fame is a powerful spur.")[30]

I should have liked to display the proud axiom *Nemo leditur nisi a seipso* ("No one suffers except by his own doing"),[31] had I not feared to offend the vast number of those who, whenever anything goes wrong for them, cry "It is not my fault." It is best to leave them this small consolation, for without it they would hate themselves; and self-hatred is soon followed by the thought of suicide.

For my part, since I have always admitted that I was the chief cause of all the misfortunes which have befallen me, I have rejoiced in my ability to be my own pupil, and in my duty to love my teacher.

History of
Jacques Casanova de Seingalt, Venetian,
written by himself at
Dux in Bohemia

CHAPTER I

In the year 1428 Don Jacobe Casanova, born at Saragossa, the capital of Aragon, natural son of Don Francisco, abducted Donna Anna Palafox from a convent on the day after she had taken her vows. He was secretary to King Alfonso.[2] He fled with her to Rome, where, after a year of imprisonment, Pope Martin III[3] gave Donna Anna a dispensation from her vows and the nuptial blessing, at the instance of Don Juan Casanova,[4] master of the sacred palace and uncle to Don Jacobe. All the offspring of this marriage died in infancy except Don Juan, who in 1475 married Eleonora Albini, by whom he had a son named Marcantonio.[5]

In the year 1481 Don Juan was obliged to leave Rome because he had killed an officer of the King of Naples.[6] He fled to Como with his wife and son, then he set out to seek his fortune. He died on a voyage with Christopher Columbus in the year 1493.[7]

Marcantonio became a good poet in the manner of Martial,[8] and was secretary to Cardinal Pompeo Colonna.[9] The satire against Giulio de' Medici[10] which can be found among his poems obliged him to leave Rome, and he returned to Como, where he married Abondia Rezzonica.

The same Giulio de' Medici, having become Pope Clement VII, pardoned him and summoned him back to Rome, where, after the city was taken and pillaged by the Imperial troops[11] in the year 1526, he died of the plague. Otherwise he would have died of poverty, for the soldiers of Charles V[12] had robbed him of all he possessed. Piero Valeriano[13] writes of him at some length in his book *De infelicitate litteratorum*.

Three months after his death his wife gave birth to Giacomo Casanova, who died at an advanced age in France as a colonel in the army commanded by Farnese[14] against Henri, King of Navarre,[15] later King of France. He had left a son in Parma, who married Teresa Conti, by whom he had Giacomo, who married Anna Roli in the year 1680. Giacomo had two sons, of whom the elder, Giovanni Battista, left Parma in the year 1712; what became of him is not known. The younger son, Gaetano Giuseppe Giacomo, also forsook his family in the year 1715, at the age of seventeen.

This is all that I have found in a notebook of my father's. What follows I learned from my mother's lips:

Gaetano Giuseppe Giacomo left his family, enamored by the charms of an actress named Fragoletta[16] who played soubrette roles. In love and without means of support, he decided to earn his living by turning his personal advantages to account. He took up dancing and, five years later, turned actor, becoming even more highly regarded for his probity than for his talent.

Whether from fickleness or because she had given him cause for jealousy, he abandoned Fragoletta and went to Venice, where he joined a troop of actors which played at the Teatro San Samuele.[17] Across the way from the house where he lodged there lived a shoemaker named Girolamo Farussi with his wife Marzia and their only daughter Zanetta, a perfect beauty at the age of sixteen. The young actor fell in love with the girl, succeeded in awakening her heart, and persuaded her to elope with him. Being an actor, he could not hope to obtain her by gaining the consent of Marzia her mother, still less that of Girolamo her father, who thought an actor an abomination. Provided with the necessary certificates and accompanied by two witnesses, the young lovers presented themselves before the Patriarch of Venice,[18] who united them in marriage. Marzia, the girl's mother, protested loudly, and the father died of grief. I was born of this marriage[19] nine months later, on April 2 of the year 1725.

The following year my mother left me in the care of hers, who had forgiven her when she learned that my father had promised never to force her to appear on the stage. This is a promise which all actors make to the daughters of bourgeois families whom they marry, and which they never keep because their wives never hold them to it. As it turned out, my mother was very glad that she had learned to act, for, being left a widow with six children nine years later, she could not have brought them up.

I was one year old, then, when my father left me in Venice to go to London to act. It was in that great city that my mother made her first appearance on the stage, and it was there that, in the year 1727, she gave birth[20] to my brother Francesco, the celebrated painter of battle pictures, who has been living at Venice since the year 1783, practicing his profession.

My mother came back to Venice with her husband toward the end of the year 1728 and, having become an actress, she continued in that career. In the year 1730 she gave birth to my brother

Giovanni, who died at Dresden toward the end of the year 1795, serving the Elector[21] as director of the Academy of Painting. In the course of the three following years, she gave birth to two girls,[22] of whom one died in infancy and the other was married in Dresden, where, in this year 1798, she is still living. I had another brother, born posthumously,[23] who became a priest and died at Rome fifteen years ago.

And now to come to the beginning of my own existence as a thinking being. In the beginning of August in the year 1733 my organ of memory developed. I was then eight years and four months old. I remember nothing of what may have happened to me before that time. This is the incident:

I was standing in the corner of a room, leaning against the wall, holding my head, and staring at the blood which was streaming to the floor from my nose. My grandmother Marzia, whose pet I was, came to me, washed my face with cold water, and, unknown to anyone in the house, boarded a gondola with me and took me to Murano. This is a densely populated island about half an hour from Venice.

Leaving the gondola, we enter a hovel, where we find an old woman sitting on a pallet, with a black cat in her arms and five or six others around her. She was a witch. The two old women had a long conversation, of which I must have been the subject. At the end of their dialogue in the Friulian language,[24] my grandmother gave the witch a silver ducat,[25] whereupon she opened a chest, took me up in her arms, put me into it, shut it, and locked the lid on me, telling me not to be afraid. *It was just the way to make me afraid*, if I had been able to think; but I was in a stupor. I kept quiet, holding my handkerchief to my nose because I was still bleeding and feeling quite unperturbed by the racket I heard being made outside. I heard alternate laughter and weeping, cries, singing, and sundry thumps on the chest. It was all one to me. Finally they took me out; my blood stops flowing. After giving me numberless caresses, this strange woman undresses me, lays me on the bed, burns simples, collects the smoke from them in a sheet, wraps me in it, recites spells over me, then unwraps me and gives me five very good-tasting sweetmeats. She next rubs my temples and the back of my neck with a sweet-smelling unguent, and dresses me again. She says that my bleeding will gradually diminish, provided I tell no one what she had done to cure me, but solemnly warns me that I will lose all my blood and die if I dare reveal her mysteries to anyone. After impressing this upon me she tells me that a charming lady will visit me the following night, and that my happiness will depend upon her, if I have the strength of mind to tell no one that I received such a visit. We left and returned home.

I had scarcely gone to bed before I fell asleep without even remembering the fine visitor I was to receive. But waking several hours later, I saw, or thought I saw, a dazzlingly beautiful woman come down by the chimney, wearing a huge pannier and a dress of magnificent material, with a crown on her head set with a profusion of stones which seemed to me to be sparkling with fire. She approached slowly, looking at once majestic and kindly, and sat down on my bed. From her pocket she drew several small boxes, which she emptied on my head, at the same time muttering words. After delivering a long discourse, of which I understood nothing, and kissing me, she left as she had entered, and I went back to sleep.

Coming to dress me the next morning, my grandmother was no sooner at my bedside than she commanded me to keep silence. She then impressed it on me that I would die if I dared to tell anyone what must have happened to me during the night. These solemn adjurations from the lips of the only woman whose influence over me was absolute, and who had accustomed me to obey her every command blindly, were why I have remembered this incident; they made me seal it away in the most secret corner of my budding memory. In any case, I felt no temptation to tell the story. I did not know whether anyone would find it interesting, or to whom I might tell it. My disease had made me dull, and very poor company; people felt sorry for me and left me alone; everyone supposed that I would not live long. My father and mother never spoke to me.

After the journey to Murano and my nocturnal visit from the fairy I still bled, but less and less; my memory developed, and in less than a month I learned to read. It would be ridiculous to attribute my cure to these two absurdities, but it would be a mistake to hold that they could not contribute to it. As for the appearance of the beautiful queen, I have always believed that it was a dream, unless it was a masquerade deliberately contrived; but the remedies for the worst diseases are not always found in pharmacy. One phenomenon or another demonstrates our ignorance to us every day. I believe it is for this reason that nothing is harder to find than a learned man whose mind is entirely free from superstition. There have never been wizards on this earth, but their power has always existed for those whom they have been able to cajole into believing them such.

Somnio, nocturnos lemures, portentaque Thessala rides ("In dreams you mock at nocturnal phantoms and Thessalian portents").[26] *Many things become real which previously existed only in the imagination; hence many effects attributed to faith may not always be miraculous. They are miraculous for those who hold that the power of faith has no limits.*

The second incident which I remember, and which concerns myself, happened to me three months after my journey to Murano, six weeks before my father's death. I record it in order to give my reader an idea of the way in which my character was developing.

One day about the middle of November I and my brother Francesco, who was two years younger than myself, were in my father's room watching him attentively as he worked at optics.

On the table I noticed a large round crystal cut in facets, and I was enchanted when, holding it before my eyes, I saw everything multiplied. Observing that no one was watching me, I seized the opportunity to slip it into my pocket.

Three or four minutes later my father rose, went to get the crystal, and, not finding it, said that one of us must have taken it. My brother assured him that he knew nothing about it and, though I was the culprit, I said the same. He threatened to search us and promised to give the liar a beating. After pretending to look for it in every corner of the room, I adroitly dropped it into my brother's coat pocket. I was instantly sorry, for I could have pretended to find it somewhere; but the crime was already committed. My father, exasperated by our fruitless efforts, searches us, finds the crystal in my innocent brother's pocket, and inflicts the promised punishment. Three or four years later I was stupid enough to boast to my brother that I had played this trick on him. He has never forgiven me and has taken every opportunity to avenge himself.

When I once related this crime in all its particulars in a general confession, my confessor rewarded me with a bit of recondite learning which I was glad to acquire. He was a Jesuit. He told me that, since I was named Giacomo, I had by this action verified the meaning of my name, for Jacob in Hebrew meant "supplanter." This was why God had changed the name of the ancient patriarch Jacob to Israel, which means "seeing." He had deceived his brother Esau.

Six weeks after this event my father was attacked by an abscess inside his head at the level of the ear, which brought him to the grave in a week. The physician Zambelli, who had begun by giving the patient oppilative remedies, thought to repair his mistake by castoreum,[27] which brought on death in convulsions. The apostem[28]

31

discharged through his ear one minute after he died; it left after killing him, as if it found nothing further to do in him. He was in the prime of life, at thirty-six years of age. He died regretted by the public, and particularly by the nobility, who conceded that he was superior to his station both by his probity and by his knowledge of mechanics. Two days before his death he sent for us all to appear at his bedside in the presence of his wife and of the Signori Grimani,[29] Venetian noblemen, as he wished to obtain their promise to become our protectors.

After giving us his blessing, he made our mother, who dissolved in tears, swear that she would bring none of his children up for the stage, on which he would never have appeared if he had not been driven to it by an unfortunate passion. She took the oath, and the three patricians gave him their words to see that it was not broken. Circumstances helped her to keep her promise.[30]

My mother, being six months gone with child, was excused from acting until after Easter. Beautiful and young as she was, she refused her hand to all who sued for it. Never losing courage, she believed that she could bring us up without assistance. She considered that her first duty was to me, not so much from any special fondness as because of my disease, which had reduced me to such a state that no one knew what to do with me. I was extremely weak, had no appetite, was unable to apply myself to anything, and looked like an idiot. The doctors argued among themselves over the cause of my disease. "He loses," they said, "two pounds of blood a week, and he can only have from sixteen to eighteen. Then where can such an abundant flow of blood come from?" One said that all my chyle turned to blood; another maintained that the air I breathed must increase the blood in my lungs by a certain amount at each respiration, and that this was why I always kept my mouth open. All this I learned six years later from Signor Baffo, a great friend of my father's.

It was he who consulted the famous physician Macoppe,[31] of Padua, who gave him his opinion in writing. This document, which I have kept, says that "our blood is an elastic fluid, which can increase and diminish in density, but never in quantity," and that my hemorrhage "could only come from the density of the mass, which relieved itself naturally, in order to facilitate its circulation." He said that I should already be dead, "if Nature, which seeks to live, had not come to her own assistance." He concluded that "since the cause of this density could only be in the air" I breathed,

CHAPTER II

*My grandmother comes to put me to board
with Doctor Gozzi. My first love.*

The Slavonian woman at once took me up to the attic and showed me my bed, the last in a row with four others, three of which belonged to boys of my own age, who were then at school, and the fourth to the maidservant, who was charged with making us say our prayers and keeping an eye on us to prevent us from indulging in the mischief and lewdness usual among schoolboys. She then took me down to the garden and told me I might walk there until dinnertime. I felt neither happy nor unhappy; I said nothing; I experienced neither hope nor despair nor even curiosity; I was neither cheerful nor sad. The only thing that troubled me was my mistress's person. Though I had no settled notion of beauty or ugliness, her face, her look, her voice, her manner of speech repelled me; her masculine features unnerved me every time I raised my eyes to her face to listen to what she was saying to me. She was tall and as heavy-set as a soldier, with a yellow complexion, black hair, and long, shaggy eyebrows. She had several long hairs on her chin, hideous half-exposed breasts which hung, with a great cleft between them, halfway down her tall body, and her age appeared to be fifty. The maidservant was a peasant who did everything. The so-called garden was an open space measuring thirty or forty paces in either direction, the only pleasant thing about it being its green color.

Toward noon I saw three boys approaching me; they chattered away at me as if we were old acquaintances, saying all manner of things which assumed a background of experience I did not possess. I said nothing in reply, but this did not dash them at all; they made me join in their innocent pleasures. These consisted in running, playing horse-and-rider, and turning somersaults. I let them initiate me into all these pastimes without protesting, until we were called in to dinner. I sit down at the table and, seeing a wooden spoon before me, I push it away and demand my silver service, which I cherished as a present from my grandmother. The maid said that since her mistress insisted on equality, I must conform to the customs of the house. This annoyed me, but I submitted. Having learned that there must be equality in everything, I ate my soup from the tureen like the others, without complaining of the speed with which my fellow boarders ate, though I was much surprised that it was sanctioned. After the very bad soup we were given a small portion of dried cod, then an apple, and dinner was over. It was Lent. We had neither glasses nor cups; we all drank from the same earthenware jug, which contained a vile beverage called *graspia*.[1] It was water in which grape-stems stripped of their grapes had been boiled. From then on I drank nothing but water. This fare surprised me, because I did not know if I was allowed to consider it bad.

After dinner the maid took me to school to a young priest named Doctor Gozzi.[2] The Slavonian woman had agreed to pay him forty soldi[3] a month. This is the eleventh part of a zecchino. He was to begin by teaching me to write. I was put with the five-year-olds, who at once fell to jeering at me.

Supper, as might be expected, was even worse than dinner. I was astonished that I was not allowed to complain of it. I was then consigned to a bed, in which the three notorious insects would not let me shut my eyes. In addition, rats ran all over the attic and jumped up on my bed, filling me with fear which froze my blood. Thus did I begin to learn what it is to be unhappy and to bear misfortune patiently. Meanwhile, the insects that were eating me up diminished the terror that the rats inspired in me, and my terror in turn made me less conscious of the bites. My soul profited from the competition between my afflictions. The maidservant remained deaf to my cries.

At the first rays of morning I left the nest of vermin. After complaining a little of all the sufferings I had endured, I asked the maid for a shirt, since the one I had on was hideous with the stains from the lice. She told me that shirts were changed only on Sunday and laughed when I threatened to complain of her to her mistress. For the first time in my life, I wept with vexation and anger when I heard my companions mocking me. They were in the same state as I was; but they were used to it. I need say no more.

Profoundly depressed, I spent the whole morning at school in a heavy doze. One of my fellow boarders told the Doctor the reason, but only to ridicule me. The good priest, whom Eternal Providence had bestowed on me, took me into another room, where, having heard my story and confirmed it with his own eyes, he was distressed to see the welts which covered my innocent skin. He quickly put on his cloak, took me to my boardinghouse, and showed the Laestrygonian[4] giantess the state I was in. Feigning astonishment, she

36

blamed the maid. She had to yield to the priest's insistence upon seeing my bed, and I was as astonished as he to see the filthiness of the sheets between which I had spent that cruel night. The accursed woman, still stoutly laying the blame on the maid, assured him that she would discharge her; but the maid, entering just then and unable to stomach the reprimand, told her to her face that the fault was hers, at the same time uncovering the beds of my three fellow boarders, which were just as dirty as mine. The mistress then gave her a slap on the face, to which the maid replied with a more vigorous one, and instantly took to her heels. The Doctor then departed, leaving me there and telling the Slavonian woman that he could not admit me to his school again until she should send me there as clean as the other pupils. I was then treated to a violent scolding, which she ended by telling me that if ever I made such a fuss over nothing again, she would turn me out of the house.

I felt completely bewildered; I was scarcely entering on conscious existence, I knew only the house in which I had been born and brought up, where cleanliness and a decent sufficiency were the rule; I found myself being ill-treated and scolded; I could not conceive that I was guilty. She flung a shirt in my face; and an hour later I saw a new maid changing the sheets, and we ate dinner.

My schoolmaster took particular pains to teach me. He had me sit at his own table, where, to convince him that I deserved the distinction, I applied myself to studying with all my power. At the end of a month I was writing so well that he set me to grammar.

The new life I was leading, the hunger I was forced to endure, and, above all, the air of Padua brought me such health as I had never conceived of before; but this very health made my hunger even more unendurable; I was as ravenous as a dog. I was growing visibly taller; I slept nine hours of the deepest sleep untroubled by any dream, except one in which I always seemed to be seated at a big table satisfying my cruel appetite. Pleasing dreams are worse than nightmares.

This ravenous hunger would finally have wasted me away if I had not made up my mind to steal and swallow anything edible I could lay my hands on when I was sure I was not observed. In a few days I ate some fifty smoked herring I found stored in a cupboard in the kitchen, to which I made my way in the dark of night, and all the sausages which were hanging in the chimney, raw and utterly indigestible as they were; while all the eggs I could find in the poultry-yard, scarcely laid and still warm, provided me with exquisite food. I even went so far as to steal food from the kitchen of my schoolmaster the Doctor. The Slavonian woman, in despair because she could not catch the thieves, discharged maid after maid. However, since I could not always find a chance to steal I was thin as a skeleton, mere skin and bones.

In five or six months I had made such rapid progress that the Doctor appointed me proctor of the school. My duties were to examine the written lessons of my thirty schoolmates, correct their mistakes, and report on them to the master with whatever comments in praise or blame they deserved. But my strictness did not last long. The lazy boys easily discovered how to mollify me. When their Latin was full of mistakes they won me over with roast cutlets and chickens and often gave me money. But I was not content with imposing a tax on the ignorant; I let my greed turn me into a tyrant. I refused my approval even to those who deserved it, when they tried to escape paying the levy I demanded. No longer able to stomach my injustice, they accused me to the master. Seeing me convicted of extortion, he dismissed me from my office. But my destiny was already about to end my cruel apprenticeship.

Taking me into his private room with him one day, the Doctor asked me if I was willing to do as he would suggest in order to leave the Slavonian woman and come to board with him. Finding me delighted by his proposal, he had me copy out three letters, of which I sent one to the Abate Grimani, the second to my friend Signor Baffo, and the third to my good grandmother. My mother was not in Venice at this period, and since my half year was about to end, there was no time to lose. In these letters I described all my sufferings, and prophesied my death if I were not rescued from the clutches of the Slavonian woman and put to board with my schoolmaster, who was willing to take me but who asked two zecchini a month.

Signor Grimani, instead of answering me, sent his friend Ottaviani to reprimand me for having let myself be inveigled. But Signor Baffo talked with my grandmother, who did not know how to write, and wrote me that in a few days I would find myself better off.

A week later that excellent woman, who loved me unfailingly to the day of her death, appeared just when I had sat down to dinner. She came in with the mistress. As soon as I saw her, I flung myself on her neck, unable to hold back my tears, in which she instantly joined. She sat down and took me on her lap. Thus encouraged, I gave her a detailed account of all my sufferings, in the presence of the Slavonian woman. Then, first showing her the beggarly table at which I was expected to find adequate nourishment, I took her to see my bed. I ended by imploring her to take me to dine with her, after six months of hunger and weakness. Undaunted, the Slavonian woman said only that she could not do more for the money she received. It was true. But who obliged her to keep a boardinghouse and so become the murderess of boys whom avarice put in her care and who needed to be properly fed?

My grandmother calmly told her to pack all my clothes in my trunk, for she was going to take me away. Delighted to see my silver table-service again, I quickly put it in my pocket. My joy was beyond words. For the first time I felt that contentment *which obliges the heart of him who feels it to forgive, and his mind to forget, all the vexations which have led to it.*

My grandmother took me to the inn where she was lodging, and where she ate almost nothing in her astonishment at the voracity with which I ate. Doctor Gozzi, to whom she sent word, appeared, and his presence prepossessed her in his favor. He was a handsome priest, twenty-six years of age, plump, modest, and ceremoniously polite. Within a quarter of an hour they agreed on everything and, after paying over twenty-four zecchini, she was given a receipt for a year in advance; but she kept me with her for three days in order to outfit me as an abate[5] and have a wig made for me, since the filthy state of my hair made it necessary to cut it off.

The three days over, she insisted on herself settling me in the Doctor's house, so that she could entrust me to the good offices of his mother, who at once told her to send me, or buy me, a bed; but the Doctor saying that I could sleep with him in his, which was very wide, my grandmother thanked him profusely for his kind con-descension. She left, and we saw her off as far as the *burchiello* in which she returned to Venice.

Doctor Gozzi's family consisted of his mother, who deeply respected him because, being born a peasant, she did not think herself worthy of having a son who was a priest, let alone a Doctor. She was ugly, old, and ill-tempered. The father was a shoemaker who worked all day and never spoke to anyone, even at table. He grew sociable only on holidays, which he spent in a tavern with his friends, returning home at midnight so drunk that he could not stand up and singing Tasso;[6] in this condition he could not bear to go to bed and became savage when anyone tried to make him. He had no discernment and no reasoning power except what wine gave him, to such a point that when fasting he was incapable of dealing with the simplest family matter. His wife said that he would never have married her if he had not been given a good breakfast before he went to the church.

Doctor Gozzi also had a sister thirteen years of age named Bettina,[7] who was pretty, lighthearted, and a great reader of romances. Her father and mother were forever scolding her for showing herself at the window too much, and the Doctor because of her fondness for reading. The girl pleased me at once, though I had no idea why. It was she who little by little kindled in my heart the first sparks of a feeling which later became my ruling passion.

Six months after I entered his house, the Doctor found himself without pupils. They all left because I was the sole object of his attentions. In consequence he resolved to establish a small boarding school for young boys; but two years went by before it became possible. During those two years he taught me all that he knew, which, to tell the truth, was very little, but enough to initiate me into all the branches of learning. He also taught me to play the violin, an art which I was able to turn to advantage on an occasion of which the reader will learn in its proper place. Without even a smattering of philosophy himself, he taught me the logic of the Peripatetics,[8] as well as cosmography according to the ancient system of Ptolemy,[9] at which I did nothing but scoff, challenging him with theories to which he could find no answers. His conduct, however, was irreproachable and, though no bigot, he was extremely strict in matters of religion; since everything was an article of faith for him, nothing presented any difficulties to his understanding. The Flood had been universal; before the disaster men had lived for a thousand years, God talked with them, Noah had built the ark in a hundred years, and the earth, suspended in air, remained motionless at the center of the universe, which God had created out of nothing. When I said, and proved to him, that the existence of nothing was absurd, he cut me short by telling me I was a fool. He liked a good bed, a pint of wine, and a cheerful household. He disliked wits and epigrams, and criticism because it easily turned to slander, and he laughed at the stupidity of people who spent time over newspapers, which, according to him, never told the truth and always said the same thing. He would say that nothing was as uncomfortable as uncertainty, and so he condemned thinking because it bred doubt.

His great passion was preaching, for which he was well qualified both by his figure and his voice. Hence his audience was composed entirely of women, though he was their sworn enemy. He did not look them in the face when he had to speak with them. According to him, the sin of the flesh was the greatest of all sins, and he became very angry when I told him it could only be the least. His sermons were stuffed with passages drawn from Greek authors, whom he quoted in Latin, and I one day told him that he should quote them in Italian, for Latin was no more comprehensible than Greek to the women who listened to him, telling their beads. My objection angered him, and from then on I did not dare remonstrate with him. He praised me to his friends as a prodigy because I had learned to read Greek all by myself without any other help than a grammar.

In Lent of the year 1736 my mother wrote to him that he would do her a favor if he would bring me to Venice for three or four days, since she had to go to Petersburg and wanted to see me before she left. This invitation gave him cause for thought, for he had never seen Venice nor good society, and he did not want to appear a novice in any respect. So we set out from Padua by the *burchiello*, accompanied by his whole family.

My mother received him with the ease of perfect good breeding, but as she was marvelously beautiful my poor master found himself in the very uncomfortable situation of having to converse with her yet not daring to look her in the face. As soon as she noticed this, she thought she would have a little fun with him. For my part, I attracted the attention of the entire company, who, having seen me almost an imbecile, were astonished to find that I had become more than presentable in the short space of two years. The Doctor was elated to see that all the credit was given to him. The first thing that shocked my mother was my blond wig, which stood out against my dark complexion and made the most crying contrast with my eyebrows and my black eyes. Upon her asking the Doctor why he did not let me wear my own hair, he answered that it was far easier for his sister to keep me clean this way. This provoked a laugh, after which he was asked if his sister was married. The laughter redoubled when, answering for him, I said that Bettina was the prettiest girl in our street, though she was only fourteen. My mother told the Doctor that she wanted to give his sister a very fine present, but on condition that she would take care of my own hair for me, and he gave her his promise. She immediately sent for a wigmaker, who brought me a wig which matched my coloring.

Everyone having sat down to cards, with the Doctor looking on, I went to see my brothers in my grandmother's room. Francesco showed me some architectural drawings, which I pretended to consider passable, and Giovanni showed me nothing; he struck me as stupid. The others were still in frocks.

At supper the Doctor, who was seated next to my mother, was extremely awkward. He would not have said a word if an English man of letters had not addressed him in Latin. He modestly replied that he did not understand English, whereupon there was a great burst of laughter. Signor Baffo saved the situation by telling us that the English read Latin in accordance with the rules for reading English. I made bold to say that they were as wrong as we should be if we read English as if we were reading Latin. The Englishman, having declared that my reasoning was prodigious, wrote down the following ancient distich and gave it to me to read:

Discite grammatici cur mascula nomina cunnus
Et cur femineum mentula nomen habet.
("Teach us, grammarians, why *cunnus* [vagina] is a
masculine noun
And why *mentula* [penis] is feminine.")[10]

After reading it aloud, I said that this time it was Latin. "We know that," said my mother, "but you must construe it." I answered that, instead of construing it, I would answer the question it put. After thinking for a little time, I wrote this pentameter: *Disce quod a domino nomina servus habet* ("It is because the slave takes his name from his master"). It was my first literary exploit, and I can say that it was at this moment that the seeds of my desire for the fame which comes from literature were sown in my soul, for the applause of the company set me on the pinnacle of happiness. The astonished Englishman, after remarking that no boy of eleven years had ever done as much, first embraced me several times and then made me a present of his watch. My mother's curiosity was aroused and she asked Signor Grimani what the verses meant; but since he understood them no better than she did, it was Signor Baffo who whispered a translation of them to her. Surprised at my knowledge, she could not resist an impulse to go and fetch a gold watch and give it to my master, whose inability to express the extremity of his gratitude to her turned the scene into high comedy. My mother, to save him from searching for a compliment to pay her, offered him her

42

cheek. All that was now required was two kisses, than which nothing is simpler and means less in good society; but the poor man was so embarrassed that he would rather have died than give them to her. He retired with his head hanging, and was left in peace until we went to bed.

He waited until we were alone in our room before pouring forth his heart. He said it was a pity that he could not publish either the couplet or my answer in Padua.

"Why?"

"Because they are obscene. But your answer is magnificent. Let us go to bed and say no more about it. Your answer is a miracle, for it is impossible that you should have any knowledge of the subject matter, to say nothing of composing verses."

So far as the subject matter was concerned, I knew it in theory from having already read Meursius[11] in secret, precisely because the Doctor had forbidden me to; but he was right to be astonished that I could compose a verse, for he himself, though he had taught me prosody, had never been able to compose one. *Nemo dat quod non habet* ("No one can give what he does not possess") is a false axiom in moral science.[12] When we left four days later my mother gave me a package containing a present for Bettina, and the Abate Grimani gave me four zecchini to buy books. A week later my mother left for Petersburg.

At Padua my good master did nothing but talk of my mother, in season and out of season, for three or four months. But Bettina became extraordinarily attached to me when she found that the package contained five ells of black sendal[13] of the sort known as "lustring," and twelve pairs of gloves. She took care of my hair so well that in less than six months I was able to leave off wearing my wig. She came to comb my hair every day, and often when I was still in bed, saying that she did not have time to wait for me to dress. She washed my face and neck and chest, and gave me childish caresses which, since I was bound to consider them innocent, made me chide myself for letting them trouble me. As I was three years her junior, it seemed to me that she could not love me with any evil intent, and this made me angry at the evil which I felt in myself. When, sitting on my bed, she told me that I was putting on flesh and, to convince me, convinced herself of it with her own hands, she roused the most intense emotion in me. I did not stop her, for fear she would become aware of my susceptibility. When she told me that I had a soft skin, the tickling made me draw away, and I was put out with myself for not daring to do as much to her, but delighted that she could not guess that I wanted to. After washing me, she gave me the sweetest kisses, all the while calling me her dear child; but despite my wanting to, I did not dare to return them. When, finally, she started making fun of my timidity, I began to return them, and even to better purpose; but I stopped as soon as I felt stimulated to go to greater lengths; I would turn my head away, pretending to look for something, and she would leave. After she left I was in despair over not having followed my natural inclination, and astonished that Bettina could do all that she did to me without producing any effect upon herself, whereas only by the utmost effort could I keep from going further. I kept promising myself that I would change my way of behaving.

At the beginning of that autumn the Doctor took three boarding pupils, one of whom was fifteen years of age and named Candiani. In less than a month he seemed to me to be on the best of terms with Bettina. This discovery caused me a feeling of which until then I had had no idea, and which I did not analyze until some years later. It was neither jealousy nor indignation but a noble disdain, which I saw no reason to condemn. For as the coarse, ignorant, stupid, ill-mannered son of a farmer that he was, unable to compete with me in anything and having the advantage of me only in having reached the age of puberty, Candiani did not seem to me to deserve being favored over me; my budding self-esteem told me that I was his superior. I was possessed by a mingled feeling of scorn and pride, directed against Bettina, whom I loved without knowing it. She divined it from the manner in which I received her caresses when she came to my bed to comb my hair; I pushed away her hands, I did not respond to her kisses, and one day, piqued because I would not answer when she asked me why I had changed, she said, as if pitying me, that I was jealous of Candiani. The reproach seemed to me an insulting calumny; I told her that I thought Candiani worthy of her as she was of him; she departed smiling, but already hatching the only plan which could secure her revenge: she must make me jealous; but since to do that, she had to make me fall in love with her, this is how she set about it.

One morning she came to my bed bringing me a pair of white stockings she had knitted herself; after dressing my hair, she told me that she had to try them on me to see if she had made any mistakes and so guide herself in knitting me more. The Doctor had gone to say his mass. Putting on the stockings, she said that my thighs were dirty and at once began washing them without asking my leave.

44

I was ashamed to let her see me ashamed, though I never imagined that what happened would happen. Seated on my bed, Bettina carried her zeal for cleanliness too far, and her curiosity aroused a voluptuous feeling in me which did not cease until it could not become greater. Thus calmed, it occurred to me that I had committed a crime and I felt that I should ask her forgiveness. Expecting nothing of the sort, Bettina thought for a moment and then said that the fault was entirely hers, but that she would make sure it would not happen again. With that she left me to my own reflections.

They were cruel. It seemed to me that I had dishonored her, had betrayed the trust of her family, had violated the law of hospitality, and had committed the most hideous of crimes, a crime for which I could not atone except by marrying her, always provided that she could bring herself to marry such a shameless creature, who was utterly unworthy of her.

These reflections were followed by the blackest melancholy, which became more intense with every passing day, for Bettina had entirely ceased to visit my bed. For the first week I thought this decision of hers perfectly justified; and in a few more days my melancholy would have become perfect love, if her behavior toward Candiani had not infected my soul with the poison of jealousy, though I was very far from believing her guilty of the same crime she had committed with me.

Some of my reflections having convinced me that what she had done with me had been deliberate, I imagined that an access of repentance was preventing her from returning to my bed; this idea was flattering to me, for it led me to conclude that she was in love. Sick of all this reasoning, I decided to encourage her by writing. I wrote her a short letter calculated to set her mind at rest, whether she believed herself guilty, or suspected me of feelings the opposite of those demanded by her self-esteem. I thought my letter a masterpiece, and more than enough to make her adore me and give me the preference over Candiani, whom I considered a brute beast unworthy of making her hesitate between him and myself for a single instant. She answered me by word of mouth a half hour later, saying that she would come to my bed the next morning, but she did not come. I was furious, but that noon at the dinner table she astonished me by asking me if I would like to have her dress me up as a girl and go with her to a ball which our neighbor the physician Olivo was giving five or six days later. The entire table applauded the idea, and I consented. I foresaw the moment when a mutual explanation would make us the closest of friends, safe from being waylaid by any sensual weakness. But Fate had decided otherwise: here is what happened to prevent the ball from taking place and to turn the occasion into a veritable tragicomedy.

One of Doctor Gozzi's godfathers, an elderly man of means who resided in the country, had suffered a long illness; believing that his end was near, he sent a carriage, with a message begging him to come at once, together with his father, to be present at his deathbed and commend his soul to God. The old shoemaker instantly emptied a bottle, dressed, and set off with his son.

The moment I saw that they had gone, not having the patience to wait until the night of the ball, I found an opportunity to tell Bettina that I would leave the door from my bedroom to the hall open and would expect her as soon as the household had gone to bed. She answered that she would not fail to come. She slept on the ground floor in a small room divided from her father's bedroom only by a partition; since the Doctor was away, I was sleeping alone in the large bedroom. The three boarding pupils lived in a room near the cellar. So I had no fear that anything would go amiss. I was very happy to be so close to the moment for which I had longed.

No sooner had I retired to my room than I bolted my door, then opened the one giving on to the hall, so that Bettina had only to push it to come in. That done, I put out my candle without undressing.

We think situations of this sort are exaggerated when we read them in romances, but such is not the case. What Ariosto[14] says of Ruggiero waiting for Alcina is a masterly depiction from nature.

I waited until midnight more or less patiently; but when I saw two and three and four hours pass without her appearing, I became furious. The snow was falling in great flakes, but I was more nearly dead from anger than from the cold. An hour before dawn I decided to go downstairs without shoes, for fear of waking the dog, and post myself at the foot of the stairway four paces from the door which should have been unlocked if Bettina had gone out by it. I found it locked. It could only be locked from inside; I thought she might have fallen asleep, but to wake her I should have had to knock loudly and the dog would have barked. From this door to the door of her room was another ten or twelve paces. Overwhelmed by disappointment and unable to settle on any course, I sat down on the bottom step. A little before dawn, chilled to the bone, numb, and shivering, I decided to go back to my room, for if the maid had found me there she would have concluded that I had gone mad.

I stand up; but at the same instant I hear a noise inside. Sure that Bettina would appear, I go to the door; it opens; but instead of Bettina I see Candiani, who gives me such a kick in the belly that I find myself stretched out flat, half buried in the snow. After which he goes and shuts himself up in the room in which his bed stood beside those of his Feltrinian[15] schoolmates.

I spring up and start off to strangle Bettina, for at that moment nothing could have saved her from my fury; but I find the door locked. I give it a great kick, the dog starts barking, and I go back upstairs to my room, shut myself in, and lie down to restore my soul and my body, for I was worse than dead.

Deceived, humiliated, wronged, become an object of scorn to the happy and triumphant Candiani, I spent three hours ruminating the direst schemes of vengeance. Poisoning them both seemed to me nothing in this moment of misery. I conceived the base plan of going to the country and telling the Doctor everything. As I was only twelve years old my mind had not yet acquired the cold ability to lay heroic plans of vengeance fathered by the factitious sentiment of honor. I was only just beginning my apprenticeship in matters of this sort.

In this state of mind, I hear at the inner door to my room the hoarse voice of Bettina's mother imploring me to come down because her daughter is dying.

Aggrieved that she should die before I killed her, I rise, go downstairs, and find her in her father's bed in frightful convulsions, surrounded by the whole family, partly undressed, and rolling from side to side. She twisted, she writhed, hitting out at random with fists and feet, and escaping by violent jerks first from one then from another of those who were trying to hold her still.

With this scene before me, and full of the events of the night, I did not know what to think. I knew neither nature nor artifices, and I was astonished to find myself a cold spectator able to maintain my self-possession in the presence of two persons one of whom I intended to kill and the other to dishonor. At the end of an hour Bettina fell asleep. A midwife and the physician Olivo arrived at the same moment. The woman said that the seizure was hysterical; the doctor that the womb had nothing to do with it. He prescribed rest and cold baths. I laughed up my sleeve at them both, but said nothing; I knew that the girl's illness could only be the result of her nocturnal labors or of the fright that my meeting with Candiani must have given her. I determined to put off my revenge until Doctor Gozzi should arrive. I was far from believing that Bettina's illness was feigned, for I thought it impossible that she could possess so much strength.

Passing through Bettina's room to return to my own and seeing her pockets on the bed there, I was suddenly tempted to secure their contents. I find a letter, I see Candiani's handwriting, I go to my room to read it, astonished at the girl's imprudence, for her mother might have found it and, being unable to read, have given it to her son the Doctor. I was now persuaded that she had gone out of her mind. But what did I not feel when I read the following words! "As your father is away, there is no need for you to leave your door open as you did the other times. When I leave the table I will go to your room; you will find me there." After reflecting for a little, I was moved to laugh and, realizing that I had been made a perfect dupe, I believed I was cured of my love. I thought Candiani deserved my forgiveness and Bettina my scorn. I congratulated myself on having learned an excellent lesson for my life to come. I even admitted that Bettina had good reason to prefer Candiani, who was fifteen whereas I was still a child. But when I remembered the kick he had given me, I continued to bear him a grudge.

At noon we were dining in the kitchen because of the cold when Bettina fell into convulsions again. Everyone went running to her except myself. I quietly finished my dinner, then returned to my studies. At suppertime I found Bettina's bed in the kitchen beside her mother's, but I paid no attention to it, any more than I did to the noise which went on all night and the confusion next morning when she went into convulsions again.

Toward evening the Doctor returned with his father. Candiani, who feared that I would take vengeance, came to ask me what I intended to do, but he fled when he saw me coming toward him knife in hand. It did not occur to me for an instant to tell the Doctor the sordid story; such a project could take shape in my nature only during a moment of wrath. *Irasci celerem tamen ut placabilis essem* ("I become angry quickly, even as I am quickly appeased").[16]

The following morning the Doctor's mother interrupted our schooling to tell her son, after much beating around the bush, that she believed Bettina's illness was the result of a spell which a witch whom she knew must have put on her.

"That may well be; but we must be sure we are not mistaken. Who is this witch?"

"It is our old maidservant; and I have just made certain."

"How?"

"I barred my door with two broomsticks in a cross so that she had to uncross them if she wanted to come in; but when she saw them she turned back and came in by another door. It is obvious that if she were not a witch she would have uncrossed them."

"It is not so obvious, my dear Mother. Have the woman come here."

"Why," he asked her, "did you not go into the room this morning by the usual door?"

"I don't know what you mean."

"Did you not see the St. Andrew's cross[17] on the door?"

"What kind of a cross?"

"It is no use your pretending not to know," said his mother. "Where did you spend last Thursday night?"

"With my niece, who has just had a baby."

"No, no. You went to the witches' Sabbath, for you are a witch. And you have bewitched my daughter."

At that the poor woman spat in her face, and the Doctor came running to hold his mother, who had raised her cane to give her a beating. But he had to run after the maid, who went down the stairs shouting to rouse the neighbors. He calmed her by giving her some money, then got together his ecclesiastical paraphernalia to exorcise his sister and find out if she was really possessed by a devil. The newness of these mysteries captured all my attention. I thought all these people either insane or idiots. I could not picture devils in Bettina's body without laughing. When we approached her bed, her breath seemed to fail, and her brother's exorcisms did not restore it. The physician Olivo appeared and asked if he was in the way; the Doctor answered that he was not if he had faith. The physician then departed, saying that he had faith only in the miracles of the Gospels. The Doctor returned to his room and when I was alone with Bettina, I whispered these words into her ear: "Take courage, get well, and count on my silence." She turned her head away without answering me, and spent the rest of the day without convulsions. I thought that I had cured her, but the next day the convulsions went to her brain. In her delirium she uttered words in Greek and Latin, after which no one doubted the nature of her illness. Her mother went out and returned an hour later with the most celebrated exorcist in Padua. He was an extremely ugly Capuchin[18] monk, named Fra Prospero da Bovolenta.

When he appeared, Bettina burst out laughing and assailed him with the most deadly insults, which delighted everyone present, since only the devil was bold enough to address a Capuchin in this fashion; but the Capuchin, hearing himself called an ignorant, stinking impostor, fell to hitting Bettina with a great crucifix, saying that he was beating the devil. He only stopped when he saw her ready to throw a chamberpot at his head, a thing which I would greatly have liked to see. "If he who has offended you with words," she said to him, "is the devil, strike him with yours, you donkey; and if it is I, learn to respect me, you clod; and be gone." At this I saw Doctor Gozzi blush.

But the Capuchin, armed from head to foot, after reading a terrible exorcism, commanded the evil spirit to tell him its name.

"My name is Bettina."

"No, for that is the name of a baptized girl."

"So you think a devil must have a masculine name? Know, ignorant Capuchin, that a devil is an angel without sex. But since you believe that he who speaks to you through my lips is a devil, promise to tell me the truth and I promise to yield to your exorcisms."

"Very well, I promise to tell you the truth."

"Do you think you are wiser than I am?"

"No; but I believe I am stronger in the name of the most holy Trinity and by the power of my sacred office."

"Then if you are stronger, stop me from telling the truth about you. You are vain of your beard; you comb it ten times a day and you would not cut half of it off to make me depart from this body. Cut it off and I swear I will depart from it."

"Father of lies, I will double your sufferings."

"I defy you to do that."

Bettina then burst out laughing so hard that I guffawed; but the Capuchin, seeing me, told the Doctor that I had no faith and he must put me out of the room. I left, telling him that he had guessed right; but I still had time to see Bettina spit on his hand when he held it out to her and told her to kiss it.

Here was this incredibly talented girl, confounding the Capuchin, yet no one was surprised because all her words were ascribed to the devil! I could not imagine what her purpose was.

After dining with us and uttering a hundred imbecilities, the Capuchin went back to the room to bestow his blessing on the possessed girl, who greeted him with a glass of some black liquid given her by the apothecary, which she flung in his face, and Candiani, who was standing beside the monk, received his share, which pleased me immensely. Bettina was right to take advantage of this moment when all that she did was attributed to the devil. As he left, Father Prospero told the Doctor that the girl was undoubtedly possessed, but that he must find another exorcist, since God did not see fit to grant him the grace of delivering her.

After he was gone Bettina spent four hours in perfect quiet and surprised us all by coming to the table to sup with us. After assuring her father, her mother, and her brother that she felt perfectly well, she told me that the ball was to take place the next day and that she would come in the morning to dress my hair like a girl's. I thanked her and told her that she had been very ill and ought to take great care of herself. She went off to bed, and we remained at table, talking of nothing but her.

When I went to my room I found the following note in my nightcap, which I answered when I saw that the Doctor was asleep. "Either come to the ball with me dressed as a girl, or I will show you a sight that will make you cry."

Here is my answer: "I will not go to the ball, for I have firmly resolved to avoid every chance of being alone with you. As for the unhappy sight with which you threaten me, I believe you have wits enough to keep your word; but I implore you to spare my heart, for I love you as if you were my sister. I have forgiven you, dear Bettina, and I wish to forget everything. Here is a note which you should be delighted to have in your hands again. You see what a risk you ran by leaving it in your pocket on your bed. My returning it to you must convince you of my friendship."

CHAPTER III

Bettina believed mad. Father Mancia.
The smallpox. I leave Padua.

Not knowing into whose hands her note had fallen, Bettina must have been in despair, so that I could not give her a surer proof of my friendship than to allay her anxiety; but my generosity, though it delivered her from one distress, was only to cause her a greater. She knew that her secret was out. Candiani's note showed that she received him every night: so her lying story, which she had perhaps invented to deceive me, was now useless. I wanted to free her from this embarrassing situation. In the morning I went to her bed; and I gave her Candiani's note with my answer.

The girl's intelligence had won her my esteem; I could no longer despise her. I regarded her as a creature led astray by her own temperament. She loved the male sex; the only harm in it was the consequences for her. Believing that I saw the matter in its true light, I had decided to act as a youth who could reason, not as a lover. It was her part to blush, not mine. The only thing I was still curious about was whether the Feltrinians had slept with her too. These were Candiani's two schoolmates.

Bettina pretended all day to be in the happiest frame of mind. In the evening she dressed for the ball; but suddenly an indisposition, whether feigned or real, made her take to her bed. The whole household was alarmed. For my part, since I knew everything, I expected new and even more lamentable scenes. I had gained an advantage over her which her self-esteem could not tolerate. Yet despite such excellent schooling before I reached adolescence, I continued to be the dupe of women until I was sixty years of age. Twelve years ago, if my guardian Genius had not intervened to help me, I would have married a silly girl with whom I had fallen in love in Vienna. Today I believe I am safe from such follies; but alas! I regret it.

The next morning the whole household was grief-stricken because the demon that possessed Bettina had conquered her reason. The Doctor told me that among her ravings were blasphemies, from which it followed that she must be possessed, for it was impossible that a girl who was merely insane would have attacked Father

Prospero as she had. He resolved to put her in the hands of Father Mancia. This was a celebrated Jacobin,[1] or Dominican,[2] exorcist, who was said never to have failed with a bewitched girl.

It was a Sunday. Bettina had eaten a good dinner, and had been out of her head all day. Toward midnight her father arrived at the house, singing Tasso and so drunk that he could not stand. He went to his daughter's bedside and, after kissing her fondly, told her that she was not mad. She answered that he was not drunk.

"You are possessed, my dear daughter."

"Yes, Father; and only you can cure me."

"Very well! I am ready."

And he becomes the theologian; he reasons on the power of faith, and on the power of the paternal blessing; he throws off his cloak; he takes a crucifix in one hand, he puts the other on his daughter's head, and begins talking to the devil in such a style that even his stupid, gloomy, ill-tempered wife cannot but shout with laughter for once. Of all who were present, only the two actors in the scene did not laugh, and this was what made it so amusing. I admired Bettina, who, naturally inclined to laugh at anything and everything, managed to maintain the utmost gravity. Doctor Gozzi was laughing too, but trying to put an end to the farce, for he considered that his father's absurdities were so many profanations against the sacredness of exorcisms. The exorcist finally went off to bed, saying that he was sure the demon would leave his daughter in peace all that night.

The next morning, just as we were getting up from table, Father Mancia makes his appearance. The Doctor, followed by the entire family, conducted him to his sister's bedside. As for me, I was so absorbed in watching and studying the monk that I scarcely knew where I was. Here is his portrait.

His stature was tall and majestic, his age about thirty years, his hair was blond, his eyes blue. His features were those of the Apollo Belvedere,[3] except that they expressed neither triumph nor presumption. Dazzlingly white, his pallid complexion intensified the redness of his lips, which disclosed his fine teeth. He was neither thin nor fat, and the sadness of his countenance made it the sweeter. His movements were slow, his manner timid, which suggested an extreme modesty of mind.

When we entered, Bettina was, or was pretending to be, asleep. Father Mancia began by taking an aspergillum and sprinkling her with lustral water. She opened her eyes, looked at the monk, and instantly closed them; then she opened them again, looked at him more closely, turned over on her back, let her arms drop, and with her head prettily inclined, sank into a sleep than which nothing could have appeared sweeter. The exorcist, who was standing, produced his service book, a stole which he put round his neck, and a reliquary which he placed on the sleeping girl's bosom. Then, with a saintly look, he asked us to kneel and pray to God to tell him if the patient was possessed or was suffering from a natural illness. He left us kneeling for half an hour, during which he kept reading in a low voice. Bettina did not stir.

Tired, I suppose, of playing this role, he asked the Doctor to hear him in private. They entered the bedroom, from which they emerged a quarter of an hour later, summoned by a great burst of laughter from the demented girl, who no sooner saw them reappear than she turned her back on them. Father Mancia smiled, dipped the aspergillum in the holy water pot several times, sprinkled us all generously, and departed.

The Doctor said that he would come back the next morning, and that he had undertaken to deliver her within three hours if she was possessed, but that he promised nothing if she was insane. Her mother said she was sure he would deliver her, and she thanked God for having granted her the grace of seeing a saint before she died. Nothing was more charming than Bettina's madness the next morning. She began by saying the wildest things a poet could invent, and did not stop upon the appearance of the exorcist, who after enjoying them for a quarter of an hour armed himself from head to foot and asked us to leave the room. He was instantly obeyed. The door was left open, but that made no difference. Who would have dared to go in? For three hours we heard nothing but the most dismal silence. At noon he called us, and we went in. There was Bettina, dejected but perfectly quiet, while the monk picked up his gear. He left, saying that he had hope and asking the Doctor to send him news of her. Bettina dined in bed, ate supper at the table, and was well-behaved the next day; but now for what happened to make me certain that she was neither insane nor possessed.

It was the day before the eve of the Purification of Our Lady.[4] The Doctor always had us receive communion at the parish church; but for confession he took us to Sant'Agostino, a church in which the Jacobins of Padua officiated. At table he told us to prepare ourselves to go to confession there on the next morning but one.

His mother said, "You should all go to confess to Father Mancia so that you can be absolved by such a holy man. I shall go to him too." Candiani and the Feltrinians agreed; I said nothing.

I was distressed by the plan; but I dissimulated, determined to prevent its execution. I believed in the secrecy of confession, and I could certainly not have made one that was false; but knowing that I was free to choose my confessor, I would never have been so stupid as to go and tell Father Mancia what had happened to me with a girl whom he would instantly have known could be none other than Bettina. I was certain that Candiani would tell him everything, and for this I was very sorry.

Early the next morning she came to my bed to bring me a neckband, and secretly handed me this letter:

"Hate me for living; but respect my honor, and a shadow of peace for which I hope. None of you must go to confession to Father Mancia tomorrow. You are the only one who can frustrate the plan, and you do not need to have me tell you how. I shall see if it is true that you feel some friendship for me."

It is beyond belief how sorry I felt for the poor girl when I read her note. Nevertheless, I replied as follows: "I understand that despite all the inviolable laws of confession your mother's plan cannot but alarm you; but I cannot see how, in order to frustrate it, you should count on me rather than on Candiani, who has declared his approval of it. All I can promise you is that I will not go with the others; but I have no power over your lover. It is you who must speak to him."

Here is the answer she handed me: "I have not spoken to Candiani again since the fatal night that made me wretched; I will not speak to him again, even if my speaking to him could restore my happiness. It is to you alone that I wish to owe my life and my honor."

I thought the girl more astonishing than any of those whom the romances I had read had portrayed as wonders. It seemed to me that she was deceiving me with unparalleled effrontery. I saw that she was trying to bind me in her chains again; and though I had no wish for them I resolved to perform the generous act of which she thought that I alone was capable. She felt sure she would succeed; but in what school had she learned to know the human heart so well? By reading romances. It may be that reading some romances causes the ruin of many girls; but it is certain that *reading good ones teaches good manners and the practice of the social virtues*.

55

So, having resolved to show the girl all the kindness of which she believed me capable, when we were about to go to bed I told the Doctor that my conscience obliged me to ask him to excuse me from going to confession to Father Mancia, and that I wished not to do differently from my schoolmates. He answered that he understood my reasons and that he would take us all to Sant' Antonio.[5] I kissed his hand. So the matter was settled, and at noon I saw Bettina come to the table with satisfaction painted on her countenance.

An open chilblain obliging me to stay in bed, and the Doctor having gone to church with all my schoolmates, leaving Bettina alone in the house, she came and sat on my bed. I was expecting this. I saw that the moment for having things out had come, and, all in all, I was not sorry.

She began by asking me if I minded her having seized the opportunity to speak to me. "No," I answered, "for you give me the opportunity to tell you that, since my feeling for you is only one of friendship, you can rest assured that from henceforth nothing I shall do can be of a nature to trouble you. So you may do whatever you please. For me to act otherwise, I should have to be in love with you; and I am that no longer. You stifled the seed of a beautiful passion in an instant. I was scarcely back in my room after the kick Candiani gave me, before I began to hate you, then I despised you, then you became indifferent to me, and finally my indifference vanished when I saw the powers of mind you possess. I have become your friend, I forgive your weaknesses, and having accustomed myself to thinking of you as you are, I have conceived the most extraordinary esteem for your intelligence. I was its dupe, but no matter: it exists, it is amazing, divine, I admire it, I love it, and it seems to me that the homage I owe it is to cherish the purest friendship for her who possesses it. Pay me in the same coin. Truth, sincerity, and no tricks. So put an end to all your nonsense, for you have already won from me all that you could ask. The mere thought of love is repugnant to me, for I can love only if I am sure of being loved without a rival. You are at liberty to attribute my stupid fastidiousness to my age; but it cannot be otherwise. You wrote me that you no longer speak to Candiani, and if I am the cause of your breaking off with him, I am sorry, believe me. Your honor demands that you try to patch things up with him; and in future I must be careful not to give him the slightest grounds for taking offense. Consider, too, that if you made him fall in love with you by seducing him in the same way, you have committed two wrongs, for it is possible that if he loves you, you have made him unhappy."

"All that you have said," Bettina answered, "is founded on a false assumption. I do not love Candiani, and I never loved him. I hated him, and I hate him, because he has deserved my hatred, and I shall convince you of it despite the appearances that speak against me. As for seduction, I beg you to spare me that base reproach. You, too, must consider that if you had not first seduced me I would never have done what I have deeply repented of doing for reasons which you do not know and which I will now explain to you. The sin I committed is great only because I did not foresee the harm it could do me in the inexperienced mind of a creature as ungrateful as yourself, who dares to reproach me with it."

Bettina wept. What she had just told me was plausible, and flattering; but I had seen too much. In addition, what she had shown me her mind was capable of made me sure that she intended to deceive me, and that her maneuver was only the consequence of her self-esteem, which would not allow her unprotestingly to accept a victory on my side which was too humiliating to her.

Not to be shaken from my idea, I answered that I believed all that she had just told me concerning the state of her heart before the little game which had made me fall in love with her; and so I promised that in future I would spare her the name of seducer. "But admit," I said, "that the violence of your flame was only momentary and that only a faint breath sufficed to put it out. Your virtue, which did not leave the path of duty except for a single hour, and which at once regained all its empire over your erring senses, is also worthy of some praise. In an instant you who adored me became insensible to all my sufferings, which I did not fail to communicate to you. It remains for me to learn how this virtue could be so precious to you, when Candiani shipwrecked it every night in his arms."

"You have now come," she said (giving me the triumphant look of one who is confident of victory), "to just the point to which I wanted to bring you. That is what I had no way of communicating to you, and what I could never tell you myself because you refused the meeting I asked of you for no other purpose than to acquaint you with the truth.

"Candiani," she went on, "declared his love to me a week after he entered our house. He asked me to consent to his father's asking my hand in marriage for him as soon as he should have finished his studies. I answered that I did not yet know him well and that I had

bedstead moved into the kitchen beside her mother's. This fever might be natural, but I doubted it. I was certain that she would never have made up her mind to recover, for that would give me too good a reason for believing that she was also deceiving me in regard to the supposed innocence of her relations with Candiani. I decided that her having her bedstead taken to the kitchen was another artifice of the same sort.

The next morning the physician Olivo, finding a high fever, told the Doctor that it would bring on incoherence, but that her ravings would come from the fever, not from devils. And in fact Bettina was delirious all day; but the Doctor, having gone over to the physician's opinion, paid no attention to his mother's protests and did not send for the Jacobin. On the third day the fever was even higher, and spots on the skin suggested smallpox, which broke out on the fourth day. Candiani and the two Feltrinians, who had not had it, were immediately sent to lodge elsewhere, so that I, who had no need to fear it, was left alone. Poor Bettina was so covered with the pestilential spots that by the sixth day it was impossible to see her skin anywhere on her body. Her eyes closed, all her hair had to be cut off, and her life was despaired of when her mouth and throat were found to be so full of spots that nothing but a few drops of honey could be introduced into her esophagus. Her only visible movement was now her breathing. Her mother never left her bedside, and I was admired when I brought my table and my notebooks there too. The girl had become a frightful object; her head was bigger by a third; her nose had vanished, and her sight was feared for even if she should recover. What I found extremely unpleasant, but bore with firmness, was her stinking sweat.

On the ninth day the parish priest came and gave her absolution and extreme unction, then he said that he left her in the hands of God. Throughout this sad scene the dialogues between Bettina's mother and the Doctor made me laugh. She wanted to know if the devil that possessed her could even now give her a fit of madness, and what would become of the devil if Bettina should die, for she did not think him fool enough to remain in such a disgusting body. She asked if he could take possession of the poor girl's soul. The poor Doctor, whose theology was Ubiquitarian, answered all her questions by statements in which there was not even a glimmer of common sense and which only confused the poor woman more and more.

The tenth and eleventh days it was feared that she would die at any moment. All her pustules had turned black and were discharging with a stench which made the air unbreathable; no one could bear up under it except myself, who was distressed by the poor creature's condition. It was in this terrible state that she awoke in me all the affection which I showed her after her recovery.

On the thirteenth day, when her fever had completely subsided, she began thrashing about because of an intolerable itching, which no medicine could more effectively have soothed than these potent words, which I repeated to her from minute to minute: "Remember, Bettina, that you are going to get well; but if you dare scratch yourself, you will be so ugly that no one will ever love you again." I challenge all the physicians in the world to find a more powerful deterrent to itching than this in the case of a girl who knows that she has been beautiful and is in danger of becoming ugly through her own fault if she scratches.

At last she opened her beautiful eyes, her bed was changed, and she was carried to her room. An abscess which developed on her neck kept her in bed until Easter. She infected me with eight or ten pustules, three of which have left an indelible mark on my face; they stood me in good stead with Bettina, who now realized that only I deserved her affection. Her skin was left covered with red spots, which did not disappear until a year had passed. She loved me afterwards without any feigning, and I loved her without ever plucking a flower which fate, supported by prejudice, had reserved for marriage. But what a wretched marriage! Two years later she became the wife of a shoemaker named Pigozzo, a base scoundrel who brought her to poverty and misery. Her brother the Doctor had to take care of her. Fifteen years later he took her with him to Val San Giorgio,[7] of which he was appointed archpriest. When I went to see him eighteen years ago I found Bettina old, ill, and dying. She expired before my eyes in the year 1776, twenty-four hours after my arrival. I shall speak of her death in its proper place.

At this same time my mother came back from Petersburg, where the Empress Anna Ivanovna[8] did not find the Italian comedy sufficiently amusing. The whole troop was already back in Italy and my mother had made the journey with Carlino Bertinazzi, Harlequin,[9] who died at Paris in the year 1783. As soon as she reached Padua she sent word of her arrival to Doctor Gozzi, who at once took me to the inn at which she was staying with her traveling companion. We ate dinner there, and before leaving she presented him with a fur and gave me a lynx-skin to give to Bettina. Six months later she had me come to Venice, in order to see me again before she left for Dresden, where she had accepted a lifetime engagement in the service of the Elector of Saxony Augustus III, King of Poland. She took with her my brother Giovanni, who was then eight years old and who wept desperately when they left, which led me to suspect that he was not especially intelligent, for there was nothing tragic about the departure. He was the only one of us who owed all that he became in life to our mother, though he was not her favorite.

After this period I spent another year in Padua studying law, of which I became a Doctor at the age of sixteen,[10] my thesis in civil law having been "*de testamentis*" ("concerning wills") and in canon law *utrum hebrei possint construere novas Synagogas* ("whether Jews may build new synagogues"). My vocation was to study medicine so that I could practice the profession, for which I felt a strong inclination, but my wish was disregarded; I was forced to study law, for which I felt an unconquerable aversion. It was alleged that the only way I could make my fortune was to become an advocate and, still worse, an ecclesiastical advocate, because I was considered to be gifted in speaking. *If the question had been given due consideration I should have been allowed to do as I wished and become a physician, in which profession quackery is even more effective than it is in legal practice.* I practiced neither profession; and it could not be otherwise. Perhaps this is why I have never wished either to employ advocates when I happened to have legal claims to present in court or to call in physicians when I was ill. *Legal squabbling ruins more families than it supports; and those who die killed by physicians are far more numerous than those who are cured. It follows that mankind would be far less wretched without these two breeds.*

Having to attend the University—which is called the Bo[11]—to hear the professors lecture had made it necessary for me to go about alone, and I was delighted, for until then I had never considered myself a free man. Wanting to enjoy to the full the freedom of which I found myself in possession, I made as many undesirable acquaintances as possible among the notorious students. The most notorious cannot but be those who are the greatest libertines, gamblers, frequenters of places of ill repute, drunkards, debauchees, seducers of decent girls, given to violence, false, and incapable of entertaining the slightest virtuous feeling. It was in the company of fellows of this kind that I began to know the world by studying it in the harsh book of experience.

The theory of behavior is useful to the life of man only as the index is useful to him who goes through it before reading the book itself; when he has

64

read it, all that he has learned is the subject matter. Such is the moral teaching which we receive from the discourses, the precepts, and the stories we are treated to by those who bring us up. We listen to it all attentively; but when we have an opportunity to profit by the various advice we have been given, we become possessed by a desire to see if the thing will turn out to be what we have been told it will; we do it, and we are punished by repentance. What recompenses us a little is that in such moments we consider ourselves wise and hence entitled to teach others. Those whom we teach do exactly as we did, from which it follows that the world always stands still or goes from bad to worse.

Aetas parentum, pejor avis, tulit nos nequiores mox daturos progeniem vitiosiorem ("The generation of our parents, worse than that of our grandparents, has created us worse again and destined soon to bring forth yet more vicious progeny").[12]

So it was that Doctor Gozzi's permission to go out by myself put me in the way of learning several truths of which up to that time I was not only ignorant but of which I did not even suspect the existence. Upon my appearance the old hands descended on me and sounded me out. Finding me inexperienced in everything, they obliged me to learn by making me fall into every trap. They made me play cards, and when they had won the little money I had they made me lose on my word, and then taught me to engage in shady dealings in order to pay up. I began to know what it was to be in trouble. I learned to be wary of all those who praise a man to his face, and never to count on the offers of those who flatter. I learned to live with brawlers, whose company must be avoided if one is not to be forever on the verge of destruction. As for professional prostitutes, I did not fall into their snares because I found none of them as pretty as Bettina; but I could not keep myself from desiring the kind of glory whose source is a courage which contemns life.

In those days the students of Padua enjoyed very large privileges. They were abuses which their antiquity had made legal; this is the original nature of almost all privileges. They differ from prerogatives. The fact is that in order to keep their privileges in force the students committed crimes. The guilty were not punished according to the rigor of the law, for the interest of the State could not allow such severity to diminish the number of students who flocked to this famous University from every part of Europe. The principle of the Venetian government[13] was to pay very high stipends to professors of great renown and to let those who came to hear their lectures live in the utmost freedom. The students were responsible only to a head of the student body called the "Syndic."[14] He was a foreign gentleman who was obliged to maintain a registry and to answer to the government for the behavior of the students. He had to give them up to justice when they broke the laws, and the students accepted his decisions because when they had a shadow of justification he also defended them. They refused, for example, to allow the customs officers to search their luggage, and the ordinary sbirri[15] would never have dared to arrest a student; they carried whatever forbidden arms they pleased; they freely seduced girls of decent family whose parents could not keep them under supervision; they frequently disturbed the public peace with nocturnal pranks: in short, they were a set of unbridled youths who asked nothing but to satisfy their whims, amuse themselves, and laugh.

In those days it happened that a sbirro entered a coffeehouse where there were two students. One of them ordered him to leave, the sbirro disregarded the order, the student fired a pistol at him and missed, but the sbirro returned the fire and wounded the student, then took to his heels. The students gathered at the Bo and, dividing up into groups, went hunting for sbirri in order to avenge the insult by massacring them; but in one encounter two students were killed. The entire body of students then assembled and swore never to lay down their arms until there were no more sbirri in Padua. The government intervened, and the Syndic undertook to persuade the students to lay down their arms if atonement were made, since the sbirri were in the wrong. The sbirro who had wounded the student was hanged, and peace was made; but during the week before the peace, since all the students were going about Padua divided into patrols, I did not want to be less courageous than the rest, no matter what the Doctor said. Armed with pistols and a carbine I went out with my fellow students every day, searching for the enemy. I was extremely disappointed that the troop of which I was a member never came upon a single sbirro. When the war was over the Doctor laughed at me; but Bettina admired my courage.

Reluctant to appear poorer than my new friends in this new life, I began spending more than I could afford. I sold or pawned all that I possessed, and contracted debts which I could not repay. These were my first vexations, and the most painful that a young man can experience.

I wrote to my good grandmother for help; but instead of sending it she came to Padua herself to thank Doctor Gozzi and Bettina, and took me back to Venice on October 1st, 1739.

At the moment of my departure the Doctor wept and presented me with his most cherished treasure. He hung about my neck a relic of some saint whose name I no longer remember, which might still be in my possession if it had not been set in gold. The miracle it performed for me was to be of service to me at a moment of urgent need. Each time I returned to Padua to complete[16] my law studies I lodged in his house; but I was always unhappy to see the scoundrel who was to marry her hanging around Bettina, who seemed to me worthy of a better fate. I was sorry that I had spared her for him. It was a prejudice I had at the time, but of which I soon rid myself.

CHAPTER IV

*The Patriarch of Venice confers minor orders
on me. My acquaintance with Senator Malipiero, with Teresa Imer, with the niece of my
parish priest, with Signora Orio, with Nanetta
and Marta, with La Cavamacchie. I become a
preacher. My adventure at Pasiano with Lucia.
Assignation on the fourth floor.*

"He has just come from Padua, where he has been studying at the
University," was the phrase used to introduce me everywhere,
which was no sooner uttered than it gained me the silent observation of my equals in rank and age, the compliments of fathers, and
the caresses of old women, among them some who were not really
old but were willing to pass as such so that they could embrace me
without impropriety. The parish priest of San Samuele,[1] whose
name was Tosello, after inducting me into his church, presented
me to Monsignor Correr, Patriarch of Venice, who gave me the
tonsure and four months later, by special favor, conferred the four
minor orders on me.[2] It was the greatest comfort to my grandmother. Good masters were immediately found so that I could
continue my studies, and Signor Baffo chose the Abate Schiavo[3]
to teach me to write a pure Italian and especially the language of
poetry, for which I had a decided bent. I found myself most comfortably lodged with my brother Francesco, who had been set to
study theatrical architecture. My sister and my posthumous brother
were living with my grandmother in another house, one that
belonged to her and in which she wished to die because her husband
had died there. The house I lived in was the same one[4] in which
I had lost my father and for which my mother continued to pay the
rent; it was large and very well furnished.

Though the Abate Grimani was supposed to be my principal
patron, I nevertheless saw him very seldom. The person to whom
I attached myself was Signor Malipiero, to whom the priest Tosello
immediately presented me. He was a Senator[5] who, not wishing
to occupy himself with affairs of state at his age, which was seventy,
led a pleasant life in his palace, eating well and every evening

entertaining a most select company made up of ladies who had all gone the pace and of men of wit and intelligence who were sure to know of the latest happenings in the city. This old nobleman was a bachelor and rich, but subject three or four times a year to extremely painful attacks of gout which at each recurrence left him stiff first in one limb, then in another, so that his entire body was crippled. Only his head, his lungs, and his stomach had been spared. He was handsome, a connoisseur of wine, and an epicure; his mind was keen; with a vast knowledge of the world, he possessed the eloquence of the Venetians and the wisdom which is the portion of a senator who has not retired until he has spent forty years governing the Republic nor ceased to court the fair sex until he has had twenty mistresses and realized that he must give up all hope of pleasing even one. Though he was almost completely crippled, his condition was not apparent when he was seated, or talking, or at table. He ate only once a day, and always alone because, having lost all his teeth, he took twice as long to eat as another would have taken to eat the same meal and he was unwilling either to hurry himself in deference to his guests or to see them waiting while he chewed his food with his sound gums before swallowing it. For this reason alone he put up with the unpleasantness of eating in solitude, much to the displeasure of his excellent cook.

The first time that my parish priest did me the honor of presenting me to His Excellency, I most respectfully impugned this reasoning, which everyone considered unanswerable. I told him that he need only invite to his table those who naturally ate twice as much as other people.

"Where are they to be found?"

"It is a delicate matter. Your Excellency must try out table companions and, when you find them to be such as you want, must have the art to keep them without letting them know the reason. For there is not a well-bred person in the world who would have it said that he has the honor of eating with Your Excellency only because he eats twice as much as another."

Realizing all the cogency of my remarks, His Excellency told the priest to bring me to dinner next day. Having found that, if I was strong in precept, I was even stronger in practice, he had me share his table every day.

Despite his age and his gout this Senator who had renounced everything except himself still nurtured an amorous inclination. He loved Teresa, the daughter of the actor Imer,[6] who lived in a house near[7] his palace, its windows being across the way from the apartment in which he slept. The girl, then aged seventeen, and pretty, willful, and a flirt, who was studying music to make a career of it on the stage, who was forever showing herself at her window, and whose charms had already intoxicated the old man, treated him cruelly. She came almost every day to pay him a visit, but she was always accompanied by her mother, an old actress who had retired from the stage to pursue the salvation of her soul and who, naturally enough, had decided to see if she could not contrive an alliance between the devil and God. She took her daughter to mass every day and insisted on her going to confession every Sunday; but in the afternoon she took her to visit the amorous old man, whose fury terrified me when she refused him a kiss on the excuse that, having performed her devotions that morning, she could not stoop to offend the very God she had eaten and who was perhaps still in her stomach. What a spectacle for me, then aged fifteen, whom the old man allowed to be the only and silent witness of these scenes! The scoundrelly mother applauded her daughter's resistance, and even made bold to lecture the votary of pleasure, who in turn did not dare to refute her maxims, which were either too Christian or not Christian at all, and had to fight down the temptation to throw anything within reach at her head. He could think of nothing to say to her. Anger took the place of concupiscence, and after they were gone he relieved himself with philosophical reflections addressed to me. Compelled to answer him and not knowing what to say, I one day suggested marriage. He astonished me by answering that she refused to become his wife.

"Why?"

"Because she does not want to incur the hatred of my family."

"Offer her a large sum of money, a position."

"She says she would not commit a mortal sin to become queen of the world."

"You must violate her or send her packing, banish her from your house."

"I am incapable of the first, and I cannot make up my mind to the second."

"Kill her."

"That is what it will come to, if I do not die first."

"Your Excellency is to be pitied."

"Do you ever go to visit her?"

70

"No, because I might fall in love with her; and if she acted toward me as I see her act here, I should be miserable."

"You are right."

After witnessing these scenes and being honored with these conversations, I became the nobleman's favorite. He admitted me to his evening receptions, which, as I have already said, were frequented by superannuated women and by men of wit. He said that they were the place for me to acquire a knowledge far more important than the philosophy of Gassendi,[8] which I was then studying at his behest instead of the Peripatetic philosophy, which he ridiculed. He laid down certain rules of conduct by which, as he showed me, I must abide if I was to attend his receptions, since the company would be astonished to see a boy of my age admitted to them. He ordered me never to speak except in reply to direct questions, and above all never to express my opinion on any subject, for at the age of fifteen I was not entitled to have one. Faithfully obeying his commands, I gained his esteem and within a few days was the pet of all the ladies who visited him. In my character of a young abate of no importance, they insisted on my accompanying them when they went to see their daughters or their nieces in the visiting rooms of the convents in which they were being educated; I went to their houses at all hours, and entered unannounced; I was scolded when I let a week go by without putting in an appearance; and when I entered the young ladies' apartments, I heard them hurrying away; but they said they were silly as soon as they saw that it was only I. I was delighted with their trustfulness.

Signor Malipiero amused himself before dinner by questioning me on the advantages I gained from being received by the respectable ladies whom I had met at his receptions, telling me before I could answer, however, that they were propriety itself and that everyone would consider me a low scoundrel if I said anything about them which reflected on the estimable reputation they enjoyed in society. Thus he inculcated the sound precept of discretion in me. It was at his palace that I met Signora Manzoni, the wife of a notary public,[9] of whom I shall have occasion to speak further on. This worthy lady inspired the greatest devotion in me. She taught me much, and gave me very sound advice; which if I had only followed it my life would not have been stormy, and so I should not today have found it worth recording.

So many fine acquaintanceships among women of fashion, as they are called, gave me a desire to please by my person and by elegance in dress; but my parish priest objected, as did my good grandmother. Taking me aside one day he told me in honeyed words that in the condition which I had embraced I should think of pleasing God by my state of mind, not men by my person: he condemned my elaborate curls and the delicate perfume of my pomade; he told me that the devil had me by the hair and that I would be excommunicated if I continued to devote such care to it, citing the words of an ecumenical council, *Clericus qui nutrit comam anathema sit* ("An ecclesiastic who grows his hair shall be anathema").[10] I replied by citing the example of a hundred abati who were not regarded as excommunicated and were left in peace, though they put on three times as much powder as I who put on only a trace of it and who used a pomade scented with ambergris which would make a woman in childbirth faint, whereas mine, which was scented with jasmine, brought me compliments from every gathering I entered. I ended by telling him that if I had wanted to stink I should have become a Capuchin, and that I was very sorry but I could not obey his commands in this particular.

Three or four days later he persuaded my grandmother to let him into my room so early in the morning that I was still asleep. She swore to me afterward that if she had known what he was going to do she would not have opened the door for him. The presumptuous priest, who loved me, softly approached and, with a pair of good scissors, pitilessly cut off all my front hair from ear to ear. My brother Francesco, who was in the next room, saw him but did nothing to stop him. In fact he was delighted for, wearing a wig himself, he was jealous of the beauty of my hair. He has been envious of me all his life, yet combining, though I know not how, his envy with affection; today this vice of his must have died of old age, like all mine.

When I awoke the work was already done. After his crime the priest departed as if nothing had happened. It was my two hands which made me realize all the horror of this unexampled butchery.

What anger! What indignation! What projects of revenge as soon as, mirror in hand, I saw the state to which the audacious priest had reduced me! My grandmother came running at my cries, my brother laughed. The old woman calmed me somewhat by admitting that the priest had gone beyond the bounds of permissible punishment.

Resolved to take my revenge I dressed, brooding over a hundred dark plans. I considered that I had a right to avenge myself in blood, without fear of the law. Since the theaters were open, I set out masked[11] and went to see the advocate Carrara, whom I had met at

Signor Malipiero's, to find out if I could bring a suit against the priest. He told me that a family had recently been ruined because the head of it had cut off a Slavonian merchant's mustache, which is far less than an entire forelock; hence I had but to command him if I wished to serve the priest on the spot with an extrajudiciary[12] which would make him tremble. I told him to do so, and to tell Signor Malipiero that evening why he had not seen me at his dinner table. It was clear that I could no longer go out unmasked so long as my hair had not grown back.

I ate a very bad dinner with my brother. My being obliged by this misfortune to forgo the delicate fare to which Signor Malipiero had accustomed me was not the least of the sufferings I had to bear because of the action of the high-handed priest whose godson I was. The fury that possessed me was so great that I shed tears. I was in despair because the insult I had suffered had a comic aspect and so put me in a ridiculous light, which I considered more prejudicial to my honor than any crime. I went to bed early, and a sound ten hours' sleep cooled my rage somewhat, but it left me no less determined to avenge myself by due legal process.

I was dressing to go to Signor Carrara's to read over the extrajudiciary, when I saw before me a skillful hairdresser whom I had encountered at Signora Contarini's. He told me that Signor Malipiero had sent him to dress my hair so that I could go out, for he wanted me to come and dine with him that same day. After looking over the damage, he laughed and said that I need only leave it to him, assuring me that he would make it possible for me to go out even more elegantly curled than before. This skillful young man made all my front hair the same length as the part which had been cut, and then dressed my hair *en vergette* to such effect that I found myself pleased, satisfied, and avenged.

I instantly forgot the insult, I went to the advocate and told him that I no longer wished for revenge, then I flew to Signor Malipiero's, where chance would have it that I found the priest, whom, despite my joy, I treated to a withering look. Nothing was said of what had happened, Signor Malipiero took in the whole scene, and the priest departed, certainly repenting of his action, for my hair was so elegantly curled that it really did deserve excommunication.

After my cruel godfather left, I did not dissemble with Signor Malipiero: I told him in so many words that I would look for another church, for I absolutely refused to remain connected with one whose priest was a man capable of going to such lengths. The wise old man told me that I was right. *This was precisely the way to bring me to do what was wanted of me.* That evening the entire company, who had already heard the story, complimented me, assuring me that my curls could not be more charming. I was the happiest of lads, and all the happier when two weeks had passed since the occurrence and Signor Malipiero had not said a word to me about going back to the church. Only my grandmother kept bothering me, insisting that I ought to go back.

But when I felt sure that my noble patron would not bring up the subject again, I was greatly surprised to hear him say that an opportunity had arisen which would make it possible for me to go back to the church and at the same time secure full satisfaction from the priest. "As president," he continued, "of the Confraternity of the Blessed Sacrament,[13] it falls to me to choose the orator to deliver the panegyric upon it on the fourth Sunday of this month, which happens to be the day after Christmas. The person I shall recommend to him is you, and I am sure that he will not dare to refuse you. What do you say to such a triumph? Does it please you?"

My surprise at his proposal was extreme, for it had never entered my head to become a preacher, still less that I had the ability to compose a sermon and deliver it. I told him I was certain he was joking; but as soon as he convinced me that he was speaking in earnest, it took him only a minute to persuade me and to make me sure that I was born to be the most famous preacher of the century as soon as I had put on flesh, for in those days I was extremely thin. I had no fear for my voice or my gestures, and so far as composition was concerned, I felt that I had more than ability enough to produce a masterpiece.

I told him that I was ready and that I could not wait to get home and begin writing the panegyric. "Though I am no theologian," I said, "I am well versed in the subject. I shall say astonishing things, and they will be new." The next day he told me that the priest had been delighted by his choice and even more by my willingness to accept this sacred task, but that he insisted that I show him my composition as soon as I had finished it, because, since the subject lay in the domain of the most exalted theology, he could not permit me to enter the pulpit unless he was certain that I had said nothing heretical. I agreed to this, and during the course of the week composed and copied out my panegyric. I still have it, and, what is more, I consider it excellent.

My poor grandmother could do nothing but weep with satisfaction at seeing her grandson an apostle. She made me read it to her, she told her beads as she listened, and declared that it was beautiful. Signor Malipiero, who did not tell his beads as he listened, told me that the priest would not like it. I had taken my text from Horace: *Ploravere suis non respondere favorem speratum meritis* ("They lamented that their merits did not meet with the gratitude for which they had hoped").[14] I deplored the wickedness and ingratitude of mankind, which had brought to naught the plan the divine wisdom had conceived for its redemption. He did not approve of my having taken my text from a moralist; but he was delighted that my sermon was not stuffed with Latin quotations.

I went to the priest's house to read it to him; he was not at home; having to wait for him, I fell in love with his niece Angela, who was working at the embroidery frame, who told me that she wanted to know me, and who, wanting a good laugh, insisted on my telling her the story of the forelock that her reverend uncle had cut off. This love determined my fate; it was the cause of two others, which were the causes of several other causes which ended by obliging me to renounce being a churchman. But let us not go too fast.

When the priest arrived he did not seem displeased to see me being entertained by his niece, who was my own age. After reading my sermon he told me that it was a very pretty academic diatribe, but that it was not suitable for the pulpit.

"I will give you one," he said, "of my own composition, which no one has seen. You shall learn it by heart, and I give you permission to say that it is yours."

"Thank you, Your Reverence. But I will deliver my own or none at all."

"But you shall not deliver this one in my church."

"You may discuss that with Signor Malipiero. Meanwhile, I shall take my composition to the censors, then to Monsignor the Patriarch, and if it is rejected I will have it printed."

"Come, come, young man! The Patriarch will agree with me."

That evening I repeated my argument with the priest to Signor Malipiero in the presence of all his guests. I was forced to read my panegyric, which was applauded on all hands. I was praised for my modesty in quoting none of the Fathers, whom at my age I could not have read, and the ladies admired me for having included not a word of Latin except my text from Horace, who, though a great libertine, nevertheless said excellent things. One of the Patriarch's nieces, who was present, said that she would speak to her uncle, to whom I was determined to appeal. Signor Malipiero told me to come and discuss the matter with him in the morning before I did anything else.

I obeyed, and he sent for the priest, who came at once. After letting him talk his fill, I convinced him by telling him that either the Patriarch would approve my sermon and I would deliver it without his running any risk; or he would disapprove of it and I would yield.

"Do not go to him," he said, "and I will approve it; I only ask you to change your text, for Horace was a villain."

"Why do you quote Seneca, Origen, Tertullian, Boethius, whom, since they were all heretics, you must consider more odious than Horace, who after all could not be a Christian?"

But I finally gave in to please Signor Malipiero, and I put in the text the priest wanted, despite the fact that it was out of keeping with my sermon. I then gave it to him, so that I should have an excuse, by calling for it the following morning, to talk to his niece.

But what really amused me was Doctor Gozzi. I sent him my sermon out of vanity. He sent it back to me, condemning it and asking me if I had gone mad. He told me that if I was allowed to deliver it in the pulpit I would bring dishonor not only on myself but also on him, who had educated me.

I delivered my sermon in the Church of San Samuele before a most select audience. I received great praise, after which it was unanimously predicted that I would become the greatest preacher of the century, since no one at the age of fifteen had ever played the role so well.

In the bag in which it is customary for the congregation to put their offerings for the preacher, the sexton who emptied it found nearly fifty zecchini, together with some love letters which scandalized the bigots. One, which was anonymous, though I thought I knew who had written it, led me into an awkward indiscretion which I think it best to spare the reader. This rich harvest when I was greatly in need of money made me think seriously of becoming a preacher, and I announced my vocation to the priest and asked him to help me. I thus gave myself the means of going daily to his house, where I fell more and more in love with Angela, who was willing to let me love her but who, showing herself to be a perfect dragon of virtue, obstinately refused to grant me the slightest favor. She wanted me to renounce my orders and marry her. I could not

76

bring myself to do this. But hoping to make her change her mind, I persisted. Her uncle had commissioned me to compose a panegyric on St. Joseph which I was to recite on the 19th of March 1741. I composed it, and the priest himself spoke of it with enthusiasm; but it was fated that I should not preach more than once on this earth. Here is the story; sorry as it is, it is only too true, though there are those who are cruel enough to find it comic.

I thought I need not take much trouble to learn my sermon by heart. I was the author of it, I knew that I knew it; and the calamity of forgetting it did not seem to me within the realm of possible things. I might forget a sentence; but I must surely be able to substitute another; and just as I never found myself at a loss when I was discoursing to a group of well-bred people, I thought it beyond probability that I could find myself stricken dumb before an audience in which I knew no one who could abash me and make me lose my reasoning powers. So I amused myself as usual, doing no more than read my composition over night and morning in order to fix it in my memory, of which I had never had reason to complain.

So on the 19th of March, the day on which I was to enter the pulpit four hours after noon to deliver my sermon, I did not have the strength of mind to deprive myself of the pleasure of dining with the Count of Montereale,[15] who was staying in my house and who had invited the patrician Barozzi, who was to marry his daughter the Countess Lucia after Easter.

I was still at table with this distinguished company when a clerk came to tell me that I was awaited at the sacristy. With my stomach full and my head the worse for wine, I set out, I hurry to the church, I enter the pulpit.

I speak the exordium perfectly, I draw breath. But after a bare hundred words of the exposition, I no longer know what I am saying or what I have to say. Determined to go on at all costs, I beat around the bush, and what finishes me off completely is a low murmur from the restive audience, only too aware of my plight. I see several people leave the church, I think I hear laughter, I lose my head and all hope of retrieving the situation. I can assure my reader that I have never known whether I pretended to faint or fainted in good earnest. All I know is that I dropped to the floor of the pulpit, at the same time hitting the wall with my head and wishing that I had split my skull. Two clergymen came and led me back to the sacristy, where without a word to anyone I took my cloak and my hat and went home. Shutting myself in my room, I put on a short coat such as abati wear in the country, and after packing what I needed in my portmanteau I went and asked my grandmother for some money, then set out for Padua to obtain my *terzarie*.[16] I arrived there at midnight and immediately went to bed in the house of my good Doctor Gozzi, to whom I took care not to give an account of my disaster. After doing all that was necessary for my doctorate in the following year, I returned to Venice after Easter, to find my misfortune forgotten; but there was no longer any question of my preaching. I was encouraged to try again, but to no purpose. I completely renounced the profession.

On Ascension Eve Signora Manzoni's husband introduced me to a young courtesan who was then causing a great stir in Venice. She was known as La Cavamacchie,[17] which means "the cleaner," because her father had practiced the cleaning trade. She wanted to be called Preato, that being her family name; but her friends called her Giulietta; it was her Christian name, and pretty enough to be recorded in history.

Her celebrity was due to the fact that the Marchese Sanvitale,[18] of Parma, had spent a hundred thousand scudi on her in return for her favors. Her beauty was the talk of Venice. Those who could manage to speak with her considered themselves fortunate, and those who were admitted into her circle more than fortunate. As I shall have occasion to speak of her more than once in these memoirs, the reader may be glad to have her story in a few words.

In the year 1735, Giulietta, then fourteen years of age, took a coat which had been cleaned to a Venetian nobleman named Marco Muazzo. This nobleman, finding her charming despite her rags, went to see her at her father's house with a well-known advocate named Bastiano Uccelli.[19] Uccelli, even more struck by her fervid imagination and gaiety than by her beauty and her fine figure, set her up in a well-furnished apartment, gave her a music master, and made her his mistress. During the Fair[20] he took her walking with him on the Liston,[21] where she amazed all the connoisseurs. Within six months she thought herself musician enough to sign a contract with an impresario, who took her to Vienna to play a castrato role in an opera by Metastasio.[22]

At this point the advocate saw fit to leave her and turned her over to a rich Jew, who gave her some diamonds and then likewise left her. In Vienna her charms won her the applause for which she could not hope from her talents, which were less than mediocre. The crowd of worshipers who went to sacrifice to the idol, and which was renewed from week to week, determined the august Maria Theresa to destroy the new cult. She sent the new goddess a command to leave the capital of Austria instantly. It was Count Bonifazio Spada who brought her back to Venice, which she left to sing in Padua. It was there that her charms won her the love of Count Giacomo Sanvitale; nothing came of it, however, for the Marchesa, who stood very much on her dignity, slapped her face in her own box over a certain remark of the artist's which she considered insolent. The insult so disgusted Giulietta with the theater that she gave it up forever. She returned to her native city. Rejoicing in the reputation of having been *sfrattata*[23] from Vienna, she could not fail to make her fortune. It had become a title. To disparage a singer or a dancer, it was only necessary to say that she had been to Vienna and had been so little acclaimed that the Empress had not thought her worth banishing.

Signor Steffano Querini delle Papozze[24] immediately became her acknowledged lover, and her fancy man three months later when the Marchese Sanvitale made her his mistress in the spring of the year 1740. He began by giving her a hundred thousand ducati correnti.[25] To prevent anyone from attributing the gift of such an extravagant sum to weakness, he said that it was scarcely enough to avenge the artist for a slap his wife had given her. Giulietta, however, would never admit the slap, and she was right: by acknowledging the Marchese's magnanimity, she would have dishonored herself. The slap would have blighted charms of whose intrinsic value she prided herself upon seeing the world convinced.

In the following year, 1741, Signor Manzoni introduced me to this Phryne[26] as a young abate who was beginning to make a name for himself. She was living near San Paterniano,[27] at the foot of the bridge, in a house belonging to Signor Piai. I found her in the company of six or seven seasoned admirers. She was sitting at her ease on a sofa, beside Signor Querini. Her appearance surprised me; in the tone of a princess, and looking at me as if I were for sale, she told me that she was not sorry to have made my acquaintance. As soon as she had asked me to be seated, I began examining her too. I found it easy to do. The room was not large, but there were at least twenty candles.

Giulietta was a tall, beautiful girl of eighteen years; her dazzling whiteness, the crimson of her cheeks, the vermilion of her lips, and the blackness and the very narrow curved line of her eyebrows impressed me as artificial. Two fine rows of teeth made one overlook the fact that her mouth was too large. So she took care always to be smiling. Her bosom was simply a broad, beautiful table, on which a fichu was artfully disposed to make one imagine that the dishes one wishes to find in such a place were indeed there; but I did not admire it. Despite her rings and her bracelets, I observed that her hands were too big and too bony, and for all the care she took not to expose her feet, a slipper which lay at the bottom of her dress made it clear to me that they were as big as she was—a graceless proportion which is displeasing not only to Chinese and Spaniards, but to all connoisseurs. A tall woman should have small feet, and such was the taste of Lord Holofernes, who otherwise would not have found Lady Judith charming. "*Et sandalia eius,*" says the Holy Spirit, "*rapuerunt oculos eius*" ("And her sandals ravished his eyes").[28] Comparing her, in the course of my careful examination, with the hundred thousand ducats which the nobleman from Parma had given her, I was astonished, for I would not myself have given a zecchino to look upon all those other beauties *quas insternebat stola* ("which her dress concealed").

A quarter of an hour after my arrival, the murmur of water struck by the oars of a gondola coming in to the landing announced the prodigal Marchese. We rose, and Signor Querini quickly left his place, blushing a little. Signor Sanvitale, who was old rather than young and who had traveled, sat down near her, but not on the sofa, which obliged the beauty to turn. I was now able to see her in full-face. I found her more beautiful so than in profile. The four or five times I paid court to her sufficed for me to tell the company at Signor Malipiero's that she could be attractive only to exhausted appetites, for she possessed neither the beauties of simple nature nor the sophistication of society nor any particular talent nor easy manners. My opinion pleased everyone present, but Signor Malipiero smiled and whispered in my ear that Giulietta would certainly be informed of the portrait I had just drawn of her and would become my enemy. He proved to be right.

I thought it strange in this notorious girl that she very seldom addressed me and that she never looked at me without peering through a concave lens to assist her myopic vision or squeezing her eyelids together, as if she did not want to give me the honor of a full view of her eyes, which were incontestably beautiful. They were blue, perfectly shaped, prominent, and illuminated by that unimaginable iridescence which nature gives only, and rarely, to youth, and which usually disappears at about the age of forty after having performed miracles. The late King of Prussia kept it until his death.

Giulietta learned of the portrait I had given of her at Signor Malipiero's. The informer was the Ragionato[29] Saverio Costantini. She said to Signor Manzoni in my presence that a great connoisseur had found some annoying faults in her, but she did not specify them. I saw that she was hitting at me indirectly, and I expected to be ostracized. However, she kept me waiting for a full hour. The conversation turned to a concert given by the actor Imer, at which his daughter Teresa had had a brilliant success. She asked me point-blank what Signor Malipiero was doing with her; I answered that he was giving her an education.

"He is quite capable of that," she replied, "for he is highly intelligent; but I should like to know what he is doing with you."

"Whatever he can."

"I am told he finds you a little stupid."

The laugh, of course, was on her side. Not knowing what to answer, I very nearly blushed and a quarter of an hour later I left, certain that I should never set foot in her house again. My account of this breach greatly amused my old Senator the next day at dinner.

I spent the summer going to indulge in Arcadian courtship with Angela at the school where she went to learn embroidering. Her parsimony in granting me favors irritated me, and I already found my love a torment. With my strong temperament, I needed a girl of Bettina's type, one who enjoyed appeasing the flame of love without quenching it. But I soon got rid of my taste for this shallow satisfaction. Having a kind of virginity myself, I felt the greatest reverence for a girl's. I thought it the Palladium[30] of Cecrops.[31] I would have nothing to do with married women. What stupidity! I was fool enough to be jealous of their husbands. Angela was recalcitrant in the highest degree, yet not a flirt. She was drying me up; I was growing thin. The pathetic and plaintive speeches I addressed to her at the embroidery frame at which she worked with two other girls, sisters and friends of hers, produced more effect on them than upon her heart, for that was too much the slave of the precept which was poisoning my life. If I had had eyes for anyone but her I should have realized that the two sisters had more charm than she did; but she had made me obstinate. She told me that she was ready to become my wife, and she believed that I could wish for nothing more. She exasperated me beyond measure when, as a mark of extreme favor, she told me that abstinence made her suffer as much as it did me.

At the beginning of the autumn a letter from the Countess of Montereale summoned me to her country place in Friuli, an estate named Pasiano.[32] She was to be entertaining a brilliant company, including her daughter, who had become a Venetian lady of patrician rank, who was intelligent and beautiful and had one eye so lovely that it made up for the other, rendered hideous by leucoma.

Finding gaiety at Pasiano, I had no difficulty in increasing it and for the time being forgetting the cruel Angela. I was allotted a room on the ground floor, giving on to the garden, where I found myself so comfortable that it did not occur to me to wonder next to whom I might be lodging. Upon my awaking the following morning my eyes were pleasantly surprised by the charming object which approached my bed to serve me my coffee. It was a very young girl, but already formed as city girls are at seventeen; she was only fourteen. White-skinned, with black eyes, her hair hanging loose, and covered only by a shift and a petticoat laced awry which exposed half of her bare leg to view, she looked at me as frankly and calmly as if I had been an old acquaintance. She asked me if I had found my bed comfortable.

"Yes. I'm sure you made it. Who are you?"

"I'm Lucia, the caretaker's daughter, I have neither brothers nor sisters, and I'm fourteen. I'm very glad you haven't a valet, for I will wait on you myself, and I am sure you will be satisfied."

Enchanted by this beginning, I sit up; she hands me my dressing gown, saying a hundred things of which I did not understand a word. I drink my coffee, as disconcerted as she was at ease, and amazed at a beauty to which it was impossible to remain indifferent. She had sat down on the foot of my bed, excusing herself for the liberty she was taking only by a laugh which expressed everything. Her father and her mother came in while I still had the coffee cup to my lips. Lucia does not budge; she looks at them as if pluming herself on the post she had assumed. They chide her gently and ask me to excuse her.

The good people say a hundred civil things to me; and Lucia goes off about her business. They praise her to me: she is their only child, their darling, the consolation of their old age; she obeys them in everything; she fears God; she is as fit as a fiddle; she has only one fault.

"What is that?"

"She's too young."

"A charming fault."

In less than an hour I am convinced that I have been conversing with probity, truth, the social virtues, and genuine honor.

Re-enter Lucia, laughing, freshly washed, with her hair done up in a way of her own, with shoes on her feet, and wearing a dress; after dropping me a rustic curtsy, she gives her mother several kisses, then goes and sits on her father's lap; I tell her to sit on the bed; but she says that such an honor is not for her when she is dressed.

The simple, innocent, and enchanting notion which I find in this answer makes me laugh. I consider if she is prettier now than she was an hour earlier, and I decide in favor of earlier. I put her above not only Angela but Bettina too.

The hairdresser enters, the respectable family departs, I dress, I go upstairs, and spend the day most amusingly, as one spends the day in the country in select company. The next morning I am scarcely awake before I ring, and once more Lucia appears before me, the same as the previous day, as astonishing in her words as in her ways. Everything in her shone under the charming varnish of frankness and innocence. I could not conceive how, being properly brought up and virtuous and not at all stupid, she did not know that she could not show herself to me in this way without risk of setting me on fire. "It must be," I told myself, "that, attaching no importance to certain little freedoms, she is not strait-laced." With this idea in mind, I decide to convince her that I appreciated her. I do not feel guilty toward her parents, for I suppose them to be as easygoing as herself. Nor do I fear to be the first to alarm her lovely innocence and to cast the dark light of evil into her soul. In short, unwilling either to be the dupe of feeling or to act unfeelingly, I decided to find out what was what. Without further ado, I extend a libertine hand toward her, and by what appears to be an involuntary movement she draws back, she blushes, her gaiety vanishes, and she turns, pretending to look for something or other, until she finds herself over her agitation. This took only a minute. She approaches again, delivered from all her uneasiness except the shame of having shown herself ill-natured and the fear of having misinterpreted an action which, on my part, might have been either completely innocent or common politeness. She was already laughing. I saw in her soul all that I have just set down, and I hastened to reassure her. Seeing that I was risking too much by acting, I resolved to devote the following morning to making her talk.

After drinking my coffee I interrupted what she was saying to me by remarking that it was cold and that she would not feel it if she came under the covers with me.

"Shan't I be in your way?"

"No, but it occurs to me that your mother might come in."

"She won't think any harm."

"Come here. But you know the risk we're running."

"Of course—I'm no fool; but you are good and, what's more, a priest."

"Then come, but first shut the door."

"No, no, for people would think I don't know what."

So she came into the place I made for her, telling me some long story of which I understood not a word, for in this position, not wishing to surrender to the movements of nature, I was the most torpid of men. Lucia's fearlessness, which was certainly not feigned, impressed me to such a point that I was ashamed to enlighten her. Finally she told me that it had just struck fifteen o'clock[33] and that if old Count Antonio came down and saw us as we then were, he would make jokes she would find annoying. "He is the kind of man," she said, "that, when I see him, I run away. I shall go now because I am not curious to see you get out of bed."

I stayed there for more than a quarter of an hour, motionless and in a condition to arouse pity for I was really in a state of violent excitement. The conversation into which I led her the next morning, without making her come into my bed, finally convinced me that she rightly deserved to be the idol of her parents, and that her freedom of mind and her uninhibited behavior had no other source than her innocence and the purity of her soul. Her artlessness, her vivacity, her curiosity, her constant blushes when she said things which provoked me to laughter and which, on her part, were wholly guileless—everything about her showed me that she was an angel incarnate who could not fail to become the victim of the first libertine who should take her in hand. I felt certain that it would not be I. The mere thought made me shudder. My own self-esteem answered for Lucia's honor to her respectable parents who, trusting in their good opinion of my morals, thus freely left her in my hands. I thought that I should become the most contemptible of men if I betrayed their confidence in me. So I chose the course of suffering and, certain of gaining the victory under any circumstances, I determined to fight, content that her presence should be the only reward of my desires.

I had not yet learned the maxim that *so long as the battle goes on, victory remains uncertain.*

I told her that I should be glad if she would come earlier and wake me even if I was asleep, because the less I slept the better I felt. Thus our two hours of conversation became three, which passed like a flash. When her mother, coming to fetch her, found her sitting on my bed, she no longer scolded her but only exclaimed over my kindness in putting up with her. Lucia gave her a hundred kisses. The kind, innocent woman begged me to teach Lucia good behavior and to cultivate her mind. After her mother left, Lucia did not consider that she was any the more free. The company of this angel made me suffer the pains of hell. Though constantly tempted to deluge her face with kisses when she laughingly brought it within two inches of mine and told me that she wanted to be my sister, I scrupulously avoided taking her hands; for me to have given her a single kiss would have blown my edifice sky-high, for I felt that I had become as inflammable as straw. When she left I was always astonished that I had won the victory; but, my appetite for laurels being insatiable, I could scarcely wait for the next morning to come so that I might renew the sweet and perilous battle. *It is shallow desires which make a young man bold; strong desires confound him.*

After ten or twelve days, at the conclusion of which I felt obliged either to make an end or become a villain, I chose to make an end, since nothing assured me that I should obtain the due reward of my villainy in the consent of the object who would have led me into it. With Lucia turned dragon when I had put her in the position of having to defend herself, the open door of the room would have exposed me to disgrace and to dreary repentance. The thought terrified me. I must make an end, and I did not know how to go about it. I could no longer resist a girl who, at earliest dawn, and wearing only a petticoat over her shift, came running to me in pure gaiety of heart to ask me how I had slept, breathing her words upon my very lips. I drew back my head, and she laughingly reproached me for being afraid when she was not. I fatuously answered that she was wrong if she believed that I was afraid of her, who was no more than a child. She answered that two years' difference meant nothing.

Unable to bear any more, yet growing more amorous every day precisely because of the schoolboy's remedy, which disarms by exhausting potency at the moment but, *irritating nature, provokes her to vengeance, which she takes by redoubling the desires of the tyrant who has subdued her,* I spent the whole night with the phantom of Lucia haunting a mind already saddened by my decision to see her the next morning for the last time. My intention of asking her face to face to return no more seemed to me magnificent, heroic, unique, infallible. I believed that Lucia would not only help me to carry out my plan, but would also hold me in the highest regard all the rest of her life.

With the first light of day she appears, dazzling, radiant, laughing, her hair down, running to me with open arms, but suddenly downcast at seeing me pale, discomposed, wretched.

"Why, what is the matter?" she asks.

"I couldn't sleep."

"Why?"

"Because I have made up my mind to inform you of a plan which, though it will make me miserable, will gain me your highest regard."

"But if it will gain you my regard, it ought to make you happy. But tell me why, having talked to me fondly yesterday, you address me today as formally as if I were a young lady. What have I done to you, Signor Abate? I'm going to fetch your coffee, and you shall tell me everything when you've drunk it. I can hardly wait to hear what you have to say."

She goes, she comes back, I drink the coffee, I am serious, her artless talk sets me laughing, which delights her; she clears away, she goes and shuts the door, for it was a windy day; then, not wanting to lose a word of what I was to tell her, she asks me to make a little room for her. I do so fearing nothing, for I believed that I was like a dead man.

After giving her a true account of the state into which her charms had put me and of all that I had suffered from my determination to resist my inclination to give her unmistakable evidence of my tender feelings, I explain to her that, unable any longer to endure the torment which her presence caused my amorous soul, I am reduced to asking her to keep out of my sight from henceforth. The unbounded truth of my passion, my desire that she should consider the expedient I had adopted to be the utmost effort of a perfect love, lent me a sublime eloquence. I depicted the terrible consequences which could make us wretched if we acted in any other way than that which her virtue and my own had obliged me to propose to her.

At the conclusion of my sermon she wiped away my tears with the front of my shift, never dreaming that by this charitable act she exposed to my view two rocks eminently adapted to make the most skillful of pilots suffer shipwreck.

After this scene in dumb show, she told me sadly that my tears distressed her and that she could never have imagined she could give me cause to shed them. "All that you have told me," she said, "has shown me that you love me very much; but I do not understand how you can be alarmed by it, whereas your love gives me infinite pleasure. *You banish me from your presence because your love makes you afraid. What would you do if you hated me?* Am I guilty because I have made you fall in love? If that is a crime, I assure you that, since I had no intention of committing it, you cannot in conscience punish me for it. Yet it is true that I am rather glad of it. As for the risks people run when they love each other, and which I know perfectly well, we are free to defy them. I am astonished that, though I am ignorant, this does not seem so difficult to me, whereas you who, according to what everyone says, are so intelligent, feel afraid. What surprises me is that, though love is not a sickness, it has made you ill, whereas its effect on me is exactly the contrary. Is it possible that I am wrong and that what I feel for you is not love? You saw me so gay when I arrived, because I dreamed of you all the livelong night; but that didn't keep me from sleeping, except that I woke five or six times to find out if it was really you I was holding in my arms. As soon as I saw it was not you, I went back to sleep to find my dream again, and I succeeded. Didn't I have good reason to be gay this morning? My dear Abate, if love is a torture for you, I am sorry. Could it be that you were born not to love? I will do whatever you tell me to; except that, even if your cure depended on it, I could never stop loving you. Yet if your cure does depend on your no longer loving me, then do all that you can, for I would rather have you alive without love than dead from loving. Only see if you cannot find some other way, for the plan you have told me about makes me wretched. Think. It may be that there is more of a choice than you suppose. Suggest another. Trust in Lucia."

This truthful, artless, natural speech showed me by how much Nature's eloquence is superior to the eloquence of the philosophic mind. For the first time I clasped this heavenly creature in my arms, saying: "*Yes, my dear Lucia; you can apply the most powerful palliative to the sickness which is devouring me; let me give a thousand kisses to that tongue of yours, to the heavenly mouth which has told me that I am happy.*"

We then spent a full hour in the most eloquent silence, except that from time to time Lucia cried out, "Oh, my God! Is it true that I am not dreaming?" Even so, I respected her in the matter of essential importance, and precisely because she offered me no resistance. This was my weakness.

"I am uneasy," she says suddenly; "I have a strange feeling." She jumps out of the bed, hurriedly sets it to rights, and sits down on the foot of it. A moment later her mother enters, shutting the door again behind her and remarking that I was right for there was a strong wind. She compliments me on my fine color, and tells her daughter she must go and get dressed to go to mass. Lucia came back an hour later to tell me that the miracle she had performed made her proud, for my present look of health made her a thousand times more certain of my love than the pitiful state in which she had found me that morning. "If your perfect happiness," she said, "depends only on me, be happy! I can refuse you nothing."

She then left me; and despite the fact that my senses were still reeling, I did not fail to reflect that I was on the very edge of the abyss and that only the greatest effort could keep me from falling into it.

After spending the whole month of September there in the country, I found myself in possession of Lucia for eleven successive nights, which, knowing that her mother was a sound sleeper, she came and spent in my arms. What made us insatiable was an abstinence which she did everything in her power to force me to renounce. She could not taste the sweetness of the forbidden fruit except by letting me eat it. She tried a hundred times to deceive me by saying that I had already gathered it, but Bettina had taught me too much for me to be taken in. I took my departure from Pasiano promising her that I would return in the spring, but leaving her in a state of mind which was to be the cause of her unhappy fate—a fate with which I sincerely reproached myself in Holland twenty years later, and with which I shall reproach myself to the day of my death.

Three or four days after my return to Venice I relapsed into all my old ways, falling in love with Angela again and hoping to achieve at least what I had achieved with Lucia. A fear which I no longer find in my nature today, a panic terror of consequences fatal to my future career, held me back from full enjoyment. I do not know if I have ever been a man of perfect probity; but I know that the sentiments I cherished in my early youth were far more delicate than those to which the course of my life has accustomed me. *An evil philosophy too greatly diminishes the number of so-called prejudices.*

The two sisters who worked at the embroidery frame with Angela were her bosom friends and the repositories of all her secrets. I had no idea, until after I had come to know them, that they condemned their friend's excessive severity. Not being conceited enough to suppose that the two girls could fall in love with me from listening to my complaints, not only did I not restrain myself in their presence, I confided my troubles to them when Angela was not there. I often spoke to them with an ardor far greater than that with which I addressed the cruel girl who quelled it in me. *The genuine lover is always afraid that the object of his love will think he is exaggerating; and fear of saying too much makes him say less than is the case.*

The mistress of the school, a sanctimonious old woman, who at first seemed quite indifferent to my unconcealed fondness for Angela, finally looked askance on my frequent visits and informed Angela's uncle, the priest Tosello, of them. In consequence he one day gently warned me that I should not frequent the house so much, since my assiduity might be wrongly interpreted and in a manner prejudicial to his niece's honor. This was a thunderbolt; but, receiving his warning without showing my emotion, I answered that I would find some other place to spend the time I was spending at the embroideress's house.

Three or four days later I paid her a polite visit, without stopping at the embroidery frame for even an instant; however, I managed to slip into the hands of the elder sister, whose name was Nanetta, a letter inside which was another for my dear Angela, in which I explained the reason which had obliged me to suspend my visits. I begged her to think of some means which might procure me the satisfaction of discoursing to her on my passion. I wrote to Nanetta that I would come the next day but one to receive the answer, which she would easily find means to give me.

The girl carried out my instructions to perfection; and on the second day following she handed me the answer as I was leaving the room, and in such way as to escape all notice.

In a brief note (for she disliked writing) Angela promised me eternal constancy and told me to do everything I should find in the letter Nanetta was writing me. Here is the translation of Nanetta's letter, which I have kept, as I have all those which will be found in these memoirs.

"There is nothing in the world, Signor Abate, that I am not prepared to do for my dear friend Angela. She comes to visit us every feast day, sups with us, and spends the night. I suggest a way for you to make the acquaintance of Signora Orio, our aunt; but if you succeed in gaining entrance to our house, I warn you not to show that you have a special liking for Angela, for our aunt would disapprove of your coming to her house to secure the opportunity of speaking to someone who is not in the family. So I suggest the following plan, which I will further as far as in me lies. Signora Orio, though a woman of station, is not rich and hence wishes to be entered in the list of noble widows who can aspire to the bounty of the Confraternity of the Blessed Sacrament, of which Signor Malipiero is president. Last Sunday Angela told her that you enjoy the affection of this nobleman, and that the best means of gaining his support would be to obtain your promise to ask him for it. She foolishly told her that you are in love with me and that you only went to our embroidery mistress's house to have an opportunity to talk with me, and that hence I could secure your interest on her behalf. My aunt answered that, since you were a priest, there was nothing to fear and that I might write to you to come to her house; but I refused. The Procuratore[34] Rosa, who is my aunt's very life, told her that I was right and that it was not proper for me to write to you, but that she herself should ask you to come and discuss an important matter with her. He said that if it was true that you were taken with me, you would be sure to come, and he persuaded her to write you the note which you will find at home. If you wish to find Angela with us, put off your visit until day after tomorrow, Sunday. If you can persuade Signor Malipiero to grant the favor my aunt asks, you will become the pet of the house. You will forgive it if I treat you badly, for I said that I did not like you. You will do well to flirt a little with my aunt, even though she is sixty. Signor Rosa will not be jealous, and you will endear yourself to the whole household. I shall arrange an opportunity for you to speak with Angela alone. I will do everything in my power to convince you of my friendship. Farewell."

I found this plan thoroughly well contrived. I received Signora Orio's note that evening; I went to her house in accordance with Nanetta's instructions; she asked me to act in her interest, and entrusted me with all the certificates of which I might have need. I gave her my promise. I scarcely spoke to Angela; I made up to Nanetta, who treated me very badly; and I won the friendship of the old advocate Rosa, who was useful to me later on.

Considering how I could obtain this favor from Signor Malipiero, I saw that my best course would be to appeal to Teresa Imer, who turned everything to her own advantage and at the same time pleased the old man, who was still in love with her. So I paid her a surprise visit, even entering her room unannounced. I found her alone with the physician Doro,[35] who at once pretended to be there only for professional reasons. He then wrote out a prescription, took her pulse, and left.

This Doro was rumored to be in love with her, and Signor Malipiero, who was jealous of him, had forbidden her to receive him and she had promised not to. Teresa knew that I was not unaware of this, and she must have been annoyed at my discovering that she made light of the promise she had given the old man. She must also fear that I would be indiscreet. It was the moment when I could hope to obtain from her all that I wished.

I told her in a few words the business which brought me to see her, and at the same time assured her that she must never think me capable of a base action. After assuring me that she wanted nothing better than to seize this occasion to convince me of her desire to oblige me, Teresa asked me to give her all the necessary certificates for the lady for whom she was to interest herself. At the same time she showed me those of another lady on whose behalf she had undertaken to speak, but she promised to sacrifice her for me. She kept her word. Only two days later I had the decree, signed by His Excellency as president of the Fraternity of the Poor.[36] Signora Orio's name was immediately included in the list for the bounties which were drawn by lot twice a year.

Nanetta and her sister Marta were the orphan daughters of a sister of Signora Orio, whose entire property consisted in the house in which she lived, of which she rented out the second floor, and a pension from her brother, who was secretary to the Council of Ten.[37] She had living with her only her two charming nieces, of whom one was sixteen, the other fifteen. In place of a servant she had a woman water-carrier who, for four lire[38] a month, came every day to do the chores for the entire house. Her one friend was the advocate Rosa, who, like herself, was sixty and was only awaiting the death of his wife to marry her. Nanetta and Marta slept together on the fourth floor in a wide bed, in which Angela too slept with them every feast day. On weekdays they all went to school to the embroidery mistress.

As soon as I was in possession of the decree which Signora Orio wanted, I made a brief visit to the embroidery mistress to give Nanetta a note in which I told her the good news that I had obtained the favor, adding that I would take the decree to her aunt the next day but one, which was a feast day. I earnestly urged her to arrange a private meeting with Angela for me.

The next day but one Nanetta was on the watch for my arrival and handed me a note, at the same time telling me to find an opportunity to read it before I left the house. I enter, and I see Angela with Signora Orio, the old advocate, and Marta. Anxious to read the note, I decline a chair and give the widow her certificates and the decree of admission to the bounties; the only recompense I ask of her is the honor of saluting her hand.

"Oh, my dearest Abate, you shall kiss me, and no one will take it amiss since I am thirty years older than you."

She should have said forty-five.

I give her the two kisses, and she tells me to go and kiss her nieces as well, who instantly took to flight, only Angela remaining to brave my audacity. The widow asks me to be seated.

"Signora, I cannot."

"Why not? What behavior!"

"Signora, I will come back."

"I won't hear of it!"

"I am under a pressing necessity."

"I understand. Nanetta, go upstairs with the Abate and show him."

"Please excuse me, Aunt."

"What a prude! Marta, you go."

"Aunt, make Nanetta obey you."

"Alas, Signora, the young ladies are right. I am leaving."

"Not a bit of it; my nieces are downright fools. Signor Rosa will show you the way."

He takes me by the hand and leads me to the requisite place on the fourth floor, and leaves me there. Here is Nanetta's note:

"My aunt will ask you to supper but you will decline. You will leave when we sit down at table, and Marta will go to light you to the street door, which she will open; but you will not go out. She will close it and come back. Everyone will believe you gone. You will go up the stairs in the dark, and then up two more flights until you reach the fourth floor. The stairs are good. You will wait there for the three of us. We will come after Signor Rosa leaves and we put our aunt to bed. It will rest with Angela herself to grant you the private interview which you desire, and all night long if she so wishes; and I hope it will be a happy one for you."

What joy! What gratitude for the fortunate chance which brought me to read this note in the very place where I was to wait in darkness for the object of my flame! Sure that I should find my way without the least difficulty, and foreseeing no obstacle, I go downstairs to Signora Orio, rejoicing in my good fortune.

CHAPTER V

An untoward night. I fall in love with the two
sisters, I forget Angela. A ball at my house.
Giulietta humiliated. My return to Pasiano.
Lucia's misfortune.

After expressing her thanks to me at great length, Signora Orio told me that in future I was to enjoy all the privileges of a friend of the family. We spent four hours laughing and joking. I made such good excuses for not staying to supper that she had to accept them. Marta was going to light the way for me; but a direct command from Signora Orio to Nanetta, whom she believed to be my favorite, obliged her to precede me, candlestick in hand. The sly vixen hurried down the stairs, opened the door, banged it shut, put out the candle and, leaving me there, ran back up to rejoin her aunt, who sharply reprimanded her for treating me so shabbily. I groped my way upstairs to the appointed place, and flung myself on a couch like a man who, having given his enemies the slip, awaits the moment of his happiness.

After spending an hour in the most pleasing reveries, I hear the street door being opened, then closed and double-locked, and ten minutes later I see the two sisters, followed by Angela. I disregard the others completely and spend two whole hours talking only with her. Midnight strikes; I am pitied for having gone supperless; but the tone of commiseration offends me; I answer that, in such happiness, it would be impossible for me to feel any lack. I am told that I am in prison, since the key to the house door is under Signora Orio's bolster, who will not open it until dawn, to go to the first mass. I am astonished that anyone should think I could consider this bad news; on the contrary, I am happy to have five hours before me and to be sure that I shall spend them with the object of my adoration. An hour later Nanetta laughs under her breath. Angela insists on knowing what she is laughing at; she whispers in her ear; Marta laughs too; I ask them to tell me why they are laughing; and finally Nanetta, looking chagrined, tells me that she has no other candle and that when this one burns out we shall be left in darkness. This news fills me with joy, but I hide it. I tell them that I am sorry on their account. I suggest that they go to bed and sleep in peace, assuring them of my respect; but this proposal sets them laughing again.

"What shall we do in the dark?"

"We'll talk."

There were four of us, we had been conversing for three hours, and I was the hero of the play. Love is a great poet: its matter is inexhaustible; but if the end at which it aims never arrives, it sinks like dough at the baker's. My dear Angela listened, but not being fond of talking, answered very little; she was not particularly clever; instead, she prided herself on showing sound common sense. To weaken my arguments she usually only launched a proverb, as the Romans fired a catapult. She drew away, or repulsed my poor hands with the most offensive gentleness, whenever love called them to its aid. Yet I continued to talk and use my hands without losing courage. But I became desperate when I saw that my too subtle arguments confused her instead of convincing her and, instead of softening her heart, troubled it. I was completely astonished to read on Nanetta's and Marta's faces the impression which the shafts I was shooting straight at Angela made on them. This metaphysical curve seemed to me out of the course of nature; it should have been an angle. Unfortunately I was studying geometry at that period. Despite the season, I was sweating great drops. Nanetta got up to carry out the candle, which would have made an unbearable stench if it had guttered out in our presence.

No sooner is it dark than my arms naturally rise to take possession of the object necessary to the state of my soul; yet I cannot but laugh when I find that Angela has seized the previous moment to make sure that she will not be caught. I spent a whole hour saying the most amusing things which love could invent to persuade her to come back and sit on the same seat. I thought it impossible that she could really be in earnest. "This joke," I said at last, "has gone on too long; it is against nature; I can't run after you, and it amazes me to hear you laughing; such strange behavior makes it seem that you are mocking me. So come and sit down. Since I have to talk to you without seeing you, at least my hands should assure me that I am not talking to the air. If you are making a mock of me, you must realize that you are insulting me, and love, I believe, should not be put to the test of insult."

"Very well! Calm yourself. I am listening to you and not losing a single word; but you must realize too that I cannot in decency permit myself to sit close to you in the dark."

94

"So you want me to stay here like this until dawn?"

"Lie down on the bed and sleep."

"You amaze me—how can you consider that possible, to say nothing of compatible with my passion? Come now! I am going to pretend I'm playing blindman's buff."

Upon that, I get up and vainly seek her all over the room. I catch someone; but it is always Nanetta or Marta, whose pride makes them name themselves at once; whereupon, stupid Don Quixote that I am, I consider it my duty to let them go. Love and prejudice prevent me from realizing the cowardice of such respect. I had not yet read the anecdotes of Louis XIII, King of France; but I had read Boccaccio.[1] I continue to hunt for her. I reproach her with her cruelty, I put it to her that she ought to let herself be found, and she answers that it is as hard for her to find me as it is for me to find her. The room was not large, and I began to be furious at never managing to catch her.

More disgusted than exhausted, I sit down and spend an hour telling the story of Ruggiero when Angelica disappeared from his sight by means of the magic ring which the lovelorn knight had all too guilelessly given her.

> Così dicendo, intorno a la fontana
> Brancolando n'andava come cieco
> O quante volte abbracciò l'aria vana
> Sperando la donzella abbracciar seco.[2]

("So saying he went stumbling around the fountain like a blind man. Oh, how often he embraced the empty air, hoping to embrace the damsel!")

Angela did not know Ariosto, but Nanetta had read him several times. She began defending Angelica and putting the blame on the simplicity of Ruggiero, who, if he had been sensible, should never have entrusted the coquette with the ring. Nanetta enchanted me; but I was too stupid in those days to make reflections which would have led me to change my conduct.

I had only an hour before me; nor could I wait for daylight, since Signora Orio would rather be dead than miss her mass. I spent this last hour talking only to Angela, trying first to persuade her, and then to convince her, that she should come and sit beside me. My soul passed through the whole scale of colors, in a crucible of which

HISTORY OF MY LIFE

the reader can have no idea unless he has been in a similar situation. After using every conceivable argument, I had recourse to prayers, then (*infandum* ["unutterable"][3]) to tears. But when I realized that they were useless, the feeling which took possession of me was *the righteous indignation which ennobles anger*. I believe I should actually have struck the proud creature who had been monster enough to keep me for five whole hours in the most cruel kind of distress, if I had not been in the dark. I showered her with all the insults which a scorned love can suggest to an enraged mind. I hurled fanatical curses at her; I swore that all my love had changed to hate, and ended by warning her to beware of me, for I should certainly kill her as soon as my eyes could see her.

My invectives ended with the darkness of night. At the first glimmerings of dawn and at the noise made by the great key and the bolt when Signora Orio opened the door to go out and put her soul in the state of repose which was a daily necessity to her, I made ready to leave, taking my cloak and hat. But, reader, I cannot depict the consternation of my soul, when, glancing at the faces of the three girls, I saw them melting into tears. In such shame and despair that I felt tempted to kill myself, I sat down again. I reflected that my brutality had driven those three beautiful souls to sobs. I could not speak. Feeling choked me; tears came to my rescue, and I indulged in them with delight. Nanetta rose and told me that her aunt must soon be back. I quickly wiped my eyes, and without looking at them or saying a word, I left and went straight home to bed, where I could not get a wink of sleep.

At noon Signor Malipiero, noticing that I was greatly changed, asked me the reason for it, and, feeling a need to unburden my soul, I told him all. The wise old man did not laugh. His very sensible remarks were balm to my soul. He knew that he was in the same situation in respect to Teresa. But he could not help laughing, nor could I, when he saw me eat with the appetite of a dog. I had not supped; but he complimented me on my excellent constitution.

Resolved not to return to Signora Orio's, about that time I defended a metaphysical thesis in which I maintained that "any being which can be conceived only abstractly can exist only abstractly." I was right; but it was easy to make my thesis look impious, and I was obliged to retract it. I went to Padua, where I was granted the degree of Doctor *utroque jure*.[4]

On my return to Venice I received a note from Signor Rosa in which he told me that Signora Orio wished me to come and see her. I went in the evening, when I was sure that I should not find Angela, whom I wanted to put out of my mind. Nanetta and Marta were so gay that they dispelled the shame I felt at appearing before them after two months; but my thesis and my doctorate substantiated my excuses to Signora Orio, whose only reason for wanting to see me was to complain of my never visiting her any more. As I left, Nanetta handed me a letter containing one from Angela. "If you have the courage," Angela's letter ran, "to spend another night with me, you will not have cause to complain, for I love you. I wish to know from your own lips if you would have continued to love me if I had consented to dishonor myself."

Here is the letter from Nanetta, who was the only intelligent one of the three girls. "Signor Rosa having undertaken to persuade you to return to our house, I wrote this letter beforehand to let you know that Angela is in despair over losing you. The night that you spent with us was cruel, I admit; but it seems to me that it should not have made you determine not to come again, at least to see Signora Orio. I advise you, if you still love Angela, to risk one more night. She will perhaps be able to justify herself, and you will leave happy. So come. Adieu."

These two letters delighted me. I saw that I could now avenge myself on Angela by treating her with the most open contempt. I went on the first feast day, with two bottles of Cyprus wine[5] and a smoked tongue in my pocket, and was surprised not to find the hardhearted vixen there. Turning the conversation to her, Nanetta said that Angela had told her that morning at mass that she could not come until suppertime. I saw no reason to doubt it, so when Signora Orio asked me to stay I did not accept. Just before the supper hour I pretended to leave, as I had the time before, and ensconced myself in the appointed place. I could not wait to play the delightful role I had planned. I felt sure that even if Angela had made up her mind to change her tactics, she would grant me no more than small favors, and these no longer interested me. My only remaining emotion was a great desire for revenge.

Three quarters of an hour later I hear the street door shut, and ten minutes after that I hear footsteps coming up the stairs, and I see before me—Nanetta and Marta.

"But where is Angela?" I ask Nanetta.

"She must have been unable either to come or to send word. Yet she must know that you are here."

"She thinks she has tricked me, and I admit I did not expect this; now you know her as she is. She is laughing at me in triumph. She used you to make me fall into the snare; and she is better off, for if she had come it would have been I who laughed at her."

"Permit me to doubt that."

"Never doubt it, my dear Nanetta; you shall be convinced of it by the delightful time we shall have tonight without her."

"In other words, as a sensible man you will make the most of second-best; but you shall go to bed here, and we will go and sleep on the couch in the other room."

"I shall not prevent you; but you would be playing a cruel trick on me, and in any case I should not go to bed."

"What! You would have the endurance to spend seven hours with us? I am sure that when you run out of things to say you will fall asleep."

"We shall see. In the meanwhile here is a tongue and here is some Cyprus wine. Can you be cruel enough to let me eat by myself? Have you some bread?"

"Yes, and we will not be cruel. We'll eat a second supper."

"It is you I ought to be in love with. Tell me, beautiful Nanetta, if you would make me unhappy as Angela does."

"Do you think I can answer such a question? Only a conceited fool could ask it. All I can tell you is that I haven't the least idea."

They quickly set three places, brought bread, Parmesan cheese, and water, and, laughing all the while, they ate with me and shared my Cyprus wine, which, as they were not used to it, went to their heads. Their gaiety became delightful. Looking at them, I was surprised at not having realized all their good qualities until that moment.

Sitting between them after our late supper, I took and kissed their hands and asked them if they were truly my friends and if they approved of the contemptible way in which Angela had treated me. They answered together that they had wept for me. "Then permit me," I said, "to feel the fondness of a true brother for you, and do you feel for me as if you were my sisters; let us exchange pledges of our affection in the innocence of our hearts; let us kiss each other and swear eternal fidelity."

The first kisses I gave them came neither from amorous desire nor from any intention to seduce them, and for their part they swore to me some days later that they returned them only to assure me that they shared my innocent feeling; but these harmless kisses soon

98

became ardent and began to kindle a fire in the three of us which must have taken us aback, for we broke off and then looked at each other in grave astonishment. The two sisters made some excuse to move away, and I remained absorbed in thought. It is not surprising that the fire which these kisses had kindled in my soul, and which was even then creeping through all my limbs, made me fall invincibly in love with the two girls on the instant. They were both of them prettier than Angela, and Nanetta's quick intelligence and Marta's gentle and artless nature made them infinitely superior to her: I felt greatly surprised that I had not recognized their qualities before that moment; but they were well-born and utterly innocent girls, and the chance which had put them into my hands must not prove to be their ruin. Nothing but blind vanity could have made me believe that they loved me; but I could well suppose that the kisses had affected them even as they had me. On this assumption it was plain to me that, in the course of the long night I was to spend with them, I should not find it difficult to bring them to concessions whose consequences would be nothing short of crucial. This thought filled me with horror. I resolved to exercise the severest restraint, and I did not doubt that I should find the strength to observe it.

They reappeared, and when I saw that their faces expressed nothing but trust and contentment, I instantly cast mine in the same mold, firmly resolving that I would not expose myself to the fire of kisses again.

We spent an hour talking of Angela. I told them I was determined not to see her again, since I was convinced that she did not love me. "She loves you," said the artless Marta, "I am sure of it; but if you do not mean to marry her you had better break with her entirely, for she is resolved not to grant you the slightest favor so long as you are only her lover: so you must either leave her or reconcile yourself to her granting you nothing."

"Your reasoning is perfect; but how can you be sure that she loves me?"

"Nothing is surer. And now that we have promised to love each other like brother and sister, I can frankly tell you why. When Angela sleeps with us, she covers me with kisses and calls me her 'dear Abate.' "

Nanetta burst out laughing and put a hand over her sister's mouth; but this artlessness so set me on fire that I had the greatest difficulty in controlling myself. Marta said to Nanetta that, since I was so intelligent, I could not fail to know what two girls who were good friends did when they were in bed together.

"Certainly, my dear Nanetta," I added, "everyone knows about these little games, and I cannot believe that your sister has been too indiscreet in making this confession."

"Well, it is done now; but one does not talk about these things. If Angela knew—"

"She would be in despair, I am sure, but Marta has given me such a proof of her friendship that I shall be grateful to her until I die. It is over and done with. I loathe Angela, I shall never speak to her again. She is false-hearted, she wants to destroy me."

"But if she loves you she has every right to want you to marry her."

"True enough; but the tactics she employs have no other aim than her own advantage, and since she knows how I suffer she cannot behave as she does unless she does not love me. Meanwhile, by a make-believe as false as it is monstrous, she assuages her beastly desires with this charming Marta, who kindly serves as her husband."

At this Nanetta's laughter redoubled; but I did not change my serious expression and went on talking to Marta in the same style, praising her admirable sincerity with the most high-flown eloquence.

Finding that the subject was giving me the greatest pleasure, I told Marta that Angela ought to play the part of her husband too; whereupon she laughed and said that she only played husband to Nanetta, which Nanetta was obliged to admit.

"But by what name does Nanetta call her husband," I asked Marta, "in her transports?"

"Nobody knows."

"So then you love someone," I said to Nanetta.

"Yes, I do, but no one shall ever know my secret."

At this, I flattered myself that Nanetta might secretly be Angela's rival. But with all this charming talk, I lost any wish to spend the night in idleness with these two girls who were made for love. I said I was very glad that I entertained only friendly feelings toward them, for otherwise I should find it extremely hard to spend the night with them without wishing to give them proofs of my love and to receive proofs of theirs, "for," I added coolly, "you are both ravishingly beautiful and more than capable of turning the head of any man whom you will allow to know you as you are." After this speech

I pretended I wanted to go to sleep. "Don't stand on ceremony," Nanetta said, "get into bed. We will go and sleep on the couch in the other room."

"If I did that, I should consider myself the most contemptible of men. Let us talk: my sleepiness will pass off. I am only sorry on your account. It is you who should get into bed, and I will go to the other room. If you are afraid of me, lock yourselves in, but you would be wrong, for I love you only with the heart of a brother."

"We will never do that," said Nanetta. "Please do as we say, and go to bed here."

"If I keep my clothes on, I shan't sleep."

"Then undress. We won't look at you."

"That doesn't worry me; but I could never get to sleep, with you obliged to stay up on my account."

"We'll go to bed too," said Marta, "but we won't undress."

"Such distrust is an insult to my integrity. Tell me, Nanetta, do you consider me a man of honor?"

"Yes, certainly."

"Well and good. Do you want to convince me of it? You must both lie down beside me completely undressed, and count on my word of honor, which I now give you, that I will not touch you. You are two and I am one—what have you to fear? Won't you be free to leave the bed if I do not behave myself? In short, if you will not promise to show me this proof of your confidence, at least when you see that I have fallen asleep, I will not go to bed."

I then stopped talking and pretended to fall asleep, and they whispered together; then Marta told me to get into bed and said they would do likewise when they saw that I was asleep. Nanetta made the same promise, whereupon I turned my back to them, took off all my clothes, got into the bed, and wished them good night. I pretended to fall asleep at once, but within a quarter of an hour I was asleep in good earnest. I woke only when they came and got into the bed, but I at once turned away and resumed my sleep, nor did I begin to act until I had reason to suppose that they were sleeping. If they were not, they had only to pretend to be. They had turned their backs to me and we were in darkness. I began with the one toward whom I was turned, not knowing whether it was Nanetta or Marta. I found her curled up and covered by her shift, but by doing nothing to startle her and proceeding step by step as gradually as possible, I soon convinced her that her best course was to pretend to be asleep and let me go on. Little by little I straightened her out, little by little she uncurled, and little by little, with slow, successive, but wonderfully natural movements, she put herself in a position which was the most favorable she could offer me without betraying herself. I set to work, but to crown my labors it was necessary that she should join in them openly and undeniably, and nature finally forced her to do so. I found this first sister beyond suspicion, and suspecting the pain she must have endured, I was surprised. In duty bound religiously to respect a prejudice to which I owed a pleasure the sweetness of which I was tasting for the first time in my life, I let the victim alone and turned the other way to do the same thing with her sister, who must be expecting me to demonstrate the full extent of my gratitude.

I found her motionless, in the position often taken by a person who is lying on his back in deep, untroubled sleep. With the greatest precautions, and every appearance of fearing to waken her, I began by delighting her soul, at the same time assuring myself that she was as untouched as her sister; and I continued the same treatment until, affecting a most natural movement without which I could not have crowned my labors, she helped me to triumph; but at the moment of crisis she no longer had the strength to keep up her pretense. Throwing off the mask, she clasped me in her arms and pressed her mouth on mine. After the act, "I am sure," I said, "that you are Nanetta."

"Yes, and I consider myself fortunate, as my sister is, if you are honorable and loyal."

"Even unto death, my angels! All that we have done was the work of love, and let there be no more talk of Angela."

I then asked her to get up and light some candles, but it was Marta who obliged. When I saw Nanetta in my arms on fire with love, and Marta holding a candle and looking at us, seeming to accuse us of ingratitude for not saying a word to her, when, by having been the first to yield to my caresses, she had encouraged her sister to imitate her, I realized all my good fortune.

"Let us get up," I said, "and swear eternal friendship and then refresh ourselves."

Under my direction the three of us made an improvised toilet in a bucket of water, which set us laughing and renewed all our desires; then, in the costume of the Golden Age, we finished the rest of the tongue and emptied the other bottle. After our state of sensual intoxication had made us say a quantity of those things which only love can interpret, we went back to bed and spent the rest of the night in ever varied skirmishes. It was Nanetta who joined in the last. Signora Orio having gone to mass, I had to leave them without wasting time on words. After swearing that I no longer gave a thought to Angela, I went home and buried myself in sleep until dinnertime.

Signor Malipiero remarked on my happy look and the dark circles around my eyes, and I let him imagine whatever he pleased but told him nothing. I went to Signora Orio's house the next day but one, and since Angela was not there I stayed for supper, then left with Signor Rosa. Nanetta found an opportunity to hand me a letter and a packet. The packet contained a piece of dough on which was the impression of a key, and the letter told me to have the key made and to come and spend the night with them whenever I wished. It also said that Angela had come and spent the next night with them and that, in the course of their usual practices, she had guessed all that had happened and that they had admitted it and reproached her with being the cause. She had treated them to the coarsest insults and sworn never to set foot in the house again. But they did not care.

A few days later, fate delivered us from Angela. She went to live in Vicenza with her father,[6] who spent two years there decorating a number of houses with frescoes. I was thus left in undisturbed possession of these two angels, with whom I spent at least two nights a week, always being expected and gaining entrance with the key they had found means to obtain for me.

About the end of the Carnival, Signor Manzoni told me that the famous Giulietta wanted to talk with me and that she had always been disappointed not to see me again. Wondering what she could have to say to me, I went there with him. After receiving me politely enough, she said that she had been told I had a splendid drawing room in my house and that she would like me to give a ball for her there at her expense. I consented at once. She gave me 24 zecchini and sent her servants to fit up my drawing room and the other rooms with chandeliers, so that I had only to see to the orchestra and the supper. Signor Sanvitale had already left, and the government of Parma had appointed a steward to manage his affairs. I saw him ten years later at Versailles, decorated with various royal orders as Grand Equerry to the eldest daughter of Louis XV, the Duchess of Parma, who, like all the French princesses, could not abide living in Italy.

My ball went well. The only guests were Giulietta's circle and, in a small room, Signora Orio with her two nieces and the advocate

Rosa whom, as people of no importance, she had allowed me to invite.

After supper, when the company were dancing minuets, she took me aside and said, "Quick! take me to your room; I've just had an amusing idea, and we'll have a good laugh."

My bedroom was on the fourth floor, and thither we repair. I observe that she immediately locks the door; I did not know what to think. "I want you," she said, "to dress me up as an abate in one of your suits, and I will dress you as a woman in my dress. We will go downstairs in these disguises and dance the quadrilles. Come, hurry, my dear friend, we'll begin by doing our hair."

Sure of making a conquest, and delighted at the novelty of the adventure, I quickly coil up her long hair and then let her make me a chignon which she arranges very neatly under her own bonnet. She puts rouge and some patches on my face, I submit with good grace, at the same time frankly letting her see that I am enjoying it, and she is pleased to grant me a sweet kiss, on condition that I should not look for anything more; I answer that everything must depend upon her. Meanwhile, I warn her that I adore her.

I lay on the bed a shirt, a neckband, a pair of drawers, black stockings, and a coat and breeches. Faced with having to drop her skirt and petticoat, she adroitly puts on the drawers and says that they fit well, but when she tries to put on my breeches she finds that they are too tight in the waist and at the top of the thighs. There is nothing for it but to unsew them in the back and, if need be, to cut the material. I undertake to do all this; I sit down on the foot of the bed and she stands with her back toward me, but she says that I want to see too much, that I am going about it clumsily, that I am taking too long, and that I touch her where there is no need to; she loses patience, she leaves me, she rips open the breeches and fixes them herself. I put my stockings and shoes on her, then slip the shirt over her head, but as I arrange the ruffle and the neckband she finds my hands too curious, for her bosom was bare. She upbraids me, she calls me vile names, but I take no notice; I was determined that she should not make a dupe of me; then too, she was a woman for whom a hundred thousand scudi had been paid, and who could not but be of interest to a thinking man. At last she was dressed and it was my turn.

I quickly take off my breeches despite her insisting that I keep them on; she has to put her shift on me herself, and then her skirt; but, suddenly turning coy, she berates me for not concealing the too visible effect of her charms upon me, and she refuses me the relief which would have calmed me in an instant. I try to give her a kiss; she resists; it is my turn to lose patience and, despite her, the result of my incontinence visibly stains the shift. She insults me, I reply in kind, and tell her that she is entirely to blame; but it is no use, she continues to sulk; however, she had to finish what she had begun and put the rest of her clothes on me.

Obviously, any respectable woman who had got herself into such a situation with me would have had amorous intentions and would not have belied them just when she saw that I shared them; but women of Giulietta's sort are governed by a perversity which makes them their own enemies. Giulietta felt she was tricked when she saw that I was not timid. My readiness seemed to her a lack of respect. She would have liked me to steal a few favors, which she would have granted me without seeming aware of it. But I was not willing to flatter her vanity to that extent.

Wearing our disguises, we went down to the drawing room, where general applause instantly put us in a good humor. Everyone supposed that I had made the conquest which had escaped me; but I was well pleased to let it be believed. I joined a quadrille with my abate, whom I was chagrined to find charming. During the evening Giulietta treated me so well that, believing she had repented of her scurvy behavior, I likewise repented of mine; but this was a momentary weakness for which Heaven was to punish me.

After the quadrille all the men felt entitled to take liberties with Giulietta in her role of abate; and on my side I did not restrain myself with the girls, who would have feared to be thought stupid if they had objected to my proceedings. Signor Querini was fool enough to ask me if I had on breeches, and I saw him go pale when I answered that I had had to give them to the abate. He went and sat in a corner of the room, and would not dance again.

The entire company having in course of time become aware that I had on a woman's shift, no one any longer doubted my good fortune, except Nanetta and Marta, who could not believe that I would be unfaithful. Giulietta realized that she had done a very stupid thing, but there was no help for it now.

As soon as we returned to my room to undress, thinking that she had repented and having, in the meanwhile, become possessed by a desire for her, I thought I could venture to kiss her and at the same time take one of her hands to convince her that I was ready to accord her all the satisfaction she deserved; but she gave me such a violent box on the ear that I very nearly returned the compliment. After that I undressed without looking at her and she did likewise. We went downstairs together; but despite the cold water with which I washed my face, the whole company could see on it the mark of the heavy hand which had struck it.

Before she left, she took me aside and told me emphatically that if I had any wish to get myself thrown out of a window, I had only to come to her house, and that she would have me assassinated if what had happened between us became known.

I gave her no cause to do either, but I could not prevent people from telling the story of our exchanging shifts. Since I was not seen at her house again, everyone thought that my absence was an atonement demanded by Signor Querini. The reader will see, six years later in these memoirs, on what occasion this notorious woman was obliged to pretend she had forgotten the entire incident.

I spent a very happy Lent with my two angels, at Signor Malipiero's receptions, and studying experimental physics at the monastery of La Salute.[7]

After Easter, having to keep the promise I had made to the Countess of Montereale and impatient to see my dear Lucia again, I went to Pasiano. I found a very different set of people from those who had been there the previous autumn. Count Daniele, who was the oldest member of the family, had married a Countess Gozzi;[8] and a rich young tenant farmer, who had married a goddaughter of the old Countess, was suffered to be present with his wife and his sister-in-law. I found supper a very long affair. I had been given the same room, and I could not wait to see Lucia, for I had made up my mind that my days of behaving like a child with her were over. . . .

Not having seen her before I went to bed, I was certain that she would be there when I woke in the morning; but instead I see only an ugly peasant woman. I ask her for news of the family, but I learn nothing for she can speak only Friulian. This is the local dialect.

I feel uneasy. What can have become of Lucia? Has our relationship been discovered? Is she ill? Is she dead? I stop asking myself questions and get dressed. If she has been forbidden to see me I will have my revenge, for one way or another I will find means to see her, and my desire for vengeance will make me do what honor prevented me from doing despite my love.

Enter the caretaker, looking woebegone. I immediately ask him how his wife and his daughter are, and when I name the latter he bursts into tears.

"Is she dead?"

"Would to God that she were!"

"What has she done?"

"She has run away with L'Aigle, Count Daniele's courier, and we do not know where."

His wife arrives in time to hear these words, which renews her grief and she faints. The caretaker, seeing me sincerely sharing his sorrow, tells me it was only a week ago that this misfortune had befallen him. "I know L'Aigle," I said. "He is a famous scoundrel. Did he ask you for her hand in marriage?"

"No, for he was sure that we would not consent."

"I am amazed at Lucia."

"He seduced her, and we did not realize until after she was gone why she was getting fat."

"Then they had been seeing each other for a long time?"

"She got to know him a month after your departure. He must have put a spell on her, for she was a perfect angel, and I believe you can bear witness to it."

"And does nobody know where they are?"

"Nobody. God knows what the wretch will do with her."

As downcast as these decent people, I buried myself in the woods to ruminate my grief. I spent two hours in the most various reflections, some of them sound, others unsound, but all beginning with *if*. *If* I had arrived, as I might easily have done, a week earlier, my loving Lucia would have confided everything to me and I should have prevented this murder. *If* I had proceeded with her as I did with Nanetta and Marta, I should not have left her in the aroused state which must have been the chief cause of her yielding to the scoundrel's desires. *If* she had not known me before she met the courier, her still innocent soul would not have listened to him. I was in despair at being forced to admit that I was the agent of the infamous seducer, that I had worked on his behalf.

> El fior che sol potea pormi fra dei,
> Quel fior che intatto io mi venia serbando
> Per non turbar, ohimè! l'animo casto
> Ohimè! il bel fior colui m'ha colto, e guasto.[9]

("And the flower which alone could raise me to the rank of the gods, the flower which I was keeping intact in order not to trouble, alas! that chaste soul, alas! he has plucked it and destroyed it.")

It is certain that if I had known where to look for her with any likelihood of finding her, I should have set off immediately. Before I knew of the disaster which had overtaken Lucia, I was proud, in my vanity, that I had been virtuous enough to leave her a virgin; and now I repented in shame of my stupid restraint. I promised myself that in the future I would behave more wisely so far as restraint was concerned. What made me most unhappy was the thought that before long, when Lucia would have sunk into unhappiness and perhaps infamy, she could not remember me without loathing and hate me as the original cause of her misfortunes. This disastrous outcome caused me to adopt a new principle of conduct, which I later carried too far.

CHAPTER VI

My grandmother's death and its consequences.
I lose the good graces of Signor Malipiero.
I no longer have a house.

[* * *]

On my return to Venice, I had to suspend my usual activities on account of the last illness of my good grandmother, whom I never left until I saw her expire.[1] She could leave me nothing, for she had given me all she possessed during her lifetime. This death had consequences which obliged me to adopt a new way of life. A month later I received a letter from my mother telling me that since there was no likelihood of her being able to return to Venice, she had decided to give up the house she had kept there. She said that she had communicated her intention to the Abate Grimani, whose wishes I was to obey. He, after selling all the furnishings, would see to it that I was settled in a good boardinghouse, and do the same for my brothers and my sister. I called on Signor Grimani to assure him that he would always find me obedient to his commands. The rent for the house was paid until the end of the year.

When I learned that at the end of the year I should be without a house and that all the furnishings were to be sold, I no longer stinted myself in my wants. I had already sold some linen and tapestries and pieces of porcelain; I set about selling mirrors and beds. I knew that I should be taken to task; but it was my father's inheritance, upon which my mother had no claim; I considered myself within my rights. As for my brothers, there would always be time to discuss it.

Four months later I received a letter from my mother dated from Warsaw and containing another. Here is a translation of my mother's letter: "I have made the acquaintance here, my dear son, of a learned Minimite,[2] a Calabrian, whose great qualities made me think of you every time he honored me with a visit. A year ago I told him that I had a son who was preparing for the priesthood but whom I had not the means to keep. He answered that my son would become his own if I could persuade the Queen[3] to appoint him to a bishopric in his native Calabria. The thing would be done, he said, if she would have the goodness to recommend him to her daughter the Queen of Naples.[4] Trusting in God, I flung myself at Her Majesty's feet, and I found favor. She wrote to her daughter, who arranged for Our

Lord the Pope[5] to appoint him to the bishopric of Martorano.[6] True
to his word, he will take you with him the middle of next year, for to
reach Calabria he has to pass through Venice. He has written to you
himself, answer him at once, send me your answer, and I will deliver
it to him. He will set you on the road to the highest dignities of the
Church. Imagine my happiness when, twenty or thirty years from
now, I see you at least a bishop. Until he arrives, the Abate Grimani
will take care of you. I give you my blessing, and I am, etc. . . . "

The Bishop's letter, which was in Latin, said the same thing. It
was full of unction. He informed me that he would stay in Venice
only three days. I answered as might be expected. These two letters
turned my head. Good-by, Venice! Absolutely certain that the highest fortune would be mine at the end of my course, I could not wait
to enter upon it; and I congratulated myself that I felt not the
slightest regret for all that I should leave behind by leaving my
country. "I have done with trifling," I told myself. "In future I
shall concern myself only with what is great and substantial." Signor
Grimani, after congratulating me to the skies on my good fortune,
assured me that he would find me a boardinghouse where I could
live from the beginning of the coming year while I waited for the
Bishop.

Signor Malipiero, who was a wise man in his fashion, and who
saw me carried away by vain pleasures in Venice, was delighted
when he saw me on the verge of setting out to fulfill my destiny
elsewhere and read my ardent delight in the eager readiness with
which I adapted myself to what circumstances had offered me. On
this occasion he gave me a lesson which I have never forgotten. He
told me that the famous precept of the Stoics, *sequere Deum* ("follow
the God"),[7] meant neither more nor less than "surrender yourself to
what fate offers you, provided that you do not feel a strong repugnance to doing so." "This," he went on, "was the demon of Socrates,
saepe revocans raro impellens ('which often forbids, seldom prompts');[8]
and this the source of the *fata viam inveniunt* ('Destiny finds the
way')[9] of the same Stoics." Herein lay the wisdom of Signor Malipiero, who had learned it without ever having studied any book but
that of man's moral nature. However, the maxims of the same
school played a part in something which happened to me a month
later, which brought me into disfavor with him, and which taught
me nothing.

Signor Malipiero believed that he could recognize in the faces of
young people signs indicative of the absolute dominion which

Fortune would exercise over them. When he saw this, he took them under his protection so that he could teach them to assist Fortune by wise conduct for, as he said with great good sense, "medicine in the hands of the foolhardy is poison, as poison becomes medicine in the hands of the wise."

Accordingly, he had three protégés for whose education he did everything in his power. One was Teresa Imer, of whose innumerable vicissitudes my readers will find some account in these memoirs. I was the second, of whom they may judge as they see fit, and the third was one of the gondolier Gardela's daughters,[10] who was three years younger than I, and so far as prettiness goes, her face did bear a most striking sign. To put her on the stage, the philosophical old man was having her take dancing lessons, "for," he said, "the ball cannot go into the pocket unless someone gives it a push." She is the Gardela who, under the name of Agata, had a brilliant success in Stuttgart. She became the first acknowledged mistress of the Duke of Württemberg[11] in the year 1757. She was charming. She was in Venice when I left and she died there two or three years ago. Her husband, Michele Dall'Agata, poisoned himself soon afterward.

One day after having all three of us dine with him he left, as he always did, to take a siesta. The Gardela girl, having to go for a lesson, left me alone with Teresa, whom, though I had never flirted with her, I still found attractive. Sitting side by side at a small table with our backs to the door of the room in which we supposed our patron was sleeping, at a certain turn in the conversation it occurred to us in our innocent gaiety to compare the differences between our shapes. We were at the most interesting point of the examination when a violent blow from a cane descended on my neck, followed by another, which would have been followed by yet more if I had not escaped from the hailstorm at top speed by running out of the room. I went home without my cloak and without my hat. A quarter of an hour later I received them both, together with a note, from the Senator's old housekeeper, who also warned me never again to dare to set foot in His Excellency's palace.

I answered at once, directly to him and in the following terms: "You struck me in anger, hence you cannot boast of having given me a lesson. By the same token, I have learned nothing. I can forgive you only by forgetting that you are wise; and that I shall never forget."

The nobleman was perhaps in the right; but for all his prudence he acted unwisely, since his servants all guessed his reason for banishing me, and so the whole town laughed over the story. He did not dare to address the slightest reproach to Teresa, as she told me some time later; but, naturally, she did not dare ask him to pardon me.

One fine morning not long before our house was to be vacated, I saw before me a man of about forty, wearing a black wig and a scarlet cloak and with a face tanned by the sun, who handed me a note from Signor Grimani directing me to put all the furniture in the house at his disposition after turning it over to him in accordance with the inventory he had with him, of which I must have a duplicate. Fetching my inventory at once, I showed him all the specified pieces of furniture when they happened to be there, and when they were not, telling him that I knew what I had done with them. Taking a high tone, the oaf said he insisted on knowing what I had done with them, to which I replied that I was not answerable to him, then, hearing him begin to bellow, I advised him to clear out in a manner which showed him that I had the whip hand in my own house.

Feeling it incumbent on me to inform Signor Grimani of this occurrence, I called on him before he had risen, but found that my man was there already and had told him the whole story. I had to swallow a severe reprimand. He next demanded that I account for the missing articles of furniture. I answered that I had sold them to keep from running into debt. After calling me a scoundrel and telling me that I had no rights over them, he ordered me to leave his house on the instant.

Beside myself with rage, I start off to find a Jew to whom I can sell whatever is left, but, deciding to stop at my house on the way, I find a bailiff at my door, who hands me a summons. I read it and discover that it was executed at the instance of Antonio Razzetta.[12] This was the man with the tanned complexion. All the doors had been sealed. I cannot even enter my bedroom. The bailiff had gone but had left a guard. I leave and go to see Signor Rosa, who, after reading the summons, tells me that the seals will be removed the next day and that meanwhile he will have Razzetta summoned before the *avogadore*.[13]

"For tonight," he said, "you must find a bed in some friend's house. This is an outrage, but he shall pay you dearly for it."

"He is acting under Signor Grimani's orders."

"That is his affair."

I went and spent the night with my angels.

The next morning the seals were removed and I went home again; Razzetta not having appeared, Rosa summonsed him in my name under penal law in order to have a warrant issued for his arrest the following day if he did not appear. Early in the morning of the third day a footman of Signor Grimani's brought me a note from his master ordering me to come to his house to talk with him; I went.

Upon my appearance he asked me harshly what I meant to do.

"To secure myself against violence under the protection of the laws, by defending myself from a man with whom I have nothing to do and who forced me to spend the night in a place of ill repute."

"In a place of ill repute?"

"Exactly. Why was I prevented from going home?"

"You are there now. But go at once and tell your advocate to stop all proceedings. Razzetta did nothing except at my order. You were very likely going to sell all the rest of the furniture. Everything has been taken care of. You have a room in San Giovanni Grisostomo in a house belonging to me, the second floor of which is occupied by La Tintoretta,[14] our leading ballerina. Have your clothes and your books taken there and come to dine with me every day. I have put your brother in a good house and your sister in another, so everything is settled."

Signor Rosa, to whom I went at once with an account of all that had happened, advised me to do whatever the Abate Grimani wished, and I followed his advice. I had received satisfaction, and my being admitted to his table was an honor. In addition I was curious about my new lodging with La Tintoretta, who was being much talked about on account of a certain Prince Waldeck[15] who was spending a great deal on her. The Bishop was to arrive in the summer, I had only six more months to spend in Venice awaiting the prelate, who was perhaps to set me on the road to the Papacy. Such were my castles in Spain. After dining that same day at Signor Grimani's, without saying a word to Razzetta who was seated beside me, I went for the last time to my fine house in the parish of San Samuele, where I had everything which I considered my rightful property carried to my new lodging by boat.

[* * *]

CHAPTER VII

Arrival of the Bishop. I leave Venice.

[* * *]

The death of his grandmother marked the beginning of a turbulent period in Casanova's life. First he entered a seminary which he soon left after quarreling with the Rector about whether or not he had shared a bed with another seminarian. Then he was imprisoned for debt in the fortress of Sant'Andrea at the behest of the villainous Razzetta and his patron, Signor Grimani. Although the fortress was surrounded by water, with characteristic daring Casanova escaped undetected for one night only in order to thrash Razzetta. This he did, returning to the prison immediately afterwards, thus providing himself with an alibi. The rest of his imprisonment he improved by conducting an affair with a fellow prisoner's wife.

By one of those twists of fortune which, as he often remarks, guided his whole career, on his release from Sant'Andrea Casanova returned to Grimani's house where he prepared his departure for Ancona en route for Martorano and his post with the new Bishop.

Three or four days later Signor Grimani informed me that the Bishop had arrived.[1] He was lodging in his Minimite monastery[2] of San Francesco di Paola. Signor Grimani himself took me to the prelate, as if I were a jewel which he cherished and which he alone had the right to display to him.

I saw a handsome monk with a bishop's cross on his chest; I would have taken him for Father Mancia had he not looked more robust and been more reserved in manner. He was thirty-four years old,[3] and he was a bishop by the grace of God, of the Holy See, and of my mother. After giving me first his blessing, which I received kneeling, and then his hand to kiss, he embraced me and called me his "dear son" in Latin, in which language he always addressed me thereafter. I was beginning to think that, being a Calabrian, he was ashamed to speak Italian; but he undeceived me when he spoke to Signor Grimani. He said that since he could not take me with him until after he had reached Rome, Signor Grimani would arrange to send me there, and that in Ancona a Minimite monk named Lazari, who was a friend of his, would give me his address and money for the journey. From Rome on we would remain together, and would go to Martorano by way of Naples. He asked me to come and see him very early the next morning so that we could breakfast together after he had said his mass. He said that he would leave on the day after that. Signor Grimani took me back to his palace, treating me all the way to a moral discourse at which I could not but laugh. Among other things he warned me that I must not study much, because in the heavy air of Calabria too much application could make me consumptive.

The next day I waited on the Bishop at daybreak. After mass and chocolate he catechized me for three hours on end. I saw clearly that he did not like me; but, on my side, I was well pleased with him; he seemed to me a thorough gentleman and in any case, since he was to guide me to the great stage of the Church, I could not but like him, for in those days, though I was very much prejudiced in my own favor, I had not a shred of self-confidence.

After the good Bishop's departure, Signor Grimani gave me a letter which he had left with him and which I was to deliver to Father Lazari at the Minimite monastery in the city of Ancona. He told me that he would send me to Ancona with the Venetian Ambassador, who was about to set out; so I must be in readiness to leave. I was delighted with all this. I could not wait to be out of his custody.

As soon as I ascertained the time when the suite of the Cavaliere da Lezze,[4] Ambassador of the Republic, was to embark, I took leave of all my acquaintances. I left my brother Francesco in the school conducted by Signor Joli,[5] the celebrated theatrical scene painter. Since the peota[6] in which I was to travel to Chioggia was not to leave the quay until daybreak, I spent the brief night in the arms of my two angels, who were certain that they would never see me again. For my part, I could not foresee what might happen, for, having abandoned myself to fate, I considered that to think about the future was effort wasted. So we spent the night between joy and sorrow, between laughter and tears. I left them the key. This love, which was my first, taught me almost nothing about the way of the world, for it was perfectly happy, unbroken by trouble of any kind, and untarnished by any interested motives. All three of us often felt impelled to raise our hearts to Eternal Providence and render thanks for the direct protection by which it had kept us safe from any accident which could have troubled the sweet peace we had enjoyed.

All my papers, and all the forbidden books I owned, I left with Signora Manzoni. This lady, who was twenty years my senior and who, believing in fate, amused herself by turning over the pages of its great book, told me with a smile that she was sure she would be giving me back all that I had deposited with her by the next year at the latest. Her predictions astonished and pleased me; since I had a great respect for her, I felt it incumbent on me to help her see them come true. What enabled her to look into the future was neither superstition nor a vain, unreasonable foreboding; it was a knowledge of the world and of the character of the person in whom she was interested. She laughed over never having been wrong.

I embarked at the Piazzetta di San Marco. On the previous evening Signor Grimani had given me ten zecchini, which he said should be more than enough to keep me through the time I should have to spend in the lazaretto of Ancona undergoing quarantine.[7] Once I was out of the lazaretto, it was not to be expected that I should need money. Since they were so sure of it, it was my duty to be as sure as they were; but I gave the matter no thought. However, I found it comforting that, unknown to anyone, I had in my purse forty fine zecchini, which greatly raised my youthful spirits. I set off with a joyful heart, regretting nothing.

On his way to Ancona, Casanova's troubles multiplied. First he met a ruffianly monk, Father Corsini, who introduced him to a brothel and a gambling den. The brothel gave him a nasty disease and the gambling den took all his money and more, leaving him destitute and ill. Another monk, Frate Steffano, who turned out to be a different sort of rogue with a passion for food and money, nevertheless came to his aid. Eventually they reached Ancona together and took up residence in the lazaretto where they were required to spend twenty-eight days in quarantine. Casanova's fortunes began to look up.

CHAPTER VIII

The lazaretto at Ancona. The Greek slave.
I go to Naples to find the Bishop, but do not find him.
Fortune provides me with the
means of going to Martorano, which I very soon
leave and return to Naples.

[* * *]

Two weeks of my regimen had cured my indisposition to the point
where I was taking an early morning walk in the courtyard; but a
Turkish merchant from Salonica arriving at the lazaretto with his
household and being lodged on the ground floor, I had to give up
my walks. My only remaining pleasure was to pass my time on the
balcony, which gave on the same courtyard, in which the Turk
strolled about. What interested me was a Greek slave girl of
astonishing beauty. She spent almost the whole day sitting at the
door of her room, knitting or reading in the shade. The heat was
extreme. When she raised her beautiful eyes and saw me, she
looked away and often, pretending surprise, rose and went slowly
back into her room, as if to say, "I did not know anyone was
looking at me." She was tall and her whole appearance showed that
she was very young. Her skin was white and her eyes black like her
hair and her brows. She dressed in the Greek fashion, which is very
voluptuous.

Unoccupied, confined to a lazaretto, and such as nature and habit
had made me, could I contemplate such an object four or five hours
every day without falling madly in love? I had heard her conversing
in *lingua franca*[1] with her master, a handsome old man who was as
bored as she was and who would come out for a few moments with
his pipe in his mouth, only to return to his room almost at once. I
would have spoken to the girl, had I not been afraid of driving her
away and never seeing her again. I finally resolved to write to her,
since nothing stood in the way of my getting a letter to her, for I had
only to drop it at her feet. But not being certain that she would pick
it up, I hit upon the following plan to avoid any risk of precipitating
an awkward situation.

Waiting for a time when she was alone, I dropped a sheet of
paper folded like a letter but on which I had written nothing,
meanwhile keeping my real letter in my hand. When I saw her

117

stoop to pick up the pretended letter, I threw her the other too. She picked them both up, put them in her pocket, and vanished. My letter ran as follows: "Angel of the East whom I adore! I shall spend the whole night on this balcony, hoping that you will come for but a quarter of an hour to hear my voice through the hole at my feet. We will speak in whispers, and to hear me you can climb up on the bale which is under the same hole."

I asked my guard to be good enough not to lock me in as he did every night, and he made no objection to granting my request, on condition, however, that he would watch me, for if I took a notion to jump down, he risked losing his head. However, he promised not to come out on the balcony.

Waiting at the appointed place, I saw her appear at midnight, just as I was giving up hope. I lay down on my stomach and put my head to the hole, which was a splintery square five or six inches across. I saw her climb on the bale; when she stood up her head was only a few feet from the floor of the balcony. She had to steady herself against the wall with one hand, for the awkward position made her totter. In this situation, we talked of ourselves, of love, of desires, of obstacles, of impossibilities, and of ruses. When I told her why I could not jump down, she said that even if I did we should be lost, for there was no way I could get back up again. Then too, God alone knows what the Turk would have done to her and to me if he had caught us. After promising me that she would come and talk with me every night, she put her hand up through the hole. Alas! I could not get my fill of kissing it. I thought I had never touched a hand so soft and so delicate. But what delight when she asked me for mine! I quickly thrust my whole arm down through the hole, and she pressed her lips to the bend of my elbow; after that she forgave my rapacious hand all that it could steal from her Greek bosom, for which I hungered far more ravenously than I had for the kisses I had just imprinted on her hand. After we parted I was delighted to see my guard sound asleep in a corner of the room.

Satisfied that I had obtained all that I could obtain in this awkward position, I waited impatiently for the next night, racking my brains for a way to make it still more delicious; but the Greek girl, thinking to the same purpose, obliged me to admit that her wits were more fertile than mine.

She was in the courtyard with her master after dinner and had said something to him to which he nodded his assent, whereupon I saw a Turkish servant and their guard drag out a great basket of merchandise and place it under the balcony; while she had another bale placed on top of two others, as if to make more room for the basket. Understanding her plan, I trembled with joy. I saw that by this maneuver she had provided the means to stand two feet higher that night. "But what of it?" I reflected. "She will be in the most awkward position imaginable, so stooped over that she cannot possibly bear it. The hole is not big enough for her to make herself comfortable by putting her whole head through it."

Raging because I could not hope to enlarge the hole, I lie down, I examine it, and I see no other course but to unnail the whole worn plank from the two beams underneath it. I go back into the room; the guard was not there. I choose the strongest among the pairs of tongs which I see; I set to work and, making several attempts, for I am constantly afraid I will be caught, I pull out the four big nails which held the plank to the beams; I can now take it up whenever I please. I leave it there and wait impatiently for night. After eating a bite or two, I post myself on the balcony.

The object of my desires arrived at midnight. Dismayed to see that it took great agility on her part to climb up on the new bale, I lift my plank, set it aside, and, lying down, offer her the whole length of my arm; she takes hold of it, climbs, and, straightening up, is astonished to find that she is in my balcony down to her waist. She brought the whole length of her bare arms into it without any difficulty. We wasted only three or four minutes congratulating each other on having independently worked for the same end. If on the previous night I had been more her master than she had been mine, on this night she commanded my entire body. Alas! stretch my arms as I would, I could not possess more than half of hers. I was in despair; but she, though she had me entirely in her hands, was ready to weep because she could satisfy only her mouth. She heaped a thousand Greek curses on the wretch who had not made the bale at least half a foot bigger. Even then we should not have been satisfied; but my hand could have soothed her ardor somewhat. Though our pleasures were sterile, they occupied us until dawn. She departed without making a sound; I put back the plank, and went to bed in great need of regaining my strength.

She had told me that since the Lesser Bairam[2] began that day and continued for three more, she could not come again until the fourth day. It was the Turkish Easter. The Lesser Bairam lasts longer than the Greater. I spent these three days watching their ceremonies and their constant bustling about.

The first night after the Bairam, when she had clasped me in her loving arms, she told me that she could not be happy unless she were mine and that, as she was a Christian, I could buy her and then wait for her in Ancona till she had finished her quarantine. I had to confess that I was poor, and at that she sighed. The next night she told me that her master would sell her for two thousand piasters,[3] that she could give them to me, that she was a virgin, and that I could convince myself of it if the bale were bigger. She said she would give me a box filled with diamonds, a single one of which was worth two thousand piasters, and that by selling the others we could live in comfort without any fear of poverty. She said that her master would not notice the theft of the box until he had completed his quarantine, and that he would suspect anyone rather than her.

I was in love with this creature; her proposal troubled me; but when I woke in the morning I hesitated no longer. The next night she came with the box, and when I told her that I could not bring myself to be an accomplice in robbery, she wept and answered that I did not love her as she loved me, but that I was a "true Christian." It was the last night. The prior of the lazaretto was to come the next day at noon to give us our freedom. Surrendering to her senses, no longer able to resist the fire which was burning her soul, the charming Greek told me to stand up, bend over, take her under the armpits, and pull her up onto the balcony. What lover could resist such an invitation? Naked as a gladiator, I stand up, I bend over, I take her under the armpits and, without needing the strength of Milo of Crotona,[4] I was pulling her up when I felt my shoulders grasped and heard the guard's voice saying, "What are you doing?" I let go, she flees, and I fall on my stomach. I have no wish to get up, and I let the guard shake me. He thought the effort I had made had killed me, but I was worse than dead. I did not get up, because I wanted to strangle him. Finally I went to bed without addressing a word to him, and even without putting back the plank.

The prior came in the morning and told us we were free. As I left, brokenhearted, I saw the Greek girl wiping away her tears.

[* * *]

As soon as I arrive [in Naples], I find someone to guide me to the place named in the address I had been given, but the Bishop is not there. I go to the Minimite monastery, and am told that he had left for Martorano, and all the inquiries I make are fruitless. He had left no orders which could possibly concern me. So there I am in the great city of Naples with eight carlini[5] in my pocket and no idea where to turn. Yet my destiny calls me to Martorano, and there I am determined to go. The distance is only two hundred miles.[6] I find several coachmen setting out for Cosenza, but when they learn that I have no trunk, they refuse to take me unless I pay in advance. I admit they are right; but I had to get to Martorano. I determine to go on foot, boldly asking for food anywhere along the way, as Frate Steffano had taught me to do. I spend two of my carlini on a meal; that leaves me with six. Told that I should take the Salerno road, I get to Portici in an hour and a half. My legs carry me to an inn where I take a room and order supper. Excellently served, I eat, go to bed, and sleep very well. The next morning I get up and go to look at the royal palace.[7] I tell the innkeeper that I will come back for dinner.

As I enter the royal palace, a man of prepossessing appearance and dressed in the fashion of the East approaches me and says that if I wish to see the palace he will show me everything and so I shall save my money. I accept, thanking him heartily, and he walks beside me. When I tell him that I am a Venetian, he answers that, as a Zantiote,[8] he is my subject. I take the compliment for what it is worth and make him a slight bow.

"I have some excellent muscat wines from the Levant,"[9] he says, "which I could sell you cheaply."

"I might buy some; but I know them well."

"So much the better. Which one do you prefer?"

"Cerigo."

"You are right. I have some which is excellent, and we shall taste it at dinner, if you will dine with me."

"Certainly, with pleasure."

"I have wine from Samos and from Cephalonia.[10] I have a stock of minerals—vitriol, cinnabar, antimony, and a hundred quintals of mercury."

"I will buy some mercury too."

It is quite naturally, and without any thought of deceit, that a young man who is new to poverty and ashamed to be poor, and who falls into conversation with a rich man who does not know him, talks of buying. I suddenly remember an amalgam of mercury made with lead and bismuth. The mercury increased by a fourth part. I say nothing; but I think to myself that if the Greek did not know this magistery,[11] I might make money from it. I felt that I must proceed with cunning and caution. I saw that if I proposed point-blank to sell him my secret, he would think it worthless; I must first surprise him with the miracle of the increase, laugh at it, and then watch him come on. *Cheating is a sin, but honest cunning is simply prudence. It is a virtue.* To be sure, it has a likeness to roguery, but that cannot be helped. He who has not learned to practice it is a fool. In Greek this kind of prudence is called *kerdaleophron*.[12] *Kerda* means "fox." After seeing the palace, we repair to the inn. The Greek takes me to his room, where he orders the innkeeper to set a table for two. In the next room he had large flagons full of muscat wine and four filled with mercury, each holding ten pounds. Having my plan sketched out in my head, I ask him for a flagon of mercury at whatever it was worth, and I take it to my room. He goes out on some business, telling me that we shall meet again at dinnertime. I go out too, and buy two and a half pounds of lead and the same quantity of bismuth. It was all that the druggist had. I go back to my room, ask the innkeeper for two large empty flagons, and I make my amalgam.

We dine in high spirits and the Greek is delighted to see that I find his Cerigo muscat exquisite. He asks me smilingly why I had bought a flagon of his mercury and I answered that he could see the reason in my room. He comes there, sees the mercury in two bottles, I ask for a piece of chamois, strain it, fill his flagon, and see him astonished by the quarter-flagon of fine mercury which I have left, together with an equal quantity of a powdered metal which he did not recognize and which was the bismuth. I greet his astonishment with a burst of laughter. I summon the waiter and send him off with the mercury I had left to sell it to the druggist. He comes back and hands me fifteen carlini.

The astounded Greek asks me to give him back his own flagon, which stood there full and was worth sixty carlini; I give it to him with a smile and thank him for having enabled me to make a profit of fifteen carlini. At the same time I tell him that early the next morning I must leave for Salerno. "Then we shall sup together again," he says, "this evening."

We spend all the rest of the day on Vesuvius, and never mention the mercury; but I saw that he was thoughtful. During our supper, he says smilingly that I might well stay over the next day and make forty-five carlini on the other three flagons of mercury he had with him. I answered him in a dignified and serious tone that I did not need them and that I had only increased one of his flagons to amuse him by a pleasant surprise.

"But," he said, "you must be very rich."

"No, for I am after[13] the method of increasing gold, and that costs us a great deal."

"Then there are several of you?"

"My uncle and I."

"What need have you to increase gold? Increasing mercury should be enough for you. Tell me, please, can the mercury you have increased be increased by as much again?"

"No. If it could, it would be a vast seedbed of wealth."

"I find your sincerity delightful."

Supper over, I paid the innkeeper and asked him to have a carriage and pair ready early in the morning to take me to Salerno. Thanking the Greek for his excellent muscat wine, I asked him for his address at Naples, adding that he would see me two weeks hence for I was determined to buy a barrel of his Cerigo. After embracing him cordially, I went off to bed, well pleased with my day's work and not at all surprised that the Greek had not proposed that I sell him my secret. I was sure that he would think it over all night and that I should see him at daybreak. In any case I had money enough to get me to Torre del Greco, and there Providence would take care of me. I thought I could not possibly make my way to Martorano by begging alms, because, such as I was, I did not arouse pity. I could interest only people ready to believe that I was not in need. That is of no use to a genuine beggar.

As I had hoped, the Greek came to my room at dawn.

"We will take coffee together," I said.

"Tell me, Signor Abate, will you sell me your secret?"

"Why not? When we meet again in Naples."

"Why not today?"

"I am expected in Salerno. Besides, the secret is worth a great deal of money and I do not know you."

"That is no obstacle, since I am well enough known here to pay you in cash. What do you want for it?"

"Two thousand once."[*][14]

"I will give you that, on condition that I shall myself increase the thirty pounds I have here with whatever material you specify to me, which I will go and buy myself."

"That is impossible, since the material is not to be had here; but at Naples anyone can get as much as he pleases."

[*] A coin worth 14 paoli. (C.'s note.)

"If it is a metal, it can be found at Torre del Greco. We can go there together. Can you tell me what the increase costs?"

"One and one-half per cent; but are you known in Torre del Greco too? For I should not wish to waste my time."

"Your doubt pains me."

He takes a pen, writes the following note, and hands it to me: "On sight. Pay the bearer fifty once in gold and charge them to my account. Panagiotti—Rodostemo. To Signor Gennaro di Carlo."

He tells me the man lives two hundred paces from the inn and urges me to go there myself. I go without waiting to be asked twice, receive fifty once and, returning to my room where he was waiting for me, put them on the table. I then tell him to come with me to Torre del Greco,[15] where we will complete the transaction, after exchanging engagements in writing. Having his own carriage, he ordered the horses harnessed and generously told me to take the fifty once.

At Torre del Greco he wrote me out a receipt in which he promised to pay me two thousand once as soon as I should have told him with what substances and by what process he could increase mercury by a fourth without impairment of its purity and of the same quality as that which I had sold at Portici in his presence.

Pursuant to this, he drew me up a bill of exchange payable in eight days at sight on Signor Gennaro di Carlo. I thereupon told him that the substances were lead, which amalgamated naturally with mercury, and bismuth, which served only to give it the fluidity it must have to pass through the chamois. The Greek went out to perform the operation in the house of some person whom he did not name. I dined alone, and in the evening I saw him looking very gloomy. I had expected as much.

"The operation is performed," he said, "but the mercury is not perfect."

"It is 'of the same quality as that which I sold in Portici.' Your receipt states that clearly."

"But it also says 'without impairment of its purity.' You must admit that its purity is impaired. It is also true that it can no longer be increased."

"I stick to the point of quality. We will go to court, and you will lose. I should be sorry to have the secret become public knowledge. If you do win, you can congratulate yourself, for you will have got my secret from me for nothing. I did not think you capable, Signor Panagiotti, of tricking me in this fashion."

124

"Signor Abate, I am incapable of tricking anyone."

"Do you know the secret, or do you not? Would I have told it to you except for the bargain we made? This will set all Naples laughing, and the lawyers will make money."

"I am already in trouble enough over the affair."

"In the meanwhile, here are your fifty once."

As I was taking them from my pocket in great fear that he would accept them, he left, saying he did not want them. We supped separately, each in his own room, divided by open war; but I knew that we would make peace. He came to me in the morning, when I was getting ready to leave and a carriage was already waiting for me. When I told him to take his fifty once, he answered that I should content myself with another fifty and give him back his bill of exchange for two thousand. We then began talking sense, and after two hours I gave in. He handed me another fifty once, we dined together, we embraced afterward, and then he presented me with a note good for a cask of muscat wine at his storehouse in Naples and with a magnificent case containing twelve silver-handled razors from the famous manufactory in Torre del Greco. We parted the best of friends. I stayed in Salerno for two days to buy shirts, stockings, handkerchiefs, and whatever I needed. I had a hundred zecchini at my disposal, I was in excellent health and proud of my exploit, in which I saw nothing with which I need reproach myself. The cunning and the quickness of mind on which I had drawn to sell my secret could be condemned only by a civic morality which has no place in the business of life. Free, rich, and certain of appearing before my Bishop a well-turned-out youth instead of a tramp, I recovered all my high spirits, and congratulated myself on having learned, at my own expense, to defend myself against Father Corsinis, swindling gamesters, mercenary women, and especially against those who praise a man to his face. I set off with two priests who were in a hurry to reach Cosenza. We did the one hundred and forty miles in twenty-two hours. The morning after I arrived in the capital of Calabria, I hired a small carriage and proceeded to Martorano.

As I traveled, I fixed my eyes on the famous *Mare Ausonium*[16] and rejoiced in being at the center of *Magna Graecia*,[17] which Pythagoras's[18] sojourn had rendered illustrious for twenty-four centuries. I looked with astonishment at a country renowned for its fertility, in which, despite the prodigality of nature, I saw only poverty, a dearth of all that delightful superfluity which alone can make life precious, and a humanity to which I was ashamed to remember that I belonged. Such is the Terra di Lavoro[19] where *labor* is held in abhorrence, where everything is sold for a song, where the inhabitants feel relieved of a burden when they find someone willing to accept their gifts of all kinds of fruits. I saw that the Romans had not erred in calling them brutes instead of Bruttii.[20] The priests who were traveling with me laughed when I confessed to my fear of the tarantula and the chersydrus.[21] I believed that the malady they communicated was even more horrible than that of Venus. The priests assured me that they were fabulous and laughed at the *Georgics*[22] of Vergil and the line which I quoted to justify my fear.

I found Bishop Bernardo da Bernardis sitting in an uncomfortable chair at a wretched table on which he was writing. He got up to raise me from my knees and, instead of blessing me, clasped me to his bosom. I saw that he was sincerely concerned when I told him that I had found no word at Naples telling me where I could come to fall at his feet, and he looked relieved when I said that I was in debt to no one and in good health.

He sighed as he told me of his feelings and his poverty, and ordered a servant to lay a third place at his table. In addition to this man, he had the most canonical of maidservants and a priest whose few words at table made me think him a great ignoramus. His house was quite large, but badly built and falling to ruin. It had so little furniture that, to provide me with a poor bed in a room near his, he had to give me one of his own hard mattresses. His wretched dinner horrified me. His attachment to the rule of his order made him keep the fast and the oil was bad. However, he was intelligent and, what is more, an honest man. He told me what greatly surprised me—that his bishopric, though it was not one of the poorest, yielded him only five hundred ducati del regno[23] a year and, still worse, he was in debt to the amount of six hundred. He said with a sigh that the only happiness he enjoyed was having escaped from the clutches of the monks, whose persecution of him had made his life a purgatory for fifteen years. All this information discouraged me, for it showed me the straits in which my presence must put him. I saw that he was disconcerted to realize what a poor present he had made me. Yet I felt that he was only to be pitied.

He smiled when I asked him if he had good books, a literary circle, or any good society in which to spend a pleasant hour or two. He admitted that in his entire diocese there was not a person who could boast of writing decently, still less of having taste and any notion of good literature, not a single real library, and no one curious enough to look into a newspaper. However, he promised me that we would give some time to letters together when the books he had ordered from Naples arrived.

That might well be; but without a good library, a circle, a spirit of rivalry, a literary intercourse, was this the country in which I must settle down at the age of eighteen? Seeing me thoughtful and almost overwhelmed by the prospect of the dreary life I must be prepared to lead with him, he tried to encourage me by telling me that he would do everything in his power to make me content.

As he had to officiate at a pontifical service the next day, I saw all his clergy and the women and men who filled his cathedral. It was then that I decided upon my course, grateful to fortune that I was in a position to do so. I saw nothing but brutes who seemed to me positively scandalized by my entire appearance. What ugly women! I told Monsignore in so many words that I felt no call to die a martyr in this city a few months hence.

"Give me," I said, "your episcopal blessing and permission to go, or come with me yourself, and I assure you that we shall make our fortunes. Resign your bishopric to those who made you such an ill present of it."

My proposal set him laughing again and again all the rest of the day; but if he had accepted it, he would not have died two years later in the prime of life.[24] The worthy man was moved to ask my forgiveness for the fault he had committed in bringing me there. Recognizing that it was his duty to send me back to Venice, and being without money and not knowing that I had any, he told me he would send me back to Naples, where a citizen to whom he would give me an introduction would give me sixty ducati del regno, with which I could go back to my native country. I accepted his offer gratefully, and hurried off to open my trunk and bring back the fine case of razors which Panagiotti had given me. I had all the trouble in the world persuading him to accept it, for it was worth the sixty ducati he was giving me. He took it only because I threatened to stay on there if he persisted in refusing it. He gave me a letter to the Archbishop of Cosenza,[25] in which he praised me and asked him to send me to Naples at his expense. So it was that I left Martorano sixty hours after I arrived, pitying the Bishop whom I left there and who shed tears as he gave me a thousand heart-felt blessings.

The Bishop of Cosenza, a man of intelligence and wealth, insisted on lodging me in his house. At table I warmly praised the Bishop of Martorano; but I railed mercilessly at his diocese and then at the whole of Calabria, in a style so cutting that Monsignore and the entire company could not contain their laughter. Two ladies, relatives of his, did the honors of his table. The younger of them saw fit to disapprove of my satirical attack on her country. She declared war on me; but I mollified her by saying that Calabria would be a ravishing country if only a quarter of its inhabitants were like her. It may have been to prove the contrary of what I had maintained that, the following evening, he had a large company to supper. Cosenza is a city in which a gentleman can have a pleasant time, for there is a rich nobility, some pretty women, and some not uncultivated men.[26] I left on the third day, with a letter from the Archbishop to the celebrated Genovesi.[27]

I had five traveling companions who struck me from the first as being pirates or professional thieves, so I was careful never to let them see that I had a well-filled purse. I always slept with my breeches on, not only for the safety of my money but as a precaution I thought necessary in a country where unnatural desires are common.

1743.

I arrived at Naples on September 16th, and at once went to deliver my letter from the Bishop of Martorano. It was addressed to Signor Gennaro Palo, at Santa Anna. This man, whose only obligation was to give me sixty ducati, read the letter and said that he would be glad to put me up, as he wanted me to make the acquaintance of his son, who wrote poetry too. The Bishop had written him that I was a sublime poet. After the usual protests, I accepted his invitation, then went and had my little trunk carried to his house. As soon as I got back, he had me shown into his room again.

I found no difficulty in answering all the questions he asked me;
what I did find most strange and curious was the prolonged laughter
which burst from his lungs at every answer I made him. My account
of the poverty of Calabria and the state of the Bishop of Martorano,
both of which I described in a way to draw tears, roused his laughter
to the point where I thought it would kill him.

He was big, fat, and red-faced. Thinking that he was mocking
me, I was ready to take offense when he finally became calm and
told me with great earnestness that I must pardon his laughter, for it
was due to a disease which ran in his family and that one of his
uncles had actually died of it.

"Died of laughing?"

"Yes. The disease, which was unknown to Hippocrates,[1] is called
li flati."[2]

"How can this be? Do hypochondriac affections, which make all
their victims melancholy, make you cheerful?"

"But my *flati*, instead of acting on the hypochrondrium,[3] affect
my spleen, which my physician holds to be the organ of laughter. It
is a new discovery."

"Not at all. Indeed, it is a very old idea."

"You don't say so! We shall discuss it at table, for I hope you will
spend several weeks here."

"I cannot. I must leave day after tomorrow at the latest."

"Then you have some money?"

"I am counting on the sixty ducati which you will have the
goodness to give me."

At this his laughter began again; he accounted for it afterward
by telling me that the idea of making me stay there as long as he
pleased had amused him. He then asked me to go and see his son
who, at the age of fourteen, was already a great poet. A maidservant showed me to his room, and I was delighted to find him a

youth of fine presence and with a manner which aroused interest at once. After greeting me most politely, he asked me to excuse him if he could not give me his entire attention, since he was busy on a canzone which must go to press the next day; a young lady who was related to the Duchess of Bovino[4] was to take the veil at Santa Chiara, and his poem was for the occasion. Considering his excuse more than legitimate, I offered to help him. He read me his canzone and, finding it full of enthusiasm and versified in the manner of Guidi,[5] I advised him to call it an ode. After praising it where it deserved praise, I ventured to correct it where I thought it needed correction, even going so far as to substitute new verses for those I considered weak. He thanked me, asking me if I were not Apollo himself, and began making a copy of it to send to the compiler. While he was copying it, I wrote a sonnet on the same subject. Paolo was delighted with it and insisted that I sign it and send it to the compiler with his ode.

While I was copying it for the second time to correct some errors in spelling, he went to his father and asked him who I was, which set him laughing until we sat down at table. A bed was made up for me in the young man's own room, an arrangement which pleased me greatly.

Don Gennaro's family consisted only of this son, a daughter who was not pretty, his wife, and two old sisters who were very devout. At supper he had some men of letters. I made the acquaintance of the Marchese Galiani, who was writing a commentary on Vitruvius[6] and was the brother of the Abate Galiani, whom I met at Paris twenty years later when he was embassy secretary to the Count of Cantillana.[7] The next day at supper I met the celebrated Genovesi, who had already received the letter the Archbishop of Cosenza had written him. He talked to me at some length of Apostolo Zeno[8] and the Abate Conti.[9] During supper he remarked that *the most venial mortal sin a regular priest could commit was to say two masses in one day to earn two more carlini, whereas a secular priest who committed the same sin deserved burning*.

The next day the nun took the veil, and the most highly praised compositions in the *raccolta*[10] were the two by Paolo and myself. A Neapolitan named Casanova no sooner learned that I was a foreigner than he became curious to meet me. Finding that I was staying with Don Gennaro, he came to compliment him on the occasion of his name day, which was celebrated the day after the nun took the veil at Santa Chiara.

After telling me his name, Don Antonio Casanova asked me if my family was originally Venetian. "I am, Signore," I answered modestly, "a great-grandson of the grandson of the unfortunate Marcantonio Casanova who was secretary to Cardinal Pompeo Colonna and who died of the plague at Rome in the year 1528, during the pontificate of Clement VII." Upon hearing this, he embraced me and called me his cousin. It was just at this moment that the whole company thought Don Gennaro would die from laughing, for it seemed impossible to laugh as he was doing and live through it. His wife gave Don Antonio a look of annoyance and said that since he was aware of her husband's disorder, he might well have spared him this absurdity; he answered that he could not have supposed it a laughing matter; I said nothing for, all things considered, I thought this scene of recognition highly comic. When Don Gennaro quieted down, Don Antonio, never losing his gravity, invited me to dinner, together with young Paolo, who had become my inseparable friend.

The first thing my worthy cousin did when I arrived at his house was to show me his genealogical tree, which began with a Don Francisco, brother of Don Juan. In mine, which I knew by heart, Don Juan, from whom I was directly descended, was born posthumously. It was possible that Marcantonio had had a brother; but when he learned that mine began with Don Francisco, of Aragon, who lived at the end of the fourteenth century, and that in consequence the whole genealogy of the illustrious house of the Casanovas of Saragossa became his own, he was so beside himself with joy that he did not know what to do to convince me that the blood which flowed in his veins was mine.

Seeing that he was curious to know what chance had brought me to Naples, I told him that, having entered the Church after my father's death, I was on my way to seek my fortune in Rome. When he introduced me to his family I thought his wife did not receive me cordially; but his pretty daughter and his still prettier niece could easily have made me believe in the fabled power of blood. After dinner he told me that the Duchess of Bovino had expressed her curiosity to know who this Abate Casanova was, and that he would consider it an honor to take me to call on her and introduce me as his relative.

Since we were alone, I begged him to excuse me, as I was outfitted only for my journey. I told him that I had to spare my purse, so that I should not arrive in Rome without money.

Delighted at my confiding my reason to him, and persuaded that it was a good one, he told me that he was rich and that I must not hesitate to let him take me to a tailor. He assured me that no one would know of it and that he would be greatly chagrined if I refused him the pleasure. I clasped his hand and said that I was ready to do whatever he wished. So he went with me to a tailor, who took all the measurements he indicated, and who the next day appeared at Don Gennaro's bringing me everything the most highborn abate would need to appear in society. Don Antonio arrived later, stayed for dinner with Don Gennaro, then took me to call on the Duchess with young Paolo. To show her graciousness she at once addressed me in the familiar form, as is the custom in Naples. She was with her very pretty daughter, then ten or twelve years of age, who some years later became Duchess of Matalona.[11] She presented me with a snuffbox of light tortoiseshell covered with arabesque incrustations in gold. She invited us to dine with her on the following day and said that afterwards we would go to Santa Chiara to call on the new nun.

When I left the Casa Bovino I went by myself to Panagiotti's warehouse to obtain the cask of muscat wine. The head of the establishment did me the favor of putting it in two small casks, of which I sent one to Don Gennaro and the other to Don Antonio. As I left the warehouse, I encountered the worthy Greek, who was glad to see me again. Was I to blush in the presence of this man whom I knew I had deceived? Not at all—on the contrary, he considered that I had acted most uprightly toward him.

At supper Don Gennaro thanked me for my valuable present without laughing. The next day Don Antonio, in return for the excellent muscat I had sent him, presented me with a cane which was worth at least twenty once, and his tailor brought me a traveling suit and a blue redingote with gold buttonholes, all of the finest cloth. I could not be better outfitted. At the Duchess of Bovino's I met the wisest of all Neapolitans, the illustrious Don Lelio Caraffa,[12] of the ducal family of Matalona, for whom the King, Don Carlos, had a particular liking and whom he honored with the name of friend.

In the visiting room at Santa Chiara, I shone for two hours, holding my own against all the nuns behind the gratings and satisfying their curiosity with my answers. If my destiny had let me remain in Naples, I should have made my fortune there; but I believed I ought to go to Rome, though I had no settled plan.

I steadfastly refused to yield to the urging of Don Antonio, who offered me the most honorable employment in several noble houses, which he specified to me, as tutor to the eldest son of the family.

The dinner at Don Antonio's was magnificent; but I was pre-occupied and angry because his wife obviously frowned on me. I noticed that she more than once looked at my coat and then whispered something to her neighbor. She had found out every-thing. There are certain situations in life to which I have never learned to adapt myself. *In the most brilliant company, if but a single member of it stares me up and down, I am undone; I become ill-tempered and stupid.* It is a weakness.

Don Lelio Caraffa offered me a liberal salary if I would remain as tutor to his nephew the Duke of Matalona, who was then ten years old. I called to thank him and begged him to become my true benefactor by giving me a good letter of introduction for Rome. He sent me two the next morning, one addressed to Cardinal Acquaviva,[13] the other to Father Georgi, a powerful churchman.[14]

I quickly made up my mind to leave when I found that my acquaintances were determined to procure me the honor of kissing the Queen's hand. It was obvious that in answering the questions she would put to me, I should have to tell her that I had just left Martorano and give her an account of the wretched bishopric which her intercession had secured for the good Minimite. Then too, Her Majesty knew my mother, there was nothing to stop her from revealing her position in Dresden; Don Antonio would be scandalized and my genealogy made ridiculous. I knew the inevit-able and unhappy results of the prejudices then current; I should have come a complete cropper. I left while it was still time. Don Antonio presented me with a watch in a tortoiseshell case inlaid with gold and gave me a letter to Don Gaspare Vivaldi,[15] whom he termed his best friend. Don Gennaro gave me sixty ducati, and his son begged me to write to him and swore eternal friendship. They all wept as they accompanied me to a coach in which I had taken the last place.

From my landing at Chioggia until my arrival at Naples, fortune had treated me outrageously. It was at Naples that I began to breathe again, and Naples was always propitious to me, as will be seen in the course of these memoirs. At Portici I went through the horrible moment when I nearly came to the end of my courage, and *for lost courage there is no remedy.* It cannot be recovered. The mind succumbs to an apathy against which nothing avails. With his letter to Don Gennaro, the Bishop of Martorano compensated me for all the harm he had done me. I did not write to him until after I reached Rome.

Busy looking at the fine Strada di Toledo[16] and drying my tears, I did not think of examining the faces of my three traveling companions until we reached the gate of the great city. The man of forty or fifty years who sat beside me had a pleasant, lively face. The two women on the forward-facing seat were young and pretty; their clothes were clean and neat, they looked jolly but at the same time respectable. We reached Aversa in complete silence, where the driver told us that he would stop only to water his mules, so we did not get out. Toward nightfall we stopped at Capua. Incredible as it may seem, I never opened my mouth all day long but listened with pleasure to the dialect of the man, who was a Neapolitan, and the beautiful speech of the two sisters, who were Romans. It was the first time in my life that I had the firmness to spend five hours in silence in the company of two charming girls or women. At Capua we were given a room with two beds, as a matter of course. The man who had sat beside me was the first to speak, looking at me and saying:

"So I shall have the honor of sleeping with the Signor Abate."

"I leave it to you, Signore," I said coldly, "to make whatever arrangement you wish." This answer brought a smile to the lips of the young lady whom I had already decided was the prettier. I considered it a good omen.

We were five at supper, for when the *vetturino* has contracted to feed his passengers, it is customary for him to eat with them. In the casual remarks at the table I found a certain good breeding and knowledge of the world. This made me curious. After supper I went downstairs to ask the *vetturino* who my traveling companions were. "The man," he replied, "is an advocate and one of the two sisters is his wife, but I do not know which."

I showed them the civility of going to bed first, and also of rising earliest and going out, so that the ladies were left the freedom of the room. I did not come back until I was summoned to take coffee. I praised it, and the more attractive of the two sisters promised me the same charming offering every day.

A barber appeared and shaved the advocate and, when he had finished, offered me the same service, but in a tone which I did not like. When I answered that I had no need of him, he replied that a beard was a dirty thing.

As soon as we were in the coach the advocate remarked that barbers were mostly an insolent lot.

"The question," said my beauty, "is whether a beard is a dirty thing or not."

"The answer is yes," said the advocate, "for it is an excretion."

"That may be so," I replied, "but it is not regarded as such; does anyone call the hair an excretion? On the contrary, its growth is stimulated and it is admired for its length and beauty."

"It follows," the lady resumed, "that the barber is a fool."

"But apart from that," I replied, "have I a beard?"

"I thought so."

"Then I will begin being shaved when I get to Rome. This is the first time anyone has accused me of needing it."

"My dear wife," said the advocate, "you should have held your tongue, for it is quite possible that the Signor Abate is going to Rome to become a Capuchin."[17]

This thrust made me laugh; but I did not want to leave him master of the field. I told him that he had guessed right, but that my wish to become a Capuchin had left me as soon as I saw his wife. Laughing too, he said that his wife was mad about Capuchins, so I should not abandon my vocation. This jest having led to more, we spent our day pleasantly until we reached Garigliano, where amusing conversation made up for a poor supper. My budding inclination was fostered by the obvious partiality of its object.

As soon as we were seated in the coach the next day, the fair lady asked me if I expected to stay in Rome for a time before going on to Venice. I answered that as I knew no one in Rome, I feared I should have a dull time. She said that foreigners were well liked there and she was sure that I would find it pleasant.

"Then may I hope that you will permit me to pay my respects to you?"

"We should consider it an honor," said the advocate.

My beauty blushed, I pretended not to notice it, and we whiled away the day in talk as pleasant as that of the day before. We stopped at Terracina, and were given a room with three beds, two of them narrow, with a wide bed between them. It went without saying that the two sisters would share the wide bed, and they got into it while the advocate and I chatted at the table with our backs turned to them. The advocate got into the bed on which he saw his nightcap, and I into the other, which was only a foot from the wide bed, on the side on which his wife was lying. All vanity apart, I could not bring myself to believe that this arrangement was entirely due to chance. I was already on fire for her.

I undress, put out the candle, and lie down, considering a plan which made me restless, for I was afraid either to adopt it or to reject it. I could not get to sleep. A faint light by which I could see the bed in which the charming woman was lying kept me from closing my eyes. God knows to what decision I should finally have come, for I had been struggling with myself for over an hour, when I saw her sit up, get out of the bed, walk softly around it, and get into her husband's. After that I heard not a sound. This action was so little to my liking, indeed it so mortified and disgusted me, that I turned over on the other side and slept until dawn, when I saw the lady back in her own bed.

I dress in a foul humor and go out, leaving them all asleep. I go for a walk and do not return to the inn until, the coach being ready to leave, the two ladies and the advocate were waiting for me.

My beauty gently reproaches me with having forgone her coffee. I offer the excuse that I had needed a walk. I spent the whole morning not only without saying a word but without ever looking at her. I complained of a bad toothache. At Piperno, where we dined, she remarked to me that my indisposition was made to order. The reproach pleased me, for it gave me the right to have things out with her.

In the afternoon I played the same role all the way to Sermoneta, where we were to spend the night and which we reached early. As it was a fine day, the lady said she would like to take a little stroll and asked me civilly if I would give her my arm. I consented at once. Politeness left me no alternative. My heart was sore. I could not wait to return to my former footing, but only after having the matter out with her, and I did not know how to precipitate such an explanation.

As soon as I saw that I was far enough from her husband, who was giving his arm to her sister, I asked her what had made her think my toothache made to order.

"I will be frank. The change in your manner was too marked, you even took great care not to look at me all day. Since a toothache could not prevent you from being polite, I concluded that it was made to order. Besides, I know that none of us gave you any cause to change your attitude."

"Yet the change must have been caused by something. You are only half sincere, Signora."

"You are mistaken, Signore. I am completely sincere, and if I gave you any cause, I do not know what it was or it is something which I should not know. Be so good as to tell me in what way I have failed you."

"In no way, for I have no right to make any claim upon you."

"But you have rights, the same rights as I have, the rights which good society grants to all its members. Speak. Be as frank as I am."

"You are in duty bound not to know the cause, or rather, to pretend not to know it—that is true. But admit at the same time that my duty is not to tell it to you."

"Excellent! Now it has all come out. But if it is your duty not to tell me the reason for your change of humor, the same duty obliges you not to reveal the change. Delicacy sometimes commands a gentleman to conceal certain feelings which might be compromising. It is a restraint on impulse, I know; but it is worth the effort when it only makes him who exercises it all the more admirable."

An argument at once so subtle and so strong made me blush for shame. I pressed my lips to her hand, saying that I admitted I was in the wrong and that she would see me at her feet, begging her to forgive me, if we were not in the street. "Then let us say no more about it," she said, and touched by my quick repentance, she gave me a look of such forgiveness that I thought I did not deepen my guilt when I took my lips from her hand and let them feed on her lovely smiling mouth.

Intoxicated with happiness, I changed from gloom to gaiety so quickly that at supper the advocate indulged in a hundred witty sallies at my toothache and the walk which had cured it. The next day we dined at Velletri, going on from there to spend the night at Marino, where despite the large number of troops we had two small rooms and a fairly good supper.

I could not have wished to be on better terms with the charming Roman. I had received only one pledge from her; but it was a pledge of the firmest love, and it assured me that, once we were in Rome, she would be wholly mine. In the coach we spoke to each other with our knees more than with our eyes, thus making sure that what we said would be overheard by no one.

The advocate had told me that he was going to Rome to conclude an ecclesiastical suit and that he would lodge with his mother-in-law near the Minerva.[18] His wife was most anxious to see her after an absence of two years, and her sister expected to remain in Rome as the wife of an employee in the Santo Spirito bank.[19] Invited to call on them, I promised that I would avail myself of the opportunity whenever my business should permit.

We had come to the dessert when my beauty, admiring the design of my snuffbox, said to her husband that she wished she had one like it. He promised that she should.

"Then buy this one, Signore," I said; "I will let you have it for twenty once. You can pay the amount to the bearer of a note of hand which you will draw up for me. He will be an Englishman to whom I happen to owe that sum and whom I am glad to have this means of repaying."

"Your snuffbox," said the advocate, "is worth the twenty once you ask, and I should be delighted to see it in my wife's possession, she would find it a pleasant reminder of you; but I will do nothing but pay you cash for it."

Seeing that I was unwilling, his wife told him that she could just as well write me the note of hand to bearer which I needed. He answered, with a laugh, that she must beware of me, for it was all a trick on my part. "Don't you see," he added, "that his Englishman is a fiction? He will never put in an appearance, and the snuffbox will be ours for nothing. This Abate, my dear wife, is a great rogue."

"I had no idea," she answered, with a look at me, "that such rogues existed." I told her sadly that I wished I were rich enough to be able to indulge in such rogueries.

But now something happened which filled me with joy. There was one bed in the room where we were eating supper and another in an adjoining closet which had no door and could only be entered from the room we were in. The two sisters naturally chose the closet. When they were in bed the advocate went to bed too, and I followed him. Before extinguishing the candle, I put my head into the closet to wish them a good night. My real reason was to find out on which side of the bed the wife was lying. I had a plan all prepared.

But what curses did I not heap on my bed when I heard the dreadful noise it made when I got into it! Feeling certain that the lady would be acquiescent even though she had promised me nothing, I wait until the advocate begins snoring, then start to get up to pay her a visit; but as soon as I try to rise, the bed begins squeaking, the advocate wakes and puts out his arm. He feels that I am there and goes back to sleep. A half hour later I try the same maneuver, the bed goes through the same *lazzi*[20] and the advocate through the other. Sure that I am there, he goes back to sleep, but the accursed blabbing of the bed makes me decide to abandon my plan. But then the most unlikely thing happens.

A great noise of people running up and down stairs, tramping back and forth, fills the house. We hear gunshots, a drum beating the alarm, cries, shouts, someone knocks at our door, the advocate asks me what is going on. I say I have no idea and will he please let me sleep. The terrified sisters ask us in Heaven's name to bring a light. The advocate gets up in his shirt to look for one, and I get up too. I go to shut the door after him, and I shut it, but the spring breaks and I find it can only be opened with the key, which I do not have. I proceed to the bed of the two sisters to hearten them amid the noise and confusion, the cause of which I did not know. While I am telling them that the lawyer will be back in a moment with a light, I obtain some substantial favors. The weak resistance emboldens me. Fearing to lose a time so precious, I bend forward and, to take the object of my affection in my arms, I let myself fall on it. The planks supporting the mattress slip and the bed collapses. The advocate knocks, the sister gets up, my goddess begs me to leave her, I cannot but yield to her prayers, I grope my way to the door and tell the advocate that, as the spring is out of order, I cannot open it. He goes downstairs to find the key. The two sisters were behind me in their shifts. Hoping I have time to finish, I put out my arms; but, feeling that I am roughly repulsed, I realize that it must be the sister. I take hold of the other. The advocate being now at the door with a bunch of keys, she begs me in God's name to go back to bed, for if her husband sees me in the dreadful state I must be in, he will guess everything. Feeling that my hands are sticky, I understand what she means, and I hurry to my bed. The sisters retire to theirs, and the advocate comes in.

He at once goes to the closet to reassure them; but he bursts out laughing when he sees them buried in the fallen bed. He urges me to go and look, but I naturally excuse myself. He tells us that the alarm was due to a German detachment having surprised the Spanish troops which were in the town and which thereupon decamped. A quarter of an hour later not a soul was left, and silence succeeded all the uproar. After congratulating me on not having stirred from my bed, he lay down again.

I waited sleeplessly for dawn so that I could go downstairs and wash and change my shirt. When I saw the state I was in, I admired my love's presence of mind. The advocate would have guessed everything. Not only were my shirt and my hands dirtied, but, I do not know how, so was my face. Alas! he would have found me guilty, and I was not as guilty as I might have been. This camisade is recorded in history; but I am not mentioned. I laugh every time I read it in the elegant De Amicis,[21] who wrote better than Sallust.

My divinity's sister sulked over our coffee; but on the face of the angel whom I loved I saw love, friendliness, and content. It is a great pleasure to feel happy. Can one be so and not feel it? The theologians say one can. Let them go mind their own business! I saw myself in possession of Donna Lucrezia (for such was her name), though I had obtained nothing from her. Neither her eyes nor the slightest of her gestures retracted anything; the ostensible reason for our laughter was the rout of the Spaniards; but that, though she did not know it, was only incidental.

We reached Rome early. At the Tower,[22] where we ate an omelette, I cajoled the advocate with the fondest advances; I called him "papa," I gave him a hundred kisses, and I predicted that he would become the father of a son, which obliged his wife to vow that she would give him one. Then I said so many charming things to my idol's sister that she had to forgive me the collapse of the bed. On leaving them I said I would visit them the next day. I was let out at an inn near the Piazza di Spagna,[23] whence the *vetturino* took them to their house near the Minerva.

So here I was in Rome, with a good wardrobe, a fair amount of money, some jewelry, and a fair amount of experience, with good letters of recommendation, completely free, and at an age when *a man can count on the help of fortune if he has a spark of courage and a face which disposes those whom he approaches to look on him with favor.* It is not beauty, but something more valuable, which I possessed but which I cannot define. I felt that I was capable of anything. I knew that *Rome was the one city in which a man who set out from nothing had often risen very high; and it is not surprising that I believed I possessed all the qualities needed to rise; my capital was an unbridled self-esteem which inexperience prevented me from mistrusting.*

The man fit to make a fortune in this ancient capital of Italy must be a chameleon sensitive to all the colors which the light casts on his surroundings. He must be flexible, insinuating, a great dissimulator, impenetrable, obliging, often base, ostensibly sincere, always pretending to know less than he does, keeping to one tone of voice, patient, in complete control of his countenance, cold as ice when another in his place would be on fire; and if he is so unfortunate as not to have religion in his heart he must have it in his mind, and, if he is an honest man, accept the painful necessity of admitting to himself that he is a hypocrite. If he loathes the pretense, he should leave Rome and seek his fortune in England. Of all these necessary qualities—I do not know if I am boasting or admitting my deficiency—I possessed only obligingness, which, without the others, is a fault. I was an interesting fool, a rather fine horse of a good breed, but unbroken or, what is worse, badly broken.

I at once took Don Lelio's letter to Father Georgi. This learned monk was esteemed by the whole city. The Pope thought highly of him because, being no friend to the Jesuits, he did not hide the fact. The Jesuits, for their part, thought themselves strong enough to disregard him.

After carefully reading the letter, he said he was prepared to be my adviser and that hence, if I wished, I might make him responsible for preserving me from misfortune, for if a man behaves himself properly he need not fear that evil will befall him. He then asked me what I wanted to do in Rome, to which I replied that it was for him to tell me.

"All in due time. So come and see me often, and conceal nothing from me, nothing, I say, of all that concerns you and happens to you."

"Don Lelio also gave me a letter to Cardinal Acquaviva."

"Then I congratulate you, for he is the one man who has more power in Rome than the Pope."

"Shall I take it to him at once?"

"No. I will speak to him about you this evening. Come here tomorrow early. I will tell you where and when you are to deliver it to him. Have you money?"

"Enough to keep me for at least a year."

"Excellent. Have you any acquaintances?"

"None."

"Do not make any without consulting me, and above all do not go to coffeehouses and eating houses, and if you must go, listen and do not talk. *Shun those who would interrogate you* and if *politeness obliges you to answer, evade the question if it can lead to any consequences.* Do you speak French?"

"Not a word."

"Too bad—you must learn it. Have you finished your studies?"

"After a fashion. But I am *infarinato*[24] enough to hold my own in a conversation."

"That is all to the good, but be on your guard, for Rome is the city of *infarinati*, and they are forever unmasking each other and bickering among themselves. I hope that when you take your letter to the Cardinal, you will be dressed as a modest abate and not in that elegant coat, which is not of a cut to placate Fortune. Good-by until tomorrow."

Very well pleased with the monk, I went to the Campo di Fiore[25] to deliver my cousin Don Antonio's letter to Don Gaspare Vivaldi. This excellent man received me in his library, where he was conversing with two respectable abati. After welcoming me most graciously, Don Gaspare asked me for my address and invited me to dinner the next day. He spoke in the highest terms of Father Georgi and, seeing me to the stairs, said that he would attend the next day to paying the sum which Don Antonio directed him to give me.

So my generous cousin was giving me more money, which I could not refuse. *It is not difficult to give, but to know how to give.* On my way home I met Father Steffano; he was the same as ever and loaded me with caresses. *I could not but feel a certain respect for this sordid freak, whom Providence had employed to save me from utter ruin.* After telling me that the Pope had granted him all that he asked, he warned me to avoid the policeman who had given me the two zecchini, for, finding that he had been deceived, he wanted his revenge. The rascal was in the right. I told Frate Steffano to persuade the officer to deposit my note with some merchant and when I knew with whom it had been left I would go and take it up. The thing was arranged in this fashion, I paid the two zecchini, and the ugly business was over.

I supped at an eating house with some Romans and some foreigners, faithfully following Father Georgi's advice. I was made to listen to some harsh criticism of the Pope and of the Cardinal Minister, who was responsible for the Papal State's being inundated by eighty thousand men, both Germans and Spaniards. What surprised me was that everyone ate meat, though it was a Saturday; but at the end of a week a number of things I observed in Rome had exhausted my capacity for surprise. There is not a Catholic Christian city in the world where people are less strict in matters of religion than they are at Rome. The Romans are like the employees at the tobacco monopoly, who are allowed to take away as much as they please for nothing. The citizens of Rome live in the greatest freedom, except for one thing: the *ordini santissimi*[26] are as much to be feared as *lettres de cachet*[27] were in Paris before the atrocious revolution.

1743.

It was on the next day, October 1st of the year 1743, that I finally made up my mind to be shaved. My down had become a beard. I felt that I must begin to renounce certain privileges of adolescence. I dressed completely in the Roman fashion, as Don Antonio's tailor had decreed that I should do. Father Georgi seemed much pleased when he saw me so turned out. After inviting me to take a cup of chocolate with him, he told me that the Cardinal had been informed of my impending visit by a letter from the same Don Lelio, and that His Excellency would receive me about noon at the Villa Negroni,[28] where he would be taking a stroll. I said that I was to dine at Signor Vivaldi's, and he advised me to visit him often.

At the Villa Negroni, the Cardinal no sooner saw me than he stopped to receive my letter, leaving the two people who were with him to walk on. He put it in his pocket without reading it. After two minutes of silence, which he spent looking at me, he asked me if I felt any inclination for politics. I answered that as yet I had not felt drawn to anything but frivolities, and that hence I could only answer for my extreme readiness to do whatever His Excellency should command me, if he found me worthy to enter his service. He at once told me to go to his palace[29] the next morning and speak with the Abate Gama,[30] whom he would inform of his intentions. "You must," he said, "set about learning French at once. It is indispensable." After asking me if Don Lelio was in good health, he left me, giving me his hand to kiss.

From there I went to the Campo di Fiore, where Don Gaspare kept me to dine with a select company. He was a bachelor and his only passion was literature. He loved Latin poetry even more than Italian and his favorite poet was Horace, whom I knew by heart. After dinner he gave me a hundred Roman scudi[31] on behalf of Don Antonio Casanova. After I signed a receipt for the amount, he said that he would be delighted to have me take chocolate with him in his library any morning.

When I left his house I went to the Minerva quarter. I could not wait to see how surprised Donna Lucrezia and her sister Angelica would be. To find the house, I inquired where Donna Cecilia Monti lived. This was her mother.

I found a young widow, who looked as if she were the sister of her daughters. I did not need to tell her who I was, for she was expecting me. Her daughters entered, and their reception of me gave me some passing amusement, for they seemed to think I was a different person. Donna Lucrezia introduced her younger sister to me, a girl of eleven, and her brother the abate, who was fifteen and as handsome as possible.

I maintained a behavior calculated to please the mother: I was modest and respectful and showed a fittingly lively interest in everything about me. The advocate arrived and, surprised to find me so greatly changed, was flattered when I remembered to address him as father. He began making jokes and I followed his lead, though not so far as to color my witticisms with the levity which had kept us laughing in the coach. "Having your beard shaved," he said, "has added one to your mind." Donna Lucrezia did not know what to make of the change in my manner. Toward nightfall I observed the arrival of some ladies who were neither ugly nor beautiful and of five or six abati who were clearly material for study. All these gentlemen listened most attentively to whatever I said, and I left them free to make what conjectures they pleased. Donna Cecilia told the advocate that he was an excellent painter but that his portraits were not good likenesses; he answered that she saw me wearing a mask, and I pretended to find his explanation mortifying. Donna Lucrezia said that I seemed to her exactly the same, and Donna Angelica maintained that the air of Rome gave foreigners a completely different appearance. Everyone applauded her aphorism, and she blushed with pleasure. After four hours I slipped away, but the advocate came running after me to tell me that Donna Cecilia wished me to consider myself a friend of the house, free to call there at any time without ceremony. I returned to my inn, hoping that I had pleased the household as much as it had enchanted me.

The next morning I waited on the Abate Gama. He was a Portuguese and appeared to be about forty years of age; his handsome countenance expressed frankness, humor, and intelligence. His affability sought to inspire trust. His speech and his manners were such that he could have passed as a Roman. He told me in honeyed phrases that His Excellency had himself given orders to his majordomo in regard to my residing in the palace. He said that I should dine and sup with him at the secretaries' table and that until I had learned French, I could, when I saw fit, occupy myself with making abstracts of letters which he would give me. He then gave me the address of the French teacher, to whom he had already spoken. He was a Roman advocate named Dalacqua, who lived directly across from the Palazzo di Spagna.[32]

After giving me these brief instructions and telling me that I could count on his friendship, he had a servant take me to the majordomo, who, after making me sign my name in a large book, at the bottom of a page filled with other names, paid me sixty Roman scudi in bank notes as three months' salary in advance. Followed by a footman he then took me up to the fourth floor and showed me my apartment. It consisted of an anteroom next to which was a bedroom with an alcove between two smaller rooms, all very nicely furnished. We then left, and the servant handed me the key and told me that he would come to wait on me every morning. He took me to the main door to make me known to the porter. Without losing an instant, I went to my inn and arranged to have my few possessions transported to the Palazzo di Spagna. This is the whole story of my sudden entrance into a house in which I would have made a great fortune if I had conducted myself in a way in which, being what I was, I could not. *Volentem ducit, nolentem trahit* ("[Fate] leads the willing, drags the unwilling").[33]

I at once went to my mentor, Father Georgi, to tell him all that had happened. He said that I could consider my career well begun and that, in the superior situation in which I found myself, my future depended entirely on how I behaved. *"Bear in mind," this wise man told me, "that to make your conduct irreproachable, you must discipline yourself; and that if anything untoward befalls you, no one will consider it either a piece of bad luck or an unavoidable calamity; these terms mean nothing; it will be entirely your own fault."*

"I am sorry, most reverend Father, that my youth and lack of experience will often make me trouble you. I shall become a burden to you; but you will find me docile and obedient."

"You will often think me too strict; but I foresee that you will not tell me everything."

"Everything, absolutely everything."

"Excuse me if I smile. You are not telling me where you spent four hours yesterday."

"It is of no importance. I made the acquaintance during my journey. I believe it is a decent house, where I can properly visit, unless you tell me it is not."

"Heaven forbid! It is a perfectly decent house, frequented by respectable people. The family is happy to have made your acquaintance. You pleased all their guests and they hope you will become a member of their circle. I heard all about it this morning. But you must not visit them constantly."

"Am I to stop going there from one day to the next?"

"No. That would be impolite. Go once or twice a week. But not regularly. You sigh, my son."

"No, no. I will obey you."

"I do not wish you to do it out of obedience, and I hope that your heart will not suffer; but, whether or no, you must conquer it. *Remember that reason has no greater enemy than the heart.*"

"Yet it is possible to reconcile them."

"There are those who think so. Beware of the *animum* of your favorite Horace. You know there is no middle course, *nisi paret imperat.*"[34]

"Yes. *Compesce catenis,*[35] he tells me, and he is right. But in Donna Cecilia's house my heart is not in danger."

"So much the better for you. For then ceasing to frequent it will not pain you. Remember it is my duty to believe what you say."

"And it is mine to follow your advice. I will go to Donna Cecilia's only occasionally."

Stricken with despair, I took his hand to kiss it, but he withdrew it and embraced me, turning away so that I should not see his tears.

I dined at the Palazzo di Spagna, sitting beside the Abate Gama at a table with ten or twelve other abati, for in Rome everyone either is or wants to be an abate. Since there is no prohibition against wearing their distinctive dress, everyone who wants to be respected wears it, with the exception of noblemen who have not entered on an ecclesiastical career. At table, where my grief kept me from saying a word, my silence was attributed to my sagacity. The Abate Gama invited me to spend the day with him, but I excused myself on the ground that I had some letters to write. I spent seven hours writing to Don Lelio, to Don Antonio, to my young friend Paolo, and to the Bishop of Martorano, who candidly answered me that he wished he were in my place.

In love with Donna Lucrezia and happy in my love, I thought that to abandon her was the blackest perfidy. To ensure the supposititious happiness of my life in the future, I was to begin by destroying my present happiness and denying my heart; I could accept this logic only by becoming a base object of contempt at the judgment seat of my own reason. I decided that when he forbade me her house Father Georgi should not have told me that it was respectable; my grief would have been less.

The next morning the Abate Gama brought me a large book filled with ministerial letters which I was to abstract to keep myself occupied. When I was ready to go out, I went to have my first French lesson; then, with the idea of taking a walk, I was crossing the Strada Condotta, when I heard my name called from a coffeehouse. It was the Abate Gama. I whispered to him that Minerva had forbidden me the coffeehouses of Rome.

"Minerva," he answered, "commands you to acquire some notion of them. Sit down here beside me."

I heard a young abate loudly recounting a true, or imaginary, incident which directly impugned the justice of the Pope, though without bitterness. Everyone laughed, and he joined in. Another, asked why he had left the service of Cardinal B., answered that it was because His Eminence claimed *not to be obliged to pay him, except for certain extra services which he demanded in his nightcap.* The laughter was general. Another came over and told the Abate Gama that if he cared to while away the afternoon at the Villa Medici,[36] he would find him there with *due romanelle*[37] who asked only a quartino.[38] This is a gold coin worth one fourth of a zecchino. Another read an inflammatory sonnet against the government and several people copied it. Another read a satire of his own composition which tore the honor of a family to shreds. In comes a pretty-faced abate. His hips and thighs make me think him a girl in disguise; I say so to the Abate Gama, who tells me that it is Beppino della Mammana,[39] a famous castrato. The Abate calls him over and laughingly says that I had taken him for a girl. He gives me a bold look and says that if I will spend the night with him he will serve me as a boy or a girl, whichever I choose.

At dinner everyone at the table spoke to me, and I thought that I had made such answers as I should. Giving me coffee in his room afterward, the Abate Gama said that all the company with whom I had dined were respectable men, then asked me if I believed I had made a good impression on them.

"I venture to think so."

"You flatter yourself. You evaded certain questions so obviously that everyone at the table was aware that you were keeping something back. No one will ask you any more questions."

"I should be sorry if they did not. Was I to make public what is my own business?"

"No, but there is always a middle course."

"So Horace tells us.[40] It is often difficult."

"*One must know how to win affection and esteem at the same time.*"

"That is my sole aim."

"God bless me! today you aimed at esteem far more than at affection. That is all very fine, but you must be prepared to fight envy and her daughter calumny; if those two monsters cannot ruin you, you will triumph. At table you demolished Salicetti,[41] who is a physician and, what is more, a Corsican. He must hold it against you."

"Was I to let him maintain that the *voglie*[42] of pregnant women cannot have the slightest influence on the skin of the fetus? I know from experience that they do. Are you of my opinion?"

"I am neither of yours nor of his, for I have certainly seen children with marks that are called 'longings'; but I cannot answer that those marks come from longings their mothers have had."

"But I can swear to it."

"So much the better for you if you know it so positively, and so much the worse for him if he denies that it is possible. *Leave him to his error. That is better than to convince him he is wrong, and make an enemy of him.*"

That evening I went to Donna Lucrezia's. They knew my news, and congratulated me. She told me that I looked sad, and I answered that I was in mourning for my time, which was no longer mine to dispose of as I wished. Her husband told her that I was in love with her, and his mother-in-law advised him not to be so sure of himself. After spending only an hour there, I returned to the palace, setting the air on fire with my amorous sighs. I spent the night composing an ode which I sent to the advocate the next morning, being certain that he would show it to his wife, who was fond of poetry and who did not know that it was my passion. I spent three days without going to see her. I studied French and abstracted letters from ministers.

His Excellency was "at home" every evening, and at these occasions the highest nobility of Rome, both men and women, were present; I did not attend. Gama told me that I should attend as he did, without putting myself forward. I went. No one spoke to me; but since I was unknown, everyone asked who I was. Gama asked me which of the ladies I thought the most charming, and I pointed her out to him; but I was sorry at once, for I saw the toady go and tell her what I had said. I saw her look at me attentively, then smile. She was the Marchesa G.,[43] whose gallant was Cardinal S. C.[44]

On the morning of a day when I had decided to spend the evening at Donna Lucrezia's, her husband appeared in my room and, after saying that I was wrong if I thought I was convincing him that I was not in love with his wife by not going to see her more often, he invited me to a light repast at Testaccio with the whole family on the following Thursday. He said that at Testaccio I would see the only pyramid in Rome.[45] He said that his wife knew my ode by heart and that she had aroused a great desire to make my acquaintance in his sister-in-law Donna Angelica's fiancé, who was a poet and would make one of the party going to Testaccio. I promised to be at his house at the appointed hour in a carriage seating two.

At that time the Thursdays in October were days for gaiety in Rome. That evening at Donna Cecilia's we talked of nothing but the excursion, and I felt that Donna Lucrezia was counting on it as much as I was. We did not know how, but, consecrated to love, we commended ourselves to its protection. We loved each other and pined because we could not exchange proofs of it.

I did not want my good Father Georgi to learn of the outing from anyone but myself. I was determined to go to him and ask his permission. I feigned indifference, and he offered no objection. Indeed, he told me that I should certainly go, it was an irreproachable family party, and in any case there was nothing against my getting to know Rome and enjoying decent diversions.

I went to Donna Cecilia's at the appointed hour in a coupé which I hired from a native of Avignon named Roland.[46] My acquaintance with this man had important consequences, which will give me occasion to speak of him eighteen years hence. The charming widow introduced her future son-in-law Don Francesco to me as a great admirer of literary men and unusually well versed in letters. Taking this description at its face value, I treated him accordingly; at the same time I thought him stupid-looking and quite without the gallantry to be expected in a young man who was about to marry an extremely pretty girl, for such Angelica was. *However, he was respectable and rich, which is worth far more than gallantry and learning.*

When we started to get into our carriages, the advocate told me that he would keep me company in mine and that the three ladies would go with Don Francesco. I answered that he would go with Don Francesco himself, since Donna Cecilia should properly fall to my share, and any other arrangement would be an insult to me; and so saying, I gave my arm to the beautiful widow, who agreed that my arrangement was in accordance with the rules of etiquette observed in the best society. I saw approval in Donna Lucrezia's eyes, *but I was amazed at the advocate, for he could not fail to know that he owed me his wife.* "Can he have become jealous?" I asked myself. If he had, I should be greatly put out; yet I hoped that at Testaccio I could make him see his duty.

The journey and the collation at the advocate's expense easily brought us to the end of the day, but the gaiety was at mine. There was none of the usual joking about my love for Donna Lucrezia, and I lavished my attentions only on Donna Cecilia. I said but a few casual words to Donna Lucrezia and not one to the advocate. I thought this the only way to make him understand that he had failed in his duty to me. When we were ready to return to our carriages, the advocate took Donna Cecilia from me and seated himself beside her in the carriage for four in which Donna Angelica and Don Francesco had already taken places; so, almost out of my mind with delight, I gave my arm to Donna Lucrezia, treating her to some inane compliment, while the advocate, laughing heartily, appeared to be congratulating himself on having tricked me.

How many things we should have said to each other before giving ourselves up to our love if time had not been so precious! But knowing all too well that we had only half an hour, we instantly became a single individual. At the summit of happiness and intoxicated with satisfaction, I was surprised to hear Donna Lucrezia's lips utter these words: "Oh, my God! what misery!" She pushes me away, rearranges her clothes, the coachman stops, and the footman opens the door.

"What is it?" I ask, restoring myself to a decent condition.

"We are home."

Every time I recall this episode, I think it fabulous, or supernatural. It is not possible to reduce time to nothing, for it was less than an instant, yet the horses were worn-out nags. We had two pieces of good luck. The first was that the night was dark, the second that my angel was seated where she had to get out first. The advocate was at the door the moment the footman opened it. Nothing can be more quickly put to rights than a woman. But a man! If I had been on the other side, I should have been in a sorry fix. She got out slowly, and it all passed off perfectly. I remained at Donna Cecilia's until midnight.

I went to bed—but how was I to sleep? I was still filled with all the fire which the too short distance between Testaccio and Rome had prevented me from returning to the Sun from which it came. It was devouring my entrails. *Alas for those who think that the pleasure of Venus is worth anything, unless it comes from two hearts which love each other and which are in perfect concord!*

I got up in time to go for my lesson. My French teacher had a pretty daughter named Barbara; the first times I went to take a lesson she was always present, and indeed she sometimes gave it to me herself, and even better than her father. A handsome youth who also came for lessons was her lover, as I did not find it hard to perceive. This youth often came to visit me, and one reason why I liked him was his discretion. I had talked to him about Barbaruccia[47] a dozen times, but though he admitted that he loved her, he always changed the subject. I ceased to mention it to him; but not having seen him for several days, either at my apartment or at the French teacher's, and Barbaruccia having ceased to appear too, I wanted to know what had happened, more out of curiosity than from any real concern.

Finally, as I was coming out of church after mass at San Carlo al Corso, I see the young man. I go up to him and reproach him for dropping out of sight. He answers that his soul was so tormented by a grievous misfortune that he did not know what he was doing; that he was on the brink of ruin; that he was desperate.

I see that his eyes are filled with tears, he makes to leave me, I hold him back, I tell him that he can no longer count me among his friends if he will not confide his troubles to me. At that he stops, leads me to a cloister, and speaks as follows:

"I have loved Barbaruccia for six months, and three have gone by since she made me certain that I was loved. Five days ago her father came upon us at five o'clock in the morning in a situation which left no doubt that we were guilty lovers. He controlled himself and left the room, but just as I was about to throw myself at his feet, he conducted me to the door of the house and forbade me ever to enter it again. The monster who betrayed us was the maidservant. I cannot ask her hand in marriage because I have a married brother and my father is not rich. I have no profession and Barbaruccia has nothing. Alas! since I have confessed all to you, tell me what state she is in. Her despair must be as great as mine, it cannot be greater. There is no way that I can get a letter to her, for she never leaves the house, even to go to mass. Alas for me! what shall I do!"

I could only condole with him, for as a man of honor I could not interfere in such a situation. I told him I had not seen her for five days, and not knowing what else to say I gave him the advice which all fools give in such circumstances: I advised him to forget her. We were on the Ripetta[48] quay, and, the distracted look with which he fixed his eyes on the waters of the Tiber making me fear that his despair would lead to some tragedy, I said that I would ask her father for news of Barbaruccia and would tell him what I learned. He implored me not to forget him.

It was four days since I had seen Donna Lucrezia, despite the fire which the excursion to Testaccio had kindled in my soul. I feared Father Georgi's mildness, and still more that he might have decided to stop advising me.

I went to see her after taking my lesson and found her alone in her room. She said sadly and tenderly that it was impossible I could not have had time to come and see her.

"Ah! my beloved! It is not time that I lack. I am so jealous of my love that I would rather die than have it discovered. I have been thinking of inviting you all to dinner at Frascati. I will send a phaeton for you. I hope that there we can be alone together."

"Yes, yes, do that; I am sure your invitation will not be refused."

A quarter of an hour later everyone came in and I proposed the excursion, entirely at my expense, for the following Sunday, the feast of St. Ursula, which was the name of my angel's younger sister. I asked Donna Cecilia to bring her, and her son as well. My invitation was accepted. I said that the phaeton would be at their door at exactly seven o'clock, together with myself in a carriage for two.

The next day, on my way downstairs after taking my lesson from Signor Dalacqua, I see Barbaruccia passing from one room to another; she gives me a look and drops a letter. I feel obliged to pick it up, otherwise the maid, who was coming up the stairs, would have seen it. The letter, which enclosed another and was directed to me, said: "If you think it wrong to give this letter to your friend, burn it. Pity an unhappy girl and be discreet." The enclosure, which was not sealed, ran: "If your love equals mine, you cannot hope to be happy without me. We can neither speak nor write to each other except by the intermediary I have made bold to employ. I am ready to do anything which can unite our fates until death. Think, and decide."

I felt greatly touched by the girl's cruel situation; but I at once made up my mind to return her letter to her the next day, enclosed in one from me in which I would ask her to forgive me if I could not render her this service. I wrote it that evening and put it in my pocket.

The next day I prepared to give it to her, but, having changed my breeches, I could not find it; so, having left it at home, I had to wait until the next day. In any case, I did not see the girl.

But the same day the poor, disconsolate lover appears in my room just after I had finished dining. He flings himself on a couch and paints such a vivid picture of his desperation that finally, fearing the worst, I cannot but soothe his grief by giving him Barbaruccia's letter. He was talking of killing himself because his heart told him that Barbaruccia had resolved to forget him. I had no other way to persuade him that his conviction was false than to give him the letter. It was my first error in this disastrous affair, committed because I was too softhearted.

He read it, read it over again, he kissed it, he wept, he flung himself on my neck thanking me for restoring him to life, and ended by saying that he would bring me his answer before I went to bed, for his mistress must be in need of the same consolation he had received. He left, assuring me that his letter would not implicate me in any way and that I was free to read it.

And in fact his letter, though it was very long, contained nothing but protestations of eternal constancy and chimerical hopes; even so, I should not have assumed the role of Mercury in the affair. To keep out of it, I need only have considered that Father Georgi would never approve of my complying.

The next morning, finding Barbaruccia's father ill, I was delighted to see his daughter sitting at his bedside. I concluded that he had probably forgiven her. It was she who gave me my lesson, though without leaving her father's side. I handed her her lover's letter, which she put in her pocket, blushing furiously. I told them they would not see me the next day. It was the feast of St. Ursula, one of the thousand martyred virgins and royal princesses. That evening at His Eminence's reception, which I attended regularly although it was only very rarely that anyone of distinction spoke to me, the Cardinal beckoned to me. He was talking with the beautiful Marchesa G., to whom Gama had reported that I thought she outshone all the other women.

"The Signora," says the Cardinal, "wants to know if you are making good progress in the French language, which she speaks to perfection."

I answer in Italian that I have learned a good deal, but that I did not yet venture to speak.

"*You must venture,*" said the Marchesa, "*but at the same time be unassuming. That will shield you from any criticism.*"

Since I had not failed to take the word "venture" in a sense which the Marchesa had presumably not intended, I blushed. Noticing it, she opened another subject with the Cardinal, and I slipped away.

At seven o'clock the next morning I was at Donna Cecilia's. My phaeton was at the door. We set off at once, in the same order as before. We reached Frascati in two hours.

This time my carriage was an elegant vis-à-vis,[49] softly uphol-
stered and so well sprung that Donna Cecilia praised it. "I shall have
my turn," said Donna Lucrezia, "on the way back to Rome."
I bowed to her, as if taking her at her word. In this way she *dissipated
suspicion by defying it.* Certain that my desire would be fully satisfied
at the end of the day, I surrender to all my natural high spirits. After
ordering a dinner which did not spare my purse, I let them take me
to the Villa Ludovisi.[50] Since we might well lose sight of one
another, we agreed to meet at one o'clock at the inn. The discreet
Donna Cecilia took her son-in-law's arm, Donna Angelica her
fiancé's, and Donna Lucrezia was left with me. Ursula went running
off with her brother. In less than a quarter of an hour we were out of
sight.

"Did you hear," she began, "how innocently I made sure of
spending hours alone with you? And it is a vis-à-vis! How clever
love is!"

"Yes, my angel, love has made our two minds one. I adore you,
and I do not go for days without coming to visit you only that I may
be sure of one day in which we shall be undisturbed."

"I did not think it possible. It is you who have done it all. You
know too much for your age."

"A month ago, my darling, I knew nothing. You are the first
woman who has initiated me into the mysteries of love. You are she
whose departure will make me wretched, for in all Italy there can be
but one Lucrezia."

"What! I am your first love! Alas for you! You will never get over
it! Why am I not wholly yours? You, too, are my soul's first love,
and you will surely be the last. Happy the woman whom you will
love after me. I am not jealous of her. I am only sorry that she
will not have a heart like mine."

Seeing my tears, Donna Lucrezia gave way to hers. Throwing
ourselves down on a lawn, we pressed our lips together, and tasted
our own tears flowing down on them. *The ancient natural philosophers
are right: Tears are sweet, I can swear to it; the moderns are but idle
chatterers.* We were sure that we had swallowed them with the nectar
which our kisses distilled from our amorous souls. We were but one
being, when I said that someone might catch us.

"Never fear. Our Geniuses are watching over us."

We were resting there quietly after the first brief combat, looking
at each other without a word and without thinking of changing our
position, when the divine Lucrezia glanced to her right.

"Look!" she said, "did I not tell you that our Geniuses were watching over us? Ah! How he stares at us! He is trying to reassure us. Look at that little demon. Nature has no greater mystery. Admire him. He is certainly your Genius or mine."

I thought she had gone out of her head.

"What are you saying, my angel? I do not understand you. What is it that I am to admire?"

"Do you not see that beautiful snake with his fiery scales and his raised head, which seems to be worshiping us?"

I look in the direction in which she was staring and see an iridescent snake an ell long which was indeed looking at us. I was far from pleased by the sight, but, not wishing to show less courage than she did, I controlled myself.

"Is it possible, my dearest," I said, "that the sight of him does not terrify you?"

"The sight of him delights me, I tell you. I am sure that such an idol is a snake only in appearance."

"And if he came writhing and hissing toward you?"

"I would clasp you even more closely to my breast and I would defy him to harm me. Lucrezia in your arms can feel no fear. Look. He is going away. Quick, quick! He is trying to tell us by his going that some of the profane are on their way here, and that we must find another lawn on which to renew our pleasures. So let us get up. Arrange your clothing."

We had scarcely risen and were walking slowly away when we saw Donna Cecilia and the advocate emerging from the adjoining walk. Neither hurrying nor avoiding them, as if it were perfectly natural that we should meet, I ask Donna Cecilia if her daughter is afraid of snakes.

"For all her intelligence, she is afraid of lightning to the point of fainting and she runs away screaming when she sees a snake. There are snakes here; but she is mistaken to be afraid, they are not poisonous."

My hair stood on end, for her words assured me that I had witnessed a miracle of love. Her children came up, and we separated again.

"But tell me," I said, "you astonishing creature, what would you have done if your husband and your mother had caught us in the act?"

"Nothing. *Do you not know that in such divine moments one is only in love? Can you suppose that you did not possess me entirely?*"

She was not composing an ode when she spoke these words.

"Do you believe," I asked her, "that no one suspects us?"

"My husband either thinks that we are not in love or pays no attention to certain little freedoms in which young people commonly indulge. My mother is intelligent, and perhaps suspects everything; but she knows that it is none of her business. Angelica, my dear sister, knows everything, for she will never be able to forget the ruined bed, but she is discreet, and besides, she has taken it into her head to feel sorry for me. She has no conception of what my passion is. Without you, my dear, I might have died without ever knowing love, for my husband has won from me only the acquiescence which it is a wife's duty to give."

"Ah! your husband enjoys a divine privilege, of which I cannot help being jealous. He clasps all your beauties in his arms whenever he pleases. No veil keeps his senses, his eyes, his soul from enjoying them."

"Where are you, beloved snake? Hasten to watch over me, and I will satisfy my lover this instant."

In this fashion we spent the whole morning, declaring that we loved each other and proving it wherever we thought we were safe from being caught.

Nè per mai sempre pendergli dal collo
il suo desir sentia di lui satollo.[51]

("No matter how long she hung on his neck, her desire for him was never satisfied.")

At my choice and delicious dinner, I was chiefly attentive to Donna Cecilia. Since my Spanish tobacco[52] was excellent, my pretty snuffbox made the round of the table several times. Once when it had reached the hands of Donna Lucrezia, who was seated at my left, her husband told her that she might give me her ring and keep it. "Done!" I said, thinking that the ring was worth less; but it was worth more. Donna Lucrezia would not hear a word. She put my snuffbox in her pocket and gave me her ring, which I put in mine since it was too small for my finger.

But suddenly we were all reduced to silence. Angelica's fiancé takes from his pocket a sonnet, fruit of his genius, which he had composed to my honor and glory, and insists on reading it. Everyone applauds, and I have to thank him, take the sonnet, and promise him another in due course. He thought that I would immediately have called for writing materials and answered him on the spot, and that there we should remain, devoting to his accursed Apollo the three hours which were destined for love. After coffee, I having settled with the innkeeper, we all scattered about the gardens of another villa, the Aldobrandini[53] if I remember rightly.

"Explain to me," I asked my Lucrezia, "out of the metaphysics of your love, how it can be that at this moment I feel as if I were about to plunge into the delights of love with you for the first time. Let us hasten to look for a spot where we shall find an altar to Venus, and let us sacrifice until we perish, even if we see no snakes; and if the Pope comes with all the Sacred College, let us not stir. His Holiness will give us his blessing."

After wandering about a little, we entered a shady walk; it was quite long, and halfway down it there was an arbor filled with turf seats, each of a different shape. We saw one which struck us. It was in the form of a bed but in addition to the regular bolster there was another, lying parallel to it about two feet away, but only a quarter as high. We looked at it and laughed. It was an eloquent bed. We instantly made ready to try its virtues. From where it stood we had a prospect of a great, solitary plain, across which even a rabbit could not have reached us unobserved. Behind the bed there was no way of approaching the walk and we saw its two ends at equal distances to right and left. No one who entered the walk could reach us in less than a quarter of an hour except by running. Here in the garden at Dux, I have seen an arbor of the same sort; but the German gardener never thought of the bed. In this happy spot we had no need to tell each other our thoughts.

Standing face to face, intensely serious, looking only into each other's eyes, we unlaced, we unbuttoned, our hearts throbbed, our hands hurried to calm their impatience. Neither of us having been slower than the other, our arms opened to clasp the object of which they were to take possession. After our first combat the beautiful Lucrezia laughed and confessed that since genius had the right to shine everywhere, it was nowhere out of place. We both applauded the happy effect of the smaller bolster. Our adventures varied after that, but though they were all good, they were all rejected to give place to others. At the end of two hours, enchanted with each other and looking most lovingly into each other's eyes, we spoke in unison, saying these very words: "Love, I thank thee."

After turning her grateful eyes for a moment on the infallible sign of my defeat, Donna Lucrezia laughed and gave me a most languorous kiss; but when she saw that she was restoring me to life, "Enough!" she cried, "a truce to triumphing! Let us get dressed." At that we hurried, but instead of keeping our eyes on ourselves, we fixed them on that which impenetrable veils were to hide from our insatiable desire. When we were fully dressed we agreed to make a libation to love, to thank him for having guarded us from being disturbed while we celebrated his orgies. A long, narrow seat without a back, which could be straddled like a riding mule, was our simultaneous choice. The combat began and was proceeding vigorously; but foreseeing that the end was too distant and the libation doubtful, we put it off until we should be face to face in the darkness of night to the music of four trotting horses.

As we slowly made our way toward the carriages, our talk was the confidences of satisfied lovers. She told me that her future brother-in-law was rich and that he had a house at Tivoli, where he would invite us to spend the night. She thought of nothing but imploring love to reveal how we could spend it together. She finally told me sadly that the ecclesiastical suit with which her husband was occupied was going so well that she feared he would obtain his judgment too soon.

We passed the two hours which we spent face to face in the carriage playing a comedy which we could not finish. Arriving at their house, we had to ring down the curtain. I should have finished it if I had not taken a fancy to divide it into two acts. I went to bed rather tired; but a good sleep restored me completely. The next day I went to take my lesson at the usual hour.

CHAPTER X

Benedict XIV. Excursion to Tivoli. Departure
of Donna Lucrezia. The Marchesa G. Barbara
Dalacqua. My bad luck and my departure
from Rome.

It was Barbaruccia who gave it to me, for her father was seriously ill. As I was leaving she slipped a letter into my pocket, then ran away so that I should not have time to refuse it. She was right, for it was not a letter to be refused. It was addressed to me and dictated by feelings of the liveliest gratitude. She asked me to tell her lover that her father was speaking to her, and that she hoped as soon as he recovered he would engage a different maid. She ended by assuring me on her oath that she would never implicate me.

Her father being kept in bed by his illness for twelve consecutive days, it was she who gave me my lessons. She aroused my interest in a way which was entirely new to me where a pretty girl was concerned. It was a feeling of pure pity, and I was flattered when I perceived that she counted upon it. Her eyes never lingered on mine, her hand never touched mine, her toilet never showed the least sign of being studied to make it pleasing to me. She was pretty, and I knew that she was susceptible; but these considerations detracted nothing from what I felt that I owed to honor and good faith, and I was very glad that she did not believe me capable of taking advantage of my knowledge that she had erred.

As soon as her father recovered he dismissed his maid and engaged another. She begged me to give her lover the news and to tell him that she hoped to win her over to their side, so that at least they could have the pleasure of writing to each other. When I promised to tell him, she took my hand to kiss it. I withdrew it and made to give her a kiss, whereupon she blushed and turned away. This pleased me. I conveyed the news of the new maid to her lover, he contrived to speak to her, and won her over to his cause, and I took no more part in the intrigue, for I clearly saw the unfortunate consequences it could have. But the harm was already done.

I seldom called on Don Gaspare, for my French studies prevented me; but I called on Father Georgi every evening; though my standing there was only that of a protégé of the monk's, I gained some reputation by it. I never spoke myself, but I found much to interest me. There was criticism without backbiting, there was talk of politics and literature; I was picking up knowledge. On leaving the wise monk's monastery, I went to the great reception at the palace of my master the Cardinal, which it was my duty to attend.

At almost every one of these, when the Marchesa G. saw me at the table where she was playing cards, she would speak a word or two to me in French, which I always answered in Italian because I felt that I ought not to make her laugh in public. A strange feeling, which I leave to the perspicacity of my reader. *I thought her charming, and I avoided her, not because I was afraid I should fall in love with her, for, in love as I was with Donna Lucrezia, that seemed to me impossible, but for fear she might fall in love with me or at least become interested in me. Was this a vice or a virtue? Solvat Apollo* ("Let Apollo find the solution"). As once before, she sent the Abate Gama to fetch me; this time she was standing and in the company of my master and Cardinal S. C. I go to her, and she surprises me with a question in Italian which I should never have expected.

"Vi ha piaciuto molto," she asks, *"Frascati?"* ("Did you like Frascati very much?")

"Very much, Signora. I never in my life saw anything so beautiful."

"Ma la compagnia con la quale eravate, era ancora più bella, ed assai galante era il vostro vis à vis" ("But the company you were with was even more beautiful, and your vis-à-vis was very smart").

My only answer was a bow. A moment later Cardinal Acquaviva said to me, kindly:

"Are you surprised that it is known?"

"No, Monsignore, but I am surprised that it is talked about. *I did not think that Rome was so small.*"

"And the longer you remain in Rome," said S. C., *"the smaller you will find it.* Have you not gone yet to kiss His Holiness's foot?"

"Not yet, Monsignore."

"You must go," said Cardinal Acquaviva.

I answered with a bow.

As we left, the Abate Gama told me that I must go without fail the next morning.

"I suppose," he said, "you sometimes put in an appearance at the Marchesa G.'s."

"You may stop supposing so, for I have never been there."

"You amaze me. She calls you over, she talks to you!"

"I will go there with you."

"I never go."

"But she talks to you, too."

"Yes, but... You do not know Rome. Go there by yourself. You must go."

"You think she will receive me?"

"Are you joking? You need not have yourself announced. Simply go in to see her when the double doors of the room she is in are open. You will find it full of people paying her court."

"Will she see me?"

"You may be sure of that."

The next day I go to Monte Cavallo,[1] and I go straight into the room where the Pope was as soon as I am told that I may enter it and that he is alone. I kiss the "holy cross" on the "most holy slipper," he asks me who I am, I tell him, and he answers that he has heard of me, and he congratulates me on my good fortune in being in the service of so eminent a Cardinal. He asks me how I had managed to enter his service, and I tell him the whole story, altering nothing, beginning with my arrival at Martorano. After laughing heartily at my account of the Bishop, he said that instead of struggling to speak to him in Tuscan I should speak to him in Venetian just as he was speaking to me in Bolognese.[2] I talked away at such a rate that he said he would be glad to have me come to see him as often as I could. I asked him for permission to read all the forbidden books, and he granted it by giving me his blessing and saying that he would have a written permission sent me gratis; but he forgot to do it.

Benedict XIV was learned, a man who liked his joke, and extremely agreeable. The second time I talked with him was at the Villa Medici. He called me over and, continuing his walk, talked in the lightest vein. He was accompanied by Cardinal Annibale Albani[3] and the Venetian Ambassador. A man of modest appearance approaches, the Pontiff asks him what he wants, the man speaks to him in a low voice, the Pope hears him out and says, "You are right, commend yourself to God." He gives him his blessing, the man goes dejectedly away, and the Pope continues his walk.

"That man," I said to the Holy Father, "was not satisfied with the answer Your Holiness gave him."

"Why?"

"Because presumably he had already commended himself to God before he spoke to you and, hearing you send him back to God again, he feels he is being sent, as the saying goes, from Herod to Pilate."[4]

The Pope burst out laughing, as did his two companions, but I kept a straight face.

"I cannot," said the Pope, "accomplish anything without the help of God."

"Very true. But this man also knows that Your Holiness is his prime minister; so it is easy to imagine how frustrated he feels now that he has been sent back to Your Holiness's master. His only resource is to go and give money to all the beggars in Rome. For a baiocco apiece they will all pray to God for him. They boast of their influence. I believe only in Your Holiness's, so I beg you to deliver me from this irritating inflammation of the eyes by dispensing me from eating fish."

"Eat meat."

"Most Holy Father, your blessing."

He gives it to me, adding that he did not dispense me from fasting.

That evening at the Cardinal's reception, I found that the news of the dialogue between the Pope and myself was out. Everyone was now eager to speak to me. What I found flattering was Cardinal Acquaviva's pleasure, which he vainly tried to conceal.

I did not fail to follow the Abate Gama's advice. I went to the Marchesa G.'s at the hour when anyone could go there. I saw her, I saw her Cardinal and a great many other abati; but I thought I must be invisible, for since the Signora did not honor me with a look, no one said a word to me. After half an hour I left. It was not until five or six days later that she told me, with the most gracious courtesy, that she had seen me in her reception room.

"I did not know that the Signora had done me the honor to notice me."

"Oh, I see everyone. I am told you have wit."

"If those who have told you so, Signora, know what wit is themselves, you have given me very good news."

"Oh, they know what it is."

"If they had never spoken to me, they would never have found it out."

"Very true. Let me see you here."

A circle had formed around us. Cardinal S. C. said that when the Signora spoke to me in French, I ought to answer her in the same language, whether well or badly. The politic Gama said to me privately that my style was too cutting and that in the end I would be disliked.

Having learned enough French, I took no more lessons. Practice would suffice to familiarize me with the language. I did not call on Donna Lucrezia except occasionally in the morning; and I went to Father Georgi's every evening. He had heard of my excursion to Frascati, and had found no fault with it.

Two days after the Marchesa had more or less commanded me to pay my court to her, I entered her reception room. Seeing me at once, she gave me a smile, which I thought it proper to answer with a low bow; but that was the end of it. A quarter of an hour later she sat down to cards and I went off to dinner. *She was pretty, and a power in Rome; but I could not bring myself to crawl. Roman manners exasperated me.*

Toward the end of November Donna Angelica's fiancé called on me with the advocate to invite me to spend a day and a night at his house in Tivoli with the same company I had entertained at Frascati; I accepted with pleasure, for since St. Ursula's Day I had not been alone with Donna Lucrezia for a single moment. I promised him I would be at Donna Cecilia's in my carriage at dawn of the appointed day. We had to start very early, since Tivoli is sixteen miles from Rome and since the large number of beautiful things to be seen there took a great deal of time. As I was to be away for a night, I asked the Cardinal himself to give me permission; when he heard with whom I was going, he answered that I was quite right to take the opportunity of seeing the wonders of the famous place in good company.

At the appointed hour I was at Donna Cecilia's door with the same four-horse vis-à-vis, and as usual she fell to my lot. Notwithstanding her irreproachable morals, the charming widow was well content that I should love her daughter. The whole family was in a phaeton for six, which Don Francesco had hired. At half past seven we stopped at a small house where Don Francesco had arranged to have an elegant breakfast ready for us which, as it was to serve us for dinner too, was ample as well. At Tivoli we should have time only for supper. So after breakfasting heartily, we returned to our carriages and reached his house by ten o'clock. I was wearing the ring Donna Lucrezia had given me, having had it remade to fit my finger. I had also had an obverse setting fitted to it, which displayed only a field of enamel with a caduceus[5] entwined by a single snake. On either side of the caduceus were the Greek letters Alpha and Omega.

This ring was the sole subject of conversation at breakfast as soon as it was seen that the reverse contained the same stones that had been set in Donna Lucrezia's ring. The advocate and Don Francesco cudgeled their brains to decipher the hieroglyph, much to the amusement of Donna Lucrezia, who knew the secret.

After half an hour spent in viewing Don Francesco's house, which was really charming, we all set off together to spend six hours seeing the antiquities of Tivoli. While Donna Lucrezia was saying something to Don Francesco, I whispered to Donna Angelica that when she became the mistress of the house I would come and spend a few days with her during the seasons of good weather.

"As soon, Signore, as I become the mistress here, the first person to whom I shall order my door closed will be you."

"Thank you for warning me, Signorina."

The joke is that I took this reprimand for nothing less than a very flattering and very clear declaration of love. I was almost paralyzed. Donna Lucrezia gave me a shake and asked me what her sister had said to me. When I told her she said very seriously that after she left I must take her sister in hand and force her to admit that she was wrong. "She pities me," she added; "it is for you to avenge me."

When I praised a small room which gave on to the orangery, Don Francesco said that I should sleep in it. Donna Lucrezia pretended not to have heard him. Since the whole party was to view the beauties of Tivoli together, we could not hope to be alone during the day. We spent six hours looking and admiring, but I saw very little. If my reader is interested in knowing something about Tivoli without going there, he has only to read Campagnani.[6] I did not get to know Tivoli well until twenty-eight years later.

Toward evening we returned to the house, exhausted and dying of hunger. An hour's rest before supper, two hours at the table, the exquisite dishes, and the excellent wine of Tivoli did so much to restore us that we needed nothing more than our beds, whether for sleep or for the rites of love.

Since no one wanted to sleep alone, Lucrezia said she would share a bed with Angelica in the room which gave on the orangery, that her husband should sleep with the Abate, and her young sister with her mother. Everyone thought the arrangement excellent. Don Francesco took a candle, conducted me to the small room I had praised, showed me how to lock the door, and bade me good night. This small room was next to the room in which the two sisters were to sleep. Angelica had no idea that I was her neighbor.

I put my eye to the keyhole and five minutes later saw them come in, accompanied by Don Francesco, who lit a night lamp for them and then left. After locking the door they sat down on the couch, where I watched them undress. Lucrezia, knowing that I could hear her, told her sister to take the side of the bed toward the window. Upon which the virgin, unaware that she was observed, takes off even her shift and in this striking array crosses to the other side of the room. Lucrezia extinguishes the night light, blows out the candles, and lies down too.

Happy moments for which I hope no longer, but whose precious memory death alone can take from me! I believe I never undressed more quickly. I opened the door and fell into the arms of my Lucrezia, who said to her sister: "It is my angel, hold your tongue and go to sleep."

She could say no more, for our clinging mouths were no longer either organs of speech or channels for respiration. Become a single being at the same instant, we did not have the strength to restrain our first desire for more than a minute; it ran its course without the sound of a single kiss or the least movement on our part. The raging fire which urged us on was scorching us; it would have burned us had we tried to restrain it.

After a short respite, ourselves the ingenious ministers of our love and jealous of the fire which it was to rekindle in our veins, we went silently, seriously, and calmly to work drying from our fields the too copious flood which had followed the first eruption. We performed this sacred service for each other with fine linen, devoutly and in the most religious silence. After this expiation we paid homage with our kisses to all the places which we had lately flooded.

It was now my part to invite my fair enemy to begin a battle whose tactics could be known only to love, a combat which, enchanting all our senses, could have no fault but that of ending too soon; but I excelled in the art of prolonging it. When it was over, Morpheus took possession of our senses and held us in a sweet death until the moment when the light of dawn showed us in each other's scarcely opened eyes an inexhaustible spring of new desires. We surrendered to them, but it was to destroy them. A delightful destruction, which we could only accomplish by satisfying them!

"Beware of your sister," I said; "she might turn and see us."

"No, my sister is charming; she loves me and she pities me. Is not that so, dear Angelica? Turn and embrace your sister, who is possessed by Venus. Turn and see what awaits you when love makes you his slave."

Angelica, a girl of seventeen, who must have passed a hellish night, asks nothing better than an excuse to turn and show her sister that she had forgiven her. Kissing her a hundred times, she confessed that she had not slept at all.

"Forgive," Lucrezia said, "him who loves me and whom I adore; come, look at him, and look at me. We are as we were seven hours ago. The power of Love!"

"Hated by Angelica," I said, "I dare not—"

"No," said Angelica, "I do not hate you."

Telling me to kiss her, Lucrezia gets on the other side of me and enjoys the spectacle of her sister in my arms, languishing and showing no signs of resistance. But feeling, even more than love, prevents me from defrauding Lucrezia of the token of gratitude which I owed her. I clasp her frenziedly, at the same time reveling in the ecstasy I saw on the face of Angelica, who was witnessing so splendid a combat for the first time. The swooning Lucrezia implores me to stop, but finding me inexorable throws me on her sister who, far from repulsing me, clasps me to her bosom so strongly that she achieves happiness almost without my participation. *It was thus that when the Gods dwelt on earth the voluptuous Anaideia,[7] in love with the soft, delightful breath of the West Wind, one day opened her arms to it and became fruitful. It was the divine Zephyrus.[8]* The fire of nature made Angelica insensible to pain; she felt only the joy of satisfying her ardent desire.

Astonished, blissfully content, and kissing us in turn, Lucrezia was as delighted to see her swoon as she was charmed to see that I continued. She wiped away the drops of sweat which dripped from my brow. Angelica finally perished for the third time, so lovingly that she ravished my soul.

However, the sun's rays coming in through the cracks in our window shutters, I left them. After locking my door, I got into bed; but only a few minutes later I heard the voice of the advocate reproaching his wife and his sister-in-law for their sloth. Then, knocking on my door and finding me in my nightshirt, he threatened to bring my neighbors in. But he left, saying he would send me a hairdresser. I lock my door again, I give my face a thorough washing in cold water, which restores me to my usual looks. An hour later I enter the drawing room, showing not a sign of anything. I am delighted to see that my fair conquests look fresh and rosy. Donna Lucrezia was perfectly relaxed, Angelica gayer than usual and radiant; but as she keeps turning uneasily now to the left, now to the right, I can see her only in profile. Seeing her smile at my vain attempts to catch her eye, which she was determined not to let me do, I tell Donna Cecilia that her daughter should not powder her face. Trapped by my calumny, she makes me rub her face with a handkerchief, and looks at me. I take it back and beg her pardon, and Don Francesco is delighted that the whiteness of his future wife's complexion has led to such a doubt.

After drinking chocolate, we go to view his fine garden, and finding myself alone with Donna Lucrezia I reproach her for her perfidy. Looking at me like a goddess, she reproaches me for my ingratitude.

"I have enlightened my sister," she says. "Instead of pitying me, she must now approve of me, she must love you; and as I am soon to go away, I leave her to you."

"But how can I love her?"

"Is she not charming?"

"She is indeed. But charmed by you I am proof against all other charms. And in any case at this time she should be entirely taken up with Don Francesco, and it is not for me to trouble the harmony of a married couple. I can tell you, too, that your sister has a very different way of looking at things from yours. Last night both she and I were victims of our senses. This is so true that I do not feel that I have been unfaithful to you. But Angelica—do you hear?—Angelica must already be regretting that she allowed nature to lead her astray."

"That may be all very true; but what distresses me is that we shall leave at the end of the month. My husband is certain he will obtain his judgment this very week. So our pleasures are over."

The news made me sad. At table I paid no attention to anyone but the generous Don Francesco, whom I promised an epithalamium for his wedding, which was to take place in January.

We returned to Rome, and during the three hours we were alone together Donna Lucrezia could never convince me that I was less in love with her than I had been before she surrendered all her treasures to me. We stopped at the small house where we had breakfasted, to eat some ices which Don Francesco had ordered made for us. We reached Rome at eight o'clock. Feeling badly in need of rest, I at once went to the Palazzo di Spagna.

Three or four days later the advocate called and took his leave of me with the utmost civility. He was returning to Naples after winning his suit. As he was to leave on the next day but one, I spent the last two evenings of his stay in Rome at Donna Cecilia's. Having learned the hour at which he was to leave, I set out two hours earlier and stopped where I supposed he would spend the night, hoping thus to have the pleasure of supping with him for the last time; but something having come up which obliged him to delay his departure for four hours, I had only the pleasure of dining with him.

After the departure of this extraordinary woman, I was left in the state of lassitude to which a young man succumbs when his heart is empty. I spent all my days in my room, making summaries of the Cardinal's French correspondence, and he was good enough to tell me that he found my extracts well chosen but that I really must not work so hard. The Marchesa G. was present and heard this most flattering compliment. After the second time I had paid my court to her she had seen no more of me. Her manner to me was cool. Hearing the Cardinal reproach me with working too much, she told him that I must be working to cure my grief at Donna Lucrezia's departure.

"You are right, Signora, I felt it very keenly. She was kind; and *she forgave me if I could not visit her often.* In any case, my friendship for her was innocent."

"I have no doubt of it, despite the fact that in your ode the poet seems to be in love."

"A poet cannot compose," said my adorable Cardinal, "without pretending to be in love."

"But if he is in love," the Marchesa replied, "he need not pretend to be."

So saying, she took my ode from her pocket and handed it to S. C., remarking that it did me honor, that it was a little masterpiece according to all the wits of Rome, and that Donna Lucrezia knew it by heart. The Cardinal smiled and handed it back to her, saying that he did not care for Italian poetry but that since she admired it she might well give herself the pleasure of translating it into French. She answered that she only wrote prose in French, and that any translation of a piece of poetry into prose could not but be bad.

"My literary endeavors," she added, with a look at me, "go no further than an occasional modest poem in Italian."

"I should consider myself fortunate, Signora, if I could obtain the favor of seeing one of them."

"Here," said her Cardinal, "is a sonnet by the Signora."

I respectfully take it and prepare to read it, when the Signora tells me to put it in my pocket and give it back to His Eminence the next day, though, she added, her sonnet did not amount to much.

"If you go out in the morning," said the Cardinal, "you can dine with me and give it back to me then."

"In that case," Cardinal Acquaviva replied instantly, "he will go out on purpose."

After a low bow which excused me from speaking, I gradually move away and go to my room, eager to read the sonnet. But before reading it, I give a moment's thought to myself, to my present situation, and to the very great progress it seemed to me I had made that evening at the reception. The Marchesa G. telling me in the clearest way possible that she has taken an interest in me!

The Marchesa G., under cover of her grandeur, having no fear of compromising herself by making advances to me in public! Who would have dared to see anything wrong in it? A young abate like myself, of no importance whatever, could only aspire to her protection, and her nature was such that she granted it chiefly to those who, though considering themselves more than worthy of it, showed no sign of laying claim to it. My modesty in this respect was perfectly apparent to everyone. Why, the Marchesa would have insulted me if she had thought me capable of imagining that she was drawn to me! Impossible! No one could be so stupidly conceited! This was so true that her Cardinal himself invites me to dinner. Would he have done so if he could possibly have thought his Marchesa found me attractive? On the contrary, he did not ask me to come and dine with him until he had gathered from what the Marchesa herself said that I was the very person they needed for an hour of talk now and again at no risk, absolutely none.

Nonsense!

Why should I put on a mask before my dear reader? If he thinks me conceited, I forgive him. I felt certain that I had attracted the Marchesa; I congratulated myself on her having taken that terrifying first step without which I should never have dared even to cast an eye on her, let alone attack her in force. In short, I did not see her as a woman I could love, and a woman well worthy of succeeding Donna Lucrezia, until that evening. She was beautiful, young, intelligent, witty, highly cultivated, well read, and a power in Rome. I decided I would pretend not to be aware of her liking for me, and to begin the next day giving her reason to believe that I loved her without daring to hope. I was certain that I should triumph. It was a course which Father Georgi himself could not but pretend to approve. I had observed with the greatest satisfaction that Cardinal Acquaviva had been pleased that Cardinal S. C. had invited me, though he himself had never so far honored me.

I take up her sonnet and read it, I find it good, flowing, facile, faultless in diction. In it the Marchesa praised the King of Prussia, who had recently captured Silesia by what amounted to a surprise attack.[9] As I copied it out, I took a fancy to compose an answer to it in which Silesia would complain because Love, the speaker in the Marchesa's sonnet, dared to applaud her royal conqueror when he was himself a declared enemy of Love.

A man who is in the habit of composing verses cannot possibly deny himself the pleasure once a happy idea has come to his mind. I thought my idea splendid, and that is what counts. I replied to the Marchesa's sonnet, using the same rhymes, and went to bed. In the morning I polished it, made a fair copy, and put it in my pocket.

The Abate Gama came to breakfast with me and congratulated me on the honor S. C. was doing me, but he warned me to be on my guard because His Eminence was extremely jealous. I thanked him and assured him that I had nothing to fear in that respect, since I did not feel the slightest inclination for the Marchesa.

Cardinal S. C. received me kindly but with a dignity calculated to make me conscious of the favor he was conferring on me.

"Did you," he at once asked me, "find the Marchesa's sonnet well turned?"

"Charming, Monsignore. Here it is."

"She is very talented. I am going to show you ten stanzas she composed, but in the strictest confidence."

"Your Eminence may be sure that I will not betray it."

He opens a secretary and hands me ten stanzas to read, of which he was himself the subject. I find them lacking in inspiration, but with some images well expressed in a passionate style. They were clearly a declaration of love. By showing them to me, the Cardinal had committed a grave indiscretion. I ask him if he has answered; he says he has not, smiles, and asks me if I will lend him my pen, but still in the strictest confidence.

"I will stake my head on that, Monsignore; but the Signora will notice the difference in style."

"She has nothing of mine; but in any case I am sure she does not think me a good poet. So your stanzas must be such that she will not find them above my ability."

"I will write them, Monsignore, and Your Eminence shall pronounce on them. If you find that you cannot do as well, Your Eminence will not deliver them."

"Excellent. Will you write them now?"

"Now? It is not prose, Monsignore."

"Try to bring them to me tomorrow."

We dined alone together at two o'clock, and he liked my appetite. He congratulated me on eating as much as he did. I answered that he flattered me too greatly and that he had outdone me. I was laughing to myself over his eccentric character and considering the advantage I could reap from it, when in comes the Marchesa, without being announced, of course. It was the first time that I had found her a perfect beauty. At her sudden appearance the Cardinal laughs because she goes and sits down beside him so quickly that she does not give him time to rise. For my part, I am left standing, as is to be expected. She talks of various things in a lively way; coffee is brought, and at last she tells me to sit down, but as if she were throwing a coin to a beggar.

"By the way, Abate, have you read my sonnet?"

"And brought it back to His Eminence. I admired it, Signora. I found it so well turned that I am sure you must have spent much time over it."

"Time?" says the Cardinal. "You do not know her."

"Without toil, Monsignore, one accomplishes nothing of value. That is why I have not dared to show Your Eminence an answer to it which I composed in half an hour."

"Show it, show it," says the Marchesa. "I want to read it."

"Silesia's Answer to Love." The title makes her blush. She becomes perfectly serious. The Cardinal remarks that love has nothing to do with it.

"Wait," says the Signora. "We must respect the ideas of poets."

She reads it aloud, and very well; she reads it over again. She finds Silesia's reproaches to Love well justified, and she explains to the Cardinal why Silesia cannot but take it ill that her conqueror was the King of Prussia. "Ah yes, of course," says the Cardinal. "I see . . . Silesia is a woman[10] . . . The King of Prussia is . . . Oh really! it is a marvelous idea."

We had to wait ten minutes for His Excellency's laughter to subside.

"I want to copy the sonnet," he said. "I must have it."

"The Abate," said the Marchesa, smiling, "will save you the trouble."

"I will dictate it to him. What is this? Wonderful! he has written it with the same rhymes as yours. Did you notice that, Marchesa?"

A glance which she gave me put the finishing touch to my falling in love with her. I saw that she wanted me to understand the Cardinal as she understood him and to be in league with her. I felt more than ready. After copying the sonnet I left them. The Cardinal said that he expected me for dinner the next day.

I went to my room and locked myself in, for the ten stanzas I had to compose were of the most peculiar nature. I had to straddle the ditch with consummate skill, for at the same time that the Marchesa would have to pretend she thought the Cardinal the author of the stanzas, she must not only know that they were mine but also know that I knew she knew it. I had to spare her pride, and at the same time make certain that she would find an ardor in my verses which could come only from my love and not from poetic imagination. I also had to keep in mind doing my best from the Cardinal's point of view, for the more well turned he found the stanzas the more he would think them worthy of his owning their authorship. The great point was to be clear, and that is precisely the most difficult thing in poetry. Obscurity, which is easier, would have passed as sublimity with the man whose good graces I must endeavor to gain. If the Marchesa in her ten stanzas described the Cardinal's excellent qualities, both physical and moral, I had to give him something of the same sort. So I composed them to all these requirements. I described her visible beauties and took care not to describe her hidden ones, and I concluded my last stanza with these two beautiful lines from Ariosto:

Le angeliche bellezze nate in cielo
Non si ponno celar sotto alcun velo.[11]

("The angelic beauties born in heaven cannot be hidden under any veil.")

Well pleased with my little effort, I went to the Cardinal's and gave it to him, saying that I doubted if he would want to acknowledge himself the author of a production which only too clearly revealed the hand of an apprentice. After reading them aloud twice, and very badly, he said that, true enough, they did not amount to much but they were what he needed; and he thanked me for having put in the two lines from Ariosto, which would show the Marchesa that he had needed their help. To console me, he said that when he copied them out he would change some verses so that they would not scan, which would make her certain that he had written them. We dined earlier, and I left to give him time to copy out the stanzas before the lady arrived.

It was on the next day, in the evening, that meeting her at the door of the Palazzo just as she was stepping out of her carriage, I gave her my arm. She told me point-blank that she would be my enemy if Rome came to know her stanzas and mine.

"I do not know what you are talking about, Signora."

"I expected you would not, but mark my words."

As soon as she reached the drawing room, I fled to my own room in despair, for I believed that she was really angry. "My stanzas," I thought to myself, "are too highly colored; they are compromising to her pride, and she does not like my knowing too much about her intrigue. She tells me she is afraid I will be indiscreet; but I am sure she is only pretending; it is an excuse for dismissing me from her favor. What would she have done if I had stripped her naked in my verses?" I was sorry that I had not. I undress, I go to bed, and a half hour later the Abate Gama knocks at my door; I pull the latchstring. He comes in saying that Monsignore wished me to come down. "The Marchesa G. and Cardinal S. C. are asking for you."

"I am sorry. Go and tell them the truth. Tell them too, if you like, that I am ill."

As he did not return, I saw that he had done his errand well.

The next morning I received a note from Cardinal S. C. informing me that he expected me for dinner, that he had been bled, that he needed to speak to me, and that I was to come early, even if I were ill—it was urgent. I could not guess the reason for his summons, but I did not anticipate anything unpleasant.

No sooner am I dressed than I hurry downstairs and go to hear mass, at which I was sure Monsignore would see me. After the mass, he took me aside and asked if I was really ill.

"No, Monsignore. I only wanted to sleep."

"You were wrong, for you are liked. Cardinal S. C. is being bled."

"I know. He mentions it in this note, in which he commands me to wait on him if Your Eminence approves."

"Very well. But it is odd. I did not know that he needed a third person."

"Will there be a third person?"

"I have no idea, and I am not curious."

Everyone thought that the Cardinal had been speaking to me of state affairs. I went to Cardinal S. C.'s, and found him in bed.

"Since I have been put on a diet," he said, "I will dine alone; but you will lose nothing by it, for the cook has not been informed. What I have to tell you is that I fear your stanzas are too well turned, for the Marchesa is mad about them. If you had read them to me as she read them, I would not have claimed them."

"Yet she believes they are by Your Eminence."

"She has no doubt of it; but what am I to do if she takes it into her head to ask me for more verses?"

"I am at your disposal, Monsignore, day and night, and you may be sure that I will die rather than betray your secret."

"I beg you to accept this small present. It is some Negrillo from Havana[12] which Cardinal Acquaviva gave me."

The tobacco was good, but what went with it was better. The snuffbox was of enameled gold. I accepted it with respect and a feeling of gratitude. *If His Eminence did not know how to compose verses, at least he knew how to give, and in a nobleman that knowledge is a far greater grace than the other.*

At noon I was surprised to see the Marchesa appear in the most elegant dishabille.

"If I had known," she said to him, "that you were in good company, I would not have come."

"I am sure," he answered, "that you will not find our Abate unwelcome company."

"No, for I believe he is honorable."

I stood there without a word, but at the same time determined to leave with my fine snuffbox at the first cutting remark she should take it into her head to make to me. He asked her if she would eat dinner, at the same time telling her that he had been put on a diet.

"Yes," she said, "but I shall not enjoy it, for I hate eating alone."

"If you will grant him the honor, the Abate will keep you company."

She answered only by giving me a gracious look. She was the first woman of high station with whom I had had anything to do. I could not become accustomed to her accursed air of patronage, which can have nothing in common with love; but I saw that in the presence of her Cardinal she could not behave otherwise. *I knew that she must know that a haughty air is unnerving.*

The table was laid near His Eminence's bed. Eating next to nothing herself, the Marchesa encouraged me by praising my excellent appetite.

"I told you," the Cardinal said, "that the Abate is my equal."

"I think," she answered, "that he is not far from it. But you are more discriminating."

At that, I ask her to tell me what reason she had for thinking me a glutton.

"I like only the choice, exquisite morsel *in everything*, Signora."

"Explain your 'in everything,'" says the Cardinal.

Venturing a laugh, I began improvising in verse, enumerating every kind of thing which deserved to be called a "choice morsel." The Marchesa applauded, saying that she admired my courage.

"My courage, Signora, is your doing, for I am as timid as a rabbit when I am not given it. *It is you who are the author of my impromptu, 'cum dico quae placent dictat auditor'*" ("when I say anything pleasing, it is my reader who has dictated it").[13]

"I admire you. For my part, even if Apollo himself should encourage me, I could not produce four lines except in writing."

"Have the courage, Signora, to trust in your Genius, and you will utter things divine."

"I agree," said the Cardinal. "Please allow me to show the Abate your ten stanzas."

"They are faulty; but I am willing, provided it remains between us."

The Cardinal then handed me the Marchesa's ten stanzas, and I read them aloud, giving them all the feeling which reading aloud can give a good piece of poetry.

"How well you read that!" said the Marchesa. "I can no longer believe that I wrote them. I thank you. But now please be so good as to give His Eminence's ten stanzas in answer to mine the same kind of reading. They are far better."

"Never believe it," he said to me. "However, here they are. *But try not to make them worse than they are by your reading.*"

There was no need for the Cardinal to ask this of me, for the verses were mine, I was incapable of reading badly, and the more so since Bacchus had increased the fire which having the Marchesa before me had kindled in my soul.

I read them in a way which delighted the Cardinal and which made the Marchesa blush at the passage wherein I described certain beauties which poetry is permitted to praise but which I could not have seen. She snatched them from me with every sign of resentment, saying that I had altered some of the verses. It was true, but I pretended not to admit it. I was aflame, and so was she. The

Cardinal had fallen asleep; she rose, made her way to the *belvedere*[14] and sat down, and I followed her. She had scarcely seated herself on the balustrade before I came and stood in front of her. One of her knees was touching the fob pocket in which I had my watch. Taking one of her hands with respectful tenderness, I told her that she had set me on fire.

"I adore you, Signora, and if you do not permit me to hope, I am determined never to see you again. Pronounce sentence on me."

"I believe you are a libertine and inconstant."

"I am neither."

With these words, I clasped her in my arms and saluted her lips with an amorous kiss, which she received without stooping to make me offer her the least violence. My famished hands now tried to open the way to complete possession; but she quickly changed her position and begged me so sweetly to respect her that I felt it my duty not only to calm my transports but also to ask her pardon. She then spoke to me of Donna Lucrezia, and she must have been delighted to find me a paragon of discretion. After that she talked of the Cardinal, trying to make me believe that she was only his good friend. We then recited beautiful passages of poetry to each other, she sitting so that I could see half of a well-turned leg, I still standing and pretending not to see it, and determined that I would wait for another day to obtain a greater favor than I had been granted on this.

We were interrupted by the Cardinal, who came out in his nightcap, *innocently asking if we had not lost patience waiting for him.*

I did not leave them until nightfall, well satisfied with my good fortune and determined to hold my budding love in check until a propitious occasion should assure me that it would be crowned with victory. From that day on, the charming Marchesa never ceased to give me tokens of her particular esteem without the slightest attempt at concealment. I thought I could count on the coming Carnival, feeling certain that the more I spared her delicacy, the more she would herself try to present me with an opening on an occasion when she could give my love, my loyalty, and my constancy their full reward. But my fortune was to take a different turn just when I least expected it and when Cardinal Acquaviva and the Pope himself were planning to give it a firm foundation. That illustrious pontiff had most warmly congratulated me on the beautiful snuffbox I had received from Cardinal S. C., at the same time never breathing a word to me about the Marchesa G.; and Cardinal Acquaviva had not concealed his pleasure when he saw the beautiful snuffbox in which his generous brother cardinal had given me a sample of his Negrillo. Seeing me so well on the road, the Abate Gama, though he congratulated me, did not dare give me any more advice; and Father Georgi, who divined the whole situation, told me that I should content myself with the favor of the Marchesa G. and take very good care not to give her up for some other acquaintance. Such was my situation.

It was on Christmas Day that I saw Barbaruccia's lover enter my room, shut the door, and throw himself on a sofa, saying that I was seeing him for the last time.

"I come only to ask you for some good advice."

"What advice can I give you?"

"Here—read this. It will tell you everything."

It was a letter from Barbaruccia and ran as follows: "I am pregnant, my dear, I can no longer doubt it. I write to tell you that I have resolved to leave Rome by myself and to die where God may please to send me if you do not take care of me. I will bear anything rather than confess to my father the unhappy state to which we have brought ourselves."

"As a man of honor," I said, "you cannot abandon her. Marry her, despite your father and hers, and then live with her. Eternal Providence will help you."

He reflects, he seems calmer, he leaves.

Anno 1744.

At the beginning of January he appears again, looking very happy.

"I have," he says, "rented the top floor of the house next to Barbaruccia's. She knows this; and tonight I will leave it by the attic window and go in through the attic window of hers. We will settle on a time when I can carry her off. My plan is laid. I have decided to take her to Naples; and since her maid, who sleeps in the attic, cannot help knowing of her elopement, I will take her with us."

"May God bless you."

A week later I see him enter my room an hour before midnight with an abate.

"What do you want with me at this hour?"

"I want to make you acquainted with this handsome abate."

I recognize Barbaruccia and am alarmed. "Did anyone see you come in?"

"No. And suppose anyone did? It is only an abate. We spend every night together."

"I congratulate you."

"The maid has already consented, she will come with us. We leave in a little while and shall be at Naples in twenty-four hours. We have a carriage to take us to the first posthouse, where I am sure they will give us horses."

"Good-by, then. I wish you happiness. I must ask you to leave."

"Good-by."

A few days later when I was walking at the Villa Medici with the Abate Gama, I hear him remark that there is to be an execution at the Piazza di Spagna that night.

"What sort of execution?"

"The Bargello[15] or his lieutenant will execute some *ordine santissimo*, either by searching some suspected house or carrying off someone who does not expect it."

"How has it become known?"

"His Eminence has to know it, for the Pope would not dare to encroach on his jurisdiction[16] without asking his leave."

"So he has asked him?"

"Yes. An *auditore santissimo*[17] came to ask his permission this morning."

"But our Cardinal could have refused."

"True, but he never refuses such a request."

"And if the person sought is under his protection?"

"In that case His Eminence sends him a warning."

A quarter of an hour later, when I had left the Abate, I began to feel very uneasy. It occurred to me that the order might concern Barbaruccia or her lover. Dalacqua's house was under the jurisdiction of Spain. I looked for the young man everywhere, but in vain, though I did not dare to go to his house or to Barbaruccia's for fear of implicating myself. Yet if I had been sure I should find him there, I would certainly have gone, but my suspicion was not firmly founded enough.

About midnight, feeling ready for bed, I go to the door to take out the key when I am surprised to see an abate come in breathless and throw himself into a chair. Recognizing Barbaruccia I lock my door; I gather what has happened and, foreseeing the consequences, consider myself lost. In my trouble and confusion I ask her no questions, I give her a piece of my mind, upbraiding her for having taken refuge in my room, and I ask her to go.

Alas! I should not have asked her, I should have forced her and even summoned help if she refused to go. I did not have the heart.

At the word "go," she flung herself at my feet, sobbing, moaning, and begging me to take pity on her. I gave in, but warning her that we were both lost.

"No one saw me enter the palace or come up here, I am sure of it; and I think I am lucky to have come here to see you ten days ago, otherwise I should never have guessed where your room is."

"Better that you should never have known! What has become of your lover the Doctor?"

"The *sbirri*[18] have carried him off with the maid. But here is the whole story:

"My lover told me last evening that a carriage[19] would be waiting at eleven o'clock tonight at the foot of the Scala di Trinità dei Monti[20] and that he would be waiting for me in it. Accordingly, an hour ago I left my house by the attic window, with the maid going ahead. I entered his house, I put on the clothes which you see, I came downstairs and started straight toward the carriage. My maid was walking ahead of me with my few belongings. Turning a corner, I notice that one of my shoe buckles has come undone, I stop and bend over to fasten it. My maid, thinking that I was still following her, went on to the carriage and got in; I was only thirty paces behind her. But then something stopped me in my tracks. The maid had scarcely got in when by the light of a lantern I see the carriage surrounded by *sbirri*, at the same time the postilion dismounts, another man takes his place and drives the carriage away at full gallop with my maid and my lover, who was certainly waiting for me in it. What could I do at that terrible moment? Since I could not go back home, I obeyed an impulse which I can only call involuntary and which brought me here. So here I am. You tell me that my action has ruined you, and all this is killing me. Find some expedient, I am ready for anything; even to ruin myself if necessary, to save you."

But as she uttered these last words she burst into sobs for which I can find no comparison. Realizing the full horror of her situation, I thought it far worse than mine; but that did not prevent me from seeing that I was on the verge of ruin, guiltless though I was.

"Let me take you to your father's feet," I said. "I feel that I have the power to convince him that he must save you from shame."

But when she hears me propose this expedient, which was the only one, I see that the poor creature is in despair. Her tears falling *in torrents*, she answers that she would rather I put her out in the street and abandoned her there. This is what I should have done, and

I considered it; but I could not bring myself to do it. What stopped me was her tears.

Do you know, my dear reader, the power of tears falling from the lovely eyes of a young, pretty girl who is respectable and *unfortunate*? Their power is irresistible. *Credete a chi ne ha fatto esperimento* ("Believe him who has had the experience").[21] It was a physical impossibility for me to turn her out. What tears! Three handkerchiefs were soaked with them in half an hour. I have never seen tears shed so uninterruptedly; if they were necessary to assuage her grief, there was never in the world a grief to equal hers.

After all these tears, I asked her what she thought of doing when daylight came. It had already struck midnight.

"I will leave the palace," she said, sobbing. "In these clothes no one will notice me; I will leave Rome; I will walk until my breath fails."

With these words she fell to the floor; I thought she was going to die. She herself put a finger to her neckband to help her to breathe, for she was choking. I saw her turning blue. I was in the most excruciating of quandaries.

After untying her neckband and unbuttoning everything that was tight on her, I brought her back to life by sprinkling her face with water. The night being extremely cold, and there being no fire in my room, I told her to get into bed and be sure that I would respect her. She answered that she believed her state was such that it could inspire only pity, but that in any case she was in my hands to do with as I would. To restore her courage and to give her blood a chance to flow freely, I persuaded her to undress and get under the covers. Since she had not the strength, I had to undress her and carry her to the bed myself. In so doing, I performed a new experiment on myself. It was a discovery. I resisted the sight of all her charms without any difficulty. She went to sleep, and so did I, lying beside her, but fully dressed. A quarter of an hour before dawn I woke her and, finding her strength restored, she did not need me to help her dress.

As soon as it was daylight, I went out, telling her to remain calm until I returned. I went out with the intention of going to her father, but I changed my mind as soon as I saw spies. I went to the coffee-house in the Via Condotti, observing that I was followed at a distance. After taking a cup of chocolate, I put some biscuits in my pocket and returned to the palace, observing that I was still followed by the same spy. I gathered from this that the Bargello, having failed to catch her, was now reduced to acting on conjectures. The porter told me, without my asking him, that a seizure was attempted during the night but that he believed it had failed. At the same moment an *auditore* of the Cardinal Vicar's asked the porter when he could speak to the Abate Gama. I saw that there was no time to be lost, and I went up to my room to decide on a course.

After making Barbaruccia eat two biscuits dipped in Canary wine, I took her to the top of the palace to an indecorous place to which no one ever went. I told her she must wait there until she heard from me, since my lackey was bound to arrive. He arrived a few minutes later. I went down to the Abate Gama's apartment, first ordering the man to bring me the key to my room as soon as he had finished cleaning it.

I found the Abate in conversation with an *auditore* of the Cardinal Vicar's. When he had finished talking with him, he came to me and at once ordered chocolate. To give me the news of the day, he told me about the Cardinal Vicar's message. His Eminence was to be asked to dismiss from the palace a person who must have taken refuge in it about midnight. "Nothing can be done," he added, "until the Cardinal is visible; if anyone has hidden in the palace without his knowledge, he will certainly have the person turned out." We then talked of the cold weather until my servant brought me the key. Seeing that I had at least an hour before me, I thought of an expedient which alone could save Barbaruccia from disgrace.

Making sure that I was unobserved, I went to the place where Barbaruccia was hiding, gave her a pencil, and made her write a note in good French, in these terms: "I am, Monsignore, a decent girl disguised as an abate. I implore Your Eminence to permit me to tell you my name in person. I trust in your magnanimity to save my honor."

"You will leave this place," I told her, "at exactly nine o'clock. You will go down three flights of stairs and you will enter the apartment on your right and pass through it to the last antechamber, where you will see a stout gentleman sitting before a brazier. You will hand him this note, asking him to deliver it to the Cardinal at once. Do not fear that he will read it, for he will not have time. As soon as he has delivered it, you may be sure that the Cardinal will let you come in at once and will hear you without a witness. Go down on your knees and tell him your whole story, perfectly truthfully, all except the fact that you spent the night in my room and that you have talked with me. Say that when you saw your lover carried off, you were frightened, you entered the palace, and went up to the top floor where, after spending an agonizing night, you felt inspired to write him the note which you sent in to him. I am certain, my poor Barbaruccia, that His Eminence will save you from disgrace in one way or another. This is your only hope of having your lover become your husband."

When she had assured me that she would carry out all my instructions to the letter, I went downstairs, had my hair dressed, changed my clothes, and, after hearing mass in the presence of the Cardinal, I went out and did not return until dinnertime.

At table this extraordinary incident furnished the sole subject of conversation. Each gave his own version of it. Only the Abate Gama said nothing, and I did likewise. What I gathered was that the Cardinal had extended his protection to the person who was sought. This was all I wanted; so, thinking that I had no further reason for fear, I silently rejoiced in the outcome of my little stratagem, which I thought a masterpiece. After dinner I asked the Abate Gama to tell me what all this business was about, and here is his answer:

"A father whose name I have not yet learned appealed to the Cardinal Vicar to prevent his son from eloping with a girl whom he planned to take out of the state. The elopement was to take place at midnight in our Piazza. After obtaining His Eminence's leave, as I told you yesterday, the Vicar ordered the Bargello to bring in his men and capture the guilty couple in the act. The order was carried out; but the *sbirri* discovered they had been tricked when, on arriving at the Bargello's and ordering the prisoners out of the carriage, instead of a girl they found a woman and indeed such a woman as no one would think of carrying off. A few minutes later a spy came to the Bargello and told him that just as the carriage was leaving the Piazza an abate had run into the Palazzo di Spagna. The Bargello at once went to the Cardinal Vicar and reported the circumstance which had been responsible for his failure to apprehend the girl, apparently mentioning his suspicion that she might be the very abate who had taken refuge in the Palazzo. The Vicar then informed our master that a girl dressed as an abate might be hiding in his palace. He asked him to have the person, whether girl or abate, turned out, unless it was someone whom His Eminence knew to be above suspicion. Cardinal Acquaviva was informed of this just before nine o'clock this morning by the Vicar's *auditore*, with whom you saw me talking this morning. He dismissed him with an

VOLUME ONE CHAPTER TEN

assurance that he would have a thorough search made and would turn out anyone in the palace who was not known to him.

"Sure enough, the Cardinal immediately gave such an order to the majordomo, who at once began carrying it out; but a quarter of an hour later he was ordered to stop the search. The reason for the counterorder can only be this:

"The Chamberlain has told me that on the stroke of nine o'clock a very good-looking abate, whom he really thought a girl in disguise, appeared before him and asked him to deliver to His Eminence a note which the abate handed him. He delivered it immediately, and no sooner had His Eminence read it than he ordered him to admit the abate, who has not left His Eminence's apartment since then. As the order to stop the search was given immediately after the abate was admitted, there is good reason to believe that the said abate is the girl whom the *sbirri* failed to apprehend and who took refuge in the palace, where she must have remained in hiding all night until she was prompted to present herself to the Cardinal."

"Even so, His Eminence may today put her into the hands not of the *sbirri* but of the Vicar."

"Not even into the hands of the Pope. You can have no idea of the power of our Cardinal's protection, and his protection has already been extended since the person is not only still in the palace but in the master's own apartment under his guard."

The story was interesting and the attention with which I listened to it was far from offending the inquisitive Gama, who would certainly have told me nothing if he knew how deeply I was involved and how great my interest in the story must be. I went to the opera at the Teatro Aliberti.[22]

The next morning Gama entered my bedroom and smilingly told me that the Cardinal Vicar knew that the abductor was a friend of mine and that the girl must be too, since her father was my French teacher.

"Everyone is certain," he said, "that you knew about the whole affair and they naturally think that the poor child spent the night in your room. I admire the prudence you demonstrated in your behavior toward me yesterday. You were so well on your guard that I would have wagered you knew nothing about it."

"Nor did I," I answered calmly and seriously. "I have learned of it only this moment from your own lips. I know the girl, but I have not seen her since six weeks ago, when I stopped taking lessons; I am much better acquainted with the young Doctor, yet he never told me anything about his plan. However, everyone is free to think what he chooses. It is natural, you say, that the girl should have spent the night in my room. *Permit me to laugh at those who take conjectures for certainties.*"

"*It is the particular vice of the Romans*, my dear friend, and those who can laugh at it are fortunate; but this slander, for I believe it to be a slander, can turn our master's mind against you."

That evening, there being no opera, I went to the reception. I found not the slightest change in the Cardinal's manner nor in anyone else's. I found the Marchesa more gracious to me than usual. It was the next day after dinner that Gama told me that the Cardinal had sent the girl to a convent, where she was being very well taken care of at His Eminence's expense.

"I am sure," he said, "that she will not leave it except to become the wife of the young man who tried to abduct her."

"I assure you," I answered, "that I shall be very glad, for both he and she are honorable and worthy of everyone's esteem."

A day or two later Father Georgi told me that the news of the day in Rome was the abortive attempt to carry off the daughter of the advocate Dalacqua; and that I was credited with having managed the entire intrigue, as he was greatly displeased to hear. I spoke to him as I had spoken to Gama, and he appeared to believe me, but he said that *Rome did not like to know things as they were but as it chose to think they must be.*

"It is known," he said, "that you went to Dalacqua's house every morning; it is known that the young man frequently called on you, and that is enough. *No one wishes to know what would scotch the slander, for slander is the delight of this holy city.* Your innocence will not prevent the business from being laid to your account forty years hence at a conclave of cardinals at which you are put up as a candidate for the Papacy."

During the following days this accursed adventure began to be a real annoyance, for everyone spoke of it to me and I clearly saw that if people listened to what I had to say and appeared to believe me, it was only because they could not do otherwise.

The Marchesa G. slyly told me that Signorina Dalacqua was under the greatest obligation to me; but what troubled me most was that, even in these last days of the Carnival, Cardinal Acquaviva had changed his old unconstrained manner toward me. No one noticed it; but I saw it beyond peradventure.

It was, in fact, at the beginning of Lent, when everyone had stopped talking about the elopement, that the Cardinal told me to go into his study with him. It was there that he treated me to the following little discourse:

"The Dalacqua affair is over, no one even mentions it now. But, leaving aside the question of whether it is a slander or not, the general verdict is that those who profited by the young man's bungling attempt to abduct the girl are you and I. All this talk is nothing to me, for if the same thing happened to me again, I would not act otherwise; nor do I wish to know what no one can oblige you to tell and what, as a man of honor, you even ought not to tell. If you knew nothing about it beforehand, by turning the girl away—always supposing that she was in your room—you would have committed a barbarous and even cowardly act, which would have made her miserable for the rest of her life and, even so, would have left you suspected of complicity and, what is worse, of disloyalty. But despite all this you can well imagine that, though I scorn all talk of the kind, I nevertheless cannot remain entirely indifferent[23] to it. Such being the case, I find myself obliged to ask you to leave not only my service but Rome as well; but I will supply you with an excuse which will preserve your honor and, what is more, such consideration as the proofs of my esteem which I have given you may have gained you. I give you permission to inform anyone you please in confidence, and even to announce to the world, that you are going away on a piece of business which I have entrusted to you.

"Consider what country you wish to go to; I have friends everywhere; I will give you such recommendations as I am certain will procure you employment. I will give you letters of introduction in my own hand; it rests with you to arrange matters so that no one will know where you are going. Come tomorrow to the Villa Negroni, prepared to tell me to what place you wish me to give you letters. You must be ready to leave in a week. Believe me, I am sorry to lose you. It is a sacrifice which I make to the greatest of all prejudices. Do not oblige me to witness your grief, I beg you."

He spoke these last words when he saw my tears, and he gave me no time to answer so that he need not see more of them; I nevertheless found the strength to compose myself and to appear in good spirits to all who saw me coming out of his office. At table everyone thought me in the best possible humor. The Abate Gama, after giving me coffee in his room, congratulated me on looking so happy. "I am sure," he said, "that it is because of your conversation with His Eminence this morning."

"You are right. But you do not know the concern which I conceal."

"Concern?"

"Yes, I am very much afraid I may fail in a difficult mission which the Cardinal entrusted to me this morning. I am obliged to hide the little confidence I feel in myself in order not to diminish the confidence His Eminence has in my small abilities."

"If my advice can be of any use to you, make free of it. However, you do very well to appear happy and calm. Is it a mission in Rome?"

"No. It involves a journey on which I must start in a week or ten days."

"In what direction?"

"Westward."

"I will not ask you any more."

I went by myself to the Villa Borghese, where I walked for two hours in desperation, for I loved Rome and, having started on the highroad to fortune, I saw myself an outcast not knowing which way to turn and with all my hopes blighted. Examining my conduct, I could not find that I was guilty; but I clearly saw that Father Georgi was right. I should not only have had nothing to do with Barbaruccia's subsequent course, I should have changed my French teacher as soon as I discovered that she was carrying on a love affair. But at my age and with my small knowledge of what misfortune meant, I could not have a caution which could only be the fruit of long experience. I considered where I ought to go, I thought about it all night and all the next morning, yet I could not decide on one place rather than another. I went back and retired to my room without any thought of supper. The Abate Gama came and told me that His Eminence wished me not to make any engagement for dinner the next day as he had business to transact with me.

I found him at the Villa Negroni, *tomando el sol*.[24] He was walking with his secretary, whom he left as soon as he saw me. Left alone with him, I gave him a full and faithful account of Barbaruccia's intrigue, omitting not the smallest detail. After this faithful narrative, I described the grief I felt at leaving him, painting it in the liveliest colors. I told him that I felt that all my hopes of fortune were dashed for my entire life, since I was certain that I could attain to it only in his service. I spent an hour talking to him in this vein, weeping most of the time; but all that I said was of no avail. He told me in the kindest manner to take courage, and when he urged me to tell him to what place in Europe I wished to go, the word which despair and resentment brought to my lips was "Constantinople."[25]

"Constantinople?" he said, falling back two steps.

"Yes, Monsignore, Constantinople," I repeated, wiping away my tears.

The prelate, who was a man of wit, though a thorough Spaniard, said not a word for two or three minutes. Then, looking at me with a smile:

"I am obliged to you," he said, "for not choosing Ispahan,[26] for I should have been at a loss. When do you wish to leave?"

"A week from today, as Your Eminence commanded me."

"Shall you embark at Naples, or at Venice?"

"At Venice."

"I will give you an adequate passport, for you will find two armies in winter quarters[27] in Romagna. So far as I am concerned, you can tell everyone that I am sending you to Constantinople, for nobody will believe you."

This piece of political acumen almost made me laugh. He gave me his hand, which I kissed, and set off to rejoin his secretary, who was waiting for him in another walk; as he left, he told me that I was to dine with him.

On my way back to the Palazzo di Spagna, considering what I had done, my astonishment at having chosen Constantinople was so great that for a moment I thought only two things were possible: either I had gone mad, or I had been impelled to bring out the name by nothing other than the mysterious power of my Genius, who was summoning me there in concert with my destiny. What surprised me was that the Cardinal had consented at once. It seemed as if his pride had prevented him from advising me to go somewhere else. He was afraid I might think he had been boasting when he told me that he had friends everywhere. To whom would he recommend me? What should I do in Constantinople? I had no idea, but go there I must. His Eminence dined alone with me and made a point of showing me the utmost kindness, as I did of showing the utmost satisfaction, for my self-esteem was stronger than my grief and would not allow me to give anyone who might be observing me the slightest cause for suspecting that I was in disfavor. The chief reason for my sadness was having to leave the Marchesa G., with whom I was in love and from whom I had obtained nothing of consequence.

On the next day but one His Eminence gave me a passport for Venice and a sealed letter addressed to "Osman Bonneval,[28] Pasha of Karamania, at Constantinople." I could have kept it to myself, but since the Cardinal had not forbidden it, I showed the address on the letter to all my acquaintances. The Abate Gama laughed and said he knew I was not going to Constantinople. The Cavaliere da Lezze, the Venetian Ambassador, gave me a letter addressed to a rich and kindly Turk who had been a friend of his. Don Gaspare asked me to write to him, as did Father Georgi. When I took leave of Donna Cecilia, she read me part of a letter from her daughter, containing the happy news that she was pregnant. I also paid a call on Donna Angelica, whom Don Francesco had married without inviting me to the wedding.

When I went to receive the Holy Father's blessing, I was not surprised to hear him tell me of his acquaintances in Constantinople. Of these the one he had known best was Monsieur de Bonneval. He directed me to give him his compliments and tell him he was sorry he could not send him his blessing. Giving me a most hearty one, he presented me with a rosary of agates connected by a thin gold chain, which might be worth twelve zecchini.

When I took leave of Cardinal Acquaviva, he gave me a purse in which I found a hundred coins of the sort the Castilians call *doblones de a ocho*.[29] They were worth seven hundred zecchini and I had three hundred. I kept two hundred and procured a bill of exchange for sixteen hundred Roman scudi on a Ragusan who had an office in Ancona and was named Giovanni Bucchetti. I took a seat in a berlin with a lady who was taking her daughter to Loreto to fulfill a vow she had made at the crisis of an illness which, but for the vow, might well have brought her to the grave. The girl was ugly. I was bored during the whole journey.

HISTORY OF MY LIFE

Volume Two

CHAPTER I

My short and too lively stay in Ancona.
Cecilia, Marina, Bellino. The Greek slave girl
from the Lazaretto. Bellino unmasks.

I reached Ancona at nightfall on the 25th of February in the year 1744 and put up at the best inn in the town. Satisfied with my room, I tell the host that I wish to eat meat. He replies that in Lent Christians eat fish. I say that the Pope has given me permission to eat meat; he tells me to show him the permission; I say that he gave it to me by word of mouth; he will not believe me; I call him a fool; he tells me to go and lodge elsewhere; and this last proposition of his, which I do not expect, astonishes me. I swear, I curse; whereupon a solemn-looking individual comes out of a room and proceeds to tell me that I *was wrong* to want to eat meat, since fish was better in Ancona; that I *was wrong* to expect the innkeeper to take my word for it that I had permission; that, if I had permission, I *was wrong* to have asked for it at my age; that I *was wrong* to have called the innkeeper a fool, since he was free to refuse to lodge me; and, finally, that I *was wrong* to raise such a row.

This man who was sticking his nose into my business unasked, and who had come out of his room only to tell me how unimaginably *wrong* I was, had very nearly set me laughing.

"Sir," I said, "I subscribe to all your accusations. But it is raining, I am extremely hungry, and I have no wish to go out looking for another lodging at this hour. So I ask you if, since our host refuses, you will provide me with supper."

"No, for I am a Catholic and hence am keeping the fast; but I will undertake to calm our ruffled host, who will give you a good supper, though of fish."

So saying, he started downstairs; and I, comparing his cool common sense with my hasty petulance, acknowledge that he is worthy of teaching me a thing or two. He comes back upstairs, enters my room, says that all is well again, that I shall have a good supper, and that he will keep me company at it. I reply that I shall consider it an honor and, to oblige him to tell me his name, I tell him mine, adding that I am Cardinal Acquaviva's secretary.

"My name," he says, "is Sancho Pico, I am a Castilian and Proveditor of the army of His Catholic Majesty, which is commanded by the Count de Gages[1] under orders from the Generalissimo, the Duke of Modena."

After exclaiming over the appetite with which I ate all that was set before me, he asked me if I had dined; and he seemed relieved when I answered that I had not.

"Will the supper you have eaten," he asked, "make you ill?"

"I have reason to hope that, on the contrary, it will do me good."

"Then you have deceived the Pope. Follow me to the next room. You will have the pleasure of hearing some good music. The first actress is lodging there."

The word "actress" arouses my curiosity, and I follow him. I see a woman rather well on in years eating supper at a table with two girls and two handsome youths. I look in vain for the actress. Don Sancho introduces her to me in the person of one of the youths, who was ravishingly handsome and could not have been more than sixteen or seventeen years old. I think at once that he is the castrato who had played the part of first actress at the theater in Ancona,[3] which was subject to the same regulations as the theaters in Rome. The mother introduces her other son, a good-looking boy too, but not a castrato, whose name was Petronio and who appeared as prima ballerina, and her two daughters, the elder of whom, named Cecilia, was studying music and was twelve years old; the other, who was a dancer, was eleven and named Marina; they were both pretty. The family came from Bologna and made a living by its talents. Affability and lightheartedness made up for their poverty.

When Bellino (for such was the name of the castrato who was first actress) rose from table he yielded to Don Sancho's urging and sat down at the harpsichord and accompanied himself in an air which he sang with the voice of an angel and enchanting *fioriture*. The Spaniard listened with his eyes closed and seemed to be in ecstasy. For my part, far from keeping my eyes closed, I was admiring Bellino's which, black as carbuncles, sparkled with a fire which burned my soul. This anomalous being had some of Donna Lucrezia's features and certain gestures reminiscent of the Marchesa G. The face seemed to me feminine. And the masculine attire did not prevent my seeing a certain fullness of bosom, which put it into my head that despite the billing, this must be a girl. In this conviction, I made no resistance to the desires which he aroused in me.

After two pleasant hours Don Sancho saw me to my room and told me that he was leaving early in the morning for Sinigaglia[4] with the Abate Vilmarcati, and would return the following day in time for supper. Wishing him a good journey, I said that I should meet him on the road, since I wished to sup at Sinigaglia that day. I was stopping in Ancona only for a day, to present my bill of exchange to the banker and get another for Bologna.

I went to bed full of the impression which Bellino had made on me and sorry to leave without having given him proof of the justice I did him in not being hoodwinked by his disguise. But the next morning I had no more than opened my door when he appears before me and offers me his brother to serve me instead of a hired manservant. I agree, he comes at once, and I send him to bring coffee for the whole family. I make Bellino sit down on my bed, intending to treat him as a girl; but his two sisters come running to me and thwart my plan. I could not but delight in the charming picture I had before my eyes: gaiety, of three different kinds, unadorned beauty, familiarity without presumption, the verve of the theater, a pretty playfulness, little Bolognese grimaces with which I was not yet familiar and which I found most charming. The two little girls were perfect living rosebuds, and more than worthy of being preferred to Bellino if I had not taken it into my head that Bellino was a girl too. Despite their extreme youth the sign of their precocious puberty was visible on their white bosoms.

The coffee came, brought by Petronio, who served us and took some to his mother, who never left her own room. Petronio was a true Giton,[5] and a professional at that. This is not unusual in outlandish Italy, where intolerance in this matter is not unreasonable, as it is in England, nor ferocious, as it is in Spain. I gave him a zecchino to pay for the coffee and made him a present of the eighteen paoli in change, which he accepted with such a mark of his gratitude as clearly revealed his tastes. It was a kiss from half-open lips, which he planted on mine in the belief that I was a devotee of the pretty practice. I had no difficulty in setting him right, but I saw no sign that he felt humiliated. When I told him to order dinner for six, he answered that he would order it only for four, since he had to keep his dear mother company, who ate in bed.

Two minutes later the innkeeper came up and said that the people I was having to dinner each ate at least enough for two, so he would serve me only if I paid six paoli apiece. I agreed. Thinking it proper to say good day to the obliging mother, I go to her room and congratulate her on her charming family. She thanks me for the eighteen paoli I had given her dear son and proceeds to confide her poverty-stricken circumstances to me.

"The impresario Rocco Argenti," she tells me, "is a hardhearted monster who has given me only fifty Roman scudi for the whole Carnival. We have spent it all, and can only get back to Bologna on foot and begging for alms on the road."

I gave her a doblon de a ocho, at which she wept for joy. I promise her another if she will tell me a secret.

"Admit," I say, "that Bellino is a girl."

"You may be sure he is not; but he does look it. So much so, indeed, that he had to submit to being examined."

"By whom?"

"By the very reverend confessor of Monsignor the Bishop."

"I will not believe a word of it until I have examined him myself."

"Very well; but in conscience I can have nothing to do with it for, God forgive me, I do not know what your intentions are."

I go to my room, I send Petronio out to buy a bottle of Cyprus wine, he gives me seven zecchini in change from a doblon I had given him, and I divide it among Bellino, Cecilia, and Marina; then I ask the two girls to leave me alone with their brother.

"My dear Bellino," I say, "I am sure that you are not of my sex."

"I am of your sex, but a castrato; I have been examined."

"Let me examine you too, and here is a doblon for you."

"No, for it is clear that you are in love with me, and religion forbids me to let you."

"You were not so scrupulous with the Bishop's confessor."

"He was old, and all he did was take a hasty look at my unfortunate condition."

I put out my hand, he pushes it away and rises. This obstinacy angers me, for I had already spent fifteen or sixteen zecchini to satisfy my curiosity. I sit down to dinner in the sulks, but the appetite of the three pretty creatures restores my good humor and I make up my mind to obtain a return for the money I had spent from the two younger sisters.

With the three of us sitting before the fire eating chestnuts, I begin distributing kisses; and Bellino, on his side, shows no want of compliance. I touch and then kiss the budding breasts of Cecilia and Marina; and Bellino, with a smile, does nothing to stop my hand from slipping behind his shirt ruffle and laying hold of a breast which leaves me in no possible doubt.

"This breast," I said, "proclaims you a girl, and you cannot deny it."

"All we castrati have the same deformity."

"So I am aware. But I know enough about it to tell the one kind from the other. This alabaster breast, my dear Bellino, is the charming breast of a girl of seventeen."

Completely on fire, and seeing that he offered no resistance to my hand, which was delighting in possessing such a breast, I make to approach it with my panting lips, which were pale from the intensity of my ardor; but the impostor, as if he had only that moment become aware of the forbidden pleasure I was enjoying, rises and walks off. I am left raging, yet unable to blame him, for I should first have had to blame myself. Needing to recover my calm, I asked Cecilia, who was his pupil, to sing me some Neapolitan songs; then I went out to see the Ragusan Bucchetti, who gave me a bill of sight on Bologna in exchange for the one I presented to him. Back at the inn, I went to bed after eating a dish of macaroni in the company of the girls. I told Petronio to have a post chaise ready for me at daybreak, as I wished to leave.

Just as I was going to shut my door, I see Cecilia, wearing little more than a shift, coming to tell me that Bellino would consider it a favor if I would take him with me as far as Rimini, where he was engaged to sing in an opera which was to be produced after Easter.

"Go and tell him, my little angel, that I am ready to do him the favor if he will first do me that of showing me, in your presence, whether he is a girl or a boy."

She goes, and comes back to tell me he is already in bed, but that if I would put off my departure for only one day he promised to satisfy my curiosity.

"Tell me the truth and I will give you six zecchini."

"I cannot earn them, for I have never seen him naked and so cannot be sure of my own knowledge; but he is certainly a boy, otherwise he would not have been allowed to sing in this city."

"Very well. I will not leave until day after tomorrow, if you will spend the night with me."

"So you love me?"

"Very much; but you must be kind to me."

"That I will, because I love you too. I'll go and let my mother know."

"You have surely had a lover."

"Never."

She came back in high spirits, saying that her mother thought me a man of honor. She fastened my door and fell into my arms with all the abandon of love. I found that she might be a virgin; but as I was not in love with her I did not catechize her. Love is the divine sauce which makes that morsel delicious. Cecilia was charming, but I had not had time to desire her; hence I could not say to her, "You have made me happy"; it was she who said it to me; but I did not feel much flattered. However, I was willing to believe her, she was tender, I was tender, I fell asleep in her arms, and when I woke, after giving her love's morning salutation, I presented her with three doblones, which could not but please her better than vows of eternal constancy. Ridiculous vows, which no man can make to the most beautiful of women. Cecilia left to carry her wealth to her mother, who wept for joy as she renewed her trust in Divine Providence.

I sent for the innkeeper and ordered him to prepare a supper for five regardless of expense. I was sure that the noble Don Sancho, who was to be back toward evening, would not refuse me the honor of supping with me. I ate no dinner; but the Bolognese family did not feel that any such abstinence was necessary to give them an appetite for supper. When I sent for Bellino and demanded that he keep his promise, he replied with a smile that the day was not over yet and that he was sure he would travel to Rimini with me. I asked him if he would like to take a walk with me, and he went to dress.

Just then in comes Marina, looking sulky, and says that she does not know how she had deserved the proof of my disfavor I was about to give her.

"Cecilia spent the night with you, you go off tomorrow with Bellino, I am the only unlucky one of us."

"Do you want money?"

"No, I love you."

"You are too young."

"Age has nothing to do with it. I am better developed than my sister."

"Then perhaps you have had a lover."

"Certainly not."

"So much the better. We'll find out this evening."

"Then I'll tell my mother to have some sheets ready for tomorrow, otherwise the maid would guess what happened."

I found these comedies in the highest degree entertaining. Coming to the port with Bellino, I bought a small barrel of oysters at the Venetian arsenal as a treat for Don Sancho, and after arranging to have them delivered to the inn, I took Bellino out to the roads with me and went on board a Venetian ship of the line which had just finished its quarantine. Finding no one I knew in it, I went on board a Turkish vessel which was making ready to sail for Alexandria.

Scarcely aboard, the first person I see is the beautiful Greek girl whom I had left in the lazaretto at Ancona seven months earlier. She was beside the old captain. I pretend not to see her and ask him if he has any fine merchandise to sell. He takes us to his cabin and opens his closets. I read in the Greek girl's eyes her joy at seeing me again. Nothing that the Turk showed me having suited me, I told him that I would be glad to buy something pretty, such as might please his fairer half. He laughs, she speaks to him in Turkish, and he goes off. She comes running and throws herself on my neck, and, clasping me to her bosom, says: "Fortune gives us this one moment." My courage being no less than hers, I sit down, accommodate her to my position, and in less than a minute do what her master had never done to her in five years. I plucked the fruit, and I was eating it; but to swallow it I needed another minute. The poor Greek girl, hearing her master coming back, left my arms and turned her back to me, thus giving me time to set myself to rights without his seeing my disordered state, which could well have cost me my life, or all the money I possessed, to bring to an amicable settlement. What amused me in this really serious situation was to see Bellino struck motionless by surprise and shaking with fear.

The knickknacks which the beautiful slave chose cost me only twenty or thirty zecchini. "*Spolaitis*,"[6] she said to me in her native language; but she ran away when her master told her she ought to kiss me. I left more sad than gay, feeling sorry for the charming creature whom, for all her courage, Heaven had obstinately determined to grant only a partial favor. In the felucca,[7] when Bellino had recovered from his fright, he said that I had shown him a prodigy which he could not believe he had really seen but which gave him a strange idea of my character; as for the Greek girl's, he was completely at a loss, unless I were to tell him that all women from her country were of the same nature. Bellino said that they must be unhappy.

"Then you must believe," said I, "that coquettes are happy?"

"I don't want either kind. I want a woman to yield to love sincerely, and to surrender after she has struggled with herself; I don't want her to give in to the first sensation a man who attracts her arouses in her and abandon herself to him like a bitch whose only law is instinct. Admit that this Greek girl certainly showed you that you were attractive to her, but at the same time gave you unequivocal proof of her animality and of an effrontery which exposed her to the shame of being refused, for she could not know that she had attracted you as much as you attracted her. She is very pretty, and it all went well; but I was terrified."

I could have calmed Bellino and put an end to his perfectly sound argument by telling him the whole story; but that would not have served my purpose. If he was a girl, it was to my advantage to convince him that I attached little importance to the great affair and that it was not worth employing trickery to prevent it from following its course unimpeded.

We returned to the inn, and toward nightfall we saw Don Sancho enter the courtyard in his carriage. I went to meet him and asked him to excuse me for having assumed that he would do me the honor of supping with Bellino and myself. Acknowledging with dignity and politeness the favor which I had been so kind as to do him, he accepted.

The choice and well-prepared dishes, the good Spanish wines, the excellent oysters, and still more the high spirits and the voices of Bellino and Cecilia, who performed duets and seguidillas[8] for us, gave the Spaniard five hours of paradise. Leaving us at midnight, he said he would only go to bed easy if I would promise to sup with him in his room the next evening, in the same company. This meant that I must put off my departure for another day. I surprised him by accepting.

I then urged Bellino to keep his promise to me; but he answered that Marina had something to say to me and that we should have plenty of time to be together the next day, and so left me. I remained alone with Marina, who happily locked my door.

More well developed, though younger, than Cecilia, the girl felt she owed it to herself to convince me that she deserved to be preferred to her sister. I could well believe it, merely from seeing the fire in her eyes. Fearing that she would be slighted by a man who might have been exhausted by the previous night, she poured out all the amorous ideas which occupied her soul; she told me in detail all that she knew how to do, she set forth all her theories, and gave me a full account of all the occasions she had had to become a past mistress in the mysteries of love, together with her notion of love's pleasures and the means she had employed to obtain a taste of them. I finally made out that she was afraid that, not finding her a virgin, I would reproach her. Her anxiety pleased me, and I amused myself by assuring her that virginity in girls seemed to me only childish imagination, since nature had not even given most of them the tokens of it. I ridiculed those who only too often made the mistake of chiding them on the subject.

I saw that my doctrine pleased her and that she came into my arms full of confidence. And in fact she proved herself superior to her sister in every way, and she was exultant when I told her so; but when she wanted to fill my cup by assuring me she would stay awake the whole night with me, I persuaded her not to, arguing that we would be the losers by it, since if we granted nature the sweet respite of sleep she would show her gratitude by the increased energy of her fire when we woke.

So, having enjoyed ourselves sufficiently and slept well, we renewed the celebration in the morning; and Marina left me well satisfied when she saw the three doblones which she happily carried to her mother, who was insatiable in contracting ever greater obligations to Divine Providence.

I went out to get money from Bucchetti, since I did not know what might happen to me on my journey before I reached Bologna. I had enjoyed myself, but I had spent too much. I still had to consider Bellino, who, if he was a girl, must not find me less generous than his sisters had done. Whether he was must inevitably come out during the course of the day; and I thought I was certain of it.

Those who say that life is only a combination of misfortunes mean that life itself is a misfortune. If it is a misfortune, then death is a happiness. Such people did not write in good health, with their purses stuffed with money, and contentment in their souls from having held Cecilias and Marinas in their arms and being sure that there were more of them to come. Such men are a race of pessimists[9] (forgive me, my dear French language!) which can have existed only among ragged philosophers and rascally or atrabilious theologians. If pleasure exists, and we can only enjoy it in life, then life is a happiness. There are misfortunes, of course, as I should be the first to know. But the very existence of these misfortunes proves that the sum of good is greater. I am infinitely happy when I am in a dark room and see the light coming through a window which opens on a vast horizon.

At suppertime I waited on Don Sancho, whom I found alone and in a very decent room. His table was laid with silver dishes and his servants were in livery. Bellino, whether from whim or as a ruse, enters dressed as a girl, followed by his two very pretty sisters but whom he totally eclipsed, and at that moment I became so sure of his sex that I would have staked my life against a paolo. It was impossible to imagine a prettier girl.

"Are you convinced," I asked Don Sancho, "that Bellino is not a girl?"

"Girl or boy, what does it matter? I think he is a very handsome castrato; and I have seen others as good-looking as he."

"But are you sure of it?"

"*Valgame Dios!*[10] I am not interested in making sure."

Respecting the Spaniard for possessing a wisdom which I lacked, I made no answer; but at table I could not take my eyes from this being whom my depraved nature impelled me to love and to believe a member of the sex to which it was necessary to my purposes that he should belong.

Don Sancho's supper was exquisite and, as was to be expected, better than mine, for otherwise he would have considered himself dishonored. He gave us white truffles, several kinds of shellfish, the best fish from the Adriatic, still champagne, Peralta, sherry, and Pedro Ximenes.[11] After supper Bellino sang in a fashion to make us lose the little reason the excellent wines had left us. His gestures, the way he moved his eyes, his gait, his bearing, his manner, his face, his voice, and above all my instinct, which I concluded could not make me feel its power for a castrato, all combined to confirm me in my idea. Yet I still needed to make certain from the testimony of my own eyes.

After duly thanking the noble Castilian, we wished him a good sleep and went to my room, where Bellino must either keep his promise to me or earn my contempt and resign himself to seeing me set off alone at dawn.

I take his hand and I make him sit down beside me before the fire, and I ask his two young sisters to leave us alone. They go at once.

"This business," I said, "will not take long if you are of my sex, and if you are of the other you will have only to spend the night with me. I will give you a hundred zecchini in the morning and we will leave together."

"You will leave alone, and you will be generous enough to forgive my weakness if I cannot keep my promise to you. I am a castrato, and I cannot bring myself either to let you see my shame or to expose myself to the loathsome consequences which convincing you of it may have."

"It will have none, for as soon as I have seen, or touched, I will myself beg you to go to bed in your own room; we will leave tomorrow the best of friends and there will be no more of this matter between us."

"No, my mind is made up: I cannot satisfy your curiosity."

At these words I am out of all patience, but I control myself and try gently to advance my hand to the place where I should find if I was right or wrong; but he uses his to stop mine from pursuing the investigation I was set on making.

"Take your hand away, my dear Bellino."

"No, absolutely not! For I see you are in a state which horrifies me. I knew it, and I shall never consent to such infamies. I will go and send my sisters to you."

I hold him back, and pretend to regain my calm; but suddenly, thinking I could take him unawares, I stretch out my arm to the bottom of his back, and my quick hand would have learned the truth from that direction if he had not parried the thrust by rising and blocking my hand, by which I was still holding on, with his, which he had been keeping over what he called his shame. It was at this moment that I saw he was a man, and believed that I saw it against his will. Astonished, angered, mortified, disgusted, I let him leave. I saw that Bellino was in truth a man; but a man to be scorned both for his degradation and for the shameful calm I observed in him at a moment when I ought not to have seen the most patent evidence of his insensibility.

A little later his sisters appeared, but I asked them to leave since I needed sleep. I told them to inform Bellino that he would leave with me and that he would no longer find me in the least curious. I fastened my door and went to bed, but very much dissatisfied, for despite the fact that what I had seen should have disillusioned me, I felt that it had not. But what more did I want? Alas! I thought about it and I could not imagine.

Next morning, after eating an excellent soup, I set off with him, and with my heart torn by the tears of his sisters and of their mother, who, mumbling paternosters and telling her beads, kept repeating "*Dio provvederà*"[12] over and over.

Belief in Eternal Providence on the part of most of those who live by practices forbidden by laws or religion is neither absurd nor feigned nor the fruit of hypocrisy; it is true, real, and, such as it is, pious, for its source is unimpeachable. Whatever ways it takes, it is always Providence which acts, and those who worship it regardless of everything else can only be good souls though guilty of sinning.

Pulchra Laverna
Da mihi fallere; da justo, sanctoque videri;
Noctem peccatis, et fraudibus objice nubem!

("Fair Laverna, let me deceive, let me appear just and good; cover my sins with darkness and my stealth with a cloud.")[13]

Such was the Latin which Roman thieves talked to their goddess in Horace's day, who, so a Jesuit told me, would not have known his language if he had said *justo sanctoque*.[14] There were ignorant men among the Jesuits too. Thieves laugh at grammar.

So now I was traveling with Bellino, who, believing that he had disillusioned me, might well hope that I would no longer be curious about him. But a quarter of an hour had not passed before he found that he was mistaken. I could not look into his eyes and not burn with love. I told him that since his eyes were a woman's and not a man's, I needed to convince myself by touch that what I had seen when he had run away was not a monstrous clitoris.

"It may be that," I said, "and I feel that I shall have no difficulty in forgiving you for such a defect, which in any case is merely a trifle; but if it is not a clitoris, I need to convince myself of it, which is a very easy matter. I no longer want to see; all I ask is to touch, and you may be sure that as soon as I am certain I will become as gentle as a dove, for once I discover that you are a man, I cannot possibly continue to love you. That is an abomination for which—God be praised!—I feel no inclination in myself. Your magnetism and, what is more, your breasts, which you abandoned to my eyes and my hands expecting that they would convince me I was mistaken, instead of doing so gave me an invincible impression which makes me still believe that you are a girl. Your build, your legs, your knees, your thighs, your hips, your buttocks are a perfect replica of the

Anadyomene,[15] which I have seen a hundred times. If after all that it is true that you are simply a castrato, permit me to believe that, knowing you look exactly like a girl, you hatched the cruel scheme of making me fall in love and then driving me mad by refusing me the proof which alone can restore me to sanity. An excellent physician, you have learned in the most diabolical of schools that the one way to make it impossible for a young man to be cured of an amorous passion to which he has succumbed is to aggravate it; but, my dear Bellino, you must admit that you cannot practice this tyranny unless you hate the person upon whom it is to produce such an effect; and, that being the case, I should use what reason I have left to hate you in the same measure, whether you are a girl or a boy. You must also be aware that your obstinate refusal to give me the certainty which I ask of you forces me to despise you as a castrato. The importance you attribute to the matter is childish and malicious. If you have human feelings, you cannot persist in your refusal, which, as the logical consequence of my reasoning, reduces me to the painful necessity of doubt. Such being my state of mind, you must finally realize that I cannot but resolve to use force, for if you are my enemy I must treat you as such without further scruples."

At the end of this too threatening harangue, to which he listened without once interrupting me, he answered only in the following few words:

"Consider that you are not my master, that I am in your hands on the strength of the promise which you sent me by Cecilia, and that you will be guilty of murder if you use force on me. Tell the postilion to stop; I will get out, and I will complain of your conduct to no one."

After this short answer, he melted into tears which reduced my poor soul to utter desolation. I almost believed that I was wrong—I say "almost," for if I had been sure of it I would have begged him to forgive me. I was unwilling to set myself up as the judge of my own cause. I withdrew into the bleakest possible silence, and found the strength of mind not to speak another word until halfway through the third post, which ended at Sinigaglia, where I intended to sup and spend the night. Before we reached there, things had to be settled. I thought there was still hope that I could make him see reason.

"We could," I said, "have parted at Rimini good friends, and that would have been the case if you had felt any friendship for me. At the price of a compliance which would have led to nothing, you could have cured me of my passion."

"It would not have cured you," answered Bellino, firmly, but with a sweetness which surprised me, "for you are in love with me whether I am a girl or a boy, and when you found that I am a boy, you would have continued to love me, and my refusals would have made you even more furious. Finding me still inexorably determined, you would have run into excesses which would later have made you shed useless tears."

"So you say, and think you are proving that your obstinacy is reasonable; but I have every right to contradict you. Convince me, and you will find me a good and loyal friend."

"You will be furious, I tell you."

"What has infuriated me is the way you deliberately displayed your charms, when, you must admit, you knew the effect they would have on me. You did not fear my amorous fury then; and do you expect me to believe that you fear it now, when all that I ask of you is to let me touch an object which cannot but fill me with disgust?"

"Ah! disgust! I am certain of the contrary. Here is my reasoning, and let it be the end of the matter. If I were a girl, I could not help loving you, and I know it. But since I am a boy, my duty is not to comply in the least with what you demand, for your passion, which is now only natural, would at once become monstrous. Your ardent nature would become the enemy of your reason, and your reason itself would soon surrender, to the point of becoming the accomplice of your frenzy, thus seconding your nature. This inflammatory revelation which you desire, which you do not fear, which you demand of me, would leave you with no control over yourself. Your sight and your touch, seeking what they cannot find, would want to avenge themselves on what they found, and the most loathsome thing that can happen between men would happen between you and me. How can you, with your intelligence, cozen yourself into thinking that when you found me a man you would cease to love me? Do you believe that after your discovery what you call my charms, which you say have made you fall in love, would vanish? No, they might even grow more powerful, and then your ardor, become merely animal, would employ every means your amorous mind could conjure up to calm itself. You would manage to persuade yourself that you could change me into a woman, or, imagining that you could become a woman yourself, you would want me to treat you as such. Led astray by your passion, your reason would invent sophism after sophism. You would say that your love for me, a man, is more reasonable than it would be if I were a girl, for you would find the source of it in the purest friendship, and you would not fail to cite me examples of such anomalies. Led astray yourself by the specious brilliance of your arguments, you would become a torrent which no dam could hold back, and I should be at a loss for words to demolish your specious reasoning, and lack the strength to repulse your furious efforts. You would finally threaten me with death, if I denied you entrance to an inviolable temple, whose gate wise nature made to open only outward. It would be a loathsome profanation, which could not be accomplished without my consent, and you would find me ready to die before I would give it."

"Nothing of the sort would happen," I answered, rather shaken by his cogent reasoning, "and you exaggerate. Yet I feel obliged to tell you, if only as a matter of form, that even if all you say should happen, it seems to me there would be less harm in allowing nature an aberration of this kind, which philosophy may well consider a mere folly without consequences, than to follow a course which will make an incurable disease of a sickness of the mind which reason would render only momentary."

Thus does the poor philosopher reason when he undertakes to reason at moments when a tumultuous passion leads the divine faculties of his soul astray. To reason rightly one must be neither in love nor in anger; for those two passions reduce us to the level of animals; and unfortunately we are never so much inclined to reason as when we are agitated by one or the other of them.

Having reached Sinigaglia in comparative calm, and the night being dark, we stopped at the posthouse inn. After having our trunks untied and brought to a good room I ordered supper. As there was only one bed I asked Bellino in a perfectly calm voice if he wished to have a fire lighted for him in another room. He surprised me by gently answering that he had no objection to sleeping in my bed.

My reader can easily imagine the astonishment I felt at this answer, which I could never have expected and which I greatly needed to purge my mind of all the dark humor which was troubling it. I saw that I had come to the dénouement of the play, and I was afraid to congratulate myself, for I could not foresee if it would be pleasant or tragic. The one thing I was sure of was that in bed he would not escape me, even if he were insolent enough to refuse to undress. Satisfied that I would be victorious, I was determined to win a second victory by leaving him alone if I found he was a man, though I did not believe it. If I found him a girl, I had no doubt that

I would be gratified by all the compliance which he ought to show, if only in reparation.

We sat down to supper; and in his words, his manner, the expression of his eyes, his smiles, he seemed to me to have become a different person.

Feeling relieved of a great burden, I got through supper more quickly than usual and we rose from the table. After sending for a night lamp, Bellino fastened the door, undressed, and got into bed. I had done the same without uttering a word. And so we were in bed together.

CHAPTER II

Bellino unmasks; his story. I am arrested.
My involuntary flight. My return to Rimini
and my arrival in Bologna.

I had scarcely got into the bed before I was overcome to see him moving toward me. I clasp him to me, I see that he is fired by the same transport. The exordium of our dialogue was a deluge of mingling kisses. His arms were first to slip down from my back to my loins. I stretch mine still lower, it is revelation enough that I am happy, I sense it, I feel it, I am convinced of it. I am right, I am vindicated, I cannot doubt it, I do not want to know how, I fear that if I speak I shall no longer be happy, or be happy as I would not wish to be, and I give myself, body and soul, to the joy which flooded my entire being and which I saw was shared. The excess of my bliss seizes all my senses with such force that it reaches the degree at which nature, drowning in the highest of all pleasures, is exhausted. For the space of a minute I remain motionless in the act of mentally contemplating and worshiping my own apotheosis.

Sight and touch, which I had thought would be the leading actors in this drama, play only secondary roles. My eyes ask no greater bliss than to remain fixed on the face of the being who held them spellbound, and my sense of touch, concentrated in my fingertips, fears to move elsewhere since it cannot imagine that it could find anything more. I should have accused nature of the most despicable cowardice if, without my permission, it had dared to leave the place of which I could feel I was in possession.

Scarcely two minutes had passed before, without breaking our eloquent silence, we set to work together to give each other fresh assurances of the reality of our mutual happiness—Bellino by assuring me of it every quarter of an hour by the sweetest moans; I by refusing to reach the end of my course again. I have all my life been dominated by the fear that my steed would flinch from beginning another race; and I never found this restraint painful, for the visible pleasure which I gave always made up four fifths of mine. For this reason nature must abhor old age, which can itself attain to pleasure, but can never give it. Youth shuns its presence, for youth's deadly enemy is age, sad, weak, deformed, hideous age, which drives it into lonely seclusion at last, and always too soon.

We finally broke off. We needed an interval. We were not exhausted; but our senses demanded that our minds be calm so that they could return to their proper seats.

Bellino, the first to break the silence, asked me if I had found him a good mistress.

"Mistress? Then you admit you are a woman? Tell me, tigress, if it is true that you loved me, how could you put off your happiness, and mine, for so long? But is it really true that you belong to the bewitching sex of which I believe I have found you to be?"

"You are the master now. Make certain."

"Yes. I need to convince myself. Good God! what has become of the monstrous clitoris I saw yesterday?"

After a complete conviction, which was followed by a long outpouring of gratitude, the fascinating creature told me her story as follows:

"My name is Teresa. The poor daughter of an employee at the Institute at Bologna,[1] I made the acquaintance of the celebrated castrato singer Salimbeni,[2] who lodged in our house. I was twelve years old and had a good voice. Salimbeni was handsome; I was delighted to find that I pleased him, and to have him praise me, and eager to learn music from him and to play the harpsichord. Within a year I had acquired a fairly good grounding and was able to accompany myself in an air, imitating the *fioriture* of the great master, whom the Elector of Saxony, the King of Poland,[3] had summoned to serve him. His reward was such as his affection made him demand of me; I did not feel ashamed to grant it to him, for I worshiped him. Men like yourself are certainly to be preferred to men like my first lover; but Salimbeni was an exception. His good looks, his intelligence, his manners, his talent, and the rare qualities of his heart and soul made him preferable to all the whole men I had known until that time. Modesty and discretion were his favorite virtues, and he was rich and generous. He could never have found a woman to resist him; but I never heard him boast of conquering any woman. In short, his mutilation made him a monster, as it could not but do, but a monster of adorable qualities. I know that when I gave myself to him he made me happy; but he did so much that I can only believe I made him happy too.

"Salimbeni had a protégé whom he was boarding in the house of a music teacher in Rimini, a boy of my own age whom his dying father had had castrated to preserve his voice, so that he could turn it to profit for the benefit of the numerous family he was leaving behind, by appearing on the stage. The boy was named Bellino and was the son of the good woman whose acquaintance you just made at Ancona and whom everyone believes to be my mother.

"A year after I first came to know this being so favored by Heaven, it was he himself who told me the unhappy news that he must leave me to go to Rome. I was in despair, even though he assured me that I would soon see him again. He left my father the charge and the means to continue the cultivation of my talent; but within a few days a malignant fever carried him off; and I was left an orphan. After that Salimbeni could no longer resist my tears. He decided to take me with him as far as Rimini and leave me to board with the same music teacher in whose house he was keeping the young castrato, the brother of Cecilia and Marina. We left Bologna at midnight. No one knew that he was taking me with him—which was easy enough, for I knew no one, and no one took any interest in me, except my dear Salimbeni.

"As soon as we reached Rimini he left me at the inn and himself went to see the music teacher and make all the necessary arrangements with him for me. But half an hour later he is back at the inn, lost in thought. Bellino had died the day before our arrival. Thinking of the grief his mother would feel when he wrote her the news, it occurs to him to take me back to Bologna under the name of the Bellino who had just died and put me to board with his mother, who, being poor, would find it to her advantage to keep the secret. 'I would give her,' he said, 'sufficient means to have you complete your musical studies, and four years from now I will bring you to Dresden, not as a girl but as a castrato. We will live there together, and no one can say anything against it. You will make me happy until I die. All that is necessary is to make everyone believe you are Bellino, which you will find easy enough, since no one knows you. Only Bellino's mother will know the truth. Her children will not suspect that you are not their brother, for they were infants when I sent him to Rimini. If you love me, you must renounce your sex and even forget it completely. You must now take the name of Bellino and leave with me at once for Bologna. Within two hours you will be dressed as a boy; all you need do is to keep anyone from knowing that you are a girl. You will sleep alone; you will keep out of sight when you dress; and when in a year or two your breasts begin to develop it will be of no consequence, for having too much bosom is a defect in which all we castrati share. In addition, before I leave you I will give you a little apparatus and teach you how to adjust it so well to the place which shows the difference of sex that the deceit will pass unnoticed if it ever happens that you have to undergo an examination. If you like my plan, you will enable me to live in Dresden with you without giving the Queen,[4] who is very devout, any occasion to object. Tell me if you consent.'

"He could be sure that I would. I could have no greater pleasure than to do whatever he wished. He had me dressed as a boy, he made me leave all my girls' clothes behind, and after ordering his servant to wait for him in Rimini, he took me to Bologna. We arrive there at nightfall, he leaves me at the inn, and goes at once to see Bellino's mother. He explains his plan to her, she assents to it, and it consoles her for the death of her son. He brings her back to the inn with him, she calls me her son, I address her as 'Mother'; Salimbeni goes off, telling us to wait. He comes back an hour later and takes from his pocket the apparatus which in case of necessity would make me pass as a man. You have seen it. It is a sort of long, soft gut, as thick as one's thumb, white and with a very smooth surface. I had to laugh to myself this morning when you called it a clitoris. It was attached to the center of an oval piece of very fine transparent hide, which was five or six inches long and two inches wide. When this is fixed with gum tragacanth to the place where sex can be distinguished, it obliterates the female organ. He dissolves the gum, tries the apparatus on me in the presence of my new mother, and I find that I have become like my dear lover. I should really have laughed if the imminent departure of the person I adored had not pierced my heart. I was left more dead than alive, with a presentiment that I should never see him again. People laugh at presentiments, and with good reason, for not everyone can hear the voice of his heart; but mine did not deceive me. Salimbeni died still a young man in the Tyrol last year,[5] with the resignation of a philosopher. I was left under the necessity of turning my talent to account. My mother thought it a good plan to continue passing me off as a man, for she hoped she could send me to Rome to sing. In the meanwhile she accepted an offer from the theater in Ancona, where she also put Petronio to dance as a girl.

"After Salimbeni, you are the only man in whose arms Teresa has truly sacrificed to perfect love; and you have but to ask and I will from this day on abandon the name of Bellino, which I loathe since Salimbeni's death and which is beginning to cause me difficulties for which I have no patience. I have appeared in only two theaters, and to be admitted to both of them I had to submit to the same degrading examination, for wherever I go people think I look so much like a girl that they will not believe I am a man until they have been convinced. Until now I have had to deal only with old priests, who were innocently satisfied with having seen, and then certified me to the bishop; but I have continually to defend myself against two kinds of people, who assail me to obtain illicit and loathsome favors. Those who, like you, fall in love with me and so cannot believe that I am a man, insist upon my showing them the truth; and that I cannot bring myself to do for fear they will want to convince themselves by touch as well; in such a case I am afraid not only that they will strip off my mask but that, becoming curious, they will want to use the apparatus to satisfy monstrous desires which may come to them. But the wretches who persecute me beyond endurance are those who declare their monstrous love to me as the castrato I pretend to be. I fear, my dear one, that I will stab one of them. Alas, my angel! Rescue me from my shame. Take me with you. I do not ask to become your wife, I will only be your loving mistress, as I would have been to Salimbeni; my heart is pure, I know that my nature is such that I can live faithfully with my lover. Do not forsake me. The affection you have inspired in me is true love; what Salimbeni inspired in me was the fondness of innocence. I believe I did not become truly a woman until I tasted the perfect pleasure of love in your arms."

Moved to tears, I wiped hers away and promised her in all sincerity that she should share my fate. Infinitely affected though I was by the extraordinary story she had told me, in which I could see nothing but truth, I yet could not convince myself that I had awakened a genuine love in her during my stay in Ancona. "How could you bear, if you loved me," I said, "to let me suffer so greatly and to give myself to your sisters?"

"Alas, my dear! Consider our great poverty, and how very hard it would have been for me to disclose myself. I loved you; but could I be sure that the liking you showed for me was not a passing fancy? When I saw you change so readily from Cecilia to Marina, I thought that you would treat me in the same way as soon as you had satisfied your desires. But I could no longer doubt of your fickle nature, and of the little importance you attached to the happiness of love, when I saw what you did with that Greek slave girl on the Turkish ship, without my presence troubling you in the least. It would have troubled you if you had loved me. I was afraid that you would scorn me afterward, and God alone knows how I suffered! You insulted me, my dear one, in a hundred different ways, but I pleaded your cause. I saw your anger and your determination to be revenged. Did you not threaten me today in the carriage? I confess that you frightened me; but do not go thinking that it was my fear which decided me to satisfy your desire. No, my dear—I had made up my mind to give myself to you as soon as you took me away from Ancona, even from the moment when I sent Cecilia to ask you if you would take me to Rimini."

"Break your engagement in Rimini, and let us go on. We will stay in Bologna only three days, you shall come to Venice with me and, dressed in the clothing of your real sex and under another name, I defy the impresario of the opera at Rimini to find you."

"I agree. Your will shall always be mine. Salimbeni is dead. I am my own mistress, and I give myself to you; you shall have my heart, and I hope that I shall be able to keep yours."

"Please let me see you once again with the strange device which Salimbeni gave you."

"At once."

She gets out of bed, pours water into a glass, opens her trunk, takes out her apparatus and her gums, dissolves them, and fits on the mask. I see something unbelievable. A charming girl, who looked it in every part of her body, and who, with this extraordinary attachment, seemed to me even more interesting, for the white pendant offered no obstruction to the well of her sex. I told her that she had been wise not to let me touch it, for it would have intoxicated me and made me become what I was not, unless she had instantly calmed me by revealing the truth. I wanted to convince her that I was not lying, and our skirmish was comical. We fell asleep afterwards and did not wake until very late.

Struck by all that I had heard from the girl's lips, by her beauty, her talent, the innocence of her soul, her feelings, and her misfortunes, the most cruel of which was certainly the false role she had been obliged to play, for it exposed her to humiliation and infamy, I determined to make her the partner of my fate, or myself the partner of hers, for we were very nearly in the same situation.

Thinking further, I saw that now that I was resolved to make her mine, and to give myself to her, I ought to set the seal of marriage on our union. According to the notions I then held, this should only increase our affection, our mutual esteem, and that of society at

212

large, which could never have considered our union legitimate or accept it as such unless it was validated by the civil law. Her talent assured me that we should never lack the necessaries of life, nor was I without hope of mine, though I did not know either in what direction or how I was to turn it to advantage. Our mutual love would have been not only impaired but reduced to nothing if the idea of living at her expense could have humiliated me, or if she could have grown proud, begun to domineer over me, and changed the nature of her feeling because, instead of seeing me as her benefactor, she had come to regard herself as my benefactress. If Teresa had a soul capable of such baseness, she deserved my utmost contempt. This I must know, I must sound her out, I must submit her to a test which would reveal her soul to me completely. With this idea in mind, I addressed her as follows:

"My dear Teresa, all that you have told me makes me sure that you love me, and your own certainty that you have become the mistress of my heart has made me so completely in love with you that I feel ready to do anything to convince you that you have not made a mistake. I must show you that I am worthy of a trust of which I know none higher, by treating you with a sincerity equal to your own. Our hearts, that is, must be placed in exactly the same position toward each other. I know you now, but you do not know me. You tell me it is all the same to you, and your trustfulness is proof of the most perfect love; but it sets me too far below you at the very moment when you believe you have made yourself even more adorable by setting me above you. You ask to know nothing, you ask only to be mine, you aspire to nothing but to possess my heart. It is noble, my beautiful Teresa, but it humiliates me. You have confided your secrets to me, I must confide mine to you. Promise me that when you have learned all, you will tell me sincerely if anything has changed in your soul."

"I swear it. I will hide nothing from you; but do not be so cruel as to tell me things that are not true. I warn you that they will accomplish nothing if you expect them to show you that I am less worthy of your love, but they will lower you a little in my soul. I should not want to find you capable of trickery. Trust in me as I trust in you. Tell me the plain truth."

"Here it is. You assume that I am rich; I am not. I shall have nothing once I have emptied my purse. You perhaps suppose that I am a man of high birth, and I am of a rank either lower than your own or equal to it. I have no talent which can earn money, no employment, no reason to be sure that I shall have anything to eat a few months hence. I have neither relatives nor friends nor rightful claims nor any settled plan. In short, all that I have is youth, health, courage, a modicum of intelligence, a sense of honor and of decency, with a little reading and the bare beginnings of a career in literature. My great treasure is that I am my own master, that I am not dependent upon anyone, and that I am not afraid of misfortunes. My nature tends toward extravagance. Such is the man I am. Now answer me, my beautiful Teresa."

"To begin with, I want you to know that I am sure that all you have told me is pure truth, and that nothing in your account surprised me except the noble courage with which you gave it to me. Know, too, that there were times in Ancona when I thought you were such as you have just described yourself to be, and that far from being frightened off, I hoped that I was not mistaken, for if I was not I had better reason to hope I might win you. But to be brief. Since it is true that you are poor, that you have nothing to rely on, and that you are even no good at economizing, permit me to tell you that all this makes me very glad, for if you love me you naturally cannot scorn the present I am about to give you. The present is the person you love. I give myself to you; I am yours; I will take care of you. Hereafter think of nothing but loving me; but it must be me alone. From this moment I am Bellino no longer. Let us go to Venice, and my talent will earn our living; and if you do not want to go to Venice, let us go wherever you please."

"I must go to Constantinople."

"Let us go there. If you are afraid you will lose me because I will be inconstant, marry me and then your right over me will be legal. I do not say that I will love you better as my husband; but it will please me to bear the flattering title of your wife, and we will laugh at it."

"Very well. Day after tomorrow at the latest, I will marry you in Bologna; for I want to make you mine by every possible tie."

"Now I am happy. We have nothing to do in Rimini. We will leave tomorrow morning. There is no use in our getting up. Let us eat in bed, and then make love."

"An excellent idea."

After spending a second night in pleasure and content, we set off at dawn; and after traveling for four hours we thought it time to eat breakfast. We were at Pesaro.[6] Just as we were entering the carriage again to continue our journey, up comes a noncommissioned officer

with two fusiliers and asks our names and then for our passports.
Bellino hands him hers; I look for mine and cannot find it. I had put
it with my letters from the Cardinal and the Cavaliere da Lezze; I
find the letters and cannot find the passport; all my searching is in
vain. The corporal makes off, after ordering the postilion to wait. A
half hour later he comes back and hands Bellino his passport, telling
him that he is free to leave; but as for me, he has been ordered to
take me to the commandant. The commandant asks me why I have
no passport.

"Because I have lost it."

"No one loses a passport."

"Indeed they do, and the proof is that I have lost mine."

"You cannot go farther."

"I came here from Rome, and I am on my way to Constantinople to deliver a letter from Cardinal Acquaviva. Here is his
letter, sealed with his arms."

"I will have you taken to Signor de Gages."

I was led into the presence of the famous General, who was
standing surrounded by his staff. After telling him what I had told
the commandant, I asked him to let me continue my journey.

"The only favor I can do you is to hold you under arrest here
until a new passport reaches you from Rome, in the same name
under which you registered here. Only a fool loses a passport, and
the Cardinal will learn not to entrust his errands to fools."

He then ordered that I be put under arrest at the principal
guardpost, which was outside the city and was called the Santa
Maria,[7] after I had written to Rome for a new passport. So I was
taken back to the posthouse, where I wrote to the Cardinal telling
him of my misfortune and begging him to send me the passport
without delay, and sent my letter off by courier. I asked him to send
the passport directly to the military secretariat. After that I embraced
Bellino-Teresa, whom this untimely mishap had plunged in gloom.
I told her to go to Rimini and wait for me there, and I made her
accept a hundred zecchini.

She wanted to stay in Pesaro; but I would not let her. I had my
trunk untied and, after watching her leave, I allowed myself to be
taken to the guardpost. These are moments when every optimist
doubts his theory; but a stoicism which it is not difficult to assume
has the power to blunt their influence for evil. What distressed me
greatly was the anguish of Teresa, who, seeing me thus torn from her
arms in the first moment of our union, almost choked with trying to

hold back her tears. She would not have left me if I had not convinced her she would see me again at Rimini within ten days. She was also well aware that she should not remain at Pesaro.

At Santa Maria the officer put me in the guardhouse, where I sat down on my trunk. He was an accursed Catalan, who did not even honor me with an answer when I told him that I had money, that I wanted a bed and a servant to attend to all my wants. I had to spend the night on a heap of straw, among Catalan soldiers, and without having eaten anything. It was the second night I spent in this fashion after delicious ones. My Genius diverted himself by treating me in this fashion in order to give me the pleasure of making comparisons. It is a harsh school; but its effect is certain, especially on men who have something of the stockfish[8] in their nature.

To close the lips of a philosopher who presumes to tell you that in the life of men the sum of pains is greater than the sum of pleasures, ask him if he would want a life in which there was neither pain nor pleasure. He will not answer you, or he will tergiversate; for if he says he would not, he likes life, and if he likes it, he admits that it is pleasant, which it could not be if it were painful; and if he says he would, he proves himself a fool, for then he must conceive of pleasure as indifference.

When we suffer, we gain the pleasure of hoping for the end of our suffering; and we are never wrong, for we have at least the resource of sleep, in which good dreams console and soothe us; and when we are happy, the thought that our happiness will be followed by misery never comes to trouble us. Pleasure, then, when it is present, is always pure; pain is always tempered.

You are twenty years old. The regent of the universe comes to you and says: "I give you thirty years of life; fifteen of them will be painful and fifteen delicious. Each fifteen will be consecutive. Choose. Do you wish to begin with the painful years or with the delicious years?"

Admit, reader, whoever you may be, that you would answer: "God in Heaven, I will begin with the fifteen unhappy years. In the certain expectation of the fifteen delicious years, I am sure that I shall have the strength to make light of my sufferings."

You see, my dear reader, the conclusion which follows from these considerations. Believe me, the wise man can never be wholly unhappy. Indeed he is always happy, says my master Horace, *nisi quum pituita molesta est* ("except when phlegm troubles him").[9]

But what man always has catarrh?

The fact is that during that accursed night at Santa Maria in Pesaro, I lost little and gained much, for, so far as Teresa was concerned, since I was sure I should be with her again in ten days, it meant nothing. What I gained was some schooling in the life of man. I gained a system against stupidity. Foresight. It is a hundred to one that a young man who has lost his purse on one occasion and his passport on another will never lose either again. And in fact neither of these misfortunes ever again befell me. They would have befallen me if I had not always been afraid that they would befall me. A fool is never afraid.

When the guard was changed the next morning, I was turned over to a pleasant-looking officer. He was French. I have always liked Frenchmen, even as I have an aversion to Spaniards. Yet I have often been gulled by Frenchmen, never by Spaniards. We should not trust our likes and dislikes.

"By what chance, Signor Abate," the officer asked me, "have I the honor to have you in my custody?"

Such language allays apprehension at once. I tell him the whole story and after hearing it to the end, he says it is very "amusing." I really found nothing "amusing" in my wretched adventure; but a man who found it "amusing" was one whom I could not dislike. He immediately put a soldier at my service who, for a price, found me a bed, chairs, a table, and everything I needed. The officer ordered my bed put in his own room.

After dinner, to which he invited me, he suggested a game of piquet,[10] and by evening I had lost three or four ducati; but he warned me that my skill was not equal to his, and still less to that of the officer who would take over guard duty the next day. He therefore advised me not to play with him, and I followed his advice. He also told me that he was having guests for supper, and that there would be a bank at faro;[11] he added that the banker would be a man against whom I ought not to play. He said he was a "Greek."[12] The players arrived, the play went on all night, the punters lost and berated the banker, who let them talk and pocketed the money, after giving his share to my friend the officer, who had put money in the bank. The banker was called Don Bepe il cadetto;[13] recognizing from his speech that he was a Neapolitan, I asked the officer why he had told me he was a "Greek." He thereupon explained the meaning of the word to me, and the lesson he read me on the subject proved useful to me afterwards.

For the next five or six days nothing happened to me. On the sixth, the same French officer who had treated me so well reappeared. When he saw me he said that he was sincerely glad to find me still there; I accepted the compliment for what it was worth. Toward evening the same players arrived; and the same Don Bepe, after winning, was treated to the epithet "sharper" and a blow from a cane, which he intrepidly pretended not to notice. Nine years later I saw him in Vienna, become a captain in the service of the Empress Maria Theresa under the name of Afflisio. Ten years after that I found him a colonel; still later I found him a millionaire, and finally, thirteen or fourteen years ago, sentenced to the galleys. He was handsome but, oddly enough, despite his good features he had the look of a gallows bird. I have seen others of the same cast of countenance—Cagliostro,[14] for example, and another man who has not yet been sent to the galleys but who will certainly not escape it, for *nolentem trahit* ("he who is unwilling is dragged").[15] If my reader is curious, I will whisper the rest into his ear.

In nine or ten days, during which I waited for my passport, which must arrive soon, the whole army came to know me and like me. I went walking even out of sight of the sentinel; no one had any fear that I would try to escape, and rightly, for I should have been a fool to think of it; but now comes one of the strangest things that has happened to me in all my life.

Walking at six o'clock in the morning a hundred paces from the guardhouse, I see an officer dismount from his horse, drop the reins on its neck, and go off somewhere. Meditating on how quietly the horse was standing there, like a trusty servant his master had told to wait for him, I approach and, for no particular reason, I pick up the reins, put my foot in the stirrup, and mount. It was the first time in my life I had ever been on the back of a horse. I do not know if I touched it with my cane or with my heels; the horse starts off like a thunderbolt, and at full gallop, when it feels my heels, with which I was pressing against it only to keep from falling off, my right foot even being out of the stirrup. The sentry at the last advanced post orders me to halt; it was an order which I was incapable of obeying. The horse keeps on. I hear musketshots, which miss me. At the first advanced post of the Austrians, my horse is stopped, and I thank God that I can dismount. The officer of hussars asks me where I am going in such a hurry, and without thinking, I answer that I cannot tell anyone except Prince Lobkowitz,[16] who was in command of the army and was at Rimini. The officer thereupon orders two hussars to mount their horses, and after mounting me on another, they take me at full gallop to Rimini and present me to the officer at the principal guardpost, who at once has me taken to the Prince.

He was alone, I tell him the unvarnished truth, at which he laughs and says that my story is none too plausible. He says that he ought to put me under arrest, but that he was willing to spare me that vexation. He summons an adjutant and orders him to accompany me outside the Porta Cesena. Then, turning to me, he says in the officer's presence that from there I could go wherever I pleased; but he tells me to take good care not to come back into his army again without a passport, for he would give me a bad time. I ask him if I may have back my horse. He answers that the horse does not belong to me.

I was sorry I had not asked him to send me back to the Spanish army.

The officer who was to take me out of the city asked me, as we passed a coffeehouse, if I would like to drink a cup of chocolate, and we went in. I see Petronio and, when the officer is speaking to someone, I tell him to pretend not to know me and at the same time ask him where he was lodging, which he tells me. When we have drunk our chocolate, the officer pays, we set off, and as we ride along he tells me his name, I tell him mine, and the story of the strange chance which accounted for my being in Rimini. He asks me if I had stopped a few days in Ancona, I answer yes, and I see him smile. He tells me that I can obtain a passport in Bologna, return to Rimini and Pesaro without any fear, and recover my trunk by paying the value of the horse to the officer from whom I had taken it. So conversing, we arrived outside the gate, and he wished me a good journey.

I am free again, with money and jewels, but without my trunk. Teresa was in Rimini, and I was forbidden to return there. I decide to hurry on to Bologna, obtain a passport, and return to the Spanish army, where I was sure that the passport from Rome would come. I could not bring myself either to abandon my trunk or to do without Teresa until the end of her engagement with the impresario of the opera at Rimini.

It was raining; I had on silk stockings, I needed a carriage. I stop under the door of a chapel to wait for the rain to end. I turn my handsome redingote inside out so as not to be recognized as an abate. I ask a peasant if he had a conveyance to take me to Cesena, and he answers that he has one half an hour's walk away. I tell him to go and fetch it, assuring him that I would wait; but then this befell me. Some forty loaded mules pass by, on their way to Rimini. It was still raining. I approach one of the mules, put my hand on its neck, really with no particular intention, and slowly keeping pace with the mule, I re-enter the city of Rimini, and since I appear to be a muleteer no one says a word to me; even the muleteers themselves may not have noticed me. In Rimini I gave two baiocchi to the first urchin I saw to show me the way to the house where Teresa was lodging. With my hair under a nightcap, my hat brim pulled down, my fine cane hidden under my reversed redingote, I looked like a nobody. As soon as I was safely in the house, I asked a maid where Bellino's mother was to be found; she takes me to her room, and I see Bellino, but dressed as a girl. She was there with the whole family. Petronio had forewarned them. After telling them the whole brief story, I made them understand the necessity for secrecy, and they each swore that no one should learn from him that I was there; but Teresa was in despair to find me in such great danger, and despite her love and her joy at seeing me again she reproves me for what I have done. She says that I absolutely must find a way to leave for Bologna and come back with a passport, as Signor Weiss[17] had advised me to do. She said that she knew him, that he was a very decent sort, and that he came to visit her every evening, and that consequently I must hide. We had time to think about it. It was only eight o'clock. I promised her that I would leave, and calmed her by telling her that I would find a way to do it without being seen by anyone. Meanwhile Petronio went to find out if any muleteers were leaving. It would be easy for me to go as I had come.

When Teresa had taken me to her room she told me that even before entering Rimini she had met the opera impresario, who immediately took her to the apartment she was to occupy with her family. Being alone with him there, she had told him that, as she was really a girl, she no longer wished to appear as a castrato, and that he would thenceforth see her only in the dress of her sex. The impresario had congratulated her. Rimini belonged to a different legateship,[18] where it was not forbidden, as it was in Ancona, for women to appear on the stage. She ended by saying that, as she was only engaged for twenty performances, to begin after Easter, she would be free at the beginning of May and so, if I could not stay in Rimini, she would come and join me wherever I wished at the end of her engagement. I answered that as soon as I had obtained a passport and so would have nothing to fear in Rimini, nothing would prevent me from spending the six weeks there with her. Knowing that Baron Weiss visited her, I asked her if it was she who had told him that I had spent three days in Ancona, and she said that she had and had even told him that I had been arrested for not having a passport. I then understood why he had smiled.

After this necessary conversation, I received the compliments of the mother and of my little wives, whom I thought less gay and less unreserved because they felt certain that Bellino, who was no longer a castrato or their brother, must have pre-empted me in the character of Teresa. They were not mistaken, and I was careful not to give them even a single kiss. I listened patiently to all the mother's lamentations, who insisted that by admitting that she was a girl Teresa had thrown away her hope of fortune, since she would have had a thousand zecchini for the coming Carnival at Rome. I said that she would have been unmasked at Rome and put in some wretched convent for the rest of her life.

Despite my state of agitation and the dangerous situation I was in, I spent the whole day alone with my dear Teresa, with whom I felt I was more in love every minute. She freed herself from my arms at eight o'clock in the evening, having heard someone arrive, and left me in the dark. I saw Baron Weiss come in and Teresa give him her hand to kiss in the style of a princess. The first news he gave her was mine; she pretended to be glad, and listened with apparent indifference when he told her he had advised me to come back to Rimini with a passport. He spent an hour with her, and I thought her adorable in everything she did, for she maintained a behavior which could not possibly kindle the least spark of jealousy in my soul. It was Marina who lit him downstairs about ten o'clock, and Teresa at once returned to my arms. We had a pleasant supper and were about to go to bed, when Petronio told us that six muleteers were leaving for Cesena with thirty mules two hours before dawn, and that he was sure if I went to the stable only a quarter of an hour before they left and drank with them, I could easily leave in their company without even trying to keep them in the dark. I felt sure he was right and instantly resolved to follow his advice, and he promised to wake me at two in the morning. He did not have to wake me. I dressed quickly and set off with Petronio, leaving my dear Teresa sure that I adored her and would be faithful to her, but uneasy about my getting away from Rimini. She wanted to give me back the sixty zecchini she had left. I kissed her and asked her what she would think of me if I took them.

When I told a muleteer, with whom I drank, that I wanted to ride one of his mules as far as Savignano, he replied that I was at liberty to do so, but that it would be best if I did not mount until I was outside of the city and had gone through the gate on foot, as if I were one of them.

This was just what I wanted. Petronio went with me as far as the gate, where I gave him a handsome token of my gratitude. My departure from Rimini went off as well as my entrance. I left the muleteers at Savignano, where, after sleeping for four hours, I took the post to Bologna and put up at a wretched inn.

In that city it took me only a day to discover that I could not possibly obtain a passport. I was told that I did not need one, and rightly; but I knew that I did need one. I decided to write to the French officer who had treated me so courteously on the second day I was under arrest, asking him to inquire at the military secretariat if my passport had arrived and, if it had, to send it to me and, meanwhile, to find out who was the owner of the horse I had absconded with, for I thought it only right that I should pay him for it. In any case, I resolved to wait for Teresa in Bologna, and I informed her of my decision the same day, begging her never to leave me without letters from her.

What I decided to do the same day after posting these two letters, the reader will see.

CHAPTER III

I lay aside my clerical garb and put on a
uniform. Teresa leaves for Naples, and I go to
Venice, where I enter my country's service.
I sail for Corfu and go ashore at Orsara to take
a walk.

At Bologna, to escape observation, I put up at an inn which no one frequented. After writing my letters and resolving to wait for Teresa there, I bought some shirts and, being far from certain that my trunk would be returned, I considered getting some clothes. Reflecting that there was now little likelihood of my achieving fortune in my ecclesiastical career, I decided to dress as a soldier in a uniform of my own invention, since I was certain that I would not be called upon to explain my business to anyone. Coming from two armies in which I had seen no dress but a soldier's respected, I wished to inspire the same respect. Then, too, I was very well pleased with the idea of returning to my country under the ensign of honor, where I had been not a little ill-treated under that of religion.

I inquire for a good tailor; I am sent one named Morte.[1] I explain to him of what cut and what colors I want my uniform made, he takes my measurements, he gives me samples of cloth, I choose, and no later than the next morning he brings me everything I need to impersonate a follower of Mars. I bought a long sword, and with my handsome cane in hand, a trim hat with a black cockade, with my hair cut in side whiskers and a long false pigtail, I set forth to impress the whole city. I at once took lodging at the Albergo al Pellegrino.[2] I have never had a pleasure in this kind equal to that which I felt when I saw myself in a mirror dressed as I now was. I decided I had been born to be a soldier, I thought I was astonishing. Certain that no one would recognize me, I relished the stories which would be invented about me when I made my appearance at the most frequented coffeehouse in the city.

My uniform was white, with a blue vest, a shoulder knot of silver and gold, and a sword knot to match. Very well pleased with my appearance, I go to the principal coffeehouse, where I take chocolate and try to read the gazette, but my thoughts were elsewhere. I was delighted to find myself the center of attention, though

I pretended to be unaware of it. I aroused such curiosity that everyone was whispering into his neighbor's ear. One brazen fellow, hoping to draw me into conversation, ventured to speak to me; but my monosyllabic answer discouraged even the most hardened questioners in the coffeehouse. After strolling for a considerable time under the finest of the arcades,[3] I went to my inn and dined alone.

When I had finished, the innkeeper came up with a book to register my name.

"Casanova."

"Your profession?"

"Officer."

"In what service?"

"None."

"Your country?"

"Venice."

"Where have you come from?"

"That is none of your business."

I am well satisfied with my answers. I see that the innkeeper has come to ask me all these questions only at the instigation of some busybody, for I knew that Bologna was a city in which people lived in perfect freedom.

The next morning I went to the banker Orsi to draw money on my bill of exchange. I took a hundred zecchini and a bill for six hundred on Venice. Then I went for a walk on La Montagnola.[4] Two days later, just as I was drinking coffee after dinner, a servant announces the banker Orsi. Surprised that he should call on me, I have him shown in, and I see that he is accompanied by Monsignor Cornaro,[5] whom I pretend not to know. After saying that he has come to offer me money on my drafts, he introduces the prelate to me. I rise, saying that I am delighted to make his acquaintance. He tells me that we had already met in Venice and in Rome; with an injured air, I answer that he was certainly mistaken. The prelate looks grave and, instead of persisting, begs my pardon, the more so since he thought he knew the reason for my reserve. After taking coffee he leaves, inviting me to come and breakfast with him the following morning.

Firmly resolved to continue denying my identity, I went. I did not want to admit that I was the person whom Monsignor Cornaro knew, because of the bogus officer's rank I had bestowed on myself. Unschooled in imposture as I was, I did not know that in Bologna I had nothing to fear.

The prelate, who at that time was only an apostolic protonotary, said, as he drank chocolate with me, that I might have very good reasons for my reserve, but that I was mistaken in not trusting him, since the affair in question did me honor. Upon my answering that I did not know to what affair he was referring, he asked me to read an article in the gazette published in Pesaro, which he had before him: "Signor Casanova, an officer in the Queen's Regiment, has deserted after killing his captain in a duel. The circumstances of the duel are not known; it is only known that the aforesaid officer took the road to Rimini, riding the horse of the other officer, who was left dead on the field."

Greatly surprised at this farrago, in which falsehood was mixed with a very small proportion of truth, I managed to keep a straight face and said that the Casanova of the article must be another man of the same name.

"Possibly, but you are certainly the Casanova I met a month ago at Cardinal Acquaviva's and two years ago in Venice at the house of my sister Signora Loredan. Furthermore, Bucchetti of Ancona gives you the title of abate in his bill of exchange on Orsi."

"Very well, Monsignore. Your Excellency forces me to admit it; I am he; but I beg you not to ask any of the further questions you have in mind. Honor compels me to observe the strictest silence."

"You have said enough and I am satisfied."

"Let us talk of something else."

After a little polite conversation, I thanked him for all his offers and left. I did not see him again until sixteen years later. I will give my reader an account of that meeting when we get there.

Laughing to myself over all unfounded stories and over the combinations of circumstances which give them a semblance of veracity, from that time on I became a great Pyrrhonist[6] in respect to historical truths. It gave me the greatest pleasure to see that my very reserve was encouraging the Abate Cornaro in his belief that I was the Casanova who was mentioned by the Pesaro gazette. I felt sure that he would write to Venice, where the incident would do me honor, at least until people learned the truth, which would then justify my denial. For this reason I resolved to go there as soon as I had received a letter from Teresa. I thought I would have her come to Venice, since I could wait for her much more comfortably there than in Bologna, and in my own country there could be nothing to prevent me from marrying her openly. Meanwhile, the fallacious tale amused me. I expected every day to see it cleared up in the gazette. The officer Casanova must be laughing over the horse the gazette writer in Pesaro had sent him off on, just as I was laughing over the whim which had taken me to dress as an officer in Bologna and which had laid the foundation for the whole story.

On the fourth day of my stay in Bologna, an express messenger handed me a thick letter from Teresa. The letter contained two enclosures. She told me that the day after I left Rimini, Baron Weiss had brought the Duke of Castropiñano[7] to see her and that, after hearing her sing to her own accompaniment on the harpsichord, he had offered her a thousand once and her traveling expenses to sing at the Teatro San Carlo[8] for a year. She must be there in May. She was sending me a copy of the contract he had drawn up for her. She had asked him to give her a week to consider it, and he had agreed. She only awaited my answer to her letter before either signing the Duke's contract or refusing his offer.

The second enclosure was a document in her own hand in which she undertook to serve me as long as she lived. She told me that if I wanted to go to Naples with her, she would meet me at whatever place I would designate, and that if I felt any aversion to going back to Naples, I must disregard her piece of good fortune and be certain that she could conceive of no good fortune and no happiness except doing all that she could to make me content and happy.

Her letter having made it necessary for me to reflect, I told the messenger to come back the next day. I was in a state of the greatest irresolution. It was the first time in my life that I found myself unable to make up my mind. Two equally strong motives in the scales kept them from inclining in one direction or the other. I could neither command Teresa to reject such good fortune, nor let her go to Naples without me, nor bring myself to go to Naples with her. The mere thought that my love could stand in the way of Teresa's prospects of fortune made me shudder; and what prevented me from going to Naples with her was my self-esteem, which was even stronger than the fire with which I burned for her. How could I bring myself to go back to Naples seven or eight months after I had left it, and appear there without any position in the world but that of a dastard living at the expense of his wife or his mistress? What would my cousin Don Antonio have said, and Don Gennaro Palo and his son, and Don Lelio Caraffa, and all my acquaintances among the nobility? The thought of Donna Lucrezia and her husband made me shudder too. If I went there and found everyone despising me, would the love which I would feel for Teresa keep me from being unhappy? Sharing her destiny, whether as husband or lover, I should find myself degraded, humiliated, and condemned to servility both by my position and as my only possible profession. The reflection that now, at the fairest time of my youth, I was about to renounce all hope of the high fortune for which I considered that I was born gave the scales such a push that my reason silenced my heart. I decided on a course which would gain me time. I wrote to Teresa to go to Naples and to be sure that I would join her there either in July or when I returned from Constantinople. I advised her to take a respectable-looking chambermaid with her, so that she could appear with decency in the great city of Naples, and to conduct herself in such a way that I could marry her without blushing. I foresaw that Teresa's fortune would owe even more to her beauty than to her talent, and knowing myself as I did, I knew that neither as a lover nor as a husband could I brook even the semblance of a rival.

My love yielded to my reason; but my love would not have been so accommodating a week earlier. I wrote to her to answer me at Bologna by the same express messenger, and three days later I received her last letter, in which she told me that she had signed the contract, that she had engaged a chambermaid who could pass as her mother, that she would leave in the middle of May, and that she would wait for me until the time came when I wrote her that I no longer thought of her. On the fourth day after receiving her letter I set off for Venice; but first for what happened to me before I left.

The French officer to whom I had written about retrieving my trunk, offering to pay him for the horse I had absconded with, or which had absconded with me, wrote me that my passport had arrived and was at the war chancellery and that he could easily send it to me with my trunk if I would go to the trouble of paying fifty doblones[9] in compensation for the horse I had taken to Don Marcello Birac, business agent for the Spanish army, who lived at an address which he gave me. He said that he had written, explaining the whole matter, to the said Birac, who, upon receiving the money, would give me a written undertaking to have my trunk and my passport delivered to me.

Delighted that all was well in this respect, I lost not a moment in repairing to the business agent, who lived with a Venetian I knew named Batagia. I paid over the money, and received my trunk and my passport on the morning of the day I left Bologna. Everyone in Bologna heard that I had paid for the horse, which made the Abate

Cornaro still more certain that I was the Casanova who had killed his captain in a duel.

To get to Venice, I had to go through being quarantined, which I was determined not to do. The quarantine was still enforced because the two governments[10] concerned were at odds. The Venetians insisted that the Pope be the first to open his frontiers to travelers, and the Pope maintained the contrary. The matter was not yet settled, and commerce suffered from it. Here is how I went about it, without fear for the result, though it was a delicate undertaking, for Venice was particularly strict in matters of health; but in those days one of my greatest pleasures was to do anything which was forbidden or at any rate difficult.

As I knew that passage was free from the State of Mantua to the State of Venice, and from the State of Modena to that of Mantua, I saw that if I could enter the State of Mantua under color of coming from Modena, all would be accomplished. I would cross the Po somewhere, and go straight to Venice. So I hired a *vetturino* to take me to Revere. This is a city on the Po, belonging to the State of Mantua. The *vetturino* told me that he could take byroads to Revere and say that he had come from Modena; but that we would be in difficulties when we were asked for a health certificate made out at Modena. I told him to say that he had lost it and to leave the rest to me. My money persuaded him.

At the Revere gate, I said that I was an officer of the Spanish army on my way to Venice to discuss a matter of great importance with the Duke of Modena, who was there at the time.

Not only was the *vetturino* not asked to produce the health certificate from Modena, but in addition to being accorded military honors I was treated with great politeness. No difficulty was made over giving me a certificate of departure from Revere, with which, after crossing the Po at Ostiglia, I went on to Legnago, where I left my *vetturino* handsomely paid and thoroughly satisfied. At Legnago I took post horses, and arrived that evening at Venice, putting up at an inn in the Rialto[11] quarter on April 12, 1744, my birthday, which in the course of my life has on ten different occasions been remarkable for some unusual event. The next day at noon I went to the Exchange, intending to engage passage on a vessel and leave for Constantinople at once; but since I found none intending to sail for two or three months, I took a room on a Venetian ship of the line which was to sail for Corfu in the course of the month. The vessel was named *Our Lady of the Rosary*, and was commanded by Captain Zane.[12]

Having thus obeyed my destiny, which according to my superstitious fancy was summoning me to Constantinople, where I felt
that I had irretrievably engaged myself to go, I set out toward the
Piazza San Marco, very curious to see and to be seen by all my
acquaintances, who could not but be surprised to see me no longer
dressed as an abate. From Revere on, I had worn a red cockade[13] on
my hat.

My first visit was to the Abate Grimani, who loudly exclaimed
when he saw me. He sees me in a military uniform when he has
every reason to think I am with Cardinal Acquaviva and on the road
to political office. He was just getting up from dinner and had a
number of visitors. Among them I notice an officer in Spanish
uniform; but I do not let that daunt me. I tell the Abate Grimani
that as I am passing through Venice, I am delighted that it gives me
the opportunity to pay him my respects.

"I did not expect to see you in this attire."

"I came to the wise decision of abandoning that of the
Church, wearing which I could not hope for a destiny capable of
satisfying me."

"Where are you going?"

"To Constantinople, to which I hope to find a quick passage
from Corfu. I am on a mission from Cardinal Acquaviva."

"Where have you come from now?"

"From the Spanish army, which I left ten days ago."

At these words I hear the voice of a young nobleman saying,
with a look in my direction, "That is not true." I answer him that
my profession does not permit me to stomach the lie direct, and, so
saying, I bow all around and leave, paying no attention to anyone
who told me to stop.

Since I had on a uniform, I considered that I should also have all
the pride and touchiness which go with it. As I was no longer a
priest, I must not pass over being given the lie. I go to call on
Signora Manzoni, whom I was most anxious to see, and her reception of me is all that I could wish. She reminds me of her predictions
and plumes herself on their accuracy. She insists on my telling her all
that has happened to me, I oblige, and she smiles and says that if I am
going to Constantinople it is more than likely that she will never see
me again.

On leaving her house, I go to Signora Orio's. It was there that
I enjoyed the surprise which greeted my appearance. She, the old
advocate Rosa, and Nanetta and Marta were as if turned to stone.

I thought the two girls had grown prettier in the last nine months, of which they vainly asked me to give them an account. The story of those nine months was not of a nature to please Signora Orio and her nieces; it would have lowered me in the estimation of those innocent souls; even so, I gave them three delicious hours. Seeing that the old lady was in raptures, I told her that she had only to say the word and she could keep me for all of the four or five weeks I had to wait for my ship to sail, by giving me a room and supper, but on condition that I should be no trouble to her. She answered that she would be happy if only she had a room, and Rosa told her that she had one and that he would undertake to get it furnished within two hours. It was the room next to the one occupied by her nieces. Nanetta said that in that case she would move downstairs with her sister and they would sleep in the kitchen; and I immediately said that, not wanting to cause them any inconvenience, I would remain at the inn where I was. Signora Orio at once told her nieces that there was no need for them to move downstairs, since they could fasten their door.

"They would not need to, Signora," I said gravely.

"I know that; but they are prudes with a high opinion of themselves."

I then made her accept fifteen zecchini, assuring her that I was rich and that it was an advantageous arrangement for me even so, for a month at the inn would cost me more. I said that I would send her my trunk and would come the next day to take supper and spend the night. I saw joy on the faces of my two little wives, who regained their empire over my heart despite the image of Teresa which was before the eyes of my soul at every moment.

The next morning, after sending my trunk to Signora Orio's, I went to the War Office; but to avoid any difficulties I went without a cockade. Major Pelodoro flung himself on my neck when he saw me in uniform. As soon as I told him that I had to go to Constantinople and that, despite the uniform he saw me wearing, I was at liberty, he said that it would be a great advantage to me to go to Constantinople with the Bailo,[14] who was to set off in two months at the latest, and that I should try to arrange it and even try to enter the Venetian service.

I thought it good advice. The Savio for War,[15] who was the same one who had made my acquaintance the year before, saw me there and called me over. He said he had received a letter from Bologna informing him of a duel which did me honor, and that he knew

I refused to admit it. He asked if I had been given a discharge when I left the Spanish service, and I answered that I could not have a discharge since I had never served. He asked how I could be in Venice without having gone through quarantine, and I answered that travelers entering by way of the State of Mantua were not quarantined. He, too, advised me to enter the service of my country.

Leaving the Doges' Palace, I found the Abate Grimani under the Procuratie[16] and he told me that my abrupt departure from his house had displeased everyone present.

"Including the Spanish officer?"

"No. On the contrary, he says that if it is true you were with the Spanish army ten days ago, you were right to act as you did; what is more, he told me that you were with it and showed me a copy of a gazette which gives an account of a duel and says that you killed your captain. Surely this is sheer invention."

"Who told you it is sheer invention?"

"Then it is true?"

"I do not say that; but it could be true, as it is true that I was with the Spanish army ten days ago."

"That is impossible, unless you violated the *contumacia*."[17]

"There was no violation. I openly crossed the Po at Revere, and here I am. I regret that I can no longer call on Your Excellency unless the person who gave me the lie accords me proper satisfaction. I could stomach insults when I belonged to a calling which professes humility, but now I belong to one which professes honor."

"You are wrong to take this tone. The person who gave you the lie is Signor Valmarana, at present a Proveditor for Health,[18] who maintains that since all entries are closed, you cannot be here. Satisfaction! Have you forgotten who you are?"

"No. I know that last year I could let myself be thought a coward, but now I will give anyone who slights me cause to repent it."

"Come and dine with me."

"No, for the officer would hear of it."

"He would even see you, for he dines with me every day."

"Very well. I will let him judge my cause."

Dining with Pelodoro and three or four officers, who all told me that I ought to enter the Venetian service, I decided to do so. A young lieutenant, whose health prevented him from going to the Levant, wanted to sell his commission;[19] he asked a hundred zecchini for it; but, beyond that, it was necessary to obtain the approval of the Savio. I told Pelodoro that the hundred zecchini were ready, and he promised to speak to the Savio on my behalf.

Toward nightfall I went to Signora Orio's, where I found my quarters very comfortably furnished. After quite a good supper, I had the pleasure of seeing the aunt herself order her two nieces to make me at home in my room.

The first night they both slept with me, and on the following nights they took turns, removing a plank from the wall and thus leaving an aperture by which the mistress of the moment came and went. We did all this very carefully and had no fear of being caught. Our doors were fastened, so, if the aunt came to see her nieces, the one who was missing would have time to go back, replacing the plank; but no such visit was ever made. Signora Orio counted on our good behavior.

Two or three days later the Abate Grimani arranged an interview between me and Signor Valmarana at the Sultana coffeehouse; he told me that if he had known that the quarantine could be eluded he would never have said that what I had said was impossible, and that he thanked me for making the fact known to him; the matter was thus amicably settled, and I always dined at the Abate Grimani's until my departure.

Toward the end of the month I entered the service of the Republic as an ensign in the Bala[20] regiment, which was at Corfu. The officer who had left it in consequence of the hundred zecchini I had paid him was a lieutenant; but the Savio for War advanced arguments to which, if I wanted to enter the service, I was obliged to yield. He promised that at the end of the year I would be promoted to the rank of lieutenant, and that I would at once be granted the leave I needed to go to Constantinople. I accepted because I wanted to serve.

The person who obtained me the favor of traveling to Constantinople with the Cavaliere Venier, who was going there as Bailo, was Signor Pietro Vendramin, the illustrious Senator. He introduced me to the Cavaliere Venier,[21] who promised to take me with him from Corfu, which he would reach a month after I did.

Some days before I left I received a letter from Teresa, telling me that the Duke who had engaged her for Naples was taking her there in person. She said that he was old, but that even if he were young, I had nothing to fear. She said that if I needed money I should draw bills of exchange on her and be sure that she would pay them even if she had to sell everything she possessed.

Another passenger on the ship which would take me to Corfu was to be a Venetian nobleman who was going to Zante[22] as Councilor. He had a very large retinue, and the captain of the vessel, after warning me that if I had to eat by myself I would not eat any too well, advised me to obtain an introduction to the nobleman, and so assure myself of being invited to his table. His name was Antonio Dolfin,[23] but he was generally known by his byname of Bucintoro.[24] He had been given the name of that magnificent ship because of his manner and the elegance of his attire.

As soon as Signor Grimani learned that I had engaged a room on the same ship in which this nobleman was going to Zante, he did not wait for me to ask before presenting me to him and thus gaining me the honor and benefit of eating at his table. Signor Dolfin said with the greatest affability that he would be happy if I would present myself to his wife, who was to sail with him. I called on her the following day, and saw before me a charming woman for her years, but totally deaf. I had nothing to hope for. She had a charming young daughter,[25] whom she left in a convent and who later became celebrated. I think she is still alive, the widow of the Procurator Tron, whose family is now extinct.

I have rarely seen a handsomer man or one who bore himself better than this lady's father, Signor Dolfin. Withal he was highly intelligent, and no less remarkable for his eloquence and perfect breeding; a dashing gamester, though he always lost, loved by every woman whose love he sought, always courageous and unruffled, in good fortune and bad. He had traveled without obtaining permission, which had brought him into disgrace with the government, so that he had entered the service of a foreign country. A Venetian nobleman cannot commit a greater crime; representations were made and he was forced to return to Venice and suffer the punishment of spending some time under "the Leads."[26]

This charming, generous, but not wealthy man had to ask the Great Council[27] for a lucrative governorship, and he was appointed Councilor for the island of Zante; but he was going there with such a suite that he could not hope to profit by it.

This noble Venetian, Dolfin, being such a man as I have described, could not make his fortune in Venice. An aristocratic government cannot hope for peace unless it is based upon the fundamental principle of equality among aristocrats. Now, it is impossible to judge of equality, whether physical or moral, except by appearances; from which it follows that the citizen who wants to avoid persecution must, if he is not like everyone else or worse, bend his every effort to appearing to be so. If he has much talent, he must hide it; if he is ambitious, he must pretend to scorn honors; if he wants to obtain anything, he must ask for nothing; if his person is handsome, he must neglect it: he must look slovenly and dress badly, his accessories must be of the plainest, he must ridicule everything foreign; he must bow awkwardly, not pride himself on being well-mannered, care little for the fine arts, conceal his good taste if he has it; not have a foreign cook; he must wear an ill-combed wig and be a little dirty. As Signor Dolfin Bucintoro had none of these qualifications, it follows that he could not make his fortune in his native country, Venice.

The day before I sailed, I did not leave Signora Orio's house. She shed as many tears as her nieces, and I shed no fewer. A hundred times over as they perished from love in my arms on that last night they said that they would never see me again, and they predicted rightly. If they had seen me again, they would have predicted wrongly. Such is all the value of prophecies!

I went on board on the 5th of May, very well off in clothing, jewels, and ready money. I had five hundred zecchini. Our ship was armed with twenty-four cannon and had a garrison of two hundred Slavonians. We sailed from Malamocco[28] to Istria during the night and dropped anchor in the port of Orsara[29] for the operation called *savorna*.[30] This means filling the bottom of the hold with a sufficient quantity of stones, for if the ship is too light it cannot be sailed properly. I landed with several others to take a walk, in spite of my knowing the ugly place, where I had spent three days not nine months before. I laughed as I reflected on the difference between my present profession and the one I had abandoned. I was sure that no one would recognize in the imposing figure I now presented the miserable abate who, but for the ill-omened Frate Steffano, would have become God knows what.

[* * *]

By way of Corfu Casanova eventually reached Constantinople where he delivered to Monsieur de Bonneval the letters with which he had been charged in Rome by Cardinal Acquaviva. Introduced by Bonneval to a number of rich and cultivated Turks, he was propositioned by one and briefly tempted by the prospect of marriage to the daughter of another. Refusing both offers, he set out again for Venice, but found himself waylaid in Corfu by his passion for intrigue, both amorous and financial. Here his luck deserted him once more. Ruined by gambling, abandoned by a new mistress and infected with venereal disease by a celebrated courtesan, he returned to Venice where he found his brother under arrest. Resigning his commission, and undeterred by past disasters, Casanova resolved to set up in business as a professional gambler. He soon lost all his remaining money and found that the only way to earn his living was to play the fiddle. His old adversary and patron, Grimani, procured him a job at the Teatro San Samuele for one scudo per day. The Casanova who had consorted on equal terms with patricians in Venice and ambassadors in Constantinople was now a musical hack—but not for long.

CHAPTER VII

*I go completely to the dogs. A piece of extra-
ordinary good luck raises me from my low
estate and I become a rich nobleman.*

After an education calculated to lead me into an honorable profession suitable for a young man who, in addition to a good grounding
in letters, was endowed with promising qualities of mind and with
those accidental personal advantages which always and everywhere
produce an impression, here I am, at the age of twenty, become a
menial journeyman of a sublime art in which, if he who excels is
admired, the mediocrity is rightly despised. I became a member of a
theater orchestra, in which position I could demand neither esteem
nor consideration and must even expect the scorn of those who had
known me as a doctor, then as an ecclesiastic, then as a soldier, and
had seen me received and made much of in polished and noble
circles.

All this I knew; but contempt, to which I could not have
remained indifferent, was not shown me. I defied it, for I knew
that it was deserved only by baseness, and with that in any form I
could not reproach myself. As for esteem, I let my ambition sleep.
Satisfied with being at no one's beck and call, I proceeded on my
way without worrying about the future. Forced to become an
ecclesiastic, and unable to succeed by any other course than that of
hypocrisy, I should have been disgusted with myself; and to continue in the military profession, I should have had to practice a
patience of which I had no reason to believe myself capable. I
considered that the profession one adopts should produce an income
sufficient to meet the necessities of life, and that the salary I should
have received in return for serving in the troops of the Republic
would not have sufficed me; for because of my upbringing, my
needs were greater than others'. Playing the violin, I earned enough
to keep myself without turning to anyone. *Happy are they who can
boast that they are self-sufficient.* My profession was not a noble one,
but I did not care. Calling everything prejudice, I soon acquired all
the habits of my degraded fellow musicians. After the performance I
went with them to a tavern, which we left only in a state of
intoxication to spend the night in some house of ill fame. When

we found it full, we forced the occupants to take to their heels, and we decamped without paying the unhappy women who had submitted to our brutality even the miserable recompense which the law accords them. These highhanded proceedings often exposed us to the most obvious dangers.

We often spent our nights roaming through different quarters of the city, thinking up the most scandalous practical jokes and putting them into execution. We amused ourselves by untying the gondolas moored before private houses, which then drifted with the current to one side of the Grand Canal or the other, and making merry over the curses the gondoliers would call down on us the next morning when they did not find their gondolas where they had moored them.

We often woke midwives and made them dress and go to deliver women who, when they arrived, called them fools. We did the same to the most celebrated physicians, whose slumbers we interrupted to send them to noblemen who, we told them, had suffered an apoplexy, and we routed priests from their beds and packed them off to pray for the souls of people in perfect health who, we said, were at death's door.

In every street through which we passed we relentlessly cut the bell cord hanging at every door; and when we happened to find a door open because someone had forgotten to shut it, we groped our way up the stairs and terrified all the sleeping inmates by shouting at their bedroom doors that the street door of the house was open. And then we decamped, leaving the house door as open as we had found it.

One very dark night we decided to overturn a big marble table which was a sort of monument. The table stood almost in the middle of the Campo Sant'Angelo.[1] In the days of the war which the Republic had fought against the League of Cambrai,[2] so the story ran, it was on this big table that the commissaries had counted out their pay to the recruits who enrolled in the service of St. Mark.

When we could get into bell towers, we thought it great sport to alarm the whole neighborhood by ringing the tocsin which announces a fire, or to cut all the bell ropes. When we crossed the canal, instead of all going together in a gondola, each of us took one, and when we got out on the other side we all ran away, to make the gondoliers, whom we had not paid, run after us.

The whole city was complaining of our nocturnal malefactions, and we laughed at the investigations which were made to discover the disturbers of the public peace. We had to keep our secret most

HISTORY OF MY LIFE

carefully, for if we had been discovered the authorities might well have given themselves the pleasure of sentencing all of us to spend some time on board the galley of the Council of Ten, which is moored opposite the two tall columns in the Piazzetta San Marco.

We were seven, and sometimes eight, for as I was very fond of my brother Francesco I often took him along with us. But fear finally tempered, and even ended, our excesses. Here is the story.

In each of the seventy-two parishes of the city of Venice, there is a big tavern called a *magazzeno*,[3] where wine is sold at retail, which stays open all night, and where one can drink more cheaply than at the other taverns in the city, where food is also provided. One can also eat at the *magazzeno* by sending out for what one wants to the pork butcher's shop, which is also regularly to be found in each parish and which is open all night. The pork butcher also keeps a cook-shop, where he prepares execrable food; but since he sells everything cheaply his establishment is of great use to the poor. In the *magazzeno* itself one never sees either members of the nobility or citizens in good circumstances, for cleanliness is not to be found there. These places are frequented only by the common people. They have small rooms containing only a table surrounded by benches instead of chairs.

It was during one Carnival, midnight had struck, we were eight, all masked, roving through the city, each of us trying to gain distinction in our comrades' eyes by thinking up some new kind of practical joke. Passing the *magazzeno* of the parish named Santa Croce,[4] we are tempted to go in for a drink. We enter, we walk about, and we find no one except three men peaceably drinking with a rather pretty woman. Our leader, who was a Venetian nobleman belonging to one of the Balbi families, said it would be a fine trick, and a new one, to carry off the poor topers in one direction and the woman in another, so that we could use her afterward at our good pleasure. He tells us his plan in detail, we approve it, he gives us our roles, and, well concealed by our masks, he leads us into the room, where, taking off his mask, certain that even so he will not be recognized, he addresses the startled men in the following words:

"On pain of death, and by order of the heads of the Council of Ten,[5] come with us at once, not making the slightest sound; as for you, my good woman, you have nothing to fear. You will be taken home."

He had scarcely finished his speech before two of our band took the woman and immediately conducted her to the place where our leader had told them to go and wait for us, and we seize the three trembling men, whose last thought is to resist us. The waiter comes running up to be paid, and our leader pays him, ordering him to say nothing, still on pain of death. We take the three men on board a large boat; our leader gets up on the poop, ordering the boatman to row at the bow. The boatman is forced to obey, not knowing where he may go, for the course depends on the man on the poop. None of us knew where our leader was going to take the three poor devils.

He takes a course to leave the canal, leaves it, and in a quarter of an hour arrives at San Giorgio,[6] where he disembarks the three prisoners, who are glad to be left there, for they must have been fearing they would be murdered. Then our leader, feeling tired, has the boatman go up on the poop and orders him to take us to San Geremia,[7] where after paying him liberally, he leaves him in his boat.

From San Geremia we go to the Campiello del Remer, in San Marcuola,[8] where my brother and another of our band were waiting for us in a corner, sitting on the ground with the woman, who was crying.

"Don't cry, my beauty," said our leader, "no harm will come to you. We will go and drink a glass in Rialto and then we will take you home."

"Where is my husband?"

"You will see him back at home tomorrow morning."

Relieved by his answer, and docile as a sheep, she came with us to the inn of the "Two Swords,"[9] where we made a good fire in an upstairs room and where, after having food and drink brought, we sent the waiter away. We then removed our masks, and we saw the woman we had carried off become all amiability at the sight of our faces and the way in which we behaved. After we had encouraged her with words and glasses of wine there befell her what she could not but be expecting. Our leader, as was only right, was the first to pay her his amorous duty, after most politely overcoming her reluctance to yield to him in the presence of us all. She chose the sensible course of laughing and letting him do as he pleased.

But I saw that she was surprised when I came forward to be the second; she thought herself obligated to show her gratitude; and when, after my turn, she saw the third, she no longer doubted of her happy fate, which promised her all the members of the band. She was not mistaken. My brother was the only one who pretended to be ill. He had no other choice, for the law among us irrevocably demanded that each of us do what another did.

After this fine exploit, we resumed our masks, paid the innkeeper, and took the happy woman to San Giobbe,[10] where she lived, leaving her only when we saw her opening her door. None of us could keep from laughing when she thanked us most sincerely and in the most perfect good faith. After that we separated and all went home.

It was not until two days later that our escapade began to be talked of. The young woman's husband was a weaver, as were his two friends. He joined with them in approaching the heads of the Council of Ten with a complaint in which he presented a completely truthful account of our action, the atrocity of which was, however, diminished by a circumstance which must have set the three judges laughing, as it did the whole city. The document said that the eight maskers had subjected the woman to no ill treatment. The two maskers who had carried her off had taken her to such-and-such a place where, the six others having arrived an hour later, they all went to the "Swords," where they spent an hour drinking. They had then taken her home, begging her to excuse them for having played a trick on her husband. The three weavers had not been able to leave the island of San Giorgio until daybreak, and when the husband reached home he found his wife in bed fast asleep; upon waking she had told him the whole story. She complained only of the great fear she had felt, and she demanded justice and exemplary punishment for it. Everything about the complaint was comical, for the husband said that the eight maskers would not have found them so easy if their leader had not used the respected name of the Council.

The complaint had three results. The first was to set the whole city laughing. The second was to send every idler to San Giobbe to hear the heroine herself tell the story. The third was to make the tribunal issue a decree promising five hundred ducati to anyone who should reveal the guilty parties, even if it were one of themselves, except only their leader. The reward would have made us tremble, if our leader, the only one among us whose character would have let him turn informer, had not been a Venetian nobleman. This rank of our leader's made me certain that, even had one of us been capable of reporting the facts to gain the five hundred ducati, the tribunal would have done nothing, since it would have had to punish a patrician. No such traitor was found among us, though we were all poor. But we were so frightened that we all mended our ways and our nocturnal expeditions came to an end.

Three or four months later the Cavaliere Nicolò Tron, who was then a State Inquisitor, astonished me by telling me the whole story of the escapade, and naming all my companions in it, one after the other.

In the middle of the spring of the following year, 1746, Signor Girolamo Cornaro, the eldest son of the house of Cornaro della Regina,[11] married a daughter of the Soranzo di San Polo family, and I was one of the fiddlers making up one of the several orchestras for the balls which were given for three days in the Palazzo Soranzo[12] on the occasion of the marriage.

On the third day, when the festivities were nearly over, I leave the orchestra an hour before dawn to go home, and as I go down the stairs I notice a senator in his red robe[13] about to get into his gondola. I see a letter drop to the ground beside him as he is drawing his handkerchief from his pocket. I advance and pick up the letter and, catching up with the imposing Signore just as he is going down the steps, I hand it to him. He thanks me, he asks me where I live, I tell him, he insists upon taking me home, I accept the courtesy he was kind enough to offer me, and take a place on the bench beside him. Three minutes later he asks me to shake his left arm: "I feel," he said, "such a numbness that I seem not to have this arm at all." I shake it with all my might, and I hear him tell me, in ill-articulated words, that he felt as if he were losing his whole leg too and that he thought he was dying.

Greatly alarmed, I open the curtain, take the lantern, look at his face, and am terrified to see that his mouth was drawn up toward his left ear and his eyes were losing their luster.

I call to the gondoliers to stop and let me get out to find a surgeon who will come at once and bleed His Excellency, who had certainly been struck by apoplexy.

I disembark. It was at the bridge by the Calle Bernardo, where three years earlier I had given Razzetta a cudgeling. I run to the coffeehouse, someone shows me where a surgeon lives. I knock loudly, I shout, the door opens, the man is wakened, I urge him to hurry, I will not let him dress, he takes his case and comes with me to the gondola, where he bleeds the dying man, and I tear up my shirt to make him a bandage.

We quickly reach his palace in Santa Marina;[14] the servants are awakened, he is removed from his gondola, carried to his apartment on the second floor, undressed, and put to bed almost dead. I tell a servant to run for a physician, he goes, the physician arrives and bleeds him again. I station myself beside his bed, considering it my duty not to leave.

An hour later a patrician who is a friend of his arrives, then I see another, they are in despair, they question the gondoliers, who tell them that I am better able to answer them than they are. They question me, I tell them all that I knew; they do not know who I am, they do not dare to ask me, and I tell them nothing. The patient lay motionless, with no sign of life but his breathing. Fomentations were applied, and the priest who had been fetched expected him to die. No visitors were admitted, the two patricians and I were the only persons who remained with him. I join them at noon in a light dinner without leaving the room. Toward evening the elder of the two patricians tells me that I may leave if I have business to attend to, since they intended to stay with the sick man all night, lying down on mattresses which they would order brought. I answer that I will sleep in the chair in which I was, since I felt certain that if I left, the patient would die, just as I felt certain that he could not die so long as I remained there. I see them exchange looks, astonished at my answer.

I learn from them as we are eating supper together that the dying nobleman was Signor Bragadin, only brother of the Procuratore of the same name.[15] This Signor Bragadin was celebrated in Venice not only because of his eloquence and his talents as a statesman but also because of the love affairs which had signalized his stormy youth. He had committed extravagances for women who had likewise committed them for his sake; he had gambled a great deal and lost a great deal, and his brother the Procuratore was his bitterest enemy because he had taken it into his head that he had tried to poison him. He had accused him of the crime before the Council of Ten, which, eight months later, had unanimously declared him innocent; but the Procuratore had not changed his opinion. This innocent man, oppressed by his unjust brother, who despoiled him of half his income, nevertheless lived the life of an amiable philosopher in the bosom of friendship. He had two friends, the men whom I saw with him: one was of the Dandolo and the other of the Barbaro family, both of them as upright and amiable as himself. He was handsome, learned, fond of a joke, and meek in disposition. His age at the time was fifty.

The physician who had undertaken to cure him, whose name was Ferro, was persuaded for reasons all his own that he could restore him to health by applying an ointment of mercury to his chest; and he was given his way. The rapid effect of this remedy, which was well received by his two friends, alarmed me greatly. Its rapidity appeared in the fact that in less than twenty-four hours the patient was troubled by a violent brain fever. The physician said that he knew the ointment would produce this effect, but that the next day its action on the brain would diminish and proceed to the other parts of the body, which needed to be stimulated both artificially and by an equilibrium in the circulation of the fluids.

At midnight Signor Bragadin was on fire and in a dangerous state of agitation; I get up, and I see him with lusterless eyes and scarcely able to breathe. I rouse the two friends from their mattresses, saying that the patient must be relieved of what would kill him. Not waiting for them to answer, I uncover his chest, I remove the plaster, then wash him with warm water, and within three or four minutes he has recovered from his agitation and is resting easy in the gentlest of sleep. We go back to bed.

The physician arrives very early in the morning and is delighted to find his patient in good condition. Signor Dandolo tells him what had been done, as the result of which he found his patient improved. The physician complains of such a liberty having been taken and asks who has played havoc with his treatment. Signor Bragadin tells him that the person who had delivered him from the mercury which was about to kill him was a physician who knew more than he did; and so saying points to me.

I do not know which of us was the more surprised, whether the physician at seeing a young man he had never seen before declared more learned than himself, or I, who did not know that I was so. I maintained a modest silence, though finding it difficult to stifle my laughter, while the physician looked at me and rightly concluded that I was a brazen charlatan who had dared to supplant him. He coldly informed the sick man that he surrendered his place to me, and he was taken at his word. He leaves, and leaves me promoted physician to one of the most illustrious members of the Venetian Senate. All in all, I was delighted. I then told my patient that all he needed was to diet and that nature would do the rest in the mild weather which would soon be upon us.

Thus dismissed, Doctor Ferro told the story all over the city; and since the patient felt better every day, one of his relatives who came to visit him said that everyone was amazed that he had been pleased to make a fiddler from a theater orchestra his physician. Signor Bragadin laughed and replied that a fiddler might well know more than all the physicians in Venice.

His Excellency listened to me as if I were an oracle. His two surprised friends accorded me the same attention. Encouraged by this obsequiousness, I spoke as a physician, I dogmatized, and I cited authors whom I had never read.

Signor Bragadin, who had the weakness to dabble in the abstruse sciences, told me one day that he thought me too wise for a young man, and hence I must have some supernatural gift. He asked me to tell him the truth. It was then that, in order not to offend his vanity by telling him he was wrong, I hit upon the strange expedient of making him, in the presence of his two friends, a confidence as false as it was extravagant, namely, that I was in possession of a numerical calculus which, when I put it a written question which I reduced to numerals, returned me an answer, likewise in numerals, which gave me the information I wanted and which no one on earth could have imparted to me. Signor Bragadin said that it was the Key of Solomon,[16] known to the uninitiated as the cabala. He asked me from whom I had learned the science, and when I answered that the person who had taught it to me was a hermit who was living on Monte Carpegna[17] when I was under arrest in the Spanish army, he said that the hermit must have bound an invisible spirit to the calculus without my knowledge, for mere numbers could not have the power to reason.

"You are in possession," he said, "of a treasure, and it rests with you to derive the greatest advantage from it."

I answered that I did not know how I could derive any great advantage from it, and the more so since the answers my calculus gave me were so obscure that I had become disgusted with it of late and almost never put any questions to it.

"Yet it is true," I added, "that if I had not constructed my pyramid[18] three weeks ago, I should not have had the happiness of knowing Your Excellency."

"How is that?"

"Having asked my oracle, on the second day of the festivities in the Palazzo Soranzo, if I should meet anyone at the ball there whom I did not wish to meet, it answered that I must leave the festival at exactly ten o'clock."[19]

Signor Bragadin and his two friends were as if turned to stone. Signor Dandolo then asked me to answer a question which he would ask me himself, and which he alone was able to interpret, since he alone knew the facts. He writes the question, he hands it to me, I read it, I understand neither the question nor the subject to which it refers, but it does not matter, I have to give an answer. If the question is so obscure to me that I cannot understand the first thing about it, I ought not to understand the first thing about the answer either. So I answer in four verses in ordinary figures, which he alone could interpret, displaying complete indifference as to the interpretation. Signor Dandolo reads them, reads them over again, shows surprise, he understands it perfectly, it is divine, it is unique, it is a heavenly treasure. The numbers are merely the vehicle, but the answer can only have come from an immortal intelligence. After Signor Dandolo, Signor Barbaro and Signor Bragadin ask questions on all sorts of subjects, they find all my answers divine, I congratulate them, and say that I am happy to be in possession of something which I had scarcely valued until then but which I would now value highly, since I saw that it put me in a position to be useful to Their Excellencies.

They then all three asked me together how long it would take me to teach them the rules of the calculus. I answered that it was a matter of very little time, and that I would do it even though the hermit had told me that if I taught it to anyone before I had reached the age of fifty I would drop dead three days afterward. "I do not," I said, "believe in his threat." Signor Bragadin then told me in the most serious tone that I ought to believe in it, and from then on none of the three again asked me to teach him the art of the cabala. They considered that if they could attach me to them, it would be the same as being in possession of the cabala themselves. Thus I became the hierophant[20] of these three men who, with all their worth and their amiability, were lacking in wisdom, since they dabbled in what are known as the chimeras of knowledge: they believed in the possibility of what was morally impossible. With me at their orders, they saw themselves in possession of the philosophers' stone, the universal medicine,[21] communication with the elemental spirits[22] and all the celestial intelligences, and of the secrets of all the governments of Europe. They also believed in magic,[23] to which they gave the specious name of occult physics.

After convincing themselves of the divinity of my cabala by questions concerning things which had happened in the past, they proceeded to make it of use to them by always consulting it concerning the present and the future, and I did not find it hard to practice divination, since I never gave an answer which did not have two meanings, one of which, however, known only to me, was not revealed until after the event. My cabala was never wrong. I now understood how easy it had been for the ancient priests of paganism to impose on the ignorant and credulous universe. But what has always amazed me is that the Holy Fathers of the Christian Church, who were not simple, ignorant men like our Evangelists, thinking that they could not deny the divinity of oracles, attributed them to the devil. They would not have thought in this fashion if they had known the art of the cabala. My three friends were like the Holy Fathers: seeing the divinity of my answers, and not being ill-natured enough to think me a devil, they believed that my oracle was animated by an angel.

These three noblemen were not only Christians perfectly loyal to their religion, they were pious and scrupulous: all three of them were unmarried, and all three had become irreconcilable enemies of women, after renouncing them. They held that such a renunciation was the chief condition which the elemental spirits enforced upon those who wished to have commerce with them. The one excluded the other.

What struck me as extremely strange when I first began to know these three patricians was that they were all highly endowed with what is known as intelligence. But a prejudiced intelligence reasons badly, and what is essential is to reason well. I often laughed to myself when I heard them talk of the mysteries of our religion and deride people whose intellectual faculties were so limited that those mysteries were incomprehensible to them. The incarnation of the Word was mere play to God, and the Resurrection was so trifling a matter that they could not think it a miracle, for the flesh being accessory, and it being impossible that God should be dead, Jesus Christ naturally had to return to life. As for the Eucharist, the real presence and transubstantiation were for them (*praemissis concessis* ["the premises being granted"]) the most obvious things possible. They went to confession every week, without feeling the least diffidence in the presence of their confessors, whose ignorance they lamented. They thought it their duty to confess only what they believed to be a sin, and on this point their reasoning was perfectly correct.

With these three noblemen who, eccentric as they were, deserved and enjoyed respect for their probity, their birth, their prestige, and their age, I thoroughly enjoyed myself, despite the fact that in their avidity for knowledge they often kept me busy for eight or ten hours a day, with the four of us shut up together and no visitors admitted. I made them my intimate friends by telling them the whole story of my life until then, which I did quite frankly, though not in every detail as I have just set it down, in order not to lead them into any mortal sins.

I know that I deceived them, and that hence I did not act toward them as a man of honor in all the rigor of the term; but if my reader is a man of the world, I ask him to think a little before considering me unworthy of his indulgence.

If I wanted my morality to be perfectly pure, I should—I am told—either not have become intimate with them or have disabused them. Disabused them? No—I answer—for I did not think myself capable of it. I should only have made them laugh; they would have called me an ignoramus and sent me packing. They would not have paid me for it, and I felt no vocation to set myself up as an apostle. As for my making a heroic resolve to leave them, as I might have done, as soon as I learned that they were visionaries, I will answer that to make it I should have had to have the morality of a misanthrope, an enemy of mankind, of nature, of good manners, and of himself. As a young man who needed to live well and to enjoy the pleasures which my constitution demanded at that age, should I have run the risk of leaving Signor Bragadin to die, should I have had the barbarity to leave these three worthy men open to the deceits of some dishonest scoundrel who might have contrived to make their acquaintance and ruined them by inducing them to undertake the chimerical operation of the Great Work?[24] In addition, an invincible self-esteem prevented me from showing myself unworthy of their friendship by my ignorance, or my pride, or my bad manners, of which I should have given them unmistakable proof if I had rejected their acquaintance.

I took the most creditable, the noblest, and the only natural course. I decided to put myself in a position where I need no longer go without the necessities of life; and what those necessities were for me no one could judge better than I. With the friendship of these three eminent persons, I became a man who would enjoy consideration and prestige in his own country. In addition, I should have the very flattering pleasure of becoming the subject of conversation and of the speculations of those who in their idleness insist on divining the causes of all the moral phenomena which they observe. No one in Venice could understand how an intimacy could exist between myself and three men of their character, they all heaven and I all earth; they most severe in their morals, and I addicted to every kind of dissolute living.

At the beginning of the summer Signor Bragadin was well enough to return to the Senate. The following is the discourse he addressed to me on the eve of the day on which he went out for the first time.

"Whoever you are, I owe you my life. Your patrons who wanted to make you a priest, a scholar, an advocate, a soldier, and then a violinist were fools who did not know you. God commanded your angel to bring you to me. I have come to know you; if you wish to be my son, you have only to recognize me as your father and from thenceforth I will treat you as such in my house until I die. Your apartment is ready, have your things brought to it, you will have a servant, and a gondola at my expense, you will eat at our table, and have ten zecchini a month. At your age my father did not give me a larger allowance. You need not think of the future; think of amusing yourself, and take me as your counselor in whatever befalls you and whatever you wish to undertake, and you will always find me your good friend."

I instantly threw myself at his feet to assure him of my gratitude, and addressed him by the sweet name of father. I swore to obey him as his son. The two other friends, who were staying in the palace, embraced me, and we swore eternal brotherhood.

That, my dear reader, is the whole story of my metamorphosis, and of the happy period which raised me at one bound from the base role of a fiddler to that of a nobleman.

CHAPTER VIII

I lead a dissolute life. Zawoiski. Rinaldi.
L'Abadie.

Fortune, she who had been pleased to give me a taste of her despotism in leading me to happiness by a road unknown to wisdom, had not the power to make me adopt such a system of conduct as would put me in a position to be dependent on no one in my life to come. I began to behave in complete disregard of anything which could set bounds to my inclinations. Once I obeyed the laws, I thought I could scoff at prejudices. I believed I could live in perfect freedom in a country which was under an aristocratic government. I should have been wrong even if Fortune had made me a member of the government. The Republic of Venice, knowing that its first duty is self-preservation, is itself the slave of the all-overriding interest of the state. The occasion arising, it is bound to sacrifice everything to this duty, in the face of which the laws themselves cease to be inviolable. But enough of this now all too familiar subject. The whole of mankind knows that true freedom exists, and can exist, nowhere. I have touched on the subject only to give my reader some idea of my conduct in my native country, where in this year I entered on a path which was to end in a state prison as inscrutable as it was impenetrable, and both precisely because it was unconstitutional. At no loss for money, endowed by nature with a striking exterior, a resolute gambler, a spendthrift, a great talker with a sharp tongue, completely without modesty, fearless, running after pretty women, supplanting rivals, and thinking no company good except such as amused me, I could not but be hated. As I was always ready to risk my own skin, I felt that I was entitled to do whatever I pleased, for anything that stood in my way I considered an evil to be challenged.

This behavior on my part could not but be displeasing to the three sages whose oracle I had become; but they dared not say a word to me. Signor Bragadin laughingly told me I was showing him the wild life he had led when he was my age, but that I must be prepared to pay the price for it, and to find myself punished as he had been when I should have reached his. Without failing in the respect

I owed him, I made a joke of his dire prophecies and went my way. But here is the first sample of his character which he gave me, in the third or fourth week of our acquaintance.

At the casino[1] of Signora Avogadro,[2] a woman whose wit and charm belied her sixty years, I met a young Polish gentleman named Gaetan Zawoiski.[3] He was waiting for money from his country and, while he waited, the women of Venice, enchanted by his handsome face and Polish manners, kept him well supplied. We became good friends; I opened my purse to him; and he opened his to me even more generously twenty years later in Munich. He was a man of honor, with only a modicum of intellect but enough to keep him happy. He died five or six years ago in Dresden, having become minister to the Elector of Trier.[4] I will speak of him in his proper place.

This charming young man, whom everyone liked and who was believed to be a freethinker because he was seen with Signor Angelo Querini[5] and Signor Lunardo Venier,[6] one day when we were in a garden on La Giudecca[7] introduced me to a beautiful foreign countess, who attracted me. We went to call on her the same evening at the Locanda del Castelletto[8] where, after introducing me to her husband, Count Rinaldi, she asked us to stay for supper. The husband made a faro bank, at which, punting with the Countess as partner, I won some fifty zecchini. Delighted to have made this brilliant acquaintance, I went to call on her by myself the next morning; her husband, after asking me to excuse her for still being in bed, had me shown in. In the conversation between us she had the art to leave me hoping for everything while granting me nothing, and when she saw me about to leave she invited me to supper. I went, I won as on the previous evening, still in partnership with her, and I returned home in love. I believed she would be kind to me the next morning; but when I went I was told she had gone out. I went again in the evening, and after she had offered me her excuses, we played, and I lost all the money I had, still in partnership with her.

After supper the outsiders left, and I remained there alone with Zawoiski, since Count Rinaldi had offered to give me my revenge. I played on my word, and he put down the cards when he found that, according to the tally, I owed him five hundred zecchini. I went home in a profound melancholy. Honor demanded that I pay my debt the next day, and I had not a soldo. Love increased my despair; I saw myself on the verge of being exposed as a pauper. My state of mind, which was visibly imprinted on my face, did not escape Signor Bragadin the next morning. He sounded me out and was so encouraging that I told him the whole story; I ended it by saying that I saw myself on the verge of dishonor and that it would kill me. He relieved me by saying that he would pay my debt that very day, if I would promise him never again to play on my word. I swore that I would not; I kissed his hand, and went out for a walk feeling very happy. I was sure that this heaven-born man would give me five hundred zecchini that afternoon, and I was delighting in the thought of the credit my promptness would bring me in the eyes of the lady, who would no longer put off granting me her favors. This was the only reason which kept me from regretting the amount; but greatly affected by my dear master's generosity, I was completely resolved not to play on my word again.

I dine very cheerfully with him and my two other friends, never mentioning the matter. A moment after we got up from the table, a man came bringing a letter and a package for Signor Bragadin. He read the letter: "Well and good!" The man left; and he told me to come to his room with him.

"Here," he said, "is a package which belongs to you."

I open it, and I find thirty or forty zecchini. Seeing my surprise, he laughs and hands me the letter to read.

"I assure Signor di Casanova that our playing last night on his word was only for fun: he owes me nothing. My wife sends him half of the gold which he lost in cash.—Count RINALDI."

I look at Signor Bragadin, who was dying with laughter at my amazement. I understand the whole thing. I thank him. I embrace him; and I promise to be wiser in the future. My soul sees the light; I am cured of my love, and I feel ashamed at having been duped by both the husband and the wife.

"Tonight," said my wise physician, "you will sup very cheerfully with the charming Countess."

"Tonight I will sup with you. You have given me a lesson such as only a master teacher can give."

"The first time you lose on your word, your best course will be not to pay."

"That would dishonor me."

"Never mind. The sooner you dishonor yourself, the more you will save, for you will have to dishonor yourself when you find that you absolutely cannot pay. So it is better not to wait for that inevitable moment."

"But it will be still better to avoid it by henceforth playing only for cash."

"Certainly, for you will save both your honor and your money; but since you are fond of gambling, I advise you never to punt. Deal. You will have the advantage."

"A small one."

"As small as you like, but you will have it. The punter is a fool. The banker reasons. 'I wager,' he says, 'that you will not guess.' The punter answers, 'I wager that I shall guess.' Which one is the fool?"

"The punter."

"Then in Heaven's name be sensible. And if you find yourself punting, and beginning to win, know that you are still only a fool if you end by losing."

"A fool? Luck changes."

"Stop as soon as you see it change, even if you have only won a soldo. You will still have won."

I had read Plato, and I was amazed to find a man who reasoned like Socrates.

The next day Zawoiski called on me very early to tell me I had been expected at supper, and that I had been praised for the promptness with which I had paid the amount I had lost. I let him believe it; and I did not see the Count and Countess again until sixteen years later in Milan. Zawoiski did not learn the whole story from my own lips until forty years later at Carlsbad. He had become deaf.

Two or three weeks after this specimen, Signor Bragadin gave me an even more telling example of his character. Zawoiski had introduced me to a Frenchman named L'Abadie, who was applying to the government for the post of inspector of all the land forces of the Republic. His appointment depended on the Senate. I presented him to my master, who promised to vote for him; but here is what happened to prevent him from keeping his word.

Needing a hundred zecchini to pay some debts, I asked him to give them to me. He asked me why I did not ask Monsieur de l'Abadie to do me the favor.

"I should not dare."

"Do not be so timid; I am sure he will lend them to you."

"I very much doubt it; but I will try."

I go to see him the next day and, after some polite opening remarks, I put the request to him; and, with no less politeness, he begs to be excused, saying all the things one says when one either will not or cannot do favors of the sort. Zawoiski arrives, I leave them, and go and tell my kind patron that my attempt had availed me nothing. He smiled and said that the Frenchman was lacking in intelligence.

1746.

It was on that particular day that the decree making him inspector of the Venetian armies was to be brought before the Senate. I pursue my usual occupations, I come home at midnight and, learning that Signor Bragadin has not yet come in, I go to bed. In the morning I go to wish him good morning, and I tell him I am on my way to congratulate the new inspector. He answers that I can spare myself the trouble, since the Senate had rejected the proposal.

"How can that be? Three days ago he was certain of the contrary."

"He was not wrong, for the decree would have been approved if I had not decided to speak against it. I demonstrated to the Senate that a sound policy would not allow us to give the post to a foreigner."

"I am surprised to hear it, for Your Excellency did not think so day before yesterday."

"I did not know him well. I discovered yesterday that the man did not have brains enough for the post he was soliciting. Can he be a man of good judgment and refuse you a hundred zecchini? His refusal loses him an income of three thousand scudi which he would be enjoying at this moment."

I go out, and come upon Zawoiski with L'Abadie, who was furious.

"If you had warned me," he said, "that the hundred zecchini would have kept Signor Bragadin quiet, I would have found a way to let you have them."

"If you had the brains of an inspector, you would have guessed it."

The man proved useful to me by telling everyone the story. Those who later needed the Senator's voice learned the means of obtaining it. I paid all my debts.

[* * *]

Puffed up by his new-found prosperity under the patronage of Signor Bragadin, Casanova was soon in enough trouble to make it prudent to leave Venice. He traveled to Milan and then to Mantua where he decided to put his occult powers to good use.

CHAPTER XI

I go to Cesena to take possession of a
treasure. I stay in Francia's house. His daughter
Genoveffa.

1748.

At the opera I was approached by a young man who, without further introduction, told me that I was at fault, as a foreigner, in not having gone to see the natural history collection of his father Antonio de Capitani, commissary and presiding judge for canon law. I answered that if he would be so good as to call for me at the Albergo San Marco I would repair the omission and cease to be at fault. The canonical commissary turned out to be as strange an eccentric as I have ever encountered. His collection of rarities consisted in the genealogy of his family, books of magic, saints' relics, antediluvian coins, a model of Noah's Ark, numerous medals, including one of Sesostris[1] and one of Semiramis,[2] and an old knife[3] of a very curious shape and covered with rust. What he kept under lock and key was the paraphernalia of Freemasonry.

"Be so good as to tell me," I said, "what there is in common between natural history and your collection, for I see nothing which has any connection with the three kingdoms."[4]

"What! Do you not see the antediluvian kingdom, the kingdom of Sesostris, and that of Semiramis?"

At this answer, I embraced him, whereupon he displays his erudition over each of his possessions, ending by telling me that the rusty knife was the one with which St. Peter had cut off Malek's[5] ear.

"You own this knife,[6] and you are not a very rich man?"

"How could the knife make me rich?"

"In two ways. First, by putting you in possession of all the hidden treasures in the territories belonging to the Church."

"That follows, for St. Peter has the key to them."

"God be praised. Secondly, by selling it to the Pope himself, if you have the chirographs which prove its authenticity."

"You mean the certificate. I should not have bought it otherwise. I have all that."

254

"Very good. To obtain this knife, I am certain that the Pope would make your son a cardinal; but he would want the sheath too."

"I haven't it; but it is not needed. In any case, I will have one made."

"It must be the very one in which St. Peter himself put the knife when God commanded him: *Mitte gladium tuum in vaginam*[7] ("Put up thy sword into the sheath"). It exists, and it is in the hands of someone who would sell it to you cheaply, unless you wish to sell him the knife, for the sheath without the knife is useless, as is your knife without the scabbard."

"How much would the sheath cost me?"

"A thousand zecchini."

"And what would he give me if I would sell him the knife?"

"A thousand zecchini."

The commissary looks at his son in amazement and asks him if he would ever have believed that anyone would offer him a thousand zecchini for his old knife. So saying, he opens a drawer and unfolds a document written in Hebrew on which there was a drawing of the knife. I pretend to be greatly impressed, and I advise him to buy the sheath.

"It is not necessary," he says, "either for me to buy the sheath or for your friend to buy the knife. We can dig up the treasures on half shares."

"Certainly not. The magistery demands that the owner of the knife *in vaginam* ['in its sheath'] be one person. If the Pope had it he could, by a magical operation of which I have knowledge, cut off one ear of any Christian king who tried to encroach on the rights of the Church."

"Very strange. It is true that the Gospel says St. Peter cut off somebody's ear."

"The ear of a king."

"Oh, not a king!"

"A king, I tell you. Inquire if Malek or Melek does not mean king."[8]

"And if I decided to sell my knife, who would give me the thousand zecchini?"

"I would. Five hundred in cash tomorrow, and the remaining five hundred in the form of a bill of exchange payable one month from date."

"That is what I call talking! Do me the honor to come and eat a dish of macaroni with us tomorrow, and we will discuss a very important matter with all the secrecy which it demands."

I accepted his invitation, and I went. The first thing he told me was that he knew where there was a treasure in the Papal State, so he would decide to buy the sheath. Certain that he would not believe me on my mere word, I took a purse from my pocket and showed him five hundred zecchini; but he replied that the treasure was worth millions. We sat down at table.

"You will not be served," he said, "on silver, but on dishes by Raffaello."[9]

"Signor Commissario, your munificence becomes your exalted rank. A fool would think that this was ugly earthenware."

"A man in very good circumstances," he told me after dinner, "who is domiciled in the Papal State, where he owns a country house in which he resides with his family, is certain that there is a treasure in his cellar. He has written to my son that he is prepared to spend whatever is necessary to obtain possession of it if he can find him a skillful magician capable of unearthing it."

The son then drew from his pocket a letter, several parts of which he read to me, asking me to excuse him for not giving me the whole letter to read, since he had promised secrecy; but without his noticing it I had already seen "Cesena," which was the name of the city from which it had been written.

"So the thing is," the canonical commissary resumed, "to arrange for me to buy the sheath on credit, for I have no ready money. You would risk nothing by endorsing my bills of exchange, for I own property; and if you know the magician you could go halves with him."

"The magician is all ready. It is myself; but if you do not begin by paying me five hundred zecchini in cash, we will proceed no further."

"I have no money."

"Then sell me the knife."

"No."

"You are making a mistake, for now that I have seen it I have the power to take it from you. However, I am too honest to want to play you such a trick."

"You have the power to take my knife? I should like to see proof of that, for I do not believe a word of it."

"Very well. Tomorrow you will no longer have it; but don't expect me to give it back to you. An elemental spirit which is at my command will bring it to me in my room at midnight, and the same spirit will tell me where the treasure is."

"Make him tell you, and you will convince me."

I thereupon called for pen and paper; I questioned my oracle in their presence, and I made it answer that the treasure was beside the Rubicon, but outside of the city. They did not know what the Rubicon[10] was; I told them it was a stream which had formerly been a river; they went for a dictionary, I saw that they were amazed when they found it was at Cesena. I then relieved them of my presence, to give them time to reason falsely. I had taken a fancy, not to steal five hundred zecchini from the poor fools, but to go with the young man and at his expense dig him up the treasure which the other fool at Cesena believed he had in his cellar. I could not wait to play the role of magician.

So when I left the good man's house I went to the public library,[11] where, with the help of a dictionary, I wrote the following piece of mock erudition: "The treasure is seventeen and one half fathoms underground, where it has lain for six centuries. Its value amounts to two million zecchini, and the treasure itself is contained in a wooden chest, the same which Godfrey of Bouillon[12] took from Matilda[13] Countess of Tuscany in the year 1081 when he came to help the Emperor Henry IV[14] to win his battle against that princess. He buried the chest where it is now before he went to besiege Rome. Gregory VII,[15] who was a great magician, having learned where the chest was buried, resolved to go and recover it in person; but death thwarted his plan. After the death of Countess Matilda in the year 1116, the Genius who presides over hidden treasures[16] set seven guards over it. On a night when the moon is full a learned philosopher can bring it to the surface of the earth by standing in the Great Circle."[17]

The next day, as I expected, I see both the father and the son in my room. I give them the history of the treasure which I had composed, and at the height of their amazement I say that I am determined to recover the treasure, of which I offer them one fourth if they will buy the scabbard. Otherwise I again threaten them that I will take the knife. The commissary says that he will decide when he sees the sheath, and I undertake to show it to him the next day. They left well satisfied.

I spent the day putting together a sheath, and a more ridiculous one would be hard to find. I boiled the thick sole of a strong boot, and I made a slit in it which the knife could not fail to enter. Then by rubbing it with sand I gave it the proper look of antiquity. The commissary could not get over his astonishment when I went to see him the next morning and had him put the knife in it. We dined together, and after dinner we settled it that his son should go with me to introduce me to the owner of the house in which the treasure was; that I should receive a bill of exchange on Bologna for one thousand Roman scudi drawn to the order of his son; but that he would not make it over to my order until I had brought up the treasure; and that the knife in the sheath should not be put into my hands until I needed it to perform the great operation. Until then his son would keep it in his pocket.

We bound ourselves to these conditions by exchanging agreements in writing, and we stipulated that we should set out on the next day but one. When we set out the father blessed his son, at the same time telling me that he was a Count Palatine[18] and showing me the certificate issued by the reigning Pope.[19] I thereupon embraced him, addressing him as Count, and I received the bill of exchange.

[* * *]

In the morning I took ship and traveled to Ferrara, and from there to Bologna and Cesena, where we lodged at the Albergo della Posta. Very early the next day we proceeded, on foot, to the house of Giorgio Francia, a rich peasant and the owner of the treasure, who lived a quarter of a mile outside the city and was not expecting such a fortunate visit. He embraced Capitani, whom he knew, and, leaving me with his family, went off to discuss the business with him.

The first thing I noticed, which I instantly recognized as *my* treasure, was the man's elder daughter. I saw her ugly younger sister, a booby of a son, a wife who ruled the roost, and three or four serving-women.

When the elder daughter, the one who attracted me at once, and who was named Genoveffa, like almost all the peasant women of Cesena, heard me say that she must be eighteen, she answered very seriously that she was only fourteen. The house had an excellent exposure and was isolated for a distance of four hundred paces in every direction. I saw with pleasure that I should be well lodged there. What troubled me was a stinking exhalation, which could not but infect the air. I ask Francia's wife where the stench comes from, and she answers that it is the smell of hemp being macerated.

"How much is your hemp worth?"

"Forty scudi."

"Here they are. The hemp is mine, and I will tell your husband to have it taken far away."

My companion called me, and I went down. Francia treated me with the respect he would have shown to a great magician, even though I did not look like one. We agreed that he should have one fourth of the treasure, the second fourth would belong to Capitani, and the remaining two fourths to me. I told him that I needed a room to myself with two beds and an antechamber in which there must be a tub for bathing. Capitani must be lodged at the opposite end of the house from mine, and in my room I must have three tables, two small and one large. In addition I ordered him to procure me a virgin seamstress between fourteen and fifteen years old. The girl must keep the secret, as must all the people in the house, for if the Inquisition[20] learned what we were about, all would be lost. I said that I would come to lodge with him the next day, that I ate two meals a day, and drank no wine but Sangiovese.[21] For breakfast, I would bring my own chocolate with me. I promised to pay him whatever expense he incurred if I failed in my attempt. The last order I gave him was to have the hemp taken away and to purge the air the same day with gunpowder. I told him to find a trustworthy man to go to the Albergo della Posta early the next morning and fetch all our luggage. He was to have a hundred candles and three torches at my disposition in the house.

We had not gone a hundred steps before Francia comes running after me to give me back the forty scudi I had given his wife for the hemp. I would not take them until he assured me that he was certain to sell it the same day for the same price. At this behavior on my part the man conceived the greatest respect for me, which became even greater when, despite Capitani, I refused the hundred zecchini he wanted to give me to pay for my journey. I saw that he was delighted when I said that on the eve of acquiring a treasure one does not even consider such trifles. The next morning we found that we were very well lodged, with all our paraphernalia at hand.

Dinner having been too copious, I told him to economize and give me only some good fresh fish for supper. After supper he came and said that he had consulted with his wife and that I could be sure of his daughter Genoveffa. After telling him to come back with her, I asked him what grounds he had for believing that he had a treasure in his house.

"In the first place," he replied, "the tradition handed down by word of mouth from father to son for eight generations. In the second place, the loud knocking underground which goes on all night. Thirdly, my cellar door opening and shutting by itself every three or four minutes, which is the work of demons we see moving about the countryside every night in the form of pyramidal flames."

"If all this is so, it is as sure as that two and two make four that you have a treasure in your house. God preserve you from putting a lock on the door which opens and shuts, you would have an earthquake which would open an abyss in the same spot, for the spirits want to be able to go in and out freely to attend to their affairs."

"Thank God that a learned man whom my father brought here forty years ago said the same thing. Great man that he was, he needed only three more days to bring up the treasure, when my father learned that the agents of the Inquisition were about to take him. He got him out of the way in a hurry. Tell me, please, why magic cannot resist the Inquisition."

"Because the monks have more devils in their service than we have. I am sure that your father had already spent a great deal with that learned man."

"Two thousand scudi or very nearly."

"More, more."

I told them to follow me; and to do something by way of magic, I dipped a napkin in water, and uttering frightful words in no known language, I washed their eyes, their temples, and their chests, though Genoveffa might not have surrendered hers to me if I had not begun with her father's hairy one. I made them swear, on a portfolio which I took from my pocket, that they had no impure diseases, and Genoveffa that she had her maidenhead. Since she blushed very red as she swore it, I was so cruel as to explain to her what the word "maidenhead" meant, and I was delighted when, telling her to repeat her oath, she said, blushing even more deeply, that she knew what it was and so did not need to swear over again. I ordered them to give me a kiss, and having smelled an insufferable stench of garlic coming from my dear Genoveffa's mouth, I instantly forbade it to them. Giorgio assured me that there would be no more of it in his house.

Genoveffa was not a perfect beauty so far as her face was concerned, for she was tanned and her mouth was too big; but her teeth were fine and her lower lip protruded in a way which made it seem intended to gather kisses. She had begun to interest me when, in washing her chest, I found that her breasts were of a firmness of which I had no conception. She was also too blonde, and her hands were too fleshy to appear soft, but I was prepared to overlook all that. My plan was not to make her fall in love with me, for that would have taken too long with a peasant girl, but to make her obedient and submissive. I decided to make her feel ashamed of showing any antagonism, and thus to assure myself of encountering no opposition. In default of love, the chief thing in undertakings of this kind is submissiveness. Grace, vice, and ecstasy are sure to be wanting; but their absence is almost made up for by the exercise of absolute domination. I told them that each of them was to sup with me in turn, the eldest first, and that Genoveffa would always sleep in my anteroom, where there would be a tub in which I would bathe my guest an hour before he sat down at table and that he must be fasting.

I gave Francia a written list of all the things he was to buy for me in Cesena the next day, but without haggling. They were a piece of white linen twenty or thirty ells long costing eight or ten zecchini, thread, a pair of scissors, needles, storax, myrrh, sulphur, olive oil, camphor, a ream of paper, pens, ink, twelve sheets of parchment, fine paintbrushes, an olive branch which could be made into a staff a foot and a half long.

Delighted with the role of magician which I was about to play, and in which I had not thought that I was so well versed, I went to bed. The next morning I ordered Capitani to go to the principal coffeehouse in Cesena every day, to listen to what people might be saying so that he could report it to me. Francia came back before noon with all the things I had ordered him to get. He assured me he had not haggled, and that the shopkeeper who had sold him the cloth would certainly go about saying that he was drunk, for he had paid at least six scudi more for it than it was worth. I told him to send me his daughter and to leave me alone with her.

I had her cut four pieces six feet long, two two feet long, and a seventh two and a half feet long to make the hood of the surplice I needed[22] for the great conjuration. I ordered her to sit down near my bed and start sewing.

"You will eat dinner here," I said, "and stay here until evening. When your father arrives you will leave us; but you will come back to sleep here after he goes."

So she ate dinner beside my bed, where her mother served her all the things I sent her, and drank only Sangiovese wine. Toward evening when her father arrived, she disappeared.

I had the patience to bathe the good man in the tub and to sit with him at the supper table, where he ate like a wolf, assuring me that it was the first time in his life he had gone twenty-four hours without eating. Drunk on Sangiovese wine, he slept until his wife appeared, bringing me my chocolate. His daughter came and sewed until evening,[23] then disappeared on the arrival of Capitani, whom I treated as I had treated Francia. The next day was Genoveffa's turn. I had awaited it with the greatest impatience.

At the appointed hour I told her to get into the tub, and to call me when she had done so, because I had to bathe her as I had bathed her father and Capitani. She went off at once without answering me, and called me a quarter of an hour later. I went to the end of the tub, looking as gentle and as serious as possible. She was on her side; I told her to lie on her back and to look at me while I pronounced the formula for the rite. She obeyed with perfect docility, and I washed her all over, in every position. As I had to give a faultless performance in my role, I found it more trying than enjoyable, and she must have found it no less trying to display indifference and to conceal the emotion which must have been aroused in her by my hand which kept washing her just where she must have felt its touch more acutely than anywhere else. I made her get out of the bath to dry her; and it was then that my zeal to do the thing properly ordered her to assume postures which very nearly made me step out of my role. A modicum of relief which I contrived to give myself at a moment when she could not see me having calmed me, I told her to get dressed.

As she was fasting she ate with a ravenous appetite, and the Sangiovese wine which she drank like water heated her so much that I no longer saw she was tanned. As soon as we were alone I asked her if she had disliked what I had made her do and she answered that, on the contrary, she had enjoyed it.

"Then I hope," I said, "that tomorrow you won't mind getting into the bath after I do, and washing me as I have washed you."

"I'll be glad to; but how will I know what to do?"

"I will tell you, and in future you will sleep in my room every night, for I must make certain that on the night of the great operation you are still a virgin."

After this announcement, Genoveffa began to be at ease with me, she looked at me with assurance, she often smiled, and she showed no more embarrassment. She went to bed, and having nothing more which could be new to me, she did not need to overcome any feeling of modesty. To offset the heat, she stripped naked, and she went to sleep. I did likewise, but feeling sorry that I had undertaken not to make the great sacrifice until the night on which I was to bring up the treasure. The operation would fail, I knew; but I knew that it would not fail because I had failed to take her maidenhead.

Genoveffa got up very early and set to work. When she had finished the surplice she spent the rest of the day making me a parchment crown with seven points, on which I painted terrifying characters.

An hour before supper I got into the tub, she came in as soon as I told her it was time, and she performed the same ablutions on me which I had performed on her the evening before, and with the same zeal and the same gentleness, giving me the same tokens of the most ardent affection. I passed a charming hour, during which I respected only the sanctuary. Having been kissed all over, she thought she should do as much for me when she found that I did not forbid it.

"I am delighted," I said, "to see that you are taking pleasure in all this. Know, my dear child, that the perfect success of our operation hangs upon nothing but the pleasure you can obtain from my presence, without the slightest constraint."

So instructed, she completely surrendered to nature, doing unbelievable things to convince me that the pleasure she experienced was beyond expression. Despite abstaining from the forbidden fruit, we feasted sufficiently to be able to sit down at table thoroughly pleased with each other. It was she who, as she was going to her bed, asked me if our sleeping together would ruin the undertaking. She came joyously into my arms when I answered that it would not, and we went at it until love itself demanded sleep. I had occasion to admire the richness of her temperament in her wonderful inventiveness.

I spent most of the following night with Francia and Capitani observing with my own eyes the phenomena of which the peasant had told me. Standing on the balcony which gave on the courtyard of the house, I heard the door opening and shutting every three or four minutes by itself, I heard subterranean knockings which followed one another regularly at the rate of three or four a minute. The sound was like that which would be made by a great bronze pestle pounded into a mortar of the same material. Taking my pistols, I stationed myself by the moving door with a lantern in my hand. I saw the door open slowly and thirty seconds later shut with a bang. I opened and closed it myself, and finding no hidden physical reason for the strange phenomenon, I decided that some trickery was afoot. I took care not to say so.

Back on the balcony again, I saw shadows coming and going in the courtyard. It could only be masses of dense, humid air; and as for the pyramidal flames which I saw gliding about the countryside, they were a phenomenon with which I was already acquainted. I let them go on believing that they were spirits guarding the treasure. The whole countryside of southern Italy is full of will-o'-the-wisps which the common people take to be devils. This is the origin of the name *spirito folletto*.[24]

It was at night . . . [25]

HISTORY OF MY LIFE

Volume Three

CHAPTER I

*I attempt my magical operation. A terrible
storm comes up. My fear. Genoveffa remains
pure. I give up, and sell the sheath to
Capitani. I decide to go to Naples. What
puts me on a different road.*

Anno 1748,[1]
the 23rd of my age.

It was on the next night that I was to perform the great operation,
for otherwise we should have had to wait for the full moon of
the following month. I was supposed to compel the gnomes to
bring the treasure to the surface at the place where I would put
my conjurations on them. I knew that the operation would fail, but
that it would be easy for me to explain the reason; meanwhile I must
continue to give a flawless performance in my role of magician,
which I very much enjoyed. I made Genoveffa work all day at
sewing together a circle of thirty sheets of paper on which I had
painted characters and terrifying figures in black. This "Great
Circle,"[2] as I called it, had a diameter of three paces. I had made a
sort of scepter from the olive branch which Giorgio Francia had
brought me. So, having everything I needed, I warned Genoveffa
that at midnight, when I came out of the circle, she must be ready
for anything. She could not wait to give me such a proof of
her obedience; but that did not lessen my feeling that I was still in
her debt.

So, having instructed her father Giorgio and Capitani to station
themselves on the balcony, not only to be ready to carry out my
orders if I called to them but also to prevent the household from
seeing what I was about to do, I take off all my profane garments; I
put on the great surplice which had been touched only by the pure
hands of the innocent Genoveffa; then I let my long hair hang loose,
I set the seven-pointed crown on my head and take the great circle
on my shoulders, and with one hand holding the scepter and the
other the very knife with which St. Peter once cut off Malek's ear, I
go down to the courtyard and, after spreading out my circle on the
ground and walking around it three times, I jump into it.

After crouching inside it for two or three minutes, I rise and stand motionless, watching a heavy black cloud which was coming up on the western horizon while thunder rumbled violently in the same direction. How I should have been admired if I had dared to predict it! The lightning grew more frequent as the cloud ascended, leaving the celestial vault without a glimmer of light; that from the lightning was enough to make the terrible darkness brighter than day.

As all this was perfectly natural, I had no reason to be surprised at it; nevertheless a beginning of terror made me wish I were in my room, and I began to shudder when I heard and saw the thunder and lightning which were following one another with the greatest rapidity. The flashes, which were all about me, froze my blood. In the terror which overtook me I persuaded myself that if the flashes of lightning I saw did not strike me down it was because they could not enter the circle. For this reason I did not dare leave it and take to my heels. But for my false belief, which was only the product of fear, I should not have remained in the circle for as long as a minute, and my flight would have convinced Capitani and Francia that, far from being a magician, I was an utter coward. The force of the wind, its frightful howling, my fear, and the cold combined to set me shaking like a leaf. My philosophical system, which I thought was proof against any assault, was gone. I recognized an avenging God who had lain in wait for me there to punish me for all my misdeeds and thus end my unbelief by death. What convinced me that my repentance was of no avail was that I absolutely could not move.

But now down comes the rain, I hear no more thunder, I see no more lightning, I feel my old courage reborn. But what a rain! It was a torrent falling from the sky through the air, which would have flooded everything if it had lasted for more than a quarter of an hour. When the rain ended both the wind and the darkness were gone. High in the absolutely cloudless sky I saw the moon, more beautiful than ever. I gathered up my circle, and after ordering Capitani and Francia to go to bed without speaking to me, I went to my room, where one glance showed me Genoveffa looking so beautiful that she frightened me. I let her dry me off without looking at her, and then in piteous tones told her to get into her bed. She said in the morning that, seeing me shivering despite the heat of the season, she had felt afraid for me.

After sleeping for eight hours I was sick of the comedy. When Genoveffa appeared I was astonished that she seemed a different person. She no longer seemed to be of a different sex from mine, since I no longer felt that mine was different from hers. At the moment an idea whose superstitiousness took nothing from its power made me believe that the girl's innocence was protected and that I should be struck dead if I dared to assail it. In the resolve which I made I had no other thought than that her father Francia would be less gulled and she less unhappy, unless, that is, the same thing happened to her which had happened to poor Lucia at Pasiano.

As soon as Genoveffa became an object of sacred terror in my eyes I determined to leave immediately. What made my resolve irrevocable was a panic yet very reasonable terror. Some peasants might have seen me in the circle and, convinced that the storm had been the effect of my magical operation, might go and accuse me to the Inquisition,[3] which would lose no time in seizing my person. Shaken by the possibility, which would have destroyed me, I sent for Francia and Capitani and told them in Genoveffa's presence that I had to put off the operation because of an agreement I had made with the seven gnomes who guarded the treasure, of which they had given me as full an account as I could wish. I left it with Francia in writing, drawn up in the following terms, and the same as the one I had given Capitani in Mantua:

"The treasure which lies here at seventeen and one half fathoms underground has been there for six centuries. It consists of diamonds, rubies, and emeralds, and a hundred thousand pounds of powdered gold. All this is contained in one chest, which is the same one which Godfrey of Bouillon took from Matilda Countess of Tuscany in the year 1081, when he went to help the Emperor Henry IV win his battle against that princess.[4] He buried the chest where it now is before he went to besiege Rome. Gregory VII,[5] who was a great magician, having learned where the chest was buried, determined to go and recover it in person; but he died before he could carry out his plan. In the year 1116, immediately upon the death of the Countess Matilda, the gnome who is the Genius presiding over hidden treasures gave it seven guardians."

After giving him this document I made him swear to wait for me, or to believe no one who did not give him an account of the treasure exactly like the one I was leaving him. I had the crown and the circle burned, ordering him to keep the other things until I should return, and I sent Capitani to Cesena at once to wait at the Albergo della Posta for the man whom Francia would send him with all our baggage.

Seeing that Genoveffa was inconsolable, I took her aside and assured her that she would see me soon. Some scruples of conscience made me feel obliged to tell her that, since her innocence was no longer necessary to the raising of the treasure, she was under no further obligation and was free to marry if the opportunity arose.

I went on foot to Cesena and to the inn, where I found Capitani ready to return to Mantua after having visited the fair at Lugo.[6] He shed tears as he told me that his father would be in despair when he saw him come back without St. Peter's knife. I gave it to him, and offered him the sheath as well if he would buy it for the 500 Roman scudi stipulated in the bill of exchange he had given me; and considering it a very good bargain he agreed at once and I gave him back the bill. I made him sign an agreement by which he undertook to return my sheath to me whenever I sent him the same sum of 500 Roman scudi.[7]

I had no use for the sheath, and no need of money; but I thought that to let him have it for nothing would dishonor me and give him an idea that I set no value on it. Chance decreed that we should not see each other until long afterward and when I was not able to give him the 250 zecchini.[8] So, as it turned out, my escapade made me the richer by that amount, while at the same time it never entered Capitani's head to complain or to believe that I had gulled him; for, with the sheath in his possession, he believed that he was master of all the treasures which might be hidden in all the Papal States.

Capitani left the next day, and for my part I would have set off for Naples without losing any time, had not something immediately happened which caused me to put off following my plan.

[* * *]

Returning to his inn in Cesena, Casanova decides to visit the theater where he recognizes among the company the Venetian Manzoni and his old adversary, Giulietta "la Cavamacchie," now supposedly married to Signor Querini but apparently under the protection of her friend and former lover, General Spada, owner of the theater.

The next morning at daybreak I am awakened by an extraordinary uproar in the public room and almost at the door of my bedroom. A minute later I hear the noise in the room next to mine. I get out of bed and quickly open my door to see what is going on. I see a troop of *sbirri*[9] at the open door of the room and in the room I see a decent-looking man sitting up in bed and shouting in Latin at the ruffians and at the innkeeper, who was there and who had dared to open his door for them. I ask the innkeeper what it was all about.

"This gentleman," he answers, "who apparently speaks only Latin, is in bed with a young woman, and the Bishop's constables have come to find out if she is his wife. It is perfectly simple: if she is, he has only to prove it to them by some certificate, and the thing will be over; but if she is not, he must put up with going to prison with the girl; but that won't happen to him, for I will undertake to patch the matter up for two or three zecchini. I will speak to their captain, and they will all go away. If you speak Latin, go in and make him see reason."

"Who forced the door of his room?"

"It was not forced; I opened it myself; it is my duty."

"It is the duty of a highway robber."

Surprised by such infamous proceedings, I cannot refrain from interfering. I enter, and I tell the man in the nightcap all the circumstances of the intrusion. He answers, with a laugh, that in the first place no one could know if whoever was in bed with him was a girl, for the person had been seen only in male attire, and that in the second place he considered that no one on earth had the right to force him to declare whether it was his wife or his mistress, always supposing that the person in bed with him was indeed a woman.

"Furthermore," he said, "I am determined not to spend a single paolo[10] to end the matter, and not to get out of bed until my door has been shut. As soon as I have dressed I will show you a pretty ending to this comedy. I will send all these robbers running with my saber."

I then see in the corner of the room a saber and a Hungarian coat which looked as if it belonged to a uniform. I ask him if he is an officer, and he answers that he had written his name and rank in the innkeeper's register. Absolutely astounded at this extraordinary state of affairs, I question the innkeeper,[11] who says that it is true, but that the ecclesiastical tribunal nevertheless had the right to inquire into any scandalous conduct.

"The insult you have just offered this officer," I tell him, "will cost you dear."

In answer to my threat they all laughed in my face. Much annoyed at being mocked by such riffraff, I ask the officer if he dares entrust his passport to me; he says that, since he has two, he can very well entrust me with one of them and, so saying, he takes it from a portfolio and hands it to me to read. It was from Cardinal Albani.[12] I see the officer's name and his rank as captain in a Hungarian regiment of the Empress-Queen. He tells me that he has come from Rome and is on his way to Parma to deliver to Monsieur Dutillot,[13] Prime Minister of the Infante the Duke of Parma, a package entrusted to him by Cardinal Alessandro Albani.

Just then a man enters the room asking me to tell the Signore in Latin that he wished to leave at once and had not time to wait for him; so that he should either settle matters with the constables immediately or pay him. He was the *vetturino*.[14]

Seeing it was obviously a plot, I asked the officer to leave the whole matter to me, assuring him that I would bring him off with honor. He told me to do whatever I pleased. I told the *vetturino* that he had only to bring up the Signore's trunk and he would receive his money. He brought up the trunk and received the eight zecchini from my hands, giving a receipt to the officer, who spoke only German, Hungarian, and Latin. The *vetturino* left at once; and the *sbirri* likewise, in great alarm, except for two, who remained in the public room.

I then advised the officer not to get out of bed until I returned. I said that I was going to the Bishop to tell him that he owed him the most complete satisfaction, and he had no doubt of it when I told him that General Spada was in Cesena; he answered that he knew him, and that if he had known he was there he would have blown out the innkeeper's brains for opening the door of his room to the *sbirri*. I quickly put on my redingote and not stopping to undo my curl-papers I went to the Bishop's palace and, raising a row, was conducted to the Bishop's room. A lackey told me he was still in bed; but not having time to wait I go in and I tell the prelate the whole story, exclaiming over the iniquity of such proceedings and railing at a police force which violated the law of nations.

He does not answer me. He calls, and orders me taken to the Chancellor's room.

I repeat the facts to the Chancellor, not measuring my words[15] and using a style calculated to irritate and not to gain favors. I threaten; I say that if I were the officer I would demand exemplary satisfaction. The priest smiles and, after asking me if I have a fever, tells me to go and talk with the captain of the *sbirri*.

Delighted that I had irritated him and so brought the matter to the point where only the authority of General Spada could, and must, end it to the honor of the insulted officer and the confusion of the Bishop, I go to the General's. I am told that he cannot be seen until eight o'clock, and I return to the inn.

The ardor with which I had embraced the affair appeared to spring from my innate sense of decency, which could not bear to see a foreigner treated in such a fashion; but what made me so hot in it was a far stronger motive. I imagined that the girl in bed beside him was very attractive; I could not wait to see her face. Shame had never permitted her to expose her head. She had heard me, and I was sure that I had made a good impression on her.

As the door of the room was still open, I enter and give the officer an account of all that I had done, assuring him that in the course of the same day he would be free to leave at the Bishop's expense, after receiving complete satisfaction at the behest of the General. I say that I cannot see him until eight o'clock. He expresses his gratitude; he tells me that he will not leave until the next day, and he pays me the eight zecchini I had given the *vetturino*. I ask him of what nationality his traveling companion was, and he answers that the person is French and understands no language but his own.

"Then you speak French?"

"Not a word."

"That's odd. Then you never talk to each other except by gestures?"

"Exactly."

"I am sorry for you. May I hope to breakfast with you?"

"Ask him if he wishes it."

So I address my request to him, and I see a tousled head appear from under the covers, revealing a smiling, fresh, attractive face which leaves me in no doubt of its sex, though the hair is cut like a man's.

Enchanted by the lovely apparition, I say that having taken up her cause without seeing her, the sight of her could only have increased my eagerness to be of use to her and my zeal. She refutes my reasoning as prettily as possible and with all the wit of her nation. I go out to order coffee and to give her time to sit up; for it had been settled that neither of them would get out of bed so long as the door of their room remained open.

The waiter having come, I go back, and I see the Frenchwoman in a blue redingote and with her hair awkwardly arranged like a man's. I am surprised by her beauty and sigh for the moment when I shall see her up. She drank coffee with us, never interrupting the officer, who was talking to me and to whom I did not listen in the ecstasy into which I was thrown by the face of this creature who did not look at me and whom the *pudor infans* ("silent shame")[16] of my dear Horace kept from uttering a single word.

At eight o'clock I go to the General's and I tell him the circumstances, exaggerating as much as possible. I say that if he does not deal with the situation, the officer considered that he must send an express to his patron the Cardinal. But my eloquence was not needed. Count Spada, after reading the officer's passport, said that, comedy though it was, he would treat it as a matter of the gravest importance. He ordered his Adjutant to go to the Albergo della Posta at once and invite the officer to dinner together with his companion, whose sex no one had been able to discover; and then to go and inform the Bishop officially that the officer would not leave until he had obtained whatever satisfaction he wished and whatever sum of money he considered proper as damages.

How I enjoyed witnessing this gratifying scene, of which, filled with justifiable vanity, I considered myself the author!

The Adjutant, preceded by me, waits on the Hungarian officer, gives him back his passport, and invites him to dinner with his companion; then tells him to put in writing the kind of satisfaction he wishes and what sum he asks in recompense for the time he has lost. I hurried to my room to provide him with ink and paper; and the brief document, in passable Latin for a Hungarian, was ready at once. The *sbirri* had vanished. The good Captain would ask for only thirty zecchini, despite all that I said to persuade him to ask for a hundred. On the score of satisfaction he was also too lenient. He insisted only upon seeing the innkeeper and all the *sbirri* asking his pardon together on their knees in the public room and in the presence of the General's Adjutant. Otherwise, if this was not done within two hours, he would send an express to Rome to Cardinal Alexander and would remain in Cesena until the answer came, with the Bishop paying his expenses at the rate of ten zecchini a day.

The Adjutant set off at once to take the document to the Bishop. A moment later in comes the innkeeper to tell the officer that he is free; but he left as fast as his legs could carry him when the officer told him he owed him a caning. After that I left them and went to my room to have my hair dressed and to change my clothes, as I was to dine with them at the General's. An hour later I saw them before me, well dressed in uniform. The lady's was simulated, and very elegant.

It was at this moment that I decided to leave for Parma with them. The girl's beauty reduced me to slavery on the spot. Her lover appeared to be sixty years of age; I thought their union very incongruous; and I imagined that I could settle everything amicably.

The Adjutant came back with a priest from the Bishop's palace, who told the officer that he would have all the satisfaction he desired in half an hour; but that he must be content with fifteen zecchini, since the journey to Parma took only two days. The officer answered that he would reduce none of his demands, and he was given the thirty zecchini, for which he refused to sign a receipt. So the matter was settled, and the welcome victory having been the fruit of my efforts, it gained me the unalloyed friendship of the couple. To see that the girl was not a man one had only to examine her figure. Any woman who thinks she is beautiful because, when she is dressed as a man, everyone takes her for a man, is not a beautiful woman.

When, toward the dinner hour, we entered the drawing room where the General was, he took pains to introduce the two officers to the ladies who were present and who laughed as soon as they saw the masquerader; but having already heard the whole story, they were surprised, for they had not expected to have the pleasure of dining with the heroes of the play. The women saw fit to treat the young officer as if he were a man, and the men paid him the homage they would have paid him if he had declared that he was a girl. The only woman who sulked was Signora Querini, for finding that she was receiving less attention, she thought that she was outshone. She addressed him only to show off her French, which she spoke fairly well. The only person who never spoke was the Hungarian officer, for no one cared to speak Latin, and the General had almost nothing to say to him in German.

An old abate who was at the table tried to justify the Bishop by assuring the General that the constables and the innkeeper had acted as they had done only by order of the Holy Office of the Inquisition. That, he told us, was why there were no bolts in rooms in inns, because foreigners were not permitted to lock themselves in. Nor were two persons of different sex permitted to sleep together unless they were husband and wife.

Twenty years later[17] in Spain I found that all rooms in inns had a bolt on the outside, so that foreigners who slept in them could be to all intents and purposes imprisoned.

CHAPTER II

I buy a fine carriage and leave for Parma with the old Captain and the young French-woman. I see Genoveffa again and present her with a fine pair of gold bracelets. My perplexities concerning my female traveling companion. Monologue. Conversation with the Captain. Private interview with the French-woman.

"It is strange," said Signora Querini to the masquerader, "that you can live together and never speak to each other."

"Why strange, Signora? We understand each other none the worse, for speech is not necessary in the business we do together."

This answer, which the General translated into good Italian for the whole company at the table, provoked a burst of laughter; but Signora Querini affected the prude: she thought it too revealing.

"I do not know," she said to the pretended officer, "of any business in which speech, or at least writing, is not necessary."

"I beg your pardon, Signora. Is not gaming a business?"

"Then you do nothing but play cards?"

"Nothing else. We play faro, and I keep the bank."

This time the laughter lasted until everyone was out of breath; and Signora Querini could not help laughing too.

"But does the bank," asked the General, "win a great deal?"

"Hardly. The stakes are so small that it's not worth counting up."

No one took the trouble to translate this answer for the worthy officer. Late in the afternoon the company broke up, and everyone wished the General, who was leaving, a good journey. He likewise wished me a good journey to Naples; but I told him that I wanted first to see the Infante, the Duke of Parma, and at the same time serve as interpreter to the two officers who could not understand each other: he answered that if he were in my place he would do the same. I promised Signora Querini that I would let her hear from me at Bologna, not intending to keep my promise.

The officer's mistress had begun to interest me when she was hidden under the bedclothes; she had attracted me when she put her head out, and far more when I saw her up; but she added the

276

finishing touch at dinner, when she displayed a kind of wit which I greatly admired, which is seldom found in Italy and often found in France. As her conquest seemed to me no difficult matter I considered how to go about achieving it. Assuming, without the least conceit, that I was better suited to her than the officer, I did not imagine that I should find him making any difficulties. I thought him one of those natures who, considering love a trifle, yield easily to circumstances, adapt themselves, and accept whatever compromises chance may offer. Fortune could not possibly provide me with a better opportunity to push my attack than making me the couple's traveling companion. There was no likelihood that I would be refused; indeed, I thought my company would be very welcome to them.

As soon as we were back at the inn I asked the officer if he intended to go to Parma by post or by carriage. He answered that, having no carriage of his own,[1] he would prefer to go by post.

"I have a carriage," I said, "and a very comfortable one; and I offer you the two back seats in it, if my company is not distasteful to you."

"It falls out perfectly. Please propose your excursion to Henriette."[2]

"Will you, Madame Henriette, grant me the honor of conducting you to Parma?"

"I should be delighted, for we will talk; but your part will not be easy since you will often have to play a lone hand."

"I shall do so with the greatest pleasure, only regretting that our journey is a very short one. We will discuss it at supper. In the meanwhile permit me to go and finish some business."

The "business" was a carriage, which I owned only in imagination. It was to the Caffè della Nobiltà[3] that I immediately went to ask where there might be a good carriage for sale. I at once heard that there was an English carriage for sale at Count Dandini's[4] and that no one would buy it because the price was too high. He asked two hundred zecchini for it, and it was only a two-seater, with a folding seat. It was just what I wanted. I find someone to guide me to the coach house, the carriage is to my liking; the Count had gone out to supper, I promise to buy it the next day, and I return to the inn well satisfied. During supper I talked to the officer only to settle it that we would leave the next day after dinner and would each pay for two horses. The long dialogues were between Henriette and myself on any number of pleasant topics, in which I admired a wit in her which was entirely new to me, for I had never conversed with a Frenchwoman. Finding her always charming and unable to suppose her anything but an adventuress, I was surprised to find her entertaining sentiments which I thought could only be the fruit of a most refined education; but when the idea came to me I dismissed it. Every time I tried to make her talk about her lover the officer she evaded my question, but in the most gracious way possible. The only question I asked her to which she felt it necessary to give me an answer was that he was neither her husband nor her father. The good man had fallen asleep. When he woke I wished them good night, and I went off to bed very much in love and very much delighted with the promising adventure, which I imagined would be full of charm and whose demands upon me I was certain that I could meet, since I had plenty of money and was completely my own master. What crowned my happiness was that I was sure I should see the culmination of the intrigue within two or three days.

The next morning very early I went to Count Dandini's. Passing a jeweler's shop, I bought a pair of gold bracelets made with Spanish links[5] such as are worn in Venice, five ells long and unusually fine. I at once thought that I would make Genoveffa a present of them.

When Count Dandini saw me he recognized me. He had seen me at Padua, in the house of his father, who, when I was a student in the university there, held the chair of Roman Civil Law. I bought the carriage, which must have cost twice as much, on condition that he would at once send for a harness maker who would bring it to me at the inn door in perfect order an hour after noon.

From there I went to Francia's, where I delighted Genoveffa beyond measure by giving her the bracelets, of which no girl in Cesena had a pair as beautiful. By this present I paid ten times more than all the expenditure the good man had made during the ten or twelve days I had passed in his house. But a present of far greater value which I gave him was to make him swear to wait for me and never trust any other magicians to bring up the treasure, even if ten years should pass before he saw me again. I assured him that at the first operation undertaken by another philosopher,[6] the guardian gnomes would make it go down twice as far, and that at thirty-five fathoms even I should find it ten times as difficult to bring it up. I said frankly that I could not tell him exactly how soon he would see me again; but that he must wait for me, for it was decreed that only I could bring up his treasure. I accompanied his oath with maledictions which, if he broke it, would bring certain ruin to his whole family. Thus, far from having to reproach myself with having deceived the good man, I became his benefactor. He did not see me again, for he died; but I am sure that his descendants are still waiting for me, for the name of Farussi by which they knew me must have remained immortal in their house.

Genoveffa saw me off to within thirty paces of the city of Cesena, and in the course of hearty embraces with which I took leave of her I saw that my fear of lightning had only had a temporary effect on me; but I was too glad not to have committed that particular piece of villainy to think of returning to it. The present I made her in twenty words was of greater consequence than the bracelets. I told her that if I put off coming back for more than three months she could set about finding herself a husband without any fear that her marriage would prevent acquiring the treasure, which I could not bring up until the Great Science should allow me to. After shedding a few tears she assured me that she would act in accordance with what I had just told her.

So ended the business of the Cesena treasure, in which instead of being a swindler I was a hero; but I dare not boast of it when I consider that if I had not been master of a purse full of gold I would have ruined poor Francia with a light heart; and I believe that any young man with a modicum of intelligence would have done the same thing. As for Capitani, to whom I sold the sheath for St. Peter's knife at rather too high a price, I have never felt any remorse over it, and I should consider myself the stupidest of men if I repented of it now; for Capitani himself thought that he had gulled me when he accepted it as security for the two hundred and fifty zecchini he gave me; and the canonical commissary, his father, valued it to his dying day more than he would have valued a diamond worth a hundred thousand scudi. Dying in that conviction, the man died rich; and I shall die poor. I leave it to the reader to decide which of us was better off.

Back at the inn I arranged everything for the short journey, the thought of which was enough to make me happy. Each time Henriette said anything to me I thought her more charming, and her intelligence enslaved me more than her beauty. I had the impression that the officer was well pleased that I should fall in love with her; and I thought I saw very clearly that the girl asked nothing better than to change lovers. I could assume as much without conceit, for aside from the fact that on the physical side I had all that an acceptable lover could have in order to hope to please, I also appeared to be very rich, even though I had no servant. I told her that, to have the pleasure of not having one, I spent twice as much and that by serving myself I was always sure to be well served; in addition, I was sure I should not be robbed and should not have a spy at my heels. Henriette understood me perfectly; and in short my future happiness intoxicated me.

The worthy officer was determined to give me the money which his share of the posts to Parma would have cost him. We dined, had our trunks put on and securely tied, and then set off after a contest of politeness over the seat beside Henriette, which he wanted me to take. He did not see that the folding seat was the one which my budding love could not but prefer to his; but I had no doubt that Henriette saw it perfectly. Seated facing her, my eyes saw her without my having to turn my head to give them that pleasure, which is certainly the greatest a lover can have among those which he cannot be denied.

In a happiness which I felt to be so great I had to endure one trial. When Henriette said amusing things which made me laugh, seeing the Hungarian distressed because he could not laugh at them too I undertook to explain the joke to him in Latin; but it often turned out that I explained it so badly that it became flat. The officer did not laugh, and I was mortified, for Henriette must suppose that I did not speak Latin as well as she spoke French; and it was the truth. In all the languages in the world what one learns last is their wit; and it is very often idiom which makes the joke. I did not begin to laugh over reading Terence, Plautus, and Martial[7] until I was thirty.

Some repair being needed to my carriage, we stopped at Forlì.[8] After a very gay supper I insisted on going to sleep in another room. During the day's journey the girl had struck me as so unpredictable that I was afraid she would leave her lover's bed and get into mine. I did not know how the Hungarian, who seemed a man of strict honor, might have taken it. I wished to obtain possession of Henriette in peace and quiet, as the result of an amicable and honorable arrangement. The girl had nothing but the male attire she was wearing, not a scrap of woman's clothing, not even a shirt. When she changed hers, she put on a fresh one of her lover's. This was something as new to me as it was puzzling.

It was at Bologna, when we were in high spirits over our supper, that I asked her by what strange chance she had become the mistress of this worthy man, whom one would expect to hear was her father rather than her husband. She answered with a smile that I should get him to tell me the story himself, in all its circumstances and perfectly truthfully. I at once told him that I was curious to hear it, and that she was willing. After making certain that it would not distress her, and making her say again that he should tell me everything, he addressed me as follows:

"An officer who was a friend of mine in Vienna having to go to Rome on a mission, I obtained a six months' leave and went with him. I eagerly availed myself of the opportunity to see the great city, assuming that the Latin language must be at least as well known there as it is in Hungary. But I was very much mistaken, for even among churchmen no one speaks it more than badly. Those who know it only claim to be able to write it; but it is true that they write it purely.

"After a month Cardinal Alessandro Albani gave my friend dispatches for Naples; and we parted; but before he left he introduced me to the Cardinal, giving me such a good recommendation that His Eminence told me that within a few days he would give me a packet and a letter addressed to Monsieur Dutillot, Minister to the Infante, the new Duke of Parma, Piacenza, and Guastalla, paying me, of course, for the journey. As I wanted to see the port which the ancients called 'Centum cellae'[9] and which is now called 'Civitavecchia,' I decided to devote these days to it and went there with my guide, who spoke Latin.

"Visiting the port, I saw an old officer disembark from a tartan[10] with this girl, dressed as you see her. She made a great impression on me. But I should not have thought of her again if the same officer had not arrived with her and put up not only in the same inn where I was lodging but in a room so situated that from my windows I saw the whole inside of it. The same evening I saw the girl eat supper with him without ever seeing them exchange a single word. At the end of their supper I saw the girl get up and leave the table, while the officer never raised his eyes from a letter he was reading. A quarter of an hour later he closed his windows, and when I saw the room in darkness I supposed he had gone to bed. The next morning I saw him go out; and this girl here, left alone in the room with a book in her hand, interested me even more strongly. I went out, and coming back an hour later, I saw the officer speaking to her, while she only answered him by a word or two at intervals, in great dejection. At that I ordered my guide to go and tell the girl masquerading as an officer that if she could give me only an hour's meeting I would give her ten zecchini. Doing my errand at once, he came back and told me that she had answered in French that she was leaving for Rome after having eaten something, and that at Rome it would be easy for me to find out how I could arrange to talk with her. My guide assured me that he would learn where she would lodge from the *vetturino* who was driving her. She left after breakfasting with the same officer; and I left the next day.

"Two days after I returned to Rome I received from the Cardinal the packet, the letter for Monsieur Dutillot, and a passport with the money for my journey, which I was free to pursue at my leisure. So I took a carriage which was going back to Parma, for eight zecchini.

"I was really no longer thinking of the girl when, two days before my departure, my guide told me that he knew where she was lodging with the same officer. I told him to try to make her the same proposal, informing her that I was leaving on the next day but one and so the thing must be done quickly. He answered me the same day that, if she knew the hour of my departure and the gate by which I would leave, she would be on my road two hundred paces outside the city and that, if I were alone, she could get into my carriage, in which we could go somewhere and talk.

"Thinking this a very happy arrangement, I sent her word of the hour and the place, which would be outside the Porta del Popolo in the direction of the Ponte Molle.[11]

"She kept her promise in every detail. As soon as I saw her I stopped the carriage, and she seated herself beside me, saying that we should have plenty of time to talk since she had decided to come and dine with me. You cannot imagine what efforts it took before I could understand her and how hard she tried to make herself comprehensible. It was by gestures. I agreed, and with great pleasure.

"So we dined together; and she refused me nothing I could ask of her; but she surprised me not a little when she would not take the ten zecchini I tried to give her, managing to make me understand that she would rather go with me to Parma, where she had something to do. Finding the adventure very much to my liking, I consented, only regretting that I could not warn her that, if she had been followed to force her to return to Rome, I was not in a position to protect her against such an attempt; I also regretted that, in our mutual ignorance of each other's language, I could not hope to entertain her with amusing talk nor entertain myself by learning of her adventures. Hence I can tell you nothing about her situation. All I know is that she wishes to be called Henriette, that she must be a Frenchwoman, that she is as gentle as a lamb, that she seems to have had a most excellent education, that she is in perfect health, and that she must be both intelligent and courageous, as appears from the examples of those qualities which she gave me in Rome and you at the General's table in Cesena. If she will tell you her story and allow you to translate it into Latin for me, say to her that she will give me the greatest pleasure, for I find that in these few days I have become sincerely her friend. To tell the truth, I shall be very much distressed when we have to part in Parma. Say to her that, instead of the ten zecchini I owe her, I will give her the thirty which, but for her, I should never have received from the Bishop of Cesena. Tell her that, if I were rich, I would give her a great deal more. Be so good as to make all this clear to her in her language."

After asking him if a faithful translation of all that he had just said to me would satisfy him and hearing him answer that he wished it to be perfectly faithful in every detail, I repeated to her word for word all that the officer had said to me.

Henriette, with a noble frankness in which there was, however, a trace of shame, substantiated everything. As for satisfying our curiosity by relating her vicissitudes to us, she asked me to tell him that he must excuse her.

"Tell him," she said, "that the same principle which forbids me to lie does not allow me to tell the truth."

As for the thirty zecchini which he had decided to give her when he left her, she asked me to tell him that she absolutely would not accept a single scudo and that he would distress her if he tried to insist.

"I want him," she said, "to let me go and lodge by myself wherever I see fit, and so far to forget me that he will not try to find out what has become of me in Parma and will pretend not to know me if he happens to meet me anywhere."

After speaking these terrible words to me in a tone as serious as it was gentle, and without any emotion, she embraced the old man in a way which expressed far more compassion than love. The officer, who did not know what words had led to the embrace, was greatly mortified when I translated them to him. He asked me to tell her that, to be willing to obey her order, he must be sure that in Parma she would have whatever she might need. Her only answer was to tell me to ask him not to feel any anxiety about her.

After this declaration we all became equally sad. We stayed there a good quarter of an hour, not only without speaking but without looking at one another. Getting up from the table to leave and wishing them good night, I saw that Henriette's face was fiery red.

As I went to bed I began talking to myself, as I always do when something by which I am greatly interested excites me. Silent thought is not enough for me. I must speak; and possibly at such moments I believe I am conversing with my demon. Henriette's unequivocal declarations confused me completely. "Who can this girl be," I asked the air, "who combines the finest feelings with an appearance of the greatest libertinism? In Parma she insists upon becoming her own mistress, and I have no reason to flatter myself that she will not impose the same law on me that she has decreed for the officer to whom she has already given herself. Farewell my hope! Who can she be? Either she is sure she will find her lover, or she has a husband in Parma, or respectable relatives, or, in a wild spirit of unbridled libertinism, she means to defy fortune to plunge her into the most terrible abyss if it will not raise her to the pinnacle of happiness by bringing her a lover who can lay a crown at her feet: that would be the project of a madwoman or a woman in despair. She has nothing, and as if she needed nothing she refuses to take anything from the officer from whom she could, without blushing, accept a small sum which in a manner of speaking he owes her. Since she does not blush for the favors she granted him without being in love with him, what shame can she feel at receiving thirty zecchini? Can she believe that it is less base to yield to the passing fancy of a man whom she does not know than to receive assistance of which she is absolutely in need to save her from destitution and the risk of finding herself in the street in Parma? Perhaps she thinks that her refusal will justify her misstep in the officer's eyes. She wants him to conclude that she took it only to escape from the man who had her in his power in Rome; and the officer could not think otherwise, for he could not suppose that he had made her fall irretrievably in love with him when he saw her at the window in Civitavecchia. So she might be right and believe that she has justified herself in his eyes; but not in mine. With her intelligence, she must have known that if she had not made me fall in love with her I would not have set off with her, and she could not have been unaware that she had only one means of deserving my forgiveness too. She might have virtues; but not the virtue which could have prevented me from claiming the usual reward which a woman owes to the desires of a lover. If she thought she could play the prude with me and make me her dupe, I ought to show her that she was mistaken."

After this monologue I decided, before I fell asleep, that I would have it out with her no later than the following morning, before we left. "I will ask her," I said to myself, "to grant me the same favors that she has granted the officer; and if she refuses I will avenge myself by showing her the most humiliating contempt even before we reach Parma." I thought it obvious that she could not refuse me tokens of real or feigned affection except by flaunting a virtue which she did not possess, and if her virtue was feigned I ought not to fall victim to it. As for the officer, I was certain, after what he had said to me, that he could have no reason to take offense at my declaration. As a sensible man, he could only be neutral.

With my mind both filled with this reasoning and convinced by it, for I thought it was framed and dictated by the ripest wisdom, I fall asleep and, in a dream which fell nothing short of the charms of reality, Henriette appears before me all smiles and, to my great surprise, with her hair dressed as a woman's. She pleads her case, and proves me wrong, in the following terms: "To demolish all the insulting sophisms you have heaped up, I have come to tell you that I love you and to prove it to you. I know no one in Parma, I am neither mad nor desperate, and I want to be only yours." After uttering these words she does not disappoint me; she yields to my amorous transports, which hers aroused.

In dreams of this sort the dreamer usually wakes an instant before the crisis. Nature, zealous for truth, will not let illusion go so far. A sleeping man is not wholly alive, and he must be alive at the moment when he can give life to a being like himself. But, oh miracle! I did not wake, and I spent the whole night with Henriette in my arms. But what a long dream! I could not know it was a dream until my waking at daybreak made it vanish. I lay there for a good quarter of an hour motionless and stupefied, going over the details of it in my astonished memory. I remembered that I had several times said in my sleep: "No, I am not dreaming"; and I should still have thought that I had not been dreaming if I had not found the door of my room bolted from inside. But for that, I should have believed that Henriette had left before I waked, after spending the night with me.

After this blissful dream I found that I was helplessly in love, and it could not be otherwise. Anyone who badly needs to eat and goes to bed without supper must, if he spends the night dreaming he is eating, wake in the morning ravenously hungry. I dressed quickly, determined to make certain of possessing Henriette before I got into the carriage, or to remain in Bologna, though letting her go on to Parma with the officer in my carriage. In order not to commit the slightest breach of good manners, I saw that before having it out with her I must talk frankly with the Hungarian Captain. I seem to hear even an intelligent reader laugh and exclaim: "Can anyone attach so much importance to such a trifle?" That reader, since he cannot be, and can never have been, in love, is right. For him it can be only a trifle.

After dressing I enter my traveling companions' room and after bidding them good morning and rejoicing with them over the good health which I saw depicted in their faces, I inform the officer that I have fallen in love with Henriette. I ask him if he would be offended if I tried to persuade her to become my mistress.

"If what obliges her," I said, "to ask you to leave her as soon as we reach Parma, and not even to inquire about her, is a lover she may have in that city, I flatter myself, if you will permit me to talk with her for half an hour alone, that I can persuade her to sacrifice her lover to me. If she refuses me I will remain here. You will go to Parma with her and leave my carriage at the posthouse, sending me a receipt here from the post master with which I can recover it at my convenience."

"After we have breakfasted," he replied, "I will go to see the Institute;[12] you will be left here alone with her; you shall speak to her. I hope that when I return in a couple of hours you will be able to tell me that you have persuaded her to do whatever you wish. If she persists in her resolve I can easily find a *vetturino* here; in that way you will keep your carriage with you. I should be infinitely happy to leave her in your custody."

Delighted to have accomplished half of the business and to find that I am not far from the end of the play, I ask Henriette if she is curious to see what is worth seeing in Bologna, and she answers that she would like to if she were dressed as a woman; but that she did not care to go about showing herself to the whole city in men's clothes. We breakfast, then the officer leaves. I tell Henriette that he is leaving me alone with her until his return because I had told him that I needed to speak with her in private.

"The order," I said, after sitting down facing her, "which you gave the Captain yesterday to forget you as soon as you have left him in Parma, to make no inquiries about you, and to pretend not to know you if he sees you anywhere—does it apply to me too?"

"It was not an order but an urgent request which I made of him, a favor which my circumstances forced me to ask of him and which, since he has no right to refuse it, I never supposed for a moment that he would make any difficulties about granting me. As for you, I would certainly not have failed to ask you to do me the same favor, if I could have supposed you were thinking of making indiscreet inquiries about me. You have shown me tokens of friendship and you can imagine that if, my circumstances being what they are, the protection which the Captain still wished to extend to me after my request to him would cause me distress because it might harm me, yours would harm me even more. If you were my friend, you should have understood all this."

"Since I am your friend, you should likewise understand that I cannot possibly leave you alone, with no money and nothing you can sell, in the middle of the street in a city in which you cannot even converse. Do you suppose that a man whose friendship you have won can abandon you after he has become aware of your situation and has heard of it from your own lips? If you believe that, you have no notion of friendship; and if the man grants you the favor you ask of him, he is not your friend."

"I am sure that the Captain is my friend, and you heard what he said. He will forget me."

"I know neither of what nature the Captain's friendship for you may be, nor how much he can rely on his own will; but I know that if he can so easily grant you the favor you asked of him the friendship he feels for you is of an entirely different nature from mine. I am prepared to tell you that not only is it not easy for me to do you the strange favor of abandoning you in the state in which I see you, but that it is impossible for me to do what you wish if I come to Parma; for not only do I feel friendship for you, I love you, and I love you in such a way that it is absolutely necessary either that complete possession of your person should make me happy or that I should remain here, letting you go to Parma with the officer; for if I come to Parma, I should become the most unhappy of men, whether I see you with a lover, or a husband, or in the bosom of a respectable family, or, finally, if I cannot discover what has become of you. 'Forget me' is quickly said. Know, Madame, that a Frenchman may be able to forget, but that an Italian, to judge by myself, has no such strange power. In short, I tell you that you must speak out now. Shall I come to Parma? Shall I remain here? One or the other. Decide. If I stay here that is the end of it. I will leave tomorrow for Naples; and I am sure that I shall be cured of the passion you have aroused in me. But if you tell me to accompany you to Parma you must, Madame, assure me that you will make me happy in the possession of your heart—no less. I wish to be your only lover, on condition, however, if you wish, that you will not make me worthy of your favors until I have been able to deserve them by my services and my attentions and by all that I will do for you with a submission of which you will never have seen the equal. Choose, before that worthy and only too fortunate man returns. I have already told him all."

"How did he answer you?"

"That he would be delighted to leave you in my care. What is the meaning of that sly laugh?"

"Let me laugh, I beg you, for I have never in my life conceived of a declaration of love being made in anger. Do you understand what it is to say to a woman in a declaration of love, which should be all tenderness: 'Madame, one or the other, choose this instant'?"

"I understand it very well. It is neither sweet nor touching as it ought to be in a novel; but this is history, and history which could not be more serious. I have never felt such an urgency. Do you realize the excruciating condition of a man in love at the moment when he must choose a course which can determine his very life? Consider that, despite all my passion, I treat you with perfect respect; that the course I will take if you persist in your resolve is not a threat but a heroic act which makes me worthy of all your esteem. The word 'choose' cannot sound harsh to you; on the contrary, it honors you, for it leaves you to decide your fate and mine. To be convinced that I love you must you see me come like an idiot weeping to you to have pity on me? No, Madame. Sure that I have qualities to deserve your heart, I refuse to ask you for pity. Go where you will; but let me leave. If, prompted by a humane feeling, you want me to forget you, permit me, by going far from you, to make it less difficult for me to recover an unhappy mastery over myself. If I come to Parma I shall go mad. Consider now, I beg you, that you would be doing me an unforgivable wrong if you said to me at this moment: 'Come to Parma, even though I ask you not to try to see me.' Do you understand that in all decency you cannot say that to me?"

"I certainly understand it, if it is true that you love me."

"Thank God! Be sure that I love you. So choose. Decide."

"Still the same tone! Do you know that you appear to be in a rage?"

"Forgive me. I am not in a rage, but in a violent paroxysm, and at a decisive moment. I cannot but resent my too freakish destiny and

288

the accursed *sbirri* of Cesena who waked me; were it not for them I should not have seen you."

"Then you are sorry you met me?"

"Have I not reason to be?"

"None whatever, for I have not yet chosen."

"I begin to breathe. I wager you tell me to come to Parma."

"Yes—come to Parma."

CHAPTER III

*I set out from Bologna a happy man. The
Captain leaves us at Reggio, where I spend
the night with Henriette. Our arrival in
Parma. Henriette resumes the dress of her
sex; our mutual happiness. I encounter some
of my relatives, but do not make myself
known.*

It was then that the scene changed. I fell at her feet, I clasped her
knees, kissing them a hundred times; no more anger, no more harsh
tones, tender, submissive, grateful, ardent, I swear that I will never
even ask to kiss her hands until I have deserved her heart. The divine
woman, who was amazed to see me pass from despair to the utmost
tenderness, tells me in a tone even more tender than mine to rise.
She said that she was sure I loved her, and that she would do
everything in her power to keep me faithful. If she had said that
she loved me as much as I loved her, she would have said no more. I
had my lips pressed to her beautiful hands when the Captain came
in. He congratulated us. I told him happily that I would go and
order the horses, and left him with her. We set off together, all three
of us well satisfied.

Halfway through the post before reaching Reggio,[1] he put it to
me that we ought to let him go on to Parma alone. He told us that if
he arrived with us he would give occasion for talk, that he would be
questioned, and that there would also be much more gossip about us
if we arrived with him. We thought his view most prudent. We
immediately decided to spend the night at Reggio and to let him go
on to Parma alone in a postchaise. We acted accordingly. After
having his trunk untied and put on the small carriage he left us,
promising that he would come and dine with us the next day.

This procedure on the worthy man's part could not be as pleasing
to Henriette as it was to me, for a certain delicacy, partly founded on
prejudice, was felt on either side. After the new arrangement, how
could we have lodged at Reggio? In all decency Henriette would
have had to sleep in a bed alone, yet she could not have kept herself,
or kept us, from realizing how absurd such a reserve would be, and
the absurdity was unfortunately of a kind which would have made

us all blush. Love is a divine child, to whom shame is so abhorrent that if he gives way to it he feels disgraced, and feeling disgraced makes him lose at least three quarters of his dignity. Neither Henriette nor I could feel perfectly happy unless we dismissed the worthy Captain's memory.

I at once ordered supper for Henriette and myself, finding the intensity of my happiness too much for my faculties; nevertheless I seemed downcast, and since Henriette seemed as downcast as I, she could not reproach me for it. We ate very little supper and talked scarcely at all, for our remarks seemed dull to us both; we vainly changed from one subject to another to find something interesting. We knew that we were going to sleep together; but we would have thought it indiscreet to say so to each other. What a night! What a woman she was, this Henriette whom I loved so greatly, who made me so happy!

It was not until three or four days after our union that I asked her what she would have done, without a scudo and knowing no one in Parma, if when I declared my love I had not gone on to tell her that I had decided to leave for Naples. She answered that in all likelihood she would have been in the most disastrous situation; but that, having been certain that I loved her, she could not but be equally certain that, unable to abandon her, I would have spoken my mind. She added that, impatient to make sure of what I thought of her, she had made me translate her resolution to the officer, knowing that he was not in a position either to oppose it or to continue to keep her with him. She said that, not having included me in the favor of forgetting her which she asked of the officer, she considered it impossible that I should not ask her if I could be of use to her, merely out of a feeling of friendship, and that then she would have made up her mind in accordance with the feelings she found that I entertained. She ended by saying that if she had gone wrong, her husband and her father-in-law were the cause of it. She called them monsters.

Entering Parma, I kept the name of Farussi; it was my mother's family name. Henriette herself wrote the name she took: "Anne d'Arci, Frenchwoman." Just as we were telling the customs officers that we had nothing new, a smart-looking young Frenchman offers me his services and says that instead of stopping at the posthouse inn I would do better to let him show me the way to D'Andremont's,[2] where I would find everything French—apartment, cooking, and wines. Seeing that Henriette was pleased with the proposal I accept, and we go on to Andremont's, where we find that we are very well lodged. After engaging by the day the lackey who had taken us there, and concluded a detailed arrangement for everything with the proprietor, I went with him to put my carriage in a coach house.

After telling Henriette that we would meet again at dinnertime, and the hired lackey to wait for me in the anteroom, I went out by myself. Certain that in a city under a new government[3] spies must be everywhere, I wanted to go out alone, despite the fact that the city, my father's birthplace, was entirely unknown to me.

I did not feel that I was in Italy: everything seemed ultramontane. I heard passers-by speaking together in French or in Spanish, those who spoke neither talked in low tones. Going here and there at random, on the watch for a shop where linen was sold and not wanting to ask where I could find it, I see one in which I notice the fat proprietress sitting in a corner behind her counter.

"Madame, I want to buy all kinds of linen."

"Monsieur, I will send for someone who speaks French."

"There is no need, for I am Italian."

"God be praised! Nothing is so unusual nowadays."

"Why unusual?"

"Don't you know that Don Filippo has arrived? And that Madame de France,[4] his wife, is on the way?"

"I congratulate you. Money is bound to flow, and everything will be in good supply."

"True enough, but everything is expensive, and we can't get used to these new ways. It's a mixture of French freedom and Spanish jealousy, which makes us dizzy. What do you want in the way of linen?"

"I warn you to begin with that I don't haggle; so beware. If you overcharge me I will not come to your shop again. I need fine linen to make twenty-four chemises for a woman, dimity to make petti-coats and corsets, muslin, handkerchiefs, and other things which I hope you have, for, being a foreigner, God knows into what hands I may fall."

"You will be in good hands if you trust to me."

"I think I may believe you; so I beg you to help me. I must also find seamstresses who will work in the lady's room, for she needs to have everything necessary made as quickly as possible."

"Dresses too?"

"Dresses, hats, mantles, in short everything, for as a woman you can imagine her stark naked."

"If she has money I promise you she shall lack nothing. I will see to it myself. Is she young?"

"She is four years younger than I am, and she is my wife."

"Ah! May God bless you! Have you children?"

"Not yet, my good woman."

"How fortunate I am! I will send out at once for the pearl of seamstresses. Meanwhile, you shall choose."

After having chosen the best she had among all the various things I asked her for, I paid the price and the seamstress arrived. I told the proprietress that I was staying at D'Andremont's, and that if she would send me a merchant with materials she would be doing me a favor.

"Are you dining at home?"

"Yes."

"That is all I need to know. Trust to me."

I told the seamstress, who was with her daughter, to follow me, carrying my linen. I stop only to buy both silk and cotton stockings, and as I enter my apartment I bring in the shoemaker, who was at the door. That was the moment of true pleasure! Henriette, to whom I had said nothing beforehand, watches everything being laid out on the table with a look of the most complete contentment, but with no other show of her satisfaction except in the praise she bestowed on the fine quality of the articles I had chosen. No heightened gaiety because of it, no base thanks or expressions of gratitude.

The hired valet had gone into my room in the apartment when I arrived with the seamstresses, and Henriette had quietly told him to go back to the anteroom in readiness to come when he was called. The linens are spread out, the seamstress begins cutting to make chemises, the shoemaker takes her measure, and I tell him to bring us up the slippers first, and he leaves. A quarter of an hour later he comes up with slippers for Henriette and for me, and the hired valet comes in with him unsummoned. The shoemaker, who spoke French, was telling Henriette comic stories. She interrupts him to ask the hired valet, who was standing there beside us, what he wanted.

"Nothing, Madame; I am here only to receive your orders."

"Didn't I tell you that when you were needed we would call you?"

"I want to know which of you is my master."

"Neither," I said, laughing; "here is your day's pay. Go."

Henriette went on laughing with the shoemaker, who, seeing that she spoke only French, proposes a language teacher. She asks him what his nationality is.

"Flemish. He is learned. His age is fifty. He is a wise man. He lodges at Bornisa's.[5] He charges three Parmesan lire[6] for a lesson if it lasts an hour and six for two hours; and he wants to be paid each time."

"Do you wish me to engage him?" she asked me.

"Please engage him; it will keep you occupied."

The shoemaker promised to send him to her the next morning at nine o'clock. While the elder seamstress was cutting, her daughter began to sew; but as only one could not do much sewing I told the woman that she would do us a favor if she would get another who could speak French. She promised to have her come the same day. At the same time she offered me her son as a hired valet, saying that he was already beginning to make himself understood in French and was neither a thief nor a gossip nor a spy. Henriette having told me that she thought I would do well to engage him, she immediately ordered her daughter to go and fetch him and also to fetch the seamstress who spoke French. So here was company to entertain my dear wife.

The woman's son was a lad of eighteen who had been to school; he was modest, and he looked honest. When I asked him his name I was much surprised to learn that it was Caudagna.

The reader knows that my father was a native of Parma, and he may remember that a sister of my father's had married a Caudagna.[7] "It would be odd," I said to myself, "if this seamstress were my aunt and if my valet were my cousin. Not a word!" Henriette asked me if I wanted the seamstress to dine with us; but I begged her not to mortify me in future by deferring to me in such trifling matters. She laughed and promised that she would not. I then put fifty zecchini in a small purse and gave it to her, saying that with it she could herself buy all the little things which I might have failed to divine that she needed. She accepted it, saying that the gift gave her the greatest pleasure.

A moment before we sat down at the table we saw the Hungarian Captain come in. Henriette ran and embraced him, calling him "Papa"; she begged him to come to dinner with us every day. The worthy man, seeing all the women at work, was delighted to find that he had placed his adventuress so well, and his joy knew no bounds when I embraced him and told him I owed him my happiness.

We dined most choicely. Andremont's cook was excellent. I discovered that Henriette was an epicure and the Hungarian a glutton; I was something of both. So, trying several of our host's wines, we ate a very enjoyable dinner. My young hired valet pleased me by serving his mother no less respectfully than he did the rest. Giannina, his sister, was sewing with the Frenchwoman. They had already dined.

At dessert I saw the proprietress of the linen shop arrive with two other women, one of whom, who was a milliner, spoke French. The other had samples for all kinds of dresses. I let Henriette choose whatever she wished in the way of caps, bonnets, and trimmings from the first; but I insisted on taking a hand in the choice of dresses, though adapting my taste to that of my beloved. I made her choose materials for four dresses, and it was I who was grateful for her willingness to accept them. The more I bound her heart to me, the more I felt that I was increasing my happiness. Thus we spent the first day, in which it was impossible to do more than we did. In the evening at supper, as she seemed to me not to be as gay as usual, I asked her why.

"My dear, you are spending a great deal of money for me, and if you are spending it to make me love you more, you are throwing it away, for I love you no more than I did day before yesterday. All that you do can please me only as I know more and more surely that you are worthy to be loved; but I have no need to be convinced of that."

"So I believe, dear Henriette; and I congratulate myself if you feel that your fondness cannot grow stronger; but know that I do as I do simply in order to love you the more; I want to see you shine in the finery of your sex, only regretting that I cannot make you shine still more. And if that pleases you, must it not delight me?"

"Certainly it pleases me; and in a way, since you have called me your wife, you are justified; but if you are not very rich you cannot but feel how I must reproach myself."

"Ah, dear Henriette! let me, I beg you, think that I am rich, and be sure that you cannot possibly be the cause of my ruin: you were born but to make me happy. Think only of never leaving me, and tell me if I may hope it."

"I wish it, my dearest; but who can be certain of the future? Are you free? Are you dependent?"

"I am free in the fullest sense of the word; and I am dependent on no one."

"I congratulate you and it rejoices my soul; no one can take you from me. But alas! you know that I cannot say as much. I am certain that I am being sought; and I know that if they catch up with me they can easily find means to gain possession of me. If they tear me from your arms I shall be wretched."

"And I will kill myself. You make me tremble. Have you reason to think this misfortune can befall you here?"

"I have reason to think it only if someone who knows me contrives to see me."

"Is it likely that the 'someone' is in Parma?"

"I think it scarcely possible."

"Then let us not frighten our love with fears, I beg you; and above all be gay, as you were at Cesena."

"Yet at Cesena I was unhappy, and I am happy now; but do not fear that you will find me gloomy, for gaiety is natural to me."

"I imagine that at Cesena you must have been constantly afraid that the French officer with whom you were living in Rome would catch up with you."

"Not in the least. He was my father-in-law, who, I am sure, did not make the slightest effort to find out where I had gone once he no longer saw me at the inn. He can only have felt very glad to be rid of me. What made me unhappy was being a burden to a man whom I did not love and with whom I could not converse. Add that I could not have the solace of thinking I was giving happiness to the man I was with, for I had only inspired a passing desire in him, which he had considered worth ten zecchini, and, when I had satisfied it, I could not but believe that I had become a burden to him, for it was obvious that he was not rich. I was unhappy for another and most painful reason. I thought it my duty to bestow caresses on him and since he had in all decency to return them, I was afraid that he was sacrificing his health to consideration: the idea distressed me, for, as we did not love each other, we were both doing violence to ourselves out of mere politeness. We lavished on courtesy what is due only to love. Another thought troubled me even more. I could not bear it that anyone should believe the good man was keeping me for his profit. That is why you cannot have been aware that you attracted me as soon as I saw you."

"What! Was it not rather because of your own self-respect?"

"No, truly; for you could have no opinion of me but the one I deserved. I made the misstep of which you know because my father-in-law was going to put me in a convent. But I beg you, do not be curious about my story."

"I will not press you, my angel. Let us love each other now, and let no fear of the future trouble our peace."

We went to bed in love, only to rise in the morning even more in love. I spent three months with her, always as much in love and constantly congratulating myself that I was so.

The next morning at nine o'clock I saw the language teacher. He was a respectable-looking man, well-mannered, modest, speaking little and well, guarded in his answers, and learned in an old-fashioned way. He began by setting me laughing when he said that the Copernican system[8] could be accepted by a Christian only as an ingenious hypothesis. I answered that it could not but be God's system since it was Nature's, and that Scripture was not the book from which Christians could learn physics. His laughter made me think him a Tartuffe;[9] but if he could amuse Henriette and teach her Italian it was all I wanted. She told him at once that she would give him six lire every day, since she wanted a two-hour lesson. Six Parmesan lire are worth thirty French sous.[10] After her lesson she gave him two zecchini to buy her new novels which were already praised.

While she was taking her lesson I chatted with the dressmaker Caudagna to find out if we were relatives. I asked her what her husband's occupation was.

"My husband is major-domo to the Marchese Sissa."

"Is your father still living?"

"No, Signore. He is dead."

"What was his family name?"

"Scotti."

"And are your husband's father and mother alive?"

"His father is dead, and his mother is still living with Canon Casanova, his uncle."

That was all I needed to know. The woman was my first cousin once removed, and her children my third cousins. Since my cousin Giannina was not pretty I kept her mother chattering. I asked her if the Parmesans were pleased to have become the subjects of a Spaniard.

"Pleased? It has put us all in a perfect maze; everything is upside down, we don't know where we are. Happy days, when the house of Farnese[11] reigned, you are no more! Day before yesterday I went to the theater,[12] and Arlecchino[13] had everybody laughing fit to burst; but guess what—Don Filippo, who's our new Duke, tried so hard to keep from laughing that he made faces; and when he couldn't hold in any longer he put his hat in front of his face so no one could see him roaring. Somebody told me that laughing spoils the grave countenance of an Infante of Spain, and that if he let it be seen they'd write to his mother[14] in Madrid and she would think it dreadful and unworthy of a great prince. What do you think of that? Duke Antonio[15]—God rest his soul!—was a great prince too; but he laughed so heartily you could hear it in the street. We're brought to such confusion as nobody would believe. For the last three months there's not a soul in Parma who knows what time of day it is.[16]

"Since God made the world the sun has always set at half past twenty-three, and at twenty-four o'clock people have always said the Angelus; and all decent people knew that was the time to light their candles. The way things are now is unbelievable. The sun has gone mad—it sets every day at a different time. Our peasants no longer know at what hour to come to market. They call it a regulation—but do you know why? Because now everyone knows that dinner is at twelve o'clock. A fine regulation! In the days of the Farnese people ate when they were hungry, and that was much better."

Henriette had no watch; I went out to buy her one. I brought her gloves, a fan, earrings, and various knickknacks, all of which pleased her. Her teacher was still there; he praised her aptitude.

"I could," he said, "have taught Madame heraldry, geography, chronology, the sphere; but she knows all that. Madame received a superior education."

The man's name was Valentin de La Haye.[17] He told me that he was an engineer and a professor of mathematics. I shall have much to say of him in these memoirs, and my reader will learn his character better from his actions than from any portrait of him that I might draw.

We dined gaily with our Hungarian. I could not wait to see my dear Henriette in women's clothes. She was to be brought a simple dress the next day, and petticoats and a few chemises had already been made for her.

Henriette's intelligence was as sparkling as it was subtle. The milliner, who was from Lyons, enters our room the next morning saying:

"Madame et Monsieur, I am your servant."

"Why," Henriette asks her, "don't you say 'Monsieur et Madame'?"

"I have always," the woman answered, "seen the first honors paid to the ladies."

"But by whom do we hope such honors will be paid us?"

"By men."

"And don't you see that women become absurd if they do not pay men the same honors as men's politeness renders them?"

They who believe that a woman is incapable of making a man equally happy all the twenty-four hours of a day have never known an Henriette. The joy which flooded my soul was far greater when I conversed with her during the day than when I held her in my arms during the night. Having read a great deal and having natural taste, Henriette judged rightly of everything and, though not learned, she reasoned like a geometrician. Since she did not pretend to intellect, she never said anything important except with a laugh which, by giving it the color of frivolity, put it within the capacity of the entire company. In this way she bestowed intelligence on those who did not have it themselves, and who adored her for it. After all, a beautiful woman without a mind of her own leaves her lover with no resource after he has physically enjoyed her charms. An ugly woman of brilliant intelligence makes a man fall so much in love that she leaves him feeling no lack. So what must I have been with Henriette, who was beautiful, intelligent, and cultivated? It is impossible to conceive the extent of my happiness.

Ask a beautiful woman who is not very intelligent if she would give some small part of her beauty for a little more intelligence. If she is frank she will say that she is satisfied with what she has. Why is she satisfied? Because, having only a little, she can have no notion of the intelligence she lacks. Ask an ugly but intelligent woman if she would change places with the other. She will answer no. Why? Because, having a great deal of intelligence, she knows that it serves her for everything.

The intelligent woman who cannot make a lover happy is the bluestocking. In a woman learning is out of place; it compromises the essential qualities of her sex; then, too, it never goes beyond the limits of what is already known. No scientific discoveries have been made by women. To go *plus ultra* ("farther") requires a vigor which the female sex cannot have. But in simple reasoning and in delicacy of feeling we must yield to women. Hurl a sophism at an intelligent woman: she cannot unravel it; but she is not the dupe of it; she tells you she is not taken in by it, and she rejects it. The man who finds it insoluble accepts it at face value, as does the bluestocking. What an intolerable burden for a man is a woman with the mind of Madame Dacier[18] for example! God preserve you from it, my dear reader!

When the seamstress arrived with the dress Henriette said that I must not be present at her metamorphosis. She told me to go out for a walk until I could come back to the house and find her no longer in disguise.

It is a great pleasure to do whatever the object of one's love commands. I went to the French bookseller's shop, where I found an intelligent hunchback. Nothing, by the way, is more uncommon than a stupid hunchback. Since all intelligent men are not hunchbacks, and all hunchbacks are intelligent, I long ago concluded that it is not intelligence which produces rickets but rickets which produces intelligence. The hunchback, with whom I at once struck up an acquaintance, was named Dubois-Chatellerault.[19] He was an engraver by profession, and director of the Duke-Infante's mint, for it was planned at the time to strike coins; but it was never done.

After spending an hour with this intelligent man, who showed me several of his engravings, I went back to my lodging, where I found the Hungarian Captain waiting for the door of Henriette's room to be opened. He did not know that she was to receive us undisguised. The door opened at last, and there she was. She receives us with perfect composure, dropping us a graceful curtsy in which there was no trace of either the overbearingness or the freedom of the soldier. It was we whom surprise and her new appearance had put out of countenance. She makes us sit down on either side of her; she looks at the Captain in a friendly way; her manner to me expresses tenderness and love, but with none of the show of familiarity which a young officer can make without dishonoring love but which is unsuitable in a well-bred woman. Her new bearing forces me to conform to it with complete good grace, for Henriette was not playing a part. She was actually the character she was representing.

In an ecstasy of admiration I take her hand to kiss it; but she draws it away, and offers me her lips, saying:

"Am I not the same?"

"No. And so little the same that I can no longer say *tu* to you. You are no longer the officer who answered Signora Querini that you played faro 'keeping the bank and the stakes are so small that it's not worth counting up.' "

"It is certain that, dressed as I am, I should not have dared say such a thing. But I am none the less Henriette, who has made three missteps in her life, the last of which, but for you, would have ruined me. Delightful misstep, the cause of my knowing you!"

These sentiments affected me so profoundly that I was on the point of throwing myself at her feet to ask her to forgive me if I had not shown her more respect, if I had taken it all too lightly, if I had conquered her too cavalierly.

Henriette, charming as ever, put an end to this too emotional scene by shaking the Captain, who seemed turned to stone. His obvious air of mortification arose from the shame he felt at having treated such a woman as an adventuress, for he could not believe that she was not what she appeared to be. He looked at her in amazement, he made her bow after bow; he seemed to be assuring her of his respect and his repentance; he was confounded. For her part, she seemed to be telling him, without a trace of reproach: "I am very glad that you know me now."

She began that same day to do the honors of the table like a woman who was accustomed to it. She treated the Captain as her friend and me as her favorite. At one moment she seemed my mistress, at another my wife. The Captain asked me to tell her that if he had seen her disembark from the tartan dressed as she now was he would not have dared to send his guide to her.

"Oh, I am sure of that," she answered him; "but it is strange that a uniform is less worthy of respect than a simple dress."

I begged her not to think ill of her uniform, for I owed it my happiness.

"As I owe mine," she answered, "to the *sbirri* of Cesena."

It is a fact that I spent that whole day in Arcadian courtship; and that when we went to bed together it seemed as if it were for the first time.

CHAPTER IV

I take a box at the opera despite Henriette's
reluctance. Monsieur Dubois comes to call, he
dines with us; trick which my mistress plays
on him. Henriette reasons on happiness.
We call on Dubois; extraordinary talent which
my wife displays there. Monsieur Dutillot.
The court gives a magnificent entertainment
in the palace gardens; our disastrous en-
counter there. I have an interview with Mon-
sieur d'Antoine, the Infante's favorite.

Madame de France, the Infante's wife, having arrived, I told Henriette that I would engage a box for every day. She had said several times that her ruling passion was music. As she had never seen an Italian opera I was surprised to hear her answer me coldly:

"You mean you want us to go to the opera every day?"

"I even think we should get ourselves talked about if we did not go; but if you will not enjoy going, my dear, you know that you are under no obligation to put yourself out. I prefer our conversations in this room to all the music in the universe."

"I am mad about music, my dear; but I cannot help trembling at the very thought of going out."

"If you tremble, I shudder; but we must go to the opera, or leave for London or somewhere else. You have only to command."

"Take a box that is not too conspicuous."

I took a box in the second tier; but as the theater was small a pretty woman could not fail to be noticed in it. I told her so, and she replied that she did not think she was in danger of being recognized, since none of the names in the list of foreigners then in Parma which I had given her to read was known to her.

So Henriette came to the opera; but in the second tier, without rouge and without a candle. It was an *opera buffa*,[1] the music to which, by Buranello,[2] was as excellent as the actors. She used her opera glass only for them, never turning it either on the boxes or the parterre. No one seemed to be curious about us; so we went home well satisfied, in the bosom of peace and love. As the finale of the second act had pleased her greatly, I promised it to her. It was to Monsieur Dubois that I went to obtain it; and thinking that she might play the harpsichord, I offered her one. She answered that she had never learned to play the instrument.

The fourth or fifth time we went to the opera Monsieur Dubois came to our box. Not offering him my seat, since I did not want to introduce him, I asked him what I could do for him. He then gave me the *spartito*[3] of the finale, for which I paid him what it had cost him. As we were opposite to the sovereigns I asked him if he had engraved them, and when he replied that he had already made two medallions of them I asked him to bring them to me in gold. He promised that he would do so, and left. Henriette did not even look at him; and this was as it should be, since I had not introduced him to her; but the next day when we were still at table he was announced. Monsieur de La Haye, who was dining with us, immediately congratulated us on our having made the acquaintance of so celebrated an artist. It was he who took the liberty of introducing him to his beautiful pupil, who then treated him to the polite remarks which it is customary to make to all new acquaintances. After thanking him for the *spartito* she asked him to procure several other arias for her. He said that he had taken the liberty to call on me to bring me the medallions in which I had shown an interest; and so saying he took from his portfolio the two which he had made. On one of them was the Infante with the Infanta, on the other the Infante. As everything about the medallions was beautiful, we praised them.

"The workmanship is priceless," said Henriette, "but the gold can be reimbursed."

He answered modestly that they weighed sixteen zecchini, and she paid him for them, thanking him and asking him to come some other day at suppertime. Coffee was brought.

As Henriette was about to put sugar into Dubois's cup, she asked him if he liked it very sweet.

"Madame, your taste is mine."

"Then you must know that I like it without sugar; and I am very glad that my taste is the same as yours."

So saying, she puts no sugar in his cup and after putting some in De La Haye's cup and in mine she puts none at all in hers. I wanted to burst out laughing, for the minx, who usually liked it very sweet, drank it bitter that day to punish Dubois for the insipid compliment he had paid her by saying that his taste was the same as hers. However, the clever hunchback would not retract. Drinking it with every appearance of pleasure, he maintained that it should always be drunk bitter.

After they left, and after laughing for a long time with Henriette over the trick she had played, I told her that she would be the victim of it, for in future she would always have to take her coffee bitter whenever Dubois was present. She said she would pretend that her doctor had ordered her to drink it sweet.

At the end of a month Henriette was speaking Italian. It was the result of practicing with Giannina, who served her as chambermaid, more than of the lessons she received from De La Haye. Lessons serve only to teach the rules of languages; to speak them, practice is necessary. We had been to the opera a score of times without making any acquaintances. We were happy in the fullest sense of the word. I never went out except with her in a carriage, and neither of us would receive callers. I knew no one, and no one knew me. After the Hungarian left, the only person who came to dine with us, when we invited him, was Dubois, for De La Haye dined with us every day.

Dubois was very curious about us; but he was intelligent enough to conceal it. One day he talked to us of how brilliant Don Filippo's court had become since Madame's arrival and of the great number of foreigners of both sexes who had attended it that day.

"Most of the foreign ladies we have seen there," he said, addressing Henriette, "are unknown."

"Perhaps if they were known they would not have put in an appearance."

"Perhaps; but I can assure you, Madame, that even if their attire or their beauty made them conspicuous, the wish of the Sovereign is entirely in favor of freedom. I still hope, Madame, to have the honor of seeing you there."

"It is very unlikely, for you cannot imagine what a ridiculous figure I think a woman cuts who goes to court without being presented, especially if she is of a station which gives her the right."

The hunchback was at a loss for an answer, and Henriette nonchalantly changed the subject. After he left she laughed with me over his thinking that he had concealed his curiosity. I told her that in all conscience she should forgive any man whose curiosity she aroused, whereupon she came to me all smiles and caressed me. Living together in this fashion, and tasting the delights of true happiness, we scoffed at the philosophy which denies that happiness can be perfect, because, it maintains, it is not enduring.

"What do they mean," Henriette said one day, "by that word 'enduring'? If they mean 'perpetual,' 'immortal,' they are right. But since man is not so, happiness cannot be so; apart from that, all happiness is enduring, for to be so it needs only to exist. But if by perfect happiness they mean a series of varied and uninterrupted pleasures, they are wrong too; for by putting between our pleasures the calm which must follow each of them after we enjoy it, we gain the time to recognize the reality of our happiness. Man can be happy only when he recognizes that he is so, and he can recognize what he is only in a state of calm. Hence, without periods of calm, he would never be happy. Hence pleasure, to be such, has to end. So what do they mean by the word 'enduring'? Every day we reach the point when, desiring sleep, we set it above all other pleasures; and sleep is the true image of death. We can only be grateful to it after it has left us.

"Those who say that no one can be happy all his life talk to no purpose too. Philosophy teaches the means to compound such happiness, if he who wishes to achieve it remains free from disease. Lifelong happiness could be compared to a bouquet composed of various flowers which would make a combination so beautiful and so harmonious that one would take it for a single flower. Is it impossible that we should spend all our lives here as we have spent a month, always in good health and lacking nothing? To crown our happiness we could, when we are very old, die together, and then our happiness would have been perfectly enduring. Death would not interrupt it but would only end it. We could be unhappy only if we assumed that we should continue to exist after our existence ended, which I think implies a contradiction. Do you agree with me?"

It was thus that my divine Henriette gave me lessons in philosophy, reasoning better than Cicero in his *Tusculans*;[4] but she admitted that such enduring happiness could be realized only in the case of two people who, living together, were in love with each other, healthy, intelligent, sufficiently wealthy, with no duties except to themselves, and having the same tastes, more or less the same character, and the same temperament. Happy the lovers whose minds can take the place of their senses when their senses need rest! Sweet sleep follows, not to end until it has restored all their faculties to equal vigor. On waking, the first to revive are the senses, eager to set the mind to work again. Man and the universe share the same condition. We could say that there is no difference between them, for if we discount the universe there is no more man, and if we discount man there is no more universe, for who could have an idea of it? Thus if we take away space we cannot imagine the existence of matter, nor, taking away the latter, can we imagine the former.

I was very happy with Henriette, and she was no less happy with me: never a moment of ill-humor, never a yawn, never did a folded rose petal come to trouble our content.

The day after the closing of the opera,[5] Dubois, after dining with us, told us that he was having the two leading singers, male and female, to dinner the next day, and that we had only to wish it and we could hear the finest pieces they had sung at the theater in the vaulted drawing room of his country house, where music lost nothing. Henriette, first thanking him heartily, answered that her health was so poor that she could make no engagements from one day to the next; and she at once turned the conversation to other subjects.

As soon as we were alone I asked her why she did not wish to allow herself the diversion of going to Dubois's house.

"I would go, my dear, and with great pleasure; but I am afraid that I may find someone at his dinner who would recognize me and so put an end to our happiness."

"If you have some new reason for being afraid, you are right; but if it is only a groundless fear, my angel, why do you take it upon yourself to give up a real pleasure? If you knew what joy I feel when I see you ravished and as if in ecstasy when you hear some beautiful piece of music!"

"Very well. I do not want you to think I have less courage than you. We will go to Dubois's directly after dinner. The singers will not sing before then. Besides, it is likely that, since he will not be counting on us, he will not have invited anyone who is curious to speak with me. We will go without telling him and without his expecting us. He said that he is at his country house, and Caudagna knows where it is."

In accordance with her reasoning, to which she had been inspired by prudence and love, which so seldom agree, the next day at four in the afternoon we went to his house. We were surprised to find him alone with a pretty girl, whom he introduced to us, saying that she was his niece, whom private reasons prevented him from letting everyone see.

Professing to be delighted to see us, he said that as he did not expect us he had changed his dinner to a small supper party, which he hoped we would honor him by attending, and that the *virtuosi*[6] would soon arrive. So it was that we were obliged to stay for supper. I ask him if he has invited many people, and he answers triumphantly that we shall be in company worthy of us, and that he only regretted that he had not invited any ladies. Henriette made him a little curtsy and smiled. I saw her looking carefree and content; but she was forcing herself. Her noble soul refused to show uneasiness; but in any case I did not believe she had any real cause for fear. I would have believed it if she had told me her whole story; and I would certainly have taken her to England, and she would have been very glad to go.

A quarter of an hour later the two singers arrived: they were Laschi[7] and La Baglioni,[8] who in those days was very pretty. Then all the people whom Dubois had invited arrived. They were all Spaniards or Frenchmen, and all at least middle-aged. There was no question of introductions, in which I admired the hunchback's tact; but since all the guests were seasoned courtiers, the breach of etiquette did not prevent them from paying Henriette all the honors of the gathering, which she received with an ease unknown anywhere but in France, and indeed only in the most exalted circles, except for certain provinces where haughtiness is too often displayed.

The concert began with a magnificent symphony;[9] then the singers performed a duet, then a pupil of Vandini's[10] played a concerto for violoncello, which was much applauded. But now for what caused me the greatest surprise. Henriette rises and, praising the young man who had played the *a solo*, she takes his violoncello from him, telling him modestly and calmly that she would do it even better justice. She sits down in his place, takes the instrument between her knees, and asks the orchestra to begin the concerto over again. Most profound silence descends on the company, and deathly fear on me; but—thank God!—no one was looking at me. For her part, she did not dare. If she had raised her beautiful eyes to mine she would have lost courage. But seeing her merely strike the pose of being ready to play, I thought it was only a joke which would end with this really charming tableau; but when I saw her make the first stroke of the bow, I thought the excessive palpitation of my heart would strike me dead. Knowing me well, Henriette had no resource but never to look at me.

But what was not my state when I heard her play the *a solo*, and when after the first movement the applause almost deafened the orchestra? The transition from fear to a satisfaction as excessive as it was unexpected produced such a paroxysm in me as the most violent fever could not do at its height. The applause had not the slightest effect on Henriette, at least visibly. Without raising her eyes from the notes, which she knew only from having followed the entire concerto while the violoncellist was playing, she did not rise until after she had played alone six times. She did not thank the company for having applauded her; but turning to the violoncellist she told him, with an air of gracious and noble courtesy, that she had never played a better instrument. After thus complimenting him, she smilingly told the audience that they must forgive the vanity which had induced her to increase the length of the concert by half an hour.

This compliment having put the finishing touch to my astonishment, I vanished to go and weep in the garden, where no one could see me. Who can this Henriette be? What is this treasure whose master I have become? I thought it impossible that I should be the fortunate mortal who possessed her.

Lost in these reflections, which increased the pleasure of my tears, I should have stayed there for a long time if Dubois himself had not come to look for me and had not found me despite the darkness of the night. He summoned me to supper. I relieved his anxiety by telling him that a momentary dizziness had obliged me to come out to cure it by taking the air.

On the way I had time to dry my tears, but not to restore their normal color to the whites of my eyes. However, no one noticed me. Only Henriette, seeing me reappear, told me by a sweet smile that she knew what I had gone to do in the garden. At table my place was opposite her.

The hunchbacked Dubois-Chatellerault, director of the Infante's mint, had assembled the most agreeable noblemen of the court at his house, and the supper which he gave them, of few but well-chosen dishes, was exquisite. Henriette being the only woman present, it was natural that all attention should be paid to her; but even if there had been others she was such as to eclipse them all. If she had astonished the entire company by her beauty and talent, she conquered them completely by her wit at table. Monsieur Dubois never said a word; considering himself the author of the play, he was proud of it and thought it his part to remain modestly silent. Henriette had the tact to be equally gracious to everyone and the intelligence never to say anything witty without including me. On my side, it was in vain that I pretended submission and the most profound respect for the goddess; she wanted everyone to understand that I was her oracle. The company might well think that she was my wife; but none of them could be sure of it from the manner in which I behaved toward her. The conversation having turned to the merits of the Spanish and French nations, Dubois was stupid enough to ask her which she preferred. The question could not have been more tactless, for half of the guests were Spanish and the other half French; for all that, she talked so well that the Spaniards wished they were French and the Frenchmen wished they were Spanish. Dubois, unquelled, asked her what she thought of the Italians, and at that I felt alarmed. A Monsieur de La Combe,[11] who was at my right, shook his head in disapproval of the question; but Henriette did not let it go unanswered.

"Concerning the Italians," she said uncertainly, "I can say nothing, for I know only one Italian, and a single example is not enough to put one nation above all others."

I should have been the stupidest of men if I had shown the least sign that I had heard Henriette's magnificent answer, and even more stupid if I had not at once dismissed the odious subject by asking Monsieur de La Combe some banal question about the wine with which our glasses were filled.

The talk turned to music. A Spaniard asked Henriette if, besides the violoncello, she played any other instrument, and she answered that it was the only one for which she had ever felt any inclination.

"I learned in the convent," she said, "in the hope of pleasing my mother, who plays it quite well; however, without a downright order from my father, supported by the Bishop, the Mother Abbess would never have allowed me to study."

"And what reasons could the Abbess allege for refusing?"

"Pious bride of Our Lord that she was, she insisted that I could not hold the instrument except by assuming an indecent posture."

At this dictum of the Abbess I saw the Spaniards bite their lips, but the Frenchmen roared with laughter. After a silence of a few minutes, Henriette having made a gesture which seemed to ask permission to rise, everyone rose, and a quarter of an hour later we left. Dubois attended her to the step of our carriage, thanking her endlessly.

I could not wait to clasp the idol of my soul in my arms. I did not give her time to answer all the questions I asked her.

"You were right," I said, "not to want to go, for you were certain to make me enemies. At this moment I must be mortally hated; but you are my universe. Cruel Henriette! You very nearly killed me with your violoncello! As I could not believe that you would have kept it a secret, I thought you had gone mad, and as soon as I heard you I had to go out to dry the tears which you forced from my heart. Tell me now, I beg you, what other accomplishments you have which you are hiding from me and in which you excel, so that when they are manifested to me for the first time they will not make me die of terror or surprise."

"No, my dear love, I have no others, I have emptied my sack, and now you know your Henriette completely. If you had not told me a month ago that you had no liking for music, I would have told you that I can play the instrument. If I had told you so, you could have got me one, and I do not wish to amuse myself with something which may bore you."

No later than the next day I went and found her a violoncello; and she was very far from boring me with it. It is impossible for a man who has no marked passion for music not to become a passionate devotee of it when the person who performs it to perfection is the object of his love. The human voice of the violoncello, which is superior to that of any other instrument, went to my heart when Henriette played it, and she was convinced of it. She offered me the pleasure every day, and I suggested to her that she should give concerts; but she was prudent enough never to consent. Despite that, the course of destiny was not to be halted. *Fata viam inveniunt* ("Fate will find the way").[12]

The day after his charming supper the ill-omened Dubois came to thank us, and at the same time to receive the praises which we bestowed on his concert, his supper, and the persons he had invited.

"I foresee, Madame, the difficulty I shall have in resisting the importunity with which I shall be asked for introductions to you."

"You will not find it very difficult, Monsieur, since your answer can be put in a very few words. You know that I receive no one."

He no longer dared speak of introductions. About this time I received a letter from the younger Capitani in which he told me that, being in possession of St. Peter's knife in its sheath, he had gone to Francia's with two learned men who were certain that they could bring up the treasure and had been surprised to find that he would not receive him. He asked me to write to him, and to go there myself, if I wanted to have my share. I did not answer him. I rejoiced that the good peasant, mindful of my instructions, was safe from the fools and the impostors who would have ruined him.

After Dubois's supper we spent three or four weeks lost in happiness. In the sweet union of our hearts and our souls not one empty moment ever came to show us that dreary specimen of misery known as a yawn. Our only outside diversion was a drive out of the city when the weather was fine. As we never left the carriage and never went anywhere, no one, either of the court or the city, had been able to make our acquaintance, despite the general curiosity about us and the desires which Henriette had inspired in all the men who had been present at Dubois's supper. She had become more courageous, and I more confident, after we found that no one had recognized her either at the theater or at the supper. She had no fear of finding the person who could reveal her identity except among the nobility.

One day when we were driving outside the Porta di Colorno,[13] we met the Infante and the Duchess on their way back to Parma. Fifty paces farther on we met a carriage in which we saw a nobleman with Dubois. Just as we would have drawn beyond them one of our horses fell. The nobleman who was with Dubois cried "Stop!" to send help to our coachman, who might need assistance. With dignified politeness he at once addressed the appropriate compliment under the circumstances to Henriette, and Dubois did not lose a moment in saying to her, "Madame, this is Monsieur Dutillot."[14] The usual bow was her answer. The horse got up, and in a minute we were on our way again. This perfectly simple meeting should have had no consequences; but it had one.

The next morning Dubois came to breakfast with us. He began by saying at once that Monsieur Dutillot, delighted with the fortunate chance which had given him the pleasure of making our acquaintance, had commissioned him to ask our permission to call on us.

"On Madame, or on me?" I answered instantly.

"On both."

"Very well," I replied; "but one at a time; for Madame, as you see, has her room, as I have mine. So far as I am concerned, it will be I who will hasten to wait on His Excellency if he has any order to give me or anything to communicate to me, and I beg you to tell him so. As for Madame, there she is, speak with her. I am only, my dear Monsieur Dubois, her most humble servant."

Thereupon Henriette calmly and with the utmost politeness told Monsieur Dubois to thank Monsieur Dutillot and at the same time to ask him if he knew her.

"I am certain, Madame, that he does not know you."

311

"You see? He does not know me, and he wants to call on me. You must admit that if I received him I should stamp myself an adventuress. Tell him that though no one knows me, I am not an adventuress; and that hence I cannot have the pleasure of receiving him."

Dubois, realizing the mistake he had made, said nothing more; and during the following days we did not ask him how the Minister had received our answer.

Another three or four weeks later, the court being at Colorno, a magnificent entertainment[15] was given—I forget on what occasion—during which everyone was allowed to walk about the gardens, which were to be illuminated all night. Dubois having frequently spoken of the entertainment, which was public, we were tempted to go to it, and Dubois himself accompanied us in our carriage. We went there the day before and put up at the inn.

Toward evening we went to walk in the gardens, where, as it happened, the sovereigns were present with a considerable suite. According to French court custom, the Infanta curtsied first to Henriette as soon as she saw her, but without stopping. I then noticed that a Chevalier of the Order of St. Louis[16] who was beside Don Filippo looked at Henriette with great attention. Retracing our steps, we met the same Chevalier halfway down the walk, whereupon, after excusing himself by a bow to us, he asked Dubois to hear something he had to say to him. They talked together for a quarter of an hour, walking behind us. We were about to leave the gardens when the same Chevalier, hurrying to overtake us, after politely begging my pardon, asked Henriette if he had the honor to be known to her.

"Monsieur, I have not the honor of knowing you."

"Madame, I am D'Antoine."[17]

"I do not remember, Monsieur, that I have ever had the honor of seeing you."

"That is enough, Madame—I beg you to forgive me."

Dubois told us that the gentleman, who had no post at court, being only the Infante's intimate friend, had asked him to present him to Madame, believing that he knew her. He had replied that her name was D'Arci and that if he knew her he had no need of his intervention in order to pay her a visit. Monsieur d'Antoine had replied that since the name D'Arci was unknown to him he had hoped that he was not making a mistake but that, wishing to resolve his uncertainty, he had taken it upon himself to approach her without being presented.

"And so," said Dubois, "now that he knows that Madame is not acquainted with him, he must be convinced that he was mistaken."

After supper I thought Henriette seemed uneasy, and I asked her if she had pretended not to know Monsieur d'Antoine.

"It was not a pretense. I know his name. It is a family well known in Provence; but I do not know him."

"Is it possible that he knows you?"

"He may possibly have seen me; but he has certainly never talked with me, for I should have recognized him."

"The meeting makes me uneasy, and it seems to me that you are not unconcerned over it. Let us leave Parma, if you will, and go to Genoa; and when my business is settled we will go to Venice."

"Yes, my dear, we shall be more at ease then. But I think we have no need to hurry."

The next day we saw the masquerades, and on the day after that we went back to Parma. Two or three days later my young valet Caudagna handed me a letter, saying that the messenger who had brought it was waiting outside for the answer.

"This letter," I say to Henriette, "makes me uneasy."

She takes it from me and, after reading it, hands it back, saying that she believes that Monsieur d'Antoine is a man of honor and that hence we have nothing to fear. Here is the letter:

"Either at your lodging, Monsieur, or at my house, or wherever you please, at whatever hour you appoint, I ask you to enable me to tell you something which should be of great interest to you. I have the honor to be your very humble and obedient etc. D'Antoine. To Monsieur de Farussi."

"I think," I said, "that I should hear what he has to say. But where?"

"Neither here nor at his house, but in the palace garden. Your answer should contain nothing but the hour at which you wish to meet him."

In accordance with her advice I wrote him that I would be in the first walk of the ducal garden at half past eleven, asking him to set another hour if the one I had named was inconvenient for him. After dressing and waiting until the time, I went to the place I had appointed for the meeting. We could not wait to know what it was all about.

At half past eleven I found Monsieur d'Antoine alone in the walk I had indicated.

"I have been compelled," he said, "to request the honor which you are doing me because I could find no safer means of conveying this letter to Madame d'Arci. I ask you to deliver it to her, and not to be offended if I give it to you sealed. If I am mistaken, it is a matter of no consequence, and my letter will not even deserve the trouble of an answer; but if I am not mistaken, only the lady herself should have the power to let you read it. That is why it is sealed. If you are truly the lady's friend, its contents cannot but be of no less interest to you than to her. May I be certain that you will deliver it to her?"

"Monsieur, I give you my word of honor that I will do so."

CHAPTER V

Henriette receives Monsieur d'Antoine. I lose
that charming woman, whom I accompany as
far as Geneva. I cross the Saint Bernard Pass
and return to Parma. Letter from Henriette.
My despair. De La Haye pursues my acquaint-
ance. Unpleasant adventure with an actress;
its consequences. I become a bigot. Bavois.

After having repeated to Henriette, word for word, what Monsieur d'Antoine had said to me, I handed her the letter, which filled four pages. After she had read it she said that the honor of two families did not permit her to let me read it, and that she was now obliged to receive Monsieur d'Antoine, who, as she had just learned, was related to her.

"So now," I said, "the last act begins. Miserable wretch that I am! What a final scene! Our happiness is coming to its end. Why did we have to stay so long in Parma? What blindness on my part! Under the present circumstances there was not a place in all Italy more to be feared than this, and I chose it above all the rest of the earth, for, except in France, I believe, no one would have been likely to recognize you anywhere. And I am all the more a wretch because it is entirely my fault!—for you had no other will than mine; and you never concealed your fears. Could I have made a more stupid mistake than to permit Dubois to visit us? I should have foreseen that the man would manage to satisfy his curiosity in the end, a curiosity which is too natural for me to blame him for it and which in any case would not have existed if I had not first aroused it and then increased it by letting him visit us freely. But what use is it to think of all this now that it is too late? I foresee the most painful outcome that I can imagine."

"Alas, my dear! I beg you to foresee nothing. Let us only prepare ourselves to be superior to whatever may happen. I will not answer this letter. It is you who must write him to come here tomorrow at three o'clock in his carriage and to send in his name. You shall be with me when I receive him; but a quarter of an hour later you shall retire to your room on some excuse. Monsieur d'Antoine knows my whole story and in what I have done wrong, but he knows, too, in what I have done right, which obliges him, as a man of honor, to protect me from any affront, and he will do nothing except with my consent, and if he sees fit to depart from the conditions I will lay down I will not go to France: we will go and spend the rest of our days together wherever you choose. Yes, my dear. But remember that inevitable circumstances may compel us to consider our separation our best course, and that then we must adopt that course in such a way that we may hope not to be unhappy. Trust in me. Be sure that I shall find a way to assure myself of all the happiness that can be supposed possible if I am reduced to accepting the idea of living without you. You must take the same precaution for your future, and I am sure you will succeed; but meanwhile let us banish sadness so far as we can. If we had left here three days ago we might have made a mistake, for Monsieur d'Antoine might have decided to give my family a proof of his zeal by making inquiries into my whereabouts which would have exposed me to violent proceedings which your love could not have tolerated; and then God knows what would have happened."

I did all that she asked; but from that moment our love began to grow sad, and sadness is a disease which in the end kills love. We often spent an hour looking at each other and not saying a word.

The next day when Monsieur d'Antoine arrived I followed her instructions to the letter. I spent six very boring hours alone, pretending that I was writing. Since my door was open the same mirror by means of which I saw them might also enable them to see me. They spent the six hours writing, often interrupting what one or the other of them was setting down by remarks which must have been crucial. I could foresee nothing but the saddest of outcomes.

After Monsieur d'Antoine left, Henriette came to my table, and she smiled when she saw that I was looking at her eyes, which were swollen.

"Tell me," she asked, "shall we go away tomorrow?"

"Yes indeed. Where shall we go?"

"Wherever you please; but we must be back here in two weeks."

"Here?"

"Alas, yes. I gave my word that I would be here when the answer comes to the letter I wrote. I can assure you that we need fear no violence. But, my dear, I can no longer bear this city."

"Alas, I loathe it! Shall we go to Milan?"

"Excellent! To Milan, then."

316

"And since we have to return here, Caudagna and his sister can come with us."

"Excellent."

"Leave it to me. They shall have a carriage to themselves, in which they will take your violoncello; but it seems to me you must let Monsieur d'Antoine know where you are going."

"On the contrary, it seems to me that I should tell him nothing about it. So much the worse for him if he can doubt that I will return. It is quite enough that I promised him I would be here."

The next morning I bought a trunk, into which she put whatever she thought she needed, and we set off, followed by our servants, after telling Andremont to lock up our apartment.

At Milan we spent two weeks, concerned with nothing but ourselves, never going out, and seen only by a tailor, who made me a coat, and a seamstress, who made her two winter dresses. I also gave her a lynx pelisse, of which she was very fond. An instance of Henriette's delicacy which greatly pleased me was that she never asked me the slightest question concerning the state of my purse. My own delicacy prompted me never to give her reason to believe that my purse was exhausted. When we returned to Parma I still had three or four hundred zecchini.

The day after our return Monsieur d'Antoine came to dine with us uninvited, and after coffee I retired as I had the first time. Their conference continued as long as the one in which Henriette had made her decision, and after the Chevalier's departure she came and told me that it was over, that her destiny decreed that we must part.

"When?" I asked her, clasping her in my arms and mingling my tears with hers.

"As soon as we reach Geneva, to which you will take me. You must set about tomorrow finding a respectable-looking woman with whom I will travel to France and the city to which I must go."

"Then we shall be together for a few days more? But I know no one except Dubois who can find you a woman of decent appearance, and I am troubled by the thought that the same woman may satisfy his curiosity concerning what you would not have him know."

"He will know nothing, for in France I will find another."

Dubois accepted the commission as a great honor, and three or four days later himself brought Henriette a middle-aged woman, passably well dressed, who considered herself fortunate to have found an opportunity to return to France. She was the widow of an officer who had recently died. Henriette told her to be in readiness to leave as soon as Monsieur Dubois sent her word. On the day before our departure Monsieur d'Antoine, after dining with us, gave Henriette a letter to read, addressed to Geneva, which he afterwards sealed and which she put in her pocket.

We set out from Parma at nightfall, and we stopped at Turin for only two hours to engage a manservant to wait on us as far as Geneva. The next day we ascended Mont Cenis[1] in sedan chairs, then descended to La Novalaise by sledge.[2] On the fifth day we reached Geneva and put up at the "Scales."[3] The next day Henriette gave me a letter addressed to the banker Tronchin,[4] who had no sooner read it than he told me he would come to the "Scales" in person to bring me a thousand louis.[5]

We were still at table when he appeared to discharge the obligation and at the same time to tell Henriette that he would give her two men for whom he would vouch. She told him that she would leave as soon as he should bring them to her and she should have the carriage she needed, as he must have learned from the letter I had delivered to him. After assuring her that she would have everything the next day, he left and we remained alone together, gloomy and pensive, as one is when the most profound sorrow weighs on the mind.

I broke the silence to say that the carriage which Tronchin would furnish her could not possibly be more comfortable than mine, and, that being so, she would be doing me a favor by keeping it for herself and letting me have the one the banker would give her; and she assented. At the same time she gave me five rolls of a hundred louis each, herself putting them in my pocket. A poor consolation for my heart, only too oppressed by so cruel a parting. During the last twenty-four hours the only eloquence we could muster was that which sighs, tears, and the tenderest embraces bestow on two happy lovers who have come to the end of their happiness and are forced by stern reason to accept the fact.

Henriette held out no illusory hopes to assuage my grief. She asked me not to make any inquiries about her and to pretend that I did not know her if, traveling in France, I should ever meet her anywhere. She gave me a letter to deliver to Monsieur d'Antoine in Parma, forgetting to ask me if I intended to return there; but I instantly resolved to do so. She asked me not to leave Geneva until after I had received a letter from her which she would write me from the first place at which she stopped to change horses. She left at daybreak, with her waiting-woman beside her and a footman on the coachman's seat and another ahead on horseback. I did not go back upstairs to our room until after I had followed the carriage with my eyes and long after I lost it from sight. After ordering the waiter not to enter my room until the horses with which Henriette was traveling should have returned, I went to bed, hoping that sleep would come to the aid of my grief-stricken soul, which my tears could not relieve.

The postilion returning from Châtillon[6] did not arrive until the following day. He gave me a letter from Henriette, in which I found only one word: "Farewell." He told me that no accident had befallen her and that she had continued her journey, taking the road to Lyons. Since I could not leave until the next morning, I spent one of the saddest days of my life alone in my room. On one of its two windows I saw written: "You will forget Henriette too." She had written the words with the point of a small diamond, set in a ring, which I had given her. The prophecy was not of a nature to console me; but in how absolute a sense had she used the word "forget"? She could really mean no more than that the wound would heal, and since that was only natural she need not have gone to the trouble of making me a distressing prophecy. No. I have not forgotten her, and it is balm to my soul every time I remember her. When I consider that what makes me happy in my present old age is the presence of my memory, I conclude that my long life must have been more happy than unhappy, and after thanking God, cause of all causes and sovereign contriver—we know not how—of all combinations, I congratulate myself.

The next day I set out for Italy with a servant whom Monsieur Tronchin gave me. Despite the unfavorable season, I took the route through the Saint Bernard, which I crossed in three days on the seven mules required for ourselves, my trunk, and the carriage intended for my beloved. A man overwhelmed by a great sorrow has the advantage that nothing seems painful to him. It is a kind of despair which also has a certain sweetness. I felt neither hunger nor thirst nor the cold which froze all nature in that terrible part of the Alps. I reached Parma in reasonably good health, purposely going to lodge in a bad inn at the end of the bridge, where I was not at all pleased to find Monsieur de La Haye lodged in a small room next to the one which the innkeeper gave me. Surprised to see me there, he addressed me a long compliment intended to make me talk; but I answered only that I was tired and that we would see each other.

The next day I did not go out except to deliver Henriette's letter to Monsieur d'Antoine. Finding, when he unsealed it, that it contained a letter addressed to me, he gave it to me without reading it. But as it was not sealed he thought that Henriette must have intended that he should read it, and he asked me for permission to do so after I had read it to myself in a murmur. Handing it back to me, he said that he and all his credit were at my disposal on any occasion. Here is a copy of the letter Henriette wrote me:

"It is I, my only love, who had to forsake you. Do not add to your grief by thinking of mine. Let us imagine that we have had a pleasant dream, and let us not complain of our destiny, for never was an agreeable dream so long. Let us boast of having succeeded in being happy for three months on end; there are few mortals who can say as much. So let us never forget each other, and let us often recall our love to renew it in our souls, which, though parted, will enjoy it even more intensely. Do not inquire for me, and if chance brings you to know who I am, be as if you did not know it. Rest assured, my dear, that I have so ordered my affairs that for the rest of my life I shall be as happy as I can be without you. I do not know who you are; but I know that no one in the world knows you better than I do. I will have no more lovers in all my life to come; but I hope that you will not think of doing likewise. I wish you to love again, and even to find another Henriette. Farewell."

The reader will see where, and under what circumstances, I met Henriette again fifteen years later.[7]

As soon as I was alone in my room all I could do was go to bed after locking my door, without even bothering to order something to eat. Such is the effect of a great sorrow. It stupefies; it does not make its victim want to kill himself, for it stops thought; but it does not leave him the slightest ability to do anything toward living. I found myself in a like state six years later—but not on account of love—when I was put under the Leads,[8] and again twenty years later, in 1786 at Madrid, when I was imprisoned at Buen Retiro.[9]

At the end of twenty-four hours I found my state of inanition not unpleasant; even the thought that, by increasing, it might cost me my life did not strike me as consoling, but it did not frighten me. I was glad to see that no one came to my room to disturb me by asking if I did not want to eat something. I was glad that, immediately after I arrived, I had dismissed the servant who had attended me when I crossed the Alps. After twenty-four hours of fasting my prostration was marked.

In these straits it was De La Haye who came and knocked at my door. I would not have answered him had he not said as he knocked that someone had the most urgent reasons for talking with me. I get up and open my door for him, then go back to bed.

"A foreigner," he says, "who needs a carriage wishes to buy yours."

"I do not want to sell it."

"Then please excuse me; but you seem very ill."

"Yes; I need to be left in peace."

"From what illness are you suffering?"

He approaches, he has difficulty in finding my pulse, he is disturbed, he asks me what I had eaten the day before; and upon learning that nothing had entered my stomach for two days, he guesses the truth and becomes alarmed. He entreats me to take some broth, with such solicitude that he persuades me. Then, never mentioning Henriette, he preaches me a sermon on the life to come and on the vanity of this mortal life, though it is our duty to preserve it since we have not the right to deprive ourselves of it. I answer nothing; but determined not to leave me, he orders a light dinner three or four hours later and, when he saw me eat it, he was exultant and he entertained me all the rest of the day with the latest news.

The next day I asked him to keep me company at dinner; and considering that I owed him my life I gave him my friendship; but in a very short time my fondness for him became unbounded because of the event which I will now recount to my reader in detail.

Two or three days later Dubois, to whom De La Haye had told the whole story, came to see me, and I began going out. I went to the theater, where I made the acquaintance of some Corsican officers who had served in the Royal Italian Regiment in the service of France,[10] and of a young Sicilian named Paterno, who was the pattern of recklessness. Being in love with an actress who scorned him, the young man kept me entertained with his description of her adorable qualities and at the same time of her cruelty toward him, whom she received in her house but whom she repulsed whenever he tried to give her evidence of his love. She was ruining him by making him spend a great deal on dinners and suppers which were shared by her numerous family but for which she gave him no credit.

After attentively examining the woman on the stage and finding that she had some merit, I became curious about her, and

Paterno was glad to take me to her house. Finding her decidedly approachable and knowing that she was poor, I had no doubt that I could obtain her favors at the cost of fifteen or twenty zecchini. I imparted my plan to Paterno, who laughed and said that she would no longer receive me if I dared make her such a proposal. He gave me the names of several officers whom she had declined to see again after they had made her proposals of the same sort; but he said he would be delighted if I made the attempt and afterwards would tell him frankly what had happened. I promised that I would tell him everything.

It was in her dressing room at the theater that, being alone with her and hearing her admire my watch, I offered it to her as the price of her favors. Handing it back to me, she replied in accordance with the catechism of her trade:

"A man of honor," she said, "can make such proposals only to whores."

I left her, saying that to whores I offered only a ducat.

When I told the story to Paterno I saw that he was triumphant; but his urgings were of no avail; I refused to attend any more of his suppers—utterly boring suppers at which, even as they were eating them, the actress's whole family laughed at the stupidity of the dupe who was paying for them.

A week or so later Paterno told me that the actress had related the incident to him exactly as I had reported it and had added that I no longer went to call on her for fear she would take me at my word if I made her the same proposal again. I asked the young scapegrace to tell her that I would call on her again, being certain not only that I would not make her the same proposal but also that I would not want her even if she were ready to give herself to me for nothing.

My young friend repeated my words so well that the actress, cut to the quick, charged him to tell me that she challenged me to visit her. Thoroughly determined to convince her that I despised her, I went to her dressing room again at the end of the second act of a play in which she had finished her role. After dismissing someone who was with her, she said she had something to say to me.

She locked her door; then, sitting on my knees, she asked me if it was true that I despised her so greatly. My answer was brief. I went to the point and, without a thought of bargaining, she surrendered at discretion. Yet duped, as I always am, by compassion, which is forever out of place when an intelligent man has to do with

322

women of this sort, I gave her twenty zecchini, which she much preferred to my watch. Afterwards we laughed together at the stupidity of Paterno, who did not know how such challenges were bound to end.

I told him the next day that I had been bored and that I would not call on her again; and, as I was no longer curious about her, this was my intention; but the reason which compelled me to keep my promise to him was that three days later I found that the wretched woman had made me the same sort of present that I had been treated to by the prostitute at O'Neilan's. Far from feeling that I had cause to complain, I considered myself justly punished for having so basely abandoned myself after having belonged to an Henriette.

I thought it best to confide in Monsieur de La Haye, who dined with me every day, making no secret of his poverty. The worthy man, who deserved respect both for his age and his appearance, put me into the hands of a surgeon named Frémont,[11] who was also a dentist. Certain symptoms which he recognized decided him to put me through the great cure.[12] Because of the season the cure compelled me to spend six weeks in my room.

1749.[13]

But during those six weeks De La Haye's company infected me with a disease far worse than the pox,[14] and one to which I thought I was immune. De La Haye, who only left me for an hour in the morning to say his prayers in church, turned me into a bigot, and to such an extent that I agreed with him that I should consider myself fortunate to have caught a disease which had brought salvation to my soul. I sincerely thanked God for having made use of Mercury[15] to lead my mind, until then wrapped in darkness, to the light of truth. There is no doubt that this change in my method of reasoning proceeded from the mercury. That impure and always very dangerous metal so weakened my mind that I thought I had reasoned most erroneously until then. I came to the point of deciding to lead an entirely different life after I was cured. De La Haye often wept with me in his satisfaction at seeing me weep as a result of the genuine contrition which, with incredible skill, he had implanted in my poor, sick soul. He talked to me of Paradise and of the things of the next world as if he had been there in person, and I did not laugh at him. He had accustomed me to renounce my reason, where to renounce it one had to be a fool. No one knew, he said to me one day, whether God created the world at the spring or at the autumn equinox.

"Granted creation," I answered, despite the mercury, "the question becomes puerile, for the season cannot be determined except in relation to some part of the earth."

De La Haye persuaded me that I must stop reasoning in this fashion, and I surrendered. He had been a Jesuit; but not only would he not admit it, he would not allow the subject to be raised with him. Here is the discourse with which he one day put the finishing touch to his seduction of me:

"After being educated at school, cultivating the sciences and the arts with some success, and spending twenty years at the University of Paris, I served in the army in the corps of engineers, and I published books, though without putting my name to them, which are still used in every school for the instruction of youth. Not being rich, I undertook the education of several youths who now shine in the world even more by their conduct than by their abilities. My last pupil was the Marchese Botta.[16] Being now without employment, I live, as you see, trusting in God. Four years ago I met the Baron de Bavois,[17] a young Swiss, a native of Lausanne, son of the general of the same name, who had a regiment in the service of the Duke of Modena,[18] and who later had the misfortune to give occasion to too much talk.[19] The young Baron, a Calvinist like his father, having no liking for the idle life he could have led at home, asked me to teach him what I had taught the Marchese Botta so that he could pursue a military career. Delighted that I could foster his honorable predilection, I left every other occupation to devote myself to him. In the conversations I had with the young man I discovered that he knew that in the matter of religion he lived in error. He remained in it only because of the consideration which he owed his family. After wringing his secret from him I easily brought him to see that it was a matter of paramount concern, since his eternal salvation depended on it. Impressed by this truth, he abandoned himself to my affection. I took him to Rome and presented him to Benedict XIV, who, after his abjuration, procured him a post in the Duke of Modena's forces, in which he is now serving with the rank of lieutenant. But since my dear proselyte, who is now only twenty-five, receives only seven zecchini a month, he has not enough to live on. His change of religion results in his receiving nothing from his parents, who are horrified by his apostasy. He would have no choice but to go back to Lausanne if I did not assist him. But alas! being myself poor and without employment, I can only assist him by the pittance I obtain for him from the purses of the charitable souls whom I know. Having a grateful heart, my pupil would like to know his benefactors; but they do not wish to be known, and they are right, for charity ceases to be a meritorious action if he who distributes it cannot keep it free from all vanity. For my part—thank God!—I have no cause for vanity. I am only too happy to be able to serve as father to a young predestinate, and to have had a share, as a weak instrument, in the salvation of his soul. This good, handsome youth trusts only in me. He writes to me twice a week. Discretion forbids me to give you his letters to read, but you would weep if you read them. It was to him that I yesterday sent the three louis which I had from you."

At the end of this speech De La Haye rose and went to the window to blow his nose and hurriedly dry his tears. Feeling moved and admiring so much virtue in De La Haye and in his pupil the Baron, who, to save his soul, had reduced himself to living on charity, I wept too. In my budding piety I told the apostle that not only did I not want the Baron to know that it was I who was helping him but I did not even want to know how much I was giving him, and that I therefore begged him to take from my purse whatever he might need, without rendering any account to me. At that, De La Haye came to my bedside with open arms and said as he embraced me that by thus obeying the Gospels to the letter, I was following the one sure road to the Kingdom of Heaven.

The mind obeys the body. With my stomach empty, I became a fanatic; the mercury must have made a hollow in the region of my brain, in which enthusiasm had taken its seat. Unknown to De La Haye, I began writing Signor Bragadin[20] and my two other friends letters about the man and his pupil which communicated all my fanaticism to them. My reader knows that this disease of the mind is infectious. I urged it upon them that the greatest good of our little society depended upon our adding these two persons to it. "It is God's will," I said, "that you should employ all your resources to find some honorable employment in Venice for Monsieur de La Haye and in the army for young Bavois."

Signor Bragadin wrote me that De La Haye could stay with us in his palace, and that Bavois could write to his patron the Pope asking him to recommend him to the Venetian Ambassador,[21] a letter from whom to the Senate conveying the Holy Father's wish would, as things now stood, assure him of a post. The affair of the

Patriarchate of Aquileia²² was then being negotiated, and the Republic, which was in possession of it, as well as the House of Austria,
which claimed the *jus eligendi*,²³ had appointed Benedict XIV to
arbitrate it. It was clear that the Senate would accord the greatest
attention to the wish of the Pontiff, who had not yet handed down
his decision.

When I received this crucial answer I informed De La Haye of all
that I had done in the matter; and I saw that he was astonished. He
instantly grasped all the force and the truth of old Senator Bragadin's
reasoning, and he sent his dear Bavois a magnificent letter in Latin to
copy and send at once to His Holiness, in the certainty that he
would be granted the favor he asked. After all, it was only a
recommendation.

CHAPTER VI

*I receive good news from Venice, to which I
return, taking De La Haye and Bavois with
me. Excellent reception from my three friends,
and their surprise at finding me a model of
devotion. Bavois leads me back to my former
life. De La Haye a true hypocrite.*

During these days I received word from Venice that the cases against me[1] had been forgotten, and at the same time a letter from Signor Bragadin in which he told me that the Savio di Settimana[2] had written the Ambassador that he could assure the Holy Father that when the Baron de Bavois presented himself steps would be taken to give him a post in the troops of the Republic, which would enable him to live honorably and to entertain the highest hopes from his own merit.

With this letter in my hand, I rejoiced the heart of De La Haye, who, seeing at the same time that since my difficulties had been resolved I would return to my native country, determined to go to Modena to have a talk with Bavois and decide on the new course of action which he should adopt in Venice in order to enter upon the road to fortune. He could have no doubt either of my sincerity or my friendship or my loyalty; he saw that I had become a fanatic and he knew that it is usually an incurable disease when the causes which have produced it remain in operation, and, by himself coming to Venice, he hoped to keep them active. So he wrote to Bavois that he was coming to see him; and two days later he took leave of me, melting into tears, praising my soul and my virtues, calling me his son, and assuring me that he had not become attached to me until after he had seen the divine mark of predestination stamped on my physiognomy. Such was his language.

Two or three days later I went to Ferrara and from there to Venice by way of Rovigo, Padua, and Fusina,[3] where I left my carriage. After a year's absence my friends received me as if I were an angel come from Heaven to make them happy. They showed the greatest impatience to witness the arrival of the two sainted souls whom I had promised them in my letters. A lodging for De La Haye was already prepared, and two furnished rooms for Bavois had also been found in the neighborhood, for political considerations did not permit Signor Bragadin to give lodging in his palace to a foreigner[4] who was not yet admitted into the service of the Republic.

But their surprise was extreme when they could not but observe the wonderful change in the life I led. To mass every day, often to sermons, my assiduity in attending the "forty hours,"[5] no casinos, a coffeehouse where the company consisted only in men of known prudence, and continual study in my room when their duties kept them out of the house. My new behavior compared with my old habits made them adore Divine Providence and its incomprehensible ways. They blessed the crimes which had obliged me to spend a year far from my country. What further astonished them was that I began by paying all my debts, without asking a soldo from Signor Bragadin, who, not having sent me anything for a year, had taken care of all my money. They were delighted to see that I had become averse to any kind of gaming.

At the beginning of May I received a letter from De La Haye in which he told me that he was about to embark with the dear son of his soul to put himself under the orders of the respectable persons to whom I had announced him.

Making sure of the hour at which the *barca corriere*[6] from Modena would arrive, we all went to meet him, except Signor Bragadin, who was at the Senate that day. He found all five of us at his palace and welcomed the two strangers as warmly as they could wish. De La Haye at once told me countless things; but I listened to him only with my ears, for Bavois engrossed my entire attention; I saw in him an entirely different person from the one I expected from the description of him which he had given me. I spent three days studying him before I could resolve upon a genuine attachment, for this is a portrait of the youth, who was twenty-five years of age:

Of middle height, handsome, very well built, blond, gay, always equable, speaking well and wittily, and expressing himself modestly and respectfully. His features were agreeable and regular, he had fine teeth, a good head of hair, elegantly curled and exhaling the scent of the excellent pomade with which he dressed it. This individual, who in neither substance nor form resembled the one De La Haye had portrayed for me, also surprised my friends. However, they were no less cordial to him on that account, nor did they form any judgment prejudicial to the good opinion they were bound to have of his morals.

As soon as I saw Monsieur de La Haye well settled in his room it fell to me to conduct the Baron de Bavois to his apartment, not very far from the Palazzo Bragadin, whither I had already had his few pieces of baggage carried. As soon as he found that he was excellently lodged in the house of a worthy citizen and his wife, who, having been well schooled beforehand, began by showing him a thousand attentions, he embraced me affectionately, assuring me of his entire friendship and of the profound gratitude he felt for all that I had done for him without knowing him and of which Monsieur de La Haye had informed him in full. I replied that I did not know to what he was referring; and I turned the conversation to the kind of life he wished to lead in Venice until the time when a post would give him an obligatory occupation. He answered that he hoped we would amuse ourselves very pleasantly, since he believed that his tastes were not different from mine. What I noticed at once was that he immediately attracted the hostess's two daughters, who were neither pretty nor ugly, but whom he at once flattered with an affability which could not but make them believe they had attracted him. I thought it common politeness. For the first day I only took him to the Piazza San Marco and to a coffeehouse until suppertime. It went without saying that he would dine and sup every day at Signor Bragadin's. At table he made an impression with apt remarks; and Signor Dandolo[7] appointed the hour on the following morning at which he would call for him to present him to the Savio for War.[8] After supper I took him to his lodging, where I left him in the hands of the two daughters of the household, who said they were delighted that the young Swiss nobleman whose arrival we had announced to them had no servant, as they had feared he might, for they undertook to convince him that he could do without.

The next morning I went to call for him with Signor Dandolo and Signor Barbaro, who were to introduce him to the Savio. We found the young Baron at his toilet under the delicate hands of the elder daughter of the house, who was dressing his hair and whose skill he praised. His room was fragrant with pomade and scented waters. My friends were in no way scandalized; but I observed their surprise, for they did not expect to see so great a show of worldliness in the convert. What almost made me burst out laughing was that, upon Signor Dandolo's remarking that if we did not hurry we should not have time to go to mass, the Baron asked him if it was a feast day. He answered that it was not, without adding any comment; but in the days that followed there was no longer any question of mass. I let them go, and we met again at dinner, where the talk was of the reception the Savio had given him; and in the afternoon my friends took him to visit their patrician relatives of the female sex, who were all pleased to see the charming young man. Thus in less than a week he had edged into society and was in no danger of being bored; but during the same week I became thoroughly acquainted with his character and his way of thinking. It would not have taken me so long if I had not entertained contrary preconceptions: Bavois loved women, gambling, and spending money, and, since he was poor, women were his chief resources. As for religion, he had none; and since he had the shining virtue of not being a hypocrite, he did not hide it from me.

"How," I asked him one day, "did you manage, being what you are, to deceive De La Haye?"

"Heaven preserve me from deceit! De La Haye knows the system I follow and my way of thinking, he knows me *funditus* ('thoroughly'). Pious as he is, he fell in love with my soul, and I let him. He has done me good; I am grateful to him, and I love him, and the more so because he never bores me by talking dogma and eternal salvation to me. It is all settled between us."

The amusing part of the business is that in the same week Bavois not only restored my mind to the state it was in when I parted from Henriette but made me blush to have been duped by De La Haye, who, though he played the role of thorough Christian to perfection, could nevertheless be nothing but a thorough hypocrite. Bavois opened my eyes, and I quickly resumed all my old ways. But let us return to De La Haye.

A man who at bottom cared for nothing but his own well-being, well on in years, and with no inclination for the sex, he was precisely the person to enchant my friends. Talking to them of nothing but God, angels, and eternal glory, always going to one church or another with them, they adored him, and they could not wait for the moment when he would reveal himself, for they imagined he was a Rosicrucian,[9] or at least the hermit of Carpegna[10] who, teaching me the cabala, had made me a present of the immortal Paralis.[11] They were distressed that, by the very words of the oracle, I had forbidden them ever to speak of my science in De La Haye's presence. This left me free to enjoy all the time I should have had to devote to their pious curiosity; and in any case I could not but fear De La Haye, for, such as I saw him to be, he would never have lent himself to my nonsense and he would probably even have tried to disabuse my friends in order to supplant me.

In the short space of three weeks I saw him obtain such an ascendancy over their minds that he was foolish enough to think not only that he had no further need of me to maintain his standing but that he had standing enough to knock me head over heels if he felt so inclined. I saw this from the different tone in which he talked to me and from the difference in his behavior. He began having private secrets with the three of them, and he had persuaded them to introduce him in houses which I did not frequent. He began giving himself airs, though always with a smile, and complaining, though in honeyed words, when I spent the night no one knew where. It began to annoy me that, when he preached me his gentle sermons at table in the presence of my friends and his proselyte, he appeared to regard me as one who was leading him astray. He did it as if in jest; but I was not taken in. I put an end to his game by going to call on him in his room and telling him frankly that, as a votary of the Gospels, I would now tell him in private what on another occasion I would say to him in public.

"What is it, my dear friend?"

"Take care in future not to treat me to any more of your jibes about the life I lead with Bavois, in the presence of my three friends. Privately, I will always listen to you gladly."

"You are wrong to take a certain jesting seriously."

"Why do you never aim at the Baron? Be prudent in future, or fear that, no less in jest, I may treat you to a reply which I spared you yesterday but which I will not spare you at the first opportunity."

During these same days I spent an hour with my three friends giving them instructions from the oracle never to do anything which Valentin (it was by his baptismal name that the oracle named him) might suggest to them without first consulting me. I had no doubt that they would obey the order. De La Haye, who did not fail to see a certain change, began to behave more sensibly. Bavois, whom I informed of my action, praised it. I was already thoroughly convinced that De La Haye had been of service to him only out of weakness—in other words, that he would have done nothing for him if he had not had a pretty face, though Bavois would never admit it. He did not have experience enough to admit it. The young man, seeing that giving him a post was constantly put off, entered the service of the French Ambassador;[12] which compelled him not only to cease visiting Signor Bragadin but also to stop seeing De La Haye because he was lodging in that nobleman's house. This is one of the most inviolable laws of the sovereign guardians of the Republic. Neither patricians nor their households may have the slightest connection with the households of foreign envoys.[13] But the step which Bavois took did not prevent my friends from soliciting a post for him; and they succeeded, as will be seen later in these memoirs.

[* * *]

Recovering from his uncharacteristic fit of piety, and leaving De La Haye to dally with another good-looking young man, Casanova plunged once more into the amorous life of Venice, to such effect that he was soon in trouble with the authorities. He resolved to visit Paris with his friend Balletti, whose parents, Mario and Silvia, were actors in that city. Casanova left Venice on June 1st, 1750, traveling to France via Ferrara.

CHAPTER VIII

My apprenticeship in Paris. Portraits.

Silvia celebrated her son's arrival by inviting her relatives to supper at her house. I was delighted to have reached Paris in time to make their acquaintance. Mario, Balletti's father, did not come to the table because he was recovering from an illness, but I met his elder sister, who was called by her stage name of Flaminia.[1] She was known in the Republic of Letters[2] for some translations; but what made me want to know her well was the story, which was current all over Italy, of the sojourn[3] which three famous men had made in Paris. The three men were the Marchese Maffei,[4] the Abate Conti,[5] and Pier Giacomo Martelli.[6] They became enemies, the story went, because of the preference to which each of them aspired in the actress's good graces, and as men of learning they fought with their pens. Martelli wrote a satire on Maffei, in which he gave him the anagrammatic name of "Femia."

As I was presented to Flaminia as a candidate in the Republic of Letters, she saw fit to honor me with her conversation. I found her repulsive in her face, her tone, her style, and even her voice; she did not quite say it, but she gave me to understand that, famous herself in the Republic of Letters, she was talking to an insect; she acted as if she were laying down the law and she considered that, at the age of seventy, she had every right to do so toward a youth of twenty-five who had added nothing to any library. To flatter her, I talked of the Abate Conti, and in a certain connection I cited two lines by that profound writer. She corrected me affably enough on the word *scevra*, which means separated, which I pronounced with the consonantal *u*, which is *v*.[7] She said that it should be pronounced as a vowel, and that I should not take it amiss to have learned the fact in Paris on my first day there.

"I am certainly eager to learn, Madame, but not to unlearn. It should be pronounced *scevra*, and not *sceura*, because it is a contraction of *scévera*."

"It remains to be seen which of us is wrong."

"You are, Madame, according to Ariosto, who rhymes *scevra* with *persevra*."

333

She was going on when her husband, who was eighty years old,[8] told her that she was mistaken. She said no more, and from that time on she told everyone that I was an impostor. Her husband was Lodovico Riccoboni, known as Lelio, the same man who had brought the Italian troupe to Paris in the year sixteen in the service of the Duke-Regent.[9] I was aware of his merit. He had been very handsome, and he rightly enjoyed the esteem of the public both for his talent and for his morals. During supper my principal concern was to study Silvia, who was praised to the skies. I found her above everything that was said of her. Her age was fifty, her figure elegant, her bearing distinguished, as were her manners; she was easy, affable, pleasant, well-spoken, obliging to everyone, full of wit yet completely unpretentious. Her face was an enigma, it was interesting and it pleased everyone, yet on examination it could not be considered beautiful; but by the same token no one had ever dared to pronounce it ugly. She could not be said to be neither beautiful nor ugly, for the fascination of her character made an instantaneous impression. So what was she? Beautiful—but in accordance with laws and proportions unknown to all except those who, feeling an occult power drawing them to love her, had the courage to study her and the capacity to discover them.

This actress was the idol of all France, and her talent was the mainstay of all the comedies which the greatest authors wrote for her, and especially Marivaux.[10] But for her, their comedies would never have come down to posterity. An actress capable of replacing her has never been found, and never will be found, for she would have to combine in herself all the aptitudes which Silvia possessed in the too difficult art of the theater—action, voice, countenance, intelligence, bearing, and knowledge of the human heart. Everything in her was nature; the art which accompanied and had perfected it all was not allowed to appear.

To be unique in every respect, she added to those which I have just mentioned a quality even without which she would have risen to the pinnacle of fame as an actress. Her life was pure. She was ready to make friends of men, but never lovers—scorning a privilege which she could have enjoyed but which would have made her base in her own estimation. For this reason she gained a reputation for respectability at an age when it would have seemed absurd and almost insulting to all women of her profession. For this reason several ladies of the highest rank honored her with their friendship even more than with their patronage. For this reason the capricious Parisian groundlings never dared to hiss her in a role which they did not like. By general and unanimous consent, Silvia was a woman above her profession.

Since she did not consider that her good conduct could be placed to her credit, for she knew that she practiced it only for the sake of her self-esteem, no pride, no show of superiority was ever seen in the relations she was obliged to have with her fellow actresses, who, content to shine by their talents, were not concerned to make themselves conspicuous by their virtue. Silvia loved them all, and she was loved by them, she did them justice publicly, and she praised them. But she was right: she had nothing to fear, none of them could cast the slightest shadow on her.

Nature cheated this unique woman out of ten years of her life. She became consumptive at the age of sixty, ten years after I met her. The climate of Paris plays these tricks on Italian women. Two years before her death I saw her play the role of Marianne in Marivaux's comedy,[11] in which she seemed to be only Marianne's age. She died in my presence, holding her daughter in her arms and giving her her last advice five minutes before she expired. She was honorably buried at Saint-Sauveur[12] without the slightest opposition from the parish priest, who said that her profession[13] of actress had never prevented her from being a Christian.

Excuse me, reader, if I have delivered Silvia's funeral oration ten years before reaching her death. When I come to that, I will spare you another.

Her only daughter, the principal object of her affection, was seated beside her at this same supper. She was only nine years old. Entirely taken up by the mother's excellences, I did not pause to make any observations on the daughter. That was to come only later. Well satisfied with my first evening, I returned to my lodgings in the house of Madame Quinson. Such was the name of my hostess.

When I woke, Mademoiselle Quinson came to tell me that there was a manservant outside, who had come to offer me his services. I see a very short man; this I find distasteful, and I tell him so.

"My shortness, Prince, will assure you that I will not wear your clothes to go gadding in."

"Your name?"

"Whatever name you please."

"What? I am asking you what your name is."

"I have none. Each master whom I serve gives me one, and in the course of my life I have had more than fifty. I will take the name you give me."

"Come now, you must have a name of your own, your family name."

"Family? I never had a family. I had a name in my youth, but in the twenty years that I have been a servant, always changing masters, I have forgotten it."

"I will call you L'Esprit."

"You do me great honor."

"Go get me change for this louis."

"Here it is."

"I see you are rich."

"Entirely at your service, Monsieur."

"Who will give me information about you?"

"The agency for servants, and Madame Quinson as well. Everyone in Paris knows me."

"That will do. I will give you thirty sous a day. I do not provide your clothing, you will sleep at home, and you will be at my orders every morning at seven o'clock."

Balletti came to see me and asked me to come to dinner and supper every day. I had L'Esprit show me the way to the Palais-Royal[14] and left him at the gate. Eager to satisfy my curiosity concerning a promenade which was so highly praised, I began by observing everything. I saw a rather fine garden, walks bordered by big trees, fountains, the whole surrounded by *high houses*, many men and women strolling, benches here and there, from which *new pamphlets*, scented waters, toothpicks, and trinkets were sold; I saw cane chairs which were rented for a sou, newspaper readers sitting in the shade, light women and men breakfasting alone and in company; coffeehouse waiters hurrying up and down a small concealed staircase behind beds of shrubbery. I sit down at a small empty table, a waiter asks me what I will have, I ask for chocolate without milk, and he brings me some which is horrible in a silver cup. I let it stand and tell the waiter to bring me coffee if it is good.

"Excellent, I made it yesterday myself."

"Yesterday? I don't want it."

"The milk in it is excellent."

"Milk? I never drink it. Make me a cup of coffee made with water, at once."

"With water? We make that only after dinner. Would you like a bavaroise?[15] Would you like a decanter of orgeat?"[16]

"Yes, orgeat."

I find it an excellent beverage, and I decide to make it my regular breakfast. I ask the waiter if there is anything new, and he answers that the Dauphine has given birth to a prince; an abbé tells him he is mad: it is a princess she has borne. A third man comes forward and says:

"I have just come from Versailles, and the Dauphine has borne neither a prince nor a princess."

He tells me that he gathers I am a foreigner, and I answer that I am an Italian, arrived in Paris the day before. He then talks to me of the court, of society, of the theater; he offers to introduce me everywhere, I thank him, I leave, and the Abbé accompanies me and tells me the names of all the light women who are strolling about. A gentleman of the robe[17] meets him, he embraces him, and the Abbé introduces him to me as learned in Italian literature; I address him in Italian, he answers wittily, and I laugh at his style and tell him the reason: he spoke exactly in the style of Boccaccio. My remark pleases him, I persuade him that it is not the way to speak, though that ancient writer's language is perfect. In less than a quarter of an hour we become fast friends, finding that we have the same inclinations. He a poet, I a poet, he interested in Italian literature, I in French, we give each other our addresses and promise to exchange visits.

I see many men and women crowded together in one corner of the garden, looking up. I asked my new friend what was remarkable there. He said that they were watching the meridian line, each with his timepiece in his hand, waiting for the moment when the shadow of the style would show exactly noon, when they would set their timepieces.

"But aren't there meridians everywhere?"

"Yes, but the most celebrated is the one in the Palais-Royal."

At that I could not help laughing.

"Why are you laughing?"

"Because it is impossible that all meridians are not the same; so this is the height of gawking."

He thought a little and then laughed too; and he gave me the courage to criticize the good Parisians. We leave the Palais-Royal by the main gate, and I see to my right a crowd in front of a shop whose sign was a civet cat.[18]

"What's this?"

"Now you will really laugh. All these people are waiting to buy snuff."

"Is it sold only in this shop?"

"It is sold everywhere; but for the last three weeks no one will have any snuff in his snuffbox except what comes from the Civet Cat."

"Is it better than others?"

"Not at all; it may even be worse; but since the Duchess of Chartres[19] made it fashionable no one will have anything else."

"What did she do to make it fashionable?"

"She stopped her carriage two or three times outside the shop, buying only enough to fill her snuffbox and openly telling the young woman who sells it that it was the best snuff in Paris; the gawkers who crowded around her told others, and everyone in Paris knew that if one wanted good snuff one had to buy it at the Civet Cat. The woman will make her fortune, for she sells over a hundred crowns' worth of it a day."

"The Duchess of Chartres probably does not know she has made the woman's fortune."

"On the contrary, the Duchess, who is very intelligent, contrived the whole thing herself; being fond of the woman, who was recently married, and considering what she could do to help her, she decided that the thing to do was just what she has done. You cannot imagine what good souls the Parisians are. You are in the only country in the world in which intelligence can make its way to fortune either if it displays itself in genuine contributions, in which case it is welcomed by intelligence, or if it imposes what is specious, in which case it is rewarded by stupidity; stupidity is characteristic of the nation, and what is astonishing is that it is the daughter of intelligence, so that it is no paradox to say that the French nation would be wiser if it were less intelligent.

"The gods who are worshiped here, though no altars are raised to them, are novelty and fashion. A man has but to run, and all those who see him run after him. They would not stop until he was found to be mad; but to find that out is to count the sands: we have madmen here who have been mad from birth and they are still accepted as wise. The snuff from the Civet Cat is a very small example of what a flock of sheep our citizens are. Our King, out hunting, came to the Pont de Neuilly[20] and wanted a drink of ratafia.[21] He stopped at the tavern there; he asked for it, and by

338

some strange chance the poor tavernkeeper had a flagon of it, and the King, after drinking a glass, saw fit to say to those around him that it was an excellent drink and asked for another. That was all it took to make the tavernkeeper's fortune. In less than twenty-four hours the whole court and the whole city knew that the ratafia at Neuilly was the best drink in Europe, for the King had said so. The most fashionable people flocked to Neuilly at midnight to drink ratafia, and in less than three years the tavernkeeper was a rich man and had a house built on the same spot, on which you will see the inscription *Ex liquidis solidum* ('From liquids, a solid'), which is quite amusing and which was given him by one of our Academicians. What saint must the fellow thank for his swift rise to a brilliant fortune? Stupidity, flightiness, love of a joke."

"It seems to me," I said, "that this approbation of the views of the King and the princes of the blood comes from an unconquerable affection in the nation, which adores them; it is so great that they believe them to be infallible."

"True. Everything that happens in France makes foreigners believe that the nation adores its King; but those among us who think see that this love of the nation for the monarch is only tinsel. How can one base anything on a love which has no basis? The court does not rely on it. The King comes to Paris, and everyone cries: 'Long live the King' because some idler has begun shouting it. It is a cry which comes from high spirits, or perhaps from fear, and which the King himself, believe me, does not take seriously. He cannot wait to get back to Versailles, where there are twenty-five thousand men to protect him from the fury of the same populace which, grown wise, might take it into their heads to cry: 'Death to the King.' Louis XIV knew them. And his knowledge cost several councilors of the Great Chamber[22] their lives when they ventured to talk of assembling the States-General[23] when the country was threatened with calamity. France has never loved her Kings, except St. Louis[24] for his piety, Louis XII,[25] and Henri IV[26] after his death. The King who now reigns said with perfect sincerity during his convalescence: *'I am amazed at these great rejoicings because I have recovered my health, for I cannot see any reason why I should be so much loved.'* This remark of our monarch's has been praised to the skies. He was actually using his reason. A philosophical courtier should have told him that he was so much loved because his surname was 'the Well Beloved.' "

"Are there any philosophers among the courtiers?"

"No—for as a courtier, a man cannot be a philosopher; but there are intelligent men who, in deference to their own interests, only champ the bit. Not long ago the King, in conversation with a courtier whom I will not name, extolled the pleasures he enjoyed when he spent the night with Madame la M.,[27] and said that he did not believe there was another woman on earth who could furnish their equal. The courtier answered that His Majesty was of that opinion because His Majesty had never been to a bordello.[28] The courtier was banished to his estate."

"The Kings of France are right, I believe, to shun summoning the States-General, for then they are in the same situation as a Pope who summons a Council."

"Not quite, but very nearly. The States-General would be dangerous if the people, who are the third estate, could counterbalance the votes of the nobility and the clergy; but that is not the case,[29] and it never will be, for it is not to be believed that policy will put the sword in the hands of madmen. The people would be glad to acquire the same influence, but there will never be either a King or a minister who will grant it to them. Such a minister would be a fool or a traitor."

The young man who, so discoursing, at once gave me a just idea of the nation, of the Parisian populace, of the court, and of the monarch, was named Patu.[30] I shall have occasion to speak of him. Still talking in the same vein, he took me to Silvia's door and congratulated me on my having the entrée to such a house.

I found the amiable actress in brilliant company. She introduced me to all her guests, telling me who each of them was as she introduced me. The name which struck me was Crébillon.[31]

"What, Monsieur!" I said to him. "Am I so quickly fortunate? For eight years you have charmed me. Listen, I beg you."

Thereupon I recite him the finest scene in his *Zénobie et Rhadamiste*,[32] in my blank verse translation. Silvia was delighted to see the pleasure which Crébillon, at the age of eighty, took in hearing himself rendered into a language which he loved more than his own. He recited the same scene in French, and he politely pointed out the places in which he said I had improved it. I thanked him, but was not taken in by his compliment. We sat down at table and, asked what I had seen of interest in Paris, I told them everything I had seen and heard, except Patu's discourse. After I had talked for at least two hours Crébillon, who had seen more clearly than any of the others the course I was taking to learn both the good and the bad of his nation, addressed me as follows:

"For a first day, Monsieur, I think you promise very well. You will make rapid progress. You tell your story excellently. You speak French in a way which is perfectly comprehensible; but all that you said, you put in Italian constructions. You make people listen to you, you arouse interest, and the novelty of your language renders your listeners doubly attentive; I will even say that your idiom is just the thing to gain their approval, for it is odd and new, and you are in the country where everything odd and new is sought after; nevertheless, you must begin tomorrow, and no later, to make every effort to learn to speak our language well, for in two or three months the same people who now applaud you will begin laughing at you."

"I believe it, and I fear it; so my principal purpose in coming here was to apply myself entirely to the French language and French literature; but how, Monsieur, am I to go about finding a teacher? I am an intolerable pupil, always questioning, curious, demanding, insatiable. I am not rich enough to pay such a teacher, even supposing that I find him."

"For fifty years now, Monsieur, I have been looking for a pupil such as you describe yourself to be, and it is I who will pay you if you will come to me for lessons. I live in the Marais,[33] in the Rue des Douze Portes, I have the best Italian poets, whom I will make you translate into French, and I will never find you insatiable."

I accepted, at a loss to express all my gratitude. Crébillon was six feet tall, overtopping me by three inches; he ate well, told stories amusingly but without laughing himself, and he was famous for his witticisms. He spent his life at home, going out very seldom, and seeing almost no one because he always had a pipe in his mouth and was surrounded by eighteen or twenty cats with which he played for the greater part of the day. He had an old housekeeper, a cook, and a valet. His housekeeper saw to everything, handled his money, and, since she never let him want for anything, he never asked her to render an account. It is a remarkable fact that Crébillon's face resembled a lion's, or a cat's, which is the same thing. He was a royal censor,[34] and he told me it entertained him. His housekeeper read him the works which were brought to him, and paused in her reading when she thought something called for his criticism; and I often laughed over his quarrels with the woman when he was of a different opinion. One day I heard her turn away someone who had come to receive his corrected manuscript:

"Come next week," she said, "for we haven't had time to look over your work yet."

I visited Crébillon three times a week for a year, and I learned from him all the French I know, but I have never been able to rid myself of Italianisms; I recognize them when I find them in others; but when they come from my pen I do not recognize them, and I am sure I shall never learn to recognize them, just as I have never known what fault in Latinity Livy[35] is taxed with.

I composed an octet in irregular measure on a certain subject and took it to Crébillon for him to correct. After reading my eight lines attentively he addressed me as follows:

"Your thought is fine and very poetic; your language is flawless; your verses are good and exactly measured; nevertheless your octet is bad."

"How can that be?"

"I have no idea. What is lacking is the 'certain something.'[36] Imagine that you see a man and find him handsome, well built, pleasing, witty, and in short perfect in your most severe judgment. A woman comes up, she looks at him, and after considering him thoroughly she leaves, telling you that he does not please her. 'But, Madame, tell me what fault you find in him.' 'I don't know.' You go back to the man, you consider him more carefully, and you find that he is a castrato. 'Ah!' you say, 'now I see the reason why the woman did not find him to her taste.' "

It was by this comparison that Crébillon made me realize why my octet could not please.

At table we talked a great deal about Louis XIV,[37] to whom Crébillon had paid court for fifteen years, and he told us some very curious anecdotes which no one knew. He assured us that the Siamese Ambassadors[38] were rogues in the pay of Madame de Maintenon. He said that he had never finished his tragedy entitled *Cromwell*[39] because the King himself had one day told him not to waste his pen portraying a scoundrel.

He talked to us of his *Catilina*,[40] and said that he considered it the weakest of all his plays, but that he would not have wanted it to be good if, to make it so, he had had to bring Caesar on the stage, for Caesar as a young man would arouse laughter, as Medea[41] would do if she were brought on the stage before she knew Jason. He praised Voltaire's talent highly, at the same time accusing him of theft, for he had stolen the Senate scene[42] from him. He said that, to do him justice, he was born with every talent for writing history but that he falsified it and filled it with fairy tales to make it interesting. According to Crébillon the Man in the Iron Mask[43] was a fairy tale, and he said that he had been assured of it by Louis XIV himself.

The play being given at the Théâtre Italien that day was *Cénie*,[44] by Madame de Graffigny.[45] I went early to get a good place in the amphitheater.[46] The ladies covered with diamonds who were entering the first-tier boxes interested me, and I observed them attentively. I had a fine coat, but since the sleeves of it were open and it had buttons all the way down everyone who saw me recognized me as a foreigner; the fashion no longer existed in Paris. While my attention was thus occupied a richly dressed man three times my size approaches me and politely asks if I am a foreigner. I say that I am, and he immediately asks me if I like Paris. I reply by praising it; and at the same moment I see entering the box at my left a woman covered with jewels but immensely stout.

"Who on earth," I ask my fat neighbor, "is that fat sow?"

"She is the wife of this fat pig."

"Ah, Monsieur, I ask a million pardons."

But the man was in no state for me to beg his pardon for, far from being angry, he was choking with laughter. I was in despair. After having a good laugh, he rises, leaves the balcony, and a moment later I see him in the box speaking to his wife. I see them both laugh, and I was on the verge of leaving when I hear him calling me:

"Monsieur, Monsieur."

I cannot refuse without being impolite, and I approach the box. Now perfectly serious, he begs my pardon with the greatest dignity for having laughed so much and most graciously invites me to come to supper at his house that evening. I thank him and tell him that I already have an engagement. But he insists and his wife joins in, and to convince them that it is not a pretext I tell them that I am invited to Silvia's.

"I am certain," he says, "that I can obtain your release, if you have no objection; I will go to her myself."

I yield, he goes; he comes back later with Balletti, who gives me a message from his mother that she is delighted to have me make such excellent acquaintances and that she expects me for dinner the next day. Balletti tells me privately that it is Monsieur de Beauchamp,[47] Receiver-General of Finances.

After the play I gave my hand to Madame and got into her carriage. In their house I found the lavishness which was the rule among all people of their sort in Paris: a great crowd of guests, a great many parties at cards, and great gaiety at table. We rose from supper an hour after midnight, and I was driven home. The house was open to me during all the time I stayed in Paris, and it was very useful to me. Those who say that all foreigners who go to Paris are bored for at least the first two weeks are right, for it takes time to make one's way in. For my part, I know that in twenty-four hours I was already kept occupied and was sure that I would enjoy myself there.

CHAPTER IX

My blunders in French, my successes, my
numerous acquaintances. Louis XV.

Casanova divided his time in Paris between actors and aristocrats but the
highlight of his stay was a visit to the court of Louis XV where he
encountered an old adversary.

[* * *]

King Louis XV, who was passionately fond of hunting, was in
the habit of spending six weeks of the autumn of every year at
Fontainebleau.[1] He was always back at Versailles by the middle of
November. The journey cost him five millions; he took with him
everything that could contribute to the enjoyment of all the foreign
envoys and his whole court. The French and Italian comedians and
his actors and actresses of the Opéra were commanded to follow
him. During these six weeks Fontainebleau was far more brilliant
than Versailles. Even so, the great city of Paris was not left without
spectacles. Opera and the French and Italian players continued
nevertheless, for there were so many actors that substitutes could
be found for those who were absent.

Mario, Balletti's father, who had completely recovered his
health, was to go there[2] with his wife Silvia and his whole family;
he invited me to go with them, offering me a lodging in a house
which he had rented, and I accepted. I could not have enjoyed a
better opportunity to become acquainted with all the court of Louis
XV and all the foreign envoys. So I at once waited on Signor
Morosini,[3] now Procurator of San Marco, then Ambassador of the
Republic to the King of France. The first day on which opera was
given he permitted me to escort him; it was a piece by Lully.[4] I was
seated in the parquet, exactly under the box occupied by Madame
de Pompadour,[5] whom I did not know. In the very first scene the
famous Lemaure[6] comes out of the wings and at her second line
gives a shriek so loud and so unexpected that I thought she had gone
mad; I give a little laugh, in all innocence, never imagining that
anyone would think it out of place. A Blue Ribbon,[7] who was in

attendance on the Marquise, asks me curtly from what country I come, and I answer curtly that I am from Venice.

"When I was in Venice I often laughed at the recitative in your operas too."

"I believe you, Monsieur, and I am equally certain that no one there ever thought of preventing you from laughing."

My rather sharp answer brought a laugh from Madame de Pompadour, who asked me if I really came from "down there."

"From where?"

"From Venice."

"Venice, Madame, is not down; it is up."

This answer of mine was thought even odder than my first, and the whole box falls to deciding whether Venice was down or up. Apparently it was concluded that I was right, and I was not attacked again. I listened to the opera without laughing, and since I had a cold I blew my nose too often. The same Blue Ribbon, whom I did not know, and who was the Maréchal de Richelieu,[8] remarked to me that apparently the windows of my room were not tightly closed.

"Beg pardon, Monsieur; they are even *calfoutrées*."

There was general laughter, and I was mortified because I realized that I had mispronounced the word *calfeutrées*.[9] I looked thoroughly humiliated. A half hour later Monsieur de Richelieu asks me which of the two actresses pleased me better in the way of beauty.

"That one."

"She has ugly legs."

"One does not see them, Monsieur, and in any case in assessing the beauty of a woman the first thing I put apart[10] is her legs."

This witticism, which I had uttered by chance and of whose implication I was unaware, gave me standing and made the company in the box curious about me. The Maréchal learned who I was from Signor Morosini himself, who told me that he[11] would be pleased to have me wait on him. My witticism became celebrated, and the Maréchal de Richelieu received me graciously. The foreign envoy on whom I waited most assiduously was Lord Keith,[12] Marshal of Scotland, who was Ambassador from the King of Prussia. I shall have occasion to speak of him.

It was on the day after I arrived in Fontainebleau that I went to court alone. I saw the handsome King on his way to mass, the whole royal family, and all the court ladies, who surprised me by their ugliness as those at the court of Turin had surprised me by their

346

beauty. But seeing a surprising beauty among so much ugliness, I asked someone what the lady's name was.

"She is Madame de Brionne,[13] Monsieur, who is even more virtuous than beautiful, for not only is there not a single story about her but she has never given the slightest occasion for slander to invent one."

"Perhaps nothing became known."

"Oh, Monsieur, at court everything becomes known."

I went on alone, prowling everywhere, even into the royal apartments, when I saw ten or twelve ugly ladies who looked as if they were running rather than walking and so awkwardly that they seemed about to fall flat on their faces. I asked where they were coming from and why they were walking so awkwardly.

"They are coming from the apartment of the Queen, who is about to dine, and they walk so awkwardly because their slippers have heels half a foot high, which makes them walk with their knees bent."

"Why do they not wear lower heels?"

"Because they think these make them look taller."

I enter a gallery and I see the King pass supporting himself with one arm around Monsieur d'Argenson's[14] shoulders. Louis XV's head was ravishingly beautiful and set on his neck to perfection. Not even a most skillful painter could draw the attitude the monarch gave it when he turned to look at someone. One felt instantly forced to love him. I thought that I saw the majesty for which I had looked in vain in the face of the King of Sardinia. I felt certain that Madame de Pompadour had already fallen in love with that countenance when she contrived to make his acquaintance. Perhaps it was not true, but the face of Louis XV[15] compelled the observer to think so.

I enter a room in which I see ten or twelve courtiers walking up and down, and a table prepared for dinner, big enough for twelve, but set only for one.

"For whom is that table?"

"For the Queen, who is about to dine. There she is."

I see the Queen of France,[16] without rouge, wearing a large bonnet, looking old and pious, thanking two nuns who set on the table a plate containing fresh butter. She sits down; the ten or twelve courtiers who were walking about station themselves before the table in a semicircle ten paces away, and I join them in the deepest silence.

The Queen begins to eat, looking at no one and keeping her eyes fixed on her plate. She had eaten some of a dish and, finding it to her taste, she returned to it, but as she returned to it she cast her eyes over the company, apparently to see if she saw anyone to whom she should justify her epicureanism. She found him and she addressed him, saying:

"Monsieur de Lowendal."[17]

At the name I see a handsome man two inches taller than myself, who, bowing and taking three steps toward the table, answers:

"Madame."

"I believe that the best ragout of all is a fricassee of chicken."

"I am of that opinion, Madame."

After this answer, which was delivered in the most serious tone, the Queen eats and the Maréchal de Lowendal falls back three steps and resumes his previous station. The Queen said no more, finished dining, and returned to her apartments.

Curious as I was to make the acquaintance of the celebrated soldier who had taken Bergen-op-Zoom,[18] I am enchanted to have done so on this occasion. Consulted by the Queen of France on the excellence of a fricassee, and giving his opinion in the same tone in which a death sentence is pronounced at a court-martial. Enriched by the anecdote, I go to regale Silvia's table with it at an elegant dinner at which I found the choicest of agreeable company.

A week or ten days later I am in the gallery at ten o'clock, forming a line with everyone else to have the ever fresh pleasure of seeing the King go by on his way to mass and the singular pleasure of seeing the nipples of Mesdames de France[19] his daughters, who were so dressed that they displayed them to everyone, together with their completely bare shoulders, when I am surprised to see La Cavamacchie, Giulietta,[20] whom I had left in Cesena under the name of Signora Querini. If I was surprised to see her, she was no less so to see me in such a place. Giving her his arm was the Marquis de Saint-Simon,[21] first gentleman of the bedchamber to Prince de Conti.[22]

"Signora Querini at Fontainebleau?"

"You here? I remember Queen Elizabeth,[23] who said: *Pauper ubique jacet*" ("The poor man makes his bed everywhere").[24]

"The comparison is excellent, Madame."

"I am joking, my friend; I have come here to see the King, who does not know me, but the Ambassador will present me tomorrow."

She takes her place in the line five or six paces above me in the direction from which the King was to come. The King enters, with Monsieur de Richelieu by his side, and I see him immediately look at the supposed Madame Querini, and as he walks along I hear him address *his friend* exactly in these words:

"We have prettier women here."

After dinner I go to the Venetian Ambassador's, and I find him at dessert with a large company, seated beside Signora Querini, who, on seeing me, says the most gracious things possible, which was extraordinary in such a nitwit who had no reason either past or present to like me, for she was aware that I knew her through and through and had been able to make her do as I wished. But I understand the reason for it all, and I make up my mind to do everything to please her and even to serve her as a false witness if that should be what she needed.

She comes round to speaking of Signor Querini, and the Ambassador congratulates her on his having rendered justice to her merit by marrying her.

"Strangely enough," said the Ambassador, "I did not know of it."

"Yet it happened more than two years ago," said Giulietta.

"It is a fact," I said to him, "for it was two years ago that General Spada introduced the Signora by the name of Querini to all the nobility in Cesena, where I had the honor to be."

"I do not doubt it," said the Ambassador, looking at me, "since Querini himself writes me of it."

When I made to leave, the Ambassador took me into another room on the pretext of showing me a letter. He asked me what was said in Venice on the subject of the marriage, and I answered that no one knew of it and that, in fact, people were saying that the heir of the house of Querini was to marry a Grimani.[25]

"I will write the news to Venice day after tomorrow."

"What news?"

"That Giulietta is really Querini, since Your Excellency will present her as such to Louis XV."

"Who told you that I shall present her?"

"She herself."

"She may have changed her mind by now."

I thereupon repeated to him the exact words I had heard from the King's lips, which showed him the reason why Giulietta no longer wished to be presented. Monsieur de Saint-Quentin,[26] the minister who secretly carried out the monarch's private commands, had gone in person after mass to tell the beautiful Venetian that the King of France had poor taste, since he had not thought her more beautiful than several other ladies at his court. Giulietta left Fontainebleau early the next morning. I discussed Giulietta's beauty at the beginning of these memoirs;[27] her countenance had extraordinary charms, but they had lost their power by the time I saw her at Fontainebleau; then, too, she painted her face white, an artifice which the French cannot forgive; and they are right, for white paint conceals nature. Yet women, whose business is to please, will continue to use it, for they always hope to find a man who is taken in by it.

After my journey to Fontainebleau I saw Giulietta again at the Venetian Ambassador's; she laughed and told me that she had been joking when she called herself Madame Querini and that in future she would be obliged to me if I would call her by her real name of Countess Preati;[28] she told me to come and see her at the Hôtel du Luxembourg, where she was staying. I went there very often to amuse myself by observing her intrigues, but I never entered into them. During the four months which she spent in Paris she drove Signor Zanchi out of his mind. He was secretary of the Venetian Embassy, an amiable, upright, and well-read man. She made him fall in love with her, he said he was ready to marry her, she flattered him, and then she treated him so badly and made him so jealous that the poor wretch lost his reason and died soon afterward. Count Kaunitz,[29] Ambassador of the Empress-Queen, was attracted by her, and so was Count Zinzendorf.[30] The intermediary in these brief affairs was an Abbé Guasco,[31] who, not being rich and being extremely ugly, could aspire to her favors only by becoming her confidant. But the man on whom she set her heart was the Marquis de Saint-Simon. She wanted to become his wife, and he would have married her if she had not given him false addresses for him to obtain information about her birth. The Preati family, of Verona, which she had appropriated, disowned her, and Monsieur de Saint-Simon, who despite his love had managed to keep his common sense, had the strength of mind to leave her. She did not come off well in Paris, and she left her diamonds in pawn there. Back in Venice, she managed to marry the son of the same Signor Uccelli[32] who sixteen years earlier had taken her out of poverty and put her on the stage. She died ten years ago.

In Paris I still went to take lessons from the elder Crébillon; nevertheless my speech, which was full of Italianisms, often made me say in company what I did not mean to say, and my remarks almost always produced very odd jokes which were repeated afterward; but my gibberish did not prevent people from forming a favorable opinion of my wit; on the contrary, it gained me some choice acquaintances. Several women who mattered asked me to come and teach them Italian, adding that it would give them the pleasure of correcting my French, and in the exchange I gained more than they did.

Madame Préaudeau,[33] who was one of my pupils, received me one morning still in bed and saying that she did not feel like taking a lesson because she had taken medicine the night before. I asked her if during the night she had *déchargé*[34] well.

"What a question! What curiosity! You are intolerable."

"Lord, Madame, why does one take a medicine if it is not to *décharger*?"

"A medicine purges, Monsieur, and does not make one *décharger*, and let this be the last time in your life that you use the word."

"I know very well, now that I think of it, that I can be misinterpreted; but say what you will, it is the right word."

"Would you like some breakfast?"

"No, Madame, I've had it. I drank a *café* with two Savoyards[35] in it."

"Good God! I am lost. What a madman's breakfast! Explain yourself."

"I drank a *café*, as I drink one every morning."

"But that is nonsense, my friend; a *café* is the shop in which it is sold, and what one drinks is a cup of it."

"Do you drink the cup? In Italy we say *un caffè*, and we have brains enough to understand that we didn't drink the shop."

"He refuses to be wrong. And the two Savoyards—how did you swallow them?"

"Dipped in the coffee. They were no bigger than those you have there on your night table."

"You call those Savoyards? Say *biscuits*."

"We call them Savoyards in Italy, Madame, for the fashion for them came from Savoy, and it is not my fault if you thought I ate two of those porters who stand at street corners to serve the public and whom you call Savoyards,[36] while they may be from some other country. In future I will say that I have eaten *biscuits*, to conform to your usage; but permit me to tell you that the term *Savoyards* fits them better."

In comes her husband; she tells him of our disagreements; he laughs and says that I am right. Her niece enters. She was a girl of fourteen, well behaved, intelligent, and extremely modest; I had given her five or six lessons, and since she liked the language and applied herself earnestly she was beginning to speak. Here is the fatal compliment which she addressed to me:

"*Signore, sono incantata di vi vedere in buona salute*" ("Sir, I am delighted to see you in good health").

"I thank you, Mademoiselle, but to translate 'I am delighted' you must say *ho piacere*. And again, to translate 'to see you,' you must say *di vivervi*, not *di vi vedere*."

"I thought, Monsieur, that the *vi* should be put in front."

"No, Mademoiselle, we put it *derrière*" ("behind").[37]

Monsieur and Madame are dying with laughter, the young lady smiling, and I speechless and in despair at having made so gross a blunder; but it was done. I take up a book, sulking and wishing in vain that their laughter would end; but it lasted more than a week. My shameless *double-entendre* spread all over Paris and made me furious; but I at last learned the power of words and for the time being my credit diminished. Crébillon, after laughing heartily, told me that I should have said *après* instead of *derrière*. But if the French laughed over the mistakes I made in speaking their language, I took my revenge by pointing out some absurd usages of theirs.

"Monsieur," I ask, "how is Madame your wife?"

"You do her great honor."

"Her honor has nothing to do with it; I am asking after her health."

A young man in the Bois de Boulogne falls from his horse; I run to pick him up, but he is on his feet and full of life.

"Have you come to any harm?"

"On the contrary, Monsieur."

"Then I take it the fall did you good."

I am calling on Madame la Présidente Charon[38] for the first time; her nephew makes a brilliant entrance; she presents me and tells him my name and country.

"What! You are an Italian, Monsieur? On my word, you make such a good appearance that I would have wagered you were French."

"Monsieur, when I saw you I very nearly fell into the same error—I would have wagered that you were Italian."

"I did not know that I looked Italian."

I was at table at Lady Lambert's,[39] someone remarked on a cornelian I had on my finger on which the head of Louis XV was engraved to perfection. My ring makes the round of the table, everyone finds the likeness striking; a young Marquise hands me back the ring, saying:

"*Is it really an antique?*"

"You mean the stone? Yes, Madame, it is."

Everyone laughs, and the Marquise, who had the reputation of being intelligent, does not see fit to ask why people are laughing. After dinner the conversation turns to the rhinoceros which was being shown at the fair at Saint-Germain[40] for twenty-four sous a head. "Let us go see it, let us go see it!" We get into a carriage, stop at the fair, and take several turns through the walks, looking for the one in which the rhinoceros was. I was the only man, I had a lady on either arm, the intelligent Marquise was preceding us. At the end of the walk where we had been told the animal was, its master was sitting at the gate to take their money from people who wished to go in. It is true that he was dressed in African costume, enormously fat, and looked like a monster; but the Marquise ought at least to have recognized that he was a man. Not a bit of it.

"Are you the rhinoceros, Monsieur?"

"Step in, Madame, step in."

She sees us choking with laughter, and, seeing the real rhinoceros, she feels obliged to apologize to the African, assuring him that she had never in her life seen a rhinoceros and so he must not be offended if she had made a mistake.

[∗ ∗ ∗]

The Duke of Maddaloni introduced me to the Roman Princes Don Marcantonio and Don Giovanni Battista Borghese[41] who were amusing themselves in Paris and living without ostentation. I observed that when these Roman princes are presented at the French court they are received only under the title of Marquis. For the same reason the Russian princes who were presented were not accorded the title of Prince; they were called *Knez*.[42] It made no difference to them, for the word means "Prince." The French court was always scrupulously particular in the matter of titles. Simply reading the gazette is enough to show it. The title "Monsieur"—which is commonly given everywhere—is used very sparingly; "Sieur" is the form of address to the untitled. I noticed that the King called none of his bishops "Bishop," he called them "Abbé." He also affected not to know any nobleman of his kingdom whose name he did not find inscribed among those who were in his service. Yet the haughtiness of Louis XV had only been inculcated into him by his upbringing, it was not natural to him. When an ambassador presented someone to him, the person so presented went home certain that the King of France had seen him, but that was all. He was the most polite of Frenchmen, especially toward ladies and toward his mistresses in public; he dismissed from his favor anyone who dared to fail in respect to them, even in the slightest; and no one more than he possessed the royal virtue of dissimulation, faithfully keeping a secret and delighted when he was sure that he knew something of which everyone else had no inkling. Monsieur d'Éon's being a woman[43] is a small example. The King alone knew, and had always known, that he was a woman, and the whole altercation between the false Chevalier and the Foreign Office was a comedy which the King allowed to play itself out simply because it amused him.

Louis XV was great in everything, and he would not have had a failing if flattery had not forced failings upon him. How could he know that he was at fault when he was always being told that he was the best of kings? About this time the Princess of Ardore gave birth to a son.[44] Her husband, who was the Neapolitan Ambassador, wanted Louis XV to stand godfather to it, and the King consented. The present he gave his godson was a regiment. The new mother would have none of it, because she did not like soldiers. The Maréchal de Richelieu told me that he had never seen the King laugh so much as when he was informed of her refusal.

At the Duchess of Fulvy's[45] I made the acquaintance of Mademoiselle Gaussin,[46] known as Lolotte, who was the mistress of Lord Albemarle,[47] the English Ambassador, a man of brilliant and most noble parts and very generous, who, one night when he was out walking with Lolotte, chided her for praising the beauty of the stars she saw in the sky, since he could not give them to her. If His Lordship had been the English envoy in France at the time of the break between his nation and the French he would have patched things up, and the unhappy war which caused France to lose the whole of Canada[48] would not have occurred. There is no doubt that the harmony between two nations most often depends upon the respective envoys whom they have at the courts which are on the verge or in danger of falling out.

As for his mistress, all who knew her had the same opinion of her. She had all the qualities to deserve to become his wife, and the greatest houses in France did not consider that she needed the title of Lady Albemarle in order to be admitted into their society, and no woman was offended to find her seated at her side because it was common knowledge that she had no title except that of His Lordship's mistress. She passed from her mother's arms into His Lordship's at the age of thirteen, and her conduct was always irreproachable; she had children, whom His Lordship recognized, and she died Countess of Érouville. I will speak of her in due course.

At this same time I met at the house of the Venetian Ambassador Signor Mocenigo a Venetian lady,[49] the widow of the English baronet Wynne, who had just come from London with her children. She had gone there to make sure of her dowry and the estate of her late husband, which could not pass to her children unless they declared that they were of the Anglican religion. She had accomplished this, and she was returning to Venice satisfied with her journey. She had with her her eldest daughter,[50] who was only twelve years old but whose character was already delineated to perfection in her beautiful face. She now lives in Venice, the widow of the late Count Rosenberg, who died in Venice as Ambassador from the Empress-Queen Maria Theresa; she shines in her native country by her discreet behavior, her wit, and her social virtues, which are of the highest. Everyone says of her that her only failing is not being rich. It is true, but no one can complain of it; she feels how great a failing it is only when it prevents her from being generous.

[* * *]

CHAPTER XI

*The beautiful O-Morphi. Imposture
by a painter. I practice cabalism for the
Duchess of Chartres.*

At the Saint-Laurent fair my friend Patu took a notion to sup with a Flemish actress named Morphy[1] and invited me to join him; I accepted. La Morphy did not tempt me; but that did not matter—a friend's pleasure is motive enough. So he offered her two louis, which were at once accepted, and after the opera we went to the beauty's house in the Rue des Deux Portes Saint-Sauveur. After supper Patu wanted to sleep with her, and I asked for a couch for myself in some corner of the house. La Morphy's younger sister, a pretty, ragged, dirty little creature, said she would give me her bed but wanted a half écu;[2] I promised it to her. She takes me to a closet in which I see only a mattress on three or four boards.

"Do you call that a bed?"

"It's my bed."

"I don't want it, and you shan't have the half écu."

"Were you going to undress for bed?"

"Of course."

"What an idea! We haven't any bedclothes."

"Then you sleep with your clothes on?"

"Certainly not."

"Very well, go to bed yourself and you shall have the half écu. I want to see you."

"All right, but you mustn't do anything to me."

"Not a thing."

She undresses, lies down, and covers herself with an old curtain. She was thirteen years old. I look at the girl; I send every prejudice packing; I see her neither slovenly nor in rags, I find her a perfect beauty. I make to examine her completely, she refuses, she laughs, she resists; but a whole écu makes her as mild as a lamb, and since her only fault is being dirty I wash her all over with my own hands; my reader knows that admiration is inseparable from another kind of appreciation, and I find the little Morphy willing to let me do whatever I please, except what I did not want to do. She warns me again. Calmed, I spent an hour telling her amusing stories; then we sat down at table.

She ate for two, but I for four. The service was of porcelain but at dessert of silver gilt, as were the candelabra, each of which held four candles. Seeing that I admired their beauty she said they were a present her friend had made her.

"Did he give you snuffers too?"

"No."

"Then I conclude that your lover must be a great lord, for great lords know nothing of snuffing."

"The wicks of our candles do not need snuffing."

"Tell me who taught you French, for you speak it too well for me not to be curious to know."

"Old La Forêt, who died last year. I was his pupil for six years; he taught me to compose verses too; but I have learned words from you which I never heard pass his lips: *à gogo, frustratoire, dorloter.*[16] Who taught them to you?"

"Good society in Paris, Madame de Boufflers[17] for example, a woman of profound intelligence who one day asked me why the Italian alphabet contained *con rond*.[18] I laughed, and did not know how to answer."

"I think they are abbreviations used in the old days."

After making punch we amused ourselves eating oysters, exchanging them when we already had them in our mouths. She offered me hers on her tongue at the same time that I put mine between her lips; there is no more lascivious and voluptuous game between two lovers, it is even comic, but comedy does no harm, for laughter is only for the happy. What a sauce that is which dresses an oyster I suck in from the mouth of the woman I love! It is her saliva. The power of love cannot but increase when I crush it, when I swallow it.

She said that she was going to change her dress and come back with her hair ready for the night. Not knowing what to do I amused myself looking at what she had in her desk, which was open. I did not touch her letters but, opening a box and seeing some condoms,[19] I quickly wrote the following verses and substituted them for what I had stolen:

Enfants de l'amitié, ministres de la peur,
Je suis l'amour, tremblez, respectez le voleur,
Et toi, femme de Dieu, ne crains pas d'être mère
Car si tu fais un fils, il se dira son père.

S'il est dit cependant que tu veux te barrer
Parle; je suis tout prêt, je me ferai châtrer.

("Children of friendship, ministers of fear, I am Love, tremble, and respect the thief. And you, wife of God, do not fear to become a mother, for if you bear a son he will say he is its father. Yet if you are determined to bar your door, speak; I am ready, I will have myself gelded.")

M. M. reappeared in a new guise. She had on a dressing gown of India muslin embroidered with flowers in gold thread, and her nightcap was worthy of a queen.

I threw myself at her feet to beg her to yield to my desires then and there; but she ordered me to hold my fire until we were in bed.

"I do not want," she said with a smile, "to be bothered with keeping your quintessence from falling on the carpet. You shall see."

With that she goes to her desk, and instead of the condoms she finds my six verses. After reading them, then reading them over again aloud, she calls me a thief and, giving me kiss after kiss, she tries to persuade me to restore the stolen goods. After reading my verses slowly aloud once more, pretending to reflect on them, she goes out on the pretext of looking for a better pen, then comes back and writes the following answer:

Dès qu'un ange me f . . . , je deviens d'abord sûre
Que mon seul époux est l'auteur de la nature.
Mais pour rendre sa race exempte des soupçons
L'amour doit dans l'instant me rendre mes condoms.
Ainsi toujours soumise à sa volonté sainte
J'encourage l'ami de me f . . . sans crainte.

("When an angel f . . . s me I am at once sure that my only husband is the author of nature. But to make his lineage free from suspicion Love must instantly give me back my condoms. Thus always obedient to his sacred will, I encourage my friend to f . . . me without fear.")

I thereupon returned them to her, giving a very natural imitation of surprise; for really it was too much.

Midnight had struck, I showed her her little Gabriel, who was sighing for her, and she made the sofa ready, saying that as the alcove was too cold, we would sleep there. The reason was that in the alcove her friend could not see us.

While waiting I tied up my hair in a Masulipatam[20] kerchief which, going round my head four times, gave me the redoubtable look of an Asiatic despot in his seraglio. After imperiously putting my sultana in the state of nature and doing the same to myself, I laid her down and subjugated her in the classic manner, delighting in her swoons. A pillow which I had fitted under her buttocks and one of her knees bent away from the back of the sofa must have afforded a most voluptuous vision for our hidden friend. After the frolic, which lasted an hour, she took off the sheath and rejoiced to see my quintessence in it; but finding, even so, that she was wet with her own distillations, we agreed that a brief ablution would restore us *in statu quo*. After that we stood side by side in front of a large upright mirror, each putting one arm around the other's back. Admiring the beauty of our images and becoming eager to enjoy them, we engaged in every kind of combat, still standing. After the last bout she fell onto the Persian carpet which covered the floor. With her eyes closed, her head to one side, lying on her back, her arms and legs as if she had just been taken down from a St. Andrew's cross,[21] she would have looked like a corpse if the beating of her heart had not been visible. The last bout had exhausted her. I made her do the "straight tree,"[22] and in that position I lifted her up to devour her chamber of love, which I could not reach otherwise since I wanted to make it possible for her, in turn, to devour the weapon which wounded her to death without taking her life.

Reduced after this exploit to asking her to grant me a truce, I set her on her feet again; but a moment later she challenged me to give her her revenge. It was my turn to do the "straight tree" and hers to grasp me by the hips and lift me up. In this position, steadying herself on her two diverging pillars, she was horrified to see her breasts splattered with my soul distilled in drops of blood.

"What do I see?" she cried, letting me fall and herself falling with me. Just then the alarm chimed.

I called her back to life by making her laugh.

"Have no fear, my angel," I said, "it is the yolk of the last egg, which is often red."

I myself washed her beautiful breasts, which human blood had never soiled before that moment. She was very much afraid that she had swallowed some drops of it; but I easily persuaded her that even if it were so, it would do no harm. She dressed in her habit and then left, after imploring me to go to bed there and to write and tell her how I was before I went back to Venice. She promised to do as much for me the next day. The caretaker would have her letter. I obeyed. She did not leave until a half hour later, which she certainly spent with her friend.

[* * *]

CHAPTER V

I give M. M. my portrait. Her present to me.
I go to the opera with her. She gambles and
replenishes my purse. Philosophical conversa-
tion with M. M. Letter from C. C. She knows
all. Ball at the convent: my exploits as Pierrot.
C. C. comes to the casino instead of M. M.
I spend an absurd night with her.

1754.

On the second day of the year, before going to the casino I went to Laura's house to give her a letter for C. C. and to receive one which made me laugh. M. M. had initiated the girl not only into the mysteries of Sappho,[1] but also into pure metaphysics. She had become a freethinker. She wrote that, not wishing to give an account of her doings to her confessor but at the same time not wanting to lie to him, she had stopped telling him anything. "He told me," she wrote, "that perhaps I confessed nothing to him because I did not examine my conscience well, and I answered that I had nothing to tell him, but that if he liked I would commit some sin on purpose, so that I could have something to tell him."

Here is a copy of the letter from M. M. which I found at the casino:

"I am writing to you in bed, my dark-haired dear, because I feel as if my hips were completely out of joint; but it will go away, for I am eating and sleeping well. What brought balm to my blood was the letter in which you assured me that the loss of yours had no ill effect. I shall be certain of it on Twelfth-night in Venice. Write me if I can count on that. I want to go to the opera. I forever forbid you egg whites in salad. In future when you go to the casino you must ask if anyone is there, and if you are told there is, you must go away; my friend will do likewise; so you will never meet; but it will not be for long, for he is mad about you and determined that you shall make his acquaintance. He says he did not believe there was a man of your vigor in the universe; but he insists that, making love as you do, you are defying death, for he maintains that the blood you spurted out must have come from the brain. But what will he say when he learns that you think nothing of it? But here is something

461

to make you laugh: he wants to eat salads of egg whites, and I am to ask you to give me some of your Four Thieves vinegar; he says he knows it exists, but it is not to be had in Venice. He told me he spent a sweet and cruel night, and he expressed a certain uneasiness for me, too, for he thought my efforts were beyond the delicacy of my sex. That may well be; but in the meanwhile I am delighted at having outdone myself and having been put to such a noble test of my strength. I love you to adoration; I kiss the air, thinking that you are there; and I cannot wait to kiss your portrait. I hope that mine will be as dear to you. I believe we are born for each other, and I curse myself when I think that I have put a barrier between us. The key which you see here is to my jewel-box. Search it; take whatever you see addressed 'To my Angel.' It is a small present which my friend wanted me to give you in exchange for the nightcap you gave me. Farewell."

The small key which I found in the letter was to a casket in the boudoir. Impatient to see the nature of the present which her friend had inspired her to give me, I go and open the little casket, and I undo the packet. I find a letter and a shagreen case. Here is the letter:

"What will make this present dear to you, my loving friend, is my portrait, of which our friend, who has two, is happy to deprive himself when he thinks that you will become its owner. In this box you will find my portrait twice concealed by two different secret devices. You will see me as a nun if you remove the bottom of the snuffbox lengthwise; and if you push the corner of it you will see a hinged cover open, under which I appear as you have made me. It is impossible, my dear, that any woman has ever loved you as I love you. Our friend encourages my passion. I cannot decide if I am more fortunate in my friend or in my lover, for it is beyond my powers to imagine anything better than either."

In the case I found a gold snuffbox, which a few traces of Spanish snuff showed had been used. Following the instructions I found her at the bottom of it, dressed as a nun, standing, and in half profile. Raising the false bottom showed her to me lying naked on a black silk mattress in the pose of Correggio's Magdalen.[2] She was looking at a Cupid who had his quiver at his feet and was seated on her nun's habit. It was a present of which I did not think myself worthy. I wrote her a letter in which she could not but find the deepest gratitude truly depicted. In the same small casket I saw all her diamonds in drawers and four purses filled with zecchini. Handsome behavior being one of my great

462

admirations, I shut the casket and went back to Venice, happy if I could only have found the will and the means to escape from the sway of Fortune by ceasing to gamble.

The jeweler gave me the medallion of the Annunciation just as I wished it to be. It was made to be worn hanging from the neck. A link through which the neck cord was to pass contained the secret device. If it was pulled hard, the Annunciation sprang up and revealed my portrait. I attached it to a gold chain of Spanish links six ells long, which made it a most noble present. I put it in my pocket and in the evening of Epiphany Day I posted myself at the foot of the fine statue which the grateful Republic had erected to the hero Colleoni after having him poisoned,[3] if backstairs history tells true. *Sit divus, modo non vivus* ("Let him be a god so long as he is not alive")[4] is a saying of the enlightened monarch which will endure as long as there are monarchs.

At exactly two o'clock[5] I saw M. M. get out of the gondola dressed, and very well masked, as a woman. We went to the opera at San Samuele, and at the end of the second ballet we went to the Ridotto, where she greatly enjoyed looking at all the patrician ladies, whose rank gives them the privilege of sitting down with their faces unmasked. After walking about for half an hour we went to the room set apart for the great bankers. She stopped at Signor Momolo Mocenigo's[6] bank; at that time he was the handsomest of all the young patrician gamesters. As there was no play at his table, he was lolling easily in front of two thousand zecchini, with his head bent toward the ear of a masked lady sitting beside him. She was Signora Marina Pisani,[7] whose adoring cavalier he was.

M. M. having asked me if I wished to play, and I having answered no, she said that she was taking me for her partner and, not waiting for me to reply, she draws out a purse and puts a roll of coins on a card. The banker, moving only his hands, shuffled, then cut, and M. M. won her card and then the paroli. The Signore pays, takes a new pack of cards, and begins whispering to the lady beside him, quite indifferent to four hundred zecchini which M. M. had already put on the same card. The banker continuing his conversation, M. M. said to me in good French: "Our stakes are not high enough to interest the Signore; let us go." So saying, she takes away her card and moves on. I pick up the money without answering the Signore, who says:

"Your masker is too intolerant."

I rejoin my beautiful gamester, who was surrounded.

She stops at the bank of Signor Piero Marcello,[8] another charming young man, at whose side was Signora Venier,[9] Signor Momolo's sister. She plays, and loses five rolls one after the other. Having no more money, she takes coins by handfuls from the pocket in which I had the four hundred zecchini, and in five or six deals she has the bank at death's door. She stops, and the noble banker congratulates her on her luck. After pocketing all the money she had won I give her my arm and we go downstairs and set off to have supper. Noticing that several busybodies were following us I took a *traghetto* gondola, and had it land where I wished. This is the way to escape from busybodies in Venice.

After eating a good supper I emptied my pockets. For my share I found I was in possession of nearly a thousand zecchini; she asked me to do hers up in rolls and put them in her little casket and keep the key to it. I finally gave her the medallion containing my portrait, whereupon she reproached me for not having done her the favor sooner. After having tried in vain to discover the secret, she was delighted to learn it, and she thought me a very good likeness.

Remembering that we had only three hours before us I urged her to undress.

"Yes," she said; "but be careful; for my friend maintains that you may die on the spot."

"And why does he think you are not in equal danger, since your ecstasies are more frequent than mine?"

"He says that the liquid which we women distill cannot come from the brain, since the womb has no connection with the seat of understanding. It follows, he says, that the child is not the mother's son in respect to the brain, which is the seat of reason, but the father's; and I think it is true. According to this system woman has at most only the quantity of reason which she needs; she has none over to give a portion of it to the fetus."

"Your lover is wise. According to this system we must forgive women all the follies they commit for love's sake, and men none. That is why I shall be in despair if I find that you have become pregnant."

"I shall know that in a few weeks, and if I am pregnant so much the better. I have decided what course I shall take."

"And what course is that?"

"To entrust myself entirely to my friend and to you. I am certain that neither of you will let me be brought to bed in the convent."

464

"That would be a stroke of fate which would determine our destiny. I should have to carry you off and take you to England and marry you."

"My friend thinks that it would be possible to bribe a physician who would declare that I was suffering from some malady of his own invention and order me to go and drink mineral waters at the springs, which the Bishop might allow. At the watering place I would be cured, then I would come back here; but I would far rather that we united our destinies until death. Could you live comfortably anywhere, as you do here?"

"Alas, no! But with you could I be unhappy? We will talk of this when it becomes necessary. So now let us go to bed."

"Let us. If I bear a son my friend will take care of him as his father."

"Could he believe that he is?"

"You can both take the credit; but some resemblance will show me the truth."

"Yes—for example if in time to come he writes pretty verses you can conclude that he is his."

"Who told you that he can write verses?"

"Admit that he wrote the six in answer to mine."

"I will not admit it. Good or bad, they are mine, and I mean to convince you of it on the spot."

"No, no. Let us go to bed, or Love will challenge Apollo to a duel."

"An excellent idea! Take this pencil and write. At the moment I am Apollo."

She then dictated the following four lines:

Je ne me battrai pas. Je te cède la place.
Si Venus est ma sœur, commune est notre race.
Je sais faire des vers. Un moment de perdu
Ne pourra pas déplaire à l'amour convaincu.

(I will not fight. I yield the ground to you. If Venus is my sister, we are kindred. I can write verses. A moment lost cannot offend a confident Love.")

I thereupon asked her pardon on my knees, admitting that she was also versed in mythology; but could I suppose that a Venetian lady of twenty-two who had been brought up in a convent could be so talented? She said that she had an insatiable desire to convince me that she deserved my heart, and she asked me if I thought her a shrewd gamester.

"Shrewd enough to make the banker tremble."

"I do not always play so high, but having taken you as my partner I defied Fortune. Why did you not play?"

"Because having lost four thousand zecchini during the last week of the year, I had no money left; but I will play tomorrow and Fortune will favor me. Meanwhile here is a little book I took from your boudoir. It is Pietro Aretino's postures. In these three hours I want to try some of them."

"That is very like you. But some of them are impossible and even silly."

"True, but four are very interesting."

It was in these labors that we spent the three hours. The chimes of the clock put an end to our celebration. After escorting her back to her gondola I went home to bed; but I could not sleep. I got up and went to pay some pressing debts. One of the greatest pleasures a wastrel can enjoy is that of paying certain debts. The money M. M. had won for me brought me luck all night, and I reached the end of the Carnival having won every day.

Going to the casino in Murano three days after Twelfth-night to put ten or twelve rolls in M. M.'s casket, I found the caretaker's wife with a letter from her for me. I had just received one from C. C. by Laura. After giving me as good news of her health as I could wish, M. M. asked me to find out if the same jeweler who had set her medallion had by any chance set a ring which displayed a St. Catherine which must also conceal a portrait; she wanted to know the secret of it. She said that it was a boarder of whom she was fond who had the ring, that it was very thick, and that the girl did not know that there must be a secret device for opening it. I answered that I would obey all her commands. But here is C. C.'s letter, which is amusing because of the quandary in which it put me. The letter from C. C. was of very recent date; M. M.'s had been written two days earlier.

"Oh, how happy I am! You love my dear friend Mother M. M. She has a medallion as thick as my ring. She can have received it only from you; it must contain your portrait. I am sure that the painter who painted her Annunciation is the same one who painted my patron saint; the jeweler must be the same one too. I feel very sure that it was you who gave it to her. Content to know all, I did not want to risk grieving her by telling her that I had discovered her secret. But my dear friend, being either more frank or more curious, did not do likewise. She told me she was certain that my St. Catherine served to cover a portrait, which must be that of the person who had given it to me. I answered that it was true my ring came from my lover, but that I did not know it could contain his portrait. She replied that if such was the case, and I was willing, she would try to find out the secret and afterward she would reveal hers to me too. Certain that she could not find the secret, I gave her my ring, saying that discovering it would please me. The nun who is my aunt sending for me just then, I left my ring with her, and she gave it back to me after dinner, saying that she had been unable to discover anything, but she was still certain the portrait must be in it. She is convinced of it, but I assure you that in this respect she will not find me obliging, for if she saw you she would guess everything and then I should have to tell her who you are. I am sorry that I must keep something from her, but I am not at all sorry either that you love her or that she loves you, and I pity you so much for being cruelly reduced to making love at a grating that I would gladly let you take my place. I should make two people happy at one stroke. Farewell."

I answered that she had guessed rightly that my portrait was in M. M.'s medallion; but I urged her to continue to keep my secret, assuring her that the fancy I had taken for her dear friend in no way detracted from the constancy of my passion for her. Thus did I equivocate, to keep up the intrigue, which I yet saw coming to its end in the closeness of their friendship.

Having learned from Laura that on such-and-such a day a ball was to be given in the large visiting room of the convent, I made up my mind to go to it masked in such a way that my two dear friends could not recognize me. I was certain that I should see them. During the Carnival in Venice nuns are allowed to have this innocent pleasure. There is dancing in the visiting room, and they remain inside, watching the festivities from behind their wide gratings. At the end of the day the festivities are over, everyone leaves, and they retire well satisfied to have been present at one of the pleasures of the laity. The ball was to take place on the day on which M. M. had invited me to sup at her casino; but that did not prevent me from going masked to the visiting room, where I was sure to see my dear C. C. as well.

Wanting to make certain that my two friends would not recognize me, I decided to mask as Pierrot.[10] There is no costume better fitted to disguise a person, provided he is neither a hunchback nor lame. The wide tunic of a Pierrot, the long, very wide sleeves, the wide trousers which come down to the heels, conceal everything distinctive in his figure by which someone who knew him intimately could recognize him. A cap which covers his whole head, his ears, and his neck hides not only his hair but also the color of his complexion, and a piece of gauze in front of the eyes of his mask prevents anyone from seeing whether they are black or blue.

So, having eaten a dish of soup, I mask after this fashion and, heedless of the cold (for the whole costume being of white linen, one cannot be more lightly clad), I board a gondola, have it drop me at a *traghetto*, and there take another gondola which conveys me to Murano. I had no cloak. In my trouser pockets I had only a handkerchief, the keys to the casino, and my purse.

I go down to the visiting room, which was full, but everyone makes way for the strange mask, whose characteristics were unknown in Venice. I walk on, assuming the gait of a booby as the nature of the mask demands, and I enter the circle of dancers. I see Punches, Scaramouches, Pantaloons, Harlequins. At the gratings I see all the nuns and all the boarders, some seated, others standing, and though I do not let my eyes linger on any of them I see M. M. and, on the opposite side, my loving C. C., who was standing up to enjoy the spectacle. I proceed around the entire circle, walking as if I were drunk, looking everyone up and down, but more looked at and studied. Everyone was trying to make me out.

I stop in front of a pretty girl disguised as a female Harlequin and rudely take her hand to make her dance a minuet with me. Everyone laughs and draws back to make room for us. The Harlequiness dances in perfect character with her costume, and I with mine: I amused the company vastly by constantly appearing to be on the verge of falling, though I always kept my balance. Each time the general apprehension was followed by laughter.

After the minuet I danced twelve furlanas[11] with extraordinary energy. Out of breath, I let myself drop and pretended to sleep, and when my snores were heard everyone respected Pierrot's slumbers. Next there was a contradance which lasted an hour and in which I thought it best not to join; but after the contradance up comes a Harlequin who, with the impertinence permissible to his character, spanks me with his lath. This is Harlequin's weapon. Having, as Pierrot, no weapon, I catch him by the belt and run about the room carrying him, he meanwhile continuing to hit me with his lath on my behind. His Harlequiness, who was the charming girl who had danced with me, comes running to rescue her friend and also hits me with her lath. At that I put the Harlequin down, snatch his lath, and take the Harlequiness on my shoulders, hitting her on the behind and running at full speed all over the room to the laughter of the company and the frightened cries of the girl, who was afraid that if I fell she would show her thighs or her drawers. But an impertinent Punch put a sudden end to the whole comical struggle. He came up behind me and tripped me so hard that I could not keep from falling. Everyone booed him. I quickly got up and, very much annoyed, began an out-and-out wrestling match with the insolent fellow. He was as tall as I am. Since he was awkward and had no resources but his brute strength, I made him bite the dust and I handled him so roughly that his coat came unbuttoned, whereupon he lost his hump and his false belly. To the sound of the clapping and laughter of all the nuns, who had perhaps never enjoyed such a spectacle, I seized the moment, dashed through the crowd, and escaped.

Dripping with sweat, I called a gondola, shut myself up in it, and had it take me to the Ridotto to avoid catching a chill. Night was falling, I was not to be at the casino in Murano until two o'clock, and I could not wait to see M. M.'s surprise when she saw Pierrot before her. So I spent the two hours playing at all the small banks, going from one to another, winning, losing, indulging in all sorts of antics in complete freedom of body and soul, sure that no one recognized me, enjoying the present and snapping my fingers at the future and at all those who are pleased to exercise their reason in the dreary task of foreseeing it.

But two o'clock strikes and reminds me that love and a delicious supper await me to bring me new pleasures. With my pockets full of silver I leave the Ridotto, I hurry to Murano, go to the casino, and enter the bedroom, where I think I see M. M. in her habit standing with her back to the fireplace. I approach to see the effect of the surprise on her face, and I am turned to stone. What I see is not M. M., but C. C. in a nun's habit; even more surprised than I am, she neither speaks nor moves. I drop into an armchair to give myself time to get over my astonishment and recover my intellectual faculties.

When I saw C. C. I was as if struck by lightning. My soul was left as motionless as my body, lost in an inextricable labyrinth.

"It is M. M.," I said to myself, "who is playing this trick on me; but how did she manage to find out that I am C. C.'s lover?

C. C. has betrayed my secret. But if she has betrayed me how dare she appear before me? If M. M. loves me how can she have deprived herself of the pleasure of seeing me and sent me her rival? It cannot be meant as a favor for no one carries doing favors to such lengths. It is meant to be a stinging, scornful insult."

My self-esteem did not fail to produce strong arguments to refute the possibility, but in vain. Shivering in the cold gloom of my disappointment, I alternately saw that I was tricked, deceived, trapped, scorned.

In this fashion I spent half an hour, bleak and silent, keeping my eyes fixed on C. C.'s face while she, too, looked at me without a word, more embarrassed and nonplussed than I, for she could at most recognize me as the same masker who had cut such capers in the visiting room.

Being in love with M. M., and having gone there only for her sake, I did not have the easy recourse open to the so-called reasonable man—I could not make the best of the situation by substituting the one for the other, despite the fact that I was far from scorning C. C., whose merits were at least as great as M. M.'s. I loved her, I adored her; but at that moment she was not the one for me to have. It would have been an outright denial of love, which could not but rouse my reason to indignation. It seemed to me that if I settled for doing the honors to C. C. I should be contemptible; it seemed to me that honor forbade me to lend myself to such deceit; in addition, I was glad both to gain the opportunity of reproaching M. M. with an indifference very far from love and of refraining from acting in a way which would ever lead her to suppose that she had done me a favor. Add that during all this time I was inclined to believe that she was in the hiding place and her friend with her.

I had to resolve on a course, for I could not think of spending the whole night there masked as I was and saying nothing. I considered deciding to leave, the more so because neither M. M. nor C. C. could be certain that the Pierrot was I; but I dismissed the idea with horror when I thought of the intense mortification C. C.'s beautiful soul would suffer if she ever learned that I was the Pierrot; it was with the greatest grief that I thought that she might even now suspect it. I was her husband; I was the man who had seduced her. These reflections lacerated my soul.

I suddenly begin to imagine that M. M. is in the secret closet and that, if she is, she will show herself when she considers the time is ripe. With this thought in mind, I decide to remain. I untie the handkerchief which bound the white mask of Pierrot to my head, and I relieve my charming C. C. from anxiety by showing her my face.

"It could only be you," she says, "but I breathe again. You seemed surprised to see me. Did you not know that you would find me here?"

"You may be sure I knew nothing about it."

"If you are displeased, I am in despair; but I am innocent."

"My adorable love, come to my arms. How can you suppose that I could be displeased to see you? You are always my better half; but I beg you to release my soul from the cruel labyrinth in which it is lost, for you could not be here unless you have betrayed our secret."

"I! I could never have done that, even if it cost me my life."

"Then how can you be here? How did your dear friend manage to discover everything? No one on earth can have told her that I am your husband. Perhaps Laura—"

"Laura is loyal. My dear love, I cannot even guess."

"But how were you persuaded to put on this disguise, to come here? You are able to leave the convent, and you have never told me so important a secret?"

"Can you believe that I would not have told you anything so important if I had ever left it? Today was the first time—two hours ago; and nothing is so simple or so natural as what made me do what I have done."

"Tell me about it, my love; my curiosity is boundless."

"Your curiosity is dear to me, and I will tell you everything. You know how fond M. M. and I are of each other; our affection could not be greater; you must be sure of it from all that I have written to you. Well, then—two days ago M. M. asked the Abbess and my aunt to let me sleep in her room instead of the lay sister, who had a bad cold and had gone to cough in the infirmary. She was given permission, and you cannot imagine how happy we were to find ourselves free for the first time to sleep together in the same bed.

"Today, a moment after you left the visiting room where you made us laugh so much, and where neither M. M. nor I could ever have imagined that it was you, she went out. I followed her, and as soon as we were alone she said she needed me to do her a service on which her happiness depended. I replied that she had only to tell me what it was. She thereupon opened a drawer and to my great surprise dressed me as you see me now. She kept laughing, and I laughed too, not knowing where the joke might end. When she saw that I was all dressed she said that she was going to trust me with a great secret, which she fearlessly confided to my loyalty. 'Know, my dear friend,' she said, 'that I was going to leave the convent tonight and not come back until tomorrow morning. But now it has been decided that it is not I who will go, but you. You have nothing to fear, and you need no instructions, for I am sure that in your situation you will not be at a loss. In an hour a lay sister will come here, I will speak to her privately, then she will tell you to follow her. Accordingly, you will go out with her by the small door and cross the garden until you reach the room which gives on the little quay. There you will get into a gondola, saying nothing to the gondolier except, "To the casino." You will be there in five minutes, you will get out, and you will enter a small room in which you will find a fire burning. You will be all alone there, and you will wait.' 'Wait for whom?' I said. 'No one. That is all you are to know. Nothing will happen to you which will offend you. Trust to me. At the casino you will eat supper and go to bed, too, if you wish, for no one will disturb you. I beg you not to ask me any further questions, for I cannot tell you more.'

"Tell me, my dear, what I could do after hearing this, and after having promised her that I would do whatever she asked? Begone, base suspicion! I laughed, and expecting only something pleasant, as soon as the lay sister came I followed her, and here I am. After being bored for three quarters of an hour, I saw Pierrot.

"I can assure you on my honor that the very moment I saw you appear my heart told me that it was you; but the next moment, when I saw you start back after looking at me closely, I knew just as clearly that you felt that you had been tricked. You sat here in such a gloomy silence that I should have thought it very wrong if I had been the first to break it, and the more so since, despite what my heart told me, I could not but fear that I was mistaken. Pierrot's mask might hide someone else—but certainly no one who could be dearer to me than you after eight months during which only force has kept me from embracing you. Now that you must be sure I am innocent, let me congratulate you on your knowing this casino. You are fortunate, and I wish you happiness. M. M. is the only woman, after me, who is worthy of your affection, the only woman with whom I can be content to share it. I pitied you; I pity you no more, and your happiness makes me happy. Kiss me."

I should have been an ingrate and a barbarian if I had not then clasped to my breast with unfeigned signs of the most sincere affection the angel of goodness and beauty who was there only for friendship's sake. But after convincing her that I considered her entirely justified, I did not fail to express my tender feelings and then to launch into theories equally reasonable and unreasonable to account for M. M.'s extraordinary behavior, which I considered very dubious and next to impossible to interpret to her credit. I told her in so many words that, apart from the pleasure it gave me to see her, it was obvious that her friend had played a vile trick on me which I could not but resent for its patent offensiveness.

"I do not see that," C. C. replied. "My dear friend must have contrived to find out, though I don't know how, that you were my lover before you met her. She might well have believed that you still love me, and she believed—for I know her soul—that she was giving us a sacred proof of perfect friendship by procuring us, without forewarning, the highest happiness for which two lovers can hope. I cannot but love her for it."

"You are right, my dear one; but your situation is very different from mine. You have no other lover, and, unable to live with you, I could not resist M. M.'s charms. I have fallen madly in love with her; she knows it; and, with her intelligence, she cannot have done what she has done except to show me her scorn for me. I admit that I feel it most keenly. If she loved me as I love her she could never have done me the excruciating favor of sending you here in her stead."

"I do not agree with you. Her soul is as great and noble as her heart is generous, and just as I am not displeased to know that you love her and are loved by her and that you have made each other happy, as appearances tell me you have, so she is not displeased to know that we love each other and indeed is delighted to have an opportunity to convince us that she approves of it. She wants you to understand that she loves you for yourself, that your pleasures are hers, and that she is not jealous of me, who am her dearest friend. To convince you that you should not be displeased that she had discovered our secret, she tells you, by sending me here, that she is satisfied that you should share your heart between her and me. You know that she loves me, and that I am often her wife or her fond husband; so, just as you do not object to my being your rival and to my often making her happy, she does not want you to suppose that her love is like hate, for such is the love of a jealous heart."

"You plead your friend's cause like an angel, my dear wife, but you do not see the thing in its true light. You have intelligence and a pure soul; but you have not my experience. M. M. loves me only to amuse herself, knowing perfectly well that I am not such a fool as to be taken in by what she has now done. I am miserable, and it is she who makes me so."

"Then I, too, should have cause to complain of her. She has shown me that she has all power over my lover and that, having made him her own, she finds no difficulty in giving him back to me. On top of that, she shows me that she scorns the affection I feel for her, by putting me in a position to show it to someone else."

"Now your argument is getting shaky. The case between her and you is entirely different. The love you and she indulge in is only a game by which you delude your senses. The pleasures you enjoy do not exclude others; what could make you jealous of each other would be a love of the same kind between women; but M. M. could not feel offended that you had a lover, just as you could not if she had one—provided in either case that the lover was not the other's."

"But that is precisely our case, and you are wrong. We are not a bit offended that you love us both. Didn't I write you that I wished I could give you my place? Does that make you think I scorn you too?"

"Your wish, my dear, to give me your place when you did not know that I was her lover arose from the fact that your love had changed into friendship, and for the time being I must be glad of it; but I have good reason to be offended if M. M. entertains the same sentiment, for I love her now and I am certain that I can never marry her. Do you understand that, my angel? Being sure that you will become my wife I am equally sure of our love, which will have time enough to be rekindled; but M. M.'s love will not return. Is it not humiliating for me if all I have done and all I have been able to do is to make myself an object of contempt? As for you, you cannot but adore her. She has initiated you into all her mysteries; you owe her eternal gratitude and friendship."

Such is the substance of our discussion, which continued until midnight, when the tactful caretaker brought us an excellent supper. I could not eat, but C. C. had a good appetite. Despite my gloom I had to laugh when I saw a salad of egg whites. She said that I was right to laugh, because the yolks, which were the best part, had been removed. I took pleasure in admiring the increase in her beauty, though I felt not the least desire to show her my feeling. I have always held that there is no merit in being faithful to a person one truly loves.

Two hours before dawn we went back to sit in front of the fire. C. C., seeing me sad, showed the most delicate respect for my situation—not a trace of provocation, no posture which deviated from the strictest decency. Her words were loving and tender, but she never once dared to reproach me for my coldness.

Toward the end of our long conversation she asked me what she was to say to M. M. when she returned to the convent.

"She expects," she said, "to see me perfectly happy and full of gratitude for her generous gift of this night. What shall I tell her?"

"The plain truth. You must not keep one word of our conversation from her, or one of my thoughts if you can remember them. You must tell her that she has made me unhappy for a long time to come."

"I should distress her too much if I told her that, for she loves you, and the medallion which contains your portrait is her dearest possession. I will do my very best to make it up between you quickly. I will send you a letter from me by Laura, unless you assure me that you will go to her house for it tomorrow."

"Your letters will always be dear to me; but you will see that M. M. will not want to have things out. There is one point on which she may not believe you."

"Yes, I know—the strength of mind we had to spend eight hours together like brother and sister. If she knows you as I know you she will think it impossible."

"In that case tell her the opposite if you wish."

"No, no! It would be a very ill-timed lie. I can dissimulate a little; but I shall never learn to lie. I love you, too, because all through this night you have not pretended that you still love me."

"Believe me, my angel, I am sick with grief. I love you with all my soul; but now I am in a situation to be pitied."

"You weep, my dear; I beg you to spare my heart. I cannot forgive myself for having said that to you; but believe that I had no intention of reproaching you. I am sure that in a quarter of an hour M. M. will be weeping too."

When the hour struck, having no more hope that M. M. would appear to justify herself, I kissed C. C., I resumed my disguise to cover my head and so shelter myself from a very strong wind whose whistlings I heard, and I hurried down the stairs after giving C. C. the key to the casino and telling her to return it to M. M.

Continuing his complex intrigues with M. M. and C. C., Casanova discovered that M. M.'s protector—the man who had watched them make love in the little casino—was Monsieur de Bernis, the French Ambassador. These two voluptuaries who had so much in common were soon friends, and the younger man came to regard Bernis as one of his patrons, which in itself deprived the four-way affair of some of its excitement. Inevitably Casanova began to take an interest in other women. In the process he made powerful enemies among the patricians, chief among them Signor Condulmer. According to Casanova, he attracted the hatred of Condulmer by making love to the wife of another patrician, Signora Zorzi, whom Condulmer himself had been courting hitherto. Whatever the truth of this claim, Condulmer was a dangerous man to cross—for a while the most dangerous possible in Venice. During eight crucial months in 1755 Condulmer was one of the three State Inquisitors, effectively the supreme powers in the city because they possessed the authority to imprison anyone they chose on their word alone.

As Casanova's troubles mounted, Signor Bragadin, who had himself been State Inquisitor, urged his protégé to take refuge in Florence, but the advice came too late. The two men were never to see one another again. The very next morning, July 26, 1755, Messer Grande—the chief policeman of the city—entered Casanova's room.

To wake, to see him, and to hear him ask if I was Giacomo Casanova took no more than the first moment. As soon as I answered that I was the person that he had named, he ordered me to give him whatever papers I had, whether written by me or by anyone else, to dress, and to go with him. I having asked him by whose authority he gave me the order, he answered that it was by the authority of the tribunal.

CHAPTER XII

Under the Leads. Earthquake.

The word "tribunal" petrified my soul, leaving me only the physical ability to obey him. My desk was open; all my papers were on the table at which I wrote, I told him he could take them; he filled a bag which one of his men brought him, and he said I must also surrender certain bound manuscripts which there was reason to suppose I possessed; I showed him where they were, and then I saw it: the jeweler Manuzzi had been the infamous spy who had accused me of having these books when he had gained entrance to my house, leading me to believe that he could arrange for me to buy diamonds and, as I said, that he could get me a purchaser for the books; they were the *Key of Solomon*,[1] the *Zecor-ben*,[2] a *Picatrix*,[3] a complete treatise on the planetary hours[4] favorable to making the necessary perfumes and conjurations for conversing with demons of all classes. Those who knew that I had these books thought I was a magician, and it rather pleased me. Messer Grande also took the books I had on my night table: Ariosto, Horace, Petrarch, the *Philosophe militaire*[5] in manuscript, which Mathilde[6] had given me, the *Portier des Chartreux*, and the little book of lubricious postures by Aretino which Manuzzi had also reported, for Messer Grande asked me for it too. The spy Manuzzi looked like an honest man, a necessary quality in his trade; his son made a fortune in Poland by marrying an Opeska[7] whom he did away with, or so they say, for I know nothing about it and even do not believe it, though I do know that he was capable of it.

While Messer Grande thus made a harvest of my manuscripts, my books, and my letters, I automatically got dressed, neither rapidly nor slowly; I made my toilet, I shaved, C. D.[8] dressed my hair, I put on a shirt with a lace ruff and my fine coat, all without thinking what I was doing and without saying a word, even as Messer Grande, who never took his eyes off me, did not dare to object to my dressing as though I were going to a wedding.

When I left my room I was surprised to find thirty or forty constables in the drawing room. They had done me the honor to think so many were needed to secure my person, whereas according to the axiom *ne Hercules quidem contra duos* ("not even Hercules against two"),[9] only two were necessary. It is strange that in London, where everyone is brave, only one man is used to arrest another, and that in my dear country, where people are cowards, thirty are sent. The reason may be that the coward who is forced to become an assailant must be more afraid than the man assailed, and the latter for that very reason may become brave; and in fact in Venice one often sees one man defend himself against twenty *sbirri* and get away after giving them a beating. In Paris I helped a friend of mine escape from forty bumbailiffs, whom we put to flight.

Messer Grande ordered me into a gondola, where he sat down beside me, keeping only four men and sending the rest away. Arrived at his headquarters, he locked me into a room after offering me coffee, which I refused. I spent four hours there during all of which I slept, waking every quarter of an hour to make water—a very strange phenomenon, for I had never suffered from strangury, the heat was excessive, and I had not supped; nevertheless I filled two large chamber pots with urine. It had been my experience on other occasions that surprise caused by an act of oppression produced the effect of a strong narcotic on me, but it was only now that I learned that it is highly diuretic. I leave it to the physicians. I had a good laugh in Prague, where I published my *Flight from the Leads*[10] six years ago, when I learned that the fine ladies considered my account of the phenomenon a piece of swinishness which I might well have omitted. I would perhaps have omitted it in talking to a lady; but the public is not a lady, and I like to be instructive. Furthermore it is not swinishness; there is nothing dirty or foul-smelling about it despite the fact that we have it in common with swine, just as we have eating and drinking, which no one has ever dubbed swinishness.

It is likely that at the same time that my terrified mind was reduced to displaying its weakness by the collapse of its thinking faculty, my body, too, as if it were in a wine press, had to expel a good part of the fluids which, in their continual circulation, activate our power to think; and that is how a terrifying surprise can bring on sudden death and—God preserve us!— send us to Paradise, for it can drive our soul from our blood.

When the Terza[11] bell rang, the chief constable entered and said he had orders to put me "under the Leads."[12] I followed him. We got into another gondola and, after taking a long way around through small canals, we entered the Grand Canal and disembarked at the Quay of the Prisons.[13] After going up several flights of stairs we

crossed a high enclosed bridge[14] which provides the communication
between the prisons and the Doge's Palace over the canal called the
Rio del Palazzo.[15] Beyond this bridge we walked the length of a
gallery, entered a room, then another, where he presented me to
a man dressed in the robe of a patrician, who, after looking at me,
said:

"È quello; mettetelo in deposito." ("That is he; put him away.")

This personage was the Secretary to Their Excellencies the
Inquisitors, the Circospetto[16] Domenico Cavalli, who apparently
felt ashamed to speak Venetian in my presence, for he pronounced
judgment on me in Tuscan. Messer Grande then turned me over to
the warden of the Leads, who was there holding a bunch of keys and
who, followed by two constables, made me go up two small flights
of stairs, proceed through a gallery, then another separated from it by
a locked door, then still another, at the end of which he used
another key to open a door through which I entered a large, ugly,
dirty garret, twelve yards long by two wide, badly lighted by a high
dormer. I supposed this garret was my prison, but I was mistaken.
The man, who was the jailer, took a thick key, he opened a heavy
door lined with iron, three and a half feet high and with a round
hole eight inches in diameter in the center of it, and ordered me to
enter just as I was looking attentively at an iron mechanism which
was fastened to the strong wall with nails and had the shape of a
horseshoe; it was an inch thick and had a diameter of five inches
from one of its parallel ends to the other. I was wondering what it
could be when he said with a smile:

"I see, Signore, that you are trying to guess what this machine is
for, and I can tell you. When Their Eminences order someone
strangled, he is made to sit on a stool with his back to this collar
and his head is placed so that the collar goes round half of his neck.
The two ends of a skein of silk which goes round the other half of it
pass through this hole leading to a winch to which they are fastened
and a man turns it until the patient has rendered up his soul to Our
Lord, for his confessor never leaves him—praise be to God!—until
he is dead."

"It is most ingenious, and I imagine, Signore, that it is you who
have the honor of turning the winch."

He did not answer. My height being five feet nine inches,
I stooped low to enter; and he locked me in. Hearing him ask me
through the grating what I wanted to eat, I answered that I had not
yet thought about it. He went away, locking all his doors again.

Overwhelmed and bewildered, I put my elbows on the sill of the grating. It was two feet in all directions, crossed by six iron bars an inch thick which formed sixteen openings five inches square. It would have lighted my cell well enough if one of the main roof timbers, a square beam a foot and a half thick and entering the wall below the dormer, which was diagonally across from me, had not cut off what light came into the garret. Having made the round of this terrible prison, keeping my head down for it was only five and a half feet high, I found, chiefly by groping, that it formed three quarters of a square twelve feet by twelve. The quarter next to the missing one was to all intents and purposes an alcove large enough to contain a bed, but I found neither a bed nor a chair nor a table nor any kind of furniture except a bucket for the needs of nature and a board fastened to the wall, one foot wide and four feet above the floor. On it I put my beautiful floss-silk cloak, my fine coat which had started its life so badly, and my hat trimmed with Spanish point lace and a white feather. The heat was extreme. In my astonishment nature led me to the grating, the only place where I could rest leaning on my elbows; I could not see the dormer, but I saw the light which illuminated the garret and rats as big as rabbits which were walking about. These hideous animals, whose sight I loathed, came directly under my grating without showing the least sign of fear. I quickly drew the inner blind over the round hole in the center of the door, for a visit from them would have frozen my blood. Sunk in the deepest reverie, my arms still crossed on the sill, I spent eight hours there motionless, silent, and never leaving my post.

When twenty-one o'clock[17] struck, I began to feel uneasy because I saw no one appearing, not even to find out if I wanted to eat, not even to bring me a bed, a chair, or at least bread and water. I had no appetite, but I thought my jailers should not know it; never in my life had I had such a bitter taste in my mouth; yet I felt certain that before the day ended someone would appear; but when I heard twenty-four o'clock strike I succumbed to something very like madness, howling, stamping my feet, cursing, and accompanying all this useless noise which my strange situation drove me to make with loud cries. After half an hour of this exercise in fury, seeing no one come, with not the slightest sign to make me imagine that anyone could have heard my ravings, and shrouded in darkness, I closed the grating, fearing that the rats would jump into the cell. I threw myself at full length on the floor after wrapping my hair in a handkerchief. Such a pitiless desertion seemed to me unthinkable, even if I had been sentenced to death. My consideration of what I could have done to deserve treatment so cruel could continue no longer than a minute, for I found no cause for arresting me. As a great libertine, a bold talker, a man who thought of nothing but enjoying life I could not find myself guilty, but seeing that I was nevertheless treated as such, I spare my reader all that rage and indignation and despair made me say and think against the horrible despotism which was oppressing me. Yet my anger and the grief which preyed on me and the hard floor on which I lay did not keep me from falling asleep; my constitution needed sleep; and when a person is young and healthy his constitution can satisfy its need without his giving it any thought.

The midnight bell woke me. That is a terrible awakening which brings regret for the nothingness or the illusions of sleep. I could not believe that I had spent three hours insensible of any discomfort. Not changing my position but still lying as I was on my left side, I put out my right arm to get my handkerchief, which my memory assured me I had placed there. As I groped along with my hand—God! what a surprise when I find another hand as cold as ice! Terror electrified me from head to foot and every one of my hairs stood on end. Never in my life was I seized with such fear, and I had never thought I was subject to it. I certainly spent three or four minutes not only motionless but unable to think. Recovering a little, I allowed myself the relief of believing that what I had touched was only a figment of my imagination; in this conviction I again stretch out my arm to the same spot and I find the same hand, which, frozen with horror and giving a piercing shriek, I grasp and drop, drawing back my arm. I shudder; but regaining control over my mind, I decide that while I was asleep a corpse had been placed near me; for I was certain that when I lay down on the floor nothing had been there. I immediately imagine the body of some innocent wretch, perhaps one of my friends, who had been strangled and laid beside me so that when I woke I should find an example of the fate which I must expect. The thought infuriates me; for the third time I extend my arm to the hand, I grasp it, and at the same moment get up, intending to pull the corpse toward me and so ascertain the fact in all its atrocity; but as I try to raise myself on my left elbow the same cold hand which I am holding comes to life, draws away, and, to my great surprise, I instantly realize that the hand in my right hand is none other than my left, which, numbed and stiffened, had lost motion, feeling, and warmth, the effect of the soft, yielding, cozy bed on which my poor self was lying.

The incident, though comic, did not cheer me. On the contrary it gave me cause to make the darkest reflections. I realized that I was in a place where if the false seemed true, realities must seem dreams; where the understanding must lose half of its privileges; where a distorted imagination must make reason the victim either of chimerical hopes or terrible despair. I at once put myself on guard against anything of that nature; and at the age of thirty years I for the first time in my life turned for help to philosophy, all the germs of which were in my soul and which I had never before had occasion either to value or to employ. I believe that the great majority of men die without ever having thought. I continued to sit where I was until eight o'clock;[18] the half-light of the new day appeared; the sun should rise at quarter past nine; I longed to see the day begin; a presentiment which I thought infallible assured me that I should be sent home; I was burning with desires for revenge which I did not conceal from myself. I seemed to be leading the people to exterminate the government and massacre the aristocrats; everything was to be brought to dust; I was not satisfied to leave the slaughter of my oppressors to executioners, it was I myself who should massacre them. Such is man: he does not suspect that what speaks such words in him is not his reason but his greatest enemy, anger.

I waited less time than I was prepared to wait; and that went some way toward calming my fury. At half past eight the profound silence of the place, the Hell of living humanity, was broken by the squeak of the bolts in the vestibules of the corridors which had to be traversed to reach my cell. I saw the jailer in front of my grating asking me if I had "time to think about what I wanted to eat." One is lucky when the insolence of a villain assumes the mask of raillery. I answered that I wanted a rice soup, boiled beef, a roast, bread, water, and wine. I saw that the churl was surprised not to hear the lamentations he expected. He went away; but a quarter of an hour later he came back to say that he was astonished that I did not ask for a bed and whatever I needed because, said he,

"If you flatter yourself that you have been put here only for one night, you are mistaken."

"Then bring me everything you think I shall need."

"Where am I to go for it? Here is a pencil and paper. Write it all down."

I wrote him instructions where to go to get me a bed, shirts, stockings, dressing gown, slippers, nightcaps, an armchair, a table, combs, mirrors, razors, handkerchiefs, the books which Messer Grande had taken from me, ink and pens and paper. When I read him the list, for the rascal could not read, he told me to cross out books, ink, paper, mirror, razor, for they were all forbidden under the Leads by the regulations, and he asked me for money to buy my dinner. I had three zecchini and I gave him one of them. He left the garret and I heard him set off an hour later. During the hour, as I learned afterward, he waited on seven other prisoners who were confined up there in cells at a distance from one another to prevent any communication.

Toward noon the jailer appeared, followed by five constables appointed to serve the state prisoners. He opened my cell to bring in the furniture I had ordered and my dinner. The bed was put in the alcove, my dinner was set out on a small table. My table service consisted of an ivory spoon which he had bought with my money, knife and fork being forbidden as were all metal implements.

"Order what you want to eat tomorrow," he said, "for I can only come here once a day at dawn. The most illustrious Secretary ordered me to tell you that he will send you suitable books, since those you want are forbidden."

"Thank him for his kindness in putting me in a cell by myself."

"I will give him your message, but you would do well not to make such jokes."

"I am not joking, for it is better, I think, to be alone than with the criminals who must be here."

"What, Signore? Criminals? I should resent that very much. There are only respectable people here, who, however, have to be sequestered from society for reasons which only Their Excellencies know. You have been put in a cell alone to increase your punishment, and you want me to convey your thanks for it?"

"I did not know that."

The ignoramus was right, as I had learned only too well a few days later. I discovered that a man shut up in solitude and deprived of any possibility of occupying himself, alone in an almost dark place, where he does not and cannot see anything except, once a day, the person who brings him food, and in which he cannot walk upright, is the most wretched of mortals. He longs for Hell, if he believes in it, only to have companionship. Confined there, I reached the point of longing for the company of a murderer, a maniac, a man with some

483

stinking disease, a bear. Solitude under the Leads drives one to despair; but to know it one must have experienced it. If the prisoner is a man of letters, give him a writing desk and paper and his wretchedness will decrease by nine tenths.

After the jailer left I put the table near the hole to get a little light, and I sat down to dine by the glimmer which came from the skylight; but I could swallow only a little soup. Having had nothing to eat for forty-five hours, it is no wonder if I was ill. I spent the day in my armchair, without accesses of fury, longing for the morrow and preparing my mind to read the books which had been so graciously promised me. I passed a sleepless night to the disagreeable noise the rats made in the garret and in company with the clock of San Marco, which, when it struck the hours, seemed to be in the room with me. A kind of torture of which few of my readers will have any knowledge caused me intolerable pain: it was a million fleas romping all over my body, avid for my blood and my skin, and piercing them with a voracity of which I had no conception; the accursed insects gave me convulsions, made my muscles contract spasmodically, and poisoned my blood.

At the first light of dawn Lorenzo[19] (for such was the jailer's name) had my bed made and the place swept and dusted, and one of his *sbirri* brought me water to wash in. I wanted to go out into the garret, but Lorenzo told me it was not allowed. He gave me two thick books, which I refrained from opening, not being certain that I could control a first burst of indignation which they might arouse in me and which the spy would have reported. After leaving me my victuals and cutting two lemons for me, he went away.

After quickly eating my soup to eat it hot, I put one book under the light which reached the hole from the dormer, and I saw that I could easily read it. I look at the title, and I see *La Cité mystique de Soeur Marie de Jésus appelée d'Agreda*.[20] I had never heard of it. The second book was by a Jesuit whose name I have forgotten.[21] He instituted a new special adoration directed to the heart of Our Lord Jesus Christ. Of all the human parts of our divine mediator, it was the heart which, according to the author, should be especially adored—the strange idea of an ignorant fool, reading the first page of whose book was enough to revolt me, for I thought that the heart was an organ no worthier than the lungs. The *Cité mystique* interested me a little.

I read everything that the extravagance of the heated imagination of an extremely devout Spanish virgin, given to melancholy, shut up in a convent, and guided by ignorant and flattering confessors, could bring forth. All these chimerical and monstrous visions were adorned with the name of revelations; in love with the Holy Virgin and admitted to her intimate friendship, she had received a command from God himself to write the life of his divine mother; the information which she needed and which no one could have read anywhere had been supplied her by the Holy Spirit.

So she began the history of the mother of God not at her birth but at the moment of her most immaculate conception in the womb of St. Anne. This Sister María of Agreda was the Superior of a convent of Franciscan nuns[22] which she founded in her own house. After narrating in detail all that her great heroine did during the nine months before her birth, she said that at the age of three years she was sweeping her house, aided by nine hundred servants, all angels, whom God had bestowed on her, under the personal command of their own prince, Michael, who came and went between her and God and God and her on their reciprocal embassies. What is striking in this book is the certainty which is borne in upon the judicious reader that there is nothing in it which the more than fanatical author could think she had invented; invention cannot go so far; everything is told in perfect good faith; they are the visions of a sublimated cerebellum which, without a trace of pride, drunk with God, believes that it reveals nothing but what the Holy Spirit dictates to it. The book was printed with the permission of the Inquisition. I could not get over my astonishment. Far from increasing or exciting in my mind a fervor or a zeal for religion, the work tempted me to regard as fabulous all that we have in the way of mysticism and of dogma as well.

The nature of the book entails certain consequences. A reader with a mind more susceptible to the miraculous and fonder of it than mine is in danger, when he reads it, of becoming a visionary and a maniacal scribbler like the virgin herself. The need to occupy myself with something led me to spend a week over this masterpiece of hyperexalted invention; I said nothing about it to the stupid jailer; but I could bear no more. As soon as I fell asleep I was aware of the plague with which Sister d'Agreda had infected my mind, weakened by melancholy and bad food. My extravagant dreams made me laugh when I recalled them in my waking hours, for I wanted to write them down, and if I had had writing materials I should perhaps have produced a work up there even madder than the one Signor Cavalli had sent me. From that time on I saw how mistaken they are who attribute a certain strength to the human mind; its strength is only relative, and a man who studied himself thoroughly would find nothing in him but weakness. I saw that though men do not often go mad, it is nevertheless true that the thing is easy. Our reason is like gunpowder, which, though very easy to ignite, nevertheless never catches fire unless fire is applied to it; or like a drinking glass, which never breaks unless it is broken. The Spanish woman's book is just what is needed to drive a man mad; but for the poison to take effect, he must be confined under the Leads alone and deprived of any other occupation.

In the month of November 1767, when I was traveling from Pamplona to Madrid, my driver Andrea Capello stopped for dinner in a town in Old Castille which was so gloomy and ugly that I felt curious to know its name. Oh, how I laughed when I was told that it was Agreda![23] "So it was here," I said to myself, "that the brain of that holy madwoman gave birth to her masterpiece, which, if I had never had anything to do with Signor Cavalli, I should never have known!" An old priest, who conceived the highest esteem for me as soon as I questioned him about the life of that fortunate friend of the mother of her Creator, showed me the very place where she had written, assuring me that the father, mother, and sister of the divine biographer had all been saints. He told me, and it was true, that Spain had solicited Rome for her canonization together with that of the Venerable Palafox.[24] It was perhaps this mystical city[25] which gave Father Malagrida[26] the desire to write the life of St. Anne, which the Holy Spirit also dictated to him; but the poor Jesuit had to suffer martyrdom for it—all the more reason for securing his canonization when the Society revives and recovers its ancient splendor.[27]

At the end of nine or ten days I had no more money. Lorenzo asked me where he should go for some, and I laconically answered: "Nowhere." What offended this ignorant, curious, and talkative man was my silence. The next morning he told me that the tribunal granted me fifty soldi[28] a day, which he was to disburse and of which he would render me an account each month, and that he would use what I had left over as I instructed him. I told him to bring me the *Gazette de Leyde*[29] twice a week and he answered that it was not allowed. Seventy-five lire a month were more than I needed, since I could no longer eat. The extreme heat and the inanition brought on by lack of food had enervated me. It was the season of the pestilential dog days; the power of the sun's rays striking on the lead plates which covered the roof of my prison kept me as it were in a sweating room; the perspiration which oozed from my epidermis streamed onto the floor to left and right of my armchair, in which I sat stark naked.

Not having once gone to stool during the two weeks I had been there, I went and I thought I should die from pains of which I had no conception. They came from internal hemorrhoids. It was there that I acquired that tormenting malady, from which I have never recovered; this keepsake, which now and again reminds me of its source, does nothing to make me cherish it. If natural philosophy does not teach us remedies to cure a number of diseases, it at least provides us with infallible means of acquiring them. However, my malady gained me compliments in Russia; it is so greatly esteemed that I did not dare to complain of it when I was there ten years later. The same thing happened to me in Constantinople, when I had a cold in the head and complained of it in the presence of a Turk; he said nothing, but he thought to himself that such a dog as I was unworthy of it.

On the same day violent chills showed me that I was attacked by fever. I stayed in bed and the next morning I said nothing about it; but on the day after, when Lorenzo found all my food still untouched, he asked me how I was.

"Perfectly well."

"No, Signore, for you do not eat. You are ill, and you will see the magnanimity of the tribunal, which will supply you with a physician, medicines, medicaments, and a surgeon, all for nothing."

Three hours later I saw him without any of his henchmen, carrying a candle, and preceding a grave personage whose imposing physiognomy informed me that he was a physician.[30] I was at the height of the fever which had been burning my blood for three days. He questioned me, and I answered that to my confessor and my physician I never spoke except without a witness. He told Lorenzo to leave. Lorenzo refused, and the learned doctor left, saying that I was in danger of death. It was what I wanted. I also felt some satisfaction in doing something which would show the pitiless tyrants who had confined me there the inhumanity of their proceedings.

Four hours later I heard the noise of bolts. The physician came in, holding a branched candlestick, and Lorenzo remained outside. I was in an extreme languor, which I found truly restful. A person who is really ill is free from the torment of boredom. I was delighted to see the villain left outside, for I could not bear him since he had explained the iron collar to me.

In a short quarter of an hour I told the learned doctor everything.

"If you want to recover your health," he said, "you must banish grief."

"Write me a prescription for that and take it to the only apothecary who can fill it. Signor Cavalli is the bad physician who gave me the *Heart of Jesus* and the *Mystical City*."

"Those two drugs may well have given you your fever and hemorrhoids; I will not abandon you."

He left after himself making me a large quantity of lemonade, which he asked me to drink frequently. I spent the night in exhaustion, dreaming of mystical extravagances.

The next morning, two hours later than usual, I saw him with Lorenzo and a surgeon who bled me. He left me a medicine which he told me to take in the evening and a bottle of broth.

"I have obtained permission," he said, "to have you moved to the garret, where it is not as hot as it is here, where the atmosphere is stifling."

"I decline the favor, for I loathe the rats, of whose existence you are not aware, and which will certainly get into my bed."

"How distressing! I told Signor Cavalli that he came very near to killing you with his books, and he said to return them to him and he would give you Boethius[31] instead. Here it is."

"He is an author who is superior to Seneca, and I thank you."

"I leave you a syringe and barley water; keep yourself amused with enemas."

He made me four visits and he pulled me through; my appetite came back. By the beginning of September I was in good health. My only real afflictions were the extreme heat, the fleas, and the boredom, for I could not always read Boethius. Lorenzo told me that I had permission to leave my cell to bathe while I was waiting for my bed to be made and the place to be swept, the only way to reduce the number of the fleas which were eating me alive. It was a respite. I took advantage of the eight or ten minutes to walk energetically; the terrified rats did not dare to show themselves. The same day on which Lorenzo allowed me this relief, he gave me an accounting of my money. He was left owing me twenty-five or thirty lire, which I was not allowed to put in my purse. I let him keep them, telling him to have masses said for me. He thanked me as fulsomely as if he himself were the priest who was to celebrate them. I did the same every month, and I never saw any receipts from a priest; it is certain that the least injustice Lorenzo could do me was to appropriate my money and say my masses himself in some tavern.

I went on in this way, persuading myself every day that I should be sent home; I never went to bed without a sort of certainty that the next day someone would come to tell me that I was free; but when, always frustrated in my hope, I began thinking that a fixed term of imprisonment might have been meted out to me, I decided that it could not end later than October 1st, the day on which the reign of the new Inquisitors[32] began. I accordingly concluded that my imprisonment would continue as long as the present Inquisitors remained in office, and that was why I had never seen the Secretary, who, if the matter had not been decided, would come to examine me, convict me of my crimes, and pronounce my sentence:[33] I thought it could not fail to be so because it was only natural—a poor argument under the Leads, where nothing is done according to nature. I imagined that the Inquisitors must have recognized their injustice in my innocence and hence were keeping me there only as a matter of form and for the sake of their reputation, but that they would certainly have to set me free when their reign ended. I even felt that I could forgive them and forget the wrong they had done me. "How," I said to myself, "could they leave me here at the disposition of their successors, to whom they could have given no sufficient grounds for condemning me?" I thought it impossible that they could condemn me and write my sentence without communicating it to me and telling me the reason for it. That the right was on my side seemed to me incontestable, and I argued accordingly; but my argument had no currency in respect to the rules of a tribunal which differs from the legal tribunals of every government on earth. When this tribunal proceeds against a delinquent, it is already sure that he is such; so what need has it to talk with him? And when it has condemned him, what need is there to give him the bad news of his sentence? His consent is not necessary; it is better, they say, to let him hope; if he is told, that will not shorten his stay in prison by one hour; the wise man tells his business to no one; and the only business of the Venetian tribunal is to judge and to sentence; the guilty person is a machine which does not need to take any part in the business in order to co-operate in it; he is a nail which, to go into a plank, needs only to be hammered.

I knew something about these practices of the colossus under whose feet I lay; but there are things on earth which no one can ever say he knows well until he has experienced them. If among my readers there is one to whom these rules appear unjust, I forgive him because, to tell the truth, they certainly appear to be so; but he should know that, once established, they become necessary, for a tribunal of this sort could not continue to exist except by virtue of them. They who keep them in force are Senators chosen from among those who are best qualified and are known as the most virtuous.[34]

On September 30th I spent the night unable to sleep; I was impatient to see the new day appear, for I felt sure that I should be set free. The pitiless men who had put me there had ended their reign. But day appeared, Lorenzo came with my food, and announced nothing new. I spent five or six days in rage and despair. I believed it was possible that, for reasons which I could not guess, it had been decided to keep me there the rest of my life. This terrible idea made me laugh, for I knew that I had the power to remain there only a very short time, once I had made up my mind to gain freedom at the risk of my life. Either they would kill me or I would succeed in it.

Deliberata morte ferocior ("Become more implacable by resolving to die"),[35] at the beginning of November I formed the plan of escaping by force from a place where I was being kept by force; it became my only thought. I began looking for, inventing, studying a hundred ways to succeed in an enterprise which many might have attempted before me but in which no one had succeeded.

During these same days a strange event showed me the pitiable state of mind to which I was reduced. I was standing in the garret looking up at the dormer; I also saw the very thick beam. Lorenzo was coming out of my cell with two of his men when I saw the enormous beam not quiver but turn toward its right side and then at once resume its original position by a slow, uninterrupted movement in the opposite direction; feeling at the same time that I had lost my balance, I was convinced that it was an earthquake shock, and the astonished constables said the same; delighted by the phenomenon, I did not say a word. Four or five seconds later the movement occurred again, and I could not keep from uttering these words: *"Un altra, un altra, gran Dio, ma più forte"* ("Another, another, great God, but stronger"). The constables, terrified by what they considered the impiousness of a desperate and blaspheming madman, fled in horror. Examining myself afterward, I saw that I had counted it among possible events that the Doge's Palace could collapse and at the same time I could regain my freedom: the falling palace was to deposit me safe, sound, and free on the beautiful pavement of the Piazza San Marco. It was thus that I began to go mad. The shock came from the same earthquake which flattened Lisbon about the same time.[36]

CHAPTER XIII

*Various occurrences. Companions. I prepare
my escape. Change of cell.*

To prepare my reader to understand my escape from such a place I must describe the premises to him. These prison cells, intended to hold state criminals, are actually in what is known as the garret of the Doge's Palace. The fact that its roof is covered not with tiles or bricks but with lead plates three feet square and a line[1] thick gives the name of the Leads to the prisons themselves. The only entrance to them is through the palace doors or through the prison building, by which I was brought in, crossing the Bridge of Sighs which I have already mentioned. One can go up to the prisons only by passing through the room in which the State Inquisitors meet; their secretary alone has the key to it, which the warden of the Leads has to return to him as soon as he has finished attending to the prisoners early in the morning. This is done at daybreak, because later the constables coming and going would be too much seen in a place filled with all the people who have business with the heads of the Council of Ten, who meet every day in the adjoining room known as the Bussola,[2] through which the constables must necessarily pass.

The prison cells are under the roof, and on opposite sides of the palace. Three are to the west, one of which was mine, and four are to the east. The gutter along the roof over those to the west gives onto the palace courtyard; the gutter to the east is perpendicularly above the canal called the Rio del Palazzo. On that side the cells are very light and one can stand upright in them, advantages lacking to the prison in which I was and which was called *il trave.*[*] The floor of my cell was directly above the ceiling of the Inquisitors' room, in which they usually assemble only at night after the daily session of the Council of Ten, of which all three of them are members.

Knowing all this as I did and having a perfect conception of the topography of the premises, the only way I could think of to escape which had any chance of succeeding was to make a hole in the floor

---

[*]The word means beam. It was the enormous beam which deprived my cell of light. (C.'s note.)

of my prison; but I should need to have instruments, a difficult matter in a place where all outside communication was forbidden and neither visits nor corresponding with anyone were allowed. Having no money to bribe a constable, I could not count on any of them. Supposing that the jailer and the two underlings who accompanied him were obliging enough to let me strangle them, for I had no arms, another constable was stationed at the door of the locked gallery, which he opened only when one of his fellows who wanted to go out gave him the password. The one thought in my mind was to escape, and not finding the way in Boethius I stopped reading him. I thought of it constantly because I was certain that I should find it only by thinking of it. I have always believed that when a man takes it into his head to accomplish some project and pursues it to the exclusion of anything else, he must succeed in it despite all difficulties; such a man will become the Grand Vizier, he will become Pope, he will overthrow a monarchy, provided that he begins early; for the man who has reached the age which Fortune disdains no longer succeeds in any undertaking, and without her help one can hope for nothing. The thing is to count on her and at the same time to defy her reverses. But this is one of the most difficult of political calculations.

In the middle of November Lorenzo told me that Messer Grande had taken a prisoner and that Secretary Businello,[3] the new Circospetto, had ordered him to put him in the worst of all the cells, so he was going to put him with me; he assured me that when he had explained to him that I had regarded having been put by myself as a favor he had answered that I must have become wiser in the four months I had been there. The news did not trouble me nor was I displeased to learn of the change of Secretary. This Signor Pietro Businello was a worthy man whom I had known in Paris when he was there on his way to London as Resident for the Republic.

An hour after the Terza bell I heard the screech of the bolts and I saw Lorenzo followed by two constables holding a handcuffed young man who was weeping. They locked him into my "home" and went off without even a word. I was on my bed, where he could not see me. His surprise amused me. Having the luck to be five feet tall, he stood upright, looking closely at my armchair, which he thought was for his own use. He sees the Boethius on the sill of the grating. He dries his tears, opens it, and disdainfully throws it down, perhaps disgusted by seeing it was in Latin. He goes to the left side of the cell and is amazed to find clothes; he approaches the alcove; he thinks he sees a bed; he puts out his hand, he touches me, and he begs my pardon; I tell him to sit down; and our acquaintance is made.

"Who are you?" I ask him.

"I am from Vicenza, my name is Maggiorin,[4] my father is coachman to the Poggiana[5] family, he kept me in school until I was eleven, where I learned to read and write, then I went to work in a wigmaker's shop, where I learned to dress hair very well. I became valet to Count XX. Two years later his only daughter came home from the convent and, dressing her hair, I fell in love with her as she did with me. After exchanging promises of marriage we surrendered to nature, and the Countess, who is eighteen as I am, became pregnant. A very devout maid discovered our relationship and the Countess's pregnancy and told her that her conscience obliged her to reveal all to her father; but my wife was able to make her keep quiet by assuring her that within a week she would have her confessor tell him the whole story. But instead of going to confession she warned me and we resolved to leave. She took a good sum of money and some diamonds which had belonged to her late mother, and we were to set off that night for Milan; but after dinner the Count sent for me, and, handing me a letter, ordered me to leave at once to deliver it directly to the person here in Venice to whom it was addressed. He spoke so kindly and calmly that I could never have suspected what happened to me. I went to fetch my cloak and in passing I said good-by to my wife, assuring her that there was nothing to fear and that she would see me back the next day. She fainted. As soon as I arrived here I took the letter to the person, who made me wait while he wrote the answer, after receiving which I went to a tavern to eat a bite and set off at once for Vicenza. But as I left the tavern the constables seized me and took me to the guardroom; I was there until the time they brought me here. I believe, Signore, that I can consider the young Countess my wife."

"You are mistaken."

"But nature—"

"Listening to nature leads a man from one folly to another until he is imprisoned under the Leads."

"Then I am under the Leads?"

"Even as I am."

He began to weep hot tears. He was a very good-looking young man, sincere, honest, and terribly in love, and I forgave the Countess, at the same time condemning the impudence of the Count, who could have had her hair dressed by a woman. In his tears and lamentations he talked of nothing but his poor Countess; he inspired me with the greatest pity. He thought someone would come back to bring him a bed and food, but I undeceived him, and I was right. I gave him some food, but he could swallow nothing. He spent the whole day complaining of his fate but only because he could not comfort his mistress and could not imagine what would become of her. She was already more than justified in my eyes, and I was sure that if the Inquisitors had been invisibly present in my cell, hearing everything the poor youth said to me, they would not only have sent him back but have married him to his mistress despite law or custom; and they might have locked up the Count her father, who had put the straw near the fire. I gave him my pallet, for though he was clean I could not but fear the dreams of a young man in love. He understood neither the magnitude of his crime nor the Count's need to have him punished in secret to save the family honor.

The next day he was brought a pallet and such a dinner as is to be had for fifteen soldi, which the tribunal allowed him "out of charity." I told the jailer that my dinner was enough for us both and that he could use what the tribunal allowed the young man to have three masses a week said for him. He gladly undertook the commission, congratulated him on being with me, and said we could walk in the garret for half an hour. I found the walking very good for my health and for my plan of escaping, which did not come to maturity until eleven months later. At the end of the rat-infested garret I saw a quantity of old household furniture lying on the floor to left and right of two chests and in front of a great pile of notebooks. I took ten or twelve of them to read for diversion. They were all criminal cases, which I found most entertaining reading, for I was free to read what in its time must have been highly secret. I saw strange answers to suggestive interrogations regarding seductions of virgins, attentions carried too far by men employed in girls' orphanages, facts about confessors who had abused their female penitents, schoolmasters convicted of pederasty, and guardians who had cheated their wards; some of them dated back two or three centuries, the style and the customs of which gave me a few hours of pleasure. Among the household implements lying about I saw a warming pan, a kitchen boiler, a fire shovel, tongs, old candelabra, earthenware pots, and a pewter syringe. I thought that some illustrious prisoner had been granted the privilege of using these implements. I also saw a sort of perfectly straight bolt as thick as my thumb and a foot and a half long. I did not touch them. The time had not yet come to look for a use for anything.

One fine day toward the end of the month my companion was taken away. Lorenzo told me he had been sentenced to the prisons known as "the Four."[6] They are within the precincts of the prison building.[7] They belong to the State Inquisitors. The prisoners who are there enjoy the privilege of calling the jailers whenever they need to; the cells are dark; but their inhabitants are provided with an oil lamp; everything is made of marble, and there is no fear of fire. I learned long afterward that poor Maggiorin remained there for five years and was afterward sent to Cerigo[8] for ten. I do not know if he died there. He was good company for me, and I realized it when, left alone again, I relapsed into melancholy. However, the privilege of walking in the garret for half an hour every day was still allowed me. I examined everything in it. One of the big chests was filled with fine paper, pieces of cardboard, untrimmed goose quills, and balls of string; the other was nailed shut. A piece of black polished marble an inch thick, six inches long, and three wide caught my eye; I took it with no particular purpose and put it under my shirts in my cell.

A week after Maggiorin left, Lorenzo told me I was likely to have a new companion. The fellow, who was by nature nothing but a gossip, began to be annoyed because I never asked him a question. His duty was not to gossip, and, having no chance to display his discretion to me, he imagined that I never interrogated him because I supposed he knew nothing; his self-esteem was hurt, and to show me that I was wrong he began to chatter without being questioned.

He told me he believed I should often have new visitors, for the six other cells each held two people who were not of a sort to be sent to "the Four." After a long time, seeing that I did not ask him what the distinction was, he said that in "the Four" there was a hodgepodge of all sorts of people whose sentences, though they did not know them, were recorded in writing; he added that those who, like myself, were in his charge "under the Leads" were all people of the greatest distinction and guilty of crimes which inquisitive persons could not guess.

"If you knew, Signore, what sort of people they are who share your fate! You would be astonished, for it's true they tell me you are intelligent; but, begging your pardon—You know there's no use your being intelligent only to be entertained here . . . You understand me . . . fifty soldi a day is something . . . they give a citizen three lire,[9] a gentleman four, and a foreign Count eight—I ought to know, for it all goes through my hands."

At this point he pronounced his own eulogy, made up entirely of negative qualities:

"I am neither a thief nor a traitor nor a miser nor cantankerous nor cruel like all my predecessors, and when I've drunk an extra pint I grow kinder; if my father had sent me to school I'd have learned to read and write and perhaps I'd be Messer Grande; but it's not my fault. Signor Andrea Diedo[10] thinks highly of me, and my wife, who's only twenty-four and who prepares your food every day, goes to speak with him whenever she likes and he has her shown right in even when he's in bed, a favor he doesn't do to any Senator. I promise you you'll have all the new arrivals with you, though not for long, for as soon as the Secretary has learned from their own lips what he needs to know he sends them on to their destination, either to "the Four" or to some fort or to the Levant or, if they're foreigners, to the frontiers of the State, for the government doesn't consider itself free to deal with the subjects of other princes unless they're in its service. The clemency of the tribunal, Signore, has no equal; and there's not another in the world which makes life so easy for its prisoners; people say it is cruel because it won't let them write or have visitors, but that's nonsense, because writing and seeing people is a waste of time; you'll tell me you have nothing to do, but we who work here can't say as much."

Such, or very nearly such, was the first harangue with which the scoundrel honored me and which, to tell the truth, I found amusing. I saw that if the man had been a little less stupid he would have been more malicious. I decided to profit by his stupidity.

The next morning they brought my new cell-mate, who was treated the first day as Maggiorin had been. I learned that I needed a second ivory spoon, for the first day the newcomer was left with nothing to eat; it was up to me to treat him.

The man, to whom I showed myself at once, made me a deep bow. My beard, which was already four inches long, was even more imposing than my figure. Lorenzo often lent me his scissors to cut my toenails; but I was forbidden to cut my beard under threat of severe penalties. One gets used to everything.

My new companion was a man of fifty, of the same height as myself, slightly stooped, gaunt, with a big mouth and long dirty teeth; he had small hazel eyes and long red lashes, a round black wig which stank with oil, and a coat of coarse gray cloth. Despite accepting my dinner he was deliberately distant; he did not say a word to me all day and I did likewise; but he changed his tactics the next day. Early in the

497

morning he was brought a bed which belonged to him and some linen in a bag. But for me, Maggiorin could not have changed his shirt. The jailer asked him what he wanted for dinner and for money to buy it with.

"I have no money."

"A rich man like you has no money?"

"I haven't a soldo."

"Very well. I will go at once and bring you a pound and a half of ration biscuits[11] and a jug of excellent water. Those are the regulations."

He brought them before he went away, leaving me with the scarecrow.

I hear him sigh, I feel sorry for him, and I break the silence.

"Do not sigh, Signore, you shall dine with me; but it seems to me you made a great mistake in coming here without money."

"I have some; but it's not the thing to tell these harpies."

"Most sagacious—if it didn't condemn you to bread and water! May I ask you if you know the reason for your being in prison?"

"Yes, Signore, I know it; and to show you how pitiful it is I will tell you my story in a few words.

"My name is Sgualdo Nobili.[12] I am the son of a peasant, who had me taught to write and who at his death left me his little house and the patch of ground belonging to it. My birthplace is in Friuli, a day's journey from Udine. A swift stream called the Corno, which too often damaged my little property, determined me to sell it ten years ago and settle in Venice. I was paid eight thousand lire for it in fine gold zecchini. I had been told that in the capital of this glorious Republic everyone enjoyed an honorable freedom and that an industrious man with a capital such as mine could live there very comfortably by lending against pledges. Sure of my thrift, my judgment, and my knowledge of the world, I determined to practice that trade. I rented a small house in the Cannaregio quarter, I furnished it, and, living by myself, I spent two untroubled years which made me richer by ten thousand lire, for, wanting to live well, I spent a thousand on my household expenses. I was sure that I should soon be ten times as rich. About that time I lent a Jew two zecchini on a number of handsomely bound books, among which I found Charron's *Wisdom*.[13] I have never been fond of reading, I had never read anything but Christian doctrine; but Charron's *Wisdom* showed me how fortunate one is who can read. This book, Signore, which perhaps you do not know, is excellent. When one has read it one finds that one does not have to read any others; for it contains everything that a human being needs to know; it rids him of all the prejudices with which he was infected in childhood; it delivers him from the terrors of a future life; it opens his eyes, it shows him the road to happiness, it makes him wise. Find a way to read it and disregard the fools who will tell you that it is forbidden."

From this discourse I knew my man, for I knew Charron, though I was not aware that he had been translated. But what books are not translated in Venice? Charron, a great admirer of Montaigne,[14] thought that he was outdoing his model, but he did not. He gave a methodical form to a number of things which Montaigne puts down without order and which, dropped here and there by that great man, did not seem liable to censure; but Charron, a priest and a theologian, was justly condemned. He has not been much read. The stupid Italian who translated him did not even know that the translation of the word *sagesse* is *sapienza*. Charron had the impertinence to give his book the title of Solomon's. My cell-mate continued:

"Freed by Charron from my scruples and all my old false impressions, I worked at my business to such effect that in six years I had nine thousand zecchini. You must not be surprised, for in this rich city gambling, debauchery, and idleness have everyone disorganized and needing money, and the wise profit by what the fools throw away.

"Three years ago a certain Count Seriman[15] made my acquaintance and, seeing what my thrift had made me, asked me to take five hundred zecchini from him, invest them in my business, and give him half the profits. He only asked a receipt, in which I undertook to return the amount to him on demand. At the end of the year I gave him seventy-five zecchini, which amounted to fifteen per cent, and he gave me a receipt, but he showed his dissatisfaction. He was wrong, for, having money enough, I did not use his in my transactions. The second year I did the same, out of pure generosity; but we went on to quarrel, so that he demanded the return of his money. I answered that I would deduct the hundred and fifty zecchini he had received; but that made him furious and he immediately served me with an extrajudiciary[16] demanding the return of the entire amount. A clever lawyer undertook my defense and gained me two years; three months ago I was offered a compromise, and I refused; but fearing violence I turned to the Abate Giustiniani, confidential agent of the Marchese di Montealegre,[17] the Spanish

Ambassador, who rented me a small house on the Lista,[18] where one is safe from surprises. I was perfectly willing to give Count Seriman back his money, but I claimed the right to deduct the hundred zecchini I had paid in legal costs for the suit he had brought against me. My lawyer came to see me a week ago with the Count's, and I showed them the two hundred and fifty zecchini in a purse, which I was prepared to give them and not a soldo more. They left, both dissatisfied. Three days ago the Abate Giustiniani sent me word that the Ambassador had seen fit to permit the State Inquisitors to send their men to my house to serve a warrant. I did not know that it could be done. I awaited their visit courageously, after putting all my money in a safe place. I would never have believed that the Ambassador would have let them arrest me as they did. At daybreak Messer Grande came to my house, demanded three hundred and fifty zecchini, and, upon my answering that I did not have a soldo, he carried me off; and here I am."

After this narrative I made my own reflections on the infamous scoundrel who had been put in my company and on the honor he had done me to think that I was a scoundrel like himself, for otherwise he would not have told me the whole story, supposing that I was one to applaud it. In all the stupid remarks he made to me for three days on end, always quoting Charron, I saw the truth of the proverb, *Guardati da colui che non ha letto che un libro solo* ("Beware of the man who has read only one book"). Charron had made him an atheist, and he openly boasted of it. An hour after the Terza on the fourth day Lorenzo came and told him to accompany him downstairs to talk with the Secretary. He dressed quickly, and instead of his own shoes he put on mine without my noticing it. He went down with Lorenzo; a half hour later he came upstairs again crying and took from his shoes two purses in which he had three hundred and fifty zecchini and which, preceded by Lorenzo, he carried to the Secretary. He came up again afterward, took his cloak, and left; Lorenzo told me later that he had been released. The next morning his clothes were sent for. I have always believed that the Secretary made him confess that he had the money by threatening him with torture—which, as a threat, may still be good for something.

On the first day of the year 1756 I received my New Year's gifts. Lorenzo brought me a dressing gown lined with fox fur, a silk coverlet stuffed with cotton, and a bearskin bag to put my legs into during the cold weather, which was as extreme as the heat I had endured in August. As he gave them to me he said that, by order of the Secretary, I could have the use of six zecchini a month to buy all the books I wanted and the *Gazette* as well, and that it was a present from Signor Bragadin. I asked Lorenzo for a pencil and wrote on a scrap of paper: *"I am grateful to the mercy of the tribunal and the virtue of Signor Bragadin."*

One must have been in my situation to understand the sentiments which this bounty aroused in my soul; in the intensity of my gratitude I forgave my oppressors and I almost abandoned my plan of escaping; so pliable is man when misfortune degrades him. Lorenzo told me that Signor Bragadin had come before the three Inquisitors and had gone down on his knees and wept as he begged them for the favor of allowing me to receive this proof of his constant affection if I was still among the living; and that they had been so touched that they could not refuse him. I immediately wrote down the titles of all the books I wanted.

One fine morning as I was walking in the garret my eyes lingered over the long bolt which was there on the floor and I considered its possibilities as a weapon of attack and defense; I picked it up and took it into my cell, putting it under my coat with the piece of black marble; as soon as I was alone I found that the latter made a perfect whetstone, for, after rubbing the end of the bolt against the marble for a long time I saw that it showed a flat edge.

Interested in this strange kind of work, in which I was a novice, and to which I was inspired by the hope of possessing a tool which must be strictly forbidden up there, and further urged on by pride in managing to produce a weapon without the necessary instruments to make it with, even exasperated by the very difficulties— for I had to rub the bolt almost in darkness, working on the sill, only able to keep the stone from slipping with my left hand, and having no oil with which to wet and soften the iron on which I wanted to put a point—I used nothing but my saliva and I toiled for two weeks filing down eight triangular facets which at their apexes formed a perfect point; the facets were an inch and a half long. The result was an octagonal stiletto as well proportioned as one could have expected from a good cutler. It is impossible to imagine the pain and boredom I suffered and the patience I needed to accomplish this distasteful piece of work with not a tool except a loose piece of stone; for me it was torture of a kind *quam siculi non invenere tyranni* ("which even the Sicilian tyrants did not invent").[19] I could no longer move my right arm and my shoulder seemed to be out of joint. The palm of my hand had become one great sore after the vessels broke; despite my pain I did not stop my work; I was determined to see it perfected.

Proud of my production and not yet having decided how and for what I might use it, I thought about hiding it in some place where it would escape even a search; I hit upon the idea of putting it in the stuffing of my armchair, not on top, however, where, by taking up the cushion, anyone could see the unevenness it would cause in the surface, but by turning the chair upside down; I then pushed the bolt into it all the way, so that for anyone to find it he would have to know it was there. Thus did God provide me with what I needed for an escape which was to be a wonder if not a miracle. I admit that I am proud of it; but my pride does not come from my having succeeded, for luck had a good deal to do with that; it comes from my having concluded that the thing could be done and having had the courage to undertake it.

After three or four days spent in reflecting on the use to which I should put the bolt which I had transformed into a pike as thick as a walking stick and twenty inches[20] long, whose excellent sharp point showed me that it was not necessary to turn iron into steel in order to give it one, I saw that I had only to make a hole in the floor under my bed.

I was sure that the room below could only be the one in which I had seen Signor Cavalli; I was sure that it was opened every morning; and I was sure that I could easily let myself down, once the hole was made, by using my bedclothes, of which I would make a sort of rope and fasten the upper end of it to a trestle of my bed. Once in the room I would remain concealed under the tribunal's great table, and in the morning, as soon as I saw the door opened, I would go out by it and be in a place of safety before I could be pursued. I thought it probable that Lorenzo left one of his constables in the room as a guard, and if that were the case I would have killed the man at once by plunging my pike into his throat. Everything was well thought out; but since the floor might be double or even triple the work could have taken me one or two months; I thought it would be very difficult to keep the constables from sweeping my cell for so long. If I had forbidden them to do it I should have made them suspicious, and the more so since, to rid myself of the fleas, I had insisted that they sweep every day, so that the broom itself would have revealed the hole to them; I had to be absolutely certain that this misfortune would not befall me.

In the meanwhile I forbade them to sweep, at the same time not saying why I forbade it. A week or ten days later Lorenzo asked me why; I said that it was because the dust rising from the floor went into my lungs and might bring on tubercles.

"We will sprinkle water on the floor," he said.

"Certainly not, for the dampness can cause a plethora."

But a week later he ordered his men to sweep; he had them carry the bed out of my cell and, on the excuse of getting the place thoroughly cleaned, he lit a candle. I saw that it was suspicion which prompted this performance; but I showed indifference. I then hit on the way to advance my plan. The next morning I bloodied my handkerchief by pricking my finger and I waited for Lorenzo in bed.

"I had such a fit of coughing," I said, "that a vein in my chest broke and made me throw up all the blood you see; have the physician sent to me."

The learned physician came, he ordered me bled and wrote me a prescription. I told him that Lorenzo had brought on my trouble by insisting on sweeping. He reproached him and said that a young wigmaker[21] had just died of consumption from the same cause, for, according to him, dust once inhaled was never exhaled. Lorenzo swore he thought he was rendering me a service and that he would never have any sweeping done again as long as he lived. I laughed to myself, because the physician could not have spoken to better purpose if he had been my confederate. The constables who heard his doctrine were delighted to learn it and counted it among their acts of charity that henceforth they only swept the cells of those who were surly to them.

After the physician left, Lorenzo asked me to forgive him and assured me that all his other prisoners were in good health despite his having their rooms swept every day. He called them "rooms."

"But it is an important matter," he said, "and I will explain it to them, for I regard you all as my children."

I really needed the bleeding; it ended my sleeplessness and cured me of the spasmodic contractions which terrified me.

I had gained a great point; but the time to begin working had not yet come. The cold was intense and my hands could not hold the pike without freezing. My undertaking demanded a man foresighted enough to avoid anything which could easily be foreseen and a spirit bold and intrepid enough to resign itself to chance in case anything foreseen did not occur. The man who must act thus is most unfortunate; but a sound political calculation teaches that for the sake of all it is expedient[22] to risk all.

The overlong nights of winter distressed me. I had to spend nineteen mortal hours in absolute darkness; and on foggy days, which are not uncommon in Venice, the light which came in through the window and the hole in the door was not enough for me to read my book by. Since I could not read I went back to thinking of my escape, and a mind always fixed on one idea can go mad. Having an oil lamp would have made me happy; I thought about it, and I rejoiced when I believed I had found a way to obtain one by a ruse. To make the lamp I had to have the ingredients which would compose it. I needed a vessel, linen or cotton wicks, oil, a flint and steel, matches, and punk. The vessel could be a small earthenware pot, and I had the one in which my eggs were cooked in butter. I managed to get Lucca oil bought for me on the excuse that salad dressed with ordinary oil made me ill. From my quilt I pulled out enough cotton to make some wicks. I pretended to be tormented by a bad toothache, and I told Lorenzo I needed some pumice stone; he did not know what it was, and I substituted a gun flint, saying that it would produce the same effect if it was soaked in strong vinegar for a day and then applied to my tooth, when it would relieve the pain. Lorenzo said that my vinegar was of the best and that I could put a flint in it myself, and he threw me three or four. A buckle on the belt of my breeches would serve me as a steel; all I still needed was sulphur and tinder, but I had no idea how to go about getting them. But here is the way I found by dint of thinking about it, and the way Fortune took a hand in it.

I had a sort of measles which, after drying up, had left scabs on my arm that made me itch uncomfortably; and I told Lorenzo to ask the physician for a remedy. The next morning he brought me a note, which the Secretary had read, in which the physician had written: "One day of dieting and four ounces of oil of sweet almonds, and the skin will be cured; or application of an ointment of flowers of sulphur; but this topical remedy is dangerous."

"I don't care about the danger," I said to Lorenzo; "buy some of the ointment and bring it to me tomorrow; or give me some sulphur, I have butter and I will make the ointment myself; have you any matches? Give me some."

He took out all the matches he had in his pocket and gave them to me. How easily one is comforted when one is in distress!

I spent two or three hours considering what I could substitute for the punk, the only ingredient I did not have and which I could not imagine an excuse for obtaining, when I suddenly remembered that I had ordered my tailor to line my taffeta coat with punk under the arms and cover it with oilcloth, to prevent the stain from sweat which, chiefly in summer, spoils all coats at that particular place. My coat was there before me, it was brand-new, and my heart pounded; my tailor might have forgotten my order, and I was between hope and dread. I had to take only two steps to make sure, and I did not dare. I was afraid I should not find the punk and would have to give up so dear a hope. I finally make up my mind, I approach the board on which I had put my coat, and, suddenly feeling that I am unworthy of such a grace, I go down on my knees praying God that the tailor had not forgotten my order. After this fervent prayer I unfold my coat, I unsew the oilcloth, and I find the punk. My joy was great. It was natural that I should thank God, since I had looked for the punk confiding in his goodness; and I did so with an over-flowing heart.

Examining my act of thanksgiving, I did not consider that I had been a fool, as I did when I reflected on the prayer I had offered to the master of all when I went to look for the punk. I would not have done it before I was put under the Leads, nor would I do it today; but being deprived of physical freedom stupefies the facul-ties of the soul. One should pray to God to grant graces, not to reverse the course of nature by miracles. If the tailor had not put the punk under the arms of my coat, I ought to have been sure that I should not find it; and if he had, I ought to have been sure that I should find it. So why was I troubling the master of nature? The meaning of my first prayer could only be: "Lord, let me find the punk even if the tailor forgot it, and if he put it in do not make it disappear." Some theologian might find my prayer pious, holy, and perfectly reasonable, for he would say it was based on the power of faith; and he would be right, just as I, who am not a theologian, am right to consider it absurd. In any case I do not need to be a great theologian to consider my act of thanks-giving praiseworthy. I thanked God that the tailor's memory had not failed him, and my gratitude was justified by the principles of a sound philosophy.

No sooner was I in possession of the punk I needed than I put oil into a pot, then a wick, and I saw a lamp. What a satisfaction it was to owe the boon only to myself and to break a most cruel regulation!

For me, there were no more nights. Farewell salad! I was very fond of it, but I did not regret it; I thought that oil was created only to give us light. I decided to begin breaking the floor on the first Monday in Lent, for during the license of the Carnival I feared visitors from day to day; and I was right. On Quinquagesima Sunday at noon I heard the noise of the bolts, and I saw Lorenzo followed by a very fat man whom I at once recognized as the Jew Gabriel Schalon,[23] celebrated for his ability to raise money for young men by ruinous deals; we knew each other, so we exchanged the usual greetings the occasion demanded. The company of this man was not of a sort to please me, but I had to be patient; he was locked in. He told Lorenzo to go to his house to fetch his dinner, a bed, and everything he needed; and he answered that they would talk about it the next day.

This Jew, who was brainless, ignorant, talkative, and stupid except in his trade, began by congratulating me on my having been chosen above all others to share his company. My only answer was to offer him half of my dinner, which he refused, saying that he ate only food which was pure and that he had every expectation of eating his supper at home.

"When?"

"Tonight. You remember that when I asked him for my bed he said that we would talk about it tomorrow. That obviously means I do not need it. Can you suppose that they would leave a man like me without anything to eat?"

"That is how I was treated."

"No doubt; but there is some difference between you and me; and, strictly between ourselves, the State Inquisitors made a blunder when they had me arrested and they must now be wondering how to set their mistake right."

"They may give you a pension, for you are a man to be treated with consideration."

"Your conclusion is very sound; for there is not a broker on the Exchange more useful than myself to domestic trade, and the Five Savi[24] have profited greatly by the advice I have often given them. My imprisonment is a strange mistake, which may well be a lucky one for you."

"Lucky? How?"

"A month will not pass before I will have you out of here. I know to whom I must speak and what to say."

"Then I count on you."

The idiotic scoundrel thought he amounted to something. He insisted on telling me what people were saying about me; and since he only reported what the greatest fools in the city could find to say he bored me. I took up a book, and he had the impertinence to ask me not to read. His passion was talking, and always about himself.

I did not dare to light my lamp, and, when night drew on, he made up his mind to accept some bread and Cyprus wine and my pallet, which had become the bed for all new arrivals. The next morning he was brought food from his house and a bed. I had this stone around my neck for eight or nine weeks,[25] for before sentencing him to "the Four" the Secretary had to talk with him several times to bring to light his shady deals and to make him cancel some illegal contracts he had made. He confessed to me himself that he had bought certain revenues from Signor Domenico Micheli[26] which could not belong to the buyer until after the death of the Cavaliere Antonio, his father.

"It is true," he said, "that the seller lost a hundred per cent on the transaction, but it must be considered that the buyer would have lost everything if the son had died before the father."

When I saw that my unwelcome companion was not leaving, I resolved to light my lamp; he promised secrecy, but he kept quiet only as long as he remained with me; for, though there were no consequences, Lorenzo learned of it. In short the man was a burden to me and prevented me from working at my escape.

He also prevented me from the reading which kept me amused; demanding, ignorant, superstitious, blustering, timid, sometimes giving in to tears and despair, he tried to make me join in his noisy remonstrances by showing me that his imprisonment was ruining his reputation; I assured him that, so far as his reputation went, he had nothing to fear, and he took my gibe for a compliment. He refused to admit that he was avaricious, and to convince him that he was I demonstrated to him that if the State Inquisitors gave him a hundred zecchini a day and at the same time opened the gate of the prison for him, he would not leave in order not to lose the hundred zecchini. He had to agree, and he laughed over it.

He was a Talmudist, as all Jews are today; and he tried to make me believe that he was very much attached to his religion because of its wisdom. Being the son of a rabbi, he was learned in its ceremonies; but in my subsequent study of the human race I have seen that the majority of men believe that the most essential part of religion is discipline.

The Jew was excessively fat and, never leaving his bed and sleeping by day, he soon could not sleep at night, while he heard me sleeping quite well. Once he took it into his head to wake me when I was in my deepest sleep.

"In God's name," I said, "what do you want? Why did you wake me? If you die, I'll forgive you."

"Alas, my dear friend, I cannot sleep, have pity on me and let us talk a little."

"And you call me your dear friend? Hateful man! I believe that your insomnia is a real torture, and I am sorry for you; but if ever you dare again to relieve your misery by depriving me of the greatest good Nature allows me to enjoy in the misfortune which over-whelms me, I will get out of my bed and come and strangle you."

"Forgive me, I beg you, and be sure that I will never wake you in future."

It is possible that I would not have strangled him, but it is certain that he put the temptation in my way. A man in prison who is in the arms of sweet slumber is not in prison, and the sleeping slave does not feel the chains of slavery, just as kings do not reign in sleep. Hence the prisoner must regard the man thoughtless enough to wake him as an executioner come to deprive him of his freedom and plunge him back into wretchedness; add that the prisoner who sleeps usually dreams that he is free and that the illusion replaces the reality for him. I heartily congratulated myself on not having begun my work before the man arrived. He demanded that the place be swept, the constables whose task it was made me laugh when they told him that it brought me to death's door; he insisted. I pretended to be ill from it, and the constables would not have carried out his order if I had objected; but my interests demanded that I should be obliging.

On the Wednesday in Holy Week Lorenzo told us that after the Terza the Signor Circospetto would come up to pay us the custom-ary Easter visit, which serves both to bring peace to the souls of those who wish to receive the Holy Sacrament and for him to learn if they have any complaint concerning the jailer's performance of his duties.

"And so, Signori," he said, "if you wish to complain of me, complain; dress yourselves fully, for that is the rule."

I ordered Lorenzo to have a confessor sent to me the next day.

So I dressed up, and the Jew did likewise, at the same time taking his leave of me because he felt sure that the Circospetto would set him free as soon as he had talked with him; he said that his presentiment was of a kind which had never deceived him. I congratulated him. The Secretary arrived, the cell was opened, the Jew emerged and fell on his knees; I heard nothing but tears and cries, which continued for four or five minutes without a word from the Secretary. He came back, and Lorenzo told me to go out. With my eight-months beard and wearing a coat designed by love and intended for the heat of July on that very cold day, I was a figure fit to inspire laughter and not to arouse pity. The terrible cold made me shake like the edge of the shadow cast by the darkness which the setting sun brings on—which annoyed me only because the Secretary might think I was shaking with fear. Since I came out of the cell stooped over, my bow was already made; I drew myself up, I looked at him neither proudly nor cringingly, without speaking or moving; the Circospetto, equally motionless, remained silent too; the mute scene between us continued for two minutes. Seeing that I said nothing, he bent his head half an inch and left. I returned to my cell, undressed, and got into bed to revive my natural heat. The Jew was astonished that I had not spoken to the Secretary, whereas my silence had said much more than he had thought he was telling him with his cowardly cries. A prisoner of my sort in the presence of his judge should never open his mouth except to answer questions.

The next day a Jesuit came to confess me, and on Holy Saturday a priest from San Marco came to give me the Holy Eucharist. Since my confession appeared too laconic to the missionary priest who heard it he saw fit to remonstrate with me before he absolved me.

"Do you pray to God?" he asked.

"I pray to him from morning to night and from night to morning, even when I am eating and sleeping, for in the situation in which I am, everything that takes place in me, even my moments of agitation or impatience or folly, can only be prayer before the divine wisdom, which alone sees my heart."

The Jesuit heard my specious sermon on prayer with a slight smile and repaid it by a metaphysical discourse of a nature quite incompatible with mine. I would have refuted it completely if, wise in his profession, he had not had the skill to astonish me and reduce me to less than the size of a flea by a sort of prophecy which awed me.

"Since it was from us," he said, "that you learned the religion you profess, practice it as we practice it, and pray to God as we taught you to do, and know that you will never leave here except on the day dedicated to the saint who is your patron."

After speaking these words he gave me absolution and left. The impression they made on me was incredible; try as I would, I could not get them out of my head. I considered all the saints I found in the calendar.

The Jesuit was the spiritual director of Signor Flaminio Corner,[27] the old Senator, then a State Inquisitor. The Senator was a famous man of letters, a great politician, very devout, and the author of works all of which were pious, extraordinary, and written in Latin.[28] His reputation was spotless.

Informed that I was to leave the place on my patron saint's day by a man who might well know, I rejoiced to have learned that I had a patron saint and to understand that he was concerned for me; but since I had to pray to him, I had to know him. Who was he? The Jesuit himself could not have told me if he knew, for he would have betrayed the secret; but "Come," I said to myself, "let's see if I can guess." It could not be St. James of Compostela,[29] whose name I bore; for it was precisely on his feast day that my door had been broken down by Messer Grande. I took the calendar and, looking for the nearest saint's day, I came to St. George,[30] a saint of some renown, but of whom I had never thought. So I settled on St. Mark, whose day came on the twenty-fifth of the month, and to whose protection I, as a Venetian, could lay some claim; so I addressed my prayers to him, but in vain. His feast day went by, and I was still there. I took the other St. James,[31] the brother of Jesus Christ, who comes with St. Philip, but I was wrong again; so I settled on St. Anthony,[32] who, or so they say in Padua, performs thirteen miracles a day; but no less in vain. In this way I passed from one to another and insensibly became accustomed to hoping in vain for protection from the saints. I was convinced that the saint in whom I should trust was my pointed bolt. Nevertheless, the Jesuit's prophecy came true. I got out of there on All Saints' Day, as my reader will see, and it is certain that, if I had one, my protector must be honored on that day, for they are all included.

Two or three weeks after Easter I was delivered from the Jew; but the poor man was not sent home; he was sentenced to "the Four," where he remained for two years, and afterwards went and finished his days in Trieste.

As soon as I was alone I went to work with the greatest eagerness. I needed to hurry before the arrival of some new guest who would insist that the place be swept. I pulled out my bed, lighted my lamp, and flung myself on the floor pike in hand, after spreading out a napkin beside me to receive the bits of wood which I excavated with the point of the bolt; the thing was to break away the board by driving the iron into it; at the beginning of my labors the fragments were no bigger than a grain of wheat, but later they became good-sized pieces. The board was of larch and sixteen inches wide; I began to dig into it where it joined the next one; there was neither a nail nor an iron clamp, and my job was perfectly straightforward. After working six hours I tied my napkin up and set it aside so that I could go and empty it the next morning behind the pile of notebooks at the end of the garret. The fragments I had broken off were four or five times bigger in bulk than the hole from which I had taken them; its circumference was roughly thirty degrees of a circle, its diameter[33] about ten inches. I put my bed back in place, and in the morning when I emptied my napkin I had no reasons to fear that my fragments would be seen.

On the second day I found under the first board, which was two inches thick, a second board which I supposed was of the same size. Never having suffered the misfortune of visitors, and always tormented by fear of it, in three weeks I succeeded in breaking completely through three boards, under which I found the kind of flooring incrusted with small bits of marble which is known in Venice as *terrazzo marmorin*.[34] It is the usual flooring of rooms in all houses in Venice which do not belong to poor people. The great noblemen even prefer *terrazzo* to parquetry. I was appalled when I saw that my bolt was not biting into it; it was in vain that I bore down and pushed; my point slipped. It discouraged me completely. Then I remembered Hannibal, who, according to Livy,[35] had opened a passage through the Alps by chopping away the rock which he had softened through the action of vinegar—a thing I had considered incredible, not so much because of the power of the acid but because of the prodigious quantity of vinegar he must have had. I thought Hannibal had succeeded in it not *aceto* ("by vinegar") but *asceta*, which in the Latin of Padua might be the same as *ascia*[36] ("ax"), and that the error might stem from the copyists. Nevertheless I poured into my excavation a bottle of strong vinegar which I had; and the next morning, whether as the result of the vinegar or of greater patience, I saw that I should succeed, for it was not a matter of breaking the small pieces of marble but of pulverizing the cement between them with the point of my implement; and I was greatly relieved when I found that the great difficulty occurred only at the surface; in four days I destroyed the entire piece of paving without damaging the point of my pike. Its facets shone even more brightly.

Under the *marmorin* flooring I found another board, as I expected; it must be the last, that is, the first counting up in the roofing of any room whose beams support its ceiling. I began my work on this board with somewhat greater difficulty because my hole had become ten inches deep. I constantly commended myself to the mercy of God. Those freethinkers who say that prayer is of no use do not know what they are talking about. I know that after praying to God I always felt stronger; and that is enough to prove its usefulness, whether the increase in strength comes directly from God or is a physical result of one's confidence in him.

On June 25th, the day on which only the Republic of Venice celebrates the prodigy of the Evangelist St. Mark's appearing in the emblematic form of a winged lion in the ducal church toward the end of the eleventh century, an event which showed the Senate in its wisdom that it was time to dismiss St. Theodore,[37] whose credit was no longer powerful enough to aid it in its plans of aggrandizement, and to take for its patron the sainted disciple of St. Paul (or, according to Eusebius,[38] St. Peter) whom God now sent it—at three hours past noon on that day, when, stark naked, running with sweat, and lying flat on my stomach, I was working at the hole, in which, in order to see, I had set my lighted lamp, I was mortally terrified to hear the shrill grating of the bolt in the door to the first corridor. What a moment! I blow out my lamp, I leave my pike in the hole, throw my napkin into it, I rise, I hastily put the trestles and the boards of my bed in the alcove, I throw the pallet and the mattresses on top of it; and not having time to put on the sheets, I fall on it as if dead just as Lorenzo is opening my cell. One minute earlier, and he would have caught me in the act. Lorenzo would have stepped on me if a cry I gave had not made him crouch back into the doorway, saying emphatically:

"My God, I pity you, Signore, for it is as hot here as in an oven. Get up and thank God, who sends you excellent company. Come in, come in, Illustrissimo Signore," he said to the unfortunate who was following him. The churl pays no attention to my nakedness, and the Illustrissimo enters, making his way around me, while, not knowing what I was doing, I gather up my bedclothes, throw them that she will not permit that—for that, according to her elder sister, was worth twenty-five louis.[3] I tell her we will haggle about it some other time; and thereupon she gives me every indication of her future consent by consenting most freely to everything I could want.

The little Helen[4] whom I had enjoyed, though leaving her a virgin, gave her sister the six francs and told her what she hoped from me. She calls me aside before I leave and says that, since she needs money, she will come down a little. I answer that I will return and talk to her the next day. I wanted Patu to see the girl as I had seen her, to make him admit that it was impossible to see a more consummate beauty. Helen, white as a lily, had everything that nature and the art of the painter could combine in the way of perfect beauty. In addition she had a beauty of countenance which instilled the most delicious peace into the soul which beheld her. She was blonde. I went there that evening, and not having reached a suitable price, I gave her twelve francs in exchange for her sister's lending her her bed, and I finally came to an agreement to keep giving her twelve francs each time until I decided to pay the six hundred. The rate of interest was usurious, but La Morphy was a Greek[5] by nature, and she had no scruples in the matter. It is certain that I would never have brought myself to pay the twenty-five louis, for I should have thought that I was the loser by it. The elder Morphy thought me the greatest of dupes, since in two months I had spent three hundred francs for nothing. She attributed it to my stinginess. Stinginess indeed! I paid six louis to have her painted naked by a German painter,[6] who produced a living likeness. She was lying on her stomach, resting her arms and her bosom on a pillow and holding her head as if she were lying on her back. The skillful artist had drawn her legs and thighs in such a way that the eye could not wish to see more. I had him write under it *O-Morphi*.[7] The word is not Homeric, but it is Greek none the less. It means "beautiful."

But what are not the secret paths of all-powerful destiny! My friend Patu wanted a copy of the portrait. Can one refuse such a thing to a friend? The same painter made it, went to Versailles, and showed it, with several other portraits, to Monsieur de Saint-Quentin,[8] who showed them to the King, who became curious to know if the portrait of the "Greek Girl" was a true likeness. If it was, the monarch claimed the right to sentence the original to quench the fire which it had kindled in his heart.

Monsieur de Saint-Quentin asked the painter if he could bring the original of the "Greek Girl" to Versailles, and he answered that he thought it perfectly possible. He called on me to tell me of the proposal, and I thought it excellent. La Morphy jumped for joy when I told her that she was to go to court with her sister under conduct of the painter and there submit to the decrees of Providence. So one fine morning she cleaned up her little sister, dressed her decently, and went to Versailles with the painter, who told her to stroll in the park until he came back.

He came back with the Groom of the Bedchamber, who told him to go to the inn and wait for the two sisters, whom he took to a garden house and shut them in. I learned the next morning from La Morphy herself that a half hour later the King came, alone, asked her if she was Greek, drew the portrait from his pocket, looked carefully at her younger sister, and said:

"I have never seen a better likeness."

He sat down, took her on his knees, caressed her here and there, and, after his royal hand had assured him that she was a virgin, gave her a kiss. O-Morphi looked at him and laughed.

"What are you laughing at?"

"Because you are as like a six-franc piece[9] as two peas."

At this ingenuousness the monarch burst out laughing and asked her if she would like to stay at Versailles; she answered that he must arrange it with her sister, and her sister told the King that nothing could make her happier. The King then left, locking them in. A quarter of an hour later Saint-Quentin came and let them out, put the younger sister in an apartment on the ground floor in the custody of a woman, and went off with the elder sister to find the German, to whom he gave fifty louis for the portrait, but nothing to La Morphy. He only took her address, assuring her that she would hear from him. She received a thousand louis, which she showed me the next day. The honest German gave me twenty-five louis for my portrait and made me another, copying it from the one Patu had. He offered to paint for me, gratis, all the pretty girls whose portraits I might wish to have. What gave me the most pleasure was seeing the joy of the worthy Flemish girl, who, gazing at five hundred double louis,[10] thought she was rich, and who considered me the first cause of her good fortune.

"I didn't expect so much, for it's true that Helen is pretty but I didn't believe what she told me about you. Is it possible, my dear friend, that you left her a virgin? Tell me the truth."

"If she was, I can assure you that she did not cease to be by my doing."

"She certainly was, for you're the only one I gave her to. What a man of honor! She was destined for the King. Who would have thought it? God disposes. I admire your virtue. Come here and let me kiss you."

O-Morphi (for so the King always called her) pleased him even more by an ingenuousness of which the monarch had no notion than by her beauty, though it was as perfect as possible. He put her in an apartment in the Parc aux Cerfs,[11] where His Majesty kept nothing short of a seraglio and which no one was allowed to enter except ladies presented at court. At the end of a year[12] the girl bore a son, who became no one knows what, for Louis XV would never hear anything about his bastards as long as Queen Marie was alive.

O-Morphi fell into disgrace after three years. The King gave her four hundred thousand francs, which she brought as a dowry to a staff officer[13] in Brittany. I saw a son from this marriage at Fontainebleau in the year 1783. He was twenty-five years of age, and he did not know the story of his mother, whose living image he was. I asked him to give her my compliments and wrote my name on his tablets.[14]

The cause of the beauty's disgrace was the malice of Madame de Valentinois,[15] sister-in-law of the Prince of Monaco. During a visit to the Parc aux Cerfs, that lady, who is well known in Paris, told O-Morphi to make the King laugh by asking him how he treated his old wife.[16] O-Morphi, who was too simple-minded, asked the King the impertinent and insulting question, which so astonished the monarch that, rising and looking daggers at her,

"You miserable wretch," he said, "who got you to ask me that question?"

O-Morphi tremblingly told him the truth; the King turned his back on her and never saw her again. The Countess of Valentinois was not seen at court again until two years later. Louis XV, who knew that he failed his wife as a husband, wanted at least to make it up to her as King. Woe to anyone who dared fail in respect to her!

Despite all the wit of the French, Paris is and will always be the city in which impostors will succeed. When an imposture is discovered everyone shrugs and laughs, and the impostor laughs even more, for he has already become rich, *recto stat fabula talo* ("the play is a hit").[17] This characteristic which makes the nation fall into a trap so easily comes from the supreme influence which fashion exercises over it. The imposture is new; so it becomes fashionable. It is enough if the thing has the power to surprise by being out of the ordinary, and everyone welcomes it for everyone fears he will look foolish if he says "It is impossible." In France alone is it true that only natural philosophers know that between the possibility and the act there is infinity, whereas in Italy the meaning of the axiom is firmly fixed in everyone's mind. A painter had a great success for a time by announcing that he could paint a person's portrait without seeing him; all that he asked was full information from the person who ordered the portrait; he had to describe the countenance to him so precisely that the painter could not possibly go wrong. The result was that the portrait was even more to the informant's credit than to the painter's; it also followed that the informant had to say that the portrait was a perfect likeness, for if he said anything else the painter alleged the most legitimate excuse: he said that if the portrait was not a good likeness the fault lay with the person who had not been able to describe the subject's countenance to him. I was surprised at Silvia's when someone retailed this piece of news, but—be it noted—without ridiculing it or casting doubt on the skill of the painter, who, so he had heard, had already painted over a hundred portraits, all excellent likenesses. Everyone said it was brilliant. I alone, choking with laughter, said it was an imposture. The man who had told the story took offense and offered to wager me a hundred louis; but I laughed again, because it was a question on which one could not wager without running the risk of being duped.

"But the portraits are likenesses."

"I do not believe it; and if they are likenesses there is trickery."

Only Silvia, who was of my opinion, accepts his proposal to go and dine at the painter's with him and myself. We go, and we see a quantity of portraits, all said to be likenesses; but since we did not know the originals it meant nothing.

"Could you paint my daughter's portrait for me, Monsieur," Silvia asked him, "without seeing her?"

"Yes, Madame, if you are sure you can describe her countenance to me."

We exchanged a look, and that was the end of it. Politeness forbade us to say more. The painter, whose name was Sanson,[18] gave us a good dinner, and his niece, who was intelligent, pleased me extremely. As I was in a good humor I held her attention by making her laugh a great deal. The painter told us that his favorite meal was supper and that he would be honored if we would often give him the pleasure of our company at it. He showed us more than fifty letters from Bordeaux, Toulouse, Lyons, Rouen, Marseilles, the writers of which ordered portraits from him, giving him descriptions of the faces they wanted him to paint; I read three or four of them with the greatest pleasure. He was paid in advance.

Two or three days later at the fair I saw his pretty niece, who reproached me for not coming to supper at her uncle's. The niece was very attractive and, flattered by her reproach, I went there the next day, and in a week or so the business became serious. I fell in love with her, and the niece, who was intelligent and was not in love, granted me nothing. Nevertheless I hoped, and I saw that I was snared.

I was drinking coffee alone in my room and thinking of her when I am visited by a young man whom I cannot place. He tells me he has had the honor to sup with me at the house of the painter Sanson.

"Ah yes, excuse me, Monsieur, I did not place you."

"That is only natural; at table you had eyes for no one but Mademoiselle Sanson."

"That may well be, for you must admit she is charming."

"It is not hard for me to admit it since, unfortunately, I know it only too well."

"Then you are in love with her."

"Alas, yes."

"Then win her love."

"That is what I have been trying to do for a year, and I was beginning to hope when you appeared and reduced me to despair."

"Who, Monsieur, I?"

"Yes, you."

"I am very sorry; but at the same time I fail to see what I can do about it."

"Yet it would not be very difficult, and if you will permit me I will myself suggest what you could do to oblige me."

"Please tell me."

"You could never set foot in her house again."

"I agree that it is the only thing I could do if I wanted very much to oblige you; but do you think that, if I did it, she would love you?"

"Oh, that is up to me. Meanwhile, do not go there again, and I will see to the rest."

"I admit that I may do you this extraordinary favor, but permit me to say that I think it strange you should have counted on it."

"Yes, Monsieur, after giving it much thought I saw that you were a man of great intelligence. I therefore made bold to conclude that you would be able to put yourself completely in my place, that you would consider the matter rationally, and that you would not wish to fight to the death with me for a young lady whom you, I imagine, do not wish to marry, whereas in my love my only object is that bond."

"And if I, too, were thinking of asking for her hand?"

"Then we should both deserve to be pitied, and I more than you, for as long as I am alive Mademoiselle Sanson will never be the wife of another."

This well-built young man, pale, serious, cold as ice, and in love, standing there in my own room deliberately saying such things to me with amazing calm, gave me occasion to think. I walked up and down for a good quarter of an hour to weigh the two courses of action dispassionately and see which of them would prove me the more courageous and the more worthy of my own esteem. I saw that the one which would best prove me the more courageous was the one which would prove to my rival that I was wiser than he.

"What will you think of me, Monsieur," I asked him firmly, "if I never set foot in Mademoiselle Sanson's house again?"

"That you pity an unhappy wretch who will always be ready to shed all his blood to show you his gratitude."

"Who are you?"

"I am Garnier,[19] only son of Garnier the wine merchant in the Rue de Seine."

"Very well, Monsieur Garnier, I will cease to visit Mademoiselle Sanson. Be my friend."

"Until death. Good-by, Monsieur."

A moment after he was gone, in comes Patu, to whom I tell the story and who declares me a hero; he embraces me, he thinks, and he says that he would have done the same in my place, but not in Garnier's place.

The Count of Melfort, then Colonel of the Orléans regiment, asked me through Camilla, sister of Corallina (the latter I no longer saw), to answer two questions by means of my cabala. I make up two answers which are very obscure but full of meanings, I seal them and give them to Camilla, who the next day asks me to go with her to a place which she will not name. She takes me to the Palais-Royal and we go up a narrow staircase to the apartment of the Duchess of Chartres,[20] who comes in a quarter of an hour later, showers the little beauty with caresses, and thanks her for having brought me to her. After a short preamble, all dignity and graciousness but without ceremony, she begins telling me all the difficulties she had found in the two answers I had given and which she had in her hand. After showing some surprise that the questions had been Her Highness's, I tell her that I know how to operate the cabala but that I am no good at interpreting it, so she must go to the trouble of asking further questions likely to produce clearer answers. So she writes down everything she could not understand and everything she wanted to know; I tell her that she must separate the questions, since one could not ask the oracle two things; she tells me to prepare the questions myself; I answer that she must write the whole with her own hand and imagine that she is interrogating an intelligence which knew all her secrets. She writes down everything she wanted to know in seven or eight questions; she reads them over to herself, and says with great dignity that she wishes to be sure that no one except myself will ever see what she has just written. I promise it on my word of honor; I read, and I see not only that she was right but that by putting them in my pocket to return them to her the next day with the answers I was in danger of compromising myself.

"I need only three hours, Madame, to do all this, and I want Your Highness to feel no anxiety. If Your Highness has anything to do, Your Highness can go and leave me here, provided that no one interrupts me. When I have finished I will seal everything; I need only know to whom I am to deliver the packet."

"To me, or to Madame de Polignac,[21] if you know her."

"Yes, Madame, I know her."

With her own hands the Duchess gave me a tinderbox so that I could light a small candle when I needed to seal, and she left and Camilla with her. I remained there, locked in; and three hours later, just as I was finishing, Madame de Polignac entered and I handed her the package and left.

The Duchess of Chartres, daughter of the Prince of Conti, was twenty-six years of age. She had in abundance the kind of intelligence which makes every woman who possesses it adorable, she was extremely animated, without prejudices, gay, witty in conversation, loving pleasure and preferring it to the hope of a long life. "Short and sweet" was an expression which was forever on her lips. In addition she was kind, generous, patient, tolerant, and constant in all her affections. With all that, she was very pretty. She carried herself awkwardly, and she laughed at the dancing teacher Marcel when he tried to correct her. She danced with her head bent forward and her toes turned in; even so, she was charming. A prime defect, which troubled her greatly and marred her beauty, was pimples, which were believed to be due to her liver but which in fact came from an impurity of the blood which finally caused her death and against which she struggled to her last breath.

The questions she put to my oracle were directed to matters which concerned her heart, and among other things she wanted to know a remedy to rid her beautiful skin of the small pimples which distressed everyone who saw her. My oracles were obscure concerning everything whose particulars I did not know; but they were not obscure concerning her malady, and it was this which made my oracle precious and necessary to her.

The next day after dinner Camilla, as I expected, wrote me a letter in which she asked me to drop everything and be at the Palais-Royal at five o'clock, in the room to which she had taken me. I went, and an old valet, who was waiting for me, set off at once and five minutes later I saw the charming Princess.

After complimenting me briefly but most graciously, she took all my answers from her pocket and asked me if I was busy; I assured her that my only business was to serve her.

"Good! I will not go out either and we will work."

She thereupon showed me all the new questions she had already prepared on all sorts of subjects and especially concerning the remedy to make her pimples disappear. What had given her confidence in my oracle was something it had told her which no one could know. I guessed, and my guess was right; if I had not, it would have made no difference. I had had the same malady, and I was physician enough to know that a forced cure of a cutaneous disease by local remedies could kill the Princess. I had already answered that she could not be cured of the marks of the malady on her face in less than a week, and that it would take at least a year of dieting to cure it radically, but that in a week she would appear to be cured. We now spent three hours finding out all that she must do. Fascinated by what my oracle knew, she submitted to everything, and a week later all her pimples disappeared. I purged her every day, I prescribed what she should eat, I forbade her any pomades, advising her instead only to wash before going to bed and in the morning with plantain water.[22] My modest oracle told the Princess to use the same wash wherever she wanted to produce the same result, and enchanted with the Intelligence's discretion, the Princess obeyed.

I purposely went to the Opéra on the day when the Princess appeared there with her complexion completely clear. After the performance she walked in the great promenade of her Palais-Royal, followed by all the principal ladies, and flattered by everyone; she saw me and honored me with a smile. I felt I was the happiest of men. Camilla, Monsieur de Melfort, and Madame de Polignac alone knew that I had the honor to be the Princess's oracle. But the day after she went to the Opéra, small pimples returned to mar her face, and I was summoned to appear at the Palais-Royal in the morning. The old valet, who did not recognize me, showed me into a delightful little room next to another in which there was a bathtub, and the Duchess came in looking rather sad, for she had pimples on her chin and her forehead. She was holding a question for the oracle, and since it was short I amused myself by making her obtain the answer herself, which surprised her when, translating the numbers into letters, she found that the angel reproached her with having broken the prescribed diet. She could not deny it. She had eaten ham and had drunk liqueurs. Just then one of her chambermaids came in and whispered something to her. She told her to wait outside for a moment.

"You will not take it amiss, Monsieur," she said, "to see someone here who is a friend of yours and discreet."

So saying, she puts all the papers which have nothing to do with her malady in her pocket and she calls. In comes a person whom I really took to be a stable boy. It was Monsieur de Melfort.

"Look," she said, "Monsieur Casanova has taught me to operate the cabala," and she showed him the answer she had obtained. The Count did not believe it.

"Then," she said to me, "we must convince him. What do you want me to ask?"

"Whatever Your Highness pleases."

She thinks, she takes an ivory box from her pocket, and she writes: *Tell me why this pomade no longer produces any effect on me.*

She constructs the pyramid, the columns, and the keys as I had already taught her to do, and when she is ready to obtain the answer I show her how to make various additions and subtractions which appear to arise from the numbers but which are really arbitrary, then I tell her to translate the numbers into letters and I go out, alleging some necessity. I come back when I think the translation has been completed, and I see the Duchess beside herself with astonishment.

"Ah, Monsieur, what an answer!"

"It may be wrong; but that can happen."

"Not at all; it is divine. Here it is: *'It has no effect except on the skin of a woman who has not had children.'* "

"I see nothing astonishing in the answer."

"Because you do not know that the pomade is the one prescribed for me by the Abbé de Brosses,[23] which cured me five years and ten months ago before I gave birth to the Duke of Montpensier.[24] I would give everything I possess in the world to learn to operate this cabala myself."

"What!" said the Count. "It is the same pomade the history of which I know?"

"The very same."

"It is astonishing."

"I should like to ask another question about a woman whom I do not wish to name."

"Just say 'the woman I have in mind.' "

She then asks what the woman's malady is, and I make her obtain the answer that she wants to deceive her husband. At that the Duchess cried out in amazement.

It was very late, and I left with Monsieur de Melfort, who had first spoken privately to Her Highness. He told me that what the cabala had answered about the pomade was astonishing; and here is the story.

"The Duchess," he said, "pretty as you see her, had her face so full of pimples that the Duke, in disgust, could not bring himself to sleep with her, hence she would never have borne a child. The Abbé de Brosses cured her with this pomade, and in all her beauty she went to the Comédie Française in the Queen's box. As chance would have it, the Duke of Chartres goes to the theater, not knowing that his wife was there, and takes a place in the King's box. He sees his wife in the opposite box, he thinks her pretty, he asks who she is, he is told that she is his wife, he does not believe it; he leaves his box, goes to see her, compliments her on her beauty, then goes back to his box. At half past eleven we were all at the Duchess's apartment; she was playing cards. Suddenly—and contrary to all precedent—a page informs the Duchess that the Duke her husband is entering her apartment, she rises to receive him, and the Duke tells her that he had thought her so beautiful at the theater that, on fire with love, he has come to ask her to allow him to get her with child. Hearing this, we all left immediately; it was in the summer of the year '46, and in the spring of '47 she gave birth to the Duke of Montpensier, who is five years old and in good health.

366

But after her lying-in the pimples came back and the pomade had no more effect."

After relating this anecdote the Count took from his pocket an oval tortoise-shell box with a very good likeness of the Duchess and gave it to me as a present from her, saying that if I wanted to have it set in gold she sent me the gold as well, and he handed me a roll of a hundred louis. I accepted it, begging him to express all my gratitude to the Princess; but I did not have the portrait set in gold, for I was greatly in need of money at the time. When the Duchess summoned me to the Palais-Royal after that there was no further question of curing her pimples, for she would never follow a diet; instead she made me spend five hours or six hours now in one corner now in another, leaving me, coming back again, having dinner or supper served to me by the old valet, who never spoke a word to me. The cabalas concerned only private matters of her own or of other people in whom she was interested, and she hit upon truths which I did not know I knew. She wanted me to teach her to operate the cabala, but she never pressed me to do it; she only had Monsieur de Melfort tell me that she would obtain me a post which would give me an income of twenty-five thousand livres if I would teach her the calculations. Alas, it was impossible. I was madly in love with her, but I never let her see the least sign of my passion. I thought such a conquest beyond me. I feared I should be humiliated by too scornful a refusal, and perhaps I was a fool. All I know is that I have always regretted that I did not speak out. It is true that I enjoyed several privileges which she might not have allowed me to enjoy if she had known that I loved her. I was afraid that I should lose them if I declared myself. One day she wanted the oracle to tell her if it was possible to cure a cancer which Madame La Pouplinière[25] had on one breast. I took it into my head to answer that the lady did not have a cancer and was in excellent health.

"What!" she said, "everyone in Paris believes it, and she consults every doctor; nevertheless, I believe the cabala."

She sees Monsieur de Richelieu at court and she tells him she is sure that Madame La Pouplinière is shamming; the Marshal, who was in on the secret, told the Duchess she was wrong, and she offered to wager him a hundred thousand francs; when she told me this, I trembled.

"Did he accept your wager?"

"No. He seemed amazed, and you know that he ought to know."

Three or four days later she told me that Monsieur de Richelieu had admitted to her that the cancer was a ruse to excite pity in her husband, to whom she wanted to return, but that the Marshal had told her he would pay a thousand louis to find out how she had discovered it.

"If you want to earn them," she said, "I will tell him everything."

"No, no, Madame—I implore you."

I feared a snare. I knew the Marshal's character; and the story of the hole[26] in the fireplace wall by which that illustrious nobleman entered the lady's house was known all over Paris. Monsieur de La Pouplinière had himself made the thing common knowledge by refusing to see his wife, to whom he gave twelve thousand francs a year. The Duchess had composed some very pretty verses on the affair; but no one outside of her own circle had seen them except the King, who was very fond of her despite the fact that she occasionally treated him to cutting witticisms. One day she asked him if it was true that the King of Prussia was coming to Paris; and the King having replied that there was no truth in it, she retorted that she was sorry because she was dying to see a king.

CHAPTER XII

My stay in Vienna. Joseph II.

In August 1752 Casanova left Paris for Dresden, where he failed to meet the King-Elector, Augustus III, or his celebrated Prime Minister, Count Brühl. He then returned to Venice via Prague and Vienna, where he had a brief but illuminating encounter with the poet Metastasio—almost forgotten today but a towering figure in the late eighteenth century.

So here I am, in the capital of Austria for the first time, at the flourishing age of twenty-eight. I had a few possessions, but scarcely any money; so I had to go slowly until the return of a letter of exchange which I at once drew on Signor Bragadin. The only other letter I had was one from the poet Migliavacca,[1] of Dresden, introducing me to the celebrated Abate Metastasio,[2] whose acquaintance I was most eager to make. I presented it to him on the next day but one, and in an hour's conversation I found him even more learned than his works proclaim him to be and with a modesty which at first I could not believe was natural; but I very quickly perceived that it was real when it vanished as soon as he recited something of his own and himself pointed out its beauties. I talked to him of his teacher Gravina,[3] and he recited five or six stanzas which he had composed on his death and which were not printed, and I saw him shed tears, touched by the sweetness of his own poetry. After reciting them to me, he added these words:

"Ditemi il vero: si può dir meglio?" ("Tell me the truth: is it possible to write better?")

I answered that only he had the right to believe it impossible. I asked him if his beautiful lines cost him much effort, and he at once showed me four or five pages filled with erasures due to his trying to bring fourteen lines to perfection. He assured me that he had never been able to compose more lines than that in a day. He then substantiated a truth which I already knew, namely, that the lines which cost a poet the most labor are those which uninitiated readers think cost him none. I asked him which of his operas he liked the best, and he said it was his *Attilio Regolo*,[4] and he added:

"Ma questo non vuol già dire che sia il migliore." ("But that does not necessarily mean it is the best.")

369

I told him that all his works had been translated into French prose[5] at Paris, and that the publisher had gone bankrupt because it was impossible to read them, and that this showed the power of his beautiful poetry. He answered that some other fool had gone bankrupt in the previous century by translating Ariosto[6] into French prose, and he laughed heartily at those who maintained, and who maintain, that a work in prose has the right to be called a poem. On the subject of his ariettas, he said that he had never written one of them without setting it to music himself, but that he usually did not show his music to anyone; and he laughed heartily at the French for believing that it is possible to fit words to a tune composed before-hand. He made a very philosophical comparison:

"It is," he said, "as if you said to a sculptor: 'Here is a piece of marble, make me a Venus which will show her expression before you have carved her features.' "

At the Imperial Library[7] I found, to my great surprise, Monsieur de La Haye with two Poles and a young Venetian[8] whom his father had entrusted to him for a good education. I embraced him several times. I thought he was in Poland. He told me that he was in Vienna on business and that he would go back to Venice in the summer. We called on each other, and as soon as I told him I had no money he lent me fifty zecchini, for which I was grateful to him. The news he told me which gave me decided pleasure was that of his friend the Baron de Bavois, who was already a lieutenant-colonel in the Venetian service. He had the good fortune to be chosen as adjutant-general by Signor Morosini, whom the Republic had appointed border commissioner[9] on his return from his embassy in France. I was delighted at the good fortune of those who could not but recognize me as first cause of it. I learned beyond doubt in Vienna that De La Haye had been a Jesuit; but no one was allowed to speak to him on the subject.

[* * *]

The Emperor Franz I was handsome, and I should have known that his physiognomy promised good fortune even if I had not seen him a monarch. He treated his wife with the utmost consideration, he did not prevent her from being prodigal, for it was only Kremnitz ducats[10] which she staked at cards or gave away in pensions, and he let her put the State in debt because he had the skill to become its creditor himself. He favored commerce because he put into his coffers a good share of the profits which it produced. He was also given to gallantry, and the Empress, who always addressed him as "Master," pretended not to notice. Perhaps she did not want it known that her charms did not suffice her husband's nature, and the more so since everyone admired the beauty of her numerous family. I saw all her Archduchesses[11] and thought them all beautiful except the eldest; among the males I studied only her eldest son,[12] whose physiognomy I found unpromising, despite the contrary opinion of the Abate Grossatesta, who also prided himself on being a physiognomist.

"What do you see in it?"

"I see conceit and suicide."

I guessed rightly, for Joseph II killed himself; and despite the fact that he did not intend it, he killed himself none the less. His conceit was the reason for his not being aware of it. What he professed to know, and did not know, made what he did know useless, and the acuity he tried to have spoiled what acuity he had. He loved to talk to anyone who, dazzled by his reasoning, did not know how to answer him, and those whose sound arguments invalidated his own he called "pedants." He told me in Laxenburg[13] seven years ago, talking of a man who had spent a fortune to buy a patent of nobility, that he despised anyone who bought one. I replied that it would be better to despise the person who sold it. He turned his back on me and from then on did not consider me worthy to hear his voice. His passion was to see people laugh, at least in their sleeves, when he told some story, for he told them well and embroidered on the circumstances amusingly; and he considered those who did not laugh at his jokes lacking in intelligence. They were precisely the people who understood them best. He preferred the arguments of Brambilla,[14] who encouraged him to kill himself, to those of the doctors whose advice to him was *Principiis obsta* ("Resist from the beginning").[15] As for the art of ruling, he did not know it, for he had no knowledge of the human heart, he could neither dissimulate nor keep a secret; he showed the pleasure he took in punishing, and he had not learned to control his counten- ance. He so far neglected this art that when he saw someone he did not know he made a grimace which rendered him very ugly, when he could have used an eyeglass instead, for the grimace seemed to say, "Who can that creature be?"

He succumbed to a malady which was most cruel in that it left him his reason until the end and because, before killing him, it showed him that his death was inescapable. He must have known the unhappiness of repenting of everything he had done and the other unhappiness of being unable to undo what he had done, partly because it was impossible and partly because he would have thought it dishonorable, for his sense of his high birth must always have remained in his soul even when it was languishing. He had the greatest esteem for his brother,[16] who reigns in his stead today, yet he had not the strength of mind to follow the important advice which he more than once gave him. With great magnanimity he gave a large reward to the intelligent physician[17] who had pronounced his death sentence, but with no less pusillanimity he had some months earlier rewarded the physicians and the charlatan who had made him believe he was cured. He also had the unhappiness of knowing that he would not be regretted; it is a most grievous thought. Another misfortune he had was not to die before the Archduchess his niece.[18] If those who were about him had really loved him, they would have spared him the dreadful news, for he was already dying and there was no need to fear that he would so far recover as to punish discretion as indiscretion; but they were afraid that his successor would not be generous to the worthy lady, who at once obtained a hundred thousand florins. Leopold would have defrauded no one.

[* * *]

CHAPTER XIV

Progress of my love affair with the beautiful
C. C.

Leaving Vienna, Casanova reached Venice "two days before Ascension Day in the year 1753" and immediately plunged back into his old ways. His quest for pleasure took him to Padua, where he was involved in an incident with the rascally "P. C." and his wife. The couple took up the acquaintance in Venice. They were to bring him many troubles but also the supreme delight of an affair with P. C.'s fourteen-year-old sister. So enamored with "C. C." did Casanova become that he persuaded his friend Signor Bragadin to ask the girl's parents for her hand in marriage.

On the next day but one P. C. came to call and told me triumphantly that his sister had told her mother that we loved each other and that, if she must marry, she could not be happy with anyone but me.

"I adore her," I answered; "but will your father give her to me?"

"I do not think so; but he is old. In the meanwhile, love. My mother is willing that she should go to the *opera buffa* with you today."

"Then we will go, my friend."

"I am obliged to ask you to do me a small favor."

"Command me."

"At the moment there is some excellent Cyprus wine for sale cheap. I can have a cask of it against a note payable in six months. I am sure I can resell it at once, and make a profit; but the merchant requires a guarantee, and is willing to accept yours. Will you sign my note?"

"With pleasure."

"Here it is."

I signed without hesitation. Who is the man in love who at that moment could have refused such a favor to one who, to revenge himself, could have made him miserable? After arranging to meet him at the same place at twenty o'clock,[1] I went to the Piazza San Marco to engage a box.[2] A quarter of an hour later I see P. C. masked and in a brand-new suit of clothes. I tell him he has done well to give up wearing his uniform and I show him the number of my box. We part. I go to the fair, I buy a dozen pairs of white gloves, a dozen pairs of silk stockings, and embroidered garters with gold clasps, which I at once put at the top of my own stockings. I am delighted to be giving this first present to my angel. After that, the hour being at hand, I hurry to the Campo dei Santi Apostoli, and I see them standing still and looking about for me; P. C. says that he has business which obliges him to leave us and that since he already knows the number of my box he will join us at the opera. I thereupon tell his sister that there is nothing for us to do but row about in a gondola until time for the Liston. She answers that she would like to go for a walk in a garden on La Giudecca,[3] I second her idea. Not having dined, as I found she had not, I tell her that we can get something to eat in the garden, and we go there in a ferry-gondola.

We go to a garden I know in San Biagio,[4] where a zecchino makes me lord and master of the place for the whole day. No one else was permitted to enter. We order what we want to eat, we go upstairs to the apartment, leave our disguises there, and go down to the garden for a walk. C. C. had on only a short taffeta bodice and a skirt of the same material; it was her entire costume. My amorous soul saw her naked, I sighed, I cursed duty and all feelings contrary to the nature which triumphed in the Golden Age.

As soon as we reached the long walk, C. C., like a young greyhound released from days of tedious confinement in its master's room and given the freedom of the fields at last—joyously obeying its instincts, it runs at top speed left and right, back and forth, returning every moment to its master's feet as if to thank him for allowing it to play so wildly—even so did C. C., who had never been granted the untrammeled freedom she was enjoying that day; she ran and ran until she was out of breath, and then laughed at the astonishment which kept me motionless and staring at her. After catching her breath and wiping her forehead she takes it into her head to challenge me to a race. The notion pleases me, I accept; but I insist on a wager.

"The loser," I say, "must do whatever the winner pleases."

"Agreed."

We set the goal of the race at the gate which gives on the Lagoon. The first to touch it will be the winner. I was certain to win; but I meant to lose to see what she would order me to do. We start. She uses all her strength, but I spare mine so that she touches the gate five or six paces ahead of me. She catches her breath, thinking up some pretty penalty to inflict on me, then she goes behind the trees and a minute later comes and says that she sentences me to find her ring, which she had hidden somewhere on her person, that I am free to look for it, and that she will think very little of me if I do not find it.

It was charming: there was mischief in it, but she was enchanting; and I must not take advantage of her, for her ingenuous confidence was something to be encouraged. We sit down on the grass. I search her pockets, the folds of her short bodice and her skirt, then her shoes, and I turn up her skirt, slowly and circumspectly, as high as her garters, which she was wearing above the knee; I unfasten them and I find nothing. I fasten them again, I draw down her skirt, and, since I am free to do anything, grope under her armpits. The tickling makes her laugh; but I feel the ring, and if she wants me to get it she has to let me unlace her bodice and touch the pretty breast over which my hand must pass to reach it; but just in time the ring drops lower, so that I had to take it from the waist of her skirt, thereby blessing both my hungry eyes and my hand, which she was surprised to see shaking.

"Why are you shaking?"

"With pleasure at finding the ring; but you owe me a revenge. You shall not beat me this time."

"We'll see."

At the beginning of the race the charming runner did not make much speed, and I was in no hurry to get ahead of her. I felt certain that I could gain the lead toward the finish and touch the gate before her. I could not suppose that she was up to the same trick; but she was. When she was thirty paces from the goal, she ran her best, and, realizing that I must lose, I fell back on an unfailing ruse. I let myself fall, crying:

"Oh, my God!"

She turns, she thinks I have hurt myself, and she comes to me. With her help I get up, groaning, and pretending that I could not stand on one foot, and she is perturbed. But as soon as I see that I am one step ahead of her, I look at her, I laugh, I run to the gate, I touch it, and I cry victory.

The charming girl was too amazed to understand what had happened.

"Then you didn't hurt yourself?"

"No—I fell on purpose."

"On purpose to fool me, counting on the kindness of my heart. I would not have believed you capable of it. It's against the rules to win by a trick, and you have not won."

"I won, because I got to the gate ahead of you, and, trick for trick, you must admit that you tried to trick me when you began running your best."

"But that's fair. Your trick, my dear friend, was outrageous."

"But it got me the victory.

" *'Vincasi per fortuna o per inganno*
Il vincer sempre fu laudabil cosa.' "[5]

("Whether victory be gained by luck or by ruse, winning has always been praiseworthy.")

"That's a maxim I have more than once heard from my brother but never from my father. But to cut it short, I admit that I lost. Pronounce my sentence, I will obey you."

"Wait. Let us sit down. I must think about it.

"I sentence you," I said thoughtfully, "to change garters with me."

"Garters? You saw mine. They're old and ugly, they're worth nothing."

"Never mind. I shall think of the object of my love twice a day, at the moment when it is always in the mind of a devoted lover."

"It is a pretty idea and it flatters me. I forgive you now for having tricked me. Here are my ugly garters."

"And here are mine."

"Oh, my dear deceiver, how beautiful they are! What a pretty present! How my dear mother will like them! They must be a present you have just received, for they are brand-new."

"No. They're not a present. I bought them for you, and I have racked my brains to find a way of persuading you to accept them. Love suggested making them serve as the forfeit for our race. Imagine my disappointment when I saw you on the verge of winning. It was love itself which suggested a trick based on what does you honor, for admit that if you had not come running to me at once it would have shown you were hardhearted."

"And I'm sure you wouldn't have played such a trick on me if you could have guessed how much it made me suffer."

"Then you feel a deep interest in me?"

"I would do anything on earth to convince you of it. As for these garters, I assure you I'll never wear any others and my brother shall never steal them from me."

"Is he capable of it?"

"Perfectly so, if this is gold."

"It is gold; but you shall tell him it is gilded copper."

"But you must show me how to fasten these pretty clasps, because my legs are thin there."

"Let us go and eat our omelette."

We needed the light repast. She became gayer, and I more in love and hence more to be pitied because of the restraint I had laid on myself. Impatient to put on her garters, she asked me to help her in perfect good faith, with no thought of evil and not a grain of coquetry. An innocent girl who, though she is fourteen years old, has never loved and never mingled with other girls knows neither the violence of desire nor exactly what excites it nor the dangers of being alone with a lover. When instinct makes her fall in love with a man she believes him worthy of all her trust, and she thinks she can only make him love her by showing him that she trusts him with no reservations. C. C. pulled her skirt up to her thighs and finding that her stockings were too short for her to put the garters on above the knee, she said that she would put them on with longer stockings; but I at once gave her the dozen pairs of pearl-gray stockings I had bought. In an ecstasy of gratitude, she sat on my lap, giving me the same sort of kisses she would have given her father when he made her such a present. I returned them, quelling the violence of my desires with a strength more than human. However, I told her that a single one of her kisses was worth more than a kingdom. C. C. took off her shoes and put on a pair of my stockings, which reached halfway up her thigh; and, supposing that I was in love with her, she thought not only that the sight would please me but that, since it was of no consequence, I would think her a fool if she attached any importance to it. The more innocent I found her to be, the less I could make up my mind to possess her.

We went downstairs again, and after strolling until nightfall we went to the opera wearing our masks, for, the theater being small, we might have been recognized. C. C. was certain that she would no longer be allowed to go out if her father discovered that she was given the privilege.

We were surprised not to see P. C. At our left was the Marchese di Montealegre,[6] the Spanish Ambassador, with his mistress Signorina Bola, and at our right a masked man and woman who, like ourselves, had never taken off their masks. They watched us constantly, but C. C., whose back was toward them, could not be aware of it. During the ballet she put the libretto of the opera on the ledge of the box, and I saw the masked man reach out and take it. Judging from this that it could only be a person whom one of us knew, I mentioned it to C. C., who at once recognized her brother. The lady could be none other than his C. Knowing the number of my box, he had taken the one beside it, and I foresaw that he intended to have his sister to supper with the woman. I did not like it; but I could not avoid it except by a direct challenge; and I was in love.

After the second ballet he came to our box with his lady, and after the usual compliments the introduction was made; and we had to go to supper at his casino. After taking off their disguises the ladies embraced, and C. fulsomely praised the beauties of my angel. At table she affected to shower her with attentions, and she, having no knowledge of the world, treated her with the utmost respect. Yet I saw that C., despite all her art, was very jealous of the budding charms which I had preferred to hers. P. C., boisterously gay, minced no words in his stupid jokes, at which only his lady laughed; my annoyance made me serious, and C. C., who understood nothing of the situation, remained silent. Our supper party was as depressing as possible.

At dessert, by which time he was drunk, he embraced his lady, challenging me to do as much to mine; I answered calmly that since I loved the Signorina I would not go so far until I had won rights over her heart. C. C. thanked me, her brother said that he did not believe us, and his lady told him to be still. At that I took from my pocket the gloves I had bought and gave her six pairs of them, presenting the other six to C. C. As I put them on for her, I kissed her beautiful arm again and again as if it were the first favor I had secured. Her brother laughed derisively and got up from the table.

He threw himself on a sofa, bringing C., who had also drunk too much, down with him and exposing her bosom to our view, while she only pretended to resist; but when he saw that his sister had turned her back on him and gone to a mirror and that his lewd behavior disgusted me, he pulled up her skirts to display for my admiration what I had already seen when she fell beside the Brenta and had handled since. For her part she slapped him in pretended punishment, but she was laughing. She wanted me to believe that her laughter deprived her of the power to defend herself; but her efforts had the contrary effect of revealing her completely. An accursed hypocrisy forced me to praise the shameless creature's charms.

But now the libertine, apparently calmed, asks her to forgive him, rearranges her dress, and changes her position; then, without changing his, he displays his bestial condition and adjusts the lady to himself, holding her astride him while she, still pretending that she was powerless in his hands, lets him perform, and performs. At that I go and talk to C. C., standing between her and them to hide the horror which she must already have seen in the mirror. Red as fire, she spoke to me of her beautiful gloves, which she folded on the mantelpiece.

After his brutal performance the scoundrel came and embraced me, and the lady embraced his sister, saying she was sure she had seen nothing. C. C. modestly answered that she did not know what there had been for her to see. But I saw that her beautiful soul was in the greatest perturbation. As for my own state, I leave it to the reader who knows the human heart to divine it. How could I bear this scene in the presence of an innocent girl whom I adored; and at the very moment when my soul was struggling between crime and virtue to defend her from myself? What torture! Anger and indig-nation set me trembling from head to foot. The infamous scoundrel believed that he had given me a great proof of his friendship. Reckoning as nothing the fact that he was dishonoring his lady and debauching and prostituting his sister, he was so blinded and infatuated that he did not understand that what he had done must have aggravated me to the point of very nearly drenching the scene in blood. I do not know how I restrained myself from cutting his throat. The only reasonable excuse he offered me two days later was that he could not imagine that when I had been alone with his sister I had not treated her just as he had treated C. After taking them home, I went to bed, hoping that sleep would calm my anger.

Upon awaking and finding that I was only indignant, my love became unconquerable. I thought C. C. was to be pitied only because I could not myself make her happy, for I was determined to do anything necessary to prevent the scoundrel from profiting in any way by her charms if I were forced to give her up. I felt I must lose no time. How horrible! What an unparalleled sort of seduction! What a strange way of winning my friendship! I seemed to be under the dire necessity of pretending to accept as tokens of friendship what could spring only from the baseness of an unbridled libertinism ready to sacrifice everything for the sake of its own continuance. I had been told that he was deeply in debt, that he had gone bankrupt in Vienna, where he had a wife and children, and he had done the same in Venice, compromising his father, who had turned him out of the house and who pretended not to know that he was still living there. He had seduced C., whom her husband refused to see, and after running through what money she had, he wanted to keep her as his mistress despite the fact that he did not know where to turn for a single zecchino. His mother, who adored him, had given him everything she possessed, even to her clothes. I expected to see him come to ask me for money again or to stand surety for him; but I was resolved to refuse him. I could not bear either the thought that C. C. was to become the cause of my ruin or the thought that she must serve as her brother's tool in supporting his debauchery.

Guided by love, I called on him the next day and after telling him that I adored his sister with the purest intentions, I made him realize what pain he had made me feel during that infamous supper. I told him that I had resolved to associate with him no longer, even if I had to renounce the pleasure of seeing his sister; but that I would find means to keep her from going out with him if he flattered himself that he could sell her to someone else.

He answered only that I must forgive him because he had been drunk and that he did not believe I loved his sister with a love which excluded possessing her. He embraced me with tears in his eyes, and just then his mother came in with her daughter to thank me for the pretty presents I had given her. I told her that I loved her only in the hope that she would grant me her hand and that to that end I would send someone to speak with her husband after I had secured a sufficient income to make her happy. So saying, I kissed her hand, unable to hold back my tears, which set hers flowing. After thanking me for the sentiments I had expressed to her, she withdrew, leaving me with her daughter and her son, who seemed turned to stone.

The world is full of mothers of this stamp, every one of them honest and endowed with all the virtues, the first of which being good faith they are nearly always the victims of the trust they repose in those whom they take to be people of probity.

My speech to the Signora astonished her daughter. But she was even more astonished when I repeated to her what I had said to her brother. After reflecting for a very short time, she told him that with any other man but myself she would have been ruined, and that she would not have forgiven him if she had been in the place of the lady he had dishonored even if she had been his wife.

P. C. wept. But the scoundrel could command his tears. The day being Whitsunday and the theaters not open, he asked me to meet him on the next day at the usual place, where he would bring his sister to me. He added, addressing us both, that since honor and love obliged him not to leave Signora C. alone, he would leave us in perfect freedom.

"I will give you my key," he said to me, "and you shall bring my sister back here after you have supped wherever you please."

He left us after giving me the key, which I had not strength of mind to refuse, and I left a moment later, telling C. C. that we would talk the next day in the garden on La Giudecca. She said that what her brother had now done was the most honorable decision he could take.

It was fulfilled the next morning; he left her with me and, burning with love, I foresaw what must happen. After engaging a box we went to our garden, where, it being Whitmonday, we found many people; but as the casino was unoccupied we asked nothing more.

We go upstairs and, certain that we should not dare take a walk, since ten or twelve parties were sitting at a number of tables in the garden, we decide to sup in the casino, not caring to go to the opera until the second ballet. So we ordered supper for later. We had seven hours before us; she said she was sure we would not be bored and, having taken off her disguise, she threw herself in my arms, saying that I had finally won her heart and soul during that terrible supper where I had been so considerate toward her. What we said was always accompanied by kisses, with which we deluged each other's faces. *But love kisses the face only to thank it for the desires it inspires; and since its desires have a different goal, love becomes irritated if that is not attained.*

"Did you see," she asked, "what my brother did to his lady when she got astride him as one rides a horse? I hurried to the mirror; but I could well imagine what was happening."

"Were you afraid I would do the same to you?"

"No, I assure you. How could I have feared such a thing, knowing how much you love me? You would have humiliated me so greatly that I could no longer have loved you. We will keep ourselves until we are married. Shall we not? You cannot imagine the joy of my soul when you spoke out to my mother. We will love each other forever. But, while I think of it, please explain the two verses on my garters."

"Are there two verses on them? I didn't know it."

"Please read them. They are in French."

As she was sitting on my lap, she unfastens one garter while I take off the other. Here are the two verses, which I ought to have read before I gave her the garters:

En voyant tous les jours le bijou de ma belle
Vous lui direz qu'amour veut qu'il lui soit fidèle.

("You who see my beauty's jewel every day, tell it that Love bids it be true.")

The verses which, though naughty, I thought were perfect, both funny and witty, made me burst out laughing and then laugh even more when I had to explain them word by word to satisfy her. Since they depended on two ideas both of which were new to her, she needed a commentary which set us both on fire. The first thing I had to tell her was that the "jewel" stood for her little such-and-such, of which I could only obtain possession by marrying her, and the second was that her garters would have the privilege of seeing it constantly if they had eyes. Blushing furiously, C. C. embraced me with all her heart and said that her jewel did not need any such flattering advice from her garters, since it knew very well that it was only for her husband.

"I am only sorry," she said after thinking a moment, "that I shall not dare show anyone my garters now. Tell me what you are thinking."

"I am thinking that those lucky garters have a privilege which I may never enjoy. Why am I not where they are! I may die of the desire I feel, and I shall die unhappy."

"No, my dear. I am in the same state as you, for you must have jewels to interest me, too, and I am sure I shall live. Besides, we can hasten our marriage. For my part, I am ready to pledge you my faith tomorrow if you wish. We are free, and my father will be obliged to consent."

"Your reasoning is sound, for his honor would demand that of him; yet I wish first to show him my respect by making an application for your hand, and our household will soon be set up. It will be a matter of a week or ten days."

"So soon? You'll see that he will say I am too young."

"And perhaps he will be right."

"No; for I am young, but not too young. I am certain, my dear, that I could be your wife."

I was burning; I could no longer resist the compelling force of nature.

"My dear one," I said, holding her clasped in my arms, "are you sure that I love you? Do you think I could fail you? Are you certain you will never repent of marrying me?"

"I am more than certain of it, dear heart; I shall never believe you capable of making me unhappy."

"Then let us marry now before God, in his presence; we cannot have a truer and more worthy witness than our Creator, who knows our consciences and the purity of our intentions. We have no need of documents. Let us pledge our faith to each other; let us unite our destinies here and now and be happy. We will have a church ceremony when we can do everything publicly."

"So be it, my dear. I promise God and you that from this moment until my death I will be your faithful wife, and that I will say the same to my father, to the priest who will bless us in church, and to the whole world."

"I make you, my dear, the same vow, and I assure you that we are truly married and belong to each other. Now come to my arms. We will complete our marriage in bed."

"Now? Is it possible that I am so near to my happiness?"

Thereupon I went out and told the hostess not to bring us supper until we called and to leave us undisturbed, for we wanted to sleep until nightfall. C. C. had thrown herself on the bed with all her clothes on; but I laughed and told her that Love and Hymen went naked.

"Naked? And you too?"

"Of course. Leave it to me."

In less than a minute I had her before my avid and covetous eyes with no veil to hide the least of her charms from me. In an ecstasy of admiration which put me beside myself I devoured all that I saw with fiery kisses, hurrying from one spot to another and unable to stop anywhere, possessed as I was by the desire to be everywhere, regretting that my mouth must move less swiftly than my eyes.

"Your beauty," I said, "is divine; it will not let me believe at this moment that I am mortal."

C. C., white as alabaster, had black hair, and her puberty was apparent only in the down which, divided into little curls, formed a transparent fringe above the little entrance to the temple of love. Tall and slender, she was ashamed to let me see her hips, which the junction of her thighs set off to perfection and whose proportions she thought faulty, whereas if they had been less full and less prominent they would have been less beautiful. Her belly scarcely showed its contours, and her breasts left nothing for either my eyes or my hands to desire. Her large black eyes, under brows not given to anger,[7] bore witness to the joy of her soul in its delight at seeing the effect of her wonderful beauty in my admiration. Her rosy cheeks, which contrasted with her whiteness, showed only two small dimples except when a sweet smile added a fraction of an inch to the length of her coral lips, which at the same time showed teeth whose whiteness surpassed that of her bosom only because it was brightened by the sheen of their enamel.

Beside myself, I began to fear either that my happiness was not real or that it could not be made perfect by an even greater enjoyment. But at that most serious moment mischievous Love gave me occasion to laugh.

"Can it be the law," said C. C., "that the husband must not undress?"

"No, my angel. And even if such a barbarous law existed I would not submit to it."

Never have I undressed more quickly. Then it was her turn blindly to obey the promptings of instinct. She did not interrupt her transports and her ardors except to ask me if it was really true that I belonged to her. She said that the statue of Beauty her father possessed proved that the first sculptor had been a man, for a woman would have made it of the opposite sex from hers.

"Great power of love!" she cried. "I feel no shame. Would I have believed it ten days ago? Please don't tickle me there, it's too sensitive."

"Dear heart, I am going to hurt you more than that."

"I am sure of it; but let nothing stop you. What a difference between you and my pillow."

"Your pillow? Are you joking? Tell me what you mean."

"It's just silliness. These last four or five nights I couldn't get to sleep unless I held a big pillow in my arms and kissed it over and over and imagined it was you. I only touched myself there, dear, just for a moment at the end and very lightly. Then a pleasure for which there are no words left me motionless and as if dead; I fell asleep and when I woke eight or nine hours later I laughed to find the big pillow in my arms."

C. C. became my wife like a heroine, as every girl in love must do, for pleasure and the assuagement of desire make even pain delicious. I spent two whole hours without ever separating from her. Her continual swoons made me immortal. Nightfall bade me resolve to suspend our pleasures. We dressed and I called for lights and supper.

What a delicious repast, even though there was not much of it! We ate gazing at each other, and we did not speak because we did not know what more to say. We found our supreme happiness in the thought that it was we who had created it and that we would renew it whenever we wished.

The hostess came up to see if we wanted anything else, and she asked us if we were going to the opera and if it was true that it was such a fine spectacle.

"Have you never gone?" C. C. asked her.

"Never—it's too expensive for people like us. My daughter is so curious about it that she would give—God forgive me!—her maidenhead to go just once."

C. C. burst out laughing and replied that she would be paying too dearly to satisfy her curiosity, and just as I was thinking of offering the woman the box I had taken she said to me that we could make the girl happy by giving her our key. I give it to her, swearing that I had had the same idea.

"Here," she said to the hostess, "is the key to a box at San Moisè, which cost two zecchini. Go to the opera at once with your daughter, and tell her to keep her maidenhead for something better."

"And here are two more zecchini," I added, "to do as you please with."

Amazed at such a liberal present, the good woman ran to take it to her daughter, while we congratulated ourselves on having made it necessary for us to go back to bed. The hostess comes back upstairs with her daughter, a beautiful and quite savory blonde, who insists on kissing the hands of her benefactors.

"She will be off at once," said her mother, "with her lover, who is downstairs, but I won't let her go alone because he's a strapping fellow. I shall go with them."

I told her to keep the gondola in which they came back, and we would take it to return to Venice.

"Really? You mean to stay here until four o'clock?"[8]

"Yes, for we were married this morning."

"This morning? God bless you!"

She goes to the bed and, seeing signs worthy of veneration, she embraces my charming initiate, congratulating her on her virtue; but

385

what amused us extremely was a sermon the woman preached to her daughter while she pointed out what, according to her, did immortal honor to C. C. and what Hymen very seldom saw on his altar. The daughter replied, casting down her blue eyes, that she was certain the same thing would happen when she was married.

"I'm sure of it too, because I never let you out of my sight. Take the basin and get some water and bring it here, for the bride must need it."

She brought up water, then they left, and the comical scene diverted my angel exceedingly. After refreshing ourselves all over, we locked ourselves in and went back to bed, where four hours passed very quickly. The last combat would have gone on longer if my wife, already grown curious, had not taken it into her head to put herself in my place and me in hers. When she thus displayed herself before my soul in a state of obsession which pronounced her ravaged by Venus, the supreme degree of pleasure seized on my senses. Left as if dead, we fell asleep; but a moment later the hostess knocked to say that the gondola was at our service. I hurried to open the door, eager to laugh at what she would have to tell us about the opera; but she left it to her daughter while she went to make us coffee. The blonde helped C. C. to dress, occasionally giving me glances which showed me beyond doubt that her mother was greatly mistaken if she thought her inexperienced.

Nothing was more telltale than my angel's eyes, which had such dark circles that they looked as if they had been bruised. The poor child had sustained a combat which had literally left her another person. After drinking some very hot coffee we told the hostess that we wanted a choice dinner for the following day. By the light of early dawn we disembarked at the Campo di Santa Sofia[9] to evade the curiosity of the gondoliers. We parted content, happy, and certain that we were well and duly married. I went to bed resolved that, by an infallible oracle, I would compel Signor Bragadin to obtain the girl's hand for me. I slept until noon; I ate dinner in bed, and I spent the rest of the day gambling and losing.

CHAPTER XV

Continuation of my love affair with C. C.
Signor Bragadin asks for the young lady's
hand for me. Her father refuses and puts her
in a convent. De La Haye. I lose at cards.
Association with Croce, which replenishes my purse.
Various incidents.

The next day I saw P. C. in my room in high spirits and taking an entirely new tone with me. He told me in so many words that he was sure I had slept with his sister and that he was delighted.

"She refuses to admit it," he said, "but that makes no difference. I will bring her to you today."

"You will be doing me a kindness, for I love her, and I shall arrange to have her father asked for her hand for me in such a way that he will not refuse."

"I should like nothing better, but I doubt it. Meanwhile, I am under the necessity of asking you to do me another favor. In exchange for a note payable in six months, I can have a ring worth two hundred zecchini which I am sure I can sell today for the same price; but unless you will stand surety, the merchant, who knows you, will not let me have it. Will you do me this favor? I know that you lost three hundred zecchini yesterday; I offer you a hundred, which you will repay me when the note falls due."

How could I refuse the wretch what he asked of me? I answered that I was ready; but that he was wrong in thus abusing the affection which bound me to his sister. We went to the merchant who had the ring and we completed the transaction. The man, whom I did not know, thought he was paying me a great compliment when he said that he was ready to give P. C. everything he had on my surety. Such was the fashion in which the scoundrel went about Venice looking for the one man in a hundred ill advised enough to grant me credit against all reason, for I had nothing. And so C. C., who should have brought me nothing but happiness, became the cause of my ruin.

C. C.'s father having gone to Treviso on business, her brother brought her to me at noon. To convince me that he was honest he gave me back the note for the Cyprus wine for which I had stood

387

surety, insisting at the same time that when next we met he would give me the hundred zecchini he had promised me.

On La Giudecca, where I at once had the garden closed, we dined in a grape arbor. I thought C. C. had become more beautiful. Friendship had been added to love, so that our perfect contentment shone in our faces. The hostess, who had found me generous, gave me game and sturgeon. The blonde waited on us at table and came to wait on us in our room when she learned that we were going to bed. After helping my wife undress she offered to take off my shoes; but I waved her away, pretending not to see her bosom, which on the excuse of the hot weather she displayed too lavishly. But could I have eyes for anyone else when I was with C. C.?

She at once asked me what was the meaning of the hundred zecchini her brother was to bring me, and I told her the whole story. She said that in future I must absolutely refuse him my signature, for, since the wretch was sunk in debt, he would involve me in his ruin, which was inevitable.

On this second occasion we found our amorous pleasures more substantial; we thought we relished them with more delicacy, we discussed them. She begged me to do everything possible to make her pregnant, for in case her father obstinately refused to let her marry so young he would change his mind when he saw her with a big belly. I had to give her a lecture on the rudiments to make her understand that her becoming a mother depended upon us only in part, but that it was likely it would happen on one occasion or another, especially when we reached the sweet ecstasy at the same time.

So, both applying ourselves sedulously and single-mindedly after two attempts which she said went very well, we spent four good hours sleeping. I called; candles were brought, and after drinking coffee we resumed our amorous labors in order to arrive together at that life-engendering death which was to ensure our happiness. But dawn having come to warn us that we must go back to Venice, we dressed in haste and left.

We did the same on Friday, but I think I should spare the reader the details of our communion, which, though always new to those who are in love, often does not seem so to those who hear it recounted. We arranged to go to the garden for the last time on Monday, the last day for masks. Death alone could prevent me from going, for it might be the last day of our amorous enjoyments.

So, having seen P. C. on Monday morning, when he confirmed the appointment for the same hour at the same place, I did not fail to be there. The first hour passes quickly, despite the impatience of him who waits; but after the first another passed, then a third, a fourth, and a fifth, and the couple for whom I was waiting did not appear. I could imagine only the most terrible disasters. But if C. C. had been unable to leave, her brother should have come to tell me so; but it was possible that some insurmountable obstacle had prevented him from going to fetch his sister. I could not go to their house for fear of missing them on the way.

It was finally on the stroke of the Angelus that I saw C. C. coming toward me, masked, but alone.

"I was sure," she said, "that you were here, and I let my mother say what she would. Here I am. You must be dying of hunger. My brother has not shown his face all day. Let us go to our garden quickly. I need to eat, and to have love console me for all that I have suffered today."

As she had told me everything I did not need to ask her any questions. We went to our garden, despite a very violent storm which, our gondola having only one oar, terrified me. C. C., who was unaware of the danger, frisked about, and the movement she imparted to the gondola put the gondolier in danger of falling into the water, which would have meant our death. I told her to keep quiet, though I did not tell her the danger we were in for fear of frightening her. It was the gondolier who shouted that if we did not sit still we were lost. We arrived at last, and the gondolier smiled when I paid him four times the fare.

We spent six hours there in a state of happiness which the reader can imagine. Sleep was not of our company. The only thought which clouded our joy was that, the season of masks[1] being over, we did not see how we could continue our amorous meetings. I promised that I would call on her brother on Wednesday morning, when she would join us as usual.

After taking leave of the kind hostess of the garden, who could not hope to see us again, we went to Venice and, after leaving C. C. at her door, I went home. The news with which I was greeted when I woke at noon was the return of De La Haye with his pupil Calvi. He was a very handsome boy, as I think I have said, but I laughed heartily at table when, encouraging him to speak, I found him a young De La Haye in miniature even to his gestures. He walked, he laughed, he looked about like him, he spoke De La Haye's French, which was correct but harsh. I thought this was going much too far. I considered it my duty to tell his tutor publicly that he must certainly rid his pupil of his affectations, for his aping him would expose him to bitter raillery. Baron Bavois came in, and after spending an hour with the boy he thought as I did. The promising boy died two or three years later. Two or three months after Calvi's death De La Haye, whose passion was forming pupils, became tutor to a young Cavaliere Morosini,[2] the nephew of the Morosini who had set Baron Bavois on the road to fortune and who was then Border Commissioner for the Republic to settle its boundary with the House of Austria, whose commissioner was Count Cristiani.[3]

In love as I was, I could no longer put off taking the step on which, as I thought, my happiness depended. After the company left I asked Signor Bragadin and his two faithful friends to grant me a hearing for two hours in our withdrawing room, where we were inaccessible. It was there that, making no exordium but *ex abrupto*, I told them that I was in love with C. C. and determined to elope with her if they could not induce her father to grant me her hand.

"It will be necessary," I said to Signor Bragadin, "to provide me with an income on which I can live and to guarantee the ten thousand ducats which the girl will bring me as her dowry."

Their answer was that if Paralis would give them all the necessary instructions they would obey. I asked nothing better. I thereupon spent two hours constructing all the pyramids they wished, and the upshot was that the intermediary who was to ask her father for the girl would be Signor Bragadin in person, because it was he who would have to guarantee the dowry by all his present and future possessions. As C. C.'s father was then in the country I told them that I would inform all three of them when he returned, since the three of them must be together when he was asked for her hand.

Well satisfied with what I had done in the matter, I called the next morning on P. C. An old woman told me that he was not at home but that the Signora would come to me at once. I see her a moment later with her daughter, both looking sad. C. C. tells me that her brother is in prison for debt and that it would be difficult to get him out since the amounts he owed were too great. Her mother weeps as she says she is in despair because she cannot support him in prison and shows me the letter he had written in which he asked her to give an enclosed letter to his sister. I ask her if I may read the letter he had written her, she hands it to me, and I find that he begs her to recommend him to me. I say, handing it back to her, that she can only write him that I can do nothing for him and at the same time I ask the mother to accept twenty zecchini, with which she could

VOLUME THREE CHAPTER FIFTEEN

help him, sending him one or two at a time. She took them only at her daughter's urging.

After this mournful scene I tell them what I have done toward obtaining C. C. as my wife. The Signora said that my measures did them much honor and were well planned; but she added that I must not hope for anything, since her husband would not give her in marriage until she was eighteen, and then only to a merchant. He was to arrive that day. As I was going, C. C. slipped a note into my hand. She wrote me that, since I had the key to the small door, I could safely come to her at midnight, sure that I would find her in her brother's room. My joy was complete, for, despite their doubts, I hoped for everything. I go home and inform Signor Bragadin that Signor Ch.,[4] C. C.'s father, is expected at any moment. He writes the note in my presence. He asked him to appoint an hour at which he could come to discuss an important matter with him. I told him to wait until the next day to send it.

Having gone to C. C.'s house at midnight, I found her waiting for me with open arms in her brother's room. After she had assured me that I had nothing to fear, that her father had returned in perfect health, and that everyone was asleep, we gave ourselves up to love; but she trembled when I told her that her father would receive the fatal note the next day. She told me what she feared, and her reasoning was sound.

"My father," she said, "who now thinks of me only as a child, will look at me with new eyes and, once he begins examining my conduct, God knows what he will do. We are even happier now than we were when we were going to La Giudecca, for we can spend every night here together; but what will my father do when he finds out that I have a lover?"

"What can he do? If he refuses me I will carry you off, and the Patriarch[5] cannot refuse us the nuptial benediction. We shall belong to each other for the rest of our lives."

"It is all that I ask, and I am ready for anything; but I know my father and I am afraid."

Two hours later I left her, promising that I would return the next night. Signor Bragadin sent his note to her father about noon. He replied that he would himself go to his palace the following day to receive his orders. About midnight I told all this to my dear C. C., who said that her father was most curious to know what Signor Bragadin, to whom he had never spoken, could want with him. Uncertainty, fear, and delusive hope made the pleasures of love much less keen during these last two hours we spent together. I was certain that when Signor Ch. returned home after hearing Signor Bragadin's proposal he would have a long talk with his daughter, and, since she must expect it, I saw that she was terrified; the pity she aroused in me pierced my heart, I could think of no advice to give her, for I could not know how her father would take the matter; she must hide from him whatever circumstances might be injurious to her virtue, at the same time she must in general tell him the truth and show herself more than ready to obey his will. In the course of these reflections I repented that I had taken the great step, precisely because its consequences would be too decisive. I could not wait to escape from the cruel uncertainty which weighed on my soul, and I was surprised to see C. C. less anxious than I was. I felt certain that I would see her the next night. The contrary seemed to me impossible.

The next day after dinner Signor Ch. called on Signor Bragadin, and I did not show myself. He left after spending two hours with him and his two friends, and I learned at once that he had said what his wife had already told me, but with an addition which was most painful for me. He said that he would send his daughter to a convent for the four years which must pass before she married. He had ended by saying that if, at the expiration of that time, I had a well-established position, he might grant me her hand. I found his answer devastating, and in the despair with which it filled my soul I was not surprised at midnight to find the small door of C. C.'s house locked from inside. I went home neither dead nor alive. I spent twenty-four hours in the cruel indecision of one who must adopt a course and does not know what course to adopt. I thought that carrying her off would now be difficult, even as, with P. C. in prison, it would be difficult to correspond with my wife, for I considered her such by a far stronger bond than one we might have contracted before the Church and a notary.

It was about noon on the next day but one that I resolved to visit Signora C., ringing at the main door of the house. A maid came down and told me that the Signora had gone to the country and it was not known when she would return. At that moment I almost gave up hope. All ways of obtaining any information were closed to me. I tried to appear indifferent when I was with my three friends; but I was the most unhappy of men. Hoping to hear something, I was reduced to visiting P. C. in prison.

Surprised to see me, he expresses the greatest gratitude. He explains the state of his debts, he tells me any number of lies, which I pretend to believe; he assures me that he will be out of prison in ten or twelve days, and he asks me to forgive him for not having given me the hundred zecchini he had promised me; but he assures me that when the time comes he will honor the note for two hundred for which I had stood surety. After letting him talk I coldly ask him for news of the family. He knows nothing, and believes there is nothing new; he says that it will be my own fault if I do not call on his mother occasionally, where I will see his sister. I promised to go, and after giving him two zecchini I left.

I racked my brains for a way to find out what C. C.'s situation was. I imagined that she was unhappy, and aware that I was the cause of it I was in despair, I loathed myself. Soon I could neither eat nor sleep.

Two days after Signor Ch.'s refusal, Signor Bragadin and his two friends went to Padua for a month on the occasion of the Fair of St. Anthony. The state of my soul and my uncertain situation did not allow me to go with them. I was left alone in the palace; but I went there only to sleep. I spent the whole day at cards, I lost constantly, I had sold or pawned everything I owned, and I owed money everywhere; I could hope for help only from my faithful friends, who were in Padua, and shame kept me from writing to them.

In this situation, which was enough to bring thoughts of suicide (it was June 13th,[6] St. Anthony's Day), while I was shaving my valet announces a woman. She enters with a basket and a letter. She asks me if I am the person whose name I saw written in the address. I see the imprint of a seal which I had given to C. C. I thought I should drop dead. To calm myself, I told the woman to wait, thinking that I would finish shaving, but my hand was shaking. I put down the razor, turn my back on the woman, unseal the letter, and read the following:

"Before writing you at length, I must be sure of this woman. I am boarding in this convent, and very well treated; and I am in perfect health, despite the anxiety of my mind. The Mother Superior has orders not to let me see anyone and not to allow me to correspond with anyone; but I am already sure that I can write to you despite her prohibition. I do not doubt your constancy, my dear husband, and I am sure that you do not doubt and will never doubt mine or my readiness to do whatever you command me to do; for I am yours. Answer only a few words, until we are sure of the messenger. Murano, June 12th."

All the letters I quote are faithful translations of the originals, which I have always kept.

In less than three weeks the girl had become an expert in moral science; but her teacher must have been love, which alone performs miracles. The moment during which a man returns from death to life can only be a moment of crisis; so I needed to sit down and spend four or five minutes returning to myself.

I asked the woman if she could read.

"Oh, Signore, if I couldn't read I'd be in a bad way. There are seven of us appointed to serve the blessed nuns of XXX[7] in Murano. Each of us takes her turn coming to Venice on her day of the week; my day is Wednesday. So a week from today I can come back and bring you the answer to the letter which, if you wish, you can write now. You can see that, since our principal errands are the letters we're given to carry, we shouldn't be wanted unless we could read the addresses on those we're entrusted with. The nuns want to be sure—and they're right—that we won't give Peter a letter they write to Paul. They are always afraid we'll make that very blunder. So you'll see me a week from today at the same hour, but give orders that you're to be waked if you're asleep, for our time is measured out *like gold*. Above all, when you deal with me you need fear no indiscretion. If I didn't know how to hold my tongue, I'd lose my employment, and what would I do then, being a widow with a son eight years old and three pretty daughters, the eldest sixteen and the youngest thirteen? You're welcome to come and see them if you come to Murano. I live on the ground floor ten paces from the bridge nearest the church, on the garden side in the alley, and the door has four steps outside and I'm always home or at the convent gate or in the visiting room or running errands, of which there are plenty. The Signorina, whose name I don't know, for she's only been with us for a week and who—God keep her in health!—is really a perfect beauty, gave me this letter, but so cleverly! . . . Oh, she must be a sly one, for three nuns who were there certainly never noticed it. She gave it to me with this note for me, which I leave you too. She tells me to be discreet. The poor child! I beg you to write her that she can be sure of it and don't be afraid to vouch for me, but not for the others, though I believe they're all honest women, for God preserve me from thinking ill of anyone; but, you see, they're all ignorant, and they certainly chatter away at least to their confessors. As for me—thank God!—I know I need account to him only for my sins, and carrying a letter from a Christian woman to a Christian man isn't one; and besides, my confessor is an old monk who—God forgive me!—I think must be deaf, because he never answers me at all; but if he's deaf, that's his business, not mine."

So it was that the woman, whom I had not intended to question, kindly saved me the trouble by telling me everything I could wish to know, simply to persuade me to use no one but herself in the intrigue. It would appear that her very chatter, which sticks in the mind, contains a sublime eloquence which persuades and instills perfect confidence.

I at once answered my dear captive, intending to write only a few lines as she told me to do; but I did not have time enough to write her a short letter; it filled four pages and it perhaps said less than she had said to me in one. I told her that her letter had saved my life, since I knew neither where she was nor if she was alive or dead. I asked her if I could hope, if not to speak with her, at least to see her. I told her that I had given the bearer a zecchino, that she must have found one herself under the seal of my letter, and that I would send her as much money as she wished if she thought it might be necessary or useful to her. I begged her not to fail to write to me every Wednesday and never to fear that she was writing at too great length, telling me not only every detail of the life she was being forced to lead but also all her ideas on the subject of breaking all the chains and destroying all the obstacles which could stand in the way of our reunion, for I belonged to her just as she told me that she belonged to me. I impressed it upon her that she must use all her ingenuity to make herself loved not only by all the nuns but also by her fellow boarders, yet without confiding anything to them or showing any resentment at having been put where she was. After praising her ingenuity in finding a way to write to me despite the Mother Superior's prohibition, I impressed it upon her that she must take the greatest care never to be caught writing to me, for then her room and her chest of drawers and even her pockets would be searched and any papers she had would be confiscated. On this account I asked her to burn all my letters. I told her to apply all the powers of her mind to the consideration that she was obliged to go to confession frequently; being certain that she would well understand what I was trying to say to her. I ended by imploring her to tell me all her sufferings, assuring her that her sorrows were of even greater concern to me than her joys.

After sealing my letter in such a fashion that the zecchino under the wax would be neither seen nor felt, I gave another to the woman, assuring her that I would reward her in the same way each time she brought me a letter from the same young lady. She wept with gratitude. She said that, since she was free to come and go there, she would give my letter to the Signorina at a time when she found her alone. Here is the note which my dear C. C. had given the woman when she entrusted the letter to her:

"It is God, my good woman, who prompts me to rely on you rather than on any of the others. Take this letter to its address and, if the person is not in Venice, bring it back to me. You must deliver it into his own hands. I am sure that you will at once be given the answer, which you will deliver to me only when you are sure that no one sees you."

Love becomes imprudent only when it is impatient to enjoy; but when it is a matter of procuring the return of a happiness to which a baleful combination of circumstances has raised impediments, love sees and foresees all that the most subtle perspicacity can discover. My wife's letter filled my soul with joy, and in an instant I had passed from one extreme to the other. I felt certain that I could carry her off even if the walls of her convent were guarded with artillery. My first thought was to find some way of quickly passing the week at the end of which I was to receive her second letter. Only gambling could distract me, and everyone was in Padua. I quickly order my valet to pack my trunk and take it to the *burchiello*[8] which was about to leave, and I instantly set off for Padua, from where, at full gallop, in less than three hours I am at the door of the Palazzo Bragadin,[9] where I see its master going in to eat dinner. He embraced me and, seeing me covered with sweat, said with a laugh that he was sure I was in no hurry. I answered that I was dying of hunger.

I brought joy to the company and it increased when I told them that I would spend six days with them. After dinner I saw Signor Dandolo shut himself up in his room with De La Haye. They spent two whole hours there. Signor Dandolo came to my bedside to tell me that I had arrived just in time to consult my oracle about an important matter which concerned him, and he gave me his question. He asked if he would do well to accept the proposal which De La Haye had just made to him. I produce the answer that he should reject it. Signor Dandolo is surprised and returns with another question. He asks what reasons he shall give him for his refusal. I suggest that he answer that he had thought he should ask my advice and, finding me opposed to the plan, wished to hear no more of it. Pleased that he could put all the odium of his refusal upon me, Signor Dandolo left. I did not know what it was all about, but I did not care to know. My satisfaction consisted in the fact that Signor Dandolo's curt refusal should teach De La Haye that he must not try to make my friends do anything except through me.

I quickly masked and went to the opera. I sat down at a faro bank, I played, and I lost all my money. Fortune showed me that she was not always on love's side. After this ill-considered performance I went to bury my sorrow in sleep.

On waking in the morning I see De La Haye, all smiles. After professing the most exaggerated regard for me, he asks me why I had dissuaded Signor Dandolo from accepting the proposal he had made to him.

"What proposal?"

"You know."

"I know nothing about it."

"He told me himself that you advised him against it."

"Very well, I advised him against it; but I did not dissuade him, for if he had been persuaded he would have had no need to ask my advice."

"As you please. May I ask your reasons?"

"First tell me what the proposal is."

"Did he not tell you himself?"

"Possibly. But if you want me to tell you my reasons I must hear the whole thing from you, for he spoke to me under my promise of secrecy. You would do the same in my place. I have always heard you say that in matters of secrecy one must always be on guard against being taken unawares."

"I am incapable of taking a friend unawares; but in general your maxim is sound. I like circumspection. Here is the story. You know that Signora Tiepolo[10] has been left a widow and that Signor Dandolo continues to court her assiduously after having courted her for ten whole years during the lifetime of her husband. The lady, who is still young, beautiful, and fresh, who has very good sense and is sweetness itself, wishes to become his wife. She chose me to confide in, and, seeing nothing that is not praiseworthy in the union, either temporally or spiritually, for you know that we are all human, I was much pleased to take the matter in hand. I even thought I saw that Signor Dandolo was inclined toward it when he said he would give me his answer today. I will tell you sincerely that I was not surprised that he should ask your advice, for it is the part of a sensible man to ask the advice of a prudent friend before he resolves upon an important and decisive step; but I was greatly astonished that such a marriage did not have your approval. Forgive me if, to improve my mind, I ask you to tell me the reasons which make your opinion so different from mine."

Delighted to have discovered everything and to have arrived in time to prevent my friend, who was goodness itself, from contracting a ridiculous marriage, I answered De La Haye that I loved Signor Dandolo and that, knowing his constitution, I was certain that marriage with a woman like Signora Tiepolo would shorten his life.

"That being so," I said, "you must admit that, as a true friend, I was bound to advise him against it. Do you remember telling me that you had never married for the same reason? Do you remember talking to me at great length in Parma in defense of bachelors? Consider too, if you please, that every man is something of an egoist, and that I am entitled to be one when I think that if Signor Dandolo should take a wife his wife's credit with him must have some weight and that whatever influence she gained over him would be at the expense of mine. So you see it would be going against nature if I should advise him to take a step which he could take only to my disadvantage. If you can show me that my arguments are beside the point or are sophistries, speak, and I will yield and make my recantation to Signor Dandolo. Signora Tiepolo will become his wife upon our return to Venice; but I warn you that I will not yield unless I am thoroughly convinced."

"I do not believe I have the power to convince you. I will write to Signora Tiepolo that it is to you that she must apply."

"Do not write that, for she will think you are making a fool of her. Do you think she is stupid enough to expect that I would consent? She knows that I do not like her."

"How can she know that you do not like her?"

"From seeing that I would never let Signor Dandolo take me to call on her. In short, as long as I live with my three friends they shall never have any wife but me. As for you, marry if you please, and I will raise no objection; but if you want us to remain friends give up your scheme of seducing them away from me."

"You are caustic this morning."

"I lost all my money last night."

"Then I chose a bad time. Good-by."

From that day De La Haye became my secret enemy; and he played no small part in my being imprisoned under the Leads two years later, not by calumniating me, for he was incapable of that, but by pious discourses to pious people. If my reader is fond of bigots,

I advise him not to read these memoirs. There was no more talk of the marriage after we returned to Venice. Signor Dandolo continued to pay his court to the widow every day, and I made my oracle forbid me ever to set foot in her house.

Don Antonio Croce,[11] a young Milanese whose acquaintance I had made in Reggio, a great gambler and an old hand at rectifying bad luck, came to call on me just as De La Haye was leaving. He said that, having seen me lose my money, he had come to offer me a way of recouping if I would go halves with him in a faro bank which he would open in his house and at which the punters would be seven or eight rich foreigners, all of whom were paying court to his wife.

"You shall put three hundred zecchini in my bank," he said, "and you shall be my croupier. I have three hundred myself; but it is not enough, for the punters play high. Come to dinner at my house today and you shall meet them all. We can play tomorrow, because it being Friday there is no opera. Be sure that we shall win very large sums, for a Swede named Gillenspetz[12] can lose twenty thousand zecchini all by himself."

Certain that the celebrated swindler did not have designs on me and sure that he knew the secret of winning, I found that I was not conscientious enough to deny him my assistance as his partner and to refuse a half share in his winnings.

CHAPTER XVI

I come into money again. My adventure at
Dolo. Analysis of a long letter from my mis-
tress. P. C. plays me a scurvy trick in Vicenza.
My tragicomic scene at the inn.

The difficulty was to find the money; but in the meanwhile I wanted to make the acquaintance of the gulls and of the idol to whom they did homage. So we went to the Prato della Valle[1] where we found Signora Croce at the coffeehouse, surrounded by foreigners. She was pretty. A secretary to Count Rosenberg,[2] the Imperial Ambassador, who was with her, was the reason why no Venetian nobleman dared to appear in her train. The ones who interested me were the Swede Gillenspetz, a man from Hamburg, an English Jew named Mendex,[3] whom I have already mentioned, and three or four others whom Croce called to my attention. We went to dine and afterwards everyone asked him to make a bank; but he excused himself, which surprised me, for the three hundred zecchini he said he had should have been enough for the skillful player he was; but he cleared my doubt when, taking me to a private room, he showed me fifty fine doblones de a ocho,[4] which amounted to exactly five hundred zecchini. On my promise that I would secure the same amount, he invited them all to supper the next day. Our agreement was that we would divide the winnings before we parted, and that he would let no one play on his word.

It was to Signor Bragadin that I turned to procure the amount, for his money box was always empty. He found a Jewish usurer who, against a note which my benefactor signed, gave me a thousand Venetian ducati[5] at five percent per month, payable at the end of a month and with the interest deducted in advance. It was the amount I needed. I went to supper, he dealt until dawn, and our shares were eight hundred zecchini each. On Saturday Gillenspetz alone lost two thousand zecchini and the Jew Mendex a thousand. On Sunday we did not play and on Monday the bank won four thousand. On Tuesday he had the company to dinner, because I had told him I must go to Venice. He made a bank after dinner, and here is what happened at the end of the afternoon.

An adjutant of the Podestà[6] entered and told him that he had orders from His Excellency to speak to him in private. They went out together and two minutes later my associate came back looking rather embarrassed and told the company that he had just received an order forbidding him to deal in his house. His lady said she felt ill and withdrew, and all the players filed out. After taking half of the money on the table, I left too. He said we would meet again in Venice,[7] for he had been ordered to leave within twenty-four hours. I expected as much, for the young man was too well known, but also for the still stronger reason that the authorities wanted people to lose their money at the gaming room in the theater, where most of the bankers were Venetian noblemen.[8]

I set off at full gallop at nightfall in very bad weather; but nothing could have held me back. I was to receive C. C.'s letter early the next morning.

Six miles from Padua my horse fell on its side, so that I was caught with my left leg under its belly. As my boots were soft, I feared that I had broken it. The postilion, who was riding ahead of me, comes running up, pulls me out, and I am delighted that I have suffered no injury; but my horse was lamed. I make use of my privilege and mount the postilion's horse, but the insolent fellow takes it by the bit and will not let me go. I prove to him that he is in the wrong; but it makes no difference; he holds me back, giving me a quantity of spurious arguments, and I have no time to lose. I fire my pistol at him point-blank, at which he makes off and I pursue my journey. At Dolo[9] I go into the stable and myself saddle a horse which the postilion, to whom I immediately gave a scudo, tells me is excellent. No one is surprised that my postilion has remained behind. It was an hour after midnight, a storm had damaged the road, and, the night being very dark, when I reached Fusina I saw the first light of dawn.

I was told that there would be another storm, but I made light of it, a four-oared boat dared the elements, and I reached home safe and sound, though roughly handled by the rain and the wind. A quarter of an hour later the woman from Murano brought me a letter from C. C., saying that she would come back in two hours for my answer.

The letter was a journal seven pages long, a translation of which would bore my reader; but here is the gist of it. Her father, returned home after talking with Signor Bragadin, had summoned her to his room with her mother and had gently asked her where she had made my acquaintance. She answered that she had talked with me five or six times in her brother's room, where I had asked her if she would consent to become my wife, to which she had replied that she was governed by her father and mother. He had then told her that she was too young to think of marrying and that in any case I had as yet no established position. After that he had gone to the room in which his son was living and had himself bolted the small door opening onto the alley and the door which gave access to his mother's room, ordering him to have me told that she had gone to the country if I came to call on her.

Two days later he told her at the bedside of her mother, who was ill, that her aunt would take her to a convent where she would remain as a boarder until she should receive a husband from the hands of her father and mother. She had answered that, being perfectly obedient to his will, she was very glad to go. He had then promised to visit her there and that when her mother was well she would go too. A quarter of an hour after this conversation she got into a gondola with her aunt, who was her father's sister and who took her to the convent in which she now was. Her bed and all her clothes had been brought the same day, and she was well pleased with her room and with the nun to whom the Abbess had entrusted her and under whose supervision she was. It was this nun who had told her that she was forbidden to receive visits and letters and to write letters, under pain of excommunication. However, the same nun had given her books and everything she needed to copy out the passages she liked; it was at night that she abused this favor by writing to me, having no fear of an excommunication which she considered unreasonable. She said that she thought the woman who carried her letters was discreet and trustworthy, and that she would remain so since, being poor, four zecchini a month would make her rich. She thanked me for the zecchini I had sent her, saying that she would let me know when she needed another from me. She told me, in a very amusing style, that the most beautiful nun in the convent loved her to distraction, that she gave her French lessons twice a day, and had forbidden her to make the acquaintance of her fellow boarders. The nun was only twenty-two years old and, as she was rich and generous, all the other nuns treated her with deference. She said that when they were alone she gave her kisses of which I could rightly be jealous if she were of a different sex. As for my plan of eloping with her, she said she did not think it would be difficult to execute it, but that it would be wiser to wait until she could tell me all about the convent building. She urged me to be true to her, saying that constancy depended upon fidelity; and she ended her letter by asking me for my portrait in a ring, but with a secret device so that no one could see it. She said that I could easily send it to her by her mother, who was well again and went alone every day to the first mass at the church of the P. S.[10] She assured me that her mother would be delighted if I would go there and speak with her. She hoped, she said, that in five or six months she would be in a condition which would scandalize and dishonor the convent if she remained there.

I answered at once, not finishing my letter until I saw the woman. Her name was Laura. After giving her her zecchino I entrusted her with a package in which were fine paper, sealing wax, and a tinderbox. She left, assuring me that my cousin was growing more beautiful every day. C. C. had told her that I was her cousin, and Laura pretended to believe it. Not knowing what to do in Venice, and my honor demanding that I go to Padua, my hurried departure from which might have given rise to such unfavorable conjectures as Croce's had done, I drank a bouillon and set off, going myself to the Roman post for a *bollettone*.[11] It was easy to foresee that my pistol shot near Fiesso[12] and the lamed horse could have put the post masters in a bad humor to the point of refusing me horses; but they had to obey when they saw what is called a *bollettone* in Italy. As for the pistol shot, I had no fear because I knew I had missed the insolent fellow on purpose. But even if I had killed him nothing would have happened to me.

At Fusina I took a two-wheeled *barella*, being extremely tired and even in no condition to ride a horse. I reach Dolo, I am recognized at once, and I am refused horses. The post master comes out and threatens to have me arrested if I do not pay for the horse I had killed. I answer that if the horse is dead I will account for it to the post master in Padua, and I hand him my *bollettone* to read. He says that since I had nearly killed my postilion none of his will serve me. I say that in that case he shall serve me himself. He laughs in my face and goes off. I then go to a notary with two witnesses, I draw up a complaint, and I threaten him with a fine of ten zecchini an hour if he persists in refusing me horses.

At that he sends out a postilion with two rampaging horses; I clearly see that the plan is to have me upset, perhaps into the river. I coldly tell the postilion that the instant he overturns me I will blow out his brains. He goes back with the horses and tells the post master that he will not serve me. Just then a courier arrives at full gallop from Padua and orders six horses for a berlin and two saddle horses. I thereupon tell the post master that he shall give no one horses before me and that if an attempt should be made to use force blood will be shed, and so saying I show him my pistols. He curses and goes off; everyone around me says he is in the wrong.

Five or six minutes later who should appear but Croce in a fine six-horse berlin with his wife, a chambermaid, and footmen in his livery! He had on an imposing uniform. He gets out, we embrace, and I pull a long face and tell him that he will not leave before I do; I explain the reason, and he says I am right. He raises a row, everybody trembles, the post master had taken to his heels, his wife comes down and orders that I be served. Croce says that I am doing well to show myself in Padua, for people were saying that I too had left it by order. He tells me that Signor Gondoin,[13] a colonel in the service of the Duke of Modena, who also made a bank in his house, had likewise been compelled to leave. I promised that I would go to see him in Venice the following week. This man, who had come into my life as if he had dropped from the sky, had won ten thousand zecchini in four sessions, of which I received four thousand nine hundred. I paid all my debts and redeemed all the possessions I had pawned; but what is more, he filled my purse.

On arriving in Padua I found all my friends greatly alarmed except Signor Bragadin, to whose custody I had entrusted my money box the day before. They believed a rumor which was going the rounds that the Podestà had also sent me an order to leave. As I was a Venetian, such an order could not be sent me. Instead of going to bed I dressed in my best to go to the opera unmasked. I told them that I must go to give the lie to everything that evil tongues had been saying about me.

"I am delighted," said De La Haye, "if everything that is being said is false, but you have only yourself to blame. Your hurried departure did you this injustice. People want to know the reason for everything, and when they do not know it they invent one. However, it is certain that you tried to kill the postilion; give thanks to God that you missed him."

"Another slander. Do you think that a pistol fired point-blank can miss?"

"But the horse is dead, and you must pay for it."

"I will not pay for it, for the postilion was ahead of me. Do you know the rules of the post? Besides, I was in a hurry. I had promised a lady to breakfast with her that morning."

He seemed annoyed when, after this dialogue, I returned to him all the money he had lent me in Vienna. A man can reason well only when he has money, unless a tumultuous passion makes him lose patience. Signor Bragadin said that I would do well to go to the opera unmasked.

On my appearance in the parterre I saw that everyone was astonished, and whoever spoke to me congratulated me, whether sincerely or not. After the first ballet I went to the gaming room and in three or four deals I won five hundred zecchini. Dying with sleep and hunger, I went home to boast of my victories. My dear Bavois borrowed fifty zecchini from me, which he never returned; but it is true that I never asked him for them.

Still thinking of C. C., I spent the whole next day having my portrait painted in miniature by a skillful Piedmontese who had come to the fair and who later made a great deal of money in Venice; he also painted me a St. Catherine[14] of the same size. A Venetian who was an excellent jeweler made the ring for me surpassingly well. The figure one saw was the saint. An almost invisible blue dot on the white enamel which surrounded her was to be pushed with the point of a pin. The saint sprang up and my portrait appeared, a very good likeness. He delivered it to me four days later, as he had promised.

On Friday, just as we were getting up from table, a letter was brought for me. I was surprised to see that it was P. C. asking me to come to him at once at the "Star" (this was the posthouse inn). He said that he had news to tell me which would interest me greatly. I thought it was something which concerned his sister and I went at once.

I found him, as I expected, with his mistress C. After congratulating him on being out of prison, I asked him what the interesting news was. He said he was certain that his sister was being boarded in a convent and assured me that he would be able to tell me the name of the convent as soon as he returned to Venice. I answered that he would be doing me a favor. But the news was only a means to get me to come and talk with him. The reason for his zeal was something else. He told me exultantly that he had sold a three-year lease on his right to supply cattle for fifteen thousand florins, and that the contracting party with whom he had made the transaction had got him out of prison by standing surety for him and had advanced him six thousand florins in the form of four bills of exchange. He at once showed them to me, all four of them honored by a name which I did not know but of whose excellent reputation he assured me.

"I want to buy," he went on, "six thousand florins' worth of silks from the manufactories in Vicenza, paying the makers by these notes, which are to my order and which I will make over to theirs. I am certain to sell the silks and make a profit of ten percent. Come with us, and I will give you silks to the value of two hundred zecchini; and thus you will be covered for the two hundred zecchini you guaranteed for me on the ring. It will take us only twenty-four hours to finish the whole business."

I should not have gone; but my wish to have the value of my guarantee in my hands overcame my judgment. I consented. "If I do not go," I said to myself, "he will sell the goods at once at a loss of twenty-five percent, and my money will be gone." So I promised to leave with them early the next day. He showed me letters of recommendation to the leading houses in Vicenza. An avariciousness which was not in my character made me fall into the trap.

So very early the next morning I am at the "Star." Four horses are harnessed. The innkeeper comes upstairs with the account and P. C. asks me to pay it; I see a bill for five zecchini, four of which had been paid out by the innkeeper, for the Signore owed them to the *vetturino* he had engaged at Fusina. I paid, with a little laugh. The scoundrel had left Venice without a soldo. We got into the carriage, we reach Vicenza in three hours and put up at the "Sign of the Hat."[15] He orders a choice dinner, then leaves me with his lady while he goes to talk with the cloth manufacturers.

Signora C. begins by treating me to reproaches which I disdain. She says that it is eighteen years since she began to love me, that we were both nine years old when we saw each other for the first time in Padua. She brings it back to me. She was the daughter of the Abate Grimani's antiquarian friend who had put me to board with the Slavonian woman. Her story makes me smile, for I recollect that her mother was fond of me.[16]

But in come some shopboys, already bringing lengths of goods. Signora C. is delighted. In less than two hours the room is full of silks. P. C. arrives with two manufacturers whom he has invited to dinner. C. flirts with them, we dine, there is a great plenty of fine wines. After dinner more goods are brought; P. C. lists them, with their prices; but he wants still more. He is promised that he shall have more the next day, though it is a Sunday.

Toward nightfall several Counts arrive; for in Vicenza all noblemen are Counts.[17] P. C. had left his letters of introduction at their houses. There were a Count Velo, a Count Sesso, and a very pleasant Count Trento; they invite us to the casino which the nobility frequented. C. is admired there. After spending two hours at the casino, P. C. invites them to sup with us. Gaiety and profusion. I was bored to death; I said nothing; no one spoke to me. I go to bed in a room on the third floor, leaving them at the table. In the morning I come down for breakfast, and until noon I see so many lengths of goods that there must be enough. P. C. tells me that the whole transaction will be completed during the course of the next day and that we are invited to a ball at which all the nobility will be present. The manufacturers with whom he had been dealing all came to dinner with us. The same profusion.

At the ball that evening I really lost my patience. Everyone talked with C. and with P. C., who said nothing worth hearing, and when I said anything no one listened. I take a lady out to dance a minuet, she dances it, but looking this way and that. A quadrille is made up, and I find I am left out and that the same lady who refused me is dancing with another man. If I had been in good spirits I would have put up with it; but I preferred to return to the inn at once and go to bed, at a loss to understand what reason the nobility of Vicenza could have to treat me in such a fashion. Perhaps I was neglected because I was not named in the letters which P. C. had presented; but the rules of politeness could not be unknown to them. I possess my soul in patience. We were to leave the next day.

The next day the tired couple slept until noon. After dinner P. C. went out to pay for the goods he had chosen. We were to leave the next day, Tuesday, early in the morning. The Counts, whom C. had enchanted, came to supper. I left them still at table, impatient for the next day to come, for I must be in Venice early on Wednesday.

In the morning the inn boy comes up and tells me that breakfast is ready in the room downstairs; I delay a little. He comes up again and tells me that my wife asks me to hurry. At the word "wife" my hand strikes the poor innocent's face while my feet kicking his belly show him to the stairs, which he descends headlong at the risk of breaking his neck.

I go down furious, I enter the room in which I am awaited, and I ask P. C. who is the blackguard who has announced me at the inn as the Signora's husband; and just as he is answering that he knows nothing about it, in comes the innkeeper with a knife in his hand and asks me why I had kicked his nephew downstairs. I ask him, pistol in hand, who had told him that I was the woman's husband. He replies that it was Captain P. C. himself who had registered the party. I thereupon seize the Captain by his coat collar, I push him against the wall, and it is the innkeeper who, dropping the knife, prevents me from breaking his head open with the butt of my pistol. The Signora, as always, appeared to be in a faint. The scoundrel did nothing but shout, *"It is not true, it is not true."* The innkeeper goes downstairs and quickly comes back with the register, and, with a murderous look, holds it under the villain's eyes, defying him to repeat that it was not he who had dictated: *"P. C., Captain in the Imperial Army, with Signor and Signora Casanova."* He answers that he had misunderstood him, at which the innkeeper hits him in the face with the book. When I see the coward swallow this insult without remembering that he had a sword and was wearing a uniform, I left the room and, going upstairs, told the innkeeper's nephew to order me a *barella* and two horses for Padua at once. Frothing with rage, I put my possessions in a traveling bag, realizing too late the unpardonable error a decent man commits when he associates with scoundrels. But in comes Signora C.

"Leave this room, for I am furious, and I should not respect your sex."

She drops into an armchair and, bursting into tears, says that she is innocent; she swears that when the shameless knave dictated the registration she was not present. The innkeeper's wife comes in and tells me the same. At that my anger begins to evaporate in words; and from my window I see the *barella* I had ordered standing ready at the door. I send for the innkeeper, to pay him whatever my share may be. He replies that, since I had ordered nothing, I owed him nothing. At this juncture in comes Count Velo.

"I wager, Signor Conte, that you thought this woman is my wife."

"The whole town knows it."

"Hell and damnation! I am astonished that you should have thought so when you know that I lodge alone in this room and when you saw me retire last night leaving her with you all."

"There are accommodating husbands."

"I am not one of them, and you are no judge of men of honor. Let us go outside and I will prove it to you."

The Count quickly made for the stairs and left the inn. C. was choking, and I felt no pity for her. But then it occurs to me that if I leave without paying anything people would laugh at the scene I had made and say I had had a share in the swindle. I order the innkeeper to bring me the bill, as I insisted on paying half of it. He goes for it at once, whereupon I am treated to a fresh surprise. Signora C., falling to her knees and weeping, says that if I abandon her she is lost, for she has neither money nor anything to pawn.

"What! Have you not four thousand scudi worth of goods?"

"They have all been taken away. Did you not know it? The bills of exchange which you saw and which we thought were as good as ready money only made the gentlemen laugh; they took back all the lengths of goods we had chosen. Is it possible?"

"The scoundrel foresaw everything, and that is why he got me to come here. But I am ashamed to complain. I did a stupid thing, and I must pay the penalty."

The bill which the innkeeper brought me came to forty zecchini, an enormous amount for three days; but the money he had paid out was included. I instantly realized that my honor demanded that I pay the whole of it, and I fulfilled the obligation on the spot, taking a receipt signed by two witnesses. I gave the innkeeper's nephew two zecchini to forgive me for having mistreated him, and I refused two to C., who sent the innkeeper's wife to ask me for them.

So ended this ugly affair, which taught me a lesson, but one which I should not have needed. Two or three weeks later I learned that Count Trento had packed off the two wretches, with whom I refused to have any further dealings. A month later P. C. was back in prison, the man who had stood surety for him having gone bankrupt. He had the effrontery to send me a long letter asking me to come to see him; but I did not even answer it. I did the same to Signora C., who was reduced to poverty.

I stopped in Padua only to get my ring and to dine with Signor Bragadin, who returned to Venice a few days afterward.

C. C.'s letter, which Laura brought me punctually the next morning, told me nothing new. In my answer I gave her a detailed account of the trick her brother had played on me, and I told her to expect her ring, explaining its secret to her.

So, following the instructions she had given me, at dawn one morning I stationed myself at a place from which I saw her mother enter the church. Kneeling down beside her I said I must speak with her, and she came to the cloister. After trying to console her and assuring her that I would remain constant in my love for her daughter until the day of my death, I asked her if she went to visit her. She answered that she expected to go on Sunday and that she was sorry she could not tell me in what convent she was. I said there was no use in my knowing and that I only begged her to tell her that my heart was hers alone and to give her the ring, which I showed her.

"It is the likeness," I said, "of her patron saint, without whose protection she will never become my wife."

She was to keep it on her finger day and night, and say a Paternoster and an Ave Maria to it every day. I said that I did the same with my patron San Giacomo, reciting a Credo to him every day.

Delighted that she could teach her daughter this new devotion, she took the ring and promised to deliver it to her. I left her, giving her two zecchini which her daughter might be glad to have to satisfy her small needs. She accepted them, at the same time assuring me that she did not lack anything she needed.

In the letter she wrote me the following Wednesday I found the quintessence of true love. She said that as soon as she was alone nothing was quicker than the point of the pin with which she made St. Catherine spring up. She then kissed my portrait a hundred times and did not leave off if someone came in, for she instantly made the cover drop over it. The nuns were all edified by her confidence in the protection of her blessed patron, whose features by some chance, all the convent said, resembled hers. She said that for that reason the nun who taught her French had offered her fifty zecchini for her ring—not for love of the saint, at whom she had laughed when she read her life, but because she looked like her. The two zecchini I had sent her were very precious to her for, since her mother had given them to her publicly, she could use them as she pleased without arousing idle speculation in those who, seeing her spending money, might wonder from where she could have received it. She liked to make "little presents" to her fellow boarders. She said that her mother had praised my Christian piety, and she ended her very long letter by asking me not to tell her any more news of her brother.

For three or four weeks her letters were about nothing but her St. Catherine, which made her shake with fear when it was in the hands of some nun who, being shortsighted, rubbed the enamel. "Where would I be," she wrote me, "if at such a moment the spring worked and the nun suddenly saw a face which certainly does not look like a saint's? Tell me what I should do."

A month after P. C. was put in prison the merchant who had sold him the ring for two hundred zecchini gave me the note, reconciling himself to losing twenty. I sent it to the wretch in his prison, who kept writing me asking for money.

Croce was the talk of Venice. He kept a fine house; he dealt at faro and cleaned out the punters. Foreseeing what would happen sooner or later, I never set foot there; but his wife having given birth to a boy[18] and asking me to stand godfather to him, I went there and stayed for supper. From then on I never set foot in his house again.

HISTORY OF MY LIFE

Volume Four

CHAPTER I

I receive an anonymous letter
from a nun and I answer it. Love intrigue.

[* * *]

1753.

On All Saints' Day, just as I was about to get into my gondola to return to Venice after hearing mass, I met a woman of the same type as Laura, who, after letting a letter drop at my feet, walked on. I pick it up and I see the same woman, satisfied that she had seen me do so, pursue her way. The letter was white and sealed with wax the color of aventurine.[1] The imprint represented a running knot. No sooner have I entered the gondola than I unseal it and read the following:

"A nun who has seen you in her church every feast day for the past two and a half months wishes you to make her acquaintance. A pamphlet which you lost and which has come into her hands assures her that you understand French. However, you may answer her in Italian, for she desires clarity and precision. She does not invite you to have her summoned to the visiting room, because before you obligate yourself to speak with her she wishes you to see her. So she will give you the name of a lady whom you can accompany to the visiting room, who will not know you, and hence will not be compelled to introduce you if by any chance you do not wish to be known.

"If this seems to you unsuitable, the same nun who writes you this letter will give you the address of a casino here in Murano where you will find her alone at the first hour of the night on the day you indicate to her; you can stay and sup with her, or leave a quarter of an hour later if you have business.

"Would you prefer to offer her supper in Venice? Let her know the day, the hour of the night, and the place to which she is to go, and you will see her leave a gondola masked, provided you are on the quay alone, without a servant, masked, and holding a candle.

"Being certain that you will answer me, and as impatient as you can imagine to read your answer, I beg you to deliver it tomorrow to the same woman who brought you this letter. You will find her an hour before noon in the Church of San Canziano[2] at the first altar on the right.

"Consider that if I had not supposed you to be well disposed and honorable, I should never have resolved to take a step which might give you an unfavorable opinion of me."

The tone of this letter, which I copy word for word, surprised me even more than its contents. I had business, but I dismissed everything to shut myself in my room and answer. Making such a request was sheer madness, yet I found a dignity in it which forced me to respect her. I was at first inclined to believe that the nun might be the one who was teaching C. C. French and who was beautiful, rich, and a flirt, and that my dear wife might have been indiscreet yet know nothing about this unheard-of step on her friend's part, and for that reason had been unable to notify me of it. But I dismissed the suspicion precisely because it pleased me. C. C. had written me that the nun who taught her French was not the only one who had a good command of the language. I could not doubt C. C.'s discretion and the candor with which she would have confessed it to me if she had confided anything at all to the nun. However, since the nun who had written me might be C. C.'s beautiful friend or might be someone else, I wrote her an answer in which I straddled the ditch as far as good manners permitted me to do so; here it is:

"I hope, Madame, that my answer in French will detract nothing from the clarity and precision which you demand and of which you set me an example.

"The subject is most interesting; it seems to me of the greatest moment under the circumstances, and obliged to give an answer without knowing to whom, do you not understand, Madame, that, not being a conceited fool, I must fear a snare? It is honor which obliges me to be on my guard. If it is true, then, that the pen which writes to me is that of a respectable lady who does me the justice to suppose me possessed of a soul as noble and a heart as well disposed as her own, she will find, I hope, that I can answer her only in the following terms:

"If you have thought me worthy, Madame, of making your acquaintance personally, your opinion of me being based only on my appearance, I consider it my duty to obey you if only to disabuse you should I by chance have involuntarily led you into error.

"Of the three arrangements which you have been so generous as to propose to me, I dare choose only the first, on the conditions which your very clear foresight has stipulated. I shall accompany to your visiting room a lady whom you will name to me and who will not know me. Hence there will be no question of introducing me. Be indulgent, Madame, to the specious reasons which oblige me not to name myself. In exchange, I promise you on my honor that your name will become known to me only that I may do you homage. If you see fit to speak to me I will answer you only with the most profound respect. Permit me to hope that you will be alone at the grating and to tell you for form's sake that I am a Venetian and free in the fullest sense of the word. The only reason which prevents me from deciding on the two other arrangements which you propose to me and which do me infinite honor is, permit me to repeat, my fear of being trapped. Those happy meetings can take place as soon as you have become better acquainted with me and no doubts trouble my soul, which abhors falsehood. Very impatient in my turn, I will go tomorrow at the same hour to San Canziano to receive your answer."

Having found the woman at the appointed place, I gave her my letter and a zecchino. The next morning I returned there and she came up to me. After giving me back my zecchino she handed me the following answer, asking me to go and read it and to come back afterward to tell her if she should wait for an answer. After reading it I went and told her that I had no answer to give her. This is what the nun's letter to me said:

"I believe, Monsieur, that I have been mistaken in nothing. Like yourself, I abhor falsehood when it can have consequences; but I consider it only a trifle when it harms no one. Of my three proposals you have chosen the one which does most honor to your perception. Respecting the reasons you may have for concealing your name, I write the Countess S.[3] what I ask you to read in the note herewith. You will seal it before having it delivered to her. She will be forewarned of it by another note. You will go to her house at your convenience; she will appoint an hour and you will accompany her here in her own gondola. She will not interrogate you, and you need give her no explanations. There will be no question of an introduction; but since you will learn my name, it will rest with you to come to see me masked whenever you wish, asking for me in the name of the same Countess. Thus we shall become acquainted without your being obliged to sacrifice any of the evening hours which may be precious to you. I have ordered the woman who brings this to wait for your answer in case you should be known to the Countess and hence unwilling to make this use of her. If my choice is agreeable to you tell the woman that you have no answer to send; whereupon she will take my note to the Countess. You may take the other to her at your convenience."

I told the woman that I had no answer to send when I was certain that I was not known to the Countess, whose name I had never heard. Here is the wording of the note I was to deliver to her:

"I beg you, my dear friend, to come and speak with me when you have time, and to name your hour to the masker who brings you this note so that he can accompany you. He will be punctual. You will greatly oblige your loving friend."

The address was to the Countess S., Riva del Rio Marin.[4] I thought the note a masterpiece of the spirit of intrigue. There was something lofty in this way of proceeding. I was made to play the role of a person who was being granted a favor. I saw it all clearly.

In her last letter the nun, showing no interest in who I was, approved my choice and tried to appear indifferent to nocturnal meetings; but she expected, and even seemed certain, that I would come and have her called to the visiting room after I had seen her. Her certainty increased my curiosity. She had reason to hope that I would do it if she was young and pretty. It was perfectly possible for me to delay for three or four days and find out from C. C. who the nun might be; but aside from its being an underhanded action, I was afraid I should spoil my chances and be sorry. She told me to call on the Countess at my convenience; her dignity demanded that she should not seem eager; but she knew that I must be so. She seemed too much at home in intrigue for me to believe her a novice and inexperienced; I feared I would repent of having wasted my time; and I prepared to laugh if I found I was with some old woman. In short, it is certain that I would not have gone had I not felt curious to see what sort of face a woman of this kind would put upon a meeting with me after she had offered to come to supper with me in Venice. Then, too, I was much surprised at the great freedom enjoyed by these holy virgins, who could so easily violate their rule of enclosure.

At three in the afternoon I sent a note in to the Countess S. She came out a minute later from the room in which she was entertaining guests and said that she would be glad if I would call at her house the next day at the same hour; and after dropping me a fine curtsy she withdrew. She was a domineering woman, beginning to fade a little but still beautiful.

The next morning, which was a Sunday, I went to mass at my usual hour, in my finest clothes and with my hair elegantly dressed, and already unfaithful in imagination to my dear C. C., for I was more concerned with displaying myself to the nun, be she young or old, than to her.

After dinner I mask and at the appointed hour go to call on the Countess, who was waiting for me. We go down, get into a commodious two-oared gondola, we arrive at the convent of the XXX[5] without having talked of anything but the beautiful autumn we were enjoying. She asks to see M. M.[6] The name astonishes me, for the bearer of it was celebrated. We go into a small visiting room, and five minutes later I see M. M. appear, go straight to the grating, open four square sections of it by pressing a spring, embrace her friend, then close the ingenious window again. The four sections made an opening eighteen inches square. Any man of my stature could have passed through it. The Countess sat down facing the nun and I on the other side in a position from which I could examine this rare beauty of twenty-two or twenty-three years at my ease. I decide at once that she must be the same nun whom C. C. had praised to me, the one who loved her dearly and was teaching her French.

Very nearly beside myself with admiration, I heard nothing of what they said. As for me, not only did the nun not once speak to me, she did not condescend to give me a single look. She was a perfect beauty, tall, so white of complexion as to verge on pallor, with an air of nobility and decision but at the same time of reserve and shyness, large blue eyes; a sweet, smiling face, beautiful lips damp with dew, which allowed a glimpse of two magnificent rows of teeth; her nun's habit did not let me see any hair; but whether she had it or not, its color must be light chestnut; her eyebrows told me as much; but what I found admirable and surprising were her hand and forearm, which I saw to the elbow: it was impossible to see anything more perfect. No veins were visible, and instead of muscles I saw only dimples. Despite all this I did not regret having refused the two meetings over a supper which the divine beauty had offered me. Sure that I should possess her in a few days, I enjoyed the pleasure of paying her the tribute of desiring her. I could not wait to be alone with her at the grating, and I thought I should have committed the worst of offenses if I had waited any longer than the next day to assure her that I had accorded her qualities all the justice they deserved. She continued not to look at me; but in the end it pleased me.

Suddenly the two ladies lowered their voices and put their heads together; as this indicated that I was one too many, I slowly walked away from the grating and looked at a painting. A quarter of an hour later they bade each other good-by, after embracing at the movable window. The nun turned away without giving me an opportunity even to bow to her. On the way back to Venice the Countess, perhaps tiring of my silence, remarked with a smile:

"*M. M. is beautiful, but her mind is even more extraordinary.*"

"I have seen the one and I believe the other."

"She did not say a word to you."

"Since I did not wish to be introduced to her, she wished to ignore my being there. It was her way of punishing me."

The Countess having made no reply, we arrived at her house without opening our mouths again. I left her at her door, because it was there that she dropped me the fine curtsy which means, "Thank you. Good-by." I went elsewhere to muse over the strange adventure, whose inevitable consequences I was eager to see.

CHAPTER II

Countess Coronini. Wounded feelings.
Reconciliation. First meeting. Philosophical
digression.

[* * *]

The next morning I went to call on Countess Coronini,[1] who chose to live in the convent of Santa Giustina.[2] She was an old woman with a long experience of all the courts of Europe and who had made a reputation by taking a hand in their affairs. The desire for repose which follows disgust had made her choose the convent as her retreat. I had been introduced to her by a nun who was a relative of Signor Dandolo. This former beauty, finding that she no longer wished to exercise her considerable intelligence in the machinations of royal self-interest, kept it entertained with the frivolous gossip with which the city in which she lived supplied her. She knew everything and, as was only to be expected, always wanted to know more. She received all the ambassadors at her grating, and in consequence every foreigner was introduced to her, and several grave Senators from time to time paid her long visits. Curiosity was always the mainspring of these visits on either side; but it was concealed under the veil of the interest which the nobility may be expected to take in whatever is going on. In short, Signora Coronini knew everything and took pleasure in giving me very entertaining lessons in morals when I went to see her. As I was to call on M. M. in the afternoon I thought that I should succeed in learning something about the nun from the well-informed Countess.

As I found it perfectly easy, after some other subjects, to bring the conversation around to that of the convents in Venice, we were soon discussing the intelligence and reputation of a nun of the Celsi[3] family, who, though ugly, exercised great influence in whatever quarter she pleased. We then spoke of the young and charming nun of the Micheli family[4] who had taken the veil to prove to her mother that she was the more intelligent of the two. Speaking of several other beauties who were said to indulge in love affairs, I named M. M. and said that she must be of the same stamp, but that she was an enigma.

The Countess smiled and answered that she was not an enigma to everybody but that she must be so to people in general.

"But what really is an enigma," she added, "is her suddenly having taken the veil when she is rich, highly intelligent, very cultivated, and, so far as I know, a freethinker. She became a nun for no reason, either physical or moral. It was sheer caprice."

"Do you think she is happy, Signora?"

"Yes, if she has not repented and if repentance does not overtake her—which, if she is wise, she will keep to herself."

Convinced by the Countess's mysterious tone that M. M. must have a lover, but resolved not to let it trouble me, I mask after dining without appetite, I go to Murano, I ring at the gate, and, with my heart racing, I ask for M. M. in the name of Countess S. The small visiting room was closed. I am shown the one I am to enter. I take off my mask, put it on my hat, and sit down to wait for the goddess. She was long in coming, but instead of making me impatient the wait pleased me; I feared the moment of our interview and even its effect. But an hour having gone by very quickly, such a delay seemed to me unnatural. Surely she had not been informed. I rise, resuming my mask, go back to the gate, and ask if I have been announced to Mother M. M. A voice answers yes, and that I had only to wait. I returned to my chair, a little thoughtful, and a few minutes later I see a hideous lay sister, who says:

"Mother M. M. is occupied the whole day."

The words were scarcely spoken before she was gone.

Such are the terrible moments to which a pursuer of women is exposed; there is nothing more cruel. They degrade, they distress, they kill. In my revulsion and humiliation, my first feeling was contempt for myself, a dark contempt which approached the limits of horror. The second was disdainful indignation toward the nun, on whom I passed the judgment she appeared to deserve. She was mad, a wretched creature, shameless. My only consolation was to think her such. She could not have acted toward me as she had done unless she was the most impudent of women, the most lacking in common sense; for her two letters, which were in my possession, were enough to dishonor her if I wanted to avenge myself, and what she had done cried for vengeance. She could only defy it if she was more than mad; her behavior was that of a raving maniac. I would already have thought her out of her mind, if I had not heard her talk rationally with the Countess.

Yet in the tumult which shame and anger aroused in my soul *affixa humo* ("fastened to the earth")[5] I was encouraged by discerning

422

lucid intervals. I saw clearly, laughing at myself, that if the nun's beauty and stately bearing had not dazzled me and made me fall in love, and if a certain amount of prejudice had not entered in as well, the whole thing would not amount to much. I saw that I could pretend to laugh at it, and that no one would be able to guess that I was only pretending.

Aware, despite all this, that I had been insulted, I saw that I must take my revenge, but that there must be nothing base in it; and no less aware that I must not give her the least opportunity to crow over having played a practical joke on me, I saw that I must not show any vexation. She had sent me word that she was engaged, and that was all. I must pretend indifference. Another time she would not be engaged; but I defied her to trap me another time. I thought I ought to convince her that her behavior had only made me laugh. I must, of course, send her back the originals of her letters, but enclosed in a short and sufficient one from me. What greatly annoyed me was that I must certainly stop going to mass at her church, for since she had no idea that I went there for C. C., she might have supposed that I would be going only in the hope that she would make some apology and would again offer me the opportunities to meet her which I had rejected. I wanted her to be certain that I scorned her. For a moment I believed that the meetings she had proposed were merely figments to deceive me.

I fell asleep about midnight with this plan in mind, and on waking in the morning I found it ripe. I wrote a letter and after writing it I put it aside for another twenty-four hours to see if, when I read it over, it would show even a trace of the wounded feelings which were tormenting me.

I did well, for when I read it over the next morning I thought it unworthy of me. I quickly tore it up. There were expressions in it which revealed that I was weak, pusillanimous, and in love, and so would have made her laugh. There were others which betrayed anger, and others which showed that I was sorry to have lost all hope of possessing her.

The next day I wrote her another, after writing to C. C. that serious reasons forced me to stop going to hear mass at her church. But the next morning I thought my letter laughable, and I tore it up. It seemed to me that I had lost my ability to write, and I did not realize the reason for my difficulty until ten days after she had insulted me. I had one.

Sincerum est nisi vas, quodcumque in fundis acescit.

("Unless the vessel is clean, whatever is put in it turns sour.")[6]

M. M.'s face had made an impression on me which could not be effaced by the greatest and most powerful of abstract beings—by Time.

In my ridiculous situation I was tempted again and again to go and tell my troubles to Countess S.; but—thank God!—I never went any farther than her door. The thought coming to me at last that the harebrained nun must be living in terror because of her letters, with which I could ruin her reputation and do the greatest harm to the convent, I resolved to send them to her with a note in the following terms. But it was not until ten or twelve days after the incident.

"I beg you to believe, Madame, that it was by an oversight that I did not immediately send you your two letters, which you will find herewith. I have never thought of departing from what I am by taking a base revenge. I am obliged to forgive you for two pieces of folly, whether you committed them naturally and unthinkingly or to mock me; but I advise you not to act in the same manner toward some other man in the future, for not everyone is like me. I know your name; but I assure you it is as if I did not know it. I tell you this though it is possible that you care nothing for my discretion; but if that is the case I am sorry for you.

"You will no longer see me in your church, Madame, and it will cost me nothing, for I will go to another; yet I think it proper that I should tell you the reason. I consider it likely that you have committed the third folly of boasting of your exploit to some of your friends, and so I am ashamed to put in an appearance. Forgive me if despite my being, as I suppose, five or six years older than you, I have not yet trampled upon all prejudices; believe me, Madame, there are some which should never be shaken off. Do not take it amiss if I give you this little lesson, after the only too substantial one which you apparently gave me only in mockery. Be certain that I will profit by it all the rest of my life."

I felt that my letter was the gentlest treatment I could give the giddy nun. I went out and, calling aside a Friulian,[7] who could not recognize me under my mask, I gave him my letter, which contained the two others, and gave him forty soldi to take it at once to its address in Murano, promising him another forty when he should come back to tell me he had faithfully done his errand. The instructions I gave him were that he should deliver the packet to the portress, then leave without waiting for an answer even if the portress told him to wait. But it would have been a mistake on my

424

part to wait for him. In our city the Friulians are as reliable and trustworthy as the Savoyards[8] were in Paris ten years ago.

Five or six days later, as I was coming out of the opera, I see the same Friulian carrying his lantern. I call him and, not taking off my mask, ask him if he knows me; after looking at me attentively he says he does not. I ask him if he had done the errand in Murano on which I sent him.

"Ah, Signore! God be praised! Since it is you I have something urgent to tell you. I took your letter as you ordered me to, and after delivering it to the portress I left despite her telling me to wait. When I got back I did not find you, but what of it? The next morning a Friulian of my acquaintance, who was at the gate when I delivered your letter, came and woke me to tell me I must go to Murano, because the portress insisted on talking to me. I went, and after making me wait for a time she told me to go into the visiting room, where a nun wished to speak with me. The nun, who was as beautiful as the morning star, kept me for an hour and more, asking me countless questions all directed to learning, if not who you are, at least some way of my discovering where I could find you; but it was all to no avail since I knew nothing about you.

"She left, ordering me to wait, and two hours later she reappeared with a letter. She gave it to me and said that if I could manage to deliver it to you and bring her the answer she would give me two zecchini; but that if I did not find you I should go to Murano every day and show her her letter, promising me forty soldi for each trip I made. Up to now I have earned twenty lire; but I am afraid she will get tired of it. You have only to answer her letter and I will earn the two zecchini."[9]

"Where is it?"

"Locked up where I live, for I am always afraid of losing it."

"Then how am I to answer it?"

"Wait for me here. You will see me back with the letter in a quarter of an hour."

"I will not wait for you, for I have no interest in answering it; but tell me how you persuaded the nun to believe that you could find me. You are a rascal. It is not likely that she would have entrusted her letter to you if you had not given her reason to expect you to find me."

"That is so. I described your coat to her, and your buckles, and your height. I assure you that for the last ten days I have looked carefully at every masker of your height, but in vain. It is your buckles there that I recognized; but I should not have recognized you by your coat. Alas, Signore! It will cost you nothing to answer only a line. Wait for me in that coffeehouse."

Unable any longer to overcome my curiosity, I decide not to wait for him but to go with him to his lodging. I did not think I was obliged to answer more than: "I have received your letter. Farewell." The next morning I would have changed buckles and sold the coat. So I go to his door with the Friulian, he goes for the letter, hands it to me, and I take him with me to an inn where, to read the letter at leisure, I engage a room, have a fire lighted, and tell him to wait for me outside. I unseal the packet, and the first thing which surprises me is the two letters she had written me and which I had thought I should return to her to set her heart at rest. At the sight I am seized by a palpitation which already heralds my defeat. Besides the two letters I see a short one signed "S." It was addressed to "M. M." I read it, and I find:

"The masker who escorted me to the convent and home again would never have opened his lips to say a word to me if I had not taken it into my head to tell him that the charms of your mind are even more winning than those of your face. He answered that he wished to become acquainted with the former and that he was certain of the latter. I added that I did not understand why you had not spoken to him; and he answered with a smile that you wanted to punish him and that since he had not wished to be introduced to you, you in your turn wished to ignore his presence. I wanted to send you this note this morning; but I could not. Farewell. S. F."

After reading the Countess's note, which neither added nor subtracted an iota from the truth, and which might be a piece of evidence for the defense, my heart beat less violently. Delighted to discover that I am on the verge of being convinced that I was wrong, I pluck up my courage, and this is what I find in the letter from M. M.:

"From a weakness which I consider thoroughly excusable, curious to know what you might have found to say about me to the Countess on your way to visit me and when you took her back home, I seized the moment when you were walking up and down in the visiting room to ask her to inform me. I told her to send me word at once, or at latest the next morning, for I foresaw that in the afternoon you would certainly come to pay me a duty call. Her note, which I send you and which I ask you to read, reached me a half hour after you were sent away. First fatal mishap. Not having received her letter when you asked to see me, I did not have the courage to receive you. Second fatal weakness, for which I can easily be forgiven. I ordered the lay sister to tell you that I was 'ill the whole day.' A perfectly legitimate excuse whether it is true or false, for it is a polite lie in which the words 'the whole day' convey all. You had already left and I could not send someone running after you when the idiotic old woman came and reported to me what she had told you, not that I was 'ill,' but that I was 'occupied.' Third fatal mishap. You cannot imagine what I wanted to say, and to do, to the lay sister in my righteous anger; but here one can neither do nor say anything. One can only be patient, dissimulate, and thank God when mistakes arise from ignorance rather than from malice. I at once foresaw in part what did indeed happen, for human reason could never have foreseen it all. I guessed that, believing you had been duped, you would be disgusted, and I felt the blackest misery since I saw no way to let you know the truth until the feast day. I was certain that you would come to our church. Who could have guessed that you would take the thing with the extraordinary violence which your letter set before my eyes? When I did not see you appear in church my grief began to be unbearable, for it was mortal, but it drove me to despair and pierced my heart when I read, ten days after the event, the cruel, barbarous, unjust letter which you wrote me. It made me wretched, and I will die of it unless you come to justify yourself immediately. You thought you had been duped— that is all you can say, and you are now convinced that you were mistaken. But even believing that you were duped, you must admit that to take the course you did and to write me the terrible letter you sent me, you must imagine me a monster not to be found among women who, like myself, are well born and have been well brought up. I send you back the two letters which you sent back to me to soothe my fears. Know that I am a better physiognomist than you are, and that what I did I did not do out of 'folly.' I have never thought you capable of a base action, even if you were certain that I had brazenly duped you; but in my countenance you have seen only the soul of shamelessness. You will perhaps be the cause of my death, or at least you will make me wretched for all the rest of my life, if you do not wish to justify yourself; since, for my part, I believe I am justified completely.

"Consider that, even if my life is of no concern to you, your honor demands that you come to talk with me at once. You must come in person to recant all that you have written me. If you do not realize the terrible effect your infernal letter must have on the soul of an innocent woman, and one who is not out of her mind, permit me to feel sorry for you. You would not have the slightest knowledge of the human heart. But I am sure you will come, if the man to whom I am entrusting this letter finds you. M. M."

I did not need to read her letter twice to be in despair. M. M. was right. I at once masked to go out of the room and speak to the Friulian. I asked him if he had spoken with her that morning and if she looked ill. He replied that he thought she looked more dejected every day. I went back, telling him to wait.

I did not finish writing to her until daybreak. Here, word for word, is the letter which I wrote to the noblest of all women, whom, drawing the wrong conclusion, I had most cruelly insulted.

"I am guilty, Madame, and as unable to justify myself as I am completely convinced of your innocence. I cannot live except in the hope of your forgiveness, and you will grant it to me when you reflect upon what made me commit my crime. I saw you, you dazzled me, and, thinking of my honor,[10] it seemed to me chimerical; I thought I was dreaming. I saw that I could not be rid of my doubt until twenty-four hours later, and God alone knows how long they seemed to me. They passed at last, and my heart palpitated when I was in the visiting room counting the minutes. At the end of sixty—which, however, as the result of a kind of impatience entirely new to me, went by very quickly—I see an ill-omened figure which, with odious brevity, tells me that you are 'occupied' for the whole day; then it makes off. Imagine the rest! Alas, it was nothing short of a thunderbolt, *which did not kill me and did not leave me alive.* Dare I tell you, Madame, that if you had sent me, even by the hands of the same lay sister, two lines traced by your pen, you would have sent me away if not satisfied at least unperturbed. This is the fatal mishap, which you forgot to cite to me in your charming and most powerful justification. The effect of the thunderbolt was the fatal one which made me see myself as duped, mocked. It revolted me, my self-esteem cried out, dark shame overwhelmed me. I loathe myself and am forced to believe that under the countenance of an angel you fostered a fiendish soul. I leave in consternation, and in the course of eleven days I lose my common sense. I wrote you the letter of which you are a thousand times justified in complaining; but—can you believe it?—I thought it courteous. It is all over now. You will see me at your feet an hour before noon.

I shall not go to bed. You shall pardon me, Madame, or I will avenge
you. Yes, I myself will be your avenger. The only thing I ask of you,
as a great favor, is that you will burn my letter or say nothing about it
tomorrow. I sent it to you only after having written you four which
I tore up after reading them, because I found expressions in them
from which I feared you would read the passion which you have
inspired in me. A lady who had duped me was not worthy of my
love, were she an angel. I was not wrong but . . . wretched! Could
I believe you capable of it after I had seen you? I will now lie down
for three or four hours. My tears will flood my pillow. I order the
bearer to go to your convent at once, so that I may be sure you will
receive this letter when you wake. He would never have found me
if I had not approached him as I left the opera. I shall have no more
need of him. Do not answer me."

After sealing my letter I gave it to him, ordering him to go to the
convent gate and to deliver it only into the hands of the nun. He
promised to do so, I gave him a zecchino, and he set off. After
spending six hours in impatience I masked and went to Murano,
where M. M. came down as soon as I was announced. I had been
shown into the small visiting room in which I had seen her with the
Countess. I went down on my knees before her; but she hurriedly
told me to get up, for I could be seen. Her face was instantly suffused
by a fiery blush. She sat down, I sat down before her; and so we
spent a good quarter of an hour looking at each other. I finally broke
the silence by asking her if I could count on being forgiven, and she
put her beautiful hand out through the grating; I bathed it with my
tears and kissed it a hundred times. She said that our acquaintance
having begun with such a fierce storm should make us hope for an
eternal calm.

"It is the first time," she said, "that we are talking together; but
what has happened to us is enough for us to believe that we know each
other perfectly. I hope that our friendship will be equally tender and
sincere, and that we can be indulgent toward each other's failings."

"When may I convince you of my feelings, Signora, outside
these walls and in all the joy of my soul?"

"We will sup at my casino whenever you please—I need only
know two days in advance—or with you in Venice, if that is not
inconvenient for you."

"It would only increase my happiness; I must tell you that I am in
easy circumstances and that, far from fearing to spend money
I delight in it and that all I have belongs to the object I adore."

"I welcome both the fact and the confidence. I, too, can tell you that I am tolerably rich and that I feel I could refuse nothing to my lover."

"But you must have one."

"Yes, I have; and it is he who makes me rich and who is completely my master. For this reason I never leave him in ignorance of anything. Day after tomorrow at my casino you shall know more."

"But I hope that your lover—"

"Will not be there? You may be sure he will not. And have you a mistress?"

"Alas! I had one, but she has been torn from me. For six months I have lived in perfect celibacy."

"But you still love her."

"I cannot remember her without loving her; but I foresee that the seduction of your charms will make me forget her."

"If you were happy I am sorry for you. She was torn from you; and you have been consumed with grief, shunning society—I divined it. But if it falls out that I take her place, no one, my dear friend, shall tear me from your heart."

"But what will your lover say?"

"He will be delighted to see me in love and happy with a lover like you. Such is his nature."

"Admirable nature! Heroism beyond my strength."

"What sort of life do you lead in Venice?"

"Theaters, society, casinos, where I defy Fortune and find her sometimes kind and sometimes not."

"At the houses of foreign ambassadors too?"

"No, because I am too closely connected with certain patricians; but I know them all."

"How can you know them if you do not see them?"

"I met them in foreign countries. In Parma I knew the Duke of Montealegre,[11] the Spanish Ambassador; in Vienna Count Rosenberg;[12] in Paris the French Ambassador,[13] about two years ago."

"My dear friend, I advise you to leave, for it is about to strike noon. Come day after tomorrow at the same hour, and I will give you the necessary instructions so that you can sup with me."

"Alone?"

"Of course."

"Dare I ask you for a pledge? For this good fortune is so great."

"What pledge do you wish?"

"To see you stand at the small window, with myself in the place where Countess S. was."

She rose and with the most gracious smile pressed the spring, and after a kiss whose harshness must have pleased her as much as its sweetness, I left her. She followed me to the door with her amorous eyes.

Joy and impatience absolutely prevented me from eating and sleeping during the whole two days. It seemed to me that I had never been so happy in love and that I was to be so for the first time. In addition to M. M.'s birth, her beauty, and her intelligence, which together constituted her true worth, bias entered in to make the extent of my happiness incomprehensible. She was a vestal.[14] I was to taste a forbidden fruit. I was to infringe on the rights of an omnipotent husband, snatching from his seraglio the most beautiful of his sultanas.

If at the time my reason had not been enslaved I should have seen very well that my nun could not be essentially different from all the pretty women I had loved in the thirteen years I had been skirmishing on the fields of love; but what man in love dwells on such a thought? If it comes into his mind he rejects it with disdain. M. M. must be absolutely different from all the women in the universe and more beautiful.

Animal nature, which chemists call the "animal kingdom," instinctively secures the three means necessary to perpetuate itself. They are three real needs. It must feed itself, and in order that doing so shall not be a labor, it has the sensation called "appetite"; and it finds pleasure in satisfying it. In the second place it must preserve its own species by generation, and certainly it would not perform that duty—despite what St. Augustine[15] says—if it did not find pleasure in doing it. In the third place it has an unconquerable inclination to destroy its enemy; and nothing is better contrived, for since it must preserve itself it must hate whatever achieves or desires its destruction. Under this general law, however, each species acts independently. These three sensations—hunger, appetite for coitus, hate which tends to destroy the enemy—are habitual satisfactions in brute beasts, let us not call them pleasure; they can only be such comparatively speaking; for they do not reason about them. Man alone is capable of true pleasure, for, endowed with the faculty of reason, he foresees it, seeks it, creates it, and reasons about it after enjoying it. My dear reader, I beg you to follow me; if you drop me at this point, you are not polite. Let us examine the thing. Man is in the same condition as the beasts when he yields to these three instincts without his reason entering in. When our mind makes its contribution, these three satisfactions become pleasure, pleasure, pleasure: the inexplicable sensation which makes us taste what we call happiness, which we cannot explain either, although we feel it.

The voluptuary who reasons disdains greediness, lust, and the brutal vengeance which springs from a first impulse of anger; he is an epicure; he falls in love but he does not wish to enjoy the object he loves unless he is sure that he is loved; when he is insulted, he will not avenge himself until he has coldly arrived at the best way to relish the pleasure of his revenge. In the result he is more cruel, but he consoles himself by the knowledge that he is at least reasonable. These three operations are the work of the soul, which, to procure itself pleasure, becomes the minister of the passions *quae nisi parent imperant* ("which, if they do not obey, command").[16] We bear hunger in order to savor culinary concoctions better; we put off the pleasure of love in order to make it more intense; and we defer a vengeance in order to make it more deadly. Yet it is true that people often die of indigestion, that we deceive ourselves or allow ourselves to be deceived in love by sophisms, and that the object we wish to exterminate often escapes our vengeance; but we run these risks willingly.

CHAPTER III

*Continuation of the preceding chapter. First
assignation with M. M. Letter from C. C. My
second assignation with the nun in my superb
casino in Venice. I am happy.*

Nothing can be dearer to the thinking man than life; yet the greatest
voluptuary is he who best practices the difficult art of making it pass
quickly. He does not want to make it shorter; but he wants amusement to render its passing insensible. He is right, if he has not failed
in any duty. They who believe that they have no duty save that of
pleasing their senses are wrong, and Horace may have been wrong
too in the passage where he told Julius Florus[1]: *Nec metuam quid de
me judicet heres, Quod non plura datis inveniet* ("Nor will I fear my
heir's judgment of me because he does not find more than I
received").[2]

The happiest of men is he who best knows the art of being happy
without infringing on his duties; and the unhappiest is he who has
adopted a profession in which he is under the sad necessity of foreseeing the future from dawn to dark of every day.

Certain that M. M. would not break her word, I went to the
visiting room two hours before noon. My expression made her
instantly ask me if I was ill.

"No," I answered; "but I may look so in the uneasy expectation
of a happiness too great for me. I have lost appetite and sleep; if it is
deferred I cannot answer to you for my life."

"Nothing is deferred, my dear friend; but how impatient you are!
Let us sit down. Here is the key to the casino[3] to which you will go.
There will be people there, for we have to be served; but no one
will speak to you and you need speak to no one. You will be
masked. You are not to go there until half past the first hour of
night,[*4] no sooner. You will go up the stairs opposite the street door
and at the top of the stairs you will see, by the light of a lantern, a
green door, which you will open to enter an apartment which you
will find lighted. In the second room you will find me, and if I am

---

[*]According to the Italian reckoning this is two hours after sunset. (C.'s
note.)

not there you will wait for me. I will not be more than a few minutes late. You may unmask, sit by the fire, and read. You will find books. The door to the casino is in such-and-such a place."

Since her description could not be more precise, I express my delight that I cannot go wrong. I kiss the hand which gives me the key and the key as well before putting it in my pocket. I ask her if I will see her in secular clothes or dressed as a saint as I now saw her.

"I leave here dressed in my habit, but at the casino I put on secular clothes. There I have everything I need in the way of masking attire too."

"I hope that you will not put on secular clothes this evening."

"Why, if I may ask?"

"I love you so much in your coif, as you are now."

"Ah, I understand. You imagine that I have no hair, so I frighten you; but let me tell you that I have a wig which could not be better made."

"Good God! What are you saying? The very name of 'wig' un-does me. But no. No, no; never doubt it—I will think you charming even so. Only be careful not to put it on in my presence. I see that you are mortified. Forgive me. I am in despair that I mentioned it to you. Are you certain that no one will see you leaving the convent?"

"You will be certain of it yourself when, making the circuit of the island in a gondola, you will see where the little quay is. It gives onto a room of which I have the key, and I am sure of the lay sister who waits on me."

"And the gondola?"

"It is my lover who vouches to me for the fidelity of the gondoliers."

"What a man your lover is! I imagine he is old."

"Certainly not. I should be ashamed. I am sure he is not forty. He has everything, my dear friend, to deserve love. Good looks, wit, a gentle nature, and perfect manners."

"And he forgives you your caprices."

"What do you mean by 'caprices'? He took me a year ago. Before him I knew no man, as before you I knew no one who inspired me with a fancy. When I told him everything he was rather surprised, then he laughed and only read me a short lecture on the risk I was running by putting myself in the power of a man who might be indiscreet. He wanted me to know who you are before

434

I went any further; but it was too late. I vouched for you, and he laughed again at my vouching for someone I did not know."

"When did you confide it all to him?"

"Day before yesterday; but completely truthfully. I showed him copies of my letters and of yours, reading which made him say he thought you were French despite your having told me that you were Venetian. He is curious to know who you are, and that is all; but since I am not curious about it you need have no fear. I give you my word of honor that I will never make the slightest attempt to find out."

"Nor I to find out who this man is, who is as extraordinary as yourself. I am in despair when I think of the bitter sorrow I caused you."

"Let us say no more about it; but console yourself, for when I think about it I conclude that you could have acted otherwise only if you were a conceited fool."

When I left she repeated the pledge of her love to me at the little window and she remained there until I was out of the visiting room.

That night at the appointed hour I found the casino without any difficulty, I opened the door and, following her instructions, I found her dressed in secular clothes of the utmost elegance. The room was lighted by candles in girandoles in front of mirrors and by four other candelabra on a table on which there were some books. M. M. seemed to have a beauty entirely different from that which I had seen in the visiting room. Her hair appeared to have been done in a chignon which emphasized its abundance, but my eyes merely glanced at it, for nothing would have been more stupid at the moment than a compliment on her fine wig. To fall on my knees before her, to show her my boundless gratitude by constantly kissing her beautiful hands, were the forerunners of transports whose outcome ought to be a classical amorous combat; but M. M. thought her first duty was to defend herself. Ah! those charming refusals! The strength of two hands repelling the attacks of a respectful and tender lover who is at the same time bold and insistent, played very little part in them; the weapons she used to restrain my passion, to moderate my fire, were arguments delivered in words as amorous as they were energetic and reinforced every moment by loving kisses which melted my soul. In this struggle, as sweet as it was painful to us both, we spent two hours. At the end of the combat we congratulated ourselves on each having carried off the victory; she in having been able to defend herself against all my attacks, I in having kept my impatience in check.

At four o'clock[5] (I am still using the Italian reckoning) she said she was very hungry and that she hoped she would not find me differing from herself. She rang, and a well-dressed woman who was neither young nor old and whose appearance betokened respectability came in and laid a table for two, and after putting everything we needed on another beside us, she served us. The service was of Sèvres porcelain.[6] Eight made dishes composed the supper; they were set on silver boxes filled with hot water which kept the food always hot. It was a choice and delicious supper. I exclaimed that the cook[7] must be French, and she said I was right. We drank only Burgundy, and we emptied a bottle of "oeil de perdrix" champagne[8] and another of some sparkling wine for gaiety. It was she who dressed the salad; her appetite was equal to mine. She rang only to have the dessert brought, together with all the ingredients for making punch. In everything she did I could not but admire her knowledge, her skill, and her grace. It was obvious that she had a lover who had taught her. I was so curious to know who he was that I said I was ready to tell her my name if she would tell me that of the happy man whose heart and soul she possessed. She said we must leave it to time to satisfy our curiosity.

Among her watch charms she had a little rock-crystal flask exactly like the one I had on my watch chain. I showed it to her, praising the essence of rose which it contained and with which a small piece of cotton was soaked. She showed me hers, which was filled with the same essence in liquid form.

"I am surprised," I said, "for it is very rare and it costs a great deal."

"And it is not for sale."

"That is true. The creator of the essence is the King of France; he made a pound of it, which cost him ten thousand écus."

"It was a present to my lover, who gave it to me."

"Madame de Pompadour sent a small flask of it two years ago to Signor Mocenigo,[9] the Venetian Ambassador in Paris, through the A. de B.,[10] who is now the French Ambassador here."

"Do you know him?"

"I met him that day, having the honor to dine with him. As he was about to set out on his journey here, he had come to take his leave. He is a man whom Fortune has favored, but a man of merit and great wit and of distinguished birth, for he is a Count of Lyons.[11] His handsome face has won him the nickname of 'Belle-Babet';[12] we have a little collection of his poems,[13] which do him honor."

Midnight had struck and, since time was beginning to be precious, we leave the table, and before the fire I become insistent. I said that if she would not yield to love she could not refuse nature, which must be urging her to go to bed after such a fine supper.

"Are you sleepy, then?"

"Not in the least; but at this hour people go to bed. Let me put you to bed and sit by your side as long as you wish to stay there, or else permit me to retire."

"If you leave me you will make me very unhappy."

"No more unhappy than I shall feel at leaving you; but what are we to do here in front of the fire until dawn?"

"We can both sleep in our clothes on the sofa you see there."

"In our clothes? So be it. I can even let you sleep; but if I do not sleep will you forgive me? Beside you, and uncomfortable in my clothes, how could I sleep?"

"Very well. Besides, this sofa is a real bed. You shall see."

With that she rises, pulls the sofa out at an angle, arranges pillows, sheets, and a blanket, and I see a real bed. She tucks my hair under a large handkerchief and hands me another so that I can do her the same service, saying that she has no nightcap. I set to work, concealing my distaste for her wig, when something totally unexpected gives me the most agreeable surprise. Instead of a wig, I find the most beautiful head of hair. She tells me, after laughing heartily, that a nun's only obligation is not to let the outside world see her hair, and after saying so she throws herself down at full length on the couch. I quickly take off my coat, kick my feet out of my shoes, and fall more on her than beside her. She clasps me in her arms, and subjecting herself to a tyranny which insults nature, she considers that I must forgive her all the torments which her resistance cannot but inflict on me.

With a trembling and timid hand and looking at her with eyes which begged for charity, I undo six wide ribbons which fastened her dress in front and, ravished with joy because she does not stop me, I find myself the fortunate master of the most beautiful of bosoms. It is too late: she is obliged, after I have contemplated it, to let me devour it; I raise my eyes to her face, and I see the sweetness of love saying to me: "Be content with that, and learn from me to bear abstinence." Driven by love and by omnipotent nature, in despair because she will not let my hands move elsewhere, I make every imaginable effort to guide one of hers to the place where she could have convinced herself that I deserved her mercy;

but with a strength greater than mine she refuses to remove her hands from my chest, where she could have found nothing to interest her. Nevertheless, it was there that her mouth descended when it detached itself from mine.

Whether from need or from the effect of lassitude, having passed so many hours unable to do anything but constantly swallow her saliva mixed with mine, I sleep in her arms, holding her clasped in mine. What woke me with a start was a loud chiming of bells.

"What is that?"

"Let us dress quickly, my dear, my love; I must get back to the convent."

"Then dress. I am going to enjoy the spectacle of seeing you disguised as a saint again."

"Gladly. If you are not in any hurry you can sleep here."

She then rang for the same woman, who I realized must be the great confidante of all her amorous mysteries. After having her hair done up, she took off her dress, put her watches, her rings, and all her secular ornaments in a desk, which she locked, put on the shoes of her order, then a corset in which, as in a prison, she confined the pretty children which alone had fed me on their nectar, and finally put on her habit. Her confidante having gone out to summon the gondolier, she flung herself on my neck and said that she would expect me the next day but one to decide on the night she would come to spend with me in Venice, where, she said, we would make each other completely happy; and she left. Very well pleased with my good fortune, though full of unsatisfied desires, I put out the candles and slept deeply until noon.

I left the casino without seeing anyone, and, well masked, went to call on Laura, who gave me a letter from C. C. which ran as follows:

"Here, my dear husband, is a good example of my way of thinking. You will find me ever more worthy to be your wife. You must believe that, despite my age, I can keep a secret and that I am discreet enough not to take your silence in bad part. Sure of your heart, I am not jealous of what can divert your mind and help you to bear our separation patiently.

"I must tell you that yesterday, going through a corridor which is above the small visiting room and wanting to pick up a toothpick I had dropped, I had to take a stool away from the wall. Picking it up, I saw through an almost imperceptible crack where the floor meets the wall your own person very much interested in conversing

438

with my dear friend Mother M. M. You cannot imagine either my surprise or my joy. Yet those two feelings instantly gave place to my fear of being seen and making some babbling nun curious. After quickly putting the stool back in its place, I left. Ah, my dear! I beg you to tell me everything. How could I love you and not be curious about the whole story of this remarkable occurrence? Tell me if she knows you, and how you made her acquaintance. She is my dear friend, of whom I told you, and whom I did not think it necessary to name to you. It is she who has taught me French and she has given me books in her room which have enlightened me on a very important matter of which few women have any knowledge. Know that but for her the terrible illness which almost killed me would have been discovered. She gave me linen and sheets; I owe her my honor; and so she learned that I have had a lover, as I have learned that she has had one too, but we were never curious about our respective secrets. Mother M. M. is an incomparable woman. I am certain, my dear, that you love her and that she loves you, and since I am not in the least jealous of her I deserve that you should tell me all about it. But I am sorry for you both, for all that either of you can do can only serve, I believe, to excite your mutual passion. The whole convent believes that you are ill; I am dying to see you. So come at least once. Farewell."

The letter made me uneasy, for I felt very sure of C. C., but the crack might betray us to others. In addition, I now had to tell my darling a lie, for honor and love forbade me to tell her the truth. In the answer which I immediately sent her I said that she must at once inform her friend that she had seen her through the crack, talking to a masker. As for my having made the nun's acquaintance, I said that having heard of her rare qualities I had had her called to the grating, announcing myself under a false name, and that consequently she must refrain from talking about me, for she had recognized me as the same man who went to hear mass at her church. As for love, I assured her that there was no such thing between us, though I agreed that she was a charming woman.

On St. Catherine's Day,[14] which was C. C.'s name day, I went to mass in her church. Going to the *traghetto* to take a gondola, I observe that I am followed. I needed to make sure of it. I see the same man also take a gondola and follow me; this could be natural; but to make certain I disembark in Venice at the Palazzo Morosini del Giardino,[15] and I see the same man disembarking too. After that I am in no more doubt. I come out of the palace, I stop in a narrow street near the Flanders post,[16] and, knife in hand, I force him into the corner of the street and, putting the point to his throat, I insist on his telling me at whose order he is following me. He would perhaps have told me all if someone had not happened to enter the street. At that he got away, and I learned nothing. But seeing that it was only too easy for a busybody to know who I was if he persisted in trying to find out, I resolved not to go to Murano again except masked or at night.

The next day, which was the one on which M. M. was to let me know how she would arrange to come to supper with me, I went to the visiting room very early. I saw her before me, displaying on her face the signs of the contentment which flooded her soul. The first compliment she paid me was on my appearing at her church after three weeks during which I had not been seen there. She told me that the Abbess had been very pleased, because she said she was sure she knew who I was. I thereupon told her the story of the spy, and my resolve not to go to mass in her church again. She replied that I would do well to show myself in Murano as little as possible. She then told me the whole story of the crack in the old flooring and said that it had already been stopped up. She said she had been warned by a boarder at the convent who was fond of her, but she did not name her.

After these few remarks I asked her if my happiness was deferred, and she answered that it was deferred only for twenty-four hours because the new lay sister had invited her to supper in her room.

"Such invitations," she said, "come seldom, but when they do one cannot refuse except at the cost of making an enemy of the person who extends the invitation."

"Can one not say one is ill?"

"Yes, but then one must receive visitors."

"I understand, for if you refuse you may be suspected of slipping away."

"No, no—slipping away is not considered possible."

"Then you are the only one who can perform the miracle?"

"You may be sure that I am the only one, and that gold is the powerful god who performs it. So tell me where you will wait for me tomorrow precisely at the second hour of the night."

"Could not I wait for you here[17] at your casino?"

"No, for the person who will take me to Venice is my lover."

"Your lover?"

"Himself."

440

"That is something new! Well then, I will wait for you in the Piazza dei Santi Giovanni e Paolo, behind the pedestal of the equestrian statue of Bartolomeo da Bergamo."[18]

"I have never seen either the statue or the square except in an engraving; but I will not fail to be there. You have told me enough. Nothing but terribly bad weather could keep me from coming; but let us hope for good. So good-by. We will talk much tomorrow evening, and if we sleep we shall go to sleep more content."

I had to act quickly, for I had no casino. I took a second rower, so that I was in the San Marco quarter in less than a quarter of an hour. After spending five or six hours looking at a number of them, I chose the most elegant and hence the most expensive. It had belonged to Lord Holderness,[19] the English Ambassador, who had sold it cheaply to a cook on his departure. He rented it to me until Easter for a hundred zecchini in advance, on condition that he himself would cook the suppers and dinners I might give.

The casino had five rooms, furnished in exquisite taste. It contained nothing that was not made for the sake of love, good food, and every kind of pleasure. Meals were served through a blind window which was set back into the wall and filled by a revolving dumb-waiter which closed it completely. The masters and the servants could not see one another. The room was decorated with mirrors, chandeliers, and a magnificent pier glass above a white marble fireplace; and the walls were tiled with small squares of painted Chinese porcelain, all attracting interest by their representations of amorous couples in a state of nature, whose voluptuous attitudes fired the imagination. Some small armchairs matched the sofas which were placed to left and right. Another room was octagonal and walled with mirrors, with floor and ceiling of the same; the counterposed mirrors reflected the same objects from innumerable points of view. The room was next to an alcove, which gave by concealed doors onto a dressing room on one side and on the other a boudoir in which were a bathtub and an English-style water closet. All the wainscoting was embossed in ormolu or painted with flowers and arabesques. After telling him not to forget to put sheets on the bed and candles in all the chandeliers and in the candelabra in each room, I ordered him to prepare a supper for two for that evening, warning him that I wanted no wines except Burgundy and champagne and no more than eight made dishes, leaving the choice to him regardless of expense. He was to see to the dessert too. Taking the key to the street door I warned him that when I came in I wished to see no one. The supper was to be ready at the second hour[20] of night and was to be served when I rang. I observed with pleasure that the clock in the alcove had an alarm, for despite my love I was beginning to succumb to the power of sleep.

After giving these orders I went to a milliner's to buy a pair of slippers and a nightcap trimmed with a double ruffle of Alençon point.[21] I put it in my pocket. Since I was to give supper to the most beautiful of all the sultanas of the Master of the Universe, I wanted to make sure the evening before that everything would be in order. Having told her that I had a casino, I must not appear to be a novice in any respect.

It was the cook who was surprised when he saw me at the second hour all alone. I instantly berated him for not having lighted candles everywhere, when, as I had told him the hour, he could be in no doubt about it.

"I will not fail to do so another time."

"Then light up and serve."

"You told me it would be for two."

"Serve for two. Remain present at my supper this first time, so that I can point out to you everything I find good or bad."

The supper came in the dumb-waiter in good order, two dishes at a time; I commented on everything; but I found everything excellent in Saxon porcelain.[22] Game, sturgeon, truffles, oysters, and perfect wines. I only reproached him with having forgotten to set out hardboiled eggs, anchovies, and prepared vinegars on a dish, to make the salad. He rolled up his eyes with a contrite look, accusing himself of having committed a great crime. I also said that another time I wanted to have bitter oranges to give flavor to the punch and that I wanted rum, not arrack. After spending two hours at table I told him to bring me the account of all that he had spent. He brought it a quarter of an hour later, and I found it satisfactory. After paying him and ordering him to bring me coffee when I should ring, I retired to the excellent bed which was in the alcove. The bed and the good supper won me the most perfect sleep. But for them, I should not have been able to sleep for thinking that on the next night I should have my goddess in my arms in that very bed. On leaving in the morning I told my man that for dessert I wanted all the fresh fruits he could find and, above all, ices. To keep the day from seeming long I gambled until nightfall and I did not find Fortune different from my love. Everything went just as

I wished. In the depths of my soul I gave thanks for it to the powerful Genius of my beautiful nun.

It was at the first hour[23] of night that I took up my post by the statue of the heroic Colleoni. She had told me to be there at the second hour, but I wanted to have the sweet pleasure of waiting for her. The night was cold, but magnificent, and without the least wind.

Exactly at the second hour I saw a gondola with two rowers arrive and disembark a masker, who, after speaking to the gondolier at the prow, came toward the statue. Seeing a male masker, I am alarmed, I slip away, and I regret not having pistols. The masker walks around the statue, comes up to me, and offers me a peaceable hand which leaves me in no more doubt. I recognize my angel dressed as a man. She laughs at my surprise, clings to my arm, and without a word between us we make our way to the Piazza San Marco, cross it, and go to the casino, which was only a hundred paces from the Teatro San Moisè.

Everything is as I have ordered. We go upstairs, I quickly unmask, but M. M. gives herself the pleasure of walking slowly through every corner of the delicious place in which she was being received, delighted that I should see all the graces of her person in every profile and often in full face and admire in her clothing what kind of man the lover who possessed her must be. She was surprised at the magic which everywhere showed her her person from a hundred different points of view at the same time even when she stood still. The multiplied portraits of her which the mirrors offered her by the light of all the candles expressly placed for the purpose were a new spectacle which made her fall in love with herself. Sitting on a stool I attentively examined all the elegance of her attire. A coat of short-napped rose velvet edged with an embroidery of gold spangles, a matching hand-embroidered waistcoat, than which nothing could be richer, black satin breeches, needle-lace ruffles, buckles set with brilliants, a solitaire of great value on her little finger and on her other hand a ring which showed only a surface of white taffeta covered by a convex crystal. Her *bautta*[24] of black blond-lace was as beautiful as possible in both design and fineness. So that I could see her even better she came and stood in front of me. I search her pockets and I find a snuffbox, a comfit box, a phial, a case of toothpicks, a pair of opera glasses, and handkerchiefs exhaling scents which sweetened the air. I attentively examine the richness and workmanship of her two watches and of her fine seals hung as pendants from chains covered with small diamonds. I search her side pockets and I find flintlock pistols with a spring firing mechanism, of the finest English manufacture.

"All that I see," I say, "is beneath you, but permit my astonished soul to do homage to the adorable being who wishes to convince you that you are really his mistress."

"That is what he said when I asked him to take me to Venice and leave me there, adding that his wish was that I should enjoy myself there and become ever more convinced that he whom I was about to make happy deserved it."

"It is unbelievable, my dear. Such a lover is one of a kind, and I can never deserve a happiness by which I am already dazzled."

"Let me go and unmask by myself."

A quarter of an hour later she appeared before me with her beautiful hair dressed like a man's but unpowdered and with side locks in long curls which came down to the bottom of her cheeks. A black ribbon tied it behind, and it fell to her knees in a hanging plait. M. M. as a woman resembled Henriette,[25] and as a man a Guards officer named *L'Étorière*[26] whom I had known in Paris; or rather she resembled the youth Antinoüs,[27] whose statues are still to be seen, if her French clothes had permitted the illusion.

Overwhelmed by so many charms, I thought I felt ill. I threw myself on the sofa to support my head.

"I have lost all my confidence," I said; "you will never be mine; this very night some fatal mishap will tear you from my desires; perhaps a miracle performed by your divine spouse in his jealousy of a mortal. I feel prostrated. In a quarter of an hour I may no longer exist."

"Are you mad? I am yours this moment if you wish. Though I have not eaten I do not care about supper. Let us go to bed."

She felt cold. We sit down before the fire. She tells me that she has no vest on. I unfasten a diamond brooch in the shape of a heart which kept her ruffle closed, and my hands feel before my eyes see what only her shirt defended against the air, the two springs of life which ornamented her bosom. I become ardent; but she needs only a single kiss to calm me, and two words: "After supper."

I ring, and seeing her alarm I show her the dumb-waiter.

"No one will see you," I say; "you must tell your lover, who may not know of this device."

"He knows of it; but he will admire your thoughtfulness and will say that you are no novice in the art of pleasing and that clearly I am not the only woman who enjoys the delights of this little house with you."

"And he will be wrong. I have neither supped nor slept here except alone; and I hate deceit. You are not my first passion, my divine love; but you will be my last."

"I am happy, my dear, if you will be faithful. My lover is so; he is kind, he is gentle; but he has always left my heart empty."

"His must be so too, for if his love were like mine he would not permit you an absence of this kind. He could not put up with it."

"He loves me, as I love you; do you believe that I love you?"

"I must believe it; but you would not put up with—"

"Say no more; for I feel that, if you will not keep anything from me, I will forgive you everything. The joy which I feel in my soul at this moment is due more to my certainty that I shall leave you wanting nothing than to my certainty that I shall spend a delicious night with you. It will be the first in my life."

"Then you have not spent nights with your worthy lover?"

"Yes, but those nights were inspired only by friendship, grati-tude, and compliance. Love is what counts. Despite that, my lover is like you. He has a natural vivacity and his wit is always ready, like yours; besides which both his face and his person are attractive, though he does not resemble you in looks. I also think he is richer than you are, though this casino might make one conclude the opposite. But do not imagine that I consider you less deserving than he because you confess that you are incapable of the heroism of permitting me an absence; on the contrary, if you told me that you would be as indulgent as he is to one of my caprices, I should know that you do not love me as I am very glad that you do love me."

"Will he wish to know the details of this night?"

"He will believe that it will please me if he asks me about it, and I shall tell him everything except some circumstances which might humiliate him."

After the supper, which she found choice and exquisite, as she did the ices and the oysters, she made punch, and in my amorous impatience, after drinking several glasses of it, I begged her to consider that we had only seven hours before us and that we should be doing very wrong not to spend them in bed. So we went into the alcove, which was lighted by twelve flaming candles, and from there to the dressing room, where, presenting her with the fine lace cap, I asked her to dress her hair like a woman. After saying that the cap

445

was magnificent she told me to go and undress in the outer room, promising that she would call me as soon as she was in bed.

It took only two minutes. I flung myself into her burning arms, on fire with love and giving her the most lively proofs of it for seven continuous hours which were interrupted only by as many quarters of an hour devoted to the most feeling talk. She taught me nothing new so far as the physical side of the performance was concerned, but any quantity of new things in the way of sighs, ecstasies, transports, and unfeigned sentiments which find scope only at such moments. Each discovery I made elevated my soul to Love, who furnished me with fresh strength to show him my gratitude. She was astonished to find herself capable of so much pleasure, for I had shown her many things which she thought were fictions. I did what she did not think she was entitled to ask me to do to her, and I taught her that the slightest constraint spoils the greatest of pleasures. When the alarm chimed she raised her eyes to the Third Heaven[28] like an idolator, to thank the Mother and the Son[29] for having so well rewarded her for the effort it had cost her to declare her passion to me.

We dressed in haste, and seeing me put the beautiful cap in her pocket she assured me that it would always be most dear to her. After taking coffee we hurried to the Piazza dei Santi Giovanni e Paolo, where I left her, assuring her that she would see me on the next day but one. After watching her get into her gondola I went home, where ten hours of sleep restored me to my normal state.

CHAPTER IV

Continuation of the preceding chapter.
Visit to the convent and conversation with M. M.
Letter which she writes me and my answer.
Another meeting at the casino in Murano in
the presence of her lover.

On the next day but one I went to the visiting room after dinner. I send for her, and she comes at once and tells me to leave, for she is expecting her lover, but that I must come without fail on the following day. I leave. At the end of the bridge I see a poorly masked masker getting out of a gondola the gondolier of which I knew and had good reason to believe was then in the service of the French Ambassador. He was not in livery, and the gondola was plain, like all gondolas belonging to Venetians. I turn and see the masker going to the convent. I feel no more doubt, and I go back to Venice delighted to have made the discovery and pleased that the Ambassador was my senior partner. I resolve to say nothing about it to M. M.

I go to see her the next day and she tells me that her friend had come to take leave of her until the Christmas holidays.

"He is going to Padua," she says, "but everything is arranged for us to sup at his casino if we wish."

"Why not in Venice?"

"No, not in Venice, until he is back. He asked me not to. He has great judgment."

"Very well. When shall we sup at the casino?"

"Sunday, if you like."

"Let it be Sunday; I will go to the casino at dusk and will read while I wait for you. Did you tell your friend that you were not uncomfortable in my casino?"

"My dear, I told him everything; but one thing greatly troubles him. He wants me to beg you not to expose me to the danger of a big belly."

"May I die if it ever entered my mind. But don't you run the same risk with him?"

"Never."

"Then we must be very careful in future. I think, since there is no masking[1] during the nine days before Christmas, I shall have to go to your casino by water, for if I go by land I could easily be recognized as the same man who went to your church."

"That is very prudent. I can easily point out the quay to you. I think you can come during Lent too, when God wants us to mortify our senses. Isn't it odd that there is a time when God approves of our amusing ourselves and another when we can only please him by abstinence! What can an anniversary have in common with the divinity? I do not understand how the action of the creature can influence the creator, whom my reason can only conceive as independent. It seems to me that if God had created man with the power to offend him, man would be justified in doing everything he forbade him to do, if only to teach him how to create. Can one imagine God being sad during Lent?"

"My divine one, you reason perfectly; but may I ask you where you learned to reason, and how you managed to break away?"

"My friend gave me good books, and the light of truth quickly dissipated the clouds of superstition which were oppressing my reason. I assure you that when I reflect on myself I think I am more fortunate in having found someone who has enlightened my mind than unfortunate in having taken the veil, for the greatest happiness of all is to live and die at peace, which we cannot hope to do if we believe what the priests tell us."

"You are very right; but permit me to wonder at you, for enlightening an extremely prejudiced mind such as yours must have been could not be the work of a few months."

"I should have seen the light much less quickly if I had been less steeped in error. What separated the true from the false in my mind was only a curtain; reason alone could draw it; but I had been taught to scorn reason. As soon as I was shown that I should set the greatest store by it I put it to work; it drew the curtain. The evidence of truth appeared with the utmost clarity, my stupid notions disappeared; and I have no reason to fear that they will reappear, for I strengthen my defenses every day. I can say that I did not begin to love God until after I had rid myself of the idea of him which religion had given me."

"I congratulate you. You were more fortunate than I. You have gone further in a year than I in ten."

"Then you did not begin by reading what Lord Bolingbroke[2] has written. Five or six months ago I was reading Charron's[3] *La Sagesse*, and I don't know how our confessor found it out. He dared to tell me at confession that I must stop reading it, I answered that since my conscience was not troubled by it, I could not obey him. He said that he would not absolve me, and I answered that I would go to communion nevertheless. The priest went to Bishop Diedo[4] to ask what he should do, and the Bishop came to talk with me and gave me to understand that I should be guided by my confessor. I answered that my confessor's business was to absolve me, and that he did not even have the right to advise me unless I asked him for advice. I told him outright that, since it was my duty not to scandalize the entire convent, if he persisted in refusing me absolution I would go to communion nevertheless. The Bishop ordered him to leave me to my conscience. But I was not satisfied. My lover procured me a brief from the Pope which authorizes me to confess to anyone I choose. All my sisters are jealous of the privilege; but I used it only once, for the thing is not worth the trouble. I always confess to the same priest, who has no difficulty in absolving me, for I tell him absolutely nothing of any importance."

So it was that I came to know her as an adorable freethinker; but it could not be otherwise, for she had an even greater need to quiet her conscience than to satisfy her senses.

After assuring her that she would find me at the casino I went back to Venice. On Sunday after dinner I had myself rowed around the island of Murano in a two-oared gondola, to see where the quay for the casino was and also the small one by which she left the convent; but I could make out nothing. I did not find the quay for the casino until during the novena,[5] and the small quay for the convent six months later at the risk of my life. We shall speak of it when we come to that time.

About the first hour of night I went to the temple of my love and, waiting for my idol to arrive, I amused myself by looking at the books which made up a small library in the boudoir. They were few but choice. They included all that the wisest philosophers have written against religion and all that the most voluptuous pens have written on the subject which is the sole aim of love. Seductive books, whose incendiary style drives the reader to seek the reality, which alone can quench the fire he feels running through his veins. Besides the books there were folios containing only lascivious engravings. Their great merit lay in the beauty of the drawing far more than in the lubricity of the poses. I saw engravings for the *Portier des Chartreux*,[6] made in England, and others for Meursius,[7] or

449

Aloisia Sigea Toletana, than which I had never seen anything finer. In addition the small pictures which decorated the room were so well painted that the figures seemed to be alive. An hour went by in an instant.

The appearance of M. M. in her nun's habit wrung a cry from me. I told her, springing to embrace her, that she could not have come in better time to prevent a schoolboy masturbation to which all that I had seen during the past hour would have driven me.

"But in that saintly dress you surprise me. Let me adore you here and now, my angel."

"I will put on secular clothes at once. It will take me only a quarter of an hour. I do not like myself in these woolens."

"No, no. You shall receive the homage of love dressed as you were when you brought it to birth."

She answered only with a *Fiat voluntas tua* ("Thy will be done") delivered with the most devout expression as she let herself fall on the commodious sofa, where I treated her with caution despite herself. After the act I helped her take off her habit and put on a plain robe of Pekin muslin which was the height of elegance. I then played the role of chambermaid while she dressed her hair and put on a nightcap.

After supper, before going to bed we agreed not to meet again until the first day of the novena when, the theaters being closed for ten days, masks are not worn. She then gave me the keys to the door giving onto the quay. A blue ribbon fastened to the window above it was to be the signal which would show it to me by day, so that I could later go there by night. But what filled her with joy was that I went to stay in the casino and never left it until her lover returned. During the ten days I stayed there I had her four times and thereby convinced her that I lived only for her. I amused myself reading, or writing to C. C., but my love for the latter had grown calm. The chief thing which interested me in the letters she wrote me was what she told me about her dear friend Mother M. M. She said that I had done wrong not to cultivate her acquaintance, and I answered that I had not pursued it for fear of being recognized. In this way I made her even more obliged to keep my secret inviolably.

It is not possible to love two objects at once, and it is not possible to keep love vigorous if one either gives it too much food or none at all. What kept my passion for M. M. always at the same pitch was that I could never have her except with the greatest fear of losing her. I told her it was impossible that, one time or another, some nun would not need to speak with her at a time when she was neither in her room nor in the convent. She maintained that it could not happen, since nothing was more respected in the convent than a nun's privilege of shutting herself up in her room and denying herself even to the Abbess. She had nothing to fear but the fatal circumstance of a fire, for then, when everything was in confusion and it was not natural that a nun would remain calm and indifferent, her absence must necessarily become known. She congratulated herself on having been able to win over the lay sister, the gardener, and another nun whom she always refused to name. Her lover's tact and his money had done it all, and he vouched for the fidelity of the cook and his wife, who together took care of the casino. He was sure of his gondoliers, too, despite the fact that one of them must certainly be a spy for the State Inquisitors.

On Christmas Eve she told me that her lover was about to arrive, that she was to go with him to the opera[8] on St. Stephen's Day and sup with him at the casino on the third day of Christmas. After saying that she would expect me for supper on the last day of the year she gave me a letter, asking me not to read it until I was at home.

An hour before dawn I packed my things and went to the Palazzo Bragadin, where, impatient to read the letter she had given me, I immediately locked myself in my room. It ran as follows:

"You nettled me a little, my dear, when day before yesterday, on the subject of my having to keep everything about my lover from you, you said that, satisfied with possessing my heart, you leave me mistress of my mind. Dividing heart and mind is a sophistical distinction, and if it does not seem so to you, you must admit that you do not love the whole of me, for it is impossible that I can exist without a mind and that you can cherish my heart if it is not in accord with it. If your love can be content with the contrary, it does not excel in delicacy.

"But since circumstances may arise in which you could convict me of not having acted toward you with all the sincerity which true love demands, I have resolved to reveal a secret concerning my lover to you, despite the fact that I know he is certain I will never reveal it, for it is treachery. Yet you will not love me the less for it. Reduced to choosing between the two of you, and obliged to deceive one or the other, love has conquered in me; but not blindly. You shall weigh the motives which had the power to tip the scales to your side.

"When I could no longer resist my desire to know you intimately I could not satisfy it except by confiding in my friend. I had no doubt of his willingness. He conceived a very favorable idea of your character when he read your first letter, in which you chose the visiting room, and he thought you showed yourself a man of honor when, after we became acquainted, you chose the casino in Murano in preference to your own. But as soon as he learned of it he also asked me to do him the favor of allowing him to be present at our first interview ensconced in a perfect hiding place from which he would not only see all that we did without himself being seen but also hear all that we said. It is a closet whose existence cannot even be guessed. You did not see it during the ten days you spent in the casino; but I will show it to you on the last day of the year. Tell me if I could refuse him the favor. I granted it; and nothing was more natural than to keep it a secret from you. So now you know that my friend witnessed all that we said and did the first time we were together. But do not take it amiss, my darling; you pleased him, not only by everything you did but also by all the amusing things you said to me. I felt very anxious when our conversation turned to the nature my lover must have to be so excessively tolerant; but fortunately all that you said could only be flattering to him. This is the complete confession of my treachery, which, as a sensible lover, you must forgive me, and the more so since it did you no harm. I can assure you that my friend is most curious to know who you are. That night you were natural and very likable; if you had known that you were being watched God knows what you would have been. If I had told you the thing it is even possible that you would not have consented, and you would perhaps have been right.

"But now I must risk everything for the sake of everything and make myself easy, knowing that I have done nothing for which I can be reproached. Know, my dear, that on the last day of the year my friend will be at the casino, and that he will not leave it until the next day. You will not see him, and he will see everything. Since you are not supposed to know, you understand how natural you must be in everything, for if you were not, my friend, who is very intelligent, might suspect that I have betrayed the secret. The principal thing you must be careful about is what you say. He has all the virtues except the theological one called faith, and on that subject you have free rein. You can talk of literature, travel, politics, and tell as many anecdotes as you please, and be sure of his approval.

"The question remains whether you are willing to let a man see you during the moments when you surrender to the furies of love. This uncertainty is now my torment. Yes or no: there is no middle course. Do you understand how painful my fear is? Do you feel how difficult it must have been for me to take this step? I shall not sleep tomorrow night. I shall have no rest until I have read your answer. I will then decide on a course in case you answer that you cannot be affectionate in someone's presence, especially if the 'someone' is unknown to you. Yet I hope that you will come nevertheless, and that if you cannot play the role of lover as you did the first time no bad consequences will ensue. He will believe, and I will let him believe, that your love has cooled."

Her letter surprised me greatly; then, after thinking it over, I laughed. But it would not have made me laugh if I had not known what sort of man it was who would witness my amorous exploits. Certain that M. M. must be very uneasy until she received my answer, I answered her at once, in the following terms:

"My divine angel, I want you to receive my answer to your letter before noon. You shall dine perfectly easy.

"I will spend the night of the last day of the year with you and I assure you that your friend, as our spectator, will see and hear nothing which can lead him to suppose that you have revealed his secret to me. Be sure that I will play my role perfectly. If man's duty is to be ever the slave of his reason, if he must, so far as he is able, permit himself nothing without taking reason as his guide, I can never understand how a man can be ashamed of letting a friend see him at a moment when he is giving the greatest proofs of love to a very beautiful woman. Such is my situation. Yet I must tell you that if you had forewarned me the first time you would have done wrong. I would have refused absolutely. I should have thought that my honor was involved; I should have thought that, in inviting me to supper, you were only the willing accomplice of a friend, a strange man dominated by this strange taste, and I would have formed such an unfavorable opinion of you that it would perhaps have cured me of my love, which at that time was only beginning to bud. Such, my charmer, is the human heart; but at present the case is different. Everything you have told me about your worthy friend has shown me his character, I consider him my friend too, and I love him. If a feeling of shame does not keep you from letting him see you fond and loving with me, how—far from being ashamed of it— can I fail to be proud of it? Can a man blush at what makes him

453

proud? I cannot, my dear, either blush over having conquered you or over letting myself be seen in moments when I flatter myself I shall not appear unworthy of your conquest. Yet I know that, by a natural feeling which reason cannot disapprove, most men feel a repugnance to letting themselves be seen at such moments. Those who cannot give good reasons for their repugnance must have something of the cat in their nature; but they can have good reasons for it and yet feel under no obligation to explain them to anyone. The chief reason is probably that a third person who is looking on and whom they see cannot but distract them, and that any distraction can only lessen the pleasure of intercourse. Another important reason could also be considered legitimate, that is, if the actors knew that their means of obtaining pleasure would appear pitiable to those who should witness them. Such unfortunates are right in not wishing to arouse feelings of pity in the performance of an act which would seem more properly to arouse jealousy. But we know, my dear, that we certainly do not arouse feelings of pity. Everything you have told me makes me certain that your friend's angelic soul must, in seeing us, share our pleasures. But do you know what will happen, and what I shall be very sorry for, since your lover can only be a most likable man? Seeing us will drive him frantic, and he will either run away or have to come out of his hiding place and go down on his knees to me, begging me to give you up to the violence of his amorous desires in his need to calm the fire which our transports will have kindled in his soul. If that happens I will laugh and give you up to him; but I will leave, for I feel that I could not remain the unmoved spectator of what some other man might do to you. So good-by, my angel; all will be well. I hasten to seal this letter, and I will take it to your casino this instant."

I spent these six holidays with my friends and at the Ridotto,[9] which at that period was opened on St. Stephen's Day. As I could not deal, since only patricians wearing the official robe[10] were allowed to make bank there, I played day and night, and I constantly lost. Whoever punts cannot but lose. The loss of four or five thousand zecchini, which was my entire wealth, only made my love stronger.

At the end of the year 1774 a law issued by the Great Council forbade all games of chance and caused the closing of the Ridotto, as it was called. The Great Council was amazed when it saw, on counting the ballots, that it had passed a law which it could not pass, for at least three quarters of those who had cast ballots had not wanted it, and yet three quarters of the ballot proved that they had wanted it. The voters looked at one another in astonishment. It was a visible miracle of the glorious Evangelist St. Mark, who had been invoked by Signor Flangini, then First Corrector,[11] now a Cardinal, and by the three State Inquisitors.

On the appointed day I arrived at the casino at the usual hour, and there was the beautiful M. M. dressed as a woman of fashion, standing with her back to the fireplace.

"My friend," she said, "has not yet come; but as soon as he is here I will give you a wink."

"Where is the place?"

"There. Look at the back of that sofa against the wall. All the flowers in relief which you see have holes in their centers which go through to the closet behind. There is a bed, a table, and everything a man needs to stay there for seven or eight hours entertaining himself by watching what is done here. You shall see it when you wish."

"Did he have it built himself?"

"Certainly not, for he could not foresee that it might be of use to him."

"I understand that the spectacle may give him great pleasure; but since he cannot have you when nature will give him the greatest need of you, what will he do?"

"That is his concern. Besides, he is free to go if he is bored, and he can sleep, but if you are natural he will enjoy it."

"I shall be, except that I shall be more polite."

"No politeness, my dear, for you will at once become unnatural. Where did you ever hear of two lovers in the fury of love thinking of being polite?"

"You are right, dear heart; but I will be delicate."

"That you may, just as you always are. Your letter pleased me. You treated the subject thoroughly."

M. M. was wearing nothing over her hair, but it was negligently dressed. A sky-blue quilted dress was her only attire. She had on ear-buttons studded with brilliants; her neck was completely bare. A fichu of silk gauze and silver thread, arranged in haste, half revealed the beauty of her bosom and displayed its whiteness where her dress opened in front. She had on slippers. Her shy and modestly smiling face seemed to be saying: "This is the person you love." What I found most unusual and what pleased me excessively was her rouge, which was applied as the court ladies apply it in Versailles. The charm of such painting lies in the carelessness with which it is placed on the cheeks.

The rouge is not meant to look natural, it is put on to please the eyes, which see in it the tokens of an intoxication which promises them amorous transports and furies. She said that she had put on rouge to please her lover, who liked it. I answered that such a taste led me to think him French. When I said this she winked at me: her friend had arrived. So it was then that the comedy was to begin.

"The more I look at your face, the more angry I am at your spouse."

"They say he was ugly."

"It has been said: so he deserves to be cuckolded, and we shall work at it all night. I have lived in celibacy for the past week, but I need to eat, for I have nothing in my stomach but a cup of chocolate and the whites of six fresh eggs which I ate in a salad dressed with Lucca oil[12] and Four Thieves vinegar."[13]

"You must be ill."

"Yes; but I shall be well when I have distilled them one by one into your amorous soul."

"I did not know that you were in need of *frustratoires*."[14]

"Who could need them with you? But my fear is reasonable, for if I miss you, I will blow out my brains."

"What does 'miss' mean?"

"In the figurative sense it means 'fail in one's purpose.' Literally it means that when I want to shoot my pistol at my enemy, the priming doesn't catch. I *miss* him."

"Now I understand you. And it would be a misfortune, my dark-haired love, but not enough to make you blow out your brains."

"What are you doing?"

"I am taking off your cloak. Give me your muff,[15] too."

"That will be difficult, for it is nailed."

"Nailed?"

"Put your hand in it. Try."

"Oh, the wretch! Is it the egg whites that gave you such a nail?"

"No, my angel, it is your whole charming person."

At that I picked her up, she held me around the shoulders to make less weight for me, and, having dropped my muff, I grasped her by the thighs and she steadied herself on the nail; but after a turn around the room, fearing what would follow I set her down on the carpet, then sat down myself and made her sit on me, whereupon she had the kindness to finish the job with her beautiful hand, collecting the white of the first egg in the palm of it.

"Five to go," she said; and after cleaning her beautiful hand in a potpourri of aromatic herbs, she gave it to me to kiss again and on the bed, and can nowhere find the shirt which decency demands that I put on. The newcomer thought he was entering Hell. He exclaimed:

"Where am I? Where are they putting me? What heat! What a stench! With whom am I?"

At that Lorenzo called him out, asking me to put on a shirt and come into the garret; he told him that he had orders to bring him a bed from his house and everything he asked for, and that until his return he could walk in the garret and that meanwhile the cell would be purged of the stench, which was only the smell of oil. What a surprise for me to hear him say that the stench was only oil! As a matter of fact it came from the lamp, which I had extinguished without snuffing it. Lorenzo did not ask me a single question about it; so he knew everything; the Jew had told him. How lucky I was that he could not have told him more! At that moment I began to feel somewhat kindly toward Lorenzo.

After quickly putting on a fresh shirt and a dressing gown, I came out. The new prisoner was writing in pencil a list of what he wanted. He was the first to speak when he saw me:

"It's Casanova!"

I at once recognized the Abate Count Fenaroli,[39] of Brescia, a man of fifty years, amiable, rich, and a favorite in the choicest society. He came and embraced me, and when I said I would have expected to see anyone else on earth up there except himself, he could not hold back his tears, which provoked mine.

As soon as we were alone I said to him that when his bed arrived I would offer him the alcove but that he should do me the favor of refusing it and that he should not ask for the cell to be swept, adding that I would tell him the reasons when there was more time. I explained the reason for the stench of oil, and after assuring me that he would keep everything secret he said that he considered himself fortunate to have been put with me. He said that no one knew what my crime was, so everyone was trying to guess it. Some said I was the head of a new religion; others said Signora Memmo had convinced the tribunal that I was teaching her sons atheism. Still others said that Signor Antonio Condulmer, one of the State Inquisitors, had had me imprisoned as a disturber of the public peace because I hissed the Abate Chiari's comedies and was planning to go to Padua on purpose to kill him.

All these accusations had some basis which gave them an air of probability, but they were all fabrications. I did not care enough about religion to be interested in founding a new one. Signora Memmo's three sons, all of them highly intelligent, were more the sort to lead others astray than to be led astray themselves, and Signor Condulmer would have been kept too busy if he had tried to lock up everyone who hissed the Abate Chiari. As for the Abate, who had been a Jesuit, I had forgiven him. The celebrated Father Origo,[40] likewise a Jesuit, had taught me how to avenge myself on him by speaking well of him at large gatherings. My praises provoked my hearers to satires, and I was avenged without any trouble to myself.

Toward evening a bed was brought, together with an armchair, linen, scented waters, a good dinner, and good wines. The Abate could eat nothing; but I did not imitate him. His bed was set up without moving mine and we were locked in.

I began by taking from the hole my lamp and my napkin, which, having fallen into the lamp, had become soaked with oil. I laughed heartily. An accident which has no consequences and which is occasioned by causes which could have tragic ones is a good reason for laughter. I put everything in order; and I lit my lamp, the story of which made the Abate laugh. We spent a sleepless night, not so much because of the million fleas which were devouring us as because our talk was so interesting that we could not bring ourselves to end it. Here is the story of his arrest, as he himself told it to me:

"Yesterday at twenty o'clock[41] a party consisting of Signora Alessandri,[42] Count Paolo Martinengo,[43] and myself boarded a gondola; we reached Fusina at twenty-one and Padua at twenty-four, intending to see the opera and return here immediately afterward. During the second act my evil genius sent me to the gaming room, where I saw Count Rosenberg, the Ambassador from Vienna, with his mask off, and ten paces from him Signora Ruzzini,[44] whose husband is about to leave for the same court as Ambassador of the Republic. I bowed to them both and I was going to leave when the Ambassador said to me loudly: '*You are very fortunate to be able to pay your court to so charming a lady; it is only at moments like this that the part I play in the most beautiful country in the world becomes my torment. Tell her, I beg you, that the laws which prevent me from speaking to her here have no power in Vienna, where I shall see her next year and where I shall make war on her.*' Signora Ruzzini, who saw that we were speaking of her, asked me what the Count had said and I repeated it to her word for word. 'Answer him,' she said, 'that *I accept his declaration of war and that we shall see which of us two is the better warrior.*' I did not think I was committing a crime by repeating her answer, which was merely a compliment. After the opera we ate a fowl and we were back here at fourteen o'clock. I was going to bed to sleep until twenty, when a *fante* brought me a note which ordered me to be at the Bussola at nineteen o'clock to hear what the Circospetto Businello, Secretary to the Council of Ten, had to say to me. Astonished by the order, which is always an ill omen, and much troubled that I had to obey it, at the appointed hour I appeared before the minister, who, without saying even a word to me, ordered me put here."

Nothing was more innocent than his offense; but there are laws in the world which one can break innocently and the transgressors of which are no less guilty for that. I congratulated him on knowing what his crime was, on his crime itself, and on the manner of his arrest, and since his offense was a very slight one I told him that he would remain with me only a week and then be ordered to go and live on his estate in Brescia for six months. He answered sincerely that he did not believe he would be left there a week—a perfect example of the man who, feeling no guilt, cannot conceive that he will be punished. I let him keep his illusion; but what I told him proved to be the case.[45] I made up my mind to be a good companion to him in order to give him as much comfort as I could in the great distress his imprisonment caused him. I sympathized in his misfortune to such a point that I entirely forgot my own during all the time he was with me.

The next morning at daybreak Lorenzo brought coffee and a big basket containing dinner for the Count-Abate, who did not understand how anyone could suppose a man would want to eat at such an hour. We were allowed to walk for an hour and then were locked in. The fleas which tormented us made him ask me why I did not have the place swept. I could not bear to have him either think me a swine or believe that my skin was thicker than his; I told him, and even showed him, everything. I saw that he was surprised, and indeed mortified because he had in a sense forced me to entrust him with so weighty a secret. He encouraged me to work and to finish the hole that day if possible, so that he could himself let me down and afterward pull up my rope; for his part, he did not wish to make his crime more serious by flight. I showed him the model of a device by which I was sure that when I had got down I could pull the sheet I had used as a rope down after me; it was a bit of stick fastened at one end to a long string. My sheet was to be secured to the trestle of my bed only by this stick, which would go into the two halves of a loop in the rope under the trestle; the string which operated the stick was to go to the floor of the Inquisitors' room, where, as soon as I found myself on my feet, I would pull on it. He had no doubt of its working, and he congratulated me on it, the more so since the precaution was absolutely necessary, since if the sheet had stayed there it would be the first thing to catch the eyes of Lorenzo, who could not come up to where we were except by passing through that room; he would look for me at once, find me, and arrest me. My noble companion was convinced that I should give up my work, since there was great danger of my being caught at it and the more so as it would take me several more days to finish the hole, which was to cost Lorenzo his life. But could the thought of purchasing freedom at the price of his life lessen my eagerness to obtain my freedom? I should have done what I did if the consequence of my escape would have been the death of all the constables in the Republic and even of the State itself. Love of country becomes nothing but a phantasm in the mind of the man whom his country is oppressing.

But my good humor did not prevent my dear companion from succumbing to moments of melancholy. He was in love with Signora Alessandri, who had been a singer and who was the mistress or the wife of his friend Martinengo, and he must have had her favors; but the more a lover is in favor, the more miserable he becomes if he is torn from the arms of the woman he loves. He sighed, tears flowed from his eyes, and he admitted that he loved a woman who combined all the virtues. I sincerely condoled with him, taking care not to comfort him by saying that love is only a trifle, a distressing sort of consolation which only fools offer to lovers; it is not even true that love is nothing but a trifle.

The week which I had predicted passed very quickly; I lost his precious companionship; but I did not give myself time to regret it. I took good care never to ask this honorable man to keep my secret; the least doubt on my part would have been an insult to his noble soul.

On July 3rd Lorenzo told him to be ready to leave at the Terza, which during that month rings at twelve o'clock. For this reason he did not bring him his dinner. During the whole week the only nourishment he took was soup, fruits, and Canary wine.[46] It was I who ate well, to the great satisfaction of my friend, who admired my cheerful temperament. We spent the last three hours vowing the tenderest friendship. Lorenzo appeared, went down with him, and reappeared a quarter of an hour later to take away all of this most amiable man's possessions.

On the next day Lorenzo gave me an accounting of his expenditures during the month of June, and I saw that he was touched when, finding that I had a balance of four zecchini, I told him that I made his wife a present of them. I did not tell him that it was the recompense for my lamp; but he may have thought so.

Devoting myself entirely to my work, I saw it reach perfection on August 23rd. The delay was caused by a very natural mishap. When, digging into the last board, always with the greatest care to make it only extremely thin, I got very close to its opposite surface, I put my eye to a small hole through which I ought to see the Inquisitors' room, as in fact I did see it; but at the same time I saw, at a very short distance from the same hole, which was no bigger than a fly, a perpendicular surface about eight inches across. This was what I had always feared: it was one of the beams supporting the ceiling. I saw that I should have to make the hole bigger in the direction away from the beam; for the latter made the space so narrow that my rather portly person could never have got through it. I had to enlarge the opening by a fourth, still always fearing that the space between the two beams would not be enough. After the enlargement a second little hole of the same size showed me that God had blessed my work. I stopped up the little holes, both to prevent the small fragments from dropping into the room and to make it impossible for a ray from my lamp to pass through and so reveal my operation to anyone who might have seen it.

I set the night before St. Augustine's Day[47] as the time for my escape, because I knew that the Great Council met on that feast and hence there would be no one in the Bussola, which was next door to the room through which I must necessarily pass on my way out. I therefore decided to leave on the night of the 27th.

At noon on the 25th something happened to me which makes me tremble even now as I record it. At noon precisely, I heard the screech of the bolts; I thought I should die. A violent palpitation of my heart, which was beating three or four inches below its proper place, made me fear that my last hour had come. I dropped into my armchair in panic. Coming into the garret, Lorenzo put his head to the grating and said in joyous tones:

"I congratulate you, Signore, on the good news I bring you."

Instantly supposing that he meant my freedom, for I knew of no other news which could be good, I saw that I was lost.

The discovery of the hole would have led to my pardon being revoked.

Lorenzo enters and tells me to come with him.

"Wait till I get dressed."

"It doesn't matter, for you are only going from this vile cell to another which is light and brand-new, where you will see half of Venice from two windows, where you can stand upright, where—"

But I could bear no more, I felt that I was dying.

"Give me some vinegar," I said. "Go and tell the Signor Secretary that I thank the tribunal for this kindness and that I beg him in God's name to leave me here."

"You make me laugh. Have you gone mad? You are to be taken out of Hell and put in Paradise, and you refuse? Come, come, you must obey; stand up. I will give you my arm and I will have your clothes and your books brought you."

Astonished and in no position to say another word, I rose, I left the cell, and I instantly felt a slight relief when I heard him order one of his men to follow him with my armchair. As always, my pike was hidden in its stuffing, and that was at least something. I wished I were also being followed by the fine hole I had made with such effort, and which I had to abandon; but it was impossible. My body moved on; but my soul remained behind.

Supporting myself on Lorenzo's shoulder, while the fellow supposed he was giving me courage with his jokes, I passed through two narrow corridors and, after going down three steps, entered a large and very light room, at the far left-hand corner of which I went through a small door into a corridor which was two feet wide and twelve long and had two grated windows to my right, through which I clearly saw the upper part of the whole section of the great city which lay on that side, as far as the Lido. But I was in no state to be consoled by a fine view.

The door of the cell was in the corner of this corridor; I saw a grated window which was opposite one of the two which lighted the corridor, so that the prisoner, though shut in, could enjoy much of the pleasant prospect. Most important of all, since the window was open, it let in a gentle, cool wind which tempered the unbearable heat and which was veritably balm to the poor creature who had to breathe in the cell, especially during this season.

I did not make these observations at the time, as the reader can well imagine. As soon as Lorenzo saw me in the cell, he had my armchair brought, and I instantly flung myself into it; then he left, saying that he would have my bed and all my belongings fetched at once.

The stoicism of Zeno,[48] the ataraxia of the Pyrrhonists,[49] present our judgment with most extraordinary images. They are praised, they are derided, they are admired, they are laughed at, and the wise admit their possibility only with restrictions. Any man who is called upon to judge of a moral possibility or impossibility has every reason to start only from himself, for if he is honest he cannot admit an inner power in anyone unless he feels the seed of it in himself. What I find in myself on this subject is that, through a power gained by great application, a man can succeed in keeping from crying out in his sufferings and can resist being swept away by his first impulses. That is all. *Abstine* ("abstain") and *sustine*[50] ("bear") are the tokens of a good philosopher, but the material sufferings which afflict the Stoic will not be less than those which torment the Epicurean, and grief will be more painful for him who conceals it than for him who obtains a real relief by complaining. The man who tries to seem indifferent to an event which determines his condition only appears to be so, unless he is an idiot or in a frenzy. He who boasts of perfect tranquillity lies, and I beg Socrates' pardon a thousand times. I will believe in Zeno completely if he will tell me that he has found the secret of preventing nature from turning pale, blushing, laughing, and crying.

I sat in my armchair like a man in a stupor; motionless as a statue, I saw that I had wasted all the efforts I had made, and I could not repent of them. I felt that I had nothing to hope for, and the only relief left to me was not to think of the future.

My thoughts rising up to God, the state in which I was seemed to me a punishment visited on me directly by him because, though he had left me time to finish my whole task, I had abused his mercy by putting off my escape for three days. It was true that I could have gone down three days earlier, but I did not think I deserved so severe a punishment for having delayed in consequence of the most prudent consideration possible, or for exercising a caution enforced on me by a forethought which, on the contrary, deserved to be rewarded, since if I had obeyed only my natural impatience I would have defied every danger.

To fly in the face of the reasoning which had made me put off my escape until August 27th, I should have had to receive a revelation; and reading María de Agreda had not turned me into an idiot.

CHAPTER XIV

Underground prisons called "the Wells."
Lorenzo's revenge. I enter into a correspondence
with another prisoner, Father Balbi; his
character. I plan my escape with him.
The method. My stratagem for sending him
my pike. Success. I am given an infamous
companion; portrait of him.

A minute later two *sbirri* brought me my bed and left, only to return at once with all my clothes; but two hours passed during which I saw no one, though the doors to my cell were open. The delay caused me much thought but I could reach no conclusion. Having everything to fear, I tried to attain a state of tranquillity such that I could resist whatever tribulation might come.

Besides "the Leads" and "the Four," the State Inquisitors had nineteen other terrible prison cells underground in the Doge's Palace; to these they sentenced criminals who had deserved death. All the highest judges on earth have always believed that by sparing the life of him who has deserved death they have shown him mercy, no matter how horrible a punishment they mete out to him instead. In my opinion it can only be mercy if it seems so to the criminal; but they do it without consulting him. It becomes injustice.

These nineteen underground prisons have every resemblance to tombs but they are called "wells"[1] because they are always flooded by two feet of sea water, which comes in through the same grated hole by which they receive a little light; these holes are only a square foot in size. The prisoner, unless he enjoys being in a salt bath up to his knees all day, has to sit on a platform where he also has his pallet and on which at dawn a jailer puts his water, his soup, and his ration biscuit, which he has to eat at once, for if he delays enormous sea rats would tear it from his hands. In this horrible prison, to which the prisoners are usually condemned for the remainder of their days, and with such food, a number of them live to extreme old age. A criminal who died about that time had been sent there at the age of forty-four. Convinced that he had deserved death, he may have thought his prison a merciful reprieve. There are those who fear nothing but death. The man's name was Beguelin;[2] he was French.

He had served with the rank of captain in the troops of the Republic during her last war with the Turks in the year 1716, and in Corfu under Field Marshal Count Schulenburg,[3] who forced the Grand Vizier to raise the siege. Beguelin served the Marshal as a spy, disguising himself as a Turk and boldly entering the enemy army; but at the same time he was spying for the Grand Vizier. Found guilty of his double espionage, he deserved death, and it was certain that the judges who sent him to die in "the Wells" showed him mercy; and the fact is that he lived for thirty-seven years. He can only have been bored and always hungry. He may have said: *Dum vita superest bene est* ("So long as life remains, it is well").[4] But the prisons I saw at Spielberg[5] in Moravia, to which clemency consigned prisoners sentenced to death and which the criminal never managed to survive for a year, are such that the death they bring *siculi non invenere tyranni* ("even Sicilian tyrants did not invent").[6]

During the two hours I waited I did not fail to imagine that I was perhaps to be taken to "the Wells." In a place where the poor wretch who is condemned to it feeds on chimerical hopes he must also feel unreasonable panic terrors. The tribunal, master of the garrets and the cellars of the great palace, might well have decreed Hell for anyone who had tried to run away from Purgatory.

I finally heard furious steps approaching. I saw Lorenzo, his face distorted by anger. Frothing with rage, blaspheming God and all the saints, he began by ordering me to give him the ax and the tools I had used to make a hole in the floor and to tell him which of his *sbirri* had brought them to me. Not stirring even a finger, I replied that I did not know what he was talking about. He orders me searched. But at that I quickly get up, I threaten the scoundrels, and, stripping naked, I told them to do their duty. He had my mattresses searched and my pallet emptied, he even made his men search the stinking chamber pot. He picked up the cushion of my armchair, and finding nothing hard in it, he threw it angrily on the floor.

"You refuse," he said, "to tell me where the tools with which you made the hole are, but someone will make you talk."

"If it is true that I made a hole in the floor, I will say that I received the tools from you and have given them back to you."

At this answer, which his men, whom he seemed to have angered, received with approbation, he shouted, he banged his head against the wall, he stamped his feet; I thought he was going mad. He went out, and his men brought my clothes, my books, my bottles, and everything except my lamp and my stone. That done, before leaving the corridor he closed the two windows through which I got a little air. I was now shut up in a small space with no opening by which the air could enter. I confess that after he left I thought I had got off cheaply. Despite his training in his trade he did not think of turning my armchair upside down. Finding that I was still in possession of my bolt, I adored Providence and I saw that I could still count on making it the means of my escape.

The intense heat and the shock of the day's events kept me from sleeping. Early the next morning he brought me wine which had turned to vinegar, stinking water, rotting salad, spoiled meat, and very hard bread; he did not have the place swept, and when I asked him to open the windows he did not even answer. An extraordinary ceremony which was begun that day consisted in a constable making the round of my cell carrying an iron bar with which he pounded the entire floor and the walls and especially under the bed. I noticed that the constable who was doing the pounding never struck the ceiling. This observation gave me the idea that I could get out by way of the roof; but to succeed in such a project demanded a combination of circumstances which did not depend upon me; for I could do nothing which was not visible. The cell was brand-new; the least scratch would have been instantly seen by all the constables when they came in.

I spent a terrible day. The intense heat began toward noon. I really believed I should be stifled. I was in nothing short of a sweating room. I could neither eat nor drink, for everything was spoiled. The weakness caused by the heat and by the sweat which came out in great drops all over my body made it impossible for me either to walk or to read. My dinner the next day was the same; the stench of the veal he brought me reached my nose at once. I asked him if he had been ordered to kill me off by hunger and heat, and he went away without answering. He did the same thing the next day. I told him to give me a pencil because I wanted to write something to the Secretary, and again he did not answer and left. I ate the soup out of spite and dipped some bread in Cyprus wine to preserve my strength and kill him the next day by plunging my pike into his throat; things had become so bad that I thought I had no other course; but the next day instead of carrying out my plan I satisfied myself with swearing to him that I would kill him when I was set free; he laughed, and left without answering. I began to believe he was acting as he did by order of the Secretary, to whom he had perhaps reported the hole. I did not know what to do; my patience struggled against despair; I felt that I was dying of inanition.

It was on the eighth day that, in the presence of his constables, I demanded in a voice of thunder that he give me an accounting of my money, calling him an infamous hangman. He answered that I should have it the next day; but before he locked my cell I grabbed up the bucket of filth and showed him by my posture that I meant to throw it into the corridor; at that he told a constable to take it and, the air having become foul, he opened a window; but after the constable gave me a clean bucket he shut the window again and left, paying no attention to my outcries. Such was my situation; but seeing that what I had obtained had been the result of the insults to which I had treated him, I prepared to talk to him even more roughly the next day.

The next day my rage cooled. Before giving me my account he presented me with a basket of lemons which Signor Bragadin had sent me and I saw a large bottle of water which I thought was fit to drink and in my dinner a chicken which looked promising; more-over, a constable opened the two windows. When he handed me my account I merely glanced at the total and told him to give the balance to his wife, except for a zecchino which I ordered him to distribute among his men, who were there and who thanked me. Left alone with me, he proceeded to deliver the following discourse calmly enough:

"You have already told me, Signore, that it was from me you obtained what you needed to make the enormous hole you made in the other cell, so I am no longer in doubt about it. But would you be so good as to tell me who gave you what you needed to make the lamp?"

"You did."

"What, again? I did not believe that intelligence consisted in audacity."

"I am not lying. It is you, and with your own hands, who gave me everything I needed: oil, gun flint, and matches—all the rest I had."

"You are right. Can you as easily convince me that I also gave you what you needed to make the hole?"

"Yes, just as easily. I received nothing except from you."

"God have mercy on me! What are you saying? Please tell me how I gave you an ax?"

"I will tell you everything if you like, but in the Secretary's presence."

"I do not wish to hear more, and I believe you. Say nothing, and remember that I am a poor man and have children."

He went away, holding his head in his hands.

I was very glad I had found the way to instill fear into the rascal, for whom it was decreed that I should cost him his life. I now realized that his own interest forbade his telling the minister anything that I had done.

I had ordered Lorenzo to buy me the complete works of the Marchese Maffei;[7] he did not want to spend the money, and he did not dare tell me so. He asked me what I could need with books when I had so many.

"I have read them all and I need new ones."

"I will arrange to have someone who is here lend you books if you will lend him yours, and so you will save your money."

"They are novels, which I do not like."

"They are learned books; and if you think you are the only one with brains here, you are wrong."

"Very well. We shall see. Here is a book I will lend to the man with brains. Bring me one too."

I gave him Pétau's *Rationarium*[8] and four minutes later he brought me the first volume of Wolff.[9] Pleased, I canceled my order to buy me Maffei; and even more pleased that he had made me listen to reason on such an important subject, he left.

Less tempted by the prospect of reading the learned work than by seizing the opportunity to begin a correspondence with someone who could perhaps help me in the plan for escaping which I had already sketched out in my mind, upon opening the book I found a piece of paper on which I read, in six well-turned verses, a paraphrase of Seneca's saying: *Calamitosus est animus futuri anxius* ("It is misery for the mind to be anxious about the future").[10] I immediately made six more verses. I had let the nail of the little finger of my right hand grow in order to clean my ears with it, I cut it to a point and made a pen of it, in place of ink I used the juice of black mulberries, and I wrote my six verses on the same piece of paper. In addition I wrote a list of the books I had, and I put it behind the spine of the same book. All books bound in boards in Italy have a sort of pocket under the binding at the back. On the spine of the same book, where the title is put, I wrote *latet*[11] ("something is hidden"). Impatient to receive an answer, the next morning I at once told Lorenzo that I had read the book through and that the person would do me a favor if he would send me another. He immediately brought me the second volume.

A loose note between the pages of the book ran as follows: "We who are together in this prison are both greatly pleased that the ignorance of a miser procures us an unparalleled privilege. I who write am Marin Balbi,[12] a Venetian nobleman and a monk of the Somaschian Order. My companion is Count Andrea Asquin,[13] of Udine, the capital of Friuli. He commands me to tell you that you are at liberty to make use of all his books, a catalogue of which you will find in the hollow of the binding. We must, Signore, employ every precaution to keep our little correspondence from Lorenzo."

That we had both hit upon the idea of sending each other catalogues and the idea of concealing a written message in the aperture at the back of the book did not surprise me, for it seemed to me to require nothing but common sense; but I thought his warning to exercise caution very strange when the letter which told all was a loose sheet. Lorenzo not only might open the book, it was his duty to do so, and, seeing the letter and unable to read, he would have put it in his pocket to get it read to him in Italian by the first priest he came upon in the street, and everything would have been discovered at its very beginning. I at once decided that this Father Balbi must be a blockhead.

I read the catalogue and on the other half of the sheet I wrote them who I was, how I had been arrested, my ignorance of my crime, and my hope that I would soon be sent home. On receiving another book, Father Balbi wrote me a letter which covered sixteen pages. Count Asquin never wrote to me. The monk entertained himself by writing me the whole story of his misfortunes. He had been under the Leads for four years[14] because, having had three bastards by three indigent girls, all of them virgins, he had had them baptized under his own name. His Father Superior[15] had admonished him the first time, threatened him the second, and the third time had lodged a complaint with the tribunal, which had imprisoned him; and the Father Superior sent him his dinner every day. His defense took up half of his letter, in which he amply displayed the poverty of his intelligence. Both his Superior, he said, and the tribunal were nothing short of tyrants, for they had no jurisdiction over his conscience. He said that, since he was sure that the bastards were his, he could not deprive them of the advantages they could derive from his name; and that their mothers were respectable though poor, for before him they had had commerce with no man. He ended by saying that his conscience obliged him to recognize publicly that the children these honest young women had given him were his, thus forestalling the slander that they were the children of others, and that in any case he could not deny nature or the fatherly love which he felt for the poor innocents. "There is no danger," he said, "that my Superior will fall into the same fault, since his pious affection is shown only to his boy pupils."

I needed no more to know my man: eccentric, sensual, a poor reasoner, malicious, imprudent, and ungrateful. After saying in his letter that he would be very unfortunate without the company of Count Asquin, who was seventy years of age and had books and money, he used up two pages abusing him to me and describing his faults and absurdities. Out of prison I would not have answered a man of his character; but up there I had to make use of everything. In the back of the book I found pencil, pens, and paper, which made it possible for me to write at my ease.

All the rest of his long letter contained the histories of all the prisoners who were under the Leads and who had been there during the four years he had spent there himself. He told me that Niccolò was the constable who secretly bought him whatever he wanted and who told him the names of all the prisoners and everything that went on in the other cells, and to convince me of it he told me all he knew about the hole I had made. "You were taken from there," he said, "to make room for the patrician Priuli Gran Can,[16] and Lorenzo spent two hours having the hole you made stopped up by a carpenter and an ironsmith, on whom he enjoined silence upon pain of their lives, as he did on all his constables. Niccolò assured me that only one day later you would have left by a method which would have caused a great scandal, and that Lorenzo could have been strangled because it was perfectly clear that, though he tried to show surprise when he saw the hole and pretended to be furious with you, it could only be he who had given you the tools to break open the floor, which you must have given back to him. Niccolò also told me that Signor Bragadin promised him a thousand zecchini if he can make it possible for you to leave and that Lorenzo is confident that he can earn them without losing his post through the protection of Signor Diedo, who is his wife's lover. He also said that none of the constables dared tell the Secretary what had happened for fear that Lorenzo would get out of it with clean hands and would then avenge himself on the informer by having him discharged. I beg you to have confidence in me and to tell me all the particulars of this business and especially how you managed to procure the necessary tools. I promise you that my discretion will be equal to my curiosity."

I had no doubt of his curiosity but much doubt of his discretion, since his very question proved him to be the most indiscreet of men. However, I saw that I had to humor him, for I thought that a creature of his sort would be just the one to do everything I told him to do and to help me regain my freedom. I spent the whole day answering him; but a strong feeling of suspicion made me put off sending him my answer; I saw that our exchange of letters might be a trick of Lorenzo's to find out who had given me the tools to break the floor and where I was keeping them. I wrote him in a few words that a big knife with which I had made the hole was under the sill of the window in the corridor leading to the cell where I now was, I having myself put it there when I came in. This spurious confidence set my mind at rest in less than three days, for Lorenzo did not search the sill and he would have searched it if he had intercepted my letter.

Father Balbi wrote me that he knew I could have the big knife, for Niccolò had told him I had not been searched before I was locked in; Lorenzo had known this, and the circumstance might have saved him if I had succeeded in escaping, for he claimed that when he received a man from the hands of Messer Grande he could not but suppose that he had already been searched. Messer Grande would have said that, having seen me get out of my bed, he was sure that I had no weapons about me. He ended his letter by asking me to send him my knife by Niccolò, whom I could trust.

The monk's rashness surprised me. When I felt sure that my letters were not being intercepted I wrote him that I was not able to repose any confidence in his Niccolò and that I could not even entrust my secret to paper. Meanwhile his letters amused me. In one of them he told me the reason why Count Asquin was confined under the Leads even though he could not move, since, in addition to his being seventy years of age, he was hampered by a big belly and by a leg he had broken long ago and which had been badly set. He said that, not being rich, the Count practiced law as an advocate at Udine and that in the city council he defended the peasantry against the nobility, who were seeking to deprive them of the right to vote in the provincial assemblies. Because the demands of the peasants disturbed the public peace the nobles had recourse to the tribunal of the State Inquisitors, which ordered Count Asquin to abandon his clients. Count Asquin replied that the municipal code authorized him to defend the constitution, and he disobeyed; but the Inquisitors had him carried off, despite the code, and confined him under the Leads, where he had been for five years.[17] Like me, he had fifty soldi a day, but he had the privilege of handling his money himself. In this connection the monk, who never had a soldo, freely denigrated his companion to me, especially on the score of avarice. He said that in the cell on the other side of the hall there were two gentlemen[18] from the Sette Comuni, also in prison for disobedience, the elder of whom had gone mad and was kept tied up. In another cell there were two notaries.[19]

About this time a Veronese Marchese,[20] of the Pindemonte family, had been imprisoned for disobeying a summons to appear. This nobleman had enjoyed great privileges, perhaps the most important of them being that his servants were allowed to deliver his letters into his own hands. He was there only a week.

When my suspicions were set at rest, my state of mind led me to reason as follows. I wanted my freedom. The pike I had was excellent; but I could not use it because each morning every corner of my cell was sounded with an iron bar, except the ceiling. So I could only hope to escape through the ceiling by having it broken from outside. Whoever was to break it could escape with me by helping me to make a hole in the great roof of the palace the same night. Once on the roof I would see what needed to be done; so the thing was to resolve and begin. I could see no resource except the monk, who, at the age of thirty-eight, though he was lacking in judgment, could carry out my instructions. So I must make up my mind to confide everything to him and think of some way to send him my bolt. I began by asking him if he wanted his freedom and if he was prepared to do everything to gain it by escaping with me. He replied that both he and his companion would be ready to do everything to break their chains; but that there was no use thinking about what was impossible; here he made me a long list of the difficulties, with which he filled four pages and which would have kept me occupied for the rest of my life if I had tried to circumvent them. I answered that I was not concerned about the general difficulties and that, having made my plan, I had thought only of solving the particular ones, which I could not entrust to paper. I promised him freedom if he would give me his word of honor to carry out my orders blindly. He promised me he would do everything.

I then wrote him that I had a pointed iron bar twenty inches long, which he was to use to break open the ceiling of his cell so that he could get out of it; and that once out, he was to break through the wall which separated us, pass through the opening he had made to a point above my cell, break it open above, and pull me out. "Once you have done all this," I said, "you will have nothing more to do, for I will do all the rest. I will get you both out, you and Count Asquin."

He answered that when he had got me out of my cell I would at best be in a prison which would differ from the first only in size. "We shall be in the garrets," he wrote, "still confined behind three locked doors." "I know that, Reverend Father," I replied, "and it is not by way of the doors that I intend we shall escape. My plan is made and I am sure of it, and all that I ask from you is carrying it out to the letter, and no objections. Think only of some way by which my twenty-inch bar can reach your hands without whoever is to bring it to you knowing that he is bringing it; and send me your ideas on the subject. In the meanwhile have Lorenzo buy you forty or fifty images of saints big enough to paper the whole inside of your cell. All these prints of religious subjects will give Lorenzo no occasion for suspecting that their only use will be to cover the hole which you will make in the ceiling and by which you will get out. It will take you several days to make the hole; and in the morning Lorenzo will see nothing of what you have accomplished the day before, for you will put the print back where it was and your work will pass unnoticed. I cannot do this, for I am under suspicion and no one would believe that I have any great reverence for prints. Do this, and think of some way to get my bar."

Thinking about it too, I ordered Lorenzo to buy me a folio Bible which had recently been printed and which contained the Vulgate[21] and the Septuagint.[22] I thought of this book, the size of which led me to hope that I could put my pike in the back of the binding and so send it to the monk; but when I received it I found that the bolt was two inches longer than the Bible, which measured exactly a foot and a half. The monk had written me that his cell was already papered with prints; and I had written him my idea about the Bible and the great difficulty due to the length of my bar, which I could not shorten except with a forge. He answered, deriding the poverty of my imagination, that I had only to send him the bolt in my fox-skin cloak. He said Lorenzo had told him that I had this fine cloak, and it would give no cause for suspicion if Count Asquin asked to see it in order to have one like it bought for him. I had only, he said, to send it to them folded up; but I was sure that Lorenzo would unfold it on the way, for a folded cloak was more awkward to carry than if it were unfolded; but in order not to discourage him and at the same time to convince him that I was less stupid than himself, I wrote him that he need only send for the cloak. The next morning Lorenzo asked me for it, and I gave it to him folded up but without the bolt. A quarter of an hour later he brought it back to me, saying that they had admired it.

The next day the monk wrote me a letter in which he admitted that he had been guilty of giving me bad advice; but he added that I had been wrong to take it. According to him, the pike was lost, for Lorenzo had brought the cloak unfolded and he must have put the bar in his pocket. So all hope was lost. I consoled him by telling him the truth, at the same time asking him to give his advice less rashly in the future. I then decided to send the monk my bolt in the Bible, but taking a precaution which would infallibly prevent Lorenzo from looking at the ends of the big volume. So I told him that I wanted to celebrate St. Michael's Day[23] with two big dishes of macaroni[24] with butter and Parmesan cheese; I wanted two dishes of it because I wanted to make a present of one to the worthy personage who lent me books. Lorenzo said that the same worthy personage wished to read the big book which had cost three zecchini. I answered that I would send it to him with a dish of macaroni; but I said that I needed the largest dish he had in his house and that I wanted to season it myself; he promised to do everything to the letter. In the meanwhile I wrapped the bolt in paper and I put it in the back of the binding of the Bible. I divided the two inches; each end of the bolt protruded from the Bible by one inch. By placing a big dish of macaroni filled with butter on the Bible, I was sure that Lorenzo's eyes would remain fixed on the butter for fear of spilling it on the Bible, and that thus he would not have time to look at the two ends of the back of the volume. I informed Father Balbi of all this beforehand, urging him to be deft when he received the macaroni from Lorenzo and to be careful not to take first the dish and then the Bible but both together, for taking the dish would expose the Bible and then Lorenzo could easily see the two protruding ends.

On St. Michael's Day Lorenzo appeared very early in the morning with a great kettle in which the macaroni were boiling; I at once put the butter on a portable stove to melt it and I got my two dishes ready, sprinkling them with Parmesan cheese, which he had brought me all grated. I took the pierced spoon and I began to fill them, adding butter and cheese with each spoonful and not stopping until the big dish meant for the monk could hold no more. The macaroni were swimming in butter, which came up to the very edge of the dish. Its diameter was almost twice the width of the Bible.[25] I picked it up and set it on the big book, which I had put beside the door of my cell, and holding it on the palms of my hands with the spine toward Lorenzo I told him to put out his arms and spread his fingers, and I admonished him to carry it with the greatest care and slowly so that the butter would not spill out of the dish and run over the Bible. As I admonished him to be careful of this most important burden, I kept my eyes fixed on his, which I was most happy to see never moved from the butter, which he was afraid of spilling. He wanted to take the macaroni and come back for the Bible afterward; but I laughed and said that if he did that, my present would lose all its beauty. He finally took it, complaining that I had put in too much butter and protesting that if it spilled on my Bible it would not be his fault. I knew that I was certain of victory as soon as I saw the Bible on his arms, for the two ends of the pike, which were now at a distance from my eyes equal to the width of the book, had become invisible for him now that he was holding it; they were next to his shoulders and there was no reason for him to raise his eyes to look at either of the ends, which had not the slightest interest for him. He could only be concerned to keep his dish horizontal. I followed him with my eyes until I saw him go down three steps to enter the corridor in front of the monk's cell, who, by blowing his nose three times, gave me the prearranged signal that everything had reached his hands in good order. Lorenzo came back and said that everything had been delivered according to my instructions. Father Balbi took a week to make a big enough opening in his ceiling, easily hiding it each day with a print which he removed and pasted up again with bread.

On October 8th he wrote me that he had spent the whole night working at the wall which separated us and that he had only managed to remove one brick; he exaggerated the difficulty of breaking out bricks held together by mortar which was too solid; he promised to continue, and in all his letters he repeated that we should make our situation worse, for we could not succeed. I answered that I was certain of the contrary.

Alas! I was certain of nothing; but I had to do as I was doing or give up my whole plan. How could I have told him that I did not know? I wanted to be out of there—that was all I knew; and the only thing in my mind was to take what steps I could to forward my escape, and not to stop until I was confronted with something insurmountable. I had read the great book of experience and I had learned from it that great enterprises were not to be talked about but executed, though with due regard for the power which Fortune exercises over all the undertakings of men. If I had imparted these lofty mysteries of moral philosophy to Father Balbi he would have said that I was mad.

His work proved to be difficult only on the first night; during those which followed, the more bricks he took out the easier it was to get out more. At the end of his work he found that he had removed thirty-six bricks from the wall.

On October 16th at eighteen o'clock,[26] just as I was amusing myself translating one of Horace's odes, I heard footsteps above my cell and then three knocks; I at once replied with another three; it was the signal we had arranged to inform each other that we had not been mistaken. He worked until evening, and the next day he wrote me that if my ceiling was only two boards thick his work would be completed that day, for each board was only an inch thick. He assured me that he would make the small circular entrance-way as I had told him to do, and that he would take great care never to go completely through the last board; this I had strongly urged on him because the least sign of a break in my cell would have raised the suspicion that it originated outside of it. He assured me that he would carry his excavation to the point at which it could be completed in a quarter of an hour. I had already settled on the next day but one as the time when I would leave my cell by night and not return to it, for with a companion I felt sure that in three or four hours I could make an opening in the great roof of the Doge's Palace and get up onto it, and then take the best means which chance offered me of getting down.

Two hours after noon on that day, which was a Monday,[27] while Father Balbi was still at work, I heard the sound of the door to the room next to my cell being opened; my blood froze; but I had strength enough left to knock twice, the alarm signal we had agreed to use, on hearing which Father Balbi was to hurry back through the hole in the wall and regain his cell. A moment later I saw Lorenzo, who asked my pardon for giving me the company of a "beggarly scoundrel." I saw a man between forty and fifty years of age, short, thin, badly dressed, with a round black wig, whom two constables proceeded to unbind. I had no doubt that he was a rogue, since Lorenzo had so characterized him in my presence and he had taken no offense at the title. I answered Lorenzo that the tribunal was lord and master; after having a pallet brought for him, he left, telling him that the tribunal allowed him ten soldi a day. My new cellmate replied:

"May God repay them!"

Overwhelmed by this fatal obstacle, I looked at the scoundrel, whose face betrayed him. I was thinking of getting him to talk, when he began himself by thanking me for the pallet which I had brought for him. I told him that he would eat with me, and he kissed my hand, asking me if even so he could have the ten soldi the tribunal allowed him, and I said that he could. He then went down on his knees, took a rosary from his pocket, and began peering all around the cell.

"What are you looking for, my friend?"

"I am looking, if you will forgive me, for some image *dell'immacolata Vergine Maria*, since I am a Christian, or at least for some poor crucifix, for I was never in such need of commending myself to St. Francis of Assisi, whose name I unworthily bear, as I am at this moment."

I could hardly keep from bursting into laughter, not at his Christian piety, which I revered, but at the way in which he had defended himself; his asking my pardon made me think he took me for a Jew; I hastened to give him the Office of the Holy Virgin,[28] whose image he kissed, then handed it back to me, modestly saying that his father, warden of a galley, had failed to have him taught to read. He said that he was a devotee of the most holy Rosary and told me a quantity of its miracles, to which I listened with the patience of an angel, and he asked my permission to recite it looking at the holy image which was the frontispiece to my Book of Hours. After the Rosary, which I recited with him, I asked him if he had dined and he said he was dying of hunger. I gave him everything I had; he devoured it all ravenously, drank all the wine I had, and when he was tipsy he began first crying and then babbling without rhyme or reason. I asked him the cause of his misfortune, and here is his story:

"My one and only passion in this world, dear master, has always been the glory of this sacred Republic and strict obedience to its laws; always attentive to the evil practices of the wicked, whose sole occupation is to deceive their prince and cheat him out of his dues and to keep their own activities concealed, and I have tried to discover their secrets and I have always faithfully reported to Messer Grande whatever I have been able to discover; it is true that I have always been paid; but the money I have received has never given me as much pleasure as the satisfaction I have felt in seeing that I was useful to the glorious Evangelist St. Mark. I have always scorned the prejudice of those who attach an evil meaning to the designation 'spy'; that name is ill-sounding only in the ears of those who do not love the government, for a spy is nothing but one who fosters the good of the State, the scourge of criminals, and the loyal subject of his prince. When I have been called upon to put my zeal into action, the feeling of friendship, which may have some weight with others, has never had any with me, still less what is called gratitude, and I have often vowed silence to wrest from someone an important secret which, as soon as I learned it, I punctually reported, assured by my confessor that I could reveal it not only because I had had no intention of keeping my oath of silence when I took it but because, where the public welfare is concerned, no oath is binding. I feel that, the slave of my zeal, I would have betrayed my father and I would have stilled the promptings of nature.

"Three weeks ago, then, I observed at Isola,[29] a small island where I was living, a great intimacy among four or five notable personages of the city whom I knew to be dissatisfied with the government because of the discovery and confiscation of a certain contraband shipment, which the principals had been obliged to expiate by imprisonment. The First Chaplain[30] of the parish, born a subject of the Empress-Queen, was in the plot, whose secret I determined to unravel. The plotters met in the evening at an inn, in a room where there was a bed; and after drinking and talking together they left. I boldly determined to hide under the bed one day when, sure that I was unobserved, I found the room open and empty. Toward evening my plotters arrived and talked about the city of Isola which they said was not under the jurisdiction of St. Mark but under that of the principality of Trieste, for it could not be regarded as a part of Venetian Istria. The Chaplain said to the leader of the plot, whose name was Pietro Paolo, that if he would sign a document and the others would do the same, he would himself wait on the Imperial Ambassador[31] and that the Empress would not only seize the city but would reward them. They all told the Chaplain they were ready, and he promised to bring the document the next day and leave at once and come here to bring it to the Ambassador. I decided to make their infamous project miscarry, despite the fact that one of the conspirators was my godfather, a spiritual relationship which gave him a claim on me more sacred and inviolable than if he had been my brother.

"After they left I had plenty of time to get away, thinking it useless to run a second risk by hiding myself the next day under the same bed. I had discovered enough. I left at midnight in a boat, and the next day before noon I was here, where I had someone write down the names of the six rebels for me, then took them to the Secretary to the State Inquisitors, telling him the facts. He ordered me to go early the next morning to Messer, who would give me a man with whom I should go to Isola to point out the Chaplain to him, for it seemed that the Chaplain would not have left by then, and after that I was to let the matter alone. I carried out his order. Messer gave me the man, I took him to Isola, I showed him the Chaplain, and I went about my business.

"After dinner my godfather sent for me to come and shave him, for I am a barber. After I had shaved him he gave me an excellent glass of refosco[32] and some slices of garlic sausage and he ate with me in good fellowship. My love for him as my godfather then filled my soul, I took his hand and, with heartfelt tears, advised him to end his acquaintance with the Chaplain and above all not to sign the document of which he knew; upon this he said to me that he was no more friendly with the Chaplain than with anyone else and he swore he had no idea what document I was referring to. I then began to laugh, I said I had been joking, and I left him, repenting that I had listened to the voice of my heart.

"The next day I saw neither the man nor the Chaplain, and a week later I left Isola and came here. I went to see Messer Grande, who instantly had me locked up; and here I am with you, dear master. I thank St. Francis that I am in the company of a good Christian who is here for reasons which I do not seek to know, for I am not curious. My name is Soradaci,[33] and my wife is a Legrenzi, daughter of a Secretary to the Council of Ten, who trampled on prejudice in order to marry me. She will be in despair not to know what has become of me; but I hope I shall stay here only a few days; I can be here only for the convenience of the Secretary, who presumably will need to question me."

After this brazen narrative, which showed me what kind of monster he was, I pretended to condole with him and, lauding his patriotism, predicted that he would be free in a few days. A half hour later he went to sleep, and I wrote the whole story to Father Balbi, urging upon him the necessity of suspending our work to await a favorable opportunity. The next day I ordered Lorenzo to buy me a wooden crucifix and a print of the Holy Virgin, and to bring me a flask of holy water. Soradaci asked him for his ten soldi, and Lorenzo scornfully gave him twenty. I ordered him to bring me four times as much wine and some garlic, for my cell-mate delighted in it. After he left I deftly took Father Balbi's letter from the book; he described his fright to me. He had returned to his cell more dead than alive and had quickly put the print back over the hole. He reflected that all would have been lost if Lorenzo had taken it into his head to put Soradaci in his garret instead of putting him with me. Lorenzo would not have seen him in the cell and he would have seen the hole.

The account Soradaci gave me of his activities led me to conclude that he would certainly have to undergo questioning, for the Secretary could not have had him locked up except on suspicion of slander or because his report was not clear. I therefore decided to entrust him with two letters which, if he had taken them to those to whom they were addressed, would have done me neither good nor harm, and which would have done me good if the traitor gave them to the Secretary in proof of his fidelity. I spent two hours writing the letters in pencil. The next morning Lorenzo brought me the image of the Virgin, the bottle of holy water, and all that I had ordered.

After feeding the scoundrel well I told him that I was under the necessity of asking him to do me a favor upon which my happiness depended.

"I count, my dear Soradaci, on your friendship and your courage. Here are two letters which I beg you to take to their addresses as soon as you regain your freedom. My happiness depends on your fidelity; but you must hide them, for if they are found on you when you leave here we are both lost. You must swear to me by this crucifix and by this Holy Virgin that you will not betray me."

"I am ready, master, to swear whatever you ask; I am under too great an obligation to you to betray you."

He began crying and protesting that he was wretched enough without my supposing him capable of treachery. After giving him a shirt and a nightcap, I took my nightcap off, I sprinkled the cell with holy water, and in the presence of the two sacred images I intoned an oath accompanied by imprecations which had no sense but were horrifying, and after several signs of the cross I made him get down on his knees and swear with imprecations which set him trembling that he would deliver the letters. After that I gave them to him, and it was he who insisted on sewing them into the back of his vest between the cloth and the lining.

I was morally certain that he would give them to the Secretary; so I used every art to write in such a style that no one would ever discover my ruse. My letters were of a nature to gain me the indulgence of the tribunal and even its esteem. I wrote to Signor Bragadin and to the Abate Grimani and I told them to set their minds at rest and not to repine over my fate, for I had reason to hope that I would soon be released. I told them that when I came out they would find that my punishment had done me more good than harm, because no one in Venice had stood in greater need of reformation than I. I asked Signor Bragadin to send me a pair of lined boots for the winter, since my cell was high enough for me to stand upright and walk about in. I did not want Soradaci to know that my letters were so innocent, for he might have taken it into his head to act like an honest man and deliver them.

CHAPTER XV

Soradaci turns traitor. How I overawe him.
Father Balbi successfully completes his work.
I leave my cell. Count Asquin's untimely
observations. The moment of departure.

Two or three days later Lorenzo came up at the Terza and took Soradaci down with him. Not seeing him return, I thought I should see no more of him; but he was brought back toward the end of the day, which rather surprised me. After Lorenzo left he told me that the Secretary suspected him of having warned the Chaplain, since the priest had never gone to see the Ambassador and no document had been found on him. He said that after a long interrogation he had been put all alone in a very small cell where he had been left for seven hours and that afterward he had been fettered again and taken to the Secretary, who tried to make him confess that he had told someone in Isola that the priest would not return there; this he could not confess, for he had never said it to anyone. The Secretary had finally rung and he had been brought back to my cell.[1]

In bitterness of soul I realized that he might well be left with me for a long time. During the night I wrote all this to Father Balbi. It was under the Leads that I learned to write in the dark.

The next morning after swallowing my broth, I wanted to make sure of what I already suspected.

"I wish," I said to the spy, "to add something to the letter I wrote Signor Bragadin; give it to me; you can sew it back in afterward."

"It is dangerous," he answered, "for someone might come in just at that moment and catch us at it."

"Let them come. Give me back my letters."

The monster then fell on his knees before me and swore that when he appeared before the terrible Secretary for the second time he was seized with a violent shaking and felt an intolerable pressure on his back just where the letters were, and the Secretary asking him what it was, he could not keep from telling him the truth, and Lorenzo having taken off his fetters and then his vest, he had unsewn the letters, which the Secretary had put in a drawer after reading them. He added that the Secretary had said that if he had delivered

538

the letters it would have been known and his crime would have cost him his life.

I then pretended to feel ill. I covered my face with my hands and flung myself on the bed on my knees before the crucifix and the Virgin demanding vengeance upon the monster who had betrayed me by violating the most solemn of all oaths. After that I lay down on my side with my face to the wall, and I had the firmness to remain there all that day without uttering a word, pretending not to hear the villain's tears and cries and protestations of repentance. I played my role wonderfully well in a comedy of which I already had the whole plot sketched out in my head. During the night I wrote Father Balbi to come at exactly nineteen o'clock,[2] and not one minute earlier or later, to finish his work, and to work for only four hours, so that he should leave without fail exactly when he heard twenty-three o'clock strike. I told him that our freedom depended on this absolute precision on his part and that he had nothing to fear.

It was the 25th of October, and the days were nearing when I must either carry out my project or abandon it forever. The State Inquisitors and even the Secretary went every year to spend the first three days of November[3] in some village on the mainland. During these three days when his masters were on vacation Lorenzo got drunk in the evening, slept until the Terza, and did not appear under the Leads until very late. It was a year earlier that I had learned all this. Prudence demanded that, if I was to escape, I must choose one of these three nights, in order to be certain that my flight would not be discovered until fairly late in the morning. Another reason for my eagerness, and one which led me to take the resolve at a time when I could no longer doubt that my companion was a scoundrel, was extremely powerful, and I think it deserves to be recorded.

The greatest relief a man in misfortune can have is the hope of soon escaping from it; he thinks of the happy moment when he will see the end of his misery, he persuades himself that it will not be long in coming, and he would do anything on earth to know exactly when it will come; but no one can know at what time something which depends on the will of another will happen, unless that other has announced it. However, in his impatience and weakness, the man comes to believe that by some occult means he can discover the time. "God," he says, "must know it, and God may permit it to be revealed to me by some omen." As soon as his curiosity has led him to this reasoning he does not hesitate to consult the omens, whether he is ready or not to believe all that they may tell him. Such was the state of mind of those who in past ages consulted oracles; such is the state of mind of those who today still question cabalas and who seek revelations in a verse of the Bible or a verse of Vergil, which has brought such fame to the *sortes virgilianae*[4] of which so many writers tell us.

Not knowing what method to use to make Destiny reveal to me through the Bible the moment at which I was to regain my freedom, I decided to consult the divine poem of *Orlando furioso* by Messer Lodovico Ariosto, which I had read countless times and which was still my delight up there. I worshiped his genius and I thought him far better suited than Vergil to foretell my good fortune.

With this idea in mind, I composed a short question in which I asked the supposed Intelligence which canto of Ariosto contained the prediction of my day of deliverance. After that I constructed an inverted pyramid made up of the numbers which resulted from the words of my question, and by subtracting nine from each pair of digits I finally came out with the number *nine*. I therefore concluded that the prediction I sought was in the ninth canto. I used the same method to discover in which stanza the prediction occurred and the resulting number was *seven*. Now eager to learn which verse of the stanza contained the oracle, the same method gave me the number *one*. So having the numbers 9, 7, 1 I took up the poem and, with my heart palpitating, found canto *nine*, stanza *seven*, first verse:

Tra il fin d'Ottobre, e il capo di Novembre

("Between the end of October and the beginning of November").[5]

The clarity of the verse and its appropriateness struck me as so amazing that I will not say I had complete faith in it, but my reader will forgive me if, for my part, I prepared to do all that I could to help verify the oracle. The strange thing is that "between the end of October and the beginning of November" there is only midnight, and it was in fact at the stroke of midnight on October 31st that I left there, as the reader will see. I beg him, after this faithful account, not to dismiss me as more superstitious than anyone else, for he would be wrong. I recount the thing because it is true and extraordinary, and because if I had disregarded it I should perhaps not have escaped. The incident will teach all those who have not yet attained wisdom that but for predictions many things that have happened would never have happened. The event does the prediction the service of verifying it. If the event does not occur the prediction becomes null and void; but I refer my kind reader to universal history, where he will find many events which would never have occurred if they had not been predicted. Forgive the digression.

And now for the way I spent the day until nineteen o'clock, meaning to strike awe into the soul of the stupid, vicious brute who was my companion, to confuse his feeble mind by astonishing images, and so make him powerless to harm me. When Lorenzo left us that morning I told Soradaci to come and eat his soup. The villain was in bed and he had told Lorenzo that he was ill. He would not have dared to come to me if I had not summoned him. He got up and, groveling on his belly at my feet, kissed them and, bursting into tears, said that unless I forgave him he would be a dead man that same day and that he already felt the beginning of the curse laid on him by the vengeance of the Holy Virgin, whom I had invoked against him; he felt griping pains tormenting his entrails and his tongue was covered with ulcers; he showed it to me and I saw that it was really covered with aphtha; I do not know if he had them the day before. I was not interested in examining him to see if he was telling me the truth; my interest was to pretend that I believed him and even to make him hope for forgiveness. I had next to make him eat and drink. The traitor might be intending to deceive me; but determined as I was to deceive him, it was a matter of finding out which of us was the cleverer. I had prepared an attack against which I was certain he could not defend himself.

I instantly assumed the countenance of a man inspired and I ordered him to sit down.

"Let us eat this soup," I said, *"and afterward I will declare your good fortune to you. Know that the Holy Virgin of the Rosary appeared to me at daybreak and commanded me to forgive you. You will not die and you will leave this place with me."*

Lost in wonder, he ate the soup with me, kneeling on the floor because there were no stools, then he sat on his pallet to hear me out. This is what I said:

"The grief which your treachery caused me kept me awake all night, because my letters, which you gave to the Secretary, would have been read by the State Inquisitors and have led to my being sentenced to stay here the rest of my life. My only consolation, I confess to you, was my certainty that you would die before my eyes within three days. With my mind full of this thought unworthy of a Christian, for God commands us to forgive, a slumber at daybreak brought me a vision. I saw this Holy Virgin, whose image you see, come to life, move, stand before me, open her mouth, and speak to me in these words: *'Soradaci is a devotee of my holy Rosary, I protect him, it is my will that you forgive him; and the curse he drew upon himself will now cease to operate. As the reward of your generous act I will command one of my angels to put on human form and at once come down from Heaven to break open the roof of this cell and take you from it in five or six days. The angel will set to work today at nineteen o'clock and he will work until half an hour before sunset, for he must return to Heaven by daylight. When you leave here with my angel you will take Soradaci with you, and you will look after him on condition that he gives up his trade of spy. You will tell him all this.'* After saying these words the Holy Virgin vanished, and I found that I was awake."

Maintaining all the gravity I could muster, I studied the countenance of the traitor, who appeared to be petrified. I then took my Book of Hours, I sprinkled the cell with holy water, and I began pretending to pray to God, from time to time kissing the image of the Virgin. An hour later the beast, who had never said a word, asked me point-blank at what hour the angel was to come down from Heaven and if he would hear him breaking open the cell.

"I am certain that he will come at nineteen o'clock, that we will hear him working, and that he will leave at twenty-three; and it seems to me that four hours of work is enough for an angel."

"You may have been dreaming."

"I am sure I was not. Are you prepared to swear to me that you will renounce being a spy?"

Instead of answering he went to sleep and did not wake until two hours later, when he asked me if he could put off giving me his oath that he would renounce his trade.

"You can put it off," I said, "until the moment the angel enters this cell to take me away with him; but I warn you that if you do not swear to give up your evil trade I will leave you here, for such is the order I received from the Holy Virgin."

I then saw his relief, for he felt sure that the angel would not come. He seemed to pity me. I could not wait to hear the nineteenth hour strike, and the comedy entertained me vastly, for I was sure that the arrival of the angel would set the brute's miserable reason tottering. The thing was infallible unless, to my great regret, Lorenzo had forgotten to deliver the book.

At eighteen o'clock I began eating dinner, and I drank water. Soradaci drank all the wine and for dessert ate all the garlic I had; it was his sweetmeat. When I heard nineteen o'clock I fell on my knees, ordering him to do likewise in a voice which made him tremble. He obeyed, looking at me like an idiot with unseeing eyes. When I heard the little noise which told me that my accomplice was passing through the wall,

"The angel is coming," I said.

I then lay down on my stomach, at the same time giving him a push between the shoulders which made him fall into the same position. The noise from the breaking was loud, and I remained there prostrate for a good quarter of an hour. Did I not have reason enough to laugh when I saw that the scoundrel had remained motionless in the same position? But I did not laugh. I was engaged in the noble work of driving him mad or at least frantic. His accursed soul could not become human except by being steeped in terror. I spent three and a half hours reading while he told the Rosary, falling asleep from time to time and never daring to open his mouth, only looking up at the ceiling when he heard the noise of the monk splitting a board. In his stupor he kept bowing to the image of the Virgin in the most comical way imaginable. At the stroke of twenty-three o'clock I told him to do as I would do, since it was time for the angel to leave; we prostrated ourselves, Father Balbi left, and we heard not another sound. When I rose the expression I saw on the villain's face betokened dread and terror rather than rational surprise.

I amused myself for a while talking with him to hear how he would reason. He said things, always weeping, the connection between which was little short of absurdity; it was a hodgepodge of ideas none of which was pursued. He talked of his sins, of his special devotions, of his zeal for St. Mark, of his duties to his prince, and it was to this merit in him that he attributed the grace which the Holy Virgin was granting him, and I had to put up with a long tale of the miracles of the Rosary which his wife, whose confessor was a Dominican, had told him. He said that he could not guess what I would do with him, ignorant as he was.

"You will be in my service and you will have everything you need, without pursuing your vile and dangerous trade of spying."

"But we cannot stay in Venice."

"Of course not. The angel will lead us to a state which does not belong to St. Mark. Are you ready to swear to me that you will renounce your trade? And if you swear, will you perjure yourself again?"

"If I swear, I will not break my oath, that is sure; but admit that if I had not perjured myself you would not have obtained the grace which the Holy Virgin has granted you. So you must be grateful to me and love me for betraying you."

"Do you love Judas, who betrayed Jesus Christ?"

"No."

"Then you see that one must loathe the traitor and at the same time adore Providence, which makes good come out of evil. You have been a scoundrel, my dear man, until now. You have offended God and the Holy Virgin, and at present I will no longer accept your oath unless you expiate your sin."

"What sin have I committed?"

"Your sin of pride in supposing that I should feel obliged to you for giving my letters to the Secretary."

"Then what must I do to expiate my sin?"

"You must do this. Tomorrow when Lorenzo comes you must remain motionless on your pallet with your face to the wall and never look at Lorenzo. If he speaks to you you must answer him, without looking at him, that you could not sleep. Do you promise to obey me?"

"I promise you that I will do all that you say."

"Promise it to this holy image. Quick!"

"I promise you, most holy Virgin, that when Lorenzo comes I will not look at him and that I will not stir from my pallet."

"And I, most holy Virgin, swear to you by the bowels of Jesus Christ your God and son, that as soon as I see Soradaci turn to Lorenzo I will run and strangle him to your honor and glory."

I asked him if he had anything to object to my oath, and he said he was satisfied with it. I then gave him something to eat and told him to go to bed because I needed sleep. I spent two hours writing an account of all this to the monk and I said that if the work was almost completed he need come to the roof of my cell again only to break through the board and enter. I told him that we would leave on the night of October 31st, and that we would be four, counting his companion and mine. It was the 28th. Early the next day the monk informed me that the small entrance-way was finished and that he needed to get on the roof of my cell again only to open it, which he was sure he could do in four minutes. Soradaci obeyed his orders perfectly. He pretended to be asleep, and Lorenzo did not even speak to him. I kept my eyes on him and I believe I should really have strangled him if I had seen him turn his head toward Lorenzo, for to betray me he would have had to do no more than give him a wink.

I spent the day treating him to sublime discourses calculated to inspire fanaticism, leaving him in peace only when I saw that he was drunk and ready to fall asleep or on the point of going into convulsions under the impact of a metaphysics equally foreign and new to his mind, which had never applied its faculties to anything but inventing some trick of his spying trade.

He gave me pause for a moment by saying that he could not understand how an angel would need to work so long to open my cell; but I at once regained the upper hand by saying that he was not working as an angel but as a man, and I added that his evil thought must have instantly offended the Holy Virgin.

"And you will see," I said, "that because of your sin the angel will not come today. You always think not like an honest, pious, devout man but like a wicked sinner who supposes he is dealing with Messer Grande and the *sbirri*."

He then began weeping, and I was delighted to see that he was in despair when nineteen o'clock struck and there was no sound of the angel arriving. I then broke into lamentations which distressed him, and I left him to suffer all day. The next day he did not fail to obey, and when Lorenzo asked after his health he answered without looking at him. He maintained the same behavior on the following day, until I finally saw Lorenzo for the last time on the morning of the 31st, having given him the book in which I told the monk to come and make the opening. This time I feared no more obstacles, having learned from Lorenzo himself that not only the Inquisitors but the Secretary too had gone to the country. I had no reason to fear the arrival of any other guest; and I no longer needed to humor my infamous companion.

But now for an apology which I should perhaps make to some reader who might think unfavorably of my religion and morals because of the way I abused our holy mysteries and the oath which I made the idiot swear and the lies I told him about the appearance of the Holy Virgin.

Since my purpose was to tell the story of my escape with all its circumstances as they really happened, I considered it my duty to conceal nothing. I cannot say that I am confessing, for I feel no sting of repentance; nor can I say that I am proud of what I did, for it was with the utmost reluctance that I made use of the imposture. If I had disposed of any better means I would certainly have given them the preference. To regain my freedom I feel that I would still do the same thing today, and perhaps a great deal more.

Nature commanded me to escape, and religion could not forbid me to do it; I had no time to lose; having a spy with me who had given me an indubitable example of his perfidy, I must make it morally impossible for him to inform Lorenzo that the roof of the cell was being broken in. What was I to do? I had only two possibilities, and I must choose. Either I must bind the villain's soul by terror, or silence him by strangling him, as any other reasonable man more cruel than I would have done. It would have been much easier for me, and I should even have had nothing to fear, for I would have said that he died a natural death and no one would have taken much trouble to discover if it was true or not. Now where is the reader who can think that I would have done better to strangle him? If there is one such, may God enlighten him; his religion will never be mine. I believe that I did my duty; and the victory which crowned my exploit may be proof that eternal Providence did not disapprove of the means I employed. As for the oath I made him that I would always look after him, thank God he himself freed me from it, for he did not have the courage to escape with me; but even if he had found the courage I confess to my reader that I should not have thought I was perjuring myself if I had not kept it. I would have got rid of the monster at the first opportunity, even if I had had to hang him from a tree. When I swore that I would always help him, I knew that his loyalty would last only as long as the frenzy of his fanaticism, which was bound to disappear as soon as he saw that the angel was a monk. *Non merta fè chi non la serba altrui* ("He does not deserve loyalty who does not observe it").[6] A man has far more right to sacrifice everything to his own self-preservation than sovereigns have to do the same to preserve the State.

After Lorenzo left I told Soradaci that the angel would come to make an opening in the roof of my cell at seventeen o'clock; "he will bring a pair of scissors," I said, "and you shall cut my beard and the angel's."

"Does the angel wear a beard?"

"Yes, you will see it. After that we will leave and go to break open the roof of the palace; and at night we will get down into the Piazza San Marco and go to Germany."

He did not answer; he ate by himself, for my heart and mind were too much occupied with my escape to leave me capable of eating. I had not even been able to sleep.

Seventeen o'clock strikes, and the angel is there! Soradaci made to prostrate himself, but I said it was no longer necessary. In less than three minutes he broke through, the perfectly round piece of board dropped at my feet, Father Balbi slid into my arms.

"Your work," I said as I embraced him, "is done; mine begins."

He delivered the pike to me and gave me a pair of scissors, which I handed to Soradaci so that he could cut off our beards at once. This time I could not keep from laughing when I saw the utter astonishment with which the brute was staring at the angel, who looked like a devil. Beside himself, he cut our beards perfectly with the points of the scissors.

Impatient to see the topography of the place, I told the monk to stay there with Soradaci, for I did not want to leave him alone; I climbed out and found that the hole in the wall was narrow, but I got through it; I came to the roof of the Count's cell, I entered it and cordially embraced the unfortunate old man. I saw a figure not fitted to encounter the difficulties and dangers which such a flight was sure to bring us on an immense sloping roof covered with lead plates. He at once asked me what my plan was, saying that he thought the steps I had taken were not sufficiently considered.

"All I ask," I replied, "is to go forward until I find freedom or death."

He said, grasping my hand, that if my idea was to make a hole in the roof and try to find a way down over the lead plates, he did not see how I could do it unless I had wings.

"I have not," he added, "the courage to go with you; I will stay here and pray to God for you."

I then went out to investigate the great roof, getting as close as I could to the sides of the loft. Managing to touch the under side of the roof at the narrowest point of the angle, I sat down among the roof timbering, with which the lofts of all great palaces are filled. I sounded the boards with the point of my bolt and I found that they were as if rotting away. At each blow I made with my pike everything it entered fell to pieces. Seeing that I could certainly make a big enough opening in less than an hour, I went back to my cell, where I spent four hours cutting up sheets, napkins, mattresses, and everything I had which would make a rope. I insisted on knotting the pieces together myself with weaver's knots, for a badly made knot could have come undone and whoever was hanging from the rope at that moment would have fallen to the ground. I saw myself in possession of a hundred *braccia*[7] of rope. In great enterprises there are certain points which decide the issue and in regard to which the leader who deserves to succeed is he who trusts no one.

After finishing the rope I made a bundle of my coat, my floss-silk cloak, some shirts, stockings, and handkerchiefs, and the three of us went to the Count's cell carrying all this with us. The Count first congratulated Soradaci on having had the luck to be put with me and to be about to follow me. His look of confusion gave me an almost irresistible desire to laugh. I no longer restrained myself; I had cast off the mask of Tartuffe[8] which I had worn all day for the past week to prevent the two-faced scoundrel from betraying me. I saw that he was sure I had deceived him, but otherwise he was completely bewildered; for he could not guess how I could have corresponded with the supposed angel to make him come and go at the hour I pleased. He heard the Count saying that we were braving the most obvious danger of perishing, and coward as he could not but be, he was already turning over a plan to excuse himself from the perilous journey. I told the monk to bundle up his things while I went to make the hole at the edge of the loft.

I needed no help to complete my opening by two o'clock[9] that night. I pulverized the boards. My aperture was twice as big as necessary, and I was able to touch the entire plate of lead. The monk helped me get it out of the way, for it either curved around the edge of the marble gutter or was riveted to it; but by pushing my pike between the gutter and the plate I got it loose, and then with our shoulders we bent it back until the opening through which we would have to pass was large enough. Putting my head out of the hole, I was distressed to see the bright light of the crescent moon, which would reach its first quarter the following day. It was an obstacle which we had to bear with patience, putting off our departure until midnight, when the moon would have gone to light the antipodes. On a splendid night, when everyone of any account would be strolling in the Piazza San Marco, I could not risk being seen walking about up there. Our shadows, stretching far over the pavement of the square, would have been seen by the strollers, they would have looked up, and our persons would have provided a most unusual spectacle which would have aroused curiosity, especially on the part of Messer Grande, whose *sbirri*, the only guardians of the great city of Venice, keep watch all night. He would instantly have found a way to send a troop of them up there, which would have ruined all my fine plans. I therefore imperiously decreed that we were not to go out until after the moon had set. I called on God for help, and I did not ask for miracles. Exposed to the whims of Fortune, I must give her as little scope as I could. If my enterprise failed, I must not have the slightest miscalculation to reproach myself with. The moon was certain to set at five, and the sun would rise at half past thirteen; we would have seven hours of total darkness in which to act.

I told Father Balbi that we would spend three hours conversing with Count Asquin; and to go to him by himself at once and let him know that I was in need of his lending me thirty zecchini which might be as indispensable to me as my pike had been in accomplishing all I had done. He did my errand and four minutes later came back and told me to go alone because the Count wanted to speak to me without witnesses. The poor old man began by gently telling me that I did not need money to make good my escape, that he had none, that he had a large family, that if I died the money he gave me would be lost, adding a great many other reasons, all calculated to hide his avarice. My answer took half an hour. I used excellent arguments but ones which have never had any power since the world began, for no orator can extirpate a passion. It was a case of *nolenti baculus* ("for him who is unwilling, the rod"), but I was not hardhearted enough to use force on the unfortunate old man. I ended by saying that if he wanted to flee with me I would carry him on my shoulders as Aeneas did Anchises;[10] but that if he wanted to remain and pray to God for us his prayer would achieve nothing, for he would be asking God to bring success to an undertaking to which he had not contributed by ordinary means. The sound of his voice called my attention to his tears, which tried my temper; he asked me if two *zecchini* would satisfy me, and I answered that I had to be satisfied with anything. He gave them to me, begging me to return them if after making a round of the great roof of the palace I took the sensible course of going back to my cell. I promised him I would do so, a little surprised that he supposed I could decide to return. I was certain that I would never go back there.

I called my companions, and we put all our equipment near the hole. I divided the hundred *braccia* of rope into two coils and we spent two hours talking and not unpleasurably recalling all our vicissitudes. The first sample Father Balbi gave me of his excellent character was to tell me ten times over that I had broken my word to him, since I had assured him in my letters that my plan was all laid and infallible, whereas it was nothing of the kind; and he brazenly told me that if he had known this beforehand he would not have got me out of my cell. The Count, with all the gravity of his seventy years, told me that my wisest course was not to go on, for the impossibility of getting down from the roof was as obvious as the danger, which might cost me my life. I said mildly that the two things which were obvious to him were far from obvious to me; but since he was an advocate by profession, here is the harangue with which he tried to convince me. What spurred him on was the two zecchini which I should have had to return to him if he had persuaded me to stay.

"The slope of the roof, covered as it is with lead plates, will not allow you to walk over it for you can scarcely stand upright on it. The roof has seven or eight dormers, but they are all barred with iron and there is no way of reaching them to stand in front of them for they are all distant from the edges. The ropes you have will be of no use to you, because you will find no place to which you could fasten one end securely, and even if you found it, a man descending from such a height cannot remain suspended by his arms or manage his own descent. So one of you three would have to put a rope around the other two, one at a time, and let them down as you let a bucket down into a well; and whoever did this would have to stay behind and go back to his cell. Which of the three of you feels inclined to perform this act of charity? And supposing that one of you is hero enough to be willing to remain behind, pray tell me on which side you will go down. Not on the side toward the square and the pillars, for you would be seen. Not on the side toward the church, for you would still be shut in. Not on the side toward the courtyard of the palace, for the Arsenalotti[11] make constant rounds there. You can only go down on the side toward the canal. You have no gondola and no boat waiting for you; so you would have to throw yourselves into the water and swim as far as Sant'Apollonia,[12] which you would reach in a deplorable state, not knowing where to go at night to put yourselves in fit condition to continue your flight. Consider that it is slippery on the leads, and if you fall into the canal you cannot hope to escape death even if you can swim, for the height is so great and the canal so shallow that the fall would crush you to death before you could drown. Three or four feet of water are not a volume of fluid sufficient to lessen the violence of the descent of a solid body falling into it. The least that could happen to you would be to find you had broken your legs or arms."

I listened to this harangue, inappropriate as it was to the exigencies of the situation, with a patience which was not like me. The monk's reproaches, hurled at me with no consideration, made me indignant and provoked me to refute them harshly; but I would have ruined what I had built up, for I was dealing with a coward quite capable of answering that he was not desperate enough to brave death and so I had only to set off by myself; and by myself I could not hope to succeed. I humored these grudging spirits by mildness. I said that I was sure I would save us though I was not in a position to tell them my plans in detail. I told Count Asquin that his sensible considerations would make me act with prudence and that my trust in God was so great that it stood me in stead of all else.

I frequently put out my hands to discover if Soradaci was still there, for he never said a word; I laughed as I thought of what he might be turning over in his malicious mind, which must know that I had deceived him. At half past four I told him to go and see where the crescent moon was in the sky. He came back and said that in a half hour it would no longer be visible, and that an unusually thick fog must be making the leads very dangerous.

"It is enough for me, my man, if the fog is not oil. Make a bundle of your cloak and some of our ropes, which we must divide equally between us."

I was then surprised to find the man at my knees, taking my hands and kissing them, and saying with tears that he begged me not to ask his death.

"I am certain," he said, "to fall into the canal; I can be of no use to you. Alas! Leave me here and I will spend the whole night praying to St. Francis for you. It is in your power to kill me; but I will never make up my mind to come with you."

The fool did not know that I thought his company would bring me misfortune.

"You are right," I said, "stay; but on condition that you will pray to St. Francis and go at once and bring all my books, which I wish to leave to the Count."

He obeyed me instantly. My books were worth a hundred scudi[13] at least. The Count said he would return them to me when I came back.

"Be sure," I answered, "that you will not see me here again, and that I am very glad this base coward has not courage enough to follow me. He would be in my way, and in any case such a coward is unworthy to share the honor of so signal an escape with Father Balbi and me. Is not that so, my brave companion?" I said to the monk, another coward in whom I hoped to arouse some sense of honor.

"Very true," he said, "always provided that he does not have cause to congratulate himself tomorrow."

I then asked the Count for pens, ink, and paper, all of which he had despite the prohibition, for prohibitions were nothing to Lorenzo, who would have sold St. Mark himself for a scudo. I then wrote the following letter, which I left in the care of Soradaci without being able to read it over, for I wrote it in the dark. I began it with a visionary motto, which under the circumstances I thought very appropriate.

Non moriar sed vivam, et narrabo opera Domini.

("I shall not die, but live, and declare the works of the Lord.")[14]

"Our Lords the State Inquisitors are bound to do everything to keep a culprit in prison by force; but the culprit fortunate enough not to be on parole must also do everything he can to gain his freedom. Their right is founded upon justice; the culprit's upon nature. Just as they did not need his consent to lock him up, so he cannot need theirs to flee.

"Giacomo Casanova who writes this in the bitterness of his heart knows that he is liable to the misfortune of being caught before he leaves the State and returned to the hands of those whose sword he seeks to flee, and in that case he appeals on his knees to the humanity of his generous judges, begging them not to make his fate still more cruel by punishing him for what he has done only at the prompting of reason and nature. He begs them, if he is taken, to return to him all his belongings which he leaves in the cell he has vacated. But if he has the good fortune to escape, he gives all that he leaves here to Francesco Soradaci, who remains a prisoner because he fears the danger to which I am about to expose myself and does not, as I do, love his freedom more than his life. Casanova begs the magnanimous virtue of Their Excellencies not to deny the wretch the gift he has made him. Written an hour before midnight without light in the cell of Count Asquin this 31st day of October 1756."

Castigans castigavit me Deus, et morti non tradidit me.

("The Lord hath chastened me sore: but he hath not given me over unto death.")[15]

I gave him the letter, warning him not to give it to Lorenzo but only to the Secretary himself, who certainly would not fail to come up. The Count told him that my letter would infallibly produce the intended effect, but that he must give everything back to me if I reappeared. The idiot answered that he hoped to see me again and return everything to me.

But it was time to leave. The moon was no longer visible. I tied half the ropes to Father Balbi's neck on one side and the bundle of his wretched clothing on his other shoulder. I did the same to myself. Both of us in our vests, with our hats on our heads, we set forth to what we might find.

E quindi uscimmo a rimirar le stelle (Dante).

("And from there we went out to see the stars again.")[16]

CHAPTER XVI

*I leave the prison. I am in danger of losing my
life on the roof. I leave the Doge's Palace.
I embark, and I reach the mainland. Danger to
which Father Balbi exposes me. Stratagem
I am obliged to use to get rid of him for a time.*

I went out first; Father Balbi followed me. I told Soradaci to put the
lead plate back where it had been and dismissed him to pray to his
St. Francis. Down on my hands and knees, I got a good grip on my
pike and, extending my arm, I pushed it slantwise into the joints
between the plates, with the result that by using my four fingers to
grasp the edge of the plate I had raised, I was able to help myself
along to the top of the roof. To follow me the monk had put the
four fingers of his right hand into the belt of my breeches near
the buckle, so that I was in the unhappy position of a beast of burden
at once carrying and drawing, and what is more while climbing a
slope wet from the fog.

Halfway up this rather dangerous ascent the monk told me to
stop because one of his bundles had come loose from his neck and
rolled down, perhaps no farther than the gutter. My first response
was the temptation to give him a good kick; it would have been
more than enough to send him hurrying after his bundle; but God
granted me the strength to resist it; the punishment would have been
too great both for him and for me, since all by myself I simply could
not have got away. I asked him if it was the bundle of ropes; but
when he said that it was the one in which he had put his black
redingote, two shirts, and a precious manuscript he had found under
the Leads and which, he insisted, would make his fortune, I calmly
told him that he must bear it patiently and go on. He sighed, and,
still clinging to my behind, he followed me.

After passing over fifteen or sixteen plates, I found that I had
reached the ridge of the roof, on which, spreading my legs, I sat
comfortably astride. The monk did likewise behind me. We had our
backs turned to the small island of San Giorgio Maggiore,[1] and two
hundred paces ahead of us were the numerous domes of the Church
of San Marco, which forms part of the Doge's Palace; it is the Doge's
chapel; no monarch on earth can boast of having one equal to it. I at

once got rid of my burdens and told my accomplice that he might do likewise. He managed well enough to put his bundle of ropes between his thighs, but his hat, which he tried to put there too, lost its balance and, after turning all the somersaults necessary to bring it to the gutter, dropped into the canal. My companion instantly succumbed to despair.

"A bad omen," he said. "Here I am, at the beginning of our enterprise, without a shirt, without a hat, and without a manuscript which contained the precious and completely unknown history of all the festivals celebrated in the palace of the Republic."

Less savage than I had been when I was climbing, I told him that the two accidents he had just experienced were far too natural for even a superstitious person to call them auguries, that I did not consider them such, and that they did not discourage me; but that they should serve him as a last warning to be prudent and obedient and to reflect that if his hat had fallen off to his right instead of to his left we should have been lost, for it would have dropped into the palace courtyard, where the Arsenalotti would have picked it up, and, concluding that there must be someone on the roof of the Doge's Palace, they would certainly have done their duty and found some way to pay us a visit.

After spending several minutes looking to right and left, I told the monk to stay there with the bundles and not to move until I returned. I set out carrying only my pike, moving along on my behind, still straddling the angle without any difficulty. I spent nearly an hour going everywhere, stopping, observing, examining; but, seeing nothing in any direction to which I could fasten one end of my rope to let myself down into a place where I should be safe, I was in the greatest perplexity. There was no use giving further thought either to the canal or to the palace courtyard. On the top of the church I could see only precipitous slopes between the domes, none of them leading anywhere which was not locked. To get beyond the church in the direction of La Canonica[2] I should have had to climb over steep curved surfaces; it was natural that I dismissed as impossible what I saw no way of doing. I had to be *bold but not foolhardy*. The exact point between them is, I believe, one of the most imperceptible middle points in philosophy.

My eyes and my thought began to dwell on a dormer which was on the side toward the Rio del Palazzo,[3] about two thirds of the way down the slope. It was far enough from the place at which I had made my exit to assure me that the loft which it lighted did not belong to the guarded precincts of the cells I had broken open. It could only furnish light to some garret, inhabited or not, above one of the palace apartments, in which when day began I should naturally find the doors open. As for the palace servants, or those of the Doge's family,[4] I was morally certain that they would have hastened to get us away and done anything except put us back in the hands of inquisitorial justice, even if they had known us to be the greatest criminals in the State. With this idea in mind, I felt impelled to inspect the front of the dormer, and I proceeded there at once by raising one leg and letting myself slide until I was more or less sitting on its small horizontal roof, which was three feet long and a foot and a half wide. I then bent well over, holding firmly to its sides, and bringing my head as close to it as I could. I saw, or rather, managed to feel, a light iron grating and behind it a window with round panes joined together by narrow slotted strips of lead. I thought nothing of the window, though it was shut; but the grating, light as it was, demanded a file, and the only tool I had was my pike.

Thoughtful, gloomy, and baffled, I did not know what to do when a very natural occurrence had the effect of an extraordinary prodigy on my astonished soul. I hope that my sincere avowal will not lower me in the eyes of my philosophical reader, if he considers that a man in a state of anxiety and distress is only half of what he can be in a state of tranquillity. The midnight bell sounding from San Marco just at that moment was the phenomenon which seized upon my mind and which, by a violent shock, delivered it from the dangerous doubt under which it was laboring. The bell reminded me that the day which was just then to begin was All Saints' Day; if I had a patron saint, he must be among them. But what raised my courage still more and actually increased my physical powers was the profane oracle I had received from my dear Ariosto: *Tra il fin d'Ottobre, e il capo di Novembre.* If a great misfortune makes a freethinker pious, it is almost impossible for him not also to become in some degree superstitious. The sound of the bell spoke to me, told me to act, and promised me victory. Lying prone up to my neck and bending my head down toward the small grating, I pushed my bolt into the frame which held it and I determined to break it and remove the grating in one piece. It took me only a quarter of an hour to smash all the wood which made up the four sides of the frame. The grating being now in my hands in one piece, I put it beside the dormer. I found it no more difficult to break away the glazed window, paying no attention to the blood flowing from my left hand, which was slightly cut by a pane I pulled out.

With the help of my bolt I used my original method to return to my position astride the pyramidal summit[5] of the roof, and I made my way to the place where I had left my companion. I found him desperate, furious, and in an atrocious humor; he reviled me because I had left him all alone for two long hours. He assured me that he was only waiting for seven o'clock to go back to his cell.

"What did you think I was doing?"

"I thought you had fallen into some chasm."

"And aren't you glad to see that I didn't?"

"What were you up to all this time?"

"You'll see. Follow me."

I tied my belongings and my rope to my neck and proceeded toward the dormer. When we came to the place where it was to our right I gave him a detailed account of all that I had done, consulting him as to how we could both get into the loft. I saw that it would be easy for one of us, because the other could let him down by means of the rope; but I did not know what means the other could employ to get down too, for I did not see how I could make the cord fast so that I could tie myself to it. If I got in and let myself go, I might break a leg, for I did not know if the jump down was too long to risk. To these sound considerations, delivered in friendly tones, the monk replied that I had only to let him down, and that then I would have all the time I needed to think out how I could rejoin him in the place to which I had lowered him. I controlled myself enough not to reproach him with all the cowardice of his answer but not enough to defer setting his mind at rest. I instantly undid my bundle of ropes; I put a loop around his chest under the armpits, I made him lie down on his belly, and I let him down feet first to the small roof of the dormer, where, still controlling the rope from my position astride the summit, I told him to get his legs inside up to the hips, supporting himself with his elbows on the roof. I then slid down the slope as I had done the first time and, lying down on my belly, I told him to let his body go without any fear for I had a firm hold of the rope. When he reached the floor of the loft he untied himself, and pulling the rope back I found that the distance from the dormer to the floor was ten times the length of my arm. It was too long a jump to risk. He said that I could throw the ropes inside; but I took good care not to follow his stupid advice. I went back to the summit, and not knowing what to do, I made my way to a place near a cupola which I had not inspected. I saw a flat terrace, paved with lead plates, next to a large dormer window closed by a pair of blinds, and in a vat I saw a heap of quicklime and beside it a trowel and a ladder long enough for me to use it to climb down to where my companion was; only the ladder interested me. I passed my rope under the top rung and, resuming my position astride the roof, I dragged the ladder to the dormer. It was now a matter of getting it in. The ladder was twelve times the length of my arm.

The difficulties I had to overcome in the process of getting the ladder in were so great that I heartily repented of having deprived myself of the monk's help. I had pushed the ladder in the direction of the gutter so that one end of it touched the opening in the dormer and the other end protruded beyond the gutter by a third of the length of the ladder. I then slid down to the roof of the dormer, I dragged the ladder sidewise and, pulling it to me, I fastened the rope to the eighth rung. I then pushed it down again and got it back in line with the dormer; then I pulled the rope toward me; but the ladder could only go in as far as the fifth rung, its top struck against the roof of the dormer and no amount of force could have made it go in any farther. It was absolutely necessary to raise the other end; raising it would lower the opposite end, and the whole ladder could be put in. I could have set the ladder across the opening, tied my rope to it, and let myself down without any risk; but the ladder would have remained where it was, and in the morning it would have shown the *sbirri* and Lorenzo the place where I might well still be.

Somehow, then, the entire ladder had to be brought into the dormer, and having no one with me I was left with no choice except making up my mind to go down to the gutter myself and raise the end of it. This is what I did, exposing myself to a danger which, but for an extraordinary intervention of Providence, would have cost me my life. I had no hesitation about letting the ladder go by slackening the rope, for there was no fear that it would drop into the canal since it was hooked to the gutter by its third rung. Holding my pike, I slid slowly to a point in the gutter beside the ladder; I put down the pike and nimbly turned so that I was directly facing the dormer and had my right hand on the ladder. The gutter sustained the tips of my toes, for I was not standing but lying on my belly. In this position I mustered strength enough to raise the ladder half a foot, at the same time pushing it forward. I had the satisfaction of seeing it go in a good foot. The reader will understand that its weight must have diminished considerably. It was now necessary to raise it two more feet to make it go in that much farther; with that done, I was sure I could get it all the way in by at once returning to the roof of the dormer and pulling on the cord which I had tied to the rung. To elevate it two feet, I rose to my knees, but the force I tried to use to push it up made the toes of my two feet slip, so that my body dropped off into space as far as my chest, till it hung from my two elbows. It was in the same terrible instant that I used all my strength and all the aid of my elbows to press my body forward and check my further descent by my ribs; and I succeeded. Taking care not to slip, I managed with the help of the rest of my arms as far as the wrists to hold myself against the gutter with my whole belly. I had no fear for the ladder, since, my two efforts having pushed it in three feet, it could not move from where it was. So, finding that I now had my wrists and my groins from my lower belly to the top of my thighs actually on the gutter, I saw that by raising my right thigh so that I could put first one knee and then the other on the gutter, I should be out of my great danger. The effort I made to carry out my plan brought on a nervous spasm, the pain from which is enough to fell the strongest of men. It seized me just as my right knee was already touching the gutter; but the painful spasm, which is called a "cramp," not only practically paralyzed me in every limb, it necessitated my remaining motionless to wait for it to go away of itself, as previous experience had taught me it would do. Terrible moment! Two minutes later I made the attempt and—thank God! —I brought one knee to the gutter, then the other, and as soon as I thought I had sufficiently recovered my breath I straightened up, though still on my knees, and raised the ladder as far as I could, and I managed to get it high enough to be on a level with the opening in the dormer. Sufficiently well acquainted with the laws of the lever and of equilibrium, I then took my bolt and, following my usual method, climbed to the dormer, where I had no difficulty getting the ladder in, my companion receiving the end of it in his arms. I threw the ropes, my clothes, and all the debris from breaking the window down into the loft and then entered it, warmly greeted by the monk, who saw to pulling in the ladder. Arm in arm, we made the round of the dark place we were in, which might have been thirty feet long and ten wide.

At one end of it we found a double door made of iron bars; turning the latch at the center, I opened it. We groped our way around the walls, and, starting to cross the place, we found a large table surrounded by stools and armchairs. We went back to where we had touched windows; I opened one, then the blinds, and by the starlight we saw chasms between domes. I did not for a moment think of climbing down; I wanted to know where I was going, and I knew nothing of this part of the palace. I closed the blinds, we left the room, and returned to the place where we had left our baggage. At the end of my strength, I dropped onto the floor, stretched out with a bundle of ropes under my head, and in my utter exhaustion of body and mind a very sweet slumber took complete possession of me; I fell so irresistibly asleep that I thought I was yielding to death, and even had I been sure that it was so, I would have made no resistance, for the pleasure I felt in falling asleep was unbelievable.

My sleep lasted three hours and a half. The piercing cries and rough shaking of the monk were what waked me. He said that twelve o'clock[6] had just struck and that it was inconceivable I should sleep in our situation. It was inconceivable to him; but my sleep had not been voluntary; it was my constitution at bay which had brought it on, and the inanition due to my having neither eaten nor slept for two days. But the sleep had restored all my vigor, and I was delighted to see that the darkness of the loft had lessened a little.

I rose, saying:

"This place is not a prison; there must be a perfectly simple way of getting out of it, which will be easy to find."

We then made our way to the end opposite the door made of iron bars and in a very narrow corner I thought I felt a door, I feel a keyhole, I thrust my bolt into it, hoping that it is not a closet. After three or four pushes I open it, I see a small room, and I find a key on a table. I try the key in the door, and I see that I have locked it. I open it and I tell the monk to go quickly for our bundles, and as soon as he brings them I lock the small door again and put the key back where it was. I leave the small room and find that I am in a gallery lined with niches full of notebooks. They were archives. I find a short, narrow stone stairway and I go down it; I find another with a glazed door at the end; I open it and I see that I am at last in a room I knew; we were in the ducal chancellery.[7] I open a window, and I see that I could easily get down, but I would be in the labyrinth of little courtyards which surround the Church of San Marco. God forfend! On a desk I see an iron instrument with a wooden handle and a round point, which the chancellery secretaries use to make holes in parchments, to which they then attach the lead seals[8] with thread; I take it. I open the desk and find a copy of a letter informing the Proveditor-General[9] in Corfu of the dispatch of three thousand zecchini for restoring the old fortress. I look to see if I can find the money, but it is not there. God knows with what pleasure I would have appropriated it, and how I would have laughed at the monk if he had dared to tell me that it was robbery. I would have considered it a gift from Providence, to say nothing of appropriating it by right of conquest.

I go to the door of the chancellery, I put my bolt into the lock, but convinced in less than a minute that my pike could not force it, I quickly decide to make a hole in one of the two leaves of the door. I choose the place where there are the fewest knots in the wood. I go to work on the board at the point where its junction with the other leaf affords me a crack, and all goes well. I made the monk force the wooden-handled instrument into the cracks I opened with the pike; then, pushing the latter as hard as I could to left and right, I broke and split and shattered the wood, heedless of the tremendous noise which my method of attack produced; the monk was trembling, for someone must be hearing it far away. I knew the danger, but I had to risk it.

In half an hour the hole was large enough, and so much the better for us that it was, for I should have had great difficulty making it any bigger. Knots to left, right, above, and below would have made it necessary for me to use a saw. The circumference of the hole was frightening, for it bristled all round with points jagged enough to tear our clothes and lacerate our skins. It was five feet up; under it I set a stool, onto which the monk climbed. He put his joined arms and his head into the hole, and I, standing behind him on another stool and taking him first by the thighs and then by the legs, managed to push him out into a dense darkness; but I did not care how dark it was, for I knew the place. When my companion was out, I threw him all my belongings, leaving nothing but the ropes in the chancellery.

I then set two stools side by side below the hole, and adding a third on top of them I climbed up on it; in this way the hole was opposite my thighs. I pushed myself into it up to the lower part of my abdomen with considerable difficulty and lacerating myself, for it was narrow; then, having no one behind to help me get farther, I told the monk to take me around the chest and pull me through without mercy and even in pieces if necessary. He obeyed my order, and I silently bore all the pain which my badly scratched flanks and thighs caused me.

As soon as I was out I quickly gathered up my clothes, went down two stairways, and had no difficulty in opening the door onto the passage in which is the great door to the Royal Stairs[10] and, beside it, the office of the Savio alla Scrittura.[11] The great door was locked, as was the one to the Hall of the Four Doors.[12] The door to the stairs was as big as a city gate; it took only a glance to show me that without a ram or a petard it was inviolable; at that moment my bolt seemed to be saying to me: "*Hic fines posuit* ['Here he has set the bounds'];[13] you have no more use for me." Precious instrument of my freedom, worthy to be hung *ex voto* on the altar of my tutelary divinity! Serene and calm, I sat down, saying to the monk that my work was ended and it was now for God or Fortune to do the rest:

Abbia chi regge il ciel cura del resto
O la Fortuna se non tocca a lui.

("Let him who rules the heavens see to the rest, or Fortune if it is not his concern.")[14]

"I do not know," I said, "if the palace sweepers will come here today, which is All Saints' Day, or tomorrow, All Souls' Day. If anyone comes I will run out as soon as I see the door opened, and do you follow in my tracks; but if no one comes I will not stir from here; and if I die of hunger I don't know what I can do about it."

At these words the poor man became furious. He called me a madman, desperate, a deceiver, a liar, and I know not what else. My patience was heroic. Thirteen o'clock[15] struck. From the moment I awoke in the loft under the dormer until that moment, only an hour had passed. The important thing which now occupied me was changing all my clothes. Father Balbi looked like a peasant, but he was unscathed: he was neither in rags nor bleeding; his red flannel vest and his violet leather breeches were not torn. But my figure inspired pity and horror. I was torn and scratched from head to foot and covered with blood. When I pulled my silk stockings off of two wounds I had, one on each knee, they both bled. The gutter and the lead plates had put me in this state. The hole in the chancellery door had torn my vest, my shirt, my breeches, my hips, and my thighs; I had terrible scratches everywhere. I ripped up some handkerchiefs and made such bandages as I could, tying them on with string, of which I had a ball in my pocket. I put on my fine coat, which on that cold day became laughable; I dressed my hair as well as I could and tied it up in the net; and, having no others, I put on white stockings, a shirt trimmed with lace, and put two more shirts, handkerchiefs, and stockings in my pocket, and I threw my breeches, my torn shirt, and everything else behind an armchair. I put my fine cloak on the monk's shoulders, which made him appear to have stolen it. I had the look of a man who, after attending a ball, has gone to some place of ill fame and there been roughed up. The bandages visible on my knees were the only thing which marred the elegance of my attire.

Thus decked out and wearing my fine hat trimmed with gold Spanish lace and a plume, I opened a window. My presence was at once noticed by some idlers in the palace courtyard, who, not understanding how a person of my appearance could be at that window at such an early hour, went and told the man who had the key to the place. Thinking he might have locked someone in the evening before without noticing it, he fetched his keys and came. I did not learn this until I was in Paris five or six months later.

Sorry that I had shown myself at the window, I sat down beside the monk, who was proceeding to treat me to some untimely remarks when I heard the sound of keys and of someone coming up the Royal Stairs. In the greatest perturbation I get up, I look through a crack in the great door, and I see a man alone,[16] wearing a black wig and no hat, calmly coming up carrying a bunch of keys in both hands. I told the monk in the most impressive tone not to open his mouth, to stand behind me, and follow me. I took hold of my pike, keeping it concealed under my coat, and I stationed myself by the door in such a position that, as soon as it was opened, I could start down the stairs. I prayed to God that the man would offer no resistance, for, otherwise, I should have to cut his throat. I was resolved to do it.

As soon as the door opened I saw that he was as if turned to stone by my appearance. Never pausing or saying a word to him, I went down as fast as I could, followed by the monk. Neither dawdling nor running, I took the magnificent "Stairway of the Giants," as it is called, disregarding the voice of Father Balbi who followed me repeating over and over:

"Let us go to the church!"

The door to the church was on the right, twenty paces beyond the stairs.

The churches of Venice do not enjoy the slightest immunity as asylums for any wrongdoer, be his offense criminal or civil; so no one goes there any more to stave off the constables who have a warrant to capture him. The monk knew this; but his knowledge was not enough to overcome the temptation. He told me afterward that what prompted him to take refuge at the altar was a religious feeling which I ought to respect.

"Why didn't you go by yourself?"

"Because I did not have the heart to abandon you."

The immunity I sought was beyond the boundaries of the Most Serene Republic;[17] I was already beginning even then to make my way to it; I was there in spirit, and I had to get my body there. I went straight to the Porta della Carta,[18] which is the royal entrance to the Doge's Palace; and looking at no one (a way to avoid being looked at), I crossed the Piazzetta, reached the quay, and got into the first gondola I found there, saying loudly to the gondolier on the poop:

"I want to go to *Fusina*, call another man quickly."

The other man came on board at once; I drop nonchalantly onto the cushion in the middle, the monk sits down on the bench, and the gondola at once leaves the quay. The person of the hatless monk wrapped in my cloak contributed not a little to my being taken for a charlatan or an astrologer.

No sooner had we rounded the Customs House[19] than my gondoliers began vigorously cutting through the waters of the great Giudecca Canal, which has to be traversed to reach either Fusina or Mestre, the place to which I really wanted to go. When I saw that we were halfway down the canal, I said to the gondolier on the poop:

"Do you think we shall be at Mestre before fourteen o'clock?"

"You told me to go to *Fusina*."

"You are mad; I said *Mestre*."

The other gondolier said I was wrong; and Father Balbi, as a good Christian zealous for the truth, told me I was wrong too. I then laughed, admitting that I might have made a mistake but that I had intended to say "to Mestre." No one answered. My gondolier said that he was ready to take me to England.

"We shall be at Mestre," he said, "in three quarters of an hour, for *we have the current and the wind in our favor.*"

I then turned and looked down the splendid canal; and seeing not a single boat and admiring the most beautiful day one could hope for, the first rays of a magnificent sun just rising above the horizon, the two young gondoliers rowing at top speed, and thinking at the same time of the cruel night I had spent, of the place where I had been the day before, and of all the coincidences which had been favorable to me, feeling took possession of my soul, which rose up to a merciful God, setting the springs of my gratitude in motion, touching me with extraordinary power and so profoundly that my tears suddenly found fullest vent to relieve my heart, which was choking from excess of joy; I sobbed, I cried like a child forced to go to school.

My charming companion, who until then had not spoken except to side with the gondoliers, thought it his duty to calm my tears, of whose noble source he was unaware; and the way he went about it did indeed make me pass in an instant from tears to a laugh so strange that, baffled by it, he confessed to me some days later that he thought I had gone mad. The monk was stupid, and his malice came from his stupidity. I saw that I was in the difficult position of having to turn it to advantage; but he came very near to being my ruin, though unintentionally, because he was stupid. He would never believe that I had ordered the gondoliers to go to Fusina when I intended to go to Mestre; he said that the idea could not have come to me until I was on the Grand Canal.

We reached Mestre. I found no horses at the posthouse; but at the Osteria della Campana[20] there were plenty of *vetturini*, who serve as well as the post. I went into the stable, and seeing that the horses were good I agreed to give the *vetturino* what he asked to be at Treviso in an hour and a quarter. Within three minutes the horses were put in, and supposing that Father Balbi was behind me, I turned to say "Get in—"

But I did not see him. I look about, I ask where he is, nobody knows. I tell the stableboy to go and look for him, determined to reprimand him even if he had gone to attend to his natural needs; for we were under the necessity of putting that off too. I am told that he is not to be found. I was like a soul in torment. I think of leaving by myself, it was the thing to do; but I listen to a weak feeling instead of to my strong reason, and I run out. I ask for him, everyone says he has been seen but no one can tell me where he may have gone; I search the arcades of the principal street, it occurs to me to stick my head into a coffeehouse, and there I see him, standing at the counter drinking chocolate and talking with the waitress. He sees me, he says she is charming and urges me to drink a cup of chocolate too; he says I must pay, for he has no money. I control myself and answer that I do not want any, telling him to hurry and gripping his arm so hard he thought I had broken it. I paid, he followed me. I was shaking with anger. I start off toward the carriage, which is waiting for me at the door of the inn; but I have scarcely taken ten steps before I meet a citizen of Mestre named Balbo Tomasi, a good man but who had the reputation of being a spy for the tribunal of the Inquisitors. He sees me, he comes up, and he exclaims:

"You here, Signore! I am delighted to see you. So you have just escaped. How did you manage it?"

"I did not escape, Signore, I was set free."

"That is impossible, for I was at the Grimani palace in San Polo last evening and I should have heard of it."

The reader can imagine the state of my soul at that moment: here I was, discovered by a man who I believed had been hired to have me arrested, which he could do by merely winking at the first *sbirro*, of which Mestre was full. I told him to speak in a whisper and to follow me behind the inn. He came, and when I saw that we were out of anyone's sight and that I was close to a little ditch beyond which there was nothing but open country, I put my right hand on my pike and my left on his collar; but he nimbly escaped me, jumped the ditch, and began running as fast as he could away from the city of Mestre, turning every now and again to kiss his hand to me by way of saying: "A good journey to you, have no fear!" I lost sight of him; and I thanked God that the man's being able to escape from my hands had prevented me from committing a crime, for I was on the verge of cutting his throat and he had no evil intentions. My situation was dreadful. I was alone, and at open war with all the forces of the Republic. I had to sacrifice everything to foresight and caution. I put my pike back in my pocket.

In all the dejection of a man who has just escaped from a great danger, I cast a look of scorn on the base coward who had seen to what a pass he had brought me, and I got into the carriage. He sat down beside me and never dared to say a word. I thought of how I could rid myself of the wretch. We reached Treviso, where I ordered the post master to have two horses ready to leave at seventeen o'clock;[21] but I did not intend to continue my journey by the post—first because I had no money, and second because I feared I should be followed. The innkeeper asked me if I wanted breakfast, and I needed it to stay alive, for I was dying of inanition; but I did not have the courage to say yes. A quarter of an hour lost could be fatal to me. I dreaded being caught and feeling ashamed of it all the rest of my life, for a man with his wits about him and a clear field should be able to defy four hundred thousand men to find him. If he does not know how to hide, he is a fool.

I went out by the San Tomasso[22] gate like a man who is going for a stroll, and after walking a mile along the highroad I made off into the fields, not intending to leave them until I was out of the Venetian State. The shortest road out of it was by way of Bassano, but I took the longest because there might be men waiting for me at the nearest point of exit and I was sure that no one would suppose that, to leave the State, I would take the road to Feltre, which was the longest way round to reach the jurisdiction of the Bishop of Trento.

After walking for three hours I sank onto the hard ground, absolutely at the end of my strength. I either had to take some nourishment or prepare to die there. I told the monk to put the cloak beside me and to go to a farmhouse which I saw and buy something to eat and bring it all to me where I was. I gave him money enough. After saying he thought I had more courage, he went off on my errand. The wretch was stronger than I was. He had not slept; but he had eaten well the day before, he had drunk a cup of chocolate, he was thin, caution and honor were not harrowing his soul, and he was a monk.

Though the house was not an inn the farmer's kindly wife sent me a peasant girl with an adequate dinner, which cost me only thirty soldi. When I felt sleep about to overtake me I started off again, with a good sense of my direction. Four hours later I stopped behind a village and learned that I was twenty-four miles[23] from Treviso. I was done in; my ankles were swollen and my shoes broken. Daylight would end in an hour. I lay down in the middle of a clump of trees and made the monk sit down beside me.

"We must go," I said, "to Borgo di Valsugana,[24] the first town beyond the borders of the Venetian State. We shall be as safe there as in London, and we will rest, but to reach the town, which belongs to the Prince-Bishop of Trento, we must take some unavoidable precautions, the first of which is that we must separate. You will go by way of the forest of Mantello,[25] I through the mountains, you by the easiest and shortest way, I by the hardest and longest, you with money, I without a soldo. I make you a present of my cloak, which you will exchange for a cape and a hat, and then everyone will take you for a peasant, for fortunately you have the look of one. Here is all the money I have left from the two zecchini I got from Count Asquin, it comes to seventeen lire, take them; you will be at Borgo tomorrow evening, and I twenty-four hours later. You will wait for me at the first inn on the left. I need to sleep in a good bed tonight, and Providence will show me the way to one, but I need to be in it peacefully, and with you I cannot be at peace. I am sure that we are now being searched for everywhere and that our descriptions have been circulated so accurately that we should be arrested at any inn which we dared to enter together. You see my deplorable condition and my absolute need to rest for ten hours. So farewell. Go, and leave me to set about finding myself a refuge somewhere nearby."

"I was already expecting," he replied, "all that you have just said to me; but my only answer is to remind you of what you promised me when I let you persuade me to break open your cell. You promised that we would never separate; so do not hope that I will leave you, your fate shall be mine and mine shall be yours. We will find a good refuge for our money and we will not go to inns; we will not be arrested."

"So you are determined not to follow the good advice I have given you."

"Absolutely determined."

"We shall see."

So saying I got up, not without effort; I took his measure and marked it out on the ground, then I drew the pike from my pocket, lay down on my left side, and began to make a small excavation, maintaining the utmost calm and answering not a word to all the questions he asked me. After working for a quarter of an hour I looked at him sadly and said that, as a Christian, I considered it my duty to warn him that he should commend his soul to God.

"For," I said, "I am going to bury you alive in this hole, and if you are stronger than I am, you shall bury me in it. This is the only course which your brute stubbornness leaves open to me. However, you can run away if you choose, for I will not run after you."

Seeing that he did not answer I went on working. I began to fear that the sorry beast, of whom I was determined to rid myself, would drive me to extremes.

Finally, whether deliberately or in terror, he came hurtling toward me. Not knowing his intention, I advanced the point of the pike; but there was nothing to fear. He said that he would do everything I wished. I then embraced him; I gave him all the money I had, and I repeated my promise to join him at Borgo. Though left without a soldo, and having two rivers to cross, I heartily congratulated myself on having been able to shake off the burden of such a man's company. With that done, I was certain that I should succeed in getting out of the State.

HISTORY OF MY LIFE

Volume Five

[* * *]

By escaping from the Doge's palace Casanova had succeeded in the most audacious feat of an audacious career, one which was to make him notorious throughout Italy and beyond. Once outside the city he was not safe until he passed out of the considerable area controlled by the Venetian Republic. This took several days. He also needed money. Such was his reputation that this had to be extracted by threats from a cowardly banker, terrified that he, too, would find himself "under the Leads" for aiding an enemy of the state. But by this time Casanova was beyond caring about the consequences of his actions. With characteristic humor he explains how the last stage of his adventure involved taking refuge for the night with the wife of a Venetian policeman while her husband was away on duty—searching for the fugitive Casanova.

Leaving Venetian territory he made for Munich and from there returned to France where he proposed to ask for help from his old acquaintance Monsieur de Bernis, now at the Ministry of Foreign Affairs. His arrival in Paris coincided with an attempt on the life of Louis XV.

CHAPTER II

The Minister of Foreign Affairs. Monsieur de Boulogne, the Comptroller-General. The Duke of Choiseul. The Abbé de Laville. Monsieur Pâris-Duverney. Establishment of the lottery. My brother comes to Paris from Dresden; he is received into the Academy of Painting.

Once more I am in the great city of Paris and, since I can no longer count on my own country, obliged to make my fortune there. I had spent two years in Paris; but since at that time my only object was to enjoy life I had not studied the city. This second time I had to pay my court to those with whom the Blind Goddess made her abode. I saw that to accomplish anything I must bring all my physical and moral faculties into play, make the acquaintance of the great and the powerful, exercise strict self-control, and play the chameleon to all those whom I should see it was my interest to please. To follow these principles I saw that I must scrupulously avoid what is known in Paris as "dubious company" and renounce all my old ways and any pretensions which could make me enemies who could easily give me the reputation of being a man not fit to be trusted with important business. As the result of these meditations I decided to practice a systematic reserve in both act and word which would lead to my being considered even more fit for affairs of consequence than I had any reason to suppose I was. As for living expenses, I could count on the hundred écus[1] a month which Signor Bragadin would never have failed to send me. It was enough. I had only to see that I was well dressed and decently lodged; but to begin with I needed a sum of money, for I had neither suits nor shirts.

So the next day I went back to the Palais Bourbon. Being sure that the porter would tell me the Minister was engaged, I went there with a note which I left for him. I announced my arrival and told him where I was lodging. To say more would have been to say too much. Meanwhile I found that wherever I went I had to tell the story of my escape; it was a task, for it took two hours; but I felt I must oblige those who were eager to hear it, for their eagerness could arise only from their lively interest in myself.

At supper at Silvia's I found all the evidence of friendship I could wish for, but in a calmer atmosphere than on the previous evening; and I was greatly impressed by the merits of her daughter. At the age of fifteen she had all the qualities which captivate. I congratulated her mother who had fostered them in her, and at the time I did not think of defending myself from her charms: I was not yet at ease enough to suppose that they could assail me. I left early, impatient to see what the Minister would say in reply to my note.

I received his answer at eight o'clock. He said that I would find him alone at two o'clock in the afternoon. He received me as I expected he would. He conveyed to me not only his pleasure over my triumph but all the joy which he felt in having an opportunity to be of use to me. He at once told me that as soon as he had learned of my escape by a letter from M. M. he had felt certain I would go nowhere but to Paris and that my first visit would be to him. He showed me the letter in which she[2] informed him of my arrest, and her last letter, in which she told him the story of my escape as she had heard it. She said that since she could no longer hope to see either of the two men on whom alone she could count, her life had become a burden to her. She lamented that she did not have the resource of devotion. She said that C. C. often came to see her and that she was not happy with the man who had married her.

Having looked through what M. M. wrote him about my escape and finding that all the details were wrong, I promised to send him the true story of it. He took me at my word, promising that he would send it on to our unfortunate friend and giving me a roll of a hundred louis[3] with the most perfect tact. He promised to keep me in mind and to let me know when he would need to speak to me. With the money I outfitted myself; and a week later I sent him the story of my escape, giving him permission to have it copied and to use it as he thought best to interest anyone who could be helpful to me. Three weeks later he sent for me and told me that he had spoken about me to Signor Erizzo,[4] the Venetian Ambassador, who had found nothing to say against me; but that, not wanting to compromise himself with the State Inquisitors, he would not receive me. I did not need him. He said that he had given my story to Madame la Marquise,[5] who knew me and with whom he would try to obtain me an interview, and in closing he said that when I went to see Monsieur de Choiseul,[6] I would be well received, as I would be by the Comptroller-General Monsieur de Boulogne,[7] with whom, if I used my head, I should be able to work out something substantial.

"He will himself," he said, "give you hints, and you will see that 'the man who is listened to is the man who obtains.' Try to think up some project profitable to the royal exchequer, avoiding anything complicated or chimerical, and if what you write is not too long I will give you my opinion on it."

I left him full of gratitude, but at a loss to find a way to increase the King's revenues. Having not the faintest notion of finances, no matter how I racked my brains all the ideas which came to me were only for new taxes, and since they all struck me as odious or absurd I rejected them all.

My first visit[8] was to Monsieur de Choiseul, as soon as I learned that he was in Paris. He received me at his toilet table, where he was writing while his hair was being dressed. The courtesy he showed me was to interrupt his letter at short intervals, asking me questions, which I answered, but to no purpose, for instead of listening he went on writing. Now and again he looked at me; but that meant nothing, for the eyes see, they do not hear. Nevertheless the Duke was a man of great intelligence.

After finishing his letter he said to me in Italian that the Abbé de Bernis had told him part of the story of my escape.

"Tell me how you managed to bring it off."

"The story, Monseigneur, takes two hours, and I have the impression that Your Excellency is in a hurry."

"Tell it to me briefly."

"It is the very shortest version of it which takes two hours."

"You can tell me the details another time."

"Without the details the story is not interesting."

"Of course. But one can abbreviate anything as much as one wishes."

"Very well. I will tell Your Excellency that the State Inquisitors had me imprisoned under the Leads.[9] At the end of fifteen months and five days I made a hole in the roof; I entered the Chancellery[10] through a dormer and broke open the door to it; I went down to the Piazza; I took a gondola which carried me to the mainland, whence I went to Munich. From there I came to Paris, where I have the honor to pay you my respects."

"But—what are the Leads?"

"That, Monseigneur, takes a quarter of an hour."

"How did you manage to make a hole in the roof?"

"That takes half an hour."

"Why were you imprisoned up there?"

"Another half hour."

"I think you are right. The interest of the thing is in the details. I have to go to Versailles. I should be glad to have you call on me from time to time. Meanwhile, think of how I can be of use to you."

On leaving him I went to call on Monsieur de Boulogne. I saw a man entirely different from the Duke in appearance, dress, and manner. He at once congratulated me on the interest which the Abbé de Bernis showed in me and on my financial abilities. I very nearly burst out laughing. He was with an octogenarian whose face bore the stamp of genius.

"Let me have your ideas, either by word of mouth or in writing; you will find me a good pupil and ready to grasp them. This is Monsieur Pâris-Duverney,[11] who needs twenty millions for his Military School.[12] The thing is to find them without burdening the State or embarrassing the royal treasury."

"There is only one God, Monsieur, who has the power of creation."

"I am not God," Monsieur Duverney replied, "yet I have sometimes created, but everything has changed."

"Everything," I answered, "has become more difficult, I know; nevertheless, I have a plan in mind which would yield the King the return on a hundred millions."

"And how much would such a yield cost the King?"

"Only the expense of collecting it."

"Then it is the nation which would supply the revenue?"

"Yes, but voluntarily."

"I know what you have in mind."

"I should be surprised, Monsieur, for I have imparted my idea to no one."

"If you are not otherwise engaged, come to dinner with me tomorrow, and I will show you your project, which is admirable but which is beset with almost insurmountable difficulties. Nevertheless, we will discuss it. Will you come?"

"I will do myself the honor."

"Then I will expect you. I am at Plaisance."[13]

After he left, the Comptroller-General praised his talent and his probity. He was the brother of Pâris de Montmartel,[14] whom secret history made the father of Madame de Pompadour, for he was Madame Poisson's lover at the same time as Monsieur Le Normand.[15]

I went to walk in the Tuileries, reflecting on the fantastic piece of luck which Fortune seemed to be offering me. I am told that twenty millions are needed, I boast that I can furnish a hundred millions without having any idea how to do it, and a famous man, thoroughly experienced in business, invites me to dinner to convince me that he already knows my plan. If he thinks he can worm it out of me I defy him to do it; when he has imparted his own plan to me I shall be at liberty to tell him whether he has guessed mine or not, and if the thing is within my comprehension I will perhaps say something new; if I don't understand a word of it, I will maintain a mysterious silence.

The Abbé de Bernis had described me as a financier only to get me a hearing. Otherwise, I should not have been admitted. I was sorry I did not at least know the jargon of the department. The next morning I took a hackney coach and, in low spirits, told the driver to take me to Monsieur Duverney's at Plaisance. It was a little way beyond Vincennes.

So here I am at the door of the famous man who had saved France after the crashes brought on by Law's[16] system forty years earlier. I find him with seven or eight gentlemen before a great fire. He announces me by my name, adding that I am a friend of the Minister of Foreign Affairs[17] and of the Comptroller-General. He then introduces me to his guests, giving three or four of them the title of Intendant of Finances.[18] I bow, and instantly fall to worshiping Harpocrates.[19]

After touching on the Seine, which was frozen more than a foot deep, on Monsieur de Fontenelle,[20] who had just died, on Damiens, who refused to confess anything, and on the five millions which his trial would cost the King, the conversation turned to the war and then to praise of Monsieur de Soubise,[21] whom the King had chosen as commander. This subject led to the cost of the war and to the resources for maintaining it and the country. I spent an hour and a half in boredom, for all their discussions were so stuffed with the technical terms of their profession that I understood nothing. After an hour and a half at table, where I opened my mouth only to eat, we went into a drawing room, where Monsieur Duverney left the company and took me to his study with a good-looking man of about fifty years of age whom he had presented to me by the name of Calzabigi.[22] A moment later two Intendants of Finances came in too. Smiling, Monsieur Duverney put in my hands a folio notebook, saying:

"There is your plan."

I see on the title page: "Lottery[23] of ninety lots, of which the winning lots, drawn each month at random, can only fall on five numbers," etc., etc. I hand it back to him and I do not hesitate an instant before telling him that it is my plan.

"Monsieur," he said, "you have been forestalled; the scheme is Monsieur de Calzabigi's."

"I am delighted to find that Monsieur and I think alike: but if you have not adopted it, may I ask you the reason?"

"Several very plausible arguments have been raised against the plan, and the answers to them have been indecisive."

"I know only one argument in the whole of nature," I answered coldly, "against which I could say nothing. That would be if the King would not allow his subjects to gamble."

"That argument has no bearing, the King will permit his subjects to gamble. But will they gamble?"

"I am astonished that there should be any doubt of it, if people are sure that they will be paid if they win."

"Then let us suppose that they will gamble if they are certain that there is money with which to pay. How is the money to be raised?"

"The royal treasury. A decree of the Council. It is enough if the King is believed able to pay a hundred millions."

"A hundred millions?"

"Yes, Monsieur. The thing is to dazzle."

"Then you think the King could lose them?"

"I suppose it possible; but after taking in a hundred and fifty millions. If you know the value of a political calculation, you can only start from there."

"Monsieur, I am not the only one. Will you not admit that at the very first drawing the King can lose an immense sum?"

"Between possibility and reality there is infinity; but I admit it. If the King loses a great sum at the first drawing, the success of the lottery is assured. It is a misfortune to be desired. Moral forces are calculated like probabilities. You know that all insurance companies[24] are rich. I will prove to you before all the mathematicians in Europe that, granted God is neutral, it is impossible that the King will not make a profit of one in five by this lottery. That is the secret. Will you admit that reason must yield to a mathematical proof?"

"I admit it. But tell me: why cannot the *castelletto*[25] guarantee the King an unfailing profit?"

"There is no *castelletto* in the world which can make it patently and absolutely certain that the King will always profit. The *castelletto* serves only to maintain a temporary balance on one number or two or three, which, being unusually overloaded, could if they came out cause the backer of the lottery a great loss. In such a case the *castelletto* declares the number closed. The *castelletto* could only make you sure of profiting by putting off the drawing until all the chances carried an equal load, and then there would be no lottery, for the drawing might not take place for ten years; and, besides that, I will tell you that under those circumstances the lottery would become a sheer fraud. What saves it from that dishonorable name is the scheduled drawing every month, for then the public is sure that the backer can lose."

"Will you be good enough to speak before the full Council?"[26]

"With pleasure."

"Will you answer all objections?"

"Every one."

"Will you bring me your scheme?"

"I will not communicate my scheme, Monsieur, until its theory is accepted and I am certain that it will be adopted and that I will receive the benefits for which I shall ask."

"But your plan can only be the same as this one."

"I doubt it. In my plan I set forth approximately how much the King will profit each year, and I prove it."

"Then it could be sold to a company which would pay the King a fixed sum."

"I beg your pardon. The lottery can prosper only under a precondition whose effect is absolutely necessary. I would not go into it to serve a committee which, to augment the profit, would set about increasing the operations, and thereby diminish the eagerness to participate. I am sure of that. The lottery, if I am to have anything to do with it, must be royal or nothing."

"Monsieur de Calzabigi is of the same opinion."

"Nothing could please me better."

"Have you capable people for the *castelletto*?"

"All I need is intelligent machines, of which there must be plenty in France."

"What do you estimate the profit will be?"

"Twenty per cent at each drawing. Whoever brings the King six francs will receive five, and the crush will be so great that, *caeteris paribus* ['other things being equal'], the whole nation will pay the monarch at least five hundred thousand francs a month. I will prove it to the Council on condition that its members are men who, once they have recognized a truth which follows from either a scientific or a political calculation, will no longer hesitate."

Delighted that I could keep my word in everything I had undertaken to do, I got up to go somewhere. When I came back I found them still standing discussing the matter among themselves. Calzabigi came to me and asked in a friendly tone if I included the *quaterna* in my plan. I answered that the public should be free to play the *cinquina*[27] too, but that in my plan I made the stake higher, because the player could not stake on the *quaterna* or the *cinquina* without also playing them as a *terno*.[28] He answered that in his plan he admitted the simple *quaterna* with a profit of fifty thousand for one. I mildly replied that there were very good mathematicians in France, who, when they found that all the chances did not yield equal gains, would profit from collusion. He then clasped my hand, saying that he hoped we could speak further. After giving my address to Monsieur Duverney I left at nightfall satisfied, and certain that I had left a good impression on the old man's mind.

Three or four days later Calzabigi appeared at my lodging, and I received him with the assurance that if I had not presented myself at his door it was because I had not dared. He said straightforwardly that the way I had spoken to the gentlemen had impressed them and that he felt certain that if I would apply to the Comptroller-General we would establish the lottery, which would be most profitable to us.

"I believe it," I answered; "but the profit they would draw from it themselves would be even greater; despite that, they are in no hurry; they have not sent for me, and in any case it is no longer my chief interest."

"You will hear something today. I know that Monsieur de Boulogne has spoken of you to Monsieur de Courteuil."[29]

"I assure you that I made no application to him."

He asked me most cordially to come and dine with him, and I accepted. Just as we were leaving I received a note from the Abbé de Bernis, who wrote me that if I could be at Versailles the next day he would arrange for me to speak with Madame la Marquise, and that I would find Monsieur de Boulogne there at the same time.

It was not vanity but policy which prompted me to give the note to Calzabigi to read. He said that I was in possession of everything I needed to force Duverney himself to start the lottery.

"And your fortune," he said, "is made, if you are not rich enough not to care. We have been moving heaven and earth for two years to get this project accepted, and we have never had anything for our pains but stupid objections, which you demolished last week. Your project must be very much the same as mine. We should join forces, believe me. Remember that, by yourself, you will encounter insurmountable difficulties, and that the 'intelligent machines' you need are not to be found in Paris. My brother[30] will take all the work on himself; use your powers of persuasion, and then be content to enjoy half the emoluments of the directorship while you amuse yourself."

"Then it is your brother who originated the plan."

"It is my brother. He is ill, but his mind is perfectly active. We will call on him."

I saw a man in bed covered with scab; but that did not keep him from eating with appetite, writing, conversing, and performing all the functions of a man in health. He did not appear in public because, in addition to the disfiguring scab, he had constantly to scratch some part of his body, which in Paris is an abomination which is never forgiven, whether the scratching is due to a disease or is simply a bad habit. So Calzabigi told me that he stayed where he was and saw no one because he itched all over and his only relief was to scratch.

"God," he said, "can have given me fingernails for no other purpose."

"Then you believe in final causes, and I congratulate you. Nevertheless I believe you would scratch even if God had forgotten to give you fingernails."

I saw him smile, and we discussed our business. In less than an hour I found that he was very intelligent. He was the elder brother and a bachelor. A great arithmetician, thoroughly acquainted with theoretical and practical finance, familiar with the commerce of all nations, versed in history, a wit, a worshiper of the fair sex, and a poet. He was a native of Leghorn; he had worked at Naples in the

Ministry, and had come to Paris with Monsieur de l'Hôpital.[31] His
brother was also very clever, but inferior to him in every respect.

He showed me a great pile of papers in which he had worked out
all the details of the lottery.

"If you think," he said, "that you can do it all without needing me, I
congratulate you; but you would be deluding yourself; for if you have
had no practical experience and if you are without trained assistants
who know what they are doing, your theory will get you nowhere.
What will you do when you have obtained the decree? When you
speak to the Council you would do well to set a date after which you
will wash your hands of the matter. Otherwise they will keep putting
you off till the Greek Kalends.[32] I can assure you that Monsieur
Duverney will be very glad to see us join forces. As for the analytical
relations between equal winnings from all chances, I will convince you
that they should not be taken into account for the *quaterna*."

Thoroughly persuaded that I should join forces with them but
without letting them know that I considered I should need their
help, I went downstairs with his brother, who was to introduce me
to his wife before dinner. I saw an old woman well known in Paris as
La Générale La Mothe[33] and famous for her former beauty and her
drops, another superannuated lady, known in Paris as Baroness
Blanche,[34] who was still Monsieur de Vaux's[35] mistress, another
who was called La Présidente,[36] and still another, pretty as an
angel, who was called Madame Razzetti,[37] from Piedmont, the
wife of a violinist at the Opéra and then on the best of terms not
only with Monsieur de Fondpertuis,[38] Master of the Revels,[39] but
also with several other gentlemen. I did not shine at dinner. It was
the first I had attended with serious business on my mind. I never
once spoke. That evening at Silvia's the company also thought me
preoccupied, despite the love which the young daughter of the
house increasingly inspired in me.

Two hours before dawn the next day I set off for Versailles,
where Minister de Bernis received me banteringly, saying he
would wager that, but for him, I should never have discovered
that I was an expert in finance.

"Monsieur de Boulogne told me that you amazed Monsieur
Duverney, who is one of the greatest men in France. Go to him at
once, and pay court to him in Paris. The lottery will be established,
and it is for you to profit by it. As soon as the King has gone hunting,
be in the private apartments,[40] and when I see the opportunity I will
'show you off' to Madame la Marquise. After that you will go to the

Foreign Affairs office and introduce yourself to the Abbé de Laville;[41] he is first secretary, he will give you a good reception."

Monsieur de Boulogne promised me that as soon as Monsieur Duverney informed him that the Council of the Military School had agreed, he would have the decree establishing the lottery issued, and he encouraged me to inform him of any other ideas which I might have.

At noon Madame de Pompadour came to the private apartments with the Prince of Soubise and my patron, who immediately pointed me out to the great lady. After curtsying to me, as was the custom, she said that she had read the story of my escape and had found it most interesting.

"Those gentlemen *up there*,"[42] she said with a smile, "are greatly to be feared. Do you visit the Ambassador?"

"I cannot better show him my respect than by not going there."

"I hope that you are now thinking of settling among us."

"Nothing could make me happier; but I need patronage, and I have learned that in this country it is accorded only to talent. That discourages me."

"I think that you need set no limit to your hopes, for you have good friends. I shall be glad to do what I can for you if I have an opportunity."

The Abbé de Laville received me very well and did not leave until he had assured me that he would have me in mind as soon as an opportunity arose. I went to dine at an inn, where a good-looking abbé came up and asked me if we might dine together. Politeness did not permit me to refuse. As we sat down at table, he congratulated me on the excellent reception which the Abbé de Laville had accorded me.

"I was there," he said, "writing a letter; but I heard almost all the kind things he said to you. May I ask you to whom you owe your introduction to the worthy Abbé?"

"If you are extremely curious to know, Monsieur l'Abbé, I will be glad to tell you."

"Oh, no, no! Pray excuse me."

After this indiscretion he spoke only of indifferent and amusing things. We left together in a "chamber pot" and reached Paris at eight o'clock, where, after promising to exchange visits and telling each other our names, we parted. He got out in the Rue des Bons Enfants and I went to supper at Silvia's in the Rue du Petit Lion. That woman among women congratulated me on my new acquaintances and advised me to cultivate them.

At home I found a note from Monsieur Duverney asking me to be at the Military School the next morning at eleven o'clock. At nine o'clock in came Calzabigi, whom his brother had sent to me with a large sheet of paper containing the arithmetical table of the entire lottery, which I could explain to the Council. It was a calculation of the probabilities which, set over against the certainties, proved what I had only stated. In substance it showed that the lottery would have come out exactly even so far as paying the winning tickets was concerned if instead of five numbers six should be drawn. Only five were to be drawn, and this made it scientifically certain that the advantage would always be one in five, which came to eighteen in ninety, which was the total number of lots in the lottery. This demonstration had the corollary that the lottery could not be maintained with drawings of six numbers, since the operating expenses amounted to a hundred thousand écus.

Thus instructed, and thoroughly persuaded that I ought to follow this plan, I proceeded to the Military School, where we at once went into conference. Monsieur d'Alembert[43] had been asked to be present as the great master of universal arithmetic. His presence would not have been considered necessary if Monsieur Duverney had been by himself; but there were some who, in order to avoid accepting the result of a political calculation, stubbornly denied its validity. The conference lasted three hours.

After my argument, which took only half an hour, Monsieur de Courteuil summarized all that I had said, and an hour was spent in nugatory objections which I easily refuted. I said that if the art of calculation in general was properly the art of finding the expression of a single relation arising from the combination of several relations, the same definition applied to moral calculation, which was as certain as mathematical calculation. I convinced them that without that certainty the world would never have had insurance companies, which, all of them rich and flourishing, laugh at Fortune and at the weak minds which fear her. I ended by saying that there was not a man at once learned and honorable in the world who could offer to be at the head of this lottery on the understanding that it would win at every drawing, and that if a man should appear with the temerity to give them that assurance they should turn him out, because either he would not keep his promise or, if he kept it, he would be a scoundrel.

Monsieur Duverney rose and said that in any case they could always abolish the lottery. After signing a paper which Monsieur

Duverney presented to them, all the gentlemen left. Calzabigi came the next morning to tell me that the thing was settled and that it was now only a matter of waiting for the decree to be issued. I promised him I would call on Monsieur de Boulogne every day and that I would have him made a director as soon as I learned from Monsieur Duverney what my emoluments were to be.

The proposal made to me, which I accepted at once, was six collector's offices and an income of four thousand francs[44] a year secured by the lottery itself. It was the return on a capital of a hundred thousand francs, which I was at liberty to withdraw if I relinquished the offices, since the capital represented my guarantee.

The decree of the Council was issued a week later. The direction was given to Calzabigi, with emoluments of three thousand francs per drawing and a yearly income of four thousand francs—the same as mine—and the main office of the enterprise in the Hôtel de la Loterie in the Rue Montmartre. Of my six offices I at once sold five for two thousand francs each, and I opened the sixth[45] in luxurious quarters in the Rue Saint-Denis, putting my valet there as chief clerk. He was a young and highly intelligent Italian who had formerly served as valet to the Prince of La Cattolica,[46] the Neapolitan Ambassador. The day for the first drawing was set, and it was announced that all winning tickets would be paid a week after the drawing at the main office of the lottery.

Within twenty-four hours I had bills out to the effect that all winning tickets signed by me would be paid at my office in the Rue Saint-Denis twenty-four hours after the drawing. The result was that everyone came to my office for tickets. My profit consisted in the six percent on receipts. Fifty or sixty clerks from the other offices were stupid enough to complain of my move to Calzabigi. He could only answer them that they were free to catch up with me by doing the same thing, but that they had to have the money.

My receipts at the first drawing[47] were forty thousand livres. An hour after the drawing my clerk brought me the register and showed me that we had to pay out seventeen or eighteen thousand livres, all on *ambi*,[48] and I gave him the money. It was very profitable for my clerk, who though he asked for nothing always accepted the tips he was given, and from whom I did not demand any accounting. The lottery made a profit of six hundred thousand francs on the total receipts, which amounted to two millions. Paris alone contributed four hundred thousand francs. I dined at Monsieur Duverney's the next day with Calzabigi. We had the pleasure of hearing him complain that he had made too much. In Paris only eighteen or twenty *terne* won; though they were small, they gave the lottery a brilliant reputation. The rage being on, we expected that the receipts at the next drawing would be twice as large. The good-natured banter to which I was subjected at table over my scheme delighted me. Calzabigi demonstrated that my inspiration had assured me of an income of one hundred and twenty thousand francs a year, which ruined all the other collectors. Monsieur Duverney replied that he had often acted on similar inspirations and that, in any case, the collectors were all free to do the same thing, for it could only make the lottery more highly thought of. The second time, a *terna* of forty thousand francs forced me to borrow money. My receipts had been sixty thousand, but I had to turn them over to the financial agent the day before the drawing. In all the great houses to which I went and in theater lobbies, as soon as people saw me they gave me money, asking me to stake for them as I chose and to give them the tickets, for they knew nothing about it. I carried tickets for large and small amounts in my pockets, from which I let people choose, and I returned home with my pockets full of money. The other collectors did not have this privilege. They were not of a sort to be accepted in society. Only I went about in a carriage of my own; it gave me a reputation and unlimited credit. Paris was, and still is, a city where people judge everything by appearances; there is not a country in the world where it is easier to make an impression. But now that I have given my reader a full account of the lottery I will mention it only as it comes up.

A month after my arrival in Paris my brother Francesco, the painter, with whom I had left Paris in 1752, arrived from Dresden with Madame Silvestre.[49] He had spent four years there copying all the finest battle paintings in the celebrated gallery.[50] We were very glad to see each other again; but when I offered him the support of all my highly placed acquaintances to get him into the Academy, he answered that he did not need influence. He painted a picture representing a battle, he exhibited it at the Louvre, and he was received[51] by acclamation. The Academy paid him twelve thousand francs for his picture. After his reception my brother became famous, and in twenty-six years he earned nearly a million; however, extravagance and two bad marriages ruined him.

[* * *]

CHAPTER IV

The Abbé de Laville. The Abbé Galiani.
Character of the Neapolitan dialect.
I go to Dunkirk on a secret mission.
I am completely successful.

The Minister of Foreign Affairs asked me if I would be interested in undertaking secret missions and if I thought I had any aptitude in that way. I replied that I would be interested in anything which I considered honest and by which I could be sure of earning money, and that so far as aptitude was concerned I left it to him. He told me to go and talk with the Abbé de Laville.

The Abbé, the First Secretary, was a man of cold temperament, a profound politician, the soul of his department, and very highly esteemed. He had served the State well as Chargé d'Affaires at The Hague;[1] in gratitude, the King gave him a bishopric on the very day that he died. It was a little too late. The heir to all he possessed was Garnier,[2] a self-made man who had been cook to Monsieur d'Argenson[3] and who had become rich by profiting from the friendship which the Abbé de Laville had always felt for him. The two friends, who were about the same age, had named each other residuary legatee in wills which they had deposited with a notary. The survivor was Garnier.

The Abbé, then, after treating me to a short discourse on the nature of secret missions and on the prudence necessary in those who undertook them, said that he would inform me as soon as anything suitable for me turned up, and he kept me for dinner. At table I met the Abbé Galiani,[4] the Neapolitan Embassy Secretary. He was a brother of the Marchese Galiani, of whom I will speak when we come to my journey to the Kingdom of Naples. The Abbé was very witty. He had an extraordinary knack for giving his most serious remarks a tinge of humor, and always with a straight face, speaking French very well with the incorrigible Neapolitan accent, which made him a favorite in all circles. The Abbé de Laville told him that Monsieur Voltaire complained that his *Henriade*[5] had been translated into Neapolitan verse in a way which made readers laugh. He replied that Voltaire was in the wrong, for the nature of the

Neapolitan language was such that it was impossible to handle it in verse except in a way which aroused laughter.

"If you can imagine it," he said, "we have translations of the Bible and the *Iliad* both of which are funny."

"I can believe it of the Bible, but I find it surprising in the case of the *Iliad*."

[* * *]

At the beginning of May[6] the Abbé de Bernis wrote me that I should go to Versailles to talk with the Abbé de Laville. The Abbé asked me if I thought I was capable of paying a visit to ten or twelve warships which were anchored at Dunkirk and becoming well enough acquainted with their commanding officers to give him a detailed report on how well they were provisioned in all respects, especially as to their supplies in general, the numbers of their crews, their stock of munitions of all kinds, their administration, and their discipline. I answered that I could try, that when I returned I would give him my report in writing, and that it would be for him to tell me if I had done well.

"Since it is a secret mission," he said, "I cannot give you any letters. I can only wish you a successful journey and give you some money."

"I do not want any money. When I return you may give me what you consider I have deserved; as for my making a successful journey, I shall need at least three days before starting, for I must get some sort of letter."

"Then try to be back before the end of the month. That is all I have to say."

On the same day I had a half hour's conversation at the Palais Bourbon with my patron, who, unable to resist praising me for my delicacy in refusing to take any money in advance, gave me another roll of a hundred louis with his usual magnanimity. From then on I never again needed to make use of the generous man's purse, not even at Rome fourteen years later.

"Since the mission is secret," he said, "I am sorry that I cannot give you a passport; but through Silvia you can obtain one on some pretext from the First Gentleman of the Bedchamber[7] now serving. You must be extremely prudent in your behavior, and above all keep clear of anything *in munere* ['in the way of bribery'],[8] for you know, I believe, that if you get into any difficulty appealing to your principal will avail you nothing. You will be disowned. The only acknowledged spies are the ambassadors. So you need to be even more reserved and circumspect than they are. If when you come back you will let me see your report before you take it to the Abbé de Laville, I will give you my advice regarding what I think you should omit from it."

Full of this business, in which I was a complete novice, I told Silvia that, as I wanted to accompany some English friends to Calais and return to Paris, she would do me a great favor if she would obtain a passport for me from the Duke of Gesvres.[9] Glad to oblige me, she wrote to the Duke, telling me that I must deliver the letter to him personally, since passports of this kind could not be issued unless they contained a description of the bearer. They were valid only in the so-called Île de France,[10] but they procured respect in all the northern part of the kingdom. So I went to him with her husband. The Duke was at his estate in Saint-Ouen.[11] No sooner had he seen me and read Silvia's letter than he had a passport issued for me; and after leaving Mario I went to La Villette to ask Madame XXX if she wanted me to take any message from her to her niece. She said that I could take her the box of porcelain figures if Monsieur Kornmann had not yet sent it. So I went to see the banker, who delivered it to me and to whom I gave a hundred louis, asking him for the same amount in a letter of credit on a reliable house in Dunkirk together with a personal recommendation, since I was going there for pleasure. Kornmann gladly did both, and I set out toward evening of the same day.

Three days later I put up at the Conciergerie[12] in Dunkirk. An hour after my arrival I gave the charming Madame P. the most pleasant surprise by delivering her box and conveying her aunt's compliments to her. Just as she was praising her husband to me and saying that he made her happy, he arrived and, delighted to see me, at once offered me a room without even asking if my stay in Dunkirk was to be long or short. After duly thanking him and promising that I would come and take potluck for dinner at his house from time to time, I asked him to show me the way to the banker to whom Monsieur Kornmann had recommended me.

Scarcely had the banker read the letter before he gave me a hundred louis and asked me to expect him at my inn toward evening, when he would introduce me to the Commandant. The latter was Monsieur du Bareil.[13] With the politeness of all Frenchmen in high office, the Commandant, after asking me the usual questions, invited me to sup with his wife, who was still at the theater. She received me as cordially as her husband had done, and having excused myself from cards, I began making the acquaintance of the company, especially of the army and navy officers. Making a point of talking about all the European navies and giving myself out to be an expert on the subject from having served in the fleet of my Republic, it took me no more than three days not only to pick up an acquaintance of all the naval captains but to become good friends with them. I rattled away about shipbuilding and the Venetian system of maneuvers, and I observed that the worthy sailors who listened to me were even more attentive when I talked nonsense than they were when I said anything sensible. On the fourth day one of the captains invited me on board his ship for dinner; whereupon all the others invited me either to breakfast or to a between-meals repast. I devoted the entire day to each of the captains who thus honored me. I showed interest in everything, I went down into the hold, I asked countless questions, and everywhere I found young officers eager to show their importance, whom I had no difficulty in pumping. I got them to confide to me whatever I needed to know for my detailed report. Before going to bed I wrote down everything good or bad I had learned during the day about the ship on which I had been. I slept only four or five hours. In two weeks I considered that I had learned enough.

[* * *]

Though clearly suspicious of Casanova's dubious reputation and raffish manners, the French authorities took note of his talent for business and gave him further commissions. He meanwhile pursued his social and amorous life in the demi-monde.

CHAPTER V

The Count of La Tour d'Auvergne and
Madame d'Urfé. Camilla. My passion for the
Count's mistress; ridiculous incident which
cures me. The Count of Saint-Germain.

[* * *]

Camilla,[1] actress and dancer at the Comédie Italienne, whom I had begun to love at Fontainebleau seven years earlier, was the woman [...] on whom I especially fastened because of the pleasures I enjoyed in her small house at the Barrière Blanche,[2] where she lived with her lover the Count of Égreville,[3] who made much of me among their guests. The brother of the Marquis de Gamaches[4] and of the Countess du Rumain,[5] he was a handsome young man, very amiable and reasonably rich. He was never so happy as when he saw a great deal of company in his mistress's house. She loved only him; but, full of intelligence and tact, she drove none of her admirers to despair; neither miserly nor prodigal in granting her favors, she made all the members of her circle adore her without having to fear either a blabbing tongue or the mortification of being cast off.

After her lover the man whom she honored with her attention above all the rest was the Count of La Tour d'Auvergne.[6] He was a nobleman of ancient lineage who adored her and who, not being rich enough to have her entirely to himself, had to be content with the share in her which she granted him. She was said to love him second best. She allowed him a modest sum for the expenses of a young girl whom she had, in a manner of speaking, given him as a present on seeing that he had fallen in love with her when she was in her service. La Tour d'Auvergne kept her at Paris with him in furnished rooms in the Rue Taranne;[7] he said that he loved her because she was a present his dear Camilla had given him; and he often took her to sup with her at the Barrière Blanche. She was fifteen years old, simple, ingenuous, without a grain of ambition; she told her lover she would never forgive him an infidelity except with Camilla, to whom she thought she must yield him because she owed her happiness to her. I fell so much in love with the girl that I often went to sup at Camilla's only in the hope of finding her there and enjoying the artless remarks with which she enchanted the entire company. I tried my best not to betray myself, but I was so mad about her that by the time supper was over I would often have become very gloomy because I saw that my passion could not be cured in the usual way. Allowing my condition to be suspected would have made me ridiculous, and Camilla would have railed at me mercilessly. But now for what happened to cure me of my passion.

As Camilla's little house was at the Barrière Blanche I sent my lackey for a hackney coach to take me home when everyone was ready to leave after supper. Since we had remained at table until an hour after midnight he told me that no coaches were to be found. La Tour d'Auvergne said that it would be no inconvenience to him to take me home, though his carriage was only for two.

"My little girl," he said, "will sit on our laps."

I accept, of course, and here I am in the carriage, with the Count at my left and Babet sitting on our thighs. Full of desire, I determine to seize the opportunity, and, wasting no time, for the coachman was driving fast, I take her hand, squeeze it, she squeezes mine, I gratefully raise it to my lips, covering it with silent kisses, and, impatient to convince her of my ardor, I proceed as my state of bliss demands that I do; but just at the moment of crisis I hear La Tour d'Auvergne saying:

"I am obliged to you, my dear friend, for a piece of your country's politeness of which I thought I was no longer worthy; I hope it is not a mistake."

At these horrifying words I put out my hand, I feel the sleeve of his coat; there is no such thing as presence of mind at such a moment, and the more so since the words were followed by a laugh which would have confounded the most hardened of men. I let go, unable either to laugh at the thing or deny it. Babet asked her lover why he was laughing so hard, and when he tried to tell her the reason laughter overcame him again, I said nothing, and I felt an utter fool. Fortunately the carriage soon stopped at my lodging, and, my lackey opening the door for me, I went in, wishing them a good night, which La Tour d'Auvergne reciprocated still laughing uproariously. As for me, I did not begin to laugh at the episode until half an hour later, for, after all, it was funny; nevertheless it depressed and vexed me, for I saw that I must expect to be the butt of many jokes.

Three or four days later I decided to go at nine in the morning and ask the obliging nobleman to give me breakfast, for Camilla had sent to inquire after my health. I did not mean to let the incident stop my visits to her, but I wanted first to know how the thing had been taken.

As soon as the charming La Tour saw me he exploded into laughter and after laughing his fill came and embraced me, mincing like a girl. I begged him, half humorously, half seriously, to forget my silly blunder, for I really did not know how to defend myself.

"Why try to defend yourself?" he answered. "We all like you, it is a very funny story, which has delighted us and delights us every evening."

"Then everyone knows of it?"

"Can you doubt that? Camilla is dying of laughter, and you must come this evening, I'll bring Babet, and she will set you laughing too, for she maintains that you made no mistake."

"She is right."

"What! she is right? Tell that to someone else. You do me too much honor, and I do not believe a word of it; but you are taking the right stand."

And it was the stand I took at table, pretending to be amazed at La Tour's indiscretion and saying that I was cured of my passion for him. Babet called me a dirty swine and refused to believe I was cured. For unfathomable reasons the episode turned me against her and attached me to La Tour d'Auvergne, who had every quality to make everyone like him. But my friendship for him very nearly had a disastrous consequence.

It was on a Monday in the foyer of the Comédie Italienne that the charming Count asked me to lend him a hundred louis, promising to return them on Saturday.

"I haven't that much. But here is my purse at your service," I said, "with ten or twelve louis."

"I need a hundred, and immediately, for I lost them last night on my word at the Princess of Anhalt's."*[8]

"I haven't that much."

"A collector of the lottery must have over a thousand."

"Of course, but my cash box is sacred; I have to turn it over to the fiscal agent a week from today."

---

*She was the mother of Empress Catherine of Russia. (C.'s note.)

"It won't keep you from turning it over, for I will return them to you on Saturday. Take a hundred louis from your cash box, and put my word of honor in their place. Do you think it worth a hundred louis?"

At that I turn my back on him, telling him to wait for me, I go to my office in the Rue Saint-Denis, I take a hundred louis, and I bring them to him. Saturday arrives, I do not see him, and on Sunday morning I pawn my ring and put the same amount in my cash box, which I turn over to the fiscal agent the next day. Three or four days later in the amphitheater of the Comédie Française, up comes La Tour d'Auvergne and apologizes. I reply by showing him my hand and saying that I had pawned my ring to save my honor. He answers gloomily that someone has failed him but that he is sure he can return the amount to me on the following Saturday:

"And I give you," he said, "my word of honor for it."

"Your word of honor is in my cash box, so you will permit me not to count on it further; you may return the hundred louis to me when you please."

At these words I saw the gallant nobleman turn as pale as a corpse.

"My word of honor, my dear Casanova," he said, "is dearer to me than life, and I will give you the hundred louis tomorrow morning at nine o'clock a hundred paces from the coffeehouse at the end of the Champs Élysées. I will give them to you privately, no one will see us, I hope that you will not fail to be there and that you will have your sword, as I shall have mine."

"I find it very regrettable, sir, that you insist on my paying so dearly for a jest. You do me infinite honor, but I would rather apologize to you, if that can prevent this unfortunate matter from going further."

"No, I am far more in the wrong than you, and the wrong can only be undone by the blood of one of us. Will you come?"

"Yes."

I supped at Silvia's in great depression, for I loved the gallant man, and I loved myself no less. I felt I was in the wrong, for my jest had really been too cutting, but it did not enter my mind not to keep the appointment.

I arrived at the coffeehouse a moment after he did; we breakfasted, he paid, and we left and walked in the direction of the Étoile. When we were sure we were not observed he handed me a roll of a hundred louis with the greatest courtesy; and, saying that one thrust should suffice on either side, he unsheathed after stepping back four paces. My only answer was to unsheathe too, and as soon as I saw that I was in measure I gave him my straight lunge, and, certain that I had wounded him in the chest, I jumped back, calling upon him to keep his word. Mild as a lamb, he lowered his sword, put his hand to his chest, and, showing it to me stained with blood, said that he was satisfied. I spoke to him with all the civility of which I was capable and which the occasion demanded, while he applied a handkerchief to his chest. I was very glad when, looking at the point of my sword, I saw that only one line[9] of it showed blood. I offered to see him home and he refused. He asked me to be discreet and to be his friend thenceforward. After embracing him in tears, I went home very sad and considerably wiser in the ways of the world. Our meeting never became known. A week later we supped together at Camilla's.

About this same time I received twelve thousand francs from the Abbé de Laville as the honorarium for the mission I had accomplished in Dunkirk. Camilla told me that La Tour d'Auvergne was in bed because of his sciatica, adding that if I liked we would pay him a visit the next day. I accepted, we went, and after breakfasting I told him gravely that if he would let me do what I wished to his thigh I would cure it, for his trouble was not what was called "sciatica" but a damp humor which I would dispel with the Talisman of Solomon[10] and five words. He laughed but told me to do whatever I pleased.

"Then I will go and buy a brush."

"I will send a servant."

"No, for I must be sure that it is bought without haggling, and I have to get some drugs too."

I went for niter, flowers of sulphur, mercury, and a small brush, and I told him I needed a small quantity of his urine, which must be fresh. His laughter and Camilla's did not impair my gravity; I handed him a glass, I drew his curtains, and he obeyed me. After making a little amalgam with it, I told Camilla to rub his thigh with her hands while I murmured a spell, but that all would be lost if she laughed. After spending a good quarter of an hour laughing, they finally prevailed on themselves to behave as I was behaving. La Tour exposed his thigh to Camilla, who, pretending she was acting a role in a play, began massaging the patient while I mumbled words which they could not possibly understand since I did not myself know what I was saying. I almost spoiled the performance myself when I saw the faces Camilla was making to keep from laughing. Nothing could be funnier. After telling them at last that there had been enough massage I dipped the brush in the amalgam and, making one continuous stroke, drew the Sign of Solomon on him—the five-pointed star composed of five lines, thus. After that I wrapped his thigh in three napkins and told him that if he could stay in bed and not unwrap it for twenty-four hours I guaranteed that he would be cured. What pleased me was that I heard no more laughter from them. They were astonished.

After this comedy, which I made up and acted with neither purpose nor premeditation, we left, and in the hackney coach on the way I told Camilla a quantity of wonderful tales, to which she listened so attentively that when I left her I saw that she was vastly impressed.

At eight o'clock in the morning four or five days later, when I had almost forgotten what I had done to Monsieur de La Tour d'Auvergne, I hear horses stopping at my door. I look out of my window, I see him dismount and come in.

"You were sure of the result," he said, embracing me, "since you did not come to see how I was getting on the morning after your amazing treatment."

"Certainly I was sure, but if I had had time you would have seen me nevertheless."

"Tell me if I am allowed to take a bath."

"No bath until you feel you are cured."

"I will obey you. Everyone is amazed, for I could not help telling all my acquaintances about your miracle. I find skeptics who laugh at me, but I let them say what they please."

"You should have kept the secret, I think, for you know Paris. Everyone will say I am a quack."

"Not everyone is so narrow-minded, and I have come to ask you to do me a favor."

"What is your pleasure?"

"I have an aunt who is not only well known but famous for her knowledge of all the abstruse sciences, a great chemist, a woman of intelligence, extremely rich, sole mistress of her fortune, and whose acquaintance can only be useful to you. She is dying to meet you, for she claims that she knows you and that you are not the man Paris believes you to be. She begged me to bring you to dinner at her house, and I hope that you will have no objection. My aunt is the Marquise d'Urfé."[11]

I did not know her, but the name d'Urfé impressed me at once, for I knew the story of the famous Anne d'Urfé,[12] who had

594

flourished at the end of the sixteenth century. The lady was the widow of his great-grandson; and I saw that, having entered the family, she might well have become versed in all the sublime doctrines of a science which greatly interested me though I considered it chimerical. I therefore answered Monsieur de La Tour d'Auvergne that I would go to his aunt's house with him whenever he pleased, but not for dinner unless there would be only the three of us.

"She has twelve people to dinner every day, and you will eat at her house with the best of Parisian society."

"That is exactly what I do not want, for I loathe the reputation of magician, which, in the kindness of your heart, you must have given me."

"Not at all; you are known and you are highly regarded. The Duchess of Lauraguais[13] told me that you went to the Palais-Royal four or five years ago and spent whole days with the Duchess of Orléans,[14] and Madame de Boufflers,[15] Madame du Blot,[16] and even Melfort[17] have spoken to me about you. You are wrong not to cultivate your old acquaintances. What you have done for me convinces me that you could have a brilliant and lucrative career. I know any number of the best people in Paris, both men and women, who have the same malady as mine and who would give you half of their possessions if you cured them."

La Tour's reasoning was sound; but since I knew that what I had done to him was only a prank which had happened to succeed I had no wish to incur publicity. I told him that I absolutely declined to make a spectacle of myself, and that he had only to tell his aunt that I would wait on her privately and not otherwise and that I left it to her to indicate the day and the hour. When I got home about midnight of the same day I found a note from the Count telling me to be at the Terrasse des Capucins at the Tuileries the next day at noon, where he would meet me to take me to dinner at his aunt's, and assuring me that we should find her door open only to us.

Meeting punctually at the appointed place and hour, we went to the lady's house the next day. She lived on the Quai des Théatins[18] next door to the Hôtel de Bouillon. Beautiful despite her age, Madame d'Urfé received me most courteously with all the easy grace of the old court in the days of the Regency.[19] We spent an hour and a half in desultory conversation, but all the while, though of course we did not confess to it, she was studying me as closely as I was studying her. Each of us was trying to trap the other into admissions. I had no difficulty in pretending to be ignorant, for I really was so. Madame d'Urfé displayed nothing except curiosity, but I clearly saw that she could not wait to parade her lore. At two o'clock the three of us were served the same dinner which was served every day for twelve. After dinner La Tour d'Auvergne left us to go and see Prince Turenne,[20] whom he had left that morning with a high fever, and then Madame d'Urfé began talking to me of chemistry, alchemy, magic, and all the things with which she was infatuated. When we came to the subject of the Great Work[21] and I guilelessly asked her if she was acquainted with the primordial substance, she did not burst out laughing, for that would have been impolite, but with a gracious smile she told me that she already possessed what was called the philosopher's stone and that she was versed in all the great operations. She showed me her library,[22] which had belonged to the great D'Urfé[23] and his wife Renée of Savoy[24] and to which she had added manuscripts which had cost her more than a hundred thousand francs. Her favorite author was Paracelsus,[25] who, according to her, had been neither man nor woman and had had the misfortune to poison himself with too strong a dose of the universal medicine.[26] She showed me a small manuscript which set forth the great operation in French in very clear terms. She said she did not keep it under a hundred locks because it was written in a cipher of which she alone had the key.

"Then, Madame, you do not believe in steganography?"[27]

"No, Monsieur; and if you will accept it I make you a present of this copy."

I took it and put it in my pocket.

From the library we went to her laboratory, which really astonished me; she showed me a substance which she had kept on the fire for fifteen years and which needed to remain there four or five years more. It was a powder of projection[28] which was to perform the transmutation of all metals into gold in one minute. She showed me a tube through which coal to keep the fire in her furnace always at the same heat came down of its own weight, so that she often went three months without entering her laboratory at no risk of finding her fire out. A small conduit underneath carried off the ashes. The calcination of mercury was child's play for her; she showed me some already calcined and said that she would demonstrate the procedure to me whenever I pleased. She showed me the tree of Diana[29] of the famous Talliamed,[30] whose pupil she was. As everyone knows, Talliamed was the learned

Maillet, who, according to Madame d'Urfé, had not died at Marseilles, as the Abbé Le Maserier[31] had led everyone to believe, but was alive, and, she added with a slight smile, she often received letters from him. If the Regent[32] of France had heeded his advice he would still be among the living. She said that the Regent had been her first friend, that it was he who had nicknamed her Égérie[33] and had himself arranged her marriage to Monsieur d'Urfé. She had a commentary by Raymond Lully,[34] which made clear everything that Arnold of Villanova[35] had written following Roger Bacon[36] and Geber,[37] who, according to her, were not dead. This precious manuscript was in an ivory casket, to which she had the key, and in any case her laboratory was closed to everyone. She showed me a cask filled with *platina del Pinto*,[38] which she could turn into pure gold whenever she pleased. It was Mr. Wood[39] himself who had given it to her in 1743. She showed me the same platinum in four different vessels, three of which contained it intact in sulphuric, nitric, and hydrochloric acid, but in the fourth, in which she had used *aqua regia*,[40] the platinum had been unable to resist. She melted it by the burning glass[41] and said that without some admixture it could be melted in no other way, which in her opinion proved that it was superior to gold. She showed me some of it precipitated by sal ammoniac, which was never able to precipitate gold.

She had an athanor[42] which had been kept burning for fifteen years. I saw that the tower of it was filled with black coals, from which I concluded that she had visited it two or three days before. When we went back to her tree of Diana I respectfully asked her if she agreed with me that it was only a toy to amuse children. She answered with dignity that she had in fact only made it to amuse herself, using silver, mercury, and spirits of niter and crystallizing them together, and that she considered her tree only a metallic vegetation which showed in little what nature could do on a great scale; but she said that she could make a tree of Diana which would be a true tree of the sun, producing golden fruits which would be gathered and continuing to produce them until the exhaustion of an ingredient which she would mix with the six "lepers"[43] in proportion to their quantity. I modestly replied that I did not believe it was possible without the powder of projection. Madame d'Urfé answered only with a gracious smile. She then showed me a porcelain bowl, in which I saw niter, mercury, and sulphur, and a plate on which was a fixed salt.[44]

"I imagine," the Marquise said, "that you know these ingredients."

"I know them," I answered, "if the fixed salt is the salt of urine."

"You are right."

"I admire your sagacity, Madame. You have analyzed the amalgam with which I painted the pentacle[45] on your nephew's thigh; but there is no tartar which can show you the words which give the pentacle its efficacy."

"What is needed for that is not tartar but a manuscript by an adept which I have in my room and which I will show you, in which the words are set forth."

I made no answer, and we left the laboratory.

We had scarcely entered her room before she took from a casket a black book, which she placed on her table, then she began looking for a piece of phosphorus; while she was searching I opened the book, which was behind her, and I saw that it was full of pentacles, and luckily I saw the very talisman which I had painted on her nephew's thigh, encircled by the names of the Planetary Geniuses[46] except for two—those of Saturn and Mars—and I quickly closed the book. The Geniuses were the same as Agrippa's,[47] which I knew, but betraying nothing, I returned to her, and a moment later she found the phosphorus, which really surprised me; but I will speak of it elsewhere.

Madame sat down on her sofa, made me sit beside her, and asked me if I knew the Count of Trèves's[48] talismans.

"I never heard of them, but I know Polyphilus's."[49]

"They are said to be the same."

"I do not believe it."

"We shall find out if you will write down the words you spoke when you painted the pentacle on my nephew's thigh. It will be the same book if I find you those words around the same talisman in this one."

"That would be proof, I admit. I will go and write them."

I wrote the names of the Geniuses; Madame found the pentacle, read out the names to me, and, pretending astonishment, I gave her my paper, where with great satisfaction she read the same names.

"You see," she said, "that Polyphilus and the Count of Trèves were masters of the same science."

"I will admit it, Madame, if your book shows the way to utter the ineffable names.[50] Do you know the theory of the planetary hours?"[51]

598

"I believe I do, but it is not necessary in this operation."

"I beg your pardon. I painted the pentacle of Solomon on Monsieur de La Tour d'Auvergne's thigh at the hour of Venus, and if I had not begun with Anael,[52] who is the Genius of that planet, my operation would have had no effect."

"I did not know that. And after Anael?"

"One must go on to Mercury, from Mercury to the Moon, from the Moon to Jupiter, from Jupiter to the Sun. You see that it is the magical cycle according to the system of Zoroaster,[53] in which I skip Saturn and Mars, which science excludes in this operation."

"And if you had operated during the hour of the Moon, for example?"

"In that case I should have gone to Jupiter, then to the Sun, then to Anael, that is, Venus, and I should have ended with Mercury."

"I see, Monsieur, that you employ the hours with remarkable facility."

"Without that, Madame, one can do nothing in magic, for one does not have time to calculate; but it is not difficult. A month's study will accustom any beginner to it. What is more difficult is the rites, for they are complicated; but one can learn them in due time. I never go out in the morning without knowing how many minutes compose the hour of that particular day, and I take care that my watch is perfectly regulated, for a minute is decisive."

"Would you be so kind as to instruct me in the theory?"

"You have it in Artephius[54] and more clearly in Sandivonius."[55]

"I have them, but they are in Latin."

"I will translate them for you."

"Will you be so obliging?"

"You have shown me things, Madame, which compel me to oblige you, for reasons which I will perhaps tell you tomorrow."

"Why not today?"

"Because I must first know the name of your Genius."

"You know that I have a Genius."

"You must have one, if it is true that you have the powder of projection."

"I have it."

"Give me the oath of the Order."

"I dare not, and you know why."

"Tomorrow I shall perhaps do away with your fears."

The oath was that of the Brothers of the Rosy Cross,[56] which is never exchanged unless the parties first know each other; so

Madame d'Urfé was afraid, and rightly so, that she might be indiscreet, and on my side I had to pretend that I felt the same fear. I thought I ought to gain time, but I knew what the oath was. It can be exchanged between men without indecency, but a woman like Madame d'Urfé must hesitate to give it to a man whom she was seeing for the first time that day.

"When we find the oath announced in our Sacred Scriptures," she said, "it is masked. 'He swore,' says the Holy Bible, 'putting his hand on his thigh.'[57] But it is not the thigh. So we never find a man taking an oath to a woman in that manner, for woman has no word."[58]

At nine in the evening the Count of La Tour d'Auvergne arrived at his aunt's and was surprised to find me still with her. He said that his cousin Prince Turenne's fever had increased greatly and that smallpox had broken out. He told her that he had come to take leave of her for at least a month, since he was going to shut himself up with the patient. Madame d'Urfé praised his zeal, and she gave him a sachet, making him promise that he would return it to her after the Prince was cured. She told him to hang it around the Prince's neck and to be certain of a harmless eruption and a sure cure. He promised, took the sachet, and left.

I then said to the Marquise that I did not know what her sachet contained, but that if it was magic I had no faith in it, for she had given him no instructions concerning the hour. She answered that it was an electrum;[59] and, that being the case, I asked her pardon.

She said that she admired my reserve, but that she thought I would not be disappointed in her circle if I would consent to make their acquaintance. She said that she would introduce me to all her friends by having me to dinner with them one at a time and that afterward I would enjoy their company together. In consequence of this arrangement I dined the next day with a Monsieur Gerin[60] and his niece, neither of whom I liked. Another day it was with an Irishman named Macartney, a physician of the old school, who bored me extremely. Another day she ordered her porter to admit a monk, who, talking of literature, said countless inane things against Voltaire, of whom I was fond in those days, and against the *Esprit des Lois*,[61] which he nevertheless refused to credit to its celebrated author, Montesquieu. He attributed it to the malice of some monk. Another day she had me to dinner with the Chevalier d'Arzigny,[62] a man of ninety, who was known as the "dean of the fops" and who, having figured at the Court of Louis XIV, displayed all its courtesy and knew its gossip. He amused me vastly; he wore rouge; his coats were adorned with the pompons of his century; he professed to be tenderly attached to his mistress, who did the honors of a small house for him where he supped every night in company with his friends, all of them charming young girls who forsook other company for his; nevertheless he was not tempted to be unfaithful to her, for he slept with her every night. This amiable though decrepit and shaky old man had such sweetness of character and such unusual manners that I believed everything he said. His cleanliness was extreme. A large posy of tuberoses and jonquils in the top button-hole of his coat, together with a strong smell of ambergris from the pomade which kept his false hair and eyebrows attached to his head—even with these, his teeth gave off an extremely strong smell, which Madame d'Urfé did not mind but which I found intolerable. Except for that, I would have sought his society as often as I could. Monsieur d'Arzigny was a professed Epicurean, with a serenity which was amazing; he said that he would undertake to receive a drubbing of twenty-four blows every morning if that could assure him that he would not die within twenty-four hours, and that the older he grew the more of a drubbing he would accept.

On another day I dined with Monsieur Charon,[63] Councilor of the Great Chamber,[64] who was her referee in a suit she was pros-ecuting against Madame du Châtelet,[65] her daughter, whom she hated. The old Councilor had been her accepted lover forty years earlier, and for that reason he felt it incumbent on him to find in her favor. The French magistrates made justice go by favors and they considered they were at liberty to favor their friends because their right to judge was theirs by virtue of the money with which they had bought it.[66] The Councilor bored me.

But on another day I greatly enjoyed the company of Monsieur de Viarmes,[67] Madame d'Urfé's nephew, a young councilor, who came to dinner at her house with his wife. The couple were likable, and the nephew was extremely witty, as all Paris knew from reading the Remonstrances au Roi,[68] of which he was the author. He told me that the business of a councilor was to oppose everything the King might do even if it was good. The reasons he alleged for the soundness of this maxim were those put forth by all minorities in collective bodies. I shall not bore my reader by repeating them.

The dinner which I found most entertaining was the one to which she invited Madame de Gergy,[69] who came with the famous adventurer, the Count of Saint-Germain.[70] Instead of eating he talked from the beginning to the end of dinner; and I listened with the greatest attention, for no one was a better talker. He made himself out to be a prodigy in everything, he aimed to amaze, and he really amazed. His tone was peremptory, but no one took it amiss, for he was learned, speaking all languages well, a great musician, a great chemist, with an attractive face and the ability to win the friendship of all women, for at the same time that he gave them paints which beautified their complexions he persuaded them to believe, not that he could make them younger—for that, he said, was impossible—but that he could keep them in their present condition by means of a water which cost him a great deal but which he gave them as a present. This very strange man, who was born to be the most arrant of impostors, would say, without being challenged and as if in passing, that he was three hundred years old, that he possessed the universal medicine, that he could do whatever he pleased with nature, that he melted diamonds and out of ten or twelve small ones made a big one no less in weight and of the finest water. These things were trifles for him. Despite his egregious boasting, his eccentricities, and his obvious lies, I could not bring myself to consider him insolent, but I did not consider him worthy of respect; I found him astonishing despite myself, because he astonished me. I shall speak of him again when the time comes.

After Madame d'Urfé had introduced me to all these people I told her that I would dine with her whenever she wished, but always with no one else present except her relatives and Saint-Germain, whose eloquence and extravagant boasting amused me. When he dined, as he often did, at the best houses in Paris he never ate anything. He said that his life depended on his diet, and people willingly put up with him, for his tales were the spice of the dinner.

I had come to know Madame d'Urfé thoroughly, while she, on her side, believed that I was a genuine adept under the mask of a man of no consequence; but she was confirmed in this chimerical opinion five or six weeks later when she asked me if I had decoded the manuscript which contained the procedure for the Great Work. I told her that I had and hence had read it and that I would return it to her, giving her my word of honor that I had not copied it.

"I found nothing new in it," I said.

"You will excuse me, Monsieur, but without the key I consider the thing impossible."

"Shall I name your key to you, Madame?"

"Please do so."

I thereupon give her the word, which belonged to no language, and I see that she is surprised. She said that it was too much, for she believed that she alone possessed the word, which she kept in her memory and had never written down.

I could have told her the truth, which was that the same calculation by which I had managed to decode the manuscript had taught me the word, but I took it into my head to tell her that a Genius had revealed it to me. It was this false confidence which put Madame d'Urfé in my power. On that day I became the arbiter of her soul, and I abused my ascendancy. Every time I recollect it I feel sorry and ashamed, and I am doing penance for it now through the obligation I have assumed to tell the truth in writing my memoirs.

Madame d'Urfé's great chimera was believing in the possibility of conversing with what are called "elemental spirits."[71] She would have given everything she possessed to acquire the art; and she had known impostors who had swindled her by making her believe they could set her on the right road. Confronted with me, who had given her such a clear proof of my knowledge, she thought she had reached her goal.

"I did not know," she said, "that your Genius had the power to force mine to reveal his secrets."

"He did not have to use force, for he knows everything by virtue of his own nature."

"Then does he know what secret I lock in my soul?"

"Certainly, and he must tell it to me if I question him."

"Can you question him whenever you please?"

"Whenever I have paper and ink; and I can even let you question him yourself by telling you his name. My Genius is named Paralis.[72] Write a question addressed to him, as if you were putting it to a mortal; ask him how I was able to decode your manuscript and you shall see how I will make him answer you."

Trembling with joy, Madame d'Urfé writes her question; I put it into figures, then into a pyramid as always, and I make her obtain the answer, which she herself puts into letters. She finds only consonants, but by a second operation I make her obtain the vowels, which she combines with the consonants, and she has a perfectly clear answer which surprises her. She sees before her eyes the word which was required to decode her manuscript. I left her, taking with me her soul, her heart, her mind, and all her remaining common sense.

603

CHAPTER VI

Madame d'Urfé's mistaken and contradictory
notions as to my power. My brother marries;
plan conceived on his wedding day. I go to
Holland on a financial mission for the gov-
ernment. I am given a lesson by the Jew Boas.
Monsieur d'Affry. Esther. Another Casanova.
I meet Teresa Imer again.

Prince Turenne having recovered from the smallpox, the Count of
La Tour d'Auvergne had left him, and, aware of his aunt's interest in
the abstruse sciences, he was not surprised to find that I had become
her only friend. I enjoyed his presence at our dinners, as I did that of
all her relatives, whose courteous manner toward me delighted me.
They were her brothers Monsieur de Pontcarré and Monsieur de
Viarmes,[1] who had just been elected Provost of the Merchants,[2] and
his son, whom I believe I have mentioned.[3] Madame du Châtelet
was her daughter; but since a suit made them irreconcilable enemies
she was never present.[4]

La Tour d'Auvergne having had to rejoin his Boulognese regiment
in Brittany at this time, we[5] dined together, with no other company,
nearly every day. Madame's servants considered me her husband; they
said that I must be, thinking it the explanation for the long hours we
spent together. Believing that I was rich, Madame d'Urfé supposed
that I had taken a post in the Military School lottery only as a mask.

According to her, I not only possessed the stone but could
converse with all the elemental spirits. Hence she believed that I
had the power to turn the world upside down and determine the
fortunes of France for good or evil, and she attributed my need to
remain unknown only to my justified fear of being arrested and
imprisoned, for that, she insisted, would necessarily follow as soon as
the Ministry managed to learn who I was. These wild ideas came
from the revelations which her Genius made to her at night and
which her heated imagination made her believe were real. Setting
them forth to me in perfect good faith one day, she said her Genius
had convinced her that, since she was a woman, I could not give her
the power to converse with the Geniuses, but that, by an operation
which I must certainly know, I could make her soul pass into the

body of a male child born from a philosophical union between an immortal and a woman or between a man and a female being of divine nature.

In lending my support to the lady's crazy notions I did not feel that I was deceiving her; for that was already done, and I could not possibly disabuse her. If in strict honesty I had told her that all her notions were ridiculous, she would not have believed me; so I took the course of drifting with the tide. I could not but enjoy letting myself be considered the greatest of all Rosicrucians and the most powerful of all men by a lady who was allied to the greatest houses in France and who, in addition, was even richer from her investments than from a yearly income of eighty thousand livres which she received from an estate[6] and from the houses she owned in Paris. I clearly saw that, if the need arose, she could refuse me nothing, and though I had laid no plan to gain possession of her wealth either in whole or in part, I did not have the strength of mind to renounce my power over her.

Madame d'Urfé was a miser. She spent barely thirty thousand livres[7] a year, and she invested her savings on the Exchange and doubled them. A broker bought her royal securities when they were at their lowest price and sold them for her when they went up. In this way she had greatly augmented her portfolio. She told me several times that she was ready to give all that she had to become a man and that she knew it depended on me.

I told her one day that it was true I could perform the operation, but that I could never bring myself to do it because I would have to take her life.

"I know that," she answered, "and I even know the kind of death to which I must submit, and I am ready."

"And what kind of death, Madame, are you pleased to believe it may be?"

"It is," she answered eagerly, "the same poison which killed Paracelsus."

"And do you believe that Paracelsus attained hypostasis?"[8]

"No. But I know the reason. He was neither man nor woman, and it is necessary to be completely one or the other."

"That is true; but do you know how the poison is made? And do you know that it cannot be made without the help of a salamander?"[9]

"That may be so, but I did not know it. I beg you to ask the cabala if there is anyone in Paris who possesses the poison."

I immediately thought that she believed she possessed it herself; and, not having hesitated to say so in my answer, I pretended to be astonished. It was she who was not astonished, and I saw her triumph.

"You see," she said, "that all I need is the child containing the male word[10] drawn from an immortal creature. I have been informed that it depends on you, and I do not believe you can lack the necessary courage because of a mistaken pity you may feel for my old carcass."

At these words I rose and I went to the window of her room, which gave onto the quay, and remained there for a quarter of an hour reflecting on her idiocies. When I returned to the table at which she was sitting she looked at me closely and said with deep feeling:

"Is it possible, my dear friend? I see you have been weeping."

I let her believe it, I sighed, I took my sword, and I left. Her carriage, which was at my disposal every day, was at the door, awaiting my orders.

My brother had been received into the Academy[11] by acclamation after exhibiting a painting he had made in which he depicted a battle and which gained the approbation of all the connoisseurs. The Academy itself wanted to own it and gave him the five hundred louis he asked for it. He had fallen in love with Corallina and would have married her if she had not been guilty of an infidelity which offended him so greatly that, to end any hope she might have of making it up, within less than a week he married a dancer[12] who appeared in the ballets at the Comédie Italienne. The wedding party was given by Monsieur de Saincy, bursar in charge of vacant ecclesiastical benefices,[13] who was very fond of the girl and who in gratitude for my brother's chivalry in marrying her got all his friends to order paintings from him, which paved the way to the considerable fortune he made and the great fame which he came to enjoy.

It was at my brother's wedding that Monsieur Kornmann, discoursing to me at length about the great scarcity of money, urged me to speak with the Comptroller-General concerning a way to remedy the situation. He said that by giving royal securities at a reasonable price to a company of brokers in Amsterdam it would be possible in exchange to acquire some other power's notes, which, not being discredited as France's were, could easily be realized. I asked him not to mention it to anybody, promising him that I would act.

No later than the next day I mentioned it to my patron the Abbé, who, considering it an excellent speculation, advised me to go to Holland[14] myself with a letter of recommendation from the Duke of Choiseul[15] to Monsieur d'Affry,[16] who could be sent several millions in royal paper to discount as I saw best. He told me to go at once and discuss the matter with Monsieur de Boulogne, and above all not to appear to be feeling my way. He assured me that, as soon as it became clear that I was not asking for any money in advance, I would be given all the letters of recommendation I wanted.

I was instantly enthusiastic. That same day I saw the Comptroller-General, who, considering my idea excellent, told me that the Duke of Choiseul would be at the Invalides[17] the next day and that I should lose no time before going to him to discuss the matter and give him the note he would write to him. He promised me he would have the Ambassador supplied with twenty millions in securities, which in any case could always return to France. I said somberly that I hoped not, if no more than a reasonable price was asked. He replied that peace was about to be made,[18] and in consequence I must dispose of them only at a very small loss and in that respect I should depend on the Ambassador, who would have all the necessary instructions.

I felt so flattered by a mission of this nature that I did not sleep all that night. The Duke of Choiseul, who was famous for moving rapidly, had no sooner read Monsieur de Boulogne's note and listened to me for five minutes than he had a clerk write a letter to Monsieur d'Affry in my behalf, which he read over and signed without reading it to me; after having it given to me sealed, he wished me a good journey. On the same day I obtained a passport from Monsieur de Berkenrode,[19] took leave of Manon Balletti and all my friends except Madame d'Urfé, with whom I was to spend the whole of the next day, and authorized my faithful clerk to sign the tickets at my office.

A month earlier a very pretty and decent girl, a native of Brussels, had been married under my auspices to an Italian named Gaetano, a dealer in secondhand goods. I had been her sponsor. The brute ill-treating her in his jealous rages, and the unhappy beauty constantly coming to me with her complaints, I had several times made peace between them. They came expecting me to give them dinner on the very day I was packing to leave for Holland. My brother and Tiretta were with me, and as I was still living in a furnished room I took them all to dinner with me at Landelle's,[20] where the food was excellent. Tiretta was in his carriage; he was ruining the ex-Jansenist,[21] who was still in love with him.

At dinner Tiretta, who was handsome and loved to clown and who had never seen the beautiful Fleming, began flirting with her outrageously. She was delighted, and we would have laughed and all would have gone well if her husband had been reasonable and polite; but, jealous as a tiger, the wretch was sweating blood. He did not eat, he kept turning white, he looked daggers at his wife, and he refused to take it as a joke. Tiretta made fun of him. Foreseeing unpleasant scenes, I tried to moderate his excessive high spirits, but in vain. An oyster dropped onto Madame Gaetano's beautiful bosom, and Tiretta, who was sitting beside her, quickly put his lips to it and sucked it in. Gaetano rose in a fury and slapped his wife so vindictively that his hand bounced back from her face to her neighbor's. Roused to rage, Tiretta seized him by the waist and stretched him out on the floor, and since, being unarmed, he took his vengeance only with his fists, we let him continue; but the waiter came up, whereupon the jealous husband left. His wife, her face disfigured by tears and blood—for she was bleeding from the nose, as was Tiretta—asked me to take her somewhere, for she thought her life would be in danger if she went home. I quickly got her into a hackney coach, leaving Tiretta with my brother. She asked me to take her to an old attorney, a relative of hers, who lived on the fourth floor of a six-story house on the Quai de Gesvres.[22] After hearing the whole unhappy story he said to me that, being poor, he could do nothing for the unfortunate girl, but that he would do everything if he had only a hundred écus. I gave them to him, and he assured me that he would set about ruining her husband, who would never be able to find out where she was. She told me she was sure he would do all that he had promised, and after expressing all her gratitude she let me go. On my return from Holland my reader will learn what became of her.

After I assured Madame d'Urfé that I was going to Holland for the good of France and that I would be back at the beginning of February, she asked me to sell some shares in the East India Company of Gothenburg[23] for her. She had sixty thousand francs' worth of them, and she could not sell them on the Paris Exchange because there was no money there; in addition she could not obtain the interest on them, which amounted to a considerable sum since it had been three years since any dividends had been declared. When I consented to do her the service she had to make me the owner of the shares through a bill of sale, which she did in due form on the same day, the transaction being certified by Tourton & Baur,[24] Place des Victoires. Back at her house I offered to give her an undertaking in writing to pay her the value of her shares on my return, but she refused. I left her, gratified to see not the slightest sign of suspicion on her face.

After obtaining a bill of exchange for three thousand florins[25] on the Jew Boas,[26] the court banker at The Hague, from Monsieur Kornmann, I set out; in two days I reached Antwerp, where I took a *jacht*,[27] which the next day brought me to Rotterdam, where I slept. On the day after I went to The Hague, where I put up at Jacquet's inn, the "English Parliament."[28] On the same day, which was Christmas Eve, I called on Monsieur d'Affry just when he was reading the letter from the Duke of Choiseul informing him about me and the business in hand. He made me stay for dinner with Monsieur Kauderbach,[29] Resident for the King of Poland and Elector of Saxony, and he encouraged me to do my best, saying, however, that he doubted if I would succeed because the Dutch had good reason to believe that peace would not be made very soon.

On leaving the Embassy I took a carriage to the house of the banker Boas, whom I found at table with all his ugly and numerous family. After looking at my bill of exchange he said that only that day he had received a letter from Kornmann praising me. He asked me why, since it was Christmas Eve, I was not going to rock the Infant Jesus to sleep; I answered that I had come to celebrate the Feast of the Maccabees[30] with him. He and his whole family applauded my answer, and he begged me to accept a room in his house. Accepting his offer, I at once sent word to my valet to come to the house with my luggage, and when I took leave of Boas after supper I asked him to find me some good piece of business by which I could make eighteen or twenty thousand florins during the short time I intended to stay in Holland. He answered seriously that he would think it over.

The next morning after I had breakfasted with him and his family he said that he had found what I wanted and took me to his study, where, giving me three thousand florins in gold and notes, he said that there was nothing to stop me from making twenty thousand florins in a week, as I had told him I wanted to do the evening before. Greatly surprised, for I had only been joking, at how easy it was to make money in that country, I thank him for his kind interest and I hear him out.

"Here," he says, "is a note which I received day before yesterday from the Mint. It informs me that four hundred thousand ducats[31] have just been struck and that the Mint is prepared to sell them at the current price of gold, which, fortunately, is not very high at the moment. Each ducat is worth five florins, two and three-fifths stuivers.[32] Here is the rate of exchange at Frankfort on the Main. Buy the four hundred thousand ducats, take or send them to Frankfort, obtaining bills of exchange on the Bank of Amsterdam,[33] and there you have just what you asked for. You make one and one-ninth stuiver per ducat, which yields you twenty-two thousand two hundred and twenty-two of our florins. Obtain possession of the gold today, and in a week your profit will be liquid. There you are."

"But," I answered, "will the directors of the Mint not demur at entrusting me with such a sum, which comes to over four million livres tournois?"[34]

"Certainly they will, if you do not buy the ducats for cash or give an equal amount in good paper."

"My dear Monsieur Boas, I have neither that much money nor that much credit."

"Then you will never make twenty thousand florins in a week. Judging from the proposal you made me yesterday evening, I thought you were a millionaire. I will have one of my sons make the transaction today or tomorrow."

After giving me this sound lesson Boas went to his office and I went to dress. Monsieur d'Affry went to the "English Parliament" to return my visit and, not finding me there, wrote me a note asking me to call on him to hear what he had to tell me. I went there, I dined with him, and I learned directly from the letter he had just received from Monsieur de Boulogne that he was not to let me dispose of the twenty millions he was to receive except at a loss of eight percent, for peace was on the verge of being made. He laughed at the idea and I did likewise. He advised me not to discuss my business with Jews, the most honest of whom was only the least dishonest, and he offered me a letter of recommendation in his own hand to Pels,[35] of Amsterdam, which I gratefully accepted; and to assist me in the matter of my Gothenburg shares he introduced me to the Swedish Ambassador.[36] He, in turn, sent me to Monsieur D. O.[37] I left on the day after St. John's Day[38] because of the convocation of the most zealous Masons in Holland. The person who invited me to attend it was Count de Tott,[39] brother of the Baron who failed to make his fortune in Constantinople. Monsieur d'Affry presented me to Her Highness the Regent, mother[40] of the Stathouder,[41] whom I thought too serious for his age, which was then only twelve. She kept dozing off. She died not long afterward, and her brain was found to be swimming in water. There I also saw Count Philipp of Sinzendorf,[42] who was looking for five millions for the Empress and who easily obtained them at five percent interest. At the theater I met a Minister of the Porte[43] who had been a friend of Monsieur de Bonneval's,[44] and I thought I should see him die from laughing before my eyes. Here is the rather comical incident:

The play being given was the tragedy *Iphigenia*.[45] The statue of Diana was in the center of the stage. At the end of one act Iphigenia entered followed by all her priestesses, who as they passed the statue all bowed low to the goddess. The candle-snuffer, a good Dutch Christian, comes out and makes the same bow to the statue. The parterre and the boxes burst out laughing, and so do I, but not hard enough to die of it. When, as in duty bound, I explained the joke to the Turk he fell into such a fit of laughter that he had to be carried to his inn, the "Prince of Orange."[46] Not to laugh at the thing at all would have proved one stupid, I admit; but one had to have a Turkish sense of humor to laugh at it so hard. Yet it was a great Greek philosopher[47] who died laughing when he saw a toothless old woman eating figs. Those who laugh much are better off than those who laugh little, for gaiety unloads the spleen and generates good blood.

Two hours before reaching Amsterdam in my two-wheeled post chaise with my servant sitting behind, I meet a four-wheeled carriage, drawn by two horses like mine and also carrying a master and servant. The driver of the four-wheeled carriage wanted my driver to make way for him, mine protested that if he did he would upset me in the ditch, but the other insisted. I address the master, a handsome young man, and ask him to order his driver to make way for me.

"I am posting, Monsieur," I say, "and furthermore I am a foreigner."

"Monsieur, here in Holland the post has no special rights,[48] and if you are a foreigner you must admit that you have no greater claim than mine, since I am in my own country."

At that I get out in snow halfway up my boots, and holding my drawn sword I tell the Dutchman to get out or to make way for me. He replied, with a smile, that he had no sword and that in any case he would not fight for such a silly reason. He told me to get back in my chaise, and he made way for me. I arrived at Amsterdam about nightfall and put up at the "Star of the East."[49]

The next day I went to the Exchange and found Monsieur Pels, who said that he would give thought to my chief business, and a quarter of an hour later I found Monsieur D. O., who at once arranged for me to speak with a broker from Gothenburg, who wanted to discount my sixteen shares on the spot, giving me twelve percent interest. Monsieur Pels told me to wait and assured me that he would get me fifteen percent. He gave me dinner, and seeing me delighted with the excellence of his red Cape wine,[50] he laughed and said that he made it himself by mixing Burgundy with Malaga. The next day I dined at the house of Monsieur D. O., who was a widower of forty and whose only daughter, Esther,[51] was fourteen. She was a beauty except that her teeth were not good. She was the heir to all the wealth of her amiable father, who adored her. With her white complexion, her black hair, which she wore unpowdered, and her eloquent, very large black eyes, she made a great impression on me. She spoke French very well; she played the harpsichord with great delicacy, and was passionately fond of reading. After dinner Monsieur D. O. showed me his house, which was not occupied, for after his wife's death he had chosen an apartment on the ground floor in which he was very comfortable. The apartment he showed me was a suite of six or seven rooms which contained a treasure in antique porcelain; the walls and the casements were entirely covered with marble plaques, each room in a different color and with floors of the same under magnificent Turkish carpets made to order for the particular rooms. The large dining room was entirely covered with alabaster, and the tables and buffets were of cedarwood. The house was entirely covered with marble plaques on the outside too. One Saturday I saw four or five housemaids washing those splendid walls; what made me laugh was that the maids all had very wide panniers, which obliged them to wear breeches, otherwise they would have afforded too interesting a sight to passers-by. After seeing the house we went downstairs, and Monsieur D. O. left me alone with his daughter in the anteroom in which he worked with his clerks; but that day there was no one there. It was New Year's Day.

After playing a sonata for harpsichord, Mademoiselle O. asked me if I was going to the concert. I replied that nothing could persuade me to go to it since I was with her.

"Are you thinking of going to it, Mademoiselle?"

"I should like nothing better than to go to the concert, but I cannot go all by myself."

"I should be very happy to escort you, but I dare not hope as much."

"You would be doing me a great favor, and I am certain that if you make the offer to my father he will not refuse you."

"Are you certain?"

"Perfectly certain; since he knows you, he would be guilty of rudeness; I am amazed that you could fear it; my father is most polite; I see that you do not know Dutch customs. In this country unmarried girls enjoy a decent freedom; they lose it only when they marry; go to him, go to him."

I go in to Monsieur D. O., who was writing, and ask him if he will do me the honor of letting me escort his daughter to the concert.

"Have you a carriage?"

"Yes, Monsieur."

"Then I need not order mine. Esther?"

"Yes, Father."

"You may get dressed. Monsieur Casanova is kind enough to take you to the concert."

"Thank you, dear Papa."

After kissing him she goes to dress, and an hour later she appears with joy on her countenance. I could only have wished she had used a little powder; but Esther was proud of the color of her hair, which made her complexion look even whiter. A transparent black fichu covered her bosom, which it revealed as just beginning to develop and too firm.

We go downstairs, I offer her my hand to help her into the carriage, and I wait, supposing that a maid or a governess will attend her; but seeing no one I get in, very much surprised. Her lackey, after closing the door, gets up behind. I thought it impossible. Such a girl alone with me! I was struck dumb. I asked myself if I should remember that I was a great libertine or if I should forget it. Esther, all animation, said we were to hear an Italian singer with the voice of a nightingale, and seeing me speechless she asked me why. I beat about the bush, but finally said that I thought her a treasure of which I did not deserve to be the guardian.

"I know," she said, "that in the rest of Europe girls are not allowed to go out alone with men, but here we are taught to behave ourselves, and we are certain that if we do not we will contrive our own unhappiness."

"Happy the man who will be your husband, and happier still if you have already chosen him!"

"Oh, it is not for me to choose him, that lies with my father."

"And if the man he chooses is not the man you love?"

"We are not allowed to love a man before we know he is to be our husband."

"Then you love no one."

"No one, and what is more I have not yet felt tempted to."

"Then may I kiss your hand?"

"Why my hand?"

She drew it away, she gave me her lips, and modestly returned my kiss with one which went to my heart, but I stopped at that when she told me she would do the same in her father's presence whenever I wished.

We arrived at the concert, where Esther found a quantity of young ladies who were friends of hers, all daughters of wealthy businessmen, some of them pretty, some ugly, and all eagerly asking her who I was. All she could tell them was my name, but she became animated when she saw a beautiful blonde nearby; she asked me if I thought her attractive; I answered, of course, that I was not attracted by blondes.

"Even so, I shall introduce her to you, for she may be a relative of yours; her name is the same, and here is her father. Monsieur Casanova," she said to him, "I beg to introduce Monsieur Casanova, a friend of my father's."

"Is it possible? I hope," he said, "I may be your friend too, but perhaps we are relatives. I am of the Naples family."

"Then we are relatives, though very distant ones, for my father was from Parma. Have you your genealogy?"

"I must have it somewhere; but to tell the truth I set little store by it, for in this country no one considers such trifles."

"Nevertheless, we can amuse ourselves with it for a quarter of an hour, and then laugh at it and keep it to ourselves. Tomorrow I shall have the honor of calling on you, and I will bring you a tree of my ancestors. Would it displease you to find the founder of your line among them?"

"I should be delighted, Monsieur, and I shall have the honor of calling on you myself at your lodging tomorrow. May I ask if you have a business establishment at home?"

"No, I am in finance and at present in the service of the French ministry. I am on a mission to Monsieur Pels."

Monsieur Casanova then beckoned to his daughter, who came at once and whom he introduced to me. She was Esther's intimate friend; I sat down between the two of them, and the concert began. After a fine symphony, a concerto for violin, and another for oboe, the Italian singer who was so highly praised under the name of Trenti appeared, taking her place behind the musician at the harpsichord. Great was my surprise when in this so-called Madame Trenti I saw Teresa Imer,[52] wife of the dancer Pompeati, whom the reader may remember. I had known her eighteen years earlier, when old Senator Malipiero had given me a caning when he caught me in some childish naughtiness with her, and I had seen her again at Venice in 1753, where we had made love once or twice, not as children but as real lovers. She had left for Bayreuth, where she was mistress to the Margrave;[53] I had promised to visit her there; but C. C. and the nun M. M.[54] had not left me time for it. Then I was confined under the Leads, and I had heard no more of her. My surprise was great to see her now at a concert in Amsterdam. I said nothing, listening to an aria which she sang with the voice of an angel, preceded by a recitative which began: *Eccoti giunta al fin, donna infelice* ("You have come at last, unhappy woman").[55]

The applause would not end. Esther told me that no one knew who the woman was, that there were countless stories about her, that she was very badly off, and that she lived by traveling to every city in Holland and singing at public concerts, the only payment she received being what the audience put into a silver plate which she carried through all the rows at the end of the concert.

"Does she find her plate well filled?"

"Not at all, for everyone here has already paid for his ticket. So she does well if she takes in thirty or forty florins. Tomorrow she will be at the concert at Leiden and the next day at The Hague and the day after that at Rotterdam, then she comes back here; she has been leading this life for more than six months now, and people are always delighted to hear her."

"Has she no lover?"

"They say she has young men in every city, but that instead of their giving her money she spends it on them, for they haven't a sou. She never wears anything but black, not only because she is a widow[56] but because of some great blow she says she has suffered. You will see her going through our row in half an hour."

Keeping my hands in my muff, I counted out twelve ducats, wrapped them in paper, and waited with my heart beating in a way which made me smile, since I could see no good reason for it.

As she went through the row in front of mine I saw that she was very much surprised when she caught sight of me; but I at once looked away and began talking with Esther. When she stopped in front of me I put the little roll on her plate without looking at her, and she moved on. But I looked closely at a little girl of four or five years who was following her and who, when she reached the end of the row, came back and kissed my hand. I was extremely surprised when I saw that the child had precisely my features. I managed to hide it, but the little girl stood there staring at me.

"Would you like some bonbons, pretty child?" I said. "Take the box too."

So saying I gave her the full box, which was only tortoise shell, but I would have given it to her if it had been gold. At that she left, and Esther laughed and said the child was the image of me.

"A striking likeness," added Mademoiselle Casanova.

"Chance," I said, "often produces resemblances for no reason at all."

After the concert I left Mademoiselle Esther O. with her father, whom we had met there, and I went to the "Eastern Star," where I was lodging. I had ordered a dish of oysters and I was about to eat them before going to bed when I saw Teresa and the little girl appear in my room. I rose to give her the ecstatic embrace which the occasion demanded, whereupon she saw fit to sink into a chair in a faint, perhaps real, perhaps feigned. As it might be genuine, I was willing to play the expected part in the scene, and I revived her with cold water and making her smell eau de Luz.[57] Restored to her senses, she began staring at me without a word. I asked her if she wanted supper, and she answered yes. I quickly ordered three places set, and we were served the usual sort of supper except that it kept us at table until seven o'clock in the morning doing nothing but tell each other our good and bad fortunes. She was acquainted with most of my recent vicissitudes, and I knew nothing of hers. So it was she who talked for five or six hours on end. Sophie[58] (for such was the name of her daughter) slept soundly on my bed until daylight. Teresa kept the most important of her disclosures, and the one which was of greatest concern to me, for the end. She said that Sophie was my daughter, and she took from her pocket the baptismal certificate which showed the date of her birth. We had been lovers in Venice at the beginning of the Fair of the Ascension in 1753, and Sophie was born at Bayreuth the end of that year; she had now just turned six. I said that I was convinced of it, and that since I was in a position to provide her with the best education I was ready to take care of her; but she replied that she was her jewel and that I would tear her soul from her body if I took her away; instead, she offered me her son, who was twelve years old and whom she did not have the means to bring up properly.

"Where is he?"

"He is boarding at Rotterdam, or I had better say in pawn there, for the man with whom he is staying will never give him to me unless I pay him all I owe him."

"How much do you owe?"

"Eighty florins. You have given me sixty-two, give me four more ducats, and my son is yours and I shall be the happiest of mothers. I will bring him to you at The Hague next week, since you say you have to go back there."

"Yes, my dear Teresa. Instead of four ducats, here are twenty. We will meet again at The Hague."

The transports of her gratitude and the joy which flooded her soul were excessive; but they did not have the power to reawaken my old fondness, or, rather, the old hankering I had had for her, for I had never loved her passionately. She embraced me for more than a quarter of an hour, with increasing demonstrations of the most ardent desire, but in vain; I returned her caresses without ever giving her the proof she sought that they came from the same source as that to which Sophie owed her birth. Teresa melted into tears, then she sighed, took her daughter, and left, after reminding me that we were to meet again at The Hague and that she would leave at noon.

Teresa was two years older than I, she was pretty, blonde, full of intelligence and talent; but her charms were no longer the same, for I should have felt their power. The story of all that had happened to her during the six years after she left Venice for Bayreuth would be worthy of my reader's attention, and I should be glad to write it if I remembered all its details. Convicted of infidelity by the amorous Margrave because of a Monsieur de Montperny,[59] she had been turned out; she had separated from her husband Pompeati and had gone to Brussels with a lover, where for a few days she had taken the fancy of Prince Charles of Lorraine,[60] who gave her a special patent granting her the direction of all theatrical performances throughout the Austrian Netherlands. With this patent she had embarked on the most extensive enterprises which had led her to spend enormous sums, so that in less than three years, after selling all her diamonds, her laces, her wardrobe, and everything she owned, she had been obliged to go to Holland to avoid being sent to prison. Her husband had killed himself in Vienna[61] during a fit of madness brought on by intestinal pains; he had opened his abdomen with a razor and had died tearing out his entrails.

The business I had in hand did not allow me to go to bed. Monsieur Casanova came to drink coffee with me and invited me to dinner, arranging to meet me at the Amsterdam Exchange,[62] which is an amazing institution to any thinking foreigner. Millionaires who look like yokels are very numerous there. A man who has only a hundred thousand florins is so poor that he does not dare do business under his own name. Monsieur D. O. invited me to dine next day at a small house he had on the Amstel; and Monsieur Casanova treated me very well. After reading my genealogy, which had stood me in such good stead at Naples, he went for his, which he found to be exactly the same, but, completely unimpressed by the fact, he only laughed—quite unlike Don Antonio in Naples, who took it with the utmost seriousness and gave me such excellent proof that he did so. However, he offered me his services and his advice in anything to do with business if I needed them. I thought his daughter pretty, but I was not struck either by her charms or her intelligence; my mind was occupied with Esther, whom I mentioned several times at table, until finally I forced Mademoiselle Casanova to tell me she was not pretty. A girl who knows she is pretty triumphs when she can silence a man who speaks in favor of one of her contemporaries who has indubitable defects. Nevertheless, the girl was Esther's intimate friend.

After dinner Monsieur D. O. told me that if I would sell my shares at fifteen percent above par, he would take them himself and I would be under no expense for either a broker or a notary. I agreed, and after turning them over to him I asked him for payment in a bill of exchange on Tourton & Baur in livres tournois and to my order. After calculating the daler[63] of the Bank of Sweden at eight livres ten sous in accordance with the rate at Hamburg, he gave me a sight bill of exchange for seventy-two thousand francs, whereas at five percent[64] I expected to receive only sixty-nine thousand. It was six percent, which won me great esteem from Madame d'Urfé, who perhaps did not expect such honesty from me. Toward evening I went with Monsieur Pels to Zaandam[65] in a boat set on a sledge with sails. I found the journey extraordinary and most entertaining. We got there surprisingly fast with a wind which took us along at fifteen English miles an hour. It is impossible to imagine a conveyance more comfortable or steadier or freer from danger. There is no one who would not be glad to take a trip around the world in such a carriage over a frozen sea, but with a stern wind, for that is the only possible course, the rudder having no effect. What greatly pleased me was the perfect timing with which two sailors lowered two sails when, having come close to the island, they had to stop the ship. This is the only moment when one may feel afraid, for the ship continued on its way for over a hundred paces even after the sails were lowered, and if there had been a delay of only a second the violence of its collision with the shore would have smashed it to pieces. We ate perch and could not take a walk because of the high wind; but I went there once again, and I say nothing about it because everyone knows the wonders of Zaandam, the hotbed of all the rich merchants who, in time, become millionaires at Amsterdam. We went back to Monsieur Pels's house in a two-horse sleigh which belonged to him. He kept me for supper, and I did not leave him until midnight. He said, with the honesty which was displayed on his countenance, that since I had become his friend and Monsieur D. O.'s I would not need the services of the Jews in my principal business but should apply directly to them.

The next morning, with the snow falling in great flakes, I went early to Monsieur D. O.'s, where I found his daughter in a very good humor. In her father's presence she began by rallying me on having spent the night at my inn with Madame Trenti.

Monsieur D. O., after saying that I need not defend myself because anyone was entitled to love talent, asked me to tell him who the woman was. I said she was a Venetian whose husband had recently killed himself, and that it was almost six years since we had last seen each other.

"The sight of your daughter," said Esther, "must have surprised you."

I replied that the child could not be mine, since her mother's husband was still alive at the time; but she continued to discuss the resemblance and to joke about my having fallen asleep the evening before when I supped at Monsieur Pels's.

"I envy anyone," she said slyly, "who has the secret of getting a good sleep, for of late I never fall asleep until I have courted it for a long time yet dreaded it, for when I wake, instead of finding my mind freer, I find it stupefied and weighed down by the indifference which comes from fatigue."

"Try, Mademoiselle, spending the night listening to the long story of some man in whom you are interested, but from his own lips. You will fall happily asleep the night after."

"Such a person does not exist. I think I need books, and the help of someone who knows them to find me interesting ones. I like history and travels, but I have to be sure that what I read is not invented. If anything makes me suspect it, I stop reading at once."

I promised to bring her some books the next day before I left for The Hague; she accepted my offer, congratulating me on the prospect I had of seeing Madame Trenti again at The Hague.

Esther's frankness set me on fire, and Monsieur D. O. laughed heartily at the way his daughter was calling me to account. At eleven o'clock we got into a sleigh and went to the small house, to which she had told me that Mademoiselle Casanova would also come with her fiancé. I saw her look pleased when I assured her that nothing could interest me more than herself.

We saw the two of them coming to meet us covered with snow. We get out; we enter a room to take off our furs; and I notice that the fiancé, after looking at me for a moment, whispers to his intended. She laughs, she goes and says something to Esther, who goes and tells her father, who laughs even more. They were looking at me, I was sure that it was about me they were talking; I pretended indifference, but that was no reason for me not to join them. Indeed, good manners demanded it.

"There may be some mistake," said Monsieur D. O.; "we really must look into it. Did anything out of the ordinary," he said, addressing me, "happen to you on your journey from The Hague to Amsterdam?"

At this question I looked at the fiancé, and I at once guessed what it was all about.

"Nothing out of the ordinary," I replied, "except meeting a fine fellow who wanted to see my carriage overturned, and I believe I see him here."

The laughter redoubled, and we embraced; but after he told the whole story in all its details Mademoiselle Casanova told him sharply that he should have fought. Esther disagreed, saying that he had shown more courage by listening to reason, and Monsieur D. O. declared that he was strongly of her opinion; but the refractory girl, after airing some romantic notions, became deliberately sulky with her lover. I chided her for it, which pleased Esther.

"Come, come," said the charming Esther gaily, "let us put on skates and lose no time amusing ourselves on the Amstel, for I fear the ice will melt."

I did not want to ask her to excuse me. Monsieur D. O. leaves us. Mademoiselle Casanova's fiancé puts skates on me, and the young ladies are ready, wearing short skirts and armed with black velvet drawers to guard against mishaps. We go down to the Amstel, and, since I was a complete novice at the sport, the reader can imagine that, having fallen abruptly on the hard ice at least twenty times, I thought I would end by breaking my back; but not a bit of it, I felt ashamed to leave off, and I stopped only when we were called in to dinner. When we got up from table I felt as if I were paralyzed in every limb. Esther gave me a jar of ointment and assured me that if I had myself rubbed when I went to bed I would feel perfectly well in the morning. She was right. Everyone laughed; I let them laugh; I realized that the whole skating party had been got up only to make me a laughingstock, and I saw nothing wrong in that. I wanted to bring Esther to love me, and I was sure that so much submission and obligingness on my part could not but set me on the road. I spent the afternoon with Monsieur D. O., letting the young people go back to the Amstel again, where they enjoyed themselves hugely until twilight.

We talked of my twenty millions, and I learned from him that I should never succeed in discounting them except with a mercantile company which would give me other papers in exchange, and that even by such a transaction I must be prepared to lose heavily. When I told him that I would like to make the transaction with the East India Company of Gothenburg he said that he would speak to a broker and that Monsieur Pels could be very useful to me.

When I woke in the morning I thought I was done for. My last vertebra, which is called the *os sacrum*, seemed to be in a thousand pieces. Yet I had had myself rubbed with almost all the ointment Esther had given me. I did not forget her wishes. I had myself driven to a bookseller's, where I bought all the books I thought might entertain her. I sent them to her, asking her to send me back all the ones she had read. She did so promptly, and, thanking me profusely, asked me to come and kiss her before leaving Amsterdam if I wanted to receive a nice present.

I went there very early, leaving my post chaise at her door. Her governess took me to her bed, where I found her in a merry mood, with a complexion of lilies and roses.

"I am certain," she said, "that you would not have come if I had not used the word 'kiss.' "

So saying, she surrendered all the charms of her face to my eager lips. Glimpsing the pink buds of her young breasts, I was about to lay hold of them, but as soon as she saw it she stopped laughing and defended herself. She said that I was well advised to go and amuse myself at The Hague with Madame Trenti, in whose care I had left a most precious pledge of my affection. I assured her that I was going to The Hague only to talk business with the Ambassador, and that she would see me again five or six days later, in love only with her. She answered that she relied on my word, and when I left her she granted me such a sweet kiss that I felt certain she would grant me everything on my return. I left very much in love and reached Boas's house at suppertime.

CHAPTER VII

*My luck in Holland. I return to Paris with
young Pompeati.*

Among the letters I received at the post I found one from the
Comptroller-General which told me that twenty millions in royal
securities were in the hands of Monsieur d'Affry, who would not
deliver them at more than an eight percent loss; and another from
my patron the Abbé de Bernis which advised me to make the most
advantageous deal I could with them and to be sure that when the
Ambassador communicated it to the Minister he would be ordered
to consent to the transaction, provided that not less was offered than
could be obtained on the Exchange at Paris.

Boas, astonished by the profitable sale I had made of my sixteen
Gothenburg shares, told me he would undertake to get the twenty
millions discounted for me in shares of the Swedish East India
Company if I would persuade the Ambassador to sign an agreement
in which I would undertake to deliver the French royal securities at
a ten percent loss, taking the Swedish shares at fifteen percent above
par, as I had sold my own sixteen. I would have consented if he had
not stipulated that I give him three months and that my contract
could be changed if peace was made. I saw at once that I would do
well to go back to Amsterdam, and I would have gone if I had not
given La Trenti my word that I would wait for her in The Hague.
She arrived from Rotterdam the next day and wrote me that she
expected me for supper. I received her letter at the theater. The
servant who brought it said that he would take me to her lodging as
soon as the play was over. After sending my lackey back to Boas's
house, I went.

I found this most unusual woman on the fifth floor of a dilapidated house with her daughter and her son. In the middle of the
room there was a table covered with a black cloth on which stood
two candles. Since The Hague was a court city I was richly dressed.
The woman, clad in black with her two children, made me think of
Medea.[1] Nothing could be prettier than the two young creatures. I
fondly embraced the boy, calling him my son. His mother told him
that from that moment on he was to consider me his father. He
recognized me as the man he had seen at Venice in May 1753, in

Signora Manzoni's house, and I was very much pleased. His stature was short, he seemed to have an excellent constitution, he was well built, and his delicate features bespoke intelligence. He was thirteen years old.

His sister stood there motionless, seemingly waiting for her turn to come. Having taken her on my lap, I could not have enough of covering her with kisses. For all her silence, she enjoyed seeing that she interested me more than her brother did. She had on only a very light petticoat. I kissed every part of her pretty body, delighted to be the man to whom the little creature owed her existence.

"Isn't this the same gentleman, dear Mother, whom we saw at Amsterdam and who people thought was my father because I look like him? But that's not possible, because my father is dead."

"True," I said, "but I can be your fond friend. Do you want me?"

"Oh, my dear friend! Let's give each other a good hug!"

After the laughter which was to be expected, we sat down at table. The heroine gave me a choice supper and excellent wine. She had not, she said, treated the Margrave better at the suppers for two with which she entertained him. Wanting to know the character of her son, whom I had decided to take with me, I talked only with him. I discovered that he was false, secretive, always on his guard, always preparing his answers in advance, and hence never giving such answers as would have come from his heart if he had followed its bidding. All this, however, was accompanied by a show of politeness and reserve which he thought was bound to please me. I told him quietly that his calculated manner might be all very well at the proper time and place, but that there were moments when a man could not be happy unless he was unconstrained and that it was only then that he would be seen to have a lovable nature, if indeed it was such. At that his mother, thinking to praise him, said that his principal quality was discretion; that she had taught him to be discreet always and in everything, and hence she was not hurt by his habit of being as reserved with her as he was with everyone else. I told her to her face that it was abominable, and that I could not imagine how a father could have any fondness—let alone a predilection—for a son who never spoke out.

"Tell me," I said to the boy, "if you feel able to promise me that you will have complete confidence in me and will under no circumstances keep any secrets from me or leave anything unspoken between us."

"I promise you," he answered, "that I will die sooner than tell you a lie."

"That is his character," his mother interrupted; "such is the horror of lying that I have inculcated in him."

"That is all very well," I answered, "but you could teach your son a different road to happiness. Instead of showing him the ugliness of falsehood, you could show him the beauty of truth. It is the only way to make oneself lovable, and in this world to be happy one must be loved."

"But," he answered, with a sly smile which I did not like and which enchanted his mother, "aren't not lying and telling the truth the same thing?"

"Certainly not, for you would only have to tell me nothing at all. The thing is to disclose your soul, to tell me everything that goes on within you and around you, and to reveal to me even what might make you blush. I will help you to blush, my dear son, and before very long you will find yourself in no danger of it; but when we know each other better we shall soon see if we suit each other, for I could never consider you my son without loving you tenderly, and I will never permit you to call me father unless I see that you love me as you might love your closest friend; as for knowing you, I will undertake to do that, for you will never be able to hide the least of your thoughts from me; but if I find it out despite you, I shall love you no longer and you will be the loser. You shall come to Paris with me as soon as I finish my business in Amsterdam, where I am going tomorrow. When I return I hope I shall find that your mother has taught you the rudiments of a new system of conduct."

I was amazed to see my daughter, who, having listened to everything I had said to her brother without batting an eye, was making vain efforts to hold back her tears.

"Why are you crying?" said her mother; *"it's stupid."*

At that the child burst out laughing, threw herself on her neck, and kissed her. I saw beyond doubt that her laughter had been as false as her feeling tears had been natural.

"Do you want to come to Paris with me too?" I asked her.

"Yes, my dear friend, but with Mamma, for without me she would die."

"What if I ordered you to go?" said her mother.

"I would obey, but away from you how could I live?"

Thereupon my dear daughter pretended to cry. That she was pretending was obvious. Even Teresa must have known it, and I

625

took her aside and told her that if she had brought up her children to be actors she had succeeded, but that in polite society they were monsters in embryo. I stopped reproaching her when I saw her crying, but real tears. She asked me to stay at The Hague a day longer; I told her I could not, and I left the room to go somewhere; but I was very much surprised on my return to hear Sophie say to me that if she was to believe I was her friend she must have a proof of it.

"What proof, my little darling?"

"Coming to supper with me tomorrow."

"I cannot, for since I have just refused the same thing to your mother she would be offended if I granted it to you."

"Oh no—for it was she who just told me to ask you."

We laughed; but when her mother called her a little fool and her brother added that he would not have committed such an indiscretion, I clearly saw the distress of her soul in the little girl's face. I hastened to reassure her, not caring if I displeased her mother by giving her a taste of new moral principles, to which she listened with wonder. I ended by promising her I would come to supper with her the next day, but on condition that she would give me only one bottle of Burgundy and three dishes.

"For you are not rich," I said.

"I know it, my dear friend, but Mamma said that you would pay for everything."

At this answer I had to hold my sides, and her mother, despite her annoyance, had to do the same. The poor woman, artful though she was, took Sophie's ingenuousness for stupidity. It was intelligence, it was a diamond of the first water which only needed someone to polish it. She said that the wine cost her nothing, that a certain V. D. R.,[2] a young man who was the son of a burgomaster of Rotterdam, provided her with it, and that he would sup with us the next evening if I had no objection. I answered, with a laugh, that I would even be glad to see him. I left after devouring my daughter with kisses. I wished that her mother would give her to me, but it was no use my asking, for I saw that she regarded her as a resource for her old age. This is the usual attitude among adventuresses, and Teresa was nothing else. I gave the mother twenty ducats to spend on dressing my adopted son and Sophie, who, in an outburst of gratitude, flung herself on my neck. Joseph wanted to kiss my hand, but I warned him that in future he was not to show his gratitude to me only by kisses. When I started to go downstairs she showed me a little room in which her children slept. I saw her meaning, but I was far from having any of my old hankering for her. Esther completely occupied me.

The next day at Teresa's I found young V. D. R. A handsome youth of twenty-two, simply dressed, neither cold nor warm, neither polite nor impolite, with no social grace. He had every right to be Teresa's lover, but none to treat me cavalierly. When she saw that he wanted to play the "man in possession" and that he offended me she took a high tone with him. After criticizing the poorness of the dishes and praising the excellence of the wines he sent her, he departed, leaving us at dessert. I, in turn, left her at eleven o'clock, assuring her that I would see her again before I set out. A Princess Galitzin,[3] née Kantemir, had invited me to dinner.

The next day I received a letter from Madame d'Urfé, who sent me twelve thousand francs in the form of a bill of exchange on Boas, saying very generously that since her shares had cost her only sixty thousand francs she did not want to profit from them. This present of five hundred louis[4] pleased me. All the rest of her letter was filled with fantasies. She said that her Genius had told her that I would come back to Paris with a boy born from philosophical intercourse and that she hoped I would take pity on her. Strange coincidence! I laughed in anticipation of the effect which the appearance of Teresa's son would have on her soul. Boas thanked me for my willingness to let him pay me my bill of exchange in ducats. Gold in Holland is a commodity. Payments are made in paper or in silver. At the moment no one wanted ducats because the agio[5] had gone up to five stuivers.

After dining with Princess Galitzin I went for my redingote and then went to the coffeehouse to read the gazettes. I saw V. D. R., who, about to begin a game of billiards, whispered to me that I might well bet on him.

This friendly advance pleased me. I thought he was sure of his skill, and I began betting; but after he lost the third game I bet against him without his knowledge. Three hours later he stopped, having lost thirty or forty games, and, thinking that I had always bet on his side, he expressed his regret. I saw that he was surprised when, showing him thirty or forty ducats, I said that, being a little doubtful of his confidence in his own skill, I had won them by betting against him. All the players laughed; he could not stand a joke; he took great offense at my jibes; he left in a rage; and a moment later I went to Teresa's because I had promised her I would. I was to leave for

Amsterdam the next day. She was expecting V. D. R., but she stopped expecting him when I told her how and why he had left the billiard room in a rage. After spending an hour with Sophie in my arms, I left her, assuring her that we would meet again in three or four weeks. On my way back to Boas's alone, with my sword under my arm, I am suddenly attacked in the brightest moonlight by V. D. R. He says he is curious to see if my sword is as sharp as my tongue. I try vainly to calm him by talking reasonably, I do not unsheathe though he has his bare sword in his hand, I say that he should not take mere jests so hard, I beg his pardon, I offer to put off my departure and beg his pardon at the coffeehouse. Not a bit of it—he is determined to kill me, and to persuade me to draw my sword he gives me a blow with the flat of his. It is the only blow I have received in my entire life. I finally draw my sword, and, still hoping to make him listen to reason, I fence with him, giving ground. He takes it for fear, and he gives a lunge which makes my hair stand on end. He pierced my cravat on the left, his sword veering off—four lines farther in, and he would have cut my throat. In my terror I jumped to one side, and, determined to kill him, I wounded him in the chest and, being sure of it, I invited him to stop. Saying that he was not yet dead, he came after me like a madman; I touched him three or four times in succession. At my last thrust he jumped back, saying that he had had enough and only begged me to leave.

I was glad when, starting to wipe off my sword, I saw that the point of it was very little stained. Boas had not yet gone to bed. When he had heard the whole story he advised me to leave for Amsterdam at once, despite my assuring him that the wounds were not mortal. My chaise being at the harness-maker's, I set off in a carriage belonging to Boas, leaving my servant orders to start the next day and bring my baggage to Amsterdam, at the "Second Bible,"[6] where I put up. I arrived there at noon, and my servant at nightfall. He had no news to tell me; but what pleased me was that nothing was heard of the matter at Amsterdam until a week later. Though simple enough, the thing could have done me harm, for the reputation of being a brawler is no way to please financiers with whom one is about to conclude profitable business.

As far as appearances went my first visit was to Monsieur D. O., but in reality it was Esther who received the homage of it. The way I had parted from her had set me on fire. Her father was not there; I found her writing at a table; she was entertaining herself with a

problem in arithmetic; to divert her I made two magic squares; they
delighted her; in return she showed me some trifles which I already
knew and in which I pretended to be interested. My good Genius
put it into my mind to perform the cabala for her. I told her to write
a question asking something she did not know and was curious
about, assuring her that by means of a certain calculation she
would receive a satisfactory answer. She laughed, and she asked
why I had come back to Amsterdam so soon. I show her how to
construct pyramids with numbers drawn from words, and all the
other ceremonies; then I have her extract a numerical answer
herself, which I have her translate into the French alphabet, and
she is astonished to read that what has brought me back to Amsterdam so quickly is love. All wonder, she says it is astonishing even if
the answer is untrue, and she wants me to tell her what masters can
teach such a wonderful calculation. I say that those who know it
can teach it to no one.

"Then how do you know it?"

"I learned it by myself from a manuscript which my father
left me."

"Sell me the manuscript."

"I have burned it. I am at liberty to teach it to only one person,
but not until I reach the age of fifty. If I teach it before then I risk
losing it. An elemental spirit who is attached to the oracle would
leave it. I learned all this from the same manuscript."

"Then you can find out all the greatest secrets in the world?"

"I should have that privilege if the answers weren't in most cases
very obscure."

"As it doesn't take long, would you have the kindness to extract
the answer to another question for me?"

She then asked what her destiny was to be, and the oracle
answered that she had not yet taken the first step on the road to it.
All wonder, Esther calls her governess and thinks she will amaze her
by showing her the two oracles; but the good Swiss woman sees
nothing extraordinary in it. In her impatience she calls her a fool.
She begs me to let her put another question, and I encourage her.
She asks what person in Amsterdam loves her most, and, using the
same method, she finds the answer that no one loves her more than
the person to whom she owes her existence. The poor, intelligent
girl then tells me with the utmost seriousness that I have made her
miserable, for she will die of grief if she cannot learn the calculation.
I do not answer, and she sees me downcast. She writes a question,

hiding the paper with her beautiful hand. I get up to leave her free; but while she is constructing the pyramid I glance at the paper as I walk by, and I read her question. After doing everything I had taught her to do, she says that I can extract the answer without having to read her question. I agree, and she blushes and asks me to do her the favor. I consent, but on condition that she will not ask me to do her the same favor again. She promises. Since, having read her question, I know that she asked the oracle's permission to show her father all the questions she put, I produce the answer that "she will be happy if she never keeps anything which is important to her a secret from her father." At that she oh'd and ah'd, finding no words strong enough to show me her gratitude. I left her to go to the Exchange, where I talked at length with Monsieur Pels about my chief business.

The next morning a handsome and very gentlemanly man came bringing me a letter from Teresa in which she introduced him to me, assuring me that if I had any business to transact he could be useful to me. His name was Rigerboos.[7] She said that V. D. R.'s five wounds were all slight, that I had nothing to fear, that no one knew anything of the affair, and that there was nothing to stop me if I needed to go back to The Hague. She said that Sophie talked about me from morning to night, and that when I came back I would be much better pleased with her son. I asked Monsieur Rigerboos to give me his address, assuring him that if the occasion arose I should have perfect confidence in his probity. A moment after he left I received a note from Esther in which she asked me, in her father's name, to come and spend the whole day with her, unless some important business prevented me. I answered that except for a transaction of which her father knew, my only important business in the world would be whatever I could do to conquer her heart. I promised to go.

I went there at dinnertime. Esther and her father were busily examining the calculation which drew rational answers from the pyramid. Her father embraced me, with joy painted on his noble countenance, saying that he was fortunate to have a daughter who had deserved my attention. When I answered that I adored her he encouraged me to kiss her, and Esther gave a cry and literally sprang into my arms.

"I have attended to everything," said Monsieur D. O., "and I have the whole day to myself. I have known from childhood, my dear friend, that the science of which you are in possession exists in the world, and I was acquainted with a Jew who made a great fortune by it. He said, as you do, that he could impart it only to one person, upon pain of losing it himself. But he put it off so long that he died without being able to impart it to me. It was a high fever which deprived him of the power. Permit me to tell you that if you do not know how to profit by your skill, you do not know what you possess. It is a treasure."

"My oracle, Monsieur, answers very obscurely."

"The answers my daughter has shown me are perfectly clear."

"It seems she is fortunate in her questions, for the answers depend upon that."

"We shall see after dinner if I have the same good fortune, if you will be so good as to work with me."

At table we talked of other things entirely, for there were some employees present, and among them his head manager, an ugly, coarse fellow, who I thought had notions about Esther. After dinner we withdrew, and, with only Esther present, Monsieur D. O. took two very long questions from his pocket. In one he wanted to know how he should go about obtaining a favorable decision from the States-General[8] in a business matter which was of great consequence to him and of which he gave the details. I answered this question very obscurely and very quickly, leaving it for Esther to put it into words; when he asked his second question I took a notion to answer it clearly. He asked what had been the fate of a ship which was known to have sailed from the East Indies on a certain date, but what had become of it was not. It should have arrived two months since; he wanted to know if it was still in existence or if it had perished, and where and how. No one had ever had any news of it. The company which owned it would be satisfied with an insurer who would give them ten percent, but they found no one. What made it almost certain that the ship was lost was a letter from an English captain who testified that he had seen it go down.

The gist of my answer, which I was stupid enough to give without apprehending any ill consequences, was that the ship still existed and had suffered no damage, and that trustworthy news of it would arrive within a week. So it was that, wanting to raise my oracle's reputation sky-high, I risked its losing it entirely. But I should have done none of this if I had guessed what Monsieur D. O. would do in consequence of my oracle. He went pale for joy. He told us that it was of the utmost importance to speak of the matter to no one, for he was planning to go and insure the vessel at the best rate possible. Aghast, I told him that I did not answer for the truth of the oracle and that I should die of mortification if I were the cause of his losing a large sum. He asked me if the oracle sometimes deceived me, and I answered that it often led to mistakes by being equivocal. Esther, seeing my uneasiness, begged her father to take no steps in the matter.

Monsieur D. O. remained lost in thought, then spoke at length, reasoning erroneously on the so-called power of numbers, and told his daughter to read him all the questions she had asked. There were six or seven of them, all short and all of a nature to be answered plainly or equivocally or humorously. Esther, who had constructed all the pyramids, shone by extracting the answers with my all-powerful help. Her father, in ecstasies at seeing her so clever, thought that she would succeed in mastering the oracle, and Esther herself made bold to believe it. After spending seven hours discussing all the answers, which were acclaimed as divine, we supped. Monsieur D. O. invited me to dine at his house on the Amstel, which I already knew. I accepted with pleasure.

Returning to my lodging, I passed a house where there was dancing, and, seeing people going in and out, I wanted to see what was doing. It was a *musicau*[9]—a dark orgy in a place which was a veritable sewer of vice, a disgrace to even the most repellent debauchery. The very sound of the two or three instruments which made up the orchestra plunged the soul in sadness. A room reeking with the smoke of bad tobacco, with the stench of garlic which came from the belches emitted by the men who were dancing or sitting with a bottle or a pot of beer to their right and a hideous slattern to their left, presented my eyes and my thoughts with a distressing image which showed me the miseries of life and the level of degradation to which brutishness could reduce pleasures. The crowd which gave life to the place was composed entirely of sailors and others of the common people, to whom it seemed a paradise which made up to them for all that they had suffered on long and painful voyages. Among the prostitutes I saw there I found not one with whom I could possibly have diverted myself for a moment. A shady-looking man who might be a tinsmith and who had the manners of a boor came and asked me in broken Italian if I wanted to dance for a sou. I declined. He pointed out a Venetian woman who was sitting there, saying that I could take her to a room upstairs and drink with her.

I approach, I think I recognize her, but the gloomy light of four unsnuffed candles does not let me make out her features. Impelled by curiosity, I sit down beside her and ask her if it is true that she is a Venetian and if it has been long since she left her native country. She answers that it has been about eighteen years. I am brought a bottle, I ask her if she wants to drink, she says yes, adding that I can go upstairs with her. I answer that I haven't time, I hand over a ducat in payment, I am given the change, which I put into the hand of the poor devil of a creature, who offers me a kiss which I refuse.

"Do you like Amsterdam better than Venice?" I ask her.

"In my own country I didn't follow this accursed trade. I was only fourteen, and I lived with my father and mother."

"Who seduced you?"

"A courier."

"In what *contrada*[10] of Venice did you live?"

"I didn't live in Venice but on an estate in Friuli not far from there."

An estate in Friuli, eighteen years, a courier—I am moved, I look at her closely, and I recognize Lucia[11] of Pasiano, but I am careful not to change my attitude of indifference. Far more than age, debauchery had withered her face and all its appurtenances. Lucia, fond, pretty, ingenuous Lucia, whom I had loved so much and whom I had spared out of delicacy, in such a state, ugly, repellent, in a brothel in Amsterdam! She drank without looking at me and without caring to know who I was. I did not feel curious to learn her story, I even thought I knew it. She said that she lived in the *musicau* and would give me pretty girls if I came to see her. I gave her two ducats and quickly left. I went to bed overwhelmed with sorrow. I thought I had spent a day of ill omen, remembering Monsieur D. O. too, who because of my silly cabala might be going to lose three hundred thousand florins. The thought, which made me despise myself, boded ill for the affection which Esther inspired in me. I foresaw her becoming my implacable enemy together with her father. A man cannot love except with the hope of being loved. The sight of Lucia in the *musicau* left an impression on me which brought me the most ominous dreams. I considered myself the cause of her misfortune. She was only thirty-two, and I foresaw a horrible future for her.

After tormenting myself and not sleeping, I get up, I order a carriage, and I put on a fine suit to go and make my bow to Princess Galitzin, who was lodging at the "Star of the East." She had gone to the Admiralty. I go there and find her in the company of Monsieur de Reischach[12] and Count de Tott, who had just received news of my friend Pesselier,[13] at whose house I had met him. I had left him very ill when I departed from Paris.

Leaving the Admiralty, I dismiss my carriage and my lackey, ordering him to be at Monsieur D. O.'s house on the Amstel at eleven o'clock. I go there on foot, and, dressed as I am, I find some of the Dutch populace hooting and whistling at me. Esther sees me from the window, a cord is pulled on the second floor, the door opens, I go in, close it behind me, and at the fourth or fifth step on my way up a wooden staircase my foot strikes against something yielding. I look, and seeing a green portfolio I stoop to pick it up, but I awkwardly give it a push, and it drops under the staircase through an opening which had been made in the front of the next step, apparently to give light to the place under the stairs. I do not stop but go on up. I am received as usual, and I explain the reason for my elaborate dress. Esther laughs at my looking like a different person, but I have the impression that they are gloomy. Esther's governess comes in and speaks to them in Dutch. I see Esther look distressed, then go and give her father a hundred caresses.

"I see," I say to him, "that some misfortune has befallen you; if my presence incommodes you, permit me to withdraw at once."

He answers that the misfortune is not great and that he has resigned himself to it, since he is rich enough to bear it with equanimity.

"I have lost," he said, "a quite well-furnished portfolio, which, if I had used my common sense, I would have left at home, for I had no need for it until tomorrow. I can only have lost it in the street— how, I don't know. It contains some sizable bills of exchange, on which I can stop payment, but also some English bank notes, of which the bearers can make what use they please. Let us thank God for all things, my dear Esther, and pray to him to keep us in health and to preserve us from still greater misfortunes. I have suffered worse blows in my life, and I have borne up. So let us say no more of this incident, which I will regard as a small bankruptcy."

I remained silent, with joy in my soul. I was sure that the portfolio was the one I had pushed through the opening, so it was not lost; but I at once thought that I would not let them recover it without some cabalistic trappings. The chance was too good a one for me to fail to use it and give my hosts a great example of the infallibility of my oracle. The idea having put me in a good humor, I said countless things which made Esther laugh and told her stories which ridiculed the French, whom she detested.

We dined very choicely and drank of the best. After coffee I said that if they liked cards I would play; but Esther said it would be a pity to waste time at that.

"I can't get enough of pyramids," she said. "May I ask who has found my father's portfolio?"

"Why not?" I said. "It's a simple question."

She framed it very briefly and the answer which came out, equally brief, told her that no one had found her father's portfolio. She ran and embraced her father, whom the answer had made sure that his portfolio would come back to him; but she was first surprised, then laughed a great deal, when I told her that any hope she had that I would go on working was vain unless she gave me at least as many caresses as she had given her dear father. At that she gave me a quantity of kisses, and she extracted the pyramid from the question which asked where the portfolio was. I elicited the words: "The portfolio dropped through the opening in the fifth step of the staircase."

D. O. and his daughter rise, greatly relieved, they go down, and I follow them. He himself shows us the opening through which the portfolio must have passed. He lights a candle, then enters a store-room, goes down an underground staircase, and with his own hands picks up the portfolio, which was lying in water exactly under the opening in the stair. We go back up and spend an hour in the most serious discussion of the divinity of the oracle and its ability to make its possessor the happiest of men. Opening the portfolio, he showed us forty Exchequer bills for a thousand pounds sterling[14] each, of which he presented two to his daughter and two to me; taking them with one hand, I gave them to the beautiful Esther with the other, telling her to keep them for me. She would not consent until I threatened not to work with the cabala for her again. To Monsieur D. O. I said that I wanted nothing from him but his friendship. He embraced me and promised I should have it to the last day of his life.

By making Esther the custodian of twenty-two thousand florins, I was certain to bind her to me. The girl had a witchery in her eyes which intoxicated me. I said to her father that the business I had most at heart was to negotiate the twenty millions at little loss. He answered that he hoped to satisfy me, but that since he would often need me with him, I should come to lodge in his house. Esther added her solicitations to his, and I accepted, taking great care to conceal all the satisfaction I felt but at the same time showing them all the gratitude I owed them.

He then went to his study to write, and, left alone with Esther, I said that I felt ready to do anything for her which lay in my power but that first of all she must give me her heart. She said that the moment when I could ask her father for her hand would come when I was staying in their house. I assured her that she would have me there the next day.

Coming back, Monsieur D. O. said that the next day we would hear a great piece of news on the Exchange. He said that he would himself take over the supposedly lost ship for three hundred thousand florins—and let them call him a fool!

"I should really be a fool," he added, "if, after all that I have seen of the divinity of the oracle, I had doubts. I will make three millions; and if I lose it will not ruin me."

Esther, dazzled by the recovered portfolio, told her father that he must act at once, and for my part I could no longer retreat. Seeing me gloomy, Monsieur D. O. assured me that he would be no less my friend if the oracle proved to be fallacious. I asked him to let me question the oracle again before he risked such a large loss, and I saw that they were both delighted by my zeal for the good of their house.

But here is yet another incident which will make some of my readers incredulous or incline them to condemn me as a thoughtless and even dangerous person. I did everything myself—the question, the pyramid, and all the rest—refusing to let Esther take any part in it. I was delighted to be in time to prevent such a slaughter and determined that I would prevent it. A double meaning, which I could bring from my pen, would have discouraged them both, and since I had it in my head I thought I had expressed it perfectly in numbers on the paper which lay before me. Esther, who had the alphabet by heart, quickly translated it into words and amazed me when she read my answer. She read these words: "In such a case as this, there is nothing to *fear*. Your regret would be too painful." Nothing more was needed. Father and daughter together ran to embrace me, and Monsieur D. O. said that when the ship appeared he would owe me a tenth of his profit. Surprise prevented me from answering him and expressing my gratitude, for I felt certain that I had written "believe" [*croire*], not "fear" [*craindre*]. I could no longer draw back.

The next day I went to stay with them in a charming suite of rooms, and on the day after that I took Esther to a concert, where she rallied me on La Trenti's not appearing at it. The girl possessed me entirely, but since she constantly refused to yield to the essential purpose of my caresses she kept me languishing.

Four or five days later Monsieur D. O. communicated to me the decision reached at a conference he had held with Pels and the heads of six other banking houses concerning my twenty millions. They offered ten millions in cash and seven in obligations yielding five and six percent, with a deduction of one percent for brokerage fees. In addition they waived all claim to the twelve hundred thousand florins which the French East India Company[15] owed to the Dutch East India Company. I sent copies of the decision to Monsieur de Boulogne and Monsieur d'Affry, demanding a prompt answer. The answer I received a week later from Monsieur de Courteuil by order of Monsieur de Boulogne was that such terms were unacceptable and that I had only to return to Paris if I could not do better, and I was again told that peace was imminent. But Monsieur D. O.'s confidence had increased extraordinarily some days before this answer arrived. The Exchange itself had received trustworthy news that the ship in question was at Madeira. Four days earlier Monsieur D. O. had bought it with all its cargo for three hundred thousand florins. What a pleasure it was when we saw him come into our room with a look of triumph which confirmed the news! He said that he had already insured it from Madeira to Texel[16] for a trifle, and that a tenth of the profit was at my disposition. But what astonished me was these exact words, with which he ended his discourse:

"You are now rich enough to establish yourself in our country with the assurance of becoming immensely wealthy in a few years simply by using your cabala. I will be your agent. Let us make one household, and if you love my daughter I give her to you if she wants you."

Joy shone in Esther's eyes, but in mine she could see only my surprise, which was so beyond measure that it left me dumb and as if stupefied. After a long silence I entered upon a wiredrawn analysis of the feelings appropriate to the situation, ending by saying that though I adored Esther I must go back to Paris before coming to a resolve; I said I was sure that I would be able to decide my fate when I returned to Amsterdam. My answer won their approval and we spent the day in high spirits. The next day Monsieur D. O. gave a splendid dinner for his friends, who only said, amid good-natured laughter, that he had learned before anyone else that the ship was at Madeira, though no one could imagine how he had come to know it.

A week after this lucky incident he gave me an ultimatum on the business of the twenty millions, the upshot of which was that France would lose only nine percent on the sale of the twenty millions, on condition that I could not demand any brokerage fees from the purchasers. I sent accurate copies of this proposal to Monsieur d'Affry by express messenger, asking him to transmit them at my expense to the Comptroller-General together with a letter in which I warned him that the transaction would fall through if he let a single day pass before giving Monsieur d'Affry whatever powers he needed in order to give me the authority to contract. I appealed with no less urgency to Monsieur de Courteuil and the Duke, informing them all that I was to be given nothing but that I would conclude the transaction nevertheless, being certain that I would be reimbursed for my expenses and that what was due me as broker would not be refused me at Versailles.

As it was Carnival,[17] Monsieur D. O. saw fit to give a ball. He invited all the most distinguished men and women in the city. I will tell my reader only that the ball was sumptuous, as was the supper. Esther danced all the contradances with me with every possible grace, and shone arrayed in the diamonds of her late mother.

We were spending the whole of every day together, in love and unhappy because abstinence tormented us. Esther would only go so far as to permit me some little theft when I went to breakfast with her. She was generous only with her kisses, which, instead of calming me, made me frantic. She told me, like all the supposedly decent girls in the universe, that she was sure I would never marry her if she let me do whatever I wanted to her. She did not think I was married, for I had assured her too often that I was a bachelor, but she had no doubt that I had some strong attachment in Paris. I admitted it, and I assured her that I was going to free myself completely so that I could be bound to her until death by the most solemn of ties. Alas! I was lying, for she could not be separated from her father, who was only forty, and I could not imagine it possible that I should settle permanently in such a country.

Ten or twelve days after sending the ultimatum I received a letter from Monsieur de Boulogne in which he said that the Ambassador had received all the necessary instructions to enable me to conclude the business, and the Ambassador told me the same. He warned me to look to my arrangements, for he would not deliver the royal securities except upon receiving 18,200,000 francs in currency.

The sad moment of parting having thus come, we did not try to restrain our tears. Esther gave me the equivalent of the two thousand pounds sterling I had left with her on the day the portfolio was found, and her father, in accordance with my instructions, gave me one hundred thousand florins[18] in bills of exchange on Tourton & Baur and on Pâris de Montmartel[19] and a receipt for two hundred thousand florins which authorized me to draw on him until the entire amount was exhausted. When I left, Esther presented me with fifty shirts of the finest linen and fifty Masulipatam[20] handkerchiefs.

It was not love of Manon Balletti but a stupid vanity, a wish to cut a figure in Paris, which made me leave Holland. The fifteen months I spent under the Leads were not enough to cure the defects of my character. "Destiny" is a word without meaning; it is we who make our destiny, despite the maxim of the Stoics: *Volentem ducit, nolentem trahit* ("[Fate] leads the willing, drags the unwilling").[21] I am too self-indulgent if I apply it to myself.

After vowing to Esther that I would see her before the end of the year I left with a commissioner of the company which had bought the French securities and, reaching The Hague, went to stay with Boas, who received me with mingled astonishment and admiration. He said I had performed a miracle and that I should hurry on to Paris, if only to enjoy the incense of congratulations. He said, however, that he was sure I could not have done what I had done unless I had convinced the company beyond doubt that peace was on the verge of being made. I replied that I had not convinced them, but that peace would certainly be concluded. He said that if I could obtain for him a positive written assurance from the Ambassador that peace would be made he would present me with fifty thousand florins in diamonds. I replied that the Ambassador's certainty on the subject could not be greater than mine but that, even so, I considered it still only a moral certainty.

The next day I concluded everything with the Ambassador; and the commissioner returned to Amsterdam.

I went to supper at Teresa's, who showed me her children very nicely dressed. I told her to go to Rotterdam the next day and wait for my arrival there to entrust her son to me, for to avoid talk I did not want to take charge of him in The Hague.

From one of Boas's sons I bought a pair of diamond earrings and several fine stones for forty thousand florins. I had to promise him that I would stay with him when I came back to The Hague, but I did not keep my word.

At Rotterdam Teresa bluntly told me that she knew for certain I had made half a million in Amsterdam and that her fortune would be assured if she could leave Holland and set herself up in London. She got Sophie to tell me that my good fortune had been the result of her prayers to God. All this made me laugh. I gave her a hundred ducats and told her that I would arrange to have her paid another hundred when she wrote to me from London. I saw that she thought the amount small, but I did not let that persuade me to give her more. She waited until I had got into my chaise to ask me for another hundred ducats, and I whispered to her that I would give her a thousand on the spot if she would let me have Sophie. After thinking for a moment she said no. I left after giving my daughter a watch. I reached Paris on the 10th of February,[22] and I took a fine apartment in Rue Comtesse-d'Artois near the Rue Montorgueil.[23]

CHAPTER VIII

*Flattering reception from my patron. Madame
d'Urfé's delusions. Madame XCV and her
family.*

During the short journey I came to the conclusion that my newly adopted son's soul was not as attractive as his person. What his mother had chiefly instilled by the education she had given him was discretion. This quality in her son was the one which her own interest demanded that he should possess above all others; but the unschooled boy carried it too far; he combined it with dissimulation, suspicion, and false confidences. Not only did he not say what he knew, he pretended to know what he did not know; to be successful, he felt that he must be impenetrable, and to that end he had acquired the habit of imposing silence on his heart and never saying anything which he had not framed in his mind beforehand. He thought he was being prudent when he gave a false impression. Incapable of friendship, he became unworthy to win friends.

Foreseeing that Madame d'Urfé would count on the boy for the accomplishment of her chimerical hypostasis and that the more I made his birth a mystery, the more her Genius would lead her to invent wild fantasies, I ordered him to conceal nothing about himself if a lady to whom I would present him showed any curiosity about his circumstances when she was alone with him. He promised to obey me. He had not been expecting that I would order him to be sincere.

My first visit was to my patron,[1] whom I found entertaining a large company; among them I saw the Venetian Ambassador,[2] who pretended not to know me.

"How long have you been in Paris?" asked the Minister, taking my hand.

"No time at all. I have just got out of my post chaise."

"Then go to Versailles, you will find the Duke of Choiseul and the Comptroller-General there. You have performed miracles, go and be adored. Come to see me afterward. Tell the Duke that I have sent Voltaire a passport in which the King appoints him a gentleman-in-ordinary."[3]

One does not go to Versailles at noon, but this was the way Ministers talked when they were in Paris. It was as if Versailles were at the other end of the street. I went to Madame d'Urfé's.

The first thing she said to me was that her Genius had told her she would see me that very day.

"Kornmann," she said, "told me yesterday that what you have done is incredible. I am sure it was you who discounted the twenty millions. Securities have gone up, and within the week there will be a circulation of at least a hundred millions. Forgive me for having ventured to make you a present of twelve thousand francs. It is nothing."

I saw no need to tell her that she was wrong. She sent word to the porter to close the door to everyone, and we began talking. I saw her tremble with joy when I coolly told her that I had brought a twelve-year-old boy with me, whom I meant to bring up in the best boarding school in Paris.

"I will put him in Viar's,"[4] she said, "where my nephews are. What is his name? Where is he? I know what the boy is. I cannot wait to see him. Why did you not come straight here?"

"I will present him to you day after tomorrow, for tomorrow I shall be at Versailles."

"Does he speak French? Until I have made all the arrangements for his schooling, you simply must leave him with me."

"We will discuss it day after tomorrow."

After stopping at my office, where I found everything in order, I went to the Comédie Italienne, where Silvia was playing.[5] I found her in her dressing room with her daughter. She said she knew I had done very well with my business in Holland, and I saw that she was surprised when I said that I had worked for her daughter. The girl blushed. After saying that I would go to supper with them I took a place in the amphitheater. What a surprise! In one of the first-tier boxes I see Madame XCV[6] with all her family. Here is the story.

Madame XCV, of Greek origin, was the widow of an Englishman to whom she had given six children, four girls[7] and two boys. On his deathbed, unable to resist his wife's tears, he declared himself a Roman Catholic; but since his children could not inherit a capital of forty thousand pounds sterling which he had in England except by declaring themselves Anglicans, she had just come from London, where she had attended to all that.[8] It was at the beginning of the year 1758.[9]

642

In the year *1753* I fell in love with her eldest daughter[10] at Padua, where I acted in a play with her, and six months later at Venice Madame *XCV* saw fit to exclude me from her society. Her daughter made it possible for me to bear the affront calmly by a charming letter, which I still cherish; besides, being then in love with M. M. and C. C., I easily forgot her. The girl, though only fifteen[11] years old, was a beauty, and to the charms of her figure she added those of a cultivated mind, the spell of which is often more powerful. The Chamberlain to the King of Prussia, Count Algarotti,[12] gave her lessons, and several young patricians hoped to conquer her heart; the one who seemed to have the preference was the eldest son of the Memmo di San Marcuola[13] family. He died four years ago as Procurator of San Marco.

The reader can imagine my surprise when, five years later, I saw the whole family. Miss *XCV*[14] recognizes me instantly, she points me out to her mother, and the latter at once beckons to me with her fan. I went to her box at once.

She receives me by saying that we are no longer in Venice, that she is heartily glad to see me again, and that she hopes I will often come to call on her at the Hôtel de Bretagne[15] in the Rue Saint-André-des-Arts, where she is staying. Her daughter treats me to the same compliment with even greater insistence; she looks a goddess, and it seems to me that after a sleep of five years my love wakes again with an increase in power equal to that which the object before my eyes had gained in the same period of time.

They tell me that they expect to spend six months in Paris before going back to Venice; I reply that I intend to make my residence in Paris, that I have just returned from Holland that day, that I am obliged to spend the next day at Versailles, and that they will see me the day after that at their lodging, eager to offer them any services in my power.

"I have heard," says Miss *XCV*, "that what you have done in Holland must make you dear to France, and I have always hoped to see you; and your prodigious escape gave us the greatest pleasure, for we were always fond of you. We learned the details of it from a sixteen-page letter you wrote to Signor Memmo, which made us shudder and laugh. As for what you accomplished in Holland, we heard of it yesterday from Monsieur de la Pouplinière."[16]

The Farmer-General himself, whom I had first met at his house in Passy[17] seven years earlier, now entered the box. After congratulating me briefly, he said that if I could obtain twenty millions for the

East India Company[18] in the same way, he would have me made Farmer-General. He advised me to get myself naturalized as a French citizen before it became generally known that I must be worth at least half a million.

"You cannot have made less."

"The business, Monsieur, will ruin me if I am denied my brokerage fee."

"You are right to speak out. Everyone is eager to make your acquaintance, and France is indebted to you, for you have made securities rise."

It was at supper at Silvia's that my soul reveled in delight. I was made as much of as if I had been a son of the house, and on my side I convinced the whole family that I wanted to be regarded as such. It seemed to me that I owed all my good fortune to their influence and their unfailing friendship. I made the mother,[19] the father, the daughter, and the two sons[20] promise to accept the presents I had for them. Since the richest one was in my pocket, I presented it to the mother, who immediately gave it to her daughter. It was a pair of earrings which had cost me six thousand florins. Three days later I gave her a small chest in which she found two pieces of superb calencar,[21] two of very fine linen, and trimmings of the Flemish needlepoint known as "English point." I gave Mario, who liked to smoke, a gold pipe, and my friend[22] a handsome snuffbox. I gave a watch to the Cadet,[23] of whom I was inordinately fond. I shall have occasion to speak of this youth, whose qualities made him superior to his station in every respect. But was I rich enough to give such substantial presents? No, and I knew it. I made them only because I was afraid I should not become rich enough. If I had been sure of it, I would have waited.

I set out for Versailles before dawn. The Duke of Choiseul received me pen in hand as he had before; his hair was being dressed. This time he laid down his pen. After a brief compliment he said that if I felt I was capable of negotiating a loan of a hundred million florins at four percent, he would give me a recommendation which would do me honor. I answered that I might consider it after I learned what recompense for what I had already done would be given me by way of encouragement.

"Everyone says you have made two hundred thousand florins."

"Saying it means nothing unless it is proved. I can claim the brokerage fee."

"True. Go and state your case to the Comptroller-General."

Monsieur de Boulogne stopped the work he was doing to receive me graciously, but when I told him he owed me a hundred thousand florins, he smiled.

"I know," he said, "that you are the holder of bills of exchange to your order for a hundred thousand écus."

"That is true, but what I own has nothing to do with what I did. I have proof of it. I refer you to Monsieur d'Affry. I have an infallible plan for increasing the King's revenues by *twenty millions* without causing any complaint among those who will provide them."

"Execute it, and I will have the King himself give you a pension of a hundred thousand francs and a patent of nobility if you will become a French citizen."

I went to the private apartments, where Madame la Marquise was having a ballet rehearsed. She greeted me as soon as she saw me and said that I was a clever negotiator whom the gentlemen "down there"[24] had not properly appreciated. She still remembered what I had said to her at Fontainebleau eight years earlier. I replied that all good things came from "up there," and that I hoped to share in them through her kind offices.

Back in Paris I went to the Hôtel de Bourbon to inform my patron of all the results of my journey. He advised me to be patient and to continue to do well; and, when I mentioned that I had seen Madame *XCV* at the theater, he said that La Pouplinière was going to marry her eldest daughter.

The news when I reached my lodging was that my son had left.

"A great lady," said my hostess, "came to call on the Count" (he had immediately been dubbed Count) "and took him away with her."

[* * *]

At Madame d'Urfé's I found my supposed son in her arms. She outdid herself in excuses for carrying him off, but I laughingly turned them aside. I told the little man that he must regard Madame as his queen and always open his heart to her. She told me she had made him sleep with her, but that she would have to forgo the pleasure if he would not promise to be better behaved in future. I thought it sublime, and I saw the young man blush. He asked her to tell him how he had offended her.

She said that Saint-Germain would dine with us; she knew that the adept amused me. He came, he sat down at the table—not to eat but to talk, as he always did. He brazenly related incredible stories, which we had to pretend we believed because he said that he had been either an eyewitness or the chief actor in them; but I could not keep from bursting out laughing when he told of something which had happened to him when he dined with the Fathers of the Council of Trent.[25]

Madame was wearing a large armed magnet[26] hanging from her neck. She claimed that at one time or another it would draw lightning down on her and thus she would go to the sun.

"There can be no doubt of it," said the impostor; "but I am the only person on earth who can give magnets a strength a thousand times greater than the usual run of physicists give them."

I said coldly that I would wager twenty thousand écus that he would not even double the strength of the one Madame was wearing. Madame prevented him from accepting the wager, and she told me privately afterward that I would have lost because Saint-Germain was a magician. I said she was right.

A few days later the self-styled magician left for Chambord,[27] one of the royal castles, where the King had given him an apartment and a hundred thousand francs so that he could work without interruption on the dyes which were to make all the cloth manufactories in France prosperous. He had won over the King by installing a laboratory at Trianon for him which often amused him, for he suffered from boredom everywhere except when he was hunting; it was the Marquise who had introduced the adept to him to teach him chemistry; for after he had presented her with the water of youth she believed everything he said. This miraculous water, taken in the quantity he had prescribed for her, did not, the worshiper of truth admitted, have the virtue of restoring youth, for that was impossible, but it had the virtue of preventing old age by keeping the body *in statu quo* for several centuries. She had told the monarch that she really felt she was not aging.

The monarch showed the Duke of Zweibrücken[28] a diamond of the first water weighing twelve carats which he wore on his finger and which he was convinced he had made himself, having been initiated into the magisterium[29] by the impostor. He said that he had melted twenty-four carats of small diamonds which had become one, and that it had later been reduced to twelve when it was polished on the wheel. Thus convinced of the adept's knowledge, he had given him the same lodging at Chambord which he had given the illustrious Maréchal de Saxe[30] for his lifetime. I heard this story from the Duke's own lips when I had the honor to sup with him and the Swedish Count of Lewenhaupt[31] at Metz at the "King Dagobert" inn.[32]

Before leaving Madame d'Urfé I told her that the boy might be the person to assure her rebirth, but that she would spoil everything if she did not wait until he had reached puberty.

She sent him to board at Viar's, giving him all kinds of teachers and the name of Count d'Aranda, despite the fact that he was born in Bayreuth[33] and that his mother had never had the slightest acquaintance with any Spaniard of that name. I did not go to see him until three or four months after he was well settled there. I was always afraid I might be subjected to some affront because of the name the visionary Marquise had given him without my knowledge.

CHAPTER X

J. J. Rousseau. I visit "Count Aranda."

About this time Madame d'Urfé took a fancy to make the acquaintance of J. J. Rousseau;[1] we went to Montmorency[2] to visit him, taking some music, which he copied wonderfully well. People paid him twice as much as they would have paid another copyist, but he guaranteed that there would be no errors. It was the way he made his living.

We found a man who reasoned well, whose manner was simple and modest, but who was entirely undistinguished either in his person or his wit. We did not find what is called a pleasant man. We thought him rather impolite, and it took no more for Madame d'Urfé to set him down as vulgar. We saw a woman[3] of whom we had already heard. She scarcely looked at us. We went back to Paris laughing at the philosopher's eccentricity. But here is a faithful account of a visit paid him by the Prince of Conti,[4] father of the Prince who was then known as the Count of La Marche.[5]

The charming Prince goes to Montmorency by himself, on purpose to spend a pleasant day talking with the philosopher, who was already famous. He finds him in the park, he accosts him and says he has come to dine and spend the day with him in unconstrained conversation.

"Your Highness will eat poor fare; I will go and order another place set."

He goes, he comes back, and after spending two or three hours walking with the Prince he conducts him to the room in which they are to dine. The Prince, seeing three places laid:

"Who," he said, "is the third person with whom you want me to dine? I thought we should dine alone together."

"The third person, Monseigneur, is another myself. It is a being who is neither my wife nor my mistress nor my servant nor my mother nor my daughter; and she is all those."

"I believe it, my dear friend; but since I came here only to dine with you, I will leave you to dine with all those other selves. Good-by."[6]

Such are the absurdities of philosophers when, trying to be remarkable, they only succeed in being eccentric. The woman was

Mademoiselle Levasseur, whom he had honored with his name, except for one letter of it, under the mask of an anagram.[7]

[* * *]

As soon as my supposed son was, according to Madame d'Urfé, well settled in Viar's boarding school, she insisted that I go with her to visit him. And to tell the truth, I was surprised.

A prince could not be better lodged, better treated, better dressed, or more respected by everyone in the establishment. She had given him all kinds of teachers, and a schooled pony so that he could learn equitation. He went by the name of Count of Aranda. A girl of sixteen or eighteen and very pretty, the daughter of Viar, proprietor of the school, never left him and announced herself as his young lordship's governess with every sign of satisfaction. She assured Madame d'Urfé that she took particular care of him, that when he woke she brought him his breakfast in bed, then dressed him, and did not leave him until she had put him to bed. Madame d'Urfé approved of all her attentions and assured her she was grateful. The little fellow could say nothing to me except that I had made his life happy. I decided to go back by myself one day to sound him out and learn on what terms he was with the pretty girl.

On the way back I told Madame that I was pleased with everything except the name Aranda, which might cause difficulties. She replied that the boy had said enough to show beyond doubt that he really had a right to bear the name.

"In my desk," she said, "I had a seal with the arms of that house; as soon as the boy saw them he seized on the seal and asked me how I happened to have the arms. I answered that I had them from the Count of Aranda himself, urging him to tell me how he could prove he was of the family; but he silenced me by saying that his birth was a secret he had sworn never to reveal to anyone."

Curious to discover the source of an imposture of which I should never have believed the young rascal capable, I went to see him by myself a week later. I found him with Viar, who, seeing that he addressed me with something very close to humility, must have thought that he belonged to me. Praising the young Count's talents in the highest terms, he said that he played the flute excellently, danced and fenced very nimbly, rode very well, and that no one was better at drawing all the letters of the alphabet. He then showed me some pens he had cut, with one, three, five, and up to eleven nibs, and urged me to examine him in heraldry, a science so necessary to a nobleman and of which no one had a better know-ledge than he.

The boy then blazoned his arms in herald's jargon, which made me laugh for I knew almost none of the terms; but I took pleasure in seeing how skillfully he wrote freehand with his various pens, which simultaneously drew as many straight and curved lines as they had nibs. I told Viar that it was all very gratifying; and very much pleased, he left me alone with him. We went into the garden.

"May I ask," I said, "what this nonsense about your calling yourself Aranda is?"

"It is nonsense, but let it pass, I beg you, for I have to do it to inspire respect here."

"It is a lie which I cannot let pass, for it may have disagreeable consequences which will involve us all. It is an imposture, my friend, of which I did not believe you capable, a feather-brained whim which may become criminal and which I do not know how to make good and save your honor after all you have said to Madame d'Urfé."

I did not end my scolding until I saw him weep and heard him implore me. He said that he would rather endure the mortification of being sent back to his mother than the shame of having to admit to Madame d'Urfé that he had lied and having to give up the name which he had claimed as his own at school. He moved me to pity. I could really do nothing to mend matters short of sending him to live under another name fifty leagues from Paris.

"Tell me," I said, "and mind you tell me the truth, what exactly is the nature of the affection of the pretty young lady who lavishes such attentions on you."

"I think, my dear Papa, that this is a time for the discretion which you and my Mamma have so often recommended to me."

"So that is it! Your objection has told me everything; but there is no place for discretion in a confession."

"Well then, Mademoiselle Viar loves me and gives me proofs of it which leave me in no doubt."

"And you?"

"I love her too; and certainly it can't be wrong for me to return her affection—she's so pretty! and her sweetness and her caresses are such that I could be insensible to them only if I were made of marble or utterly ungrateful. I have told you the truth."

With this avowal, which had already corrupted me, the young man blushed furiously. I was too much interested to change the subject. The charming young girl, in love, demonstrative, holding the little fellow in her arms, making him return her ardors, rose into my mind to beg my indulgence, and she had no difficulty in gaining it. I needed to make him continue his narrative to learn if he had nothing to reproach himself with in the response which it seemed to me he could not but accord to so pretty a girl.

So, assuming that kindly manner in which there is no shadow of reproach:

"Then," I said, "you have become the charming girl's little husband?"

"She tells me so every morning and every evening, and then I enjoy seeing how happy it makes her when I call her my little wife."

"And you are not afraid someone will catch you?"

"That is up to her."

"You are in each other's arms as God made you?"

"Yes, when she comes to put me to bed, but she only stays an hour at most."

"Would you like her to stay longer?"

"Not really, because after I've made love I can't help falling asleep."

"I imagine she is your first mistress in the fine art of love."

"You may be sure of that."

"And if she becomes pregnant?"

"She has assured me it is impossible, and when she told me the reason she convinced me; but in a year or two we both think she would have to fear it."

"Do you think she has had another lover before you?"

"Oh no, I'm sure she hasn't."

This whole dialogue only had the effect of making me irretrievably in love with his young mistress. I left him after asking him at what hour she brought him his breakfast. I could neither disapprove nor put obstacles in the way of the mutual affection of their two young hearts; but I thought the least recompense they owed me for my tolerance was to let me witness their amorous ecstasies at least once.

[* * *]

If the account of his success in Holland is to be believed, it might have seemed that a glittering career was now open to Casanova in the service of France, but this was not to be. Instead he was drawn back to the world of courtesans and gamblers, charlatans and confidence tricksters which was his natural milieu. While pursuing a profitable association with the absurd Madame d'Urfé, he crossed swords with her friend, the self-styled Comte de Saint-Germain—Casanova hated rivals—and with several other such counts and barons who prowled the inns and gaming rooms of Europe looking for an easy profit. In trouble with the police, up to his ears in debt and embroiled in petty but complicated law suits, Casanova took his usual way out of trouble and left the country, moving first to Holland and then, via Germany, to Switzerland where he decided to become, of all things, a monk. The impulse did not last. But he did find himself greatly taken by the Protestant simplicity of the country, which gave a special charm to its women . . .

HISTORY OF MY LIFE

Volume Six

CHAPTER V

Soleure. Monsieur de Chavigny. Monsieur and
Madame. . . . I act in a play. I feign illness
to forward my good fortune.

[* * *]

Casanova stayed first in Zurich and then left for Soleure in pursuit of a
mysterious "Amazon" whom he met by pretending to be a waiter.

At the post station in Soleure[1] I found a letter from Madame d'Urfé
enclosing one from the Duke of Choiseul addressed to Monsieur de
Chavigny, Ambassador. It was sealed, but the name of the minister
who had written it was on the outside. I hire a carriage by the day, I
dress as I would for Versailles, I go to the door of the Ambassador's
residence, he is not receiving, and I leave the letter for him. It was a
feast day, I go to the last mass, where I do not see the beautiful lady,
and after taking a little stroll I return to my inn. An officer was
waiting for me with an invitation from the Ambassador to dine "at
the Court."[2]

Madame d'Urfé wrote me in her letter that she had gone straight
to Versailles and that she was sure the Duchess of Gramont[3] had
persuaded the minister to write a most efficacious letter for me. I was
very glad, for I intended to play the role of an important personage.
The Marquis de Chavigny had been the French Ambassador in
Venice thirty years[4] before this time; I knew a great deal about
him and I could scarcely wait to make his acquaintance.

I go at the appointed hour, I am not announced, as soon as the
double doors are opened for me I see the handsome old man come to
meet me, and I hear him address me in the most obliging and courtly
terms. He introduces all his entourage to me; then, pretending to have
misread my name, he takes from his pocket the Duke of Choiseul's
letter and reads aloud the passage in which he asks him to show me
every consideration. He makes me sit down at his right on a sofa, and
he asks me only such questions as oblige me to say that I am traveling
simply for pleasure, that the Swiss nation is in several respects superior
to all others, and that this moment is the happiest of my life since it has
procured me the honor of his acquaintance.

Dinner is served, and His Excellency gives me the place beside
him and on his right. There were fifteen or sixteen places at the

table, and each guest was served by a footman in the Ambassador's livery. The conversation turning that way, I said to him that he was still spoken of in Venice with the fondest admiration.

"I shall always remember," he said, "the kindnesses which were shown me during my whole term as Ambassador; but be so good as to name those who still speak of me. They must be very old."

It was just what I wanted. Signor Malipiero had informed me of events during the Regency[5] which had gained him great credit; and Signor Bragadin had told me about his love affair with the celebrated Stringhetta.[6]

His cook was excellent; but the pleasure of talking to him led me to neglect that of eating. I saw him redden in his delight; he said to me as we rose from the table that he had never dined with greater pleasure at Soleure and that my recalling his Venetian gallantries to him had made him young again. He embraced me and asked me to spend all my time at his house, day and night, as long as I remained in Soleure. In his turn he talked much of Venice; after praising its system of government he said there was not a city in the world where one could eat better fare, even on fast days, only provided one made sure to procure good oil and foreign wine. About five o'clock he invited me to take a drive with him in a vis-à-vis,[7] getting into it first so that I should have to take the forward-facing seat.

We got out at a pretty country house, where we were served ices. On the way back to the city he said that he entertained a large company every evening, both men and women, and he hoped that, so far as it lay in his power, I would not be bored. I could scarcely wait to see the company; I thought it impossible that I should not see Madame... among them.

People began to arrive. Many of the women were ugly, some passable, and none pretty. Card games were arranged, and I was put at a table with a young blonde and an ancient dame who pretended to wit. Bored and not once opening my mouth, I lost five or six hundred counters. When the time came to pay, the old hand told me they came to three louis.

"Three louis?" I said.

"Yes, Monsieur. Two sous a counter. Did you think we were playing for coppers?"[8]

"On the contrary, Madame. I thought it was for twenty sous,[9] since I never play for less."

She left my boast unanswered, but she blushed.

After walking around the room and not seeing the beauty I hoped to find, I prepared to leave. The Ambassador had retired. I see two ladies talking together and looking at me; I recognize them as the ones I had seen at Zurich with Madame . . . ; I avoid them, and leave.

The next morning one of the Ambassador's household officials comes to tell me that His Excellency is coming and has sent me word so that he will be certain to find me. I said I would wait for him. I tried to think how I could get information about Madame . . . from him, but he saved me the trouble.

A quarter of an hour later I receive the worthy nobleman as it becomes me to do. After some desultory talk he smiled and said he was about to tell me the most unlikely thing imaginable, but he informed me in advance that he did not believe a word of it. After this preamble he said that two ladies who had seen me at the reception, and whose names he told me, had come to his room after I left to warn him to beware, because I was the waiter at the inn at Zurich.

"You waited on them at table ten days ago when they were on their way to perform their devotions at Our Lady of the Hermits—they are sure of it; and they say that yesterday, on the other side of the Aar, they met your fellow waiter, who had apparently run away with you, God knows why. They said that as soon as you realized last evening that they recognized you, you slipped away. I laughed and answered that I would be sure they were mistaken even if you had not brought me a letter from the Duke of Choiseul, and that I would have them to dinner with you today. I said that you might well have disguised yourself as a waiter in the hope of obtaining the favors of one of their party. They said the supposition was ridiculous, that you were nothing but a potboy with a knack for carving a capon and a deft hand at changing everyone's plate; and that they are ready to compliment you on your talents if I will permit it. I replied that they would make you laugh and me too. If there is any truth in this tale be so good as to tell me all the circumstances."

"Every one, and gladly. But we must observe a certain discretion, for it is a comedy which might be injurious to a person whom I would rather die than harm."

"So the story is true? You make me most curious."

"True and not true. I hope that Your Excellency does not believe I am the waiter at the 'Sword.' "

"No. I should never believe that. You played the part."

"Precisely. Did they tell you there were four of them?"

"I know that. There was the beauty too; and now I see the whole thing. You are quite right, discretion is essential, for her reputation is spotless."

"That I did not know. What happened is perfectly innocent, but it might be told with additions which could injure the honor of that charming woman, whose merits filled me with admiration."

I then told him the whole story, ending by saying that I had come to Soleure only to make her acquaintance and, if possible, to court her.

"If it is not possible," I said, "I will leave in three or four days, but not before seeing the two blabbers covered with ridicule, for they must know very well that the waiter was only a mask. They cannot pretend not to know it, except for the express purpose of putting an affront on me and injuring Madame, who was very ill advised to let them into the secret."

"Softly, softly! So many things at once! Let me embrace you. Your story really delights me. Leave it to me. You shall not go away, my dear friend; you shall court Madame. Permit me to laugh. I have been young, and a pair of beautiful eyes has often made me disguise myself too. Today at table with those two mischief-makers you shall prick their bubble, but good-naturedly. The thing is so innocent that even Monsieur ... will laugh over it. His wife cannot but know that you love her, I presume?"

"She must have seen into my soul even though I did no more than take off her boots."

"Funnier and funnier."

He went away laughing, and at the door of his carriage he embraced me for the third time. Certain, as I could not but be, that Madame ... had told her three companions everything she knew before returning to Zurich, the ... joke[10] with which the two harridans had gone to the Ambassador struck me as both malicious and perfidious; but my heart's interests obliged me to let their calumny pass as wit.

At half past one I enter the Embassy and after making my most humble bow to the Ambassador I see the two ladies. I ask the one who looked the more malicious, who limped, and whose name was F., if she recognizes me.

"Then you admit you are the waiter at the inn in Zurich."

"Yes, Madame. I was for an hour, to have the honor of seeing you close by; and you punished me by never addressing a word to me; I hope I shall not be so unfortunate here, and that you will permit me to pay court to you."

"This is amazing. You played the waiter so well that no one could have guessed you were playing a part. We shall now see if you play your present role as skillfully; and if you will come to call on me I shall be honored."

After this compliment the whole company learned the story; and just then Madame ... arrives with her husband. She sees me and instantly says to him:

"There's the waiter at Zurich."

The worthy man thanks me most politely for having done his wife the honor of taking off her boots. I see that she has told him everything and I am glad. Monsieur de Chavigny seated her on his right, and my place at the table proved to be between the two women who had calumniated me.

Though they both repelled me, I flirted with them, having the firmness scarcely ever to look at Madame ..., who was even more beautiful than she had been in riding clothes. Her husband did not seem either jealous or as old as I had supposed. The Ambassador invited them both to his ball, and he asked her to play the heroine in *L'Écossaise*[11] again, so that I could tell the Duke of Choiseul I had been well entertained at Soleure. She replied that there were two actors missing; he offered to play Lord Monrose and I instantly said I would play Murray. The arrangement infuriating my table companion F., for it left her to play the hateful role of Lady Alton, she let fly a shaft at me.

"Why isn't there a waiter's part in the play?" she said. "You would act it wonderfully well."

"But you," I replied, "will teach me to act the part of Murray still better."

The Ambassador settled on a day five or six days later, and the next morning I was sent my short part. The ball having been announced as in my honor, I returned to my inn for another suit, and I reappeared in the ballroom dressed with the utmost elegance.

I opened the ball, dancing the minuet with a woman who must have had precedence over all the others, then I danced with them all; but the wily Ambassador arranged for me to dance the contra-dances with Madame ..., and no one could object. He said that Lord Murray must dance with no one but Lindane.

At the first pause in the contradance I told her that I had come to Soleure only for her, that but for her I should never have been seen as a waiter, and that hence I hoped she would permit me to pay court to her. She said that there were reasons which forbade her to receive visits from me, but that opportunities to see each other could not fail to arise if I did not leave at once and would refrain from showing her certain attentions which must give rise to talk. Love, readiness, and prudence together could not have made me a more satisfying answer. I promised her all the discretion she could ask. On the instant my love became of heroic mold and thoroughly determined to make secrecy its law.

Having declared that I was a novice in the art of the theater, I asked Madame F. to instruct me. I went to her in the morning, but she thought it was only an excuse. By going, I was paying court to Madame . . . , who was perfectly aware of my motive for acting as I did. She[12] was a widow between thirty and forty years of age, with a malicious temperament, a yellowish complexion, and an awkward walk, because she tried to conceal the fact that she was lame. She was forever talking, and, since she tried to display a wit which she did not possess, she bored me. Nevertheless I had to pretend I was in love with her. She made me laugh one day when she said she would never have thought I was timid by nature after seeing me play the role of waiter so well at Zurich. I asked her what made her suppose me timid, and she did not answer. I had made up my mind to break with her after we had acted *L'Écossaise*.

Our first performance was attended by all the best people in the city. Madame F. was delighted to inspire loathing in her role, being sure that her own person had no part in producing the effect. Monsieur de Chavigny drew tears. People said he had played his part better than Voltaire[13] did. But my blood froze when in the third scene of the fifth act Lindane said to me: "What! You! You dare to love me!"[14] She uttered the seven words so strangely, in a tone of such deliberate scorn, even stepping momentarily out of her part, that the whole audience applauded wildly. The applause nettled and disconcerted me, for I thought her manner had trespassed on my honor. When silence was restored and I, as my role prescribed, had to answer her with, "Yes, I adore you, and I must,"[15] I brought out the words in a tone so moving that the applause redoubled: *Bis, bis* from four hundred voices forced me to repeat them.

But despite the applause we decided at supper that we did not know our parts well enough. Monsieur de Chavigny said that the second performance would be put off until the next day but one and that on the morrow we would hold a private rehearsal at his country house, where we would dine. We congratulated each other on our acting. Madame F. said that I had played my role well, but that I had done even better as the waiter, and the laugh was on her side; but I had it on mine when I replied that she had played Lady Alton excellently, but that it could hardly be otherwise since it required no effort on her part.

Monsieur de Chavigny told Madame . . . that those in the audience who had applauded her for the passage in which she expressed amazement that I should love her had been wrong, since by putting scorn into the words she had stepped out of her part, for Lindane could not but have a high regard for Murray.

The Ambassador came next day to fetch me in his carriage, saying that there was no need for me to use mine. All the actors were assembled at his country house. He at once said to Monsieur . . . that he believed he had settled his business and that they would talk about it after they had dined and rehearsed the play. We sat down at table; and afterward we got through the whole rehearsal without once needing to be prompted. Toward nightfall he told the company that he expected them all for supper at Soleure, and everyone left except Monsieur . . . , with whom he had business to discuss. I had no carriage. At the moment of departure I had a most pleasant surprise:

"Ride in my carriage with me," said the Ambassador to Monsieur . . . , "and we will discuss our business. Monsieur de Seingalt[16] will have the honor of escorting your lady in yours."

I at once give my hand to that miracle of nature, who gets in with an air of the greatest indifference, warmly pressing my hand. So there we are, sitting face to face.

A half hour went by like a minute; but we did not waste it talking. Our mouths joined and did not separate until we were ten paces from the door of the Embassy. She got out first. Her flushed face terrifies me. It not being her natural color, we would reveal our crime to every eye in the room. Her honor did not permit me to expose her in such a state to the scrutiny of Madame F., who would have felt even more triumphant than humiliated by a discovery of such consequence.

It was Love who made me think of a unique expedient, and Fortune, who often favored me, who saw to it that I had in my pocket a small box containing a sternutative.[17] I urged her to take a pinch of it at once, and I did the same. The excessive dose began to produce its effect halfway up the stairs, and we continued to sneeze for a good quarter of an hour; the blame for her tattletale redness was put entirely on her sneezes. When they stopped she said she no longer had a headache but that in future she would beware of taking such a violent remedy. I saw Madame F. lost in thought, but she dared say nothing.

This foretaste of my good fortune decided me to stay in Soleure for as long as it might take me to crown my happiness. I immediately determined to rent a country house. Any man in my situation and endowed with a heart would have made the same resolve. I saw before me a perfect beauty whom I adored, whose heart I was certain I possessed, and whom I had barely touched; I had money, and I was my own master. I thought it far more reasonable than my notion of becoming a monk at Einsiedeln. I was so full of my happiness, present and to come, that I dismissed all thought of "what people would say." I left everyone at the table and sought out the Ambassador a minute after he withdrew. As a man of the world, I could not conscientiously deny the lovable old man his right to a confidence which he had so signally deserved.

As soon as we were alone he asked me if I had profited by the favor he had done me. After kissing his noble countenance several times I told him all in these five words: "I can hope for everything." But when he heard the story of the sternutative the compliments he lavished on me were endless, for the lady's greatly changed physiognomy could have raised the suspicion of a struggle. After my narrative, which made him laugh heartily, I told him that, being under the necessity of crowning my happiness and at the same time sparing the lady's honor, and having nothing better to do, I wanted to rent a country house in which I would calmly wait for Fortune to favor me. I said that I looked to his good offices to obtain me a furnished house, a carriage at my disposal, two manservants, a good cook, and a housekeeper-chambermaid who would attend to my linen. He said that he would look into it. The next day our play went very well, and on the day after he imparted his plan to me as follows:

"I see, my dear friend, that in this intrigue your happiness depends upon your satisfying your passion without in any way injuring Madame ... 's good name. I am even sure you will leave at once without having obtained anything if your departure is necessary to her peace of mind. This will show you that I am just the man to advise you. If you really want not to be found out, you must refrain from the taking of the least step which could make anyone who does not believe that there is such a thing as an action without meaning suspect the truth. Even the most speculative mind cannot take the brief interview which I arranged for you yesterday to be anything but the effect of the purest chance, and the incident of the sternutative foils the deductions of the most penetrating malice, for a lover who wants to make the most of an occasion favorable to his passion does not begin by bringing on convulsions in his beauty's head when a fortunate chance has placed her in his power, and no one can guess that a sternutative was used to hide a reddened face, for it is not often that consummation produces that effect and that a lover foresees it to the point of carrying such a stimulant in his pocket. So what has already happened is not enough to reveal your secret. Monsieur ... himself, who, though he does not want to show jealousy, is nevertheless jealous of his wife, cannot have seen anything out of the way in my having him drive back to Soleure with me, for it is beyond all likelihood that I should wish to be your Mercury, while naturally and in accordance with the rules of the most ordinary politeness, which he has never refused to honor, his dear wife was the person who, on the return journey here, should occupy the place in my vis-à-vis which I kindly let him occupy himself, because of the interest I took in his important business.

"After this long exordium, which I have delivered in the style of a secretary of state speaking in council, let us come to the conclusion. Two things are necessary to set you on the road to fruition. The first, which concerns you, is to contrive to make Monsieur ... your friend without ever giving him cause to suspect that you have designs on his wife. The second, which concerns the lady, is to do nothing which can be observed without making the reason for it known to everyone. So I say to you that you shall not take this country house until, between us, we have hit upon a perfectly plausible reason of a nature to throw dust in the eyes of speculation. I thought of such a reason yesterday when I was considering your case.

"You must pretend to be ill, and think of an illness of which what you say to him will leave the doctor in no doubt. Fortunately I know a doctor whose passion is prescribing country air, with baths of his own composition, for almost every disease. He is to come here one of these days to take my pulse. You shall summon him to your inn for a consultation and give him two louis; I am certain he will at least prescribe the country for you and will tell the whole town that he will surely cure you. Such is Herrenschwandt's[18] way, though he is a learned man."

"What! Is he here? He is a friend of mine.[19] I met him in Paris at Madame du Rumain's."

"This is his brother. Think up an illness which is fashionable and won't disgrace you. We will find the house afterward, and I will give you a young man who will cook excellent dishes for you."

Choosing an illness cost me some thought. I gave Madame . . . an outline of my plan in the wings, and she approved of it. I begged her to find some way by which we could write to each other, and she said she would try. She said that her husband had the highest opinion of me, and that he had seen nothing wrong in my having been in her coupé with her. She asked me if Monsieur de Chavigny had taken her husband with him because it had happened that way or on purpose, and I answered: "On purpose." She raised her beautiful eyes to heaven and bit her lip.

"Are you sorry, my charmer?"

"Alas! . . . no."

Three or four days later the doctor came to see the last performance of *L'Écossaise* and dine at the Ambassador's. He having complimented me at dessert on my look of good health, I said that looks were deceptive and I asked him for a consultation. Delighted that he had been mistaken, he promised me an hour the next day at my inn. He came, and I told him what God put into my mouth.

"I suffer every night," I said, "from amorous dreams which wear me out."

"I know the complaint, Monsieur, and I will cure you of it by two remedies. The first, which you may not much like, is to go and spend six weeks in the country, where you will not see objects which, by stimulating the seventh pair of nerves, bring on the lumbar discharge which must also make you very melancholy when you wake."

"So it does."

"Oh, I know that! The second remedy consists in cold baths, which will keep you amused."

"Are they far from here?"

"They are wherever you please, because I will write you a prescription for them at once. The apothecary will make them up for you."

After writing his prescription and accepting my two louis he left, and before noon the whole town had heard of my illness and my decision to make a stay in the country. Monsieur de Chavigny joked about it at table, telling Herrenschwandt he should forbid me to receive calls from ladies. Monsieur F.[20] said I should be forbidden certain miniatures of which my jewel box was full. Monsieur . . . , who was an anatomist, pronounced the doctor's reasoning splendid. I publicly asked the Ambassador to be so good as to find me a country house, and a cook because I liked to eat well.

Tired of playing a false role which I considered no longer necessary, I stopped calling on Madame F. She took it upon herself to reproach me in no uncertain terms for my inconstancy, saying that I had hoodwinked her. She said she knew all, and she threatened vengeance. I replied that she had nothing to avenge herself for, since I had never wronged her, but that if she was planning to have me murdered I would demand guards. She replied that she was not Italian.

Delighted to have got rid of the viper, I could now turn all my thoughts to Madame . . . . Monsieur de Chavigny, active as ever on my behalf, made Monsieur . . . believe that I was just the person to persuade the Duke of Choiseul, Colonel-General of the Swiss Guards,[21] to pardon a cousin[22] of his who had killed his man in a duel at La Muette.[23] He had told him I could do anything through the Duchess of Gramont; and, informing me of all this, he asked me if I would undertake to apply for the pardon and if I thought I might be successful. It was the sure way to gain Monsieur . . . 's entire friendship. I replied that I could not be certain I would succeed, but that I would gladly undertake it.

He then arranged to have the whole case explained to me in his presence by Monsieur M . . . , who brought all the documents stating the circumstances of the *factum*, which was perfectly simple, to my inn.

I spent most of the night writing a letter intended to persuade first the Duchess of Gramont and then the Duke her father;[24] and I wrote to Madame d'Urfé that the well-being of the Rosicrucian Order depended upon the King's pardoning the officer, who had been obliged to leave the kingdom because of the duel.

The next morning I took the Ambassador the letter which was to be seen by the Duke. He judged it excellent and told me to go and show it to Monsieur . . . , whom I found in his nightcap. Full of gratitude for the interest I was taking in his concerns, he thanked me effusively. He said that his wife was still in bed and asked me to wait and breakfast with her, but I asked him to make her my excuses, for since the post left at noon I had little time.

So I went back to my inn, where I sealed my letters and sent them to the post; then I went and dined alone with the Ambassador, who was expecting me.

After praising my prudence in refusing to wait until Madame ... was up and assuring me that her husband must have become my bosom friend, he showed me a letter from Voltaire thanking him for having played the role of Monrose in *L'Écossaise*, and another from the Marquis de Chauvelin,[25] who was then staying with Voltaire at "Les Délices."[26] He promised to visit him before leaving for Turin, where he was to be Ambassador.

After dinner I went back to my room to dress, for there was to be a reception and supper at "the Court" that day. Such was the name given to the residence of the French Ambassador in Switzerland.

CHAPTER VI

My country house. Madame Dubois.
Base trick which the lame harridan plays on me.
My grievous misfortunes.

As I enter the drawing room I see Madame ... in a corner, poring over a letter. I go to her and apologize for not having waited to breakfast with her; she replies that I did right and adds that if I have not yet taken the country house I need I can do her a favor by deciding on the one her husband will propose to me, probably during supper that evening.

She could say no more, for she was summoned to take a hand at quadrille.[1] I excused myself from playing. At table everyone talked to me about my health and the baths I was to take in a country house I intended to rent. As his wife had forewarned me, Monsieur ... told me about one near the Aar which was charming.

"But," he said, "it has to be rented for at least six months."

I replied that, provided I liked it and should be free to leave when I pleased, I would pay for the six months in advance.

"It has a reception room than which there is none finer in the whole canton."

"So much the better; I'll give a ball in it. Let us go to see it tomorrow morning at the latest. I will come to your house for you at eight o'clock."

"I look forward to it."

Before going to bed I ordered a four-horse berlin, and at eight o'clock I found Monsieur ... ready. He said that he had tried to persuade his wife to come with us, but that she was a slug-a-bed. In less than an hour we reached the fine house,[2] and I thought it marvelous. There were master's rooms enough to lodge twenty. In addition to the reception room, which I admired, there was a retiring room hung with choice engravings. A large garden, a fine orchard, waterworks and fountains, and excellent facilities for baths in the main building. After approving of everything we went back to Soleure. I asked Monsieur ... to make all the arrangements so that I could move in the next day. I saw his wife, who appeared delighted when her husband told her I had liked the house. I said I hoped they would often do me the honor of dining there, and Monsieur ... gave me his word for it. After paying him the hundred louis which were the rent for six months, I embraced him and went, as always, to dine with the Ambassador.

I at once said that in deference to the suggestion his wife had made to me beforehand I had rented the house Monsieur . . . had proposed, and he thought well of it.

"But," he said, "do you really mean to give a ball there?"

"Certainly I do, provided my money can buy me everything I need."

"You'll have no difficulty about that, for you can turn to me for anything your money won't buy you. I see you want to be lavish. In the meanwhile you shall have two menservants, the housekeeper, and the cook; my major-domo will pay them and you can reimburse him; he is honest. I'll come to eat with you from time to time, and I shall listen with pleasure to the delightful story of your current intrigue. I think most highly of the young woman; her conduct is beyond her years, and the proofs of love she gives you must make you respect her. Does she know that I know everything?"

"She knows no more than that Your Excellency knows we love each other, and she takes no exception to that, for she is certain of your discretion."

"She is a charming woman."

An apothecary to whom the doctor sent me left the same day to compound the baths which were to cure me of a disease I did not have; and two days later I went myself, after ordering Leduc to follow with all my luggage. But I was not a little surprised when, on entering the apartment I was to occupy, I saw a young woman, or perhaps a girl, with an extremely pretty face approach me and start to kiss my hand. I draw it back, and my astonished look makes her blush.

"Do you belong to the household, Mademoiselle?"

"His Excellency the Ambassador's major-domo engaged me to serve you as housekeeper."

"Pardon my surprise. Let us go to my bedroom."

As soon as I am alone I tell her to sit down beside me on the couch. She replies in the gentlest and most modest fashion that she could not accept such an honor.

"As you will; but I hope you will make no objection to eating with me when I ask you to, for it bores me to eat alone."

"I will obey you."

"Where is your room?"

"There. It was the major-domo who showed it to me; but it is for you to give what orders you please."

The room was behind the alcove which contained my bed. I go into it with her, and I see dresses on a sofa; next to it a boudoir with all the usual array of petticoats, bonnets, shoes, and slippers, and a fine open trunk in which I see an abundance of linen. I look at her, I try to penetrate her serious manner, I approve of her reserve, but I think I had better subject her to some close questioning, for she was too interesting and too well dressed to be a mere chambermaid. I presume it is a trick Monsieur de Chavigny has played on me, for such a girl, whose age could not be more than twenty-four or twenty-six and who possessed the wardrobe I saw, seemed to me more fit to be the mistress of a man like myself than his housekeeper. I ask her if she knows the Ambassador and what wages she is to have, and she answers that she knows the Ambassador only by sight and that the major-domo had told her she would be paid two louis a month besides meals in her room. She said she was from Lyons, a widow, and that her name was Dubois.

I leave her, unable to decide what will happen, for the more I looked at her and talked with her, the more interesting I found her. I go to the kitchen, and I see a young man kneading dough. His name was Durosier. I had known his brother when he was in the service of the French Ambassador[3] in Venice. He said my supper would be ready at nine o'clock.

"I never eat alone."

"I know that."

"How much are you paid a month?"

"Four louis."

I see two likely-looking, well-dressed menservants. One of them says he will bring me what wine I order. I go to the small bathhouse, where I find the apothecary's apprentice preparing the bath I am to take on the morrow and every day.

After spending an hour in the garden I go to the caretaker's, where I see a numerous family, among them some not unpromising daughters. I spend two hours talking with them, delighted that everyone speaks French. As I wanted to see the whole of my house, the caretaker's wife took me everywhere. I returned to my apartment, where I found Leduc unpacking my luggage. After telling him to give my linen to Madame Dubois, I went to write. It was a pretty study, facing north, with one window. A ravishing view seemed made to inspire the soul of a poet with the most felicitous ideas engendered by the freshness of the air and the palpable silence which soothes the ear in a smiling countryside. I felt that, to enjoy the simplicity of certain pleasures, a man must be in love and fortunate in love. I congratulated myself.

I hear a knock. I see my beautiful housekeeper, who, with a smile quite unlike the one worn by a person who is about to complain, asks me to tell my valet to treat her politely.

"How has he been rude to you?"

"Perhaps not at all by his lights. He wanted to kiss me, I refused, and he, thinking it was his right, became a trifle insolent."

"In what way?"

"He laughed at me. Excuse me, Monsieur, if I resented it. I don't like being sneered at."

"You are right, my dear helpmate. Sneering always comes from either stupidity or malice. Leduc shall be told at once that he is to respect you. You shall sup with me."

Leduc coming to ask me some question half an hour later, I told him he must treat Madame Dubois with respect.

"She's a prude—she wouldn't let me kiss her."

"As for you, you're a blackguard."

"Is she your chambermaid or your mistress?"

"Perhaps she is my wife."

"Well and good. I will go and amuse myself at the caretaker's."

I was well satisfied with my little supper and with an excellent Neuchâtel[4] wine. My housekeeper was accustomed to wine from "La Côte,"[5] which was delicious too. In short, I was well pleased with the cook, with my housekeeper's modesty, and with my Spaniard, who changed her plate for her without putting on airs. After ordering my bath for six o'clock in the morning I told my servants to retire. Thus left alone at table with the too beautiful woman, I asked her to tell me her story.

"My story is very short. I was born in Lyons. My father and mother brought me to Lausanne with them, or so they have told me, for I do not remember it myself. I know I was fourteen when my father, who was coachman to Madame d'Hermenches,[6] died. The lady took me into her household, and three or four years later I entered the service of Lady Montagu[7] as a chambermaid, and her old footman Dubois married me. Three years later I was left a widow at Windsor, where he died. The air of England threatening me with consumption, I asked my generous mistress to let me leave her service, which she granted me, paying for my traveling expenses and giving me some valuable presents. I went back to my mother's house in Lausanne, where I entered the service of an English lady who was very fond of me and who would have taken me to Italy if she had not become suspicious of the young Duke of Roxburghe,[8] who showed signs of being in love with me. She loved him, and she thought I was secretly her rival. She was wrong. She gave me a quantity of presents and sent me back to my mother's, where I have lived for two years by the work of my hands. Monsieur Lebel,[9] major-domo to the Ambassador, asked me four days ago if I wished to enter the service of an Italian nobleman as housekeeper and told me the conditions. I accepted, since I have always had a great desire to see Italy; that desire was the reason for my folly; and here I am."

"What folly?"

"Coming to you without knowing you beforehand."

"Then you would not have come if you had known me beforehand?"

"Certainly not, for I shall no longer be able to find service with a woman. Do you think you are the kind of man to have a housekeeper like me without people's saying that you have me for something else?"

"I expect as much, for you are very pretty and I scarcely look a milksop; but I do not care."

"I wouldn't care either, if my station in life allowed me to defy certain prejudices."

"Which is to say, my beauty, that you would like to go back to Lausanne."

"Not now, for that would be unjust to you. People might believe you had offended me by being too free, and you yourself might reach a wrong conclusion about me."

"What conclusion, if you please?"

"You would conclude that I want to make an impression on you."

"That might be, for your sudden and unreasonable departure would annoy me greatly. Even so, I am sorry for you. Thinking as you do, you can neither want to stay with me nor leave. Yet you must decide one way or the other."

"I have already decided. I shall stay, and I am almost certain that I shall not regret it."

"I like your hope; but there is one difficulty."

"Will you be so good as to explain?"

"I must, my dear Dubois. I cannot abide either melancholy or certain scruples."

"You will never find me melancholy; but please let us come to an understanding on the article of scruples. What do you mean by scruples?"

"I like that. In common usage the word 'scruple' means a superstitious malice which sees vice in an act which may be innocent."

"If an act leaves me in doubt I am not inclined to put a bad construction on it. My duty only bids me watch over myself."

"You have read a good deal, I should think."

"It's the one thing I do, really, for otherwise I'd be bored."

"Then you have books?"

"Many. Do you understand English?"

"Not a word."

"I'm sorry, for they would entertain you."

"I don't like romances."

"No more do I. I like that. What, may I ask, made you decide so quickly that I am romantic?"

"And I like that! Your outburst delights me, and I am glad I have got you to laugh at last."

"Excuse me if I laugh, because—"

"Because me no becauses. Laugh in season and out of season; you'll never find a better way to handle me. I should say you've hired yourself out to me too cheaply."

"I have to laugh again, for it lies with you to increase my wages."

I rose from the table very much surprised by this young woman, who seemed in a fair way to find the chink in my armor. She could reason; and in this first dialogue she had already drained my resources. Young, beautiful, elegantly dressed, and intelligent—where she would lead me I could not guess. I was eager to talk with Monsieur Lebel, who had procured me such a piece of household furniture.

After clearing the table and taking everything into her room, she came to ask me if I used curl papers under my nightcap. It was Leduc's province; but I gladly gave her the preference. She managed it very well.

"I foresee," I said, "that you will serve me as you did Lady Montagu."

"Not quite; but since you do not like melancholy, I must ask you a favor."

"Ask it, my dear."

"I would rather not wait on you in your bath."

"May I die if the thought has entered my head. It would be a scandal. Leduc shall do it."

"Then pray forgive me, and I make bold to ask you another favor."

"Tell me freely whatever it is you want."

"May I have one of the caretaker's daughters sleep with me?"

"If it had ever occurred to me I swear I would have asked you to do just that. Is she in your room?"

"No."

"Go and fetch her."

"I'll do it tomorrow, for if I went now people would start inventing reasons. Thank you."

"You are prudent, my dear. And be sure I will never stand in the way of your being so."

She helped me to undress, and she must have found me perfectly modest; but thinking of my behavior before I fell asleep I saw that it did not spring from virtue. My heart was Madame . . .'s, and the widow Dubois had rather overawed me; perhaps I was her dupe, but I did not dwell on the thought.

In the morning I rang for Leduc, who told me he had not expected to have the honor. I called him a fool. After taking a cold bath I went back to bed, ordering him to bring two cups of chocolate. My helpmate entered, in a very fetching dishabille and all smiles.

"You are in good spirits, my beautiful housekeeper."

"In good spirits because I am very glad to be with you, I slept well, I've been for a walk, and in my room there's a very pretty girl, who will sleep with me."

"Call her in."

I laughed when I saw a girl as ugly as she seemed to be shy. I told her she would drink chocolate with me every morning, and she showed that she was pleased, saying that she liked it very much. In the afternoon Monsieur de Chavigny came and spent three hours with me, and he was satisfied with the whole house but greatly surprised by the housekeeper Lebel had provided for me. He had said nothing to him about her. He thought it was the perfect cure for the love which Madame . . . had inspired in me. I assured him that he was wrong. He addressed her with the utmost politeness.

No later than the next day, just as I was about to sit down at table with my helpmate, a carriage enters my courtyard and I see Madame F.

get out of it. I am surprised and annoyed, but I could not avoid going to meet her.

"I did not expect you would honor me with a visit, Madame."

"I came to ask you to do me a favor, after we have dined."

"Then come at once, for the soup is on the table. Permit me to present Madame Dubois. Madame de F.," I say to the latter, "will dine with us."

My helpmate did the honors of the table, playing the role of hostess like an angel, and Madame F., despite her pride, put on no airs. I did not speak twenty words during the whole dinner nor bestow any attentions on the madwoman, for I was impatient to learn what kind of favor she wanted to ask of me.

As soon as the widow Dubois left us, she told me bluntly that she had come to ask me to let her have two rooms for three or four weeks. Greatly surprised by her effrontery, I reply that I cannot grant her the favor.

"You will grant it, for the whole town knows that I have come here to ask it."

"And the whole town will know that I have refused you. I want to be alone and entirely free; any company at all would be burdensome."

"I will not burden you in any way; you need not even know that I am in your house. I shall not consider it impolite if you do not inquire after my health, and I will not inquire after yours even if you fall ill. I will have my maid cook for me in the small kitchen, and I will not walk in the garden when I know you are there. The apartment for which I ask you is the two last rooms on the second floor, which I can enter and leave by the small stairway without being seen and without seeing anyone. Now tell me if, in strict politeness, you can refuse me the favor."

"If you knew even the rudiments of politeness you would not ask it of me, and you would not insist after hearing me refuse you."

She does not answer, and I stride up and down the room like a maniac. I consider having her put out the door. I think I have the right to treat her as insane, then I reflect that she has relatives, and that she herself, treated without any consideration, will become my enemy and perhaps take some horrible revenge. Finally I think that Madame . . . would disapprove any violent means I might resolve upon to get rid of the viper.

"Very well, Madame," I say, "you shall have the apartment, and an hour after you enter it I will go back to Soleure."

"Then I accept the apartment, and I will move into it day after tomorrow, and I do not believe you will be so foolish as to go back to Soleure on that account. You would set the whole town laughing."

So saying, she rose and left. I let her go without stirring from where I was; but a moment later I repented of having yielded, for her errand and her effrontery were equally beyond all bounds. I called myself stupid, a coward, a fool. I ought not to have taken the thing seriously, I should have laughed at it, made a mock of her, told her clearly that she was mad and forced her to leave, calling in the caretaker's whole family and my servants as witnesses. When I told the widow Dubois what had happened she was amazed. She said behavior of that sort was incredible, and that my giving in to such high-handed proceedings was equally so, unless I had very strong reasons for what I had done.

Seeing that her reasoning was sound, and not wanting to tell her anything, I took the course of saying no more to her on the subject. I went for a walk until suppertime, and I remained at table with her until midnight, finding her ever pleasanter company, full of intelligence and most amusing in all the little stories she told me about herself. Her mind was extremely unprejudiced, but she maintained that if she did not follow the principles of what are called prudence and honor she would be made unhappy. So her good behavior resulted rather from her philosophy than from her virtue; but if she had not been virtuous she would not have had the firmness to practice her philosophy.

I considered my encounter with the F. woman so extraordinary that I could not keep from going the next morning early to regale Monsieur de Chavigny with it. I told my helpmate that she might dine without waiting for me if she did not see me back by the usual hour.

The Ambassador had been informed that Madame F. was coming to see me, but he burst out laughing when I told him how she had succeeded.

"Your Excellency finds it comic, but not I."

"So I see; but, believe me, you must pretend to laugh at it too. Act at all times as if you did not know she was in your house, and she will be sufficiently punished. People will say she is in love with you and that you will have none of her. I advise you to go and tell the whole story to Monsieur... and invite yourself to stay for dinner with him. I have talked with Lebel about your beautiful housekeeper. He meant no harm. Having gone to Lausanne an hour after

I charged him to find you a respectable chambermaid, he remembered it, spoke of you to La Dubois, and the thing was done. It is a lucky find for you, because when you fall in love she won't keep you languishing."

"I don't know, for she has principles."

"I am sure you will not be taken in by them. I will come to you for dinner tomorrow and will enjoy hearing her talk."

"Your Excellency will afford me the greatest pleasure."

Monsieur ... greeted me warmly and at once congratulated me on the admirable conquest[10] which was sure to make my stay in the country a pleasure. Though she suspected the truth, his wife congratulated me too; but I saw that they were both astounded when I told them the whole story in detail. Monsieur ... said that if the woman really became a burden to me I need only ask the government to serve her with an immediate order never to set foot in my house again. I replied that I did not want to employ that resource, since, in addition to being dishonorable to her, it would prove me a weakling, for everyone must know that I was master in my own house and that she could never come to lodge there without my consent. His wife said thoughtfully that I had done well to let her have the apartment and that she would go to call on her, for she had herself told her she would have an apartment in my house the next day. I said no more about it, and, invited to take potluck with them for dinner, I stayed. Since I had shown Madame ... nothing but ordinary politeness, her husband could have no suspicion that we were in communication. She seized an opportunity to tell me that I had done well to let the spiteful woman have the apartment and that I could invite her husband to come and spend two or three days with me after Monsieur de Chauvelin, who was expected, had gone. She also said that the wife of the caretaker of my house was her nurse, and that she would write me through her when the need arose.

After calling on two Italian Jesuits who were passing through Soleure and inviting them to dinner the next day, I went home. My helpmate kept me entertained until midnight with philosophical problems. She was devoted to Locke.[11] She said that the faculty of thought was not a proof of the spirituality of our soul, since God could give the property of thought to matter. I laughed heartily when she said there was a difference between thinking and reasoning.

"I think," I said, "that you would be reasoning well if you let yourself be persuaded to go to bed with me, and you think you are reasoning very well in refusing."

"Believe me," she answered, "that between a man's reason and a woman's there is the same difference that there is between the two sexes."

We were drinking our chocolate at nine o'clock the next morning when Madame F. arrived. I did not even go to the window. She dismissed her carriage and went to her apartment with her chambermaid. Having sent Leduc to Soleure to wait for letters for me, I asked my helpmate to dress my hair, saying that we should have the Ambassador and two Italian Jesuits for dinner. I had already told my cook to prepare good fast-day and meat dishes, it being a Friday. I saw that she was delighted, and she dressed my hair perfectly. After shaving, I offered her my first salutation of the day, and she accepted it with good grace, though she refused me her beautiful lips. It was the first time I kissed her cheeks. Such was the footing on which we lived together. We loved each other, and we were virtuous; but she must have suffered less than I did because of the coquetry which is only too natural to the fair sex and often stronger than love.

Monsieur de Chavigny arrived at eleven o'clock. I had not invited the Jesuits to dinner before consulting him, and I had sent my carriage for them; while waiting we went for a stroll. He asked my housekeeper to join us as soon as she had seen to all her domestic duties. He was one of those men whom France, when she was a monarchy, kept to send, at the proper time and as circumstances demanded, to win over the powers she wished to have embrace her interests. Such was Monsieur de l'Hospital,[12] who was able to gain the heart of Elisabeth Petrovna,[13] such the[14] Duke of Nivernais,[15] who did as he pleased with the Court of St. James's[16] in 1762, such were a number of others whom I knew. Walking in my garden, the Marquis de Chavigny found in my housekeeper all the qualities necessary to make a young man happy; and she enchanted him completely at table, where she overwhelmed the two Jesuits with sallies informed by a humor which was never unkind. After spending the whole day with the greatest enjoyment, he went back to Soleure, asking me to dine with him as soon as he sent me word that Monsieur de Chauvelin had arrived.

That agreeable man, whose acquaintance I had made at the Duke of Choiseul's in Versailles,[17] arrived two days later. He at once recognized me and introduced his charming wife,[18] who did not know me. Since chance put me at the table beside Madame . . . , I was in such high spirits that I said most amusing things. Monsieur de Chauvelin said that he knew some very pleasant stories about me.

"But," replied Monsieur de Chavigny, "you do not know the Zurich story"; and he told it to him.

Monsieur de Chauvelin said to Madame . . . that, to have the honor of serving her, he would have turned coachman, but Monsieur . . . replied that I was far more squeamish, for the lady who had made such an impression on me was staying as my guest in a house I had rented in the country.

"We will pay you a visit," Monsieur de Chauvelin said to me.

"Yes," Monsieur de Chavigny answered, "we will all go together."

And he instantly asks me to lend him my beautiful reception room to give a ball in no later than the following Sunday.

It was thus that the old courtier kept me from undertaking to give the ball myself. It was a piece of braggadocio which would have done me harm. I should have infringed on the right, which was the Ambassador's alone, to entertain these illustrious foreigners during the five or six days they were planning to spend in Soleure; and, besides being a blunder, it would have let me in for a great deal of expense.

In connection with the plays which were acted at Monsieur Voltaire's, the conversation turned to *L'Écossaise*, and my table companion was praised, and blushed, and became as beautiful as a star. The Ambassador invited us all to his ball the next day. I returned home madly in love with the charming woman whom Heaven had destined from birth to cause me the greatest grief I have ever suffered in my life. I leave my reader to judge.

My helpmate had gone to bed when I returned, and I was glad of it, for Madame . . . 's eyes had not left me a grain of reason. She found me sad the next morning, and she rallied me on it with wit tempered by kindness. While we are breakfasting Madame F.'s chambermaid suddenly appears and hands me a note. I tell her I will send an answer. I unseal it and I find:

"The Ambassador has sent me an invitation to his ball. I have replied that I did not feel well, but that if I felt better by evening I would go. I think that since I am in your house, I should go with you or not at all. So if you do not wish to do me the favor of escorting me, I beg you to do me that of saying I am ill. Excuse me if I have thought I might break our agreement in this one instance, for it is a case of at least making a show of good manners in public."

Furious, I take a pen and write:

"You have seized, Madame, on a good subterfuge. It will be announced that you are ill, for I beg to forgo the honor of escorting you, on the principle of enjoying complete freedom."

My housekeeper laughed at the note the lady had written me and declared that she had deserved my reply. I sealed it and sent it to her. I spent a very pleasant night at the ball, for I talked a great deal with the object of my passion. She laughed at my answer to Madame F.'s note, but she disapproved of it—"for," she said, "the poison of anger will circulate through her veins, and God knows what ravages it will make when it bursts out."

I spent the next two days at home, and very early on Sunday the Ambassador's servants came to bring everything needed for the ball and the supper, and to make all the arrangements for the orchestra and for lighting the whole house. The major-domo came to make his bow to me while I was at table. I had him sit down, and I thanked him for the fine present he had made me by giving me such a pleasant housekeeper. He was a handsome man, no longer young, honest, witty, and with his trade at his fingertips.

"Which of you two," he asked us, "is the worse fooled?"

"Neither of us," said the widow Dubois, "for we are equally satisfied with each other."

The first to arrive, about nightfall, was Madame . . . , with her husband. She spoke very politely to my helpmate, without showing the least surprise when I said she was my housekeeper. She said it was my bounden duty to take her to see Madame F., and I had to obey. She received us with every appearance of good will, and she went out for a stroll with us, escorted by Monsieur . . . . After a turn around the garden Madame . . . told me to take her to her nurse.

"But who is your nurse?"

"The caretaker's wife," Monsieur . . . answered; "we will wait for you in Madame's apartment."

"Tell me something," she said on the way. "Your housekeeper certainly sleeps with you."

"No, I swear it. I can love no one but you."

"If that is the case you ought not to keep her, for no one can believe it."

"I do not care, so long as it is not you who believes me to be in love with her."

"I will believe nothing but what you tell me. She is very pretty."

We call on the caretaker's wife, who, addressing her as "daughter," gives her countless caresses; then she goes off to make us a lemonade. Left alone with her, I could do no more than give her fiery kisses, which rivaled hers. She had on only a very light petticoat under a taffeta dress. God, what charms! I am sure that her excellent nurse would not have come back so soon if she could have guessed how much we needed her to delay. But not a bit of it. Never were two glasses so quickly filled with lemonade!

"It was all made, was it?"

"No, Monseigneur; but I am quick."

The innocence of the question and the answer made my beautiful angel burst out laughing. On the way back to Madame F.'s she said that since time was always against us we must wait to seize it until her husband decided to spend three or four days with me. I had already invited him, and he had promised to come.

Madame F. set preserves before us and praised them, especially a quince marmalade which she begged us to taste. We excused ourselves, and Madame ... trod on my foot. She told me afterward that she was suspected of having poisoned her husband.

The ball was magnificent, as was the supper at two tables, each laid for thirty, in addition to the buffet at which more than a hundred people ate. I danced only one minuet with Madame de Chauvelin, having spent almost the whole night talking with her husband, who was highly intelligent. I presented him with my translation of his short poem on the Seven Deadly Sins,[19] which greatly pleased him. When I promised to visit him in Turin he asked me if I would bring my housekeeper with me, and, on my answering no, he said I was making a mistake. Everyone thought her charming. She was urged to dance, but in vain; she told me afterward that if she had accepted, all the women would have hated her. She danced very well.

Monsieur de Chauvelin left on Tuesday, and at the end of the week I received a letter from Madame d'Urfé telling me she had spent two days at Versailles pursuing the matter in which I was interested. She sent me a copy of the pardon signed by the King in favor of Monsieur ... 's cousin. She said that the minister had already sent it to his regiment, thus restoring the culprit to the rank he had held before the duel.

Scarcely have I received her letter before I order my horses harnessed to take me to Monsieur de Chavigny with the news. My soul was flooded with joy, and I did not hide it from the

Ambassador, who congratulated me in the most flattering terms, for through my intervention Monsieur... had obtained, without spending a copper, what he would have paid very dearly for if he had been obliged to buy it. To make the thing appear even more important, I asked the Ambassador to tell the news to Monsieur... himself. He instantly sent him a note asking him to come at once.

The Ambassador received him by handing him a copy of the pardon, at the same time saying that he was indebted for it entirely to me. The worthy man, beside himself with contentment, asked me how much he owed me.

"Nothing except your friendship; but if you wish to give me a token of it, come and spend a few days with me, for I am dying of boredom. The thing you asked me to do for you must have been very easy, for you see how quickly you have been satisfied."

"Very easy? I have been working for a year, moving heaven and earth, and not succeeding; and in two weeks you have accomplished everything. My life is at your disposal."

"Embrace me, and come to see me. I consider myself the happiest of mortals when I can oblige such men as you."

"I must be off now to tell my wife, who will jump for joy."

"Yes, go to her," said the Ambassador, "and come to dinner tomorrow with just the four of us."

The Marquis de Chavigny, an old courtier and a man of intelligence, made some reflections on the court of a monarch, where nothing was easy or difficult in itself, for the one was constantly becoming the other. He knew Madame d'Urfé from having courted her when the Regent loved her in secret. It was he who had nicknamed her Égérie[20] because she said she learned everything from a Genius who was with her every night she slept alone. He then talked to me of Monsieur..., who must have conceived the greatest friendship for me. He was persuaded that the sure way to reach a woman who had a jealous husband was to conquer the husband, because friendship by its very nature excluded jealousy.

The next day at the dinner for four, Madame..., in her husband's presence, showed me a friendliness equal to his, and they promised to come and spend three days with me during the following week.

I saw them arrive one afternoon without having sent me word. When I saw her chambermaid get out of the carriage too, my heart leaped for joy; however, its transports were moderated by two unpleasant announcements: the first, conveyed to me by

Monsieur..., was that he must return to Soleure on the fourth day; the second, conveyed by Madame..., was that Madame F. must constantly be of the company. I at once took them to the apartment which I had chosen for them and which was the most suitable for my plans. It was on the ground floor on the opposite side of the house from mine. The bedroom had an alcove with two beds separated by a partition in which there was a communicating door. It was entered through two anterooms, the door to the first of which gave on the garden. I had the key for all these doors. The chambermaid was to sleep in the room above their bedroom.

Obedient to my goddess's decree, we called on Madame F., who received us very cordially, but who, on the excuse of leaving us free, declined to spend all of the three days in our company. However, she saw fit to yield when I told her that our agreement should be in force only when I was alone. My housekeeper supped in her room without my having had to tell her to do so, and the ladies did not ask about her. After supper I escorted Madame and Monsieur to their apartment, after which I could not avoid escorting Madame F. to hers; but I excused myself from being present at her evening toilet, despite her urging. When I wished her good night she said with a knowing look that after I had behaved so well I deserved to attain what I desired. I made no answer.

The next day toward nightfall I told Madame... that, having all the keys, I could enter her room and her bed at any hour. She replied that she expected to have her husband with her, for he had treated her to the flatteries he always bestowed on her when he had that in mind; but that it could be the next night, for he had never yet wanted to amuse himself two days in succession.

Toward noon we saw Monsieur de Chavigny arrive. A fifth place was quickly laid; but he protested loudly when he learned that my housekeeper was to dine alone in her room. The ladies said he was right, and we all went to make her lay by her needlework. She was the soul of our dinner; she kept us wonderfully entertained with amusing stories about Lady Montagu. When no one was within earshot Madame... told me it was impossible that I did not love her. After saying that I would show her otherwise I asked her to confirm her permission for me to spend two hours in her arms.

"No, my dear, for he told me this morning that the moon changes today at noon."

"Then he has to have permission from the moon to discharge his duty to you?"

"Exactly. According to his astrology, it is the way to preserve his health and to have a boy by the will of Heaven, for if Heaven does not take a hand I see no likelihood of it."

I could only laugh and resign myself to waiting for the next day. When we were taking our stroll she said that the sacrifice to the moon had been made, and that to be perfectly safe and free from any fear she would persuade him to make an extra one, after which he would fall asleep. So, she added, I could come an hour after midnight.

Sure that my happiness was imminent, I surrender to the joy which such a certainty inspires in a lover who has long been in a state of desire. It was the only night in which I could hope, for Monsieur . . . had decided to sleep in Soleure the next day; I could not expect a second night which might have been more animated than the first.

After supper I escort the ladies to their apartments, then retire to my room and tell my helpmate to go to bed, since I have much writing to do.

Five minutes before one o'clock I leave my room, and, the night being dark, I grope my way around half the house. I go to open the door of the apartment in which my angel was; but I find it open, and it does not occur to me to ask why. I open the door of the second antechamber, and I feel a grip. The hand she puts over my mouth tells me I must not speak. We let ourselves fall on the wide couch, and I instantly attain the height of my desires. It was the summer solstice. Having but two hours before me, I did not lose a minute; I used them in giving reiterated proofs of the fire which was devouring me to the divine woman I was sure I held in my arms. I thought that her decision not to wait for me in her bed had been supremely farsighted, since the sound of our kisses might have waked her husband. Her furies, which seemed to exceed mine, raised my soul to heaven, and I felt certain that of all my conquests this was the first in which I could rightly take pride.

The clock tells me I must leave; I get up after giving her the sweetest of kisses, and I return to my room, where I surrender to sleep in perfect contentment. I wake at nine o'clock, and I see Monsieur . . ., who with the greatest satisfaction shows me a letter he had just received from his cousin, telling him his good news. He asks me to come and take chocolate in his room, since his wife is still

683

at her toilet. I quickly put on a dressing gown, and, just as I am starting off with Monsieur . . . , in comes Madame F., who thanks me in a tone of great glee and tells me she is going back to her house in Soleure.

"Wait a quarter of an hour, we are to breakfast with Madame . . . ."

"No, I have just wished her good morning, and I am off. Good-by."

"Good-by, Madame."

No sooner has she left than Monsieur . . . asks me if she has gone mad. There was reason to think so, for, having been treated with perfect politeness, she ought at least to have waited until evening and left with Monsieur and Madame.

We went to take breakfast and indulge in commentaries on her sudden departure. Then we set out to stroll in the garden, where we found my housekeeper, whom Monsieur . . . approached. I thought Madame seemed a trifle depressed, so I ask her if she slept well.

"I did not go to sleep until four o'clock, after sitting up waiting for you in vain. What mishap kept you from coming?"

This question, which I could not possibly expect, freezes my blood. I look at her, I do not answer, I cannot shake off my surprise. It leaves me only when I am horror-struck, guessing that the woman I had held in my arms was F. I instantly withdraw behind the hedge to recover from an agitation which no one can rightly conceive. I felt that I was dying. To keep from falling I leaned my head against a tree. The first idea which came to me, but which I instantly dismissed, was that Madame . . . meant to disavow our meeting; any woman who gives herself to a man in a dark place has the right to deny it, and it may be impossible to convict her of lying; but I knew Madame . . . too well to suppose her capable of such perfidy, of a baseness inconceivable to any woman on earth except those veritable monsters who are the horror and shame of the human race. At the same moment I saw that if she had told me she had waited in vain merely to enjoy my surprise, she would have been lacking in delicacy, for in a matter of this sort the slightest doubt is already a degradation. So I saw the truth. F. had supplanted her. How had she managed it? How had she known? It was something to be reasoned out, and reasoning does not follow from an idea which oppresses the mind until the oppression has lost the greater part of its power. So I am left with the horrible certainty that I have spent two hours in the company of a monster from hell, and the thought which kills me is that I cannot deny having felt happy. That is what I cannot forgive myself, for the difference between the one woman and the other was immense and subject to the infallible tribunal of all my senses; however, sight and hearing could not enter in. But that is not enough for me to forgive myself. Touch alone should have sufficed me. I cursed Love, Nature, and my own cowardly weakness in consenting to receive into my house the monster who had dishonored my angel and made me despise myself. At that moment I sentenced myself to death, but fully determined, before I ceased to live, to tear to pieces with my own hands the Megaera[21] who had made me the most wretched of men.

While I am plunged in this Styx[22] Monsieur ... appears, asking me if I feel ill, and is horrified to see my pallor; he says that his wife had been uneasy over it; I reply that I had left her because of a slight attack of dizziness, and that I already felt well again. We rejoin them. My helpmate gives me *eau des Carmes*[23] and says playfully that what had affected me so strongly was Madame F.'s departure.

When I was again with Madame ... and at a distance from her husband, who was talking with the widow Dubois, I said that what had troubled me was that what she had said was certainly a joke.

"I was not joking, my dear; so tell me why you did not come last night."

At this answer I thought I should drop dead. I could not bring myself to tell her the reality, and I did not know what I should invent to justify myself for not having gone to her bed as we had agreed. Somber and speechless, I was in this state of irresolution when Dubois's little maid came to give her a letter which Madame F. had sent by express messenger. She opens it and gives me the enclosure, which was addressed to me. I put it in my pocket, saying that I will read it at my convenience, they do not urge me, they laugh. Monsieur ... says it is love; I let him chatter on, I gain control of myself; dinner is announced, we go; I cannot eat, but it is laid to my indisposition. I could not wait to read the letter, but I had to find the time. After we get up from table I say that I feel better, and I take coffee.

Instead of getting up the usual game of piquet, Madame ... says that it is cool in the covered walk and we should take advantage of it. I give her my arm, her husband gives his to the widow Dubois, and we go.

As soon as she was certain they could not hear what she had to tell me, she began as follows:

"I am sure you spent the night with that evil woman, and I may, though I don't know how, be compromised. Tell me all, my dear, this is my first intrigue; but if I am to learn from it I must know everything. I am sure that you loved me; alas, do not leave me now to believe that you have become my enemy!"

"Good heavens! I your enemy!"

"Then tell me the whole truth, and above all before you read the letter you have received. I implore you in Love's name to hide nothing from me."

"Here is the whole story in a few words. I enter your apartment at midnight, and in the second anteroom I feel a grip, a hand over my mouth tells me not to speak, I clasp you in my arms, and we fall on the couch together. Do you understand that I must be certain it is you, that I cannot possibly doubt it? So, never saying a word to you, and never hearing you speak to me, I spent the two most delicious hours I have spent in all my life; accursed two hours, the memory of which will make this world hell to me until my last breath. At a quarter past three o'clock I left you. You know all the rest."

"Who can have told the monster that you would come to my room at one o'clock?"

"I have no idea."

"Admit that, among the three of us, I am the most to be pitied and perhaps the only one who is unhappy."

"In God's name never believe that, for I am planning to go and stab her and then kill myself."

"And in the scandal which will follow, to leave me the most unfortunate of all women. Let us be calm. Give me the letter she wrote you. I will read it among the trees, you shall read it afterward. If they saw us reading it we should have to let them read it too."

I give it to her, and return to Monsieur . . . , whom my helpmate was convulsing with laughter. After our dialogue I felt a little more sane. The assurance with which she had insisted on my giving her the monster's letter had pleased me. I was curious about it, yet I felt loath to read it. It could only enrage me, and I feared the effects of a righteous anger.

Madame . . . rejoined us, and after we had separated again she handed me the letter, telling me to read it alone and in a calm frame of mind. She asked me to give her my word of honor that I would do nothing in the matter without first consulting her, sending her word of all my ideas through the caretaker's wife. She said we need not fear that F. would tell what had happened, since she would be the first to publish her own shame, and that our best course was to dissimulate. She made me still more curious to read the letter by saying that the harpy gave me a warning which I must not ignore.

What pierced my soul during my angel's very sensible discourse was her tears, which streamed from her eyes without any distortion of her beautiful face. She tried to moderate my all too visible distress by mingling smiles with her tears; but I saw only too well what was taking place in her noble and generous soul not to understand the pitiable state of her heart from her certainty that the vile F. knew beyond peradventure that there was an illicit understanding between us. It was this which made my despair unbounded.

She left at seven o'clock with her husband, whom I thanked in words so unfeigned that he could not doubt that they sprang from the purest friendship, and really I was not deceiving him. What natural sentiment can prevent a man who loves a woman from feeling the most sincere and affectionate friendship for her husband, if she has one? Many laws only serve to increase prejudices. I embraced him, and when I started to kiss Madame's hand he generously asked me to do her the same honor. I went to my room impatient to read the letter from the harpy who had made me the most wretched of men. Here it is, in a faithful copy, except for a few expressions which I have corrected:

"I left your house, Monsieur, sufficiently content, not because I had spent two hours with you, for you are not different from other men and in any case my whim was only something to amuse me, but because I have avenged myself for the public marks of contempt which you have shown me, for I have forgiven you the private ones. I have avenged myself on your scheming by unmasking your designs and the hypocrisy of your..., who in future can no longer look down on me with the show of superiority which she borrowed from her pretended virtue. I have avenged myself by making her wait up for you all last night, as she must have done, and by the comic dialogue between you this morning in which you must have let her know that I had appropriated what was intended for her, and by your no longer being able to believe her a miracle of nature, for if you took me for her I cannot be in any way different from her, and hence you must be cured of the mad passion which possessed you and made you adore her in preference to all other women. If I have opened your eyes you are indebted to me for a good deed; but I dispense you from any gratitude, and I even permit you to hate me,

687

provided your hatred leaves me in peace, for if in future I consider your behavior insulting I am capable of coming out with the whole story, having nothing to fear on my account, for I am a widow, my own mistress, and in a position to laugh at what anyone may say about me. I need no one. Your . . . , on the other hand, is obliged to keep up a front. But here is a warning I give you, to convince you that I am kind.

"Know, Monsieur, that for ten years I have had a slight indisposition which I have never been able to cure. You did enough last night to contract it; I advise you to take remedies at once. I warn you, so that you will be careful not to transmit it to your beauty, who in her ignorance might give it to her husband, and to others, which would make her miserable, and I should be sorry, for she has never harmed me or wronged me. Since I thought it impossible that the two of you would not cuckold the dear man, I came to stay in your house only to convince myself by clear evidence that my conclusion was not unfounded. I carried out my plan without needing anyone's help. After spending two whole nights in vain on the couch which you well know, I resolved to spend a third there too, and it crowned my enterprise with success. No one in the house ever saw me, and my chambermaid herself does not know the purpose of my nocturnal wanderings. Hence it lies with you to bury the episode in silence, and I advise you to do so.

"P.S.—If you need a doctor, impress discretion upon him, for it is known in Soleure that I suffer from this little ailment, and people might say you got it from me. That would be insulting."

The calculated insolence of this letter struck me as so out of all proportion that it almost made me laugh. I knew perfectly well that F. could only hate me, after the way in which I had treated her; but I should never have believed that she could carry her revenge to such lengths. She had given me her disease; I could not yet see the symptoms, but I had no doubt of it; the misery of having to cure it already possessed me. I had to give up my love affair, and even go away to be cured to avoid the gossip of malicious tongues. The prudent decision I reached in two hours of dark meditation was to say nothing, but with the firm determination to have my revenge the moment an opportunity arose.

Having eaten nothing at dinner, I really needed to sup well and get a sound sleep. I sat down at table with my helpmate, whom, in the sorrow of my soul, I never once looked in the face all through supper.

CHAPTER VII

The preceding chapter continued.
I leave Soleure.

But as soon as the servants had gone and we were left sitting face to face, the young widow, who was beginning to love me because I made her happy, took it upon herself to make me talk.

"Your sadness," she said, "is not like you, and it frightens me. It might relieve you to confide your concerns to me. I ask it only because you interest me; I might be able to help you. Be sure of my discretion. To encourage you to speak freely and to have some confidence in me, I can tell you everything I now know about you without having made any inquiries or used any of the other means by which an indiscreet curiosity could pry into what it is not for me to know."

"Very well, my dear. Your frankness pleases me; I see that you are my friend, and I am grateful to you for it. So begin by telling me frankly all that you know about the things which are troubling me at this moment."

"Gladly. You and Madame ... are lovers. Madame F., who was here, and whom you treated very badly, played some spiteful trick on you, which, I think, very nearly resulted in a misunderstanding between you and Madame ...; then she left your house with a rudeness which nothing can condone. This upsets you. You fear there will be further consequences; you are painfully aware that you must decide on a course; your heart and your mind are at odds, passion and sentiment war in you. I'm not sure. I am only guessing. What I am sure of is that yesterday you looked happy, and today I feel you are to be pitied, and I feel it because the friendship you have inspired in me could not be greater. I outdid myself today keeping Monsieur ... amused, I tried my best to entertain him, so that he would leave you free to talk with his wife, who seems to me well worthy to possess your heart."

"All that you have said is true; your friendship is precious to me, and I value your intelligence. Madame F. is a monster who has made me wretched in order to avenge herself for my scorn; and I cannot take any revenge on her. Honor forbids me to tell you more; besides, neither you nor anyone else can possibly give me advice which could lift the burden of my grief from me. I may well die of it, my dear; but meanwhile I beg you to remain my friend and always to talk to me with the same sincerity. I will always listen to you attentively. This is the way in which you can be useful to me, and I shall be grateful to you for it."

I spent a cruel night, which has always been a most unusual thing for a man of my temperament. Righteous anger alone, mother of the desire for revenge, has always sufficed to keep me awake, and sometimes, too, the announcement of a great happiness which I did not expect. Intense satisfaction deprives me of the comfort of sleep, and of appetite as well. Otherwise, even in the greatest anguish of mind, I have always eaten well and slept still better; in consequence, I have always extricated myself from situations to which, but for that, I should have succumbed. I rang for Leduc very early; the little girl came to tell me Leduc was ill and that Madame Dubois would bring me my chocolate.

She came, and she said I looked like a corpse and that I had done well to forgo my baths. No sooner had I drunk my chocolate than I vomited it up, for the first time in my life. It was my helpmate who had made it for me; otherwise I should have believed that F. had poisoned me. A minute later I vomited all that I had eaten for supper and, with great effort, a bitter, green, viscous phlegm which convinced me that the poison I had vomited had been administered by black rage, which, when it is strong enough, kills the man who denies it the revenge it demands. It was demanding F.'s life, and, but for the chocolate which drove it out, it would have killed me. Exhausted by my efforts, I saw my helpmate crying.

"Why are you crying?"

"I don't know what you may think."

"Be easy, my dear. I think that my condition is gaining me the continuance of your friendship. Leave me, for now I hope to sleep."

And in fact I woke restored to life. I was happy to find that I had slept for seven hours. I ring, my helpmate comes in and tells me that the surgeon from the next village wants to speak with me. She had come in very sad; suddenly I see her become cheerful, I ask her the reason, and she says that she sees me brought back to life. I tell her we will dine after I have heard what the surgeon has to say. He comes in and, after looking all around the room, whispers in my ear that my valet has the pox. I burst out laughing, for I expected something terrible.

"My dear friend, take care of him and spare no expense; I will recompense you generously; but next time don't put such a long face on your confidences. How old are you?"

"Eighty in a few days."

"God preserve you!"

As I feared that I was in the same condition, I felt sorry for my poor Spaniard, who, after all, was having the accursed plague for the first time, whereas I was at something like my twentieth.[1] It is true that I was fourteen years older than he.

My helpmate, coming back to dress me, asks me to tell her what the old fellow had said to make me laugh so hard.

"Gladly; but first tell me if you know the meaning of the word 'pox.' "

"I do. One of Lady Montagu's couriers died of it."

"Excellent; but pretend you don't know. Leduc has it."

"Poor fellow! And is that what made you laugh?"

"It was because the surgeon made such a mystery of it."

After combing my hair she said that she, too, had a great confidence to make to me, after which I must either forgive her or dismiss her on the spot.

"More trouble! What the devil have you done? Out with it!"

"I robbed you."

"What! When? How? Can you give it back? I didn't think you were a thief. I never forgive thieves, or liars either."

"How hasty you are! Yet I am sure you will forgive me, for I robbed you only half an hour ago, and I will restore it to you this minute."

"If it was only half an hour ago, you deserve a plenary indulgence, my dear; now give me back what you have no right to keep."

"Here it is."

"F.'s letter? Have you read it?"

"Of course. That was my theft."

"Then you have stolen my secret, and the theft is of the gravest because you can't restore what you took. O my dear Dubois, you have committed a great crime."

"I know it. Such a theft cannot be made good; but I can assure you that what I took shall remain in me as if I had utterly forgotten it. You must forgive me, quickly, quickly."

"Quickly, quickly! You are a strange creature. Quickly, quickly, then, I forgive you, and I embrace you; but in future refrain not only from reading but even from touching my papers. I have secrets[2] which I am not free to divulge. So forget the horrors you have read."

"Listen, please. Permit me not to forget them, and you may be the gainer. Let us discuss this terrible business. It made my hair stand on end. The monster has dealt your soul a mortal blow and your body another, and the foul creature has got Madame . . . 's honor in her keeping. This, my dear master, I think her greatest crime; for, despite the affront, your love will survive, and the disease the harridan has given you will go away; but Madame . . . 's honor, if the foul creature does what she threatens to do, is lost forever. So do not order me to forget, but on the contrary let us discuss the situation and try to find a remedy. Believe me, I am worthy of your trust and I am sure that before long I shall win all your esteem."

I thought I was dreaming when I heard a young woman of her station in life talk to me more sensibly than Minerva did to Tele-machus.[3] It took no more than what she had just said to gain her not only the esteem for which she hoped but my respect as well.

"Yes, my dear friend," I said, "let us consider how to deliver Madame . . . from the danger which threatens her, and I am grateful to you for believing that it is not impossible. Let us think of it and talk of it day and night. Continue to love her, and forgive her for her first misstep, guard her honor, and pity my state; be my true friend, cease to use the odious title of 'master,' and replace it by that of 'friend'; I shall be that to you so long as I live, I swear it. Your wise words have won my heart; come to my arms."

"No, no, there's no need for that; we are young and we could only too easily be led into offending. To be happy I want only your friendship, but I do not want it for nothing. I want to deserve it by convincing proofs which I shall give you of mine. I will go and order dinner served, and I hope you will feel perfectly well after it."

So much discretion astonished me. It might be assumed; for after all to counterfeit it the widow Dubois had only to know its prin-ciples; but that was not what troubled me. I foresaw that I should fall in love with her and risk becoming the dupe of her morality, which her self-esteem would never let her abandon even if she fell in love with me in the full sense of the word. So I decided to leave my budding love unfed. Leaving it forever in infancy could not but make it die of boredom. Boredom kills the young. At least such was my hope. I forgot that it is impossible to feel nothing but friendship for a woman whom one thinks pretty, whom one sees constantly, and whom one suspects of being in love. Friendship at its apogee becomes love, and, relieving itself by the same sweet mechanism which love needs to make itself happy, it rejoices to have become stronger after the fond act. This is what befell the fond Anacreon[4] with Smerdies, Cleobulus, and Bathyllus.[5] A Platonist[6] who maintains that one can be merely the friend of a pleasing young woman with whom one lives is a visionary. My housekeeper was too attractive and too intelligent; it was impossible that I should not fall in love with her.

We did not begin to talk until we had eaten a good dinner, for there is nothing more imprudent and dangerous than talking in the presence of servants, who are always malicious or ignorant, who misunderstand, who add and subtract, and who think they are privileged to reveal their masters' secrets without being taken to task for it because they know them without having been entrusted with them.

My helpmate began by asking me if I was sufficiently convinced of Leduc's loyalty.

"He is, my dear, a rascal at times, a great libertine, brave, even daring, quick-witted and ignorant, a brazen liar whom no one but myself can shake. With all his faults the scoundrel has one great good quality—whatever orders I give him he carries out blindly, braving any danger to which his obedience may expose him; he defies not only the cudgel but even the gallows if he sees it only in the distance. When I am traveling and it becomes necessary to know if I can risk fording a river in my carriage, he undresses without a word from me and sounds the bottom swimming."

"That will do. He is all you need. I announce to you, my dear friend—for so you will have me call you—that Madame ... has nothing more to fear. Do as I tell you, and if Madame F. will not behave herself she will be the only one to be dishonored. But without Leduc we can do nothing. However, we must first learn the whole story of his pox, for there are several things which could thwart my plan. So go at once and find out from him yourself, and above all learn if he has told the servants about his misfortune. After you have learned everything, order him to keep the strictest silence concerning your interest in his illness."

Not racking my brains to guess her plan, I immediately go up to Leduc's quarters. I find him alone and in bed, I sit quietly down beside him and promise to get him cured provided he will tell me, without deviating from truth in anything, every least circumstance of the disease he had caught. He said that on the day he had gone to

Soleure to fetch my letters he had dismounted halfway along the road to drink a glass of milk at a dairy where he had found an accommodating peasant girl who in only a quarter of an hour had bestowed on him what he instantly showed me. What was keeping him in bed was a great swelling of one testicle.

"Have you confessed this to anyone?"

"To no one, for I should be laughed at. Only the surgeon knows of my illness; but he doesn't know whom I caught it from. He told me he would rid me of the swelling at once, and that I can wait on you at table tomorrow."

"Very good. Continue to say nothing."

As soon as I repeated all this to my Minerva, she asked me these questions:

"Tell me if Madame F. can really swear that she spent those two hours on the couch with you."

"No, for she neither saw me nor heard me speak."

"Good. Then answer her infamous letter at once, saying that she has lied because you never left your room, and that you are going to make all necessary inquiries in your household to learn who the poor wretch is whom she infected without knowing him. Write, and send her the letter this instant; and in an hour and a half you shall send her a second letter, which I will now write and you shall copy."

"My charming friend, I see your ingenious plan; but I gave Madame . . . my word of honor that I would take no steps in the matter without telling her beforehand."

"Then there's nothing for it but to break your word of honor. It is love which keeps you from going as far as I do; but everything hinges on speed and on the time between the first letter and the second. Do it, my dear friend, and you shall know the rest when you read the letter I am going to write. Write the first one now."

What made me act was nothing short of an enchantment, which I cherished. Here is a copy of the letter I wrote in the firm persuasion that my helpmate's plan was unparalleled:

"The shamelessness of your letter is as surprising as the three nights you spent convincing yourself that your vile suspicion had a foundation. Know, monster from hell, that I did not leave my room, so you spent the two hours with God alone knows whom; but I may find out, and I will inform you. Give thanks to Heaven that I did not unseal your infamous letter until Monsieur and Madame . . . had gone. I received it in their presence, but scorning the hand which had written it I put it in my pocket, and neither of them asked about

694

it. If they had read it I would certainly have pursued you and killed you with my own hands, woman unworthy of life. I am perfectly well, but I have no intention of convincing you of it to prove that it was not I who enjoyed your carcass."

After showing it to the widow Dubois, who approved of it, I sent it to the wretch who had made me wretched. An hour and a half later I sent her this one, which I simply copied without adding a word to it:

"A quarter of an hour after I wrote to you the surgeon came to tell me that my valet needed his services because of a discharge he had recently contracted and symptoms which showed that he had absorbed the venomous poison of the pox. I ordered him to take care of him; and later I went alone to see the patient, who, not without some reluctance, confessed to me that it was from you he had received the fine gift. He told me that, having seen you enter Madame . . .'s apartment alone and in the dark after he put me to bed, he became curious to see what you were doing there, for if you had wished to call on the lady herself, who at that hour must be in bed, you would not have gone in by the door onto the garden. After waiting an hour to see if you would come out, he decided to go in too when he saw that you had left the door ajar. He swore to me that he did not go in with any idea of enjoying your charms, which I had no difficulty in believing, but to see if it was not some other man on whom that good fortune was being bestowed. He assured me that he nearly shouted for help when you seized him, putting one hand over his mouth, but that he changed his mind when he found himself pulled down on the couch and covered with kisses. He said that, feeling certain that you took him for someone else, he had done his duty by you for two hours on end in a manner which should have earned him a very different reward from the one you gave him, whose dismal symptoms he saw the next day. He left you, still without having spoken, at the first ray of dawn, fearing he would be recognized. Nothing could be easier than that you should have taken him for me, and I congratulate you on having enjoyed in imagination a pleasure which, being what you are, you would certainly never have obtained in reality. I warn you that the poor fellow is determined to pay you a visit, and that I cannot stop him; so be gentle with him, for he might tell the story, and you must realize the consequences of that. He will himself acquaint you with his demands, and I advise you to grant them."

I sent it to her, and an hour later I received her answer to the first letter, which, having contained only ten or twelve lines, was not long. She said that my scheme was ingenious, but that it would get me nothing, since she was sure of the facts. She defied me to visit her within a few days to convince her that the state of my health was different from hers.

At supper my helpmate told me stories meant to cheer me up, but I was too gloomy to respond to them. We were now to take the third step which was to crown our work and drive the shameless F. to the wall; and since I had written the two letters in obedience to her instructions, I saw that I must obey her to the end. It was she who told me what orders I was to give Leduc when I summoned him to my room in the morning. She wanted to have the satisfaction of hiding in the alcove behind the curtains so that she could herself hear me tell him what to do.

So, having summoned him, I asked him if he was fit to ride to Soleure on an errand which was of the utmost importance to me.

"Yes, Monsieur; but the surgeon insists that I begin taking baths tomorrow."

"So you may. You will leave at once for Madame F.'s in Soleure, you will not have yourself announced as coming from me because she must not know that I have sent you to her. Say that you need to speak with her. If she will not receive you, wait in the street; but I think she will receive you, and even without witnesses. You will tell her that she has given you the pox without your asking her for it, and that you insist on her giving you the money you need to regain your health. You will tell her that she kept you at work for two hours in the dark without recognizing you, and that but for the nasty present she gave you, you would never have spoken; but that, finding yourself in the state which you will show her, she should not blame you for having come to her. If she resists, threaten to take her to court. That is all. You will come back without losing a minute to tell me what she answers you."

"But if she has me thrown out of the window, I shan't be back very soon."

"You need have no fear of that; I give you my word for it."

"It is a strange errand."

"You are the only person in the world who can carry it off."

"I am ready; but there are a few questions I need to ask. Has the lady really got the pox?"

"Yes."

"I'm sorry for her. But how am I to tell her she gave it to me when I've never talked with her?"

"Talking isn't the way it's given, you nincompoop. You spent two hours with her in the dark and without talking; she will learn that she gave it to you when she thought she was giving it to someone else."

"Now I begin to see it. But if we were in the dark, how can I know it was she I was with?"

"You saw her go in; but you can be sure she will not ask you any questions."

"I will be off at once. I'm more curious than you are to hear what she'll answer me. But here is something else I need to know. She may try to haggle over the money she is to give me for a cure; and in that case please tell me if I shall be content with a hundred écus."

"That's too much in Switzerland; fifty are enough."

"It's not much for two hours' work."

"I'll give you another fifty."

"That sounds more like it; I am off, and I think I understand everything. I won't say so, but I'll wager it's you to whom she gave the present, that you are ashamed of it and want to deny it."

"Possibly. Keep your mouth shut and go."

"Do you know, my friend, that he is a clown in a thousand?" said my helpmate, coming out of the alcove. "I almost burst out laughing when he told you he wouldn't be back soon if she had him thrown out of the window. I am sure he will do the thing marvelously well, and by the time he gets to Soleure she will already have sent off her answer to the second letter. I'm very curious to see it."

"You are the author of this farce, my dear; it is sublime, plotted in masterly fashion. One would not attribute it to a young woman with no experience in intrigues."

"Yet it is my first, and I hope it will succeed."

"If only she doesn't challenge me to show her that I am well."

"But you feel well so far, I think."

"Very well."

"It would be a good joke, if it weren't true that she must at least have the whites."[7]

"In that case I should have no fears for my health; but what would happen to Leduc? I cannot wait to see the end of the play, for the peace of my mind."

"You shall write it, and send it to Madame . . . ."

"There's no doubt of that. You understand I must say I am the author; but I will not cheat you out of the reward your work deserves."

"The reward I want is for you to have no more secrets from me."

"That's odd. How can you be so interested in my concerns? I cannot see you as naturally curious."

"That is an ugly fault. You will only make me curious when I see that you are sad. Your considerate behavior toward me is the reason I am fond of you."

"I am really touched, my dear. In future I promise I will confide to you anything that can keep you from being uneasy."

"Oh, how happy I shall be!"

An hour after Leduc left, a man arrived on foot and gave me a letter from F. and a package, saying that he was to wait for the answer. I told him to wait outside. My helpmate being present, I asked her to read the letter and myself went to the window. My heart was pounding. She called me when she had read it and said that all was well. Here is the letter:

"Whether all that you tell me is true or is an invention of your scheming mind—of which, unfortunately for you, all Europe is informed—I accept as true what I cannot deny has the appearance of truth. I am in despair that I have harmed an innocent person, and I willingly pay the penalty. I beg you to give him the twenty-five louis which I send you; but will you be generous enough to use all your authority as his master to bind him to the strictest silence? I hope so, for, knowing me as you do, you must fear my vengeance. Consider that if the story of this farce comes out I can easily put it in a light which will cause you distress and open the eyes of the honest man whom you are deceiving; for I will never let it drop. As it is my wish that we do not meet again, I have found an excuse to visit my relatives in Lucerne tomorrow. Write me if you receive this letter."

"I am sorry," I said to my helpmate, "that I made Leduc go, for she is a violent woman and something regrettable may happen."

"Nothing will happen. Send back her money at once. She will give it to him in person, and your revenge will be complete. She can have no more doubts. You will know all when he comes back in two or three hours. Everything has gone perfectly, and the honor of the charming and noble woman whom you love is completely safe. You have now only the unpleasant certainty that you bear the wretched creature's disease in your blood; but I think it is no great matter and can easily be cured, for persistent whites cannot be called the pox, and indeed it is not often, as I learned in London, that the whites are transmitted. We can also be very glad that she leaves tomorrow for Lucerne. Laugh, my dear friend, I beg you, for our play is still a comedy."

"Alas, it is a tragedy. I know the human heart; Madame . . . can no longer love me."

"It is true that some change—but this is not the time to think of that. Quick, answer her in a few lines and send her back the twenty-five louis."

Here is my brief answer:

"Your base suspicion, your horrible plan for revenge, and the shameless letter you wrote me are the reasons for your present repentance. Our messengers crossed, and it is not my fault. I send back your twenty-five louis. I could not stop Leduc from going to see you; but you can easily appease him. I wish you a good journey, and I promise to avoid any chance of seeing you. Learn, wicked woman, that the world is not entirely peopled by monsters who set traps for the honor of those who hold honor dear. If at Lucerne you see the Papal Nuncio,[8] mention me to him and you will learn what opinion Europe holds of my mind. I can assure you that my valet has told no one the story of his present indisposition, and that he will continue not to tell it if you have received him well. Good-by, Madame."

After having the widow Dubois read my letter, of which she approved, I sent it off with the money.

"The play is not yet over; we still have three scenes: the Spaniard's return, the appearance of your painful symptoms, and Madame . . .'s astonishment when she learns the whole story."

But two hours pass, then three and four, then the whole day, and Leduc does not appear, and I am thrown into real anxiety, although the widow Dubois, never yielding an inch, kept saying he could only be so late because he had not found F. at home. There are characters incapable of foreseeing disaster. Such was I until the age of thirty when I was imprisoned under the Leads. Now that I am entering my dotage everything I foresee is black. I see it in a wedding to which I am invited, and at the coronation[9] of Leopold II, I said: *Nolo coronari* ("I do not want to be crowned"). Accursed old age, fit to inhabit hell, where others have already placed it: *tristisque senectus* ("wretched old age").[10]

At half past nine, by the light of the moon, my helpmate saw Leduc riding up at a walk. I had no candle, she stationed herself in the alcove. He came in, saying that he was dying of hunger.

"I waited for her," he said, "until half past six, and, when she saw me at the foot of the stairs, she said she had nothing to say to me. I replied that it was I who had something to say to her, and she stopped to read a letter which I saw was in your handwriting, and she put a package in her pocket. I followed her into her room, where, finding no one present, I told her she had given me the pox and that I asked her to pay the doctor for me. I was getting ready to show her proof, but, looking away, she asked me if I had been waiting for her long; and when I replied that I had been in her courtyard from eleven o'clock, she went out, and, having learned from the servant whom it seems she sent here the hour at which he had got back, she returned and, closing the door, gave me this package, saying that I would find twenty-five louis in it to cure me if I was sick and adding that if I loved my life I must refrain from talking to anyone at all on the subject. I left, and here I am. Is the package mine?"

"Yes. Go to bed."

My helpmate then came out in triumph, and we embraced. The next morning I saw the first symptom of my wretched disease; but three or four days later I saw that it amounted to very little. A week later, after taking only *eau de nitre*,[11] I was entirely rid of it—quite unlike Leduc, who was in a very bad state.

I spent the whole morning of the next day writing to Madame . . . , telling her in great detail all that I had done despite the promise I had made her. I sent her copies of all the letters, and everything necessary to prove to her that F. had left for Lucerne convinced that her revenge had been entirely imaginary. I ended my twelve-page letter by confessing that I had just found I was ill but assuring her that in two or three weeks I should be completely well. I gave my letter to the caretaker's wife with the greatest secrecy, and on the next day but one I received eight or ten lines from her telling me that I would see her during the week with her husband and Monsieur de Chavigny.

Alas for me! I had to renounce any idea of love; but the widow Dubois, my only companion, who, Leduc being ill, spent every hour of the day with me, was beginning to preoccupy me too greatly. The more I abstained from attempting anything, the more I fell in love with her, and it was in vain I told myself that by dint of seeing her constantly and letting nothing come of it I should at last become indifferent to her. I had presented her with a ring, saying that I would give her a hundred louis for it if she ever wanted to sell

700

it, and she assured me that she would not dream of selling it until she was in need after I had dismissed her. The idea of dismissing her seemed nonsense. She was unspoiled, sincere, amusing, with a natural intelligence which enabled her to reason in the soundest manner. She had never loved, and she had married an old man only to please Lady Montagu.

She wrote to no one but her mother, and I read her letters to please her. Having asked her one day to show me the replies, I could not help laughing when she said she did not answer her because she had never learned to write.

"I thought she was dead," she said, "when I came back from England, and it made me very happy when I reached Lausanne and found her in perfect health."

"Who escorted you?"

"No one."

"It is unbelievable. Young, with the figure you have, well dressed, thrown in the company of so many different kinds of people, young men, libertines, for they are everywhere—how were you able to defend yourself?"

"Defend myself? I never needed to. The great secret is never to look at anyone, to pretend not to hear, not to answer, and to lodge alone in a room, or with the hostess when one happens on a decent inn."

She had not had an adventure in all her life, she had never strayed from her duty. She had never had the misfortune—so she put it—to fall in love. She kept me amused from morning to night without a sign of prudery, and we often addressed each other as *"tu."* She talked to me admiringly of Madame . . . 's charms, and she listened with the utmost interest when I recounted my vicissitudes in love, and when I came to certain descriptions and she saw that I was concealing some too piquant circumstances, she urged me to tell her everything plainly with a charm so potent that I had to satisfy her. When my overfaithful descriptions were too much for her, she burst out laughing, got up, and after putting her hand over my mouth to keep me from going on, she ran away to her room, where she locked herself in to prevent me, she said, from coming to ask her for what at those moments she was only too desirous of granting me; but she did not tell me all this till we were in Bern. Our great friendship had reached its most dangerous period just when F. tainted me.

After supper on the day preceding the one on which Monsieur de Chavigny unexpectedly came to dine at my house with

Madame ... and her husband,[12] my helpmate asked me if I had been in love in Holland. I thereupon told her what had happened to me with Esther; but when I came to my examining her *labia minora* to find the little mark which she alone knew, my charming house-keeper ran to me to stop my mouth, shaking with laughter and falling into my arms. At that I could not refrain from searching her so-and-so for some mark, and in her spasms of laughter she could offer me very little resistance. Not being able to proceed to the great conclusion because of my health, I begged her to help me to a crisis which had become a necessity for me, at the same time doing her the same sweet service. It lasted scarcely a minute, and our curious eyes took their amorous but inactive share in it. After it was over she said, laughing but at the same time serious:

"My dear friend, we love each other, and if we are not careful we shall not long confine ourselves to mere trifling."

So saying, she rose, gave a sigh, and after wishing me good night went off to sleep with the little girl. It was the first time that we let our senses carry us away. I went to bed knowing that I was in love and foreseeing all that was bound to happen to me with this young woman, who had already gained a very strong hold on my heart.

We were pleasantly surprised the next morning to see Monsieur de Chavigny with Monsieur and Madame .... We strolled until dinnertime, then sat down at table with my dear Dubois, by whom I thought my two male guests were enchanted. Strolling after dinner, they never left her side; and for my part I had all the time I needed to repeat to Madame ... the whole story I had written her, though I did not tell her it was Dubois who deserved the credit, for it would have mortified her to learn that her weakness was known to her.

Madame ... told me that she had taken the greatest pleasure in reading the whole account simply because F. could no longer believe she had spent the two hours with me.

"But how," she asked, "were you able to spend two hours in that woman's company without knowing, even despite the dark, that it was not I? I am humiliated that the difference between her and me had no effect on you. She is shorter than I am, much thinner, and what amazes me is that her breath is foul. Yet you were deprived only of sight, and everything escaped you. It is unbelievable."

"I was intoxicated with love, my dear; then, too, the eyes of my soul saw only you."

"I understand the power of imagination, but imagination should have lost all its power in the absence of one thing which you knew beforehand you would find in me."

"You are right; it is your beautiful bosom, and when I think today that all I had in my hands was two flabby bladders I want to kill myself."

"You were aware of it, and it did not disgust you?"

"Sure that I was in your arms, how could I find anything in you disgusting? Even the roughness of the skin and the too commodious retiring room did not have the power to make me doubt or to lessen my ardor."

"What are you saying! Loathsome woman! Foul, stinking sewer! I cannot get over it. Could you forgive all that in me?"

"Since I believed I was with you, everything could not but seem divine."

"Not at all. Finding me such, you should have thrown me on the floor, even beaten me."

"Ah, my love! How unjust you are now!"

"That may well be, my dear, I am so angry with the monster that I do not know what I am saying. But now that she has given herself to a servant, and after the mortifying visit she could not refuse, she must be dying of shame and anger. What amazes me is her believing him, for he is four inches shorter than you; and can she really believe that a valet could do the thing as you must have done it to her? I am sure that she is in love with him even now. Twenty-five louis! It's obvious. He would have been satisfied with ten. How lucky that the fellow was so conveniently ill! But did you have to tell him everything?"

"How can you think so! I let him suppose she had arranged to meet me in the anteroom and that I really spent two hours with her. Reasoning from what I ordered him to do, he saw that, in my disgust at knowing I was infected, and being in a position to deny the whole thing, I had hit on a plan which would punish her, avenge me, and keep her from ever boasting that she had possessed me."

"It's a delightful comedy. The fellow's impudence is astonishing and his boldness even more so, for F. could have lied about being ill, and then you see what a risk he took."

"It occurred to me, and it gave me some qualms, for I was perfectly well."

"But now you are under treatment, and I am the cause of it. I am in despair."

"My illness, my angel, is trifling. It is a discharge resembling the one called the whites. I drink nothing but *eau de nitre*; I shall be well in a week or ten days, and I hope—"

"Ah, my dear!"

"What?"

"Let us think of it no more, I implore you."

"That is a revulsion which may be very natural when love is not strong. Alas for me!"

"No—I love you, and you would be unjust if you ceased to love me. Let us be fond friends and no longer think of giving each other proofs of it which might be fatal to us."

"Accursed and infamous F.!"

"She has gone, and in two weeks we, too, will leave for Basel, where we shall remain until the end of November."

"The die is cast, and I see that I must submit to your decision, or rather, to my destiny, for everything that has happened to me since I came to Switzerland has been disastrous. What consoles me is that I have been able to save your honor."

"You have won my husband's esteem, we shall always be true friends."

"If you must leave I see that I had better leave before you. That will make the horrible F. even more convinced that our friendship was not illicit."

"You think like an angel, and convince me more and more that you love me. Where will you go?"

"To Italy, but first I shall stop in Bern and then in Geneva."

"So you will not come to Basel, and I am glad, because people would talk. But, if you can, look happy during the few days you are to be here, for sadness does not become you."

We rejoined the Ambassador and Monsieur . . . , whom the widow Dubois's talk had not left time to think of us. I reproached her for being so chary of her wit when she was with me, and Monsieur de Chavigny told us he thought we were in love; whereupon she took him up, and I continued to walk with Madame . . . .

"That woman," she said, "is a masterpiece. Tell me the truth, and before you leave I will show you my gratitude in a way which will please you."

"What do you wish to know?"

"You love her and she loves you."

"I think so, but until now—"

"I do not want to know more, for if it is not yet done it will be done, and that comes to the same thing. If you had told me you did not love each other I should not have believed you, because it is impossible for a man of your age to live with such a woman and not love her. Extremely pretty, very intelligent, gay, with a ready tongue—she has everything to enchant, and I am sure you will find it hard to part from her. Lebel has done her a bad turn, for her reputation was excellent; but now she will not find employment with decent people."

"I shall take her to Bern with me."

"An excellent idea."

Just as they were leaving I said that I would come to Soleure to bid them good-by, since I had decided to leave for Bern in a few days. Reduced to giving up all thought of Madame . . . , I went to bed without supping, and my helpmate felt she should respect my grief.

Two or three days later I received a note from Madame . . . telling me to come to her house at ten the next day and ask to stay for dinner. I obeyed her exactly. Monsieur . . . said he would be delighted, but that he had to go to the country and could not be sure he would be back until one o'clock. He added that if I wished I could keep his wife company until he returned, and as she was at her embroidery frame with a girl I accepted on condition that she would not let me interrupt her work.

But toward noon the girl went away, and, left alone, we went to enjoy the fresh air on a terrace adjoining the house where there was an arbor from which, sitting at the back of it, we could see all the carriages that entered the street.

"Why," I instantly said, "did you not procure me this happiness when I was in perfect health?"

"Because then my husband believed you had only played the waiter for my sake and that I must dislike you; but your behavior has made him perfectly easy, to say nothing of your housekeeper, with whom he believes you are in love and whom he loves so much himself that I think he would gladly change places with you for a few days at least. Would you consent to the exchange?"

Having only an hour before me, and it no doubt the last in which I could convince her of the constancy of my love, I threw myself at her feet, and she put no obstacles in the way of my desires, which to my great regret had to be held in check, never going beyond the limits prescribed by the consideration I owed her blooming health.

In what she allowed me to do, her greatest pleasure must certainly have consisted in convincing me how wrong I had been to be happy with F.

We ran to the other end of the arbor and into the open when we saw Monsieur...'s carriage enter the street. It was there that the worthy man found us, excusing himself for having been gone so long.

At table he talked to me almost constantly about the widow Dubois, and he did not seem satisfied until I told him I intended to take her to her mother's arms in Lausanne. I bade them farewell at five o'clock in order to call on Monsieur de Chavigny, to whom I told the whole story of my cruel adventure. I should have thought it a crime not to tell the lovable old man the whole of the charming comedy which he had done so much to set in motion.

Admiring the widow Dubois's quick intelligence—for I concealed nothing from him—he assured me that, old as he was, he would consider himself happy if he could have such a woman with him. He was very much pleased when I confided to him that I was in love with her. He said that without going from house to house I could take my leave of all the good society in Soleure by attending his evening assembly, not even staying for supper if I did not want to get home too late; and that is what I did. I saw my beauty, expecting that in all probability it would be for the last time; but I was mistaken. I saw her ten years later; and in the proper place my reader shall learn where, how, and on what occasion.

[* * *]

Leaving Soleure with his "helpmate," Casanova traveled from Bern to Basel and then to Lausanne. There he and the helpmate went their separate ways. Desolate at the parting, Casanova put up as usual at the "Scales" inn on the Lausanne–Geneva road. It was August 20, 1760. Going to the inn window he saw written on a pane the words "you will forget Henriette too," just as they had been scratched there with a diamond ring thirteen years earlier on the occasion of another parting. Stunned by the coincidence, Casanova was overcome with mingled emotions: remorse, regret, the sense of loss and passing years. He consoled himself with a visit to Voltaire.

CHAPTER X

*Monsieur de Voltaire; my discussions with the
great man. A scene at his house in connection
with Ariosto. The Duke of Villars.
The Syndic and his three beautiful girls.
Argument at Voltaire's. Aix-en-Savoie.
The Marquis Desarmoises.*

"This," I said to him, "is the happiest moment of my life. At last I see my master; it is twenty years, Monsieur, since I became your pupil."

"Honor me with another twenty, and then promise to bring me my wages."

"I promise; but, on your side, promise to wait for me."

"I give you my word for it, and only death—not I—will break my word."

A general laugh greeted this first Voltairean sally. It was in the nature of things. The function of such laughter is to encourage one disputant, always at the expense of the other; and he to whom the laughers give their suffrage is always sure to win; they constitute a claque which operates in good society too. I expected as much, but I hoped that my turn would come to let fly at him. Two newly arrived Englishmen are introduced. He rises, saying:

"These gentlemen are English. I wish I were."

A poor compliment, for it forced them to answer that they wished they were French, and perhaps they did not want to lie, or they should be ashamed to tell the truth. A man of honor, I think, has the right to put his own country above all others.

No sooner has he sat down again than he returns to me, saying politely, but still with a laugh, that as a Venetian I must certainly know Count Algarotti.[1]

"I know him, but not by virtue of being a Venetian, for seven eighths of my dear fellow countrymen are unaware that he exists."

"I should have said 'as a man of letters.' "

"I know him from having spent two months with him at Padua[2] seven years ago; and I admired him principally because I discovered that he admired you."

"We are good friends; but to deserve the esteem of all who know him he does not need to admire anyone."

"If he had not begun by admiring, he would not have achieved fame. Admiring Newton, he succeeded in making it possible for ladies[3] to talk about light."

"Did he really succeed?"

"Not as well as Monsieur de Fontenelle in his *Pluralité des mondes*;[4] but he can be said to have succeeded."

"That is true. If you see him in Bologna, be so good as to tell him that I am awaiting his letters on Russia.[5] He can send them to me in care of the banker Bianchi in Milan. I am told that Italians do not like his Italian."

"I can well believe it: his style, in all his Italian writings, is his alone; it is infected with gallicisms; we think it pitiful."

"But do not French turns of expression make your language more beautiful?"

"They make it intolerable, just as a French stuffed with Italian expressions would be, even if it were written by you."

"You are right, one must write purely. Livy has been taken to task; his Latin has been said to be tainted with Patavinity."[6]

"The Abate Lazzarini[7] told me, when I was beginning to write, that he preferred Livy to Sallust."[8]

"The Abate Lazzarini, author of the tragedy *Ulisse il giovane*?[9] You must have been very young, and I wish I had known him; but I knew the Abate Conti,[10] who had been Newton's friend and whose four tragedies cover the whole of Roman history."

"I, too, knew and admired him. When I was with those great men, I congratulated myself on being young; today, here with you, I feel as if I dated from day before yesterday, but it does not humiliate me; I wish I were the youngest member of the human family."

"You would be better off than if you were the oldest. May I ask to what branch of literature you have devoted yourself?"

"To none; but perhaps the time will come. In the meanwhile I read as much as I can, and I indulge myself in studying humanity by traveling."

"That is the way to know it, but the book is too big. The easier method is to read history."

"History lies; one is not certain of the facts; it is boring; and studying the world on the run amuses me. Horace, whom I know by heart, is my guidebook, and I find him everywhere."

"Algarotti knows all of him by heart too. You are certainly fond of poetry?"

"It is my passion."

"Have you written many sonnets?"

"Ten or twelve which I like, and two or three thousand which I may not even have reread."

"The Italians are mad about sonnets."

"Yes—provided one can call it madness to wish to bestow on a given thought a harmonious measure capable of putting it in the best light. The sonnet is difficult, Monsieur de Voltaire, for we may neither extend the thought for the sake of the fourteen lines nor shorten it."

"It is the bed of the tyrant Procrustes.[11] That is why you have so few good ones. We have not one,[12] but that is the fault of our language."

"And of the French genius, too, I believe, which supposes that expanding a thought makes it lose all its brilliance and force."

"And you are not of that opinion?"

"I beg your pardon, it is a matter of the nature of the thought. A witticism, for example, is not enough for a sonnet."

"Which Italian poet do you love best?"

"Ariosto; and I cannot say that I love him better than the rest, for he is the only one I love. Yet I have read them all. When, fifteen years ago, I read your strictures on him,[13] I at once said that you would retract when you had read him."

"I am grateful to you for thinking I had not read him. I had read him; but, being young, having an inadequate knowledge of your language, and being prejudiced by the Italian writers who worship your Tasso, I unfortunately published an opinion which I sincerely thought was my own. It was not. I worship your Ariosto."

"I breathe again. So have an excommunication pronounced on the book in which you ridiculed him."

"All my books are excommunicated already; but I will now give you good proof of my retraction."

It was then that Voltaire astonished me. He recited by heart the two great passages in the thirty-fourth and thirty-fifth cantos of the divine poet in which he tells of Astolpho's conversation with St. John the Apostle,[14] never skipping a line, never pronouncing a word except in accordance with strict prosody; he pointed out their beauties to me, with reflections which only a truly great man could make. One could have expected nothing more from the greatest of all the Italian commentators. I listened to him without breathing, without once blinking my eyes, hoping in vain to catch him in a mistake; turning to the company, I said that I was overwhelmed with astonishment, and that I would inform all Italy of my wonder and the reason for it.

"All Europe," he replied, "shall be informed by me of the most humble amends which I owe to the greatest genius she has produced."

Insatiable for praise, the next day he gave me his translation of Ariosto's stanza: *Quindi avvien che tra principi e signori.*[15] Here it is:

> *Les papes, les césars apaisant leur querelle*
> *Jurent sur l'Évangile une paix éternelle;*
> *Vous les voyez demain l'un de l'autre ennemis;*
> *C'était pour se tromper qu'ils s'étaient réunis:*
> *Nul serment n'est gardé, nul accord n'est sincère;*
> *Quand la bouche a parlé, le coeur dit le contraire.*
> *Du ciel qu'ils attestaient ils bravaient le courroux,*
> *L'intérêt est le dieu qui les gouverne tous.*

("Popes and monarchs, ending their division, swear eternal peace on the Gospels; tomorrow you see them enemies; it was to deceive each other that they had assembled: no oath is kept, no agreement is sincere; when the mouth has spoken, the heart says the opposite. They dared the wrath of the heaven which they called to witness; interest is the god which governs them all.")

At the end of Monsieur de Voltaire's recitation, which brought him the applause of all present, though not one of them understood Italian, Madame Denis,[16] his niece, asked me if the famous passage her uncle had declaimed was one of the finest in the great poet.

"Yes, Madame, but not the very finest."

"Then judgment has been handed down as to the very finest?"

"Certainly—otherwise Signor Lodovico would not have received his apotheosis."

"I did not know he had been beatified."

At that all the laughers, with Voltaire at their head, were on Madame Denis's side—I alone excepted, who remained perfectly serious. Voltaire, nettled by my gravity:

"I know," he said, "why you do not laugh. You claim that it is by virtue of a superhuman passage that he was called 'divine.' "

"Precisely."

"What passage is it?"

"The last thirty-six stanzas of the twenty-third canto, which give a technical description of the way Orlando went mad. Since the beginning of the world no one has known how a person goes mad except Ariosto, who was able to write it, and who toward the end of his life went mad too.[17] Those stanzas, I am certain, have made you shudder; they inspire horror."

"I remember them; they make love terrible. I cannot wait to read them again."

"Perhaps Monsieur will be so kind as to recite them to us," said Madame Denis, with a sly glance at her uncle.

"Why not, Madame, if you will have the goodness to listen."

"Then you have taken the trouble to learn them by heart?"

"As I have read Ariosto through two or three times a year ever since I was fifteen years old, he has fixed himself in my memory from beginning to end with no effort on my part and, as it were, despite me, except for his genealogies and his historical passages, which tire the mind without touching the heart. Only Horace has remained imprinted entire in my soul, despite the often too prosaic verses in his Epistles."

"We can allow you Horace," added Voltaire; "but Ariosto is a great deal, for it is a matter of forty-six long cantos."

"Say fifty-one."[18]

Voltaire remained silent.

"Come, come," said Madame Denis, "let us have the thirty-six stanzas which make one shudder and which earned their author the appellation of 'divine.' "

I thereupon recited them, but not in the style of declamation which we use in Italy. To please, Ariosto has no need to be thrown into relief by a monotonous singsong on the part of the person who delivers him. The French are right in finding this singsong intolerable. I recited them as if they were prose, animating them by voice, eyes, and the varying intonation necessary to express feeling. My audience saw and felt feeling expressed. They saw and felt the effort I made to hold back my tears, and they wept; but when I came to the stanza:

Poichè allargare il freno al dolor puote
Che resta solo senza altrui rispetto
Giù dagli occhi rigando per le gote
Sparge un fiume di lacrime sul petto

("Because he who is alone, with no one to consider, may give the reins to his grief, from his eyes he pours a stream of tears which flow down his cheeks to his breast"),[19]

my tears burst from my eyes so impetuously and abundantly that everyone present shed tears too, Madame Denis shuddered, and Voltaire ran to embrace me; but he could not interrupt me, for Orlando, to go completely mad, had to discover that he was in the same bed as that in which Angelica had lately lain in the arms of the too fortunate Medoro,[20] which happened in the following stanza. My plaintive and mournful tone gave place to the tone of terror inspired by the madness whose prodigious force drove him to ravages such as only an earthquake or lightning could cause. At the end of my recitation I somberly received the congratulations of the entire company. Voltaire exclaimed:

"It is what I have always said: to draw tears, one must weep oneself; but to weep, one must feel, and then the tears come from the soul."

He embraced me, he thanked me, and he promised to recite the same stanzas to me the next day and to weep as I had done. He kept his word.

Pursuing the subject of Ariosto, Madame Denis said it was astonishing that Rome had not put him on the Index. Voltaire replied that, on the contrary, Leo X[21] had issued a bull excommunicating all who dared to condemn him. The two great families of Este and Medici[22] found it to their interest to support him:

"But for that," he added, "the one line on Constantine's donation of Rome[23] to Sylvester,[24] which says that it *puzza forte* ('stinks strongly'),[25] would have been enough to bring an interdict on the poem."

I said that, begging his pardon, the line which had caused even more of an outcry was the one in which Ariosto throws doubt on the resurrection of the whole human race at the end of the world.

"Speaking of the hermit who tried to prevent Rodomonte from capturing Isabella, Zerbino's[26] widow," I said, "Ariosto describes the African as tiring of his preaching, seizing him, and throwing him so far that he breaks him to pieces against a rock, where he is instantly killed and remains in a sleep such

> *Che al novissimo dí forse fia desto.*

('That he perhaps may wake on the last day.')

"That *forse* ('perhaps'), which the poet inserted only as a rhetorical ornament, caused an outcry which would have made the poet laugh heartily."

"It is a pity," said Madame Denis, "that Ariosto did not abstain from his hyperboles."

"Be quiet, my niece; they are all deliberate and all of the greatest beauty."

We talked on other subjects, all of them literary, and the conversation finally turned to *L'Écossaise*, which had been acted at Soleure. The whole story was known. Voltaire told me that if I would act in his house he would write Monsieur de Chavigny to persuade Madame ... to come and act Lindane and that he would take the part of Monrose. I declined, telling him that Madame ... was at Basel and that in any case I had to leave the following day. At that he protested vehemently, roused the whole company against me, and maintained that my visit became an insult if I did not stay for at least a week. I replied that, having come to Geneva only for him, I had nothing else to do there.

"Did you come here to talk to me or to hear me talk?"

"Principally to hear you talk."

"Then stay here three days at least, come to dine with me every day, and we will talk."

I said I would do so, and then took my leave to go to my inn, for I had a great deal of writing to do.

A Syndic[27] of the city, whom I will not name and who had spent the day at Voltaire's, came a quarter of an hour later, asking me to let him sup with me.

"I was present," he said, "at your argument with the great man, though I said nothing. I hope I may have you to myself for an hour."

I embraced him and, asking him to excuse me for receiving him in my nightcap, said that he could spend the whole night with me if he wished.

The amiable man spent two hours with me, never speaking of literature, but he had no need of that to please me. He was a great disciple of Epicurus and Socrates; capping anecdotes, outdoing each other in laughter, and talk about every kind of pleasure to be procured in Geneva kept us occupied until midnight. When he left, he invited me to sup with him the following evening, assuring me that our supper would be amusing. I promised to wait for him at my inn. He asked me not to mention our engagement to anyone.

The next morning young Fox came to my room with the two Englishmen whom I had seen at Monsieur de Voltaire's. They proposed a game of quinze[28] with stakes of two louis, and, having lost fifty louis in less than an hour, I stopped. We made a tour of Geneva and at dinnertime went to "Les Délices."[29] The Duke of Villars[30] had just arrived there to consult Tronchin,[31] who had kept him alive by his art for ten years.

During dinner I said nothing; but afterward Voltaire made me talk about the Venetian government, knowing that I must bear it a grudge. I disappointed his expectation; I attempted to prove that there is no country on earth in which one can enjoy greater freedom. Seeing that the subject was not to my liking, he took me out to his garden, which he told me he had created. The principal walk ended at a stream; he said it was the Rhone, which he was sending to France. He made me admire the fine view of Geneva and the Dent Blanche,[32] which is the highest of the Alps.

Deliberately turning the conversation to Italian literature, he began talking away on the subject with great wit and erudition, but always ending with an erroneous judgment. I did not contradict him. He spoke of Homer, Dante, and Petrarch, and everyone knows what he thought of those great geniuses. His inability to refrain from writing what he thought harmed him. I only said that if these authors had not deserved the esteem of all who studied them they would not have been given the high place they held.

The Duke of Villars and the famous physician Tronchin joined us. Tronchin—tall, well built, handsome, polished, eloquent though not talkative, a learned natural scientist, a wit, a physician, favorite pupil[33] of Boerhaave, and without either the jargon or the charlatanism of the pillars of the Faculty—captivated me. His principal medicine was only diet; but to prescribe it he had to be a great philosopher. It was he who cured a consumptive of venereal disease by the mercury which he gave him in the milk of a she-ass which he had subjected to thirty rubbings by the strong arms of three or four porters. I write this because I have been told it, but I find it hard to believe.

The person of the Duke of Villars caught all my attention. Examining his bearing and his face, I thought I saw a woman of seventy[34] dressed as a man, thin, emaciated, weak, but who in her youth might have been beautiful. His blotched cheeks were covered with rouge, his lips with carmine, his eyebrows were blackened, his teeth were false, as was the hair which was glued to his head by quantities of pomade scented with ambergris, and in his top button-hole was a large bouquet which came up to his chin. He affected grace in his gestures, and he spoke in a soft voice which made it difficult to understand what he said. Withal he was very polite, affable, and mannered in the style of the Regency.[35] I have been told that when he was young he loved women, but that in his old age he assumed the modest role of wife to three or four handsome minions, each of whom in turn enjoyed the honor of sleeping with him. The Duke was the Governor of Provence. His whole back was gangrened, and according to the laws of nature he should have died ten years earlier; but Tronchin kept him alive by diet, feeding the sores, which if they had not been fed would have died and taken the Duke with them. This is truly to live by art.

I went with Voltaire to his bedroom, where he changed his wig and the bonnet he wore over it to keep from catching cold. On a large table I saw the *Summa*[36] of St. Thomas and some Italian poets, among them the *Secchia rapita* of Tassoni.[37]

"It is," he said, "the only tragicomic poem which Italy possesses. Tassoni was a monk, a wit, and a learned genius as a poet."

"The rest perhaps—but not learned, for, ridiculing the Copernican system, he says that, following it, one could not arrive at the theory either of lunations or of eclipses."

"Where does he say anything so stupid?"

"In his *discorsi academici.*"[38]

"I haven't them, but I will get them."

He wrote down the title.

"But Tassoni," he went on, "criticized your Petrarch[39] very well."

"And thereby disgraced his taste and his reading, as did Muratori."[40]

"Here he is. Admit that his erudition is immense."

"Est ubi peccat" ("He is sometimes wrong").[41]

He opened a door, and I saw an archive of nearly a hundred bulky packages.

"That," he said, "is my correspondence. You see nearly fifty thousand[42] letters, which I have answered."

"Have you copies of your answers?"

"Of most of them. It is the duty of a valet whom I keep for no other purpose."

"I know printers who would give a great deal of money to possess themselves of this treasure."

"Beware of printers when you are ready to give something to the public, if you have not already begun."

"I will begin when I am old."

And in this connection I quoted a macaronic verse of Merlin Cocai.[43]

"What is that?"

"It is a verse from a famous poem[44] in twenty-four cantos."

"Famous?"

"And what is more, worthy to be; but to appreciate it one must know the Mantuan dialect."

"I shall understand it. Have it sent me."

"I will present it to you tomorrow."

"I shall be obliged to you."

We were fetched from there, and we spent two hours in conversation with the company, in which the great, brilliant poet kept everyone amused, always applauded though satirical and often caustic, but always laughing and never failing to raise a laugh. He maintained a princely establishment, and only at his house did one find choice fare. He was then sixty-six years of age and had an income of a hundred and twenty thousand livres. They who said and say that he became rich only by cheating the booksellers are mistaken. On the contrary, the booksellers cheated him badly, except the Cramers,[45] whose fortune he made. He gave them all his works for nothing, and thus it was that they circulated so widely. At the time I was there he gave them *La Princesse de Babylone*,[46] a charming tale which he wrote in three days.

My Epicurean Syndic came to the "Scales" for me as he had promised. He took me to a house on the right-hand side of the next street, which runs uphill. He presented me to three young ladies,[47] two of them sisters, and all made for love though one could not call them beautiful. An easy and gracious welcome, intelligent faces, and a promise of gaiety which was not disappointed. The half hour before supper was spent in decent but unrestrained conversation; during supper, however, the Syndic having set the tone, I foresaw what would happen after supper. The day being hot, on the pretext of cooling ourselves, and being sure that no one would come to interrupt us, we were soon very nearly in the state of nature. I should have given offense if I had not followed the example of the four others. What an orgy! We rose to such a pitch of gaiety that, having recited Grécourt's[48] *Y grec*, I took it upon myself to demonstrate to the three girls in turn why the decree *Gaudeant bene nati* ("Let the well-born rejoice") had been promulgated. I saw the Syndic pluming himself on the present of my person which he had made to the three girls, who, from what I saw, must have fared very poorly with him, whose concupiscence affected only his head. It was their sense of obligation which an hour after midnight made them give me an ejaculation I really needed. I repeatedly kissed the six fair hands which humbled themselves to the task, which is always humiliating to any woman made for love, but which could not be so in the farce we had played, for having had the kindness to spare them, I had, with the help of the voluptuous Syndic, done them the same service. They thanked me endlessly, and I saw that they were in raptures when the Syndic invited me for the next day.

But it was I who thanked him again and again when he saw me to my inn. He told me that he alone had been responsible for bringing up the three girls, and that I was the first man whose acquaintance he had allowed them. He begged me to continue to be on my guard against making them pregnant, for it would be a fatal misfortune for them in a city as captiously strict on the point as Geneva.

The next day I wrote Monsieur de Voltaire an epistle in blank verse, which cost me more trouble than if I had rhymed it. I sent it to him with Teofilo Folengo's[49] poem; and I made a great mistake in sending it, for I should have known he would not like it. I then went to Mr. Fox's, where the two Englishmen offered me my revenge. I lost a hundred louis. After dinner they left for Lausanne.

Having learned from the Syndic himself that his three girls were not rich, I went to a jeweler to have six doblones de a ocho[50] melted, ordering him to make me three balls of two ounces each immediately. I knew how I could go about giving them to the girls without humiliating them.

At noon I went to Monsieur de Voltaire's, who was not visible, but Madame Denis made up to me for it. She had a sound intelligence, excellent taste, learning without pretension, and a great dislike for the King of Prussia. She asked me for news of my beautiful housekeeper, and she was very glad to hear that the Ambassador's major-domo had married her. She asked me to tell her how I had escaped from the Leads, and I promised to satisfy her request some other day.

Monsieur de Voltaire did not come to the table. He did not appear until about five o'clock, carrying a letter.

"Do you know," he asked me, "the Marchese Albergati Capacelli,[51] Senator of Bologna, and Count Paradisi?"[52]

"I do not know Paradisi, but I know Signor Albergati by sight and reputation; he is not a Senator but a 'Forty,'[53] born in Bologna, where the Forty are fifty."

"Heaven preserve us! What a riddle!"

"Do you know him?"

"No; but he sends me Goldoni's[54] plays, Bologna sausages, the translation of my *Tancrède*,[55] and he is coming to see me."

"He will not come, he is not so foolish."

"What do you mean by that? Though it is true that coming to see me is foolish."

"I am talking about Albergati. He knows he would be the loser by it, for he enjoys the idea you may have of him. He is sure that if he comes to visit you, you will see his nothingness or his whole bag of tricks, and good-by illusion! In other respects he is a worthy gentleman with an income of six thousand zecchini and theatromania.[56] He is a good actor and the author[57] of prose comedies which are not funny."

"You paint a pretty picture of him. But how can he be both forty and fifty?"

"As noon at Basel is eleven o'clock."[58]

"I understand—just as your Council of Ten numbers seventeen."[59]

"Even so. But the accursed Forty of Bologna are another matter."

"Why accursed?"

"Because they are not answerable to the Exchequer, and so they commit all the crimes they please and go to reside outside the State, where they still live on their revenues."

"That's a blessing, not a curse; but let us continue. No doubt the Marchese Albergati is a man of letters."

"He writes well, for he knows his language; but he bores his reader because he enjoys the sound of his own voice and he is diffuse. And he has nothing in his head."

"He is an actor, you said."

"Excellent when he plays something of his own, especially in the part of the lover."

718

"Is he handsome?"

"On the stage, but not in ordinary life. His face has no expression."

"But his plays are liked?"

"Not at all. They would be booed if people understood them."

"And what do you say of Goldoni?"

"He is our Molière."

"Why does he call himself poet to the Duke of Parma?"[60]

"To give himself a title, for the Duke knows nothing about it. He also calls himself an advocate,[61] but he is one only *in posse*. He is a good writer of comedies, and that is all. I am his friend, and everyone in Venice knows it. In society he does not shine, he is as insipid and sweet as marshmallow."

"So someone wrote me. He is poor, and he wants to leave Venice. The owners of the theaters where his plays are performed must not like that."

"There was talk of giving him a pension; but the decision went against it. It was thought that if he had a pension he would stop working."

"Cuma[62] refused Homer a pension for fear that all blind people would demand one."

We spent the day very pleasantly. He thanked me for the *Macaronicon*[63] and promised to read it. He introduced a Jesuit[64] whom he had in his service, saying that his name was Adam but that he was not the first of men; and I was told that, amusing himself playing backgammon with him, when he lost he often threw the dice and the dicebox in his face.

I was scarcely back at my inn in the evening before I received my three gold balls, and a moment later I saw my dear Syndic, who took me to his orgy.

On the way he discussed the sense of modesty which prevents our displaying the parts which from childhood we have been taught to keep covered. He said that modesty of this kind could often derive from a virtue; but that the virtue was weaker than the force of education, since it could not resist an attack when the aggressor knew what he was about. The easiest strategy, in his opinion, was not to admit its existence, to show that one had no regard for it and ridicule it; the thing to do was to surprise it by setting the example, leaping the barriers of shame, and victory was certain; the boldness of the attacker made the modesty of the person attacked vanish instantly.

"Clement of Alexandria,"[65] he said, "a man of learning and a philosopher, said that the modesty which seems so firmly rooted in women's minds was really only in their underclothes, because as soon as they were persuaded to take those off not a shadow of it remained."

We found the three young ladies, lightly clad in linen dresses, sitting on a large sofa, and we sat down in front of them on armless chairs. The half hour before supper was devoted to charming badinage like that of the evening before and to quantities of kisses. It was after supper that the combat began.

As soon as we were sure that the maid would not come to interrupt us again, we made ourselves comfortable. The Syndic began by taking from his pocket a package of English coveralls, praising that admirable defense against a misfortune which could give rise to dread repentance. They knew of it, and they seemed satisfied, laughing at the shape which the inflated instrument took before their eyes, when I said that I certainly loved their honor even more than their beauty, but that I could never consent to seek happiness with them by wrapping myself in a piece of dead skin.

"Here," I say, taking from my pocket the three gold balls, "is what will safeguard you against any untoward consequences. After fifteen years' experience I am in a position to assure you that with these balls you have nothing to fear and that in future you will not need these miserable sheaths. Honor me with your complete confidence in this respect, and accept this small present from a Venetian who adores you."

"We are grateful to you," says the elder of the sisters; "but how does one use this pretty ball to avert a disastrous big belly?"

"All that is necessary is for the ball to be in the cabinet of love during the combat. It is an antipathic virtue in the metal which prevents pregnancy."

"But," remarks the cousin,[66] "the little ball may easily slip out of the place before the action is over."

"Not at all, when one knows how to go about it. There is a posture which will prevent the ball from coming out by its own weight."

"Show us," says the Syndic, taking up a candle to light me when I put the ball in place.

The charming cousin had said too much to withdraw and refuse the proof which her cousins wanted. I placed her at the foot of the bed in such a way that it was impossible for the ball, which I inserted, to fall out; but it fell out after the act, and she saw that I had cheated her, but she pretended not to notice it. She picked up the ball, and she challenged the two sisters to do as much. They underwent the operation with every sign of interest.

The Syndic, having no faith in the virtue of the ball, would not trust it. He limited his pleasure to looking on, and he had no reason to complain. After half an hour's respite I began the ceremonies again without the balls, assuring them that they ran no risk, and I kept my word.

When I left, I saw the three girls overwhelmed; they felt they had contracted obligations to me and had given me nothing. Bestowing countless caresses on the Syndic, they asked him how he had guessed that I was the man who deserved to be let into their great secret.

As we were leaving, the Syndic urged the three girls to ask me to stay another day in Geneva for their sake, and I assented. He was to be occupied the next day. For my part I really needed a day's rest. He saw me to my inn, treating me to the most flattering compliments.

After sleeping soundly for ten hours I felt fit to go and enjoy Monsieur de Voltaire's charming company; but the great man was pleased on that day to indulge in raillery, ill-humored jests, and sarcasm. He knew that I was to leave the next day.

He began at table by saying that he thanked me for my present of Merlin Cocai, certainly made with good intentions, but that he did not thank me for the praise I had bestowed on the poem, since I had been the cause of his wasting four hours reading nonsense. My hair stood on end, but I controlled myself. I replied quite calmly that on another occasion he might find it worthy of the greater praise which he himself could bestow. I cited several examples of the inadequacy of a first reading.

"True enough—but as for your Merlin, I leave him to you. I have put him beside Chapelain's[67] La Pucelle."

"Which pleases all competent critics, despite its versification. It is a good poem, and Chapelain was a poet; his genius has not escaped me."

My statement could not but offend him, and I should have known it after he told me that he would put the Macaronicon I had given him beside La Pucelle. I knew, too, that a filthy poem by the same name, which was widely circulated, was supposed to be by him; but since he disavowed it[68] I thought he would conceal the pain which my frankness must have caused him; but not a bit of it— he contradicted me sharply and I became no less sharp. I told him that Chapelain had the merit of making his subject agreeable without currying the favor of his readers by filth and impiety.

"Such," I said, "is the opinion of my master Monsieur de Crébillon."[69]

"You cite a great judge. But in what is my confrère Crébillon your master?"

"He taught me to speak French in less than two years. To show him my gratitude I translated his *Rhadamiste*[70] into Italian Alexandrine verse. I am the first Italian who dared to adapt that meter to our language."

"The first, if you will pardon me, was my friend Pier Jacopo Martelli."[71]

"Pardon *me*."

"Why, I have his works,[72] printed at Bologna, in my room."

"You can only have read verses of fourteen syllables[73] without alternating masculine and feminine rhyme. Yet he believed he was imitating Alexandrines, and his preface made me laugh. Perhaps you did not read it."

"Monsieur, I have a passion for reading prefaces. Martelli proves that to Italian ears his verses sound the same as Alexandrines do to the French."

"He is egregiously wrong, and I ask you to be the judge. Your masculine verse has only twelve syllables and your feminine thirteen; all Martelli's verses have fourteen, except those which end in a long syllable, which at the end of a verse always counts as two. Observe that Martelli's first hemistich is always and forever of seven syllables, whereas in the French Alexandrine it is forever and always of six. Either your friend Pier Jacopo was deaf or he had a bad ear."

"Then in the theory of your verse you follow all our rules?"

"All of them, despite the difficulty; for nearly all our words end in a short syllable."

"And how was your new meter received?"

"It was not liked, because no one knew the way to recite my verses; but when I delivered them myself in our literary circles I triumphed."

"Do you remember a passage from your *Rhadamiste*?"

"As many as you please."

I then recited to him the same scene which I had recited to Crébillon in blank verse ten years earlier, and he seemed impressed. He said that the difficulty was not perceptible, and it was the greatest compliment he could pay me. In his turn he recited a passage from his *Tancrède*, which I believe he had not then published and which was later rightly judged a masterpiece.

We should have ended on good terms, but a line of Horace which I quoted to applaud one of his ideas led him to say that Horace was a great master of the drama because of his precepts, which would never grow stale.

"You break only one of them," I said, "but you break it like a great man."

"Which one?"

"You do not write *contentus paucis lectoribus* ('satisfied with a few readers')."[74]

"If Horace had had to fight superstition he would have written for everyone, as I do."

"You might, it seems to me, spare yourself the trouble of fighting it, for you will never succeed in destroying it, and even if you did, pray tell me with what you would fill its place."

"I like that! When I deliver the human race from a ferocious monster which devours it, can I be asked what I will put in its place?"

"It does not devour it; on the contrary, it is necessary to its existence."

"Loving the human race, I should wish to see it happy as I am, free; and superstition cannot be combined with freedom. What makes you think that servitude can make a people happy?"

"Then you would wish to see sovereignty in the people?"

"God forbid! One alone must govern."

"Then superstition is necessary, for without it the people will never obey the monarch."

"No monarch—for the name makes me see despotism, which I must hate as I do servitude."

"Then what would you have? If you want the ruler to be one man, I can only consider him a monarch."

"I want him to command a free people, then he will be its leader, and he cannot be called a monarch, for he can never be arbitrary."

"Addison[75] tells you that such a monarch, such a leader, is not among possible beings. I am for Hobbes.[76] Between two evils, one must choose the lesser. A people without superstition would be philosophical and philosophers will never obey. The people can be happy only if they are crushed, downtrodden, kept in chains."

"If you have read me you will have found the proofs by which I demonstrate that superstition is the enemy of kings."

"If I have read you! I have read and reread you—and especially when I am not of your opinion. Your first passion is love of humanity. *Est ubi peccas* ('You are sometimes wrong').[77] That love blinds you. Love humanity, but you can only love it as it is. It is incapable of the benefits you would lavish upon it; and, giving them, you would only make it more unhappy and more wicked. Leave it the monster which devours it; the monster is dear to it. I never laughed so much as when I saw Don Quixote[78] having a very hard time defending himself from the galley slaves to whom he had just magnanimously given their freedom."

"Are you Venetians free?"

"As free as it is possible to be under an aristocratic government. The freedom we have is not as great as that which the English enjoy, but we are content. My imprisonment, for example, was an outright act of despotism; but knowing that I had myself abused my freedom, at certain moments I considered that they had been right to imprison me without the usual formalities."

"At that rate no one is free in Venice."

"Possibly; but grant that, to be free, it is enough to believe that one is so."

"I will not so easily grant it. Even the aristocrats who are members of the government are not free—for example, they cannot travel without permission."

"It is a law to which they deliberately subjected themselves in order to preserve their power. Would you say that a Bernese is not free because he is subject to the sumptuary laws?[79] It is he himself who is the lawmaker."

It was to change the subject that he asked me where I had come from.

"From Roche. I should have been very sorry to leave Switzerland without seeing the famous Haller. I am paying homage to my learned contemporaries—and you will be the savory at the end of the feast."

"You must have enjoyed Monsieur Haller."

"I spent three excellent days with him."

"I congratulate you. One should go down on one's knees to that great man."

"I think so too; you do him justice, and for his sake I regret that he is not so fair to you."

"So! Then possibly we are both mistaken."

At this answer, whose whole merit is in its quickness, all the company applauded.

There was no more talk of literature, and I played a silent part until, Monsieur de Voltaire having withdrawn, I went up to Madame Denis and asked her if she had any commissions for me in Rome.

I left rather well pleased that on this last day I had reduced the gladiator to reason. But I was left with a grudge against him which for ten years made me criticize everything I read, old or new, which the great man had given or was giving the public. I repent of it now, despite the fact that when I read what I published against him[80] I find that my censures were based on sound reasoning. I should have kept quiet, respected him, and doubted my own judgments. I should have reflected that but for the raillery with which he offended me on the third day I should have thought him sublime in everything. This reflection alone should have kept me silent, but an angry man always believes he is right. Reading me, posterity will number me among the Zoiluses,[81] and the very humble amends I make him today will perhaps not be read.

HISTORY OF MY LIFE

Volume Seven

CHAPTER VII

Florence. I meet Teresa again. My son. La Corticelli.

[* * *]

From Switzerland Casanova made for Aix and then for Marseilles, Toulon and Genoa. Each port of call provided him with a mistress—sometimes two—including a nun in Aix: he seems to have been partial to nuns. Eventually he found himself in Florence where there was an unexpected and not altogether happy meeting with an old friend.

In Florence I found lodgings near the Ponte alla Carraia[1] at Doctor Vannini's,[2] who told me at once that he was "unworthily" a member of the Accademia della Crusca.[3] I took an apartment the windows of which looked out on the embankment of the Arno, next to a beautiful terrace. I also took a town carriage and a hire lackey, immediately dressing the coachman and the lackey in the blue and red livery of Signor Bragadin. I did not want to impose on anyone, but I wanted to make an impression. The next day I went out alone on foot, wearing a redingote, to see Florence and be seen by no one, and in the afternoon I went to the theater[4] to hear the Arlecchino Roffi,[5] whose reputation was greater than his talent, and to judge the Florentine style of delivery, which was highly praised and which I did not like. Only Pertici[6] pleased me. Unable to sing any longer because he had grown old, he had turned actor.

The next day I presented myself to the banker Sasso Sassi, on whom I had a large letter of credit, and after dining alone I dressed for the occasion and went to the opera in the Via della Pergola,[7] taking a seat in a box near the orchestra more to see the actresses than to hear the music, which has never transported me.

But what a surprise when I see the prima donna! I instantly recognized Teresa,[8] whom, after she dropped the mask of Bellino, I had left in Rimini at the beginning of the year 1744—the very Teresa whom I would certainly have married if Signor de Gages had not had me put under arrest. Seventeen years later I see her on the stage, beautiful, fresh, and she seems to me just as young as when I had left her. I thought her a miracle; I was decided that it must be someone else, when, singing an aria, she happens to turn her eyes on me, and from then on they never leave my face. That convinced me that I was not mistaken. At the end of her aria she goes off, and she is scarcely in the wings before she turns and signals me with her fan to come and speak to her.

I leave the box with my heart beating in a way for which I did not understand the reason; for, preserving the happiest memory of Teresa, I felt no guilt toward her except for not having answered her last letter, which she had written me from Naples thirteen years before. I made my way to the pit, more curious to see what the consequences of the interview would be than to learn all that must have happened to her in the course of seventeen years, which, in those days, seemed to me a century.

I come to a door through which one went up to the stage, and I see her at the top of a short stairway giving orders to the door-keeper to let me enter. I approach her and we both remain mute. I take her hand and I put it against my chest so that she can feel my heart, which seemed to be trying to leap out.

"I cannot do as much here," she said, "but I thought my surprise would send me falling into the orchestra, and I do not know, my dear friend, how I managed to finish my aria. Alas! I have to sup out, I shall not sleep tonight; I expect you tomorrow at eight o'clock. Where are you staying?"

"At Vannini's."

"What name are you using?"

"The same."[9]

"When did you arrive here?"

"Yesterday."

"Shall you remain long in Florence?"

"As long as you wish."

"Are you married?"

"No."

"Accursed supper! What a day! Leave me, I have to go on. Good-by until tomorrow at seven."

A moment earlier she had said "at eight." I go to the parterre, and I remember that I have asked her neither her name nor her address; but I could easily find out all that. She was playing the part of Mandane.[10] At this distance I seem to see her even better, and I find her without an equal in the action with which she animated her recitative. I ask a very well-dressed young man who is sitting beside me the name of so great an actress.

"Then you have arrived in Florence only today?"

"Yes, Signore."

"Well then, her name is the same as mine because she is my wife; and my name is Cirillo Palesi,[11] at your service."

I bow to him, and I remain mute and as if I had fallen from a great height. He might have considered it impertinent if I had asked him where he lived. Teresa married to this handsome young man! And it is precisely her husband I bump into when I want to inquire about her!

I have not the strength to stay through the opera. I cannot wait to be alone so that I can reflect on this fantastic adventure, on the visit I was to make to the married Teresa the next morning at seven, for I must go by what she had said last, and on what her husband will say to me when he sees me. I feel my old fire rekindled, and I think I am not sorry to have found her married.

I go out, and I tell my lackey to call my carriage; he replies that I cannot have it until nine o'clock. The weather was so cold that the coachman had gone to the stable.

"Then we will walk. Tell me," I said, "what is the name of the *prima virtuosa*?"

"Her name was Lanti; but for the last two months it has been Palesi. I can tell you there is nothing to be done there. She is rich, and she married a young man who has nothing and no profession."

"Where does she live?"

"At the end of this street. We shall pass her door. She lives on the second floor."

After that I said no more to him, so that I could devote my attention to the route I was to take alone the next morning.

I ate scarcely a bite and went to bed at once, ordering Leduc to call me at six o'clock.

"It is not light until seven."

"I know that."

"Very well."

So at seven o'clock I am at the door of my first great passion. I go up to the second floor, I ring, and a woman who opens the door for me asks me if my name is Casanova.

"Yes."

"The Signora told me that you would come at eight o'clock; but it does not matter, go into this room, I will wake her."

Five or six minutes later I see her husband approach me politely in his nightcap, saying that his wife was getting up and would come; but I nearly laughed when, after staring at me for a time, he said:

"Was it not you, Signore, who asked me my wife's name yesterday evening?"

"I am the man, I thought I knew her, and my good luck saw to it that I should ask her husband. The friendship, Signore, which I shall always feel for you will be the same as that which I have always felt for her."

But there she is, beautiful as a star. She enters with open arms, I open mine, and we embrace like two fond friends, or like lovers enjoying the happiness of a moment for which they have longed. After a brief pause for thought, we embrace again, then she tells her husband to sit down. She draws me to a sofa, letting her tears flow freely, I cannot hold back mine; but a moment later, wiping our eyes, we happen to turn them on Signor Palesi's face, and we cannot help bursting out laughing. His amazement was too comic.

"You see my father," she said to him, "and more than my father, for I owe him everything. Happy moment, which I have awaited for ten years!"

Hearing me called "father," her husband stared at me again; but the emotion of the situation did not permit me to laugh. I was not quite two years older than Teresa; but fondness takes the name of father to mean whatever it chooses.

"Yes, Signore," I said, "she is my daughter, she is my sister, an angel without sex, she is a living treasure, and she is your wife.

"I did not," I said to her, "answer your last letter—"

"I know everything. You were in love with a nun, you were imprisoned under the Leads, and when I was in Vienna I heard of your prodigious escape. A false presentiment made me certain that I should see you there. Afterward I learned of your vicissitudes in Paris and Holland; but after you left Paris I could get news of you from no one. But here we are, and I shall die content. When I tell you all that has happened to me during these ten years you will hear some fine tales. Now I am happy. There is Signor Palesi, of Rome, who married me two months ago; we love each other, and I hope you will be his friend as you are mine."

I then rose to embrace him, and he came to meet me, though with extreme embarrassment, for he could not imagine what attitude he should assume toward me, who was now father, now brother, now friend. He did not know if he must be prepared to put up with me as the lover of his dear wife. It was she who, to reassure him, went and embraced him most heartily, making me the spectator of a second scene which I pretended to find very agreeable, but which annoyed me, for in that half hour Teresa had rekindled in me all the fire with which I had begun to burn for her at Ancona when Don Sancho Pico[12] introduced me to her.

Signor Palesi asked me if I would be pleased to breakfast, joining them for a cup of excellent chocolate which he whipped himself, and I replied that I was passionately fond of chocolate. He went off at once to make it.

Thereupon Teresa fell into my arms, saying:

"Let us embrace a hundred times this first day, my dear friend, and afterward leave it at that, since such is the decree of destiny. Tomorrow we shall meet again only as two fond friends; our transports at this happy moment are too well justified for us to restrain them."

After satisfying some of our fire, finding that we were as we had been when we parted in Rimini, we breathed again, and we resumed our places.

After reflecting a little:

"You must know," she said, "that I am still in love with my husband and determined never to deceive him. What I did just now did not depend upon me, and we must both forget it. It is over. Let it suffice us to know that we still love each other, and to have no possible doubt of it. In future, my dear friend, let us avoid any opportunity to be alone together. Does that make you sad?"

"I find you bound, and I am free. We would not have parted again; you have just rekindled all my old fire; I am the same, and happy that I have been able to prove it to myself and unhappy that I can no longer hope to possess you; I find you not only married but in love. Alas! I have delayed too long; but if I had not stopped in Genoa I should be equally unhappy. You shall know all when occasion serves. Meanwhile, I will obey no other laws than those you will prescribe for me. Your husband, I believe, does not know our story; so I must let nothing out, must I not?"

"Nothing; for he has no knowledge of my affairs, and I am very glad he shows no curiosity about them. He knows, like everyone else, that I made my fortune in Naples, where I say I went at the age of ten. Such things are falsehoods which harm no one, and which in my profession I must prefer to a number of truths which would injure me. I claim I am twenty-four—what do you say to that?"

"I would say you are telling the truth, though I know you are thirty-two."

733

"You mean thirty-one. When I met you I could not have been more than fourteen."

"I thought it was fifteen."

"Possibly; but tell me, please, do I look more than twenty-four?"

"I swear that you do not even look that. But in Naples—"

"In Naples a gazetteer might know everything; but nobody listens to such people. But I am waiting to see you at what will be one of the most interesting moments in your life."

"One of the most interesting moments in my life? When?"

"Permit me to say no more. I want to enjoy your surprise. But let us speak of something essential. How are you off? If you need money I am in a position to return yours to you with all the interest you can demand. My husband controls nothing; all that I have is my own. I have fifty thousand ducati del regno[13] at Naples, and the same amount in diamonds. Tell me how much you need. Quick, for the chocolate is coming."

Such was Teresa. Deeply moved, I was about to throw myself on her neck before answering her, when the chocolate arrived. Her husband entered, followed by a chambermaid who was a beauty and who carried three cups of chocolate on a silver-gilt tray. Palesi kept us entertained while we were drinking it, wittily describing the nature of his surprise when he saw that the man who had got him out of bed at seven o'clock was the same one who had asked him his wife's name the previous evening at the theater. Teresa's laughter, accompanied by mine, was not displeasing to the Roman, who I thought appeared jealous only for propriety's sake.

Teresa said that at ten o'clock a rehearsal of all the arias from the new opera was to be held at her house, that I was welcome to remain for it and dine with her afterward, and to spend the whole day there if I had nothing better to do. I replied that I would not leave her until after supper to let her go to bed with her fortunate husband. At these words Signor Palesi cordially embraced me, as if to say that he was grateful to me for not having raised obstacles to his exercising his rights.

He was no more than twenty or twenty-two years old, he was blond, and too good-looking for a man, for, such as he was, all mankind of either sex owed him approbation. I could not but forgive Teresa for having fallen in love with his pretty face, for I knew the power of a beautiful countenance only too well; but I disapproved of her having made him her husband, for a husband acquires sovereign rights.

Teresa's young chambermaid came in and said that my carriage was at the door.

"Will you permit my hire lackey to come in?" I asked Teresa. "Who," I said to the scoundrel, "ordered you to come here with my carriage?"

"No one; but I know my duty."

"Who told you I was here?"

"I guessed it."

"Go call Leduc and come here with him."

I told Leduc to pay him for three days, to take away his livery, and ask Doctor Vannini for another valet of the same stature who did not "guess." When the impertinent fellow begged Teresa to intervene for him, she told me I had done well.

At ten o'clock I saw all the actors and actresses arrive, together with a number of devotees of music, who all kissed her hand and whom she received most graciously. The rehearsal, which went on for three hours, bored me to extinction. I spent my time talking with Palesi, whom I liked for his never asking me where or when or how I had known his wife.

At the end of the rehearsal one of the actresses, a girl from Parma named Redegonda,[14] who had a male role and sang well, stayed for dinner with Teresa, and a moment later a young ballerina from Bologna named Corticelli,[15] whom she had also invited, arrived and at once kissed her hand. The girl's budding charms struck me; but, being full of Teresa at the moment, I paid her no special attention. After another moment I see a very stout old abate, of a bland and smiling countenance, who enters with stately steps and, looking at no one but Teresa, approaches and kisses her hand, going down on one knee in the Portuguese fashion. Gracious and smiling, Teresa makes him sit at her right; I was at her left. I at once recognize the Abate Gama,[16] whom I had left in the household of Cardinal Acquaviva[17] in Rome seventeen years earlier; but I give no sign of it. He had aged greatly, but it was he. The philandering old man, who had eyes only for Teresa, treated her to stale compliments and had not yet looked at anyone. Hoping that he will not recognize me, I avoid looking at him and I flirt with La Corticelli. Teresa calls me to order, saying that the Signor Abate wishes to know if I recognize him. At that I look at him, I pretend surprise, I rise, and I ask if I have the pleasure of seeing the Abate Gama.

"Himself," he replies, rising and taking me by the head to give me a number of kisses, in perfect accord with the combination of subtle policy and great curiosity which I knew to make up his character and which I have portrayed for my reader in the first volume of these memoirs.

After this beginning it can be imagined that we talked endlessly. He gave me news of Barbaruccia, of the Marchesa G., of Cardinal S. C.,[18] and he told me how he had passed from the service of Spain to that of Portugal, in which he still continued; but suddenly a figure appears which absorbs and bewilders all the faculties of my soul. A youth of perhaps fifteen or sixteen, but with the sort of maturity which an Italian can attain at that age, enters and bows to the whole company. I being the only person present who did not know him, Teresa presents him to me unabashed, saying:

"He is my brother."

I receive him as I should, but flabbergasted, not having had time to recover myself. This supposed brother of Teresa's was the image of me, except that he was not as dark; I instantly see that he is my son; nature had never been more indiscreet; it was the surprise which Teresa had promised me, and which she had cunningly arranged so that she should have the pleasure of seeing it in my face. In her first letters from Naples she had never written me that she was pregnant, and it had never occurred to me that she might be.

It seemed to me that Teresa should have avoided this meeting, for everyone present had eyes, and no more was needed to discern that the youth must be either my son or my brother. I give her a glance, but she turns away; the youth was looking at me in such confusion that he paid no attention to what his sister was saying to him. The others simply looked back and forth from his face to mine, and, convinced that he was my son, could only conclude that I had been the intimate friend of Teresa's mother, if it was true that she was his sister, for at the age she appeared to be it was impossible to suppose that she was his mother. Nor was it possible to conclude that I was Teresa's father, for I looked almost as young as she did.

What began to please me greatly was the youth's fine bearing and the intelligence he showed as he discoursed in the Neapolitan dialect, which he spoke very markedly. Teresa had me dine between herself and him. I found him well informed and with manners such as a Neapolitan upbringing rarely bestows. Teresa told him he should begin speaking Tuscan.

"It is only six months," she said to me, "since he left the custody of the man who brought him up and who taught him everything he knows, and especially music, which is his passion. You shall hear him at the harpsichord. I am eight years his elder."

Whether it was nature, prepossession, self-esteem, or whatever the reader may please, I rose from the table so enchanted with this son of Teresa's that I embraced him with such affection that the whole company applauded. I invited Teresa to dine with me the next day, together with everyone present.

"I too?" La Corticelli asked.

"You too."

After dinner the Abate Gama told me to choose between having him to breakfast or coming to breakfast with him the next morning, because he was dying to spend two hours alone with me. I invited him to my inn.

As soon as everyone had left, Don Cesarino (for such was the handsome youth's name) asked me if I would take him to the promenade with me. I embraced him and replied that he could go in my carriage with his brother-in-law, for I must not leave his sister alone. Palesi agreed.

As soon as we were alone I congratulated her on Cesarino.

"He is," she replied, "the happy fruit of our love. Happy, because he has everything to make him so. It is the same Duke[19] with whom I left Rimini who provided for his upbringing; I confided my secret to him as soon as I found that I was pregnant. I was delivered without anyone's knowing it, and it was he who sent him to nurse at Sorrento and had him baptized by the name of Cesare Filippo Lanti. He left him there until he was nine, then put him to board with a competent man, who saw that he received an excellent education and taught him music. From his earliest childhood he has always known me as his sister, and you cannot imagine my joy when I found that the older he grew the more he looked like you. I always considered him a sure pledge of our union, certain that it would take place as soon as we met again, for every time I looked at him I thought it impossible that he would not produce the same effect on your soul as he did on mine. I was sure that you could not refuse to make such a charming creature your legitimate son by marrying his fond mother.

"When the Duke died,[20] I left Naples, leaving him to board in the same place under the protection of Prince della Riccia,[21] who never thought him anything but my brother. Your son commands a capital of twenty thousand ducati del regno, the interest on which is paid to me and of which he does not know; but I let him want for nothing. My heart bleeds because I cannot tell him I am his mother; for I think he would love me all the more. You cannot imagine the pleasure I felt today when I saw your surprise and afterward observed how quickly you fell in love with him."

"And the resemblance?"

"It pleases me. Can it lead people to believe anything except that you were my mother's lover? Let it be so. My husband believes that is the source of the friendship between us, at which he might well have taken offense this morning when he saw our transports. He told me last night that Cesarino might be my brother on his mother's side but not on his father's, for he had seen his father at the theater and he could certainly not be mine. If I have children by Palesi all my property will go to them on my death; and if not it will go to Cesarino. My property is in trustworthy hands, even if Prince della Riccia should die."

She then took me to her bedroom, where she opened a strong-box which contained all her jewels and over fifty thousand ducati in good securities. In addition she had a large quantity of plate, and her talent, which assured her of leading roles in any theater in Italy.

I asked her if our son had yet had a love affair.

"I do not think so," she answered; "but I think my chambermaid is in love with him. I will keep my eyes open."

"Give him to me. I will teach him the way of the world."

"Ask anything of me, but leave me your son. Know that I never kiss him for fear of going mad. If you knew how good he is and how much he loves me, for I satisfy all his wishes. What will people say in Venice four months from now when they see the Casanova who escaped from the Leads become twenty years younger?"

"So you are going to Venice for La Sensa?"[22]

"Yes; and you are going to Rome?"

"And to Naples, to see my friend the Duke of Matalona."[23]

"I know him. He already has a son[24] by the daughter of the Duke of Bovino,[25] whom he married, a charming woman who was able to make a man of him. Everyone in Naples knows he was impotent."

In such talk we passed the day until Cesarino arrived with his brother-in-law. At supper my son won all that he had not earlier conquered of my paternal affection. He was sprightly and had all the Neapolitan vivacity. He wanted me to hear him at the harpsichord, at which he accompanied himself in some Neapolitan songs which made us laugh heartily. Teresa did nothing but look from him to me and from me to him, then she embraced her husband and exclaimed that to be happy in this world one must be in love.

So I spent that day, which was one of the happiest of my whole life.

CHAPTER VIII

La Corticelli. The Jewish impresario cudgeled.

At nine o'clock the next morning the Abate Gama was announced; he began by weeping for joy to see me, after so many years, in such good health and in the prime of life. The reader sees that he must have praised me to my face. However intelligent one may be, however well one may know those who practice it, having one's ears tickled is gratifying. The mild-mannered Abate, extremely amiable and without an iota of malice, but curious both by nature and by his occupation—such, in short, as I have portrayed him in my first volume—did not wait for any urging on my part to tell me his whole story for the past seventeen years, making it a lengthy business by recounting its various episodes in all possible detail. He had passed from the service of Spain to that of Portugal, and as Secretary of Embassy to Commander Almada,[1] he had been obliged to leave Rome because Pope Rezzonico[2] would not allow His Most Faithful Majesty[3] to punish the Jesuits who, though they had only broken his arm, had intended to kill him.[4] Gama traveled about Italy, corresponding with Almada and the famous Carvalho[5] and waiting for the end of the quarrel so that he could return to Rome; that was his whole story. But the eloquent Abate made it last for an hour, expecting that I would pay him in the same coin with a detailed account of my adventures; we both displayed our talent— the Abate by lengthening out his story, I by shortening mine, not without the minor pleasure of balking his curiosity. He asked me perfunctorily what I was going to do in Rome, and I replied that I was going to see the Pope to ask him to persuade the State Inquisitors[6] to pardon me. It was not true; but if I had told him truthfully that I was going there simply to amuse myself he would not have believed me. He who tells the truth to unbelieving ears prostitutes truth; it is murder. The Abate asked me to do him the favor of corresponding with him, and I promised to do so; then he told me that he was in position to show me his friendship by introducing me to the Marchese Botta-Adorno,[7] then Governor of Tuscany,[8] who was said to be a friend of the Emperor Francis I,[9] then reigning, and I replied that he would be doing me a great honor. He brought up the subject of Teresa, whereupon he found me constipated; I told him that she was a child when I had known her family in Bologna, and that her brother's resemblance to me could only be chance. On my table he saw something very well written, and he asked me if it was my secretary who had such a good hand. Costa, who was present, answered him in Spanish that it was he. The Abate then exhausted himself in compliments, ending by asking me to send Costa to him to copy some letters. I did not hesitate to answer that I urgently needed the young man all day. He wanted him only in order to make him talk. Such are the curious.

Curiosity, which moralists refuse to number among the passions, is a noble quality of mind whose laudable object is to know all of nature: *nihil dulcius quam omnia scire* ("nothing is sweeter than to know all things"); however, it is a thing of the senses, for it can arise only from perception and sensation. But curiosity is a vice when it seeks only to pry into the affairs of others, whether the man possessed by it tries to obtain knowledge of them directly or indirectly, whether he tries to discover them in order to be of service to the person he sounds or to use what he discovers for his own advantage; it is always a vice, or a disease, for the mind of a man curious by nature is never at rest. Discovering a secret is perpetrating a theft. I am not speaking of the kind of curiosity which, relying on the abstruse sciences, tries to know the future or things which are not in nature; it is the daughter of ignorance and superstition, and they who dally with it are fools; but the Abate Gama was no fool; he was curious by nature, and he was paid to be curious. Having some visits to make, he left me, promising that he would return at dinnertime.

Doctor Vannini brought me a new hire valet, vouching for him. He was from Parma and of the same height as the first; I told Leduc to give him the livery. I warned the innkeeper-academician that I wanted a creditable dinner, and I was served accordingly.

The first to arrive was La Corticelli, together with her mother, who went by the name of "Signora Laura,"[10] and her brother, a violinist who looked like a girl. Her mother told me that she never let her daughter dine alone with strangers. I replied that in that case she had only to go home or to leave her there and accept two scudi to dine with her son wherever she pleased. She took the two scudi and departed, saying she felt sure she was leaving her in good hands.

Her daughter made such amusing comments on this little dialogue between her mother and myself, laughing so heartily, that it was on that very day I began to love her. She was thirteen years of age, and looked only ten; she was well built, extremely fair, gay, with a sense of humor; but I do not know how or with what in her I could have fallen in love. She begged me to protect her against the Jewish opera impresario.[11] In the contract he had given her he had undertaken to have her dance a *pas de deux* in the second opera, and he had not done so. She asked me to force the Jew to abide by his undertaking. I promised to send the Jew word to come and talk with me.

The next to arrive was the Parmesan actress Redegonda, tall and beautiful. Costa, who was Parmesan too, told me she was the sister of my hire valet. In two or three minutes of questioning I found Redegonda worthy of attention. The Abate Gama arrives, and he congratulates me on finding me between the two pretty girls. I make him take my place, and he begins flirting with them; they laugh at him, but he persists. I saw that he thought he was pleasing them; and I well understood that vanity could prevent him from knowing he was making himself ridiculous; but I did not foresee that when I reached his age I might be like him. Indeed, I did not give it a thought. Unhappiness is the lot of the old man who does not know what he is or understand that the same sex which he attracted in his youth cannot but scorn him as soon as he shows that he still has pretensions though age has deprived him of all the qualities required to please.

My beautiful Teresa arrived last, with her husband and Cesarino, who had on a very fine coat; I embraced him after fulfilling the same obligation to his mother; and I sat down at table between them. The Abate Gama took the place between Redegonda and La Corticelli, and it was he who enlivened the meal with his witty remarks. I laughed to myself, seeing how attentively my hire valet changed his sister Redegonda's plate, while she plumed herself on being entitled to honors to which he could not aspire; she seized an opportunity to say to me:

"He's a good lad who, unfortunately, has no talent."

I had purposely put in my pocket an enameled gold box on the cover of which was my portrait, painted on the enamel in the form of a medallion and a very good likeness. I had had it made in Paris as a present for Madame d'Urfé; and I had not given it to her because the painter had made me too young. I had filled the box with the excellent Havana snuff which Monsieur de Chavigny[12] had given me and which Teresa liked very much, and I was waiting for her to ask me for some so that I could take it from my pocket.

It was the Abate Gama, who had some very good snuff in a box from Orihuela,[13] who passed it to Teresa, and she passed him some of hers in a snuffbox of light-colored tortoise shell, encrusted all over with gold, than which nothing could be handsomer. Gama finds fault with Teresa's snuff; I pronounce it good, but I venture to say that mine is better. With that I take out my snuffbox and offer her a pinch, holding it open. She could not see the portrait. She agrees that the snuff is excellent.

"In that case, Signora, shall we exchange?"

"Gladly. Give me a piece of paper."

"There's no need for that. Snuff is exchanged in whatever boxes it happens to be in."

So saying, I put Teresa's box in my pocket, and I hand her mine closed. When she sees the portrait she gives a cry which startles the company, and she cannot refrain from printing a kiss on the medallion.

"Look," she immediately says to Cesarino. "It is your portrait."

Cesarino looks at it in astonishment, and the box makes the round of the table. Everyone says it is my own portrait made ten years earlier but that it could pass for Cesarino's. Teresa is mad about it and swears the box shall never leave her hands, she gets up from the table and embraces her dear brother several times. I saw that the Abate Gama's politic mind was busily drawing conclusions from the little incident. He left toward nightfall, saying that he expected me for breakfast the next morning.

I spent the day flirting with Redegonda and Teresa, who, seeing that the girl attracted me, advised me to speak out and promised to invite her to visit her whenever I liked. But Teresa did not know her well.

The next morning the Abate Gama gave me a cup of exquisite chocolate; he said that he had sent word to Marshal Botta and that he would come for me at four o'clock to present me to him. Then, as ever the slave of his curiosity, he politely reproached me for having said nothing about my great wealth in my brief account of my adventures.

"My wealth, Signor Abate, is not great; but I have friends whose purses are open to me."

"If you have true friends you are rich. But they are very scarce."

Leaving him, I went to visit Redegonda, to whom I would gladly have given the preference over La Corticelli. She received me in a room in which I saw her mother, her uncle, and three or four children, her brothers and sisters.

"Have you not another room in which to receive your friends?"

"I do not need another room, for I have no friends to receive."

"Have the room and you will have friends. This one is all very well for receiving relatives, but not people who, like myself, come to pay homage to your charms and your talent."

"My daughter, Signore," said her mother, "has very little talent and no charms."

"Yet I find her most pleasing."

"That is an honor for her, and she will receive you whenever you come to see her, but in no other room than this."

"Here I am afraid I inconvenience you. Good-by, Signora."

I went to Teresa's and told her about my visit, and we laughed over it. She said she would be glad to see me at the opera in her *camerino*,[14] which I could enter by giving a testone[15] to the man who stood guard at the little stairway leading to the stage.

The Abate Gama came to fetch me to introduce me to Marshal Botta. I saw a man in every way worthy of respect. He was famous because of the Genoese affair.[16] He was commanding the Austrian army in person when the people of Genoa, angry at the presence of foreigners who were there only to subjugate their country, revolted and drove them out of the city. But for that the ancient Republic would have perished. He was with some Florentine ladies and gentlemen, whom he left in my honor. He talked to me of Venice like a man who knew my country well, and, after making me talk at length about France, he seemed satisfied. In his turn he talked of the Russian Court, where he had been when Elisabeth Petrovna, who still reigned, so easily ascended the throne of her father,[17] Peter the Great. He said that only in Russia did politics know the art of using poisons.

At the hour when the opera began, the Marshal withdrew, and everyone left. After taking home the Abate, who naturally assured me that I had made a very good impression on the Marshal, I went to the opera too, where, at the price of a testone, I went up to Teresa's *camerino*, to find her pretty chambermaid dressing her. She advised me to go to Redegonda's *camerino*, where, as she had to dress as a man, she might let me see charming things.

I had myself shown to it, and her mother did not want me to stay, for her daughter was just then dressing in male attire; but when I assured her I would turn my back she gave me permission, saying that I could sit at her toilet table. Now there was a large mirror on the toilet table, which admirably enabled me to see for nothing all of Redegonda's most private treasures, especially when she awkwardly put her legs into her breeches. She lost nothing by it, for I would have signed any conditions in order to obtain her favors. I thought it impossible she did not know that, seated where I was, I must see everything, and the idea increased my flame. I turned when her mother gave me permission, and, in her disguise as a man, admired this girl of twenty-one who was perfectly proportioned and five feet tall.

As soon as Redegonda was dressed she went out; whereupon I was able to talk with her privately in the wings.

"I am on fire," I said, "charming Redegonda, and I feel that I shall die if you do not make me happy. Do not pretend: as you know that in your mirror I saw the whole of you, and I cannot imagine you capable of having set me aflame only to drive me to despair."

"What can you have seen? I don't know what you're talking about."

"Come now. It's possible; but answer me. That's what matters. What am I to do to have you?"

"To have me? I do not understand such language. I am a decent girl."

"I believe it; and you must believe that after you have loved me you will not be anything else. Speak out, for I must know my fate this instant."

"I cannot say anything but that you are at liberty to come to see me."

"At what hour will you be alone?"

"Alone? Never."

"Very well, then, let your mother be present; it will not matter. If she is wise she will pretend not to see, and I will give you a hundred ducati each time."

"Really, either you are mad or you do not know me."

When, a quarter of an hour later, I recounted the whole incident to Teresa she advised me, after laughing heartily, to go at once and offer the mother the hundred ducati, and, if she refused them, to consider it good riddance and try my luck elsewhere.

I go back to the *camerino*, where she is alone.

"Signora, I am a foreigner, and I shall leave in a week or ten days; I am rich and in love with your daughter. Will you bring her to sup with me this evening, and be obliging? I will give you a hundred zecchini, and after that you shall ruin me."

"To whom do you think you are speaking? Your effrontery amazes me. Inquire who I am, and inquire into my daughter's behavior. You are the first person in the world who has dared to address me in such a manner."

"Then good-by, Signora."

"Good-by, Signore."

I find Redegonda in the wings, and I repeat the dialogue to her word for word. She bursts out laughing.

"Did I do right, or wrong?"

"More right than wrong; but if you love me come to see us."

"Come to see you now!"

"Why not? Who knows?"

"Who knows? You do not know me. Hope poisons me, my beautiful Redegonda; that is why I spoke to you clearly."

Determined to put the girl out of my mind, I went to sup with Teresa, where I spent three delicious hours which made my soul rejoice. The next day, having a great deal of writing to do, I did not go out, and toward evening I saw La Corticelli before me with her mother and her brother. She had come to hold me to my promise that I would protect her against the Jewish impresario who would not let her dance the *pas de deux* as he had undertaken to do in the contract. I said she should come to breakfast with me the next morning and I would talk to the Jew in her presence, provided he would come; I promised to send for him. Needing to finish my letters and to refrain from eating, I told Costa to serve them supper.

After finishing my correspondence, feeling in the mood for amusement, I have the little madcap sit beside me and I flirt with her in a fashion to which Signora Laura could make no objection; but I am a little surprised when the youth comes to join in.

"You are not a girl," I say.

Thus apostrophized, the rascal shows me that he is a boy, but in such a scandalous way that his sister, who was sitting on my lap, gives a great burst of laughter and throws herself into her mother's arms at the other end of the room, where, after eating a good supper, she had respectfully retired. When he sees his sister gone, the little scoundrel treats me to a gesture which annoys me, and I give him a light box on the ear. I rise and I ask Signora Laura for what purpose she has brought me this catamite. The only answer she gives me is:

"Isn't he a very pretty boy?"

I told her to leave, giving the Giton[18] a scudo to make up to him for the box on the ear. He took it, kissing my hand.

745

I went to bed laughing over the incident, for, such as nature made me, the wristband game[19] could never have been anything but the consequence of an intoxication produced by a great friendship.

The next morning I sent Costa to the Jew with a message asking him to come and hear something I had to tell him. A little later La Corticelli arrived with her mother, and the Jew came as we were breakfasting.

After setting forth La Corticelli's grievance to him, I read him his contract and I told him quietly that I could easily find means to make him abide by his undertaking. After offering various excuses, whose insubstantiality La Corticelli herself proved to him, he ended by promising me he would see the ballet master that day and instruct him to have her dance with a partner whom he named to me and who, by her account, would be very glad to compose a *pas de deux* for her. After thus settling the matter, I let them leave.

I went to the Abate Gama's, to go on to dinner at Marshal Botta's, who had sent us an invitation. It was at this dinner that I made the acquaintance of the Chevalier Mann,[20] the English Resident, who was the idol of Florence, a man of wealth, amiable, a great lover of the arts, and with excellent taste. The next day I paid him a visit, and in his small garden, the furnishings of his house, his pictures, and his choice books, I saw the man of genius. After returning my visit he invited me to dinner, and he was kind enough also to invite Signora Palesi, her brother, and her husband. After dinner Cesarino delighted the company at the harpsichord. The conversation turning to resemblances, the Chevalier Mann showed us some miniature portraits of amazing beauty. Shortly before she left, Teresa told me gravely that she had kept me in mind.

"I told Redegonda," she said, "that I would come for her and keep her for supper with me and send her home afterward. Come to supper too, have your carriage wait at my door, and you shall be the one to take her home. You will have her alone with you only a few minutes, but that is something. I would wager that you will find her submissive."

"You shall hear the whole story tomorrow. I will not fail to be at your supper."

I got there at nine o'clock. Teresa receives me as one receives an unexpected friend, I tell Redegonda that I congratulate myself on finding her there, and she replies gaily that she had not expected to have the pleasure of seeing me. At supper no one had any appetite; only Redegonda ate very heartily and laughed a great deal at all the stories I told her. After supper Teresa asks Redegonda if she wishes to have a sedan chair sent for or if she will let me take her home; she replies that, if I will be so kind, there is no need for a sedan chair. This answer makes me sure of everything. Good nights are said, embraces exchanged, I give her my arm, which she presses, we go down, her brother opens the carriage door; Redegonda gets in, I get in after her, and when I go to sit down, I find the place taken, I hear a great shriek of laughter and Redegonda saying to me:

"It's my mother."

I should have made a joke of it, but I did not have the strength. Redegonda sat down on her mother's lap. I coldly asked her why she had not come upstairs to supper with us. When we reached her door the *virtuosa*'s mother said I might come up, but I excused myself, and for good reason. If she had done the slightest thing to annoy me I would have boxed her ears, and the man they had in the house looked too much like a cutthroat.

In my fury, I think of going to La Corticelli's; the hour was unwonted, and I had never been there; but no matter. I needed to calm myself, and I was almost certain I should find the Bolognese girl accommodating and Signora Laura unable to resist money.

My lackey shows me the way to her room.

"That will do. Go and wait for me in the carriage."

I knock, I knock again, the family wakes:

"Who is there?"

I give my name, the door is opened, I enter in darkness, and I hear Signora Laura say she is going to light a candle, and that if I had let her know she would have waited up for me despite its being so cold; and in fact I felt as if I were in an icehouse. I hear La Corticelli laughing, I grope for her bed, I find it, I put in my hand, and I touch the too obvious tokens of the male sex. I guess it is her brother, and I see him by the light of the candle her mother has lighted. I see his sister lying in the same bed laughing, with the covers drawn up to her chin because, like her brother, she was stark naked. Despite my freedom from prejudice on the subject, such infamous behavior disgusts me.

"Why," I ask Signora Laura, "do you not keep your son in bed with you?"

"What harm can I fear? They are brother and sister."

"It is not good."

The catamite makes off and gets into his mother's bed, and La Corticelli says in her Bolognese dialect, which immediately sets me laughing, that it was neither good nor bad, since she loved her brother only as a brother and he loved her only as a sister. She ended by saying that if I wanted her to sleep alone I had only to buy her a bed, which she would take with her when she went back to Bologna.

Talking and gesticulating, she unwittingly let me see a third of her nudity, and I saw nothing worth seeing, nevertheless it was ordained that I should fall in love with her skin, for it was all she had. If she had been alone I would have gone further with her; but, her mother and her brother being there, I feared scenes which might anger me. I gave her ten zecchini to buy herself a bed, and I left her.

I took refuge in my inn, cursing all the execrable mothers of *virtuose*.

I spent the whole of the next morning with Monsieur Mann in the gallery,[21] where in the course of five or six visits I saw marvels in the way of paintings, statues, and engraved gems. Before going to dine with the Abate Gama, whom I had invited, I went to tell Teresa the story of my two adventures of the night before, and we laughed over them. She said that if I absolutely needed a girl I had only to take La Corticelli, who certainly would not keep me languishing.

At table the Abate Gama, talking politics in good earnest, asks me if I would be willing to represent the Court of Portugal in a certain matter at the congress which, all Europe believed, was to be held in the city of Augsburg.[22] He assured me that if I did well in the post, which he would be glad to solicit for me, I could be sure that if I went to Lisbon afterward I could get whatever I might want from the Court. I replied that he would find me ready to undertake anything of which he thought me capable, that he had only to write to me, and that I would see to it that he always had my address. It was at that moment that I first felt the strongest possible desire to become a diplomat.

That evening at the opera I talked to the ballet master, to the dancer who was to be my protégée's partner, and to the Jew, who confirmed his promise that she should dance the *pas de deux* three or four days later and every day for the rest of the Carnival. La Corticelli told me she already had a bed and invited me to supper with her. I promised I would go.

Being sure that I would pay for everything, her mother had sent out to a cookshop for a supper for four, which was good enough, and several flagons of the best Florentine wine; in addition there was a clarified wine called "ogliatico" or "aleatico,"[23] which I found excellent, but the mother, the son, and the daughter, who were not accustomed to drinking so well, became tipsy. The mother and son went off to bed without ceremony, and the little madcap did likewise, urging me to follow her example. I did not dare, the cold was intense, there was no fire in the room, and her bed had only one cover; if I had undressed I should have caught a cold. She gave herself to me and tried to assure me that I was her first lover, and I pretended to believe her. I left after spending two hours with her, promising to spend the following night with her on condition that she would heat the room with a brazier and would buy another cover, and I left her fifty zecchini.

The next day a letter which I received from Grenoble interested me greatly. Valenglart wrote me that La Roman had left for Paris with her aunt, having become convinced that if they did not go what the horoscope declared could never come true.

So they would never have gone there if I had not taken it into my head to cast them a fantastic horoscope, for even if astrology had been a science I knew nothing about it. We find countless events in real history which would never have occurred if they had not been predicted. This is because we are the authors of our so-called destiny, and all the "antecedent necessities" of the Stoics are chimerical; the argument which proves the power of destiny seems strong only because it is sophistical. Cicero laughed at it. Someone whom he had invited to dinner, who had promised to go, and who had not appeared, wrote him that since he had not gone it was evident that he had not been *iturus* ("going to go"). Cicero answers him: *Veni ergo cras, et veni etiamsi venturus non sis* ("Then come tomorrow, and come even if you are not going to come").[24] At this date, when I am conscious that I rely entirely on my common sense, I owe this explanation to my reader, despite the axiom, *Fata viam inveniunt* ("Destiny finds the way").[25] If the fatalists are obliged by their own philosophy to consider the concatenation of all events necessary, *a parte ante* ("a priori"), what remains of man's moral freedom is nothing; and in that case he can neither earn merit nor incur guilt.[26] I cannot in conscience admit that I am a machine.

Having gone to the theater to see La Corticelli rehearse her *pas de deux*, I saw her in possession of a fine pelisse. When the other ballerinas caught sight of me they treated me to scornful looks; but my favorite, proud of being preferred, came to speak to me and give me playful pinches.[27]

At supper I found that Signora Laura had provided a large brazier and another cover on the bed. She showed me all the things her daughter had bought for herself and complained that she had not provided clothes for her brother. I pacified her by giving her six zecchini.

In bed I found the girl neither in love nor passionate but amusing. She made me laugh, and I found her accommodating. She needed no more to keep me constant. I gave her a watch and promised to sup with her on the next day but one. By then she should have danced her *pas de deux*.

But I was surprised when I saw her appear only in ensembles.

I go to sup with her as I had promised, and I find her wretched; she tells me, with tears, that I must avenge her for the insult, that the Jew put the blame on the tailor but he was lying. I try to calm her by promising her everything, I spend several hours with her, and I go back to my inn resolved to avenge her after making inquiries.

The next morning early I send Costa to tell the Jew to call on me. He answers that he knows what I want, and that if La Corticelli was not dancing in this opera she would dance in the next.

I then saw what had to be done, but I also saw that I must pretend to take the thing lightly. I summoned Leduc, I told him the whole story, saying that I would be dishonored if I did not avenge myself. I told him that he alone could give me the satisfaction of arranging a good cudgeling for the scoundrel, who by breaking his word to me had given me such an obvious proof of his disregard. I promised him twenty zecchini. I impressed the importance of secrecy on him. He asked me for twenty-four hours before he gave me a positive answer.

The next morning he came to my bedside to tell me that during the preceding day he had devoted himself entirely to acquiring a knowledge of the Jew's person and of the house in which he lived, asking information from no one.

"Today," he said, "I will not let him out of my sight; I shall know at what hour he goes to bed, and tomorrow you shall hear the rest."

"Be prudent, and before you entrust the business to anyone consider carefully."

The next day he tells me that if he goes home at the same hour and takes the same road, he will have the cudgeling before he gets to bed.

"What men have you chosen?"

"No one but myself, on whom I can rely, and you shall not give me the twenty zecchini until the whole town is telling the story. After cudgeling him I will go back for my redingote where I will have left it and I will re-enter the inn by the back door, going off to bed without anyone seeing me. Even Costa will be able to swear that I cannot possibly be the man who cudgeled him if anyone should say so. However, I will have pistols in my pocket in case I have to defend myself."

The next morning he comes to dress my hair and I see he is calm. But as soon as he sees that I am alone he gives me the news that the thing is done.

"The Jew," he said, "instead of running threw himself on the ground, his shouts brought a few people, and I slipped away. I don't know if I killed him, for two blows landed on his head."

"I should be sorry if you did."

I was invited to dinner at Teresa's, where the guests were Signor Sassi, the first castrato, and the Abate Gama. I hear the pretty story told. I say I am sorry, though he is a scoundrel. The castrato says he is not sorry, and that he is sure people will say it was he who made him the present.

"They are saying," the Abate said to me, "that it is you who had it done, and for good reason."

"It will not be easy to discover who is behind it," I replied, "for the rascal has gone too far with many decent people."

The subject was dropped at last, and we dined in high spirits.

The Jew got up from bed a few days later with a plaster on his nose, and the thing was generally attributed to me; but when nothing was discovered the affair was finally forgotten. Only La Corticelli, as wild with joy as she was scatterbrained, talked as if she were sure it was I who had avenged her and was furious with me for refusing to admit it.

[* * *]

Intending to make a long stay in Florence, Casanova soon found himself in his usual trouble with the authorities who ordered him to leave Tuscany. This he did, traveling first to Rome, where he renewed old acquaintances, and then on to Naples, where he discovered yet another of his children.

CHAPTER X

My short but enjoyable stay in Naples.
The Duke of Matalona, my daughter, Donna
Lucrezia. My departure.

It is impossible either to express or to conceive how greatly my soul rejoiced when I found myself once more in Naples, where eighteen years earlier I had made my fortune on my return from Martorano.[1] I had gone there only to pay the Duke of Matalona the visit which I had promised him when he was in Paris; but before waiting on that nobleman I wanted to inquire after all my old friends.

So I went out early on foot, first to make myself known to the banker who was Belloni's correspondent. After accepting my letter of credit he gave me the number of bank notes I asked for, assuring me that no one should know anything of our dealings.

Leaving his place of business, I went to the house in which Don Antonio Casanova[2] had lived. I was told that he was living on an estate he had bought near Salerno, and of which he bore the name with the title of Marchese. I go and inquire after Palo;[3] he had died and his son was living at Santa Lucia with a wife and children. I intended to go to see him, but I never found the time for it. I next ask where the advocate Castelli[4] is living; he was the husband of my dear Donna Lucrezia, with whom I had been so much in love at Rome; I could scarcely wait to see her, and I was in ecstasy at the thought of the pleasure we should feel when we met again. I am told that he has long been dead and that his widow lives twenty miles from Naples. I promise myself that I will visit her. I knew that Don Lelio Caraffa[5] was still alive and resided in the Palazzo Matalona.[6]

So I go to dine, then I dress and take a hackney carriage to the Palazzo Matalona. The Duke was still at table; but no matter, I am announced; he comes out to see who it is, he recognizes me, he gives a cry, he embraces me, he at once does me the honor to address me in the second person singular, he introduces me to his wife, who was a daughter of the Duke of Bovino,[7] and to all the very numerous company. I tell him that I have come to Naples only to pay him the visit I had promised him in Paris.

"Then it is only right that I should put you up; let someone go at once to the inn at which Casanova *s'est débarqué* ['disembarked'] and bring all his luggage here and, if he has a carriage, put it in my stable."

I accept.

A fine-looking man who was at the table no sooner heard the name Casanova than he said to me gaily:

"If you bear my name, you must be a bastard of my father's."

"Not of your father's," I replied, "but of your mother's."

My riposte is applauded, the man comes and embraces me, and the misunderstanding is explained. Instead of hearing "Casanova," he had heard "Casalnuovo,"[8] and the gentleman was none other than the Duke of that fief.

"You know," the Duke of Matalona said to me, "that I have a son."[9]

"I was told so, and I found it hard to believe; but now I am no longer surprised. I see a princess who could not fail to perform the miracle."

The Duchess blushes, without vouchsafing me a look, but the company clap their hands, for it was well known that before his marriage the Duke of Matalona was supposed to be impotent. His son is summoned, I say that he looks like him; a cheerful monk who was seated beside the Duchess says he does not, and she coldly gives him a slap in the face, which he receives with a laugh.

In less than half an hour my banter endeared me to the entire company with the marked exception of the Duchess, who maintained a deliberate haughtiness which took the ground from under my feet. She was beautiful, but lofty as the clouds, deaf and mute in season and out of season, and always in control of her eyes. I labored for two days to persuade her to converse with me, and finally, despairing of success, I left her to her pride.

The Duke showed me to my apartment and, seeing my Spaniard, asked me where my secretary was, and when I said he was the Abate Alfani, who had assumed the office so that he could stay in Naples incognito, he replied that he had been well advised to do so, for he had cheated a great many people with his pretended antiquities.[10]

He took me to see his fine stable, where there were superb horses, then his picture gallery, then his library, and finally his private apartment and his choice books, which were all forbidden. After that he made me swear not to breathe a word of what he was going to read me. It was a scathing satire[11] on the whole court, of which I understood nothing. I never kept a secret more faithfully.

"You shall come with me," he said, "to the Teatro San Carlo,[12] where I will introduce you to the most beautiful ladies in Naples, and to which you may go whenever you wish; when you want to be completely free you shall go to my box on the third tier, which is always open to my friends. In that way the opera will cost you nothing. I will also introduce you at my mistress's box, to which you may go when you please."

"What, my dear Duke! You have a mistress?"

"Yes, for form's sake, for I love only my wife; nevertheless people believe I am in love with her and am even jealous because I never introduce anyone to her and do not allow her to receive visitors."

"And the Duchess, young and charming as she is—does not object to your having a mistress?"

"My wife cannot be jealous of her, because she knows that I am impotent with all the women on earth except with her."

"I take it you are not joking, but I find it hard to believe. Can a man have a mistress he does not love?"

"But I do love her, for she is divinely intelligent and she amuses me; but she does not interest me physically."

"That is possible; I suppose she is ugly."

"Ugly? You will see her this evening. She is pretty and only seventeen years old, she speaks French, her mind is unprejudiced, and she is well-bred."

At the hour for the opera he takes me to the great theater, he introduces me to several ladies, all of them ugly. In the great middle box I saw the very young King,[13] surrounded by many members of the nobility dressed richly but without taste. The whole parterre and all the boxes were full, the latter all covered with mirrors and illuminated inside and out because of an anniversary.[14] The effect was most striking.

He takes me to his private box on the third tier and introduces me to his friends; they were the most brilliant minds in Naples. I laughed to myself at those who do not believe that the intelligence of a nation is far more dependent on its climate than on education.[15] Such critics should be sent to Naples. What intelligence! Boerhaave,[16] the great Boerhaave, if he had been in Naples, would have known the nature of sulphur far better from its effects on plants, and even more clearly from its effects on animals. Nowhere but in that country is water the only remedy needed to cure any number of diseases which, in our country, would be deadly without the art of pharmacy.

The Duke, who had vanished, returns and takes me to the box in which his mistress was seated in company with a respectable-looking woman. As he enters he says:

"Leonilda mia, ti presento il cavalier Don Giacomo Casanova veneziano amico mio" ("My Leonilda, I beg to introduce my friend the Chevalier Don Giacomo Casanova, of Venice").

She receives me affably and modestly, and she renounces the pleasure of listening to the music for that of talking with me. When a girl is pretty it takes but a moment to find her so; if her charms must be examined to elicit a favorable judgment they become dubious. Donna Leonilda was striking. I smiled, glancing at the Duke, who had told me that he loved her as a father loves his daughter and that he kept her only for fashion's sake; he understands me, and he says I must believe what he had told me. I reply that it is incredible, and with a sly smile she says that *anything that is possible is credible.*

"I admit that," I said, "but one is free to believe or not believe when a thing seems unlikely."

"Exactly; but I think believing is quicker and easier. You arrived in Naples yesterday, it is incredible, yet it is true."

"What is incredible about it?"

"Can anyone believe that a stranger would come to Naples at a time when everyone there is in terror?"

"And indeed I felt afraid until this moment, but now I have no fear at all. If you are in Naples St. Januarius[17] cannot but protect it. You laugh?"

"I am laughing at an amusing idea. If I had a suitor with a face like St. Januarius's he would reap no favors."

"Is the saint so very ugly?"

"You can decide that for yourself when you see his statue."

The bantering tone which she had taken was one which was but a step from friendship and frankness. The charms of the mind are superior to the spell of beauty. I bring up the subject of love, and she discourses on it in masterly fashion.

"If love," she says, "is not followed by possession of the loved object it can only be a torment, and if possession is forbidden one must not allow oneself to love."

"I agree, and the more so because even the enjoyment of a beautiful object is not a true pleasure if it has not been preceded by love."

"And if love has preceded it, it accompanies it—of that there is no doubt. But one may doubt if love follows it."

"That is true, for possession is often the death of love."

"And if it is not dead in both the persons who love each other, that is murder, for the one of them in whom love survives is left unhappy."

"That is indubitable, Madame,[18] and from this argument, based on the most irrefutable dialectic, I must infer that you condemn the senses to perpetual starvation. That is cruel."

"God preserve me from such Platonism. I condemn love without enjoyment as severely as I do enjoyment without love. I leave you to draw the inference."

"Love and enjoy, enjoy and love, turn and turn about."

"Exactly."

My conclusion set her laughing, and the Duke kissed her hand. The duenna, who did not understand a word of French, listened to the opera; but I!

I was beside myself. These things were being said by a seventeen-year-old girl as pretty as a Cupid. The Duke now recited a ribald epigram by La Fontaine on enjoyment and desires, which is found only in the first edition[19] and of which the first four lines are as follows:

La jouissance et les désirs
Sont ce que l'homme a de plus rare,
Mais ce ne sont pas vrais plaisirs
Dès le moment qu'on les sépare.

("Enjoyment and desires are man's rarest possessions, but they cease to be true pleasures as soon as they are separated.")

I said that I had translated the epigram, with the six following lines, into Italian and Latin, and that in Italian it had taken me twenty lines to say what La Fontaine said in ten, whereas I said it all in six in my Latin translation. Donna Leonilda said she was sorry she did not know Latin.

In polite Neapolitan society the first token of friendship which a gentleman or a lady bestows on a new acquaintance is to use the second person singular in addressing him. Both parties are then more at their ease; but this mode of address entails no diminution in the respect which they owe each other.

Donna Leonilda filled me with admiration; if one does not recover from it, it becomes adoration, then irresistible love. The opera, which lasted five hours, came to its end without my realizing how long it was.

After the young prodigy left with her duenna the Duke told me that we must part unless I liked gambling.

"I am not averse to it with the right sort of players."

"Excellent. Then come with me. You will be with ten or twelve men of my stamp at a faro bank, then a cold supper; but it is a secret, for gambling is forbidden. I will vouch for you."

He takes me to the Duke of Monteleone's[20] and up to the fourth floor, where, after passing through ten or twelve rooms, I find myself in one in which a mild-looking banker was dealing; before him were silver and gold coins to the value of three or four hundred zecchini. The Duke makes me sit down beside him, introducing me as his friend. I go to take out my purse, but I am told that play there is on one's word and that one pays at the end of twenty-four hours. The banker gives me a *livret*[21] and a basket in which, between singles and doubles, there are a thousand counters. I say that each counter will be worth a Neapolitan ducat; that completes the ceremonies. In less than two hours I lose my whole basket, and I stop. Then I sup very gaily. The supper consisted of an enormous dish of macaroni and ten or twelve dishes of various sorts of shellfish. On the way home I never gave the Duke time to indulge in those condolences on one's losses which are always irksome. I kept him delightfully occupied with talk of Donna Leonilda.

Early the next morning the Duke sent me word that if I wanted to go to kiss the King's hand with him I must dress for the occasion. I put on a coat of rose-colored short-napped velvet embroidered with gold spangles, and I kissed the King's hand, which was swollen with chilblains.[22] He was nine years old. The Prince of San Nicandro[23] brought him up as far as in him lay, but he became an accomplished monarch, affable, tolerant, just, and generous, although too unceremonious, which, in a king, is a serious fault.

I had the honor of dining at the right of the Duchess, who, after looking at my coat, felt obliged to say that she had seldom seen a finer.

"By such means, Signora, do I attempt to preserve my person from too thorough a scrutiny."

She smiled. When we rose table the Duke took me downstairs with him to the apartment of his uncle Don Lelio, who remembered me well. I kissed the venerable old man's hand, asking him to forgive my youthful escapades. He told his nephew that eighteen years earlier he had chosen me to be the companion of his studies,[24] and he was very glad to hear me give a brief account of all my vicissitudes in Rome when I was in the service of Cardinal Acquaviva.[25]

After an hour of conversation he asked me to come to see him often.

Toward evening the Duke told me that if I wanted to go to the opera buffa at the Fiorentini[26] it would please his mistress if I went to see her in her box, and he gave me the number of it; he said that he would come for me toward the end of the performance and that we would sup together as we had done on the previous evening.

I did not need to order horses harnessed. There was always a coupé in the courtyard awaiting my orders.

At the Teatro dei Fiorentini I found the opera already begun. I enter the box in which Donna Leonilda was sitting, and she receives me with these honeyed words:

"*Caro Don Giacomo*, it is a great pleasure to see you again."

She saw fit not to address me in the second person singular. The girl's alluring features struck me as being not unfamiliar, but I could not remember what young woman it was of whom she reminded me. Leonilda was a beauty; her hair was light chestnut, a color which is above suspicion, and her beautiful black eyes at once listened and questioned. But what enchanted me, and what I found entirely new, was that when she told a story she spoke with her hands, her elbows, her shoulders, and often with her chin. Her tongue did not suffice her to express all that she wanted to convey.

The conversation turning to La Fontaine's epigram, which I had not wanted to recite to her entire because it was licentious, she said that it could only provoke a smile.

"I have a room," she said, "which the Duke has had hung for me with Chinese designs representing a quantity of the postures in which the people of that country make love. We go there sometimes, and I assure you[27] they do not arouse the slightest sensation in me."

"That may be due to a defect in temperament, for when I see things of that sort well drawn they set me on fire; and I am amazed that when you look at them with the Duke you do not feel tempted to put some of them into practice."

"We feel only friendship for each other."

"That is not easy to believe."

"I could swear that he is a man; but I could not swear that he is capable of giving a woman any substantial proof of love."

"He has a son."

"True. And, according to him, he can love only his wife."

"That is nonsense, for you are a woman to inspire desires, and a man who could be familiarly in your company without his senses responding to it ought to kill himself."

"I am delighted, *caro Don Giacomo*, to learn that you love me, but since you are staying in Naples only a few days you will easily forget me."

"A curse on gaming, for we could spend charming evenings together."

"The Duke told me that you lost a thousand ducati without flinching last night. I take it that you are unlucky."

"Not always, but when I play on the same day on which I have fallen in love I am sure to lose."

"You will win this evening."

"Today I made my declaration; I shall lose again."

"Then don't play."

"They would say I'm afraid of losing or that I have no money."

"Then I hope you will win, and that you will come and tell me so at my house tomorrow morning. You can come with the Duke."

He arrives, and he asks me if I have enjoyed the opera. It is she who answers that we can tell him nothing about the opera because we had spent the whole time talking of love. She asks him to bring me to her house the next morning so that I can tell her I have won. The Duke replies that it is his turn, that he will be the dealer, but that he will bring me to breakfast with her whether I win or lose.

We left, and we went to the same place, where all the players were waiting for my Duke. It was a company of twelve, each of whom provided the bank in turn. They insisted that this made their chances equal. The idea made me laugh. Nothing is more difficult than to establish equality among players.

The Duke of Matalona takes his place, draws out his purse, and puts two thousand ducati in gold, silver, and bank notes on the table, asking the company to excuse him if he is doubling the amount of the bank in compliment to the stranger.

"Then I, too," I said, "will risk two thousand ducati, and no more, for at Venice people say that the prudent player must never lose more than he can win. So each of my counters will be worth two ducati."

So saying, I take from my pocket ten bank notes of a hundred ducati each and give them to the banker who had won them from me the evening before. War is declared, and in less than three hours, staking only on one card and with the utmost prudence, I lose my entire basket. That ended it. I had some twenty-five thousand ducati; but I had declared that I would not lose more, I was ashamed to go back on my word. I have all my life been dismayed by losing, but I have always had the strength of mind to conceal it; my natural gaiety was doubled precisely because it was forced by art. This has always gained me the good will of the company and opened resources to me. My appetite for supper was none the worse, and my ebullience made me think of so many laughable things to say that I succeeded in entirely dissipating the low spirits of the Duke of Matalona, who was in despair at having won so large a sum from a stranger who was his guest and whom people might think he had entertained only in order to win his money. He was the perfection of courtesy, lavish, rich, generous, and a man of honor.

On the way back to his palazzo he could not bring himself to say that he was not in need of money, that he would give me all the time I wanted to pay him; he rightly feared to wound my feelings; but before he went to bed he could not refrain from writing me a short note in which he said that if I needed credit at his banker's he would stand surety for me for whatever amount I might require. I replied that I was duly sensible of his courtesy and that if I should be in need of money I would accept his generous offer.

The next morning I went to his room early to embrace him and remind him that we were to breakfast with his beautiful mistress. He put on morning dress, as I had done, and we walked to the Fontana Medina[28] and the pretty house near it in which the angel lived.

She was still in bed, not naked but sitting up, modestly charming, beautiful as the day, wearing a dimity corset laced with wide rose-colored ribbons. She was reading *Le Sopha*, by the elegant Crébillon the Younger.[29] The Duke sat down on the foot of her bed, while I could only stand in a sort of daze, looking at her enchanting face, which I seemed once to have known and even to have loved. It was the first time that I saw her well. Laughing to see me so distracted, she told me to sit down in a small armchair at her bedside.

The Duke said that I was very glad to have lost two thousand ducati to him, for my loss made me sure that she loved me.

"*Caro il mio* Don Giacomo, I am sorry I told you that you would win, you would have done better not to play: I should love you just as much, and you would be richer by two thousand ducati."

760

"And I two thousand ducati the poorer," said the Duke with a smile.

"But I shall win this evening, charming Leonilda," I said, "if you will grant me some favor today. Otherwise I shall lose my soul and die in a very few days here at Naples."

"In that case, dear Leonilda," said the Duke, "you must grant him some small token."

"That I cannot."

The Duke told her she might dress and come to breakfast in the Chinese room, and she began to obey him at once, being neither too generous in what she let us see nor too miserly in what she managed to hide from us—a procedure which is sure to set any man on fire who has already been captivated by a woman's pretty face and intelligence and manners. Nevertheless I saw her beautiful bosom; it was a theft, but one which I could never have committed if she had not permitted it. On my side, I pretended I had seen nothing.

During the moments of distraction which a woman permits herself when she is dressing, she maintained with much ingenuity that a sensible girl should be more chary of her favors with a man whom she loves than with one whom she does not love, for the simple reason that she must always be afraid of losing the former while she has no interest in keeping the latter.

I said that in time she would find the contrary to be true in my case; and she replied that I was wrong.

The Chinese designs which covered the room in which we breakfasted were admirable rather for their coloring and their drawing than for the amorous acts they represented.

"On me," says the Duke, "they have no effect whatever"; and, so saying, he shows us his nullity. Leonilda does not look, but I was shocked; however, I concealed it.

"I am," I said, "in the same case, but I do not care to convince you of it."

The Duke says he does not believe it, he puts out a hand, and he finds that I am not lying; he shows his astonishment, and, withdrawing his hand, says that I must be as impotent as he is. I deny his conclusion and I say that to convince him of the contrary I had only to look into Leonilda's eyes, he asks her to look at me, she turns and fixes her eyes on mine, the Duke puts out his hand to the place of proof once more, and he finds he is wrong. He makes to uncover me, but I oppose him; he persists, he laughs, and I let him go on; in a sweet access of ardor I seize Leonilda's hand and, never taking my eyes from hers, I press it to my lips, and the Duke withdraws his wet hand, exclaiming, laughing, and getting up to fetch a towel. Leonilda has seen nothing, but she succumbs to uncontrollable laughter, as do I and the Duke. It was one of those delicious little games which so effectually stimulate Love, who, ever a child, revels in the play and laughter whose nectar makes him immortal. In playing it all three of us transgressed certain limits, though we managed to remain within certain others. We ended it with embraces, and Leonilda's lips pressed to mine sent me away with the Duke, plunged in the intoxication of the love which fetters the mind.

On the way I told the Duke that I would not see his mistress again unless he would relinquish her to me, declaring that I was prepared to marry her and give her a dowry of five thousand ducati.

"Speak to her, I will raise no objection. You shall learn from herself what property she has."

I went to dress, and when the bell rang went down to dinner. The Duchess was surrounded by a large company. She had the goodness to say she was sorry I had had bad luck.

"Fortune, Signora, is changeable; but your kind concern is bound to bring me luck. I shall win this evening."

"I doubt it, your opponent this evening will be Monteleone, who is very lucky."

Reflecting on the state of my gambling ventures after dinner, I decided to play for cash, first so that, in case I was overwhelmed, I should not endanger my honor by losing more on my word than I could pay, secondly in order to relieve the banker of any fear that I would be short when I was cleaned out for the third time, and thirdly in the hope that the change of system would also change my luck.

I spent four hours at the San Carlo in Leonilda's box, finding her more elaborately dressed and more brilliant than she had been on the previous days. I told her that the love she had inspired in me was of a kind which could tolerate neither rivals nor delay nor the slightest possibility of future inconstancy.

"I have told the Duke that I am prepared to marry you, giving you a dowry of five thousand ducati."

"What was his answer?"

"That I should make the proposal to yourself, and that he will raise no objection."

"And we will leave together."

762

"At once. After that only death can separate us."

"We will talk tomorrow morning. You will make me happy."

The Duke arrives, she tells him that there is no more question of anything between us but marriage.

"Marriage," he replied, "is the one thing in the world which must be considered the most before it is undertaken."

"But not too much, for as long as one is considering it one does not marry; in any case we have no time for that, since Don Giacomo has to leave."

"If it is to be a marriage," he said to me, "you can put off your departure, or return after becoming formally engaged to my dear Leonilda."

"No putting it off, my dear Duke, and no returning. We have made up our minds, and if we are mistaken we shall have all the time we need to repent."

The Duke laughs, he says we will discuss it the next day, and we go to our circle, where we find the Duke of Monteleone dealing with a well-stocked bank before him.

"I have bad luck," I said to him, "when I play on my word, so I hope you will permit me to play for cash."

"As you please—it makes no difference. I have made you a bank of four thousand ducati, so that you can recoup your losses."

"And I promise to break it or to lose four thousand."

So saying, I draw from my pocket six thousand ducati, in paper as always, I give two thousand to the Duke of Matalona, and I begin playing for a hundred ducati. After a very long session I broke the bank; and, the Duke of Matalona having left, I returned to his palazzo alone. When I told him the good news the next morning he embraced me and advised me always to play for cash. A great supper which the Princess della Valle[30] was giving would keep our circle of players from meeting that day. So we went to say good morning to Donna Leonilda, putting off discussing our marriage until the morrow, and we spent the rest of the day looking at the wonders of nature in the environs of Naples. At the great supper I saw the highest nobility of Naples, and great lavishness.

The next morning the Duke told me that I could go alone to his mistress's, where, having business, he would come later, and I went; but he did not come. For this reason we could settle nothing in the matter of our marriage. I spent two hours alone with her; but, as I felt I must be ruled by her inclinations, she found me amorous only in words. When I left her I again swore that it rested entirely with her to leave Naples with me, bound by marriage to my destiny until death.

The Duke asked me, with a smile, if, after spending the whole morning alone with his mistress, I still wanted to marry her.

"More than ever. What have you in mind?"

"Nothing. And since that is how things stand we will talk tomorrow."

That evening at Monteleone's I found a personable-looking banker with much gold before him; the Duke told me he was Don Marco Ottoboni.[31] He was holding the cards in his left hand, and he drew the card very well with his right, but he held the pack so tightly in his hand that I could not see it.

I decide to play for a ducato. With persistent bad luck, I lost only eighteen or twenty ducati after five or six deals. The banker politely asks me why I am staking such small sums against him.

"Because," I reply, "when I do not see at least half the pack I am afraid I shall lose."

The next night I broke the bank of the very amiable and very rich Prince del Cassaro,[32] who asked me to give him his revenge, inviting me to supper at a pretty house he had at Posilipo,[33] where he lived with a *virtuosa*[34] with whom he had fallen in love at Palermo. He also invited the Duke of Matalona and three or four others. This was the only occasion on which I dealt at Naples. I made him a bank of six thousand ducati, after telling him that, as I was on the eve of my departure, I would play only for cash. He lost ten thousand ducati and stopped only because he had no more money. Everyone made off, and I would have stopped too if the Prince's mistress, who was playing on her word after losing thirty or forty once,[35] had not been in arrears another hundred. I continued to deal, hoping that she would recoup; but I finally put down the cards at two o'clock in the morning, saying that she should pay me in Rome.

Since I was determined not to leave Naples without having seen Caserta,[36] and since Donna Leonilda was of the same mind, the Duke sent us there in a very comfortable carriage drawn by six mules, whose trot was faster than a horse's gallop. During the journey I first heard the voice of her duenna.

It was on the day after our journey to Caserta that we settled the particulars of our marriage in a conversation which lasted two hours.

"Leonilda there," said the Duke, "has her mother living on an estate not far from the city with an income of six hundred ducati a year which I settled on her for life when I bought a piece of

property which her husband left her; but Leonilda is not dependent on her. She relinquished her to me seven years ago, and I at
once gave her a life annuity of five hundred ducati, which she will
bring you as her dowry together with all her diamonds and a fine
wardrobe. Her mother has confided her entirely to my love and to
my word of honor that I would arrange an advantageous marriage for
her. I had her educated, and when I became aware of her cast
of mind I cultivated it, freeing her from all prejudices except the
one which makes it a girl's duty to keep herself for him whom
Heaven has destined to be her husband; and you can be certain that
you will be the first man whom my dear Leonilda will clasp to her
bosom."

I told him to have the deed for her dowry drawn up and to add to
it five thousand ducati del regno, which I would pay over to him
when the marriage contract was signed; he said that he would
guarantee them himself by a mortgage on a country house which
was worth twice as much, and, turning to Leonilda, who was
weeping for joy, he said that he would send for her mother, who
would be delighted to sign her marriage agreement.

Her mother was living at Sant'Agata in the household of the
Marchese Galiani.[37] It was a day's journey from Naples. He said that
he would send his carriage for her the next day, that the day after
that we would sup together, and on the following day we would
settle everything with the notary and would go at once to the little
church in Portici, where a priest would marry us, he undertaking to
secure a dispensation from publishing the banns. On the day after
the wedding her mother would return to Sant'Agata with us, we
would dine with her there, and we would continue our journey
with her blessing.

At this conclusion to his discourse, I shuddered, then I laughed;
but Leonilda, for all her intelligence, fell fainting into the arms of the
Duke, who revived her, calling her his "dear daughter" and kissing
her again and again. At the conclusion of the scene we all three dried
our tears.

From that day on I did not play again. I had won fifteen thousand
ducati, I considered myself a married man; it was my part to conduct
myself with prudence.

The next day, at supper with Leonilda and the Duke after the
opera at the San Carlo,

"What will my mother say," she asked me, "when she sees you
tomorrow evening?"

"She will say that you have done a foolish thing to marry a stranger whom you have known for only a week. Have you written her my name, my country, my situation, my age?"

"I wrote her these three lines: *'Come tomorrow, my dear Mama, to sign my marriage contract with a man whom I receive from the hands of His Grace the Duke and with whom I shall leave for Rome on Monday.'* "

"And here are my three lines," said the Duke: " *'Come at once, my dear friend, to sign your daughter's marriage contract and give her your blessing, for she has wisely chosen a husband who could be her father.'*"

"That's not true," said Leonilda, coming to my arms; "she'll think you're an old man, and I don't like it."

"Is your mother old?"

"Her mother," said the Duke to me, "is a charming and very witty woman no more than thirty-seven or thirty-eight years old."

"What is she doing in Galiani's house?"

"Being an intimate friend of the Marchesa, she lives with her family, but she pays board."

The next morning, having various small matters of business to dispose of and needing to go to my banker to give him all my bank notes and obtain his draft on Rome, only excepting the five thousand ducati I was to pay over at the signing of the contract, I told the Duke to expect me at Leonilda's about suppertime.

At eight o'clock I enter the room, in which they were standing with their backs to the fireplace, the Duke between the mother and the daughter.

"Ah! There he is!"

I look first at the mother, who, the instant I appear, gives a piercing cry and sinks onto the sofa. I stare at her, and I see Donna Lucrezia Castelli.

"Donna Lucrezia!" I say, "how happy I am!"

"Let us recover our breath, my dear friend. Sit down here. You are going to marry my daughter."

I sit down; I understand it all; my hair stands on end, and I sink into the gloomiest silence. The astonishment was Leonilda's and the Duke's; they saw that we knew each other; but beyond that they could not go. I think of that past time and of Leonilda's age, and I see that she could be my daughter; but I considered that Donna Lucrezia could not be sure of it, for she was living with her husband, who was not yet fifty and who loved her. I rise, I take a light, and asking the Duke and Leonilda to excuse me, I request the mother to go into the next room with me.

The woman I had so greatly loved in Rome has scarcely sat down beside me before she says:

"Leonilda is your daughter,[38] I am sure of it; I have never considered her anything else, my husband himself knew it, and he made no protest; he adored her. I will show you her baptismal certificate, and after seeing the date of her birth you can calculate for yourself. My husband never touched me in Rome, and my daughter was not born prematurely. Do you remember that my late mother must have read you a letter in which I wrote her that I was pregnant? That was in the January of 1744. In six months she will be seventeen. It was my dear husband himself who gave her the name Leonilda Giacomina at the baptismal font, and when he played with her he always called her Giacomina. This marriage, my dear friend, horrifies me, yet you can understand that I will not oppose it, for I should not dare tell the reason. What do you think? Have you really the courage to marry her? You hesitate. Can it be that you have consummated the marriage before contracting it?"

"No, my dear friend."

"I breathe again."

"She has none of my features."

"That is true. She looks like me. You weep, dear friend."

"Who would not weep? I am going into the other room, and I will send you the Duke. You understand that he must be told all."

I enter, and I tell him to go and speak with Donna Lucrezia. Leonilda, aghast, comes and sits on my lap and asks me what is the matter. My distress keeps me from answering, she kisses me, trembling, and she sheds tears with me. We remained there mute for half an hour, until the Duke returned with Donna Lucrezia, who, alone of the four of us, had assumed a reasonable attitude.

"But my dear daughter," she said to Leonilda, "this unpleasant mystery must be revealed to you; and it is from your mother herself that you shall learn it. Do you remember what name my late husband often called you, when, holding you in his arms, he caressed you?"

"He called me 'charming Giacomina.'"

"That is the name of this gentleman here. He is your father. Go and kiss him as a daughter, and if he has been your lover forget your crime."

It was then that the pathos of the tragedy undid us. Leonilda ran to embrace her mother's knees, and, despite the tears which choked her, said:

"I have never loved him except as a daughter."

The scene then became dumb show, except that the sound of the tears and kisses of the two admirable creatures gave it life, while the Duke and I, the supremely interested witnesses of the spectacle, were like two marble statues.

We remained at table for three hours, always sad, always talking, and passing from reflection to reflection on this more unhappy than happy recognition, and we separated at midnight unaware that we had eaten nothing.

We knew that the next day at dinner we should discuss the incident more coolly and sensibly; we were sure that nothing would stop us from taking the wisest course, and without any difficulty, for there was no other.

On the way the Duke talked aloud to himself, making countless reflections on what moral philosophy may denominate "prejudice." That the union of a father with his daughter is horrible by nature no philosopher will make bold to say; but the prejudice in this regard is so strong that one must have a thoroughly depraved mind to trample it underfoot. It is the fruit of a respect for the laws which a good education has inculcated in a noble soul; and, so defined, it is no longer prejudice, it is duty.

This duty can also be considered natural in that nature inspires us to grant to those we love the same goods which we desire for ourselves. It would seem that what is most conducive to reciprocity in love is equality in everything, in age, in situation, in character; and at first sight one does not find this equality between father and daughter. The respect which she owes to him who had given her being raises an obstacle to the kind of affection she must feel for a lover. If the father takes possession of his daughter by virtue of his paternal authority, he exercises a tyranny which nature must abhor. Our natural love of good order likewise causes reason to regard such a union as monstrous. The offspring of it are bound to be marked by confusion and insubordination; in short, such a union is abhorrent from every point of view; but it is no longer so when the two individuals love each other and have no knowledge that reasons which have nothing to do with their mutual affection ought to prevent them from loving each other; and incestuous relations, the eternal subjects of Greek tragedies, instead of making me weep make me laugh, and if I weep at *Phèdre*,[39] it is Racine's art which makes me do so.

I went to bed, but I could not sleep. The sudden transition I had to make from carnal to fatherly love caused all my moral and

768

physical faculties the deepest distress. I slept for two hours, after deciding that I would leave the next day.

On waking and finding my decision very wise, I go to communicate it to the Duke, who was still in bed. He replied that everyone knew I was soon to leave and that such haste would be interpreted unfavorably. He advised me to take a broth with him and to consider my projected marriage a joke.

"We will," he said, "spend these three or four days gaily, and we will apply our minds to dismissing the gloomy aspects of this untoward incident and even giving it a comic cast. I advise you to renew your affair with Donna Lucrezia. You must have found her as she was eighteen years ago; she cannot possibly have been better."

This little discourse reduces me to reason. To forget the projected marriage was certainly the best course I could take; but I was in love, and the object of love is not like some piece of merchandise for which, when one cannot have it, one can easily substitute another.

So we went to Leonilda's together, the Duke in his usual spirits, but I pale, undone, the perfect picture of gloom. What immediately surprises me is to find gaiety. Leonilda flings herself on my neck, calling me "dear Papa," her mother addresses me as "dear friend," and my eyes and my soul are held captive by her face, in which eighteen years had been unable to harm a single feature.

We enact a mute scene, embracing each other again and again at intervals; Leonilda gives me, and receives, any quantity of kisses, regardless of what desires they may arouse in us; it was enough for her to be certain that, knowing who we were, we should be able to resist them. She was right. One grows used to everything. It was shame which dissipated my gloom.

I tell Donna Lucrezia about the strange welcome her sister had accorded me in Rome, and we begin laughing; we recollect the night at Tivoli,[40] and the remembered images soften us. After a short silence I tell her that if she would like to come to Rome with me simply to visit Donna Angelica I would undertake to bring her back to Naples at the beginning of Lent. She promises to give me an answer the next day.

Dining between her and Leonilda, and having to forget the latter, it is not surprising that all my old flame was rekindled. Whether it was due to her gay banter, or to my need to love, or to the excellence of the dishes and the wines, at dessert I offered her my hand.

"I will marry you," I said, "and the three of us will set off together on Monday, for now that Leonilda is my daughter I cannot leave her in Naples."

At this proposal my three table companions looked at one another, and no one answered me.

After dinner, overtaken by sleepiness, I had to lie down on the bed, and I did not wake until eight o'clock, when I was surprised to see only Donna Lucrezia, who was writing. She comes to me, she says I have slept for five hours, and that she had not gone to the opera with her daughter and the Duke so that I should not be left alone.

Recollecting an old love in the presence of an adorable woman reawakens it, desires are rekindled, and the strength with which they return is boundless. If the two persons are still in love, neither yields to the other in eagerness; they feel as if they were regaining possession of a treasure which belongs to them and which a series of harsh circumstances has long forbidden them to enjoy. Such we became in an instant, with no preamble, no idle talk, no preliminaries, and even with no feigned attacks, in which one or the other cannot but be playing a role. Immersed in the sweetness of a happy silence, we surrendered ourselves to the one true author of nature, to love.

I was the first to break the silence during the first intermission. If a man has a mind which sees the amusing side of things, will it not continue to be of the same cast during the delightful repose which follows an amorous victory?

"Here I am again," I said, "in the charming country which undid me to the sound of gunfire and drums the first time I dared to explore it in the dark."[41]

She could not but laugh, and, memory joining in, we recollected in turn all that had happened to us at Testaccio and Frascati and Tivoli.[42] We passed them in review only to laugh, but what are the subjects for laughter which two lovers who are alone together bring up except an excuse to celebrate the festival of love once more?

At the end of the second act, in the enthusiasm which love crowned and content leaves in the soul,

"Let us," I said, "be each other's until death; let us thus assure ourselves that we will die happy; we are of the same age, and we can even hope to die at the same time."

"It is my dearest wish, but stay in Naples and leave Leonilda to the Duke. We will frequent society, we will find her a husband worthy of her, and our happiness will be complete."

"I cannot settle in Naples, my dear. Your daughter was ready to leave with me."

"Say 'our daughter.' I see that you wish you were not her father. You love her."

"Alas! I am very sure that my passion for her would be stilled as long as I could live with you; but I answer for nothing if you should not be there. She is charming, and her mind captivates me even more than her beauty. Being sure that she loved me, I renounced attempting to seduce her only for fear of making her distrust me. Such an apprehension on her part might have lessened her fondness. I aspired to her esteem, I did not want to trouble her innocence. I wanted to possess her only legitimately and with a right equal to hers. My dear, we have created an angel. I cannot understand how the Duke—"

"The Duke is impotent. Now you understand all."

"How can he be impotent? He has a son."

"He is impotent, I tell you."

"Nevertheless—"

"Nevertheless. He is impotent, and he knows it."

"Let me see you as I did at Tivoli."

"No, for a carriage is stopping."

How Leonilda burst out laughing when she saw her mother in my arms! She gave us countless kisses. The Duke arrived a moment later, and we supped very gaily. He declared me the happiest of mortals when I told him I should spend the night honorably with my wife and my daughter; and he was right: I was the happiest of mortals in those days.

Quand'ero in parte altr'uom da quel ch'io sono.

("When I was in part a different man from the man I am.")[43]

After he left, it was Leonilda who undressed her mother, while, after wrapping my hair in a kerchief, I threw my clothes into the middle of the room. She tells her daughter to get into bed beside her.

"Your father," she says, "will confine his attention to your mother."

"And I," she replies, "will give mine to you both"; and, on the other side of the bed she undresses completely and gets in next to her, saying that as her father I was at liberty to see all my handiwork. Her mother is proud of her, she praises her, and she rejoices to see that I find her beautiful. It sufficed her that she was in the middle and that it was only upon her that I extinguished the fire with which she saw that I was burning. Leonilda's curiosity delighted me to the soul.

"So is that what you did," she asked me, "when you engendered me eighteen years ago?"

But the moment which leads Lucrezia to the death of love has come, just when, to spare her, I feel it my duty to withdraw. Moved to pity, Leonilda sends her mother's little soul on its flight with one hand and with the other puts a white handkerchief under her gushing father.

Lucrezia, grateful for her daughter's fond ministrations, turns her back to me, clasps her in her arms, gives her countless kisses, then, turning to me again, says in moving tones:

"There, look at her, she is unstained, touch if you want to, nothing has suffered harm, she is as I made her."

"Yes," said Leonilda, laughing, "look at me and kiss Mama."

Alas! I loved her mother, otherwise nothing would have saved her from my fury. The combat began again and did not end until we fell asleep.

What waked us was the rays of the sun.

"Go and draw the curtain, dear daughter," says her mother.

At that Leonilda, naked as my hand, obediently goes to draw the curtain, showing me beauties of which, when one is in love, one has never seen enough. Alas! Coming back to bed, she lets me bestow my kisses on all that I saw; but as soon as she sees me on the edge of the precipice she slips away and gives me to her mother, who receives me with open arms and imperiously orders me to not spare her but to make her another Leonilda. At the end of the encounter, which was a very long one, I believed I had obeyed her, but my blood, which she saw when I yielded to exhaustion, left her doubtful.

"You have accustomed me," she said, "to this frightening phenomenon."

After assuring the innocent Leonilda that it was of no consequence, we dressed, and the Duke of Matalona arrived. It was Leonilda who gave him an account of all our nocturnal labors. In the wretchedness of his impotence he could not but congratulate himself on not having witnessed them.

Determined to leave the next day so that I should be in Rome in time to enjoy the last week of the Carnival, I used all my powers of persuasion on the Duke to assure myself that a present I had determined to bestow on Leonilda would not be refused. It was the dowry of five thousand ducati which I would have given her if she could have become my wife. The Duke decided that her being my daughter was all the more reason why she should accept the amount as a dowry. She accepted it, smothering me with caresses and making me promise that I would come back to Naples to see her when I learned that she was married. I promised, and I kept my word.

Since I had decided to leave the next day, the Duke wanted me to see all the Neapolitan nobility in his palazzo at a great supper of the kind I had seen at the Princess della Valle Piccolomini's. So he left me with my daughter, saying that we would meet again at the supper. We dined together, and we spent the rest of the day within the bounds prescribed to a father and daughter. The large amount of blood I had lost the night before may have contributed to my share in our abstention. We did not embrace until the very last moment of our parting, which the mother felt as keenly as did the daughter.

I went off to dress for the supper. When I took leave of the Duchess, she addressed me in these words:

"I am sure that you will always recollect Naples with pleasure."

No one could doubt it. After showing my generosity to the Duke's household, I left as I had arrived. That nobleman, who died three or four years later, escorted me to the door of my carriage.

HISTORY OF MY LIFE

Volume Eight

Casanova continued his travels round the great cities of Europe, sometimes moving on when the authorities expelled him and sometimes of his own volition. The brisk tempo of his prose reflects his restless character and inquiring mind. But now he had a long-term plan, at once knavish and humorous, to give some shape to his travels. He proposed to gratify the crazy Madame d'Urfé's desire to become a man and achieve supreme wisdom, by using his own magic arts, thus benefiting himself in some unspecified way. Of course Casanova knew that he could grant the Marquise neither of her wishes, but he also knew she was mad enough to think that they had been granted if so persuaded by him. And even if the plan did not work, it had the kind of impish effrontery which seems to have appealed to him almost more than success.

To put the scheme into effect he needed the help of a young woman—the virgin conventionally required by complex spells. In his scam at Cesena, the intact Genoveffa had played this part. Now he had a new companion, La Corticelli, who, if by no means the genuine article, was at least young enough and sharp enough to act the part.

The two chapters containing this section of the narrative were lost from Casanova's manuscript and are therefore printed in italic as the translator's indication that they are taken from a secondary source.

[* * *]

CHAPTER III

*I return to Paris with La Corticelli, trans-
formed for the occasion into the Countess
Lascaris. The abortive hypostasis. Aix-la-
Chapelle. Duel. Mimi d'Aché. La Corticelli
betrays me, but only to her own undoing.
Journey to Sulzbach.*

Having nothing further to do in Metz, I took leave of my new acquaintances, and on the next day but one I slept at Nancy, whence I wrote to Madame d'Urfé that I was returning with a virgin, the last descendant of the Lascaris[2] family which had reigned in Constantinople. I asked her to receive her from my hands at a country house which belonged to her family, where we should have to remain for some days to perform certain cabalistic ceremonies.

She replied that she would expect me at Pont-Carré,[2] an ancient castle

777

four leagues from Paris, and that she would there receive the young princess with all the cordiality she could wish for: "I have all the more reason to do so," she added in the exaltation of her insanity, "because the Lascaris family is connected with the D'Urfés, and because I am to be reborn from the offspring of this favored virgin." I saw that my course should be not to cool her enthusiasm but to hold it in check and moderate its manifestations. So I immediately wrote to her on the subject, explaining why she must treat her as no more than a countess, and I ended by announcing that we should arrive, with the young Lascaris's governess, on Monday in Holy Week.

I spent ten or twelve days in Nancy, instructing my young scatterbrain and convincing her mother that she must content herself with being the most humble servant of the Countess Lascaris. I found it a very difficult task; I had not only to make it plain that her hope of affluence depended on her complete submission, I even had to threaten that I would send her back to Bologna alone. I was sorely to repent of my persistence. The woman's obstinacy was an inspiration of my Good Genius, who wanted to guard me against the greatest mistake I have made in all my life!

We arrived at Pont-Carré on the appointed day. Madame d'Urfé, whom I had informed in advance of the hour of our arrival, had the drawbridges of the castle lowered and stood in the gateway surrounded by her entire household, like a general ready to surrender the place to us with all the honors of war. The dear lady, who was insane only because she had an excess of intelligence, gave the pretended princess a reception so flattering that she would have been astounded by it if I had not taken care to forewarn her. She embraced her three times with truly maternal tenderness, addressed her as her "very dear niece," and recited her own genealogy and that of the house of Lascaris to show her how she came to be her aunt. What most pleasantly surprised me was that my Italian madcap heard her out with polite dignity and did not once laugh, though the whole comedy must have struck her as extremely funny.

As soon as we had retired to the apartment the fairy performed some mysterious fumigations, and censed the newcomer, who received the homage with all the modesty of an opera goddess and then threw herself into the arms of the priestess, who received her with the greatest enthusiasm.

At table the Countess was animated, gracious, talkative, which won her the heart of Madame d'Urfé, who was not at all surprised to hear her chatter away in French. Madonna Laura, who knew only her native Italian, was not present. She had been given an excellent room, where her meals were brought to her and which she never left except to go to mass.

The castle of Pont-Carré was a sort of fortress, which, in the days of the civil wars,[3] *had withstood more than one siege. It was square, as its name indicated, flanked by four crenelated towers, and surrounded by a wide moat. The rooms were huge and richly furnished, but in the old fashion. The air was infested with venomous gnats, which ate us up and produced extremely painful swellings on our faces, but I had undertaken to spend a week there, and I should have found it hard to invent a pretext for shortening the time. Madame d'Urfé had a bed for her niece set up beside her own, and I was not afraid she would attempt to assure herself of her virginity, for the oracle had forbidden it, upon pain of destroying the effect of the operation, which we fixed for the fourteenth day of the April moon.*

On that day we supped temperately, then I went to bed. A quarter of an hour later Madame d'Urfé brought me the virgin Lascaris. She undressed her, perfumed her, draped her in a magnificent veil, and, when she had put her beside me, remained, wishing to be present at the operation which was to result in her being reborn nine months later.

The act was consummated in due form, and when that was done Madame d'Urfé left us alone for that night, which was very well employed. After that night the Countess slept with her aunt until the last day of the moon, at which time I was to ask the oracle if the young Lascaris had conceived by my efforts. It might well be the case, for nothing had been spared to achieve that end; but I thought it wiser to make the oracle reply that the operation had failed because the youthful D'Aranda had seen the whole performance from behind a screen. Madame d'Urfé was in despair; but I comforted her by a second answer in which the oracle told her that what it had been impossible to accomplish during the April moon in France could be accomplished outside of the kingdom during the May moon, but that she must send the prying youth, whose influence had been so adverse, a hundred leagues from Paris for at least a year. The oracle also stipulated how D'Aranda was to travel: he must have a tutor, a manservant, and all his appurtenances in perfect order.

The oracle had spoken; no more was needed. Madame d'Urfé at once thought of an Abbé whom she liked, and D'Aranda was sent to Lyons,[4] *with a warm letter of recommendation to her relative, Monsieur de Roche-baron.*[5] *The lad was delighted to travel and never learned anything of the little slander I had permitted myself in order to get him out of the way. What made me take this action was not empty whim. I had seen beyond perad-venture that La Corticelli was in love with him and that her mother was fostering the intrigue. I had twice surprised her in her room with the youth, who was interested in her only as a young adolescent is interested in all girls; and my disapproval of my Italian accomplice's designs became, in Signora Laura's mind, an unwarranted opposition to her daughter's inclination.*

Our business now was to think of some place abroad where we could go to repeat the mysterious operation. We decided on Aix-la-Chapelle, and in five or six days everything was in readiness for the journey.

La Corticelli, angry with me for having spirited away the object of her love, reproached me vehemently and from then on began to behave badly toward me; she even went so far as to indulge in threats if I would not summon back the "pretty boy," as she called him.

"You have no right to be jealous," she said, "and I am my own mistress."

"Quite so, my beauty," I replied, "but I have a right to prevent you from behaving like a prostitute in the situation in which I have placed you."

Her mother flew into a rage and told me that she wanted to go back to Bologna with her daughter; and to soothe her I promised I would take them both there after our journey to Aix-la-Chapelle.

However, I did not feel easy, and, fearing difficulties, I hastened my departure. We left one May day in a berlin in which I accompanied Madame d'Urfé, the pretended Countess Lascaris, and a maid, her favorite, named Brougnole.[6] A two-seated cabriolet followed us; it was occupied by Signora Laura and another maid. Two menservants in full livery sat on the outside seat of the berlin. We rested one day in Brussels and another in Liège. At Aix[7] we found a great number of distinguished foreigners, and at the first ball Madame d'Urfé presented my Lascaris to two Princesses of Mecklenburg[8] as her niece. The pretended Countess received their embraces calmly and modestly, and she attracted the particular attention of the Margrave of Bayreuth[9] and of the Duchess of Württemberg,[10] who together took possession of her and did not leave her until the end of the ball. I was on tenterhooks for fear that my heroine would betray herself by some piece of theatrical repartee. She danced with a grace which won her the attention and applause of the whole company; and it was I who was complimented on her performance. I suffered martyrdom, for I thought the compliments were malicious; it was as if everyone had divined the ballerina disguised as a countess, and I believed I was dishonored. Having found an opportunity to speak privately to the young madcap, I begged her to dance like a young lady of station and not like a ballet girl, but she was proud of her success and had the impudence to answer that a young lady might well be able to dance like a dancer and that she would never dance badly to please me. This behavior so disgusted me with her that, had I known how, I would have got rid of her then and there; but I silently swore that she would escape nothing by waiting; and, be it a vice or a virtue, vengeance never ceases to burn in my heart until it has been satisfied.

On the morning after the ball Madame d'Urfé made her a present of a *casket containing a very fine watch set with brilliants, a pair of diamond earrings, and a ring adorned with a rose diamond weighing fifteen carats. All together they were worth sixty thousand francs. I took charge of them, lest it should occur to her to leave without my consent.*

Meanwhile, to ward off boredom, I gambled, I lost my money, and I made bad acquaintances. The worst of them all was a French officer named D'Aché,[11] *who had a pretty wife and an even prettier daughter. The girl very soon captured the place in my heart on which La Corticelli by now had only a slight hold; but as soon as Madame d'Aché saw that I preferred her daughter she refused to receive my visits.*

I had lent D'Aché ten louis; so I thought I could complain to him of his wife's behavior toward me; but he curtly replied that if I went to the house only for his daughter, his wife was in the right; that his daughter was a girl who could well find a husband, and if my intentions were honorable I had only to declare them to her mother. Nothing in all this was offensive except his tone, and I took offense at it; however, knowing that he was a coarse brute, a drunkard, and always ready to fight over a "yea" or a "nay," I decided to say nothing and forget his daughter, not wanting to become involved with a man of his kind.

I was in this frame of mind and almost cured of my fancy for his daughter, when, four days after our conversation, I entered a billiard room where D'Aché was playing with a Swiss named Schmit,[12] *an officer in the Swedish service. As soon as D'Aché saw me he asked me if I would bet him the ten louis he owed me. The game was just beginning; I replied:*

"Yes, that will make it twenty or nothing. I accept."

Toward the end of the game D'Aché, seeing that he was losing, made an unfair stroke so obvious that the marker told him so to his face; but D'Aché, for whom the stroke won the game, takes the money which was in the stake bag and puts it in his pocket, paying no attention to the marker's adjurations or to those of his opponent, who, seeing that he has been cheated, makes to hit the blackguard across the face with his cue. D'Aché, who had warded off the blow with his arm, instantly draws his sword and runs at Schmit, who was unarmed. The marker, a sturdy young man, caught D'Aché around the waist and prevented murder. The Swiss leaves, saying:

"We shall meet again."

The scoundrel, who had cooled down, looks at me and says:

"Now we are quits."

"Very much so."

"I'm glad of that; but, the devil take it, you could have spared me an insult which dishonors me."

"So I could, but I was under no obligation to do it. Besides, you must know what your rights are. Schmit was without his sword, but I believe he is a man of mettle, and he will give you satisfaction if you have courage enough to return his money to him, for, after all, you lost."

An officer whose name was De Pienne[13] took me aside and said that he would himself pay me the twenty louis which D'Aché had pocketed, but that Schmit must give him satisfaction, sword in hand. I did not hesitate to promise him that the Swiss would fulfill the obligation, and I undertook to bring him an affirmative reply the next day in the place where we then were.

I had no doubt that I should do as I had said. A gentleman who carries a weapon must always be ready to use it, whether in avenging an insult to his honor or in giving satisfaction for an insult he may have offered. I know that this is a prejudice which, rightly or wrongly, is called "barbaric," but there are social prejudices to which no man of honor can deny allegiance, and Schmit impressed me as being a thorough gentleman.

I went to him at daybreak the next morning; he was still in bed. As soon as he saw me,

"I am sure," he said, *"that you have come to ask me to fight D'Aché. I am more than ready to burn powder with him, but on condition that he shall first pay me the twenty louis he stole from me."*

"You shall have them tomorrow morning, and I will be with you. D'Aché's second will be Monsieur de Pienne."

"Well and good. I shall expect you here at daybreak."

I saw De Pienne two hours later, and we arranged the meeting for six o'clock in the morning on the following day, with two pistols. We chose a garden half a league from the city.

At daybreak I found my Swiss waiting for me at the door of his lodging, humming the *"Ranz-des-Vaches,"* of which his fellow countrymen are so fond. I thought it a good omen.

"You have come," he said. *"Let us be off."*

On the way he said:

"I have never fought except with a gentleman, and I find it hard to kill a scoundrel; that should be work for a hangman."

"I understand," I said, *"that it is very distasteful to risk one's life against such people."*

"I risk nothing," said Schmit with a laugh, *"for I am certain to kill him."*

"Certain?"

"Perfectly certain, because I shall make him tremble."

He was right. The secret is infallible when one knows how to employ it and when one is in the right against a coward. We found D'Aché and De Pienne at the appointed place, and we saw five or six people who could have been there only out of curiosity.

D'Aché took twenty louis from his pocket and handed them to his opponent, saying:

"I may have been mistaken, but I mean to make you pay dearly for your brutality."

Then, turning to me:

"I owe you twenty louis," he said.

I did not answer him.

Schmit, having put his money in his purse with the utmost calm, and making no reply to the other's boasting, took his station between two trees about four paces apart, drew a pair of dueling pistols from his pocket, and said to D'Aché:

"You have only to place yourself at ten paces' distance and fire first. The space between these two trees is the place where I choose to walk back and forth. You may walk too, if you wish, when it is my turn to fire."

No one could have explained his intentions more clearly or have spoken more calmly.

"But," said I, "we must decide who is to have the first shot."

"There is no need of that," said Schmit, "I never fire first; in any case the gentleman has that right."

De Pienne placed his friend at the specified distance, then he retired with me, and D'Aché fired at his opponent, who was slowly walking back and forth without looking at him. Schmit turned around with the greatest composure and said:

"You missed me, sir; I was sure you would; try again."

I thought he was mad, and I expected some kind of discussion between the parties. But not a bit of it. D'Aché, thus given leave to take the second shot, fired and again missed his opponent, who, without a word, but in a firm and confident manner, fired his first shot into the air, then, aiming at D'Aché with his second pistol, hit him in the center of the forehead and stretched him dead on the ground. Putting his pistols back in his pocket, Schmit instantly set off, unaccompanied, as if he were continuing his walk. I left two minutes later, when I was certain that the unfortunate D'Aché was lifeless.

I was in a daze, for such a duel seemed to me a dream, something out of a romance, rather than a reality. I could not get over it, for I had not detected the slightest change on the impassive countenance of the Swiss.

I went to breakfast with Madame d'Urfé, whom I found inconsolable, for it was the day of the full moon, and at exactly three minutes past four o'clock I was to accomplish the mysterious creation of the child from whom she was to be reborn. But the divine Lascaris, who was to be the chosen vessel, was writhing on her bed, feigning convulsions which would make it impossible for me to accomplish the work of fecundation.

On hearing an account of this disaster from the heartbroken Madame d'Urfé, I affected a hypocritical grief, for the dancer's spitefulness served my turn to perfection, first because she no longer aroused the slightest desire in me, second because I foresaw that I could make use of the incident to avenge myself and punish her.

I lavished consolations on Madame d'Urfé, and, after consulting the oracle, I found that the young Countess Lascaris had been defiled by a black Genius, and that I must go in search of the predestined girl whose purity was under the protection of the higher Geniuses. Seeing the mad Madame d'Urfé perfectly content with the oracle's promises, I left her and went to see La Corticelli, whom I found on her bed, with her mother beside her.

"So you are suffering from convulsions, my dear," I said.

"No, I am perfectly well; but I shall go on having them until you give me back my jewel casket."

"You have become naughty, my poor child, and it has come from taking your mother's advice. As for the casket, if you continue to behave in this way you may never get it back."

"I will tell all."

"No one will believe you, and I will send you back to Bologna without a single one of the presents Madame d'Urfé has given you."

"You will have to give me back the casket when I announce that I am pregnant—as in fact I am. If you do not satisfy me I shall go and tell the old fool everything, no matter what may happen."

Greatly surprised, I stared at her without saying a word, but I was considering how best to get rid of the impudent wench. Signora Laura said, with perfect calm, that it was only true that her daughter was with child, but that it was not by me.

"Then who made her pregnant?" I asked her.

"Count N . . . , whose mistress she was in Prague."

I did not think it possible, for she showed no signs of being with child, but, even so, it might be the case. Forced to think of some course which would foil the scoundrelly pair, I left the room without a word and shut myself up with Madame d'Urfé to consult the oracle concerning the operation which was to make her happy.

After a quantity of questions more obscure than the oracles which the Pythia delivered from her tripod at Delphi,[14] the interpretation of which I consequently left to my poor infatuated Madame d'Urfé, she herself discovered—and I took great care not to contradict her—that the young Lascaris had gone mad. Fostering all her fears, I succeeded in making her read in the reply of a cabalistic figure that the princess had failed to answer our expectations because she had been defiled by a black Genius hostile to the Rosicrucian Order; and, being now well launched, she added of her own motion that the girl must be pregnant with a gnome.

She then drew up another figure to learn how we were to go about attaining our end without fail, and I so directed her that she found she must write to the moon.[15]

This extravagance, which should have brought her back to reason, filled her with joy. Her enthusiasm was that of a mystic in ecstasy, and I became certain that even if I had tried to prove the groundlessness of her hopes I should have wasted my breath. At most she would have concluded that a hostile Genius had corrupted me and that I was no longer a perfect Rosicrucian. But I was far from undertaking a cure which would have been so disadvantageous to me and of no use to her. If nothing else, her infatuation made her happy, and no doubt a return to the truth would have made her the reverse.

In short, she received the command to write to the moon all the more joyously because she knew the devotions in which that planet delights and the form of ceremony with which it must be approached; but she could not perform it without the help of an adept, and I knew that she counted on me. I said that I would be hers to command, but that we must wait until the first phase of the coming moon, which fact she knew as well as I did. I was very glad to gain some time, for, having lost a great deal at cards, I could not leave Aix-la-Chapelle before I received the sum represented by a bill of exchange which I had drawn on Monsieur D. O.[16] in Amsterdam. In the meanwhile we agreed that, since the young Lascaris had gone mad, we would pay no attention to anything she might say in her insane fits, for, her mind being in the power of the evil Genius who had taken possession of her, it was he who put the words into her mouth.

However, her condition deserving our pity, we agreed that, to lighten her lot as much as possible, she should continue to eat with us, but that in the evening, when we rose from supper, she should go to bed in her governess's room.

After having thus disposed Madame d'Urfé not to believe anything La Corticelli might say to her, and to give her whole thought to the letter she must write to the Genius Selenis,[17] *who inhabits the moon, I set seriously about finding means to replace the money I had lost, which the cabala could not do for me. I pawned La Corticelli's casket for a thousand louis, and went to deal at an English club,*[18] *where I could win much more than I could with Frenchmen or Spaniards.*

Three or four days after D'Aché's death his widow wrote me a note asking me to call on her. I found her with De Pienne. She told me in sorrowful tones that, her husband having contracted many debts, his creditors had seized everything, so that she could not pay the expenses of a journey to throw herself and her daughter on the mercy of her family in Colmar.

"You are," she went on, "the cause of my husband's death; I ask you for a thousand écus; if you refuse me I will sue you in court, for, the Swiss officer having left, there is no one else I can sue."

"What you have permitted yourself to say surprises me, Madame," I rejoined coldly, "and but for my respect for your misfortune, I should reply with the acerbity which your behavior cannot but inspire in me. In the first place I have not a thousand écus to throw away, and even if I had them, your threatening tone would be little calculated to induce me to make such a sacrifice. In addition, I am curious to see how you could possibly go about suing me. As for Monsieur Schmit, he fought like a brave man and a gentleman, and I have yet to understand what you could gain by suing him if he had remained here. Good-by, Madame."

I had scarcely got fifty paces from the house, when I was joined by De Pienne, who said that before Madame d'Aché sued me it was for us to go to some private place and cut each other's throats. Neither of us was wearing a sword.

"Your intention is scarcely flattering," I said calmly; "indeed, it has a certain brutality which does not encourage me to involve myself with a man whom I do not know and to whom I owe nothing."

"You are a coward."

"I might be one if I imitated you. What you may think of me leaves me completely indifferent."

"You will be sorry."

"Perhaps, but meanwhile I give you due warning that I never go about without a pair of pistols in good condition and that I know how to use them. Here they are," I added, drawing them from my pocket and cocking the one in my right hand.

At sight of them the bully gave a curse and fled in one direction while I made off in the other.

Not far from where this scene had taken place I ran into a Neapolitan named Militerni,[19] then a Lieutenant-Colonel and Aide-de-Camp to the Prince of Condé, who was in command of the French army. Militerni was a man who enjoyed life, always ready to oblige and always short of money. We were friends, and I told him what had just happened.

"I should be sorry," I said, "to become involved with De Pienne, and if you can dispose of him for me I promise you a hundred écus."

"It can doubtless be done," he replied; "I will tell you more tomorrow."

And in fact he came to me the next morning and announced that my cutthroat had left Aix at daybreak in obedience to a formal order from his military superior, and at the same time he gave me an unrestricted passport from the Prince of Condé.

I admit that I was gratified by the news. I have never feared to cross swords with the first comer, though I have never sought the barbarous pleasure of shedding a man's blood; but this time I felt an intense aversion to involving myself with a man whom I had reason to believe was no more scrupulous than his friend D'Aché. So I heartily thanked Militerni, at the same time giving him the hundred écus I had promised him, which I considered too well spent to regret them.

Militerni, a past master at jesting and a tool of Marshal d'Estrées,[20] was not without either intelligence or education; but he lacked discipline and, to some extent, refinement. Withal, he was a most agreeable companion, for he was imperturbably good-humored and he had a considerable knowledge of the world. Made a Field Marshal in 1768, he went to Naples and married [21] a rich heiress, whom he left a widow a year later.

The day after De Pienne left, I received a note from Mademoiselle d'Aché asking me, on behalf of her mother, who was ill, to call on her. I replied that she would find me at such-and-such a place at an hour which I specified, where she could tell me whatever she wished.

I found her at the appointed place with her mother, who came despite her pretended illness. Complaints, tears, reproaches—nothing was spared. She called me her "persecutor," and said that the departure of De Pienne, her only friend, had reduced her to despair, that she had pawned all her possessions, that she had no further resources, and that I, being rich, ought to help her if I was not the basest of men.

"I am far from being insensible to your misfortunes, Madame, and though I am not so to your insults I cannot refrain from telling you that you proved yourself the basest of women by inciting De Pienne, who may be an honorable man, to murder me. In short, rich or not, though I owe you nothing, I will give you what you need to take your things out of pawn, and

787

I may even escort you to Colmar myself; but you must consent to my giving your charming daughter some first proofs of my love here and now."

"And you dare to make this horrible proposal to me?"

"Be it horrible or not, it is the proposal I make you."

"Never."

"Good-by, Madame."

I called the waiter to pay for the refreshments I had ordered, and I put six double louis in the girl's hand, but the proud mother, seeing it, forbade her to accept them. I was not surprised, despite her indigence, for the mother was charming and indeed a better prize than her daughter, and she knew it. I should have given her the preference, and so have ended all protest—but whim! In love, there is no accounting for it. I felt that she must hate me, and the more so because, since she did not love her daughter, she was humiliated to find her a preferred rival.

My departure leaving me still holding the six double louis which pride or pique had refused, I went to the faro bank and decided to sacrifice them to Fortune; but that capricious goddess, as haughty as the proud widow, refused them as she had done, and, having left them five times on one card, I very nearly broke the bank then and there. An Englishman named Martin offered to go halves with me; knowing him to be a good player, I accepted his proposal, and in eight or ten deals we managed so well that, after taking the casket out of pawn, I found not only that my other losses were made good but that I was also ahead by a considerable sum.

In the meanwhile La Corticelli, thoroughly angry with me, had revealed everything to Madame d'Urfé, telling her the true story of her life, of our acquaintance, and of her pregnancy. But the more truth she put into her account, the more the good lady was confirmed in her idea that the girl was mad, and she only laughed with me over the supposed insanity of my Italian traitress. She put all her trust in the instructions which Selenis was to give her in his answer.

For my part, however, being unable to overlook the girl's behavior, I decided to send her to eat in her mother's room, seeing to it that I alone kept Madame d'Urfé company and assuring her that we should easily find another chosen vessel, since the young Lascaris's madness made her wholly unfit to participate in our mysteries.

It was not long before the widow D'Aché, under the stress of need, found herself obliged to give me her Mimi; but I conquered her by kindness and, in the beginning, by so far respecting appearances that she could pretend to know nothing. I redeemed all the things she had pawned; and, satisfied with her behavior, though her daughter had not yet yielded entirely to my ardor, I *formed the plan of taking them both to Colmar with Madame d'Urfé. To persuade the lady to perform this good action without suspecting its real motives, it occurred to me to make her receive the order from the moon in the letter she was awaiting from that planet; I was certain that, under such circumstances, she would obey blindly.*

The way in which I contrived the exchange of letters between Selenis and Madame d'Urfé was as follows.

On the day determined by the phase of the moon we went to sup together in a garden outside the city,[22] where, in a room on the ground floor, I had prepared everything necessary for the ceremony; I had in my pocket the letter which was to come down from the moon in reply to the one which Madame d'Urfé had carefully prepared and which we were to send to its address. A few paces from the ceremonial chamber I had arranged to have a large bath filled with the perfumes pleasing to the luminary of the night, which we were to enter together at the hour of the moon, which on that day was an hour after midnight.

When we had burned the aromatics and sprinkled the perfumes appropriate to the worship of Selenis and recited the mystic prayers, we undressed completely, and, holding my letter concealed in my left hand, with my right I escorted her to the edge of the bath, in which was an alabaster cup filled with spirits of juniper, which I ignited, meanwhile uttering cabalistic words which I did not understand and which she repeated after me, handing me the letter addressed to Selenis. I burned the letter in the juniper flame on which the full moon was shining, and the credulous Madame d'Urfé assured me that she had seen the characters she had written ascending along the luminary's rays.

After that we got into the bath, and the letter which I held concealed in my hand, written in silver on glazed green paper, appeared on the surface of the water ten minutes later. As soon as Madame d'Urfé saw it she took it up reverently and left the bath with me.

After drying and perfuming ourselves, we dressed again. When we were in a state of decency I told Madame d'Urfé that she might read the letter, which she had laid on a perfumed white satin cushion. She obeyed, and a visible gloom descended on her when she read that her hypostasis was put off until the arrival of Querilinte, whom she would see with me at Marseilles in the spring of the following year. The Genius further told her that the young Countess Lascaris could only do her harm, and that she must leave it to me to get rid of her. He ended by ordering her to instruct me not to leave in Aix a woman who had lost her husband and who had a daughter whom the Geniuses had destined to be of great service to our Order. She was to arrange for her to travel to Alsace with her daughter and not let them out of her sight until they had arrived there, so that our influence would protect them from the dangers by which they were threatened if they were left to themselves.

Madame d'Urfé, who, her madness aside, was extremely kindhearted, recommended the widow to me with all the warmth of fanaticism and humanity and was extremely impatient to learn their whole story. I coldly told her whatever I thought proper to strengthen her in her resolve and promised to introduce the ladies to her as soon as possible.

We returned to Aix, and we spent the rest of the night together, discussing all the matters which filled her imagination. Everything being favorable to my plans, I devoted myself entirely to arranging for the journey to Alsace and to obtaining complete possession of Mimi after having so well deserved her favors by the service I was doing her.

The next day I was lucky at cards, and, to crown my day, I went to enjoy the grateful surprise of Madame d'Aché when I informed her that I had decided to take her to Colmar myself with her Mimi. I said that I must begin by introducing them to the lady whom I had the honor of accompanying, and I asked her to be ready the next day, for the Marquise was impatient to make her acquaintance. I clearly saw that she found it hard to convince herself that what I was telling her was true, for she assumed that the Marquise was in love with me, and she could not reconcile that idea with Madame d'Urfé's eagerness to put me in the company of two women who might well be dangerous rivals.

I went for them the next day at an hour we had agreed upon, and Madame d'Urfé received them with a cordiality which must greatly have surprised them, for they could not know that they owed it to a recommendation direct from the moon. The four of us dined together, and the two ladies conversed like women of the world. Mimi was charming, and I paid her particular attention, of which her mother well knew the reason and which the Marquise attributed to the esteem in which the Rosicrucians held her.

In the evening we all went to the ball, where La Corticelli, always bent on causing me every possible annoyance, danced in a manner forbidden to well-born young ladies. She performed entrechats à huit, *pirouettes, caprioles, mid-leg* battements—*in short, all the acrobatics of an opera ballet girl. I was in torment! An officer who perhaps did not know that I gave myself out to be her uncle, or perhaps only pretended not to know it, asked me if she was a professional dancer. I heard another officer behind me saying that he thought he had seen her dance at the theater in Prague during the last Carnival. I realized that I must hasten my departure, for I foresaw that the wretched girl would end by costing me my life if we remained in Aix.*

Madame d'Aché having, as I said, the manners of good society, completely won the approval of Madame d'Urfé, who thought that she saw a new favor from Selenis in her amiability. Feeling that, after the services I was doing her in so marked a manner, she owed me some gratitude, Madame d'Aché pretended not to feel well and left the ball first, so that when I took her daughter home I found myself alone with her and under no constraint. Taking advantage of this favorable circumstance, I spent two hours with Mimi, who proved to be so amenable, so willing, and so passionate that when I left her I had nothing more to desire.

On the third day I furnished the mother and daughter with traveling clothes, and, in an elegant and roomy berlin which I had secured, we all set out happily from Aix. A half hour before leaving I made an acquaintance the consequences of which were disastrous later on. A Flemish officer, whom I did not know, accosted me and described his destitute situation so feelingly that I could not help giving him twelve louis. Ten minutes later he brought me a note in which he acknowledged his indebtedness and stated the time at which he would repay me. The note showed me that his name was Malingan.[23] My reader shall learn the sequel ten months hence.

Just as we were leaving I directed La Corticelli to a four-seated carriage in which she was to travel with her mother and two maids. She shook from head to foot; her pride was wounded, and for a moment I thought she would go out of her mind; tears, insults, curses—nothing was spared. I remained unmoved, and Madame d'Urfé, laughing over the insane vagaries of her supposed niece, showed that she was very glad to be seated opposite me and beside the protégée of the powerful Selenis; while Mimi seized every opportunity to show how happy she was to be in my company.

We arrived at Liège the next day at nightfall, and I suggested to Madame d'Urfé that we spend the following day there, for I wanted to hire horses to travel to Luxembourg by way of the Ardennes; it was a detour in which I indulged myself in order to possess my charming Mimi the longer.

[* * *]

We set off again the next day and spent two days crossing the Ardennes.[24] It is one of the strangest landscapes in Europe, a vast forest whose tales of ancient chivalry furnished Ariosto with such beautiful pages on the subject of Bayard.[25]

Amid this immense forest, which contains not a single city, and which one must nevertheless cross to get from one country to another, one finds almost none of the comforts or even the necessities of life.

One would search it in vain for vices and for virtues and for what we call "manners." The inhabitants are without ambition, and, unable to have correct ideas of the truth, they hatch monstrous notions concerning nature, the sciences, and the powers of men who, in their opinion, deserve the epithet "wise." It is enough to be a physician to gain the reputation of being an astrologer, and still more a magician, among them. Yet the Ardennes are well populated, for I have been assured that they contain twelve hundred churches. The inhabitants are kindly, even obliging, especially the girls; but in general the fair sex does not deserve that epithet there. In this vast district, the entire length of which is watered by the Meuse, lies the city of Bouillon,[26] a hole if ever there was one, but in my time it was the freest city in Europe. The Duke of Bouillon[27] was so jealous of his jurisdictional rights that he preferred his prerogative to all the honors which could have been paid him at the Court of France.

We stopped one day at Metz, where we paid no visits, and in three days we arrived at Colmar, where we left Madame d'Aché, whose good graces I had won. Her family, who were very well off, received both mother and daughter with the greatest affection. Mimi shed many tears when we parted, but I comforted her by promising to see her again before long. Madame d'Urfé, whom I had prepared for the separation, felt it very little, and for my part I did not find it hard to console myself. At the same time that I congratulated myself on having contributed to the happiness of the mother and daughter, I bowed to the secret counsels of Providence.

The next day we went to Sulzbach,[28] where Baron Schaumbourg,[29] an acquaintance of Madame d'Urfé's, gave us a cordial reception. I should have been bored in the dreary place had it not been for cards. Madame d'Urfé, feeling in need of company, encouraged La Corticelli to hope for the return of my good graces and, with them, of hers. The wretched creature, who had used every means to cross me, seeing how easily I had foiled her plots and how deeply I had humiliated her, had changed her role: she had become docile, obliging, and submissive. She hoped to regain some part of the esteem which she had so completely lost, and she thought that victory was at hand when she saw that Madame d'Aché and her daughter had remained behind in Colmar. But what she had most at heart was neither my friendship nor the Marquise's, but the casket, for which she no longer dared to ask me and *which she was not to see again. By her pleasantries at table, which made Madame d'Urfé laugh heartily, the madcap managed to inspire some twinges of desire in me; but the compliments of that kind which I paid her did not lead me to lessen my severity in the least; she always slept with her mother.*

CHAPTER IV

*I send La Corticelli to Turin. Helena initiated
into the mysteries of Love. I pay a visit to
Lyons. I arrive in Turin.*

[* * *]

Need had forced me to forgive La Corticelli to some extent, and when I came home early, after supping with the rattlebrained creature and Madame d'Urfé, I would spend the night with her; but when I came home late, which happened rather often, I slept alone in my own room. The hussy likewise slept alone in a small room adjoining her mother's, through which one had to pass to enter hers.

Having come home an hour after midnight and not feeling sleepy, after putting on my dressing gown I take a candle and go to visit my beauty. I was somewhat surprised to find the door of Signora Laura's room ajar, and just as I was about to go in, the old woman reached out and caught me by my dressing gown, begging me not to enter her daughter's room.

"Why?" I said.

"She was very ill all evening, and she needs sleep."

"Very well, I will sleep too."

So saying, I give the old woman a push, I enter the girl's room, and I find her in bed with someone who hides under the coverlet.

After contemplating the tableau for a moment I began laughing, and, sitting down on the bed, I asked her who the fortunate mortal was whom it was my duty to throw out the window. Beside me on a chair I saw the person's coat, breeches, hat, and cane; but, having good pistols in my pockets, I knew I had nothing to fear; however, I did not want to make a noise.

Trembling all over, she took my hand and implored me with tears in her eyes to forgive her.

"He is a young nobleman," she said, "whose name I do not know."

"A young nobleman whose name you do not know, you cheat? Very well! He shall tell it to me himself."

As I utter the words I take a pistol and, with one vigorous hand, uncover the bird who should not have laid in my nest if he expected to escape punishment. I saw a young man whom I did not know, with his head wrapped in a madras kerchief but otherwise naked as a little Adam, as was my vixen. He turned his back to reach for his undershirt, which he had

794

thrown down beside the bed, but, seizing his arm, I kept him from moving, for the mouth of my pistol spoke an irresistible language.

"*Who are you, my fine young gentleman, if I may ask?*"

"*I am Count B.,*[1] *Canon of Basel.*"

"*Do you think you are performing an ecclesiastical function here?*"

"*Oh no, Monsieur, I beg you to forgive me and Madame too, for the guilt is entirely mine.*"

"*That is not what I asked you.*"

"*Monsieur, Her Ladyship the Countess is perfectly innocent.*"

I was in a fortunate frame of mind, far from being angry, I could scarcely keep from laughing. The tableau had a certain charm for me, because it was at once comic and voluptuous. The combination of the two cowering nudities was genuinely lascivious, and I remained in contemplation of it for a good quarter of an hour, uttering not a word and trying to resist the strong temptation I felt to get into bed with them. I overcame it only because I feared that I should find in the Canon a fool incapable of worthily playing a role which, in his place, I should have sustained to perfection. As for La Corticelli, since it never cost her anything to change on the instant from tears to gaiety, she would have played hers ravishingly; but if, as I feared, I had found myself dealing with a fool, it would have degraded me.

Convinced that neither of them had divined what was taking place in my mind, I rose, ordering the Canon to dress.

"*This incident,*" *I said to him,* "*must never be divulged; but you and I will at once repair two hundred paces away and engage each other at point-blank range with these pistols.*"

"*Ah, Monsieur,*" *my gentleman cried,* "*take me wherever you like and kill me if you please, for I was not born to fight.*"

"*Really?*"

"*Yes, Monsieur; and I took orders only to escape that fatal obligation.*"

"*Then you are a coward who will take a cudgeling?*"

"*Anything you please; but you would be a barbarian, for love blinded me. I entered this room only a quarter of an hour ago; Her Ladyship was asleep and so was her waiting woman.*"

"*Tell that to someone else, liar!*"

"*I had only just taken off my undershirt when you came in, and before that I had never been face to face with this angel.*"

"*That,*" *said the wench,* "*is as true as the Gospels.*"

"*Do you know that you are two shameless scoundrels? And you, my fine Canon, seducer of girls, you deserve that I should have you grilled like a little St. Lawrence.*"[2]

Meanwhile the wretched Canon had put on his clothes.

"Follow me, Monsieur," I said in a tone calculated to freeze him, and I led him into my room.

"What will you do," I asked him, "if I forgive you and let you leave this house without a stain on your honor?"

"Ah, Monsieur, I will leave in an hour at the most and you will never see me here again; and wherever you meet me in future you will be sure to find me a man ready to do anything to serve you."

"Very well. Go, and in future remember to take better precautions in your amorous adventures."

After thus sending him off, I went to bed thoroughly satisfied with what I had seen and what I had done; for it left me with a perfectly free hand in respect to the little cheat.

As soon as I got up the next morning I went into La Corticelli's room and ordered her, calmly but peremptorily, to pack her things, forbidding her to leave her room until she got into the carriage.

"I will say I am ill."

"Do as you please, but no one will pay any attention, no matter what you say."

Without waiting for her to protest further, I went to Madame d'Urfé and, telling her the story of the night and enlarging on the comic side of it, I made her laugh heartily. It was just what I needed to put it into her mind to ask the oracle what we should do after this flagrant proof of the young Lascaris's having been polluted by the black Genius in the guise of a priest. The oracle replied that we must leave the next day for Besançon, that from there she must go to Lyons with all her servants and wait for me, while I took the young Countess and her governess to Geneva, where I would arrange to have them sent back to their native country once and for all.

The amiable visionary was delighted with the decree and saw in it only a proof of the kindness of her good Selenis, who thus afforded her the pleasure of seeing young D'Aranda[3] again. As for me, we agreed that I should meet her in the spring of the next year to perform the great operation which would cause her to be reborn from herself as a man. She considered the operation infallible and perfectly consonant with common sense.

Everything was ready for the next morning, and we left, Madame d'Urfé and I in the berlin, La Corticelli, her mother, and the two maids in the other carriage. When we reached Besançon Madame d'Urfé left me, taking her servants with her, and the next day I set out for Geneva with the mother and daughter. I put up, as always, at the "Scales."

During the whole journey not only did I not address a word to my companions, I did not even honor them with a look. I had them eat with a *valet from Franche-Comté*[4] *whom I had decided to engage on Baron Schaumbourg's recommendation.*

I called on my banker to ask him to find me a reliable vetturino[5] to take *two unaccompanied women in whom I was interested to Turin. At the same time I gave him fifty louis for a bill of exchange on that city.*

Back at the inn, I wrote to the Cavaliere Raiberti,[6] *sending him the bill of exchange. I told him that three or four days after receiving my letter he should expect the arrival of a Bolognese dancer and her mother with a letter of introduction. I asked him to put them to board in a decent house and to pay the charges on my account. At the same time I said he would do me a great favor if he could arrange for her to dance, even gratis, during the Carnival, and told him to warn her that if I heard anything to her discredit when I arrived in Turin I would abandon her.*

The next day one of Monsieur Tronchin's clerks came, bringing me the vetturino, *who said that he would be ready to leave as soon as he had dined. After confirming the agreement he had made with the banker, I sent for the two Corticellis, and I said to the* vetturino:

"Here are the two persons whom you are to convey, and they will pay you *immediately after they arrive in Turin, safe and sound with their baggage, in four and a half days, as specified in the contract, one copy of which they will take with them and you the other."*

An hour later he came to load the carriage.

La Corticelli *dissolved into tears. I was not cruel enough to let her go without some consolation. She had been sufficiently punished for her bad behavior. I had her dine with me, and, handing her the letter of introduction to Signor Raiberti and twenty-five louis, eight of which were for the usual expenses, I told her what I had written to that gentleman, who, in accordance with my instructions, would see that she wanted for nothing. She asked me for a trunk in which there were three dresses and a magnificent mantle, which Madame d'Urfé had intended to give her before she went mad; but I told her we would talk about it in Turin. She did not dare to mention the jewel casket, and only wept; but she aroused no pity in me. I left her far better off than I had taken her; for she had beautiful dresses, linens, jewels, and a very fine watch I had given her. It was more than she had managed to deserve.*

At the moment of leaving I escorted her to the carriage, less for politeness' *sake than to commend her to the* vetturino *again. When she had gone, feeling relieved of a great burden, I went to call on my Syndic,[7] whom my readers will not have forgotten. I had not written to him since my stay in Florence; he must have put me out of his mind, and I looked forward to enjoying his surprise. And in truth it was extreme; but after the first moment he threw himself on my neck, embraced me a dozen times, shedding tears of joy, and finally said that he had lost all hope of seeing me again.*

"What are our dear little friends doing?"

"They are as well as can be. You are still the subject of their conversations and of their fond regrets; they will be mad with joy when they learn that you are here."

"You must not let them wait to hear the news."

"Certainly not; I shall go and tell them that we will all sup together this evening. By the way, Monsieur de Voltaire has let the Duke of Villars have his house and has gone to live at Ferney."[8]

"That's all the same to me, for I do not intend to visit him[9] *this time. I shall stay here two or three weeks, and I devote them entirely to you."*

"You will make several people happy."

"Before you go out, be so kind as to let me have writing materials for three or four letters; I will make good use of my time until you come back."

[* * *]

That evening, as the Syndic and I were on our way to visit our pretty cousins, I saw a fine English carriage for sale, and I exchanged it for mine, giving a hundred louis to boot. While I was bargaining for it, the uncle of the beautiful theologian[10] *who maintained theses so learnedly, and to whom I had given such sweet lessons in physiology, recognized me, came to embrace me, and invited me to dine at his house the next day.*

Before we reached the dwelling of our lovable young friends the Syndic informed me that we should find with them a very pretty girl who had not yet been initiated into the sweet mysteries.

"So much the better," I said. "I will act accordingly, and perhaps I shall be the one to initiate her."

I had put in my pocket a jewel box in which I had a dozen very pretty rings. I had long known that such trifles take one very far.

The moment when I met those charming girls again was, I confess, one of the most agreeable in my life. In their welcome I saw joy, satisfaction, candor, gratitude, and love of pleasure. They loved one another without jealousy, without envy, and without any of those ideas which could have made them think less well of themselves. They considered themselves worthy of my esteem precisely because they had lavished their favors on me without any thought of degradation and under the impulsion of the same feeling which had drawn me to them.

The presence of their new friend obliged us to limit our first embraces to the conventional demonstrations which are called "decent," and the young novice granted me the same favor, blushing and not raising her eyes.

After the usual remarks, the commonplaces of which one delivers oneself after a long absence, and a few double meanings which made us laugh and gave the young Agnes[11] matter for thought, I told her that she looked as beautiful as a Cupid, and that I would wager that her mind, no less beautiful than her ravishing figure, was free from certain prejudices.

"I have," she answered modestly, "all the prejudices which are inculcated by honor and religion."

I saw that I must be careful not to shock her, use tact, and play for time. It was not a fortress to be taken by assault in a sudden attack. But, as usual, I fell in love with her.

The Syndic having spoken my name,

"Ah," cried the girl, "then are not you, Monsieur, the gentleman who two years ago discussed some very strange questions with my cousin, the pastor's niece?[12] I am very glad to have the opportunity to make your acquaintance."

"I am happy to make yours, Mademoiselle, and I hope that when she spoke of me your charming cousin said nothing to prejudice you against me."

"Quite the contrary, for she esteems you highly."

"I shall have the honor of dining with her tomorrow, and I shall not fail to thank her."

"Tomorrow? I shall arrange to be there, for I am very fond of philosophical discussions, though I dare not put my word in."

The Syndic praised her prudence and her discretion so warmly that I clearly saw he was in love with her and that, if he had not yet seduced her, he must be looking far and wide for a way to accomplish it. The beautiful girl was named Helena.[13] I asked the young ladies if the beautiful Helena was our sister. The eldest replied with a sly smile that she was a sister but that she had no brother, and, having thus enlightened me, ran to embrace her. After that the Syndic and I outdid ourselves paying her honeyed compliments, saying that we hoped to become her brothers. Helena blushed, but answered not a word to all our gallantries. Having then displayed my jewel box and seen all the young ladies enchanted by the beauty of my rings, I managed to persuade them to choose the ones they liked best, and the charming Helena followed her companions' example and paid me with a chaste kiss. Soon afterward she left us, and we were once again able to enjoy our old freedom.

The Syndic had good reason to be in love with Helena, for the girl possessed not only all that is required to please but all that is needed to inspire a violent passion; but the three friends had no hope that they could prevail upon her to join in their pleasures, for they insisted that her feeling of modesty in the presence of men could not be conquered.

We supped very gaily, and after supper we returned to our sports, the Syndic, as usual, being merely the spectator of our exploits and very well satisfied to be no more than that. I passed the three nymphs in review twice in succession, cheating them for their own good and sparing them when I was forced to yield to nature. At midnight we parted, and the good Syndic saw me to the door of my lodging.

The next day I went to dinner at the pastor's, where I found a number of guests, among them Monsieur d'Harcourt[14] and Monsieur de Ximénès,[15] who told me that Monsieur de Voltaire knew I was in Geneva and hoped to see me. I answered him only by a low bow. Mademoiselle Hedwig, the pastor's niece, paid me a very flattering compliment which pleased me less than the sight of her cousin Helena, who was with her and whom she presented to me, saying that, having become acquainted, we should not lack opportunities to meet. It was what I most wanted. The twenty-year-old theologian was beautiful and appetizing, but she did not have that je ne sais quoi which is so piquant, the something of bitter-sweet which heightens even voluptuousness. However, her friendship with her cousin was all that I needed to enable me to inspire a favorable feeling in that young lady.

We had an excellent dinner, during which the conversation turned only on indifferent matters; but at dessert the pastor invited Monsieur de Ximénès to put some questions to his niece. Knowing this scholar by reputation, I expected some problem in geometry, but I was mistaken, for he asked her if a mental reservation suffices to justify the person who makes it.

Hedwig modestly replied that, despite the case in which a lie might become necessary, a mental reservation was always a fraud.

"Then tell me how Jesus Christ could say that the time at which the world would end was unknown to him."[16]

"He could say it because he did not know."

"Then he was not God?"

"The conclusion is false because, God having all power, he has the power to be ignorant of futurity."

The word "futurity,"[17] so aptly coined, seemed to me sublime. Hedwig was enthusiastically applauded, and her uncle went around the table to embrace her. I had a very natural objection on the tip of my tongue, and one which, arising out of the subject, might have embarrassed her; but I wanted to ingratiate myself with her and I said nothing.

Monsieur d'Harcourt was next urged to question her, but he replied with Horace, nulla mihi religio est.[18] *Thereupon Hedwig, turning to me, said that she could not help thinking of the amphidromia,[19] a pagan festival:*

"But I wish," she added, "that you would ask me a question concerning something difficult which you could not resolve yourself."

"You make it easy for me, Mademoiselle."

"So much the better, you won't have to think so hard."

"I am trying to think of something new. I have it. Will you grant me that Jesus Christ possessed all the qualities of mankind in the highest degree?"

"Yes, all, except its weaknesses."

"Do you reckon the procreative power among its weaknesses?"

"No."

"Then be so kind as to tell me what would be the nature of the creature which would have been born if Jesus Christ had seen fit to give the woman of Samaria a child."

Hedwig turned fiery red. The pastor and the entire company looked at one another, and I fixed my eyes on the beautiful theologian, who was thinking. Monsieur d'Harcourt said that we must send for Monsieur de Voltaire to resolve so thorny a question; but, Hedwig raising her eyes with a meditative look which seemed to declare her ready to answer, everyone fell silent.

"Jesus Christ," she said, "had two perfect natures in perfect equilibrium; they were inseparable. So if the woman of Samaria had had carnal knowledge of our Redeemer she would certainly have conceived; for it would be absurd to suppose so important an act in a God without admitting its natural consequence. At the end of nine months the woman of Samaria would have given birth to a male, not a female, child; and this creature, born of a human woman and a man-God, would have been one fourth God and three fourths man."

At these words all the company clapped their hands, and Monsieur de Ximénès admired the logic of the calculation; then he said:

"As a natural consequence, if the Samaritan's son had married, the children issuing from his marriage would have possessed seven eighths of humanity and one eighth of divinity."

"Unless he had married a goddess," I added, "which would have markedly changed the proportions."

"Tell me," Hedwig went on, "exactly what proportion of divinity the child would have had in the sixteenth generation."

"Wait a moment and give me a pencil," said Monsieur de Ximénès.

"There is no need to calculate," I said; "he would have had a particle of the spirit which animates you."

Everyone echoed this gallantry, which was not displeasing to her to whom I addressed it.

The beautiful blonde set me on fire by the charms of her mind. We rose from the table and gathered around her, and she demolished all our compliments with the most perfect courtesy. Having taken Helena aside, I asked her to induce her cousin to choose one of the rings from my box, which I had taken care to refill the evening before; the charming girl willingly undertook the commission. A quarter of an hour later Hedwig came to show me her hand, and I was pleased to see the ring she had chosen; I kissed her hand with delight, and she must have guessed, from the ardor of my kisses, all that she had inspired in me.

That evening Helena gave the Syndic and the three friends an account of all the questions which had been asked at dinner, not forgetting the slightest detail. She spoke easily and with grace; I did not once need to prompt her. We begged her to stay for supper, but, taking the three friends aside, she convinced them that she could not; but she told them she would be able to spend two days at a country house they had on the lake, if they would themselves ask her mother to permit it.

At the Syndic's request the three friends called on her mother the next day, and on the day after they set out with Helena. That evening we went to supper with them, but we could not spend the night there. The Syndic was to take me to a house not far away where we would be very well lodged. That being so, we were in no hurry; and the eldest, eager to please her friend the Syndic, told him that he might leave with me whenever he pleased and that they were going to bed. So saying, she took Helena's arm and led her to her room, and the two others went to theirs. A few minutes after they left, the Syndic entered the apartment to which Helena had gone, and I repaired to the two other girls.

I had spent scarcely an hour between my two little friends when the Syndic appeared and interrupted my erotic diversions by asking me to leave.

"What have you done with Helena?" I asked him.

"Nothing, she is an intractable fool. She hid under the covers and refused to look at the amusements in which I indulged with her friend."

"You should have addressed your attentions to her."

"I did so, but she repulsed me time after time. I am exhausted. I have given up, and I am sure I shall get nowhere with the wildcat unless you undertake to tame her."

"How am I to do that?"

"Go to dine with them tomorrow; I shall not be there, for I have to spend the day in Geneva. I will come for supper, and if we could get her tipsy!"

"That would be a pity. Leave it to me."

So the next day I went by myself and asked them if I might dine with them, and they entertained me in the full sense of the word. When we went for a walk after dinner the three friends, anticipating my wish, left me alone with the beautiful recalcitrant, who resisted my caresses and my pleadings and almost made me lose all hope of taming her.

"The Syndic," I said, "is in love with you; and last night—"

"Last night," she interrupted me, "last night he amused himself with his old sweetheart. I have no objection to everyone's acting as he pleases and sees fit; but I wish to be left free in my own acts and tastes."

"If I could succeed in possessing your heart, I should consider myself happy."

"Why do you not invite the pastor to dinner somewhere with my cousin? She would take me with her, for my uncle is fond of all those who love his niece."

"I am very glad to know that. Has she some man who is in love with her?"

"Not one."

"How is that possible? She is young, pretty, gay, and, what is more, highly intelligent."

"You do not know Geneva. Her intelligence is precisely the reason why no young man dares declare himself her lover. Those who might be attracted by her person avoid her because of her mind, for they would be left with nothing to say in the middle of a conversation."

"But are the young men of Geneva so ignorant?"

"Generally speaking. However, it is only right to say that many of them have received good educations and done well in their studies; but taken as a whole, they have a great many prejudices. No one likes to pass for a fool or an ignoramus; and then the young men here simply do not run after intelligence or a good education in a woman. Far from it. If a young lady is intelligent or well educated, she has to hide it carefully, at least if she hopes to marry."

"I see now, charming Helena, why you did not open your mouth during your uncle's dinner."

"I know that I have no talents to hide. So that was not the reason which made me silent that day, and I can tell you, without vanity as without shame, that it was pleasure which kept my mouth closed. I admired my cousin, who talked of Jesus Christ as I might talk of my father and who did not fear to show her knowledge of a subject which any other girl would have pretended not to understand."

"Pretended, even though she knew more about it than her grandmother."

"It is part of our ways, or rather of our prejudices."

"You reason admirably, my dear Helena, and I already sigh for the dinner party which your kindness has suggested to me."

"You will have the pleasure of being with my cousin."

"I know her merits, beautiful Helena; Hedwig is amiable and interesting; but, believe me, it is especially because you will be present that the thought of the dinner delights me."

"What if I did not believe you?"

"You would be wrong, and you would cause me great sorrow, for I love you dearly."

"Despite that, you tried to deceive me. I am sure that you have given tokens of your affection to the three young ladies, whom I greatly pity."

"Why?"

"Because none of them can suppose that you love only her."

"And do you think such delicacy of feeling makes you happier than they?"

"Yes, I do; though in this matter I am completely inexperienced. Tell me frankly if you think I am right."

"Yes, I think you are."

"You charm me; but if I am right, admit that by trying to associate me with them you do not give me such a proof of love as would convince me that you love me as I should wish to be convinced of it."

"Oh, I admit that too, and I sincerely ask your pardon. But now, divine Helena, tell me how I am to go about inviting the pastor to dinner."

"It is not difficult. Simply go to his house and invite him; and if you want to be sure that I shall be present, ask him to invite me with my mother."

"Why with your mother?"

"Because he was very much in love with her twenty years ago and still loves her."

"And where can I give the dinner?"

"Is not Monsieur Tronchin your banker?"

"Yes."

"He has a fine pleasure house on the lake; ask him for it for a day; he will lend it to you gladly. Do that, but say not a word about it to the Syndic or his three friends; we will tell them afterward."

"But do you think your learned cousin tolerates my company?"

"More than tolerates it, you may be sure."

"Very well, it will all be arranged tomorrow. You are to return to the city day after tomorrow, and I will set the dinner for two or three days later."

The Syndic joined us toward nightfall, and we spent the evening gaily. After supper, the young ladies having gone to bed as on the previous evening, I went into the room of the eldest while my friend went to see the two younger sisters. I knew that whatever I might undertake in order to bring Helena to terms would be unavailing; so I confined myself to a few kisses, after which I wished them good night, then I went to pay the younger sisters a visit. I found them sleeping soundly, and the Syndic in solitary boredom. I did not cheer him when I told him I had not been able to obtain a single favor.

"I see beyond doubt," he said, "that I shall be wasting my time with that little idiot, and in the end I shall have to make the best of it."

"I think," I replied, "that it is your most advisable course, and the sooner the better, for dangling after an insensible or capricious beauty is being her dupe. Good fortune should be neither too easy nor too difficult."

The next morning we went to Geneva together; and Monsieur Tronchin seemed delighted to be able to do me the favor I asked of him. The pastor accepted my invitation and said he was sure I would be glad to make the acquaintance of Helena's mother. It was easy to see that the worthy man cherished a tender feeling for the lady, and, if she reciprocated it a little, that could only be favorable to my plans.

I expected to go to supper that evening with the three friends and the charming Helena in the house on the lake, but a letter brought by an express messenger obliged me to leave for Lausanne at once; my former housekeeper, Madame Lebel, whom I still love, invited me to sup with her and her husband. She wrote me that she had no sooner received my letter than she had persuaded her husband to take her to Lausanne; she added that she was sure I would leave everything to give her the pleasure of seeing me again. She told me the hour at which she would arrive at her mother's.

Madame Lebel is one of the ten or twelve women whom I loved the most fondly in my happy youth. She had everything one could ask to make a happy marriage if it had been my destiny to enjoy that felicity. But with my character I may have done well not to bind myself irrevocably, though at my present age my independence is a sort of slavery. If I had married a woman intelligent enough to guide me, to rule me without my feeling that I was ruled, I should have taken good care of my money, I should have had children, and I should not be, as now I am, alone in the world and possessing nothing.

But let us renounce digressions on a past which cannot be recalled; since I am happy in my memories, I should be mad to create useless regrets.

Having calculated that, by leaving at once, I could reach Lausanne an hour before my dear Dubois, I did not hesitate to give her that proof of my esteem. I must tell my readers here that, though I loved the woman, occupied as I then was with another passion, no hope of amorous pleasure entered into my haste. My esteem for her would have sufficed to hold my love in check, but I also esteemed Lebel, and I should never have allowed myself to risk clouding the happiness of two such friends.

I hastily wrote the Syndic a note, saying that important and unexpected business obliged me to leave for Lausanne, but that on the next day but one I should have the pleasure of supping with him and the trio of friends in Geneva.

At five o'clock I reach the house of Madame Dubois, dying of hunger. The good woman's surprise at seeing me was extreme, for she did not know that her daughter was coming to visit her. Without spending much time on compliments, I gave her two louis to procure us a supper such as I needed.

At seven o'clock Madame Lebel arrived with her husband and an eighteen-months-old child, whom I had no difficulty in recognizing as mine without his mother's telling me so. Our interview was entirely happy. During the ten hours we spent at table we bathed in joy. At day-break she set out for Soleure, where Lebel had business. Monsieur de Chavigny[20] sent me countless compliments. Lebel assured me that the Ambassador showed his wife innumerable kindnesses, and he thanked me for the present I had made him in relinquishing her to him. I could see for myself that he was happy and that he made his wife happy.

My dear housekeeper talked to me of my son. She said that no one suspected the truth, but that she knew the state of the case, as did Lebel, who had religiously observed the agreement not to consummate their marriage until the two stipulated months had passed.

"The secret," said Lebel, "will never be known, and your son will be my heir, either alone or with my children if I have any, which I doubt."

"My friend," his wife said to him, "there is someone who suspects the truth, and will suspect it the more as the child grows; but we have nothing to fear on that score; the person is paid to keep the secret."

"And who, my dear Lebel," I asked her, "is this person?"

"It is Madame de . . . ,[21] who has not forgotten you, for she speaks of you often."

"Will you be so good, my dear, as to convey my compliments to her?"

"Gladly, my friend, and I am sure she will be delighted."

Lebel showed me my ring, and I showed him her wedding ring, giving him a splendid watch with my portrait for my son.

"You shall give it to him, my friends," I said, "when you consider that the time has come."

We shall meet this child again at Fontainebleau twenty-one years hence.[22]

I spent more than three hours giving them a detailed account of all that had happened to me during the twenty-seven months since we had seen one another. As for their story, it was not long; their life had the uniformity which befits untroubled happiness.

Madame Lebel was still beautiful; I did not find her changed at all; but I had changed. She declared that I was less fresh and less gay than I had been when we parted; she was right, the ill-omened Renaud had played havoc with me and the false Lascaris had caused me great concern.

After the tenderest embraces the couple set off for Soleure and I went back to dine in Geneva; but, badly needing rest, far from going to supper with the Syndic and his three friends, I wrote him that, being indisposed, I should not have the pleasure of seeing him until the morrow, and I went to bed.

The next day, which was the eve of the day I had set for my dinner at Tronchin's country house, I ordered the innkeeper to furnish me with a repast in which he was to spare no expense. I did not forget to stipulate the best wines, the finest liqueurs, ices, and everything needed for a punch. I told him that we should be six, for I foresaw that Monsieur Tronchin would be of the company. I was not mistaken, for he was there at his charming house to do us the honors of it, and I had no difficulty in persuading him to stay. In the evening I thought it best to let the Syndic and his three friends into the secret of the dinner in the presence of Helena, who pretended to know nothing about it, saying that her mother had told her that she would take her to dinner somewhere.

"I am delighted," she added, "to learn that it is to be nowhere but in Monsieur Tronchin's pretty house."[23]

My dinner was such that the greatest epicure could have asked nothing better, and Hedwig really furnished all its charm. The astonishing girl discoursed on theology so pleasantly, and made reason so attractive, that it was impossible not to feel the strongest persuasion even when one was not convinced. I have never seen a theologian able to attack and discuss the most abstruse points of that science with such facility, copiousness, and true dignity as that young and beautiful girl, who set me completely on fire during the dinner. Monsieur Tronchin, who had never heard Hedwig, thanked me again and again for procuring him such a pleasure, and, obliged to leave just when we rose from table, he invited us to repeat the occasion on the next day but one.

A thing which greatly interested me during dessert was the encomium which the pastor delivered in commemoration of his old fondness for Helena's mother. His amorous eloquence waxed in proportion as he moistened his throat with champagne and Cyprus wine or with liqueurs from the Indies. Her mother listened to him with satisfaction and matched him glass for glass; the young ladies, however, had drunk only sparingly, as had I. Nevertheless the variety of beverages and especially the punch had produced their effect, and my beauties were a little tipsy. Their gaiety was charming but extreme. I took advantage of this general well-being to ask the two superannuated lovers' permission to take the young ladies for a stroll in the garden at the edge of the lake, and it was granted with all cordiality. We went out arm in arm and a few minutes later were out of everyone's sight.

"Are you aware," I asked Hedwig, "that you have won Monsieur Tronchin's heart?"

"I should not know what to do with it. Besides, the honest banker asked me rather stupid questions."

"You must not suppose that everyone is able to ask them within your compass."

"I must tell you that no one ever asked me one which pleased me as much as yours did. A stupid and bigoted theologian who was at the end of the table appeared to be scandalized by your question and still more by my answer."

"Why, may I ask?"

"He insists that I should have answered you that Jesus Christ could not have impregnated the woman of Samaria. He said he would explain the reason to me if I were a man, but that since I was a woman, and especially an unmarried girl, he could not permit himself to say things which might suggest ideas to me when I reflected on the composite God-man. I wish you would tell me what the fool would not."

"I am willing, but you must allow me to speak to you clearly and to suppose that you are acquainted with the construction of a man."

"Yes, speak clearly, for there's no one here to hear us; but I must confess that I know nothing about the construction of a man except from theory and reading. No practical knowledge, of course. I have seen statues, but I have never seen, still less examined, a real man. And you, Helena?"

"I have never wanted to."

"Why not? It is good to know everything."

"Very well, charming Hedwig, your theologian was trying to tell you that Jesus was not capable of an erection."

"What is that?"

"Give me your hand."

"I feel it, and it is as I had imagined it would be; for without this phenomenon of nature man could not impregnate his spouse. And that fool of a theologian maintains that it is an imperfection!"

"Yes, for the phenomenon arises from desire; witness the fact that it would not have taken place in me, beautiful Hedwig, if I had not found you charming, and if what I see of you did not give me the most seductive idea of the beauties I do not see. Tell me frankly if, on your side, feeling this stiffness does not cause you a pleasant excitation?"

"I admit it, and precisely in the place you are pressing. Do not you, my dear Helena, feel as I do a certain itching here while you listen to the very sound discourse to which Monsieur is treating us?"

"Yes, I feel it, but I feel it very often where there is no discourse to excite it."

"And then," I said, "does not Nature oblige you to relieve it in this fashion?"

"Certainly not."

"But it does!" said Hedwig. "Even in sleep our hand goes there instinctively; and without that relief, I have read, we should be subject to terrible maladies."

Continuing this philosophical discussion, which the young theologian sustained in a masterly manner and which gave her cousin's beautiful complexion all the animation of voluptuous feeling, we arrived at the edge of a superb basin of water with a flight of marble stairs down which one went to bathe. Though it was chilly our heads were heated, and it occurred to me to ask them to dip their feet in the water, assuring them that it would do them good and that, if they would permit me, I would have the honor of taking off their shoes and stockings.

"Why not?" said the niece. "I'd like it."

"So should I," said Helena.

"Then sit down, ladies, on the top step." And they sit, and I, placing myself on the fourth step below, fall to taking off their shoes and stockings, praising the beauty of their legs, and for the moment showing no interest in seeing anything above the knee. I took them down to the water, and then there was nothing for it but that they should pull up their dresses, and I encouraged them to do so.

"Well," said Hedwig, "men have thighs too."

Helena, who would have been ashamed to show less courage than her cousin, was not slow to follow her example.

"Come, my charming Naiads,"[24] I said, "that is enough; you might catch cold if you stay in the water longer."

They come up the stairs backward, still holding up their skirts for fear of wetting them; and it was my part to dry them with all the handkerchiefs I had. This agreeable office allowed me to see and to touch in perfect freedom, and the reader will not need to have me swear that I made the most of the opportunity. The beautiful niece told me that I was too curious, but Helena accepted my ministrations in a manner so tender and languishing that I had to use all my will to keep from going further. Finally, when I had put on their shoes and stockings, I said that I was in raptures at having seen the secret beauties of the two most beautiful girls in Geneva.

"What effect did it have on you?" Hedwig asked me.

"I do not dare tell you to look; but feel, both of you."

"You must bathe too."

"That is impossible, getting ready takes a man too long."

"But we still have two full hours to stay here with no fear of anyone coming to join us."

Her answer made me see all the good fortune which awaited me; but I did not choose to expose myself to an illness by entering the water in the state I was in. Seeing a garden house a short distance away and certain that Monsieur Tronchin would have left it unlocked, I took them there, not letting them guess my intention.

The garden house was full of pot-pourri jars, charming engravings, and so on; but what was best of all was a fine, large couch ready for repose and pleasure. Sitting on it between the two beauties and lavishing caresses on them, I told them I wanted to show them what they had never seen, and, so saying, I exposed to their gaze the principal effective cause of humanity. They stood up to admire me; whereupon, taking them each by one hand, I gave them a factitious consummation; but in the course of my labors an abundant emission of liquid threw them into the greatest astonishment.

"It is the word," [25] *I said, "the great creator of mankind."*

"How delicious!" cried Helena, laughing at the designation "word."

"But I too," said Hedwig, "have the word, and I will show it to you if you will wait a moment."

"Sit on my lap, beautiful Hedwig, and I will save you the trouble of making it come yourself, and I will do it better than you can."

"I believe you, but I have never done it with a man."

"Nor have I," said Helena.

Having made them stand in front of me with their arms around me, I made them faint again. Then we all sat down, and, while I explored their charms with my hands, I let them amuse themselves by touching me as they pleased, until I finally wet their hands with a second emission of the humid radical, which they curiously examined on their fingers.

After restoring ourselves to a state of decency, we spent another half hour exchanging kisses, then I told them they had made me half happy, but that to bring their work to completion I hoped they would think of a way to grant me their first favors. I then showed them the little protective bags which the English invented to free the fair sex from all fear. These little purses, whose use I explained to them, aroused their admiration, and the beautiful theologian told her cousin that she would think about it. Become intimate friends and well on the way to becoming something more, we made our way toward the house, where we found the pastor and Helena's mother strolling beside the lake.

Back in Geneva, I went to spend the night with the three friends, and I took care to keep my victory over Helena concealed from the Syndic; for the news would only have renewed his hopes, and he would have wasted his efforts and his time. Without the beautiful theologian, even I would have obtained nothing from her, but since she greatly admired her cousin she would have feared to fall too far below her if she refused to imitate her in the freedoms which, in her, were the measure of her freedom of mind.

Helena did not come that evening, but I saw her the next day at her mother's, for politeness demanded that I go to thank the widow for the honor she had done me. She received me in the friendliest fashion and introduced two very pretty young ladies who were boarding in her house and who would have interested me if I had intended to make a long stay in Geneva; but since I had only a few days to spend there, Helena deserved all my efforts.

"Tomorrow," the charming girl said, "I shall be able to tell you something at Monsieur Tronchin's dinner, and I think that Hedwig will have hit upon a scheme for satisfying your desires in perfect freedom."

The banker's dinner was admirable. He took great pride in showing me that the repast provided by an innkeeper can never rival one offered by a rich householder who has a good cook, a choice cellar, beautiful silver, and porcelain of the finest quality. We were twenty at table, and the occasion was in honor both of the learned theologian and of myself in my role of wealthy stranger who spent his money freely. Among the guests I found Monsieur de Ximénès, who had come from Ferney expressly to be present, and he told me that I was expected at Monsieur de Voltaire's; but I had stupidly made up my mind not to go there.

Hedwig shone. The guests gained consideration only by their questions. Monsieur de Ximénès asked her to do her best to justify our first mother for having deceived her husband into eating the fatal apple.

"Eve," she said, "did not deceive her husband; she only cajoled him, in the hope of giving him an added perfection. Besides, Eve did not receive the prohibition from God himself, she had received it from Adam; in what she did there was only cajolery, not deceit; then, too, it is probable that her womanly good sense refused to let her think the prohibition serious."

At this answer, in my opinion full of sense, intelligence, and tact, two learned Genevans, and even the young prodigy's uncle, began muttering. Madame Tronchin gravely told Hedwig that Eve had received the prohibition from God himself, as had her husband; but the young lady replied only by a humble:

"I beg your pardon, Madame."

Madame Tronchin, turning to the pastor in alarm:

"What do you say, Monsieur?"

"Madame, my niece is not infallible."

"I beg your pardon, dear Uncle, but I am as infallible as Holy Scripture when I speak in accordance with it."

"Quick, a Bible! let us see!"

"Hedwig, my dear Hedwig . . . you are right after all. Here is the passage.[26] The prohibition preceded the creation of the woman."

Everyone applauded, but Hedwig, calm and modest, did not change her expression; only the two learned men and Madame Tronchin could not recover their calm. Another lady having asked her if, in good conscience, one could believe that the story of the apple was allegorical, she said:

"I do not think so, Madame, for the allegory could be applied only to copulation, and it is established that it did not take place between Adam and Eve in the Garden of Eden."

"But the learned hold different opinions on that point."

"So much the worse for those who deny it, Madame; for Scripture speaks clearly on the point; it says in the first verse of the fourth chapter that Adam did not know Eve until after his expulsion from the terrestrial paradise, and that then she conceived Cain."

"Yes, but the verse does not say that Adam did not know Eve until then, hence he could have known her before."

"That I cannot admit, for if he had known her earlier she would have conceived, since I should find it absurd to suppose that the act of generation could take place between two creatures proceeding immediately from the hands of God, and hence as perfect as it is possible for a man and a woman to be, without its natural effect following."

This answer made the whole company clap, and everyone whispered words of commendation for Hedwig into his neighbor's ear.

Monsieur Tronchin asked her if one could establish the immortality of the soul by reading only the Old Testament.

"The Old Testament," she replied, "does not teach that doctrine; but without its being mentioned there, reason establishes it; for what exists must necessarily be immortal, since the destruction of a real substance is contrary to nature and reason."

"Then I will ask you," the banker resumed, "if the existence of the soul is established in the Bible."

"The idea of it is inescapable. Where there is smoke there is always fire."

"Tell me if matter can think."

"That I shall not tell you, for it is not within my competence; but I will tell you that, believing God to be all-powerful, I cannot find any adequate reason for inferring his inability to give matter the faculty of thinking."

"But what do you believe yourself?"

"I believe that I have a soul by means of which I think; but I do not know if after my death I shall remember through my soul that I had the honor of dining at your table today."

"Then you believe that your memory may not be a part of your soul? But in that case you would no longer be a theologian."

"One can be a theologian and a philosopher, for philosophy harms nothing, and to say 'I do not know' does not mean 'I know.' "

Three quarters of the guests exclaimed in admiration, and the beautiful philosopher enjoyed seeing me smile with pleasure as I listened to the applause. The pastor wept for joy and whispered to Helena's mother. Suddenly, turning to me,

"I should like," he said, "to hear you ask my niece a question."

"Yes," said Hedwig; "but let it be new or none at all."

"You put me in a quandary," I replied, "for how am I to be sure that what I ask you is new? Nevertheless, tell me, Mademoiselle, if, to comprehend a thing, one must consider its principle."

"There is no comprehending it otherwise; and that is why God, having no principle, is incomprehensible."

"God be praised, Mademoiselle! your answer is what I hoped it would be. That being admitted, be so good as to tell me if God can know his own existence."

"Now I'm at the end of my rope; I don't know how to answer. What a cruel question, Monsieur!"

"Then why did you ask me for something really new?"

"But that's only natural."

"I thought, Mademoiselle, that the newest thing would be to put you in a quandary."

"What a compliment! Gentlemen, be so good as to answer for me and teach me."

Everyone beat about the bush, but no one said anything conclusive. Then Hedwig, entering into the discussion again, said:

"Nevertheless, I think that, since God knows all things, he must know his own existence; but please do not ask me how that is possible."

"Good," I said, "very good! and no one can say any more on the subject."

All the guests thought me a flattering atheist, so superficially are people of fashion accustomed to judge; but I did not care whether I was an atheist or a believer in their eyes.

Monsieur de Ximénès asked Hedwig if matter had been created.

"I do not recognize the word 'created,' " she said. "Ask me if matter was formed, and I will answer in the affirmative. The word 'created' cannot have existed, for the existence of the thing itself must precede the formation of the word which designates it."

"Then what meaning do you give to the verb 'to create'?"

" 'To make out of nothing.' You see the absurdity, for you must suppose the precedent nothing. . . . I am delighted to see you laugh. Do you think that nothing is susceptible of creation?"

"*You are right, Mademoiselle.*"

"*Now, now,*" said a guest, frowning, "*not entirely, not entirely.*"

Everyone burst into laughter, for the contradicter seemed not to know what to say.

"*Tell me, please, Mademoiselle, who your teacher was in Geneva,*" said Monsieur de Ximénès.

"*My uncle there.*"

"*No, no, my dear niece, for may I die if I ever told you all that you have brought out today. But, gentlemen, my niece has nothing to do; she reads, thinks, and reasons, perhaps too boldly; but I love her because she always ends by saying she knows nothing.*"

A certain lady, who until then had not spoken, politely asked her to define "*spirit.*"

"*Madame, your question is purely philosophical; so I will tell you that I know neither spirit nor matter well enough to be able to define them satisfactorily.*"

"*But in accordance with the abstract idea you must have of the real existence of spirit—since, admitting a God, you cannot but have an idea of what spirit is—tell me how you suppose that it can act on matter.*"

"*One cannot build solidly on an abstract idea. Hobbes*[27] *calls them 'empty ideas'; one can entertain them, but one should let them alone, for when one tries to explore them one ends in confusion. I know that God sees me, but I should make myself wretched if I tried to convince myself of it by reasoning, for, arguing from our perceptions, we must admit that one can do nothing without organs; now since God cannot have organs, for we conceive him as a pure spirit, philosophically speaking, God cannot see us any more than we can see him. But Moses and several others saw him, and I believe it without examining it.*"

"*You are well advised to do so,*" I said, "*for if you examined it you would find it impossible. But if you read Hobbes you risk becoming an atheist.*"

"*I have no fear of that, for I cannot even conceive the possibility of atheism.*"

After dinner everyone wanted to compliment the truly astonishing girl, so that I could not speak with her alone even for a moment to tell her of my love; but I went aside with Helena, who said that her cousin was to go to supper at her mother's with the pastor the next day.

"*Hedwig,*" she added, "*will stay, and we will sleep together, as we do every time she comes to sup with her Uncle. The question, then, is whether, for the sake of spending the night with us, you will be willing to hide in a place which I will show you tomorrow morning at eleven o'clock. Come at that hour to call on my mother, and I will find an opportunity to show you your hiding place. You will not be comfortable there, but you will be safe, and if you become bored, you can entertain yourself by remembering that we shall be thinking a great deal about you."*

"Shall I stay hidden long?"

"Four hours at most, because at seven o'clock the street door is closed and is not opened again except to people who ring."

"And if I had to cough in the place where I shall be, would it be heard?"

"It is possible."

"That is a great difficulty. All the rest is nothing; but no matter, I will risk everything for the sake of the greatest happiness, which I accept with my whole heart."

The next day I called on the widow, and Helena, as she showed me out, pointed to a closed door between the two flights of stairs.

"At seven o'clock," she said, "you will find it unlocked, and when you are inside you must bolt it shut. When you come, take care to choose a moment to enter it when no one will see you."

At a quarter to seven I was already shut in the closet, where I found a chair—a piece of good luck, for otherwise I should have been able neither to lie down nor to stand erect. It was a miserable hole, and I knew from the smell that it was used to store hams and cheeses; but there were none in it at the time, for I took pains to grope to left and right to find my bearings a little in the thick darkness. Shuffling cautiously along in all directions, I felt something soft, I put my hand on it, and recognized linen. It was a napkin in which there was another and then two plates between which was a fine roast chicken and a piece of bread. Directly beside it I found a bottle and a glass. I was grateful to my beautiful friends for having thought of my stomach; but I had dined well, and rather late by way of precaution, so I put off paying my respects to the cold repast until the hour of fulfillment should be more nearly come.

At nine o'clock I set to work, and since I had neither a corkscrew nor a knife I had to break the neck of the bottle with a brick which I was luckily able to pull out of the rotting floor which supported me. It was an old Neuchâtel[28] wine, and delicious. In addition, my chicken was truffled to perfection, and the two stimulants showed me that my nymphs had some notion of physiology or that chance had seen fit to serve my turn. I should have spent my time patiently enough in this retreat had it not been for the rather frequent visits of one or another rat, which announced its presence by its loathsome smell and caused me nausea. I remembered that I had suffered the same annoyance at Cologne on a like occasion.

At last ten o'clock struck, and a half hour later I heard the voice of the pastor as he went downstairs talking; he charged Helena not to play any tricks with his niece during the night and to sleep soundly. I then remembered Signor Rosa, who, twenty-two years earlier, left Signora Orio's[29] house in Venice at the same hour; and, reflecting upon myself, I found that I had changed greatly without becoming more reasonable; but if I was less sensible to pleasure I thought that the two beauties who awaited me were far superior to Signora Orio's nieces.[30]

In my long career as a libertine, during which my invincible inclination for the fair sex led me to employ every method of seduction, I turned the heads of several hundred women whose charms had overwhelmed my reason; but what was always my best safeguard is that I was always careful not to attack novices, girls whose moral principles or whose prejudices were an obstacle to success, except in the company of another woman. I early learned that what arouses resistance in a young girl, what makes it difficult to seduce her, is lack of courage; whereas when she is with a female friend she gives in quite easily; the weakness of the one brings about the fall of the other. Fathers and mothers believe the contrary, but they are mistaken. They commonly refuse to entrust their daughter to a young man, whether for a ball or a walk; but they yield if the girl has one of her friends as a chaperone. I repeat for their benefit: they are mistaken; for if the young man knows how to go about it their daughter is lost. A false shame prevents both girls alike from offering an absolute resistance to seduction, and as soon as the first step has been taken the fall comes inevitably and quickly. If the friend permits the theft of the slightest favor in order to save herself from blushing, she will be the first to urge her friend to grant a greater one, and if the seducer is skillful the innocent novice will, without realizing it, have gone too far to turn back. Then, too, the more innocent a girl is, the more unacquainted she will be with the methods and the end of seduction. Without her being aware of it, the lure of pleasure draws her on, curiosity enters in, and opportunity does the rest.

It is possible, for example, that without Helena I should have succeeded in seducing the learned Hedwig; but I am sure that I should never have conquered Helena if she had not seen her cousin grant me freedoms and take liberties with me which they must have regarded as the very reverse of what modesty and decorum demanded of a well-brought-up girl.

Since, though I do not repent of my amorous exploits, I am far from wanting my example to contribute to the corruption of the fair sex, which deserves our homage for so many reasons, I hope that my observations will foster prudence in fathers and mothers and thus at least deserve their esteem.

Soon after the pastor left, I heard three soft knocks on the door of my hiding place. I opened it, and a hand as soft as satin took mine. All my *senses reeled. It was Helena's hand, she had electrified me, and that moment of happiness had already repaid me for my long wait.*

"Follow me quietly," she whispered as soon as she had closed the door again, but in my happy impatience I clasped her fondly in my arms, and, making her feel the effect which her mere presence produced on me, I also assured myself of her complete docility.

"Restrain yourself, my friend," she said, "and let us go up quietly."

I groped my way after her, and, at the end of a long, dark corridor, she led me into an unlighted room, closing the door behind us; then she opened the door to another room, where there was a light and in which I saw Hedwig almost undressed. She came to me with open arms as soon as she saw me, and, kissing me ardently, expressed the most lively gratitude for my having been so patient in so dreary a prison.

"My divine Hedwig," I said, "if I did not love you to distraction I would not have stayed a quarter of an hour in that dreadful hole; but you have only to say the word and I will spend four hours there every day as long as I remain here. But let us not waste time, my friends; let us go to bed."

"You two go to bed," said Helena; "I will spend the night on the couch."

"No, no, my cousin!" cried Hedwig, "you must not think of it. Our destinies must be one and the same."

"Yes, divine Helena, yes," I said, going to embrace her, "I love you both equally; and all this ceremoniousness only makes us lose precious time during which I could prove my fond ardor to you. Do as I do. I shall undress and get into the middle of the bed. Come quickly to my sides, and you will see if I love you as you deserve to be loved. If we are safe here I will keep you company until you tell me to leave; but I implore you not to put out the light."

Quick as a wink, philosophizing the while on shame with the beautiful theologian, I offered myself to their gaze in the nudity of a second Adam. Blushing, perhaps fearing to lose my esteem by too much holding back, Hedwig let the last veil of modesty fall, citing St. Clement of Alexandria,[31] who says that shame resides only in the shift. I eulogized her beauties, the perfection of her forms, hoping thus to encourage Helena, who was undressing slowly; but an accusation of false modesty from her cousin had more effect than all my prodigal praises. And at last the Venus appears in the state of nature, at a loss how best to employ her hands, covering part of her most secret charms with one and a breast with the other, and seeming to be aghast at all that she cannot hide. Her bashful confusion, the struggle between expiring modesty and voluptuousness, held me spellbound.

Hedwig was taller than Helena, her skin was whiter, and her bosom twice as full; but Helena had more animation, smoother forms, and a bosom modeled after that of the Medicean Venus.[32]

When Helena, emboldened little by little, arrived at a parity with her cousin, we spent a few moments admiring one another, then we went to bed. Nature spoke imperiously, and we asked nothing better than to obey. Having donned a protective covering which I did not fear would break, I made Hedwig a woman, and, when the sacrifice was completed, she said, covering me with kisses, that the moment of pain was nothing in comparison with the pleasure.

Helena, six years younger than Hedwig, soon had her turn; but the finest fleece I have ever seen offered some resistance; she parted it with her two hands and, jealous of her cousin's success, though she could not be initiated into the mystery of love without a painful rupturing, she uttered only sighs of happiness, responding to my efforts and seeming to rival me in tenderness and ardor. Her charms and her motions made me shorten the sweet sacrifice, and when I left the sanctuary my two beauties saw that I needed rest.

The altar was cleansed of the victims' blood and we performed a salutary ablution together, delighting in serving one another.

My existence was renewed under their agile and curious hands, and the sight filled them with joy. I then told them how much I needed to renew my happiness during all the time I was to remain in Geneva, but they sighed and said it was impossible.

"In five or six days we may be able to arrange another such joyful meeting; but that will be all. Invite us," said Hedwig, "to supper at your inn tomorrow, and chance may give us the opportunity for a sweet theft."

I agreed to do so.

The mood taking us again, since I knew my nature and cheated them when I saw fit, I filled their cup of happiness for several hours, changing from one to the other five or six times before I exhausted my powers and reached the paroxysm of consummation. Between times, seeing them docile and eager, I made them assume all the most difficult of the Aretine's postures,[33] which inexpressibly amused them. We lavished our kisses on whatever aroused our admiration, and once when Hedwig had her lips fastened to the mouth of the pistol the charge exploded and poured over her face and her bosom. She was completely delighted, and, in the role of eager student of physiology, entertained herself by watching out the end of the eruption, which they declared a wonder. The night seemed short to us, though we had not wasted a minute of it, and at daybreak the next morning we had to part. I left them in bed, and I had the good luck to leave the house without being seen.

After sleeping until noon I got up and, having made my toilet, I went to call on the pastor, whom I treated to a fervent eulogy of his charming niece. It was the best way of getting him to come to supper the next day at the "Scales."

"We are in the city," I said, "so we can remain together as long as we wish; but try to bring the amiable widow and her charming daughter."

He promised to do no less.

That evening I went to see the Syndic and the three friends, who inevitably found me a trifle cold. I pretended I had a bad headache. I told them I was giving a supper for the learned theologian, and I invited them to attend it with the Syndic; but I had foreseen that the latter would decline because it might give rise to talk.

I saw to it that the most exquisite wines were the chief ingredient of my supper. The pastor and his lady drank heartily, and I encouraged their inclination to the best of my ability. When I saw that they had reached the point to which I wished to bring them, with their heads slightly muddled and entirely occupied with their old memories, I made a sign to the two beauties, who left the room as if in search of a place to which to retire. Pretending to show them the way to it by going out with them, I took them into another room, telling them to wait for me.

Going back and finding my two veterans completely occupied with each other and scarcely aware that I was there, I made punch, and, after serving them, I said I would take some to the young ladies, who were amusing themselves looking at engravings. I did not lose a minute, and I made several appearances which they found most interesting. Such stolen pleasures have an inexpressible charm. When we were more or less satisfied, we all went back together and I proceeded to mix another bowl of punch. Helena praised the engravings to her mother, urging her to go and look at them with us.

"I don't care to," she said.

"In that case," Helena resumed, "let us go and look at them again."

Finding her ruse delightful, I left with my two heroines, and we accomplished prodigies. Hedwig philosophized on pleasure, saying that she would never have known it if I had not chanced to make her uncle's acquaintance. Helena said nothing; but, more voluptuous than her cousin, she swooned like one of Venus's doves, and returned to life only to die an instant later. I admired this amazing capacity, though it is common enough; she passed from life to death fourteen times while I was accomplishing a single operation. It is true that I was running my sixth race, and that, to enjoy her happiness, I sometimes slowed my own pace.

Before we parted I promised I would call on Helena's mother every day for the sake of learning which night would be the one I could spend with them before I left Geneva. We parted at two o'clock in the morning.

Three or four days later Helena hurriedly told me that Hedwig would sleep with her that night and that she would leave her door open at the same hour.

"I will be there."

"And I will be there to lock you in, but you will be in the dark because the maid might notice a light."

I was prompt, and as ten o'clock struck I saw them come in full of joy.

"I forgot to tell you," said Helena, "that you would find a chicken here."

I was hungry, I devoured it in an instant, and then we gave ourselves to happiness.

I was to leave on the next day but one. I had received two letters from Signor Raiberti. In one of them he told me that he had followed my instructions in regard to La Corticelli; and in the other that she would probably be engaged to dance during the Carnival as first figurante. I had nothing more to do in Geneva, and, in accordance with our arrangement, Madame d'Urfé was waiting for me in Lyons. I had to go there. In this posture of affairs, the night that I was to spend with the two charming girls was my last business in Geneva.

My lessons had borne fruit, and my two pupils had become past mistresses in the art of receiving and giving pleasure. But during the intervals joy gave place to sadness.

"We shall be wretched, my friend," said Hedwig, "and we would be ready to follow you if you would provide for us."

"I promise you, my dears, that I will return before the end of two years," I said; and they did not have to wait so long.[34] We went to sleep at midnight and, waking at four o'clock, resumed our sports until six. A half hour later I left them, completely exhausted, and I spent the whole day in bed. In the evening I went to see the Syndic and his young friends. There I found Helena, who had the wit to pretend to be no more saddened by my departure than the others, and, the better to hide her stratagem, she let the Syndic kiss her as he did the three friends. For my part, imitating her trick, I begged her to convey my farewells to her learned cousin and ask her to excuse me for not going to take leave of her in person.

I left very early the next morning and arrived at Lyons the following evening. I did not find Madame d'Urfé there; she had gone to Bresse,[35] where she had an estate. I found a letter from her telling me that she would be very glad to see me there, and I went there without losing a moment.

She received me in her usual fashion, and I at once informed her that I must go to Turin to wait for Federico Gualdo,[36] then head of the Rosicrucian Order, and I made the oracle reveal to her that he would come to Marseilles with me and there would make her happy. It followed from this oracle that she must not think of returning to Paris before we had seen each other. The oracle further told her that, until she heard from me, she was to wait in Lyons with the little D'Aranda, who lavished caresses on me, begging me to take him to Turin. The reader can well imagine that I managed to put him off.

Back in Lyons, it took Madame d'Urfé two weeks to get me fifty thousand francs which I might need for my auspicious journey. During the two weeks I became well acquainted with Madame Pernon,[37] and I spent a considerable sum of money at the establishment of her husband, a rich manufacturer, for materials for an elegant wardrobe which I had made. Madame Pernon was beautiful and intelligent. She had a Milanese lover named Bono,[38] who acted as agent for a Swiss banker by the name of Sacco.[39] It was through Madame Pernon that Bono arranged to have his banker give Madame d'Urfé the fifty thousand francs which she then gave me. She also gave me the three dresses which she had promised to La Lascaris, but which La Corticelli never saw. One of the dresses was of rarely beautiful sable. I left Lyons accoutered like a prince and set out for Turin, where I was to find the famous Gualdo, who was none other than the perfidious Ascanio Pogomas whom I had sent there from Bern. I thought it would be easy for me to make the clown play the role I had in mind for him. I was cruelly deceived, as my reader will see.

[* * *]

Arriving in Turin at the beginning of December,[40] I found La Corticelli at Rivoli,[41] where Signor Raiberti had told her to expect me. She gave me a letter from that amiable man, in which he told me the address of the house which he had rented for me, since I did not want to stay at an inn, and in which I immediately installed myself and my possessions.

[* * *]

By this stage in his life Casanova was constantly revisiting old ground and renewing acquaintance. Despite the extent and frequency of his travels, he lived in a small world. Passing through Aix he encountered Henriette, elsewhere other former mistresses, and everywhere the same cast of cardsharps, pimps, and fast women.

The only fixed points in this strange universe were Signor Bragadin; Casanova's scattered family; and Madame d'Urfé. Although they never saw one another again after Casanova's imprisonment in Venice, Signor Bragadin continued to finance him until the patrician died, eleven years after his protégé's escape. The writer probably had more feeling for Bragadin than he did for his siblings. He liked one brother, the painter, but loathed another, the Abate, who—in a very typical complication—also happened to be the father of Casanova's mistress. He encountered both brothers in

Paris when he passed through that city to collect his son, the would-be Count d'Aranda, en route for London where D'Aranda's mother was now working.

In Paris he also caught up with Madame d'Urfé, who never lost faith in her pet magician, however long his absences. Madame d'Urfé now had another reason for being pleased to see him. Despite her age, she believed herself to be pregnant by Casanova. On his last visit they had engaged in various "Rosicrucian" ceremonies, including ritual bathing and sexual intercourse under a full moon, in order to facilitate her rebirth as a man in the form of her own child. Even Casanova, acting as surrogate for the spirit who was to impregnate the Marquise, found this a daunting task. Madame d'Urfé had been beautiful in youth but she was now approaching sixty and aging fast. The omnivorous but fastidious Casanova notes that he was especially repelled by sagging flesh. To make matters worse, the need to bolster his reputation as a reliable guide to the other world—or was it just bravado?—had made him tell Madame d'Urfé that the spirits required them to consummate the union three times. Fortunately, these same spirits had also insisted that Casanova's mistress be present during the rites, so the great lover was able to complete the task by thinking of her.

HISTORY OF MY LIFE

Volume Nine

CHAPTER VI

I drive my brother the Abate from Paris.
Madame du Rumain recovers her voice
through my cabala. A bad joke. La Corticelli.
I take young D'Aranda to London. My arrival
in Calais.

Madame d'Urfé received me with a joyful cry, at once telling young D'Aranda to hand me the sealed note she had given him that morning. I unseal it, and I read, after that day's date: *"My Genius told me at daybreak this morning that Galtinarde is leaving Fontainebleau and that he will come to dine with me today."*

This is a fact. Countless things of the same sort have happened to me in my lifetime, such as would turn any other man's head. They amazed me, but, God be praised, they did not make me lose my power of reasoning. People cite instances in which they have guessed something before it happened; but they never mention countless other instances in which they have foretold something which never came to pass. Six months ago I was fool enough to bet that a bitch would give birth to five puppies, all female, the next day, and I won. Everyone was amazed, except myself.

Of course I expressed my admiration for the prophetic powers of Madame d'Urfé's Genius, and I rejoiced at the good health she was enjoying during her pregnancy. Certain that I would arrive, she had sent word to all the people who were to dine with her that she was ill. We dined with young D'Aranda, and spent the rest of the day alone together deciding how best to set about bringing the little fellow to the point of going to London willingly. The oracle's answers were all obscure, since I did not myself know what course to take. Madame d'Urfé's reluctance to tell him to go was so strong that I could not presume upon her obedience to that extent. I put off the decision until another day, and I left, assuring her that I would go to dine with her every day until I set out for London. I went to the Comédie Italienne,[1] where I saw Madame du Rumain,[2] who was delighted to see me back in Paris and who begged me to come to call on her the next day, for she was in the greatest need of my oracle. But my surprise was great when I saw the ballet, and La Corticelli among the dancers. I was tempted to speak to her, not from any feeling of love but because I was curious to learn her adventures. On my way out of the theater I saw Balletti,[3] who had retired from the stage and was living on his pension; he told me where she lived, the sort of life she was leading, and the state of her finances. She was in debt, and could not pay her debts.

"Hasn't she acquired a lover?"

"She had several; but she deceived them all, and she is in poverty."

I go to sup at my brother's, who was living near the Porte Saint-Denis,[4] curious to learn how he had received the Abate.[5] He is delighted to see me again, as is his wife, and he tells me that I have arrived in time to persuade our brother the Abate to leave the house of his own free will, for otherwise he had made up his mind to put him out.

"Where is he?"

"You will see him in a moment, for we are about to have supper, and eating is his chief employment."

"What has he done to you?"

"There he is, he's coming downstairs. I will tell you all in his presence."

Astonished to see me and to see that I do not look at him, he greets me politely and then asks me what I have against him.

"I consider you a monster. I have the letter which you wrote to Passano. According to your testimony, I am a cheat, a spy, a coin clipper, and a poisoner."

He does not answer and sits down at the table.

My brother speaks to me in his presence as follows:

"When the gentleman came to me, I received him gladly; my wife was delighted to make his acquaintance; I gave him the room above this one, and I told him that my house would be his. After that, to curry favor with us, he said that you are the greatest scoundrel alive on the face of the earth, and to prove it, he told us that, having carried off a girl from Venice to marry her in Geneva, he went to see you in Genoa, he and his lady having not a shirt to their backs and being reduced to begging. It is true, he told us, that you immediately rescued him from poverty by clothing him and thereafter letting him want for nothing; but you traitorously obtained possession of her by putting her in the company of two other girls you had, you took her to Marseilles with you, sleeping with her and with the other girl in his presence, and you finally drove him out of Marseilles, giving him, to be sure, a few louis, but discourteously and simply as charity. He ended his story by telling us that, the crime he had committed in Venice preventing him from returning there, he needed us until he could find a way to support himself by his talents and his priestly profession. As for his talents, he told us that he could teach Italian; but we laughed because he does not speak French and because I was sure he had a very poor knowledge of Italian. So we thought it best to confine our efforts to his being a priest, and the next day my wife spoke to Monsieur de Saincy,[6] the bursar in charge of vacant ecclesiastical benefices, to obtain an introduction for him to the Archbishop of Paris, who, upon receiving a favorable report on his conduct, could employ him in his service, after which he could hope to be given a good benefice. To that end he would have to attend our parish church, and I spoke to the parish priest of Saint-Sauveur,[7] who promised to show him every consideration and at once to appoint an hour for him to say mass, for which he would give him the usual fee of twelve sous. When we informed the Signor Abate here of what we had done for him in four days, he became angry. He told us that he was not a man to put himself to the trouble of saying mass for twelve sous, and that he certainly would not pay court to the Archbishop in the hope of entering his service, for he had no intention of serving. We concealed our feelings. The fact is that in the three or four weeks he has been here he has turned the house topsy-turvy. A manservant of whom I was fond has left because of him, my wife's chambermaid, who took care of her linen, and whom he upbraided for no reason, left yesterday, and our cook, who does not want him in her kitchen, threatens to give notice if we have not authority enough to forbid him to enter it."

"What does he want in the kitchen?"

"To find out the menu for the day; to taste stews; to jabber away at the good woman, telling her what he thought was not good the day before. In short, our brother is an intolerable individual. I am delighted that you have arrived, for I hope that between us we will find a way to send him, tomorrow and no later, to mind his own f . . . ing business."[8]

"Nothing easier," I replied. "If he wants to stay in Paris, he is free to do so; but you must send his rags to a furnished room tomorrow, and at the same time have him served with a police order forbidding him, as a disturber of your peace, ever to set foot in your house again. If he wants to go away, let him say so, and I undertake to pay for his journey this evening before I leave here."

"Nothing could be more humane. Well, what do you say?"

"I say," replies the Abate, "that it is the way he drove me out of Marseilles. It is exactly his style. Violence. Despotism."

"Thank God, you monster, that instead of giving you a beating I give you money. You tried to get me hanged in Lyons."

"Where is Marcolina?"

"You make me laugh. I have no accounts to render to you. Hurry up. Choose."

"I will go to Rome."

"Very well. For a man traveling alone the journey costs only twenty louis; but I will give you twenty-five."

"Where are they?"

"Just a moment. Paper, pen, and ink!"

"What are you going to write?"

"Bills of exchange on Lyons, Turin, Genoa, Florence, and Rome, and to take you to Lyons tomorrow you will have a paid place in the diligence. You will have five louis in Lyons, another five in Turin, five in Florence, and five in Rome, and here in Paris not a sou from me. Good-by, my sister. I am staying at the Hôtel de Montmorency. Good-by, Cecco."[9]

"I will send our excellent brother's trunk to you tomorrow."

"A very good idea. If I am not there, have it delivered to my manservant. Leave the rest to me."

"I will send it at eight o'clock."

The next morning the trunk came, and the Abate too. I had him given a room, and I told the proprietor that I would be responsible for the Abate's board and lodging for three days and no longer. He wanted to talk to me, and I put him off until the next day. I instructed my servant not to let him enter my room, and I went to Madame du Rumain's.

"Everyone is asleep," said the Swiss; "but who are you? for I have an order."

"I am So-and-so."

"Come into my lodge and amuse yourself with my niece. I will be back."

He comes back and he takes me to the chambermaid's room; she gets up cursing.

"What is the matter?"

"You might have come at noon. Madame got home at three o'clock in the morning. It's not nine yet; but she'll be sorry, I'm going to wake her."

I go in, and she thanks me for having had her waked just as I am asking her to excuse me for it.

"Raton, bring us writing materials, and leave us. You are not to come until I call you. I am asleep for everyone on earth."

"I shall go and sleep too."

"Monsieur, how is it that the oracle has deceived us? Monsieur du Rumain is still alive,[10] he was to have died six months ago; it is true that he is not well; but we will ask about that later. The urgent thing now is something else. You know that music is my chief passion and that my voice was celebrated both for its strength and its range. I have lost it, my dear friend; it is three months since I have been able to sing. Monsieur Herrenschwandt[11] has given me every remedy in the pharmacopoeia, and nothing can bring it back to me; I am in despair over it, I am only twenty-nine[12] years old, I am unhappy, it was the only pleasure which made life dear to me. Ask the oracle, I beg you, for a remedy to give me back my voice as soon as possible. How happy I should be if I could sing tomorrow, for instance; I shall have a great number of people here, and everyone would be astonished. If the oracle is willing I am sure it can be done, for there is nothing wrong with my chest. Enough! that is my question. It is a long one, but so much the better. The answer will be long too, and I like long answers."

There were times when I liked long questions too, for they gave me time while I was constructing the pyramid to think of what I might answer. What the case required was a remedy for a trifling disorder; but I did not know one, and the honor of the oracle demanded that I give one. I was sure that a healthy regimen would restore her vocal cords to their original state; but it is not the part of an oracle to repeat what any incompetent doctor knows enough to say. So reflecting, I decide to take the course of ordering her to perform a ceremony of worship to the Sun at an hour which would oblige her to follow a regimen which would cure her, without my having to prescribe it for her.

So the oracle told her that she would recover her voice in twenty-one days, if she would begin on the day of the new moon and perform a ceremony to the rising Sun every morning in a room which had at least one window facing the east. To perform this ceremony, a second oracle instructed her, she must have slept for seven hours, and, before going to bed, must bathe in honor of the Moon, keeping her legs in warm water up to the knee. As for the liturgies appropriate to these ceremonies, I told her which psalms she was to read while bathing in order to secure beneficent influences from the Moon, and which ones she was to read before the closed window at the instant when the Sun rose. The oracle's consideration in ordering that the window should be closed greatly pleased the lady, for there might be a wind which would make her catch cold. Lost in admiration of the divinity of this magical remedy, she promised she would punctually carry out all of the oracle's instructions if I would be so good as to bring her the drugs needed for the fumigations.

I promised all that she asked, and to show her my zeal I told her that on the first day I would perform the fumigations myself so that she could learn the method, for the nature of the two ceremonies demanded that no woman be present at them. The manner in which she received my offers showed that she was deeply touched. We had to begin the next day, which was that of the new moon, and I went to her house at nine o'clock; for in order to sleep seven hours before worshiping the rising Sun she had to go to bed before ten. I was sure that what would make her recover her voice was the new regimen, and I was right in my expectation. It was at London that she gave me the news in a letter which came from her heart. This lady, whose daughter married Monsieur de Polignac,[13] loved pleasure, and, frequenting great supper parties, she could not always enjoy perfect health. She had lost the beauty of her voice. Having recovered it by a magical operation, she laughed when she found people who told her that magic was a chimerical science.

At Madame d'Urfé's I found a letter from Teresa,[14] young D'Aranda's mother. She wrote me that she would be obliged to take the step of coming to fetch her son herself if I did not bring him to her, and that she expected a definite reply at once. I told the boy that his mother would be at Abbeville in a week and that she wanted to see him.

"She must be granted the pleasure," I said; "you shall come with me."

"Gladly; but if you go to London with her, with whom shall I return to Paris?"

"Alone," said Madame d'Urfé, "preceded by a postilion."

"On horseback. Oh, how I shall enjoy that!"

"But you shall ride only eight or ten stages a day, for you need not risk your life riding at night."

"I will dress as a courier."

"Yes, I will have a fine jacket made for you, and chamois breeches, and I will give you a splendid parchment[15] with the arms of France."

"I'll be taken for a courier for the Cabinet, and I will say I am coming from London."

I then pretended to object, saying that a horse might fall and break his neck. By persisting in my opposition I made sure that he would come, for Madame d'Urfé, having suggested the plan in the first place, naturally became the one to whom he must appeal for the favor. I refused to hear a word of it for three days before I granted it to him on condition that he would not travel on horseback but would come with me. Sure that he would return to Paris, he insisted on taking only two or three shirts with him; but sure, on my side, that once I had got him as far as Abbeville he would not escape me, I had his trunk with all his clothes sent to Calais,[16] where we should find it on our arrival. In the meanwhile Madame d'Urfé had a complete courier's outfit made for him and a pair of strong boots which he needed to protect his legs in case of a fall. So it was that this difficult undertaking was made easy by chance.

I spent that afternoon with the banker Tourton & Baur[17] arranging to have my money in London distributed among several bankers, to whom he sent me, as I requested, with strong letters of recommendation. I wanted to make numerous acquaintances.

As I left the Place des Victoires, I thought of La Corticelli,[18] and curiosity took me to call on her. She was living on the Rue de Grenelle Saint-Honoré[19] in a furnished apartment. She was astonished to see me. After a long silence, seeing that I said nothing, she wept, then she said:

"I should not be unhappy if I had never known you."

"You would be just as unhappy, but in some different way, for your misfortunes are the result of your bad conduct. But what are they?"

"Unable to bear being in Turin after you dishonored me——"

"If you go on in that style I shall leave; for I have not come here to defend myself, but rather to hear the voice of your repentance."

"And I repent; but it is none the less true——"

"Good-by."

"Very well, I will tell my story and not say what I think. Sit down. I fled from Turin with Droghi;[20] he was in the corps de ballet, I don't know if you knew him; he used to come to La Pacienza's;[21] he loved me; I let him give me a child. When you arrived in Turin I was pregnant. At my wit's end to decide on a course, for Droghi had no money and did not want to confess our situation to anyone, I gave my lover one of my watches and a ring to sell, and we left. We came here, but we stayed only a week. On the promenade of the Palais-Royal we found Santini,[22] who was going to London with D'Auberval[23] to dance in the opera at the Haymarket;[24] he needed a couple; he gave us a good contract without knowing what we could do, and we left. At London we were not liked, and if we had sued we should have lost, for it was plain to see that I was pregnant, and as for Santini everyone knew that he was a tailor who didn't know how to dance a step. I gave him all my jewels to sell, and so we came back. In the two months we were in London we got twenty guineas[25] into debt, though we lived like beggars, and those barbarians would not even take up a collection for me.

"Santini had a relative in Versailles, a valet at the Court, and when he told him how hard put to it he was to provide for my lying-in at all comfortably, he offered him a lodging; he accepted, and I went to lie in at Versailles, giving birth prematurely to a dead infant after being on the verge of death myself. I came back here, reduced to possessing only one dress. The pantaloon Collalto[26] saw me, became my lover, took care of me, and one day, angry with Santini, who wanted to play the master, he slapped him and turned him out. He was right, for Santini should have shown him respect. Santini went I don't know where, and Collalto got me an engagement at the Comédie Italienne[27] and gave me my freedom. In a short time I had five or six lovers keeping me one after the other, all of whom left me for trumped-up reasons, for after all I was not married to them. Collalto himself left me, angry at finding himself ill with the same disease which I had. He ought to have forgiven me and arranged to have me cured; but men are all like you, merciless. Again I sold everything I had, and I signed a bill of exchange for four hundred francs which, having fallen due, and I not being able to pay it, was protested, and a seizure was executed on my furniture because it was believed to be mine. The seizure lasted only twenty-four hours because the landlord, informed of the fact, was able to assert his rights; but he will have it taken away in two or three days if I do not pay him his month in advance, as I have always done. I haven't a sou, and, to make matters worse, I have been dismissed from the Comédie Italienne. In a week I will no longer appear there. I cannot count on another lover, for everyone knows

I am ill; I am in the hands of the streetwalkers who prowl on the Rue Saint-Honoré at night. That is the true picture of the state in which you find me."

After this dreadful story she buried her face in a dirty handkerchief to catch a flood of tears. I was as if turned to stone, beside myself, and under the mortifying necessity of recognizing that I was one of the causes of the horrible abyss in which I saw the wretched girl sunk. Pity commanded me to do something for her at once.

"What course have you thought of taking?"

"You mock me. I don't know what taking a course means. To decide on a course one at least has to have money. I shall be arrested tomorrow. I shall go to prison and die there. God's will be done. Listen! someone is coming here. Wait."

She rises and goes out; I hear her talking; the person leaves; she comes back, and she tells me that she has given twenty-four sous to a streetwalker who had brought her a man.

"I told her," she said, "that I have company and that I am engaged for the whole night."

My horror increases; I tell her that I do not think I am capable of relieving her misfortunes either with my purse or with my advice.

"What would you do if you had money?"

"If I had enough of it, I would go and get cured."

"And after that?"

"If I had any left, I would go to Bologna, where I would earn my living by my profession, having perhaps grown wiser."

"But where would you go to be cured, since spies would have you arrested?"

"I have no idea. If Collalto had not abandoned me!"

"Ah, poor Corticelli! You are lost, and permit me to tell you that you are wrong to console yourself by attributing the cause of your misfortunes to others and not to yourself. I would never have abandoned you if you had not acted toward me like the worst of enemies. Dry your tears! I will say no more. I leave, and I promise I will come back tomorrow or the next day and tell you where you shall go to be cured without anyone being able to find you; I will pay whatever it may cost. After you are cured you shall have money enough to go to Bologna; and after that may God bless you! You will not see me again."

At that the poor girl could thank me only by sobbing and holding my hands clasped in hers, which were trembling from the excess of emotion which what I had said to her had aroused in her soul.

I stayed there until the outburst was over. At the end of the scene I gave her four louis, and I left in anguish of heart.

Having undertaken to rescue the poor girl from the abyss into which she had fallen, I thought of going to an honest surgeon whom I knew, and who alone could tell me how I could set about putting La Corticelli in an inaccessible place until she was cured. He was my erstwhile surgeon Faget,[28] who lived on the Rue de Seine.[29] I take a hackney carriage, I go there, I find him at table with his family; I ask him to finish his supper and then to go to his office with me to hear what I have to say. I tell him the whole story. She is to be cured in six weeks. No one is to know her; she will pay in advance. How much must she pay? She is poor. I am doing a work of charity.

Faget's only answer is to write a note, address it, and hand it to me unsealed, saying:

"The thing is done."

The note ordered the man to whom it was addressed, at the end of the Faubourg Saint-Antoine,[30] to take in the person who would give it to him, and who would pay him a hundred écus, and to dismiss her six weeks later safe and sound. He added that the patient had reasons for not being seen by anyone. Delighted to have finished the business so quickly and so successfully, I go home, I sup, and I go to bed, declining to listen to my brother. I send him word that he can talk to me at eight o'clock. I needed to rest.

At eight o'clock he comes into my room and, stupid as ever, tells me that he had wanted to acquaint me with his plan before I went to bed in order to give me all night to think it over.

"There was no need of that. Do you want to stay in Paris, or go to Rome?"

"Let me have the money for the journey, and I will stay in Paris, giving a written undertaking not to go to see my brother again, or you if you are here. That should suit you just as well."

"You are a fool, for only I can judge what does or does not suit me. Leave my presence at once. I have not time to listen to you. Either Paris without a sou, or twenty-five louis to take you to Rome, parceled out as I see fit."

I call Clairmont and have him turned out of the room. On my way out I tell the proprietor again that the next day is the last on which I will pay for the Abate. I was in a hurry to have done with La Corticelli and her troubles. I went in a hackney carriage to the house in the Faubourg Saint-Antoine of which Faget's note gave me the address, in order to see the place where the wretched girl was to do penance for six weeks. I find an elderly man with his wife, both of whom seem honest people, and after giving him Faget's letter to read I tell him that the girl will come without losing any time, and that I had come to see everything. At that he shows me a small room with a bed, a bath, three or four chairs, a table, a wardrobe, all very clean. He says that she will eat alone, and that unless her illness is very complicated he will have her cured at the end of six weeks. He shows me the doors of seven or eight rooms like the one we are in, four of which, he tells me, are occupied by sick girls, all more or less under the same condition of secrecy and whose names he does not know. I pay him a hundred écus, he writes the receipt in Faget's name, and I tell him he is to give the room in which we are to the person who will come to him with the receipt and the same letter from Faget. After that I go to the Palais-Royal,[31] where I happen upon a Venetian named Boncousin,[32] who tells me that he has come to open a rooming house in Paris, hoping thereby to make his fortune.

"Relying on what?"

"On two girls whom you know."

"Who are they?"

"I will not tell you. Come to supper with me, and you shall see them. Here is my address. But you shall pay for the supper, for I am not rich."

"Very well, I will come the day after tomorrow, for today and tomorrow I am engaged."

"Will you give me the money now, so that I shall be sure of it?"

"Gladly; but I did not suppose you had grown so poor. Here are six francs."

"It is very little, if you want to sup well."

"I will pay the rest after the supper. Good-by."

I knew that the man was a scoundrel. He had an inn in Venice. I should not have gone if I had not been curious about the two girls I was supposed to know. I go to dine at Madame d'Urfé's, and immediately after dinner I go to La Corticelli's to comfort her. I find her in bed. She disgusts me by showing me her illness; I tell her what I have done for her and I give her the surgeon's receipt and the letter. I tell her she has only to take a hackney carriage and go there by herself, promising that I will go to see her once before I set off for London and will leave her another hundred écus, which should be enough to take her to Bologna as soon as she is cured. Full of gratitude, she tells me that she will go after dark the next day

without saying anything to her maid, whom she will send somewhere so that she can take her shifts and her one remaining dress
with her in a bag, and she asks me for two louis more to redeem
some clothing which she had in pawn.

Delighted to have rescued La Corticelli from her sad plight, I go
to see Madame du Rumain, who had taken leave of all her acquaintances for three weeks. She was a woman of the greatest probity, as
polite and polished as possible, but with a manner so oddly affected
that it often made me laugh heartily; she talked of the Sun and the
Moon as if they were sovereigns whose acquaintance she was about
to make. Talking to me one day of the happiness of the saved after
death, she said that in heaven the happiness of souls must consist in
their loving God "to distraction." I brought her all the drugs and
herbs needed to make the perfumes; I told her what psalms to recite;
at eight o'clock we ate a light supper together, then she ordered her
chambermaid to shut her door and to expect me at ten o'clock,
when she was to put me to bed in a room on the third floor which
she had had made ready for me, instructing her to let me enter her
room at five o'clock in the morning. At half past nine o'clock
I myself put her legs in the bath, the water in which had become
warm, I showed her how to prepare the perfumes herself on the
following days, I had her recite the psalms, then I dried her legs
myself, laughing a little at her expressions of gratitude, and after
seeing her to her bed, I went off to bed myself, waited on by her
chambermaid, who, young and charming and merry, made me
laugh by saying that if I had become her mistress's chambermaid it
was only right that she should become mine. I wanted to make free
with her; but she ran away, saying that I must save myself in order to
be on my mettle with her mistress at five o'clock. She was mistaken.

The next morning at five o'clock I found Madame punctually
putting on her shoes and stockings. We went into the adjoining
room, from which we could have seen the rising Sun if the Hôtel de
Bouillon[33] had not been in the way; but it did not matter. She
performed her devotions with the air of a priestess. After that she sat
down at her harpsichord, assuring me that she would find it very
hard to occupy nine-hour mornings for three weeks in succession,
for she did not dine until two. We breakfasted at nine o'clock, and
I left her, promising that I would see her again before I set off for
London.

I went to the Hôtel de Montmorency to dress, and Clairmont
made me laugh by describing my brother's state of alarm because I had

not come home to sleep. He was curling my hair when I saw him come in. I rose quickly, asking him, "Paris or Rome?" and he replied, "Rome." At that I told him to wait outside. When I was dressed I had him summoned, and just then my brother the painter came in with his wife to say that they had come to ask me for dinner. I wrote a note to Madame d'Urfé begging her to pardon me if I could not go there; and I told my brother that he had come in time to see the execution of the Abate, who had finally made up his mind to go to Rome however I chose to send him. I sent Clairmont to the office of the Lyons diligence to reserve and pay for a place for him; then in less than half an hour I wrote him four drafts for five louis each—one on Signor Bono in Lyons, another on Signor Zappata in Turin, another on Signor Sassi in Florence, and the last for Belloni in Rome.

"What assurance have I," the fool asked me, "that these gentlemen will pay me the money on sight of these notes?"

"If you are not sure of it, leave them with me, but for good and all. You are always impertinent to your benefactors."

Clairmont came, bringing a ticket for a paid place in the diligence which left at dawn the next day. I gave it to him and I bade him good-by.

"I can dine with you."

"I do not want you. Go and dine with Passano, monster! You sign your name as a witness that I am a coin clipper, and you dare to speak to me? Clairmont, turn him out."

It was unbelievable, but it was true. My sister asked me what I had done with the girl I had carried off.

"I sent her to Venice with ten thousand écus."

"That is all very well, but think of the pain the Abate must have felt when he saw you sleeping with her."

"Fools are made to suffer pain. Did he tell you that she would never let him give her a kiss, and that she beat him?"

"Not at all. He told us she adored him."

After spending three or four hours pleasantly, I took my sister-in-law to the opera,[34] and her husband went home. She complained to me bitterly. In all the six years[35] he had been married to her he had never been able to consummate the marriage.

"I am told," she said, "that I could ask for an annulment, and I cannot because I am mad enough to love him. He is up to his ears in debt, and if I made him give me back my dowry I should ruin him. But, knowing himself, why did he deceive me by marrying me? He is a traitor."

She was right. But my brother said it was not his fault, and that he had hoped that marrying her would put an end to his impotence. After her death he married another woman,[36] who punished him. She reduced him to having to flee from Paris and leave her everything he possessed. I will say more on the subject twenty years hence.[37]

The next morning early my brother the Abate left. I did not see him again until I was in Rome six years later. I will say more on the subject when I come to that time. I spent the day at Madame d'Urfé's, where I finally consented to young Trenti's[38] returning to Paris from Abbeville on horseback, and I set my departure for three days later. I went to the Français[39] to see a new play, which failed.[40] The author wept bitterly; to console him his friends said that only the machinations of the opposition had made it fail; but that did not make up to him for the money the failure would cost him.

Curiosity made me go to the address at which Boncousin had told me he was staying with two girls who knew me. It was on the Rue Montmartre;[41] the house door, the entry, and the floor were indicated; my coachman drove round and round several times, but could never find the house. I get out to look for it on foot, address in hand; a shopkeeper tells me that two foreign girls had arrived at the house next to hers not long since and that they must be living on the fourth floor. I go up, and I ask the woman who opens the door to me for news of two Venetian girls who must have come to lodge with her.

"Lord! I have fifteen, and God damn my soul if I know what country they come from. Come in, and you shall ask them yourself."

This makes me laugh, and I find a flock of wenches making a great racket and coming to me with exclamations as soon as I appear. I beg all the wild creatures to calm themselves, and I do not even think of asking for the Venetian girls for whom I was looking, for it was a b.....[42] However, I talk to them all, and except for one, who was English, I find that they are all French. The mistress of the establishment comes to ask me if I want to sup with one of them, I consent, I decline to choose, I put myself in her hands, asking her to give me the one she thought would be most likely to please me.

She gives me one, who immediately takes charge of me, leads me to a room, and a moment later supper is brought and clean sheets are put on the excellent bed. I look at my table companion, and she does not please me. However, I hide the fact, I treat her pleasantly, I eat well, I sit at the table a long time, I send for champagne; having seen me cold to all her cajoleries, she thinks that I want to see her intoxicated; and she is obliging enough to get drunk. By the third bottle she no longer knew what she was saying or what she was doing. She undresses and lies down on the bed as nature made her, she invites me, she comes to me, I let her do what she will, and for the first time in my life I have the pleasure of seeing that she cannot make me become a man. Adèle, Marcolina, my niece P. P., Clementina, and the others were still too present to my memory. The hussy was young, pretty, and well built; but she became nothing when I compared her to the others. At three o'clock in the morning I went home, very well pleased with myself and not at all troubled by the poor idea of my valor with which I must have left the girl.

The next day after dining with Madame d'Urfé I took a hackney carriage to go to see La Corticelli in her retreat without being recognized. I found her sad, but well pleased with her situation and with the gentleness of the surgeon and his wife. I was assured that she would be completely cured. She told me that she had fled from the Rue de Grenelle at nine o'clock, carrying all her clothes with her, and that her maid must be in despair, for she was in debt to her. I gave her twelve louis, and I promised to send her twelve more when she wrote to me from Bologna; and she promised to do so; but the unfortunate girl died while she was under treatment.[43] I learned of it two months later by a letter which Faget wrote me to London, in which he told me that he did not know how to send the twelve louis which she had left to a Signora Laura, whom I must know. I sent the honest man an address at which he was able to dispatch them to her.

[∗ ∗ ∗]

After taking leave of Madame d'Urfé and assuring her that I would not fail to keep all my promises, I took the youth with me in a hackney carriage, together with his strong boots, which he admired to adoration. I took him to the Hôtel de Montmorency, whence we set out toward evening. He had begged me to travel at night, because he was ashamed to be seen dressed as a courier and not to be on horseback. On the third day we arrive at Abbeville. I order dinner, he asks me where his mother is, I reply that we will inquire for her, and I invite him to go with me to see the cloth manufactory of the Messieurs van Robais.[44]

"But we can find out in a minute whether my mother is here or not."

"Well, if she is not here we will continue our journey, and we shall meet her on the road. We shall certainly meet her before we get to Boulogne."

"Go to see the manufactory, and meanwhile I will sleep."

"As you please."

I go. An hour and a half later I return to the inn, and I do not see the lad. Clairmont was asleep.

"Where is he? I want to dine."

"He rode off at a gallop to fetch the dispatches which you forgot in Paris."

I summon the post master, I tell him that if he does not bring him back to me he can count on being ruined, for he should not have given him a horse except by my order. He calms me and assures me that he will have him overtaken before he reaches Amiens. He gives the order to a postilion, who laughs when he sees that I am uneasy.

"I'd catch him," he says, "even if he left before dawn. He left only an hour and a half ago; he cannot have traveled more than two stages; I travel three in the same time. You will see me with him at six o'clock at the latest."

"You shall have two louis for drink."

I could not eat dinner. I felt ashamed to find myself tricked in this manner by an inexperienced youth. I threw myself on my bed, where I slept until the postilion waked me by bringing in the culprit, who looked like a corpse. Without a word to him, I ordered that he be locked in a room in which there was a good bed, that he be given supper, and that the innkeeper should make himself responsible for him until early the next morning, when I should leave for Boulogne and Calais. I had to let him rest, for he was exhausted. The postilion caught up with him halfway through the fifth stage, not far from Amiens. He had been as docile as a lamb. The next morning I summoned him, and I asked him if he wanted to come to London with me of his own free will or bound hand and foot.

"Of my own free will, I give you my word of honor; but on horseback, and riding ahead of you, for otherwise I should be dishonored. No one must be able to say that you set up a hue and cry after me, as if I had robbed you."

"I accept your word of honor. Order another saddle horse on my behalf. Come and embrace me."

Perfectly content, he mounted and, keeping ahead of me all the way, he stopped in Calais at the "Golden Arm,"[45] where he was astonished to find his trunk. I arrived an hour after him.

CHAPTER VII

My arrival in London. Mrs. Cornelys. I am
presented at Court. I rent a furnished house.
I make many acquaintances. English morality.

I had scarcely arrived before I summoned the innkeeper and had
him give me a receipt for my post chaise, which I was leaving with
him, countersigning it, and I at once chartered a packet boat[1] so that
it should be at my orders whenever I pleased. Only one was
disengaged, another was for all passengers who paid six francs
a head. I paid six guineas[2] in advance for it, obtaining a receipt,
for I had been told that it was at Calais that one began to be in the
wrong in all disputes in which one could not produce visible
and palpable proof of one's rights. Before the tide falls Clairmont
sees to taking all my luggage on board, and I order supper. The
innkeeper warns me that louis do not pass current in England, and
he changes mine into guineas without taking any profit. I admired
his honesty, for the guinea was worth seventeen sous more than the
French louis.

Young D'Aranda-Trenti had resigned himself. He stayed with me
quietly, proud to have shown me his prowess on horseback. We sit
down at table, and I hear the sound of English words at the door of
my room. The innkeeper enters and tells me that it is a courier of the
Duke of Bedford,[3] the English Ambassador, who was about to arrive
on his way back to London, coming from Versailles. The courier was
arguing with the master of the packet I had chartered; he told him he
had chartered it by letter and that he could not dispose of it; the other
replied that he had not received the letter and no one could prove
the contrary against him. At that I congratulate myself on having the
packet. I go to bed, and early the next morning the innkeeper comes
to tell me that the Ambassador had arrived at midnight and that his
valet wished to speak to me. I have him shown in and he tells me on
behalf of His Lordship, who was in a hurry to get back to London,
that if I would relinquish the packet to him I should be at liberty
to make the passage to Dover just the same. I then take a pen, and
I write my answer in these words:

"My Lord the Duke may dispose of the whole of my packet, except for
the space necessary for three people together with my small amount of

baggage. I eagerly seize the opportunity to make this small gift to the English Ambassador."

The valet comes back to tell me that the Ambassador thanks me but that he wishes to pay.

"That is impossible, for the fee has been paid."

"He will give you back the six guineas."

"Tell His Lordship that the freedom of the boat is his without paying, but not otherwise; for I do not sell merchandise which I have bought."

A half hour later the Duke himself is announced and enters to tell me graciously that I am in the right, but that he is not wrong to refuse the too great favor which I wish to do him. I agree, with a mortified air, but I do not budge from my position.

"There is," he says, "a middle course. If you will take it, I shall be no less obliged to you. We will each pay half."

"I will take it, My Lord; it is I who shall be obliged to you for the honor you do me. I will not leave until you are ready."

He put three guineas on my chest of drawers without showing them to me, and he left, thanking me. I told the master of the packet to put His Lordship and all his effects on board, and I took no part in the disputes in which he engaged with the Ambassador's officers in order to get his money. It was not my affair.

We crossed the Channel in two hours and a half with the strongest of winds. The next day the search by the customs officers to see if I had any contraband articles struck me as extremely tedious, impertinent, indiscreet, and even indecent; but I had to put up with it and conceal my feelings, for an offended Englishman who has the law on his side is much more impertinent than[4] a Frenchman.

The island called England is a different color from that which one sees on the surface of the Continent. The sea is extraordinary, for being part of the Atlantic Ocean, it is subject to the ebb and flow of the tides;[5] the water of the Thames has a different flavor from that of all the rivers on earth. Horned animals, fish, and everything one eats has a different taste from what we eat, the horses are of a species of their own even in their shape, and men have a character not found elsewhere and common to the whole nation, which make them think themselves superior to all others. This is a supposition common to all nations; each thinks itself the first. They are all right.

I immediately saw the great cleanliness, the substantial fare, the beauty of the countryside and of the great roads; I admired the beauty of the carriages supplied by the post to travelers who have not one of their own; the reasonableness of the posting charges, the ease with which it is possible to pay them, the rapidity of travel, always at a trot, never at a gallop, and the construction of the cities through which I had to pass on my way from Dover to London. Canterbury and Rochester[6] have a large population, though their breadth is nothing in proportion to their length. We arrived in London toward nightfall, eighteen hours after leaving Dover, at the house of Mrs. Cornelys. This was the name assumed by Teresa, daughter of the actor Imer, later wife of Pompeati, the dancer, who had killed himself[7] in Vienna, cutting his belly open with a razor and tearing out his bowels in an instant.

This Signora Pompeati, who in Holland had taken the name of Trenti, had in London taken that of Cornelys, in honor of her lover Cornelius Rigerboos, whom she ruined, of whom I have spoken in my fourth volume.[8] I arrived, then, at the door of her house on Soho Square,[9] opposite that of the Venetian Resident, who lives on the other side of the same square. My arriving at her house was in obedience to the orders she had given me in her last letter. I had written her the day on which I hoped to see her.

I get out, leaving her son in the carriage, thinking that I shall see her at once; but the porter tells me to wait. Two minutes later a manservant brings me a letter in which Mrs. Cornelys tells me to go on to stay at a house to which the servant will show me the way and where she will come to supper with me. I find nothing strange in this. She might have reasons for it. I get in again, and the postilions arrive at the house on the street near the Square to which the servant directs them. A Frenchwoman, named Raucour[10] and excessively fat, and two menservants come to meet us; the stout woman embraces Mr. Cornelys[11] and rejoices at his safe arrival, dropping me a cold curtsy. In less than a quarter of an hour Clairmont, shown the way by La Raucour, puts all my luggage in a room which had a closet through which I could enter the apartment on the front, consisting of three fine rooms, in which the same Raucour had had My Lord Cornelys's trunk put, while he stood there open-mouthed and at a loss to answer when she said to him:

"These two valets are yours, and I am your most humble servant."

I return to my room through the same closet, and though seeing that I am not only badly lodged but lodged as an inferior, I control myself, a rare occurrence, and I do not say a word; I only ask Clairmont where his room is, so that he can go to it and dispose of his trunk, which was there with all of mine. After going, he comes to tell me that the fat lady had shown him his bed in a room in the attic where one of Master Cornelys's two menservants slept. Clairmont, who knew me, was astonished to hear me answer calmly:

"Very well, take your trunk there."

"Shall I unpack yours?"

"No. Leave that until tomorrow."

Still concealing my feelings, I go back to the room of my master, who was looking exhausted because he had tried to ride a stage on horseback and had never succeeded in making his mount gallop. He was listening to Madame Raucour, who, sitting beside him, was giving him an account of his mother Mrs. Cornelys's splendid position, her extensive enterprises, her immense credit, the magnificent mansion she had had built, the thirty-three servants she kept, two secretaries, six horses, country house, and I know not what.

"How is my sister Sophie?"[12]

"Is her name Sophie? She is called Miss Cornelys. She is a beauty, Sir, a prodigy of intelligence, grace, and talents; she sings, she plays at sight on all instruments, she dances, she speaks three languages and writes them correctly, she has her own governess and her own chambermaid. It is a pity she is too small for her age, for she is eight years old."

She was ten;[13] but since the woman was talking without vouch-safing me a look, I said nothing. My Lord Cornelys, who needed to go to bed, asked her at what time supper was served, and she replied:

"At ten o'clock and no sooner."

For Mrs. Cornelys was busy with her lawyer until then because of a great lawsuit she had against Sir Frederic Fermer.[14] I thereupon go to my room and, saying nothing, take my hat and cane and set out for a walk. It was only seven o'clock. Careful not to lose my bearings, I walk at random, and a quarter of an hour later I enter a crowded coffeehouse. It was the "Prince of Orange,"[15] notorious for those who frequented it, who were the dregs of all the scoundrelly Italians who were in London. I had been told of it in Lyons, and I had intended never to go there; it was dark, and chance led me there; nor did I ever set foot in it again. I sit down by myself, I order a lemonade; and a man sits down near me to take advantage of the light which was on my table to read a printed sheet. I see that it is in Italian. The man was crossing out letters with a pencil and putting the correction in the margin. "An author," I said to myself. I notice that he crosses out a letter in the word *ancora* and puts an *h* in the margin, to indicate that he wants it to be printed "anchora." I cannot restrain myself. I tell him that the word *ancora* has been spelled without an *h* for four centuries.

"I agree, but I am quoting Boccaccio,[16] and one should be exact in quotations."

"You are right, pray excuse me. You are a man of letters?"

"In a very small way. I am Martinelli."[17]

"Not in a small way at all. I know you by reputation. You are related to Calzabigi,[18] and he has talked to me about you. I have read some of your satires."[19]

"May I ask to whom I am speaking?"

"My name is Seingalt. Have you finished your edition of the *Decamerone*?"[20]

"I am still at work on it, and always trying to increase the number of my subscribers."[21]

"If you would like to add me—"

"You do me honor."

He thereupon gives me a ticket, and seeing that it was only a guinea, I ask him for another, I pay him, and I rise to leave, saying that I hope to see him again at the same coffeehouse. I ask him its name, and he tells me, astonished that I do not know it; but he is even more astonished when I tell him that I have just arrived in London for the first time.

"Then you will have difficulty finding your way back to where you are staying, and I will accompany you."

No sooner have we left than he very frankly warns me that the "Prince of Orange," to which chance had led me, is the most disreputable coffeehouse in London.

"But you go to it."

"I can go to it with the safe-conduct of Juvenal's verse: *Cantabit vacuus coram latrone viator* ['The traveler with an empty purse will sing when he meets a robber'].[22] The rogues have no way of getting their teeth into me. I do not speak to them; and they do not speak to me. I have been here for five years, I seek patronage only from Lord Spencer,[23] I occupy myself with literary work,[24] I am single, I earn enough to live in a furnished room and take my dinner at a tavern. I have a dozen shirts and this coat, and I am in good health; *nec ultra deos lacesso*" ("nor do I importune the gods for more").[25]

Such a man, speaking Tuscan with the greatest purity,[26] pleases me. On the way I ask him how I should go about finding a good lodging, and after learning what accommodations I want and how long I intend to stay in London, and what sort of life I want to lead, he advises me to take a whole house for myself, fully furnished and with all the kitchenware and tableware I should need, as well as table linen and bed linen.

"You will be given the inventory," he says, "and as soon as you obtain a surety, you will be lord and master there, domiciled like an Englishman and responsible only to the laws."

I ask him to tell me of such a house; and he at once enters a shop; he speaks to the proprietress, he writes, and then he comes out after copying everything I needed from an *Advertiser*.[27] It was the locations where houses such as I wanted were to be found. The nearest to where we were was in a broad street called Pall Mall,[28] and we went to see it. An old woman who opened the smaller door to us as soon as he knocked showed us the ground floor and the three upper floors. Every floor had two front rooms—each with a closet, which goes without saying in London—and two at the back. In each apartment there were two beds, one in the room and one in the closet. Everything was scrupulously clean—porcelain, mirrors, bell-pulls; it was perfection. In a very large cupboard in the room on the ground floor in which the old woman slept there was all the linen, and in another were the silver services and services of porcelain and china. In the kitchen there was an ample supply of pots and pans, and in the underground apartment, which I did not expect, there was furniture enough to lodge a whole family, and a cellar and storerooms to hold everything necessary for a well-run house. The rent was twenty guineas a week. I told Martinelli that the house pleased me and that I wanted to take it at once, so that I could move into it whenever I pleased.

As soon as he translated my decision to the old woman, she told him that if I wanted to keep her as housekeeper,[29] I need not have a surety, it being enough for her if I would always pay her the week's rent in advance; but that if I wanted to put someone else in charge of the house she would need at least two days to go over the inventory with whomever I should appoint and who, in that case, would have to give surety. I replied that I would keep her on condition that she would engage a maid, whom I would pay and who would take orders directly from her, but who must speak French or Italian in addition to English. She promised me that she would have the maid the next day; I paid her for four weeks in advance, and she gave me a receipt under the name of the Chevalier de Seingalt; I never used any other name in London. Martinelli, delighted to have been of use to me, left me when, seeing that I was in my street, I thanked him and wished him good night. I returned to Mrs. Cornelys's, who was still awaited though ten o'clock had just struck. Young Cornelys was asleep on the sofa.

So it was that, despite all those who say that London is a chaos in which a stranger who arrives there needs at least three days to find himself a lodging, I was excellently lodged two hours after I arrived. I was also delighted to have made the acquaintance of Martinelli, of whom I had had a most favorable opinion for six years. He had given me the address of his room, which was above the "Prince of Orange," and that of his printer. Profoundly shocked by the way in which the Cornelys had received me in London, I awaited her impatiently, resolved, however, to put a good face on it.

Three knocks (signifying the mistress of the house) sound at last, and from the window I see her alight from a sedan chair, I hear her coming quickly up the stairs, she enters, she shows that she is glad, and indeed delighted, to see me, but she does not come running to embrace me; she has forgotten how she parted from me at The Hague;[30] she throws herself on her son, she takes him in her arms, she covers him with kisses, which he accepts sleepily and returns coldly, saying:

"My dear Mama, my dear Mama."

I tell her that he is tired and that, for people who need rest, she has kept us waiting too long. Supper is announced, and she does me the honor to take my arm to go in to it in a room which I had not seen. She has the fourth place removed, I ask her for whom it was; and she tells me that it was for her daughter, whom she had left at home because as soon as she had told her that I had arrived with her brother she had asked her if I was in good health.

"And you punished her for that?"

"Certainly, for it seems to me that she should be first interested in her brother's health and in yours only afterward. Do you think I am right?"

"Poor Sophie. I feel sorry for her. Gratitude has more power over her than the ties of blood."

"It is not a matter of feeling, but of accustoming young people to speaking as they should."

She talked a great deal to her son, who never gave her anything but studied answers, always with his eyes cast down, and with respect but with no sign of affection. She told him that she was working to leave him rich after her death, and that she had made me bring him back because he was old enough to help her and to share her work in the house she kept; and at that he asked her what sort of work it was in which she wanted him to share.

"I give," she said, "twelve suppers and balls a year for the nobility and twelve for the citizenry at two guineas a head, and I often have five or six hundred people; the outlay is immense, and, alone as I am, it is impossible that I should not be robbed, for since I cannot be everywhere I have to put my trust in people who perhaps abuse it, but now that you are here, you can oversee everything, my dear son, keep everything under lock and key, write, handle the cash, make payments, take receipts, and go all through the house to see if the ladies and gentlemen are properly served, in short, perform the functions and act the part of master in a house in which you will actually be so as my son."

"Then you believe, my dear Mother, that I shall be able to do all that?"

"Yes, for you will learn."

"It seems to me impossible."

"One of my secretaries will come to live with you in this house, which I have taken for the purpose, and he will instruct you in everything. For a year you will do nothing but learn English and come to my assemblies so that I can introduce you to all the most important people in London; and little by little you will become English; everyone will talk of Mr. Cornelys."

"Cornelys?"

"Yes, that is your name."

"My name? I'll go and write it down so that I shan't forget it."

Thinking that he was joking, she looked at me in some surprise. She told him to go to bed, which he did at once, thanking her. Left alone with me, she said that she thought him badly brought up and too small for his age, and that she saw she must begin, perhaps too late, to have him given a different education.

"What has he learned in six years?"

"He could have learned all the branches of knowledge, for he was in the best boarding school in Paris; but he learned only what he wanted to—playing the flute, riding horseback, fencing, dancing the minuet well, changing his shirt every day, answering politely, making a charming appearance, telling a story prettily, and dressing with elegance. That is all he knows. Since he would never apply himself, he hasn't the shadow of an acquaintance with literature, he cannot write, he cannot figure, he does not care whether he knows or not that England is an island of Europe."

"That makes six lost years. My daughter will laugh at him. But it is I who have brought her up. He will be ashamed when he sees how much learning she has at the tender age of eight; she knows geography, history, languages, music, and she talks with the greatest intelligence. All the ladies are forever snatching her from one another. I keep her in a drawing school all day, she comes home only at nightfall. On Sundays she dines here, and if you will do me the favor of coming to dinner at my house on Sunday, you will see that I have not exaggerated."

It was a Monday. I say nothing; but I find it strange that she does not think me impatient to see her, that she does not tell me to come to supper at her house the next day, that she has not brought her to supper with her. She tells me that I have come to London in time to see the last assembly of that year,[31] which she was giving for the nobility, who in two or three weeks would go to spend the summer in the country.

"I cannot give you a ticket," she said, "for I can give them only to the nobility; but you can come to it, and, by keeping near me as a friend of mine, you will see everything. If I am asked who you are I will say that you are the person who took care of my son in Paris and who has come to bring him back to me."

"I am most grateful to you."

We remained at table talking until two o'clock in the morning; she gave me a full account of her lawsuit against Sir Frederic Fermer. He claimed that the house which she had had built,[32] and which cost ten thousand guineas, belonged to him, for it was he who had given her the money; but he was in the wrong, according to the law she cited, for it was she who had paid the workmen and it was to her that they had given the receipts; hence the house belonged to her; "but the money," said Fermer, "did not belong to you." She challenged him to prove it, to produce a single receipt. "It is true," said the honest woman, "that you more than once gave me a thousand guineas at a time; but it was generosity on your part, and nothing strange in a rich Englishman, since we loved each other, we were living together."

This lawsuit, which in two years she had won four times, and which did not end because of the legal chicanery Fermer employed to challenge her victory, had cost Mrs. Cornelys a great deal, and at the time we were talking there was an appeal which would take it to the Court of Equity,[33] where, *beati possidentes* ("blessed are they who are in possession"),[34] it would be fourteen or fifteen years before a decision was handed down. She told me that the suit dishonored Fermer, and I well understood that; but I could not understand how she could suppose it was to her honor; yet that was what she sincerely believed. Among the different subjects on which we touched in three hours of conversation she never asked me if I was comfortably lodged; she did not care to know if I intended to stay in London for some time and what I thought I might do there, and she offered me neither her services nor her credit, for she told me with a laugh that she never had a penny in her purse. She took in more than twenty-four thousand pounds sterling[35] a year; but in these first three years she had spent more than eighty thousand. Even so, she told me, she expected to finish paying all her debts the following winter.

Mrs. Cornelys having shown no curiosity concerning my affairs, I amused myself by telling her nothing about them. She saw no sign of wealth on me; I had only a perfectly plain watch, all my diamonds were in my jewel case. I went off to bed, annoyed but not angry, for at bottom I was very glad to have discovered her bad character. Despite the impatience I felt to see my daughter, I resolved not to see her until Sunday, going to dine at her mother's house, as, for politeness' sake, she had invited me to do.

The next morning at seven o'clock I told Clairmont to put all my belongings into a carriage, and when this was done I went to tell my poor young man, who was still in bed, that I was going to lodge in Pall Mall in the house of which the address was written on the card which I left him.

"What! You are not staying with me?"

"No, for your mother forgot to put me up."

"So she did. I want to go back to Paris."

"Don't do anything so stupid. Consider that now, being in your mother's house, you are in your own, and that in Paris you may no longer find a roof. Good-by. I shall dine with you Sunday at your mother's."

Clairmont arranged all my belongings in my new house in less than an hour. I went out wearing a *frac*,[36] and I took Signor Zuccato,[37] the Venetian Resident, the letter I had from Signor Morosini, the Procurator; he read it, and he said coldly that he was very glad to have made my acquaintance. I asked him to present me at Court, and my request set him laughing. I let him laugh, and I did not set foot in his house again. I went to take my letter from the same Procurator to Lord Egremont,[38] who was ill; I left it for him. A few days later he died. Some time afterward his widow married Count Brühl[39] Martinskirchen, who is still in London as Minister of the Elector of Saxony.[40] I went to call on the Count of Guerchy,[41] the French Ambassador, with a letter from the Marquis de Chauvelin,[42] who gave him such an account of me that he invited me to dine with him on the next day, saying that he would present me at the Court of St. James's[43] on Sunday after chapel.[44] At the Ambassador's table the next day I made the acquaintance of the Chevalier d'Éon,[45] his Secretary of Embassy, who later caused such a stir all over Europe. The Chevalier was a woman who, before becoming a diplomat, had been a captain of dragoons. Despite his considerable knowledge of diplomacy and his masculine manner, I suspected that he was some-thing less than a man. His drama began soon afterward, when Monsieur de Guerchy, who was given a leave of absence, left London. During this week I presented myself to all my bankers, in whose hands I had at least a hundred thousand écus. They accepted the drafts, and in virtue of my letters of recommendation from Messrs. Tourton & Baur, they offered me their personal services. I went to the Covent Garden[46] and Drury Lane[47] theaters, unknown to everyone, and to taverns for dinner, in order to accustom myself gradually to English ways. Mornings I went to the Exchange,[48] where I made several acquaintances; it was there that the broker Bosanquet,[49] whom I had asked to find me a good servant who, besides English, could speak Italian or French, brought me a Negro whose honesty he guaranteed. It was Bosanquet, too, who got me an English cook who could speak French and who moved into my house at once with his whole family, and it was he who introduced me to several strange confraternities of which I will speak at the proper time and place. During this same week I also arranged to be initiated into the select bagnios,[50] where a rich man goes to bathe, sup, and sleep with a choice prostitute. It is a magnificent festival, which costs six guineas in all; economy can reduce it to four; but economy spoils pleasure.

On Sunday at eleven o'clock I dressed elegantly, and, wearing my fine rings, my watches, and my order hanging from my neck on a red ribbon, I went to Court, making my way to the last ante-chamber, where I found the Count of Guerchy. I went in with him, and he presented me to George III,[51] who spoke to me, but in a voice so low that I could reply only by bowing. But the Queen[52] made up for it. I was delighted to see the Venetian Resident among those who were paying their court. As soon as Monsieur de Guerchy spoke my name, I saw that the Resident was surprised, for in his letter the Procurator had called me Casanova. The Queen having at once asked me what province of France I was from, and having learned from my answer that I was a Venetian,[53] looked at the Venetian Resident, who showed by a bow that he had no objection to make. She asked me if I knew the Ambassadors who had left six weeks earlier, and I replied that I had spent three days with them in Lyons, where Signor Morosini had given me letters for Lord Egremont and the Resident. She said that Signor Querini had said many things which made her laugh.

"He told me," she said with a laugh, "that I am a little devil."

"He meant, Madam, that Your Majesty has the wit of an angel."

I should have been glad if she had asked me for what reason[54] it was not Signor Zuccato who was presenting me, for I would have answered in a way which the Resident would not much have enjoyed. After the Court I got into my sedan chair again and was carried to Mrs. Cornelys's house on Soho Square, where I was invited for dinner. A man dressed to appear at Court would not dare to walk through the streets of London; a porter, a loafer, a scapegrace from the dregs of the people would throw mud at him, laugh in his face, push him to make him say something offensive, all in order to have an excuse for engaging him in a fist fight. The democratic spirit prevails in the English people, even far more than it does today in the French; but the power of the constitution holds it in check. In short, the spirit of rebellion is prevalent in every great city, and the great task of wise government is to keep it dormant, for if it wakes it is a torrent which no dam can hold back.

The sedan chair stops at the door of Mrs. Cornelys's house, I tell my Negro, whose name was Jarba,[55] to dismiss my chairmen; I go in, I am conducted upstairs to the second floor, where, after passing through twelve or fourteen rooms, I am shown into that in which Mrs. Cornelys was sitting with two Englishwomen and two Englishmen. She received me with a politeness expressive of the most familiar friendship, and after making me sit down beside her she continued her conversation with her four visitors, speaking English and telling neither them who I was nor me who they were. When her major-domo came to announce that dinner was served, she ordered the children brought down. At sight of Sophie I run to her impulsively to take her in my arms and kiss her; but, following her instructions, she draws back and, dropping me a low curtsy, she pays me a compliment which she has learned by heart, to which I am tactful enough not to reply, for fear of leaving her with nothing to say. Mrs. Cornelys then presents her son to the gentlemen, and tells them that it was I who have brought him back to her after six years during which I had taken charge of his education; she says this in French, and I see with pleasure that everyone present speaks French.

We sit down at table—she between her two children and I, facing her, between the two Englishwomen, one of whom, though no longer young, at once delighted me with her wit. It was with her that I conversed when I saw that Mrs. Cornelys spoke to me only casually and that Sophie, who turned her beautiful eyes from one member of the company to another, never looked at me; she quite obviously passed me over; she was carrying out a command which I thought as absurd as it was rude. Angry to find that I felt offended, and determined not to allow myself to show it, I engage the English ladies and gentlemen in an amusing conversation on the customs I had observed in England, though without the slightest tinge of criticism, thus setting them laughing and making them find me an agreeable companion; and in my turn I never look at Mrs. Cornelys.

The lady next to me, after examining the beauty of my laces, asks me what is new at Court.

"Everything seemed new to me, Madam, for I never saw it before today."

"Did you see the King?" Sir Joseph Cornelys[56] asks me.

"My son," says his mother, "one never asks such questions."

"Why not, my dear Mother?"

"Because the question may be displeasing to the gentleman."

"On the contrary," I said, "it pleased me. For six years I have been teaching him always to ask. A boy who never asks anything always remains ignorant."

Mrs. Cornelys sulks and says nothing.

"You still have not told me," the young fellow takes me up, "if you saw the King or not."

"Yes, my dear boy, His Majesty spoke to me, but I do not know what he said, whereas the Queen spoke very clearly."

"Who presented you?"

"The French Ambassador."

"Excellent!" said his mother. "But you must admit that the last question is too much by far."

"Addressed to someone else, but not to me, who am his friend. You see that the answer he obliged me to give does me honor. If

I had not wanted it known that I went to Court I should not have come to dine here dressed as I am."

"You are right. But since you like to be questioned, I will also ask you why you had yourself presented by the French Envoy and not by the Venetian one."

"Because the Venetian Envoy declined to do it; and he was in the right."

With much other conversation, this brought us to dessert, and my daughter had not yet said a word.

"My dear daughter," her mother said, "do say something to Monsieur de Seingalt."

"I shouldn't know what to say, my dear Mother. But ask him to say something to me, and I will answer as well as I can."

"Very well, my pretty child," I said, "tell me what you are studying at present."

"Drawing, and if you like I will let you see some of my work."

"I shall see it with pleasure; but please tell me in what way you think you have offended me, for you look guilty."

"I? I have certainly done nothing at which you could take umbrage."

"You speak to me without looking at me. Are you ashamed of having beautiful eyes? And now you are blushing. What crime have you committed?"

"You are embarrassing her," her mother said to me.

"Answer him that you have committed no crime, but that it is out of respect and modesty that you do not stare at the people to whom you speak."

She made no answer.

After a short silence the company rose, and the little girl, after dropping a curtsy, went to fetch her drawings and came to me.

"Mademoiselle, I will look at nothing unless you will look at me."

"Come now," her mother said, "look at Monsieur."

"This time," I said to Sophie, "I recognize you. And do you remember having seen me before?"

"Though it was six years ago, I recognized you as soon as you came in."

"How can you have recognized me if you never looked at me? If you knew, my angel, what unforgivably bad manners it is not to look at the person to whom one speaks! Who can have taught you such a bad lesson?"

At that the child looked at her mother, who had gone to the window. When I saw that I had sufficiently avenged myself, and that the English guests had understood everything, I began looking at her drawings and praising everything in detail, congratulating her on her talent and complimenting her mother for giving her so good an education. She was filled with pride by the praise I bestowed now on her daughter, now on herself, and there was an end to lowered eyes. Sophie, seeing that she was free to look at me, constantly availed herself of the unspoken permission; in her physiognomy I saw a beautiful soul, and I silently pitied her for having to live under the domination of her mother, who was a fool. She sat down at the harpsichord, she sang in Italian, after that she accompanied herself on the guitar in some short airs, then her mother[57] wanted her to dance a minuet with her brother, who had learned it in Paris, and who danced very badly because he held himself badly; and his sister, after embracing him, told him so. She danced it at once with me, and her mother, after declaring the minuet superb, told her that she should let me embrace her, which I did, taking her on my lap and giving her all the kisses she deserved, which she returned with all the affection I could wish. Her mother simply laughed, and she embraced her fondly too when, after leaving me, she went to ask her if she was displeased.

She showed me the great room she had had built for balls and for giving supper to four hundred persons all seated at a single horse-shoe-shaped table. I was easily persuaded that there was not a bigger room in London. The last assembly was to be given before Parliament closed, five or six days later. She had in her service more than twenty maids and ten or twelve footmen. All these vermin robbed her, she said, but she could not do without them, so it was unavoidable. I left Mrs. Cornelys, admiring her courage and wishing her good fortune.

I had myself carried to St. James's Park[58] to call on Lady Harrington;[59] I had a letter for her;[60] [. . .] she lived within the precincts of the Court, for which reason she entertained at her house every Sunday; play was allowed there, for the Park was under the royal jurisdiction. Everywhere else no one dares to play or to give concerts;[61] spies who walk the streets of London listen carefully to hear what sort of noise is being made in the drawing rooms of private houses, and if they suspect there is play or that someone is singing they hide wherever they can and, as soon as they see the door open, they slip in, and they hale to prison all the bad Christians who dare thus fail to respect the most sacred Sabbath, which, however, it is permissible to sanctify by going to taverns to entertain oneself with bottles and the prostitutes with which London swarms.

At Lady Harrington's I go upstairs, I send in my letter, she has me shown in at once, and I find myself among twenty-five or thirty people, men and women, I make my bow to Her Ladyship, who at once tells me that she had seen me with the Queen and that she wished to see me at her house too. For at least three-quarters of an hour I was the only speaker, answering the questions which are invariably the lot of the arriving foreigner. Lady Harrington, still beautiful at the age of forty, famous in London for her influence and for her gallantries, at once introduces me to her husband and her four adolescent daughters, all of them charming: the Ladies Isabella and Amelia Stanhope—I have forgotten the name of the third.[62] She asks me why I have come to London at the time when everyone goes to the country, and I reply that I expect to spend a year there. That leaves her nothing to reproach me with, and she says that so far as it lies in her power she will introduce me to all the pleasures of her country.

"You will see all the nobility," she says, "on Thursday at Soho Square; I can give you a ticket. Here it is. There will be supper and a ball. It costs two guineas."

I give them to her; and she writes on the ticket "Paid, Harrington." I do not tell her that I have just dined with Mrs. Cornelys.

She gets up a game of whist[63] for me, and she asks me if I have letters addressed to other ladies. I tell her that I have a very odd one which I intend to present to the lady the next day. "The letter is the lady's portrait."

"Have you it with you?"

"Yes, My Lady."

"May I see it?"

"Why not? Here it is."

"It is the Duchess of Northumberland.[64] Let us go and give it to her. We will wait until the rubber is scored."

Lord Percy had given me the portrait on the day I had dined with him, saying that it would serve me as a letter of introduction when I presented it to his mother in London.

"Here, Duchess," Lady Harrington said to her, "is a letter of introduction which this gentleman is commanded to deliver to you."

"Ah, yes! He is Monsieur de Seingalt. My son wrote to me; I am delighted to see you. I hope that you will come to my house. I receive company three times a week."

"Then permit me, Your Ladyship, to deliver my precious letter to you in your house."

"Gladly—you are right."

I played whist at very small stakes, and I lost fifteen guineas, which I paid at once, whereupon Lady Harrington took me aside to give me a lesson worthy to be recorded.

"You lost," she said, "and you paid in gold; I take it that you have no bank notes with you."

"I beg your pardon, My Lady, I have notes for fifty and a hundred."

"You should have changed one and paid with it, or have waited until another day to pay. Here in England paying in gold is a little unmannerly, though pardonable in a foreigner, who cannot know our customs; but try not to let it happen again. You saw that the lady smiled."

"Who is she?"

"Lady Coventry,[65] sister of the Duchess of Hamilton."[66]

"Should I apologize to her?"

"Certainly not. She may be well pleased, for she gains fifteen shillings[67] by it."

I thought it a rather barbed remark. But Lady Coventry was an extremely beautiful brunette. I made the acquaintance of Lord Hervey,[68] the conqueror of Havana, an amiable and witty man. He had married Miss Chudleigh,[69] and had had the marriage annulled. This celebrated Chudleigh was maid of honor to the widowed Princess of Wales;[70] she later became Duchess of Kingston. Her strange adventures are well known. I shall speak of her at the proper time and place. I went home well enough pleased with my day. On the next I began eating at home, and I was well satisfied with my English cook, who, besides his country's favorite dishes, which he gave me every day, gave me fowl and very delicate French ragouts. What pained me a little was that I was alone; I had neither a pretty mistress nor a friend, and in London one can invite a gentleman to dine with one at a tavern, where he pays his share, but not to dinner at one's own table. People laughed when I said that I ate at home because at the taverns soup was not served. I was asked if I was ill. The Englishman is a meat-eater.[71] He eats scarcely any bread, and he insists that he is economical because he saves himself the expense of soup and dessert; which led me to say that an English dinner has neither beginning nor end. Soup is considered a great expense, because even the servants will not eat the beef from which broth has been made. They say it is fit only to give to dogs. The salt beef which they serve instead of it is excellent. I tried to get used to their beer; but I had to give it up after a week. The bitter taste it left in my mouth was intolerable. The vintner whom Bosanquet had sent me supplied me with French wines which were excellent because they were natural; but I had to pay high prices for them.

On Monday morning Martinelli came to see me. I had been settled in my house for a week, and I had never seen him; I asked him to share my soup, and having learned from him that he had to go to the Museum[72] and remain there until two o'clock, I went with him to see the famous collection which does such honor to the English nation. I made the acquaintance of Dr. Maty,[73] of whom I later had reason to think highly. I will speak of him when the time comes. At two o'clock we went to dinner, and Martinelli proved to be an excellent companion, for he instructed me in the customs of the country I was visiting, to which I must conform if I wanted to live well there. *Dum fueris Romae, Romano vivito more* ("When in Rome, do as the Romans do").[74]

I told him of my blunder in paying in gold what I should politely have paid in paper, and after laughing at it a little, he showed me that it was not only evidence of the prosperity and wealth of the nation, which gave its paper the preference over gold, but also a proof of its blind confidence in its Bank,[75] in which it was convinced that there was all the real value of all the notes which circulated in the three kingdoms.[76] This preference for paper over gold was also remarkable because of the advantage of five pounds in a hundred which the guinea had over the pound sterling and which the English disregarded. You owe someone a hundred guineas and you pay him a hundred pounds sterling in paper; he says nothing, though he is the loser by it, and he thanks you. By this policy the English nation has doubled its legal tender. All the wealth it possesses in cash serves it to carry on external commerce, and it carries on internal commerce with the tokens which represent the same real wealth.[77]

After dinner I went with Martinelli to the play at the Drury Lane Theater. At the beginning of the performance the groundlings in the pit, seeing that they had been cheated because the promised play was not being given, raised a row; Garrick,[78] the celebrated actor who was buried twenty years later[79] in Westminster Abbey, came forward and tried in vain to talk to the groundlings and calm them, he was howled down, he had to withdraw, and the raging mob shouted "Every man for himself!" and at that I saw the King, the Queen, and everyone else leave their boxes, make their way out, and abandon the theater to the rage of the angry populace, which carried out its purpose amid laughter. In less than an hour everything but the walls was torn down. After this accomplishment the democratic animals all went to get drunk on spirits at the taverns. In two or three weeks the whole auditorium was rebuilt, and bills were put up announcing the first performance. When the curtain rose Garrick appeared to beg the indulgence of the public; but just as he was beginning his apology a voice from the pit shouted "On your knees!" and the cry, repeated by a hundred mouths, forced the Roscius[80] of England to kneel. There was a burst of applause, and it was all over. Such is the populace of London, which mocks the King, the Queen, and all the Princes when they appear in public; so they very seldom let themselves be seen.

Four or five days after making the acquaintance of Sir Augustus Hervey, I came upon him in the Green Park,[81] just as he had finished speaking with someone.

"Who," I asked him, "is that gentleman?"

"He is the brother of Lord Ferrers,[82] who was executed by the common hangman two months ago for killing his valet."

"And you speak to him? Is he not dishonored?"

"Dishonored for that? It would be absurd. Even his brother is not dishonored. He paid with his life for breaking the law, he owes nothing. He is a gentleman who played high. I know of no penalty in our constitution which dishonors. It would be tyrannical. I can calmly break any law, provided that I am ready to submit to the penalty enjoined for breaking it. It is a trifle mad, I admit, but it is my privilege. Dishonor would attach only to a criminal who, to avoid the penalty due for his crime, should have done cowardly or base things unworthy of a gentleman."

"For example?"

"Persuading the King to grant him mercy, asking pardon of the people, any number of things."

"Running away?"

"No, for escaping is a brave act. Observe that, to run away, a brave man needs nothing but his own faculties, whether moral or physical: he fights against death, which he risks by escaping: *Vir fugiens denuo pugnabit* ['The man who runs away will fight again']."[83]

"Then what do you think of highway robbers?"

"They are vermin whom I detest, for they inconvenience society; but at the same time I pity them when I think that their trade keeps the scaffold always before their eyes. You leave London by yourself in a hackney carriage to visit a friend who lives in a village two or three miles away. Halfway there, an agile man jumps on the step of your carriage and demands your purse, holding a pistol to your chest. What do you do then?"

"If I have a pistol I kill him, and if not I give him my purse, calling him a base assassin."

"You would do wrong. If you kill him the law will sentence you to death, for you have not the right to dispose of an Englishman's life; and if you call him a base assassin he will answer that he is not, for he does not attack you from behind, and, by attacking you from the front, he offers you the choice. It is honorable in him, for he could kill you. You can, as you give him the purse he demands, reproach him for living by a vile trade, and he will admit it. He will tell you that he will hold off the gallows as long as he can, but that he knows it is inevitable. He will thank you afterward, and he will advise you never to drive out of London except with an armed servant on horseback, for then a needy robber will not dare to attack you. We English, who know that these vermin exist in our country, travel with two purses, a small one to give to the robbers we may encounter and another with the money we need."

What was I to reply to this discourse? I thought it reasonable. The island called England is a sea in which there are sandbanks, those who navigate it must voyage with due caution. Sir Augustus's lesson pleased me greatly.

Passing from subject to subject, he pitied the fate of the thief who, after stealing seventy thousand pounds sterling on the rise and fall of stocks, and fleeing to France where he thought he was safe, had nevertheless been recently hanged in London.[84]

"A year ago," he said, "the King demanded him from the Duke of Nivernais,[85] the Ambassador of Louis XV, among the conditions of the peace. The Duke, who is witty, answered the Minister[86] that his master would have no objection to ridding France of a thief by restoring him to his country; and in due course he was sent to us, and the nation, delighted to see a compatriot who had dared to cheat it brought to the gallows, was greatly obliged to the acumen of Lord Halifax,[87] who made our neighbors buy peace at the price of a condition so humiliating to them, for they violated the law of nations in respect to the wretch."

"And so seventy thousand pounds were recovered?"

"Not a penny."

"How was that?"

"Because what he stole was not found in his possession. Apparently he left the little treasure in the hands of his wife,[88] who lives in great comfort and who, pretty and rich enough, can marry again very advantageously."

"I am amazed that she has been let alone."

"What could be done to her? You can understand that she would never have admitted that her late husband had left the money with her. There was not even any thought of making a search to recover the amount. The law against thieves orders them hanged; it says nothing about the stolen property, for it supposes that it has disappeared. Then too, if a distinction were made between thieves who restored what they stole and those who did not restore it, there would have to be two laws and two different penalties, and you see what confusion would follow. In any case it seems to me that two penalties should not be inflicted for the same crime; the penalty of the gallows suffices without adding to it the restitution of the stolen property, if it is not liquid and in a condition to be claimed by the person who owned it before the theft, for afterward the thing stolen no longer belongs to him; it is the thief who has become the owner of it, by violence it is true, but that does not keep him from being really the owner of it, for he can dispose of it. Such being the case, everyone must take great care to keep what is his, for once it has been stolen from him, he sees that restitution is too difficult. I took Havana from Spain, a great theft executed by superior force, and it was given back[89] because I could not put the island of Cuba in my purse, as I did forty million piasters,[90] which were never even mentioned."

After being treated to several specimens of equally sublime doctrine, I went with him to the Duchess of Northumberland's, where I made the acquaintance of Lady Rochefort,[91] whose husband had just been appointed Ambassador to Spain.[92] The lady was one of three whose notorious gallantries daily supplied the busybodies of the great city with agreeable stories. The Duchess told me that she looked for her son to return every day.

On the day before the assembly at Soho Square Martinelli dined with me, and the subject having come up, he talked to me of

Mrs. Cornelys and of the debts with which she was burdened, because of which she was reduced to not daring to go out of her house except on Sundays, on which day debtors could not be arrested. The enormous expenditures in which she indulged, and which were not necessary, put her in straits which must soon reduce her to the last extremity. She owed, he told me, four times as much as she possessed, even counting in her house, of which a lawsuit in progress made her ownership doubtful.

CHAPTER VIII

Mrs. Cornelys's assembly. Adventure at
Ranelagh House. Disgust with English courtesans.
The Portuguese Pauline.

I go to Mrs. Cornelys's assembly, giving my ticket at the door to her secretary, who writes down my name. I see her, and she congratulates me on having been admitted to the assembly by ticket, saying that she had been sure she would see me there. Lady Harrington arrives; she was one of her great patrons; she tells her that she has a good number of guineas to give to her, and, seeing me in conversation with her, she adds that she had imagined we were acquainted but had not ventured to mention it to me.

"Why, My Lady? I consider it an honor that I have long known Mrs. Cornelys."

"I believe it," she said with a laugh, "and I congratulate you. You must certainly know this charming girl too."

With that she takes Sophie in her arms, kisses her, and tells me that if I love myself I ought to love her too, because she has exactly my countenance. She takes her by the hand, and she leads her into the crowd, taking my arm. It was then that I had to listen patiently to innumerable questions put to Lady Harrington by women and men who had not yet seen me.

"Is this not Mrs. Cornelys's husband, just arrived?"

"No, no, no," Lady Harrington said to all the busybodies; and I was bored for, to compliment me, everyone said that no child had ever resembled its father as the little Cornelys resembled me, and I asked her to let the child go; but she was too much amused to do me the favor.

"Stay with me," she said, "if you want to meet everyone."

And she sat down, making me sit at her side and keeping the little girl standing in front of her. The mother comes to pay court to the lady, and, having to answer the question if I am her husband, she makes up her mind and says that I am only an old friend and that everyone has good reason to be surprised at the great resemblance between her daughter and me. Everyone laughs and replies that it is not surprising at all; and Mrs. Cornelys, to change the subject, says that the child has learned to dance the minuet to perfection.

"We shall see," said Lady Harrington; "send for a fiddler."

Since we were in a side room and the ball had not yet begun, a fiddler comes; wishing the child to do herself honor, I take her out, and the minuet succeeds in earning great applause from the on-lookers. The ball began, and continued until dawn without a break, for people went to eat in the side rooms in groups at all hours. I met all the nobility and all the royal family, for they were all there except the King, the Queen, and the Princess of Wales. Mrs. Cornelys had taken in more than twelve hundred guineas, but her expenditure was enormous too, with no attempt to economize and no measures to prevent theft of every kind. Mrs. Cornelys exhausted herself presenting her son to everyone, while he stood like a victim, not knowing what to say and doing nothing but make low bows, which, delivered to all and sundry, and in England, became the height of awkwardness. I felt sorry for him. In this role of an underling, which he was playing for the first time in his life, he was the most embarrassed youth on earth.

Taken home, I slept all that day, and the next day went to dine at the "Star" Tavern,[1] where I had been told that the prettiest and choicest girls in London were to be found. I had heard this at the reception of a certain Lord Pembroke[2] in Soho Square, who had told me that he went there very often. I enter the tavern, I ask a waiter for a private room. The host, observing that I do not speak English, addresses me in French, sits down with me, orders what I want, and I am so surprised by his polite, grave, and solemn manner that I cannot pluck up courage to tell him that I want to dine with a pretty English girl. I finally tell him in a roundabout way that I do not know if Lord Pembroke has deceived me in saying that I could have the prettiest girls in London there.

"No, Monsieur, he did not deceive you, and if that is what you want you can have as many as you please."

He calls "Waiter,"[3] whereupon a neat young man appears, whom he orders to send a girl for my service, as if he were ordering him to bring me paper and ink. The waiter leaves, and ten minutes later in comes a girl, whose appearance I dislike. I tell the host plainly that she does not please me.

"Give a shilling for the chairmen, and send her away. No one stands on ceremony in London, Monsieur."

I order the shilling given, and I ask for another girl, but a pretty one. The second arrives, worse than the first. I send her away. I also send away the third, the fourth, the fifth, and so on up to the tenth, delighted to see that, far from displeasing the host, my fastidiousness amuses him. I say I want no more girls, I want to dine; but I tell him I am sure the waiter had been making game of me to please the chairmen.

"That may be so, Monsieur; they always do it when they are not told the name and address of the girl who is wanted."

Toward nightfall I go to St. James's Park, I see that it is a day for Ranelagh House;[4] I was curious to see the place, it was far away, I take a carriage, and, alone without a servant, I go there to amuse myself until midnight and to try to make the acquaintance of some pretty girl. The Ranelagh Rotunda pleases me greatly, I eat bread and butter and drink tea, I dance a minuet or two, but make no acquaintances. I see very pretty girls and women, but I dare not make direct advances to any of them. Bored, I decide to leave about midnight, and I go to the door, thinking I shall find my hackney carriage, for I had not paid for it; but it was gone; there I was, cursing in vain; no one could find the carriage I was asking for, and I did not see how I was to get home. A pretty woman who saw the straits I was in and who had been there five or six minutes waiting for her carriage said to me in French that if I lived not far from Whitehall[5] she could take me to my door. I told her where I lived; her carriage arrives; one of her lackeys opens the door, we get in, and she orders her coachman to drive to my house in Pall Mall.

In the carriage, which was very comfortable, I profusely express my gratitude, I tell her my name, I say I am surprised that I had not made her acquaintance at the assembly in Soho. She tells me that she has arrived from Bath[6] that day; I pronounce myself fortunate, I kiss her hands, then her pretty face, then her beautiful bosom, and finding, instead of resistance, only the sweetest yieldingness and the laughter of love, I have no more doubts, and I give her the greatest proof that I find her perfectly to my taste. Making bold to suppose, from the ease with which she had let me have my way, that she had not found me displeasing, I beg her to tell me where I may go to pay my most assiduous court to her during all the time I shall spend in London, and she replies that we shall meet again. I do not urge her, and in no time I am back at my house, very well pleased with the adventure. I had spent two weeks without seeing her anywhere, when I found her at last in a house to which Lady Harrington had told me to go and introduce myself, giving her name; it was the house of the elderly but illustrious Lady Betty Germaine.[7] She was not at home, but she was to return in a few minutes. I see the beauty who had brought me home from Ranelagh, busy reading a newspaper; it occurs to me to ask her to introduce me. So I go to her, she interrupts her reading, hears me out, and politely replies that she cannot introduce me since she does not know me.

"I told you my name, Madame. Do you not remember me?"

"I remember you perfectly; but such escapades are no ground for claiming acquaintance."

So strange an answer left me dumbfounded. She went on quietly reading her newspaper; Lady Betty Germaine arrived. For two hours the philosophical beauty amused herself talking to others, showing not the slightest sign of being acquainted with me, but answering me politely when the conversation gave me an opportunity to address her. She was a noblewoman whose reputation in London was of the highest.

One morning at Martinelli's, on whom I had never called before, I asked him who a wench was who kept kissing her hand to me from a window on the opposite side of the street; I was surprised when he told me that she was the dancer Madame Binetti.[8] Less than four years had passed since, at Stuttgart, she had done me a great service; I did not know that she was in London. I take leave of Martinelli to go to see her all the more eagerly when he tells me that she is not living with her husband, though he is to dance with her at the Haymarket Theater.[9]

"I recognized you at once," she said, receiving me. "I am surprised, my dear doyen, to see you in London."

She called me "doyen" because I was the oldest of all her acquaintances. I said that I had had no idea she was there, and that I could not have seen her dance for I had arrived three days after the opera closed.

"How is it that you are no longer living with your husband?"

"Because he plays, he loses, and he sells everything I own. Then too, a woman of the theater, if she lives with her husband, cannot hope to have a rich lover coming to visit her. Living alone as I do, all my friends can come to see me without fearing anything."

"What should they fear from Binetti? I never thought he was jealous or unduly particular."

"Nor is he. But you must understand that in England there is a law which empowers a husband to have a lover of his wife's arrested if he catches him *in flagrante* with her. He needs only two witnesses. It is enough if he finds him sitting on the bed with her, or in a position which might indicate that he has done something with her which only her husband has a right to do. The law sentences such a lover to pay the husband who claims to have been cuckolded half of what he owns. Several rich Englishmen have been caught in this way, and that is why they do not go to visit married women, especially if they are Italian."

"Then, far from complaining, you should be very glad that he is so accommodating, for, being perfectly free, you can receive whomever you please and grow rich."

"My dear doyen, you do not know the whole of it. As soon as he supposes I have had a present from some man who has come to see me, and of whose visit his spies have informed him, he comes at night in a sedan chair and threatens to turn me out into the street if I do not give him all the money I have. You do not know the base scoundrel."

I gave her my address, asking her to come to dine at my house whenever she pleased, only letting me know the day before. It was another lesson for me on the subject of going to see women. In England there are very fine and very good laws, but they are such that they can too easily be abused. The obligation of jurors to enforce them to the letter and not otherwise has the result that, since many of them are not written clearly enough, they are given an interpretation the very opposite of that which has usually been placed upon them, and so the judge finds himself in a quandary. For this reason new laws and new glosses on the old ones are made in Parliament every day.

Lord Pembroke, having seen me at the window, came up to call on me. After being shown over my house and learning that I had a cook, he congratulated me and said that there was not a nobleman in London, except those who always lived there, to whom it would have occurred to maintain an establishment like mine. He calculated roughly that, if I wanted to dine and sup with friends, I would spend three hundred pounds a month. He said in passing that I ought to keep a pretty girl on the third or fourth floor, who would cost me very little, and that since I was a bachelor people who came to know of it would consider me very sensible.

"Do you keep one in your house, My Lord?"

"No, no, for it is my misfortune that as soon as I have slept with a woman or a girl I can no longer put up with her, so I have a new one every day, and without being as comfortable as you, I spend four times as much as you do. Observe that I am a bachelor and that I live in London like a stranger, never eating at home. I am amazed that you are content to eat alone nearly always, for I know my fellow countrymen."

"I do not speak English, I like soup, French dishes, and the best wines; so I cannot put up with your taverns."

He laughed when I told him that at the "Star" Tavern I had sent away eight or ten girls, and that he had been the reason for it.

"I did not tell you the names," he said, "of the girls I send for."

"You should have done so."

"But since they did not know you they would not have come, for they are at the disposal neither of the chairmen nor the waiters. Promise me that you will pay them as I do, and I will sign you notes with their names at once. When they see my name you shall have them, I assure you, even here if you wish."

"Here, by all means, I like that much better. Write me the notes at once and set the price, giving the preference to girls who speak French."

"That's a pity, for the prettiest ones speak only English."

However, after thinking for some time, he wrote five or six addresses and signed them with his name. I copied all the girls' names on a separate sheet, setting down the money I was to give them for spending the night or three or four hours with me. It was four guineas or six and, in the case of one of them, twelve.

"Then she's twice as pretty as the others?"

"That's not the reason; it's because she cuckolds a Duke, a peer of Great Britain, who gives her plenty of money but who touches her only once or twice a month."

I asked him if he would someday do me the honor of tasting my cook's fare, and he said he would, but taking potluck.

"And if you do not find me at home?"

"I'll go to a tavern."

Having nothing to do that day, I sent Jarba with one of His Lordship's notes to one of the two girls whom he had rated at four louis,[10] instructing him to tell her that it was for dinner alone with me, and she came. Despite my wanting to find her attractive, she pleased me only enough for a little toying after dinner. When she saw four guineas she left well satisfied. The second girl at four guineas supped with me the next day. She had been very pretty; but I found her gloomy and too meek; I could not bring myself to make her undress. On the third day at Covent Garden I saw an attractive girl, I addressed her in French, and I was delighted to hear her answer; I asked her if she would sup with me, and she asked me what present I would give her.

"I will give you three guineas."

"That will do."

At the end of the play we sup there, I find her charming, I ask her address, and I find that she is one of the three whom His Lordship had rated at six louis. Her name was Kennedy.[11] The other two were sisters; their name was Garrick; they pleased me only briefly. I kept the last, the twelve-guinea one, to crown the feast, and I did not find myself inclined to cuckold the Peer.

The next day I went to see him[12] early, telling him the whole story of the six sultanas whose acquaintance he had procured me.

"I am delighted that Kennedy pleased you, and that she does not know that I gave you her name. I have learned what your taste is. She was the favorite of Berlendis,[13] Secretary to the Venetian Ambassadors. I was able to sleep with her only once."

This Lord Pembroke was young, handsome, rich, and full of wit. He got out of bed, and wanting to take a walk, told his valet to shave him.

"I do not," I said, "see a sign of a beard."

"You will never see one on my face, for I am shaved three times a day."

"How do you manage three?"

"When I change my shirt I wash my hands, and when I wash my hands I wash my face too, and a man's face is washed with a razor."

"At what hours do you perform these three ablutions?"

"When I get up; when I come home to go out to dinner or the opera; and when I go to bed, for the girl who is with me must not find my face unpleasant because of a beard."

I praised his fastidiousness. I noticed that his valet really only drew the razor over his skin, which took less than a minute. I left him, as I had some writing to do. He asked me if I was dining at home, and I said that I was. I thought that he might come; and I guessed right. I instructed my cook to do himself honor, but not to let it appear that it was because I expected anyone.

La Binetti knocked at noon, and, delighted to find me at home, came into my room, saying that she had come to take potluck with me.

"You have done me a great favor, for it bores me always to be alone."

"This time my husband will torture himself and still not guess where I have dined."

The woman still pleased me. She was then thirty-five years of age; but no one would suppose her more than twenty-two or twenty-three. Her whole person had powerful charms, and her fine teeth and splendid lips forced the critical to admit that her mouth was not too large; in addition she had a playfulness which delighted everyone.

At half past one Lord Pembroke enters my room, and he and La Binetti utter simultaneous cries of surprise. I learn from His Lordship that he has been in love with her for six months, that he has written her ardent letters, and that she had always scorned him; and I learn from her that she would never listen to him because he was the most dissolute nobleman in all England, and that it was a pity because he was also the most amiable. The kisses which followed these explanations showed the contentment of the two parties. Praises were bestowed on chance, whose sacred minister I was declared to be, and we sat down at table, where we enjoyed exquisite dishes, both English and French. His Lordship swore that he had nowhere dined as well all that year, and condoled with me for not having company every day. La Binetti was as much of a trencherman and an epicure as His Lordship, and, after sitting at table two hours, we rose in high spirits and with a great desire to make love; but La Binetti was too well versed in the great game to be weak with the Englishman: countless kisses, but nothing more.

Busying myself over books which I had bought, I let them talk together privately as much as they pleased, and to prevent them from asking me to invite them to dinner together another day, I said that I hoped chance would often grant me such favors. At six o'clock La Binetti had herself carried to the Park,[14] from where she would go home on foot, His Lordship went home to dress, and I went to Vauxhall,[15] where I found Monsieur Malingan, the French officer to whom I had opened my purse at Aix-la-Chapelle.[16] He told me he had something to say to me, and I gave him my address. I found there a man too well known, the Chevalier Goudar[17] by name, who talked to me at some length about gaming and girls; and Malingan introduced to me, as a man of rare parts who could be very useful to me in London, a person some forty years of age, with a Greek countenance, under the name of Mr. Frederick,[18] son of the late Theodore,[19] self-styled King of Corsica, who fourteen years earlier had died destitute in London after coming out of prison, to which he had been confined six or seven years for debt. I should have done better not to go to Vauxhall that day.

To enter the enclosure named Vauxhall one paid only half[20] what one paid at Ranelagh House; but the pleasures to be had there were great. Good food, music, strolls in dark walks where the bacchantes were to be found, and strolls in lantern-hung walks where one saw the most famous beauties in London, from the highest rank to the lowest, side by side.

Amid so many pleasures I was bored because I did not have a dear mistress in my bed and at my table, and I had already been in London for five weeks. My house was the perfect place to keep a mistress in discreetly and comfortably; Lord Pembroke was right: possessing the virtue of constancy, I needed only that to make me happy. But how was I to find in London the girl exactly to my taste and of a character like that of one of the women I had so greatly loved? In London I had already seen fifty girls whom everyone thought pretty, and I had found not one among them who had completely won me over. I thought of it continually. A strange idea came to me, and I acted upon it.

I went to talk to the old woman who was the caretaker of my house, and, with the maid whom I paid for the purpose acting as my interpreter, I told her that I wanted to rent the third and fourth floors of my house in order to have company, and that, though I had the right to do so, I would make her a present of half a guinea a week. So I told her to put up a notice at my door in the following terms, which I wrote out for her on the spot:

"Third-floor or fourth-floor furnished apartment to be let cheaply to a young lady alone and her own mistress who speaks English and French and who will receive no visitors either by day or by night."

The old Englishwoman, who had sown her wild oats, laughed so hard when my maid explained the notice to her in English that I thought she would die of coughing.

"Why do you laugh so hard, my good woman?"

"I laugh because your notice couldn't be better calculated to make people laugh."

"Then you think no one will come to rent the apartment?"

"On the contrary, I'll have girls coming all day to see what it means. I'll leave it to Fanny to get rid of them. Just tell me how much I am to ask per week."

"I will settle the price myself in conversation with the young lady. Think again, and you'll see that there won't be so many girls, because I want her to be young, speaking English and French, and, what is more, respectable, for she is absolutely forbidden to receive visits, even from her father and mother."

"But there will still be a great crowd gathered at our door to read the notice."

"So much the better."

The notice was put up the next day and, as the old woman had said, I saw that all the passers-by read it and reread it two or three times, then walked on, smiling. The first two days no one inquired; but on the third day Jarba came to tell me that the strange notice was announced in the *St. James's Chronicle*,[21] in a piece in which the writer made a very witty commentary on it. I told him to bring me a translation of it. The commentator said that the apartment on the second floor of the house with the notice must be occupied by the tenant of the third and fourth floors, who thus sought to procure himself an agreeable companion, sure of being alone in virtue of the condition which was part of the contract. He said that he ran the risk of being the victim of it, for he might find a very pretty girl who, having obtained the apartment cheaply, would use it only to sleep in, or even to go to only once or twice a week, and who might even refuse to receive the landlord if he took it into his head to pay her a visit.

This well-argued commentary pleased me, for it armed me against surprises. That is why the English newspapers are engaging; they chatter about everything that happens in London and they have the art of making trifles interesting.

Lord Pembroke was the first to come and laugh with me over my notice; then Martinelli came to tell me that my notice might be my undoing, for in London there were girls intelligent enough to come on purpose to turn my head.

A full account of all the girls who came for a week or ten days to see the two apartments, and to whom I refused them on various pretexts, is not worth writing. It goes without saying that I found all those whom I dismissed unprepossessing; I saw old women who said they were young, hussies, trollops, saucy wenches, until finally, one day when I was at table, I saw appear before me a girl between twenty-two and twenty-four years of age, tall, simply but neatly dressed, with a noble and serious countenance, beautiful in every way, with black hair and a pale complexion. She enters, making me a very humble curtsy which forces me to rise; she asks me to remain seated and, to oblige me to do so, accepts a chair. I offer her sweetmeats, for she had already impressed me, and she very modestly refuses.

She tells me, not in the French in which she had begun, but in the purest Italian it is possible to speak, and without any foreign accent, that she would like to take a room on the fourth floor and that she hoped I would not refuse her, for she thought she was still young and she would have no difficulty in submitting to the other conditions.

"You are free to use only one room, but the whole apartment will be yours."

"Though your notice says 'cheap' the whole apartment would still be too dear for me, for I cannot spend more than two shillings a week for lodging."

"That is exactly the price I have set for the whole apartment, and four for the third floor; so you see, Signorina, that the whole apartment is yours. The housemaid will take entire care of your room, you can trust her to get you what food you need, and she will have your linen washed. She will also run errands for you, so that you need not go out to attend to trifles."

"Then I will give my maid notice," she said, "and I am not sorry, for she has been robbing me—no more than pennies, but that is still too much for my means; and I will tell your maid what to buy for me every day in the way of food, which she is never to exceed, giving her tenpence a week for her trouble."

"She will be satisfied. I can even say a word in your favor to my cook's wife, who can supply you with dinner and supper for the same money you would spend sending out for your meals."

"I do not think that is possible, for I am ashamed to tell you what I spend."

"If you spend only twopence a day, I would tell her to give you only twopence' worth. I beg you not to be ashamed of having the uprightness to regulate your expenditure by your resources. I advise you to content yourself with the food you can have from my kitchen, where they are always at a loss for what to do with left-overs; and I promise you I will take no part in it. I will only say a word for you to my cook, and I hope you will not object to my taking an interest in you. Wait a moment, and you will see how naturally the whole thing will be attended to."

I call Clairmont, and I tell him to send up the maid and the cook's wife.

"Tell me," I said to the latter, "at what price you can give dinner and supper in her room to this young lady, who is not rich and who wants only food to keep her alive."

874

"I could feed her very cheaply, for you almost always eat alone and you have enough prepared for four."

"Very good. In that case I hope you will feed her for what she says she wants to spend."

"I can spend only fivepence a day."

"And for fivepence a day she will feed you."

I told the maid to have the notice removed at once and to do everything necessary in the rooms which she chose to occupy on the fourth floor. As soon as they had left, she told me that she would go out only to hear mass on feast days at the chapel of the Bavarian Minister,[22] and once a month to see the person who gave her three guineas to live on. I replied that she was free to go out without accounting for it to anyone. She ended by asking me never to bring anyone to her apartment, to order the portress never under any circumstances to let anyone go up to see her, and even to say that she did not know her if anyone should come inquiring for her. I assured her that the order would be given, and she left, saying that she would come back at once with her trunk. She stopped at the old woman's quarters to pay her for the week and take a receipt. After she left I told all my household to treat the young lady with all possible deference and courtesy, for what she had confided to me obliged me to show her perfect respect. I learn that she had come and gone in a sedan chair, and it surprises me a little. The old woman sent me word to beware of a trap.

"What trap? I risk nothing if she is respectable, and if I fall in love with her, so much the better, it is what I want. I need only a week to know her inside out. What name did she give you?"

"Here it is: 'Mistress Pauline.'[23] She came here pale, and she left red as fire."

Very well pleased to have found such a treasure, I feel content. I did not need a woman to satisfy my temperament, I needed to love and to find great worth in the object which interested me, on the score of both beauty and of qualities of soul; and my budding love gained in strength if I saw that the conquest would cost me effort. I relegated the possibility of failure to the category of impossibilities; I knew that there was not a woman in the world who could resist constant attentions and all the assiduities of a man who wants to make her fall in love with him.[24]

I went to the play; and when I returned to the house the maid told me that the lady had taken a small back room which was fit only to lodge a servant; but that she had managed nevertheless by not unpacking her big trunk, for there were only a small table, four chairs, and no chest of drawers. She had supped and drunk water, and she had asked her to tell the cook's wife that soup and one dish were enough for her; she had replied that she must take what she was given and that she, the maid, would eat what was left over. After that she had sat down to write, and when she had left her she had locked her door.

"What does she take in the morning?"

"I asked her that, and she said that she ate only a little bread."

"You shall tell her tomorrow morning that the custom of this house is that in the morning the cook makes a present of breakfast to all the people living in it, whether they want coffee or tea or a plate of soup, and tell her that if she refuses the gift it might displease me; but you are not to tell her that I ordered you to tell her so. Here is a crown[25] for you, which I will give you every week so that you will show her every attention. Before I go to bed I will give you a note to carry up to her tomorrow morning, in which I will ask her to leave the servant's room she is occupying and take one in which she will be more comfortable."

I wrote to her in such terms that she felt obliged to move into a large room; but she remained at the rear of the house. She told me, too, that she had accepted the breakfast of coffee with milk. Wanting to have her dine and sup with me, I was dressing to pay her a visit and to ask her the favor in a way which would make it impossible for her to refuse, when Clairmont announced that young Cornelys wished to speak with me. I received him, laughing and thanking him for the first visit he had paid me during the six weeks we had been in London.

"Mama would never let me come; I can't stand any more. Read this letter, and you will find something which will surprise you. She herself just wrote it in my presence."

I open it and I find the following:

"Yesterday a bailiff[26] waited until my door was open, entered my house, and arrested me. I had to follow him, and I am in prison in his house; but if I do not furnish security today, he will take me tonight to the real prison of King's Bench.[27] The security is for two hundred guineas,[28] which I owe for a bill of exchange which has fallen due and which I could not pay. Get me out of here at once, my kind friend, for tomorrow I may have the misfortune to see several other creditors, who will have me committed, and if that happens I am lost. Prevent my ruin and that of my innocent family. As a foreigner you cannot stand surety for me; but you have only to say a word to some householder, and you will find him ready. If you have time to stop in where I am, come, and you shall hear that if I had not signed the bill of exchange I could not have given the ball, for all my silver and china were in pawn. My son has the address of the house in which I am held."

Determined to let her go to ruin, I take a pen and I write her in a few words that I am sorry for her, that I have not time to go to see her, and that I should be ashamed to ask my friends to stand surety in the matter of a bill of exchange which had fallen due and the payment of which could not honestly be refused. I seal the letter, I give it to the youth, who wants to leave me the address of the bailiff's house, which I refuse. He goes away gloomily, with a lackey who was waiting at my door for him.

I tell Clairmont to go up to Mistress Pauline's and ask her if I may come to see her. She sends me word that it is for me to say; I go up, and I find her well lodged, with books and writing materials on a table, and on the chest of drawers clothes which indicated neither poverty nor even straitened circumstances. It is she who begins by saying that she is infinitely grateful for the kindness I show her, and I answer her bluntly that it is I who am in need of her.

"What can I do, Signore, to show you my gratitude?"

"You can put yourself to the trouble, Signora, of honoring me with your company at table whenever I have no guests, for, when I am alone, I eat like a wolf and my health suffers from it. If you do not feel inclined to grant me this favor, you will excuse me for having asked it of you, but the arrangements I have made for you in my house will remain in force despite your refusal."

"I shall have the honor, Signore, of eating with you whenever you are alone and you send to tell me so. The only thing that troubles me is that I am not sure if my company can be of use to you or at least entertain you."

"There is no doubt of that, Signora; I am grateful to you, and I assure you that you will never repent of having shown me this kindness. I even hope that it will be I who will entertain you. You inspired the most lively interest in me yesterday. We shall dine at one o'clock."

I did not sit down, I did not look at her books, I did not ask her if she had slept well; the only thing I noticed was that when I entered her room I found her pale and that her cheeks were crimson when I left her.

I went for a walk in the Park, in love with her, and firmly resolved to do everything on earth to make her love me, determined that I would owe nothing to mere compliance. My curiosity to know who she might be was extreme; certainly she could only be Italian; but I had promised myself that I would not importune her with the slightest question—a romantic idea, but one which comes into the mind of a man who is thinking of using all possible means to capture the heart of an unknown object in which he is greatly interested.

As soon as I was back at the house Pauline came down without my having sent her word, and this politeness pleased me; so I thanked her heartily for it; since we had half an hour before us I asked her if she had any cause to complain of her health; and she replied that nature had given her so good a constitution that she had never in her life suffered the slightest indisposition, except at sea, where the waves upset her stomach.

"Then you have traveled by sea?"

"Inevitably, for England is an island."

"You are right, but I could suppose that you are English."

"That is true."

On the table in front of the sofa on which we were sitting there was an open chessboard, and, Pauline toying with the pawns, I asked her if she knew the game.

"I play it, and even well, I am told."

"And I badly. Let us play. My defeats will amuse you."

We begin, and at the third move Pauline checkmates me; my king can neither protect himself from her attack nor withdraw. She smiles. We begin again, and she checkmates me at the fifth move, and with that she enchants me by laughing heartily. I feed my budding love, observing how perfect her laughter shows her teeth to be, how much beauty it adds to her face, how capable her soul, which could feel such gaiety, must be of happiness. I rejoice to think that I will contribute to it with all my power. We begin the third game, which Pauline plays inattentively and which we abandon to go to table; but scarcely have we sat down before Clairmont announces Miss Cornelys and Madame Raucour.

"Tell them I am at dinner and shall not leave the table for three hours, so they can take themselves off!"

But a minute later little Sophie, forcing her way upstairs, comes running in and goes down on her knees before me, bursting into tears and unable to speak, for her sobs stifled her. Touched by this melancholy tableau, I take her on my knees, I dry her tears, I soothe her by saying that I know what she wants and that I will do whatever she asks. At these words Sophie passes from gloom to contained joy; she embraces me, calling me her father, her dear father, she makes me weep; I tell her that I will see to everything after dinner, and that she will strengthen my resolve if she will dine with me. At that Sophie goes to embrace Pauline, who was crying too without knowing why, and we begin dinner. Sophie asks me to have dinner served to Madame Raucour, whom her mother had forbidden to enter my presence.

But everything which Sophie said to me during that dinner, while Pauline, listening in amazement, never spoke a word, surprised me. Reasoning as if she were twenty years of age, she did nothing but condemn her mother's conduct and call herself unfortunate because her duty obliged her to submit to her authority and obey her every order blindly.

"Then you do not love her?"

"How should I love her if she keeps me in fear? I am afraid of her."

"Then what made you cry before dinner?"

"The pity I feel for our whole family. Her telling me that only I could touch your heart, that I was her only hope."

"And you were sure that you would persuade me?"

"I hoped to, remembering what you said to me at The Hague. My mother tells me that I was only three years old then, but I know I was five.[29] It was she who ordered me not to look at you when I spoke to you; but you thwarted her. Everyone tells her that you are certainly my father, and at The Hague she told me so herself; but here she tells me I am Monsieur de Montperny's[30] daughter."

"But, my dear Sophie, your mother does herself wrong and she insults you, since she tries to make you pass for illegitimate whereas you are the legitimate daughter of Pompeati, the dancer, who killed himself in Vienna and who, when you were born, was living with her."

"Then if I am this Pompeati's daughter, you are not my father?"

"Of course not, for you cannot be the daughter of two fathers."

"But how is it that I look so much like you?"

"Simply by chance."

Pauline, who was spellbound by our dialogues, said very little to her; but she constantly kissed her. She asked me if the lady was my wife, and when I replied that she was, she called her "dear Mama," which made her laugh heartily. At dessert I gave her four fifty-pound bank notes, saying that she could give them to her mother but that it was to her that I made a present of them.

"With that amount, my dear Sophie, your mother can sleep in her own room tonight."

"Write her that it is to me that you give them, for I should not dare tell her so myself."

"My dear child, I cannot write her that, for it would be to triumph over her in her affliction. Can you understand that?"

"Yes, very well."

"You may tell her that she will be doing me a great favor as often as she sends you to dine or sup with me."

"Oh, write that, please! Dear Mama," she said, looking at Pauline, "ask my papa to write that, and I will dine with you very often."

At that Pauline, laughing unrestrainedly and addressing me as "husband," gravely asked me to write the words on a slip of paper, for they could only show her mother that I loved Sophie, and increase the esteem she ought to feel for her, and I complied. Sophie left with joy in her soul, after covering us with kisses.

"It has been a long time since I laughed so much," Pauline said to me, "and I don't think I ever had a pleasanter dinner in my life. The girl is a rare jewel, and the poor little thing is unhappy. She would not be so if I were her mother."

I then told her who she was, and the reasons I had for showing her mother that I despised her.

"I laugh to think of her telling her that she found you at table with your wife."

"She will not believe it, for she knows too well that marriage is a sacrament which I detest."

"Why?"

"Because it is the tomb of love."

"Not always."

Pauline sighed, lowering her beautiful eyes and changing the subject. Her asking me if I expected to stay long in London, to which I replied that I expected to stay there nine or ten months, justified me, I thought, in asking her the same question, and she replied that she had no idea, for her return to her country depended on a letter.

"May I ask you what your country is?"

"I foresee that I shall have no secrets from you if you show any interest in them; but please let us allow a few days to pass. I only

880

began to know you today, and in a way which entitles you to my
respect."

"I shall be most flattered if I can win your esteem; but as for respect
I am not too fond of it, for it excludes friendship. I aspire to yours, and
I warn you that I will try to trap you into according it to me."

"I think you are too clever at that, and I beg you to spare me.
The great friendship which I might conceive for you would make
me unhappy when we part, a thing which may happen any day and
which I cannot but desire."

We finished our game, and after it she asked my permission to go
up to her room. I should gladly have spent the whole day with her,
for I had known very few women with a manner so sweet and
gentle. I spent the rest of the day at La Binetti's, who at once asked
me for news of Lord Pembroke. She was angry.

"He is a horrible man," she said, "who wants a new woman
every day. What do you think of that?"

"I envy him his luck in being able to obtain one."

"He gets them because women are fools. He caught me because
he took me by surprise at your house. Otherwise he would never
have had me. You laugh?"

"I laugh because he has had you; you have had him too, so the
score is even."

"It is not even, you don't know what you're talking about."

At eight o'clock I went home, and Pauline came down at once.
The maid was obeying her order by notifying her immediately. "If
Pauline," I said to myself, "has planned to make me fall in love by
showing me attentions, we are of the same mind and the thing is
done." We sat down at table at nine o'clock and stayed there until
midnight. I told her amusing stories. When she left she said I made
her too forgetful of her misfortunes.

Lord Pembroke came to take breakfast the next morning and to
congratulate me on the removal of my notice. He confessed that he
was curious to meet my tenant; but I said it was impossible because
she was of a solitary disposition and only put up with me because she
could not do otherwise. He did not insist. I told him that La Binetti
loathed him for his inconstancy, and it made him laugh.

"Shall you dine at home today?"

"No, My Lord."

"I understand."

Martinelli came to amuse me by reading me in Italian three or
four notices like mine which appeared in an *Advertiser* published

in the City. They were humorous parodies of mine. One said that there was an empty apartment suitable for a young and pretty lady who was leaving her husband because he objected to her having cuckolded him on the day after their wedding; it named the house in which the apartment was located, and said that the fugitive would pay only six shillings a week, but for that amount she would have board and the master of the house to sleep with her every night. The other notices were in the same style and all of them indecent. The freedom of the press is greatly abused in London. Martinelli politely did not mention my tenant. It was Sunday; I asked him to take me to mass at the Bavarian Envoy's. I thought I should see Pauline there, but I did not see her. She took, as she told me later, a place where she could not be seen. The church was full of people, and Martinelli pointed out to me a number of lords and ladies who were Catholics and did not hide the fact.

One of Mrs. Cornelys's lackeys handed me a letter just as I was entering my house. She said that she could go out without fear on holy days, and that she wanted to come to dinner with me. I told him to wait. I at once went to Pauline's rooms to ask her if she wanted to dine with Mrs. Cornelys, and she said that she had no objection, provided that she did not bring any men with her. So I wrote her to come without any men. She came with Sophie, who this time did not hesitate to stay in my arms. Mrs. Cornelys, embarrassed by Pauline's presence, took me aside to express her gratitude, which she did with tears, and to impart to me various chimerical ideas which filled her head, all of them calculated to make her rich in a short time. It was Sophie who enlivened our dinner. I could not help telling Mrs. Cornelys that Pauline was a foreign lady to whom I was renting an apartment.

"Then she's not your wife?" Sophie asked me.

"No, I am not so fortunate; I was joking."

"In that case I want to sleep with her."

"When?"

"When Mama will let me."

"We must see," I said, "if the lady wants you."

"She is sure of me," said Pauline, embracing her.

"Very well, Madame, I will leave her with you; I will send La Raucour to fetch her tomorrow morning."

"Tomorrow at three o'clock will be time enough. She shall dine with us."

At that Sophie went to her mother and gave her countless kisses. The woman had no idea of the pleasure it gives one to inspire love.

After Mrs. Cornelys left, I asked Pauline if she would like to go for an excursion with the little girl and myself, somewhere outside London where no one would see us, and she replied that prudence forbade her to go out with anyone at all; so we spent the whole day at home without being bored in the least. Sophie sang Italian, French, and English airs, in which she would have accompanied herself if she had had a harpsichord. She sang English duets with Pauline, which gave me the greatest pleasure. We supped in the same high spirits, and toward midnight I took them up to the fourth floor, telling Sophie that I would come up to breakfast with her if she would wait for me in bed, for I wanted to see if she was as pretty in bed as when she was dressed, and she promised to wait for me. I did not dare ask Pauline to grant me the same favor. So at eight o'clock I found her already up, though in chamber attire.

Sophie, all smiles, hid under the covers when she saw me appear; but as soon as I threw myself down beside her on the bed and began tickling her she put out her little face, which I covered with kisses, and I took advantage of my paternal rights to see exactly how she was built everywhere and to applaud everything she had, immature as it was. She was very small, but ravishingly built. Pauline saw me give her all these caresses without the least thought of evil, but she was wrong. If she had not been there, the charming Sophie would have had in one way or another to quench the fire which her miniature charms had kindled in her papa.

Very well pleased with her, I told her to get up, and we breakfasted very gaily. I spent the whole morning in this way with the two objects who delighted my heart, and after dinner, La Raucour having come to fetch the little girl, I remained with the grown-up Pauline, who was beginning seriously to set me on fire. So far I had not only not embraced her, I had not even taken her by the hand. Sitting beside her after my daughter left, I took one of her hands, pressing my lips to it, and asking her if she was married. She answered yes.

"Have you," I asked, "experienced the love of a mother?"

"No, but I can well imagine it. I have a husband, who has not yet slept with me."

"Is he in London?"

"No, he is very far from here. Let us not speak of him, I beg you."

"Tell me only if, when I lose you, it will be that you may rejoin him."

"Yes. I assure you, that unless you send me away, I will not leave your house except to leave England, and I will not leave this happy island except to go to be happy myself in my country with the husband I have chosen."

"My charming Pauline, I shall remain here unhappy, for I love you, and I fear that I will displease you if I give you the fondest proofs of it."

"Alas, I beg you to control yourself, for I am not my own mistress, either to yield to love, or to resist it if you do not spare me."

"I will obey you, but I shall languish. How can I be so unhappy when I have the good fortune to please you?"

"I have duties, my dear friend, which I cannot neglect without becoming an object of contempt to myself."

"I should consider myself the most traitorous, the most horrible of men, the most unworthy to be loved by a woman worthy of love, if I could esteem her less for making me happy by yielding to an inclination which I had myself inspired in her."

"I am glad of that. Nor do I believe you capable of it; but let us calm ourselves, remembering that we may be obliged to part to-morrow. Admit that our parting would be far more painful. If you do not admit it, it shows that your love is not of the same nature as mine."

"Of what nature, then, is the love which I have had the happiness to inspire in you?"

"It is such that its consummation seems to me only secondary."

"Then what is primary?"

"Living together in the most perfect harmony."

"That is a happiness which I possess, and which you possess. We both enjoy it from morning to night. Why can we not also be indulgent to the secondary, which will take only a few minutes of our time, which will bring our loving souls a peace and a quietude which are necessary to us? Admit, too, that this secondary thing supplies the food which keeps the primary in good health."

"I admit it, but admit, too, that the same food is most often deadly to it."

"One cannot believe that, my dear friend, when one loves; and I am in that situation. Can you yourself believe that, having me fond and amorous in your arms, you would love me less afterward?"

"No, I do not believe it; and it is precisely for that reason that I fear to make the moment of our parting intolerable."

"I must yield to your powerful reasoning, my charming Pauline. I should like to see with what you nourish your exalted intelligence. I should like to look at your books. Shall we go upstairs? I shall not go out."

"With pleasure, but you will be baffled."

"How?"

"Let us go."

We go up, I approach her books, and I find that they are all in Portuguese, except Milton in English, Ariosto in Italian, and La Bruyère's *Characters*[31] in French.

"All this, my dear Pauline, gives me a high idea of you; but why this preference for Camoëns[32] and all these other Portuguese writers?"

"Because I am Portuguese."

"You Portuguese? I thought you were Italian. At your age you know five languages, for you must also speak Spanish."

"That goes without saying."

"What an education!"

"I am twenty-two years old, but I knew those languages at eighteen."

"Tell me who you are. Tell me everything."

"Everything, and at once, trusting in you without fear, for if you love me you can do me nothing but good."

"And what are all these manuscript notebooks?"

"My story, which I have written here. Let us sit down."

[* * *]

There is debate among scholars about whether Casanova invented Pauline's story, and even Pauline herself. Both conform rather too closely to the sentimental drama of noble young love frustrated by a stern father which was so popular in the eighteenth century. For that reason we have omitted Pauline's narrative from this selection. On the other hand, Casanova's account contains convincing circumstantial details, including the advertisement in the St. James's Chronicle. Whether true or not, the real interest of this episode lies less in the story Pauline tells, which could come straight out of a contemporary novel, than in Casanova's ingenious and characteristic way of introducing her into his house.

Inevitably, Casanova fell in love with Pauline and the two began an affair which he describes as a testimony to the power of her storytelling. But on 1 August, 1763, just a few weeks after he placed his advertisement in the St. James's Chronicle, they both received fateful letters. Pauline's summoned her home. Casanova took her to Calais, deputing his servant Clairmont to escort her the rest of the way. They reached Lisbon successfully, but Clairmont was drowned on the way back. Returning to London from Calais, Casanova found himself comparing his new friend with Henriette. Although he had parted from the French girl fifteen years earlier, he decided that she had left a stronger impression on his mind, which made him conclude, not that he loved her more, but that his faculties must be declining.

Perhaps he was disturbed by the contents of his own letter from Madame du Rumain announcing the death of Madame d'Urfé, who seems to have died from the effects of her own patent medicine. The elderly Marquise had left a will declaring herself pregnant, bequeathing her property to the child and appointing Casanova its guardian. Madame d'Urfé's daughter quickly had the will set aside and claimed a substantial inheritance, leaving Casanova to mourn the loss of his friend and, among other valuable properties, the four hundred thousand francs discovered in her portfolio.

CHAPTER X

Peculiarities of the English. Castel-Bajac.
Count Schwerin. My daughter Sophie in
boarding school. My reception at the Thinkers'
Club.[1] *La Charpillon.*

I did not go out until two days later, but sad, preoccupied, and like a man who had only just arrived. I entered a coffeehouse where twenty people were reading the newspaper. Not understanding English, I sat there quietly watching those who came and went. A merchant who spoke French said to another, who was reading, that So-and-so had killed himself and that he had done well because his affairs were in such disorder that he could only live in poverty.

"You are mistaken, I was present yesterday when his effects were inventoried, for he was in debt to me too, and we all agreed that he had done a stupid thing, for he could have waited another six months before he killed himself, even without putting his affairs in order."

The calculation making me laugh, I went to the Exchange to draw some money. I find Bosanquet, who at once gives me what I ask for; and seeing, on my way out of the room in which I signed the receipt, a man whose countenance aroused my curiosity, I ask him who he is.

"He is a man who is worth a hundred thousand pounds."

"And that other one?"

"He is worth nothing."

"But what I want you to tell me is their names."

"I don't know them. A name means nothing. Knowing a man consists in knowing what amount he commands; for what does his name matter? Ask me for a thousand pounds and give me a receipt for them in my presence under the name of Attila,[2] and that is enough for me. You will repay me not as Seingalt but as Monsieur Attila, and we will laugh."

"But when you sign bills of exchange—"

"That is different, for I have to sign them with the name that the drawer gives me."

I leave him, and I go to the Park; but before entering it I want to change my bank note into coins. I enter the establishment of a fat merchant, a great trencherman whose acquaintance I had made at a tavern, and I ask him to give me guineas for my twenty-pound note, which I threw down on his counter.

"Come back in an hour," he says, "for at the moment I haven't a penny."

"Very well, I will come back on my way out of the Park."

"Take your note; you shall give it to me when I give you the cash."

"It makes no difference. Keep it. I do not doubt your honesty."

"That is madness, my friend, for if you leave me the note I will not give you the cash, if only to teach you a lesson in how to live."

"I do not believe you are capable of so dishonest an act."

"Nor am I; but in the case of something as simple as a bank note, which is no inconvenience to you in your pocket, and left here without your having received the cash, I could more easily persuade myself that I had given you the cash, despite anything you might say to me, than believe you were so stupid as to leave me the note without receiving it."

"You are right."

I go to the Park; I see Martinelli, and I thank him for having sent me his *Decamerone*.[3] He congratulates me on my reappearance in the world, and on the beautiful young lady whose slave I had become, whom Lord Pembroke had seen and found charming.

"What? What? Where did he see her?"

"With you in a carriage and four, at full trot on the road to Rochester,[4] only three or four days ago."

"Very well, I can now tell you that I took her to Calais and that I shall not see her again."

"Shall you rent your apartments again?"

"Never. I was too greatly punished for it, though love treated me well. Come to dine with me whenever you like."

Going toward Buckingham House,[5] I see in the shrubbery to my left a piece of indecency which surprises me. Four or five people at different distances were attending to their needs and showing their behinds to the passers-by.

"It is disgusting," I said to Martinelli; "those pigs should be facing us instead."

"Not at all, for then people would recognize them and would certainly look at them, whereas, showing us their arses as they do, they force us, unless we are especially interested in that part of the body, not to look in that direction."

888

"Your reasoning is excellent, my friend, but since it is something new for a foreigner, you will excuse me."

"You will have noticed that an Englishman who, walking in the street, needs to make water does not, as we do in our country, go and piss in somebody's doorway or his alley or his courtyard."

"So I have observed. They turn to face the middle of the street and piss there. But people going by in carriages see them, and that is as bad, I think."

"Who tells the people in carriages that they have to look?"

"Very true."

We go to the Green Park, where we come upon Lord Pembroke on horseback; he stops and exclaims when he sees me; I can imagine why, and I tell him that I regained my freedom four days since, and that I felt lonely at my excellent table.

"I am rather curious. I may come today."

He leaves, and, counting on it, I go home to order him a good dinner. Martinelli could not come; but he takes me out of the Park by a gate which I did not know, and he goes far enough with me to put me on the right road.

At the end of a street we see a crowd, at the center of which something curious must have been happening, for everyone was craning his neck to see. Martinelli approaches, stays there a few minutes, then tells me that I shall hear something strange.[6]

"The whole crowd," he said, "is eagerly watching a brave man who will probably die in a quarter of an hour from a blow on the temple he received in a fist fight with another man."

"Is there no remedy?"

"A surgeon who is there maintains that he will not die if he is allowed to bleed him."

"Who can forbid him?"

"That is what is astonishing. The people who forbid him are two men who have bet twenty guineas on his living or dying. One of them said, 'I wager he dies,' the other wagered that he would not die, and the wager was on. There stands the surgeon, wanting to bleed him; the man who wagered he would die will not let him, for if he lives the other will demand his twenty guineas. They refuse to hear of any compromise, so the man may die because of their accursed wager."

"By God, there's an unfortunate man and a pair of pitiless bettors."

"The Englishman has his own ideas on the subject of betting. There is a confraternity or a club called 'The Bettors,'[7] and if you are curious I will get you introduced there."

"Do they speak French?"

"Undoubtedly, for they are men of intelligence and distinction."[8]

"And what do they do?"

"They talk, and when one of them denies something that the other puts forth as a fact, if the other challenges him to bet he must bet, on pain of a fine which goes into the club treasury and which the members divide among them at the end of the month."

"My dear friend, introduce me to this delightful club, which will make me rich, for I shall not hesitate to speak out when I am of a different opinion, and I will not speak at all unless I am sure of what I am saying."

"Be careful, for they are sharp."

"But let us get back to the man who is dying from that blow in a fist fight. What will be done with the man who killed him?"

"His hand will be examined; and if it is found to be 'dangerous,'[9] he will be hanged; if they find his hand is like yours and mine, all that will happen to him is that his hand will be branded."

"I am at a loss; please explain to me. How is a 'dangerous' hand recognized?"

"When it is found to have been branded. Then it is certain that the man has killed another, and when his hand was branded he was warned to be careful not to kill still another, for he would go to the gallows."

"But if the man with the 'dangerous' hand—since there is such a thing—is attacked?"

"He shows his hand; and then everyone is bound to respect him and let him alone."

"And if he is forced?"

"Then he defends himself, and if he kills it means nothing, provided that he has witnesses."

"Fist fighting can easily cause death. I am surprised that it is permitted."

"It is only permitted on a wager. If the two who fight have not thrown a coin or two on the ground before fighting, which is proof positive of a wager, if death results the killer is sentenced to the gallows."

"O laws, O customs!"[10]

It was thus that I learned to know this proud nation. I had a good dinner prepared for the noble Lord, and he did not fail to come to it. Though only the two of us were present, our dinner lasted a long time, for I wanted commentaries on all the fine things I had learned that morning, and especially on the Bettors' Club. The amiable Lord advised me not to join it unless I was prepared to remain perfectly silent for at least a month.

"But if I am asked a question?"

"Evade it."

"Evade it? No doubt I shall do so if I am asked my opinion and I am unable to give it; but in the contrary case, when I am sure, the devil himself won't be able to make me keep still. They are not scoundrels, I hope?"

"Scoundrels? They are all noble, learned, rich, and epicures; but pitiless in accepting and in offering bets."

"But is the treasury well stocked?"

"Very poorly, for rather than pay the fine any one of them would rather lose his stake. Who will introduce you?"

"Martinelli."

"Yes, he will speak to Spencer,[11] who is a member. I have not wanted to join."

"Why?"

"Because I don't like to argue. But you are a strange man."

"What makes you say so?"

"A month shut up with a woman who was in London for fourteen months and whom no one could ever get to know or even to find out what her country is, and who was known only to you, a foreigner—it's something to nettle us all."

"How did you know that she was here for fourteen months?"

"Because she first lived in the house of an honest widow, where several people saw her; but she would never let anyone make her acquaintance. Your notice brought her into your hands."

"Unluckily for me, for I shall never love another woman."

"Oh, there'll be another in a week. Perhaps tomorrow, if you will come to dine with me in the country. I made the engagement by chance yesterday in Chelsea,[12] where a Frenchwoman who is a beauty asked me to give her dinner. I have sent my orders, and I have informed five or six of my friends who are fond of play."

"Play for stakes?"

"Of course."

"Does the charming Frenchwoman like to play?"

"No, but her husband does."

"What do you call him?"

"It is he who calls himself the Count of Castel-Bajac."[13]

"A Gascon."[14]

"Yes."

"Thin, tall, dark, and marked with smallpox."

"Just so. I am delighted that you know him. Isn't it true that his wife is a beauty?"

"I have no idea, for it was six years ago that I made his acquaintance, and I did not know that he was married then. I will come, and I am very glad to be of the company. However, I give you one warning: say nothing if he pretends not to know me. He may have good reasons for doing so. I can tell you a story in confidence tomorrow which is not to his credit. I did not know he was a gamester. I will be careful in the company of the bettors, and you, My Lord, be careful in tomorrow's company."

"I will give your Negro my address."

He rode away, and I went to see Mrs. Cornelys, who had written me a week earlier that her daughter was ill, and who complained that she had twice been told that I was not at home when she knew I was there. My only excuse was that I was in love, and she had to allow it; but Sophie's condition alarmed me. She was in bed with continual fever, extremely thin, and looking at me with eyes which told me that she was dying of grief. Her mother was in despair, for she loved her dearly; I thought she would murder me when I told her in the patient's presence that if she died it would be she who had killed her. At that the child said, "No, no," and flung her arms around her mother's neck and soothed her; but before leaving I took her aside and told her that Sophie was dying because she made her too afraid of her and treated her with unbearable tyranny.

"Send her to boarding school for two years," I said, "with nice girls of good family; tell her so this evening, and you will see that tomorrow she will be better."

She replied that a good boarding school, including instruction, cost a hundred guineas a year. I said that, after seeing what school it was, I could pay the master or mistress a year in advance from my own purse. At this offer, the woman, who was really in poverty despite her luxurious style of living, embraced me with tokens of the liveliest gratitude.

"Come with me this instant," she said, "and tell your daughter the news yourself. I want to see her face."

"Gladly."

"My dear Sophie," I said as I entered, "your mother is persuaded that a change of air will restore you to health. If you will go to one of the finest boarding schools in London for a year or two, I will lend her a hundred guineas at once."

"I can only obey my dear mother."

"It is not a matter of obedience. Would you like to go to boarding school? Answer me frankly."

"But would it please my mother?"

"Very much, my dear daughter, if you will go willingly."

"Most willingly."

The child's face became red as fire. I left her, asking her to let me have news of her. I went home to think sadly of Pauline.

The next morning at ten o'clock Jarba asked me if I had forgotten that I was engaged to dine at Lord Pembroke's.

"No, indeed. It is only ten o'clock."

"Very true. But we have twenty miles to travel."

"Twenty miles?"

"Yes, here is the address he left with me. We have to go to Saint Albans."[15]

I think it odd that His Lordship had not told me so; but such are the English. I travel post, which is not difficult in London, for there are post offices everywhere, and I go to his house in Saint Albans in less than three hours. Nothing is finer than the English roads, and nothing more attractive than the English countryside, it lacks only the vine. It is a peculiarity of the very fertile soil of the island that it cannot yield wine. Lord Pembroke's house was not of the largest, but big enough to lodge twenty masters. The lady had not yet arrived; he shows me his gardens, his baths, his gazebos, his underground hothouses for growing fruits out of season; and among other things he showed me a cock, chained in a coop, which really looked ferocious.

"What is that? It's a fine cock, but chained! Why?"

"Because he is ferocious. He loves hens, and he would run away in search of them, and he would kill all the cocks they belong to."

"And why do you condemn him to celibacy?"

"So that he will be in good condition to fight. Look, here is the list of his victories."

He opens a drawer, and he takes out a long sheet of paper on which he had recorded all the fights from which he had emerged the victor after killing his opponent. There were more than thirty of

them. He shows me his very bright steel spurs. The cock shook
when he saw them, and I could not help bursting into laughter. All
on fire, the bird raised his feet to have the spurs put on. After that he
shows me his steel helmet.

"But with these advantages he is sure to defeat his opponent."

"Not at all, for when he is fully armed he scorns an unarmed
opponent."

"You amaze me, My Lord."

"You will no longer be amazed when you read this."

From a fourth drawer he takes a list showing his entire genealogy.
He could prove twenty quarters of nobility, in the male line of
course, for if he could have proved them in the female line too,
His Lordship would have hung at least the Maltese Cross[16] around
his neck. He told me that he had cost him two hundred guineas, but
that he would not sell him for a thousand. I asked him if he had
offspring; and he replied that he was working at it, but that it was
difficult; I do not remember what difficulties he alleged. The English constantly offered my eager curiosity delightful peculiarities.

But up drives a carriage with a woman and two men. I see the
scoundrel Castel-Bajac, and a thin man whom Castel-Bajac introduced to His Lordship as Count Schwerin,[17] nephew of the celebrated Field Marshal,[18] killed on what is called the field of honor. An
English General Beckw . . . ,[19] who commanded a regiment in the
service of the King of Prussia, and who was one of the guests, pays
him compliments and says that he had died in his presence; the
modest nephew then takes from his pocket the bloodstained ribbon
of the Black Eagle[20] which the Marshal was wearing when he
received his death wound.

"His Majesty,"[21] he informed the company, "permitted me to
keep it."

"But your pocket," said an Englishman who was present, "is not
the proper place for it."

His Lordship at once took possession of Madame. I examine her,
and in comparison with Pauline she seems to me to be nothing.
Whiter of complexion because she was blonde, less tall, and without
the slightest air of nobility, she does not interest me. When she
laughed all her beauty vanished. It is a great misfortune for a pretty
woman when laughter makes her ugly—the same laughter which
often has the power to make an ugly woman beautiful.

Lord Pembroke, whose place it was to do so, introduced his
friends to the lady and the gentlemen, and when he names me,

Castel-Bajac, who could have pretended not to know me under the name of Seingalt, expresses his pleasure and embraces me.

We dine in high spirits on English fare, we drink punch, and it is Madame who insists on a little game of faro. His Lordship never plays; so it is General Beckw... who offers to make a bank to amuse the company. He puts down a hundred guineas and eight or nine hundred more in bank notes. He politely distributes twenty counters to each punter, saying that each counter is worth half a guinea. Wanting to stake gold against gold, I accept no counters. At the third deal Schwerin was the first who, having lost his twenty counters, asks for twenty more. The banker tells him that he carries no one on his word. The Field Marshal's nephew does not answer and stops playing. At the following deal the same thing happens to Castel-Bajac. Being seated beside me, he asks my permission to take ten guineas from me. I coldly reply that he would bring me bad luck, and I push away his hand. Madame says that her husband had forgotten to bring his portfolio. An hour later the General lays down the cards, and I take my leave, asking His Lordship and the entire company to dine at my house the next day.

I was back at home by eleven o'clock, without having encountered any highwaymen, as I had expected to do. I had a small purse containing six guineas at their disposition. I had been taught that lesson. I had my cook waked and told him that I should have twelve people to dinner the next day. It was the first fine dinner I was giving. I found a note from Mrs. Cornelys telling me that she would come to dine with me on the following Sunday with "our" daughter, and that we would go to see the boarding school in which she intended to put her.

Lord Pembroke arrived first at my house with the beautiful Frenchwoman, in a carriage which barely seated two. The crowding was favorable for love. The others arrived one or two at a time, and the last were the Gascon and the Prussian.

We sat down at table at two o'clock, and we rose at four, all well pleased with my cook and even more so with my vintner, for despite the souls of forty bottles which we had in our bodies, none of us was drunk.

After coffee the General invited the whole company to sup at his house, and Madame Castel-Bajac asked me to make a bank. Not waiting to be urged, I made one of a thousand guineas, half in gold, half in bank notes. Having neither counters nor slips, I said that

I would accept only gold against gold, and that I would stop when I saw fit, without announcing the last deal.

I was delighted to see that the two foreign Counts[22] paid their little debts to the General in bank notes. I changed two of the same notes which they offered me into guineas, and I changed the two notes they had given him for the General. I put these four notes aside under my snuffbox, and play began. Having no croupier, and allowing all the punters to stake, I had to deal very slowly. It was the two Counts who occupied my attention, for they always made mistakes to their own advantage. It annoyed me. Both of them having had the misfortune to lose, and both of them being, luckily for me, out of bank notes, Castel-Bajac took from his pocket a bill of exchange for two hundred pounds and threw it to me, asking me to discount it for him; I reply that I know nothing about bills of exchange. An Englishman looks at it, then hands it back to me, saying that he knows neither the drawer nor the drawee nor the endorser. "I am the endorser," says the Gascon, "and I think that suffices." Everyone laughs, except myself. I politely hand it back to him, saying that he can discount it at the Exchange. He leaves, muttering insults, and Schwerin follows him.

After the departure of the sharpers I continued dealing quietly until very late in the night. When I stopped I was the loser, because of the General, who I saw was having too good luck. Before leaving he took me aside with His Lordship to ask him to see to it that the two swindlers should not come to his house the next night, for if the Gascon had said to him half of what he had dared to say to me he would have had him shown out by the window. His Lordship replied that he could give the message only to his wife. I ask him if the four notes which had come from them, and which I had, might be forged. Seeing that they are brand-new, he replies with a laugh that it is possible.

"What would you do to make sure?"

"I would send them to the Bank[23] to be changed."

"And if the Bank found that they were forged?"

"I would put up with it, or I would have the man who gave them to me arrested."

After giving me the General's address, he left with the lady.

The next day at the Bank I was surprised by the cold indifference with which an unassuming man to whom I had given my four notes, asking him to give me guineas for them, handed them back to me, saying that they were forgeries. He smiled when I asked him to examine them a little more closely. He told me to return them to the person who had given them to me and make him pay me in good money, which I should not find it difficult to do.

I knew very well that it was in my power to have the scoundrels put in prison; but, feeling reluctant to do so, I decide to go to His Lordship's to learn where they were staying. His Lordship was still asleep, one of his footmen takes me to their lodging, and my presence surprises them. I tell them coolly enough that, the four notes they had given me being forgeries, they should at once give me forty guineas. Castel-Bajac replies that he has no money; but that the thing amazed him.

"I can only," he said, "return them to the person who gave them to me, always provided that the notes you have there are the ones we gave you."

At this counterproposal the blood rushes to my head, and I leave them. The same footman, who was waiting for me, takes me to a place where, after being put on oath, I am given a bill[24] which authorizes me to have them arrested. I go to the Alderman,[25] who undertakes to see to it, then I go home very much put out by the shameful business. I found Martinelli, who had come to ask me for dinner. I gave him an account of the matter, not telling him that the scoundrels were to be arrested. The philosopher said that, if he were in my place, he would burn the forged notes. Such heroism may have been mere boasting, but his advice was good. I did not follow it. Thinking to cheer me up, he said that he had agreed with Lord Spencer on a day for my introduction to the Thinkers' Club, and I replied that I no longer wanted to join it. One often feels resentment toward a wise man who gives one good advice which one has not the courage to follow.

Toward nightfall I went to the General's, where I found the Countess sitting on Lord Pembroke's lap. We supped gaily; the two wretches did not appear, and no mention was made of them. Getting up from supper, we went into another room, where the table for faro was ready. The General dealt until daybreak, and I went home having lost two or three hundred guineas. I went to bed, and I did not wake until very late.

A man was announced, I had him shown in, and, finding that he spoke only English, I had to summon Jarba to interpret for me. He was the chief constable, who told me that if I would pay for his journey he was sure he could arrest Castel-Bajac at Dover, for which place he had left at noon; he was sure to arrest him before nightfall.

I replied, giving him a guinea, that the other would be enough for me, and that he should let the Gascon go to the devil.

The next day being a Sunday, the only day on which the extraordinary Mrs. Cornelys could go about in London, I had her to dinner at my house with my daughter, who, delighted to be on the eve of escaping from her mother's hands, had recovered her health. The boarding school was in Harwich,[26] and we went there after dinner.

The mistress of the establishment was a Catholic noblewoman who, despite her sixty years, still looked fresh and displayed wit and the manners of good society. Having been forewarned by Lady Harrington's recommendation, she gave the young Cornelys the most gracious reception. She had fifteen or sixteen girls at board, the eldest of whom was barely thirteen years of age. I saw them all in the garden, playing innocently together. When Her Ladyship introduced Sophie to them, saying that she was to become their fellow boarder, they all hastened to give her the fondest caresses. Five or six of the young ladies, and one of them more especially, seemed to me angels incarnate, and two or three of them were so ugly that they frightened me. These two extremes are seen in England more than anywhere else. My daughter was shorter than any of the others, but her little face was so pretty that she did not lose courage. She at once made up to all of them, talking with them as if she had known them for a long time. When Her Ladyship invited us to go through the house, they all followed us.

Each girl had a small room next to another which was separated from hers by a half-wall and in which lived a fellow boarder with whom she could talk. They ate four at a table, and six maids took care of them all. They had all kinds of masters, who came to give them lessons in a large room in which I saw harpsichords, harps, guitars, and tables on which there was everything needed for lessons in drawing. Thinking that I was Sophie's father, all the girls talked to me, and I saw that those who could not yet venture to speak French or Italian were mortified. I was in ecstasies. Their short dresses, with an English-style whale-bone corset which left their bosoms entirely bare, put my soul in a stupor.

After going over the whole house, we went with only the head-mistress into a room where Mrs. Cornelys gave her the hundred guineas for a year in bank notes and took a receipt. They agreed that the little girl should enter as soon as she came with her bed and her few necessaries. Her mother took care of it all on the following Sunday.

Very early the next day the Alderman's man came to tell me that Count Schwerin was a prisoner in his house, and he gave me a note in which he asked me to come to speak with him. I decided to go when the man told me he had not a penny and that, the charge being one of forged bank notes, he was going to take him to Newgate.[27] I could not quite stomach the idea of letting him go to the gallows. So I went there, and I cannot describe how much I suffered at the sight of his endless tears, his despairing gestures, his admission of his crime, and the basenesses to which he descended to move me to pity. He swore that the notes had been given him by Castel-Bajac, but that he knew from whom he had bought them and that he was ready to tell me the person's name if I would set him free. I said that if he named the person from whom they came he was sure not to be hanged, but that I would keep him in prison nevertheless, sending him fourpence a day until he gave me my money. At that his cries began again, while he swore that he was in utter poverty and showed me his empty pockets. He then offered me, as security, his bloodstained ribbon of the Black Eagle, and I took it into my head that I should like to have it.

So I accepted it, giving him a receipt and undertaking to return it to him when he gave me forty pounds sterling. I wrote out my waiver, I paid the costs of his imprisonment, I burned the forged notes in his presence, and I let him go.

Two days later I saw the self-styled Countess Castel-Bajac appear at my house to tell me that, her husband and her lover having left, she did not know where to turn. She also complained bitterly of Lord Pembroke, who had also abandoned her after she had given him clear tokens of her affection. I said that he would have made a mistake to leave her before that, for he must have considered that she owed him something. She replied that it was true he had given her a good lesson. It finally appeared that, if I wanted to get rid of her, I had to give her what she needed to rejoin her wretched lover in Calais, for she swore to me that she did not want to see Castel-Bajac again, who in any case was not her husband. The reader will see these two persons reappear on the scene three years hence.

About this same time a tragicomic incident did not fail to afford me amusement.

An Italian came to me with a letter from my friend Balletti. He recommended the bearer of the letter to me, Signor Costantini[28] by name, a native of Vicenza, who was in London on business of great importance of which he would inform me. He asked me to be of use to him in any way in my power. Being myself the only judge of the extent of my powers and of my willingness to employ them, I told Signor Costantini that I greatly esteemed the friend who had sent him to me, and that hence he could count upon me.

"Signore," he said, "I arrived in London yesterday evening, and the long journey having cost me all the money I had, I now command only two guineas, but I know that my wife is here, she is rich, and I can easily find out where she lodges. You know that, as her husband, I can dispose of whatever she possesses."

"I know nothing about it."

"Then you do not know the laws of this country?"

"I do not."

"Too bad; but it is none the less true. I intend to go to her house tomorrow and turn her into the street with the dress she has on and nothing more, for all her furniture, her clothes, her diamonds, in short everything she possesses, is mine. May I ask you to be with me when I stage this fine scene?"

Very much surprised by the situation, and even more so by his proposal, I ask him if he had told my friend Balletti of the matter. He replies that he has confided in no one, and that I am the first person to whom he has spoken of it.

I could not dismiss him as mad, for he had not the slightest appearance of being so, and seeing, furthermore, that the law which he cited very likely existed in England, I answered him briefly that I did not feel inclined to help him in his enterprise, of which in any case I completely disapproved, unless his wife had stolen from him all the things of which he alleged that she was then in possession.

"No, Signore. She stole nothing from me but my honor, and when she left me she possessed nothing but her talent. She came here, and she has made a great fortune. Am I not right to seize it, if only to punish her and avenge myself?"

"That may be so, but since you seem to me a sensible man I ask you what you would think of me if I consented without further ado to be your companion in an enterprise which, despite your arguments, I consider cruel. Add that I might know your wife and might even be her friend."

"I will tell you her name."

"I beg you to say no more, though I am not acquainted with any Signora Costantini."

"She has changed her name; she calls herself Calori[29] and she sings in the opera at the Haymarket."

"Now I know who she is, but you are wrong to have told me her name."

"It was because I do not doubt your discretion. I am going at once to find out where she lives. That is the chief thing."

He left me, drying his tears, and I pitied him. Nevertheless I was annoyed that he had confided his secret to me. Three or four hours later I went to see La Binetti,[30] who, after telling me that La De Amicis,[31] when she left London, had gone completely mad over the impresario Mattei,[32] who did not love her, told me all the stories I wanted to hear about all the *virtuose*[33] who were then in London. When she came to La Calori, she told me she had had several lovers who had given her a great deal, but that at the moment she had no one but the celebrated violinist Giardini,[34] with whom she was in love. I asked her where she came from and if she was married, and she replied that she was from Vicenza and that she did not believe she was married.

I had almost stopped thinking about this ugly matter when, three days after my conversation with La Binetti, I received a note from King's Bench Prison,[35] which I was surprised to find signed with the name Costantini. The unfortunate man told me that he considered me the only friend he could have in London, and so he hoped that I would have come to see him, at least to give him some good advice.

Thinking it all very strange, and not understanding how it was possible, I take a hackney carriage and I hurry to King's Bench. I find him in despair, with an old English attorney who spoke Italian and whom I knew. Costantini had been arrested on the previous evening on account of several notes to order drawn by his wife, which she had not paid when they fell due. According to these notes his wife appeared to owe the bearers about a thousand guineas. The attorney who was there was the depositary of the notes, which belonged to names which I did not know. There were five of them. He had come to propose some arrangements to the prisoner.

Very much surprised by this infamous trick, which I should not have believed to be such if I had not learned from La Binetti that La Calori, far from being in debt, was rich, I asked the attorney to leave, for I needed to talk with Signor Costantini privately.

"I am arrested," he says, "for debts of my wife's, and I am told that I must pay them because I am her husband."

"It is a trick your wife is playing on you. She found out that you are in London."

"She saw me from her window."

"Why did you put off executing your plan?"

"I would have carried it out this morning; but could I believe that my wife was in debt?"

"Nor is she. These notes are false. They were predated, they were drawn only yesterday. It is a bad business, which may cost her dear."

"But I am in prison."

"Stay there, and count on me. We shall meet again tomorrow."

Indignant at this scurvy trick, and determined to take up the cudgels for the unfortunate man, I go to tell Monsieur Bosanquet the whole story; he replies that tricks of the kind were extremely common in London and that ways of dealing with them had long been known there. He ended by saying that if I took an interest in the prisoner, he would put him in the hands of an advocate who would clear him, and who would make his wife and her lover, who had apparently instigated the thing, repent of trying it. I replied that I was interested in the man, and I asked him to act and even to stand surety for him if that was necessary, being myself ready to vouch for him. I gave him the man's name, and he advised me to take no further steps in the matter.

Five or six days later he came to tell me that Master Costantini had left the prison, and even England, or so the advocate who had undertaken his defence believed.

"How was that?"

"It is perfectly simple. His wife's lover himself, foreseeing the storm, must have persuaded him to accept a sum of money on condition that he would leave, and the poor wretch agreed. So the thing is over; but it is a bit of news which will arouse laughter and which will be read in the papers, and it will even be said that Giardini did very well when he advised Signorina Calori to play this fine part."

I learned later from La Binetti that she had him given two hundred guineas. I was very well pleased, and I wrote Balletti the whole story. Some years later I came upon La Calori in Prague.

A Flemish officer who had served in France and to whose assistance I had come at Aix-la-Chapelle[36] had paid me several visits and had even dined at my house two or three times, and I was sorry that I had not yet, as in duty bound, gone to call on him at his lodging at least once; he made me blush when, running into me in London, he politely reproached me for it. He had his wife and daughter with him. A modicum of curiosity also made me want to go there. It was my evil Genius who took me there, for my good one always kept me from doing so.

When he saw me he fell on my neck, and as soon as he introduced me to his wife, calling me his savior, I had to accept all the compliments which rogues pay to decent people whom they hope to dupe. Five or six minutes later I see an old woman come in with a pretty girl. Monsieur Malingan introduced me, saying that I was the Chevalier de Seingalt of whom he had often spoken to them. The young lady, pretending surprise, said that she had known a Monsieur Casanova who looked very much like me; I replied that that, too, was my name, but that I did not have the happiness to remember her.

"I, too," she said, "had another name then; it was Augspurgher, though now my name is Charpillon;[37] and since you saw me and spoke to me only once, it is easily possible that you have forgotten me, the more so since I was then only thirteen years old. Some time afterward I came to London with my mother[38] and my aunts; we have been here now for four years."

"But where did I have the happiness of speaking with you?"

"In Paris, at the Palais Marchand,[39] you were with a charming lady; you gave me these buckles" (and so saying, she showed them to me on her shoes); "then, encouraged by my aunt, you did me the honor to embrace me."

I then remember her perfectly [. . .].

"Mademoiselle, I remember the occasion very well, and I remember you, but I do not recognize your aunt."

"This lady is her sister, but if you will be good enough to come to tea with us, you shall see her. We are living in Denmark Street,[40] Soho. I will show you that I wrote down the very flattering compliment you paid me."

CHAPTER XI

*La Charpillon and the fatal effects of my
acquaintance with her.*

At the name Charpillon I take from my portfolio the letter which the
Procurator Morosini had given me at Lyons and I hand it to her.

"What do I see! My dear Ambassador! And in all the three
months you have been in London you have never thought of
bringing me his letter?"

"It is true; I should have inquired; but since the Ambassador
showed no particular eagerness, I have neglected this little duty, and
I am grateful to the chance which enables me to perform it."

"Then come to dine with us tomorrow."

"I cannot, for Lord Pembroke told me to expect him."

"In company, or by himself?"

"By himself."

"I am glad of that. Expect me, too, with my aunt. Where do you
live?"

I give her my address, assuring her that she will do me both an
honor and a favor, and I am surprised to see her laugh.

"Then you are the Italian," she says, "who two months ago
posted on the door of his house at this address the strange notice
which set everyone laughing?"

"I am he."

"I am told that it cost you dear."

"On the contrary. I owe that notice my happiness."

"It follows that, now that the lady has gone, you must be
unhappy. No one knows who she was. Do you really make a secret
of it?"

"Certainly; and I would rather die than reveal it."

"Ask my aunt if I didn't want to go to ask you for a room. But
my mother would not let me."

"What need have you to find a cheap lodging?"

"None whatever; but I felt a need to laugh and to punish the
audacious author of such a notice."

"How would you have punished me?"

"By making you fall in love with me and then treating you so
that you suffered the pains of hell. Oh, how I should have laughed!"

"Then you believe it is in your power to make any man you choose fall in love with you, basely planning in advance to become the tyrant of him who has paid your charms the homage which is their due? It is the project of a monster, and it is unfortunate for men that you do not look like one. I shall profit by your frankness to be on my guard."

"In vain. Unless you forgo seeing me."

Since she smiled while maintaining this dialogue, I took it as it was natural to take it; but admiring in her a kind of intelligence which, together with her charms, at once convinced me that she did indeed have the power to make any man love her. It was the first sample of it which she gave me that first day on which I had the misfortune to make her acquaintance.

It was on that fatal day at the beginning of September 1763 that I began to die and that I ceased to live. I was thirty-eight years of age. If the perpendicular line of ascent is equal in length to that of descent, as it should be, on this the first day of November in the year 1797 I think I can count on nearly four years of life,[1] which in accordance with the axiom *motus in fine velocior* ("motion is increased in speed toward the end")[2] will pass very quickly.

La Charpillon, whom all London knew, and who, I believe, is still alive,[3] was a beauty in whom it was difficult to find a defect. Her hair was light chestnut, her eyes blue, her complexion of the purest white, and her stature almost equal to Pauline's, counting in the two inches she would gain when she became twenty, for at that time she was only seventeen. Her bosom was small but perfect, her hands dimpled, slender, a little longer than most, her feet tiny, and her manners assured and well-bred. Her sweet, open countenance bore witness to a soul distinguished by delicacy of feeling and to the nobility of manner which is usually due to birth. It was on these two points that Nature saw fit to lie in her appearance. She ought rather to have told the whole truth there, and lied in all the rest. The girl had deliberately planned to make me unhappy even before she had come to know me; and she told me so.

I left Malingan's house, not like a sensual man who, having a passion for the sex, cannot but feel overjoyed to have met a girl with whom, having recognized her rare beauty, he feels sure that he will easily satisfy all the desires she has inspired in him, but stupefied and surprised that the image of Pauline, which I still had before my eyes, and which, each time I saw a woman who could lay claim to please me, imperiously entered my mind to make me scorn her, did not have the power to render this Charpillon incapable of taking me by surprise. I forgave myself, concluding that what had enchanted me was only novelty and the combination of circumstances, and that disenchantment would soon follow. "I shall cease," I told myself, "to find her marvelous as soon as I have slept with her; nor will that be long in coming."

How could I imagine that she would make difficulties? She had invited herself to dinner with me; she had been the dear friend of the Procurator, whom she had certainly not kept languishing and who must have paid her, for he was neither handsome nor young enough to have made her fall in love with him. Without even flattering myself that I could please her, I knew that I had money, that I was not stingy, and that she would not resist.

Lord Pembroke had become my friend after the charity I had shown Count Schwerin and my restraint in not demanding half of the amount from the General. He had told me that we would arrange a party which would give us a pleasurable day.

When he arrived and saw four places laid he asked me who the two others who would dine with us were, and he was surprised when he learned that they were La Charpillon and her aunt, and that she had invited herself as soon as she had known that it was he who was to dine with me.

"The girl having made me want very much to have her," he said, "I finally found her at Vauxhall one night with her aunt, and I offered her twenty guineas if she would come for a stroll with me in a dark walk. She consented, asking for the money in advance, and I was kind enough to give it to her. She came into the walk; but she immediately dropped my arm, and I did not find her again."

"You should have slapped her face in public."

"I should have brought trouble on myself, and everyone would have laughed at me. She's a fool, whom I now despise. Are you in love with her?"

"I am curious about her, as you were."

"She is a scheming wench who will do everything she can to trap you."

She arrives, and she says the most charming things possible to His Lordship, scarcely looking at me. She laughs; she herself recounts the trick she had played on him at Vauxhall, and she twits him with stupidity for giving her up because of a joke which, on the contrary, should have led him to love her the more.

"Another time," she said, "I will not run away from you."

"That is possible, for I will not pay you in advance."

"Fie! 'Pay' is an ugly word which dishonors you."

His Lordship praised her wit and only laughed at all the impertinent things she said to him in her pique at the indolent lack of attention which he accorded her remarks. After dinner she left us, after making me promise to come to dinner with her on the next day but one.

I spent the whole of the following day with the amiable Lord, who introduced me to the English bagnio,[4] an entertainment which costs a great deal and which I shall not describe, for it is well known to all those who have spent some time in London and have been willing to pay six guineas to enjoy its pleasures. We had two very pretty sisters, whose name was Garrick.

On the appointed day I went to La Charpillon's to dinner, as I had promised to do. She introduces me to her mother, who, though ill and haggard, comes back to my memory at once. In the year 1759 a Genevan named Bolomay[5] had persuaded me to sell her some jewelry for six thousand francs. She had given me two bills of exchange drawn on the same Genevan by herself and her two sisters; her name was Augspurgher. The Genevan who had accepted the bills had gone bankrupt before they fell due, and the three Augspurgher sisters had disappeared a few days later. So I am greatly surprised to find them in England, and still more surprised to be brought to their house by La Charpillon, who, knowing nothing of this underhanded dealing by her mother and her aunts, had not told her that Monsieur de Seingalt was the Casanova to whom they owed six thousand francs.

"Madame, I have the pleasure of recollecting you," were the words I said to her.

"Monsieur, I recollect you too. That scoundrel Bolomay—"

"Let us not speak of it, Madame; we will leave it for another day. I see that you have been ill."

"Deathly ill, but I am better now. My daughter did not announce you by your name."

"I beg your pardon: it is mine, as was the name I had in Paris, when I made her acquaintance without knowing that she was related to you."

Thereupon the grandmother, who was named Augspurgher like her daughter, comes in with the two aunts; and a quarter of an hour later three men arrive, one of whom was the Chevalier Goudar, whom I had known in Paris;[6] of the two others, whom I did not know, one was named Rostaing[7] and the other Coumon.[8] They were the three friends of the house, all of them professional sharpers, whose office was to bring in dupes and thus provide the means of subsistence which in turn provided theirs. It was to this infamous gang that I saw myself introduced, and although I was aware of it at once, I neither fled nor promised myself that I would never set foot in the place again. I thought that I risked nothing if I remained on the defensive and nursed no intention but that of entering into a relationship with the daughter; I considered these people merely creatures who had nothing in common with my undertaking. At table I fell in with the general atmosphere, I set the tone, I led them on, I was led on, and I became convinced that I would accomplish the whole of my purpose with no difficulty. The only thing which displeased me was a request which La Charpillon made of me after asking me to excuse her for having given me poor fare at her house. She asked me to invite her to supper with the entire company and to appoint the day. I immediately asked her to name it herself, and after consulting the scoundrels, she named it. Four rubbers of whist, at which I constantly lost, brought us to supper-time, and toward midnight I went home, bored and in love with La Charpillon.

Nevertheless I had the strength not to go to see her during the two following days. The third day being the one she had appointed for supper at my house, at nine o'clock I saw her with her aunt.

"I have come," she said, "to breakfast with you and to discuss a piece of business."

"Now, or after we have breakfasted?"

"Afterward, for we must be alone."

In the ensuing private conversation, after informing me of her family's situation at the time, she said that they would cease to be in straits if her aunt, who was in the other room, had a hundred guineas. With that amount she would compound the "balm of life" which would make her fortune. She discoursed on the virtues of the balm, on the large sales of which there could be no doubt in London, and on the profit which I myself would make, since, as was only right, I should have a half share with her in the enterprise; aside from all that, she said that, on receiving the hundred guineas, her mother and her aunts would undertake in writing to repay me the same amount at the end of six months. I replied that I would give her a definite answer after supper.

So saying, and being alone with her, I assume a lighthearted manner, the manner which a polished man assumes, when, in love, he wants to find his way to the favors to which he aspires, and I begin making the appropriate motions on the large sofa on which we were seated; but La Charpillon, with the same lightheartedness, resists my every movement and repeatedly forbids my gently caressing hands to do anything they would; she refuses me hers, she tears herself from my arms, turning her head away when she sees mine within range of giving her a kiss, and finally she gets up and, all smiles, goes to join her aunt in the other room. Forced to smile too, I follow her, and a minute later she leaves, bidding me good-by until that evening.

Left alone and reflecting on this first scene, I find it natural, to be expected, and, above all, in view of her need of the hundred guineas for which she had already asked me, not at all unpromising. I saw very well that I could not hope for her favors unless I gave her the money, and certainly I had no thought of haggling; but she must see too that she should not have it if she took it into her head to play the prude. It was for me to take such measures as would guarantee me against being tricked. Not wanting to dine, I go to walk in the Park, and toward nightfall I am home again.

The company arrives, it is not late, the beautiful child asks me to make a small bank for them, and, after bursting out laughing, which she does not expect, I decline.

"A game of whist, at least," she says.

"Then you are not in a hurry for my answer concerning the matter of which you know?"

"Of course I am. So you have made up your mind."

"Yes, come."

She follows me into the other room, where, after making her sit down on the same sofa, I tell her that I have the hundred guineas and that they are at her disposal.

"You must give them to my aunt, otherwise the gentlemen would think that I had obtained them from you by shameful concessions."

"Very well, I will give them to your aunt; you may count on it."

After these words I made the same approaches to her which I had made that morning, but always to no purpose. I ceased to press her when she said that I would never get anything from her either with money or by force; but that I could hope everything from her friendship when she saw that, being alone with her, I was gentle as a lamb. At that I got up, and she followed me.

Feeling my bile rising, I saw that I could conceal it only by joining in the whist game which had already been arranged. She was in very high spirits, and it annoyed me. Beside me at the table, she exasperated me by a hundred freedoms which would have raised me to the seventh heaven if she had not twice rebuffed me that same day. When the company was leaving she called me aside to say that she would send her aunt to me in the other room if I had really decided to give her the hundred guineas. I replied that it would be necessary to write and that the time was not suitable for it, and when she asked me to fix a time I said, showing her a purse full of gold pieces, that the time would come when she made it come.

Reflecting after she left that the young hussy had undoubtedly laid a deliberate plan to cheat me, I prepared to renounce my pursuit. The failure humiliated me, but I saw a certain courage in accepting it. To distract myself I the next day began going to my daughter's boarding school, taking a basket of sweetmeats with me. I rejoiced Sophie's soul, as well as those of her schoolmates, with whom she shared them all. But the pleasure I felt was greater than theirs. I went there nearly every day. The journey took only an hour and a quarter.[9] I brought them all sorts of trinkets and small articles of attire which delighted them; Her Ladyship was politeness itself to me, and my daughter, who openly called me her dear papa, made me every day more convinced that I had won her heart as I had given her life. In less than three weeks I congratulated myself that I had forgotten La Charpillon and had replaced her by innocent affections, though one of Sophie's schoolmates pleased me a little too much for me to find myself entirely free from amorous desires.

In this state, one morning at eight o'clock I saw before me the coquette's favorite aunt, who said that her niece and the entire family were mortified that I had not put in an appearance since the supper I had given them, and especially herself, to whom her niece had given the hope that I would provide her with the means to compound her "balm of life."

"Yes, Madame, I would have given you a hundred guineas, if your niece had treated me like a friend. She refused me favors which even a Vestal[10] would have granted me, and you know that she is no Vestal."

"Permit me to laugh. She is lighthearted, a bit of a scatterbrain, she gives herself only when she is sure she is loved. She told me everything. She loves you, but she fears that your love is only a passing fancy. She is in bed with a bad cold, and she thinks she has a slight fever. Come to see her, and I am sure you will not leave dissatisfied."

At these words all the desire which I had felt to possess the girl reawoke; and after a good laugh at myself for it, I asked her at what hour I should go there to be sure of finding her in bed. She said to go immediately, and to knock only once. I told her to go and wait for me.

How gratified I was to see that I was about to succeed in possessing her and that I had made sure I should not be tricked, for, having put my case to her aunt, and having her on my side, I had no more doubts.

I quickly put on a redingote, and in a quarter of an hour I am at her door. I knock once, and the aunt comes tiptoeing to open the door and tell me to come back in half an hour, for, having to take a bath, she was already naked in her tub.

"Damn it! one lie after another! The excuse is trumped up. I don't believe a word of it."

"Truly I am not lying, and if you promise to behave I will take you to her room on the fourth floor. She can say what she pleases to me afterward, I'll pay no attention."

"To her room? And she is in the bath? Are you deceiving me?"

"No. Follow me."

She goes up, I follow her. She opens a door, she pushes me in, then she shuts it, and I see La Charpillon stark naked in the tub; pretending to think that it is her aunt, she asks her to bring her towels. She was in the most seductive position that love could ask; but no sooner has she seen me than she crouches down and gives a cry.

"Don't cry out, for I am nobody's dupe. Be still."

"Go away."

"No. Let me recover myself."

"Go away, I say."

"Be quiet, and fear no violence."

"My aunt shall pay me for this."

"She is an excellent woman and she will find a true friend in me. I will not touch you, but straighten up."

"What! Straighten up?"

"Take the position you were in when I entered."

"Certainly not, and I beg you to leave."

By dint of trying to double up more effectively, she displayed an even more seductive picture, pretending to trust in gentleness to persuade me to go, after seeing that anger had failed her. But when, though I promised not to touch her, she saw me resolved to quench as well as I could the fire she knew she had kindled in my soul, she turned her back on me, determined that I should neither think that she could take pleasure in seeing me, nor myself get any pleasure from the thought. I knew all this, but needing to recover my sanity, I had to sink to anything to appease my senses, and I was not sorry to see the cheat take effect very quickly. Just then the aunt came in, and I left without saying a word, rather glad to have acquired a feeling of contempt which assured me that feelings of love would have no more power over me.

The aunt overtook me at the door, and, asking me if I was pleased, told me to step into the parlor.

"Yes," I said, "very pleased to have made your acquaintance, and here is your reward."

So saying, I threw her a hundred-pound bank note to make her "balm of life" with, not bothering to wait for the receipt which she offered to give me. I was not brazen enough to give her nothing, whereas the ba..[11] was more than sufficiently so to guess that I should not dare leave her unrewarded.

Back at home, after thoroughly considering what had happened and deciding that I was the victor, I rejoiced; and, recovering all my good humor, I felt certain that I would never again set foot in the house of those women. There were seven of them, counting two maidservants. Their need to subsist had led them to adopt the course of rejecting no means to that end, and when in their councils they concluded that they had to employ men, they confided in the three I have named, who in their turn would have had no means of subsistence without them.

Thinking only of amusing myself, going to the theaters, to the taverns in the neighborhood of London, and to the boarding school where my daughter was, I happened to meet her at Vauxhall with her aunt and Goudar, five or six days after the scene by the bathtub. I tried to avoid her, but she at once came up to me, gaily reproaching me for my bad manners. I answered her harshly; but, pretending not to notice it, she entered an arbor, inviting me to drink a cup of tea with her. I said that I felt more inclined to sup, and she replied that in that case it was she who would accept an invitation from me. I am willing; I order for four, and to all appearances we are the best of friends. Her remarks, her gaiety, her charms, the power of which I had experienced, once again displaying themselves before my weak soul, now all the weaker from drink, I propose a stroll in the darker walks, hoping, I add, that she will not treat me as she had treated His Lordship. She replies sweetly enough, and with an appearance of sincerity which very nearly deceived me, that she wanted to be mine entirely and in the light; but that first she must have the satisfaction of seeing me call on her every day, like a true friend of the household.

"You shall see me there without fail, but now come into the walk and give me a little proof of your intentions."

"No! Absolutely not!"

At that I left her, refusing to take her home, and I went home to bed a little tipsy.

The next morning I heartily congratulated myself on her not having taken me at my word. The power which the creature had gained over me was irresistible and I was convinced that I had no other means of saving myself from becoming her dupe except either not to see her or to continue to see her and renounce enjoying her charms. The second course seeming to me impossible, I decided on the first; but the wench had determined not to let me put it into practice. The way in which she went about accomplishing her purpose must have been the result of her regular discussions with her whole infamous coterie.[12]

At home a few days after the little supper at Vauxhall, I saw before me the Chevalier Goudar, who began by congratulating me on my wise decision to see no more of the Augspurghers.

"For," he said, "if you had continued to go there you would have fallen more and more in love with the girl, and she would have reduced you to beggary."

"Then you must think me a great fool. If I had found her accommodating, she would have found me grateful, but without going beyond my means in the proofs of it I should have given her; and if I had found her cruel I could any day have done what I have done already, and so she would never have reduced me, as you think, to beggary."

"Then you are firmly resolved not to see her again?"

"Yes, firmly."

"Then you are no longer in love with her?"

"I was in love with her, and I have learned how to cure myself of it. In a few days I shall have forgotten her completely. I was no longer thinking of her when the devil contrived that I should meet the four of you in Vauxhall."

"There you are! Be persuaded that the true way to be cured of an unhappy love is not to flee the seductive object, for, when one lives in the same country, it is only too easy to cross her path everywhere."

"What other way is there?"

"Enjoying her. It is possible that La Charpillon does not love you; but you are rich, and she has nothing. You could have had her for a certain sum of money, and you would have been far more pleasantly cured when you had found her unworthy of your constancy, for, after all, you know what she is."

"I would gladly have taken that course if I had not clearly seen her plan."

"You would have frustrated it by coming to an agreement with her. You should never have paid in advance! I know the whole story."

"What can you know?"

"I know that she has cost you a hundred guineas, and that you have not had a single kiss from her. For that amount you could have had her in bed. She herself boasts of having tricked you."

"She lies. I made her aunt a present of the amount, which she needs, she tells me, to make her fortune."

"Yes, to compound her 'balm of life'; but admit that, but for her niece, she would never have received it."

"I admit it; but tell me, please, what leads you to come to say these things to me today, you who are of her coterie?"

"What brings me here, I swear to you, is nothing but friendship for you, and as for your saying that I am of her coterie, I will set you right by telling you the incident which made me acquainted with the girl, and with her mother, her grandmother, and her two aunts.

"Sixteen months ago," he went on, "happening to be at Vauxhall, I saw the Venetian Ambassador, the Procurator Morosini, walking alone. He had just arrived to congratulate the King on his accession to the throne in the name of his Republic. Seeing His Excellency delighting in watching the young London beauties who were strolling here and there, it occurred to me to go to him and say that all those beauties were at his command and that he had only to throw his handkerchief at whichever one of them he was pleased to choose. My remark making him laugh, and continuing to stroll with me while I assured him that I was not joking, he asked me, pointing to a girl, if he could have her too.

914

Not knowing her, I told him to continue his stroll, saying that I would join him presently with the answer. Having no time to lose, and certain, from her manner, that I was not about to make my proposal to a Vestal, I approach the girl and the lady who was with her, and I tell her that the Ambassador is in love with her and that I will bring him to her if she feels inclined to encourage his newborn passion. The aunt says that a nobleman of his rank could only honor her house if he came to it to make her niece's acquaintance. They give me their name and address, and the thing is done. I leave them, and before rejoining the Ambassador I happen upon a great connoisseur whom I ask who a certain Mademoiselle Charpillon, of Denmark Street, Soho, may be."

"So it was La Charpillon?"

"None other. He tells me that she is a Swiss girl who is not yet a public woman but who to all appearances soon will be, for she is not rich and has a numerous family, all females. I at once overtake the Venetian, and telling him that his business is done, I ask him at what hour on the next day I may introduce him to the beauty, warning him that, since she has a mother and aunts, she will not receive him alone. He has no objection to that; he is even glad that she is not a public woman. He appoints an hour at which I am to go with him, incognito, in a hackney carriage, and I leave him. After informing the girl and her aunt of the hour, and adding that she must pretend not to know who he is, I go home. The next day I introduced him to them, and after spending an hour in perfectly decent conversation with the girl and her aunt without making any proposal, we left. On the way the Ambassador told me that he wanted to have her on the conditions which he would give me at his residence the next day in writing, and not otherwise.

"The conditions were that Mademoiselle should go to live in a small furnished house, which would cost her nothing and in which she was to receive no one. His Excellency would arrange for her to receive fifty guineas a month and would pay for supper whenever he chose to go to sleep with her. He instructed me to find him the house, if the contract, which must be signed by the girl's mother, was agreed to, and to act quickly. In three days I did and settled everything, but demanding a written agreement from the mother that she would give me her daughter for one night after the departure of the Ambassador, who it was known would remain in London only a year."

At this point Goudar took from his pocket the agreement, which I read and reread with as much surprise as pleasure. Then he went on as follows:

"At the end of the year the Ambassador left, and the girl was free. She had Lord Baltimore,[13] Lord Grosvenor,[14] the Portuguese Envoy Saa, and several others, but none of them as his acknowledged mistress. I press the mother to make her give me a night, as she had agreed to do in writing; but she refuses to take me seriously, and the girl, who does not love me, laughs in my face. I cannot have her arrested, for she has not reached the required age; but in a few days I shall obtain a warrant for her mother's arrest, and all London will laugh. Now you know why I constantly go to her house; but you are wrong if you believe that I am involved in the plots which are hatched here. However, I can assure you that they are considering how to get you into their toils again, and that they will succeed if you are not very careful."

"Tell the mother that I have another hundred guineas at her disposal if she can arrange for me to spend a night with her daughter."

"Do you really mean that?"

"I do indeed, but I will not pay the money until the thing is done."

"That is the one sure way not to be taken in. I undertake the commission with pleasure."

I kept the brazen scoundrel to dinner with me. He was a man who, in the sort of life I was leading in London, could not but be useful to me. He knew everything, and he told me any number of amorous anecdotes which I was very glad to hear. He was, besides, known as the author of several works[15] which, though bad, showed that he had a certain wit. He was then writing his *Chinese Spy*, composing five or six letters a day at the coffeehouses at which he chanced to be. I amused myself by writing a number of them[16] for him, for which he was most grateful to me. The reader will see in what condition I found him some years later in Naples.

No later than the next day I am surprised in my room by La Charpillon herself, who, not gay but serious, tells me that she has not come for breakfast but to demand an explanation from me; at the same time she introduces Miss Lorenzi,[17] I bow to her.

"What explanation do you want, Mademoiselle?"

At these words Miss Lorenzi thinks it proper to leave us alone. She was ugly. It was the first time that I had seen her. I told Jarba to bring her breakfast and to tell the portress that I was at home to no one.

"Is it true, Monsieur, that you sent the Chevalier Goudar to tell my mother that you would give her a hundred guineas for a night with me?"

"It is true. Are a hundred guineas not enough?"

"I will thank you not to jest. It is not a question of bargaining. It is a question of learning if you think you have the right to insult me, and if you think I am one to put up with it."

"If you feel that you have been insulted I admit that I am in the wrong; but I did not expect as much. To whom was I to address myself? For directly to you leads to nothing. You are too fond of deceiving, and you exult only when you break your word."

"I told you that you should never have me either by violence or for money, but only when you have made me fall in love with you by your attentions. Now prove to me that I have failed to keep my word to you. It is you who have failed in your duty to me by your trick of surprising me when I was in the bath, and yesterday by sending to ask my mother to deliver me over to your brutality. Only a scoundrel would undertake that errand for you."

"Goudar a scoundrel? He is your best friend. You know that he loves you, and that he procured the Ambassador for you only in the hope of having you. The written agreement which is in his possession proves your wrongdoing. You are in debt to him. Pay him, and then call him a scoundrel if you can find yourself innocent by some other ethics than his. Do not cry, Mademoiselle, for I know the source of your tears. It is impure."

"You do not know it. I tell you I love you; and it is a cruel thing for me to find myself treated in this way by you."

"If you love me, you have chosen a very poor way to make me believe it."

"As you have to convince me of your esteem. You began with me as you would have done with a prostitute, and yesterday as if I were an animal without a will of my own, the mere slave of my mother. It seems to me that if you had any consideration you should at least have asked me directly, and not by the mouth of a vile go-between but in writing. I would have[18] answered you in writing, and then there would have been no possibility of deceit."

"Imagine that I did write to you; what would your answer have been?"

"Observe my frankness. I would have promised to satisfy you, without a word about the hundred guineas, simply on condition that you would pay court to me for only two weeks, coming to my house and never asking the slightest favor of me. We should have laughed, you would have become one of the family, we should have gone to promenades and plays together, and at last, having made me madly in love with you, you would have had me in your arms as you would have deserved to have me, not from compliance but from love. I am astonished that a man like you can be content that a girl whom he loves should give herself to him as an act of compliance. Do you not consider it humiliating, on the one side as well as on the other? I feel ashamed when I think—and I admit it to you—that I have never yet been moved by more than compliance. Alas for me! Yet I feel that I was born to love, and I believed that you were the man whom heaven had sent to England to make me happy. You have done the very opposite. No man has ever seen me cry. You have even made me unhappy at home, for my mother will never have the sum you offered her, even if it were to cost me only one kiss."

"I am truly sorry to have hurt you; but I see no way of mending it."

"Come to our house; that will mend it; and keep your money, which I despise. If you love me, come and conquer me like a reasonable lover and not like a brute; I will help you do it, for you must be sure now that I love you."

This harangue won me over. I gave her my word that I would pay court to her every day and be for her what she wanted me to be; but not for longer than the time she had prescribed. She confirmed her promise, and her brow cleared. She rose, and when I asked her to give me one kiss as a pledge of her good faith, she said with a laugh that I must not begin by violating our conditions. I agreed, and I begged her pardon. She left me in love, and hence full of repentance for all my past conduct toward her. *Amare et sapere vix deo conceditur* ("To love and be wise is scarcely granted to a god").[19]

The adjurations and the arguments to which she treated me, and of which the account I have just given is but a feeble representation, would perhaps have had no power if she had sent them to me in a letter; but delivered *viva voce* they could not but put me in chains. In a letter I should have seen neither her tears nor her captivating features, which all pleaded for her before a judge already corrupted by the God of Love. I began going to see her late in the afternoon of that same day, and in the reception I was given, instead of seeing that they were mocking me in my defeat, I thought I heard applause for my heroism.

Quel che l'uom vede Amor gli fa invisibile
E l'invisibil fa veder Amore.

("Love makes what a man sees invisible, and Love makes him see what is invisible.")[20]

I spent the whole of the two weeks without ever taking her hand to kiss it, and I never entered her house without bringing her a costly present, which she made of inestimable value by her enchanting grace and her show of boundless gratitude. In addition, to make the time pass more quickly I arranged some diversion every day, either at one of the theaters or on the outskirts of London. The two weeks must have cost me at least four hundred guineas. The last day finally came.

In the morning I timidly asked her, in her mother's presence, if she intended to spend the night in my house, or at home in her own bed with me. Her mother replied that we would decide that after supper. I agreed, not daring to point out to her that at my house the supper would have been tastier, and hence more costly and more inviting to love.

After supper the mother told me to leave with the company and to come back later. Although laughing to myself at this secrecy, I obeyed; and, returning, here I am at last in the parlor, where I see the mother and the daughter and a bed on the floor. I am free at last of any fear of being duped; but I am surprised that the mother, wishing me good night, asks me if I will pay the hundred guineas in advance.

"For shame!" said her daughter.

And the mother left. We locked the door.

It was the moment when my love was to begin its escape from slavery. So I go to her with open arms, but, though without harshness, she draws away, asking me to get into bed first while she makes ready to do likewise. I yield to her will, I undress, I get into bed, and, on fire with love, I see her undress, and when she has nothing on but her shift I see her blow out the candles.

Left in darkness, I complain, I say that it is impossible, she replies that she can sleep only in the dark. I think it base, but I control myself. Knowing that modesty could not enter in, I begin to foresee all the resistances whose purpose is to sour the pleasures of love, but I hope to overcome them.

No sooner do I feel that she is in bed than I approach to clasp her in my arms, but I find her worse than dressed. Crouched in her long shift, her arms crossed, and her head buried in her bosom, she let me talk as much as I will and never answers a word. When, tired of talking, I determine to act, she remains motionless in the same position and defies me to do it. I thought her behavior was meant to be a joke; but at last I am convinced that it is nothing of the sort. I see that I am duped, a fool, the most contemptible of men, as I see that the girl is the vilest of whores.

In such a situation love easily becomes rage. I lay hold of her as if she were a bolt of goods, but I can accomplish nothing; it seems to me that her accursed shift is the reason for it, and I succeed in tearing it open behind, from the top to her buttocks; thereupon, my hands becoming claws, I count on the most brutal violence on my part, but all my efforts were vain. I made up my mind to stop when I found my strength exhausted and when, having grasped her neck in one hand, I felt a strong temptation to strangle her.

Cruel night, heartbreaking night, during which I talked to the monster in every possible key: gentleness, anger, reasonableness, remonstration, threats, rage, despair, prayers, tears, vilification, atrocious insults. She resisted me for three whole hours without ever answering me, and without ever straightening up except once to prevent me from doing something which would in a way have avenged me.

At three o'clock in the morning, amazed, stupefied, feeling my head on fire, I decided to dress in the dark. I opened the door to the parlor, but finding the street door locked, I raised a row, and a maidservant came to open it for me. I walked home, accompanied by a night watchman[21] whom I went to Soho Square to find. I at once got into bed, but irritated Nature avenged herself by refusing me the rest I needed. When it grew light I took a cup of chocolate, which my stomach refused to keep down, and an hour later my shivering announced a fever which did not subside until the next day, leaving me unable to move my limbs. Ordered to stay in bed and to diet, I was sure that I should recover my strength in a few days; but what was balm to my soul was my certainty that I was cured of my insane love, for I felt that I was free from any thought of revenge. Shame had made me loathe myself.

The morning on which I had succumbed to the fever, I had ordered my manservant to shut my door to everyone, to announce no visitors to me, and to put any letters which might come for me into my desk, for I did not want to read them until I had recovered my health. It was on the fourth day that, feeling a little better, I asked Jarba for my letters. Among those which had come by post I find one from Pauline, who writes me from Madrid that Clairmont had saved her life in crossing a river, and that, not thinking she could find another servant as faithful, she had decided to keep him until she reached Lisbon, whence she would send him back to me by sea. At the time I thought she had done well; but as it turned out she caused me to lose Clairmont. I learned four months later that the ship on which he had taken passage had been wrecked, and, not seeing him again, I believed, as I believe today, that he was drowned.

Among the letters which had come by the "penny post"[22] I found two from La Charpillon's mother and one from herself. In the first of the two letters which the infamous mother wrote me on the morning after the night I had spent with her daughter, she told me, not knowing that I was ill, that her daughter was in bed with a high fever and covered with bruises from the blows I had given her, which obliged her to sue me in court. In the second letter, written the next day, she said she had learned that I was ill like her daughter and that she was sorry to hear it, her daughter herself having admitted to her that I might have reason to complain of her, but that she would justify herself at our first interview. The letter from La Charpillon was written on the third day. She said she confessed that she had been so much in the wrong that she was surprised I had not strangled her when I had her by the neck, and she swore that she would not have resisted it, for such was her duty in the cruel dilemma in which she had found herself. She said that, feeling certain that I had resolved not to go to her house again, she begged me to receive her at mine once only, since she was eager to inform me of something which would be of interest to me and which she could communicate to me only by word of mouth. In a note which Goudar had written me that morning at my door, he said that he had something to say to me and that he would come back at noon. I at once ordered him admitted.

The extraordinary man began by amazing me with a detailed account of all that had happened to me with La Charpillon during the four hours she had spent in bed with me, even down to the torn shift and the moment when she thought I would strangle her. He said that he had been informed of the entire scene by her mother, to whom the girl had given an exact account of everything. He said that she had not had fever, but that it was true that her whole body was covered with black marks, obvious signs of the blows she had received, and that her mother's great regret was that she had not received the hundred guineas, which I would certainly have paid in advance if her daughter had insisted.

"She would have had them in the morning," I said, "if she had been amenable."

"She had sworn to her mother that she would not be, and do not hope to have her without her mother's consent."

"But why does she not consent?"

"Because she maintains that as soon as you have enjoyed her you will leave her."

"That might be so; but after I had rewarded her adequately, whereas now she is left without being able to hope for anything more."

"Is that your firm resolve?"

"Most firm."

"It is your best course; but I want to show you something which will surprise you. We shall meet again in an hour."

An hour later he comes back, followed by a porter who brought an armchair[23] covered by a piece of cloth up to my room. As soon as we were alone Goudar uncovered the chair and asked me if I would like to buy it. I replied that I should not know what to do with it, besides which it was an unattractive piece of furniture.

"Nevertheless," he said, "the price asked for it is a hundred guineas."

I reply with a laugh that I would not give three for it, and this is what he then said to me:

"The chair you see here has five springs, all of which operate at the same time as soon as a person sits down in it. Their action is very rapid. Two seize the person's two arms and hold them fast; two more, lower down, take hold of his legs, spreading them as far apart as possible, and the fifth raises the back of the seat in such a way that it forces the seated person onto his coccyx."

After telling me this, Goudar sits down, the springs operate, and I see him held by the arms, and otherwise in the same position in which an obstetrician would put a woman whose labor he wanted to make easy.

922

"Get La Charpillon to sit here," he said, "and your business is done."

After laughing my fill, I tell him I do not want to buy it but that he will do me a favor if he will leave it[24] with me for only a day.

"Not even an hour unless you buy it, and the owner of the contrivance is waiting for me a hundred paces from here."

"Then return it to him and come back for dinner."

He told me what I had to do at the back of the chair to make the springs return to their places and so set him free. He covered it with the cloth again, he summoned the porter, and he left.

The action was infallible, and it was not avarice which kept me from buying the contrivance, for it must have cost its owner far more, but the fear which it inspired in me after I reflected a little. The crime could have cost me my life in the view of English judges, and besides I could not have brought myself deliberately to obtain possession of La Charpillon by force, still less by the action of this formidable contrivance, which would have made her die of fear.

At dinner I told Goudar that, La Charpillon having proposed to pay me a visit, I should have liked to keep the mechanical chair to convince her that I could have had my will of her if I had wanted to. I showed him the letter she had written me, and he advised me to let her pay the visit, if only for curiosity's sake.

Feeling in no hurry to receive the wench with those black marks on her face and bosom, which she would only have paraded to make me blush for my brutal fury, I spent eight or ten days without making up my mind to receive her, Goudar coming every day to inform me of the results of the councils held by the crew of females who were resolved to live only by trickery. He told me that La Charpillon's grandmother was a Bernese woman who had taken the name of Augspurgher without any right to it, being only the mistress of a citizen so named, by whom she had had four daughters; La Charpillon's mother was the youngest of them. This youngest daughter, who was pretty enough, having indulged in conduct not consonant with the wise regulations of the Swiss Government, had been the cause of a decree of exile from the canton for the entire family, which had gone to settle in Franche-Comté,[25] where they had lived for a time on the profits of the "balm of life," the manufacture of which the grandmother directed.

"It was there that La Charpillon was born. Her mother gave her that name, I do not know why, saying that her father was a Count of Boulainvilliers,[26] whose mistress she had been for three months.

La Charpillon becoming pretty, her mother concluded that her great good fortune awaited her in Paris, and went there to live; but four years later, seeing that the sale of her balm did not suffice to support her, that La Charpillon, being still too young, did not find a man of substance to keep her, and that the debts she had incurred threatened her with prison, she decided to go to live in London, so advised by Monsieur Rostaing, who had become her lover and who, also burdened with debts, had to flee from France. Five or six months after her arrival in London the mother nearly died from the overdose of mercury she took to cure her of the cruel disease with which Rostaing admits that he infected her.

"Coumon is a Languedocian, an intimate friend of Rostaing's, who serves him, as he does the whole family, by bringing dupes whom he picks up in the coffeehouses of London to their house for games at whist. The profit is always honorably and equally divided into six parts; but what La Charpillon earns from the temporary relations into which she enters in the great nocturnal gatherings in the gardens of London is buried in secrecy; however, I know that her mother supports Rostaing."

Such is the story I learned from Goudar. The man introduced me to the most celebrated courtesans in London, and above all to Kitty Fisher,[27] who was beginning to go out of fashion. In a potshop where we were drinking a bottle of strong beer,[28] which is better than wine, he introduced me to a girl who served there, sixteen years of age, whom I thought a wonder of nature. She was Irish and a Catholic, and her name was Sarah.[29] I wanted to have her, but he would never permit it. He himself was trying to get possession of her, and he told me he was jealous of her. He did in fact get possession of her some time later, and the following year he left England with her. Then he married her. She is the same Sarah Goudar who shone at Naples, Florence, Venice, and elsewhere, always with him, and of whom I will speak four or five years hence. He had hatched the scheme of giving her to Louis XV, putting an end to the domination of Madame Du Barry, but a *lettre de cachet*[30] sent him running. Happy days of the *lettre de cachet*, alas, you are gone forever!

When La Charpillon, after looking in vain for a reply to her last letter, saw two weeks pass without hearing a word about me, she resolved to return to the assault. This must have been the result of an extremely secret council, for Goudar had told me nothing about it.

She was announced as having arrived at my door alone in a sedan chair, a thing so extraordinary that I at once decided to receive her. I saw her before me just as I was taking chocolate; I do not rise, I do not offer her any; but she modestly asks me for some, sitting down beside me and putting out her face for me to kiss, which she had never done before. I turn my head away, but this utterly unexpected refusal does not disconcert her:

"It is," she says, "these still visible marks from the blows you gave me which make my face distasteful to you."

"You lie, I never struck you."

"It makes no difference, your tiger's claws left bruises all over my body. Look, for you run no risk that what you see will have the power to seduce you. Besides, it is nothing you have not seen before."

So saying, the scheming wench rises and shows me the whole surface of her body marked here and there with bruises which were still livid despite their age. Coward that I was, why did I not turn my eyes away? Because she was beautiful, and because I loved her charms, and because charms would not deserve their name if they were not more powerful than a man's reason. I pretended to look only at the bruises. Fool that I was! She already knew that I was tasting the poison and even gulping it down; but suddenly she rearranges her clothing and sits down beside me again, sure that I wished the exhibition would continue longer; but I control myself and I say coldly that it had been her own fault if I had hurt her so badly, and that this was so true that I could not even be sure that I had done it.

"I know," she said, "that it is all my fault, for if I had been affectionate, as I ought to have been, I could now show you only the traces of kisses; but repentance blots out crime. I come to ask your forgiveness. May I hope for it?"

"You have it already. I hold nothing against you, and it is I who repent; but I have not yet been able to forgive myself. That is all. Now that you know all, you can leave and cease both to count on me and to trouble my peace in future."

"It shall be as you wish; I know all, it is true; but it is you who do not know all, and you shall know it, if you will permit me to spend another half hour with you."

"Since I have nothing to do, you may stay and say what you have to say."

Despite the haughty role which reason and honor laid it upon me to play, I was greatly touched and, what is far worse, I felt inclined to believe that the girl had come to me again not to deceive me but to persuade me that she loved me, and that she wanted at last to deserve my becoming her fond lover. The speech she made to tell me what I did not know required no more than a quarter of an hour, and she used two, constantly interrupting it by tears and countless digressions. The gist of it was that her mother had made her swear by her soul's salvation that she would spend the night with me as she had spent it, and that she had obeyed her. She offered to be mine as she had been Signor Morosini's, living with me, seeing no more of her mother or any of her relatives, and visiting no one except the people I wanted her to visit, while I was to allow her a certain sum each month, which she would turn over to her mother to keep her from troubling her with actions at law, since she was not old enough to claim independence.

She dined with me, and she made this proposal toward nightfall, when, having seen her listen unprotestingly while I said everything to her that she deserved to hear, I had become calm and resolved to expose myself to temptation once again. A little while before she left I said to her that we could live together as she had proposed, but that I absolutely insisted on sealing the bargain with her mother, and so she should see me at her house the next day. I saw that she was surprised.

It is clear that she would that day have granted me anything I could desire, and that in consequence there would have been no question of resistance in the future and that I should have been safe from any trickery. Then why did I not do what was no less than a duty I owed to myself? Because love, which makes a man a fool, persuaded me that, having that day been the creature's judge, it would have been base in me if I had gone on to become her lover. She must have left with a feeling of contempt and a determination to avenge herself for my coldness. But a man in love cannot see his mistakes until he is no longer in love. Goudar was amazed the next day when I told him of her visit. I asked him to find me a small furnished house for rent by the month in Chelsea, and he undertook to do so. That evening I went to see the scheming wench at her house, but in a sober mood, of the absurdity of which she must have been fully aware. As she was alone with her mother, I hastened to tell the latter my plan: a house in Chelsea, to which her daughter would go to live and in which I should be the master, and fifty guineas a month for her to use as she saw fit.

"I do not care to know," the mother replied, "what sum you will give her a month; but I insist that when she leaves my custody to live elsewhere she shall give me the hundred guineas she should have received from you when you went to bed with her."

I replied that she would give them to her. The girl said that, while the house was being found, she hoped that I would come to see her. I promised I would do so.

No later than the next day Goudar came to tell me that there were a score of houses for rent in Chelsea, and that I should do well to go there with him and have the pleasure of choosing. We went, I chose, and I paid ten guineas in advance for a month, taking a receipt and obtaining acceptance of all the conditions I wanted to stipulate. In the afternoon of the same day I went to seal the bargain with the mother in the daughter's presence, making them both sign the agreement, whereupon I told the daughter to pack her things and come with me. She quickly filled a trunk with her clothes, I had it taken to my new house in a hackney carriage, and a half hour later she appears, ready to leave with me. The mother asks me for the hundred guineas, I give them to her, having no fear of being tricked, for all the girl's possessions were already in my house. We leave, and we arrive in Chelsea, where she declares the house very much to her liking. We take a stroll until nightfall, we talk, we sup in high spirits, then we go to bed, where she grants me some favors sweetly enough, but as soon as I want to proceed to the heart of the matter I am disappointed to encounter difficulties. She alleges reasons of nature, I reply that I do not consider that condition repellent enough to keep me from proving my love to her; but she resists, raising objections which, though groundless, her sweetness and her caresses persuade me to admit, and she puts me to sleep.

On waking in the morning and seeing her sleeping, it occurs to me to convince myself that she had not been lying, and I quickly unlace what prevented me from seeing; she wakes and tries to stop me, but it was too late. I gently reproach her for deceiving me, and she sees me ready to forgive her and my love eager to confirm her pardon; but it is she who refuses to forgive me for having taken her by surprise. She is angry, I try to calm her, and at the same time to force her to yield, she will not, she opposes force to force, and, knowing her tricks, I determine to make an end, but calling her all the names she deserved. She begins to dress, laughing at me so impertinently I am driven to slap her face and give her a kick which knocks her out of the bed; she screams, she stamps her feet, the caretaker comes up, she opens the door to him, she speaks to him in English, with blood streaming from her nose. The man who, as my good luck would have it, spoke Italian, told me that she wanted to leave, and that he advised me not to try to stop her, for she could lodge a very serious complaint, in which case he would have to testify against me. I replied that she could go to the devil if she pleased. She then finished dressing, and after staunching the blood and washing her face, she left in a sedan chair. I spent a long hour there without moving, unable to decide upon anything. I pronounced myself unworthy to live, and I found the girl's behavior incomprehensible and incredible. I finally decided to have the scheming wench's trunk put in a hackney carriage and to go back to my house, where, overwhelmed by melancholy, I went to bed after ordering my door closed to all visitors.

I spent twenty-four hours in reflections, all of which ended by convincing me of my mistakes and making me despise myself. I believe that what follows after a long period of despising oneself is a despair which leads to suicide.

Just as I was going out, Goudar arrived and told me to go back upstairs, for he had something important to say to me. After telling me that La Charpillon was at home,[31] and, having one cheek swollen and black, let no one see her, he advised me to send her her trunk and to give up any claims I might have upon her mother, for she was in the right and determined to ruin me by a calumny which could both ruin me and cost me my life. The reader can easily imagine its nature,[32] and everyone knows how easy it is to make it effectual in London. He said that he had been urged by the mother herself, who did not want to injure me, to act as mediator. After spending the whole day with the man, complaining to the top of my bent like the utter fool I was, I told him to assure the mother that I had no intention of keeping her daughter's trunk, but that I wanted to know if she would have the courage to receive it from me in person.

He undertook to deliver my message, but rightly saying that he felt sorry for me. He said that I was about to walk into their toils again, and that he pitied me; but I did not believe that she would have the courage to receive me, for, according to the agreement she had signed, she would at least have to give me back a hundred guineas; but, contrary to my expectation, Goudar came and reported with a laugh that Madame Augspurgher hoped that I would always continue to be the good friend of her house. I went there at nightfall, I had the trunk put in her parlor, and I spent an hour there without ever opening my mouth, looking at La Charpillon, who was sewing and who now and again pretended to dry her tears, who never raised her eyes to my face, and who two or three times loosened the bandage round her head so that I could see in what a state my slap had put her face.

I continued to go there every evening, always without speaking to her, until I saw that every sign of the damage I had done her was gone. During those five or six days my repentance for having had the temerity to disfigure her produced upon my too kindly soul the fatal effect of leading me to forget all her misdeeds and making me so much in love with her that, had she but known it, she could have stripped me of all I had and reduced me to beggary.

Seeing her prettiness restored, and dying to have her in my arms once again, sweet and caressing as I had had her, even though it had been imperfectly, I sent her a magnificent pier glass made in one piece, and a tea and coffee service for twelve of Dresden china, writing her a loving note in which I called myself the basest of men. She replied that she expected me for supper alone in her room, when she would give me, as I deserved, the most unmistakable tokens of her fond gratitude.

Certain that my good fortune now awaited me, I thought I saw that I should long since have attained it if I had been clever enough to attack her on the side of sentiment. In the blind intoxication of enthusiasm, I decided to put in her hands the two bills of exchange for six thousand francs which Bolomay had made over to my order and which gave me the right to send her mother and her aunts to prison.

Enchanted by the happiness which awaited me and by the heroic feelings which made me worthy of it, I go to her house at supper-time, and I am at once very glad not to see the two sharpers, whom I mortally hated. She receives me in the parlor, her mother being present, and I see with pleasure the pier glass over the fireplace and the Dresden china service set out in order on the mantelpiece. After countless fond expressions, she invites me to go up to her room, and her mother wishes us a happy night. We go up, and after a suffi-ciently appetizing supper, I take the two bills of exchange from my portfolio and tell her the whole story of them. I end by saying that I am putting them[33] in her hands to make her certain that, as soon as she has decided to be my mistress without reservations, I will endorse them to her order, and to assure her that I am far from thinking of using them to avenge myself for the base treatment I had received from her mother and her aunts. I only stipulate that she shall promise me that they will not leave her hands. She praises my generous act in the highest terms, she promises everything, and she goes and puts them in her jewel case. After that I think I may begin to give her proofs of my passion, and I find her gentle; but as soon as I try to persuade her to crown my flame, she resists, she presses me to her bosom, and she commands her tears to flow. I control myself. I ask her if she will change her mind in bed, she sighs, then she says no. I was not stricken dumb, I was entirely deprived of the power of speech. A quarter of an hour later I rose, and, with an appearance of the greatest calm, I took my cloak, my hat, and my sword.

"What!" she said. "Do you not want to spend the night with me?"

"No."

"Shall we see each other tomorrow?"

"I hope so. Good-by."

I left that accursed house, and I went home to bed.

CHAPTER XII[1]

Continuation of the preceding chapter,
but far stranger.

The next morning at eight o'clock Jarba announces her.

"She has dismissed her chairmen," he says.

"Say that I am asleep and tell her to go away."

But just then she comes in, and Jarba leaves us.

"Be so good," I say quietly, "as to give me back the two bills of exchange which I put in your hands last night."

"I haven't them with me; but why do you want me to give them back?"

At this question, which could only be answered by an explanation in full, I demolished the dike by which the black humor which was poisoning me was confined to the region about my heart. It escaped like a torrent, manifesting itself in invectives and terrible threats. It was an explosion which continued for a long time, and which my nature needed to preserve my life. When, disgracing my reason, my tears began to flow, she seized the opportunity to tell me that she had promised her mother that she would never give herself to anyone in her own house, and that she had now come to mine only to convince me that she loved me and that her desires were equal to those I felt, and indeed she would never leave it, if such was my wish.

The reader who thinks that, at this declaration, all my anger should have vanished, and that I should instantly have made myself sure of her sincerity and the submission inseparable from it, is mistaken. He does not know that the passage from irritated love to black anger is short and swift, while the passage from anger to love is long, slow, and difficult. The distance is the same; but when anger is seconded by indignation, a man becomes absolutely incapable of any fond feeling. To brute hatred indignation adds noble scorn, which, sprung from reason, strengthens him and makes him invincible. Its duration depends on his temperament. It does not yield until it no longer exists. My temperament was such that, in me, simple anger lasted only a moment: *irasci celerem tamen ut placabilis essem* ("I become angry quickly, even as I am quickly appeased"),[2] but when indignation has entered in, my proud reason has always made me inflexible until forgetfulness supervened to restore me to my original state.

When La Charpillon on that occasion offered herself completely to my desires, she knew, she was certain, that my anger or my pride would keep me from taking her at her word. This sort of knowledge, reader, is the daughter of philosophy in you and in me; but in a coquette it is the daughter of nature.

The young monster left me toward nightfall, to all appearances mortified, downcast, and disconsolate, saying only these few words:

"I hope you will come back to me as soon as you have come back to yourself."

She spent eight hours with me, during which she interrupted me only five or six times to deny suppositions on my part which were true but which it was vital to her not to let pass. I never troubled to have dinner brought, but it was so that I should not have to eat with her.

After she left I found myself in a condition in which my only need was to rest; but I took a bowl of broth, then I slept fairly well. On waking I found that I was calm, and, recollecting the previous day, I thought that La Charpillon had repented of her wrongdoing, of which I thought I had seen her convinced when she left. It seemed to me that I had become indifferent to her and to everything to do with her. Such was the state to which the God of Love brought me in London

Nel mezzo del cammin di nostra vita

("In the mid way of our life")[3]

at the age of thirty-eight. It was the end of the first act of my life. The second closed on my departure from Venice in 1783. The third will apparently close here,[4] where I am amusing myself writing these memoirs. The comedy will then have ended, and it will have had its three acts. If it is hissed, I hope that I shall not hear anyone tell me so; but I have not yet informed my reader of the last scene of this first act, and it is, I believe, the most interesting.

Chi ha messo il piè sull'amorosa pania
Cerchi rittrarlo, e non v'inveschi l'ale,
Che non è in somma amor se non insania
A giudizio de' savj universale.

("Let him who has set his foot on the birdlime of love try to draw it back, and not entangle his wings in it, for love is nothing but madness, according to the universal judgment of the wise.")[5]

I went to walk in the Green Park, where I saw Goudar coming to meet me. I needed the scoundrel. He said that he had come from La Charpillon's, where he had found everyone in high spirits, and that though he had several times brought the conversation around to me he had never succeeded in getting a word out of them. I told him that I despised her, together with her whole family, and he praised me. He came to dine with me, then we went to the Walsh[6] woman's, where the celebrated Kitty Fisher came to wait for the Duke of xx, who was to take her to a ball. She had on over a hundred thousand crowns' worth of diamonds. Goudar told me I could seize the opportunity to have her for ten guineas, but I did not want to do so. She was charming, but she spoke only English. Accustomed to loving only with all my senses, I could not indulge in love without including my sense of hearing. She left. La Walsh told us that it was at her house that she swallowed a hundred-pound bank note on a slice of buttered bread which Sir Richard Atkins,[7] brother of the beautiful Mrs. Pitt,[8] gave her. Thus did the Phryne[9] make a present to the Bank of London.[10] I spent an hour with Miss Kennedy, who had lived with the Venetian Secretary of Embassy Berlendis.[11] She became drunk and indulged in all sorts of wantonness; but the image of La Charpillon, which was always with me, left me no appetite for possessing the charming Irishwoman. I returned to my house, melancholy and discontented. It seemed to me that I ought to renounce La Charpillon for ever; but, in consideration of my own honor, I should not leave her with the victory or with reason to boast that she had got the two bills of exchange from me for nothing. I resolved to make her give them back to me, either willingly or by force. I had to find a way to do it; and here is what made me believe that I had found it.

Monsieur Malingan, at whose lodging I had made the infernal creature's acquaintance, came to invite me to dinner there. Since he had dined at my house more than once with his wife and daughter, I could not refuse him, the more so since he asked me to send him two dishes prepared by my excellent cook. However, I did not agree to go until I had asked him who the persons were whom he had invited. He named them, and, not knowing them, I promised

I would go. It was on the next day but one. I found there two young ladies from Liège, one of whom very soon interested me; it was she who introduced her husband, whom Malingan had not introduced to me, and another young man who I thought was paying court to the other lady, who she said was her cousin. The company being to my liking, I was hoping to spend a pleasant day, when, just after we all sat down at table, in comes La Charpillon, who gaily says to Madame Malingan that she would not have come to ask her for dinner if she had known she had so many guests. She was warmly received, and was given the place at my left; at my right was the lady from Liège whom I had already found very agreeable.

I saw that I was caught. If La Charpillon had arrived before dinner was served, I should have found some excuse to leave; but it was too late for that. The course I adopted all through the dinner was to disregard the intruder completely and to devote all my attention to the lady from Liège. After we rose from the table Malingan gave me his word of honor that he had not invited her, and I pretended to believe him.

The two ladies and gentlemen were to embark for Ostend three or four days later, and, speaking of their departure, the agreeable lady said that she was sorry to leave England without having seen Richmond.[12] I at once asked her to grant me the favor and the honor of showing it to her no later than the next day, and, not waiting for her to answer me, I invited her husband, her cousin, and, one after the other, the entire company, except La Charpillon, at whom I did not even look. The excursion was applauded and the invitation accepted.

"Two carriages seating four," I added, "will be ready tomorrow morning at eight o'clock, and there will be exactly eight of us."

"And I will make the ninth," said La Charpillon, fixing her eyes on my face with unexampled effrontery, "and I hope, Monsieur, that you will not turn me away."

"Certainly not, it would be impolite. I will precede you all on horseback."

"No, no! I will hold Mademoiselle Émilie on my lap."

She was Malingan's daughter. A quarter of an hour later I leave the drawing room to attend to something and, coming back, I encounter the brazen hussy, who says that I have insulted her most outrageously, and that I owe her amends or she will avenge herself.

"Begin," I said, "by giving me back my bills of exchange, and we will discuss the matter afterward."

934

"You shall have them tomorrow."

About ten o'clock I leave the company, after promising that I will not go on horseback and that the two carriages will be at Malingan's house, where we will all breakfast. I made all the arrangements accordingly.

The next morning after breakfast Malingan, his wife, his daughter, and the two gentlemen got into one carriage, and I had to get into the other with the two beautiful ladies and La Charpillon, who appeared to have become the married lady's intimate friend. The arrangement could not but put me in a bad humor. We arrived at Richmond in an hour and a quarter, and after ordering a good dinner we went to see the apartments, then the gardens, the weather being superb. It was autumn.

The informality of our stroll affording her the opportunity, La Charpillon comes up to me and says that she wants to give me back my bills of exchange at her house. At that I reproach her with her constant course of deceit, her base character, and her infamous behavior, I call her a who . . . ,[13] I name the men with whom she has been, I swear to her that I hate her, and that it is she who must fear my vengeance; but she was well versed in her trade, she let me talk, holding my arm and smiling, but asking me to speak softly, for I might be heard. I was heard, and I was glad of it.

At noon we went to dinner, and La Charpillon, sitting beside me, indulged in innumerable wanton words and gestures, all intended to make everyone believe that she was in love with me, and not caring if anyone thought she was hurt by the scorn which I showed for all her advances. She really made me angry, for no one could help concluding that I was a fool and that she was openly mocking me. I suffered a great deal at that dinner.

After dinner we returned to the garden, and La Charpillon, stubbornly determined to triumph, clings to my arm, and, knowing all the sites, after a few turns she takes me to the maze.[14] It was here that she wanted to put her powers to the test. She pulls me onto the grass with her, and launches a full-scale amorous attack, with expressions of passion and the fondest love. By displaying the most interesting part of her charms to my sight, she finally succeeded in seducing me; but I still do not know if it was love or a strong desire for revenge which determined me to surrender. However that may be, everything made me sure that she was to be mine, that she could not wait to prove it to me, and that she certainly had no idea of putting any obstacle in my way.

With this thought in mind, I become gentle and tender, I recant, I ask her a thousand pardons, I swear that I will no longer demand that she give me the bills of exchange, and that all that I possess is hers, and after these preliminaries, signed and confirmed by fiery kisses, I think I see that she herself invites me to gather the laurel of victory, but just at the very moment when I am certain that I shall possess her, she curvets and throws me out of the saddle.

"What now! What insane behavior!"

"Enough of this, my dear friend. I promise to spend the night at your house, in your arms."

She was still in them as she spoke the words; but my soul, my blood, the tumult of my heart left me unable to do anything but satisfy myself. Holding her clasped in my left arm with all the strength which the extreme of fury gave me, I take from my pocket a knife with a pointed blade, I unsheathe it with my teeth, and I put the point of it to her throat, which was bare except for a thin collar. I threaten to kill her if she moves.

"Do whatever you will. I ask you for nothing but my life; but after you have satisfied yourself I will not leave this place. I shall have to be taken to the carriage by force, and nothing shall stop me from telling the reason for it."

She did not need to threaten me, for I had recovered my reason the moment after the one which had decided me to cut her throat. I rose without answering her by a single word, and after picking up my knife, my hat, and my walking stick, I set out to find my way back from the bowling green[15] where I had been within a hair's-breadth of my ruin.

Can anyone believe that she followed me, that she took my arm, as if nothing had happened? It is impossible that a seventeen-year-old girl can be what she was without having gone through a hundred skirmishes of the same sort. Once the feeling of shame is overcome, she grows used to it, and she glories in it. When we rejoined the company I was asked if I had felt ill; but no one noticed the least change in her.

We returned to London, where, saying that I felt indisposed, I thanked the company and went home.

This episode made the strongest impression on my mind. I could not sleep. I knew beyond doubt that if I did not resolve to avoid every chance of seeing the girl I was absolutely lost. Her countenance cast a spell which I could not resist. So I decided not to see her again; but at the same time, ashamed of the weakness I had shown in entrusting the two bills of exchange to her and in letting myself be tricked every time she had promised to return them to me, I wrote her mother a note in which I advised her to force her daughter to send them back to me, or to prepare for proceedings on my part which would make her suffer.

After sending her the note I went out to distract myself, and after dining at a tavern I went to see my daughter at her boarding school, then I returned home, where Jarba handed me a sealed letter which had come by the "penny post." I open it, and I see that it is signed Augspurgher. It was the answer from La Charpillon's mother. Here is what it contained: "I am very much surprised that you should address yourself to me to obtain the two bills of exchange for six thousand French livres which you say you deposited with her. She has just told me that she will return them to you in person when you have grown wiser and have learned to respect her."

Reading this impertinent letter sent the blood to my head so violently that I forgot my morning's resolution. I put pistols in my pocket and I make my way to Denmark Street, Soho, intending to cane the wench into giving me back my letters. I had taken the pistols only to keep the upper hand of the two sharpers who supped there every night. I arrive in a fury, but I walk past the door, for I see the hairdresser waiting to be admitted. This hairdresser was a handsome young man who went every Saturday after supper to put up her hair in curl papers. Going to the nearest street corner, I stop, reflecting that I should do better to wait until the hairdresser was gone. Taking my stand just around the corner, a half hour later I see Rostaing and Coumon come out of the house, and I am very glad of it. It meant that supper was over. I hear eleven o'clock cried, and I am surprised that the hairdresser is staying so late. Three quarters of an hour later I see a maidservant come out with a candle in her hand, looking for something which must have fallen out of the window. I enter without compunction, I open the door to the parlor, which was two steps from the street door, and I see, in the words of Shakespeare, the "beast with the two backs"[16] stretched out on the sofa: La Charpillon and the hairdresser. On my appearance the wench gives a cry, her fancy man breaks away from her; but my stick begins descending on him without mercy or reprieve, and without leaving him time to rearrange his clothing. La Charpillon was trembling between the wall and the end of the sofa, not daring, by leaving there, to face the rain of blows from my stick, which might descend on her. The uproar brings the maids, then the aunts, then the paralytic mother; the hairdresser flees, and the three furies let fly at me with insults and imprecations which I find so unjustified that my righteous wrath descends on the furniture. The first objects I broke to pieces were the handsome pier glass and the china service I had given them. Their words angering me more and more, I smashed chairs to bits by hitting them against the floor; then, picking up my cane, I announced that I would break their heads open if they did not stop shouting. Quiet then fell.

Having thrown myself down on the sofa, for I was exhausted, I order the mother to give me my bills of exchange; but just then in comes the night watch.[17] To this night watch, which consists of a single man who walks about his district all night carrying a lantern and a long stick, is entrusted the safety and the peace of the whole vast city. There is one such everywhere. No one dares not to respect him. Putting three or four crowns into his hand, I told him to go away. He left, I shut the door, and, returning to the sofa, I again demanded my bills of exchange from Madame Augspurgher.

"I haven't them, ask my daughter for them."

"Send for her."

The two maids say that, when I began breaking up the chairs, she had fled by the street door, and that they did not know where she might have gone. At this news, the mother and the aunts are in tears:

"My daughter alone at midnight in the streets of London!"

"My niece is lost, where has she gone?"

"Accursed be the hour when you came to England to make us all wretched!"

Thinking of the terrified girl running through the streets at that hour, I tremble.

"Go," I say coldly to the two maids, "and look for her in the neighbors' houses, you will certainly find her. Come back and bring me news that she is safe, and you shall each have a guinea."

They went out, and one of the aunts followed to tell them where they might find her.

But when they saw that I was taking a part in the search for the girl, that I was alarmed by the danger in her running away, then it was that their complaints, their reproaches began again with all the more vigor. I remained there without a word, not only seeming to tell them that they were right, but on the way to being convinced myself that all the fault was mine. I waited impatiently for the maids to return. They finally arrive an hour after midnight. Breathless, and showing every sign of despair, they say they have searched everywhere, she is nowhere to be found. I give them two guineas nevertheless, and I remain there motionless and in terror, reflecting on what a dreadful part the horrible fear which my fury must have inspired in her might play in the disappearance of the unfortunate girl. How weak and stupid is a man in love!

Extremely affected by the disastrous turn of events, I do not hide my sincere repentance from the old cheats. I implore them to have her sought for everywhere as soon as the next day dawns, and to let me know instantly, so that I can hasten to beg her forgiveness on my knees and never see her again as long as I live. In addition I promise to pay for all the furniture I have broken, and to leave my bills of exchange in their hands, signing a receipt with my name. Having thus, to the eternal shame of my reason, made honorable amends to those whose souls laughed at honor, I left, promising two guineas to the maid who should bring me the news that the unfortunate girl had been found.

At the door I found the watch, who was waiting to see me home. Two o'clock had struck. I flung myself on my bed, where six hours of sleep, though broken by hideous phantasms and agonizing dreams, probably saved me from losing my reason.

At eight o'clock in the morning I hear a knocking, I run to the window, and I see one of my enemies' maids; with my heart pounding I shout that she is to be shown up, and I breathe again when I learn that Miss Charpillon had just come home by sedan chair, but in a pitiable condition. She had at once gone to bed.

"I came at once to tell you the news, not for the two guineas, but because I pity you."

The word "pity" takes me in at once; I give her the two guineas, I make her sit down near me, and I ask her to tell me all the details of her return. I feel certain that the maid is honest, that she has my interests at heart, and that if need be she will serve me faithfully. I am very far from suspecting that she may have an understanding with the mother. But how could I be so excessively stupid? It was because I needed to be so.

She began by telling me that her young mistress loved me and that she only played a part in deceiving me because her mother insisted on it.

"I know that, but where did she spend the night?"

"She took refuge with a shopwoman beyond Soho Square, where she spent the whole night, sitting uncomfortably in the shop. She has just gone to bed with a high fever. I am afraid it will have consequences, for she is in her critical days."

"That is not true, for with my own eyes I saw the hairdresser—"

"Oh, that makes no difference. He is not so particular."

"She is in love with him."

"I do not think so, though she often spends hours with him."

"And you tell me she loves me?"

"Oh, that has nothing to do with it."

"Tell her that I will go to spend the day at her bedside, and bring me her answer."

"I will send the other maid."

"No. She does not speak French."

She left, and, not having seen her reappear, at three o'clock in the afternoon I resolve to go myself to see how she is. Scarcely have I knocked once before her aunt comes to speak to me at the door and asks me not to come in, swearing that if I come in I will either kill or be killed. Her two friends were there, furiously angry with me, and the poor girl was delirious from a burning fever. She did nothing but cry out, "There is my murderer, there is Seingalt. He wants to kill me. Save me."

"In God's name, go away."

I go home, in despair and certain that I have been told the simple truth. Sunk in melancholy, I spend the whole day without eating, for I cannot swallow, and the whole night unable to sleep, with violent chills. I drank strong spirits, hoping to make myself drowsy. All was in vain; I vomited bile, I felt very weak, and the next morning at nine o'clock I went to La Charpillon's door, which was opened only a crack, as on the day before. The same shameless aunt came to say, absolutely forbidding me to enter, that the poor girl had had two relapses, that she was in convulsions and delirious, that she still constantly thought she saw me in the room, and that Dr. So-and-so said that if her condition grew worse during the next twenty-four hours she would die.

"She was having her menses," she said, "and the fright stopped them. It is terrible."

"Accursed hairdresser!"

"Youthful weakness! You should have pretended not to see anything."

"G.d d . . n it !¹⁸ What are you saying? You Swiss filth! You think that is possible? Take this."

I left, giving her a ten-pound note. Coming out of the street, I meet Goudar; I tell him, I beg him, to go to see how La Charpillon is, and to come to spend the whole day with me if he can. My expression terrifies him, he goes; and an hour later he came to tell me that the whole household was in despair, for the girl's life was in danger.

"Did you see her?"

"No. They told me that she kept throwing herself out of the bed stark naked, and that no one could see her."

"Do you believe it?"

"A maid who has always told me the truth assured me that she had gone mad because her period had stopped. In addition she has a continual fever and convulsions. I believe it all, for it is the usual consequence of a great fright in a girl who is in her critical period. She said you are the cause of it."

I then told him the whole story, describing the inability to control myself which came over me when I saw the hairdresser. Goudar could only say that he was sorry for me; but hearing that I had not been able either to eat or to sleep for forty-eight hours, he wisely told me that such grief could cost me my life or my reason. I knew it, and I saw no remedy for it. He spent the day with me, and he was useful to me; I could not eat, but I drank a great deal; unable to sleep, I spent the night pacing back and forth in my room, talking to myself like a madman.

I kept sending my Negro all day to find out how she was; and he always brought me back ill-omened answers. On the third day I go to her door myself at seven o'clock in the morning. After I have been kept waiting in the street for a quarter of an hour the door is opened part way, and I see the weeping mother, who, not letting me in, tells me that her daughter is on her deathbed. Just then a thin, pale, tall old man comes out, saying to her in Swiss German that there is nothing to do but to trust in God and obey his will. I ask her if he is the physician; she replies that the time for a physician has passed, that he is a minister of the Gospel, and that there is another upstairs.

"She can no longer speak; in an hour at the most she will be no more."

At that moment I feel as it were an icy hand clutching my heart. I let her burst into tears, and I leave saying that it is true that I was the ultimate cause of her daughter's death, but that she was the first cause of it. My trembling legs take me home, resolved to give myself the death which I thought the surest. In accordance with this terrible determination, at which I arrive with perfect coolness, I order my door shut to everyone. Then I go to my room, I put my watches, rings, snuffboxes, purse, and portfolio in my strongbox, which I put in my desk. I then write a short letter to the Venetian Resident, in which I tell him that after my death all my possessions are the property of Signor Bragadin.[19] I seal my letter, I lock it up in the same desk with the strongbox in which I had all my money, my diamonds, and my jewels, and I put the key in my pocket, in which I keep only two or three guineas in silver. I also put in my pocket my good pistols, and I go out, firmly intending to drown myself in the Thames at the Tower of London.[20] In accordance with this resolve, formed and fostered not by anger or love but in the cold light of reason, I go to a shop to buy as many lead balls as my pockets could hold and the weight of which I could manage to carry as far as the Tower, to which I intended to go on foot. I set out for it, and, reflecting on what I am about to do, I conclude that I could take no wiser course, for, if I remained alive, I should be in hell every time the image of La Charpillon arose in my memory. I even congratulate myself on its costing me no effort whatever to adopt this course; in addition I rejoice that I am just enough to punish myself, having found myself guilty of the unforgivable crime of cutting short the life of a charming object which Nature had created for love.

I walked slowly because of the immense weight I was carrying in my pockets, which assured me that I should die at the bottom of the river before my body could reappear by rising to the surface. Halfway across Westminster Bridge,[21] I come upon Sir Wellbore Agar,[22] a rich and amiable young Englishman who enjoyed life by catering to his passions. I had made his acquaintance at Lord Pembroke's in Saint Albans, then he had dined at my house, then at General Beckwith's, and we had always spent our time together very gaily, conversing on topics dear to the young. I see him, and I try to pretend that I do not see him, but he comes and catches me by the lapels.

"Where are you bound? Come with me, unless you are going to get someone out of prison, and we will have a good laugh."

"I cannot. Let me go."

"What is the matter with you, my dear friend? I do not recognize you."

"Nothing is the matter."

"Nothing is the matter? You don't see your expression. You are on your way, I swear, to do something disastrous. It's plain from your face. There's no use denying it."

"I tell you there's nothing the matter. Good-by. I will go with you some other day."

"Come now, my friend! You have a black look. I won't leave you. I will go with you."

He looks at one side of my breeches, and he catches a glimpse of a pistol, he looks at the other, he sees the mate to it, he takes my hand, he says he is sure I am going to fight, and that, as my friend, he insists upon looking on, assuring me that he will not try to interrupt the meeting. I assure him with a smile that I am not going to fight, and, without thinking what it would lead to, I find myself saying that I was only going for a walk.

"Excellent," says he. "In that case I hope my company will be agreeable to you, as yours is precious to me. We'll dine at the 'Cannon.'[23] I will go now to send someone to tell the girl who was to dine with me alone to bring along a young French-woman who—Goddamme!—[24] is charming. We will make two couples."

"My dear friend, pray excuse me, I am sad, I need to go somewhere by myself to get over it."

"You shall go tomorrow, if you still need to, but I assure you that three hours from now you will be gay. If not, I will keep you company in your gloom. Where do you intend to dine across the river?"

"Nowhere, for I am not hungry. I've eaten nothing for more than three days. I can only drink."

"You amaze me. Now I see the whole thing. It's a cholera morbus which can make you lose your mind, as one of my brothers did, who died of it."

The young man, so insistent, arguing so justly, seems to me not lightly to be dismissed. "I could," I said to myself, "carry out my plan after we part. The most I risk is living five or six hours longer;

Credete a chi n'ha fatto esperimento

('Believe him who has had the experience'),[25]

says Ariosto."

The reader can believe me when I say that all those who have killed themselves because of a great grief have only anticipated the madness which would have overcome their reason if they had not become their own executioners, and that hence all those who have gone mad could have escaped that misfortune only by killing themselves. I did not come to my resolve until I should have lost my reason if I had waited only one day more. Here is the corollary. A man should never kill himself, for it is possible that the cause of his grief will cease before madness sets in. This means that those whose souls are strong enough never to despair of anything are fortunate. My soul was not strong, I had lost all hope, and I was going to kill myself like a man of wisdom. I owe my salvation only to chance.

When Agar hears that I was going to the other side of the bridge only to amuse myself, he says that I may just as well turn back, and I let him persuade me; but a half hour later, unable to walk any longer because of the lead in my pockets, I ask him to take me to some place where I can wait for him, for I am completely exhausted. I gave him my word that I would wait for him at the "Cannon," and I went there. When I was safely in the tavern, I emptied my pockets of the too heavy packets, putting them in a closet.

While waiting for the pleasant young man, I reflected that he might prove to be the cause which would annul my suicide. He had already prevented it, for he had delayed it. "That being so," I reasoned to myself, not like a man who hoped but like a man who foresaw, "it is possible that Agar, Esquire,[26] is the being to whom I shall be indebted for my life." It remained for me to determine whether he was doing me good or evil. The conclusion to which, in accordance with my philosophy, I came again was that, in respect to absolute and decisive acts, we are our own masters only up to a certain point. I considered that in a certain sense it was by force that I found myself sitting there in the tavern waiting for the young Englishman to return, for it is certain that, taking only moral force into consideration, I had had to yield to force.

A quarter of an hour after he returned, the two young light-o'-loves, one of whom was French, came, bringing gaiety written on their charming faces. They were made for joy; they lacked nothing of all that could kindle desires in the coldest of men. I was fully aware of their merits, but since I did not give them the reception to which they were accustomed when men found them pleasing, they began to think me an invalid.[27] Though I was at death's door, I felt an assertion of my self-esteem which forced me to play a role resembling that of the man I ought to be. I gave lifeless and cheerless kisses, and I asked Agar to tell the English girl that if I were not half dead I should find her charming. They condoled with me. A man who has neither eaten nor slept for three days is certainly insensible to the seductions of Venus. Words would not have persuaded them if Agar had not told them my name. I had a reputation, and I saw that they were filled with respect. All three of them put their hopes in the influence of Bacchus. I was more than sure that they were mistaken.

The dinner being in the English style, that is, without soup, I was absolutely unable to swallow either a bit of roast beef[28] or a little pudding.[29] I ate nothing but some oysters, drinking some rather good Graves and enjoying Agar's skill in keeping them both occupied. At the height of the gaiety he suggested that the English girl dance the hornpipe[30] naked, and she consented, provided that we could find some blind musicians[31] and that we would all undress too. I said to Agar that I would do whatever he wanted, but that I could neither dance, for I could not stand on my legs, nor become such as the charms of our two heroines ought to make me. I was excused on condition that if the spectacle brought me to life I would follow their example, and the two girls swore that it would not escape them. The blindmen were found, they came; and we locked ourselves in.

While the blindmen, who had sat down, tuned their instruments, the two beauties and the athlete, who was twenty-five years of age, put themselves in the state of nature, and the performance began. It was one of those moments in which I learned many truths in this world. In that one I saw that the pleasures of love are the effect, and not the cause, of gaiety. The three bodies were magnificent, the dancing, the posturings, the gestures seductive; but no emotion told me that I was sensible to them. The male dancer maintained his conquering appearance even as he danced; I was astonished that I had never made the experiment on myself. After the dance he paid them both homage, going from one to the other, and he did not stop until he saw that Nature, in need of rest, declared him incapable. The Frenchwoman came to see if I showed any sign of life, and, finding me powerless, said that it was all over with me.

The girls dressed, and I asked Agar to give the French woman four guineas for me and to pay for everything, for I had only some small change. Could I have guessed that morning that, instead of going to drown myself, I should make one at so charming a party? My indebtedness to the Englishman made me put off my suicide until the next day. When the girls were gone, I wanted to leave

Agar, but he would not let me. He insisted that I looked better than I had in the morning, that the oysters which I had eaten and had kept down showed that I was in need of distraction, and in short that I could be well the next day and eat dinner if I went with him to spend the night at Ranelagh House.[32] He persuaded me to go there. I left the waiter at the "Cannon" my six packets, telling him that I would come back for them the next morning at nine o'clock, and I got into a hackney carriage with Agar to obey the Stoic maxim which had been inculcated into me in my happy youth: *Sequere Deum* ("Follow the God").[33]

We enter the fine rotunda, which was full of people, with our hats pulled down over our eyes. We had our arms around each other's shoulders. I stop for a moment to wait until a woman who was dancing a minuet in front of me with marked grace, and only whose back I saw, should turn to repeat the same steps in the opposite direction. What made me want to see her face was that she had on a dress and a hat exactly like a dress and a hat which I had given to La Charpillon; in addition, she was of the same stature; but this last observation did not concern me, for at that moment La Charpillon must be dead or at least on her deathbed. The dancer, then, starts off in the other direction; I look at her, and I see La Charpillon herself. Agar told me afterward that at that moment he thought I would fall down in an epileptic fit: the arm I had around his shoulders shook and contracted spasmodically.

I overcome my surprise and my spasm by a salutary doubt. There may be only a resemblance. The young woman, her attention fixed on her partner, had not noticed me; I remain where I am, waiting for her to come back in my direction, when I should see her only a step away and face to face; but just then she raises her arms to make her curtsy at the end of the minuet, and I go up to her as if I wanted to take her for the next dance. She looks at me, and she at once turns and walks away. I say nothing, and certain of the fact, I feel that I must go to sit down. A cold sweat instantly bathed my whole body. Agar, convinced that I am on the verge of a fit, advises me to take a cup of tea, to which I reply by asking him to leave me alone and to go and amuse himself.

The revolution which, in less than an hour, had taken place in my entire being made me fearful of its consequences, for I was shaking from head to foot and a violent palpitation of the heart made me doubt if I could stand even if I dared to rise. How the strange paroxysm would end terrified me, I could not but think that it would kill me.

946

My fear was not groundless. Having proved unable to bring me to my death, it gave me a new life. What a prodigious change! Feeling that I had grown calm, I fixed my eyes with pleasure on the rays of light which made me ashamed; but my feeling of shame assured me that I was cured. What contentment! Having been immersed in error, I could not recognize it until after I had emerged from it. In the dark one sees nothing. I was so amazed at my new state that, not seeing Agar reappear, I began to believe that I should not see him again. "That young man," I said to myself, "is my Genius, who assumed his appearance to restore me to my senses."

It is certain that I should have been confirmed in this insane idea if I had not seen him reappear an hour after he left me. Chance might have decreed that Agar should find some girl who would have persuaded him to leave Ranelagh House with her. I should have gone back to London alone, but certain that I had not been saved by Agar. Should I have recovered my senses if I had not seen him until some days later? I do not know. Men easily go mad. There has always been a seed of superstition in my soul, of which I am certainly not proud.

Agar finally comes back, in high spirits but very uneasy about my condition. He is astonished to see me glowing with health and surprised to hear me making amusing comments on the objects which took my fancy in the beautiful rotunda.

"My friend," he said, "you are laughing, you are no longer sad."

"No. I am hungry, and I need to ask a great favor of you, if you have not some important business tomorrow which will prevent your granting it."

"I am free until day after tomorrow, and entirely at your service."

"Here is what I have in mind. I owe you my life—my life, I tell you. But, for your gift to be complete, I need to have you spend tonight and all day tomorrow with me."

"I am yours to command."

"Then walk about, and come back for me whenever you are ready."

"Let us go at once, if you like."

"Let us go."

On the way I tell him nothing. When we enter my house I find nothing new except a note from Goudar, which I put in my pocket. It was an hour after midnight. We are served supper, and Agar is surprised to see me eat with ravenous appetite. He laughs and congratulates me. After supping well, he goes to bed and I do likewise. I sleep very soundly until noon; I go to breakfast in his room, and I tell him every detail of the whole horrible story, which would have ended with my death if I had not happened to meet him halfway across Westminster Bridge, and if he had not read my terrible resolve in my distracted countenance. At the end of the story I take his hand, I open my desk, I make him read my will, and, retrieving my purse, I give him the five or six guineas I owe him. After that I unseal Goudar's note, which contained only these few words:

"I am sure that the girl in question, far from being on her deathbed, has gone to Ranelagh with Lord Grosvenor."

Agar, young but very sensible, is thunderstruck. Convinced that he had saved my life, he congratulates himself, and we embrace. The character of La Charpillon and her mother's perfidy seem to him beyond belief, and as for the bills of exchange whose loss I regretted because, having them, I could have taken some slight revenge by sending her mother and her aunts to prison, he said that it was still in my power to have them arrested and force them to restore them to me, and the more so since I had kept the letter from the mother acknowledging the debt and admitting that I had only consigned them to her daughter on deposit.

I at once resolved to have them arrested, but I did not tell him so. After spending the whole day in high spirits with me, he left to sup with his mistress. I swore him eternal friendship, and I owed it to him. The reader will see hereafter the punishment the kind young man had to undergo for having served me so well.

Full of vigor the next morning, gay as a man who has just won a great victory, I go to the attorney who had served me in my case against Count Schwerin,[34] and he, after hearing the facts, told me that I was justified and that my right to have the scheming woman arrested was unquestionable. So I went to Holborn,[35] where I made a statement on oath, and I received the order to have the mother and the two aunts arrested. The man who had arrested Schwerin was willing to serve me again in the arrest of the women; but he did not know them, and he had to know them. He was sure he could obtain entrance to their house and take them by surprise; but he also had to be sure that the women he arrested were the ones named in the warrant.

"There might," he said, "be other women with them."

His objection was justified; so, having no one who could do the thing, for Goudar would never have undertaken it, I resolved that I would myself show the man into the house at an hour when I could be sure that the malefactors would all be together in the parlor.

I told him to be waiting in Denmark Street at eight o'clock, with a hackney coach at his orders, and to enter as soon as the door was opened for him. I assured him that I would enter at the same time, and that I would turn them over to him myself; and the thing was done accordingly in every particular. He entered the parlor with one of his constables, followed by me. I at once pointed out the mother and the two aunts to him, then I hurried away, for La Charpillon, dressed in mourning, standing with her back to the fireplace, though I only glanced at her, terrified me. I believed, and I felt, that I was cured; but the wound having only just healed over, I do not know what would have happened if at that moment she had had the presence of mind to throw herself on my neck and beg me to spare her mother and her aunts. As soon as I saw them all touched by the powerful rod,[36] I left, relishing the pleasure of vengeance, and almost certain that they would find no one to go bail for them; their p..s,[37] who were there, were petrified.

The pleasure of revenge is great, and those who procure it are happy when they taste it; but they were not happy when they sought it. The happy man is the impassive man,[38] who, not knowing what it is to hate, never thinks of avenging himself. The animosity with which I had the three women arrested, and the terror in which I left their house as soon as I saw the girl, prove that I was not yet free. To be so completely, I had to forget her.

The next morning Goudar came to me in high spirits, showing every sign of great contentment. He said that what I had had the courage to do proved either that I was cured of my passion or that I was more in love than ever. He had just come from La Charpillon's, where he had found only the grandmother, in despair and consulting an advocate.

He said that he had arrived at their house just as I was leaving it, and that he had stayed there until they had had to resign themselves to being taken to the house of the man who was executing my warrant. They had refused to go; they had insisted that he should wait until morning, when they were certain to find sureties, and their two bravoes had drawn their swords to prevent the man from using force; but the brave officer of the police had disarmed them and carried away their swords together with the three prisoners. The girl had wanted to go too, to keep them company; but she had left them in order to take every possible step to keep them from going to prison. Meanwhile the bailiff had them under guard at his house.

Goudar ended by saying that, as their friend, he would pay them a visit, and that if I were willing to enter into some arrangement he would be glad to act as mediator. I thanked him, and I said that the only way by which the women could get out of prison was to give me my money.

Two weeks[39] passed without my hearing anything more of the matter. No protests on their part, and no proposals for an arrangement. La Charpillon went to dine with them every day, and it was she who paid for their keep. It must have cost her a great deal, for they occupied two rooms and their cruel host did not allow them to send out for meals. If they had not agreed to it, he would have taken them to King's Bench.[40] Goudar said that La Charpillon had told her mother and her aunts that she would never bring herself to come to me to ask for their freedom, even if she were sure that merely speaking to me would reduce me to doing whatever she wanted. In her eyes I was the most loathsome of monsters. I went to see my daughter nearly every day, and I had completely recovered my good spirits.

During these two weeks I had looked everywhere for Agar in vain, and at last I was pleasantly surprised to see him enter my room one morning with a friendly and smiling countenance.

"Where on earth have you been hiding?" I asked him. "I have looked everywhere for you and not found you."

"It is Love, my dear friend, who has kept me in his impenetrable prison. I have come to bring you money."

"On whose behalf?"

"On the part of the Augspurgher ladies. Give me a receipt and the necessary declaration, for I am to go myself to restore them to the arms of the unhappy Charpillon, who has done nothing but weep for two weeks."

"I know her tears; but I wonder that she should have chosen as her protector the man who freed me from her chains. Does she know that I owe you my life?"

"All she knew was that we were at Ranelagh together on that evening you saw her dance when you thought she was dead; but she heard the whole story from me after she had made my acquaintance."

"I take it that she came to you to persuade you to speak to me in her favor."

"Not a bit of it. She came to tell me that you are a monster of ingratitude, for she loved you and she gave you unmistakable proofs of her affection; but now she loathes you."

"God be praised! But it is strange that she should have made you fall in love with her in order to obtain her revenge on me. My dear friend, she is fooling you, for it is you whom she is punishing."

"In any case it is a sweet punishment."

"I want you to be happy, but take care of yourself!"

Agar counted me out two hundred and fifty guineas, and I canceled my bills of exchange and renounced all my claims in writing. He went away satisfied. After this, did I not have reason to believe that the whole matter was ended? But I was sadly mistaken.

About that time the Hereditary Prince of Brunswick,[41] now the reigning Duke, married Princess Augusta, the King's sister. The Common Council,[42] having resolved to make him an English citizen and to give him the accompanying prerogatives, the Goldsmiths' Company[43] enrolled him among its members, having the Lord Mayor[44] and the Aldermen[45] give him the diploma in a gold box. The Prince, who was the first gentleman of our world, added this new luster to his nobility, which dated back fourteen centuries.

On this occasion Lady Harrington arranged that Mrs. Cornelys should make two hundred guineas. She lent her house in Soho Square to a cook who gave a ball and supper for a thousand persons[46] at three guineas a head. The groom, the bride, and the entire royal family, except the King and Queen, were present. For my three guineas I, too, was among the guests, but standing with six hundred others, the long tables in the great hall having accommodated only four hundred. I saw Lady Grafton[47] seated beside the Duke of Cumberland,[48] and astonishing all the other ladies by wearing her hair without powder and combed straight down in front so that it covered half of her forehead. They all exclaimed at it. They said that she was out of her mind, insane, absurd, and deserved to be booed, for she was making herself ugly; but in less than six months dressing the hair à la Grafton became general; it crossed the water and spread all over Europe, where it still persists, having, however, most unjustly, lost its name. It is the only fashion which can boast an antiquity of thirty-four years, though it was howled down on its first appearance. As in the case of spectacles in general, first receptions are to be distrusted. They are often wrong. A great many excellent plays, both French and English, failed at their first performances.

At this supper, for which the man who had produced it had received three thousand guineas, there was all

Che puote cor pensar può chieder bocca

("That the heart could imagine and the mouth desire")[49]

in the way of both food and drink; but, since I did not dance and was not in love with any of the beauties who decorated the festival, I left at one o'clock in the morning. It was a Sunday, that sacred day on which in London no one fears prison except criminals. Nevertheless, this is what befell me.

Splendidly dressed, I was going home in a carriage, my Negro Jarba being up behind with another manservant whom I had recently engaged. The carriage has scarcely entered my street when I hear someone call my name:

"Good evening, Seingalt."

I put out my head and I reply:

"Good evening."

I instantly see men armed with pistols, two at the right, two at the left, and two others who had stopped the carriage; I hear them call out:

"By order of the King!"

My servants ask them what they want, and one of them replies that they mean to take me to Newgate Prison, for Sunday is no protection to criminals. I ask what crime I have committed; I am told that I shall learn that in prison. My Negro says that I have the right to know it before I go there; they answer that the judge is asleep; and he retorts that I will wait until he gets up, and the passers-by, who had stopped at the disturbance, cry out that I am in the right. The head constable gives in and takes me to his quarters in the City.[50] I found myself in a large room on the ground floor, in which there were nothing but some benches and large tables. My servants, after dismissing the carriage, came to keep me company, whereupon the six constables, declaring it their duty not to leave me, had me told that I must have food and drink brought for them. I ordered Jarba to satisfy them and to be mild and polite. I had to prepare to spend five hours there. The hour of the hearing was seven o'clock.

Having committed no crime, I could be there only as the result of a calumny, and knowing that justice in London was equitable, I was perfectly at ease, resolved to put up peaceably with a misfortune which could only be of short duration. If I had obeyed the old maxim, which I knew well, never to answer an unknown voice which addresses one at night, I should have avoided this misfortune, but the error was committed, so I could only be patient. I amused myself with humorous reflections on my swift passage from the most brilliant assembly in London to the infamous company in which I found myself, richly dressed as I was.

Dawn came at last, and the proprietor of the pot house[51] where I was came downstairs to see who the criminal who had spent the night under his roof might be. His anger at his henchmen, who had not waked him to give me a room, made me laugh again, for he saw himself the loser by at least a guinea, which he would have made me pay for his courtesy. Someone finally announced that the magistrate[52] was sitting and that it was time to bring me into his presence. A sedan chair was called to carry me, for, dressed as I was, the mob would have thrown me into the gutter if I had gone on foot.

I enter a large room, where I find myself among fifty or sixty persons who at once fix their eyes on the barbarian who dares to show himself clad in such offensive finery.

At the far end of the room I see, seated in a raised armchair, the person who was apparently to inform me of what crime I was accused. He was the "sergens-fil," whom I prefer to call the "Criminal Court Magistrate." The accusations were read to him, he was addressed, he replied; and he hurriedly dictated the sentences, for the poor man was blind. He had a black bandage two inches wide which went around his head and covered his eyes. Since he could not see, it made no difference to him if they were covered. Someone beside me encouraged me, saying that he was a just judge, a man of intelligence, kind-hearted, and the author of several celebrated novels. In short, the man was Mr. Fielding.[53]

When my turn came the secretary who was beside him whispered it to him and, the complaint apparently naming me "Casanova, Italian," he called me by that name, telling me in perfect Italian to come forward for he had something to say to me. At that I made my way through the crowd and, arrived at the bar, I said:

"*Eccomi, Signore*" ("Here I am, My Lord").

All of the following dialogue between the honest magistrate and myself was conducted in Italian, and I wrote it down word for word the same day. I am happy to give my reader the following faithful and literal translation of it.

"Signor di Casanova, Venetian, you are sentenced to the prisons of His Majesty the King of Great Britain for the rest of your natural life."

"I am curious, Sir, to know for what crime I am sentenced. Will you be so good as to inform me of it?"

"Your curiosity is justified, Signor Venetian. In our country the courts do not consider that they have the right to sentence a person without informing him of his crime. You are accused, and the accusation is supported by two witnesses, of having attempted to scar a girl's face. It is she who calls upon the law to safeguard her against this outrage, and the law must safeguard her against it by sentencing you to prison. So prepare to go there."

"Sir, it is a calumny. It is possible, however, that, examining her own conduct, she may fear I might think of committing that crime. I can swear to you that I have never thought of such a base act."

"She has two witnesses."

"They are false ones. Who is this girl?"

"She is Miss Charpillon."

"I know her, and I have never given her anything but tokens of affection."

"Then it is not true that you intend to disfigure her?"

"It is false."

"In that case I congratulate you. You shall dine in your own house; but you must furnish two sureties. Two householders must vouch to us that you will never commit this crime."

"Who will dare to vouch that I will never commit it?"

"Two honest Englishmen whose esteem you have earned and who know that you are not a rogue. Send for them, and if they arrive before I go to dinner you shall be set free at once."

I go out at once, and the constables take me back to the place in which I had been. I give my servants in writing all the names of householders I can remember, charging them to tell them the reason which obliged me to inconvenience them. I urge them to make haste, and they leave. They were to come back before noon; but they did not come back, so the magistrate went to dinner. However, I comforted myself with the knowledge that he would sit after dinner too. But suddenly I hear most unpleasant news.

The chief constable, accompanied by an interpreter, comes to tell me that he is there to take me to Newgate.[54] This is the prison in London to which only the lowest and most miserable criminals are sent. I tell him through the interpreter that I am waiting for sureties, and that he can take me to prison at nightfall if they do not come. He refuses to do so. He says that as soon as my sureties arrived I would be fetched from the prison, so it should make no difference to me. The interpreter whispers to me that the man was certainly paid by the other side to do me the injury of putting me in prison, and hence that it was in my power to remain where I was by giving him money. I ask how much, and after speaking with him privately he comes to tell me that ten guineas would persuade him to keep me where I am until nightfall. I at once had him reply that I was curious to see Newgate Prison. So a hackney coach was sent for, and I was taken there.

Upon my entrance into that inferno, a crowd of wretches, some of whom were to be hanged within the week, applauded my arrival, at the same time jeering at my fine array. Seeing that I do not speak to them, they become angry and begin treating me to insults. The jailer[55] quiets them, assuring them that I do not speak English, and he takes me to a room, informing me of what it will cost me and of the prison rules, as if he were sure I was to stay there a long time.

But a half hour later in comes the same man who wanted to make ten guineas by keeping me in his house and who tells me that my sureties are waiting for me before the magistrate and that my carriage is at the door. I thank God, I go downstairs, and once more I am before the man with the bandaged eyes. I see there Mr. Pagus,[56] my tailor, and Maisonneuve,[57] my vintner, who greet me and congratulate themselves on being able to do me this small service. Not far from me I see La Charpillon with Rostaing, an attorney, and Goudar. My sureties go to give their names to a clerk, who questions them and who then goes to speak to the magistrate, who approves them and informs them of the amount for which they are to stand surety for me. They sign, and the magistrate immediately tells me to sign for twice the amount for which my sureties had signed, and at the same time affably tells me that I am free. I go to the clerk's table to sign, asking him how much the security comes to, and he replies that it comes to forty guineas, my sureties having vouched for twenty each. I sign, saying to Goudar that Miss Charpillon's beauty would perhaps have been rated at ten thousand if the magistrate had seen her. I ask the names of the two who had served as her witnesses, and I am shown the names of Rostaing and Bottarelli.[58] I cast a disdainful look at Rostaing, who was there, pale as a corpse; a feeling of pity keeps me from looking at La Charpillon. I asked the clerk if I had to pay the costs, and he answered no, which gave rise to a dispute between him and the attorney employed by the beauty, who stood there in the utmost mortification because she could not leave until the costs of my arrest were paid. During this time I saw three or four other Englishmen arrive, who had come to stand surety for me. They all begged me to forgive the English laws, which were too often hard upon foreigners. I finally got home, eager to go to bed after spending a day which was one of the most tiresome of my whole life.

CHAPTER XIII

Bottarelli. The avenging parrot. Pocchini.

The first act of my comedy having ended in this fashion, the second began the next day. As I get out of bed, I hear a noise at my door, I go to the window to see what it is, and I see Pocchini,[1] the infamous scoundrel who had robbed me at Stuttgart [...]. He was trying to enter without waiting to be announced, and just then he saw me. I told him that I could not receive him, and I closed the window.

A quarter of an hour later in comes Goudar with a copy of an English newspaper called the *St. James's Chronicle*, in which there was a brief account of my adventure, beginning with my arrest as I left Soho Square and ending with my return to my house a free man by virtue of security amounting in all to eighty pounds sterling. My name and La Charpillon's were disguised; but Rostaing's and Bottarelli's were given in full,[2] the writer of the account praising them. I asked Goudar to take me at once to see Bottarelli, whose acquaintance I wanted to make. Martinelli, who arrived at the same time, insisted on going with me too.

On the fourth floor of a dilapidated house we enter a room where we see the picture of poverty, composed of a woman, four children, and a man writing at a table. The man was Bottarelli. He rises, I ask him if he knows me, he answers no, whereupon I tell him that I am the Casanova whom his testimony had sent to Newgate the day before.

"Signore, I am sorry for it; but look at my family. I was in need of two guineas; I will serve you for nothing when you wish it."

"Are you not afraid you will be hanged?"

"No, Signore, for a false witness is not sentenced to the gallows. The law provides that we shall be deported; but nothing is harder in London than to convict a witness of having testified falsely."

"I am told that you are a poet."

"Yes, Signore. I have lengthened the *Didone*[3] and shortened the *Demetrio*."[4]

I left the scoundrel after giving his wife a guinea from pure charity. She gave me a copy of a book by her husband entitled *The Secret of the Freemasons Exposed*.[5] He was a monk in Pisa, his native city, which he had left with her, a nun. He had married her in London.

[* * *]

Strolling about the city one morning, I came to a place called the "Parrot Market."[6] Seeing a pretty one in a brand-new cage, I asked what language it spoke, and I was told that, being very young, it spoke none. I gave the ten guineas which were asked for it and I sent it home. Resolved to teach it a few interesting words, I decided to put it near my bed and constantly say to it in French, "Miss Charpillon is more of a whore than her mother." I began the thing as a joke, and certainly with no malicious intention. In less than two weeks the obedient parrot learned the few words so well that it repeated them from morning to night, with the addition that, after uttering them, it gave a great burst of laughter, a thing which I had not meant to teach it.

It was Goudar who said to me one day that if I sent my parrot to the Exchange I could certainly get it sold for fifty guineas. I at once adopted his happy idea, not in a spirit of avarice but in order to have the pleasure of calling the scheming creature who had treated me so ill a wh ...,[7] and at the same time to be safe from the law, which is extremely severe in that respect.

So I entrusted the business to Jarba, my parrot being an appropriate piece of merchandise for an Indian.

For the first two or three days my parrot, which spoke French, did not have a large audience; but as soon as someone who knew the heroine noticed the praise which the indiscreet bird bestowed on her, the circle grew bigger, and people began bargaining for the right to own the cage. Fifty guineas appeared to be too much. My Negro wanted me to sell the whole thing more cheaply; but I would never consent to it. I had fallen in love with my avenger.

How I laughed when, at the end of seven or eight days, Goudar told me what effect my talking parrot, offered for sale on the London Exchange, had had upon La Charpillon's family. Since the person who was selling it was my Negro, no one had any doubt that it belonged to me and that I had taught it to speak. He said that the girl not only was not offended by the thing but that she thought it very amusing and laughed at it all day. The ones who were in despair were her aunts and her mother, who had consulted several advocates on the subject, all of whom had replied that there were no laws to punish a calumny the author of which was a parrot, but that they could make the joke cost me very dear if they could prove that the parrot was my pupil. For this reason Goudar warned me that I must be careful not to boast that the bird had gone to school to me, for two witnesses could ruin me.

The ease with which false witnesses can be found in London is really scandalous. One day I saw a notice put up in a window and bearing in capital letters the one word "witness." It meant that the person who lived in the apartment was a professional witness.

An article in the *St. James's Chronicle* said that the ladies who considered themselves insulted by the parrot must be very poor and entirely friendless, for if they had bought the parrot as soon as they learned of its existence the story would scarcely have become known. It said that the thing could only be a revenge, and, without naming me, it said that the author of it deserved to be an English-man. Happening to encounter Agar, I asked him why he did not buy the parrot. He replied, laughing at first but then becoming serious, that the parrot amused everyone who knew the persons concerned, and he refused to say more. Jarba at last found a buyer, and he brought me fifty guineas. Goudar told me that it was Lord Grosvenor.[8] That nobleman loved La Charpillon, but as an occa-sional diversion and no more. This jest concluded my acquaintance with the coquette, whom I later often encountered in London at promenades and theaters without even remembering what had happened to me on her account, so indifferent had I become to her.

[* * *]

Recovered from the effects of his infatuation, Casanova embarked on a round of affairs, by turns sentimental and cynical. He was especially taken with "a Hanoverian woman and her five daughters" even though the "daughters" were described by the man who introduced them as "Charpillons." A complicated amorous tangle ensued. But Casanova was spending a great deal of money on his pleasures and it was not long before he became involved in a financial tangle, too. The details are irrelevant: what matters is that he was soon in danger of a forgery charge. Forgery was then a capital offense in England, with penalties rigorously enforced in what was already the world's financial center.

In such a crisis there was only one course of action: flight. Crossing the Channel, he made for Brussels, whence he moved on to Germany, eventually finding himself in Berlin. Casanova, who prided himself on his ability to mix easily with the great, naturally considered it a positive duty to introduce himself to the King of Prussia. Fortunately, he had an entrée to the Prussian Court through an old acquaintance, the Earl Marischal. In Berlin he also found Calzabigi, his erstwhile confederate in the Paris lottery. Yet again he hoped to make his fortune.

HISTORY OF MY LIFE

Volume Ten

CHAPTER IV

Lord Keith. Appointment with the King
of Prussia in the garden of Sans Souci.
My conversation with the monarch. La Denis.
The Pomeranian cadets.

It was on the fifth day after my arrival in Berlin that I presented myself to the Earl Marischal, who after the death of his brother was called Keith.[1] I had last seen him in London, on his way from Scotland, where he had been repossessed of his properties, which had been confiscated when he had followed King James. The King of Prussia had had influence enough to obtain this grace for him. He was then living in Berlin, resting on his laurels, enjoying his retirement, always in the King's favor, and taking no more part in anything at the age of eighty years.

Simple in his manner, as he had always been, he told me that he was glad to see me again, immediately asking me if I was passing through Berlin or if I intended to remain there for some time. My vicissitudes being known to him in part, I said that I should be glad to settle there if the King, giving me some employment suitable to my small talents, would graciously take me into his service. But when I asked him for his countenance in the matter, he said that his speaking to the King about me beforehand would do me more harm than good. Priding himself on knowing men better than anyone else, he liked to judge them for himself, and it very often happened that he found desert where no one else had suspected it, and vice versa. He advised me to write him that I aspired to the honor of speaking with him.

"When you speak with him," His Lordship said, "you may tell him in passing that you know me, and then I think he will ask me about you, and I know that what I shall reply will not harm you."

"I, unknown as I am, write to a King with whom I have no connection! It would not enter my mind to do such a thing."

"Do you not wish to speak with him? That is the connection. There should be nothing in your letter but the declaration of your wish."

"Will he answer me?"

"Have no doubt of it. He answers everyone. He will write you where and at what hour he will be pleased to see you. Do it. His Majesty is now at Sans Souci.[2] I am curious to learn what sort of conversation you will have with a monarch who, as you see, acts in a manner which proves that he has no fear of being taken in."

I did not delay for a single day. I wrote to him in the simplest style, though most respectfully. I asked him when and where I might present myself to His Majesty, and I subscribed myself "Venetian," dating my letter from the inn where I was staying. On the next day but one I received a letter written by a secretary, but signed "Fédéric."[3] He wrote me that the King had received my letter and had ordered him to inform me that His Majesty would be in the garden of Sans Souci at four o'clock.

I go there at three, dressed in black. I enter the courtyard of the palace by a small door, and I see no one, not a sentinel, not a porter, not a footman. Everything was in the deepest silence. I go up a short flight of stairs, I open a door, and I find myself in a picture gallery.[4] The man in charge of it offers me his services, but I thank him and decline, saying that I am waiting for the King, who had written me that he would be in the garden.

"He is," he said, "at his chamber concert, at which he is playing the flute, as he does every day immediately after his dinner. Did he give you an hour?"

"Yes, four o'clock. Perhaps he has forgotten."

"The King never forgets. He will come down at four o'clock, and you had better go to wait for him in the garden."

I go there, and soon afterward I see him, followed by his reader Catt[5] and a pretty spaniel. Scarcely has he seen me before he approaches, and, taking off his old hat with a mocking look, he names me by my name and asks me in a terrifying voice what I want with him. Surprised by this reception, I am at a loss; I look at him, and I say nothing.

"What is this? Speak. Are you not the man who wrote to me?"

"Yes, Sire; but I no longer remember anything. I thought that the King's majesty would not dazzle me. It shall not happen another time. The Lord Marischal should have warned me."

"So he knows you? Let us walk. What did you want to talk to me about? What do you think of this garden?"

At the same time that he asks me what I want to say to him, he tells me to talk to him about his garden. To anyone else I should have replied that I had no knowledge of gardens; but to a King, who supposed that I was a connoisseur, I should have appeared to be giving the lie. So, at the risk of giving him a specimen of my bad taste, I replied that I thought it magnificent.

"But," he said, "the gardens of Versailles are far finer."

"No doubt, Sire, if only because of the fountains."

"True; but if there are no fountains here it is not my fault. I have spent three hundred thousand crowns in vain to bring water here for them."[6]

"Three hundred thousand crowns? If Your Majesty spent them all at once, the fountains should be here."

"Aha! I see you are a hydraulician."

Was I to tell him that he was mistaken? I was afraid of offending him. I bent my head. Which is to say neither yes nor no. But the King did not care—thank God—to converse with me on that science, of which I knew not even the first principles. Without pausing for so much as a moment he asked me what the forces of the Republic of Venice were at sea in time of war.

"Twenty rated ships, Sire, and a great number of galleys."

"And for land forces?"

"Seventy thousand men, Sire, all subjects of the Republic, taking only one man per village."

"That is not true. You seem to want to make me laugh by talking such nonsense to me. But you are certainly a financier. Tell me what you think about taxes."

It was the first conversation I had had with a King. Observing his style, his outbursts, his sudden shifts, I thought I was called upon to play a scene of Italian improvised comedy, where, if the actor is at a loss, the groundlings hiss him. So I answered the proud King, assuming the financier's arrogance and adjusting my expression to match, that I could talk to him about the theory of taxation.

"That is what I want, for the practice does not concern you."

"Considered as to their effects, there are three kinds of taxes, one of which is ruinous, the second necessary, unfortunately, and the third always excellent."

"I like that. Go on."

"The ruinous impost is the royal tax, the necessary one is the military, the excellent one is the popular."

"What does all that mean?"

I had to take my time, for I was making it up.

"The royal tax, Sire, is the one which the monarch imposes on his subjects to fill his coffers."

"And it is always ruinous, you say."

"Without doubt, Sire, for it destroys circulation, the soul of commerce and the support of the State."

"But you consider the military tax necessary."

"But unfortunately so, for war is certainly a misfortune."

"Perhaps. And the popular?"

"Always excellent, for the King takes it from his subjects with one hand and with the other pours it into their bosom in very useful institutions and in measures calculated to increase their happiness."

"You doubtless know Calzabigi?"

"I ought to know him, Sire. Seven years ago we established the Genoese lottery in Paris."

"And in what category do you put that tax, for you will grant me that it is one?"

"Yes, Sire. It is a tax of the excellent kind when the King assigns the profit from it to the support of some useful institution."

"But the King may lose by it."

"One time in ten."

"Is that the result of certain calculation?"

"As certain, Sire, as all political calculations."

"They are often erroneous."

"I beg Your Majesty's pardon. They are never so when God is neutral."

"It is possible that I think as you do on the subject of moral calculation, but I do not like your Genoese lottery. I consider it a swindle, and I should not want it even if I had material proof that I should never lose by it."

"Your Majesty thinks like a wise man, for the ignorant people could not risk their money in it unless they were carried away by a fallacious confidence."

After this dialogue, which, all in all, does only honor to the intelligence of that illustrious monarch, he vacillated; but he did not find me at a loss. He enters a peristyle[7] enclosed by a double colonnade, and he stops before me, looks me up and down, then, after thinking a moment:

"You are," he says, "a very fine figure of a man."

"Is it possible, Sire, that after a long, rigorously scientific dissertation Your Majesty can see in me the least of the qualities which are the glory of your grenadiers?"

After a kindly smile, he said that since Lord Marischal Keith knew me he would speak to him about me, then he saluted me, taking off his hat, as he never failed to do, no matter to whom, with the greatest generosity.

Three or four days later the Earl Marischal gave me the good news that I had won the King's favor, and that His Majesty had told him that he would think about giving me some employment. Extremely curious to see at what he would employ me, and nothing urging me to go elsewhere, I decided to wait. When I did not sup at Calzabigi's the company of Baron Treyden at my hostess's table afforded me great pleasure, and, the weather being extremely fine, walking in the park made the whole day pass agreeably for me.

Calzabigi very soon obtained permission from the King to operate the lottery on the responsibility of anyone he chose, paying him six thousand crowns in advance at each drawing; and he at once reopened his receiving offices, after brazenly informing the public that the lottery would operate on his responsibility. His lack of credit did not prevent the public from staking, and in such numbers that the receipts gave him a profit of nearly a hundred thousand crowns, with which he paid a good share of his debts; and he took back the obligation for ten thousand écus which he had executed for his mistress, giving her the amount in cash. The Jew Ephraim[8] took the ten thousand écus, guaranteeing her the capital and paying her interest at six per cent.

After this lucky drawing Calzabigi had no difficulty in finding guarantors for a million divided into a thousand shares, and the lottery continued for two or three years without calamities; even so, Calzabigi went bankrupt and returned to Italy to die. His mistress married and returned to Paris.

During this time the Duchess of Brunswick,[9] the King's sister, came to pay him a visit with her daughter, whom the Crown Prince married the next year.[10] On this occasion the King came to Berlin and had an Italian opera performed for her at the small theater in Charlottenburg.[11] On that day I saw the King of Prussia dressed as a courtier, wearing a coat of lustrine with gold braid on all the seams and black stockings. His appearance was most comical. He entered the theater with his hat under his arm and escorting his sister, leading her by the hand and drawing the looks of all the spectators, for only the very old could remember seeing him appear in public except in a uniform and boots.

But at the performance what surprised me was to see the celebrated Denis[12] dance. I did not know that she was in the King's service, and, strong in the warrant of a very old acquaintance with her, I at once decided to pay her a visit in Berlin the next day.

When I was twelve years old my mother, having to leave for Saxony, had me come to Venice for a few days with my kind Doctor Gozzi.[13] Having gone to the theater, what seemed to me very surprising was a girl eight years old who, at the end of the play, danced a minuet with enchanting grace. The girl, whose father was the actor who played the part of Pantalone,[14] so charmed me that I afterward entered the box in which she was undressing to pay her my respects. I was dressed as an abate, and I saw her greatly surprised when her father told her to stand up so that I could embrace her. She did so most graciously, and I was most awkward. But I was so filled with happiness that I could not help taking from a woman who was selling jewelry there a small ring which the little girl had thought pretty but too expensive, and making her a present of it. She then came and embraced me again, with her face full of gratitude. I paid the woman the zecchino which was the price of the ring, and I went back to my Doctor, who was waiting for me in a box. My heart was in a pitiful state, for the zecchino I had given for the ring belonged to my master the Doctor, and although I felt that I was desperately in love with Pantalone's pretty daughter, I felt even more strongly that what I had done could not have been more foolish, not only because I had spent money which was not mine but because I had spent it like a dupe to obtain only a kiss.

Obliged the next day to account to the Doctor for his zecchino, and not knowing where to borrow it, I spent a most uneasy night; but the next day it all came out, and it was my mother herself who gave my master the zecchino; but I still laugh today when I think of how ashamed it made me feel. The same woman who had sold me the ring at the theater came to our house when we were dining. Showing pieces of jewelry which were declared too expensive, she praised me, saying that I had not thought the price of the ring I had given the Pantaloncina[15] too high. No more was needed to bring an accusation down on me. I thought I should end it all by asking to be forgiven and saying that it was love which had made me commit the crime, assuring my mother that this was the first and last it would make me commit. At the word "love" everyone did nothing but laugh, and I was so cruelly made fun of that I firmly resolved that it should be the last love of my life; but thinking of Giovannina, I sighed; she was so named because she was my mother's godchild.[16]

After giving me the zecchino, she asked me if I wanted her to invite her to supper; but my grandmother objected, and I was grateful to her for it. It was on the next day that I went back to Padua with my master, where Bettina[17] easily made me forget the Pantaloncina.

After this incident I never saw her again until that evening in Charlottenburg. Twenty-seven years had passed. She must have been thirty-five years of age. Had I not learned her name, I should not have recognized her, for at the age of eight her features could not be formed. I could not wait to see her alone in her room and to learn if she remembered the incident, for I did not think it possible that she could recognize me. I asked if her husband Denis was with her, and I was told that the King had banished him[18] because he ill-treated her.

So the next day I am driven to her house, I send in my name, and she receives me politely, saying, however, that she did not believe she had ever had the pleasure of seeing me anywhere before.

It was then that I gradually awakened the greatest interest in her by talking to her of her family, her childhood, and the grace by which she enchanted Venice when she danced the minuet; she interrupted me to say that she was then only six years old, and I replied that she could not have been more, as I was only ten when I fell in love with her.

"I could never tell you so," I said, "but I have never forgotten a kiss you gave me at your father's order in return for a little present I made you."

"Say no more. You gave me a ring. You were dressed as an abate. I have never forgotten you either. Is it possible that it is you?"

"It is I."

"I am delighted beyond measure. But since I do not recognize you, it is impossible that you should recollect me."

"Certainly, for if I had not been told your name I should not have thought of you."

"In twenty years, my dear friend, the face takes on a different form."

"Say rather that at the age of six one's features are not yet molded."

"You can be a good witness that I am only twenty-six years old, despite the evil tongues which make me ten more."

"Let them talk. You are in the flower of your years and made for love; and I consider myself the happiest of men now that I have been able to tell you that you are the first to have inspired amorous feelings in my soul."

After this exchange, we quickly became affectionate; but experience had taught us both to stop where we were and to leave anything else until later.

La Denis, still young, beautiful, and fresh, reduced her age by ten years; she knew that I knew it, nevertheless she wanted me to accept it, and she would have hated me if, like an idiot, I had chosen to demonstrate a truth to her which she knew as well as I did. She did not care about what I was bound to think, she left that to me. It is even possible that she considered I should be grateful to her for giving me a warrant, by her very plausible lie, to rid myself of ten years as she was doing, and she declared herself ready to bear witness for me if the occasion arose. Diminishing their ages is a sort of duty for women of the theater, principally because they know that, despite all their talent, the public turns against them when it becomes known that they are old.

Considering the fine sincerity with which she had let me see her weakness a very good omen, I had no doubt that she would be kind enough to accept my fond addresses and not make me languish long. She showed me over her whole house, and seeing her lodged with the greatest elegance in every respect, I asked her if she had a particular friend, and she replied with a smile that everyone in Berlin believed that she had, but that everyone was wrong about the principal characteristic of the friend she had, for his relation to her was more that of a father than of a lover.

"Yet you deserve a real lover, and I think it impossible that you can do without one."

"I assure you that I do not give it a thought. I am subject to convulsions, which are the bane of my life. I wanted to go to the baths at Teplitz,[19] where I am assured that I should be cured of them, and the King refused me permission; but I shall have it next year."

She saw that I was ardent, and thinking that I saw her pleased by my restraint, I asked her if she would take it amiss if I visited her frequently. She replied with a laugh that, if I did not mind, she would say she was my niece or my cousin. At that I said to her, without laughter, that it could be true, and that she was perhaps my sister. The arguments for this probability leading us to speak of the fondness which her father had always felt for my mother, we proceeded to caresses which, between relatives, have never been suspect. I took my leave when I felt that I was about to carry them too far. Showing me to the stairs, she asked me if I would dine with her on the next day. I accepted.

Returning to my inn on fire, I reflected on the concatenation of events, and at the end of my reflections I thought that I paid my debt to Eternal Providence by admitting to myself that I was born fortunate.

When I arrived at La Denis's the next day, all the people she had invited to dinner were already there. The first who fell on my neck to embrace me was a young dancer named Aubry,[20] whom I had known in Paris as a member of the *corps de ballet* at the Opéra, then at Venice as leading serious dancer and famous for having become the lover of a most illustrious lady and at the same time the paramour of her husband, who otherwise would not have forgiven his wife for setting up as his rival. Aubry played against the two of them, and he had so shown his mettle that he slept between the husband and the wife. At the beginning of Lent the State Inquisitors sent him to Trieste. Ten years later I find him at La Denis's, where he introduces his wife to me, also a dancer, and known as La Santina,[21] whom he had married in Petersburg, whence they were on their way to spend the winter in Paris. After Aubry's compliments I see approaching me a fat man who says that we were friends twenty-five years before, but that we were so young that we could not recognize each other.

"We knew each other in Padua," he said, "at Doctor Gozzi's, and I am Giuseppe dall'Oglio."[22]

"I remember. You were engaged for the service of the Empress of Russia[23] as a very accomplished violoncellist."

"Exactly so. I am now on my way back to my country, not to leave it again; and this is my wife, whom I introduce to you. She was born in Petersburg, and she is the only daughter of the famous violin teacher Madonis.[24] In a week I shall be in Dresden, where I look forward with particular pleasure to embracing Signora Casanova, your mother."[25]

I was delighted to find myself in this choice company, but I saw that recollections twenty-five years old were displeasing to my charming Madame Denis. I turned the conversation to the events in Petersburg which had raised the great Catherine to the throne, and Dall'Oglio told us that, having taken some part in the cons-piracy,[26] he had prudently decided to ask permission to resign his post;

but that he had become rich enough to be able to spend all the rest of his life in his native country without needing anyone.

La Denis then told us that only ten or twelve days earlier she had been made acquainted with a Piedmontese named Odart,[27] who had also left Petersburg after having directed the entire conspiracy. The reigning Empress had ordered him to leave, making him a present of a hundred thousand rubles.[28]

He had bought an estate in Piedmont, thinking that he should live a long life there in peace and prosperity, for he was only forty-five years old; but he chose the wrong place. Two or three years later a thunderbolt entered his room and killed him in an instant. If the blow fell on him from an all-powerful and invisible hand, it was not that of the Guardian Genius of the Russian Empire seeking to avenge the death of the Emperor Peter III, for if that unhappy monarch had lived and reigned he would have been the cause of countless misfortunes.

Catherine, his wife, recompensing them generously, sent away all the foreigners who helped her to rid herself of a husband[29] who was her enemy, and the enemy of her son[30] and of the whole Russian nation; and she showed her gratitude to all the Russians who had helped her to ascend the throne. She sent on their travels all the noblemen who had reasons not to like the revolution.

It was Dall'Oglio and his pretty wife who made me think of going to Russia if the King of Prussia did not give me such employment as I wanted. They assured me that I should make my fortune there, and they gave me excellent letters.

After they left Berlin I became La Denis's lover. Our intimacy began one evening after supper when she was seized by a fit of convulsions which lasted all night. I spent it at her bedside, and the next morning I received the recompense rightly due to constancy. Our amorous relation continued until I left Berlin. Six years later I renewed it in Florence, and I will speak of it when I come to that time.

A few days after Dall'Oglio left, she was kind enough to take me to Potsdam to show me everything worth seeing there. No one could find anything to object to in our intimacy, for she had already told the world in general that I was her uncle, and I always called her my dear niece. Her protector the General[31] had no doubt that she was such, or pretended not to doubt it.

At Potsdam we saw the King parading his First Battalion, every soldier of which had a gold watch in the fob of his breeches. It was thus that the King rewarded the courage with which they had subjugated him as Caesar subjugated Nicomedes[32] in Bithynia. No secret was made of it.

The room in which we slept at the inn where we put up faced a corridor through which the King passed when he left the palace. The window blinds being closed, our hostess told us the reason for it. She said that La Reggiana,[33] a very pretty dancer, stayed in the same room in which we were, and that the King having seen her stark naked as he went by one morning had immediately ordered her windows shut; that had been four years earlier, but they had never been opened again. He was afraid of her charms. His Majesty, after his amour with La Barberina,[34] became entirely negative. Later we saw in the room in which the King slept portraits of La Barberina, of La Cochois,[35] sister of the actress whom the Marquis d'Argens[36] married, of the Empress Maria Theresa before her marriage, with whom his desire to be Emperor had made him fall in love.

After admiring the beauty and elegance of the apartments in the palace, it was surprising to see how he himself was lodged. We saw a small bed behind a screen in one corner of the room. No dressing gown and no slippers; the valet who was there showed us a nightcap which the King put on when he had a cold; usually he kept on his hat, which must have been awkward. In the same room I saw a table in front of a sofa, on which were writing materials and some half-burned notebooks;[37] he told us that it was the history of the last war, and that the accident which had set fire to the notebooks had so annoyed His Majesty that he had abandoned the work. But he must have taken it up again later, for after his death it was published,[38] and it was little esteemed.

Five or six weeks after my brief conversation with the famous monarch, the Earl Marischal told me that the King offered me a post as tutor to a new corps of noble Pomeranian cadets[39] which he had just established. Their number being set at fifteen, he wanted to give them five tutors; thus each tutor would have three of them, and would have a salary of six hundred crowns and board with his pupils. The fortunate tutor thus needed the six hundred crowns only for clothing. His only duty would be to accompany them everywhere, and to Court too on gala occasions, wearing a gold-laced coat. I must make up my mind as quickly as possible, for four were already appointed, and the King did not like to wait. I asked His Lordship where the academy was, so that I could go to see the place, and I promised him a reply no later than the next day but one.

I needed a self-possession which was not in my nature to keep from laughing at this absurd proposal from a man in other respects so intelligent. But my surprise was still greater when I saw the quarters of these fifteen gentlemen from prosperous Pomerania. I saw three or four drawing rooms almost without furniture, a number of rooms in which there was nothing but a wretched bed, a table, and two wooden chairs, and the young cadets, all twelve or thirteen years of age, ill combed, ill dressed in uniforms, and all with the countenances of peasants. I saw them cheek by jowl with their tutors, whom I took to be their valets, and who looked at me closely, not daring to imagine that I was the colleague whom they expected. Just as I was thinking of leaving, one of the tutors puts his head out a window and says:

"The King is arriving on horseback."

His Majesty comes upstairs with his friend Q. Icilius[40] and goes to inspect everything. He sees me, and he says not a word to me. I had the glittering cross of my order on a ribbon around my neck[41] and an elegant taffeta coat. I was dumbfounded when I saw the great Frederick in a sort of fury looking at a chamber pot which was near a cadet's bed and which displayed to the curious eye the tartarous sediment which must have made it stink.

"Whose bed is this?" said the King.

"Mine," replied a cadet.

"Very good, but it is not you I am angry with. Where is your tutor?"

The fortunate tutor thereupon presented himself, and the monarch, addressing him as "clodhopper," gave him a thorough dressing down. The only consideration he showed him was to tell him he had a servant at his orders, and that it was his duty to see that the place was kept clean.

[* * *]

Casanova took the hint: there was clearly nothing for him in Berlin. Perhaps stimulated by his recent conversations about Catherine the Great, he decided to try his luck in St. Petersburg instead.

CHAPTER V[1]

*Departure from Riga and my arrival
in Petersburg. I go everywhere.
I buy Zaïre.*

I left Riga on December 15th, in atrociously cold weather, but I did not feel it. Traveling day and night, shut up in my Schlafwagen,[2] which I never left, I arrived there in sixty hours. This speed was due to the fact that at Riga I had paid in advance for all the stages, so that I received a post passport from the Governor of Livonia, who was a Marshal Braun.[3] The journey is about equal to the one from Lyons to Paris, for the French league is about equal to four versts[4] and a quarter. On the coachman's seat I had a French manservant, who offered me his services as far as Petersburg gratis, asking only for permission to ride in front of my carriage. He served me very well, poorly clad though he was, bearing up under three nights and two days of very severe cold and nevertheless remaining in good health. I did not see him again in Petersburg until three months after my arrival, when, covered with gold braid, he sat beside me at the table of Count Chernichev,[5] as *uchitel*[6] to a young Count who was sitting beside him. I shall have occasion to speak of the office of *uchitel* in Russia. The word means "tutor."

Young Lambert, lying beside me in my Schlafwagen, did nothing but eat, drink, and sleep, without ever saying a word to me, for he could only talk in his stutter about mathematical problems, in which I was not interested at every hour of the day. Never the least attempt at a joke or at an amusing or critical observation on what we saw; he was boring and stupid; which gave him the privilege of never being bored. At Riga, where I presented him to no one because he was not presentable, all he did was to go to a fencing school, where, having picked up an acquaintance with some idlers, he went to a pothouse to get drunk on beer with them; I did not know how he got the small amount of money he needed for it.

During all the short journey from Riga to Petersburg I stopped only a half hour at Narva,[7] where it was necessary to show a passport which I did not have. I told the Governor that, being Venetian and traveling only for my pleasure, I had never thought I should need a passport, my Republic not being at war with any power and there being no Russian envoy in Venice.[8]

"If Your Excellency nevertheless finds difficulties," I said, "I will go back where I came from; but I will complain to Marshal Braun, who gave me a post passport, knowing that I had obtained a passport from no power."

The Governor thought for a little, then he gave me a sort of passport, which I still have, with which I entered Petersburg not only without being asked if I had any other but without my luggage being searched. From Caporya[9] to Petersburg there is nowhere to eat or sleep except in a private house which does not belong to the post. It is a desert in which not even Russian is spoken. It is Ingria,[10] where the people speak a special language which has nothing in common with other languages. The peasants of the province amuse themselves stealing what little they can from travelers who lose sight of their carriages for a moment.

I arrived in Petersburg just when the first rays of the sun were gilding the horizon. As we were exactly at the winter solstice, and I saw the sun appear, at the end of a vast plain, at precisely twenty-four minutes after nine o'clock, I can assure my reader that the longest night in that latitude lasts eighteen hours and three quarters.

I went to lodge in a wide, handsome street called the Million-naya.[11] At a very reasonable rent I was given two rooms in which I saw not a piece of furniture; but two beds, four chairs, and two small tables were brought at once. I saw immensely big stoves; I thought it would take a great quantity of wood to heat them, but the fact proved to be exactly the contrary; only in Russia is the art of building stoves known, as the art of making cisterns or wells is known only in Venice. When it was summer I examined the inside of a big rectangular stove twelve feet high and six feet wide which was in the corner of a large room; inside it I saw, from the grate where the wood was burned to the top of it, where the pipe began by which the smoke first escaped, to escape afterward through the chimney—I saw, I say, channels[12] all of which led upward in serpentine bends. These stoves keep the room which they heat warm for twenty-four hours by means of the hole at the top, which is at the end of the large pipe and which a servant closes, by pulling a cord, as soon as he is sure that all the smoke from the wood is gone. As soon as he sees, through the small window at the bottom of the stove, that all the wood has become embers, he shuts in the heat above and below. Very rarely is a stove heated twice a day, except in the houses of great noblemen, where the servants are forbidden to shut the stoves at the top. The reason for this prohibition is very wise. It is as follows:

If it happens that a master, arriving tired from hunting or a journey and needing to go to bed, orders his servant to heat the stove, and if the servant, either by inadvertence or from haste, shuts the stove before all the smoke is gone, the sleeping man does not wake again. He commits his soul to his creator in three or four hours, moaning and not opening his eyes. Whoever first enters the room in the morning finds the air heavy, stifling, he sees the man dead, he opens the window at the bottom of the stove, a cloud of smoke bursts out of it, he opens the door and the windows, but the man does not revive, he looks in vain for the servant, who has run away, but who is found with astonishing ease and who is hanged without mercy, though he swears that he did not do it on purpose. An excellent policy, for were it not for this wise law, any servant could poison his master with impunity.

After coming to terms both for heat and for food, and finding everything cheap (which is no longer the case, everything there being now as dear as in London),[13] I bought a chest of drawers, and a large table at which I could write and to put my books and papers on.

The language which I found known to everyone in Petersburg, except the common people, was German, which I understood with difficulty but in which I expressed myself about as I do today. Immediately after dinner my landlord told me that there was a masked ball at Court, gratis, for five thousand people. The ball went on for sixty hours. It was a Saturday. The landlord gives me a ticket, which was necessary and which the masker had only to show at the entrance to the Imperial Palace.[14] I decide to go to it; I had the domino which I had bought in Mitau. I send for a mask, and chairmen carry me to the Court, where I see a great number of people dancing in several rooms in which there were orchestras. I walk through the rooms, and I see buffets at which all those who were hungry or thirsty were eating and drinking. Everywhere I see joy, freedom, and the great profusion of candles which lighted all the places to which I went. As I should expect, I find it all magnificent, superb, and worthy of admiration. Three or four hours passed very quickly. I hear a masker saying to another near to him:

"*There's the Empress, I am sure; she thinks no one can recognize her; but you will see Grigori Grigorievich Orlov*[15] *in a moment; he has orders to*

977

follow her at a distance; he is wearing a domino not worth ten kopecks,[16] *like the one you see on her."*

I follow him, and I am convinced of it, for I hear more than a hundred maskers say the same thing as she passes, all of them, however, pretending not to recognize her. Those who did not know her bumped against her in making their way through the crowd, and I imagined the pleasure she must take in the assurance it gave her that she was not recognized. I often saw her sit down among people who were conversing in Russian, and who were perhaps talking of her. In so doing she exposed herself to unpleasantness, but she had the rare satisfaction of hearing some truths, which she could never flatter herself that she heard spoken by those who were paying court to her without masks. At a distance from her I saw the masker who had been given the name of Orlov, though he never lost sight of her; but in his case everyone recognized him because of his great stature and the way he always kept his head bent forward.

I enter a room in which I see a contradance in the form of a quadrille, and I am pleased to find it being danced perfectly in the French manner; but what takes my attention from it is a man who enters the room alone disguised in the Venetian manner, bautta,[17] black cloak, white mask, cocked hat as in Venice. I feel sure that he is a Venetian, for a foreigner never succeeds in dressing exactly as we do. He comes by chance to watch the contradance beside me. It occurs to me to accost him in French; I say that I had seen many men in Europe disguised in the Venetian manner, but never one so successfully as he, to the point that one would take him for a Venetian.

"I am Venetian."

"Like myself."

"I am not joking."

"Nor am I."

"Then let us speak Venetian."

"Speak, I will answer you."

He then speaks to me, and I see from the word *Sabato*, which means Saturday, that he is not Venetian.

"You are," I say, "a Venetian, but not from the capital, for you would have said *Sabo*."

"I admit it; and from your language I judge that you may be from the capital. I thought the only Venetian in Petersburg was Bernardi."[18]

"You see that it is possible to be mistaken."

"I am Count Volpati,[19] of Treviso."

"Give me your address and I will call on you and tell you who I am, for I cannot tell you here."[20]

"There it is."

I leave him, and two or three hours later what attracts me is a girl in a domino, who was surrounded by several maskers and who was speaking Parisian in falsetto in the style of the balls at the Opéra.[21] I do not recognize her by her voice, but from her language I am sure that she is someone I know, for there were the same catchwords, the same exclamations, which I had made fashionable in Paris wherever I went at all frequently: "Oh, how agreeable!" "The dear man!" A number of these phrases, which I had originated, arouse my curiosity. I stay there, not addressing her, having the patience to wait until she unmasks to steal a look at her face; and at the end of an hour I am able to do it. She has to blow her nose; whereupon, to my great surprise, I see La Baret,[22] the stocking seller at the corner of the Rue Saint-Honoré, whose wedding party at the Hôtel d'Elbeuf[23] I had attended seven years earlier. What had brought her to Petersburg? My old love reawakens, I approach her, and I say in falsetto that I am her friend from the Hôtel d'Elbeuf.

It stops her short, she does not know what to say to me. I whisper into her ear "Gilbert," "Baret," truths which could be known only to her and to a lover; she begins to become curious, she talks only to me; I talk to her of the Rue des Prouvaires, she sees that I know everything about her, she rises, she leaves the company she was with and comes to walk with me, begging me to tell her who I am when I assure her that I had been her fortunate lover. She begins by asking me to tell no one what I knew about her, she says that she left Paris with Monsieur de Langlade, Councilor of the Parlement of Rouen, that she had left him later for a comic opera impresario[24] who had brought her to Petersburg as an actress, that she called herself Langlade, and that she was being kept by Count Rzewuski,[25] the Polish Ambassador.

"But who are you?"

Certain, by then, that she could not refuse me amorous visits, I showed her my face. Mad with joy as soon as she recognized me, she said that it was her good angel who had brought me to Petersburg, for Rzewuski having to return to Poland, it was only on a man like myself that she could count to enable her to leave Russia, where she could no longer bear to be and where she had to practice a profession for which she felt she was not born, for she could neither act nor sing. She gave me her address and an hour, and I let her pursue her way about the ball, extremely delighted to have made this discovery.

I went to a buffet, where I ate and drank very well, then I returned to the crowd, where I saw La Langlade talking with Volpati. He had seen her with me and he had gone to pump her to find out who I was; but, preserving the secrecy which I had enjoined on her, she had told him I was her husband, and she called to me by that name, saying that the masker refused to believe it was true. The young madcap's confidence was of the sort that is made at a ball. After several hours I was ready to go back to my inn; I took a sedan chair, and I went to bed, intending not to rise until it was time to go to mass. The Catholic church was served by Recollect monks,[26] who wore long beards. After sleeping deeply, I am surprised, when I open my eyes, to see that it is not yet light. I turn over on the other side, I go back to sleep, but I wake again a quarter of an hour later, and I feel sorry for myself because I can only sleep in short naps. When day appears I rise, thinking that I had spent a very bad night; I call, I dress, I send for a hairdresser, and I tell the servant to hurry, for, it being Sunday, I want to go to mass; he replies that it is Monday, that I had spent twenty-seven hours in my bed; I understand, I laugh, and I persuade myself that it is true, for I felt I was dying of hunger. That is the only day which I can say I really lost[27] in my life. I had myself carried to the house of Demetrio Papanelopulo, who was the Greek banker with whom I had a credit of a hundred rubles a month. I found myself very well received, on Signor dall'Oglio's[28] recommendation; he invited me to come to dine with him every day, and he at once paid me the month which was already due, showing me that he had honored the draft I had executed in Mitau. He found me a manservant, for whom he vouched, and a carriage by the month for eighteen rubles, which came to a little more than six zecchini. The cheapness of it astonished me; but it is no longer so today. He insisted that I dine there that day, and it was at his table that I made the acquaintance of young Bernardi, the son of the one who had been poisoned because of suspicions the story of which it is not for me to tell.[29] The young man was in Petersburg trying to obtain payment of the sums for which his late father was the creditor for diamonds which he had sold to the Empress Elizabeth. He was lodging at Papanelopulo's, and he ate his meals there, paying him board. Count Volpati came after dinner and told of the encounter he had had at the ball with an unknown man who must be Venetian and who had promised to call on him. Since he knew me only by name, he supposed it could only be I as soon as the banker introduced me to him, and I did not deny it.

The Count was about to leave; he was already in the *Gazette*, as was the custom in Russia, where no one was given a passport until two weeks after the public was informed that he was about to leave.[30] For this reason the merchants very easily give credit to foreigners, and foreigners think twice before they contract debts, for they can hope for no grace. Bernardi could not wait to be rid of Count Volpati, who was the lover of a dancer named La Fusi,[31] with whom he could not hope to accomplish anything until after his departure. This Fusi, after Volpati left, managed things so well with the young, inexperienced man in love that she got him to marry her, which did him the greatest harm in the eyes of the Empress, who had him paid and would not listen to those who solicited some post for him. Two years after I left he died, and I do not know what became of his widow.

The next day I took a letter to the then Colonel Pyotr Ivanovich Melissino,[32] now a General in the Artillery. The letter was from Signora dall'Oglio, whose lover he had been. He received me very well, he presented me to his extremely agreeable wife, and he invited me to supper once and for all. His house was managed in the French style; there was gaming, and afterward everyone supped informally. There I met his elder brother,[33] who was Procurator of the Synod[34] and who was married to a Princess Dolgoruki; the game played was faro; the company was made up of people who could be relied on neither to go about complaining of their losses nor boasting of their winnings; thus it was certain that the Government would not find out that the law against gaming was being broken. The person who kept the bank was a Baron Lefort, the son of the celebrated one.[35] The one I saw there was then in disgrace because of a lottery he had set up in Moscow at the coronation of the Empress, and for which she herself had provided the funds to amuse her Court. The lottery having gone bankrupt because of a lack of management, calumny had laid the disaster to the Baron by raising the suspicion that he was the guilty party. I played for small stakes, and I won a few rubles. Supping beside him, I improved the acquaintance, and, seeing him at his own house later, he informed me of his vicissitudes. Speaking of gaming, I praised the noble indifference with which Prince xxx had lost a thousand rubles to him. He laughed, and he told me that the exalted gamester whose noble disinterest I had admired did not pay.

"But honor?"

"Honor is not lost here on that account. There is a tacit understanding that a person who loses on his word pays if he wants to, and if he does not want to that is his privilege. The person who won from him would make himself ridiculous by demanding payment."

"It is a system which entitles the banker to refuse to carry anyone on his word."

"Nor does the gamester take offense at it. He leaves, or he puts pledges on the table. There are young scions of the highest nobility who have learned to cheat and who boast of it; a Matiushkin[36] defies all the foreign sharpers to win from him. He has just obtained leave to travel for three years. He says he is sure he will come back to Russia very rich."

At Melissino's I made the acquaintance of a young officer of the Guards named Zinoviov,[37] a relative of the Orlovs, who introduced me to the English Envoy Macartney,[38] a handsome young man of great intelligence, who had the weakness to fall in love with Mademoiselle Shitrov,[39] one of the Empress's ladies in waiting, and the boldness to get her with child. The Empress considered this English freedom an impertinence, forgave[40] the young lady, who danced very well at the Imperial Theater, and had the Envoy recalled. I met the brother of the lady in waiting, already an officer,[41] a handsome youth of great promise. At the exalted spectacle of a performance at the Court itself, at which I saw Mademoiselle Shitrov dance, I also saw Mademoiselle Sievers dance; she is now Princess N. N.,[42] whom I saw four years ago at Dresden with her daughter, who was very well brought up and clever at drawing. Mademoiselle Sievers enchanted me. I fell in love with her without ever being able to tell her so, for I was never introduced to her. She danced to perfection. The castrato Putini[43] enjoyed her good graces, which he certainly deserved both by his talent and his intelligence. He even lodged at Count Sievers's. It was the castrato Putini who brought to Petersburg the Venetian chapelmaster Galuppi,[44] called Buranello, who arrived there the next year, when I was leaving.

Demetrio Papanelopulo introduced me to the Cabinet Minister Olsuviev,[45] heavy and fat, full of wit, and the only man of learning I knew in Petersburg, for he had not become learned by reading Voltaire but by having gone to Uppsala to study[46] in his youth.

That rare man, who loved women, wine, and choice viands, invited me to dine at Locatelli's[47] at Ekaterinhof,[48] an imperial residence which the Empress had given to the old theatrical impresario for his lifetime. He was astonished when he saw me; but I was even more so to see that he had become a caterer, for that was what he did at Ekaterinhof, where, for a ruble a head, without wine, he gave excellent meals to all who went there. Monsieur Olsuviev introduced me to another Secretary of the Cabinet, Teplov,[49] who was fond of handsome youths, and whose virtue was that he had strangled Peter III, who had kept the arsenic from killing him by drinking lemonade. The person who introduced me to the third Secretary of the Cabinet, Yelagin,[50] who had spent twenty years in Siberia, was the dancer Mécour,[51] his mistress, to whom I had brought a letter from La Santina,[52] whose acquaintance I had made when she passed through Berlin. A letter from Dall'Oglio which I took to Luini,[53] a castrato musician very skilled in his art, handsome and extremely agreeable, gained me a most cordial reception in his house, where the table was exquisite. La Colonna,[54] who was first singer, was his mistress. They lived together to torment each other. I did not see them in agreement even one day. It was at his house that I made the acquaintance of another castrato, well versed in his art and agreeable, whose name was Millico[55] and who, constantly going to the house of the Master of the Imperial Hunt, Naryshkin,[56] mentioned me to him so often that the amiable nobleman, who had some smattering of letters, wanted to make my acquaintance. He was the husband of the celebrated Maria Pavlovna.[57] It was at the Master of the Hunt's magnificent table that I made the acquaintance of the *kaloyer*[58] Platon,[59] now Archbishop of Novgorod, then preacher to the Empress. This Russian monk understood Greek, spoke Latin and French, he was intelligent, he was handsome; it was natural that he should make his fortune in a country where the nobility have never condescended to intrigue for ecclesiastical dignities.

I took a letter from Dall'Oglio to Princess Dashkov,[60] who lived three versts from Petersburg, exiled from the Court when, after helping the Empress to mount the throne, she expected to share it with her. Catherine humbled her ambition. I found her dressed in mourning because of the death of the Prince her husband, who had died in Warsaw. It was she who spoke of me to Monsieur Panin[61] and who three days later wrote me a note in which she said that I could go to see him whenever I wished. I thought it admirable behavior on the Empress's part: she had disgraced Princess Dashkov, but she did not prevent her chief Minister from paying court to her every evening. I heard from people worthy of credence that Count Panin was not Princess Dashkov's lover but her father. The Princess is today the President of the Academy of Sciences. Its learned members would blush to have a woman at their head if they had not found her a Minerva. What is still wanting in Russia is the spectacle of some celebrated woman commanding its armies.

A thing which I saw[62] with Melissino, and which struck me, was the ceremony of the blessing of the waters on the Day of the Epiphany, performed on the Neva covered with five feet of ice. The children are baptized by immersion, being plunged into the river through a hole made in the ice. On that particular day, it happened that the pope who was doing the immersing let the child he was putting into the water slip from his hands.

"Drugoi," he said.

That is, "Give me another one"; but what I found wonderful was the joy of the father and mother of the drowned child, who certainly could only have gone to Paradise, having died at that fortunate moment.

I took the letter from the Florentine Signora Bregonzi,[63] who had given me supper in Memel, to the friend whom she had assured me I could persuade to be useful to me. The friend was a Venetian named Signora Roccolino;[64] she had left Venice to sing on the stage in Petersburg, knowing no music and never before having practiced the profession. The Empress, after laughing at her for her folly, sent her word that there was no position for her; but what did Signora Vincenza (for so she was called) do then? She struck up an intimate friendship with a Frenchwoman, the wife of one Proté,[65] a French merchant who lodged at the Master of the Hunt's. This woman, who was in possession of that nobleman's heart, was at the same time the confidante of his wife Maria Pavlovna, who, not loving her husband, was delighted that the Frenchwoman freed her from the obligation of submitting to her matrimonial duties if he took it into his head to demand them of her. But La Proté was the most beautiful woman in Petersburg. In the flower of her age, to all the graces of gallantry she joined the most refined taste in dress. No woman could adorn herself as she did; extremely gay in company, she united all voices in her favor; when La Proté was mentioned in Petersburg everyone was jealous of the Master of the Hunt's good fortune in possessing her. Such was the woman whose confidante Signora

Vincenza had become. She invited to her house the men who were in love with her and who were worthy of consideration, and La Proté never failed to go there. Signora Vincenza did not scruple to accept the presents which gratitude procured her from one direction or another.

As soon as I saw Signora Vincenza I recognized her; but, at least twenty years having passed since what had happened between us had taken place, she showed no surprise that I had forgotten it, and she took care not to remind me of it. Her brother, whose name was Montellato, was the man who, one night when I was leaving the Ridotto,[66] came to murder me in the Piazza San Marco, and it was in her house that a plot had been hatched which would have cost me my life if I had not jumped out the window into the street. She gave me exactly the reception which one gives to a dear fellow country-man, an old friend whom one encounters far from home; she told me her misfortunes in detail, and at the same time she boasted of her courage. She needed no one, she said, and she lived gaily with the most agreeable women in Petersburg.

"I am amazed," she said, "that, dining at the Master of the Hunt Naryshkin's as often as you do, you have not met the beautiful Madame Proté, she is the Master of the Hunt's heart and soul; come and take coffee with me tomorrow, and you will see a prodigy."

I go there, and I find her above praise. Being no longer rich, I use my wit to make an impression on her; I ask her what her name is, she says that it is Proté, I reply that she thereby declares herself to be *"pro me"*; I explain the pun[67] to her; I jest, I tell her stories, I let her know that she has set my soul on fire, I do not despair of coming to be happy in time, and the acquaintance is made. From then on I never went to the Master of the Hunt's without going to her room before and after dinner.

About this time, the Polish Ambassador having returned to Warsaw, I had to break off my liaison with La Langlade, who accepted an advantageous proposal which Count Bryus[68] made her. I then ceased to go to her house. That charming woman died six months later of smallpox. I longed to make progress with La Proté. To that end, I gave a dinner at Locatelli's in Ekaterinhof, to which I invited Luini with La Colonna, a Guards officer named Zinoviov,[69] La Proté, and Signora Vincenza with a vio-linist who was her lover. The gaiety of the dinner having set the guests on fire, after coffee each cavalier tried to disappear with his lady, profiting by which I began to take possession of the beauty, without, however, coming to the heart of the matter because of an interruption. We all went out to see what Luini, who had gone hunting, would bag in the park; he had brought his guns and his dogs for the purpose. Having left the imperial residence a hundred paces behind with Zinoviov, I point out to him a peasant girl whose beauty was surprising; he sees her, he agrees, we walk toward her, and she runs away to a hut, which she enters; we enter it too, we see her father, her mother, and the whole family, and she herself in a corner of the room, like a rabbit afraid that the dogs it saw would devour it.

Zinoviov—who, parenthetically, is the man who spent twenty years in Madrid as the Empress's envoy—talks to the father in Russian for a long time; I see that the subject is the girl, for her father calls her and I see her come forward obediently and sub-missively and stand before the two of them. A quarter of an hour later he leaves, and I follow him, after giving the fellow a ruble. Zinoviov tells me that he had asked the father if he would give her into service, and that the father had replied that he would be willing, that he must get a hundred rubles because she still had her maiden-head.

"You see," he said, "that there is nothing to be done."

"What do you mean? Suppose I were willing to give the hundred rubles?"

"Then you would have her in your service, and you would have the right to go to bed with her."

"And if she did not want it?"

"Oh, that never happens. You would have the right to beat her."

"Then suppose that she is willing. I ask you if, after enjoying her and finding her to my liking, I could go on keeping her."

"You become her master, I tell you, and you can even have her arrested if she runs away, unless she gives you back the hundred rubles you paid for her."

"And if I keep her with me, how much a month must I give her?"

"Not a copper. Only food and drink, and letting her go to the bath every Saturday so that she can go to church on Sunday."

"And when I leave Petersburg can I make her go with me?"

"Not unless you obtain permission and give security. Though she has become your slave, she is still first of all the slave of the Empress."

"Excellent. Arrange it for me. I will give the hundred rubles, and I will take her with me, and I assure you I will not treat her as a slave; but I put myself in your hands, for I should not want to be cheated."

"I will strike the bargain myself, and I assure you that I shall not be cheated. Do you want me to do it at once?"

"No, tomorrow; for I do not want the company to know of it. Tomorrow morning I will come to your house at nine o'clock."

We all returned to Petersburg together in a phaeton, and the next morning at the appointed hour I was at Zinoviov's, who was delighted to do me this small favor. On our way he said that if I liked, in a few days he would get me together a seraglio of as many girls as I could want. I gave him the hundred rubles.

We arrive at the peasant's hut, the girl being there. Zinoviov explains the matter to him, the peasant thanks St. Nicholas[70] for the good fortune he has sent him, he talks to his daughter, I see her looking at me, and I understand that she says yes. Zinoviov then tells me that I must assure myself that she is a virgin, since in signing the agreement I must state that I had bought her for my service as such. My upbringing made me reluctant to insult her by examining her; but Zinoviov encouraged me, saying that I would be doing her a favor by enabling myself to testify to the fact to her parents. At that I sat down and, taking her between my thighs, I explored her with my hand and found that she was intact; but to tell the truth I would not have called her a liar even if I had found her maidenhead gone. Zinoviov counted out the hundred rubles to the father, who gave them to his daughter, whereupon she put them in her mother's hands, and my manservant and the coachman came in to sign as witnesses to what they did not know. The girl, whom I at once gave the name Zaïre,[71] got into the carriage and drove to Petersburg with us dressed as she was in coarse cloth and without a shift. After thanking Zinoviov I stayed at home for four days, never leaving her until I saw her dressed in the French style, simply but neatly. My martyrdom was not knowing Russian; but it was she who, in less than three months, learned Italian—very badly, but well enough to tell me whatever she wanted to. She began to love me, then to be jealous; once she came very near to killing me, as my reader will see in the next chapter.

CHAPTER VI

Crèvecoeur. Baumbach. Journey to Moscow.
Continuation of my adventures in Petersburg.

On the same day that I took Zaïre home with me I dismissed
Lambert. He got drunk every day, I no longer knew what to do
with him. There was no opening for him except as a common
soldier. I obtained a passport for him, and I gave him what money
he needed to return to Berlin. Seven years later in Görz[1] I learned
that he had entered the Austrian service.

Zaïre, having become so pretty by the month of May that,
wanting to go to Moscow, I did not dare to leave her in Petersburg,
I took her with me, dispensing with a manservant. The pleasure I
took in hearing her talk to me in Venetian was inconceivable.[2] On
Saturdays I went to the Russian baths[3] to bathe with her in company
with thirty or forty other people, both men and women and all stark
naked, who, looking at no one, supposed that no one looked at
them. This lack of modesty had its source in innocence of intention.
I was amazed that no one looked at Zaïre, who seemed to me the
original of the statue of Psyche which I had seen in the Villa
Borghese.[4] Her breasts were not yet developed, she was in her
thirteenth year; nowhere did she show the indubitable imprint of
puberty. Snow white as she was, her black hair made her whiteness
even more brilliant. But for her accursed jealousy, which was a daily
burden to me, and the blind faith she had in what the cards which
she consulted every day told her, I should never have left her.

A young Frenchman with a handsome face, whose name was
Crèvecoeur[5] and who showed that he had had an upbringing
worthy of his birth, arrived in Petersburg with a Parisian girl
whom he called La Rivière,[6] young and not ugly, but who had no
talent, and no education except that which is acquired by all girls in
Paris who offer their charms for sale. The young man came to bring
me a letter from Prince Charles of Kurland, who said no more to me
than that if I could be of use to the couple he would take it as a favor.
He brought me the letter, accompanied by his fair lady, at nine
o'clock in the morning, just as I was breakfasting with Zaïre.

"It is for you to tell me," I said, "in what way I can be of use
to you."

988

"By admitting us to your company, by introducing us to your acquaintances."

"As for my company, I am a foreigner, it amounts to very little. I will go to see you, you shall come to me when you like, and I shall find it a pleasure; but I never eat at home. As for my acquaintances, you must see that, as a foreigner, I should go beyond what is permissible if I presented you and Madame. Is she your wife? I shall be asked who you are and what has brought you to Petersburg. What am I to say? I am surprised that Prince Charles did not send you to others."

"I am a gentleman from Lorraine. I came here to amuse myself; Mademoiselle Rivière there is my mistress."

"I cannot imagine to whom I can introduce you on those grounds, and in any case I think that you can see the customs of the country and amuse yourselves without needing anyone. The theaters, the promenades, even the pleasures of the Court are open to all. I imagine that you are not short of money."

"On the contrary, I have no money, and I expect none from anyone."

"And I have none left either; and you astonish me. How can you have been so foolish as to come here without money?"

"It is she who says that we need none except from day to day. She made me leave Paris without a copper, and until now she seems to be right. We have managed to live everywhere."

"Then it is she who has the purse."

"My purse," she said, "is in the pockets of my friends."

"I understand, and I see that you must find friends in all the inhabited globe; if I had a purse, for friendship of that kind I would open it to you too. But I am not rich."

Baumbach,[7] of Hamburg, whom I had known in England, from which he had fled because of debts, had come to Petersburg, where he had had the good fortune to enter the military service; son of a rich merchant, he had a house, servants, and a carriage, he liked prostitutes, good food, and play, he got into debt in all directions. He was ugly, lively, and filled with the spirit of libertinism. He arrives at my lodging just in time to interrupt the conversation I had begun with the strange young woman whose purse on her travels was in her friends' pockets. I introduce Monsieur and Madame, telling him everything except the matter of the purse. Baumbach, in ecstasies over the encounter, makes advances to La Rivière, who receives them in the manner of her trade, and in a quarter of an hour I laugh to see that she was right. Baumbach invites them to dine at his house the next day, and begs them to go with him that very day to Krasni-Kabak,[8] where he will give them an informal dinner; he asks me to be one of the party, and I accept. Zaïre asks me what is afoot, for she does not understand French, and I tell her. She says that since it is to be a party at Krasni-Kabak, she wants to go there too, and I say that she may, for it was pure jealousy and I feared the consequences, which consisted in ill-humor, tears, and fits of despair, which had more than once driven me to beat her; it was the best way to convince her that I loved her. After the beating she became affectionate little by little, and peace was made with the rites of love.

Baumbach, very well pleased, went to attend to some business, promising to return at eleven o'clock, and while Zaïre got dressed, La Rivière treated me to a discourse intended to convince me that so far as knowledge of the world went I was the most ignorant of men. What astonished me was that her lover was not at all ashamed of the role he played. The only excuse he could offer me was that he was in love with the wench; but I could not accept it.

Our party was gay. Baumbach talked only to the adventuress, Zaïre sat on my lap the greater part of the time, Crèvecoeur ate, laughed in season and out of season, and went for a walk; the beauty challenged Baumbach to play quinze[9] for twenty-five rubles, which he lost very gallantly and which he paid her, obtaining nothing in exchange but a kiss. Zaïre, very glad to have been on an excursion during which she feared I would be unfaithful to her, said a thousand amusing things to me about the Frenchwoman's lover, who was not jealous of her. She could not understand how she could bear having him so sure of her.

"But I am sure of you, and yet you love me."

"That is because I have never given you reason to think me a wh...."[10]

The next day I went to Baumbach's alone, being sure that I should find there some young Russian officers, who would have annoyed me too much by flirting with Zaïre in their language. At Baumbach's I found the traveling couple, and the two Lunin brothers,[11] then Lieutenants, now Generals. The younger of the two brothers was blond and pretty as a girl; he had been loved by the Secretary of the Cabinet Teplov,[12] and, like an intelligent youth, he not only defied prejudice, he deliberately set about winning the affection and esteem of all men of position, in whose company he was always to be found, by his caresses. Having supposed the

Hamburger Baumbach to have the same inclination which he had found Monsieur Teplov to possess, and not being mistaken, he would have thought it insulting to me not to make me of their company. With this idea in mind he took a place beside me at table, and he lavished such pretty attentions on me during dinner that I really thought he was a girl in men's clothing.

After dinner, when I was sitting before the fire between him and the traveling Frenchwoman, I declared my suspicion to him, but Lunin, jealous of the superiority of his sex, immediately displayed his, and, curious to know if I would remain indifferent to his beauty, he laid hold on me, and thinking himself convinced that he had pleased me, put himself in a position to make himself and me happy. And it would have happened if La Rivière, angry that a youth should infringe on her rights in her presence, had not taken him by the waist and forced him to put off his exploit to a more suitable time.

The struggle made me laugh; but not having been indifferent to it I saw no reason to pretend that I was. I told the wench that she had no right to interfere in our business, which Lunin took to be a declaration in his favor on my part. Lunin displayed all his treasures, even those of his white bosom, and defied the wench to do as much, which she refused, calling us b . . . . . .; we replied by calling her a wh . . . ,[13] and she left us. The young Russian and I gave each other tokens of the fondest friendship, and we swore that it should be eternal.

The elder Lunin, Crèvecoeur, and Baumbach, who had gone for a walk, came back at nightfall with two or three friends who easily consoled the Frenchwoman for the poor entertainment we had given her.

Baumbach made a bank at faro, which continued until eleven o'clock, when he had no more money, and we supped. After supper the great orgy began. La Rivière held her own against Baumbach, the elder Lunin, and his friends the two young officers. Crèvecoeur had gone to bed. I and my new friend alone appeared to keep our heads, calmly watching the encounters which quickly succeeded one another, each different from the last, and of which poor Crèvecoeur's mistress always bore the brunt. Offended that she interested us only as spectators, she from time to time vented her spleen against us in the most cruel sarcasms; but we laughed at them. Our attitude was like that of two virtuous old men who look with tolerance on the extravagances of unbridled youth. We parted an hour before dawn.

I arrive at my lodging, I enter my room, and by the purest chance I avoid a bottle which Zaïre has thrown at my head and which would have killed me if it had struck me on the temple. It grazed my face. I see her throw herself down in a fury and beat her head on the floor; I run to her, I seize her, I ask her what is the matter with her, and, convinced that she has gone mad, I think of calling for help. She calms her frenzy, but bursting into tears and calling me "murderer" and "traitor." To convict me of my crime she points to a square of twenty-five cards, in which she makes me read in symbols the whole of the debauch which had kept me out all night. She shows me the wench, the bed, the encounters, and even my sins against nature. I saw nothing; but she imagined that she saw everything.

After letting her say everything necessary to relieve her furious jealousy, I threw her accursed abracadabra into the fire, and, looking at her with eyes in which she could see both my anger and the pity I felt for her, and telling her in so many words that she had very nearly killed me, I declare that we must part for ever on the morrow. I say it was true that I had spent the night at Baumbach's, where there was a wench, but I naturally deny all the excesses she accused me of. After that, needing sleep, I undress, I get into bed, and I go to sleep, despite everything that, lying down beside me, she did to win her pardon and assure me of her repentance.

After five or six hours I am awake, and, seeing her sleeping, I dress, thinking how best to get rid of a girl who, one day or another, might very well kill me in her jealous rages. But how could I carry out my intention when I saw her on her knees before me, despairing and repentant, begging me to forgive her, to take pity on her, and assuring me that in future I should find her as gentle as a lamb? The upshot of it was that, taking her in my arms, I gave her unmistakable tokens of the return of my affection, on condition, which she swore to fulfill, that she would not consult the cards again as long as she lived with me. I had decided to go to Moscow three days after this occurrence, and I filled her with joy by assuring her that I would take her with me. Three things in particular had made the girl love me. The first was that I often took her to Ekaterinhof to see her family, where I always left a ruble; the second was that I had her eat with me when I invited people to dinner; the third was that I had beaten her two or three times when she had tried to keep me from going out.

Strange necessity for a master in Russia: when the occasion arises, he has to beat his servant! Words have no effect; nothing but stirrup leathers produce one. The servant, whose soul is only that of a slave, reflects after the beating, and says: "My master has not dismissed me, he would not have beaten me if he did not love me, so I ought to be attached to him."

Papanelopulo[14] had laughed at me when, at the beginning of my stay in Petersburg, I said to him that, being fond of my Cossack, who spoke French, I wanted to attach him to me by kindness, chastising him only with words when he drank himself senseless on spirits.

"If you do not beat him," he said, "the day will come when he will beat you."

And it happened. One day when I found him so much the worse for drink that he could not wait on me I thought it best to scold him in harsh words, threatening him only by raising my walking stick. As soon as he saw it in the air, he ran at me and seized it; and if I had not instantly knocked him down he would certainly have beaten me. I dismissed him then and there. There is no better servant in the world than the Russian, tireless at work, sleeping on the threshold of the room in which his master sleeps so that he can run to him as soon as he calls, always submissive, bandying no words with him even when he is clearly in the wrong, and incapable of stealing from him; but he becomes a monster or an imbecile when he has drunk a glass of spirits, and it is the vice of all the common people. A coachman exposed to the severest cold, often all night long, at the door of a house where he is keeping watch over his horses, knows no other way of maintaining his resistance than to drink brandy. If he drinks two glasses of it he may fall asleep on the snow, where he sometimes does not wake again. He dies frozen. The misfortune of losing an ear, the whole nose except the bone, a piece of cheek, a lip, frequently occurs if one is not careful. A Russian saw that I was about to lose an ear one day when I arrived at Peterhof[15] in a sleigh, the cold being very dry. He at once rubbed me with a handful of snow until the whole cartilage which I was going to lose came back to life. Asked how he had known that I was in danger, he said that is easy to know, for the part attacked by the cold turns extremely white. What surprised me, and what I still find incredible today, is that the lost part sometimes comes back. Prince Charles of Kurland assured me that he lost his nose one day in Siberia, yet he got it back again the following summer. Several muzhiks[16] assured me of the same phenomenon.

During this time the Empress had a commodious wooden amphitheater built, as large as the whole square in front of her

palace, which was built by the Florentine architect Rastrelli.[17] The
amphitheater, intended to accommodate a hundred thousand spectators, was the work of the architect Rinaldi,[18] who had been in
Petersburg for fifty years and who never wanted to return to his
native Rome. In the interior of this edifice Catherine intended to
give a tournament for all the valiant cavaliers of her Empire. There
were to be four quadrilles, in each of which a hundred warriors,
richly clad in the costume of the nation they represented, were to
contend, jousting against each other on horseback, for prizes of great
value. The whole Empire had been informed of the magnificent
festival, which was to be given at the sovereign's expense; and the
Princes, Counts, and Barons began to arrive from the most distant
cities with their fine horses. Prince Charles of Kurland had written
me that he would arrive too. It had been decided that the day on
which the festival would take place would be the first day of fair
weather; and nothing was more sensible, for a whole fair day
without rain or wind or threatening clouds is a very rare phenomenon in Petersburg. In Italy we count on good weather; in Russia
they count on bad. I laugh when Russians traveling in Europe talk
of their fine climate. It is a fact that during the whole of the year
1765 there was not one fine day in Russia; the irrefutable proof of
which is that it was impossible to hold the tournament.[19] The
wooden structure of the amphitheater was covered over, and it
was held the next year. The horsemen spent the winter in Petersburg; those who did not have money enough to stay went home.
One of the latter was Prince Charles of Kurland.

Everything being arranged for my journey to Moscow, I got into
my Schlafwagen with Zaïre, with a manservant who spoke Russian
and German up behind. For eighty rubles an *izvozchik*[20] contracted
to take me to Moscow in six days and seven nights with six horses. It
was cheap, and, not taking the post, I could not expect to travel
faster, for the journey was seventy-two Russian stages, which made
five hundred Italian miles[21] more or less. It seemed to me impossible, but that was his business.

We left when the cannon shot from the citadel told us that day
was done; it was toward the end of May, when one no longer sees
any night in Petersburg. But for the cannon shot which announces
that the sun had sunk below the horizon, none would know it. One
can read a letter at midnight there, the moon does not make night
lighter. People say it is beautiful, but it annoyed me. This continual
day lasts for eight weeks. During that time no one lights candles. It is

different in Moscow. Four and a half degrees of latitude less than at Petersburg make a candle always necessary at midnight.

We reached Novgorod in forty-eight hours, where the *izvozchik* allowed us five hours' rest. It was there that I saw something which surprised me. Invited to drink a glass, the coachman looked very gloomy, he told Zaïre that one of his horses would not eat, and he was in despair, for he was sure that, not having eaten, it could not go on. We all go out with him, we enter the stable, and we see the horse listless, motionless, with no appetite. Its master began haranguing it in the gentlest of tones, giving it looks of affection and esteem calculated to inspire the animal with sentiments which would persuade it to eat. After thus haranguing it, he kissed the horse, took its head in his hands and put it in the manger; but it was useless. The man then began to weep, but in such a way that I was dying to laugh, for I saw that he hoped to soften the horse's heart by his tears. After weeping his fill, he again kisses the beast and again puts its head in the manger; but again to no purpose. At that the Russian, in a towering rage at such obstinacy in his beast, swears vengeance. He leads it out of the stable, ties the poor creature to a post, takes a big stick, and beats it with all his strength for a good quarter of an hour. When he can go on no longer, he takes it back to the stable, puts its head in the trough, whereupon the horse eats with ravenous appetite, and the *izvozchik* laughs, jumps up and down, and cuts a thousand happy capers. My astonishment was extreme. I thought that such a thing could happen only in Russia, where the stick has such virtue that it performs miracles. But I have thought that it would not have happened with a donkey, which stands up under a beating much more stubbornly than a horse. I am told that today blows are not as much in fashion in Russia as they were at that time. The Russians, unfortunately, are beginning to become French.[22] A Russian officer told me that, from the time of Peter I, who, when he was displeased, rained blows from his stick on his Generals, the Lieutenant had to receive his Captain's blows with submission, the Captain the Major's, the Major the Lieutenant-Colonel's, the latter the Colonel's, who in turn had to receive them from the Brigadier-General. All this has changed today. I learned this at Riga from General Voeikov,[23] who had been brought up by the great Peter and who was born before the birth of Petersburg.[24]

I think I have said nothing about that city, which is today so celebrated and whose existence I still consider precarious, when I think of it today. It required a genius like that of that great man, who amused himself by giving the lie to Nature, to think of building a city which was to become the capital of his whole immense Empire in a place where the terrain cannot be less favorable to the labors of those who doggedly try to make it fit to hold up the palaces which are every day built there of stone, at enormous expense. I am told that the city has reached maturity today, to the glory of the great Catherine; but in the year 1765 I saw it still in its infancy. Everything seemed to me ruins built on purpose. The streets were paved in the certainty that they would have to be repaved six months later. I saw a city which a man in a hurry must have had built in haste; and in fact the Czar gave birth to it in nine months. But the nine months were its time of coming to birth; the child had perhaps been conceived long before. Contemplating Petersburg, I reflected on the proverb: *Canis faestinans caecos edit catulos* ("A bitch in a hurry bears blind pups");[25] but a moment later, admiring the great design, I said, with utmost respect: *Diu parturit leaena sed leonem* ("The lioness is long in giving birth, but she bears a lion").[26] A century from now I prophesy a magnificent Petersburg, but raised at least twelve feet, and then the great palaces will not fall into ruin for lack of piling. The barbarous architecture brought there by the French architects and fit only to build houses for marionettes will be proscribed; and Monsieur Betskoi,[27] a man of intelligence be it said, will no longer exist to give the preference over Rastrelli and Rinaldi to a Delamotte,[28] a Parisian who astonished Petersburg by constructing a four-story house the wonderful thing about which, according to him, was that no one could either see or guess where the staircases were.[29]

We arrived in Moscow as our man had promised us we should do. It was not possible to arrive there more quickly, traveling always with the same horses; but by post one goes there rapidly.

"The Empress Elizabeth," a man who was there said to me, "made the journey in fifty-two hours."

"I can well believe it," said a Russian of the old school, "she issued an ukase in which she prescribed the time, and she would have got there still faster if the time she prescribed had been shorter."

It is a fact that in my day it was not permitted to doubt the infallibility of an ukase; whoever ventured to doubt that an ukase, which means "decree," could be carried out was considered guilty of lèse-majesté. In Petersburg I was crossing a wooden bridge with Melissino, Papanelopulo, and three or four others, when, one of them hearing me criticize the meanness of the bridge, said that it would be built of stone by the day of a certain public function on which the Empress was to cross it.[30] Since it was only three weeks to the day, I said it was impossible; a Russian, looking at me askance, said that it was not to be doubted, for there had been an ukase; I was going to reply, but Papanelopulo pressed my hand and made me a sign to say nothing. In the end the bridge was not built, but that did not put me in the right, for, ten days before the day, the Empress issued a second ukase in which she decreed that it was her good pleasure that the bridge should not be built until the following year.

The Czars of Russia have always used, and still use, the language of despotism in everything. One morning I saw the Empress dressed in men's clothing to go riding. Her Grand Equerry, Prince Repnin,[31] was holding the bridle of the horse she was to mount, when the horse suddenly gave the Grand Equerry such a kick that it broke his ankle. The Empress, with a look of astonishment, ordered the disappearance of the horse and announced that death would be the punishment of anyone who dared in future to bring the offending animal before her eyes. The title which is still given today to all Court posts is a military title, which shows the nature of the government. The Empress's head coachman has the rank of colonel, as does her head cook; the castrato Luini had the rank of Lieutenant-Colonel, and the painter Torelli[32] had only the rank of captain, since he had only eight hundred rubles a year. The sentinels who stand with crossed muskets at the inner doors of the Empress's apartments ask the person who wants to enter what his rank is, to learn if they are to uncross their muskets to let him go in; the word is *Kakoi rang?* ("What rank?") When I was asked this question for the first time, and the meaning was explained to me, I was at a loss; but the officer who was there asked me how much I had a year, and when I answered him that I had three thousand rubles he at once gave me the rank of general, and I was allowed to pass. It was in this room that a moment later I saw the Empress stop at the door and take off her gloves to give the two sentinels her beautiful hands to kiss. It was by this sort of informal behavior that she kept the affection of this body of guards, which was commanded by Grigori Grigorievich Orlov, and on which the safety of her person depended in case of a revolution.

Here is what I saw the first time that I followed her to her chapel where she was going to hear mass. The *protopapas*, or bishop,[33] received her at the door to offer her the lustral water, and she kissed his ring at the same time that the prelate, decorated with a beard two feet long, bent his head to kiss the hand of his sovereign, who was at once his mistress in things temporal and his patriarch. During the whole mass she showed no sign of devotion; hypocrisy was unworthy of her, with a smiling glance she dignified now one now another of the congregation, from time to time speaking to her favorite, to whom she had nothing to say; but she wanted to glorify him by showing all who were present that it was he whom she distinguished and set above all others.

One day as she left the opera house, where Metastasio's *Olimpiade*[34] had been performed, I heard her say these exact words:

"The music of this opera has given everyone the greatest pleasure, and so I am delighted with it; but I was bored listening to it. Music is a beautiful thing, but I do not see how one can love it passionately, unless one has nothing important to do and to think about. I am having Buranello[35] brought here now; I am curious to see if he will be able to make music become something to interest me."

This is the style in which she always spoke. I will report in the proper place what she said to me on my return from Moscow. We lodged at a good inn, where I was given two rooms and where my carriage was put in a stable. After dinner I engaged a two-seated carriage, and I took a hire valet who spoke French. My carriage was for four horses, for the city of Moscow is made up of four cities,[36] and one has to drive great distances through unpaved or badly paved streets if one has many visits to make. I had five or six letters, and I wanted to leave them all; sure that I should not get out of the carriage, I took with me my dear Zaïre, who, a girl of thirteen, was curious about everything. I do not remember what feast the Greek Church was celebrating that day, but I still remember the deafening ringing of bells which I heard in every street, for I saw churches everywhere. Wheat was being sown then for the harvest in September, and we were laughed at for sowing it eight months earlier than they did, whereas not only is it unnecessary but it can only make the harvest smaller. I do not know who is right, but it is possible that we are all right.

I took to their addresses all the letters I had received in Petersburg from the Master of the Hunt, from Prince Repnin, from my banker Papanelopulo, and from Melissino's brother. The next morning I received visits from all the persons to whom I had been sent. They all invited me to dinner with my dear girl. I accepted the dinner of the first to come, who was Monsieur Demidov,[37] and

998

I promised all the others that I would go to them in turn on the following days. Zaïre, instructed in the role she was to play, was enchanted to show me that she deserved the distinction I was conferring on her. Pretty as a little angel, wherever I took her she was the delight of the company, who did not care to inquire if she was my daughter, my mistress, or my servant. In this respect, as in many others, the Russians are an admirable people. Those who have not seen Moscow cannot say that they have seen Russia, and those who have known Russians only in Petersburg do not know the Russians, for at Court they are all different from what they are by nature. In Petersburg they can all be considered foreigners. The citizens of Moscow, and especially the rich ones, pity all those whom rank, interest, or ambition has "expatriated"; for their father-land is Moscow, and they consider Petersburg nothing but the cause of their ruin. I do not know if this is true, but I say what they say.

At the end of a week I had seen everything: manufactories, churches, old monuments, natural-history collections, libraries, which did not interest me, the famous bell,[38] and I observed that their bells are not hung so that they swing, like ours, but immovably. They are rung by a rope fastened to the end of the clapper. I found the women prettier in Moscow than in Petersburg. They are gentle by nature and very accessible, it is enough to offer to kiss their hands to obtain the favor of a kiss on the lips. As for the fare, I found it profuse and without delicacy. Their table is always open to all their friends; and a friend brings five or six people to dinner without notice, sometimes even arriving when dinner is ended. It is unheard of for a Russian to say: *"We have dined, you have come too late."* They have not the baseness of soul required to utter those words. It is for the cook to see to it, and dinner begins over again; the master or the mistress makes much of the *gosti*.[39] They have a delicious drink[40] the name of which I have forgotten, but better than the sherbet[41] one drinks in Constantinople in the houses of all the great nobles. They do not give their servants, who are very numerous, water to drink, but a concoction which is not unpleasant to the taste, which is healthy and nutritious, and so cheap that with a ruble they make a large cask of it. I observed the great devotion they all have for St. Nicholas.[42] They pray to God only through the intercession of this saint, whose image must stand in a corner of the room in which the master of the house receives visitors. The person who enters bows first to the image, then to the master; if the image by some chance is not there, the Russian, after looking all over the room for it, is nonplussed, does not know what to say, and loses his head. The Russian is in general the most superstitious of all Christians. His language is Illyrian,[43] but his liturgy is entirely Greek; the common people do not understand a word of it, and the clergy, themselves ignorant, are delighted to keep them in ignorance. I was never able to make a *kaloyer* who spoke Latin understand that the only reason why we Romans, when we sign ourselves with the cross, move our hand from the left shoulder to the right, while the Greeks move theirs from right to left, is that we say *spiritus sancti* while they say, in Greek, *agios pneuma*.

"If you said *pneuma agios*," I said to him, "you would sign yourselves as we do, or we would do it as you do if we said *sancti spiritus*."

He replied that the adjective had to be before the substantive, because one could not utter the name of God without preceding it by an honorific epithet. Of this caliber are almost all the differences which separate the two sects, to say nothing of a great number of lies, which I found among them as among us.

We returned to Petersburg in the same way in which we had come from it; but Zaïre would have wished me never to leave Moscow. Being with me at every hour of the day and the night, she had become so much in love that I was distressed when I thought of the moment when I should have to leave her. The day after my arrival I took her to Ekaterinhof, where she showed her father all the little presents I had given her, telling him in great detail all the honors she had received as my daughter, which made the good man laugh heartily.

The first piece of news which I heard at Court was of an ukase ordering the building of a temple, to be dedicated to God, in the Morskaya,[44] opposite the apartment in which I was living. It was Rinaldi whom the Empress had chosen to be the architect of it. Philosopher[45] that he was, he had told her that he must know what emblem he was to put above the portal of the temple, and she replied that he was to use no emblem, simply writing GOD in large letters there, in whatever language he chose.

"I will put a triangle."

"No triangle. GOD, and that is all."

Another piece of news was the flight of Baumbach, who had been caught at Mitau, where he believed he was safe; but Monsieur de Simolin[46] had arrested him. The poor fool was in custody and his case was serious, for it was a matter of desertion. However, he was

spared the full penalty and sent to garrison in Kamchatka.[47] Crèvecoeur and his mistress had left with some money, and a Florentine
adventurer named Bilioti[48] had fled, taking eighteen thousand rubles
from Papanelopulo; but a certain Bori, Papanelopulo's familiar spirit,
had caught him in Mitau too, and had brought him back to Petersburg, where he was in prison. During these days Prince Charles of
Kurland arrived, and he sent me word of it at once. I went to call on
him at the house in which he was staying, which belonged to
Monsieur Demidov, who, owning iron mines, had taken it into
his head to have the house built entirely of iron. Outside walls,
stairway, doors, flooring, partitions, ceiling—everything was of iron,
except the furniture. He did not fear fire. The Prince had brought
with him his mistress, ill-humored as ever, whom he could no
longer put up with because she was really intolerable, and he was
to be pitied, for he could only get rid of her by giving her a husband,
and a husband such as she demanded was not to be found. I paid her
a visit, but she bored me so much with her complaints of the Prince
that I did not go back again. When the Prince came to see me and
saw my Zaïre, and reflected how little my happiness, and hers, cost
me, he learned how every sensible man who needs to love should
keep a concubine; but man's stupid hankering after luxury spoils
everything and turns every sweet to bitterness for him.

I was thought happy, I liked to appear so, and I was not happy.
From the time of my imprisonment under the Leads I had become
subject to internal hemorrhoids which troubled me three or four
times a year, but at Petersburg it became serious. An intolerable pain
in the rectum, which returned every day, made me melancholy and
wretched. The octogenarian physician Sinopaeus,[49] whom I told of
it, gave me the unhappy news that I had an incomplete fistula, of the
sort called blind, a sinus which had formed in my rectum. There was
no remedy but the cruel lancet. According to him I must make up
my mind to undergo the operation at once. The first thing was to
find out the height of the sinus, and to that end he came to my
lodging on the day after I had confided in him, with a good surgeon
who examined my intestine by introducing a lint probe covered
with oil into my anus; drawing it out, he learned its height and
extent by observing the place on the probe where the little stain
from the running humor of the fistulous cavity had remained. The
little cavity of my sinus, the surgeon told me, was two inches away
from the sphincter; the base of the sinus might be very big; my pain
came from the fact that the acrid lymph which filled the sinus was

corroding the flesh to open a way of escape, which would make my
fistula complete and the operation easier. After this opening which
nature would bring about, he said, I should be relieved of the pain
but be much more inconvenienced by the continual flow of pus
which I should have in the region. He advised me to be patient and
to wait for this beneficial effect of nature. He said, thinking that it
would comfort me, that complete fistula in the anus was a very
common complaint throughout the province in which the excellent
water of the Neva was drunk, for it had the faculty of purifying the
body by forcing out the noxious humors. For this reason everyone
in Russia who suffers from hemorrhoids is congratulated. My incomplete fistula, by obliging me to live in accordance with
a regimen, was perhaps good for my health.

The Colonel of Artillery Melissino invited me to a review three
versts from Petersburg, where the Commanding General, Alexis
Orlov, was to give dinner to the principal guests at a table set for
eighty. The party were to see a drill with the cannon which was
supposed to fire twenty times a minute. I went with the Prince of
Kurland, and I admired the exact fulfillment of the expectation. The
field cannon, served by six artillerymen and loaded by them twenty
times in one minute, fired as many shots while advancing toward the
enemy. I saw it, holding a watch with a second-hand. In three
seconds, the cannon was swabbed out at the first, loaded at the
second, and fired at the third.

At the big table I found myself beside the French Secretary of
Embassy,[50] who, wanting to drink in the Russian fashion and
thinking that Hungarian wine was as light as champagne, drank it
to such purpose that when he rose from table he could not stand.
Count Orlov set things to rights by making him go on drinking until
he vomited, and then he was carried off asleep.

In the high spirits which reigned at the dinner I enjoyed some
samples of the country's wit. *Fecundi calices quem non fecere disertum*
("Who has not been made eloquent by many cups?").[51] Since I did
not understand Russian, Monsieur Zinoviov, who was seated beside
me, explained all the witticisms of the guests which were followed
by applause. They were delivered, glass in hand, as a toast to
someone, who must reply in the same strain.

Melissino rose, holding a large goblet filled with Hungarian
wine. Everyone fell silent to hear what he would say. He toasted
his General, Orlov, who was opposite him at the other end of the
table. Here is what he said:

"May you die on the day you find yourself rich."

The applause was general. He was praising Monsieur Orlov's great generosity. He might have been criticized, but in lively company one does not consider so curiously. I thought Orlov's reply more sensible and more noble, though no less Tartarian,[52] for it, too, had to do with death. Rising in his turn, holding a big goblet,

"May you never die," he said, *"except by my hands."*

Still louder clapping.

The wit of the Russians is forceful and striking. They care nothing for subtlety or elegance of expression; they go to the point roughshod.

At this same time Voltaire had sent the Empress his *Philosophy of History,*[53] written for her and dedicated to her in a dedication six lines long. A month later a whole edition of the same work, three thousand volumes in all, arrived by water and disappeared entirely in a week. All the Russians who could read French had the book in their pockets. The leaders of the Voltaireans were two very intelligent noblemen, a Stroganov[54] and a Shuvalov.[55] I saw some verses by the former as fine as those of his idol, and twenty years later a superb dithyramb[56] by the latter; but the subject of it was the death of Voltaire, which seemed to me very strange, for a poem of that genre was never used for a sad subject. In those days Russians with pretensions to literature, whether they were noblemen or the more lettered among the military, knew, read, and praised only Voltaire, and, after reading all that Voltaire had published, believed that they were as learned as their idol; I told them that they should read the books from which Voltaire had taken his learning, and they would perhaps come to know more than he. "Beware," a wise man said to me in Rome, "of arguing with a man who has read only one book."[57] Such were the Russians in those days; but I have been told, and I believe it, that they are profound today. In Dresden I knew Prince Beloselski,[58] who, after being Ambassador in Turin, returned to Russia. The Prince was determined to geometrize the human intelligence; he analyzed metaphysics; his little book classified the soul and reason; the more I read it, the more highly I admire it. It is a pity that an atheist can put it to wrong use.

But here is a sally of Count Panin's, tutor to Paul Petrovich,[59] heir presumptive to the Empire, who was so submissive to him that, at the opera, he did not dare to applaud an air sung by Luini until he had given him permission.

When the courier bringing the news of the sudden death of Francis I,[60] the Roman Emperor, arrived, the Empress was at Krasnoe-Selo,[61] the Count-Minister was in the palace at Petersburg with his august pupil, who was then eleven years of age. The courier came at noon to deliver the dispatch to the Minister, who stood facing those who were present at his audience, of whom I was one. Paul Petrovich was at his right. He unseals the dispatch, he reads it in a low voice, then he says, addressing no one in particular:

"Here is important news. The Roman Emperor has died suddenly. Full Court mourning, which Your Highness," he said to the Prince, looking at him, "will wear three months longer than the Empress."

"But why am I to wear it longer?"

"Because, as Duke of Holstein, Your Highness has a seat in the Diet of the Empire, a privilege," he added, turning to the bystanders, "which Peter I so greatly desired and was never able to obtain."

I observed the attention with which the Grand Duke listened to his mentor, and how well he managed to hide the joy he felt. This method of instruction pleased me greatly. Give ideas to the young mind, and leave it to disentangle them. I praised it to Prince Lobkowitz,[62] who was there, and who carried my reflections even further. Prince Lobkowitz made everyone like him; he was preferred to his predecessor Esterházy,[63] and that is saying a great deal, for Esterházy had won all hearts. Prince Lobkowitz, with his high spirits and his affability, was the life of every occasion which he attended. He was paying court to the Countess Bryus,[64] who was the reigning beauty, and no one believed that he was unsuccessful.

At that time a great infantry review[65] was held twelve or fourteen versts from Petersburg; the Empress was there, with all the ladies of the Court and the principal courtiers; two or three villages near the place had houses, but so few that it was very difficult to obtain lodgings in them; even so, I wanted to attend it, partly to satisfy Zaïre, who was ambitious to show herself in my company. The festivities were to go on for three days, there were to be fireworks made by Melissino, a mine was to blow up a fort, and there were to be a number of military maneuvers on a great plain, which should furnish a most interesting spectacle. I went there in my Schlafwagen with Zaïre, having no doubt that I should obtain the lodging, whether good or bad, which I needed. It was at the time of the solstice, and there was no night.

We arrive at eight o'clock in the morning at the place where, on this first day, the maneuvers went on until noon, and afterward we stop in front of a tavern, where we have food brought to us in the carriage, for the place was so full that we could not have found room. After dinner my coachman goes everywhere to look for some sort of lodging, but none is to be found. What of it?—not wanting to go back to Petersburg, I decide to lodge in my carriage. That was what I did for all the three days, and what was declared excellent by all those who had spent a great deal and who had been very poorly lodged. Melissino told me that the Empress had declared my expedient very sensible. My house, of course, was movable, and I placed myself at the points which were always the safest and the most convenient in respect to the place where the maneuvers were to be held on that particular day. In addition my carriage was expressly made to afford perfect comfort on a mattress, for it was a sleeper. I was the only person who had such a carriage at the review; visits were paid me, and Zaïre shone in doing the honors of the house in Russian, which I was very sorry I did not understand. Rousseau, the great J. J. Rousseau, ventured to declare the Russian language a dialect of Greek.[66] So stupid a mistake does not seem to be consonant with a genius so rare, yet he fell into it.

During the three days I often conversed with Count Tott,[67] the brother of the one who then held a post in Constantinople, who was known as Baron de Tott. We had first known each other in Paris, then in The Hague, where I had the good fortune to be useful to him. He was then away from France in order to avoid difficulties into which he would have run with his fellow officers at the Battle of Minden.[68] He had come to Petersburg with Madame Soltikov,[69] whose acquaintance he had made in Paris and with whom he had fallen in love. He lodged in her house, he went to Court, where he was well regarded by everyone. He was very gay, his mind was well furnished, and he was also a handsome young man.[70] Two or three years later he was ordered by the Empress to leave Petersburg, when the war against the Turks was brought on by the troubles in Poland.[71] It was claimed that he was maintaining a correspondence with his brother, who was then working at the Dardanelles to prevent the passage of the Russian fleet commanded by Alexis Orlov. I do not know what became of him after he left Russia.

He greatly obliged me in Petersburg by lending me five hundred rubles which I have never had an opportunity to return to him, but I am not dead yet.

During these days Monsieur Maruzzi,[72] a Greek man of business who had been a merchant in Venice and who had given up business in order to become a free man, arrived in Petersburg, was presented at Court, and, having a pleasant countenance, was introduced to all the great houses. The Empress distinguished him because she was considering making him her Chargé d'Affaires in Venice. He paid court to Countess Bryus; but his rivals did not fear him; rich though he was, he was afraid to spend, and in Russia avarice is a sin which women do not forgive.

During this time I made journeys to Tsarskoye-Selo, Peterhof, Oranienbaum, and Kronstadt;[73] one should see everything when one goes anywhere and wants to say one has seen everything. I wrote on several subjects in an attempt to enter the civil service, and I presented my productions, which were seen by the Empress; but my efforts were useless. In Russia only men who are expressly sent for are regarded. Those who go there by their own choice are not esteemed. Perhaps this is right.

CHAPTER VII

I see the Czarina. My conversations with that
great sovereign. La Valville. I leave Zaïre. My
departure from Petersburg and my arrival in
Warsaw. The Princes Adam Czartoryski and
Sulkowski. The King of Poland, Stanislaus
Poniatowski, called Stanislaus Augustus I.
Theatrical intrigues. Branicki.

I was thinking of leaving at the beginning of the autumn, and both
Monsieur Panin and Monsieur Olsuviev kept telling me that I ought
not to go until I could say that I had spoken to the Empress. I replied
that I regretted it too, but that, having found no one who would
present me, I could only complain everywhere of my bad luck.

It was finally Monsieur Panin who told me to take a walk early in
the Summer Garden,[1] where she went very often and where,
meeting me by chance, it was likely that she would speak to me.
I gave him to understand that I should like to meet Her Imperial
Majesty on a day when he was with her. He named the day, and
I went there.

Strolling by myself, I looked at the statues bordering the walk,
which were of inferior stone and very badly executed, but which
became comic by reason of the names engraved on them. A weeping
statue offered the reader the name of Democritus, a laughing one
was Heraclitus, an old man with a long beard was named Sappho,
and an old woman with shrunken breasts was Avicenna.[2] They were
all in the same style. Just then I see, halfway down the walk, the
sovereign advancing, preceded by Count Grigori Orlov and followed by two ladies. Count Panin was at her left, and she was
speaking to him. I stand aside to let her pass, and as soon as she is
within range she asks me, with a smile, if the beauty of the statues
had greatly interested me; I reply, following her, that I thought they
had been put there to impose on fools or to arouse laughter in
people who had some acquaintance with History.

"All I know," she replied, "is that my worthy aunt,[3] who in any
case was not one to trouble about investigating trifles of the sort, was
imposed on; but I hope that you have not found everything you
have seen in our country as absurd as these statues."

I should have offended against both truth and good manners if, to this frankness on the part of a lady of her caliber, I had not shown her that in Russia what was laughable was nothing in comparison with what was admirable; and thereupon I entertained her for more than an hour on everything of every sort which I had found remarkable in Petersburg.

The course of my remarks having led me to mention the King of Prussia, I pronounced a eulogy on him, but at the same time respectfully taking the monarch to task for his habit of never letting the person who was answering a question he had put to him finish his answer. She then gave a gracious smile, and she asked me for an account of the conversations I had had with him, and I told her everything. She was kind enough to say that she had never seen me at the *courtag*.[4] This *courtag* was a concert of instrumental and vocal music, which she gave in her palace every Sunday after dinner and to which everyone could go. She walked up and down at it, and she spoke to those to whom she wished to accord that honor. I said that I had been to it only once, it being my misfortune that I was not fond of music. She then said, smiling and looking at Monsieur Panin, that she knew someone else who had the same misfortune. She meant herself. She stopped listening to me to speak to Monsieur Betskoi, who was approaching, and, Monsieur Panin having left her, I also left the garden, delighted with the honor I had been accorded.

Of medium stature, but well built and with a majestic bearing, the sovereign had the art of making herself loved by all those who she believed were curious to know her. Though not beautiful, she was sure to please by her sweetness, her affability, and her intelligence, of which she made very good use to appear to have no pretensions. If she really had none, her modesty must have been heroic, for she had every right to have them.

Some days later Monsieur Panin told me that the Empress had twice asked him for news of me, and that he was sure I had pleased her. He advised me to watch for opportunities to meet her, and he assured me that, having already had a taste of my quality, she would signify to me that I should approach her whenever she saw me anywhere, and that if I wanted employment, she might think of me.

Though I did not myself know for what employment I might be fitted in a country which, furthermore, I did not like, I was nevertheless very glad to know that it might be easy for me to obtain some sort of access to her Court. With this idea in mind, I went to the garden every morning. Here is a full account of the second conversation I had with her. Seeing me from a distance, she sent me word by a young officer to approach her.

As there was talk everywhere of the tournament which the bad weather had prevented from being held, she asked me, for the sake of asking me something, if a show of the sort could be given in Venice, and I answered by discoursing at some length on the sort of shows which could not be given there, and on those which were given there[5] and which could not be given anywhere else, which amused her; and in this connection I said that the climate of my native country was more fortunate than that of Russia, for fair days were common there, while in Petersburg they were very rare, despite the fact that foreigners found the year there younger than anywhere else.

"That is true," she said, "for in your country it is eleven days older."

"Would it not be," I went on, "an act worthy of Your Majesty to adopt the Gregorian calendar?[6] All the Protestants conformed to it, and England did so too, fourteen years ago, excising the last eleven days of February, and she has already gained several millions by it. In this general agreement Europe is astonished that the old style remains in force here, where the sovereign is the visible head of her Church, and where there is an Academy of Sciences. It is thought, Madame, that the immortal Peter, who ordered that the year should begin on the first of January,[7] would also have ordered the abolition of the old style, if he had not thought he should conform to England, which was then the moving spirit of all the commerce of your vast Empire."

"You know," she said, affably and slyly, "that the great Peter was not a learned man."

"I believe, Madame, that he was a great deal more. The monarch was a true and sublime genius. What served him instead of learning was a delicate tact which led him to judge rightly of all that he saw and thought could increase the happiness of his subjects. It was the same genius which always kept him from making a misstep, and which gave him the strength and the courage to root out abuses."

The Empress was about to answer me, when she saw two ladies to whom she sent word to approach.

"I will answer you with pleasure on another occasion," she said, and turned to the ladies.

The "other occasion" arrived a week or ten days later, when I thought that she no longer wished to speak to me, for she had seen me and had not sent to summon me.

She began by telling me that what I wanted her to do for the glory of Russia was already done.

"All the letters," she said, "which we write to foreign countries, and all the public acts which may be of interest to History, we countersign with the two dates, one under the other, and everyone knows that date which is in advance by eleven days is the modern one."

"But," I ventured to object, "at the end of this century the extra days will become twelve."

"Not at all, for that has also been done. The last year of this century, which, in accordance with the Gregorian reform, will not be bissextile[8] among you, will not be so among us either. Thus no real difference remains between us. Is it not true that this reduction suffices as soon as it stops the progress of the error? It is even fortunate that the error is one of eleven days, for that being the number which is added every year to the epact,[9] we can say that your epact is ours, with only the difference of a year. We even have it together during the last eleven days of the tropical year.[10] As for the celebration of Easter, we must leave it to take care of itself. You have the equinox set at the twenty-first of March, we have it at the tenth, and the same objections which the astronomers make to you, they make to us; sometimes it is you who are right, sometimes it is we, for after all the equinox often arrives one, two, or three days later or earlier; and as soon as we are sure of the equinox, the law of the March moon[11] becomes of no account. You see that you are often not in agreement even with the Jews, whose embolism[12] is said to be perfect. To conclude, this difference in the celebration of Easter does not disturb public order or the due maintenance of it, or cause any change in the important laws pertaining to government."

"What Your Majesty has just said is very wise and fills me with admiration; but Christmas——"

"It is only there that Rome is in the right, for you were going, I think, to tell me that we do not celebrate it during the days of the solstice, when it should be celebrated. We are aware of it. Permit me to say to you that it is a carping observation. I prefer letting this slight error remain to causing all my subjects great pain by removing from the calendar eleven days which would take away their birthdays or their name days from two or three million souls, and even from them all, for it would be said that with unheard-of despotism I had deprived everyone of eleven days of life. People would not complain aloud, for that is not the way here, but they would whisper to

VOLUME TEN CHAPTER SEVEN

one another that I am an atheist and that I am clearly attacking the infallibility of the Council of Nicaea.[13] This laughably simple-minded criticism would not make me laugh. I have much more agreeable things to laugh at."

She had the pleasure of seeing me surprised and of leaving me in my surprise. I felt certain that she had studied the subject on purpose to dazzle me, or that she had conferred with some astronomer after I had mentioned the reform to her in our last conversation. Monsieur Olsuviev told me some days later that it was quite possible that the Empress had read some little treatise on the subject which said everything about it that she had said to me and even more, and that it was also possible that she was perfectly well versed in the subject.

With great modesty of manner, she expressed her opinion precisely, and her mind seemed as imperturbable as her humor, whose even tenor was shown by her smiling countenance. Since she had made a habit of it, it could not cost her much effort; but that takes nothing from the merit of the thing, for to do it one must have a strength above the ordinary impulses of human nature. The Empress's bearing, the very opposite of that of the King of Prussia, showed me a genius far greater than the latter's. The kindly exterior by which she offered encouragement assured her of profiting, whereas the other, with his brusqueness, was in danger of being the loser by it. Catherine, with her undemanding manner, could demand more and obtain it. When one examines the life of the King of Prussia one admires his courage, but one sees at the same time that, but for the aid of Fortune, he would have been defeated, and when we examine that of the Empress of Russia we do not find that she counted much on the help of the blind goddess. She accomplished things which, before she mounted the throne, appeared great enterprises to all Europe; it seems that she wanted to convince all Europe that she found them small.

In one of those modern journals in which the journalist abandons his proper function to draw the reader's attention to himself, making bold to reveal his thoughts without a care for the reader whom they may offend, I read that Catherine II died happy,[14] as she had lived. She died, as everyone knows, a sudden death. Now this journalist, calling such a death happy, informs us, without telling us, that it is such a death which he would wish for himself. That is all very well—every man to his taste; and we can wish it to him since that is what he wants. But if, for such a death to be happy, it is necessary to suppose that the person whom it suddenly strikes wished for it, who told him that Catherine desired it? If he supposes the desire in her because of the profound intelligence which everyone attributed to her, we might ask him by what right he decides that a profound intelligence must regard a sudden death as the happiest of all deaths. Is it because he so regards it himself? But if he is not a fool, he ought to fear he may be wrong; and if he is in fact wrong, he is proved a fool. So the journalist is convicted of being a fool whether he is wrong or not wrong. To know which he is, we should have to question the late Empress today.

"Are you well satisfied, Madame, to have died a sudden death?"

"What nonsense! You could only put such a question to a woman in despair or to a woman who, because of her poor constitution, had to fear a painful death after a long and cruel illness. I was happy, and I was in very good health. No greater misfortune could befall me, for it is perhaps the only one which, not being a fool, I had no reason ever to expect. The misfortune prevented me from finishing a hundred things, which I should very easily have finished if God had granted me the least little illness the slightest symptom of which could have made me foresee the possibility of my death; and I can assure you that, to prepare myself for it, I should not have needed to have my doctor predict it to me. But not a bit of it. It was an order from Heaven which obliged me to set out on the greatest of journeys, without leaving me time to pack my things, when I was not ready. Am I to be called happy in having succumbed to this death because I did not have the grief of seeing it arrive? Those who suppose that I should not have had the strength to resign myself peacefully to a law of nature common to all mortals must have seen in me a cowardice with which, to tell the truth, I do not believe I ever in my life gave anyone reason to suspect that I was tainted. In short, I can swear to you today, naked spirit as you see me, that I should confess myself satisfied and happy if the too severe decree of Heaven had granted me only twenty-four hours of good sense before my last moment. I should not complain of its injustice."

"What, Madame! You accuse God of injustice?"

"How could I do otherwise, since I am damned? Do you believe it possible that a damned soul, even if on earth it had been the guiltiest of the living, can consider just a decree which condemns it to be unhappy for all eternity?"

"Indeed I consider it impossible, for recognizing the justice of your sentence would to a certain extent console you."

She spoke to me of the customs of the Venetians, of their love for games of chance, and in that connection she asked me if the Genoese lottery was established there.

"I was urged," she said, "to permit it in my domains, and I should have consented; but on condition that the amount risked should never be less than a ruble, in order to keep the poor from playing, who, incapable of reckoning, think it is easy to get a *terno*."

In reply to this observation, which was based on profound wisdom, I made her a very low bow. This was the last conversation I had with that great lady, who was able to reign for thirty-five years without ever making a crucial mistake and without ever departing from moderation.

Not long before I left, I gave an entertainment at Ekaterinhof for all my friends, with a fine display of fireworks which cost me nothing. It was a present from my friend Melissino; but my supper at a table for thirty was exquisite and my ball brilliant. Despite the slimness of my purse, I thought it incumbent on me to give my good friends this token of my gratitude for all the kindnesses they had shown me.

Since I left with the actress Valville,[20] it is here that I must tell my reader how I made her acquaintance.

I went all alone to the French theater, and I took a seat in a third-tier box beside a very pretty lady who was there all alone and whom I did not know. I speak to her, now to criticize, now to praise the work of an actress or actor, and she always replies with an intelligence as seductive as her charms. Enchanted by her, toward the end of the play I make bold to ask her if she is Russian.

"I am a Parisian," she replied, "and an actress by profession. My stage name is Valville, and if you do not know me I am not surprised, for I arrived here only a month ago, and I have acted only once, in the role of the soubrette in *Les Folies amoureuses*."[21]

"Why only once?"

"Because I did not have the good fortune to please the sovereign. But since I am engaged for a year she ordered that I be paid the hundred rubles which are due me every month, and at the end of the year I shall be given a passport, my journey will be paid for, and I will leave."

"I am sure that the Empress thinks she is doing you a favor by paying you when you do not have to work."

"She must certainly think so, for she is not an actress. She does not know that, by not acting, I lose more than she gives me, for I am forgetting my profession, which I have not yet learned completely."

"You should let her know that."

"I wish she would grant me an audience."

"That is not necessary. You certainly have a lover."

"No one."

"It is unbelievable."

No later than the next morning I send her a note in the following terms:

"I wish, Madame, to enter upon a liaison with you. You have inspired in me desires which trouble me and which I challenge you to satisfy. I ask you to invite me to supper, wanting to know in advance how much it will cost me. Having to leave for Warsaw next month, I offer you a place in my sleeping carriage, which will cost you only the inconvenience of letting me lie beside you. I know how to obtain a passport for you. The bearer has orders to wait for an answer, which I hope to read in terms as clear as those of this note."

Here is her answer, which I received two hours later:

"Having, Monsieur, the great art of breaking off any liaison with the greatest ease when I find it ill assorted, I have no difficulty in consenting to enter into one. In regard to the desires I have inspired in you, I am sorry that they trouble you, for they flatter me, and I could bring myself to satisfy them only in order to make them stronger. As for the supper which you ask of me, you will find it ready this evening, and we will bargain afterward for what follows it. The place which you offer me beside you in your sleeping carriage will be precious to me if, in addition to my passport, you have influence enough to get my journey to Paris paid for me. I hope that you will not find my terms less clear than yours. Good-by, Monsieur, until this evening."

I found La Valville all alone and very pleasantly lodged; I approached her, and she received me as if we were old friends. Proceeding at once to what interested her more than anything else, she said she would consider herself fortunate to leave with me, but that she doubted if I could get the necessary permission. I repeated that I was sure of it if she would present such a petition to the Empress as I would write for her, and she promised to present it, giving me ink and paper to write it at once. Here it is, in a few lines:

"Madame, I beg Your Imperial Highness to consider that, remaining here for a year doing nothing, I should lose my art all the more easily since I have not yet learned it completely. Hence your generosity becomes more harmful than useful to me; it would fill me with gratitude if Your Imperial Highness would carry it so far as to give me permission to leave."

"What?" she said. "No more than that?"

"Not one word more."

"You say nothing about the passport or the money for the journey, and I am not rich."

"Present this petition, and either I am the greatest fool on earth or you will have not only the money for your journey but all your salary for a year."

"That would be too much."

"It is certain. You do not know the Empress, and I know her. You must have it copied, and present it in person."

"I will copy it myself. My hand is very legible. I really feel as if I had composed it myself, for it is exactly in my style. I believe you are more of an actor than I am, and I want to begin studying under you this very evening. Let us have supper."

After a light and sufficiently choice supper, which La Valville seasoned with countless amusing Parisian expressions which I knew well enough, she made no difficulty about granting me the rest. I went downstairs only for a moment to dismiss my carriage and tell my coachman what to say to Zaïre, whom I had already told that I might go to Kronstadt and spend the night there. He was a Ukrainian, of whose loyalty I had more than once had proof; but I saw at once that, if I became La Valville's lover, I could no longer keep her with me.

In this actress I found the same character and the same qualities which one finds in all French girls who, having charms and some sort of education, consider that merit enough to entitle them to belong to only one man; they want to be kept, and the title of mistress is far more flattering to them than that of wife.

During the intermissions she told me some of her adventures, which made me guess her whole story, which was not long. The actor Clairval,[22] who had gone to Paris to recruit a troupe of players[23] for the Court at Petersburg, having met her by chance and found her intelligent, had convinced her that she was a born actress, even though she had never had any notion of it. The idea had dazzled her, and she had signed the agreement and received one from the recruiter without even troubling to look at his credentials. She had left Paris with him and with six others, actors and actresses, among whom she was the only one who had never in her life appeared on the stage.

"I thought," she said, "that just as among us a girl enters the Opéra in the chorus or the ballet without ever having learned to sing or dance, one joined a company of actors in the same way. How could I have thought anything else when an actor like Clairval told me that I was born to shine on the stage and proved it to me by taking me with him? Before giving me a written engagement he insisted only on hearing me read and making me learn two or three scenes from different plays, which he had me act in my room with him, who, as you know, plays valets to admiration; and certainly he did not mean to deceive me. He deceived himself. Well, two weeks after we arrived here I made my debut, and I got what they call a 'slap in the face,' about which I really don't care, for I don't feel it."

"Perhaps you were afraid."

"Afraid! Just the contrary. Clairval told me that if I had been able to show a little fear the Empress, who is kindness itself, would have thought it her duty to encourage me."

I left her in the morning after seeing my petition written out in her hand and excellently copied. She assured me that she would present it herself the following morning, and I accepted her invitation to a second supper for the day when I should have parted from Zaïre, whose story I told her. She praised my discretion.

French girls who have sacrificed themselves to Venus, if they have intelligence and some education, are all of the same stamp as La Valville; they have neither passion nor temperament, and so they do not love. They are accommodating, and their project is always one and the same. Able to break off a liaison at will, they enter into one with the same facility and always in a smiling humor. This is not from stupidity, but from a deliberate system. If it is not the best one, it is at least the most convenient.

Back at my lodging, I found Zaïre apparently calm, but sad; this displeased me more than anger, for I loved her; but I had to make an end and prepare to suffer all the grief which her tears would cause me. Knowing that I must leave and that, not being Russian, I could not take her with me, she was concerned about what was to become of her. She would belong to the man to whom I should give her passport, and she was very curious to know who he would be. I spent the whole day and the night with her, giving her tokens of my affection and of the grief I felt at being obliged to part from her.

The architect Rinaldi, a man of sense, who was seventy years of age[24] and who had been in Russia for forty, was in love with her; he had told me several times that I should be doing him the greatest favor if I would leave her to him on my departure, offering to give me twice what she had cost me, and I always answered him that I would never leave Zaïre to anyone with whom she would not have wanted to be of her own free will, since I intended to make her a present of the amount I should be paid by the person who acquired her. This did not please Rinaldi, for he did not venture to suppose that he pleased her; yet he hoped.

He came to me on the morning which I had decided should see the end of the business, and, speaking Russian very well, he explained to the girl all that he felt for her. She replied in Italian that, since she could belong only to the person to whom I should leave her passport, it was to me that he should address himself, and that in any case she had no inclination in the matter, neither disliking nor feeling a fondness for anyone. Unable to get a more affirmative answer from her, the worthy man left after dining with us, hoping little, but still asking for my good offices.

After he was gone I asked her to tell me sincerely if she would hold it against me if I left her to that worthy man, who would certainly treat her as if she were his own daughter.

Just as she was about to answer, I was handed a note from La Valville, in which she asked me to come to her at once, to hear some news which would please me. I immediately ordered horses put to my carriage.

"Very well," said Zaïre in a perfectly calm voice, "go about your business, and when you come back I will give you a definite answer."

I found La Valville very happy. She had waited for the Empress on her way from the chapel to her apartment, and, asked by her what she was doing there, she had given her the petition. She had read it as she walked on, and with a sweet smile had told her to wait. Three or four minutes later, having written on it, she had had the petition returned to her, addressed to the Secretary of the Cabinet Yelagin.[25] Inside it she had written four lines in Russian, which Monsieur Yelagin had himself translated for her, she having at once gone to him with the petition. The Empress ordered him to deliver to the actress Valville a passport, her salary for a year, and a hundred Dutch ducats for her journey. She was certain to receive it all in two weeks, because she could not receive the passport from the police until two weeks after an announcement of her departure was published.

The grateful Valville showed me how much my friend she was, and we settled the time of our departure. I had mine announced in the city *Gazette* three or four days later. Having promised Zaïre that I would come home, and being curious what her answer would be, I left her, assuring her that I would live with her as soon as I had put the girl I had to leave in Petersburg in good hands.

After supping with me in a very good humor, Zaïre asked me if, when he took her, Signor Rinaldi would pay me back the hundred rubles I had given her father; I answered that he would.

"But now," she said, "it seems to me I am worth much more, since you are leaving me all that you have given me and since I can make myself understood in Italian."

"I see that, my little dear; but I don't want it said that I made a profit on you, and the more so because I have already decided to make you a present of the hundred rubles I shall receive upon giving him your passport."

"Since you want to make me such a fine present, why do you not rather put me back in my father's hands with my passport? Don't you see that that would be still more generous? If Signor Rinaldi loves me, you have only to tell him to come to see me at my father's house. He speaks Russian too, they will agree on a price, and I will not object. Shall you be sorry if he does not get me so cheaply?"

"Certainly not, my dear child; on the contrary, I shall be very glad to have been of use to your family, for after all Signor Rinaldi is rich."

"That will do, and you will always be dear to my memory. Let us go to bed. You shall take me to Ekaterinhof no later than tomorrow morning. Let us go to bed."

That is the whole story of my parting from the girl who was the cause of my leading a more or less regular life in Petersburg. Zinoviov told me that, if I had furnished security, I could have left with her, and that he would himself have done me the favor. I declined, thinking of the consequences. I loved her, and it would have been I who became her slave; but it may be that I should not have reflected so sagely if at the same time I had not fallen in love with La Valville.

Zaïre spent the morning getting her things together, now laughing, now crying, and she saw my tears each time she left her trunk to come and kiss me.

When I left her at her father's, giving him her passport, I saw her whole family on their knees before me, addressing me in terms which are due only to the divinity. But Zaïre looked very much out of place in the hovel, for what they called a bed was only a big straw mattress on which the whole family slept together.

When I told Signor Rinaldi what had happened he took it in good part. He said that he hoped to have her, and that, if he had the girl's consent, he would easily agree on the price with her father; and he began going to see her the next day; but he did not get her until after I left; he was generous to her, and she stayed with him until he died.

After this sad parting La Valville became my only mistress, and in three or four weeks I was ready to leave with her. I took into my service an Armenian merchant who lent me a hundred ducats and who cooked well in the oriental fashion. I got a letter of recommendation from the Polish Resident[26] to Prince Augustus Sulkowski,[27] and another from an Anglican clergyman[28] to Prince Adam Czartoryski;[29] and having put a good mattress and bed covers in my sleeping carriage, I lay down in it with La Valville, who found this way of traveling as agreeable as it was comical, for we were actually in bed.

We stopped at Caporya[30] the next day to dine, having a plentiful supply of food and good wines in my carriage. Two days later we met the famous chapelmaster Galuppi, surnamed Buranello, who was going to Petersburg with two friends and a *virtuosa*. He did not know me, and he was greatly surprised to find at the inn where he stopped a good Venetian dinner and a man like myself who received him with a compliment in our mother tongue. He embraced me again and again when I told him my name.

The rain having spoiled the roads, it took us a week to get to Riga, where I did not find Prince Charles of Kurland. We took four more days to get to Königsberg, where La Valville, who was expected in Berlin, had to leave me. I let her have my Armenian, to whom she gladly paid the hundred ducats I owed him. Two years later I found her in Paris, and I will speak of her in the proper place. We parted very gaily, and none of the sad reflections which usually accompany partings such as ours came to trouble our good humor. We had been lovers only because we had attached no importance to love; but we felt the most sincere friendship for each other. It was at Klein-Roop, a place not far from Riga, where we stopped and spent the night, that she offered me her diamonds and all the money she had. We lodged at Countess Löwenwolde's,[31] to whom I had brought a letter from a Princess Dolgoruki.[32] The Countess had in her service, as governess of her children, the pretty Englishwoman, Campioni's wife, whom I had met in Riga the year before. She told me that her husband was in Warsaw and lodging at Villiers'.[33] She gave me a letter in which she begged him to think of her. I promised her I would have money sent to her, and I kept my word. I found little Betty as charming as ever, but still ill-treated by her cruel mother, who seemed to be jealous of her.

At Königsberg I sold my sleeping carriage, and, being now alone, I engaged a place in a four-seated carriage and went to Warsaw. My three companions were Poles who spoke only German; so I was thoroughly bored during all the six days it took me to make the unpleasant journey. I went to lodge at Villiers', where I was sure I should find my old friend Campioni.

I found him doing well, and well lodged. He kept a dancing school, and a considerable number of pupils, male and female, brought him enough to live on comfortably. He was delighted to have news of Fanny and the children, and he sent her money; but he did not think of having her come to Warsaw, which was what she wanted. He assured me that she was not his wife. He told me that the famous Marquis d'Aragon[34] had left Warsaw after losing all the money he had won in Russia to sharpers sharper than himself; but the person who had made a great fortune was Tomatis,[35] who was the manager of the *opera buffa* and of a Milanese dancer named Catai[36] who, by her charms far more than her talent, was the delight of the city and the Court; but Tomatis controlled her completely. Games of chance being permitted, he named to me the gamesters who had set up shop there. One was a Veronese woman named Giropoldi, who lived with a Lorrainese officer named Bachelier,[37] who kept the bank at faro. A dancer who had been the mistress of the famous Afflisio in Vienna brought in the customers. La Giropoldi passed her off as a virgin; however, she was the woman by whom Afflisio had had a daughter whom he had educated at the Conservatorio dei Mendicanti[38] in Venice and who was with him in Bologna when he was arrested by order of the Archduke Leopold, Grand Duke of Tuscany, who sent him to end his days in the galleys. Another sharper who had set up shop with a Saxon woman was Major Saby,[39] of whom I have spoken during my second stay in Amsterdam. Baron Sainte-Hélène[40] was there too; but his principal talent consisted in getting into debt and persuading his creditors to wait; he was staying in the same inn with his wife, a pretty and honest woman, who would have nothing to do with his business.

He told me of several other adventurers, and I was very glad to be informed at once of all these people, whose company I must avoid for my own advantage.

The next day I engaged a hire lackey and a carriage by the month, a necessity in Warsaw, where it was impossible to walk. It was toward the end of the month of October 1765.

My first step was to take the letter from the Anglican clergyman to Prince Adam Czartoryski, General of Podolia. He was sitting at a large table covered with notebooks and surrounded by forty or fifty people, in a huge library which he had made his bedroom. Yet he was married to an extremely pretty Countess Fleming,[41] whom he had not yet got with child, because, she being too thin, he did not love her.

After reading the letter, which was four pages long, he said to me most politely in choice French that he had the highest regard for the person who had sent me to him and that, being very busy, he asked me to come to supper with him, "if I had nothing better to do."

I return to my carriage and am driven to the door of Prince Sulkowski, who had then been appointed Ambassador to Louis XV. The Prince was the eldest of four brothers, and had a profound intelligence and any number of projects, all admirable, but all in the style of those of the Abbé de Saint-Pierre.[42] Being on the verge of leaving to go to the Cadet Corps, he read the letter, then he told me that he had a great deal to say to me. He added that "if I had nothing better to do" he would take it as a favor if I would come to dine with him alone at four o'clock. I replied that I would do myself that honor.

From there I went to a merchant named Kempinski, who, on Papanelopulo's instructions, was to pay me fifty ducats a month. My lackey having told me that there was a rehearsal of a new opera at the theater, to which anyone might go, I went to it, and I spent three hours there known to no one and knowing no one. I found the actresses and the dancers pretty, but most of all La Catai, who appeared as prima ballerina and did not know how to make a step but was generally applauded, especially by Prince Repnin,[43] the Russian Ambassador, whose word was law.

Prince Sulkowski kept me at table for four mortal hours, pumping me about everything except what I could know. His specialty was policy and commerce, and, finding me at a loss, he shone. He took a liking to me, I believe, precisely because he never saw in me anything but admiration.

About nine o'clock, "having nothing better to do"—the phrase which I found on the lips of all the great Polish noblemen—I called on Prince Adam, who, after announcing my name, made me acquainted with all his guests by theirs. They were Monseigneur Krasicky,[44] Prince-Bishop of Warmia; the Grand Notary to the Crown Rzewuski,[45] whom I had seen in Petersburg as the lover of the unfortunate Langlade, who soon after died of smallpox; the Palatine of Vilna, Oginski,[46] and General Ronikier,[47] and two others whose names I have forgotten; the last person he named to me was his wife, whom I found very charming. A quarter of an hour later I see a fine-looking nobleman enter, and everyone rises. Prince Adam names me, and at once says to me very coldly:

"It is the King."

This way of confronting a stranger with a King is certainly not one to take away his courage or to dazzle him with majesty, but it is still a surprise, and its too great simplicity is unnerving. At once dismissing the idea that it might be a trick, I advanced two paces, and, when I was about to kneel, His Majesty put out his hand for me to kiss with an air of the greatest affability. Just as he was going to ask me the usual questions, Prince Adam gave him the long letter from the Anglican clergyman, who was very well known to him. After reading it the charming sovereign, still standing, began asking me questions, all of them concerning the Empress and the principal personages of her Court, to which I replied with details which he showed interested him greatly. A quarter of an hour later supper was announced, and the King, still listening to me, led me to the table and made me sit at his right. The table was round. Everyone ate except the King, who presumably had no appetite, and I, who would have had none even if I had not dined at Prince Sulkowski's, so gratified was I by the honor of keeping the whole company listening to me alone.

After rising from table the King commented on everything I had said, with a grace and in a style than which nothing could have been more winning. When he withdrew he said to me that he would always see me at his Court with very great pleasure. When I was about to leave, Prince Adam said that if I wanted him to present me to his father I had only to come to his house about eleven o'clock the next day.

The King of Poland was of medium stature, but very well built. His face was not handsome, but intelligent and interesting. His eyesight was poor, and when he was not speaking one might have thought him melancholy; but when he spoke his eloquence shone, and when the subject on which he was speaking allowed it he inspired gaiety in all those who heard him by the keenness of his wit.

Well enough satisfied with this beginning, I returned to my inn, where I found Campioni with an agreeable company of girls and gamesters, who had not yet finished supper. After staying there an hour, more from curiosity than from enjoyment, I retired.

The next morning at the appointed hour I made the acquaintance of that rare man, the magnificent Palatine of Russia.[48] He had on a dressing gown and was surrounded by gentlemen all in the national costume, all booted, all with mustaches, their heads bare and shaven. He stood among them, talking now to one, now to another, affably but seriously. As soon as his son, who had mentioned me to him beforehand, spoke my name the Palatine unbent, giving me a reception in which I saw neither pride nor familiarity. Though not what is called a fine figure of a man, he had a handsome countenance and great dignity, and was well spoken. He neither intimidated nor encouraged; this enabled him to know as he was the man with whom he wished to become acquainted. After hearing that in Russia I had done nothing but amuse myself and become acquainted with the Court, he concluded that I had come to Poland only for the same purpose, and he said that he would make it possible for me to meet everyone. He said that, being a bachelor and alone, he would be pleased if I would eat at his table morning and night every day when I did not have some other engagement.

Withdrawing behind a screen, he had himself dressed, then, after showing himself in the uniform of his regiment, which was in the French style, and wearing a blond wig with a pigtail and long side whiskers in the manner of the late lamented King Augustus III,[49] he made a bow which included everyone, and he retired to the inner apartments, which were the lodging of the Palatiness his wife, who had not yet wholly recovered from an illness to which she would have succumbed but for the ministrations of the physician Reumann, who was a pupil of the great Boerhaave. The lady was a Dönhoff,[50] an extinct family, as the last heir of which she had brought the Palatine an immense dowry. It was when he married her that he resigned the Cross of Malta. He had won his wife by a duel with pistols on horseback, in which, after receiving the lady's promise that she would grant him her heart, he had the good fortune to kill his rival. From this marriage he had only Prince Adam and a Princess, today a widow, named Lubomirska,[51] and at that time Straznikowa from the name of the office her husband held in the royal army.

It was the Prince Palatine of Russia and his brother,[52] who was Grand Chancellor of Lithuania, who were the first fomenters of the troubles in Poland, which was then only just born. Discontented with the little esteem in which they were held at Court, where the King had no will but the pleasure of his favorite, Count Brühl,[53] the Prime Minister, the two brothers assumed the leadership of the conspiracy, which sought nothing less than to dethrone the King and put on the throne, under the protection of Russia, a young man, their nephew, who, having gone to Petersburg in the suite of an Ambassador,[54] had succeeded in gaining the good graces of the Grand Duchess, who soon afterward became Empress and who died in this year 1797.[55] The young man was Stanislaus Poniatowski, the son of Constance Czartoryska, their sister, and of the famous Poniatowski,[56] the friend of Charles XII.[57] Fortune decreed that he did not need a conspiracy to mount a throne[58] of which *dignus fuisset si non regnasset* ("he would have been worthy if he had not reigned").[59]

The King who was to be dethroned died, and then the conspirators acted openly; and I will not repeat to my reader the events which put Stanislaus on the throne, which on my arrival in Warsaw he had occupied for nearly two years. I found Warsaw brilliant. Preparations were then being made to hold the Diet,[60] and everyone was eager to see what it would reveal in regard to Catherine II's pretensions in recompense for all that she had done to make it possible for Poland to give herself a Piast King.[61]

At dinnertime I found at the Russian Palatine's three tables laid for thirty or forty each. I was told that this was a daily occurrence. The luxury of the Court was nothing compared to that which shone at the Prince Palatine's. Prince Adam told me that I was to take a place every day at the table at which his father sat. On that day he presented me to the pretty Princess his sister,[62] and to a number of Palatines and Starosts,[63] having later gone to make my bow to whom, in less than two weeks I became known in all the great houses and hence was invited to all the great banquets and balls which were given almost every day in one house or another.

Not having money enough to frequent the gamesters, or to obtain a tender acquaintance with some girl of the French or the Italian theater, I took a fancy to the library of Monseigneur Zaluski,[64] the Bishop of Kiowia, and especially to himself. I spent almost every morning there, and it was from him that I received authentic documents concerning all the intrigues and secret plots whose purpose was to overthrow the entire old system of Poland, of which that prelate was one of the principal supporters. But his constancy was unavailing. The prelate was one of those whom agents of the Russian despotism carried off under the eyes of the King, too weak to dare to resist, and sent to Siberia.[65] This happened some months after my departure.

Thus the life I led was very regular. I spent the afternoons at the Russian Prince Palatine's to make up his table at *tressetti*,[66] an Italian game for which he had a great liking and which I played well enough for the Prince never to be so well pleased as when he could have me as his partner.

But despite my good behavior and my economy, three months after I arrived I was in debt, and I had no resources. Fifty sequins[67] a month which I received from Venice did not suffice me. Carriages, lodging, two servants, and the necessity of being always well dressed kept me in straits, and I did not want to confide in anyone. I was right. A man in need who asks help from a rich man loses his esteem if he obtains it, and wins his scorn if he refuses it.

But here is how Fortune sent me two hundred ducats. Madame Schmidt,[68] whom the King had his reasons for lodging in the palace, sent me word to sup with her, adding that the King would be there. At the supper I saw with pleasure the charming Bishop Krasicky, the Abate Ghigiotti,[69] and two or three others, who were amateurs of Italian literature. The King, whom I never saw in a bad humor in company, and who, besides, was very well read and knew all the classics as no King ever knew them, brought up some anecdotes of ancient Roman writers, citing manuscript scholiasts who left me with nothing to say and whom His Majesty was perhaps inventing. Everyone talked; I was the only one who, being in a bad humor and not having dined, ate like an ogre, replying only in monosyllables when politeness demanded it. The conversation having turned to Horace, and each of the company quoting one or two of his maxims and giving his opinion on the profound philosophy of the great poet of reason, it was the Abate Ghigiotti who forced me to speak, saying that unless I was of his opinion I ought not to remain silent.

"If you take my silence," I said, "as confirmation of the preference you accord to that thought of Horace's over several others, I will take the liberty of saying that I know others which give nobler expression to a courtier's policy, for *nec cum venari volet poemata panges* ("if he wants to go hunting, do not compose

verses"),[70] which pleases you so much, is after all only a satire, and
not at all a delicate one."

"It is difficult to combine delicacy with satire."

"Not for Horace, who even pleased Augustus by doing it,
which is to the credit of the monarch who, by the protection he
accorded to the learned, made his name immortal and inspired
crowned sovereigns to emulate him by taking his name and even
disguising it."

The King of Poland, who on his accession to the throne had
taken the name Augustus, became serious and could not refrain from
interrupting me.

"Who, pray," he asked me, "are the crowned sovereigns who
took the name of Augustus in disguise?"

"The first King of Sweden,[71] who called himself Gustavus; it is
a perfect anagram of Augustus."

"Most amusing. It is an anecdote worth relating. Where did you
find it?"

"In a manuscript of a professor at Uppsala which I saw at
Wolfenbüttel."

The King, who at the beginning of supper had also cited
a manuscript, thereupon began laughing heartily. But after laughing
his fill he returned to the subject, asking me in what well-known
maxims of Horace's—leaving manuscripts aside—I found marked
evidence of a delicacy which made his satire agreeable.

"I could quote several, Sire, but here is one, by way of example,
which seems to me very beautiful and, above all, modest. *Coram rege*,
he says, *sua de paupertate tacentes plus quam poscentes ferent*."[72]

"That is true," said the King, and Madame Schmidt asked the
Bishop to translate the passage.

" 'In the King's presence,' " he replied, " 'those who do not
speak of their need will obtain more than those who speak of it.' "

The lady said that the maxim did not seem to her satirical. After
having spoken so much, it was for me to be silent. And the King
himself turned the conversation to Ariosto, saying that he wished we
might read him together. I replied, making him a bow, with Horace:
Tempora queram ("I hope the time may come").[73]

It was on the next day, as he came away from mass, that the
generous and too unfortunate Stanislaus Augustus, giving me his
hand to kiss, put into mine a carelessly made packet, telling me to
thank Horace and to say nothing about it to anyone. In it I found two
hundred gold ducats, and I paid my debts. From that day on I went

almost every morning to the so-called "wardrobe,"[74] where the King, while his hair was being dressed, spoke freely to those who went there only to amuse him. But he never thought of reading Ariosto. He understood Italian, but not enough to speak it, still less to appreciate the great poet. When I think of this prince and of the great qualities I found him to possess, it seems to me impossible that he committed so many errors as a king. Outliving his country[75] is perhaps the least of them. Not finding a friend who would kill him, I venture to say that he should have killed himself; but he did not need to seek his executioner in a friend, for, had he imitated Kosciuszko,[76] a single Russian would have sufficed to send him to immortality.

Warsaw became very brilliant during the Carnival. Foreigners came there from every corner of Europe for no other reason than to see the fortunate mortal who had become a king despite the fact that no one could have guessed that he would become one when he was in the cradle. After seeing him and speaking with him everyone admitted that he gave the lie to those who called Fortune blind and foolish. But his eagerness to show himself was extreme. I saw him become uneasy when he knew there were some strangers in Warsaw whom he had not yet seen. No one needed to be presented to him, for the Court was open to all, and when he saw people he did not know he was the first to speak to them.

Here is something which happened to me toward the end of January, and which it seems to me I should record, however the reader may judge of my way of thinking. It was a dream, and I have already confessed somewhere that I have never been able to keep from being a trifle superstitious.

I dreamed that, dining in good company, one of the guests threw a bottle in my face which covered it with blood, and that having instantly run my sword through the body of the aggressor I got into a carriage to leave. That is all; but here is what reminded me of the dream that same day.

Prince Charles of Kurland, who had arrived in Warsaw during this time, invited me to go to dinner with him at Count Poninski's,[77] then Major-Domo to the Crown, the man who later occasioned much talk, was created a Prince, and then was proscribed and cruelly slandered. He kept a good house in Warsaw, and he had a very agreeable family. I had never called on him, because he was in favor neither with the King nor with his relatives.

Halfway through the dinner a bottle of champagne burst without anyone touching it, and a splinter, striking my forehead, cut a vein, from which the blood, spurting rapidly, quickly flowed over my face, my coat, and the table. I get up with all the others; quick, a bandage; the cloth is changed, and everyone sits down to finish dinner. That is all.

I am dumbfounded, not by the incident, but because I recollect the dream, which, but for the little mishap, I should never have remembered. Someone else would perhaps have told the company the whole dream, but I have always been too afraid of being taken for a visionary or a fool. I did not even pay much attention to it myself, for my dream differed from what had happened in its most important circumstances. Two more of them were verified a few months later.

La Binetti, whom I had left in London, arrived in Warsaw with her husband and the dancer Pic.[78] They had come from Vienna, and they were on their way to Petersburg. She brought a letter of recommendation to the King's brother,[79] the Prince and General in the Austrian service, who was then in Warsaw. I learned all this at supper at the Prince Palatine's on the day she arrived, from the mouth of the King himself, who said that he wanted to persuade them to stay in Warsaw so that he could see them dance, for which he would pay them a thousand ducats.

Impatient to see her and to be the first to give her this good news, I went to see her at Villiers' inn[80] very early the next morning. Very much surprised to find me in Warsaw, and still more so by the news I gave her that Fortune was sending her a thousand ducats, she called Pic, who seemed to doubt it; but a half hour later Prince Poniatowski himself came to inform her of His Majesty's wish, and she granted it. In three days Pic arranged a ballet, and the costumes, the scenery, the orchestra, the supporting dancers were all supplied by the diligent Tomatis, who had unlimited powers and who spared nothing to please his generous master. The couple were so well liked that they were engaged for a year and given carte blanche; but this was taken in very bad part by La Catai, for not only did La Binetti eclipse her but she took away her admirers. For this reason Tomatis saw to it that La Binetti was subjected to several annoying occurrences on the stage, which made the two leading dancers relentless enemies. Within ten or twelve days La Binetti had a house furnished with the utmost elegance, plain plate, silver-gilt dishes, a cellar with exquisite wines, an excellent cook, and a crowd of admirers, among others the Stolnik Moczynski[81] and the Podstoli to the Crown Branicki,[82] the King's friend, who lodged in an apartment next to his.

The audience at the theater was divided into two parties, for La Catai, though her talent was nothing in comparison with that of the new arrival, felt under no obligation to yield the precedence to her. She danced in the first ballet, and La Binetti in the second, and those who applauded the former were mute upon the appearance of the latter, and the party of the latter made not a sound when the former danced. My obligations to La Binetti were very strong and of very long standing; but my duty was even stronger toward La Catai, who had on her side the whole Czartoryski family, all their relatives by marriage, and all who were dependent on them; among others, Prince Lubomirski,[83] Straznik to the Crown, who honored me with his approbation on every occasion, and who was her principal admirer. Now it is obvious that I could not desert to La Binetti without earning the scorn of all those to whom it was incumbent on me to show the greatest deference.

La Binetti reproached me bitterly, and it was in vain that I explained my reasons to her. She insisted that I stop going to the theater, telling me, without condescending to explain herself further, that she was preparing to be revenged on Tomatis in a way which would make him repent of all the rudeness he continued to show her. She called me the oldest of all her acquaintances, besides which I still loved her and I cared nothing for La Catai, who, though prettier than La Binetti, was subject to epileptic fits.

Here is the cruel way in which she made poor Tomatis feel the first effect of her hatred.

Xavier[84] Branicki, Podstoli to the Crown, Chevalier of the White Eagle,[85] Colonel of a regiment of Uhlans, still young, with a handsome face, who had served six years in France, and the King's friend, who had just come from Berlin, where he had treated with the great Frederick as envoy from the new King of Poland, was La Binetti's principal lover. It is to him that she must have confided her grievances, and it is he whom she must have charged to avenge her on a man who, as director of the theater, let slip no opportunity to make things unpleasant for her. Branicki, on his side, must have promised her he would avenge her, and, if the opportunity were long in coming, to create it. This is the course of events in all affairs of the kind, and no other conjectures are more probable. But the way the Pole went about it is unique and most extraordinary.

On February 20th Monsieur Branicki went to the opera and, contrary to his custom, after the second ballet he went to the stage box in which La Catai was undressing to make his bow to her.

Tomatis was the only person with her, and he remained there. He thought, as she did, that, having broken with La Binetti, he had come to assure her of a conquest to which she was indifferent; nevertheless, she was very polite to a nobleman whose homage was not to be scorned except at great risk.

When La Catai was ready to go home, the opera being already over, the gallant Podstoli offered her his arm to escort her to her carriage, which was at the door, and Tomatis followed her. As it happened, I was at the door too, waiting for my carriage; snow was falling in great flakes. La Catai arrives, the door of the vis-à-vis[86] is opened, she gets in, and Monsieur Branicki gets in too, and Tomatis is left there motionless and astounded. The nobleman tells him to get into his carriage and follow him; Tomatis replies that he will ride in no carriage but his own, and he asks him to be good enough to get out. The Podstoli shouts to the coachman to drive on, Tomatis orders him to stay where he is, and the coachman obeys his master. Thereupon the Podstoli, obliged to get out, orders his hussar to slap the offender's face, an order which was carried out to the letter and so rapidly that poor Tomatis was not given time to remember that he had a sword which he could at least have plunged into the body of the brute who had thus insulted him. He got into his vis-à-vis and he went home, where, apparently with no choice but to stomach the slap, he could not eat supper. I had been invited there; but after witnessing this more than scandalous incident I did not have the heart to go. I went home, sad and thoughtful, afraid that I had myself received at least some small part of the infamous slap. I wondered whether the insult could have been planned with La Binetti, and, examining the succession of events, it seemed to me impossible, for neither La Binetti nor Branicki could have foreseen Tomatis' display of bad manners.

CHAPTER VIII

My duel with Branicki. Journey to Leopol and
return to Warsaw. I receive the King's order
to leave. My departure with the unknown
young woman.

Reflecting at home on this sorry event, I decided that, in entering Tomatis' vis-à-vis, Branicki had not gone beyond what the laws of gallantry permitted. He had acted without ceremony; he would have done the same thing if Tomatis had been his intimate friend; he could foresee an Italian jealousy, but he could not foresee that Tomatis would oppose him in any such way as he did; had he foreseen it, he would not have laid himself open to the insult unless he was determined to kill the man who dared to put it upon him. As soon as he received it, nature urged him to seek vengeance, and he chose the vengeance which came into his mind: a slap! It was too much, but it was less than if he had killed him. People would have said that he had murdered him, even though Tomatis had a sword too, for Branicki's servants would not have given him time to unsheathe it.

Nevertheless, I concluded that Tomatis should have killed the servant, even at the risk of losing his own life on the spot. It demanded less courage of him than the courage which enabled him to force the Podstoli to the Crown to get out of his carriage. It seemed to me that Tomatis had made a great mistake in not foreseeing that Branicki would resent the insult violently, and hence in not immediately putting himself on guard when Branicki received it. The whole blame, in my opinion, fell upon La Catai, who should never have let the Podstoli hand her into the carriage.

The next morning the thing was the news of the day in good society everywhere. Tomatis remained indoors for a week, vainly begging the King and all his patrons for vengeance, and obtaining it nowhere. The King himself did not know what kind of satisfaction he could procure for the foreigner, for Branicki maintained that he had returned insult for insult. Tomatis told me in confidence that he would surely have found a way to avenge himself, if it would not have cost him too dear. He had spent forty thousand sequins on the two spectacles,[1] which he would infallibly have lost if, by taking vengeance, he had made it necessary for him to leave the Kingdom. The only thing which consoled him was that the regard shown him by the great families whose favor he enjoyed was redoubled, and that the King himself, at the theater, at the tables at which they were together, on the promenades, and everywhere, spoke to him and was extremely gracious to him.

La Binetti alone relished the occurrence and triumphed. When I went to see her she rallied me by condoling with me on the misfortune which had befallen my friend, as she called him; she bored me, but I could neither be certain that Branicki had acted only at her instigation, nor guess that she bore a grudge against me too; but even if I had known it I should not have taken her seriously, for the Podstoli could do me neither good nor harm. I never saw him, I had never spoken to him, he could have no hold on me. I did not even see him at the palace, for he was never there at the hours when I went there; and he never came to the Prince Palatine's, not even in the suite of the King when he came there for supper. Monsieur Branicki was a nobleman whom the whole nation detested, for he was completely Russian,[2] a great supporter of the dissidents,[3] and the enemy of all those who would not bow under the yoke which Russia wanted to lay on the ancient constitution. The King loved him because of their old friendship, for he was under personal obligations to him, and for political reasons.[4] The monarch had to straddle the ditch, for he had as much to fear from Russia, if he declared himself opposed to the settlement which had been agreed upon, as he had to fear from his country, if he had acted openly in accordance with it.

The life I was leading was exemplary, no love affairs, no gaming; I worked for the King, hoping to become his secretary, I paid my court to the Princess Palatine, who liked my company, and I played *tressetti* with the Palatine against any two others whom chance brought. On the fourth of March, on the eve of the feast of St. Casimir,[5] which was the name of the King's elder brother,[6] the Prince and Grand Chamberlain, there was a great dinner at Court, and I went to it. After dinner the King asked me if I was going to the theater that day. A comedy in Polish was to be given for the first time. This novelty interested everyone, but it was a matter of indifference to me, for I did not understand a word of Polish; I told the King so.

"Never mind that; come to it. Come in my box."

At these words I bowed, and I obeyed. I was standing behind his chair. After the second act there was a ballet in which the

Piedmontese dancer La Casacci[7] so pleased the King with her dancing that he clapped his hands—an extraordinary favor. I knew her only by sight; I had never spoken to her; she was not without talent; her great admirer was Count Poninski, who, every time I went to dine with him, reproached me for going to call on other dancers and never going to La Casacci's, where one was very well received. After the ballet it came into my head to leave the King's box and go by way of the stage to La Casacci's little box and congratulate her on the justice the King had done to her talents. I pass La Binetti's box, which was open, and I stop for a moment; Count Branicki, who was said to be her lover, enters, and, making a bow, I leave, and I enter La Casacci's box; surprised to see me in her presence for the first time, she reproaches me pleasantly; I pay her compliments, I promise I will call on her, and I embrace her. During the embrace Count Branicki enters; it had been only a minute since I had left him in La Binetti's box; it was clear that he had followed me; but why? To pick a quarrel; he had a grudge against me. He was with Bisinski,[8] Lieutenant-Colonel of his regiment. Upon his appearing, I rise, both out of politeness and to leave; but he stops me by addressing me in these words:

"I entered here, Monsieur, at a bad moment for you; it seems that you love this lady."

"Certainly, Monseigneur, does not Your Excellency consider her worthy of love?"

"Perfectly so; and what is more I will tell you that I love her, and that I am not of a humor to put up with rivals."

"Very well! Now that I know it, I will no longer love her."

"Then you yield to me?"

"On the instant. Everyone must yield to such a nobleman as you."

"Very well; but a man who yields takes to his legs."[9]

"That is a trifle strong."

As I utter the words I go out, looking at him and showing him the hilt of my sword, three or four officers who were there being witnesses to the whole incident. I had not yet taken four steps outside the box when I hear myself honored with the title of "Venetian coward"; I turn, saying to him that, outside the theater, a Venetian coward could kill a Polish bravo, and I go down the great stairs which gave on to the street. I wait there a quarter of an hour, hoping to see him come out and to make him unsheathe his sword, not being, like Tomatis, restrained by the fear of losing forty thousand sequins; but not seeing him, and perishing from the cold, I call my servants, I have my carriage brought up, and I am driven to the Prince Palatine's where the King himself had told me he was to sup.

Alone in my carriage, my first impulse having subsided a little, I congratulate myself on having resisted his violence, not having drawn my sword in La Casacci's box, and I even feel very glad that the bully had not come down, for he had Bisinski with him armed with a saber, who would have murdered me. The Poles, though generally polite enough nowadays, still keep a good deal of their old nature; they are still Sarmatians or Dacians[10] at table, in war, in the fury of what they call friendship. They refuse to understand that, a man alone being a match for another man, it is not permissible to go in a gang to cut the throat of someone who is alone and whose quarrel is with only one man. I clearly saw that Branicki had followed me, urged on by La Binetti and resolved to treat me as he had treated Tomatis. I had not received a slap, but it was almost the same thing; three officers had been witnesses that he had sent me about my business, and I recognized that I was dishonored. The power to bear that stigma not being in my nature, I felt certain that I should decide on a course, but I did not know which one. I needed full satisfaction, and I considered how best to obtain it, but by some moderate means which would leave me with a foot in both camps. I got out at the house of the King's uncle, Prince Czartoryski, Palatine of Russia, determined to tell the King the whole story and leave it to His Majesty to force Branicki to beg my pardon.

As soon as the Palatine sees me he gently reproaches me for having kept him waiting a little too long, and we sit down to play our usual game of *tressetti*. I was his partner.[11] At the second game which we lose, he reproaches me with my mistakes, he asks me where my mind is.

"Four leagues from here, Monseigneur."

"When one plays *tressetti*," he replied, "with a gentleman who plays for the pleasure of playing, one is not allowed to have one's mind four leagues away."

So saying, the Prince throws his cards on the table, rises, and goes walking about the room. I remain at the table, nonplussed, then I go to the fireplace. It could not be long before the King would be there. A half hour later the Chamberlain Pernigotti[12] arrives and tells the Prince that the King could not come. This announcement rends my soul; but I conceal my feelings. Supper is ordered; it is served, I take my usual place at the Palatine's left; we were eighteen or twenty at the table. The Palatine showed that he was displeased with me. I did not eat. Halfway through supper in comes Prince Kaspar Lubomirski,[13] Lieutenant-General in the Russian service, and sits down at the other end of the table, facing me. As soon as he sees me he condoles with me in a loud voice on what had happened to me.

"I am sorry for you," he says. "Branicki was drunk; and from a drunken man a gentleman cannot receive an insult."

"What happened, what happened?"

Such was the reply of the whole table. I say nothing. Lubomirski is questioned, he answers that since I am saying nothing it is for him to say nothing too. The Palatine then stops scowling and asks me amicably what had happened between me and Branicki.

"I will tell you everything in detail after supper, Monseigneur, in a corner of this room."

The conversation turned upon indifferent matters until the end of the meal, and when the company rose, the Palatine, whom I followed, went to the small door by which he was accustomed to retire. In five or six minutes I tell him the whole story. He sighs. He condoles with me, and he says I was justified in having my mind four leagues away when I was playing.

"I ask Your Highness to advise me."

"I never give advice in affairs of this kind, for they demand that one do a great deal or do nothing."

After this dictum, which proceeded from wisdom itself, he enters his apartment. I thereupon go for my fur, I get into my carriage, I go home, I go to bed, and my naturally good constitution makes me enjoy a sleep of six hours. Sitting up at five o'clock in the morning, I consider what course I am to take. "A great deal or nothing." I immediately reject the "nothing." So I must make a choice among the "great deal." I find only one: to kill Branicki or force him to kill me, if he will honor me with a duel, and in case, not wanting to fight, he cheats me out of a duel, to murder him, taking my measures carefully and even risking losing my head on the scaffold afterward. In this determination, and having to begin by proposing a duel four leagues from Warsaw, since the Starosty[14] extended four leagues in every direction and duels were forbidden within it on pain of death, I write him the following note, which I now copy from the original, which I still have.

"March 5, 1766, at 5 o'clock in the morning. "Monseigneur, yesterday evening at the theater Your Excellency wantonly insulted me, having neither a right nor a reason to behave to me in that fashion. That being so, I conclude that you hate me, Monseigneur, and that hence you would be glad to remove me from the number of the living. I can and I will satisfy Your Excellency. Be so good, then, Monseigneur, as to call for me in your carriage, and to take me where my defeat cannot make you guilty under the laws of Poland, and where I may enjoy the same advantage if God so far helps me that I kill Your Excellency. I should not, Monseigneur, make this proposal to you were it not for the idea I have formed of your generosity. I have the honor to be,

"Monseigneur, Your Excellency's very humble and very obedi-ent servant Casanova"[15]

I send my lackey to take this letter to him an hour before dawn at his apartment in the palace, next to the King's. I tell my servant to deliver it into no hand but his, and, if he was asleep, to wait until he woke to obtain a reply. I waited for it only half an hour. Here is a copy of it:

"Monsieur,

"I accept your proposal; but you will have the goodness to tell me at what hour I shall see you. I am, Monsieur, entirely your very humble and very obedient servant, Branicki, Podstoli C. P."[16]

Delighted with my good fortune, I instantly reply that I will be at his apartment the next day at six o'clock in the morning, to go with him to settle our quarrel in a safe place. He replies, asking me to name the arms and the place, adding that the whole affair must be ended in the course of the day. I thereupon send him the length of my sword, which was thirty-two inches, saying that the place depended upon him, provided it was outside the Starosty. He replies at once by this note, which was the last:

"Pray come to see me at once, Monsieur, and you will do me a favor. In consequence I send you my carriage. I have the honor to be, etc."

I reply by only four lines to tell him that, having a great deal to do, I had to spend the whole day at home, and that, having decided that I would not go to him unless I was sure that we should go to fight at once, he must excuse me if I sent him back his carriage.

An hour later the nobleman himself arrives at my lodging, he enters my room, leaving his suite outside and sending away two or three people who were there to speak with me. After shutting and bolting the door, he sat down on my bed, in which I was finding it more convenient to write. Not understanding what this meant, I take up two pocket pistols which I had on my night table.

"I have not come here to kill you, but to tell you that when I accept a proposal to fight I never put it off until the next day. So we shall fight today or never."

"I cannot do it today. It is Wednesday, the day of the post; I must finish something which I must send to the King."

"You shall send it after we have fought. You will not be left dead, believe me, and in any case, if you succumb, the King will forgive you. A man who is dead is beyond the reach of any reproach."

"I have a will to make, too."

"Now it's a will! So you fear you will die. Fear it no longer. You will make your will fifty years from now."

"But what objection can Your Excellency have to putting off our duel until tomorrow?"

"I do not want to be cheated. We shall both of us be put under arrest today by order of the King."

"It is impossible, unless you inform him."

"I? You make me laugh. I know that trick. You shall not have challenged me in vain. I want to give you satisfaction; but today or never."

"Very well. This duel is too dear to my heart for me to give you an excuse for not fighting it. Come to fetch me after dinner; for I need all my strength."

"With pleasure. For my part, I prefer to sup well afterward. But by the way, what is this about the length of your sword? I want to fight with pistols. I do not draw swords with unknown people."

"What do you mean, 'unknown'? I can give you twenty witnesses in Warsaw that I am no fencing master. I will not fight with pistols, and you cannot oblige me to do so, for you gave me the choice of weapons, and I have read your letter."

"Well, strictly speaking you are right, for I know that I gave you the choice; but you are too much of a gentleman not to fight with pistols if I assure you that you will be greatly obliging me. It is the least favor you can do me. I will tell you further that one risks less with pistols, for one usually misses one's shot, and I assure you that if I miss you we shall fight with swords as much as you please. Will you grant me this pleasure?"

"I like your way of putting it, for I find it witty. I feel inclined to grant you this barbarous pleasure, and, at the cost of some effort, I am even able to share in it. So," I went on, "I accept the new arrangement for our duel, upon these precise conditions. You will come with two pistols, which you will have loaded in my presence, and I shall be allowed to choose mine. But if we miss each other, we shall fight with swords until the first blood, and no longer, if that is what you want, for I feel ready to go on until death. You will come to fetch me at three o'clock, and we shall go where we are safe from the laws."

"Excellent. You are a man one can like. Permit me to embrace you. Give me your word of honor that you will say nothing to anyone, for we should be arrested."

"How can you think I would take that risk, when I would travel leagues on foot to deserve the honor you are kind enough to do me?"

"So much the better. Then it is all settled. Good-by until three o'clock."

This dialogue is authentic, and has been known to everyone for the past thirty-two[17] years. As soon as the insolent bravo left me I put into a sealed envelope all the papers which belonged to the King, and I sent a servant to fetch the dancer Campioni, in whom I had perfect confidence.

"Here is a packet," I said to him, "which you will return to me this evening if I am alive, and which you will take to the King if I am dead. You can guess what is afoot, but remember that if you speak I am dishonored, and that I further declare to you that you will not have a more bitter enemy in the world."

"I understand perfectly. If I were to disclose the affair to those who would certainly put a stop to it, it would be said that it was at your instigation. I want you to come out of it with honor. The only advice I make bold to give you is not to spare your opponent, even if he were the emperor of the world. Your respect could cost you your life."

"I know that from experience."

I ordered a tasty dinner, and I sent to the Court for some excellent Burgundy wine; Campioni dined with me. The two young Counts Mniszek,[18] with their Swiss tutor Bertrand,[19] came to pay me a visit while I was at table, and were witnesses to my good appetite and my unusual gaiety. At a quarter before three o'clock I asked everyone to leave me alone, and I went to the window to be ready to go down as soon as the Podstoli arrived at my door.

I saw him at a distance in a berlin[20] with six horses, preceded by two grooms on horseback who were leading two saddle horses, by two hussars, and by two aides-de-camp. Four menservants were up behind his carriage. He stops at my door, I quickly go down from my fourth floor, and I see that he is accompanied by a Lieutenant-General and by a chasseur, and, with one foot on the step of the carriage, I turn to my servants and I order them not to follow me and to stay in the house and wait for my orders. The Podstoli says to me that I may need them; I reply that if I had as many as he has I would bring them, but that, having only this wretched pair, I prefer to put myself in his hands unattended, sure that he will provide me with attendance if I need it. He replies by giving me his hand as a pledge that he will take care of me before himself. I sit down, and the carriage drives on. He had given the order in advance, for no one said a word. It would have been absurd if I had asked where we were going. These are moments when a man must watch over himself. The Podstoli saying nothing, I thought it my part to ask him some inconsequential questions.

"Do you expect, Monseigneur, to spend the spring and summer in Warsaw?"

"I expected so yesterday; but you may keep me from doing it."

"I hope that I shall not interfere with any of your plans."

"Have you ever served as a soldier?"

"Yes; but may I inquire why Your Excellency asks me the question, because——"

"For no reason, no reason at all. I asked it simply to say something."

At the end of a half-hour's drive the carriage stops at the entrance to a beautiful garden.[21] We get out, and, followed by all the Podstoli's suite, we go to a green arbor which was not green on the fifth of March, at one end of which there was a small stone table. The chasseur puts on the table two pistols a foot and a half long, takes from his pocket a bag of powder, then a pair of scales. He unscrews the pistols, weighs the powder and the balls, then loads them, screws them to the mark, and crosses them. Branicki, unperturbed, invites me to choose. The Lieutenant-General asks him in a loud voice if it is a duel.

"Yes."

"You cannot fight here; you are within the Starosty."

"That does not matter."

"It matters a great deal, I cannot be a witness; I am on guard at the castle, you have taken me by surprise."

"Enough. I will be responsible for everything; I owe this gentleman a satisfaction."

"Monsieur Casanova, you cannot fight here."

"Then why have I been brought here? I defend myself anywhere, even in a church."

"Lay your account of the matter before the King, and I assure you he will take your side."

"I will do so gladly, General, if His Excellency will only say to me in your presence that he is sorry for what happened between us yesterday."

At my proposal Branicki gives me a black look and says in an angry voice that he has come there with me to fight, not to parley. I then say to the General that he can bear witness that, so far as it lay in my power, I wanted to avoid the duel. He withdraws, with his head in his hands. Branicki urges me to choose. I throw off my fur, and I take up the first pistol which comes to hand. Branicki, taking the other, says that he guarantees on his honor that the pistol I am holding is perfect. I reply that I shall test it on his head. At this terrible reply he turns pale, he throws his sword to one of his pages and shows me his bared chest. However unwillingly, I see that I must do the same, for my sword was my only weapon after the pistol. I show him my chest too, and I fall back five or six paces, the Podstoli does likewise. We could not fall back farther. Seeing him determined, as I was, with the mouth of his pistol toward the ground, I take off my hat with my left hand, asking him to do me the honor of firing at me first, and I put my hat on. Instead of firing at once, the Podstoli lost two or three seconds drawing himself up and hiding his head behind the butt of his pistol; but the situation did not demand that I wait upon his every convenience. I fired at him at the same instant that he fired at me, and there was no doubt of it, for all the people in the nearby houses said that they heard only one report. When I saw him fall, I quickly put in my pocket my left hand, which I felt was wounded, and, throwing down my pistol, I ran to him; but what was not my surprise when I saw three naked sabers raised against me in the hands of three noble assassins, who would instantly have made mincemeat of me where I had dropped to my knees beside him, if the Podstoli had not turned them to stone by shouting in a voice of thunder:

"Villains, respect this gentleman."

At that they withdrew, and I went to help him get up, putting my right hand under his arm while the General helped him on the other side. In this fashion we took him to an inn which was a hundred paces from the garden. The Podstoli walked very much bent over, and stealing curious glances at me, for he could not understand where the blood came from which he saw streaming over my breeches and my white stockings.

No sooner have we entered the inn than the Podstoli throws himself into a big armchair, he stretches out, his clothes are unbuttoned, his shirt is raised as far as his stomach, and he sees that he is wounded to the death. My ball had entered his abdomen at the seventh true rib on the right and had gone out under the last false rib on the left. The two holes were ten inches apart. The sight was alarming: it seemed that the intestines had been pierced and that he was a dead man. The Podstoli looks at me and says:

"You have killed me, and now get away, for you will lose your head on the scaffold: you are in the Starosty, I am a high officer of the Crown, and here is the ribbon of the White Eagle. Get away at once, and if you have no money take my purse. Here it is."

The full purse drops, I put it back in his pocket, thanking him and saying that I have no need of it, for if I was guilty of killing I would instantly lay my head on the steps of the throne. I said that I hoped his wound would not be mortal, and that I was in despair over what he had forced me to do. I kiss his forehead, I leave the inn, and I see neither carriage nor horses nor servants. They had all gone to fetch a doctor, a surgeon, priests, relatives, friends. I find myself alone and without a sword in a countryside covered with snow, wounded, and not knowing the way back to Warsaw. In the distance I see a sleigh with two horses, I shout, the peasant stops, I show him a ducat, and I say:

"Varsaw."[22]

He understands me, he raises a mat, I lie down in the sleigh, and to keep me from being splashed he covers me with the mat. He drives at a fast canter. Half of a quarter of an hour later I meet Bisinski, Branicki's faithful friend, on horseback, riding at full gallop, with his bare saber in his hand. If he had paid any attention to the sleigh he would have seen my head, and he would certainly have cut me in two like a reed. I arrive in Warsaw, I have the peasant drive me to Prince Adam's palace to ask him for sanctuary, and I find no one. I decide to take refuge in the Recollect[23] monastery, which was a hundred paces away. I dismiss my sleigh.

I go to the door of the monastery, I ring, the porter, a pitiless monk, opens the door, sees me covered with blood, supposes that

I have come to save myself from the law, tries to shut his door, but I do not give him time. A kick in the belly knocks him down, legs in the air, and I go in. He shouts for help, some monks arrive, I tell them that I want sanctuary, and I threaten them if they refuse to grant it. One of them speaks, and I am led to a room which looks like a dungeon. I submit, sure that they will change their minds in a quarter of an hour. I ask for a man to go to summon my servants, who come at once, I send for a surgeon and Campioni. But before they arrive, in comes the Palatine of Podlasie,[24] who had never spoken to me but who, having fought a duel in his youth, seized the opportunity to tell me the details of it as soon as he heard the honorable details of mine. A moment later I saw the Palatine of Kalisz[25] come in, with Prince Jablonowski,[26] Prince Sanguszko,[27] the Palatine of Vilna, Oginski, all of whom at once began reviling the monks who had lodged me like a galley slave. They excused themselves by saying that I had got in by maltreating the porter; which made the princes laugh, but not me, for I was suffering a great deal from my wound. They at once gave me two fine rooms.

Branicki's ball had entered my hand through the metacarpus under the index finger, and, after breaking my first phalanx, had lodged there; its force had been weakened by the metal button on my waistcoat and by my abdomen, which it had slightly wounded near the navel. The ball had to be extracted from my hand, which was causing me great discomfort. A surgeon and adventurer named Gendron, who was the first to be found, came to extract it by making a cut on the opposite side, which made my wound twice as long. While he performed this painful operation on me, I told the princes the whole story, having no difficulty in concealing the agony which the unskillful surgeon caused me when he put in the pincers to take hold of the ball. Such is the power of vanity over the human mind.

After the surgeon Gendron left, the Prince Palatine's arrived and took charge of me, undertaking to get rid of the other, whom he called a vagabond. At the same moment in came Prince Lubomirski, the husband of the daughter of the Prince Palatine of Russia, who astonished us all by telling us everything that had happened immediately after my duel. As soon as Bisinski, having arrived at Wola, saw his friend's dreadful wound, and did not see me, he set off like a madman, swearing that he would kill me wherever he found me. He went to Tomatis' house, finding him in company with his mistress, Prince Lubomirski, and Count Moczynski. He asked Tomatis where I was, and as soon as he heard Tomatis reply that he knew nothing about it, he fired a pistol at his head. Upon this murderous act, Moczynski took him around the waist to throw him out the window, but Bisinski got free of him by three strokes of his saber, one of which slashed his face and knocked out three of his teeth.

"After that," Prince Lubomirski went on, "he took me by the collar, holding a pistol to my throat and threatening to kill me if I did not take him out to his horse in the courtyard so that he could leave without fear of Tomatis' servants. Which I instantly did. Moczynski went home, where he will have to remain for a long time under the care of a surgeon, and I went home to observe all the confusion into which the city has been thrown because of your duel. It is rumored that Branicki is dead, and his Uhlans are looking for you on horseback, galloping everywhere to avenge their Colonel by butchering you. A good thing for you that you are here! The Grand Marshal[28] has surrounded the monastery with two hundred dragoons, on the pretext of making sure you do not escape; but really to prevent that frenzied mob from forcing their way into the monastery to butcher you here. Branicki is in great danger, the surgeons say, if the ball pierced his intestines, and they are sure of his life if they were not touched. They will know which is the case tomorrow. He is lodging at the Grand Chamberlain's,[29] not having dared to go to his apartment at Court. However, the King went to see him at once. The General who was present at the duel says that what saved your life was your threat to Branicki that you would wound him in the head. Having tried to protect his head, he put himself in an awkward position, and he missed you. But for that, he would have pierced your heart, for he fires at the sharp edge of a knife and cuts the bullet in two. The other piece of good fortune you had was your not being seen by Bisinski, who could not suppose that you were under the mat in the sleigh."

"The great good fortune I had, Monseigneur, was that I did not kill Branicki, for I should have been butchered on the spot if he had not said three words which stopped his friends, who already had their sabers raised over me. I am sorry for what has happened to Your Highness and to the kind Count Moczynski. If Tomatis was not killed by Bisinski's shot, it shows that his pistol was empty."

"I think so too."

Just then an officer of his household brings me a note from the Palatine of Russia. "See," he writes me, "what the King has just sent me, and sleep in peace." Here is what I read in the note the King wrote to him, which I have kept. "Branicki, my dear Uncle, is in a very bad way, and my surgeons are with him to give him all the help of their art; but I have not forgotten Casanova. You can assure him of his pardon, even if Branicki should die."

I printed a respectful kiss on the note, and I showed it to the noble company, who expressed their admiration for a man truly worthy of his crown. I needed to be left alone, and they left me. After they went, my friend Campioni gave me back my packet and shed tender tears over the event which did me immortal honor. He had stayed in a corner, where he had heard everything.

The next day visitors came in crowds, together with purses filled with gold from all the magnates who were opposed to Branicki's faction. The household officer who presented me with the purse on behalf of the nobleman or the lady who sent it to me said that, being a foreigner, I might be in need of money, and that on that assumption his master or mistress took the liberty of sending me some. I expressed my thanks and refused the purse. I sent back at least four thousand ducats, and I prided myself on it. Campioni declared my heroism absurd, and he was right. I repented of it afterward. The only present I accepted was the dinner for four persons which Prince Adam Czartoryski sent me every day; but I did not eat. *Vulnerati fame crucientur* ("The wounded must be made to suffer the pangs of hunger")[30] was the favorite maxim of my surgeon, who was no genius. The wound in my abdomen was already suppurating, but on the fourth day my badly swollen arm and the blackening of my wound, which threatened gangrene, made the surgeons decide, after conferring together, that my hand must be amputated. I learned this strange news early in the morning when I read the *Court Gazette*, which was printed at night after the King had signed the manuscript. I laughed heartily at it. I laughed in the faces of all those who came that morning to condole with me, and just as I was making fun of Count Clary,[31] who was trying to persuade me to let them perform the operation, in came not the surgeon but the surgeons.

"Why three of you, gentlemen?"

"Because," said the one who regularly attended me, "before proceeding to amputation I wanted to have the consent of these learned men. We shall now see what state you are in."

He removes the bandage, he draws out the drain, he examines the wound, its color, then the livid swelling, they speak together in Polish, then the three of them together tell me in Latin that they will cut off my hand at nightfall. They are all in high spirits, they tell me

I have nothing to fear, and that it will make me sure of recovering. I reply that I am the lord and master of my hand, and that I will never allow them to perform this absurd amputation.

"There is gangrene present, and tomorrow it will rise into the arm, and then we shall have to cut off the arm."

"Very well then, you will cut off my arm; but in the meanwhile, to judge by what I know about gangrene, I saw none in me."

"You do not know more about it than we do."

"Go away."

Two hours later begin the tiresome visits of all those whom the surgeons had told about my obstinacy. The Prince Palatine himself writes me that the King was astonished at my want of courage. It was then that I[32] wrote the King that I did not know what to do with my arm without my hand and, that being the case, I would let my arm be cut off when the gangrene became visible.[33]

My letter was read by everyone at Court. Prince Lubomirski came to tell me that I had been wrong to make so light of those who were concerned for me, for after all it was impossible that the three best surgeons in Warsaw should be deceived in so simple a matter.

"Monseigneur, they are not deceived, but they think they can deceive me."

"To what purpose?"

"To flatter Count Branicki, who is very ill, and who perhaps needs this comfort in order to recover."

"You will permit me not to believe anything so unlikely."

"But what will you say when I am proved to be right?"

"If that happens I will admire you, and you will be praised for your firmness; but it must happen first."

"We shall see this evening if the gangrene has attacked my arm, and tomorrow morning I will have my arm cut off. I give Your Highness my word for it."

In the evening the surgeons who come are not three but four; they unwrap my arm, which was twice its natural size, I see that it is livid to the elbow; but when the drain is taken out of the wound I see that the edges of it are red and I see pus; I say nothing. Prince Sulkowski and the Abbé Gourel,[34] of the Prince Palatine's household, were present. The four surgeons decide that, the arm being infected, they are no longer in time to amputate the hand, and so the arm will have to be cut off at the latest the next morning. Tired of arguing, I tell them to come with the necessary instruments, and that I will submit to the operation. They go off very well pleased, to take the news to Court, to Branicki's, to the Prince Palatine's; but the next morning I ordered my servant not to let them enter my room; and the thing was over. I kept my hand.[35]

On Easter Sunday I went to mass with my arm in a sling, though I did not wholly recover the use of it until eighteen months later. My cure took only twenty-five days. Those who condemned me found themselves obliged to praise me. My firmness did me immortal honor, and the surgeons had to admit that they were all either completely ignorant or extremely imprudent.

But another little incident also amused me on the third day after the duel. A Jesuit came to speak to me privately in the name of the Bishop of Poznan,[36] of which diocese Warsaw was a part. I send everyone out of the room, and I ask him what he wants.

"I come at the behest of Monseigneur" (he was a Czartoryski, and brother to the Palatine of Russia), "to absolve you from the ecclesiastical censures you have incurred by fighting a duel."

"I have no need of that, for I do not admit it. I was attacked, and I defended myself. Convey my thanks to Monseigneur; yet if you wish to absolve me of the sin without my confessing it, you are free to do so."

"If you do not confess the crime, I cannot absolve you of it. But do this: Ask me for absolution in case you fought a duel."

"With pleasure. If it is a duel, I ask you to absolve me, and I ask you for nothing if it is not one."

He gave me absolution with the same ambiguity. The Jesuits were admirable at finding subterfuges for everything.

Three days before I go out the Grand Marshal to the Crown withdrew the troops which were at the doors of the monastery. On going out (it was Easter Sunday) I went to mass, then to Court, where the King, giving me his hand to kiss, let me go down on one knee; he asked me (it was prearranged) why I had my arm in a sling, and I replied that it was because of an attack of rheumatism; he replied that I should beware of catching it again. After seeing the King, I told my coachman to take me to the door of the mansion in which Count Branicki was staying. I thought I owed him a visit. He had sent a lackey every day to inquire how I was doing; he had sent me back my sword, which I had left on the field of battle; he was to stay in bed for at least six more weeks because it had been necessary to enlarge the two wounds, in which the packing had become embedded, preventing his recovery. I owed him a visit. Then too, people were calling to congratulate him on the King's having appointed him Lowczy (which means Master of the Royal Hunt) on the previous day. The post ranked below that of Podstoli, but it was lucrative. It was jestingly said that the King had not given it to him until after seeing that he was an excellent shot; but that day I was a better shot than he.

I enter his anteroom; the officers, the lackeys, the chasseurs are surprised to see me. I ask the Adjutant to announce me to Monseigneur if he is receiving. He does not answer, he sighs, and he goes in. A minute later he comes out, he orders both leaves of the door opened, and he tells me to go in.

Wearing a dressing gown of some gold-glazed stuff, Branicki was lying in bed with his back supported by pillows with rose-colored ribbons. Pale as a corpse, he took off his nightcap.

"I have come, Monseigneur, to ask you to pardon me for not having been able to overlook a trifle to which, were I wiser, I should have paid no attention. I have come to tell you that you have honored me far more than you offended me, and I ask your protection in the future against your friends, who, not knowing your character, believe they must be my enemies."

"I admit," he replied, "that I insulted you, but you will likewise admit that I have certainly paid for it in my own person. As for my friends, I will declare myself the enemy of all those who will not respect you. Bisinski has been banished and stricken from the roster of the nobility, and it was rightly done. As for my protection, you do not need it, the King esteems you as I do and as do all those who know the laws of honor. Be seated, and in the future let us be good friends. A cup of chocolate for Monsieur. So you are cured?"

"Completely, except for the joint, the use of which I shall not recover for a year."

"You put up a good fight against the surgeons, and you were right to tell someone that the fools thought they would be pleasing me by leaving you with only one hand. They measure another's heart by their own. I congratulate you on having routed them and kept your hand; but I have never been able to understand how my ball could have gone into your hand after wounding you in the abdomen."

Just then I was served chocolate, and the Grand Chamberlain came in, looking at me with a smile. In five or six minutes the room was filled with ladies and gentlemen who, having learned that I was with the Lowczy, and curious to hear what we would say to each other, had come to be present at our dialogue. I saw that they did not expect to find us on such good terms, and that they were delighted by it. Branicki took me back to the subject which had been interrupted.

"How could my ball have entered your hand?"

"You will permit me to assume the same position?"

"Whatever you like."

So I rise, and displaying myself as I had been, he understands.

"You should," a lady[37] said to me, "have held your hand behind your body."

"I was more concerned, Madame, with keeping my body behind my hand."

"You meant to kill my brother, for you aimed at his head."

"God forbid, Madame; it was to my interest to leave him alive, so that he could defend me, as he did, against those who were with him."

"But you told him you would aim at his head."

"That is what one always says; but the wise man aims at the center of the target; the head is at the edge. Accordingly, when I raised the muzzle of my pistol I stopped it just before it would have gone beyond the middle line."

"That is so," said Branicki; "your tactics are better than mine, you taught me a lesson."

"The lesson Your Excellency gave me in heroism and coolness is one far more worth learning and applying."

"It is obvious," his sister Sapieha resumed, "that you must have practiced a great deal with the pistol."

"Never. It was my first unlucky shot; but I have always had a clear idea of the straight line, the accurate eye, and the hand which does not shake."

"That is all that is needed," said Branicki; "I have all that, and I am delighted that I did not shoot as well as I usually do."

"Your ball, Monseigneur, broke my first phalanx. Here it is, flattened by my bone. Permit me to return it to you."

"I regret that I cannot give you back yours."

"Your wound is getting better, I am told."

"My wound is healing with great difficulty. If I had done what you did that day, the duel would have cost me my life. From what I hear, you dined very well."

"The cause of it was my fear that the dinner would be my last."

"If I had dined, your ball would have pierced my intestines, whereas, they being empty, it only grazed them."

What I learned for certain was that, as soon as he knew he was to fight at three o'clock, Branicki went to mass, confessed, and communicated. The confessor had to absolve him when he told him that his honor obliged him to fight. All this was still in accordance with the ancient code of chivalry. As for me, perhaps more, perhaps less a Christian than Branicki, I addressed God in only these few words: *"Lord, if my enemy kills me, I am damned; so save me from death."* After a number of cheerful and interesting remarks, I took leave of the hero to call on the nonagenarian Grand Marshal to the Crown, Bielinski[38] (Countess Salmour[39] was his sister), who, by virtue of his office, is the only administrator of justice in Poland. I had never spoken to him, he had defended me from Branicki's Uhlans, he had spared my life, it was my duty to kiss his hand.

I send in my name, I enter, he asks me what I want of him.

"I come to kiss the hand which signed my pardon, Monseigneur, and to promise Your Excellency that I will be wiser in future."

"I advise you to be so. But as for your pardon, go thank the King, for if he had not asked me to grant it I should have had you beheaded."

"Despite the circumstances, Monseigneur?"

"What circumstances? Is it true or not true that you fought a duel?"

"It is not true; for I fought only because I was forced to defend myself. What I did could be called a duel if Count Branicki had taken me out of the Starosty, as my first challenge instructed him to do, and as we had agreed to do. So I believe that Your Excellency, properly informed, would not have had my head cut off."

"I do not know what I should have done. The King directed me to pardon you; it shows that he thought you deserve it, and I congratulate you. If you will come to dine with me tomorrow, I shall be pleased to see you."

"You shall be obeyed, Monseigneur."

The old man was renowned and very intelligent. He had been the great friend of the famous Poniatowski, the King's father. The next day at table he talked to me at length about him.

"What a comfort it would have been for Your Excellency's worthy friend if he had lived long enough to see the crown on his son's head!"

"He would not have wanted it."

The energy with which he made this reply showed me his soul. He was of the Saxon faction.[40] The same day I went to dine[41] with the Prince Palatine, who said that reasons of policy had prevented him from going to see me at the monastery; but that it should not make me doubt his friendship, for he had thought of me.

"I am having an apartment made ready for you here," he said. "My wife enjoys your company; but the apartment will not be ready for six weeks."

"Then I will use the time, Monseigneur, to pay a visit to the Palatine of Kiowia,[42] who did me the honor to send me an invitation."

"Through whom did he transmit the invitation?"

"The Starost Count Brühl,[43] who is in Dresden and whose wife is the Palatine's daughter."

"You will do well to make this little journey now, for your duel has made you many enemies, who will seize every occasion to get you into a quarrel, and Heaven preserve you from fighting again. Heed my warning. Be on your guard, and never go about on foot, especially at night."

I spent two weeks going to dinners and suppers to which I was invited, and at all of which I was summoned to tell the story of the duel in the greatest detail. The King was often present, always pretending not to listen to me; but once he could not refrain from asking me if, being in my native country Venice, and receiving an insult there, I would have challenged the insulter to a duel, supposing that he was a Venetian patrician.

"No, Sire, for I should have guessed that he would not come to fight."

"What would you have done then?"

"I should have champed the bit. But if the same Venetian patrician dared to insult me in a foreign country, he would account to me for it."

Having gone to call on Count Moczynski, I found La Binetti there; she vanished as soon as she saw me.

"What has she against me?" I asked Moczynski.

"She is the cause of the duel, and you are the cause of her losing her lover, for Branicki will have nothing more to do with her. She hoped he would treat you as he did Tomatis, and you nearly killed her bravo. She openly criticizes him for having accepted your challenge; but he will not see her again."

This Count Moczynski was as agreeable as possible, he was more than intelligent; but, generous to the point of prodigality, he was ruining himself at Court by making presents. His wounds were beginning to heal. The person who should have been the most attached to me was Tomatis; but, quite the contrary, he was no longer as pleased to see me as he had been before the duel. He saw in me a man who tacitly reproached him for cowardice and for preferring money to honor. He would perhaps have liked it better if Branicki had killed me, for then the author of his dishonor would have become the most odious person in all Poland, and people would perhaps have more easily forgiven him for the freedom with which he continued to show himself in the great houses with a stain on his honor which rendered him contemptible, despite the good society which made much of him and which he frequented; for it was obvious that all the favor he enjoyed came from the fanatical admiration which La Catai owed rather to her beauty and her sweet and modest manner than to her talent.

Determined to pay a visit to the malcontents who had recognized the new King only under compulsion, and several of whom had even refused to recognize him, I set out with Campioni, in order to have the companionship of a man who loved me and who had courage, and with one manservant. I had two hundred sequins in my purse, one hundred of which the Palatine of Russia had given me privately and in such an obliging way that I should have done very wrong to refuse them. I had won the other hundred backing Count Clary in a game of quinze which he played against a Starost Sniatinski,[44] who was light-heartedly ruining himself in Warsaw. Count Clary, who never lost when playing a two-handed game, that day won two thousand ducats from him, which the young man paid the next morning. Prince Charles of Kurland had left for Venice, where I had recommended him to my powerful friends, with whose treatment of him he had reason to be very well satisfied. The Anglican clergyman who had recommended me to Prince Adam had then arrived in Warsaw from Petersburg. I dined with him at the Prince's; the King, who knew him, was present by his own wish. There was also talk at that time of Madame Geoffrin,[45] an old friend of the King's, who was about to arrive in Warsaw at the invitation and the expense of the King himself, who, despite the difficulties which his enemies made for him, was always the soul of all the social occasions which he honored with his presence. He said to me one day when I chanced to find him sad and thoughtful that the crown of Poland was the crown of martyrdom. Yet this King, to whom I give all the praise which is his due, was weak enough to let calumny prevent him from making my fortune. I had the pleasure of convincing him that he was mistaken. I shall speak of it in the proper place, an hour or two hence.

I arrived at Leopol[46] six days after leaving Warsaw, because I stopped for two days at the young Count Zamojski's, the Ordynat of Zamosc,[47] who had an income of forty thousand ducats and was subject to epileptic fits. He told me that he was ready to give all that he possessed to the doctor who could cure him. I pitied his young wife. She loved him, and she did not dare to go to bed with him, for his affliction descended on him precisely when he tried to give her tokens of his fondness; she was in despair because she had to refuse his urgings and even to run away when he insisted. This magnate, who died not long afterward, lodged me in a very handsome apartment in which there was nothing. It is the Polish way; a gentleman is supposed to travel with everything he needs.

[* * *]

With his departure from Warsaw Casanova had exhausted the possibilities of exotic cities in eastern Europe and Russia as sources of income and amusement. It was time to return to more familiar stamping grounds in the west. He made for Paris via Prague and Dresden, managing on the way to have himself expelled from Vienna by Maria Theresa. But even Paris was soon too hot to hold him: after a series of public scandals he was ordered out by the King's lettre de cachet. Casanova had now been deported from most of what then counted as the world's great cities—in some cases twice. Where was he to go next? Scandinavia held no charms for him; unlike that other Venetian adventurer, Da Ponte, he never seems to have considered America. That left only Madrid—at this time as strange and remote as Moscow, and almost as inaccessible.

CHAPTER XII

My journey to
Madrid. The Count of Aranda. Prince della
Cattolica. The Duke of Losada. Mengs. A ball.
La Pichona. Doña Ignacia.

At Pamplona the carter Andrea Capello took charge of me and my baggage, and we set out for Madrid. The first twenty leagues did not tire me, for the road was as good as in France. It was a monument which honored the memory of Monsieur de Gages,[1] who, after the Italian war, was made Governor of Navarre. He had, I was told, had the fine road built at his expense. This famous general, who twenty-four years earlier had had me arrested,[2] thus found the true way to gain immortality and to deserve it. As a great soldier he had won laurels only to declare himself a famous destroyer of the human race; but this fine road declared him its benefactor. His fame was permanent and secure.

But after such a fine road I cannot say that I found a bad one, for I found none at all. Uneven stony climbs and descents, where one nowhere saw the least sign to indicate that carriages passed there. Such was the whole of Old Castile.[3] No one supposes that travelers who are fond of comfort think of going to Madrid by that route, so I was not surprised to find only wretched inns[4] fit to lodge muleteers who lodge with their mules. Señor Andrea was careful to choose the most habitable places for me, and after procuring everything his mules needed he would go through the village finding me something to eat. The master of the miserable establishment at which we stopped did not stir; he showed me a room and told me that I was at liberty to sleep in it, and a fireplace in which I was free to make a fire if I went to fetch the wood myself and to cook what I wanted to eat, not even troubling to tell me where I could go to buy it for my money. On leaving in the morning I paid him the small sum he asked for my lodging and a *peseta por el ruido*, "a small coin for the noise."[5] He smoked the *cigarro*[6] and his poverty stood him in the stead of riches, provided that the departing stranger could not say that he had bestirred himself in the slightest to wait on him. What causes this is an indolence mingled with pride; one is a Castilian, one must not lower oneself to wait on a *gabacho*;[7] this is the title which the whole Spanish nation confers on a foreigner. This word *gabacho* is much more insulting than the "dog" which the Turks apply to us and the "French dog"[8] which the English apply to all foreigners. It goes without saying that the nobility and people polished by travel or education do not think in this way. The foreigner who has good introductions and who behaves himself properly finds reasonable people in England as well as in Spain and in Turkey.

I slept the second night in Agreda. It is called a city. It is a prodigy of ugliness and gloom. It is a place where a man whom some employment does not keep busy cannot but go mad, suffer from black bile, and become a visionary. It is there that Sister María de Agreda went mad to the point of writing the life of the Blessed Virgin dictated by herself. I had been given her work to read under the Leads, and my reader may remember that the visionary's dreams very nearly made me lose my mind.[9] We traveled twenty leagues a day. One morning I thought I was preceded by ten or twelve Capuchins who were moving more slowly than the mules harnessed to my carriage. We pass them, I look at them, and I see that they are not Capuchins but women of all ages.

"What is this?" I asked Señor Andrea. "Are these women mad?"

"Not at all; they wear the Capuchin habit from devotion, and I am sure that not one of them has on a shift."

It was the more likely because shifts in Spain are very rare, but the notion of wearing the Capuchin habit to be more pleasing to the Creator struck me as very strange indeed.

Here is an adventure which amused me.

At the posthouse of a city not far from Madrid I am asked for my passport, I hand it over, and I get out of my carriage to amuse myself. I see the chief official angry with a foreign priest who wants to go on to Madrid and who has no passport for the capital. He showed one with which he had been to Bilbao,[10] and the official was not satisfied. The priest was a Sicilian, he was being badgered; I take an interest in him, I ask him why he has put himself in this predicament, and he replies that he had not thought that he needed a passport to travel in Spain once he was there.

"I want to go to Madrid," he said, "where I hope to enter the household of a grandee[11] as his confessor. I have a letter to him."

"Show the letter, and you will certainly be allowed to pass."

"You are right."

From his portfolio he takes the letter, which was not sealed, he shows it to the official, who unfolds it, looks at the signature, and exclaims when he reads the name Squillace.[12]

"What, Abate! you are going to Madrid recommended by Squillace, and you dare to show his letter?"

The clerks, the police who were there, as soon as they understand that the Abate had no recommendation but one from the Minister who was the object of the entire nation's hatred, and who would have been stoned to death if the King had not arranged his escape, raise their sticks and begin to bestow a sound beating on the wretched Abate, who would never have expected such a lamentable effect from a letter of recommendation from a man upon whose favor he hoped to construct the edifice of his fortune.

This Squillace was sent by the King, who loved him, as Ambassador to Venice, where he died at a great age. He was a man to be hated by all the subjects of the monarch, whose Minister of Finance he would have liked to be, for to increase receipts he was pitiless in regard to taxes.

The door of the room which the innkeeper gave me had a bolt outside, and nothing inside which I could use to fasten my door when I went to bed; the door opened and shut only by means of the latch. I said nothing for the first night and the second; but on the third I told my carter that I would not put up with it. He replied that I should have to put up with it in Spain; since the Holy Inquisition[13] must always be able to send to see what foreigners might be doing at night in their rooms, foreigners must not have the means to lock themselves in.

"What can your accursed Holy Inquisition be curious to know?"

"Everything. To see if you eat meat on a fast day. To see if there are several people of both sexes in the room, if the women sleep alone or with men, and to learn if the women who sleep with men are their legitimate wives, and to be able to take them to prison if their marriage certificates do not speak in their favor. The Holy Inquisition, Señor Don Jaime,[14] is ever on the watch in our country for our eternal salvation."

When we met a priest who was carrying the blessed sacrament to a dying person Señor Andrea stopped and imperatively told me to get out of the carriage and kneel, even in the mud if there was any; I had to obey. The great uproar in matters of religion at that time in the two Castiles[15] was over breeches without a codpiece. Those who wore them were taken to prison, and the tailors were punished;

nevertheless both wearers and tailors persisted, and the priests and monks vainly wore out their throats in their pulpits inveighing against such indecency. A revolution was expected which would have set all Europe laughing; but fortunately the thing was settled without bloodshed. An edict was promulgated, and printed copies of it were displayed on every church door. It said that no one would be allowed to wear breeches so made except the executioner. The fashion then went out, for no one wanted either to be thought an executioner or to avail himself of such a privilege.

Thus learning, little by little, to know the country among whose people I was to live, I arrived at Guadalajara, Alcalá, and Madrid. Guadalajara and Alcalá! What are these words, these names, in which I hear only the vowel *a*? It is because the language of the Moors, whose country Spain had been for several centuries, had left a quantity of words there.[16] Everyone knows that the Arabic language abounds in *a*'s. The learned are even not unjustified in deducing thence that Arabic must be the oldest of all languages, since *a* is the easiest of all the vowels, because it is the most natural. Hence it is not just to regard as barbarisms the words in the beautiful Spanish language in which there are no other vowels: ala, achala, Aranda, Almada, Acara, bacala, Agapa, Agrada, Agracaramba, Álava, Alamata, Albadara, Alcántara, Alcaraz, Alcavala,[17] and a thousand more, which have the effect of making the Castilian language richer than all languages, a richness which, as the reader easily understands, can consist only in synonyms, since it is as easy to imagine words as it is difficult to find new qualities and as it is impossible to create things. However that may be, the Spanish language is beyond contradiction one of the most beautiful in the world, sonorous, energetic, majestic, to be pronounced *ore rotundo* ("with rounded mouth"),[18] capable of the harmony of the most sublime poetry, and which would be equal to Italian for music if it had not the three guttural letters[19] which mar its sweetness, despite all that is said by the Spaniards, who, naturally, are of a different opinion. They must be allowed to go on saying so; *quisquis amat ranam ranam putat esse Dianam* ("he who loves frogs thinks that Diana is one").[20] Nevertheless, to unprejudiced ears its tone makes it seem more imperative than any other language.

As I entered by the Puerta de Alcalá,[21] I was searched, and the greatest attention of the officials was directed to books; they were disappointed when I was found to have only the *Iliad* in Greek. It was taken from me, and it was brought to me three days later in the

Street of the Cross,[22] at the coffeehouse where I went to lodge,[23] despite Señor Andrea, who wanted to take me elsewhere. A reliable man had given me this address in Bordeaux. A ceremony to which I was subjected at the Alcalá gate annoyed me greatly. A clerk asked me for a pinch of snuff. I give it to him; it was rappee.

"Señor, this snuff is accursed in Spain."

So saying, he throws all my snuff into the mud and gives me back my snuffbox empty.

Nowhere is there such strictness in the matter of snuff as there is in Spain, where, nevertheless, the contraband trade flourishes more than elsewhere. The spies of the tobacco monopoly, which especially protected by the King, are everywhere on the watch to discover people who have foreign snuff in their boxes, and when they find them they make them pay very dearly for their daring. This indulgence is forgiven only to foreign envoys; the King knew it and had to put up with it; but he did not allow them to use it in his presence. For his part, he put into his big nose only a big pinch of his Spanish snuff in the morning when he got out of bed, and he took no more of it all day. Spanish snuff is excellent when it is pure, but it is rare. On my arrival no good Spanish snuff was to be had. What had been found among the effects of the late Queen[24] had all been sold, and I had to go three or four weeks without taking snuff, except when I went to visit the fat Prince della Cattolica,[25] who, to give me an especial mark of his affection, received me, after the first time, seated on his commode, where he remained all morning and where he began the business of the day as soon as, left alone, he fell to writing his dispatches. In any case, Spaniards prefer rappee to their snuff, just as many of us prefer the Spanish. What pleases mankind is everywhere what is forbidden. A way of making men of a certain cast of mind do their duty would be to forbid them to do it; but lawmaking is nowhere philosophical.

Fairly well lodged, all I lacked was a fire; the cold was dry and more penetrating than in Paris, despite the forty degrees of latitude. The reason is that Madrid is the highest city[26] in all Europe. Those who go there from some city on the seacoast insensibly ascend, I believe, to an altitude of a thousand toises.[27] In addition, the city is surrounded by distant mountains and by hills close by, as a result of which when the wind blows it is bitterly cold. The air of Madrid is bad for all foreigners because it is pure and rarefied; it is good only for Spaniards, all of whom are thin, undersized, and susceptible to cold to the point that when there is the slightest wind even in

August they do not expose themselves to it without being wrapped up to the eyes in great woolen cloaks. The minds of the men in that country are limited by an infinity of prejudices, those of the women are in general comparatively unprejudiced; and both men and women are subject to passions and desires as keen as the air they breathe. All the men dislike foreigners, and they are unable to allege one good reason for it, for their dislike springs from nothing but an innate hatred; add to this hatred a scorn which can certainly arise only from the fact that the foreigner is not a Spaniard. The women, who recognize the injustice of this hatred and scorn, avenge us by loving us, but taking great precautions, for the Spaniard, jealous by nature, is determined to have a reason for his jealousy as well. He has bound his honor to the slightest slip on the part of the woman who belongs to him; in this way he conceals the cowardice of a timorous soul under the respectable veil which envelops the sanctuary of honor and even of religion. Superstitious to excess, he cannot be cured of it, for he does not know that he is so. Gallantry in that country can only be a mystery, for its goal is an enjoyment which is above everything else and which is also forbidden. Hence secrecy, intrigue, and the trouble of a soul which hesitates between the duties imposed by religion and the force of the passion which struggles against them. The men of that country are generally more ugly than handsome; but the women are very pretty, burning with desires, and all ready to lend a hand in schemes intended to deceive all those who surround them to spy on their doings. The lover who most boldly faces and defies dangers is the one they prefer to all those who are timid, respectful, guarded. Their coquetry makes them want to keep them, but at bottom they despise them. In the public walks, in churches, at the theaters, they speak with their eyes to those to whom they wish to speak, possessing that seductive language to perfection; if the man, who must understand it, can seize the occasion and take advantage of it, he is sure to be successful; he need not expect the slightest resistance; if he neglects the opportunity or does not profit by it, it is not offered him again.

Needing to live in a comfortably warm room, since the brazier made me ill and there was no fireplace, I asked for a stove; and with great difficulty I found someone intelligent enough to make me one, following my instructions, of heavy tin with a long pipe which went out one of my windows to join another very long one which ascended to the gutter on the roof. The workman, proud of having succeeded, made me pay a great deal for his trial piece. During the first days until my stove was built I was told where I should go to warm myself an hour before noon and stay there until dinnertime; it was a place called the Gate of the Sun;[28] it was not a gate, but it was so named because it was there that the beneficent luminary, prodigal of his wealth, distributed the heat of his rays to all who went to walk there to warm themselves and thus enjoy their influence. I saw a large number of men of fashion walking about, either alone and rapidly, or slowly and talking to their friends; but I did not care for this sort of hearth. Needing a servant who spoke French, it was an endless task to find one; I did find him at last, but at a very high price, for he was what is called in Madrid a page; I could make him neither get up behind my carriage, nor carry packages anywhere for me, nor light me at night with a torch or a lantern. He was a man thirty years of age, with a face which could not be uglier. As a page, he was better fitted for the duties of his office being ugly than if he had been handsome, for he was not one to make the husbands of the ladies whom he went to serve jealous for fear they would fall in love with him. A woman of a certain station in Madrid does not dare to go out in a carriage unless she is accompanied by a so-called page, who sits up in front and who is with her only to spy on her. Such a rascal is more of a hindrance to a seduction than a duenna,[29] who is by nature a tyrant over the girls she guards. So, since I could find no one else, it was a fellow of this stamp whom I had to take into my service.

I delivered all my letters, beginning with the one by which Princess Lubomirska presented me to the Count of Aranda. The Count was then more powerful in Madrid than the King himself. It was he who in a single day had banished all the Jesuits in all Spain,[30] he had been able to proscribe hats with turned-down brims and cloaks coming down to the heel;[31] he was President of the Council of Castile,[32] he was all-powerful, he never went out except followed by one of the King's bodyguard, whom he always had eat at his table. As was to be expected, he was hated by the whole country, but he did not care. A man of profound intelligence, a great politician, bold, determined, reasoning correctly, a great epicurean, maintaining appearances, doing in his house everything that he forbade in other houses, and not caring if people said so. This rather ugly nobleman, who squinted to the point of deformity, received me rather coolly.

"What have you come to do in Spain?"

"To learn by observing the manners and customs of an estimable nation which I do not know, and at the same time to profit by my feeble talents if I can make myself useful to the government."

"To live here decently and quietly you do not need me, for if you behave in accordance with the laws which maintain order in the city no one will trouble you. As for your wish to use your talents to make your fortune, address yourself to the Ambassador of your Republic;[33] he will present you, and you can make yourself known."

"The Venetian Ambassador will do me no harm, but he will do me no good either, for I am in disfavor with the State Inquisitors. I am sure he will not receive me."

"In that case you can hope for nothing at Court, for the King will first ask the Ambassador about you. If the Ambassador will not present you, I advise you to think of nothing but amusing yourself."

I call on the Neapolitan Ambassador,[34] and he tells me the same thing; the Marquis of Mora,[35] the most amiable of all Spaniards, is of the same opinion. The Duke of Losada, Grand Steward to His Catholic Majesty and his favorite, sorry that he could do nothing despite his good will, advises me to try to obtain admission to the residence of the Venetian Ambassador and to do what I could to gain his support, despite a disgrace of which he could pretend to be unaware since he did not know the reasons for it. I prepare to follow the wise old man's advice, so I write a strong letter to Signor Dandolo[36] in Venice, in which I asked him for a letter of recommendation to the Ambassador himself, which would oblige him to lend me his countenance at Court despite the State Inquisitors. My letter was so composed that it could be shown to the State Inquisitors themselves, and should have a good effect.

After writing this letter I go to the residence of the Venetian Ambassador, and I present myself to Signor Gasparo Soderini,[37] the Secretary of Embassy, a man of intelligence, prudent and honest, but who nevertheless took it upon himself to say that he was astonished that I had had the audacity to present myself at the Ambassador's residence.

"I present myself, Signore, in order not to have to reproach myself with the fault of not presenting myself, for I have done nothing which can make me suppose myself unworthy of it. I should think myself far more audacious if I stayed in Madrid without presenting myself here at least once than if I had never presented myself. In the meanwhile I am glad to have taken this step, which I regard as a duty, and I leave unhappy and disappointed to have learned that if the Ambassador thinks as you do he will consider temerity what is only an act of respect on my part. If, further-more, the Ambassador is of the opinion that he may not do me the honor to receive me because of a private quarrel which exists between the State Inquisitors and myself, and the nature of which he cannot know, permit me to be surprised, for he is not here as Ambassador of the State Inquisitors but of the Republic, of which I am still a subject, for I defy him to tell me what crime I can have committed to make me unworthy of being so. I believe that if my duty is to respect in the Ambassador the image and the representative of my sovereign,[38] his duty is to extend his protec-tion to me."

Soderini had blushed at this discourse, which too clearly set forth palpable truths. He asked me why I did not write the Ambassador everything I had just said to him.

"I could not write him that before I knew if he would receive me or not; now that I have reason to believe that he thinks as you do, I will write to him."

"I do not know if His Excellency thinks as I do, and despite what I have said to you it is possible that you still do not know what I think; but meanwhile write to him, and you may be given a hearing."

Back at my lodging, I the same day wrote His Excellency everything that I had said to the Secretary of Embassy; and the next day Count Manuzzi[39] was announced to me. I see a handsome, rather well-built youth who makes a very good impression. He said that he lodged at the Ambassador's, who, having read my letter, had sent him to tell me that, having reasons for not receiving me publicly, he would nevertheless be delighted to talk with me in private, for he knew me and esteemed me. The young man told me that he was a Venetian, that he knew me by reputation from having heard his father and mother talk of me many times, lament-ing my misfortune. I finally understand that the young Manuzzi whom I had before me was the son of the Giovanni Battista Manuzzi who had served the State Inquisitors as a spy in order to get me imprisoned under the Leads, the same man who had cleverly obtained from me the books of magic I had and which were apparently the incriminating evidence which, without any other legal proceedings, had brought on me the terrible punishment to which I had been subjected. I tell him none of this, but I see that it is he; I knew his mother, who was the daughter of a valet in the service of the Loredan[40] family, and his father, who, as I said in my account of my imprisonment under the Leads, was a poor jeweler. I ask him if he is called Count in the Ambassador's household, and he says that he is, because he was in fact one by virtue of a patent he had received from the Elector of the Palatinate. He frankly tells me the truth about everything, and since he was aware that I knew of Ambassador Mocenigo's inclination, he does not hesitate to tell me with a laugh that he is his antinatural mistress. He assures me that he will do everything in his power for me; and it was all that I could ask, for such an Alexis was bound to obtain whatever he wanted from his Corydon.[41] We embrace, and he leaves, saying that he expects me after dinner at the palace in the Calle Ancha[42] to take coffee with him in his room, to which the Ambassador would certainly come as soon as he sent him word that I was there.

I went there, and the Ambassador gave me a very gracious reception, speaking with feeling of his regret that he dared not receive me publicly, for it was true that he could have done everything, and even taken me to Court without compromising himself, for he was under no obligation to know anything of the summary treatment I had received from the State Inquisitors, but he feared to make enemies. I replied that I hoped soon to receive a letter from someone which would tell him, on behalf of the Inquisitors themselves, that he could countenance me without fear, and he replied that in that case he would present me to all the Ministers.

The Ambassador was the Mocenigo who afterward got himself so much talked about in Paris because of his unfortunate inclination for pederasty, and who was later sentenced by the Council of Ten to spend seven years in the fortress of Brescia[43] for having tried to leave Venice for Vienna, where he had been appointed Ambassador, without first having been given permission to leave by the Cabinet. The Empress Maria Theresa had intimated that she did not want such a man in her capital, and in Venice it had been proving difficult to make the appointee understand the situation, when, by committing the error of trying to leave without permission, he made it possible for the Senate to appoint another Ambassador[44] to Vienna, who had the same taste as Mocenigo but who confined himself to women.

At Madrid he was liked, despite its being common knowledge that he was of the wristband clique,[45] and his often being seen driving through the streets of Madrid with his paramour. I laughed when a Spanish grandee told me at a ball that everyone knew that

Manuzzi played the part of wife to His Excellency the Ambassador; he did not know that the wife was the Ambassador, to whom Manuzzi played husband. The same inclination was shared by Frederick II, King of Prussia, and by nearly all the men of Antiquity, who were called "hermaphrodites" to designate their two passions. However, Mocenigo kept Manuzzi at a distance and did not have him dine with him when he gave formal dinners.

I had already called two or three times on the painter Mengs,[46] who for six years had been in the service of His Catholic Majesty at an excellent salary, and he had given me fine dinners with his friends. His wife was in Rome with his whole family, he was alone with his servants, lodged in a house which belonged to the King, and respected by everyone, for he talked with His Majesty whenever he pleased. At his house I made the acquaintance of the architect Sabatini,[47] a very talented man, whom the King had summoned from Naples to make Madrid clean, whereas before he arrived it was the dirtiest and most stinking city in the universe. Sabatini had constructed drains and subterranean conduits, and had had latrines built in fourteen thousand houses. He had become rich. He had married by proxy the daughter of Vanvitelli,[48] another architect, who was in Naples and who had never seen him. She had arrived in Madrid at the same time that I did. She was a beauty eighteen years of age, who had no sooner seen her husband than she had said she would never consent to become his wife. He was neither young nor handsome. However, the charming girl decided to swallow the pill when he told her that she would have to choose between him and a convent. Afterward she had no cause to repent, for she found in him a rich husband, tender and considerate, who granted her all the decent freedom she could want. I went to their house a great deal. *Brûlant pour elle, et soupirant tout bas* ("Burning for her and sighing inaudibly"),[49] for aside from the fact that the wound Charlotte had made in my heart had not yet healed over, I was beginning to feel discouraged to see that women no longer welcomed me as they had done in the past.

I began going to the theater which was a hundred paces from the house in which I lived, and to the masked balls, which the Count of Aranda had established in Madrid in a hall built for the purpose called "Los Caños del Peral."[50] The Spanish theater was full of absurdities, but it did not displease me. I saw some *autos sacramentales*,[51] which soon afterward were forbidden in Madrid, and I observed the shamelessness of a base police administration in the way in which the *aposentos*, as they call the boxes, were constructed. Instead of having boards in front, which prevents people in the parterre from seeing the man's legs and the ladies' skirts, all the boxes were open, having, instead of boards, only two pillars which supported the rail. A precisian who was sitting next to me said devoutly that it was a very wise regulation and declared it surprising that the same policy was not in force in Italy.

"Why do you think it surprising?"

"It is surprising because a lady and gentleman, being sure that people in the parterre do not see their hands, might put them to evil use."

"What use?"

"*Valgame Dios* ['God help me']! The lady could do the *puñete*[52] to the gentleman."

After laughing heartily, and finding out what the *puñete* was, I told him that the Italians and the French did not dirty their minds with such suspicions. In a large box with a grating opposite the stage sat *los padres* of the Inquisition, to make sure that the audience and the actors indulged in nothing contrary to morality. All of a sudden I heard the voice of the sentinel who was at the entrance to the parterre shout: "Dios!" At the sound the whole audience, men and women, and the actors who were on the stage, broke off, fell to their knees, and remained there until a bell which was being rung in the street was no longer heard. The bell indicated that a priest was going past carrying the viaticum to a sick person. The people of Spain are edified by everything which proves that in all that they do they never lose sight of religion. There is not a courtesan who, being with her lover and yielding to amorous desire, decides to perform the act without first having put a handkerchief over the crucifix and turned the pictures of saints to face the wall. Anyone who laughed at it, a man who called the ceremony absurd and superstitious, would be considered an atheist, and the courtesan would perhaps denounce him to the authorities.

Any man in Madrid who goes to an inn with a woman and orders dinner in a private room is accommodated at once; but the headwaiter of the inn always remains present throughout the dinner so that he can swear afterward that the two people did nothing in the room but eat and drink. Despite these prohibitions, and even because of these prohibitions, profligacy runs riot in Madrid. Both men and women think of nothing but making all surveillance fruitless. All the women have a disease which they call "the whites," but men incautious enough to expose themselves to it find at the end of twenty-four hours that it is nothing less than white. This malady is general among the women, and I was assured that even nuns are afflicted with it without ever having wronged their divine spouse in any way.

The masked ball became my favorite pleasure. The first time I went to it, alone and wearing a domino, merely to see what it was, it cost me only a doubloon; but all the other times it cost me four. This was in consequence of a discourse to which I was treated by a masker in a domino, a man of perhaps sixty years, who happened to sit beside me in the room in which one supped. Seeing that I was a foreigner from the difficulty I had in making myself understood by the waiter, he asked me where my female masker was.

"I have no women with me, I came alone to see this charming establishment, where a pleasure and an orderliness reign which I had not expected to find in Madrid."

"Very well; but to enjoy this fine spectacle you must come with a companion, for you seem to be a man to enjoy dancing, and, alone, you cannot dance, for every woman you see here has her *parejo* ['partner'] who will not let her dance with anyone else."

"In that case I will come and never dance, since I do not know a woman in this city whom I can invite to come to the ball with me."

"As a foreigner you can obtain the company of a woman or a girl much more easily than a Spaniard from Madrid. Under the new regime of gaiety and freedom introduced by the Count of Aranda, the ball which you see has become the passion of all the women and girls in Madrid. You see here some two hundred of them dancing, for I do not count those who remain in the boxes, and it is certain that four thousand girls who have no lover who will or can bring them here are at home crying, for as you know all women are forbidden to come here alone. Now, I am certain that, if you give merely your name and your address, there is not a mother or a father who will have the heart to refuse you their daughter if you present yourself to ask for the honor of offering her the pleasure of the ball, sending her domino, mask, and gloves, and going to fetch her in a carriage, in which you will undertake, of course, to bring her back home."

"And if I am refused?"

"You bow and leave, and afterward the girl's father and mother are very sorry they have refused you, for she cries, falls ill, and goes to bed, cursing and swearing at their tyranny and calling God to witness that she has never seen you in her life and that nothing was more innocent than your request."

This novel discourse, which had the stamp of truth, and which already raised my spirits by the prospect that it would introduce me to some rare adventure, for which I still had an appetite, both interested me and authorized me to ask the masker who thus addressed me in very good Italian some questions. I thank him, and I promise him I will apply the fine lesson he has given me and will inform him of the outcome and of the acquaintance he will have led me to make, for I would consider the next morning to which of all the beauties in Madrid I would throw my handkerchief. He replies that he will be delighted to hear everything, and that I should find him every evening in a box to which he would take me to introduce me to the lady who was in it then and who would also be there on the following nights. More than obliged by such politeness, I tell him my name, I pay for my supper at the posted price, I follow him, and we enter a box in which are two women and an elderly man; he introduces me as a foreigner of his acquaintance; all goes smoothly, they speak French, they discuss the fine ball, I offer my comments, I make some remarks bright enough to please the company; one of the two ladies, who still showed signs of a great, faded beauty, asks me which *tertulias* ("receptions, circles") I frequent, and when she hears me say that I usually go nowhere she invites me to go to her house, saying that her name is Pichona[53] and that everyone knows where she lives. I promise her I will go there.

The great spectacle which enchanted me came toward the end of the ball, when to the music of the orchestra, after general applause, a dance for couples began than which I had never seen anything wilder or more interesting. It was the fandango,[54] of which I thought I had an accurate notion, but I was very much mistaken. I had seen it danced only in Italy and France on the stage, where the dancers did not perform one of the national gestures which make the dance truly seductive. I cannot describe it. Each couple danced face to face, never taking more than three steps, striking the castanets, which are held in the fingers, and accompanying the music with attitudes than which nothing more lascivious could possibly be seen. Those of the man visibly indicated love crowned with success, those of the woman consent, ravishment, the ecstasy of pleasure. It seemed to me that no woman could refuse anything to a man with whom she had danced the fandango. The pleasure I took in watching it made me exclaim aloud; the masker who had brought me there told me that to have a true idea of the dance one had to see it performed by *gitanas* ("gypsy girls") with a man who also danced it to perfection. I asked if the Inquisition had no objection to make to a dance which set the soul on fire, and I was told that it was absolutely forbidden, and that no one would have dared to dance it if the Count of Aranda had not given his permission for it. I was told that when he took it into his head not to give the permission everyone left the ball dissatisfied; but that on the other hand everyone left praising him when he permitted it.

The next morning I ordered my infamous page to find me a Spaniard whom I would pay to teach me to dance the fandango, and he brought me an actor, whom I engaged to give me lessons in the Spanish language; but in three days the young man taught me the motions of the dance so well that, by the testimony even of Spaniards, there was no one in Madrid who could boast that he danced it better than I.

Three days later there was a ball, and I wanted to do justice to the lesson the masker had taught me. I wanted neither a public courtesan nor a married woman. Nor could I think of some rich or well-born lady, who would have refused me and have found me ridiculous into the bargain. It was St. Anthony's[55] day—the one who is called "St. Anthony the Great" and who is depicted with a pig; I pass by the Church of La Soledad,[56] and I enter it to hear a mass, still thinking of finding a *pareja* for the next day, which was a Wednesday. I see a tall girl coming out of a confessional, beautiful, with an air of contrition and keeping her eyes cast down. She kneels in the middle of the church, directly on the floor, of course, for that is the fashion in Spain. Imagining that she must dance the fandango like an angel, I set my heart on having her as my partner at my début at Los Caños del Peral. To find out where she lives, I think of following her, she seemed neither rich, nor noble, nor a prostitute. At the end of the mass the priest distributes the eucharist, I see her rise, go to the altar, receive it devoutly, then take a place apart to finish her prayers. I had the patience to wait until the end of the second mass. She goes out with another girl, and I follow them at some distance; at the end of a street the one on whom I had no designs leaves her and goes upstairs to her home, mine retraces her steps some twenty paces, enters another street, and then a house which had only two stories. I cannot be mistaken, I see the name of the street, del Desengaño,[57] I walk for half an hour so that she shall not think I followed her. Thoroughly prepared to be refused and to leave with a bow afterward, as the masker had told me to do, I go upstairs, I ring at the only door I see, I am asked who is there, I reply "peaceable people," which in Madrid is the password which the henchmen of the Inquisition, who inspire terror, never use. The door is opened, and I see a man, a woman, the girl in question, and an ugly one.

Speaking Spanish very badly but well enough to be understood, with my hat in my hand, and a serious and respectful manner, I say to the father, without even looking at the devout beauty, that, being a foreigner and having no *pareja*, I had come to his house by chance to ask him for permission to take his daughter, if he had one, to the ball, assuring him that I was a man of honor and that I would bring her back to him as he had entrusted her to me at the end of the evening.

"Señor, there is my daughter, but I do not know you, and I do not know if she wants to go to the ball."

"If you will permit me to go, my Father and my Mother, I should think myself fortunate."

"Then you know this gentleman?"

"I have never seen him, and I think it almost impossible that he should have seen me anywhere."

"I swear to you that I have never seen you."

The man asks me my name and my address, and he promises to give me his answer at dinnertime, if I dine at home. I ask him to excuse the liberty I had taken, I leave begging him not to fail to give me his answer, for if he will not let me have his daughter I shall have to look for another *pareja* at random, knowing none but rich girls who were all engaged.

I go home, and exactly an hour later, just as I was about to dine, I see my man. I ask him to sit down, I send away my page, and as soon as he sees we are alone he says that his daughter will accept the honor I am so good as to offer her, but that her mother will come too and will sleep in the carriage and wait for her. I reply that she would be free to do so, and that I was only sorry that she would be cold in the carriage. He says that she will have a good cloak, and he tells me that he is a shoemaker by trade.

"Then please measure me for a pair of shoes at once."

"I do not dare, for I am a hidalgo.[58] Taking someone's measure would debase me, I am a *zapatero de viejo* (cobbler),[59] and so, not being obliged to touch anyone's feet, I neither derogate from my nobility nor wrong my birth."

"Then will you mend these boots for me?"

"I will return them to you so that you will think them brand-new; but I see that they need much work, it will cost you a peso duro."[60]

It was a hundred French sous. I tell him that I am perfectly satisfied with the price, he takes the boots, and he leaves, absolutely refusing to dine with me.

Here was a cobbler who despised shoemakers who in their turn must have looked down on him. The lackeys in livery in France despise valets, because they are obliged to help their masters at moments when they must lower themselves to perform menial services.

The next day I sent a man with dominoes, masks, and gloves to my devout beauty, neither going there myself nor using my page, whom I could not bear, and at nightfall I got out at her door from a closed carriage which seated four. I found her all ready, her face prettily flushed with animation. We got into the carriage with her mother, who had on a great cloak, and we got out at the entrance to the ballroom, leaving her mother in the carriage. On the way the daughter told me that her name was Doña Ignacia.[61] The dancing had already begun, and there was a great crowd.

HISTORY OF MY LIFE

Volume Eleven

CHAPTER I

*1768. My amour with Doña Ignacia, the
gentleman-cobbler's daughter. My imprisonment
in Buen Retiro and my triumph. I am
recommended to the Venetian Ambassador by a
State Inquisitor of the Republic.*

I enter the ballroom with the beautiful Doña Ignacia, we take
several turns around it, everywhere meeting the guard of soldiers
with fixed bayonets who were walking slowly about, ready to
apprehend any who should break the peace by quarreling. We
dance minuets and contradances until ten o'clock, then we go to
supper, both remaining silent, she, perhaps, in order not to encourage me to take liberties, I because, speaking very little Spanish, I did
not know what to say. After supper I go to the box where I was to
see La Pichona,[1] and I see only maskers whom I did not know. We
go back to dancing, until permission to dance the fandango[2] is at last
given, and I fall to with my *pareja*,[3] who danced it very well and who
is surprised to find herself so well accompanied in it by a foreigner.
At the end of the seductive dance, which had set us both on fire,
I escort her to the place where refreshments were served, I ask her if
she has been pleased with me, and I tell her that she has made me so
much in love with her that I should die if she did not find a way to
make me happy and confide it to me, assuring her that I was a man
to run all risks. She replies that she could not think of making me
happy except by becoming happy herself, and that she would write
me how I could accomplish that in a letter which she would sew
between the cloth and the lining of the hood of her domino, and so
I must put off sending for it until the next day. Telling her that she
will find me ready for anything, I escort her outside, I go to find the
carriage with her beyond the *plazuela*,[4] where I had left it. We get
into it, her mother wakes, the coachman drives off, I take both her
hands, intending nothing but to kiss them; but, supposing that I was
going to subject her to something which she considered too much,
she holds them in so strong a grip that I should have sought in vain
to free them if I had attempted it. Still grasping my hands, she gives
her mother an account of all the pleasures she had enjoyed at the
ball; she did not release them until, as we entered the Calle del

Desengaño,[5] her mother told the coachman to stop, for she did not want to give the neighbors occasion to gossip by getting out at her own door. She asked me not to get out, and, after thanking me, they walked to their house. I at once went home and to bed.

The next day I sent for the domino, in which I found Doña Ignacia's letter where she had said it would be. In her letter, which was very short, she told me that Don Francisco de Ramos[6] would call on me at my lodging, that he was her lover, and that it would be from him that I should learn the way to make her happy, for my happiness could be only the consequence of hers.

Don Francisco lost no time. My page announced him to me the next morning at eight o'clock. He told me that Doña Ignacia, with whom he talked every night from the street, she being at her window, had confided to him that she had gone to the ball with me and her mother, and that, being certain that I could have conceived only a fatherly fondness for her, she had persuaded him to present himself to me, assuring him that I would treat him as if he were my son. So it was she who gave him the courage to unbosom himself to me and to ask me to lend him a hundred doblones,[7] which could put him in a position to marry her before the end of the Carnival. He told me that he was employed in the office of the Mint,[8] and that his salary, which was then very small, would be increased later, that his father and mother were in Toledo, that he would be alone in Madrid with his dear wife, and that he would have no other friend than I, never even imagining that I could have any inclination toward Doña Ignacia except that which a father could have toward a daughter.

I replied that he had divined my feelings, but that for the moment I did not have the hundred doblones, and that I did not even know how long it might be before I could have that amount. I assured him of my discretion, and, telling him that I should be pleased whenever he honored me with a call, I saw him leave extremely disappointed. He was a young man perhaps twenty-two years of age, ugly and ill built. Making light of what had happened, for I felt only a passing fancy for Doña Ignacia, I went to pay my homage to La Pichona, who had so cordially invited me to call on her the first time I had attended the ball. I had made inquiries about her. I had learned that she had been an actress, and that she owed her wealth to the Duke of Medina Celi,[9] who, having gone to see her one day when it was very cold, found that she had no brazier because she had no money to buy charcoal. The Duke, who was extremely rich, feeling ashamed to have called on a woman so poor, the next day sent her a silver brazier containing a hundred thousand pesos duros[10] in gold, which came to fifty thousand zecchini. So since that time she had lived very comfortably and received good company.

I go to call on her, she receives me cordially, but I see that she is very sad. I tell her that I had not failed to go to her box, and that I had not found her. She replies that the Duke of Medina Celi had died[11] on that day after three days' illness, and, since he was her only friend, she had not had the strength to go out.

"Was he very old?"

"No, sixty. You saw him yourself. He didn't look his age."

"Where did I see him?"

"Wasn't it he who brought you to my box?"

"That man? He didn't tell me his name. That was the first time I saw him."

His death shocked me. All his possessions went to a son,[12] who, as might be expected, was a great miser. But his miserly son in his turn had a son who was a spendthrift.

This is what I have observed always and everywhere. The miser's son is a spendthrift, and the spendthrift's son is a miser. It seems to me natural that the characters of the father and the son are in perpetual contradiction. An intelligent author[13] tries to ascertain the reason why a father usually loves his grandson far more than his son: he thinks he has found it in nature. It is natural, he says, that a man should love the enemy of his enemy. It seems to me that, advanced as a generalization, this is a barbarous reason, for, beginning with myself, I have found that the son loves his father. I grant, however, that the father's love of his son is infinitely greater than the son's of his father. I was told that the House of Medina Celi had thirty hats,[14] which means thirty grandeeships of Spain.

A young man who frequented the coffeehouse, to which I never went, came upstairs to my room without much ceremony to offer me his services in a country which was new to me and with which he was very well acquainted.

"I am," he said, "Count Marazzani,[15] of Piacenza, I am not rich, I have come to Madrid to seek my fortune; I hope to be made one of His Majesty's[16] Bodyguard. I have been waiting for a year, and, while waiting, I amuse myself. I saw you at the ball with a beauty whom no one knows. I do not want to know who she is; but if you like variety, I can introduce you to all the choicest women in Madrid."

In reply to this discourse, I ought, if I had been wise, to have treated the impertinent Count very coldly; but I was tired of pretending to be wise; there was an intolerable void in my heart; I needed, as I had needed several times before, a charming passion. I gave the Mercury[17] a good reception, I urged him to show me beauties worthy of my attention, excluding both those whom it was too easy to approach and those who were too difficult of access, for I did not want to get myself into trouble in Spain. *Nolo nimis facilem, difficilemque nimis* ("I want a woman neither to give in too easily nor to resist too much").[18] He tells me to go to the ball with him, and he promises he will arrange for me to have all the beauties who interest me, despite any current lovers they might have. Since the ball was to be on that day, I promise to go with him; he asks me for dinner, I invite him. After dinner, on his telling me that he has no money, I give him two pesos duros, and I agree to meet him in the ballroom. It was this very forward man, who was ugly and had lost one eye, who spent the whole night with me and who pointed out to me fifteen or twenty beauties, telling me their stories. He showed me one who pleased me, and whom he promised me I should enjoy in the house of a bawd he knew, to which he would have her go; and he kept his word; but he made me spend a great deal, and in comparison I found the pleasure too small. I needed to love, and I did not find a woman to capture my heart.

Toward the end of the Carnival Don Diego, *zapatero de viejo*,[19] Doña Ignacia's father, brought me my boots and compliments from his wife and daughter, who still talked of the pleasure she had enjoyed at the ball, congratulating herself on the respect I had shown her. I told him that she was a girl as worthy of respect as she was beautiful, who deserved a great fortune, and that, if I did not call on her, it was because I was afraid I might injure her reputation. He replied that her reputation was above the reach of slander, and that he would take it as an honor whenever I would come to his house. It was as much as to urge me to do so; I said that the Carnival was about to end, and that if Doña Ignacia would like it I would take her to the ball again; he told me to go to his house for my answer.

Curious to see with what countenance I should be met by the pious girl who wanted to make me hope for everything after her marriage, making me pay an exorbitant amount beforehand, I go there the same day, and I see her, rosary in hand, with her mother, while her father mended old shoes. I laughed to myself at having to accord the "Don" to a cobbler, who refused to be a shoemaker because he was a hidalgo.[20] Doña Ignacia politely gets up from the floor, where she was sitting with her legs crossed, as African women sit. This custom was a vestige of the Moorish manners of Old Spain. In Madrid I have seen noble ladies, even at Court, sitting in this posture on the floor of the Princess of Asturias's[21] antechamber. They sit so in church, too, and it is with surprising nimbleness that they pass from sitting to kneeling and thence to standing, all in an instant.

Doña Ignacia, thanking me for the honor I was doing her, said that but for me she would never have seen the ball, and that she did not hope to see it again, for she was sure that in four weeks I must have found an object worthy of my attention. I reply that I had found no one worthy to be preferred to her, and that if she wanted to go to another ball I should escort her again with very great pleasure. Her father and her mother consent, we speak of the domino, she says that her mother will go to get her one, I give her a doblón, she leaves at once to go for it, for the ball is to be that day; and, Don Diego having gone somewhere, I am left alone with the daughter, to whom I say that she had but to say the word and I would be hers, for I adored her, but that she would never see me if she was thinking of making me languish.

"What can you want from me, what can I give you, since it is my duty to preserve my innocence for the man who is to be my husband?"

"You must yield to my ardor without resisting me in the slightest, and be sure that I will respect your innocence."

I then launch an attack on her, gently and politely, but she defends herself vigorously and with a seriousness which is not to be denied. I leave her, assuring her that she will find me submissive and respectful throughout the night, but not tender and loving, which would be far better. Blushing scarlet, she replies that her duty obliged her to resist me despite herself. This metaphysical flight on the lips of a pious Spanish woman pleased me excessively; it was a matter of conquering duty, of destroying the notion of it, and then she would herself declare her readiness. I must make her argue, and carry her by storm the moment I saw her at a loss to answer me.

"If your duty," I said, "forces you to repulse me despite yourself, it follows that your duty is a burden to you, it is your mortal enemy. If it is your enemy, why do you cherish it, why do you yield it the victory? For your own sake, begin by trampling this insolent duty underfoot."

"That is impossible."

"It is perfectly possible. Think of yourself; be calm and shut your eyes."

"Like this?"

I thereupon quickly attack her in the weak place; but no sooner am I there than she repulses me, yet not roughly, and with less seriousness. She says that it is in my power to seduce her, but that if I love her I ought to spare her that shame. I then make her understand that an intelligent girl could feel ashamed only if she yielded to a man whom she did not love; but that if she loved, love, being alone responsible, justified her for everything.

"If you do not love me," I say, "I scorn you."

"But what am I to do to convince you that if I let you have your way it is from love, and not from a shameful compliance?"

"Let me do whatever I want to, and my self-esteem will help you to make me believe that you love me, without your troubling yourself to tell me so."

"Admit that, since I cannot be certain of it, I must refuse you everything."

"I admit it, but you will see me sad and cold."

"That will grieve me."

At that, my bold hands gained the advantage, hers let me guide them where I would, and my pleasure came to a fruition which she did nothing to disavow. Perfectly satisfied, for by way of a beginning I could expect nothing more, I gave myself up to a gaiety in which she had never seen me and which aroused hers. Her mother arrived with a domino and gloves, I declined to take the change from the doblón, and I left to come back for her later, as I had done the first time. The first step having been taken, Doña Ignacia saw that she would be making herself ridiculous if she opposed my advances and refused to respond when I talked to her at the ball about ways to procure us the pleasure of spending some nights together. Nature and reason, together with self-esteem, showed her that her one thought must be to keep me by making me constant. She found me entirely different from what I had been at the ball the first time, solicitous, tender, attentive, and at supper concerned to see that she was served whatever she liked best: I forced her inwardly to applaud herself for having decided to yield. I filled her pockets with sweetmeats, I put two bottles of ratafia[22] in mine to give to her mother, who was asleep in the carriage; I begged her to accept a doblón de a ocho,[23] which she refused without haughtiness, only asking me confidently to give it to her lover when he came to call on me.

"How shall I make sure not to offend him?"

"Tell him that it is the first of the hundred he asked you for. He is poor, and I am certain that at this moment he must be in despair because he has not seen me at my window; he may spend the whole night in the street. I will tell him tomorrow night that I came to the ball with you only to please my father."

Convinced that she had resolved to give herself to me, I found the girl dancing the fandango with me so voluptuously that she could not have promised me everything more eloquently in words. What a dance! It burns, it inflames, it carries away. Nevertheless, people tried to assure me that the majority of Spanish men and women who dance it mean no harm by it. I pretended to believe them. Before getting out of the carriage at her house, she asked me to go to mass at La Soledad[24] on the next day but one at eight o'clock. I did not tell her that it was there that I had seen her the first time, receiving the sacrament. She also asked me to come that evening to her house, where she would give me a letter if she could not manage to be alone with me.

Having slept until noon, when I woke I saw Marazzani, come to dine with me. He had watched me all evening at the ball, and, always in disguise, he had seen me sup with Doña Ignacia. He said that, trying to find out who she was, he had questioned all the connoisseurs in Madrid, and I patiently put up with his extremely indiscreet curiosity; but when he told me that if he had money he would have had me followed, I talked to him in a way which made him turn pale. He at once begged my pardon, promising that he would permit himself no more curiosity about her. He proposed a party with a well-favored and celebrated courtesan named Spiletta, who did not sell her favors cheaply, and I refused. Doña Ignacia occupied me entirely. I thought her very worthy to succeed to Charlotte.[25]

I arrived at La Soledad before her; she saw me in the corner of a confessional as soon as she entered with the girl who had been her companion the first time. She came and knelt down two paces from me; she never looked at me; the one who constantly examined me was her friend, who was extremely ugly but of the same age. I saw Don Francisco in the church, so I left it before Doña Ignacia did. He joined me, and he congratulated me somewhat bitterly on the good fortune I had had to go to the ball a second time with the sovereign of his soul. He confessed that he had followed us all night, and that he could have left the ball well enough pleased if he had not seen us dance the fandango, for he had thought we looked too much like a pair of happy lovers. I told him with a laugh that love was subject to delusions, and that as an intelligent man he should not allow his soul to harbor any suspicions. At the same moment, begging his pardon, I gave him a doblón de a ocho as a payment on account. He accepts it, utterly astonished, he calls me his father, his good angel, and he promises me eternal gratitude. He leaves, assuring me he was certain that, as soon as I could, I would give him the entire sum he needed in order to marry Doña Ignacia after Easter, for the Carnival was about to end, and weddings were forbidden in Lent.

Toward nightfall I called on the shoemaker, who at once treated me to some of the excellent ratafia which I had given to Doña Antonia, his wife, who, together with her daughter, did nothing but talk of the obligation under which the Count of Aranda had laid the nation by what he had done.[26]

"Nothing," said Doña Antonia, "is more innocent than a ball, nothing is better for the health, and it was forbidden before that great man occupied the exalted post in which he can do whatever he pleases, and yet he is hated because he banished *los padres de la Compañía*,[27] and he forbade heel-length cloaks and *sombreros gachos*.[28] But the poor bless him, for all the money which the ball at los Caños del Peral[29] brings in goes to the poor."

"And so," said Don Diego the cobbler, "those who go to the ball do a work of charity."

"I have two cousins," Doña Ignacia said to me, "girls who, so far as their conduct goes, are angels. I told them I had been to the ball with you, and, since they are poor, they had no hope of going; you could easily make them happy by inviting them to go with me on the last day of the Carnival. Their mother would let them come, and the more willingly because the ball ends at midnight in order not to infringe on Ash Wednesday."

"I am ready, my good Doña Ignacia, to give you so innocent a pleasure. In that case the Señora would not have to spend the night in the carriage waiting for you."

"You are very kind; but you must be introduced to my aunt, who is a woman who carries religion to the point of scrupulosity. When she has made your acquaintance I am sure that she will not object when I propose the party to her, for one sees in you a man of good conduct who cannot have the slightest evil designs on her daughters. Go there today; they live in the first house in the next street, where you will see a small sign on the door saying that laces are mended there. Take some laces with you in your pocket, and say that it was my mother who gave you their address. Tomorrow morning on my way home from mass I will do the rest, and you shall come here at noon to learn how we can all meet on the last day of the Carnival."

I did all this in accordance with Doña Ignacia's instructions. I took some laces to her cousins, and the next day my beauty told me that everything was arranged. I told her that I should have all the dominoes at my inn, that the three of them had only to come there together, going in by the back door, that we would dine in my room, that we would mask afterward to go to the ball, and that after the ball I would see them all home. I said that I would dress the elder of her cousins as a man, for she would look just like one, and that she should tell her so beforehand; she said with a laugh that she would not tell her, but that she was sure she would do whatever I told her to do.

The younger of the two cousins was ugly, but she had the look of her sex. The ugliness of the elder was surprising. Extraordinarily tall, she looked like an ill-favored man dressed as a woman. The contrast amused me, for Doña Ignacia was a perfect beauty and seduction itself when she sent her pious airs to the devil.

I saw to having dominoes and everything necessary in a closet adjoining my room, without my page knowing anything about it; and on Tuesday morning I gave him a peso duro with which to go and spend the last day of the Carnival wherever he pleased, telling him that he need not be back to serve me until the next day at noon. I bought myself a pair of shoes, I ordered a good dinner for four at an inn nearby, and I arranged for the waiter in the coffeehouse to wait on me. I also got rid of Marazzani by giving him enough to go to dine wherever he pleased, and I prepared to laugh myself and to inspire laughter in Doña Ignacia, whom love was certain to make my mistress that day. The party was a complete novelty, consisting of three pious girls, two of them revoltingly ugly, and the third, as pretty as possible, whom I had already initiated and who had become softened and tamed.

They came at noon, and until one o'clock, when we sat down at table, I treated them to nothing but sage and moral discourses with much unction. I had wine from La Mancha,[30] which was exquisite but which is as strong as Hungarian wine. The poor girls were not used to spending two hours at table and not rising until their appetites were satisfied. Unaccustomed to unmixed wine, they did not get drunk, but they became heated and succumbed to a gaiety such as they had never felt before. I told the elder cousin, who might be twenty-five years of age, that I was going to dress her as a man, and I saw that she was terrified. Doña Ignacia told her that she was very lucky to have the pleasure, and the younger cousin reflected that it could not be a sin.

"If it were a sin," I said to them, "do you think I would propose it to you?"

Doña Ignacia, who knew the Legendary by heart, said that the glorious St. Marina[31] had spent her whole life dressed as a man, and to this erudition the tall cousin surrendered. I thereupon pronounced the most fulsome eulogy on her intelligence, thus challenging her to convince me that I was not mistaken in attributing a great deal of it to her.

"Come with me," I said to her, "and you others wait here, for I want to enjoy your surprise when you see her appear before you transformed into a man."

She came, though it cost her an effort, and, after laying out all her male attire before her, I made her begin by taking off her slippers and stockings, putting on white stockings and the shoes which fitted her best. I sat down before her, telling her that she would sin mortally if she suspected that my intentions were less than decent, for, since I could be her father, it was impossible that I should have any of that kind. She replied that she was a good Christian, but not a fool. I pulled on her stockings myself, then put on the garters, saying that I should never have believed that she had either such a well-shaped leg or such white skin, and she laughed. Flattered by my praise, she did not dare to object to the reason I insisted on having for praising her thighs, which, however, I would not touch, a restraint which edified her. The fact is that they were beautiful and magnificent. I saw, as so many times before, that *sublata lucerna nullum discrimen inter feminas* ("when the lamp is taken away, all women are alike").[32] A true proverb so far as physical enjoyment goes, but false and very false in regard to love. The soul's lodestone lies in the face; this may be a strong proof that man has a soul entirely different from that of animals.

After praising the sanctimonious girl's beautiful thighs, which, however, I did not display to my view except to a certain point, I handed her my breeches, rising and turning my back to give her perfect freedom to put them on and button them to the waist. I was not surprised that they fitted her well, despite the fact that I was five inches taller than she.[33] Women differ very greatly in form from men in that region.

I handed her a shirt, and I again turned away, which perhaps displeased her, for by so doing I deprived her of a compliment; I saw afterward that she deserved one. She told me that she was finished when she had not yet buttoned her collar; she had a beautiful, firm bosom, she saw that I was looking at it, and she was grateful to me because I did not commit the indiscretion of letting her know I had seen it by praising it. I put a waistcoat on her, and, looking her over from head to foot, I said that anyone who looked at her between the thighs could see that she was belying her sex.

"Will you permit me," I asked her, "to arrange your shirt better at that point?"

"Please do," she said, "for I've never dressed in men's clothes."

At that I sat down before her where she stood, and I unbuttoned her breeches to gather together the shirt and put the bunch of material where she had nothing and where, as a man, she ought to have something. My eyes already had permission to see; but touch also had to enter in somewhat. I did it so quickly, so gravely, and so much as if by accident that the tall cousin would have been very much in the wrong to object and even to let me know that she had been aware of it. I put on her domino, her hood, and her mask, and I exhibited her. Her sister and Doña Ignacia complimented her; she could not but be taken for a man by the most knowing.

"It is your turn," I said to the younger cousin.

"Go," the elder said to her, "for Don Jaime is *el más honesto de todos los hombres de España* ['the most well behaved of all the men in Spain']."

I did not have much to do to the younger cousin, for it was only a matter of putting on her domino; nevertheless, I advised her to change her stockings, she agreed, and, when she turned her back to me to put them on at her ease, I let her do as she would. I could not hope to see anything unusual. The white handkerchief with which she covered her bosom was a little soiled, I offered her a clean one; she accepted it, but she insisted on taking off the soiled one and putting on mine herself, again turning round; I did not care. After putting on her mask, I opened the door and exhibited her. Doña Ignacia, at once noticing the stockings and the handkerchief, asked her if I was skillful at dressing and undressing. She replied that she had not needed me. It was now Doña Ignacia's turn, for I had saved her to crown the feast.

As soon as she was in the closet I did to her what she already expected. She surrendered with an air which seemed to tell me that she surrendered only because she could not resist. Being in exactly the same situation, I stopped a minute later to spare her honor; but at the second round I saw that she was born for love; I kept her for a good hour. She told her cousins that she had had to resew the whole front of her domino.

At sunset we went to the ball, where on this privileged day the Count of Aranda had given general permission for the fandango; but the crowd was so big that it was impossible to find room to dance it. At ten o'clock we supped, and we walked about until the two orchestras stopped playing. Midnight struck, and, the holy season of Lent beginning, orgies had to give place to it.

After I had escorted the girls to my room to have them leave their dominoes, we went to take the cousins home. Doña Ignacia having told me that she needed to drink coffee, I took her back to my room again, sure of keeping her for a couple of hours in perfect freedom. It was obvious that she had the same desire. I leave her in my room to go downstairs and tell the waiter to make me coffee at once, and I see Don Francisco, who asks me point-blank to do him the favor of letting him join me and Doña Ignacia, whom he has seen go upstairs to my apartment with me. I had the strength to conceal my fury. I told him that I was his to command, and that I was sure his unexpected visit would give Doña Ignacia the greatest pleasure. I enter before him, and I announce him to the beauty, congratulating her on the pleasure she must feel at seeing him at such an hour. I would have wagered that her power of dissimulation would have been at least equal to mine, but not a bit of it: in her resentment she told him that she would not have asked me for coffee if she had thought she would find him there, and she called him an indiscreet boor for having dared to inconvenience me at such an hour. I thought I must go to the defense of the poor devil, who was so dumbfounded that he looked as if he were about to breathe his last. I tried to calm Doña Ignacia by telling her that it was quite natural that Don Francisco should be at the coffeehouse at that hour on the last night of the Carnival, that he had seen us only by chance, and that it was I who had invited him to come upstairs, thinking it would please her. She pretended to yield to my arguments, and it was she who told him to sit down; but she said not another word to him, talking only to me about the ball and thanking me for the pleasure which, as a courtesy to her, I had afforded her dear cousins.

After drinking coffee Don Francisco thought it his part to take his leave. I told him that I hoped to see him sometimes during Lent; but Doña Ignacia would only grant him a slight bow. After he left she told me sadly that the unlucky meeting would prevent her from having the pleasure of spending an hour with me, for she was sure that Don Francisco was either in the coffeehouse or playing the sentinel somewhere, and that by making light of his curiosity she would risk incurring his vengeance.

"So take me home, and if you love me come to see me during Lent. The trick that madman has played on me will cost him tears, and I may even send him packing, for I encourage his love from my window only in order to get married. Are you persuaded that I am not in love with him?"

"Very much persuaded, my beautiful angel, and even convinced. I esteem you too greatly not to be so. You have made me happy; I must believe that I am loved as much as I love you."

Doña Ignacia hastily gave me a fresh proof of it, and I took her home, assuring her that as long as I remained in Madrid she should be the only object of my attentions. I dined the next day at Mengs's; and on the next day but one at four o'clock a scoundrelly-looking man approaches me in the street and tells me to go with him to a cloister, where he had something to tell me which should be of great interest to me. I go there, and when he sees that no one can hear us, he tells me that the Alcalde Messa[34] will pay me a visit that same night with all his constables, "of whom," he says, "I am one.

"He knows that you have forbidden weapons under the mat which covers the floor of your room in the corner behind the stove, he knows or he thinks he knows several other things about you which authorize him to arrest you and, after confiscating your forbidden weapons, to take you to the prison for those who are sentenced to go away to work in the *presidios*.[35] I warn you of all this because I believe you are a man of honor, and not of a sort to be subjected to such misfortunes. Do not make light of my warning. Take your measures at once, put yourself in a place of safety, and avoid this insult."

I believed the man because it was true that I had weapons under the mat; I gave him a doblón; and instead of going to Doña Ignacia's I returned to my apartment, where I took the pistols and the spring carbine which I had under the mat, and, so armed, wrapped in a long cloak, I went to the house of the painter Mengs after leaving word in the coffeehouse that my page should be sent to me there as soon as he arrived. In Mengs's house I was safe, for it belonged to the King.

The painter, an honest, ambitious, proud man, but suspicious and on his guard in respect to anything which could compromise him, did not refuse me asylum for the night; but he told me that I must think the next day about finding another lodging, for he was certain that there must be stronger reasons for what was to happen to me than my having forbidden weapons in my room, and that, having no information, he could take no responsibility. He gives me a room, we sup together alone, talking of nothing but the situation, I constantly repeating that I was guilty of nothing, he never answering me except to say that, if I was guilty of nothing but having in my room the weapons I had brought to him, I ought to have disdained the man who had come to give me the alarm, and not have rewarded him with a doblón, I ought not to have stirred from my room, I ought not to have taken my weapons elsewhere, for, with my intelligence, I should know that every man in his own room was free by natural right to keep firearms if he chose. I replied that by going to his house I had only wanted to avoid the unpleasantness of going to spend a night in prison, for I was sure that the spy to whom I had given the doblón had told me the truth.

"Tomorrow," I said, "I will go to lodge elsewhere; however, I grant that you are right on one point: I agree with you that I ought to have left my pistols and my carbine in my room."

"And you ought to have stayed there yourself. I didn't know you took fright so easily."

While we were arguing in this fashion, in comes my landlord to tell me that the Alcalde Messa with twenty constables had come to search my apartment, had had the door opened by a locksmith, had had his men look everywhere, he did not know for what, and, after finding nothing, had had it locked again, had sealed it, and had left, sending my page to prison, for, said the Alcalde, he must have warned me that he was coming to visit me, for otherwise I would not have taken refuge in the house of the Cavaliere Mengs, where he could not go to take me into custody.

On hearing this narrative Mengs admits that I had not been wrong to believe the man who had warned me; and he says that I ought to go the next day to speak with the Count of Aranda, and above all to insist on the injustice of sending my page to prison, for he was innocent.[36]

Mengs continues to sympathize with my innocent page.

"My page," I reply impatiently, "must be a rascal, for, if the Alcalde suspects that he is guilty of having warned me of his visit, it shows that the Alcalde knew that he must have had knowledge of it. Now, I ask you if my page can be anything but a scoundrel when he knows such a thing and does not warn me of it; and I ask you if he can know it unless he has himself been the informer and the spy, for after all he was the only person who knew where my weapons were hidden."

Mengs, angry to find himself proved wrong, left me and went off to bed.

The next morning early the great Mengs sent his valet to me with shirts, stockings, underdrawers, collars, handkerchiefs, scents, and powder *à la maréchale*.[37] His housekeeper brought me chocolate, and his cook came to ask me if I had permission to eat meat. A prince by his ceremoniousness invites a guest not to leave his house, but a private person who is equally ceremonious drives him away. I expressed thanks for everything, I accepted only a cup of chocolate and a handkerchief. I had had my hair dressed, my carriage was at the door; I was in Mengs's room to wish him good morning and thank him, assuring him that I would not return to his house until I believed I was free. Just then an officer arrives and asks Mengs if the Cavaliere di Casanova[38] is in his house. I answer him:

"Here I am."

"Then, Monsieur, I advise you to come with me of your own free will to the guardhouse at Buen Retiro,[39] where you will be held a prisoner, for at the moment I cannot use force, this being a royal house. But I warn you that in less than an hour the Cavaliere Mengs who is here present will have an order to turn you out, and you will be taken to prison with a publicity which will greatly displease you. So I advise you to come with me, quietly and without protest. You must also deliver to me the firearms which you have in your room."

"Monsieur Mengs can give you my weapons, which have traveled with me for eleven years and which I carry to defend myself from murderers. And I will come with you after I have written four notes, which will take me only half an hour."

"I can neither wait nor allow you to write; but you will be allowed to write when you are in prison."

"That will do. I shall obey with a submissiveness which I would not show if I could oppose force with force. I shall remember Spain when I am back in Europe and come upon decent people, my equals, who may feel tempted to journey there."

I embraced the Cavaliere Mengs, who looked mortified, his valet put my weapons in my carriage, into which I got with the officer, who was a captain and who had the bearing and manners of a perfect gentleman.

He took me to the Palace of Buen Retiro. It was a castle which the royal family had abandoned. It served only as a prison for those who were said to be guilty, and its apartments had become barracks. It was there that Philip V had been accustomed to retire with the Queen[40] during Lent to prepare to take the sacrament at Easter.

As soon as the officer left me at the guardhouse, where he consigned me to a barbarous captain who was on duty, a corporal took me inside the castle to a huge room on the ground floor, which was a prison only for those who were in it who were not soldiers. I found there a very trying stench, twenty-five or thirty prisoners, ten or twelve soldiers. I saw ten or twelve very wide beds, some benches, no table, no chairs. I asked a soldier for paper, pen, and ink, giving him an écu to buy it all for me and bring it to me at once. He took the écu with a laugh, he went away, and he did not come back. The soldiers whom I asked what had become of him laughed in my face. But what struck me was to see that among my companions were my page and Count Marazzani, who told me in Italian that he had been there for three days and that he had not written to me because he had a strong presentiment that he would see me with him. He said that in less than two weeks we should be taken from there and sent, well guarded, to work in some fortress, where, however, we could write our justifications and hope to be released in three or four years and obtain a passport to leave Spain.

"I hope," I replied, "that I shall not be condemned before I have been heard."

"The Alcalde will come tomorrow, and will question you and write down your answers. That is all. After that you will perhaps be sent to Africa."

"Have you been accused yet?"

"They dealt with me for three hours yesterday. I was asked who the banker was who gave me money to live on. I replied that I knew no banker, that I had lived by borrowing money from my friends, waiting all the while for a definite reply as to whether I was accepted or rejected as a bodyguard. I was asked why the Parmesan Ambassador[41] did not know me, and I replied that it was because I had never presented myself at the embassy. I was told that unless the Parmesan Ambassador vouched for me, I could never be a bodyguard, and that I ought to know it, whereupon the Alcalde said that His Majesty would give me an employment which I could pursue without needing to be vouched for by anyone, and they left me. I foresee everything. If the Venetian Ambassador[42] does not claim you, you will be treated as they treat all the others."

Concealing everything, swallowing my bitter saliva, and not believing that the treatment with which Marazzani threatened me was in the realm of possibility, I sat down on a bed, which I left three hours later, seeing myself covered with lice, the mere sight of which is enough to turn the stomach of an Italian and a Frenchman, but not of a Spaniard, who laughs at these little annoyances. Fleas, bedbugs, and lice are three insects so common in Spain that they have reached the point of not troubling anyone. They are considered, I believe, to be a sort of neighbor. I remained motionless, in the deepest silence, devouring all the bilious humor which was circulating and poisoning my fluids. There was no sense in talking, what made sense was to write, and the means to do so were not given me. I had perforce resigned myself to waiting for what would certainly happen to me in twenty-four or thirty hours.

At noon Marazzani told me that I could order dinner by giving money to a soldier he knew and for whose honesty he vouched, adding that he would be glad to eat a good meal with me, since for three days he had been living on bread, water, garlic, and a wretched soup. I replied that I did not want to eat and that I would not give so much as a copper to anyone again until the soldier to whom I had given an écu returned it to me. He then protested loudly over the deception, which was manifest robbery, but everyone laughed in his face. My page then spoke to him, begging him to ask me to give him money, for he was hungry and had not a copper; I told him to tell him that I would give him nothing, for in prison he was no longer in my service. So I saw all my fellow prisoners eat the wretched soup and bread and drink water, except two priests and a man who was addressed as *corregidor* ("magistrate"), the three of whom ate well.

It was at three o'clock that one of the Cavaliere Mengs's servants brought me a dinner which would have fed four amply. He wanted to leave the dinner and come back in the evening to take away the dishes and bring me supper; but in the evil humor in which I was I did not want to have to bestow my leavings either on the rabble whose companion I had become or on the soldiers. I made the servant wait, and I ate and drank, setting everything out on a bench; then I told him to take everything that was left back to the house and not to return until the next day, for I did not want supper. The servant obeyed, and the rabble treated him to catcalls. Marazzani said to me harshly that I might at least have kept the bottle of wine. I did not answer him.

At five o'clock Manuzzi[43] entered gloomily with the officer of the guard. After he had condoled with me and I had thanked him, I asked the officer if I was permitted to write to those who could not leave me in this plight except because they knew nothing of it, and, he having answered me that it would be tyranny not to let me do so, I asked him if it was within the rights of a soldier, to whom I had given an écu to buy me some paper at eight o'clock that morning, to steal my money and disappear.

"What soldier?"

I ask his name of everyone, and so does he, but in vain; no one has the least idea, the guard had been changed. The officer promises me that he will have my écu returned to me and the soldier punished. The officer at once has writing materials, a table, and a candle brought me, and Manuzzi promises me that at eight o'clock he will send a servant in the Ambassador's livery to take my letters and deliver them to their addresses, assuring me that the Ambassador will act for me privately, for he did not think he could do so openly. Before they leave I take from my pocket three écus, and I tell the rabble that I will give them to those who will tell the name of the soldier who had stolen the écu from me. At that, Marazzani was the first to name him, two others bore him out, and the officer, who knew him, wrote down his name, laughing a little, and learning to know me. I was spending three écus to recover one. They left, and I fell to writing. The patience I had to show is unbelievable. Some came to read what I was writing and, when they did not understand it, demanded that I explain it. One came to snuff my candle, and put it out. I imagined I was in the galleys, and I bore it without complaining. A soldier had the impertinence to tell me that if I would give him an écu he would make everyone keep quiet, and I did not answer him. But despite all these damned souls I finished my letters and sealed them. There was no art in my letters. They breathed the venom which was circulating in my soul.

I wrote the Ambassador Mocenigo that he was obliged by his position to defend a subject of his prince whom the ministers of a foreign power were murdering in order to seize everything he possessed. I told him to reflect that he could not refuse me his protection unless he knew how I could have broken the laws of the Republic, for my difference with the State Inquisitors arose from nothing but the fact that Signora Zorzi preferred me to Signor Condulmer,[44] who, jealous of my good fortune, had had me imprisoned under the Leads.

I wrote to Señor Manuel de Roda,[45] a learned man, the Minister of Grace and Justice, that I did not want his grace but only his justice.

"Serve God, Monseigneur, and your master the King, by preventing the Alcalde Messa from murdering a Venetian who has done nothing contrary to the laws and who came to Spain only in the belief that he was coming to a country inhabited by honest men and not by murderers whom the posts they are given authorize to murder with impunity. The man who writes to you has in his pocket a purse filled with doblones, and is imprisoned in a room in which he has already been robbed. He fears that he will be murdered tonight for the sake of his purse and everything he possesses."

I wrote the Duke of Losada to inform the King his master that certain servants of his, without his knowledge but in his name, were murdering a Venetian who had broken no law; whose only crime was to be rich enough not to need anyone so long as he remained in Spain. I put it to him that he ought to ask the King to send an order at once which would prevent such a murder.

The strongest of my four letters was the one I wrote to the Count of Aranda. I told him that if the murderers ended by killing me I should believe before I died that it was by his order, because I had vainly told the officer who arrested me that I had come to Madrid with a letter from a Princess recommending me to him.

"I have done nothing," I told him. "What compensation am I to receive, when you have me released from this inferno, for the ill treatment I have already undergone? Either have me released at once, or order your executioners to dispatch me quickly, for if they take it into their heads to send me to a *presidio*, I will kill myself first with my own hand."

Keeping copies of my letters, I dispatched them by the Ambassador's lackey, whom the all-powerful Manuzzi did not fail to send me. But I spent the cruelest of nights. The beds were full, but even had they not been, I should not have wanted to get into one. I asked in vain for straw, but even if it had been brought me I should not have known where to put it. The floor was soaked with urine, for, with two or three exceptions, no one had a chamber pot. Burning with anger, I would not spend a copper for some small comfort, and my giving three écus to have the officer told the name of the thieving soldier had only irritated the rabble all the more. I spent the whole night sitting on a bench without a back.

At seven o'clock in the morning Manuzzi came in. I at once asked him to arrange for me to go to the guardroom with himself and the officer to eat something, for I felt that I was dying; and it was done at once. I drank some chocolate, and I made their hair stand on end with my account of my sufferings. Manuzzi told me that my letters could not be taken to their addresses except in the course of the day; and he said with a laugh that I had written the Ambassador a harsh letter. I then showed him copies of the others, and the inexperienced young man said that the proper tone for obtaining what one asked for was mildness. He did not know that there are situations in which it is absolutely impossible for a man to use a mild tone. Manuzzi whispered to me that the Ambassador would dine that day at the Count of Aranda's, and that he had promised him he would speak to him privately in my favor; but that he was afraid that my ferocious letter would have irritated the Spaniard. I warned him not to say anything to the Ambassador about my letter.

An hour after he left, just when, sitting among the rabble, I was pretending not to notice the impertinences addressed to me on the score of my haughtiness, which offended them all, I see Doña Ignacia, accompanied by her father the noble cobbler, come in with the kind captain who had done me so many favors. Their visit wounded me to the soul, but I had to make the best of it, and gratefully, for it proceeded from merit, magnanimity, virtue, and humanity in the worthy man and in the pious and amorous Doña Ignacia who were paying it to me.

Though sadly, and in very bad Spanish, I managed to make them understand how deeply I felt the honor they were doing me. Doña Ignacia never said a word; it was the only way she had to keep the tears from welling from her beautiful eyes; but Don Diego summoned all his eloquence to tell me that he would never have come to see me if he was not absolutely certain that a mistake had been made, or that it was some horrible calumny, of the kind which deceives judges for a few days. From this he drew the conclusion that in a few days I would be released from this foul place and that I would receive a satisfaction proportionate to the insult which had been put upon me. I replied that I hoped so; but what surprised me, and touched me to the soul, was what this very poor man did when he left, embracing me. He put into my hands a roll, whispering to me that there were twelve doblones de a ocho in it, which I should return to him when I could. My hair stood on end. I whispered to him that I had fifty in my pocket which I did not dare show him because I feared the thieves by whom I was surrounded. At that, he put his roll back in his pocket, and he wept. I promised to visit him as soon as I should be set free. He went; he had not sent in his name. He was well dressed, he was taken to be a man of substance. Such characters are not uncommon in Spain. The noble, heroic act is the craze of the Castilian.

Mengs's servant came at noon with a dinner which was more choice and less abundant; which was what I wanted. I ate in his presence in half an hour, and he went away, carrying my compliments to his master. At one o'clock a man entered and told me to come with him. He took me to a small room, in which I saw my carbine and pistols. The Alcalde Messa, seated at a table covered with notebooks, with two clerks, told me to sit down; then he ordered me to reply truthfully to all his questions, for my answers would be written down. I told him that I understood very little Spanish, and that I would never answer anything except in writing to a person who would question me in Italian, French, or Latin. This reply, uttered in a firm voice, astonished him. He talked to me for a whole hour, I understood everything he said, but all that he ever got by way of reply was:

"I do not understand what you are saying. Find a judge who knows one of my languages, and then I will answer; but I will not dictate; I will write my answer myself."

He grew angry, I paid no attention to his outbursts. Finally he gave me a pen, and he told me to write in Italian my name, my rank, and what I had come to Spain to do. I could not refuse him that satisfaction, but I wrote only a score of lines:

"I am So-and-so, a subject of the Republic of Venice, a man of letters, moderately rich; I am traveling for my pleasure; I am known to the Ambassador of my country, to the Count of Aranda, to Prince della Cattolica, to the Marqués de Mora, to the Duke of Losada; I have not broken the least of His Catholic Majesty's[46] laws, and nevertheless I find myself being murdered, and confined with criminals and thieves by ministers who would deserve to be treated far more harshly than I. If I have done nothing against the laws, His Catholic Majesty must know that he has no

right over me except to order me to leave his domains, and I will obey the instant I receive that order. My weapons which I see here have traveled with me for eleven years, I carry them only to defend myself against highway robbers, and at the Puerta de Alcalá they were seen in my carriage and they were not confiscated; which shows that their confiscation now is only a pretext to murder me."

After writing this document I give it to the Alcalde, who sends for a man who faithfully translates the whole of it into Spanish for him. The Alcalde rises, looks at me with eyes venomous with anger, and says:

"Valgame Dios ['So help me God'], you will repent of having written this document."

So saying, he has me escorted back to the room in which I had been, and he leaves.

At eight o'clock Manuzzi came to tell me that the Count of Aranda had been the first to ask the Ambassador if he knew me, and that the Ambassador had told him nothing but good about me, ending by assuring him that he was sorry he could not be of use to me in the matter of an affront to which I had been subjected, because I was in disfavor with the State Inquisitors. The Count of Aranda replied that a great affront had indeed been put on me, but it was not such as to make an intelligent man lose his head.

" *'I should have known nothing about it,' he said to him, 'if he had not written me a furious letter, and he wrote others in the same style to Don Manuel de Roda and to the Duke of Losada. He is in the right, but one does not write such letters.'* That is all he said to him."

"Then my troubles are over, if it is true that he said I am in the right."

"You may be sure that he said it."

"If he said it he will do what is right, and, as for my letters, everyone has his style. I became angry and maddened because I have been treated like a dog; look at this room, I have no bed, and, running with urine as it is, I cannot lie on the floor; I shall spend a second night sitting on this bench without a back. Do you think it possible that I do not want to eat the hearts of all my executioners? If I do not leave this inferno tomorrow I will kill myself or go mad."

Manuzzi understood that I could not but be in a state of desperation; he promised he would come to see me early the next morning, and he advised me to pay for a bed. I would not take his advice. The lice horrified me, and I feared for my purse, my watch, my snuffbox, and everything I had. I spent a terrible night dozing on the same bench, constantly starting awake when, losing my balance, I was on the verge of falling into the stinking filth on the floor.

Manuzzi came at eight o'clock and I saw that he was really terrified at the sight of my face. He had come in a carriage, bringing with him some excellent chocolate, which he ordered heated, which I drank with pleasure, and which gave me a little courage. But the door opens, and in comes an officer, followed by two others. The first officer asks for me; I approach him, saying that it is I.

"His Excellency the Count of Aranda," he says, "is outside, and greatly regrets the misfortune which has befallen you. He learned of it yesterday from the letter you wrote him. If you had written to him at once, nothing would have happened to you."

I told him the story of the soldier who had robbed me of an écu. He asked who he was, and as soon as he was informed of everything he summoned the captain, reprimanded him, ordered him to give me an écu, which I accepted with a laugh, and to send someone to find the soldier so that he could be flogged in my presence. The officer was Count Rojas,[47] Colonel of the regiment which was at Buen Retiro. I then told him in detail the whole story of my arrest and all the sufferings I had endured in the accursed place in which I had been put. I told him that if I were not given back my freedom, my weapons, and my honor in the course of that day, I would kill myself or go mad, for a man had to lie down once a day, and I had not been able to lie either on a bed or on the floor because of the filth he would have seen if he had arrived an hour earlier.

I saw the worthy man surprised by the fury with which I spoke to him. Noticing it, I asked him to excuse me, assuring him that when I was not overcome by rage I was entirely different. Manuzzi told him what my natural temperament was, and the Colonel condoled with me. He sighed, and he gave me his word of honor that I should leave the place in the course of the day, that my weapons would be returned to me, and that I would sleep in my own bed.

"After that," he said, "you shall go to thank the Count of Aranda, who has come here purposely and who has ordered me to tell you that you shall not return to your lodging until afternoon, for His Excellency wants you to have a satisfaction sufficient to restore your peace of mind and make you forget this insult, if it is one, for what is done in the name of the law insults no one, and in your case the Alcalde Messa was deceived by the scoundrel who was in your service."

"There he is," I said. "I ask you as a favor to have him removed from here, since he is known to be a monster."

He went out, and two minutes later two soldiers came to take him, and I did not see him again. I never troubled to learn what had become of the wretch. It was then that he had me go to the guard-room to see the flogging which was given the thieving soldier. I saw the Count of Aranda forty paces from me, walking up and down followed by a number of officers and one of the King's Bodyguard. All this kept us occupied for two hours and a half. Before leaving, the Colonel invited me to dine at his house with Mengs when he next invited him. I had to return to the room, where I found a folding bed set up on planks, which looked clean. A noncommissioned officer told me it was for me, and I instantly lay down on it, but Manuzzi, before leaving me, embraced me again and again. I was convinced that he was my true friend, and it still saddens me when I think that I did him a wrong for which I am not surprised that he never forgave me, for I have never been able to forgive myself for it. [. . .]

After this scene the rabble in the room no longer dared to look at me. Marazzani came to my bedside to beg for my good offices, but I did not let him suppose that I had any influence. I said that in Spain a foreigner was doing a great deal if he was able to look after himself. I was brought dinner as usual, and at three o'clock the Alcalde Messa came to tell me to go with him because, having made a mistake, he had received an order to escort me back to my apartment, where he hoped that I should find everything I had left there. At the same time he showed me my carbine and my pistols which he handed to one of his men to carry to my room. The officer of the guard gave me back my sword; the Alcalde, in a black cloak, took his place at my left and, followed by thirty constables, escorted me to the coffeehouse in the Calle de la Cruz, where he removed the seal on the door of my room, which the landlord came to open, and where I was easily able to tell the Alcalde that everything was as I had left it. He said to me as he left that, if I had not had a traitor in my service, I should never have been led to believe that His Catholic Majesty's ministers were murderers.

"Anger, Señor Alcalde, made me write the same thing to four ministers. I believed it, and I no longer believe it. Let us forget everything; but admit that, if I had not known how to write, you would have sent me to the galleys."

"Alas, it is possible."

I washed, and I changed all my clothes; more from duty than from affection, I paid a visit to the truly noble cobbler, who, on seeing me, called himself the most fortunate of men and the most foresighted, for he was certain that a mistake must have been made; but Doña Ignacia was beside herself with joy, for she had felt none of her father's certainty. When he learned what kind of satisfaction I had received, he said that a Grandee of Spain could ask no more. I invited them to come to dine with me somewhere as soon as I sent them word, and they promised to do so. Gratitude having entered in, I found myself much more in love with Doña Ignacia than I had been before.

On leaving the Calle del Desengaño I went to see Mengs, who, knowing Spain, expected anything rather than to see me. But when he heard the story of the whole day, in which I had had so many triumphs, he congratulated me as he should. He was in gala dress, a very unusual thing; and he told me that he had gone to see Don Manuel de Roda, hoping to be useful to me with him, but that he had not been able to speak to him. He gave me a letter from Venice which he had received that day, and which I quickly unsealed, recognizing Signor Dandolo's[48] hand; in it I find a sealed letter, addressed to Signor Mocenigo, Ambassador. Signor Dandolo wrote me that, after reading the enclosed letter, the Ambassador would no longer fear to displease the State Inquisitors by giving me introductions, for the person who had written him the letter recommended me to him in the name of one of the three Inquisitors.[49] At that, Mengs says that it is in my power to make my fortune in Spain, provided that I behave myself, and especially now that the ministers were under an obligation to treat me in a way to make me forget the outrage to which I had been subjected. He advises me to take the letter to the Ambassador that very moment, and to use his carriage, for after sixty hours of continual torture I could not stand. Needing to go to bed, I excuse myself from returning to his house for supper, but I promise to dine there the next day. The Ambassador was not in. I leave the letter with Manuzzi, and I go home, where I go to bed to enjoy ten hours of the deepest sleep.

Manuzzi comes very early in the morning, with his face the picture of joy, to bring me the news that Signor Girolamo Zulian[50] wrote the Ambassador on behalf of Signor da Mula that he could introduce me everywhere, for my quarrel with the tribunal was in no way prejudicial to my honor.

"The Ambassador expects to present you at Court at Aranjuez[51] next week, and he wants you to dine with him today with a large company."

"I am engaged to dine with Mengs."

"I shall go to invite Mengs at once, and, if he declines, you must disappoint him, for you must be aware of the fine effect your entrance at the Ambassador's is bound to produce on the day after your triumph."

"You are right. Go to Mengs; and I will dine at the Ambassador's."

CHAPTER II

Campomanes. Olavides. Sierra Morena.
Aranjuez. Mengs. The Marchese Grimaldi. Toledo.
Signora Pelliccia. Return to Madrid and to the
house of Doña Ignacia's father.

In the principal vicissitudes of my life particular circumstances combined to make my poor mind a trifle superstitious. I feel humiliated when, reflecting upon myself, I recognize this truth. But how can I help it? It is in the nature of things that Fortune should do to a man who surrenders himself to her whims what a child does to an ivory sphere on a billiard table when he pushes it one way and another, only to burst out laughing when he sees it fall into a pocket; but it is not in the nature of things, it seems to me, that Fortune should do to such a man what a skillful player, who calculates the force, the speed, the distance, and the regularity of the reaction, does to the billiard ball; it is not in the nature of things, as I conceive it to be, that I should do Fortune the honor to believe that she is skilled in geometry, or that I should posit in that metaphysical being the physical laws to which I find that all nature is subject. Despite this reasoning, what I observe astonishes me. The very same Fortune I ought to regard with contempt, as synonymous with chance, becomes an object to be respected, as if she wanted to reveal herself to me as a goddess, in the most decisive events in my life. She has amused herself by constantly showing me that she is not blind, as people say; she has never cast me into the depths except to raise me proportionately high, and she seems never to have made me rise very high except to give herself the pleasure of seeing me fall. It seems that she has exercised absolute dominion over me only in order to convince me that she reasons and that she is the ruler of all things; to convince me of it, she employed striking means to compel me to act, and to make me understand that my will, far from declaring me free, was only an instrument which she used to make what she would of me.

I could not hope to attain to anything in Spain without the help of my country's Ambassador, and he, in his pusillanimity, would never have dared to do anything without the letter which I presented to him; and the letter would have led to nothing if it had not arrived precisely at the moment when my arrest, and the reparation which the Count of Aranda ordered to be given me, had made my adventure the talk of the day.

The letter made the Ambassador blush for not having acted in my favor before it arrived; but he did not despair of making people believe that the Count of Aranda had given me such ample reparation only because he had demanded it. His favorite, Count Manuzzi, had brought me an invitation to dinner from him, and luck would have it that I was engaged to dine with Mengs. Manuzzi had the good sense to go to Mengs with an invitation from the Ambassador, which greatly flattered the vain man with whom I had taken refuge, though in vain. The invitation became in his eyes a token of gratitude, which made up to him for the mortification he had suffered from having to let me be taken from his house. After accepting the invitation, and learning from Manuzzi that I had already been invited, he wrote me a note to tell me that he would come for me in his carriage at one o'clock.

I went to call on the Count of Aranda, who, after making me wait a quarter of an hour, came out with some papers.

"The thing is over," he said to me serenely, "and I believe that you can be satisfied. Here are four letters, which I return to you to read."

I see my three letters to him, to the Duke of Losada, and to the Minister of Grace and Justice.

"Why, my Lord, must I read these letters? This is the statement submitted to the Señor Alcalde."

"I know that. Read them all, and you will see that, despite your having been entirely in the right, it is not allowable to write in such a way."

"I beg your pardon. A man who has resolved to kill himself, as I had done, cannot write otherwise. I thought that everything done to me was by Your Excellency's order."

"You did not know me. However, you will go to thank Don Manuel de Roda, who wants to make your acquaintance without fail, and I will take it as a favor if you will go sometime at your convenience to the Alcalde, not to apologize to him but to say something pleasant which will make him forget the insulting things you say to him in your statement. If you inform Princess Lubomirska[1] of this affair, tell her that as soon as I heard of it I set it to rights."

After having thus done my duty to the Count of Aranda, I called on Colonel Rojas, who told me in so many words that I had made a great mistake to tell the Count of Aranda that I was satisfied.

"What could I demand?"

"Everything. The Alcalde's resignation. A sum of money in compensation for what you were made to suffer in that horrible place. You are in a country where you do not need to hold your tongue unless you have to deal with the Inquisition."

Colonel Rojas, who is now a general, is one of the most amiable men I met in Spain.

I returned to my apartment, and Mengs came to fetch me. The Ambassador paid me countless attentions, and heaped praise on the painter Mengs for having tried, by giving me asylum in his house, to save me from a misfortune which would overwhelm any man. It was at table that I gave a detailed account of all that I had suffered at Buen Retiro, and of the conversation I had just had with the Count of Aranda, who had returned my letters to me. Everyone wanted to read them, and everyone expressed his opinion. The guests were the French Consul, the Abbé Béliardi,[2] Don Rodrigo de Campomanes,[3] who was very celebrated, and the equally celebrated Don Pablo de Olavides.[4] Each of them gave his opinion on my letters, which the Ambassador condemned, calling them ferocious; but Campomanes maintained that my letters, which contained no insults, were just what was needed to make the reader see that I was in the right, even if he were the King. Olavides and Béliardi were of the same opinion. Mengs was of the Ambassador's, and invited me to go to stay in his house and so have done with the calumnies of spies, of which Madrid was full. I did not accept Mengs's invitation until after I had been urged for some time and after having heard the Ambassador himself say that I really must give the Cavaliere Mengs that satisfaction for, in addition to its being a great honor to me, it would be a satisfaction which was due to him.

What really pleased me at the dinner was making the acquaintance of Campomanes and Olavides. They were both men of an intelligence very uncommon in Spain, for, though not learned, they were well aware of all the prejudices and abuses which accompany religion there, and they not only publicly mocked them, they acted openly to destroy them. It was Campomanes who had furnished the Count of Aranda with all the matter of complaint against the Jesuits, whom the Count had driven out of Spain in one day. Campomanes squinted, the Count of Aranda squinted, and the General of the

Jesuits squinted; at table I laughed at the dissension among the three strabismics,[5] one of whom, as was only to be expected, had been crushed by the two others. I asked Campomanes why he hated the Jesuits, and he replied that he hated them no more than he did the other religious orders, which, if he could have had his way, he would have destroyed one and all. He was the author of everything that had been published against the mortmains,[6] enjoying, as he did, the friendship of the Venetian Ambassador, who had communicated to him all that the Senate had done against the monks—information which Campomanes would not have needed if he had read and put into practice all that our Fra Paolo Sarpi[7] wrote on the subject in perfect honesty. Far-seeing, courageous, active, Treasurer of the Supreme Council of Castile, of which Aranda was President, Campomanes was recognized to be a man who did not act as he did from private interest, but for the good of the State. So the statesmen respected and valued him; but the monks, the priests, the bigots, and all the rabble infected with the fear of offending God and the saints by acting against the temporal interests of the ecclesiastics and the beneficiaries of mortmain hated Campomanes with a mortal hatred. The Inquisition must have sworn to destroy him, and everyone said that in two or three years Campomanes would either have to become a bishop or be shut up in the prisons of the Inquisition for life. This prediction was fulfilled only in part. Campomanes was imprisoned by the Inquisition four years later,[8] remained in prison for three years, and did not leave it until he made a formal retraction. His friend Olavides was treated more harshly;[9] and even the Count of Aranda would not have escaped the horrible monster's fury if, profoundly intelligent and foresighted, he had not asked to be appointed Ambassador to France,[10] which the King at once granted him, glad thus to find himself rid of the obligation to hand him over to the accursed fury of the monks.

Carlos III, who died mad,[11] as almost all kings must die, had done things which even those who knew him could not believe, for he was weak, gross, stubborn, excessively devoted to religion, and inalterably determined to die a hundred deaths before he would stain his soul with the smallest of mortal sins. Everyone sees that such a man must have been completely the slave of his confessor. The excesses committed by the Jesuits[12] in Portugal, the Indies, and France had already made them hated and openly condemned in all the four quarters of the globe; and the crime of the Jesuit confessor of Don Fernando VI,[13] which had brought about the ruin of

Ensenada,[14] had taught his successor Carlos III that he must not have a Jesuit as his confessor, since the interest of the State demanded the destruction of *los Teatinos*.[15]

So they were called in Spain, and the Theatines were called *Cayetanos*.[16]

The same confessor, then, who quieted all the King's scruples against the great operation of destroying a whole religious order, was also obliged to yield to the King and give him the reins when, at the same time, the Count of Aranda showed him that he must set limits to the excessive power of the Inquisition, whose great work was to keep Christians in ignorance and to maintain in force abuses, superstitions, and the *pia mendacia* ("pious falsehoods");[17] the confessor's policy could not but give him the reins. He was certain that he could plunge the King back into the abyss of superstition whenever he pleased; and he succeeded. However, I was never able to learn if, two years after my departure, the King was given a new confessor,[18] for, unhappily for poor mankind, it is decreed that a pious king will never do anything but what his confessor will let him do, and it is obvious that the confessor's chief interest can never be the good of the State, since religion, as it exists, is directly opposed to it. If I am told that a wise king can always keep matters of State out of his confession, I will admit it; but I am not talking of a wise king, for if he is such, as a Christian he need go to confession only once a year and hear the voice of his confessor only in the words he utters to absolve him; if the king needs to talk with him to clear up doubts he is a fool; doubts and scruples are the same thing; he who goes to confession should know his religion before he goes to it. No doubts, no discussions with his confessor. Louis XIV would have been the greatest king on earth, greater than Frederick II, King of Prussia, if he had not had the weakness to chatter with his confessors.

At that time the Spanish Cabinet was engaged in a promising undertaking. A thousand families had been brought from various Swiss cantons and been sent to live in the fine deserted countryside called *las sierras de Morena*,[19] a name famous in Europe, being well known to all who have read Cervantes' masterpiece, the magnificent romance which tells the story of Don Quixote. Nature had endowed the place with all the gifts which should have made it populous, an excellent climate, fertile soil, pure water, advantageous situation, for the *sierras* (which means "mountains") are between the Kingdoms of Andalusia and Granada; nevertheless this beautiful countryside, this vast and delicious abode, was deserted. The King of Spain resolves that for a limited time he will make a present of the products of the soil to colonists, he invites them to come, paying for their journey, they come, they go there, and the Government makes every effort to lodge them and to set up an excellent administration for them, both spiritual and temporal. This enterprise had the support of Señor Olavides, a man of intelligence and education. It was he who conferred with the ministers in Madrid to establish order in the settlement, to provide it with judges who would render prompt justice, with priests of course, for these Swiss were all Catholics, with a governor, with artisans in all the necessary trades to build houses, churches, and above all a theater or circus in which to give bullfights, a favorite spectacle in Spain, and so beautiful, so humane, so natural, and so reasonable that the thinkers of that country cannot understand how there can possibly be nations in the world who can do without it. So in the Sierra Morena the worthy emigrants from Switzerland found a huge circular amphitheater, so that on certain days they could enjoy that delicious spectacle.

Don Pablo de Olavides in the memorials which he had presented for the greater prosperity of the promising colony had said that all establishments of monks should be excluded, and he gave very good reasons for it; but even if he had demonstrated it infallibly, compass in hand, it took no more to make every monk in Spain his enemy, and even the Bishop[20] of whose diocese Morena was a part. The priests of Spain said that he was right, but the monks cried out against such impiety, and persecutions were already beginning; and the subject was raised at the Ambassador's table.

After letting them talk as long as they pleased, I said as modestly as I could that the colony would vanish like a dream within a few years, for several reasons both material and moral. The principal reason which I alleged was that the Swiss was a mortal of a different species from other men.

"He is," I said, "a plant which, transplanted from the soil in which it was born, dies. The Swiss are subject to a disease called *Heimweh*,[21] which means 'return,' what the Greeks called *nostalgia*;[22] when they are away from their country, after a certain period of time the disease overtakes them, the only remedy is returning to their country; if they do not employ it they die."

I said that it might be worth trying to combine them with another colony of Spanish men and women, in order to bind them by marriages; I said that at least in the beginning they must be given Swiss priests and judges, and above all they must be declared free from all inquisition into matters of conscience, for the true Swiss had customs and laws in regard to making love[23] which were inseparable from their nature, and ceremonies of which the Spanish church would never approve, which would make the disease of *Heimweh* attack them in a very short time.

My discourse, which Don Olavides at first took to be only banter, in the end persuaded him that all I had said might be true. He asked me to set down my reflections in writing, and to communicate any thoughts I might have on the subject only to him. I promised to give him all my ideas to read, and Mengs set a day when he could dine at his house. It was on the next day that I had my few belongings carried to Mengs's, and that I began working on the subject of the colonies, treating them from the point of view both of the natural sciences and of philosophy.

The next day I went to call on Don Manuel de Roda, who—a very rare thing in Spain—was a man of letters. He was fond of Latin poetry, he had some appreciation of Italian poetry, but he gave the preference to the Spanish. He received me with great courtesy, he asked me to come to see him, and he expressed his regret for the vexation my imprisonment in Buen Retiro had caused me. The Duke of Losada congratulated me on the Venetian Ambassador's speaking well of me to everyone, and encouraged me to think that I might draw profit from my talents by proposing myself for some employment in which I could be useful to the Government, and he promised me his full support. Prince della Cattolica had me to dinner with the Venetian Ambassador. In three weeks, lodging at Mengs's and often dining at the Ambassador's, I made a quantity of valuable acquaintances. I thought of finding employment in Spain, for, receiving no letters from Lisbon, I did not dare to go there simply on the chance that something would turn up. The Portuguese lady[24] no longer wrote to me, I had no way of knowing what had become of her.

To pass the evenings I had fallen into the habit of calling on Signora Sabatini,[25] on a Spanish lady who had a *tertulia*, that is, whose evening receptions were frequented by men of letters, all of them paltry, and on the Duke of Medina Sidonia,[26] Master of the Horse to the King, man of letters, sound and reliable, to whom I had been presented by Don Domingo Varnier,[27] valet to the King, whose acquaintance Mengs had procured me. I often went to see Doña Ignacia, but since I could never be alone with her I was bored.

When I found an opportunity to tell her that she should think of some excursion with her ugly cousins, for in the country I could give her proofs of my constancy, she replied that she wanted it as much as I did, but at that season she must banish all such ideas, for Holy Week was drawing near, God had died for us, we must think not of criminal pleasures but of doing penance. After Easter we could think of our love. Such is the character of almost all the pious beauties in Spain.

Two weeks before Easter the King of Spain left Madrid for Aranjuez with the whole Court. The Venetian Ambassador invited me to go there to stay in his house, so that he could have a good opportunity to present me. On the day before we were to leave, I succumbed to a fever as I sat beside Mengs in his carriage on the way to visit the widow of the painter Amigoni.[28] The fever, which came on with chills such as it is impossible to conceive, made me shake so much that my head struck the roof of the carriage. My teeth were chattering, I could not utter a word. Mengs, in terror, ordered the coachman to return home at speed, I was quickly put to bed, where four or five hours later a violent sweat which continued for ten or twelve hours without intermission expelled from my body at least twenty pints of water, for it ran over the floor after passing through two mattresses and a straw pallet. Forty-eight hours later the fever ended, but weakness kept me in bed for a week. On the Saturday before Easter I took a carriage and went to Aranjuez, where I was very well received and very well lodged by the Ambassador; but a small pustule which, on leaving Madrid, I had near the place where I had had the fistula was so much irritated on the road by the jolting of the carriage that when I arrived in Aranjuez in the evening it made me extremely uncomfortable. During the night the pustule swelled to the size of a big pear, so that, the day being Easter, I could not get up to go to mass. In five days the tumor became an abscess as big as a melon; it terrified not only the Ambassador and Manuzzi but an old French surgeon of the King's, who swore that he had never seen the like. As for me, being the only one who was not terrified, for the abscess caused me no pain and was not hard, I told the surgeon to open it. I described to him, in the presence of a physician, the kind of fever I had just had in Madrid, and I convinced him that the abscess could come only from a quantity of lymph which had accumulated in that place and which, as soon as it was discharged, would leave me in perfect health. The physician having declared my reasoning sound, the surgeon exercised his art; he made a six-inch opening, after putting under me a large sheet folded thirty-two times. Though my abscess could have contained only a pint of liquid, it is none the less true that the lymph which left my body through it in the course of four days was as abundant as that which had come out of me as sweat during the fever I had had at Mengs's house. At the end of the four days almost no trace remained of the opening which the surgeon had made. I had to stay in bed because of my weakness; but I was very much surprised when I received in my bed a letter from Mengs which an express messenger brought me. I open it, and here is what I find in bad Italian, which I have before me now:

"Yesterday the priest of my parish posted on the door of his church the names of all those who are lodged in his district and who, not believing in God, did not take the sacrament at Easter. Among the names I saw yours, and I had to swallow a reproof from the priest, who said bitterly that he was surprised to see that I granted hospitality to heretics[29] in my house. I did not know what to answer him, for it is true that you could have stayed in Madrid one day longer and done the duty of a Christian, if only because of the consideration you owed me. What I owe to the King my master, the care I must take to preserve my reputation and my peace in the future oblige me meanwhile to inform you that my house is no longer yours. On your return to Madrid you will go to lodge where you please, and my servants will deliver your belongings to whomever you authorize to come for them. I am, etc.... Antonio Rafael Mengs."

This letter had such an effect on me that Mengs would certainly not have written it with impunity if he had not been seven long Spanish leagues[30] distant from me. I told the messenger to go. He replied that he was ordered to wait for my answer, whereupon I tore the letter in two, and I told him it was all the answer such a letter deserved. At that he left in great surprise. Without losing time, and in the heat of my anger, I dressed and I went in a sedan chair to the church in Aranjuez, where I confessed to a Franciscan monk, who gave me the sacrament at six o'clock the next morning. The monk had the goodness to write me a certificate that I had been confined to bed from the moment of my arrival *al sitio*,[31] and that despite my weakness I had done my Easter duty at his church, having confessed to him the day before. He then told me the name of the parish priest who had posted me on the door of his church.

Back at the Ambassador's house, I wrote the priest that the certificate I was sending him would make him understand the reason which had obliged me to put off receiving the sacrament at Easter, in consequence of which I asked him to remove my name from the list in which he had unjustly had the kindness to dishonor me. I asked him to take the enclosure to the Cavaliere Mengs.

I wrote Mengs that I deserved the insult he had put on me by turning me out of his house, since I had been stupid enough to do him the honor of going there; but as a Christian who had just done his Easter duty I must not only forgive him but teach him a verse known to all men of honor, but not to him, which said: *Turpius ejicitur quam non admittitur hospes* ("It is more shameful to turn out a guest than not to admit him").[32]

After sending off my letter I told the whole story to the Ambassador, who answered me only that Mengs was esteemed for nothing but his talent, for in other respects all Madrid knew that he was full of absurdities. The man had lodged me in his house only from vanity, at a moment when all Madrid, the Count of Aranda, and the ministers were sure to hear of it and when many would believe that it was partly out of respect for him that I had been escorted back to my lodging. He even told me, in an access of pride, that I should have made the Alcalde Messa escort me not to the coffeehouse where I was staying,[33] but back to his house, since it was from his house that I had been taken away. He was a man ambitious for fame, a great worker, jealous, and the enemy of all the painters of his time who could pretend to a talent equal to his, and he was wrong, for, though a great painter in coloring and drawing, he did not have the very first qualification to make a great painter, namely, invention.

"Just as," I said to him one day, "every great poet must be a painter, so every painter must be a poet."

He took my dictum in bad part, for he wrongly thought that I had uttered it only to reproach him with his deficiency. He was extremely ignorant, and he wanted to pass for learned; he was a drunkard, lascivious, bad-tempered, jealous, and avaricious, and he wanted to pass for virtuous. A great worker, he found it necessary not to dine, for he liked to drink until his reason was totally extinguished. This was why, when he was invited to dine anywhere, he drank only water.

He spoke four languages, all of them badly; but he refused to admit it. He had begun to hate me a few days before I left Madrid because chance had shown me too much of all his failings, and because he had been too often obliged to admit the justice of my criticisms. His ill breeding made him resent being under vital obligations to me. I one day prevented him from sending a memorial to the Court, which was to have been seen by the King and in which he signed himself *el más ínclito* when he wanted to call himself "the most humble"; I told him that he would be laughed at, for *ínclito* did not mean "humble" but "illustrious"; he flew into a rage, he said I must not imagine I knew Spanish better than he did, and he was in despair when someone who arrived told him that he ought to thank me, for so gross an error would have made him eternally ridiculous. Another time I prevented him from sending a critical comment on a diatribe by someone who said that we had not on earth a single antediluvian monument. Mengs had thought he would confound the author by writing in the margin that the ruins of the Tower of Babylon[34] were still to be seen: a twofold blunder, because the pretended ruins are not visible, and, even if they were, the building of that unique tower took place after the Flood. When he found himself convinced, he erased his note, but hating me with all his heart, for he was certain that I must know the full extent of his ignorance. He had a mania for discussing metaphysical problems; his passion was reasoning on beauty in general and defining it, and the things he said on the subject were enormously stupid.

Excessively splenetic, in his fits of rage he beat his children even at the risk of crippling them. I more than once snatched his eldest son[35] from his hands at moments when I thought I should see him tear him to pieces with his teeth. He boasted that his Bohemian father, a bad painter, had brought him up stick in hand, and, having himself become a good painter by this treatment, he was convinced that he must deliberately use the same means to make his children become something. He took offense when someone wrote to him and he saw in the address neither his title of Cavaliere[36] nor his Christian names. I told him one day that I had not felt offended when he failed to add the title of Cavaliere to my name, in the addresses of the letters he had written me at Florence and Madrid, and that I nevertheless had the honor to have been decorated with the same order as he. He made no answer. As for his Christian names, his reason for valuing them was very strange. He said that, since he was named Anton Raphael, and was a painter, people who failed to give him those names refused him, according to his mad idea, the qualities in painting of Antonio da Correggio[37] and Raffaello d'Urbino,[38] which he united in himself.

I one day ventured to tell him that I thought the hand of one of the principal figures which I saw in a painting of his was faulty because the fourth finger was shorter than the index finger. He told me it ought to be so, and he showed me his hand; I laughed and showed him mine, saying that I was sure my hand was formed like that of all the children descended from Adam.

"Then from whom do you suppose I am descended?"

"I have no idea; but it is certain that you are not of my species."

"It is you who are not of mine, nor of that of the rest of mankind, for the hands of men and women are generally constructed like mine."

"I wager a hundred pistoles you are wrong."

With that he rises, throwing his palette and brushes on the floor, he rings, his servants come up, he looks at their hands, and he is furious to see that they all have the fourth finger longer than the index. That time—a most unusual thing—I saw him laugh and end the argument with a jest:

"I am delighted that I can boast I am unique in something."

A sensible thing which Mengs said to me one day, and which I have never forgotten, was the following: he had painted a Magdalen whose beauty was really surprising. For ten or twelve days he had said to me every morning:

"This evening the picture will be finished."

He worked on it until evening, and the next day I found him still working on the same picture. So one day I asked him if he had been wrong the day before when he had told me that the painting was already finished.

"No," he replied, "it might seem to be finished in the eyes of ninety-nine out of a hundred connoisseurs who examined it; but the one who most interests me is the hundredth, and I look at it with his eyes. Understand that there is not a picture in the world which is finished more than relatively. This Magdalen will never be finished until I stop working on it, but it will not really be so, for it is certain that if I worked on it another day it would be more finished. Understand that even in your Petrarch there is not one sonnet which can be called really finished. Nothing of what comes from the hands or the minds of men is perfect in this world except a mathematical calculation."

I embraced my dear Mengs after hearing him talk to me in this fashion; but I did not embrace him on another day when he told me he wished he had been Raffaello d'Urbino. He was his great painter.

"How," I asked him, "can you want to have been? Such a desire is contrary to nature, for having existed, you would exist no longer. You cannot entertain that desire unless you imagine yourself enjoying its fulfillment in the bliss of Paradise, and in that case I congratulate you."

"Not at all: I should like to have been Raffaello, and I should care nothing about existing today, either in body or in soul."

"That is absurd. Think about it. You cannot have that desire and at the same time have the faculty of thought."

He flew into a rage and treated me to insults which made me laugh. Another time he compared the work of a poet composing a tragedy with that of a painter composing a picture in which the whole tragedy was depicted in a single scene. After analyzing a great number of differences, I ended by telling him that the tragic poet had to employ all the attention of his soul even in the smallest details, whereas the painter could employ colors on the surfaces of the objects and at the same time discuss various subjects with friends around him.

"This proves," I said, "that your painting is more the work of your hands than a product of your soul. That fact proves its inferiority. Find me a poet who can tell his cook what he wants for supper while composing epic verse."

Mengs worsted in an argument became brutal; he declared himself insulted. Yet the man, who died before the age of fifty years,[39] will go down to posterity as a philosopher, a great stoic, learned, and endowed with all the virtues—and all because of his biography,[40] which one of his inordinate admirers wrote and had printed in beautiful type in a large quarto volume dedicated to the King of Spain. It is a tissue of falsehoods. Let us leave him for the present, and speak of my own concerns. [...]

I still had to stay in bed because of my weakness. Manuzzi managed to induce me to go with him to Toledo to see all the antiquities which still exist in that ancient city. We were to be back in Aranjuez on the fifth day. He was eager to be away because the Ambassador was to give a great dinner for all the ministers, which, not having been presented, he could not attend.

"My exclusion," he said, "will not be remarked on when it is known that I am not in Aranjuez."

Thoroughly persuaded, and delighted to see Toledo, I set out with him early the next day, and we were there by evening. At the gate of that capital of New Castile, which is on top of a mountain, I saw a naumachia.[41] The Tagus, which carries gold, surrounds it on two sides. We lodged well enough for that country at an inn on a great square, and we went out in the morning with a guide, who took us to the Alcázar:[42] it is the Louvre of Toledo, the great royal palace in which the King of the Moors lived. Its majestic name could have no other vowel than the queen of the alphabet. After that we went to the cathedral,[43] worthy to be seen for the riches it contains. I saw the tabernacle in which the holy sacrament is carried in procession on Corpus Christi, so heavy that thirty men are used to carry it. The Archbishop of the city has an income of three hundred thousand écus, and its clergy has four hundred thousand. A canon, showing me vessels in which there were relics, said that in one of them were the thirty coins which Judas had received for selling Our Lord; I asked him to show them to me, and, looking at me balefully, he replied that the King himself would not dare to admit to such curiosity. The priests in Spain are a rabble which it is necessary to treat with more respect than anywhere else. The next morning we were shown some collections[44] of curiosities of natural history and medicine, where we were at least permitted to laugh. We were shown a dissected dragon, "which proves," the owner of it said to me, "that the dragon is not a fabulous animal"; and after the dragon we were shown a basilisk, whose eyes, instead of terrifying us, made us laugh. This grave nobleman showed us a Freemason's apron, assuring us that the person who had presented it to his father had been a member of a lodge.

"Which proves," he told us, "that those who say that the sect has never existed and does not exist are wrong."

On my return to Aranjuez, finding myself in very good health, I began paying my court to all the ministers, and the Ambassador presented me to the Marchese Grimaldi,[45] with whom I had several conferences on the subject of the Sierra Morena, where the colony was doing badly. The Swiss families could not thrive there. I gave him a plan intended to show him that the colony should be composed of Spanish families.

"Spain," he said, "is scantily populated everywhere; so it would be necessary to impoverish one place in order to enrich another."

"Not at all, for ten male emigrants who die in Asturias without marrying because of their poverty would die in the Sierra Morena after producing fifty children, and those fifty children in the next generation would produce two hundred, who would produce a thousand, and all would be well."

My project was being studied, and the Marchese Grimaldi assured me that if the thing was done I should be appointed governor.

An Italian *opera buffa* was delighting the Court, except the King,[*] who had no liking for music. He cared for nothing but hunting. An Italian musician, who enjoyed the Venetian Ambassador's patronage, wanted to compose the music for a new drama, flattering himself that he would deserve universal applause and receive substantial presents in recompense for his work. The time was too short to write to Italy; I offered to write one for him then and there, I was taken at my word, and the next day I gave him the first act. The chapelmaster composed the music for it in four days, and the Venetian Ambassador invited all the ministers to the rehearsal of the first act in the great hall of his palace. The music was declared in exquisite taste; the two other acts were already written, he hurried, and in two weeks my opera[46] was performed, and the musician had reason to be well content. As for me, I was considered to be above a poet who worked to be paid; I was paid in applause. And to tell the truth, I should have thought myself insulted if payment had been offered me. It was enough for me to see the Ambassador delighted to have me in his entourage, and to see myself valued by the ministers as a man capable of contributing to the pleasures of the Court.

The composition of the opera had necessitated my making the acquaintance of the actresses. The leading one was a Roman named Pelliccia.[47] Her talent was mediocre, she was neither pretty nor ugly, she squinted a little. Her sister, who was younger than she, was pretty; yet the pretty one attracted and interested nobody; the elder made herself liked by all who spoke to her. She had magic in her face; her squint eyes were touching, her subtle, modest laughter charmed; her easy manner gained her the good will of all.

She had a husband who was a painter, but a bad one, a well-meaning, rather ugly man, whose manner was more that of her servant than of her husband. He was extremely submissive to his wife, and she treated him with consideration. The woman did not inspire love in me, but true friendship. I went to see her every day, I wrote words for her for Roman airs which she sang with much grace, she received me unreservedly and with no artifice, as if I had been her friend from childhood.

---

[*] The King of Spain had the face of a sheep, and the sheep is the animal which has no idea of oral harmony. If one listens to the voices of a hundred sheep in a flock, one will hear a hundred different semitones. (C.'s marginal note.)

One day when there was to be a rehearsal of a short act for which I had written the words, I talked to her on the stage about the great names of the personages who were present, and who had come only to hear the new music which was to be performed. The impresario of the opera, who was named Marescalchi,[48] had contracted with the Governor of Valencia[49] to spend the month of September in that city with his troupe to play comic operas in a small theater which the Governor of that Kingdom had had built expressly for the purpose. The city of Valencia had never seen an Italian *opera buffa*, the impresario Marescalchi hoped to make a great fortune there. La Pelliccia wanted to obtain from some great nobleman of the Court a letter of recommendation for Valencia, and, knowing none of them, she asked me if she could address herself to the Venetian Ambassador in the hope that he would favor her by asking someone for a letter for her. I advised her to go and ask for one from the Duke of Arcos,[50] who was twenty paces from us and who kept his eyes fixed on her.

"There stands a great nobleman, my dear, who is dying to oblige you in some way; go yourself now and ask him to do you the favor; I am sure he will not refuse you; it is no more than asking him for a pinch of snuff."

"I haven't the courage. Present me."

"No, no—that would spoil everything. He mustn't even imagine that it is I who gave you the advice. Do as I say; seize the moment; he is there in the wings, all alone, and he looks at no one but you. After I have left you—one minute after—approach him, and ask him for the favor; you will be granted it."

I go toward the orchestra, and a minute later I see the Duke advance toward the actress and speak to her politely and decently, and, in the course of the conversation, I notice that La Pelliccia blushes as she says something to him; I see the Duke with the air of a man who consents, and I see him draw back his hand, which La Pelliccia wanted to kiss. The thing is done. After the opera she told me that he had promised she should have the letter for which she had asked him on the day the opera was first performed. He kept his word. He gave her a sealed letter addressed to a merchant in the city, whose name was Don Diego Valencia.[51] She was not to go there until September; so there was time enough. We were in the middle of May. [. . .]

I amused myself in Aranjuez by frequently seeing Don Domingo Varnier, the King's valet, a valet of the Prince of Asturias, who now reigns,[52] and a chamberwoman to the Princess, who was adored and who had had the strength of mind to get a great deal of cumbersome etiquette done away with and to change the solemn and serious tone at Court for a pleasant affability. I was charmed to see His Catholic Majesty dine every day at eleven o'clock, always eat the same thing, go hunting[53] at the same hour, and return with his brother,[54] too exhausted to do anything. The King was very ugly, but he was handsome in comparison with his brother, whose face was positively frightening. The King's brother never traveled without an image of the Blessed Virgin which Mengs had made for him. It was a painting two feet high by three and a half feet wide. The Blessed Virgin was seated on the grass and had her bare feet crossed in the Moorish fashion; her most holy legs were visible halfway up the calves. It was a painting which excited the soul by way of the senses. The Infante was in love with it, and he took to be devotion what was nothing but the most criminal of voluptuous instincts, for it was impossible that, when he contemplated the image, he did not burn with longing to have in his arms, warm and alive, the goddess whom he saw painted on the canvas. But the Infante never suspected it. He was delighted to be in love with the mother of his God. For him this love was the assurance of his eternal salvation. Such are the Spaniards. Objects intended to interest them must be striking, and they never interpret anything except in a way favorable to their dominant passion.

In Madrid, before going to Aranjuez, I saw a picture of the Blessed Virgin suckling the Infant Jesus. Her bare breast, excellently painted, fired the imagination. The picture was the retable of the high altar of a chapel in the Carrera de San Gerónimo.[55] The chapel was filled all day with pious men who went there to worship the mother of God, whose representation was perhaps interesting only because of her beautiful bosom; the offerings given at the sanctuary were so abundant that, in the century and a half during which the painting had been there, a great number of gold and silver lamps and candelabra had been made and a considerable income set aside for the maintenance of these objects, which fed on oil and wax. At the door of the chapel there were always a quantity of carriages and a soldier with fixed bayonet to keep order and prevent quarrels among the coachmen, who were constantly arriving and leaving, for there was not a nobleman who, passing the sacred place in his carriage, did not order his coachman to stop so that he could get out and go, if only for a moment, to do homage to the goddess and contemplate *beata ubera quae lactaverunt aeterni patris filium* ("the blessed paps which suckled the son of the eternal father").[56] Since I knew men, this devotion did not surprise me; but here is what surprised me on my return to Madrid at the end of May in the same year 1768.

Having to pay a visit to the Abate Pico,[57] I order the coachman to avoid the Carrera because of the carriages which might be in front of the chapel and delay my journey. The coachman replies that for some time there have been few carriages there, so he continues on his way, and, sure enough, I see only two or three. Getting out at the Abate's, I ask the coachman the reason for this suspension of devotion, and he replies that men are getting more wicked every day. I make light of his reason, and, after drinking some of his excellent chocolate with the illustrious and intelligent Abate, I ask him the reason why the chapel was losing its reputation. He bursts out laughing, and he asks me to excuse him if he does not dare tell me the reason; but he asks me to go myself and receive the indulgence, and he assures me that my curiosity will be allayed. I went there the same day, and in an instant I saw it all. The Blessed Virgin's bosom was no longer visible. A handkerchief painted by the most criminal of all painters had spoiled the superb picture. There was nothing to be seen—not even the nipple, not the suckling mouth of the Child God, not the bulge of the breast, so that the Virgin, who, before the alteration, had a reason for gazing at her son's divine lips as they sucked the ambrosia, now seemed to look at nothing but the wretched handkerchief with which, contrary to the laws of costume, a profane brush had made her as ugly as the picture. This disaster had happened at the end of the Carnival. The old chaplain having died, the new one saw fit to call the most beautiful and most holy of all the bosoms God has created scandalous. As a fool, the chaplain may have been right, but as a Spanish Christian, he was wrong, and the falling off in the offerings must already have made him repent. My reflections on this incident, and my insatiable curiosity to know men by making them talk, impelled me to call on the chaplain, who, as I saw it, must be old and stupid.

I go there one morning, and I find a priest thirty years of age, extremely lively and prepossessing, who, though he does not know me, at once offers me a cup of chocolate, which I refuse, as a foreigner must do in Spain, for not only is it usually bad, but it is pressed upon one everywhere and at all hours of the day with such urgency that if one accepted I believe one would die of it.

Without making a long exordium, I go to the point, I tell him that I am passionately devoted to painting and that I am distressed at his having had a superb picture ruined.

"That may be so, but its beauty was precisely what made it unfit to represent a woman whose appearance should excite the soul to adore and contemplate her immaculateness, and never to sensual passion. Let all beautiful pictures perish if all of them together can cause the smallest mortal sin."

"Who gave you permission to commit this murder? The State Inquisitors in Venice, even Signor Barbarigo,[58] though very devout and a theologian, would have had you imprisoned under the Leads. Love of the bliss of Paradise must not injure the fine arts, and I am sure that St. Luke the Evangelist, as a painter,[59] is speaking against you to the Blessed Virgin, whose portrait, as you must know, he painted with only three colors."

"Sir, I needed to ask no one's permission. It is I who have to say mass every day at this altar,[60] and I am not ashamed to tell you that I could not consecrate; you will forgive me my weakness. That beautiful breast troubled my imagination."

"Who obliged you to look at it?"

"I did not look at it, and the enemy of God presented it to my mind nevertheless."

"Why did you not rather mutilate yourself, like the wise Origen,[61] *qui se castravit propter regnum coelorum* ['who castrated himself for the sake of the Kingdom of Heaven']?[62] Believe me, your genitals, too weak because it seems they are too strong, are not worth the painting you have destroyed."

"Signore, you insult me."

"Not at all, for I have no such intention. Either ask the Cavaliere Mengs to make you a new picture of the Blessed Virgin such as will inspire the devotion of her devotees, whom you have very much offended, or renounce a benefice which you were not born to enjoy."

"I will do neither."

The young priest showed me to the door so unceremoniously that I left certain that he was plotting some Spanish revenge on me through the terrible Inquisition. It occurred to me that he could easily find out my name and make difficulties for me. So I at once resolved to forestall the blow. About this time I had made the acquaintance of a Frenchman named De Ségur,[63] who had just come out of the prisons of the Inquisition, where he had been confined for three years. His crime was that he had on a table in the drawing room of his house a stone basin, to which he went every morning to wash his hands and face. On the edge of the basin there was a statue of a naked child a foot and a half high. The statue was filled with water, which he caused to come out of the child's little virile member as from a faucet, when he wanted to wash. To someone who deifies everything the child might well appear to be the image of our Redeemer, for the sculptor had surrounded its head with the kind of crown which is called a halo and which sculptors and painters affix to the heads of saints. Poor Ségur was accused of impiety before the Inquisition, it was judged a crime that he should dare to wash with water which might seem to be the Saviour's urine. The jest cost him three years of penitence. *Aliena spectans doctus evasi mala* ("Taught by those which befell others, I avoided misfortunes").[64]

I presented myself to the Grand Inquisitor,[65] who was a bishop. I told him all that I had said to the chaplain, repeating every word but suppressing my bantering tone, and I ended by asking his pardon if by any chance the chaplain could have been offended. I assured him of my orthodoxy. I should never have believed that the Grand Inquisitor in Madrid would be an agreeable man, though his face was as ugly as possible. The prelate did nothing but laugh from the beginning to the end of my narrative, for he would not hear me as if in confession. He said that the chaplain was himself guilty and absolutely incapable of fulfilling his function, for, by supposing others to be as weak as himself, he had done grave harm to religion; he said that I had nevertheless done wrong to go there and irritate him. Since I had had to tell him my name, he ended by reading me, still with a smiling countenance, an accusation against me drawn up by someone who had witnessed the occurrence. He gently chided me for having called the Duke of Medina Sidonia's Franciscan confessor an ignoramus because he had refused to grant that a priest should say mass a second time on a feast day even after dining, if his sovereign, who had not heard it, ordered him to say it.

"You were right," the Bishop said, "but even so you should not have called the Duke's confessor an ignoramus in his presence. For the future, avoid all arguments on the subject of religion, in respect to both doctrine and discipline. I can tell you, so that when you leave Spain you will take with you a true idea of the Inquisition, that the parish priest who posted your name among those of the excommunicated was reprimanded, for it was his duty to inform you beforehand and above all to find out if you were ill, and we know that you really were so."

At these words I kissed his hand, going down on one knee, and I left well enough satisfied.

Let us return to Aranjuez, for what I have just written happened on my return to Madrid. As soon as I learned that the Ambassador could not lodge me in Madrid, where I thought of staying, for I was hoping for the governorship of Sierra Morena, I wrote to my good friend the cobbler Don Diego that I needed a well-furnished room with a good bed, closet, also a servant, an honest man who would be willing to ride behind my carriage, and a carriage engaged at so much a month, which, if he would vouch for me, I would pay in advance. I informed him what I wanted to pay for my apartment, and I asked him to write to me as soon as he had found it for me, for I should not leave Aranjuez until I knew where I was to go when I arrived in Madrid. The cobbler answered me at once that he was sure he could do what I wanted, and that he would inform me of the place as soon as he had found it.

The *población* ("colonization") of Sierra Morena occupied me a good deal, for I was writing on the maintenance of order, which was the chief requisite for making the colony prosper. My writings, which were only demonstrative arguments, were valued by the Minister Grimaldi and flattered the Ambassador Mocenigo, for he thought that if I succeeded in going to govern the colony it could only increase the reputation of his embassy. My labors, however, did not keep me from amusing myself, and above all from frequenting the courtiers who could acquaint me with the characters of the individuals who made up the royal family. Don Varnier, a frank, reliable, intelligent man, gave me all the information I wanted.

I asked him one day if it was true that the King's attachment to Gregorio Squillace[66] was due to his loving, or having loved, his wife, and he assured me that it was a slander imagined by those who stated as true whatever had some semblance of truth.

"If the epithet 'the Chaste,'" he said, "is to be added to the name of a king by the mouth of Truth, and not by adulation, it has never become any king better than it does Carlos III. He has never in his life had to do with another woman than the late Queen, and that not so much because it was the duty of a husband but because it was the duty of a Christian. He does not want to commit a sin because he does not want to sully his soul and because he does not want to suffer the shame of admitting his weakness to his confessor. In the best of health, strong, vigorous, having never in his life had the slightest illness, not even a fever, he has a temperament which makes him very much inclined to the act of Venus, for as long as she lived he never for one day failed to pay his marital duty to the Queen. On the days when it was forbidden him for cleanliness' sake, he tired himself more than usual at hunting, to calm the impulses of concupiscence. Imagine his despair when he found himself a widower, and resolved to die rather than to suffer the humiliation of taking a mistress. His resource was to hunt, and to keep himself so occupied every hour of the day, that he has no time left to think of a woman. It was difficult, for he likes neither to write nor to read nor to listen to music or to light conversation. Here is what he did, what he does, and what he will do until he dies. At seven o'clock he dresses, he goes to the wardrobe, his hair is dressed, and he prays until eight. He goes to mass, he drinks his chocolate, then he takes a pinch of Spanish snuff, which he pushes into his big nose; it is the one pinch of snuff he takes each day. At nine o'clock he works with his ministers until eleven, he dines alone until a quarter to twelve, and until twelve he goes to see the Princess of Asturias. At twelve he gets into his carriage, and he goes hunting. At seven he eats a bite wherever he happens to be, and at eight he returns to the castle so tired that he often falls asleep before he gets into bed. In this way he never needs a woman. He thought of remarrying, and he asked for Madame Adélaïde of France,[67] who, having seen his portrait, absolutely refused him. That annoyed him, and he has not thought of marrying since. Woe betide anyone who should propose a mistress to him."

Speaking of whether his character was humane or severe, kindly or harsh, Don Domingo said that his ministers were right to keep him inaccessible, for if someone managed to take him by surprise and beg for some favor, he made it a point of honor never to refuse anything, for it was only then that he felt he was the King.

"Believe me, the most intractable, the most difficult of sovereigns are those who give public audience to all comers. They are the ones who are the most often deceived; nothing can be got from them; their one thought is always to refuse what a petitioner asks for. The inaccessible sovereign, on the other hand, when someone manages to speak to him, listens attentively and considers how best to let him have what he asks for. The place where Carlos III is often found alone is out hunting. There he is in a good humor, and he takes pleasure in satisfying the person who speaks to him. His great fault is his firmness, for in him it is obstinacy; when he wants something done, and has supposed it possible, done it must be; failures do not discourage him. His consideration for his brother the Infante is very great; he can refuse him nothing; but he insists on being always the master. It is thought that he will grant him permission to contract a marriage of conscience,[68] for he fears that he will damn himself and he has no love for bastards. The Infante has already fathered three."

At Aranjuez I observed the immense number of people who were there waiting on the ministers to obtain posts.

"They all return home after the King's journey," said Don Domingo, "without having obtained anything."

"Then they are asking for impossibilities?"

"Not at all. They ask for nothing. 'What do you want?' a minister asks them. 'What Your Excellency thinks will be suitable for me.' 'But what can you do?' 'I don't know. Your Excellency can look into my talents, my capacity, and give me the employment for which Your Excellency may consider me fit.' 'Away with you, I haven't the time.'"

But so it goes everywhere. Carlos III died mad; now the Queen of Portugal has gone mad.[69] The King of England was mad, and has, they say, recovered.[70]

I took leave of the Venetian Ambassador three days before his departure, and I hastily embraced Manuzzi, who never failed to give me proofs of most sincere friendship. I have to admit it, to my confusion. Don Diego, the cobbler, had written me that for the money I wanted to spend I should also have a Biscayan maid-servant,[71] who, when I wished, would cook for me well enough. The address he sent me was that of a house in the Calle de Alcalá.[72] I left Aranjuez in the morning, and I arrived at my lodging early in the afternoon. Aranjuez is the same distance from Madrid as Fontaine-bleau is from Paris.[73]

I arrive, I get out, I go to the second floor, I find the Biscayan maid, who spoke French, I look at my apartment, and I find, besides the closet, a second room with a bed in which to put up a friend if I wished; I praise the cobbler. I have my belongings brought up; my lackey arrives, and he seems to be honest; I praise Don Diego. Curious to see the skill of the cook from Bilbao,[74] I order her to prepare supper for me, without company, and I offer her money, whereupon she tells me that she has some, and that she will give me the bill the next day. I go out with my manservant to fetch my belongings from Mengs's. His valet delivers everything to mine, who goes for two porters, and sets off. I do not ask if Mengs is at home, I try to give his valet a doblón, and he refuses it.

I go at once to the Calle del Desengaño to see both Doña Ignacia and her father, whom I had to thank and to reimburse, and I find no one. A woman next door tells me that he has moved. I am astonished that he did not write to tell me so, and I go back to my lodging in the Calle de Alcalá, which was three hundred paces distant. I arrange everything as I want it in my room, I ask Felipe (such was my valet's name) where Don Diego had gone to lodge, and he answers that it is far away and that he will take me there the next day. I ask him where my landlord lives, and he says it is on the floor above me, but that I can be sure he will not make the slightest noise. He had gone out, and would not come home until ten o'clock.

I have everything I need to write with set out on a small table, telling Felipe to go away and not come back until nine o'clock to serve my supper. I order him to fetch me some wine from where I knew it was good, and I fall to writing. At nine o'clock he comes to tell me that my supper is served in the other room, I go there with a ravenous appetite, for I had eaten nothing, and I am astonished to see a small table ready laid, with a cloth of a cleanliness which I had not yet seen in Spain in the houses of the citizenry. But the supper finally proves to me that Don Diego is a hero. The cook from Bilbao cooked like a Frenchwoman. Five dishes, *criadillas*,[75] which I loved to distraction, everything excellent—it seemed to me impossible that I should have such a good cook into the bargain, though I was paying a good deal for the apartment.

Toward the end of supper Felipe told me that my landlord had come home, and that, if I would permit it, he wanted to see me.

"Let him come in."

I see the cobbler and his daughter. He had rented the house expressly to lodge me.

CHAPTER III

My amour with Doña Ignacia. Signor
Mocenigo returns to Madrid.

You ill-fated Counts and Marquises who are pleased to crush the self-esteem of a man who by his lofty acts tries to convince you that he is as noble as you, beware of him if you succeed in denying his claims, in humbling him; fired by a just disdain, he will tear you limb from limb, and he will be in the right. Respect the man who, calling himself a gentleman though he is not one in your terms, imagines that to play the part he must do lofty deeds. Respect the man who gives nobility a definition which makes you laugh. He does not say that it consists in a series of generations from father to son, of which he himself is the latest heir; he makes light of genealogies. He defines the gentleman by saying that he is a man who demands respect and who believes that there is no way to be respected but to respect others, to live decently, to deceive no one, never to lie when the person who is listening to him believes that he is speaking sincerely, and to put his honor above his life. This last part of his definition of the gentleman should make you fear that he will kill you like an assassin if you succeed in dishonoring him by treachery or by surprise. In the physical world anything which strikes is subjected to the same force in reaction; but in the moral world the reaction is stronger than the action. The reaction from being imposed upon is scorn; the reaction from scorn is hatred; the reaction from hatred is murder, as it is from a stain which covers with dishonor a man who wants to be honored and who does everything to deserve it.

The cobbler Don Diego saw that he might have made himself ridiculous in my eyes when he had told me that he was noble; but, feeling that he was truly so in the meaning which he gave to the word, he wanted to convince me more and more that he had not imposed on me. The noble deed he had done[1] for me at Buen Retiro had already shown me the nature of his soul; but that was not enough for him, he wanted to go on in the same way. He finds one of my letters laying a servile task on him, such as anyone can perform more or less competently, and he is not content to serve me as a banker, for example, would have done. He forms the plan of himself becoming the tenant-in-chief of a house, in order to rent the best part of it to me. He sees that he can do this without exceeding his resources, and even at a profit eventually, assuming that his apartment would not remain unoccupied long; and he does it; and he enjoys my surprise, sure that the esteem I should conceive for him would show that I rated his magnanimous act at its due value.

He was not mistaken; I gave him every proof of it in avowals of friendship. I saw Doña Ignacia proud of what her father had done. We sat for an hour, talking, emptying a bottle, and we made all our business arrangements. The only thing I would not grant him, and on which I made him yield, was that I would not have the Biscayan woman at his expense. I rented his apartment for six months, paying the whole sum in advance; and I asked him to let the cook continue to think that it was not I who paid her but he; I asked him also to pay her what she would spend to provide me with meals every day, at least until the Ambassador arrived. In addition, having assured him that it was a real penance for me to eat alone, I invited him to dine and sup with me every day, and hence to order my Biscayan always to prepare meals for two persons. He tried in vain to think of excuses, he had to accept my conditions, reserving the right to be represented by his daughter when, having much work to do, he had not time to dress to dine with me. It is easy to understand that this last condition was not displeasing to me; and indeed I expected it.

I went upstairs to his lodging the next morning. This third floor was the attic, which was, however, divided into four sections by partitions. In the large room in which he worked at repairing shoes and boots with an apprentice, he had his bed, in which he slept with his wife. In the adjoining room, which was smaller, I saw Doña Ignacia's bed, a stool to kneel on before a great crucifix, a picture four feet high representing St. Ignatius of Loyola,[2] whose young and handsome face inspired fleshly love, and rosaries and prayer books, with a pail full of holy water. Another smaller room was occupied by her very ugly younger sister, whom I believe I have not yet mentioned, and the fourth was the kitchen, in which there was an alcove containing the cook's bed. He told me that he was more comfortably lodged than in the other house, and that the apartment he rented me paid him four times the rent of the whole house.

"But the furniture—"

"In four years it will all be paid for. This house will be my daughter's dowry, and it is to you that I owe this excellent investment."

"I am very glad of it; but it seems to me that you are making brand-new shoes there."

"That is true; but observe that I am working on the last which was given me, so that I am obliged neither to put them on the feet of the person who is to wear them nor to be concerned as to whether they fit him or not."

"How much are you paid for them?"

"A peso duro[3] and a half."

"More than the usual price, I think."

"Certainly; but the difference between the shoes I make and those which are made by ordinary shoemakers *de nuevo* is very great, both in the quality of the leather and the good workmanship."

"I will have a last made, and you shall make me shoes, if you please; but I warn you that they must be of the finest leather you have and with soles of grain morocco."

"It costs more and does not last as long."

"That makes no difference. In summer I have to wear very light shoes."

I at once had a last made, and it was he who worked for me until I left. He said he would sup with me, but that at dinner I should have his daughter, and I replied that I should value his daughter's company as highly as his own.

I called on the Count of Aranda, who, though coldly, received me well enough. I gave him an account of everything I had done at Aranjuez, and of the trouble which the parish priest and Mengs had made for me together.

"I heard of it. This second scrape was worse than the first, and I should not have known how to get you out of it if you had not quickly done what you did, which obliged the priest to cross out your name at once. Just now people are putting up placards which they think will upset me; but they are wrong. I am perfectly calm."

"What do they want of Your Excellency?"

"They want me to permit long cloaks and slouch hats. Didn't you know that?"

"I arrived yesterday."

"That accounts for it. Don't come here at noon on Sunday, for according to yesterday's placard this house will be blown up."

"I am curious to see how high it will go. I shall have the honor to be in your reception room at noon."

"I think you will not find yourself alone."

I went there, and I never saw it so full. The Count talked to everyone. On the last placard, which threatened the Count with death if he did not withdraw his decrees, there were two very forceful verses, which in Spanish have a particular wit and grace. The man who had written the placard, and who was sure to be hanged if he were to be found out, said:

Si me cogen me horqueran
Pero no me cogeran

("If they catch me they will hang me,
but they will not catch me")

Dining with me, Doña Ignacia constantly let me know how glad she was to have me in her house; but she remained completely unresponsive to the amorous pleas which I made to her when Felipe, after serving a dish, went upstairs to fetch another. She blushed, she sighed, and, forced to speak, she begged me to forget all that had happened between us during the Carnival. I smiled, saying that I was sure she knew it was not in my power to forget that I had loved her while I still loved her. I added, half seriously, half tenderly, that, even if it were in my power, I should not want to forget it all. Since I knew that she was neither inconstant nor a hypocrite, I saw very well that her reserve was due to nothing but the resolves she had made to live in future in the grace of her God, whom she had too greatly offended by loving me; but I knew what to expect, and that her resistance could not last long. However, I had to proceed step by step. I had had to do with other pious women, whose temperaments were not as strong as hers, who did not love me as much, and whom I had nevertheless conquered. I felt sure of Doña Ignacia.

After dinner she remained with me for a quarter of an hour, never seeing me amorous. I dressed after taking a siesta, and I went out without seeing her, and when, after supper, she came downstairs to join her father, who had supped with me, I treated her with the utmost gentleness, showing no sign that I had taken offense at her resolve to love me no more. The next day I acted in the same way. She told me at dinner that she had dismissed Don Francisco during the first days of Lent, and she asked me not to receive him if he came to call on me.

The next day, which was Pentecost, after calling on the Count of Aranda, whose palace was to be blown up, I went home, where

Don Diego, very neatly dressed, dined with me; I did not see his daughter. I asked him if she was dining out, and he replied with a laugh which was not Spanish that she had shut herself up in her room, where she was apparently keeping the feast of the Holy Ghost by praying; but that she would certainly come down to sup with me, since he was invited to sup at his brother's house, where he would remain until at least midnight.

"My dear Don Diego, do not stand on ceremony, I beg you, for I am speaking to you sincerely. Before you go out, tell Doña Ignacia that I willingly relinquish my rights in favor of those which God may have over her conscience. Tell her that if she finds it a burden to interrupt her devotions to sup with me, she shall sup with me another day. I shall not mind supping alone. Will you tell her that?"

"Since you wish it, I will tell her so."

After the siesta I saw him in my room, telling me contentedly that Doña Ignacia would be glad to take advantage of the freedom I granted her that day, in which she would see no one.

"That's the way to behave! I'm delighted. Tomorrow I shall thank her."

I had to exercise a great deal of self-control to answer him thus, for such excessive devotion displeased me and even made me fear that I should lose the love which attached me to the charming girl and the esteem I felt for her. However, the worthy Don Diego very nearly made me laugh when, as he left, he told me that an intelligent father must forgive excessive devotion in his young daughter, as he must a strong amorous passion. Could I expect so odd a dictum from the lips of a Spanish cobbler?

It was raining and windy, I decided not to go out. I told Felipe to dismiss my carriage and to go away after telling the cook that I would not sup until ten o'clock. I sat down to write. It was Doña Ignacia's mother who brought me a light. But suddenly I had a promising idea. When the Biscayan came at ten o'clock to say that my supper was on the table, I told her to take it away, for I did not feel like eating.

At eleven o'clock I went to bed, and I slept better. The next morning at nine Doña Ignacia entered my room to tell me how sorry she had been when she learned that morning that I had not supped.

"All alone, sad, and disconsolate, I did well to abstain from eating supper."

"You look downcast."

"I shall look better when you wish it."

The hairdresser came in, she left me. I went to the splendid mass at the Buen Suceso,[4] where I saw the most beautiful courtesans in Madrid. I dined well with Don Diego, who at dessert told his daughter that she had been the cause of my not supping. She replied that it would not happen again. I asked her if she wanted to go to Nuestra Señora de Atocha[5] with me, and she expressed her readiness, looking at her father, who told her that true devotion was inseparable from cheerfulness and from the confidence one should have in God, in oneself, and in the probity of the decent people with whom one had to do, and, that being so, she should believe that I could be an honest man despite my not having had the good fortune to be born a Spaniard.

This conclusion made me burst out laughing, which was not taken in bad part. Doña Ignacia kissed her father's hand and asked me frankly if I would take her cousin with me too.

"What need," her father asked her, "have you of your cousin? I answer for Don Jaime."[6]

"I am obliged to you," I said, "but if her cousin would like to come, and if Doña Ignacia wants her, I shall enjoy it all the more, provided it is her elder cousin, whose character pleases me better than that of the younger."

This arrangement made, her father left, and I sent Felipe to the stable to have four mules harnessed; Doña Ignacia, looking at once content and contrite, asked me to forgive her her weaknesses.

"Everything, my beautiful angel, provided that you too will forgive me for loving you."

"Oh, my dear friend! I am afraid I shall go mad if I continue to fight a battle which rends my soul."

"No battle, dear heart. Either love me as I love you, or ask me to leave your house and never again to appear in your sight. I shall have the strength to obey you; but I warn you that you will not be happy."

"That I know. No, no. Remain where you are, this house is yours; but now allow me to tell you that you are mistaken when you suppose that my elder cousin has a better character than the younger one. I know what made you think so on the last night of the Carnival; but you do not know all. The younger is a goodhearted creature, and, ugly though she is, she succumbed to a man who was able to touch her heart; but the elder is ten times uglier, and her spite because she has never been able to win anyone's love makes her malicious. Let me tell you that she believes you love her, and that she nevertheless speaks ill of you; she says you are a seducer, that I was unable to resist you, but that you will not succeed with her."

"Tell me no more, I beg you; we must punish her. Send for the younger one."

"Very well. Thank you."

"Does she know that we love each other?"

"Alas, yes."

"Why did you tell her so?"

"She guessed it, but she has a kind heart, and she only pities me. She wants us to perform a devotion together to the Blessed Virgin at La Soledad,[7] which will cure us both of a love which damns us."

"Then she is in love too?"

"Yes, but unhappily, poor child, for she alone loves. Imagine what torture!"

"Indeed it is. I pity her, for, such as she is, I do not know a man who would want her. If ever there was one, there's a girl who shouldn't love. But you——"

"But I. Say no more. My soul is exposed to a greater danger than hers, for I do not know if I am pretty, but I am courted; I must either resist or be damned; and there are men whom it is impossible to resist. God is my witness that during Holy Week I went to see a girl who had smallpox, hoping that I should catch it and become ugly. God did not will it, and then my confessor at La Soledad reprimanded me severely, and gave me a penance I should never have expected."

"Tell me what it was, please."

"Yes, I can tell you. After telling me that a beautiful face is the sign of a beautiful soul, and that it is a gift from God, for which the person who is granted it must thank him every day, for beauty is a charm which recommends the possessor of it to everyone; it followed, he went on, that by having tried to become ugly I had made myself unworthy of the gift which God had given me, and had become guilty of ingratitude to the Creator. So he told me that as a penance for my crime I must put a touch of rouge on my cheeks whenever I think I am too pale. I had to promise him I would, and I bought a pot of rouge; but until now I have not felt any need to use it. Add that my father might notice it, and then I should feel extremely embarrassed if I had to tell him that it is at my confessor's bidding."

"Is your confessor young?"

"He is seventy."

"Do you tell him all the particulars of your sins of weakness?"

"Of course! I tell him everything, for every particular, however small, is a mortal sin."

"Does he question you?"

"No, for he knows that I tell him everything. It is a great torment, a great shame; but it must be borne. I have had this confessor for two years; before him I had one who was unbearable. He asked me things which made me indignant, which insulted me. I left him."

"What did he ask you?"

"Oh, please excuse me from telling you."

"What need have you to go to confession so often?"

"What need? Would to God that I did not need it! Yet I go only once a week."

"That is too often."

"It is not too often, for when I am in mortal sin I cannot sleep. I am afraid I shall die while I am sleeping."

"I am sorry for you, my dear, for the fear must make you unhappy. I have a privilege which you have not. I count much more than you do on the mercy of God."

Her cousin arrived and we left. Nothing is more certain than that a devout girl who does the work of the flesh with her lover feels a hundred times more pleasure than a girl who is without prejudices. This truth is too much in the nature of things for me to think it necessary to prove it to my reader.

We found many carriages at the entrance to the small church, which consequently was filled with the devout of both sexes and every rank. I saw the Duchess of Villadarias,[8] famous for her andromania. When the uterine fury seized her nothing could restrain her. She laid hands on the man who aroused her instinct, and he had to satisfy her. It had happened to her several times in public places, and the people who were present had had to flee. I had met her at a ball, she was still pretty and fairly young; she was on her knees when I entered with my two devout companions, and she at once fixed her eyes on me, as if trying to recognize me, for she had seen me only in a domino. My pious charges, delighted to be there, prayed for half an hour, then got up to leave, and the Duchess got up too. Outside of the church, she asked me if I knew her; and when I named her she asked me why I did not go to see her and if I called

on the Duchess of Benavente.[9] I said that I did not, but I assured her
that I would go to make my bow to her.

On our way to take a walk in Los Balbazes,[10] I explained to the
two cousins the nature of the Duchess's malady. Doña Ignacia, in
horror, asked me if I would keep my word to her, and I saw her
breathe again when I answered no.

I laugh when I think of certain facts which a paltry philosophy
insists on putting among problems, whereas they have been solved
ever since reason has existed. The question is put which of the two
sexes has more reason to be interested in the work of the flesh in
respect to the pleasure obtained from performing it. The answer has
always been the female sex. Homer made Jupiter and Juno dispute
on the subject;[11] Tiresias,[12] who had been a woman, handed down a
correct decision, but one which is laughable because it seems that
the two pleasures are weighed in a pair of scales. A summary
judgment has led practical minds to declare that the woman's pleasure must be greater because the feast is celebrated in her own house,
and this reason is very plausible, for she has only to let the thing be
done, without exerting herself; but what makes the truth palpable to
the mind of a physiologist is that if the woman did not have more
pleasure than the man, nature would not have her play a greater part
in the thing than he; she would not have more to do than he, and
more organs, for, taking into consideration only the sack which
women have between the rectal intestine and the bladder, which is
called the womb and which is an organ absolutely foreign to her
brain and hence independent of her reason, it is certain that one can
perfectly well conceive the birth of a human being without a man's
having sown the seed of it, but never unless a receptacle has contained it and brought it to the condition of being able to resist the air
before it sees the light.

Now it is well to reflect that this creature the womb,[13] which has
only one issue, which connects it with the vagina, becomes furious
when it finds that it is not occupied by the matter for which nature
has made it and placed it in the most crucial of all the regions of the
female body. It has an instinct which does not listen to reason; and if
the individual in which it is situated opposes its will it raises the devil
and inflicts most violent disorders on the tyrant who will not satisfy
it; the hunger to which it is subject is far worse than canine;[14] if the
woman does not give it the food it demands through the channel
which she alone controls, it often becomes furious and so gains an
ascendancy over her which no strength can resist. It threatens her

with death, it makes her an andromaniac like the Duchess I have named, another Duchess whom I knew in Rome twenty-five years ago, two great Venetian ladies, and twenty more, who all together led me to conclude that the womb is an animal so self-willed, so irrational, so untamable that a wise woman, far from opposing its whims, should defer to them, humbling herself and submitting by an act of virtue to the law to which God had subjected her at her birth. Yet this ferocious organ is susceptible to a degree of management; it is not malicious except when a fanatical woman irritates it: to one such it gives convulsions; another it drives mad; another it turns into a mirror or a monster of piety, St. Theresa,[15] St. Agreda;[16] and it makes a quantity of Messalinas,[17] who, however, are not more unfortunate than the innumerable women who spend their nights half sleeping, half awake, holding in their arms St. Anthony of Padua,[18] St. Aloysius Gonzaga,[19] St. Ignatius,[20] and the Infant Jesus. It is to be noted that these poor unfortunates tell everything in confession to the priest or the monk who governs their consciences; and that very rarely does the sacred tyrant disabuse them. He fears to uproot the plant by cultivating it.

After examining all these evils to which we men are not subject, I ask if it is to be presumed that Nature *semper sibi consona* ("always in conformity with herself"),[21] never in error in her reactions and her compensations, has not given the female sex a pleasure equal in intensity to the vexatious evils which are attached to it. What I can affirm is this: the pleasure which I have felt when the woman I loved made me happy was certainly great, but I know that I should not have wanted it if, to procure it, I had had to run the risk of becoming pregnant. The woman takes that risk even after she has experienced pregnancy several times; so she finds that the pleasure is worth the pain. After all this examination I ask myself if I would consent to be born again as a woman, and, curiosity aside, I answer no. I have enough other pleasures as a man which I could not have as a woman, and which make me prefer my sex to the other. However, I admit that, to have the great privilege of being reborn, I would be satisfied, and I would bind myself in writing, especially today, to be born again not only as a woman but as an animal of any species; provided, of course, that I should be reborn with my memory, for without that it would no longer be I.

At Los Balbazes we ate ices. My two young ladies returned to my lodging very well satisfied with the pleasure I had procured them that day without offending the Lord God, whom they loved with all their hearts, despite his forbidding them to love a man who was not their husband. Doña Ignacia, whom I loved very much, and who was such as to be loved by the most fastidious of men, delighted that she had spent the whole day in my company without my making any attempt on her, but apparently fearing that I would not observe the same restraint at supper, asked me to have her cousin sup with us; I consented, and even with pleasure. The cousin was as stupid as she was ugly, her one quality was that she was kind and sympathetic; she was the same age as Doña Ignacia; after she had confided to me that she had told her all that had happened between us, I did not mind her being present at our meetings; she could be no obstacle to me. Doña Ignacia thought that I would not dare to attempt anything in her presence.

A third place had already been laid at the table, when I heard someone on the stairs. She said it was her father; I went to the door myself to ask him to come down and sup with us; he accepted with pleasure. The man was likable. The moral maxims which he uttered from time to time amused me; he made it a point of honor to parade his confidence; he believed that I loved his daughter, but in all honor, relying on my probity or on her piety; I always thought that he would have considered himself insulted and would never have left her alone with me if he had discovered that during the Carnival we had already done all that love had commanded us to do.

So it was he who kept up the conversation at table, seated beside his niece and opposite his daughter, who was next to me. It was very hot, I asked him to take off his coat so that I should be free to do likewise, and to persuade his daughter to sup as if she were in her own room, and, so far as his daughter was concerned, he managed it without too much difficulty, for she had a very beautiful bosom, but he had his hands full getting his niece to do the same thing; she finally gave in, very much ashamed to display nothing but bones under a dark skin; but I did her the kindness never to look at her. Doña Ignacia told her father how much she had enjoyed the adoration at Nuestra Señora de Atocha, and our visit to Los Balbazes, then she told him that she had seen the Duchess of Villadarias, who had invited me to call on her. At that the worthy man began discoursing on the lady's malady in a jesting vein, and mentioned a number of cases, which he and I discussed at length, and which the two cousins pretended not to understand. The good wine from La Mancha kept us at table for two hours; he told his niece that she could sleep with his daughter in the room next to mine, in which there was a wide bed, his daughter's bed in her room upstairs being very narrow and the night being torrid. I told them it would be an honor. Doña Ignacia blushed and said to her father that it would not be proper, for the room was separated from mine only by a door of which the upper half was glazed. I looked at Don Diego and smiled.

The worthy man then treated his daughter to a harangue which almost made me laugh. He reproached her with her pride, her maliciousness, her piety, her suspicious nature. He said that I must be at least twenty years older than she, and that her suspicion was a greater sin than any that she could have committed by some small amorous favor which she might have brought herself to grant.

"I am sure," he said, "that on Sunday you will forget to accuse yourself of the sin of having suspected that Don Jaime was capable of doing anything improper."

She looked at me, asked me to excuse her, and said that she would go to bed where we were. The cousin said nothing against it, and the father went upstairs very well pleased to have given me another proof of his nobility.

I decided to punish myself in order to exacerbate the love of Doña Ignacia, who loved me and who had perhaps determined on a resistance which would have grieved me. I bade them good night in the sweetest of terms, assuring them that they could be at their ease, and I went to my room, where I at once got into bed after putting out my candle. But I at once got up again to see if they might not take advantage of the opportunity to display their secret beauties, which they had no need to suspect that I was observing. The ugly cousin talked in a low voice to Doña Ignacia, who was already about to take off her petticoat, and a moment later she blew out the candle. I went to bed. The next morning at six o'clock I get up, and through the glass panes I see the bed made and the room tidied; not a sign of the two cousins. It was the third day of Whitsun week, they had certainly gone to mass at La Soledad.

Doña Ignacia came home alone at ten o'clock, I was writing, being dressed and ready to go out to mass at eleven. She told me that she had spent three hours in church with her cousin, whom she had left at her door.

"I imagine you went to confession."

"No. I went to it on Sunday, and I will go next Sunday too."

"I am delighted that your confession will not be longer on my account."

"You are mistaken."

"Mistaken! I understand you. Let me tell you that I will not be a party to our damning ourselves for mere desires. I did not come to your house either to torment you or to become a martyr. What you did with me on the last day of the Carnival made me fall completely in love with you, and you horrify me when I think that my affection and yours have become something of which you repent. I spent a very bad night, and I must take care of my health. I must think of forgetting you, and I must begin by avoiding your presence. I will keep your house, but tomorrow I will begin to lodge elsewhere. Believe me, if you know your religion as you should, you must approve of my decision. Inform your confessor of it on Sunday, and you will see that he will approve of it."

"What you say is true, but I cannot consent to it. It is for you to say if you will leave me, I will bear it in silence; I will let my father say what he will, but I tell you that I shall be the unhappiest girl in all Madrid."

After these words she lowered her beautiful eyes, she shed tears, and she touched my heart.

"Doña Ignacia, I love you, and I hope that the passion you have inspired in me will not be the cause of my damnation; I can neither see you without loving you nor love you without giving you the proofs of it which love imperiously orders me to give you in the way which my happiness demands. If I go away, you say that you will be unhappy, and I cannot bring myself to do it; if I remain and you do not change your behavior, it is I who will be unhappy and who will even lose my health. Now tell me what I must do. Am I to go or to stay? Choose."

"Stay."

"Then you will be kind and loving to me, as you were before, perhaps for my misfortune."

"Alas! I have had to repent of it and to promise *God* that I would not succumb to it again. I tell you to stay because I am sure that in a week or ten days we will become so used to each other that I will love you only as a father or a brother, and you will be able to clasp me in your arms as if I were your sister or your daughter."

"And you say you are sure of that?"

"Yes, my dear friend, sure of it."

"You are deceiving yourself."

"Let me deceive myself. Will you believe that I am happy in deceiving myself?"

"Good God! What do I hear? I see that it is true. Oh, ill-omened piety!"

"Why 'ill-omened'?"

"Nothing, my dear friend; it would take me too long, and I might endanger—— Let us say no more about it. I will remain in your house."

I went out unfeignedly distressed, more on the girl's account than on mine, though I saw myself cheated of what she would have granted me if she had not been under the domination of a misunderstood religion. I saw that I must get her out of my head, for even if I had the luck to enjoy her again one day, taking her by surprise at some moment when my words or my caresses had troubled her soul, Sunday would come, and a new promise to her confessor would send her back to me sullen and intractable. She admitted that she loved me, and she hoped she could come to love me in a different way. A monstrous desire, which can exist in a sincere soul only if it is the slave of a religion which makes it see crime where nature cannot allow crime to be.

I return home at noon, and Don Diego thinks he is pleasing me by dining with me. His daughter does not come down until the dessert. I ask her to sit down, politely, but gloomily and coldly. Don Diego asks her if I had got up during the night to go to her bed, he laughs at her, she replies that she had not insulted me by the slightest suspicion and that her hesitation had been only from force of habit. I put an end to her explanations by praising her modesty and assuring her that she would have reason to guard herself against me if the laws of duty did not have more power over me than the desires inspired in me by her charms. Don Diego pronounced this declaration of love sublime and worthy of a knight of the ancient Round Table. I had to laugh. His daughter told him that I was mocking her, and he replied that he was sure I was not and that he even believed I had known her for some time before I came to his house to ask to take her to the ball. At that she swore he was wrong.

"You have sworn it in vain," I said. "Your father knows more about it than you do."

"What! You had seen me? But where?"

"At La Soledad, when you had received the Blessed Sacrament and were coming out of the church after the mass with your young cousin, whom you met at the door. I followed you at a distance, and you can guess the rest."

Doña Ignacia was as dumbfounded as her father was triumphant and proud of his perspicacity. He said that he was going *a los toros* ("to the bullfights"), that it was a delightful day, and that one must go early, for all Madrid would be there. I had never been to a bullfight, he advises me to go, and he tells his daughter to go with me. She asks me fondly if her company will give me pleasure. I reply that it will, but on condition that she will take her cousin with her, for I was in love with her. Her father bursts out laughing; his daughter says she believes it; she sends for her, and we go to the great amphitheater[22] outside the Puerta de Alcalá, which was to be the scene of the magnificent and cruel festival which is the delight of the nation. There was no time to lose. Nearly all the boxes were either occupied or engaged. We took places in one in which there were only two ladies, one of whom, to my amusement, was the same Duchess of Villadarias whom we had seen the day before at the Atocha. My young ladies sit in front, as was only right, and I on a higher bench directly behind the Duchess, who thus had her head between my knees.

She compliments me in French on the fortunate chance which made us meet at churches and spectacles. Doña Ignacia was beside her, she praises her, she asks me if she is my mistress or my wife, and I reply that she is a beauty for whom I sighed in vain. She laughs, she refuses to believe it, and she begins talking to Doña Ignacia and treating her to the most charming sallies on love, supposing that she is as well versed in the subject as herself. She whispers to her, the other blushes, the Duchess becomes ardent, she laughs heartily, she tells me that she is the most beautiful young lady in Madrid, she says that she will not ask me who she is, but that she will be happy if I will go to dine in her house in the country with the delightful girl. I promise to go, for I cannot do otherwise, but I decline to set a day. However, she makes me promise that I will visit her the next afternoon at four o'clock. What terrified me was that she said she would be alone. It indicated a formal assignation—with all its consequences; she was pretty, but she was too notorious; my visit would have occasioned too much talk. The bullfight began, and with it silence fell, for the spectacle absorbs all the attention of the true Spaniard.

A bull comes out of a small door in a fury, and swiftly enters the arena, then stops and looks to right and left, as if to discover who can be challenging it. It sees a man on horseback who gallops toward it with a long lance in his hand; the bull runs to meet him, and the *picadero*[23] gives it a thrust of his lance, avoiding it; the angered bull pursues him, and if it has not plunged one of its horns into the horse's belly at the first encounter it does so at the second or the third or the fourth, and often at each of them, so that the horse runs about the arena spilling out and dragging its entrails, covering the ground with the blood which spurts from its wounds, until it falls dead. It is seldom that the bull receives a lance thrust so well placed that it drops dead on the spot. When that happens those who preside over the festival grant the bull to the brave and skillful *picadero* who has killed him.

It very often happens that a bull in its rage kills the horse and its rider. This atrocity is watched without compunction; it makes the foreigner shudder. After one bull, another is sent in, as well as another horse. What distressed me at this barbarous spectacle, which I attended several times, is that the horse, with which I sympathized far more than with the bull, was always sacrificed, slaughtered by the cowardice of its wretched rider. What I admired in the cruel spectacle was the nimbleness and daring of the Spaniards who run about the arena on foot against the raging bull, which, though held back by men who control it with ropes, nevertheless does not fail to attack now one, now another of those who wound it and who then escape its fury without ever turning their backs to it. These bold men have no defense but an unfolded black cloak fastened to the end of a pike. When they see that the bull is ready to charge at them, they hold out the pike, showing the bull the spread cloak; the outwitted animal then turns from the man to charge at the cloak, and the challenger escapes with astonishing agility. He runs, turning somersaults and making dangerous leaps, sometimes jumping over the barriers. This occupies the spectator and may give him some pleasure, but, taking everything into consideration, the spectacle struck me as gloomy and terrifying. It is expensive. The receipts often come to four or five thousand pistoles. In every city in Spain there is an amphitheater built for these combats. When the King is in Madrid the whole Court attends except himself, who prefers hunting. Carlos III went hunting every day of the year except Good Friday.

On the way back to my apartment the two cousins thanked me endlessly. I kept the ugly girl to supper and she remained to spend the night, as on the day before; but Don Diego dined out and our supper was a sad occasion, for, being in a bad humor, I could find nothing amusing to say. Doña Ignacia too became gloomy and thoughtful when, on her asking if I would really go to see the Duchess, I replied that it would be bad manners on my part not to go.

"We will go to dine with her in the country one day too," I said.

"Certainly not!"

"Why?"

"Because she is mad. She whispered things to me at which I should have taken offense if I had not reflected that she thought she was doing me honor by treating me as her equal."

We rose from table and, having dismissed Felipe, we sat on the balcony to wait for Don Diego and also to enjoy a little breeze which, in the hot weather we were having, was delicious. Seated beside each other on the tiles, enlivened by the good food we had eaten, excited by love, invited by the mysterious darkness which, without preventing lovers from seeing, makes them hope that they will be seen by no one, we looked at each other amorously. I let my arm fall on Doña Ignacia, and I pressed my lips to her beautiful mouth. Letting me clasp her more closely, she asked me if I should go to see the Duchess the next day.

"No," I said, "if you promise me you will not go to confession Sunday."

"What will my father confessor say if I do not go?"

"Nothing, if he knows his business. But let us discuss it a little, I beg you."

We were both in the most decisive posture, and the cousin, who had seen us ready to surrender ourselves to love, had retired to the corner of the balcony, where she stood with her back to us. Without stirring, without changing my position, without drawing back my hand, which was enjoying the palpitation of her amorous heart, I ask her if at this moment she is thinking of repenting on Sunday of the tender sin she is already prepared to commit.

"No, I am not thinking now of the confusion I shall feel when I confess it; but if you make me think of it, I reply that I shall certainly confess it."

"And after you have confessed it will you continue to love me, as you do at this moment?"

"I must hope that God will grant me the strength not to offend him again."

"I must warn you, my dear friend, that if you continue to love me God will not grant you the strength. But since I foresee that, on your side, you will endeavor to deserve that grace, I am in despair, for I foresee too that at least on Sunday evening you will refuse to commit the sweet sin with me which we are about to commit at this moment."

"Alas, my dear friend! That is true! But why think of it now?"

"My dear heart, your quietism is a far more heinous sin than the work of the flesh which love makes so precious to us. I cannot be your accomplice in a sin which my religion forbids, despite the fact that I adore you and that I am at this moment the happiest of men. One thing or the other, then. Either promise me that you will stop going to confession for as long as I remain in Madrid, or allow me now to make myself the unhappiest of mortals by retiring, for I cannot truly surrender myself to love when I am thinking of the pain which your resistance will cause me on Sunday."

While preaching her this terrible sermon, I tenderly clasped her in my arms, giving her every kind of caress in all the effervescence of love; but before coming to the act I again asked her if she promised me she would abstain from going to confession on Sunday.

"Oh, my dear friend, now you are cruel, you make me unhappy. I cannot in conscience promise you that."

At this reply I become motionless, I proceed no further, I deliberately make her unhappy in order to put her in a condition to be perfectly happy in the future; it costs me an effort, but I bear everything, being certain that my pain will not last long. Doña Ignacia, whom I had nevertheless not pushed away, is in despair to see me inactive; modesty forbids her to urge me openly; but she allows herself to redouble her caresses, to reproach me with seduction and cruelty. Just then her cousin turns and tells us that Don Diego is entering the house.

We having returned to a decent position, and the cousin having sat down beside me, Don Diego paid his respects to me, then he left, wishing us a good night's sleep. I did the same in the saddest tone to the charming Doña Ignacia, whom I adored, whom I pitied, and whom I had to treat in this way in order to make her as happy as I was.

After putting out my candles I spent half an hour spying on her through the glass panes. Sitting in an armchair with a look of the utmost dejection, she never answered a word to all that her cousin said to her, which I could not hear. The cousin having gone to bed, I thought she would make up her mind to come to mine, and I got into it; but I was mistaken. The next morning very early they left my room, and Don Diego came down at noon to dine with me and to tell me that his daughter was suffering from a very bad headache so that she had not even gone to mass. She was in bed in a state of collapse.

"She must be persuaded to eat something."

"On the contrary. She will be well this evening if she eats nothing, and she will sup with you."

After taking a siesta, I went to keep her company, sitting down beside her and, for three whole hours, saying to her everything that such a lover as I could say to a girl whom he must force to change her behavior in order to make her happy; and she kept her eyes closed through it all, never answering me, only sighing when I said something very touching to her. I left her to go for a walk in the Prado San Jerónimo,[24] telling her that if she did not come down to sup with me I should take it that she no longer wanted to see me. Frightened by my threat, she came to table when I no longer expected her, but pale and weak. She ate very little, and she never said a word, because she was convinced, and she did not know what to say to me. The tears which now and again welled from her beautiful eyes, though her pretty face never underwent the least contraction, pierced my soul. The pain she caused me was incredible; I thought I could not bear it, for I loved her, and I had no diversion in Madrid which could make up to me for this abstinence. Before going up to her room, she asked me if I had paid the Duchess the visit I had promised her, and she seemed less sad when I told her I had not gone there, of which Felipe could assure her, for it was he who had delivered the letter in which I asked the lady to excuse me for not being able to have the honor of paying my court to her that day.

"But you will go some other day."

"No, my dear friend, for I see that it would grieve you."

I tenderly kissed Doña Ignacia, sighing, and she left me as unhappy as she was herself.

I saw very well that what I demanded of her was far too much; but I had reason to hope that I should bring her to terms, for I had had proof of her great inclination to love. I did not think it was with God that I was vying for her, but with her confessor. It was she herself who had told me that she would feel in a false position toward her confessor if she stopped going to confession; and, full of probity and feelings of Spanish honor, she could neither bring herself to deceive her confessor nor resolve to combine her love with what she believed she owed to her religion. She thought rightly.

On Friday and Saturday she did no more and no less. Her father, who had seen that we were in love with each other, made her dine and sup with me, counting on her sense of duty and on mine. He did not come down except when I sent him an invitation to do so. On Saturday evening his daughter left me more sadly than ever, turning her head away when I wanted to give her the kiss which I thought would assure her of my constancy. I saw what was in the wind. She had to go to receive the Blessed Sacrament the next day. I admired the candor of her soul, I pitied her, seeing the battle which the two passions must be fighting within her. I began to feel afraid, and to repent that I had acted in a way which would make me lose the whole because I had not been content with a part.

Wanting to convince myself of the thing with my own eyes, the next morning I get up early, I dress unaided, and I wait for her to go out. I knew that she would go to fetch her cousin; I leave the house after her, I go straight to La Soledad, and I take my stand behind the sacristy door, from where I saw everyone who was in the church and where no one could see me. A quarter of an hour later I see the two cousins come in, pray together, rise, and separate. One goes to wait near one confessional, the other near another. I watched only Doña Ignacia. When her turn came she entered the box, and I saw the confessor, after giving an absolution to his right, bend his head to the left to listen to Doña Ignacia. The confession bored me, revolted me, for it never ended; what could she be saying to him? I saw the confessor speaking to his penitent from time to time. I was on the verge of leaving. It had been going on for an hour. I had heard three masses. At last I see her rise. I had already seen her ugly cousin at the high altar, receiving the Eucharist.

Doña Ignacia, with her eyes lowered and the look of a saint, goes and kneels on my side of the church, where I cannot see her; I suppose she is hearing the mass which is being said at the altar four paces from her. I expected to see her, at the end of the mass, at the high altar to receive the Sacrament, but not a bit of it. I see her rejoin her cousin at the church door and leave. "It is love. She made a sincere confession," I said to myself, "she confessed her passion, her confessor demanded sacrifices of her which she could not promise him, and the monster, true to his calling, refused her absolution. I am lost. What will happen? My peace, and the peace of this worthy girl, truly devout and ardently in love, demand that I leave her father's home. Wretch! I should have contented myself with having her from time to time by surprise. Today I shall see her dining with me in tears. I must deliver her from this hell."

I go home extremely sad, extremely displeased with myself, and I dismiss the hairdresser because I want to go to bed, I tell the Biscayan cook not to serve me dinner until I call her; I hear Doña Ignacia come in, I do not want to see her, I lock my door, I get into bed, and I sleep until one o'clock. I get up, I order dinner served and send word that the father or the daughter is to come down and dine with me, and I see the daughter, wearing a black bodice with silk ribbons at every seam. In all Europe there is not a more seductive garment when the woman has a beautiful bosom and a narrow waist. Seeing her so pretty, noticing her serene manner, I cannot keep from complimenting her. Not expecting to see her in this mood, I forget the kiss which she had refused me the night before, I embrace her, and I find her as gentle as a lamb. But Felipe was coming down, I say nothing to her, and we sit down at table. I reflect on the change, I weigh it, I conclude that the Spanish girl has jumped the ditch; she has made up her mind. Now I am happy; but I must say nothing, pretend to know nothing, and watch her come to me.

Without concealing anything of the content which was flooding my soul, I talk to her of love whenever Felipe leaves me free, and I see her not only untrammeled but ardent. Before we get up from table she asks me if I still love her, and, in ecstasy at my reply, she asks me to take her to *los toros*. Quick, the hairdresser! I put on a taffeta coat with Lyons embroidery[25] which I had never worn, and we go to the bullfight on foot, not having the patience to wait for my carriage and being afraid that we shall not find places; but we find two in a big box, and she is glad not to see me, as she had done the time before, next to her rival. After the bullfight, the day being delightful, she wants me to take her to the Prado, where we find all the most fashionable people of both sexes in Madrid. Holding my arm, she seemed proud to display herself as mine, and she filled me with joy.

But along comes the Venetian Ambassador, on foot as we were, with his favorite Manuzzi, and meets us. They had arrived from Aranjuez that day, and I knew nothing about it. They accost me with all the Spanish ceremoniousness, and the Ambassador pays me a compliment which is infinitely flattering to Doña Ignacia, who pretends not to have heard it. After accompanying us for a time, he leaves, saying that he will be glad if I will come to dine with him the next day.

Toward nightfall we go to eat ices, and we return to the house, where we find Don Diego, who congratulates his daughter on being in a good humor and on having spent an enjoyable day with me. I ask him to sup with us, he accepts, and he amuses us with countless little tales of gallantry, each of which reveals more of his noble character. But before he goes up to his room these are the exact words, literally translated, with which he surprised me:

"Amigo Don Jaime, I leave you to enjoy the coolness of the night with my daughter on the balcony, I am delighted that you love her, and I assure you that, to become my son-in-law, you have only to do what is necessary to enable me to declare myself certain *de vuestra nobleza* ['of your nobility']."[26]

"I should be only too happy, my charming friend," I said to his daughter as soon as he left us alone, "if that were possible, but I must tell you that in my country only those are styled noble whose birth gives them the right to govern the State. I should be noble if I had been born in Spain; but such as I am, I adore you, and I have reason to believe that you will make me entirely happy here and now."

"Yes, my dear friend, entirely; but I want to be so too. No infidelity."

"None. On my word of honor."

"Come, then," she said. "Let us shut the door to the balcony."

"Let us wait a quarter of an hour. Put out the candles, and do not shut the door. Tell me, my angel, whence comes[27] my happiness? I should never have expected it."

"If it is a happiness, you owe it to a tyranny which was driving me to despair. God is good, and he does not want me to become my own executioner, I am sure. When I told my confessor that it was absolutely impossible for me to stop loving you, and at the same time possible for me not to do anything wrong with you, he told me that I could not have such confidence in myself, and the more so since I had already been weak. That being the case, he wanted me to promise him that I would not be alone with you again. I told him that I could not promise him that, and he refused to absolve me. I suffered that indignity for the first time in my life with a firmness of mind of which I did not believe myself capable, and, putting myself in the hands of God, I said: 'Lord, thy will be done.' While hearing mass, I made my decision. As long as you love me, I will be yours alone, and when you leave Spain I will find another confessor. What comforts me is that my soul is perfectly at peace. My cousin, to whom I told everything, is astonished; but she is very unintelligent. She does not understand that I am led astray only for the moment."

After this declaration, which made me see all the beauty of her soul, I took her in my arms and I led her to my bed, where she remained with me, free from any scruples, until the first rays of dawn. She left me more in love than ever.

[* * *]

This was the high point of Casanova's stay in Madrid. From then on it was only a matter of time before his life followed its familiar downward spiral of intrigue, scandal and financial embarrassment. Although he had taken his usual care to cultivate the great men of Madrid, the Spanish authorities, aware of his reputation, had remained aloof, while the Venetian Ambassador, Mocenigo, himself in a delicate situation, was careful to keep their relationship on an informal footing.

Disaster struck when Casanova alienated his main ally at the embassy, the Ambassador's lover Manuzzi. Casanova and Manuzzi had become involved with a small-time card-sharp passing himself off as the Baron de Fraiture. For reasons of his own, De Fraiture persuaded Manuzzi that Casanova had betrayed him by revealing that Manuzzi was not really a count—and that, by implication, his other credentials were dubious. Given Manuzzi's relationship with the Ambassador in a country which was fiercely hostile to homosexuality, he could not afford a scandal of any kind. He dropped Casanova forthwith. Manuzzi's hostility closed the doors of the Venetian embassy, the withdrawal of the embassy's unofficial support alarmed the authorities, and Casanova was soon on his way to the Pyrenees.

Many things were to happen before he got there. In Valencia he began an affair with the Viceroy's mistress, the tempestuous Nina, who impressed even Casanova with the extravagance of her behavior; in Barcelona he crossed swords once more with the sinister Ascanio Pogomas, who managed to have him imprisoned; and before leaving Spain he narrowly escaped assassination by unknown assailants.

Perhaps in search of a quieter life, he crossed the border into France and settled for a while in Aix. His stay at a tavern in that city coincided with the arrival of a Spanish cardinal on his way to Rome for the election of a new Pope—a less significant event for Casanova than another encounter in the tavern.

CHAPTER VI

My stay in Aix-en-Provence; serious illness;
the unknown woman who takes care of me.
The Marquis d'Argens. Cagliostro. My depar-
ture. Letter from Henriette. Marseilles.
History of La Nina. Nice. Turin. Lugano.
Madame de . . . .

My room being separated from His Eminence's only by a very thin
partition, I heard him at supper severely reprimanding someone
who must be his principal servant and in charge of their journey.
The reason which provoked the Cardinal's just anger was that the
man economized at dinner and supper as if his master were
the poorest beggar in Spain.

"My Lord, I do not economize at all, but it is impossible to spend
more, unless I make the innkeepers charge me twice the proper
prices of the meals they give you, which you yourself declare to
abound in everything you can want in the way of game, fish,
and wines."

"That may be so, but with a little ingenuity you could send
messengers ahead to order meals in places where I then would not
stop, and which would be paid for nevertheless, you could have
dishes prepared for twelve when we would only be six, and above all
you could see to it that three tables are always served, one for us, one
for my officers, and the third for my servants. I see here that you tip
the postilions only twenty sous; I blush for it; in addition to what is
prescribed for the guides, you must give at least an écu each time,
and when you are given change from a louis you must leave it on the
table. I have seen you put it in your pocket. That sort of thing is
beggarly. It will be said at Versailles, at Madrid, at Rome—for
everything becomes known—that Cardinal de la Cerda is a beggar
or a miser. Understand that I am neither. Either stop dishonoring
me, or leave."

Such is the character of the great Spanish nobleman; but, all in
all, the Cardinal was right. I saw him set off the next day. What a
man! Not only was he short, ill-built, tanned, but his face was so
ugly and so common-looking that I understood his need to make
himself respected by lavishness and to distinguish himself by his

1148

decorations, for otherwise he would have been taken for a groom. Any man who has a revolting exterior must do everything to keep the eyes which see him from examining his person. External ornaments are an excellent remedy for this sorry gift of nature. Display is the only weapon which the ugly command to fight beauty.

The next day I inquired for the Marquis d'Argens.[1] I was told that he was in the country, visiting his brother the Marquis d'Éguilles,[2] President of the Parlement; and I went there. The Marquis, famous rather for the unvarying friendship with which the late Frederick II[3] honored him than for his writings,[4] which no one reads any longer, was already old. Very voluptuous, a perfect gentleman, amusing, amiable, a determined Epicurean, he lived with the actress Cochois,[5] whom he had married and who had proved worthy of it. As a wife, she considered it her duty to be her husband's first servant. In any case, the Marquis d'Argens was deeply learned, thoroughly versed in Greek and Hebrew, endowed by nature with a most excellent memory, and hence full of erudition. He received me very well in consequence of what his friend Lord Marischal[6] had written to him, he at once presented me to his wife and to President d'Éguilles, his brother, an illustrious member of the Parlement of Aix, moderately rich, a lover of literature, whose virtuous life followed rather from his character than from his religion—which is saying a great deal, for he was sincerely devout, though a man of intelligence. A friend to the Jesuits to the point of himself being a Jesuit "of the short robe,"[7] as it is called, he dearly loved his brother, pitying him and hoping that efficacious grace would bring him back to the bosom of the Church. His brother smilingly encouraged him to hope, and they both took care not to offend each other by talking of religion. I was presented to the numerous company, which consisted of relatives, both men and women, all of them amiable and polished, as are all the Provençal nobility, which possesses these attributes in the highest degree. There was a small stage on which plays were performed, the fare was excellent, there were strolls in the garden despite the season. In Provence winter is unpleasant only when it is windy; unfortunately a north wind blows very often.

A lady from Berlin, the widow of a nephew of the Marquis d'Argens, was there with her brother, whose name was Gotzkowski.[8] Very young and very gay, he had thrown himself into all the pleasure afforded by the President's house, without paying any attention to all the religious devotions which were performed every day. A professed heretic when he happened to think of the Church, and playing the flute in his room when everyone in the house was attending the mass which the Jesuit confessor of the whole family celebrated every day, he laughed at everything; but the same was not true of the young widow his sister. Not only had she turned Catholic, she had become so devout that the whole household considered her a saint. It had been the Jesuit's doing. She was not more than twenty-two years of age. I learned from her brother that her husband, whom she adored, dying in her arms and lucid until his last moment, like all who die of consumption, had said to her, as his last words, that he could not hope to see her again in eternity unless she made up her mind to become a Catholic.

His words having thus been engraved in her memory, she had determined she would leave Berlin to visit her relatives on her late husband's side. No one had dared to oppose her wish. She persuaded her nineteen-year-old brother to accompany her, and, as soon as she was in Aix and her own mistress, she confided her vocation to her relatives, all of them devout believers. The disclosure had brought joy to the house; she was made much of, she was caressed, she was assured that there was no other way for her to see her husband again *in body* and in soul, the Jesuit had been able to "proselytize" her, as the Marquis d'Argens said to me, without needing to "catechumenize" her, for she had already been baptized and she had abjured. This budding saint was ugly. Her brother at once became my friend. It was he who, coming to Aix every day, introduced me at every house.

We were at least thirty at table. Excellent fare without profusion, the tone of good society, restrained and polished conversation which excluded not only equivocal allusions to the game of love but anything which could bring it to mind. I noticed that when such a remark escaped the Marquis d'Argens all the women made wry faces, and the father confessor quickly changed the subject. I should never have supposed that the man was either a Jesuit or a confessor, for, dressing as an abbé does in the country, he looked and acted neither part. The Marquis d'Argens had told me what he was. However, his presence in no way damped my natural gaiety. I told in decent terms the story of the image of the Blessed Virgin giving suck to the Infant Jesus, to which the Spaniards lost all their devotion when the scrupulous parish priest had her bosom covered by too opaque a veil. I cannot explain what it was about the tone I gave my narrative which made all the ladies laugh. Their laughter so displeased the Jesuit that he took it upon himself to inform me that it was not permissible to tell stories in public which could bear an indecent interpretation. I thanked him by bowing, and the Marquis d'Argens, to change the subject, asked me what was the Italian name for a large force-meat pie which Madame d'Argens was serving and which the whole company declared excellent. I replied that we should call it *una crostata*, but that I did not know the name for the *béatilles* ("titbits") with which it was filled. They were little sausages, sweetbreads, mushrooms, artichoke hearts, fatted goose livers, and I know not what else. The Jesuit declared that by calling them *béatilles* I was making a mock of eternal bliss.[9] I could not keep from laughing loudly, and Monsieur d'Éguilles saw fit to come to my defense by saying that in good French *béatilles* was the generic term for all titbits of the sort.

Having thus differed from the director of his conscience, the Marquis wisely thought it best to talk of something else, and unfortunately he put the fat in the fire by asking me what Cardinal I thought would be made Pope.

"I would wager," I replied, "that it will be Father Ganganelli,[10] for he is the only Cardinal in the conclave who is a monk."

"By what necessity must it be a monk who is elected Pope?"

"Because only a monk is capable of committing the excess which Spain demands of the new Pontiff."

"You mean the suppression of the Jesuit order?"

"Exactly."

"Her demand will not be met."

"I hope so, for in the Jesuits I love my teachers; but I greatly fear it. I have seen a terrible letter. But aside from that, Cardinal Ganganelli will be Pope for a reason which will make you laugh but which is nevertheless very strong."

"What reason is that? Tell us, and we will laugh."

"He is the only Cardinal who doesn't wear a wig, and observe that since that Holy See has existed no Pope has ever worn a wig."

Since I said all this playfully, there was much laughter; but afterwards I was called on to speak seriously concerning the suppression of the order, and, when I repeated all that I had learned from the Abate Pinzi,[11] I saw the Jesuit turn pale.

"The Pope," he said, "cannot suppress the Jesuit order."

"Apparently, Abate, you did not study under the Jesuits, for their dictum is that the Pope can do everything, *et aliquid pluris* ['and somewhat more']."

Everyone thereupon thought that I did not know I was talking to a Jesuit; he did not answer me, and we spoke of other things. I was urged to stay for the performance of *Polyeucte*;[12] but I excused myself. I returned to Aix with Gotzkowski, who told me his sister's whole story and acquainted me with the characters of several members of Monsieur d'Éguilles's circle, with the result that I saw I could never adapt myself to it. But for this young man, who introduced me to some very agreeable people, I should have gone to Marseilles. Assemblies, suppers, balls, and very pretty girls made me spend the whole of the Carnival and part of Lent in Aix, always with Gotzkowski, who went back and forth from the country nearly every day to join me in parties of pleasure.

I had presented a copy of Homer's *Iliad* to Monsieur d'Argens, who knew Greek as well as he knew French, and an *Argenis*[13] in Latin to his adopted daughter,[14] who knew Latin. My *Iliad* had Porphyry's[15] scholia; it was a rare edition and very well bound. He had come to Aix to thank me, and I had to go again to dine in the country. Returning to Aix in an open chaise against a very strong north wind and without an overcoat, I arrived there chilled to the bone; and instead of going to bed I went with Gotzkowski to call on a woman who had a daughter fourteen years of age and beautiful as a star, who defied all the connoisseurs to make her see the light. Gotzkowski had tried the thing several times and had never succeeded; I laughed at him because I knew it was buffoonery[16] on the minx's part, and I went there with him that evening, determined to succeed, as I had done in England and at Metz. [. . .]

So we both set about the enterprise like seasoned warriors, the girl being at our disposal and, far from resisting, saying that she asked nothing better than that some man should rid her of her tiresome burden. Having at once seen that the difficulty we encountered came from her holding herself in a wrong posture, I should either have beaten her, as I had done to one of her sort in Venice twenty-five years earlier, or else have left; but not a bit of it, like a fool I determined to triumph over her by force, imagining that I was raping her. The age for exploits of that sort was long behind me. After vainly exhausting myself for two hours on end, I returned to my inn, leaving my friend there. I went to bed with a very severe pain in my right side, and after sleeping for six hours I woke feeling as ill as possible. Pleurisy had set in. An old physician who took care of me refused to bleed me. A violent cough began to torment me; the next morning I began spitting blood, and the disease made such strides in six or seven days that I confessed and received the last sacraments. It was on the tenth day, after I had been in a torpor for three, that the skillful old physician vouched for my life and assured all those who were concerned for me that I would recover; but I did not stop spitting blood until the eighteenth day. I then began a convalescence which lasted three weeks, and which I found more trying than the illness, for a sick person suffers but is not bored. To be bored without doing anything takes intelligence, and an invalid has almost none. During the whole of this acute illness I was cared for and waited on day and night by a woman whom I neither knew nor had any idea who had sent her to me. In the state of apathy in which I was, I never tried to find out where she had come from; I saw that I was served to perfection, I waited to be cured in order to reward her and dismiss her. She was not old; but she was not of a figure to make me think of amusing myself; she had continued to sleep in my room until she saw that I was cured, and it was after Easter that, beginning to go out, I thought of paying her and sending her away.

When I dismissed her, well recompensed, I asked her who had sent her to nurse me, and she replied that it had been my physician. She left. Some days later I thanked the physician for having found me the woman, to whom I perhaps owed my life, and he replied that she had deceived me, for he did not know her. I asked the innkeeper's wife if she knew her, and she said she did not. No one could tell me either who the woman was or at whose instigation she had come to me. I did not learn it until I left Aix, and the reader will learn it in a quarter of an hour.

After my convalescence I did not fail to go to the post for my letters; and here is a strange piece of news which I learned by reading a letter from my brother, who wrote me from Paris in reply to the letter I had written him from Perpignan. He thanked me heartily for the letter I had written him because he had learned from it that I had not been murdered on the frontier of Catalonia.

"The person," he wrote me, "who gave me the fatal news as beyond doubt is one of your best friends, Count Manuzzi, an attaché at the Venetian Embassy."

Reading this revealed everything to me. My "best friend" had carried revenge so far as to hire three cutthroats to take my life. It was at that point that he made his first mistake. He was so sure of my death that he announced it as having already happened; if he had waited, he would have seen that, by announcing it before he was certain of it, he unmasked himself. When I came upon him in Rome two years later, and tried to convince him of his baseness, he denied everything, saying that he had received the news of it in Barcelona. [. . .]

The company at the public table being excellent, I dined and supped there every day. One day at dinner there was talk of a pair of pilgrims, a man and a woman, who had just arrived, who were Italians, who had come from Santiago de Compostela[17] on foot, and who must be persons of high rank, for, when they entered the city, they had distributed a great deal of money among the poor. The lady, we were told, was charming, only eighteen years of age; very tired, she had gone to bed at once. They were staying at our inn; we all became curious about them. As an Italian, it was for me to lead the band of us to visit the pair, who must be either fanatical zealots or rogues.

We find the female pilgrim sitting in an armchair, with the look of a person tired to exhaustion, and claiming our attention by her extreme youth, her beauty, which her melancholy increased, and a crucifix of some yellow metal, six inches long, which she held in her hands. She puts it down when we appear, and she rises to greet us graciously. The male pilgrim, who was fastening cockle shells[18] to his short cloak of black oiled cloth, does not stir; he seemed, glancing at his wife, to be telling us that we should be concerned only for her. He appeared to be five or six years older than she, he was short, well enough built, and his not unhandsome face expressed boldness, effrontery, cynicism, and deceit, in all which he differed entirely from his wife, whose countenance breathed nobility. The two strange creatures, who spoke French only well enough to make themselves understood with difficulty, showed their relief when I spoke to them in Italian. She told me that she was a native of Rome, and she did not need to tell me so, for her pretty speech assured me of it; as for him, I put him down as a Sicilian, despite his telling me that he was from Naples. His passport, dated at Rome, gave his name as Balsamo;[19] hers was Serafina Feliciani, a name which she never changed. [. . .]

She told us that she was going back to Rome with her husband, glad to have made her devotions to St. James of Compostela and to Our Lady of the Pillar,[20] having gone there on foot and returned the same way, always living on alms, having vainly sought poverty in order to have and to gain more merit in the eyes of God, whom she had so greatly offended in her lifetime.

"It was in vain," she said to me, "that I never asked for more than a copper, I was always given silver and gold, so that, to fulfill our vow, whenever we entered a city we always had to give the poor all

1154

the money we had left, which, if we had kept it, would have made us guilty of failing to trust in Eternal Providence."

She told us that her husband, who was very strong, had not suffered, but that she had endured the greatest torments, having always to travel on foot and sleep in bad beds, almost always fully dressed for fear of contracting some skin disease of which it would prove very difficult to be cured.

It seemed to me likely that she mentioned this detail only to make us curious to see the cleanliness of her skin elsewhere than on her arms and hands, whose whiteness and perfect cleanliness she let us see gratis in the meanwhile. Her face had only one defect: her slightly rheumy eyelids marred the tenderness of her beautiful blue eyes. She told us that she intended to rest for three days and then leave for Rome, traveling by way of Turin to make her devotions at the adoration of the Most Holy Sudary.[21] She knew that there were several of them in Europe, but she had been assured that the true one was the one to be seen in Turin; it was the very cloth which St. Veronica had used to wipe the sweating[22] face of our Saviour, who had left the imprint of his divine countenance on it.

We left very well pleased with the pretty pilgrim, but doubting her devotion. As for me, still weak from my illness, I formed no designs on her; but all those who were with me would gladly have supped with her, if they had thought that her favors would await them afterward. The next morning the male pilgrim came to ask me if I would rather come up to breakfast with his wife and himself, or if they should come down; it would have been impolite to answer "Neither"; so I said I should be glad if they would come down. It was at this breakfast that, when I asked him what his profession was, the pilgrim replied that it was making drawings in ink in what is called "chiaroscuro." His ability consisted only in copying an engraving, and not at all in invention; but he assured me that he excelled in his art, for he could copy any engraving so accurately that he defied anyone to find the slightest difference between the copy and the original.

"I congratulate you. It is an admirable talent, with which, since you are not rich, you can earn a good living wherever you may be pleased to settle."

"Everyone tells me that, and everyone is mistaken. With my talent a man starves. Practicing my profession, I work a whole day in Naples and Rome, and I earn only a half a testone;[23] that is not a living."

After this explanation, he showed me some fans he had decorated, than which nothing could be more beautiful. It was done with ink, and they looked as if they were engraved. To convince me, he showed me the copy he had made from a Rembrandt,[24] which, if anything, was more beautiful than the original. Yet, excellent at his craft though he was, he swears to me that it does not bring him in enough to live; but I do not believe him. He was one of these lazy geniuses who prefer a vagabond life to hard work. I offer him a louis for one of his fans, and he refuses it, begging me to accept it gratis and to take up a collection for him at the public table, for he wanted to leave on the next day but one. I accepted his present, and I promised to make the collection for him.

I got together fifty or sixty écus for him, which his wife came to receive in person at the table, where we were still sitting. Far from acting immodestly, the young woman had an air of virtue. Invited to write down her name for a chance in a lottery, she excused herself, saying that in Rome girls who were brought up to be decent and virtuous were not taught to write. Everyone laughed, except myself, for, feeling sorry for her, I did not want to see her put to shame; but the thing made me certain that she must be a peasant.

It was she who, the next morning, came to my room to ask me for a letter of recommendation for Avignon, and I immediately wrote two for her, one to Monsieur Audifret, banker, the other to the proprietor of the "Saint-Omer" inn.[25] After supper that evening she gave me back the letter to Monsieur Audifret, saying that her husband had told her that he did not need it. At the same time she urges me to examine the letter she has returned and make sure that it is the one I had given her, and after looking at it I say there is no doubt that it is the same. At that she laughs and tells me I am mistaken, for it is only a copy. I refuse to admit it. She sends upstairs for her husband, who, with my letter in his hand, convinces me of the amazing imitation, which was much more difficult than copying an engraving. I expressed my admiration, saying that he could draw great profit from his talent; but that if he was not careful it could cost him his life.

The couple left the next day. [. . .] As I write this, he is in prison, which he will never leave, and his wife is perhaps happy in a convent. I have heard that he is dead.[26]

As soon as my health was perfectly restored I went to take leave of the Marquis d'Argens at the house of President d'Éguilles. After dinner I spent three hours with the learned old man, who kept me well amused with countless anecdotes of the King of Prussia's private life, all of which would be new if I had the time and the wish to publish them. He was a monarch who had great qualities and great weaknesses, like nearly all great men; but the weaknesses were less in weight and in bulk. The King of Sweden who was assassinated[27] provoked hatred and then defied it to do its worst. He had the soul of a despot, and he had had to be one in order to satisfy his ruling passion, which was to get himself talked about and to be accounted a great man. His enemies all willingly risked death in order to deprive him of life. It would seem that he should have foreseen his fate, for his acts of oppression always drove his victims to desperation.

The Marquis d'Argens presented me with all his works.[28] When I asked him if I could really boast that I had them all, he said that I had, except the account of a period of his life which he had written in his youth[29] and allowed to be printed, and which he now regretted having written.

"Why?"

"Because with the mania of wanting to write the truth, I made myself eternally ridiculous. If the urge ever comes to you, resist it as you would a temptation; for I can assure you that you will repent, because as a gentleman you cannot write anything but the truth, and as an honest writer you are obliged not only not to leave anything that may have happened to you unrecorded, but also not to spare yourself in all the sins you have committed, while, as a sound philosopher, you must bring out all your good actions. You must blame and praise yourself by turns. All your confessions will be taken at face value, and you will not be believed when you tell truths which are to your credit. Besides all that, you will make enemies when you have to reveal secrets which will do no honor to the people who will have had dealings with you. If you do not give their names, they will be guessed, which comes to the same thing. Believe me, my friend, if a man may not talk about himself, still less may he write about himself. It is permitted only to a man whom slander forces to justify himself. Believe me: never think of writing your biography."

Convinced by his solid arguments, I promised him that I would never be guilty of that folly; nevertheless, I began my biography seven years ago, and by now I have promised myself that I will finish it, although I am already repentant. I write in the hope that my history will never be published; I flatter myself that in my last illness, grown wise at last, I will have all my notebooks burned in my presence. If that does not happen, the reader will forgive me when he learns that writing my memoirs was the only remedy I thought I could employ to keep from going mad or dying of chagrin over the vexations to which I was subjected by the scoundrels who inhabited Count Waldstein's castle[30] at Dux. By keeping myself busy writing ten or twelve hours a day, I have prevented black melancholy from killing me or driving me mad. We will speak of this when the time comes.[31]

On the day after Corpus Christi[32] I left Aix for Marseilles; but before leaving I must say something about the procession with which the feast is celebrated in every Catholic Christian city, but which at Aix-en-Provence has features so peculiar that any stranger whom they do not amaze must be a dolt. As everyone knows, at this procession the Being of Beings, displayed in body and spirit in the Eucharist and carried by the Bishop, is escorted by all the religious and secular confraternities. This is the case everywhere, and I will say no more about it. But what deserves to be observed and recorded, and what cannot but surprise, are the masquerades, the antics, and the buffoonery which are indulged in and performed. The Devil, Death, the Deadly Sins, most comically dressed, fighting one another in their rage at having to pay homage to the Creator on that day; the shouts, the catcalls, the booing of the populace deriding these personages, and the din of the songs with which the crowd mockingly hail them, playing all kinds of tricks on them, make up a spectacle far more unbridled than the Saturnalia[33] and than anything which we read was anywhere indulged in by the most frantic paganism. All the peasants from five or six leagues around are in Aix on that day to honor God. It is his feast day. God goes in procession only once a year; he has to be entertained, made to laugh on that day. This is implicitly believed, and anyone who should question it would be impious, for the Bishop, who cannot but be aware of what goes on, is himself the ringleader in it. Monsieur de Saint-Marc,[34] an important member of the Parlement, solemnly told me that it was excellent, for the day brought at least a hundred thousand francs into the city. Recognizing the cogency of his argument, I said not a word to the contrary.

During all the time I stayed in Aix, I constantly thought of Henriette.[35] Already knowing her real name, I had not forgotten the message she had sent me by Marcolina, and I was always expecting to find her at some gathering in Aix, at which I should have played toward her whatever role she wished. I several times heard her name spoken in different connections, but I took care not to question the person who had mentioned it, for fear of suggesting that I knew the lady. I always thought that she must be in the country; and, determined to pay her a visit, I had stayed on in Aix after my severe illness only in order to arrive at her house in perfect health. So I left Aix with a letter in my pocket in which I announced my arrival, intending to stop at the door of her country house, send it in to her, and not to get out of my carriage until she invited me to do so.

I had instructed the postilion accordingly. It was a league and a half before the Croix d'Or.[36] We arrive there. It was eleven o'clock. I give my letter to a man who had come to see what we wanted, and he tells me that he will send it to her.

"Madame is not here?"

"No, Monsieur. She is in Aix."

"Since when?"

"For the last six months."

"Where does she live in Aix?"

"In her town house. She will be here in three weeks to spend the summer, as she always does."

"Will you be so good as to let me write a letter?"

"You have only to get out, and I will open Madame's apartment for you. You will find everything you need there."

I get out, and no sooner have I entered the house than I am surprised to see the woman who had taken care of me during my illness.

"Do you live here?"

"Yes, Monsieur."

"Since when?"

"For the past ten years."

"And how is it that you came to nurse me?"

"If you will go upstairs, I will go up too, and I will tell you the truth."

She told me that her mistress had sent for her and had ordered her to go to the inn in which I was lying ill, to enter my room boldly, and to take care of me as if it were of her own self, and that if I should ask who had sent her she should answer that it was the physician.

"What! The physician told me he had no idea who you are."

"He may have told you the truth, and he may have been ordered by Madame to answer you as I did. I know nothing more; but I am amazed that you did not see Madame in Aix."

"It is certain that she receives no one."

"You are right, but she goes everywhere."

"It is astonishing. I must have seen her, and I cannot understand how I can have failed to recognize her. You have been with her for ten years. Has she changed? Has she had some illness which has changed her features? Has she aged?"

"On the contrary. She has put on flesh. To see her, you would think she was a woman of thirty."

"I will write to her."

She leaves; and, astonished to the point of confusion by this extraordinary situation, I consider if I can, if I should, go to Aix at once, that very day. "She is at home; she receives no one; who can prevent her from receiving me? If she does not receive me, I will go away; but Henriette still loves me; she sent me a nurse; she is hurt by my not having recognized her; she knows that I have left Aix, she is sure that I am here at this moment, and she is waiting for the last act of the play to bring me to her house. Shall I go, or shall I write to her?"

I decide to write and to tell her that I will wait in Marseilles for her answer, to be addressed to me at the post office. I give my letter to my nurse, and money to send it at once by express messenger, and I go to dine in Marseilles. Not wanting to be known, I go to lodge at a poor inn, where I am very glad to see Signora Schizza, Nina's[37] sister. She had arrived there from Barcelona with her husband three or four days before, and she was about to leave for Leghorn. She had dined, her husband was not there, I was extremely curious to learn a great many things, I asked her to come to talk with me in my room until my dinner was brought.

"What is your sister doing? Is she still in Barcelona?"

"My sister is still in Barcelona, but she will not stay there long, for the Bishop will not have her either in his city or in his diocese, and the Bishop is more powerful than Count Ricla.[38] She returned from Valencia only as a woman who cannot be refused passage through Catalonia on her way back to Italy; but one does not stay nine or ten months in a city through which one is only passing. She will certainly leave within a month; but she is not sorry; for she is certain that the Count will keep her lavishly wherever she goes, and she may succeed in ruining him. Meanwhile she is well pleased to have ruined his reputation."

"I have some idea of the way her mind works, but after all she cannot be the enemy of a man who by now must already have made her rich."

"Not a bit of it. She has nothing but some diamonds. But do you suppose the monster can feel gratitude? Do you suppose she has human feelings? She is a perfect monster, and no one knows better than I that she is a monster because she cannot be anything else. She forced the Count to commit innumerable injustices for no other reason than that all Spain should talk about her and know that she has made herself the mistress of his body, his wealth, his soul, and his will. The more flagrant the injustices she makes him commit, the more certain she is that she will be talked about, and that is all she wants. Her obligations to me are beyond reckoning, for she owes me everything, even her life, yet she is so wicked that, instead of having my husband confirmed in his appointment with an increase in salary, which would have cost her only a word, she had him dismissed."

"I am amazed that, with such a character, she treated me so generously."

"Yes, I know the whole story; but if you knew it too you would not feel in the least grateful to her for what she did for you. She paid your expenses at the inn and in the Tower only to convince people in general that, to the Count's shame, you were her lover, and everyone in Barcelona knows that there was an attempt to murder you at her door and that the cutthroat whom you wounded died."

"But she cannot have ordered my murder, or been an accomplice in it, for that would be against nature."

"That I know; but is there anything in Nina which is not against nature? What I can tell you for certain is what I saw with my own eyes. During the hour the Count spent with her she did nothing but talk about you, your intelligence, your good manners, comparing the Spaniards with you to their disadvantage. The Count, annoyed, kept telling her to have done and talk of something else; but it was no use; in the end he left cursing you, and two days before what happened to you he told her that he would do her a favor she did not expect; and I can assure you that when we heard the shot a moment after you left she said with the utmost calm that it was certainly the favor the unfortunate nobleman had promised her. I told her that you might have been killed; and she replied that it was so much the worse for the Count, for his turn would come to find the man who would kill him. She began laughing at the thought of the sensation the news would produce in Barcelona the next day. However, at eight o'clock the next morning I saw her very well pleased when your servant came to tell her that you had been arrested and taken to the Citadel."

"My servant! I never knew that he had any communication with her."

"You were not meant to know it; but I assure you that the man loved you."

"I was convinced of it. But go on."

"She then wrote the proprietor of your inn a note which she did not show me but in which she must have ordered him to supply you with everything you needed. Your servant told us that he had seen your bloodstained sword and the hole in your cloak, and she was very glad to hear it; but never believe that it was because she loved you, for she said that, having escaped being murdered, you might take your revenge. What puzzled us was to guess on what pretext the Count had had you arrested.

"That evening we did not see him. He came the next day at eight o'clock, and the infamous creature received him with smiles and an air of the greatest contentment. She said she had heard that he had had you imprisoned, and that he had done well, for he could only have done it to safeguard you from what might be attempted against you by the same enemies who had tried to take your life. He replied drily that your being arrested had nothing to do with what had happened to you that night. He said that you were in custody for only a few days, for your papers would be examined, and you would be set free as soon as nothing was found in them to make you deserve a more rigorous imprisonment. She asked him who the man you had wounded was; and he replied that the police were making inquiries, for neither a wounded man nor any traces of blood had been found. He told her that your hat had been found and had been sent to you. I left her alone with him until midnight. Three days later everyone knew that you had been imprisoned in the Tower. That evening she asked the Count the reason for it, and he replied that all three of your passports might be forged, since the one you had from the Venetian Ambassador, dated at San Ildefonso, could not but be so. Everyone knew that, since you were in disfavor with your country, it was impossible that your Ambassador had given you a passport; and it was certain that, if the Venetian one was forged, the ones from the King and the Count of Aranda must be forged too, for foreigners are not given passports unless they first present one from their country's Ambassador. He[39] said that, on this supposition, you had to be strictly confined, and that you would not be released until your passports came back from the Court confirmed by those who were responsible for them. That was all.

"It was the arrest of the painter Pogomas which made us certain that it could only be he who had denounced you to the Government as a forger, to avenge himself for your having had him turned out of our house. The painter remained under arrest in the Citadel, and we thought that he must be being held to substantiate his accusation. This reasoning made us suppose that you would be released as soon as we learned that Pogomas had been removed from the Citadel only to be sent to Genoa. This meant that your passports had returned from the Court recognized as authentic; however, seeing that you were still kept there, Nina no longer knew what to think, and the Count made no reply to her further questions concerning your imprisonment. False as she is, she approved of his secrecy, respecting the reasons he might have for keeping silent on the subject.

"We finally learned that you had been unconditionally released. Nina was sure she would see you in the parterre and would triumph in her box before an audience which would consider her the person who had obliged the Captain-General to restore you to freedom. She was preparing to show herself in her box in her most splendid attire, when she was astonished to learn that there would be no more performances for three days. It was not until that evening that she learned from the Count himself that your passports and your papers had been returned to you and that you had been ordered to leave; she praised her mad lover's prudence. She saw that you would not dare go to her house, and she believed that you must have received secret orders, even to being forbidden to write to her, when she saw that you had gone without writing her a note. She said that if you had had the courage to ask her she would have left with you. But she was greatly surprised when she learned from your manservant a week later that you had only escaped the cutthroats by a sort of miracle. She laughingly told the Count the story, to which he replied that he knew nothing about it. Give thanks to God that you were able to leave Spain alive. Your becoming acquainted with the monster in Valencia should have cost you your life; the state of misfortune in which you find me is her doing, and God is justly punishing me for having brought her into the world."

"What do you mean?"

"I mean what I say. Nina is my daughter."

"Is it possible? Everyone thinks she is your sister."

"She is my sister too, for she is the daughter of my father."

"What! Your father loved you?"

"Yes, I was sixteen years old when he made me big with her. She is the child of sin; and a just God decrees that it shall be she who punishes me. My father died to escape her vengeance; but perhaps I shall cut her throat before she cuts mine. I should have strangled her in the cradle."

Overcome with horror, I did not know what to say to this dreadful narrative, the truth of which was not to be doubted. I asked her if Nina knew that she was her daughter, and she replied that her father himself had told her so when she was eleven years old, and that it was the same worthy father who had had her virginity and who would certainly have given her a child too if he had not died in the same year.

On hearing this second outrage committed by the charlatan Pelandi,[40] I could not help laughing. The man had the misfortune to fall in love with his daughters and his granddaughters. I thought to myself that, in a state of nature, the thing would not arouse horror, and that all the horror that was felt for it came only from education and force of habit. I asked the woman how Count Ricla had come to fall in love with Nina.

"Listen. It is not a long story, and it is a strange one. She had no sooner arrived in Barcelona two years ago, coming from Lisbon, where she had left her husband Bergonzi, than she was engaged as a figurante in the ballets because of her beautiful face, for, so far as talent goes, she can't dance a step. All she can do is make the turning leap called *rebaltade*; when she makes it she has the pleasure of hearing the parterre applaud her because they see her underdrawers up to the waist. You must know that there is a theatrical regulation here which makes any dancer who shows her drawers to the audience in a caper liable to a fine of an écu. Nina, who knew nothing about it, did her *rebaltade*, the audience applauded, she did another, even higher, and at the end of the ballet the censor told her that at the end of the month she would be docked two écus because of her shameless capers. She cursed and swore, but she could not get the better of the law. Do you know what she did the next day to avenge herself? She appeared without drawers, and she did her *rebaltade* the same as ever, which raised a storm of laughter in the parterre such as had never been heard in Barcelona. Count Ricla, who, in his stage box, had seen her better than anyone, being equally overcome by horror and admiration, told the censor, for whom he sent at once, that the audacious flouter of the law must be exemplarily punished otherwise than by fines.

" 'Meanwhile,' he said, 'have her brought to me.'

"Whereupon Nina marches into the Viceroy's box with her impudent air and asks him what he wants with her.

" 'You are a shameless creature who has failed in respect to the public and the laws and who deserves to be severely punished.'

" 'What have I done?'

" 'You made the same jump as you did day before yesterday.'

" 'That is true, but I did not break your Catalan law, for no one can say that he saw my drawers. To make sure that no one would see them, I didn't put any on. Could I do any more in obedience to your accursed law, which has already cost me two écus? Answer me.'

"The Viceroy and all the grave personages of his entourage had to make an effort to keep from laughing, for, as you know, gravity does not countenance laughter. The diabolical Nina was in the right after all, and to discuss whether the law had been broken or not would have entailed bringing up the most laughable details in order to prove Nina twice guilty. So the Viceroy merely told her that if she ever took it into her head to dance without underdrawers again she would be sent to prison on bread and water for a month. She obeyed.

"A week later a new ballet of my husband's was given which pleased the audience so much that an encore was demanded. The Count sent word that the audience was to be satisfied, and the dancers, male and female, were told in their dressing rooms to return to the stage and take their positions. Nina, who had nearly undressed, tells my husband that he will have to do without her. It was not possible; she had a role which was necessary to the ballet. She laughs at his arguments, she refuses. My husband tells the censor for what reason he cannot satisfy the audience; the censor goes into Nina's box, he tries to persuade her, he does not succeed, he scolds her, he threatens her, it is no use; he speaks roughly to her; at that Nina gets up and pushes him out the door so forcefully that the little fellow almost falls down. He repairs to His Excellency's box, tells him what has happened, and two soldiers instantly go to bring Nina before the Governor as she is, not in her shift, but in a state of undress to offend decency and to prove the undoing of a man who, if he was to punish her, did not need to see her so nearly naked. You know how beautiful the vixen is. In an unsteady voice the Governor says what he has to say to her, but Nina boldly tells him in so many words that he can have her killed but that he cannot make her dance.

"'To the devil with Spain, the audience, and the whole earth, I do not want to dance, and you are in the wrong to try to force me to, since it is not in my contract that I must appear in the same ballet twice on the same evening; and I am so outraged by your tyrannical proceedings and the insult you have put upon me by an act of abominable despotism that I now tell you that I will not dance on this stage either tonight or tomorrow or ever. I do not ask a copper of you, let me go home, and know that I am a Venetian and free. I admit that, despite that, you can subject me to all kinds of ill-treatment. I will bear it firmly, and if you do not have me killed I will avenge myself by going to proclaim to all Italy how you treat decent women in your country.'

"The astonished Governor declared that Nina was mad. He sent for my husband again and told him to give the ballet without her, and not to count on her in future, for she was no longer engaged. He then told Nina to go, and gave orders that she was not to be interfered with. She went back to her box, where she dressed and returned to our house, where she was living. My husband gave the ballet as well as he could, but the Governor, Count Ricla, found that he had fallen violently in love with the shameless creature. She had a valuable ring, which she was thinking of selling in order to return to Italy at once.

"It was Molinari,[41] a very bad singer, who came the next morning to tell her that His Excellency wanted to see her on the next day at a small country house, to assure himself that she was not mad, or that, having spoken to him as he had never in his life been spoken to before, she was so. It was just what Nina wanted; she felt sure that she would complete her conquest of him. She told Molinari to tell His Excellency that he would find her well-behaved and amenable. That first interview, under Molinari's proc .... ship,[42] was followed by all the rest. To keep the nobleman and assure herself that he will never escape from her chains, she ill-treats him from time to time, and thus she makes him happy when she is gracious to him. He cannot leave her."

This is all that I learned from the incestuous Schizza, who was then perhaps forty years of age. [...]

The next day I found Henriette's answer at the post office. Here is a copy of it:

"Nothing, my old friend, is more like a romance than our meeting at my country house six years ago and our present encounter twenty-two years[43] after our parting in Geneva. We have both aged. Will you believe that, though I still love you, I am very glad that you did not recognize me? It is not that I have become ugly, but putting on flesh has given me a different countenance. I am a widow, happy, and well enough off to tell you that if you should be short of money with the bankers you will find it in Henriette's purse. Do not come back to Aix to recognize me, for your return might give rise to speculation; but if you come back some time hence, we can see each other, though not as old acquaintances. I feel happy when I think that I may have helped to prolong your life by putting with you a woman whose kind heart and whose fidelity I knew. I am very glad that she told you all. If you would like to maintain a correspondence with me, I shall do all that I can to make it a regular one. I am very curious to know what you did after your escape from the Leads. I promise, now that you have given me such strong proof of your discretion, that I will tell you the whole story of what brought about our meeting at Cesena,[44] and of my return to my country. The first is a secret from everyone. Only Monsieur d'Antoine[45] knows a part of it. I am grateful to you for not having made any inquiries about me here, though Marcolina[46] must have told you all that I asked her to. Tell me what became of that charming girl. Farewell."

Her letter made up my mind for me. Henriette had grown wise; the force of temperament had diminished in her as it had in me. She was happy, I was not. If I went back to Aix for her, people would have guessed things which no one should know; and what would I have done? I could only become a burden to her. I wrote her a long letter in reply, and I accepted the correspondence which she proposed. I gave her a general account of all my vicissitudes, and she told me all the details of her life in thirty or forty letters which I shall add[47] to these memoirs if Henriette dies before me. She is still alive today, old and happy.

[* * *]

I left Marseilles alone, having taken a place in a carriage which was going to Antibes, and from there I went to Nice, where I joined company with an Abate to go to Turin by way of the

Colle di Tenda,[48] which is the highest of all the Alps. Going by this route, I had the satisfaction of seeing the beauty of the country which is called Piedmont. I arrived in Turin, where the Cavaliere Raiberti[49] and the Comte de la Pérouse[50] received me with the greatest satisfaction. They both found me aged, but after all I could only be relatively so at my then age of forty-four years. I struck up a close friendship with Sir XXX,[51] the English Envoy, a charming man, well read, rich, with excellent taste, who kept a choice table, whom everyone loved, among others a Parmesan dancer named Campioni,[52] than whom it was difficult to see a prettier woman.

As soon as I told my friends my idea of going to Switzerland to print at my expense a confutation in Italian of the *History of the Venetian Government* by Amelot de la Houssaye, they all eagerly undertook to find me subscribers who would pay me in advance for a certain number of copies. The most generous of all was the Comte de la Pérouse, who gave me twenty-five Piedmontese gold pistoles for fifty copies. I left a week later with two thousand Piedmontese lire in my purse for copies thus paid for in advance, which enabled me to print the entire work, which I had sketched out in the Tower in the Citadel of Barcelona, but which I had to write in full with the author whom I wanted to refute at hand, together with the *History of Venice* by the Procurator Nani.[53] Provided with these books, I set out, resolved to go to have my work printed in Lugano, where there was a good press and no censorship. In addition I knew that the proprietor of the press was a man of letters, and that there was excellent fare there and good society. Not far from Milan, very near to Varese, where the Duke of Modena went to spend the season, close to Coire, to Como, to Chiavenna, and to Lake Maggiore, in which were the famous Borromean Islands, I should be in a place where I could very easily amuse myself; I went there, and I at once went to lodge at the inn which was considered the best. Its proprietor was Taglioretti,[54] who immediately gave me the best of all his rooms.

The next morning I went to see Doctor Agnelli,[55] the printer, who was a priest, a theologian, and a man of good reputation. I made a formal agreement with him, in which he promised to give me four sheets a week, each in twelve hundred copies, I undertook to pay him each week, and he reserved the right of censorship, hoping, however, that he would always be of the same opinion as I. I began at once by giving him a preface and a foreword which would keep him busy for a week, after choosing my paper and prescribing the size I wanted, large octavo.

When I got back to the inn for dinner the innkeeper announces the Bargello,[56] who wanted to speak to me. The Bargello was the chief constable. Though Lugano belonged to the thirteen cantons, its police had the same organization as those of Italian cities. Curious to know what this ill-omened personage could want with me, and in any case having no choice but to listen to him, I have him shown in. Hat in hand, he tells me that he has come to offer me his services, to assure me that, though a foreigner, I should enjoy every privilege in his city with no fear for my safety in the streets if I had enemies or for my personal liberty if I had difficulties with the Venetian Government.

"I thank you, and I am sure that what you tell me is true, for I know that I am in Switzerland."

"I make bold to tell you that the custom is that all foreigners who come here, and who want to be sure that the asylum they are granted is inviolable, pay a trifling sum in advance, either by the week or the month or the year."

"And if they should not want to pay?"

"They could not count themselves safe."

"Very good. I will tell you that I fear nothing, and that consequently I count myself safe, and more than safe, without going to the trouble of paying."

"Excuse me, but I know that you are on bad terms with the State of Venice."

"You are mistaken, my friend."

"Oh, no I'm not."

"See if you can find someone who will wager two hundred zecchini that I have nothing to fear from Venice, and I will put them up in an hour."

The Bargello is taken aback, the innkeeper, who was present, tells him that he may well be mistaken, and he leaves in great astonishment. The innkeeper, very glad to have overheard the dialogue, told me that, since I intended to stay in Lugano three or four months, I might well show the Captain, or High Bailiff, who was equivalent to the Governor and who had all authority, the courtesy of going to call on him. He was, he said, a very honest and amiable Swiss gentleman, with a young wife who was very intelligent and as beautiful as possible.

"Oh, in that case I assure you I will go there tomorrow."

Toward noon the next day I go there, I am announced, I enter, and I see Monsieur de $=^{57}$ with his charming wife and a little boy five or six years old. We stand there motionless, staring at one another.

[∗ ∗ ∗]

"I will decide nothing before I talk with him, for the whole thing seems strange to me."

"I will tell him to come and talk with you."

In comes a young Frenchman in uniform, spruce, cocky, not unprepossessing, who tells me just what the coachman had told me, and ends by saying he is sure I will not refuse to take his wife with me.

"Your wife, Monsieur?"

"Oh, thank God you speak my language! Yes, my wife, who is English and not at all demanding. She will be no trouble to you."

"Very well. I should not want to delay my departure. Can she be ready at five o'clock?"

"You can be sure of it."

The next morning at the appointed hour I see her in the carriage. I pay her a brief compliment; I sit down beside her, and we set off.

[∗ ∗ ∗]

This seems the appropriate moment to leave Casanova, about to embark, full of hope, on yet another adventure. It is a characteristic moment, too, for a restless man who is always on the move, always leaving or arriving some-where.

The memoirs continue for another fourteen chapters, introducing us to new characters and recalling the familiar faces of allies and antagonists, offspring and mistresses. The final pages describe stays in Turin, Naples, Rome and Trieste as the writer worked nearer and nearer to his starting point in Venice. Finding himself able to do the State there some service, he hoped perhaps that the Venetians would allow him to end his days in his native city. It was not to be. He did receive pardon of a sort, but perhaps it was impossible for such a man to settle to a comfortable old age. Casanova is not a name we could ever associate with the concept of "home." Instead he journeyed on, eventually coming to a forced halt at the castle of Dux in Bohemia where, starved of his usual pleasures, he embarked on his memoirs. As usual, he made himself comfortable and, as usual, he was soon involved in hostilities with the other residents. Without Casanova to describe these battles in detail, we can only speculate about their nature. The memoirs break off abruptly in Volume 12, chapter x with the words "and three years later I saw her in Padua, where I resumed my acquaintance with her daughter on far more tender terms." We can imagine the rest.

TEXTUAL NOTE

Casanova and His Memoirs

1   *Biographical*

Giacomo Girolamo Casanova—or Jacques Casanova de Seingalt, as he later called himself—was born at Venice on April 2, 1725, the first child of Gaetano and Zanetta Casanova, née Farussi. The name Casanova is Spanish, and there may be some truth in Giacomo's claim that his father was descended from a certain Don Jaime Casanova who had fled from Spain to Rome in 1428 with an heiress whom he had abducted from a convent. Whatever Gaetano's descent may have been, at the age of nineteen he fell in love with an actress, broke with his parents, and became first a dancer and then an actor. By so doing he sacrificed any possible pretensions to rank. For in the eighteenth century the almost hysterical adulation bestowed on favorite performers was bought at the price of their social degradation. This was so true that when, in 1724, Gaetano won the heart of Zanetta Farussi, the young people did not dare to ask Zanetta's shoemaker father for his consent to their marriage, for even the shoemaker considered an actor "an abomination"; instead, they eloped, whereupon the shoemaker "died of grief." This semi-pariahdom into which Giacomo was born was a strong factor in shaping both his personality and his career.

More than almost any other country in Europe, Venice—Republic though it was in name—was in fact the private preserve of a small aristocracy. By 1733, Zanetta, who had followed her husband onto the stage, had borne him four more children and was six months pregnant with another. At this juncture Gaetano was attacked by an abscess of the brain. Knowing that he was doomed, and concerned to provide for his wife and children, he took the only course open to a moneyless pariah: he determined to secure them protection and patronage among the aristocracy. As an actor in the Grimani theater, he naturally turned to its owners the Grimani family, whose name had been listed in the "Golden Book" of Venetian patricians from the year 1297.

Noblesse oblige. The three brothers Michele, Alvise, and Zuane Grimani responded to his appeal and, two days before his death, solemnly promised in the presence of his family to become their protectors. So began the long line of Casanova's patrons.

It was Giacomo's welfare which had been of particular concern to his dying father. Now eight years old, the boy had suffered from hemorrhages since his birth and, according to his own account, was mentally backward. His earliest recollection dated only from shortly before this time. Of his three official protectors, it was Alvise Grimani who took Giacomo in hand. In consultation with another patrician, the poet Giorgio Baffo, it was decided to send the boy to board in Padua, where he would be tutored by the priest and Doctor of Civil and Canon Law Antonio Gozzi. If he proved capable of learning, he was later to be sent to the University of Padua to prepare for a career in the Church.

The experiment was partly successful: Giacomo became a good scholar, he attended the University (1738–1741), graduated, and later received minor orders. But to a career in the Church he eventually proved recalcitrant. For while Gozzi was trying to lead him toward it, the priest's younger sister Bettina was teaching him his real bent. In this his first love affair, it was the girl who was the seducer. After that one apprenticeship, he took the role himself. From then on the stages of his life are punctuated by women.

In Venice, to which he returned to play the role of a young ecclesiastic in 1740, it was first two sisters with whom he conducted a simultaneous affair. At the same time his promising talents acquired him a new patron in the Senator Alvise Malipiero. It was one more step toward his being accepted in the society to which alone he could look for advancement.

Meanwhile his mother, who was acting in Poland and there enjoyed the good graces of the Queen, found Casanova still another patron in the person of a Calabrian monk for whom her influence secured a bishopric in his native province. Casanova traveled to Martorano to join him (1743), stopping on the way, however, to engage in the first of the shady deals which were later to make him unwelcome in most of the capitals of Europe. But he was so appalled by the Bishop's poverty and the bleakness and rusticity of the place that he renounced the post which was offered him. After a visit to Naples, where a poem of his composition was published and attracted notice, he set out for Rome. He was now determined to win the fame which "rewards the practice of literature."

In Rome (1744) he managed to make the acquaintance of the Pope and to secure the patronage of a Cardinal. But the inevitable woman appeared; there was a scandal, and Casanova had to leave the city. Neither Constantinople, to which, in a moment of hurt feelings and bravado, he had asked the Cardinal to send him, nor Corfu (1744–1745) brought him anything but amatory successes. Indeed, it was in Corfu that he developed the unfortunate taste for gambling which plagued him all his life. (He once played piquet for forty-two consecutive hours.)

Back in Venice again (1746), he was reduced to earning his living by playing the violin in a theater orchestra, when an almost unbelievable series of coincidences brought him another possible patron in Senator Matteo Bragadin. Casanova improved the opportunity by pretending to a knowledge of the occult sciences; this consolidated his position to such effect that Bragadin was on the verge of legally adopting him. Again scandal interfered. But this time it was of a more serious nature. Casanova was summoned to appear before the dreaded tribunal which judged offenses against religion and morals. He suspected, too, that his dabbling in magic was being investigated by the still more dreaded Inquisition. Bragadin advised him to "bow to the storm"; and early in 1749 Casanova again fled.

He was only twenty-four. But what was to be the pattern of his life was now set: patrons; mistresses; anything, however dubious, which promised to bring him a luxurious living—and, always, the desire for literary fame. The course of it took him to the chief cities of Europe: Lyon (1750), where he became a Freemason; Paris (1750–1752), where he met writers and actors and began to write plays; Dresden and Prague; Vienna (1753), where he met the eminent court poet and librettist, Metastasio, but found the city sadly "intolerant of the votaries of Venus." Then Venice again (1755–1756), where this time the most celebrated episode in the memoirs occurred: his imprisonment and escape from the State prison known as "the Leads."

He fled first to Germany; then returned to Paris (1757), where he published a poem and founded and directed a lottery. To Holland next (1758–1759) on a dubious financial mission for the French government. Then back to Paris, where he rented a house and started a silk manufactory, but from which the ensuing complications, coupled with the pregnancy of one of his titled mistresses, drove him to seek refuge in The Hague (1759).

Further journeys took him to Geneva (1760), where he visited Voltaire; to Rome again (1761), where he found a new patron in Cardinal Gianfranco Albani; to Modena (1761) and Turin (1762), from both of which he was expelled; to London (1763–1764), where he was presented at court and from which he had to flee because of a false bill of exchange, carrying with him as a souvenir his fourth case of gonorrhea. From there he took a roundabout route to Berlin (1764), where Frederick the Great offered him a post as one of the five tutors to the newly established Pomeranian Cadet Corps. But Casanova was aiming higher. The fortune that had eluded him so long, he was now convinced he would find in Russia. He reached St. Petersburg in December 1764, was presented to Catherine the Great, but was not offered a post. "In Russia," he concluded, "only foreigners who are sent for expressly are esteemed."

And he left for Warsaw (1765–1766). What hopes he had there were dashed when he was drawn into a duel with a nobleman and, in the course of the publicity which followed, he was accused of having absconded from Paris with a large sum of money belonging to the lottery. The accusation was false; so too was the perhaps even worse one that he had been a strolling actor in Italy. Nevertheless, the King banished him from Poland. He left, for once after paying his debts, but—not for the first time—with a new mistress whom he had conquered on the day before his departure.

Vienna (1766), and another expulsion—this time ostensibly because he had broken the law against gambling, but really because the news of his banishment from Poland had reached the stern Empress Maria Theresa. Then Paris again (1767), where the death of his mistress in childbirth and news of the death of his oldest patron, Senator Bragadin, were followed by his banishment from France "by the King's good pleasure." The reason alleged was that he had threatened a young nobleman; but the truth of the matter was that his various dubious practices were catching up with him.

Another country? And his stay in Spain (1767–1768), despite a term of imprisonment (which he improved by writing a polemic in three volumes on the history of Venice), for once did not end in banishment. He left Barcelona of his own free will and so far restored to the grace of the Republic that the Venetian Ambassador gave him a passport.

Even so, he was still an exile from his native city. But he seems now to have determined to find some way to return there. The polemic on Venetian history (which he published at Lugano in 1769) was probably intended to soften the Venetian State Inquisitors toward him. From now on he turned more and more to literary work, avoiding the shady dealing which had brought him into disrepute. His travels now never took him far from Venice. In 1771 he was in Florence, making a translation of the Iliad. From 1772 to 1774 he was in Görz, working on a "History of the Troubles in Poland."

Then at last, in September 1774, he was pardoned.

Back in Venice in November of the same year, by 1776 he had found regular employment as a spy for the State Inquisitors. This activity he pursued, alternating it with literary work, until 1782. In that year a satire of his composition against a Venetian patrician resulted in his second, and final, banishment from Venice.

After a brief and profitless stay in Paris, he returned to Vienna (1783–1784), where he became secretary to the Venetian Ambassador Marco Foscarini, but where, more importantly, he gained the friendship of Count Waldstein. On the death of Foscarini (1784), Waldstein provided for Casanova's declining years by appointing him librarian of his castle at Dux in Bohemia.

Here Casanova continued to write, first collaborating with Da Ponte on the libretto for Mozart's *Don Giovanni*, then producing, among other things, the five volumes of his philosophical romance, *Icosameron* (1788). In the same year he first tried his hand at autobiography with his *Histoire de ma fuite*, an account of his escape from "the Leads."

In 1789, as "the only remedy to keep from going mad or dying of grief" in the boredom of his exile at Dux, he began writing his memoirs. Despite interruptions caused by other literary work (including a polemic and two mathematical treatises) and by an enormous correspondence with some of the most distinguished men of the period, he kept doggedly at his "remedy." At his death nine years later (June 4, 1798), though he had written 4545 manuscript pages, he had brought his autobiography down only to the summer of 1774.

But that summer had ushered in one of the happiest moments of his life: the moment when he received his pardon from the Inquisition and prepared to return to Venice. It is our loss—but perhaps his gain—that death spared him from going on to tell the story of one more shattered hope.

II   *The Publishing History of the Memoirs*

Despite the fact that he had maintained—and no doubt believed—that his native Italian was "unquestionably superior to French in richness, beauty, and energy,"* Casanova wrote his memoirs in French. He gives his reason in his Preface (written in 1797): "I have written in French instead of in Italian because the French language is more widely known than mine." Another passage implies that he intended to publish them during his lifetime. And in fact he proposed their publication to one of his correspondents in the same year. Nothing came of the proposal. And a year later he was dead.

No more was heard of the memoirs until 1820. In December of that year a certain Friedrich Gentzel offered the manuscript to F. A. Brockhaus, founder of the still existing publishing house of the same name (then in Leipzig, now in Wiesbaden). In the course of the negotiations it came out that Gentzel was acting for the owner of the manuscript, Carlo Angioloni. Angioloni was a grandson of Casanova's younger sister Maria Maddalena, who had married a German musician named Peter August and lived in Dresden. (Casanova visited her there whenever he was in that city.) Angioloni's father—also named Carlo—had married Maria Maddalena's daughter Marianna in 1787, and had been one of those who attended Casanova during his last illness at Dux.

Brockhaus bought the manuscript of the memoirs in January 1821. He first published them in a German version, translated—and heavily adapted—by Wilhelm von Schütz. This German version came out in twelve volumes, from 1822 to 1828. French translations of it soon began to appear. To counter them, Brockhaus decided to publish the original.

His literary advisers, however, as well as the taste of the time, suggested that the manuscript needed editing. This task Brockhaus entrusted to a certain Jean Laforgue, a professor of French at Dresden. The first four volumes of Laforgue's version appeared at Leipzig in 1826–1827, under the title *Mémoires de J. Casanova de Seingalt écrits par lui-même*. The German censorship having raised difficulties, the next four volumes were published at Paris in 1832; and—the French censorship having done likewise—the last four volumes appeared in Brussels in 1838.

III   *Laforgue and the Text of the Memoirs*

These volumes bore on their title pages the notice "Édition originale." In the narrow sense this means "first edition," but it implies

---

Le Messager de Thalie (1780), No. 3.

that the printed text conforms with the original manuscript. Laforgue's instructions from the publisher had been different.

Some of what he did, he admits in his Preface:

"The liberty which we have allowed ourselves, and which we considered to be indispensable, is the revision of the manuscript in two respects. To begin with, Casanova wrote in a language which was not his own, and he wrote as he felt, calling a spade a spade without periphrasis. Hence the original, as the author left it, is full of grammatical errors, Italianisms and Latinisms; these had to be removed to make it suitable for printing. . . .

"Then too, since the taste of the present century . . . is no longer that of a century fertile in evil and since obscenities have been relegated to their due place in proportion as a sound philosophy . . . has purified taste . . . it is indispensable to prune away all the expressions and to veil all the images which the great majority of readers would find intolerable today. But . . . the editor has been careful to take from situations only their nudity, by casting over too voluptuous images a veil which robs the narrative of none of its zest."

As for Italianisms, Laforgue is right in accusing Casanova of them. However, with a few exceptions, they are more a matter of practically transliterating Italian technical terms into French than of idiom. At any rate, in this day and age even those stern guardians of their language the French are willing to read what Casanova wrote. As for Latinisms, these can only be charged in respect to some constructions to which Casanova frequently has recourse and which go back to the narrative style of the Roman historians. That style had been drummed into Casanova from boyhood. I think that, faced with the task of handling an enormous amount of material, he saw the style for what it is—an incomparable instrument for getting over the ground of narration—and used it for precisely that purpose, despite the fact that some of its constructions have an odd effect in a modern language. As for grammatical errors, there are not as many as Laforgue implies, and those which occur are rather the result of haste than of ignorance.

In the more important matter of "casting a veil," Laforgue's practice varies widely. There are simple substitutions. For example, where Casanova writes, "The only thing I was still curious about was whether the Feltrini had slept with her too," Laforgue writes, "had shared her favors too." But there are also wholesale omissions. A particularly heinous instance occurs in the scene of the simultaneous seduction of the two sisters Marta and Nanetta.[*] Here Laforgue entirely suppresses the crucial passage:

"Little by little I straightened her out, little by little she uncurled, and little by little, with slow, successive, but wonderfully natural movements, she put herself in a position which was the most favorable she could offer me without betraying herself. I set to work, but to crown my labors it was necessary that she should join in them openly and undeniably, and nature finally forced her to do so. I found this first sister beyond suspicion, and suspecting the pain she must have endured, I was surprised. In duty bound religiously to respect a prejudice to which I owed a pleasure the sweetness of which I was tasting for the first time in my life, I let the victim alone. . . . "

So much, at least by implication, Laforgue admitted that he had done. But there was more. According to the late Mr. F. A. Brockhaus,[†] Laforgue went beyond his instructions:

"Casanova was a Venetian and a man of the Old Régime, a good Christian and very far from sharing the ideas of the French Revolution. Laforgue, hostile to the Church and a disciple of revolutionary thought, did not hesitate to change Casanova's work to accord with his own ideas. He even went so far as to add a number of passages, without the publisher's authorization."

Two examples will suffice. Where Casanova writes that in Rome Papal ordinances "are as much to be feared as *lettres de cachet* were in Paris before the atrocious Revolution," Laforgue makes it: "as *lettres de cachet* were before the Revolution which destroyed them and which showed the world the general character of the nation." So much for revolutionary ardor. As for anticlericalism, referring to his first meeting with the pretended castrato Bellino, Casanova writes: "His two sisters . . . were . . . more than worthy of being preferred to Bellino if I had not taken it into my head that Bellino was a girl too."

[*]Vol. 1, pp. 93f.
[†]In his Publisher's Preface to the Brockhaus-Plon edition. (The full bibliographical details of this edition, on which the present translation is based, are given further on.)

Laforgue seizes the opportunity and writes: "would certainly have gained my preference over Bellino if I had seen in the latter only the miserable outcast of humanity, or, rather, the deplorable victim of sacerdotal cruelty."

Mr. Brockhaus's statement that Laforgue added a number of unauthorized passages still seems to refer to his revolutionary and anticlerical propaganda. The fact is that he added a great many which have no such bearing. And here we come to the worst, and the most pervasive, of Laforgue's meddlings. He is constantly distorting Casanova's psychology by adding motivations and sentiments which Casanova either left to be inferred or, more often, simply did not have in mind at all.

For example, at the beginning of the scene of the seduction of the two sisters, already quoted in part above, Casanova writes: "They had turned their backs to me and we were in darkness. I began with the one toward whom I was turned, not knowing whether it was Nanetta or Marta." Between these two sentences, Laforgue interpolates: "I therefore acted at random." Now, Casanova was seldom at a loss to act, and often *chose* to act at random. The *pis-aller* implied by Laforgue's "therefore" is—therefore— entirely Laforgue's conception and not at all Casanova's. Then, in obedience to another of his manias—that of insisting upon making everything more accurate than Casanova saw fit to make it— Laforgue goes on to transform "the one toward whom I was turned" into "the one who was lying on my right."

Again, Casanova writes: "Don Sancho's supper was exquisite and, as was to be expected, better than mine, for otherwise he would have considered himself dishonored. He gave us white truffles, several kinds of shellfish," and so on. Here Laforgue's interpolation is again not only obtrusive, it actually obscures—or indeed contradicts—the motivation given by Casanova. Between the two sentences Laforgue inserts: "Then too, men in general are never satisfied with what is good; they want the best, or, more precisely, the most."

One more example may suffice to indicate the pervasiveness of Laforgue's gratuitous psychologizing. The scene is from one of the episodes in Casanova's lengthy siege of his first aristocratic mistress, Signora F. The phrases I have put in italics in this quotation from Laforgue have no equivalents in Casanova's text:

"I would often *be indiscreet enough* to remain behind the curtain of the window of my room, looking at her when she thought *herself perfectly certain* that nobody saw her; but *the thefts which I made from this position amounted to very little; for, whether because she suspected that I saw her, or because it was habitual in her, she was so circumspect* that even when I saw her in bed *my happiness did not go beyond* her charming head."

But if Laforgue falsifies by his interpolations, he falsifies no less by his suppressions. These, too, are legion; and everywhere their effect is to reduce Casanova's concrete descriptions—his visual, olfactory,[*] tactile, psychological details—to a series of mannerly abstractions.

Here is the same passage as Casanova wrote it (with the italics this time indicating Laforgue's suppressions):

"I often stood behind the curtains of the window *farthest from those of her bedroom* so that I might see her when she believed that she was seen by no one. *I could have seen her* getting out of bed and have possessed her in my amorous imaginings; and she *could have granted my passion that relief* without compromising herself in any way. Yet this was just what she did not do. *It seemed to me that she had her windows open only to torture me.* I saw her in bed. *Her maid came to dress her, and stood in front of her in such a way that I could no longer see her. . . . I was certain that she knew I saw her; but she would not give me the small pleasure of making a gesture which could have led me to suppose she was thinking of me.*"

Laforgue's Casanova merely moons; Casanova's Casanova thinks, and sees.

A defender of Laforgue[†] maintains that he deserved praise for having "pruned the text very little and with the utmost tact" and for having "brought light where there was obscurity, ambiguity or possible misunderstanding" and "fluidity where the reader's interest was mired in a chaos of undisciplined words." Now that we know what Casanova wrote,[‡] the first article cannot stand. The charges

---

[*]Casanova writes in his Preface: "As for women, I have always found that the one I was in love with smelled good."

[†]Octave Uzanne, in the "Essai apologétique" which he contributed to the edition of the memoirs published under the editorship of Raoul Vèze (*Mémoires de J. Casanova de Seingalt écrits par lui-même*, Paris, Éditions de la Sirène, 1924–1934).

[‡]Uzanne did not. He was allowed to consult the manuscript "only superficially and under the eye of its owner."

implied against Casanova as a stylist in the other two are true. He is often obscure—though not often so obscure that a little patience will not disentangle his meaning; his constructions are sometimes little short of "chaotic."

On the negative side, the genuine text gives the impression that Casanova wrote at top speed. Everything is secondary to somehow getting down the memories which crowded into his mind. Did he not have behind him sixty-five years of a life more full of incident than the lives of twenty ordinary men? Determined to recapture it in the minutest detail, he let the chips of awkwardness, ambiguity, carelessness fall where they might. I have not thought it any part of my duty as a translator to gloss over these defects. They are a small price to pay for the vividness which he achieves at his best and which is one of the most brilliantly positive accomplishments of the memoirs as Casanova wrote them. "Memoirs," in fact, is too pale a term. The final impression—which his faults, indeed, rather accentuate than diminish—is that Casanova is not recollecting his life, but reliving it.

IV   *The New Text*

As if the vicissitudes of editing and adaptation had not been enough, the original manuscript itself came very near to being destroyed during the Second World War.

"Preserved in twelve cartons and deposited for safe-keeping in a bunker beneath the [Brockhaus] premises in Leipzig, a bomb effected a direct hit on the superstructure.... When it became at length possible to penetrate to the bunker the manuscript was found to be intact and undamaged except for some slight mildewing. It was then transported on bicycles to the vaults of the one bank remaining in Leipzig. With the appearance of the American Army in 1945 Brockhaus was offered a truck for the removal of the firm to Wiesbaden. Stowing in it the Casanova manuscript and such of the firm's most precious possessions as it would contain, the whole was removed ... to Wiesbaden."[*]

Brockhaus's announcement, made in February 1960, that Casanova's memoirs were at last to be published as he wrote them created a sensation in the literary world. Among others, Émile

[*]J. Rives Childs, in *Casanova Gleanings*, Vol. III (1960), p. 1.

Henriot, Hubert Juin, and Paul Guimard in France, Hermann Kesten in Switzerland, Marc Slonim in the United States greeted what one of them called "the literary event of the century."[*] "An event of outstanding importance," wrote J. Rives Childs, and added: "There is hardly an example in the history of literature of a work of the importance of the *Memoirs* having been withheld in its original version for more than 160 years since completion, with readers dependent during that time on either truncated texts or adaptations."[†]

The present translation is made from Casanova's text, as given in the new edition published jointly by the houses of Brockhaus and Plon.[‡] However, if the term "Édition originale" was a misnomer as applied to Laforgue's version, the "Édition intégrale" ("complete edition") which appears on the title pages of the Brockhaus-Plon publication is not quite accurate. The differences between the printed text and the manuscript were explained by the late Mr. F. A. Brockhaus in his Publisher's Preface:

"1. The manuscript consists of ten volumes of different sizes. The first edition (1826–1838)[§] divided the whole into twelve volumes of approximately equal length. The present edition preserves this division—that is, two volumes in one double-volume—as well as the division into chapters and their titles, which the author frequently failed to supply....

"2. The author...died before he could complete his work, which accounts for the following:

"(a) At two points in the manuscript, the text appears in two different versions, which makes it possible to follow the author's method of work. The passages in question are Chapters VII–XII of Volume III and Chapter III of Volume IX of the first edition (corresponding to Chapters IX–XIV of Volume III and Chapter IX of Volume VII of the manuscript).... The present edition gives only the version which can be considered the more detailed and which is also to be found in the first edition....

---

[*]Paul Guimard, in *Arts* (Paris), No. 765 (March 9–15, 1960), p. 1.
[†]Childs, *loc. cit.*
[‡]Jacques Casanova de Seingalt Vénitien, *Histoire de ma vie*. Édition intégrale (12 vols. in 6, Wiesbaden and Paris, F. A. Brockhaus and Librairie Plon, 1960–1962). Previous English translations, including Arthur Machen's, have been made from Laforgue's version.
[§]I.e., Laforgue's.

"(b)   Two chapters are missing both from the manuscript and from the first edition. They are Chapters IV and V of Volume XII of the first edition (corresponding to Chapters IV and V of Volume X of the manuscript). However, a summary of them was found, which the author[*] entitled 'Extrait,' and which was first published in the French periodical *L'Ermitage* in ... 1906. This summary appears in the present edition, printed in italics ....

"(c) In addition, Chapters I–IV of Volume VIII of the first edition (which correspond to Chapters X–XIII of Volume VI of the manuscript) are no longer present in the latter. Laforgue undoubtedly had them at his disposal, but they have since disappeared for some unknown reason. In the present edition they appear in italics ...."

In addition, Casanova's spelling and punctuation are modernized.[†]

The notes to the present translation are based on those supplied for the Brockhaus-Plon edition by Dr. and Mrs. Arthur Hübscher and on the notes in the currently appearing German translation[‡] by its editor Professor Erich Loos. They are intended to identify persons brought on the stage, or even merely mentioned, in the memoirs and to elucidate Casanova's historical and other references for the general reader.[§]

Brooklyn, New York,   *Willard R. Trask*
February 1966

---

[*]I.e., Casanova.

[†]A facsimile edition of the manuscript is promised "if a sufficient number of subscribers can be found."

[‡]Giacomo Casanova, *Geschichte meines Lebens* ... herausgegeben und eingeleitet von Erich Loos, ... übersetzt von Heinrich von Sauter (Berlin, Propyläen Verlag, 1964 ff.).

[§]In large part, they go back to the notes supplied by a number of Casanova specialists—notably Gustav Gugitz—for the La Sirène edition. The notes to that edition, in their full form, are still indispensable to any thorough student of Casanova.

NOTES

N.B. Cross references lacking Volume details are to current Volume.

Volume One

1   Altered from Cicero to Trebatius, *Lett. famil.* VII, 6: *Quis ipse sibi sapiens prodesse non quit, nequidquam sapit.*

2   *Stoics:* School of philosophy founded at Athens in 308 by Zeno.

3   *Petrarch:* Francesco Petrarca (1304–1374), Italian poet and humanist.

4   Petrarch, *Canzoniere, In morte di Madonna Laura*, VIII, 63.

5   Horace, *Epist.*, I, 2, 62.

6   Horace, *Epist.*, II, 2, 137.

7   Misquoted after Pliny the Younger writing to Tacitus: *Equidem beatos puto, quibus deorum munere datum est aut facere scribenda, aut scribere legenda; beatissimos vero, quibus utrumque* (*Epist.*, VI, 16).

8   *Diamond of the first water cut in England:* Unless C. is being ironical here, he is mistaken: the art of diamond cutting was never practiced to any extent in England; its centers were Antwerp (from the 15th century) and Amsterdam (from the 16th century).

9   Altered from Martial, XII, *praep.: Si quid est enim in libellis meis quod placeat, dictavit auditor.*

10 Cicero, *Tusculan. disp.*, V, 38.

11 Lucretius, *De rerum natura*, I, 305: *tangere enim et tangi nisi corpus, nulla potest res.*

12 Altered from Horace, *De arte poetica*, 25–26: *Brevis esse laboro, obscurus fio.*

13 Vergil, *Bucolica*, II, 25–26.

14 Horace, *Epist.*, I, 19, 6.

15 *Olla podrida:* A Spanish dish, a mixture of various meats and vegetables, with seasonings.

16 *Locke:* John Locke (1632–1704), English philosopher.

17 Altered from *Acta apostol.*, 17, 28: *In ipso enim vivimus, et movemur et sumus.*

18 *Amphiaraus:* A renowned diviner in Argos, one of the Argonauts.

19 Altered from Aeschylus, *Seven against Thebes*, 592.

20 *Cicero:* Marcus Tullius Cicero (106–43 B.C.), Roman orator, statesman, and author. The reference is to his *Tusculans* (*Tusculanae disputationes*), written in 45–44 B.C., after the death of his daughter Tulliola.

21 *Theophrastus:* Native of Eresus in Lesbos, disciple of Aristotle.

22 *Livy: Titus Livius* (ca. 59 B.C.–A.D. 17), the great historian of the Roman Republic.—*Patavinity:* Dialect of Patavium (Padua), Livy's native city.

23 *Algarotti:* Francesco Algarotti (1712–1762), popular Italian writer, influenced by Fontenelle and the earlier French rationalists.

24 *Republic of letters:* The concept of the "republic of letters" goes back to the 16th-century humanists.

25 *Presiding judges:* Allusion to the Académie Française and its official function as guardian of the language.

26 *Lully:* Jean Baptiste Lully (1632–1687), French composer, of Italian origin.

27 *Rameau:* Jean Philippe Rameau (1683–1764), French composer and musical theorist.

28 *Franciade:* Period of the French Republican calendar, comprising four years of which three were common and the fourth bissextile. In his *A Leonard Snetlage*, [Dresden?] 1797, C. examined the new words used in France after the Revolution by means of a criticism of Snetlage's *Nouveau Dictionnaire François*.

29 Cf. note 1 and the epigraph to Chap. I.

30 Ovid, *Ex Ponto*, IV, 2, 35.

31 Altered from Seneca; cf. Cornelius Nepos, *Vita Pomponii Attici: Sui cuique mores fingunt fortunam.*

CHAPTER I

1 Cf. Preface, p. 5 and p. 16.

2 *King Alfonso:* Alfonso V el Magnanimo (1396–1458), King of Aragon from 1416 to 1458 and, as Alfonso I, King of Naples from 1442.

3 *Martin III:* Not Martin III (942–946) but Martin V (Odo Colonna, 1368–1431), who was Pope from 1417 to 1431.

4 *Don Juan Casanova:* Juan Casanova, Spanish theologian and Dominican monk, Bishop of Cerdona and Elna, made a cardinal in 1430.

5 *Marcantonio:* Marco Antonio Casanova (1476–1526 or 1527). His poems, scattered in various collections, were for the most part brought together in Volume III of the *Deliciae poetarum Italorum.*

6 *King of Naples:* Fernando I (1423–1494), King of Naples from 1458 to 1494.

7 *1493:* Don Juan Casanova must, then, have died during Columbus' return from his first voyage to America (August 3, 1492–March 15, 1493).

8 *Martial:* Marcus Valerius Martialis (first century A.D.), Roman poet, master of the pointed epigram.

9 *Pompeo Colonna:* 1479–1532, Cardinal from 1517.

10 *Giulio de' Medici:* 1478–1543, Pope as Clement VII from 1523 to 1534.

11 *Imperial troops:* The reference is to the troops of Charles V (Spanish and German mercenaries) who fought in Italy in the second war against François I of France (1526–1529). The pillage of Rome (*Sacco di Roma*) did not occur until 1527.

12   *Charles V:* 1500–1558, King of Spain 1516, Emperor from 1519 to 1555 (abdication).

13   *Piero Valeriano:* Latinized name of Giovan Pietro delle Fosse (1477–1560), Italian scholar, poet, and humanist. The work quoted, *De infelicitate litteratorum,* was first printed in Venice in 1620.

14   *Farnese:* Alessandro Farnese (1545–1592), celebrated commander in the service of Philip II of Spain.

15   *Henri, King of Navarre:* Henri Bourbon (1553–1610), later King Henri IV of France.

16   *Fragoletta:* Diminutive of the Italian *fragola* (*fravola*), "strawberry." Sobriquet of the comic soubrettes of the *commedia dell'arte* in the 17th century. The reference here is to Giovanna Balletti, née Benozzi (1662–ca. 1750).

17   *San Samuele:* Venetian theater built in 1655, destroyed by fire in 1747, rebuilt in 1748, demolished toward the end of the 18th century.

18   *Patriarch of Venice:* The title of Patriarch was adopted by the Bishop of Venice in 1451. The Patriarch here referred to was Pietro Barbarigo, Patriarch from 1706 to 1725.

19   *Of this marriage:* In his *Né amori né donne* (Venice, 1782), C. alludes to his being the fruit of illegitimate relations between Zanetta and Michele Grimani.

20   *She gave birth:* According to other sources, Francesco Casanova was said to have been the son of the Prince of Wales, whose mistress Zanetta was.

21   *The Elector:* Friedrich August III (1750–1827), Elector from 1763, King of Saxony 1806–1827; he founded the Academy of Painting in 1764.

22   *Two girls:* Faustina Maddalena (1721–1736) and Maria Maddalena Antonia Stella (1732–1800).

23   *Posthumously:* Gaetano Alvise (1734–1783). It follows that C. revised this first chapter in 1798.

24 *Friulian:* Friulian is not an Italian dialect, but is one of the Rhaeto-Romanic languages. Friuli is a district of northeastern Italy, at the foot of the Carnic Alps. The name is derived from that of the Roman city of "Forum Julii." However, most Italians consider Friulian one of their dialects.

25 *Silver ducat:* 160 soldi or 8 lire.

26 Altered from Horace, *Epist.*, II, 2, 209: *Somnio, terrores magicos, miracula, sagas, nocturnos lemures portentaque Thessala rides?*

27 *Castoreum:* Sebaceous excretion of the beaver, used as an antispasmodic.

28 *Apostem:* External tumor with suppuration.

29 *Grimani:* Venetian patrician family, first documented in 1297. The reference here is to Alvise (Alvisio) Grimani, who was an abate, and to his brothers Michele and Zuane (Giovanni).

30 *Promise:* However, C.'s sister Maria Maddalena appeared on the stage in Dresden in 1752.

31 *Macoppe:* Alexander Knipps-Macoppe (1662–1743), born in Padua of a family originally from Cologne; practiced and taught medicine in Padua.

32 *Signor Baffo:* Giorgio Baffo (1694–1768), Venetian patrician and poet. His works were printed after his death: *Raccolta universale delle opere di Giorgio Baffo* (4 vols., Cosmopoli, 1789). C. characterizes his work further on.

33 *State Inquisitors:* The three *Inquisitori di Stato* (one of the Doge's councilors and two Senators) elected annually from the Council of Ten. From the 15th century on they exercised virtually unrestricted authority in the maintenance of public order.

34 Tacitus: *Annals*, IV, 34.

35 *Burchiello:* Large gondolalike boat, well appointed and furnished. The *burchiello* sailed every day between Venice and Padua by the Brenta Canal.

36 *Camerino:* Cabin.

37 *Slavonian colonel:* The militia of the Venetian Republic was made up partly of Slavonian soldiers recruited in the Venetian

territories in Dalmatia and Istria, whose Slavic inhabitants were called, in Venetian, *schiavoni*, a name which was abolished, as humiliating, in 1797.

38 *Zecchini:* The zecchino was a gold coin taking its name from the Zecca, the mint at Venice. Its value was 22 Venetian lire.

CHAPTER II

1 *Graspia:* Water mixed with grape pomace.

2 *Doctor Gozzi:* Antonio Maria Gozzi (1709–1783), Doctor of Civil and Canon Law, abate at Padua, from 1750 parish priest of Cantarana, from 1756 archpriest of Val San Giorgio, a village south of Padua.

3 *Soldi:* The soldo di Venezia, also called baiocco veneziano, was minted down to the end of the Republic. After Napoleon introduced the French monetary system, it was replaced by the coin of 5 centesimi, still called soldo today.

4 *Laestrygonian:* Man-eating giants, neighbors of the Cyclops (*Odyssey*, X, 118–124).

5 *As an abate:* At this period an abate was a young man destined for the Church but who had not yet taken vows or received more than minor orders. He dressed in black, and was forbidden to duel and dance. There were a great many of them in the 18th century, and their status was little different from that of laymen (cf. the French *abbé*).

6 *Tasso:* Torquato Tasso (1544–1595), poet, author of *Rinaldo* (1562), *Gerusalemme liberata* (1565–1575), *Aminta* (1573); the *Gerusalemme* was still widely popular in the 18th century.

7 *Bettina:* Bettina Gozzi (who, with her brother the Abate Antonio Maria, was the only survivor of the twelve children of Vincenzo Gozzi and Apollonia Businari) was born in 1718.

8 *Peripatetics:* Disciples and followers of Aristotle.

9 *Ptolemy:* Claudius Ptolemaeus (ca. 100–178), Greek geographer, astronomer, and mathematician at Alexandria. His cosmography is contained in his principal work, the *Megale syntaxis* (better known under its abbreviated Arabic title of *Almagest*).

10 The lines are the beginning of an epigram by the 16th-century Dutch Neo-Latin poet Johannes Secundus.

11 *Meursius:* Johannes Meursius (1613–1654), Dutch archaeologist. The obscene work *Joannis Meursii Elegantiae latini sermonis, seu Aloisiae Sigeae Toletanae Satyra Sotadica de Arcanis Amoris et Veneris*, published in Holland about 1680, at first passed as a Latin translation made by him from a Spanish text; its real author was Nicolas Chorier (1609–1692).

12 *Moral science:* As opposed to the physical sciences. Here, in modern terms, "psychology."

13 *Sendal:* A soft, light, glossy silk fabric in use from the 9th to the 18th century.

14 *Ariosto:* Ludovico Ariosto (1474–1533), author of *Orlando furioso* (finished 1532).—*Ruggiero:* One of the heroes of the *Orlando furioso.*—*Alcina:* An enchantress who seduces Ruggiero. The passage referred to: VII, stz. 23–27.

15 *Feltrinians:* Original, *Feltrins;* natives of the city or district of Feltre.

16 Horace, *Epist.*, I, 20, 25.

17 *St. Andrew's cross:* A cross shaped like the letter X.

18 *Capuchin: Ordo Fratrum Minorum Sancti Francisci Capucinorum*, one of the three main branches of the Franciscan order, founded in 1525 and confirmed by Clement VII in 1528. Their name comes from the hood (*cappuccio*) which forms part of their habit.

CHAPTER III

1 *Jacobin:* Name formerly given to the Dominicans in France, from the name of their first monastery, Saint-Jacques, in Paris.

2 *Dominican: Fratres Praedicatores*, one of the great mendicant orders, founded in 1206 by St. Dominic (ca. 1175–1221) and confirmed in 1216.

3 *Apollo Belvedere:* The well-known Greek statue in the Vatican, discovered in the 16th century under Pope Julius II (1503–1513).

4   *Purification of Our Lady:* Celebrated Feb. 2.

5   *Sant'Antonio:* Called "Il Santo," the principal church in Padua, built from 1232 to 1307 and containing the tomb of St. Anthony. Renovated in 1749.

6   Ariosto, *Orlando furioso*, I, stz. 56.

7   *Val San Giorgio:* Cf. note 2 to Chap. II.

8   *Anna Ivanovna:* 1693–1740, niece of Czar Peter the Great, Czarina from 1730.

9   *Harlequin:* Arlecchino, stock character of the *commedia dell'arte*, a sly manservant from Bergamo.—*Carlo Antonio Bertinazzi* (1710–1783), well-known Italian actor friend of D'Alembert and of Pope Clement XIV.

10   *Sixteen:* C. was enrolled in the University of Padua on Nov. 28, 1737, at the age of twelve. The rudiments now taught in secondary schools were then a part of the university curriculum. To obtain the *laurea* (the degree of Doctor), studies had to be pursued for four consecutive years. Venetian law students often spent them, either entirely or in part, at Venice in an advocate's office, in which case they went to Padua regularly to obtain their certificates of assiduity. This is what C. appears to have done after he left Padua in October 1739.

11   *Bo:* Familiar name for the University of Padua (founded 1222), the main building of which was constructed, from 1494 to 1552, on the site of an inn called *Il Bue* or *Il Bo* (At the Sign of the Ox).

12   Horace, *Carm.*, III, 6, 46–48.

13   *The Venetian government:* Padua formed part of the Republic of Venice from 1406 to 1797.

14   *Syndic:* Jurisdiction over the University of Padua was in the hands of the mayor (*podestà*) assisted by the rector and two syndics (*sindachi*) chosen by the students from among the professors. There was a syndic for the "legists" (law students) and another for the "artists" (students in theology, philosophy, and medicine).

15   *Sbirro:* Minor representative of public authority in Italy (police officer, constable).

16   *Complete:* See note 10.

CHAPTER IV

1   *San Samuele:* San Samuele Profeta, a small church situated near the Palazzo Malipiero, where C. was baptized in 1725 and received the tonsure on Feb. 14, 1740. The priest was Giovanni Tosello (1697–1757), later canon at San Marco.

2   *The four minor orders:* C. received them Jan. 22, 1741, from the hands of Monsignore Antonio Francesco Correr (1676–1741).

3   *Abate Schiavo:* Biagio Schiavo (1676–1750), a well-known writer of the period.

4   *The same one:* In the Calle della Commedia, now Calle del Teatro; C.'s brother and sister were living in the Calle delle Monache.

5   *Senator:* The Senate of the Venetian Republic handled affairs of state. It was composed of 120 elected Senators and of a larger number of high officials. The reference here is to the patrician and Senator Alvise Gasparo Malipiero (1664–1745).

6   *Imer:* Giuseppe Imer (died 1758), well-known actor and impresario, born in Genoa; friend of Carlo Goldoni. His daughter Teresa made her debut as a singer at Venice in 1742, then appeared in various European cities, and became a theatrical manager in the Austrian Netherlands; in 1760, under the name of Mrs. Cornelys, she opened a pleasure resort known as "Carlisle House" in London.

7   *House near:* In the Corte del Duca.

8   *Gassendi:* The Abbé Pierre Gassendi (1592–1655), French mathematician, philosopher, and scientist; he opposed the Aristotelianism of the schools and defended a mechanistic theory of nature.

9   *Notary public:* From 1514 there were 66 notaries public at Venice; they were employed in the Avogaria (the office of the Avogadari del comun; cf. Chap. VI, n. 13) and in other magistra-

cies. *Giovanni Maria Manzoni* (1702–1786) was a Venetian notary public from 1740 to 1760; he married Catterina Capozzi (or Capoccio) (1706–1787) in 1729.

10   *Anathema:* Several councils expressed themselves to the same effect, for example, the Third Council of Carthage (397) and those of Constantinople (692) and Rome (721).

11   *I set out masked:* The theater season in Venice, and with it the right to wear masks, began in October (later at the beginning of November) and, with the exception of nine days before Christmas, ended at the same time as the Carnival. Venetian maskers wore not only a mask proper but also a sort of hood, which in this case would hide C.'s shorn hair.

12   *Extrajudiciary:* The so-called *estragiudiziale* was a letter in which the plaintiff exhorted his opponent to come to an understanding in order to avoid having to appear before a court. The extrajudiciary had to be registered with a notary public.

13   *Confraternity of the Blessed Sacrament:* The confraternities of the Blessed Sacrament, pious associations of laymen, became so numerous in the 16th century that practically every parish church in Italy had its own confraternity.

14   Horace, *Epist.*, II, 1, 9.

15   *Count of Montereale:* Antonio di Montereale married his daughter Lucia to the Venetian patrician Zuane Piero Barozzi in 1741.

16   *Terzarie:* Certificates of assiduity given to students by professors *pro hac tertia partia studii*, in January, March, and May. (Cf. note 10 to Chap. III.)

17   *La Cavamacchie:* By her right name, Giulia Ursula (Giulietta) Preato (1724–ca. 1790), singer and courtesan in Venice. C. says further on that she was fourteen years old in 1735; but according to her birth date she was only eleven.

18   *Marchese Sanvitale:* Giacomo Antonio Sanvitale (1699–1780), statesman, minister to the Duke of Parma. (C. mistakenly calls him "Count" two paragraphs later.)

19   *Bastiano Uccelli:* Sebastiano Uccelli (born 1695), Venetian notary, godfather to Carlo Goldoni. His son Francesco Antonio Uccelli married Giulia Ursula Preato in 1752.

20 *Fair:* La Fiera della Sensa, the great fair held on Ascension Day, a festival celebrated with great splendor at Venice to commemorate the conquest of Istria and Dalmatia.

21 *Liston:* A walk, dedicated to amorous intrigue, on the Piazza. Goldoni refers to it in his *Donne gelose.*

22 *Metastasio:* Pietro Antonio Metastasio, pseudonym for Trapasso (1698–1782), celebrated author of opera librettos and court poet in Vienna.

23 *Sfrattata:* Banished. C. misspells it as *sfratata,* which means "unfrocked."

24 *Steffano Querini delle Papozze:* 1711–1757, Venetian patrician. A member of the family had acquired the village of Papozzo, near Ferrara, in 1255; hence the name Querini delle Papozze.

25 *Ducati correnti:* The ducato corrente of Venice, money of account (6 lire, 4 soldi).

26 *Phryne:* Phryne of Thespiai, the most famous hetaira in Athens in the 4th century B.C. She served as Praxiteles' model for his statues of Aphrodite.

27 *San Paterniano:* San Paterniano Vescovo, a very old church in the San Marco quarter. Demolished in 1871.

28 Judith XVI, 11.

29 *Ragionato:* Title of officials (now *ragioniere*) who had studied at the Collegio dei Ragionati, attended by *cittadini* (townsmen enjoying citizenship). *Saverio Costantini* was director of the public lottery in Venice.

30 *Palladium:* Image of Pallas Athene, dropped from heaven by Zeus; in general, the image of the tutelary deity of a city.

31 *Cecrops:* Legendary founder and first king of Athens, whose original name was Kekropia.

32 *Pasiano:* The village of Pasiano is some ten miles south of Pordenone.

33 *Fifteen o'clock:* The Italian method of reckoning time (in use until the end of the 18th century) began with the Angelus, half an hour after sunset. In September the sun set about seven

o'clock; hence fifteen o'clock was about ten in the morning. The clocks in church towers struck only from 1 to 12.

34 *Procuratore:* Advocate. The profession of advocate was highly regarded in Venice; there were even patrician advocates. *Marco Niccolò Rosa* (born 1687) practiced law in Venice; married Caterina Orio.

35 *Doro:* Leonardo Doro, well-known physician in Venice at the period.

36 *Fraternity of the Poor:* C. writes *Fraterne*, from Italian *fraterna* = confraternity. It would seem that at San Samuele the Confraternity of the Poor and the Confraternity of the Blessed Sacrament were the same. (Cf. note 13 to this chapter.)

37 *Council of Ten:* The highest tribunal of the Venetian Republic. Originally of ten members (whence its name), it later came to include the Doge, his six councilors, and ten elected Senators.

38 *Lire:* The lira veneziana, silver coin minted from 1472. Value: 10 gazzette or 20 soldi.

CHAPTER V

1 *Boccaccio:* Giovanni Boccaccio (1313–1375), Italian writer and humanist, author of the *Decameron.* C.'s reference to Louis XIII is probably an error; he doubtless had in mind the anonymous *Chroniques scandaleuses de Louis XI* (1423–1483).

2 Ariosto, *Orlando furioso*, X, stz. 9. (C.'s ms. erroneously has "*fortuna*" instead of "*fontana*.")

3 *Infandum:* Aeneas's first word when he tells Dido of his recent misfortunes. Vergil, *Aeneid*, II, 3: *Infandum, regina, jubes renovare dolorem.*

4 *Utroque jure:* Doctor's degree in civil and canon law. (Cf. Chap. III, n. 10.)

5 *Cyprus wine:* A sweet, heavy wine, much in demand in Italy in the 18th century, imported to Venice directly from Cyprus.

6 *Her father:* The painter Iseppo Tosello (died 1755).

7 *The monastery of La Salute:* Santa Maria della Salute, church, monastery, and seminary of the Somaschians, built from 1631 to 1656 by Longhena.

8 *Countess Gozzi:* Emilia Teresa Gozzi, sister of the celebrated writers Gasparo and Carlo Gozzi. She married Count Giovanni Daniele di Montereale in 1743.

9 Ariosto, *Orlando furioso*, VIII, stz. 77. C. has altered the lines slightly.

CHAPTER VI

1 *Expire:* Marzia Farussi died on March 18, 1743.

2 *Minimite: Fratres Minimi*, a mendicant order following a stricter version of the Franciscan rule, founded by Francesco di Paola (1416–1507) as a community of hermits in Calabria in 1435, and established as a monastic order in 1454. The order, which was flourishing in the 18th century, still exists, chiefly in Italy and Spain.—The "learned Minimite" referred to was Bernardo da Bernardis (1699–1758), from 1739 to 1743 Vicar General in Poland, made Bishop of Martorano on May 16, 1743.

3 *The Queen:* Elisabeth Maria Josepha (1669–1757), Queen of Poland, wife of Augustus III.

4 *Queen of Naples:* Maria Amalia Walburga, wife (from 1738) of Carlo IV Borbone, King of Naples (as Carlos III, King of Spain from 1759).

5 *The Pope:* Benedict XIV (Prospero Lambertini), Pope from 1740 to 1758.

6 *Martorano* (also Martirano): Calabrian town south of Cosenza, some twelve miles from the coast.

7 Cicero, *De fin.* III, 22, attributes it to one of the Seven Sages. Seneca calls it an old precept (*De vita beata*, XV, 5); see also Seneca, *Ad Lucilium epist. moral.*, ep. 16.

8 Cicero, *De divinatione*, I, 54.

9 Vergil, *Aeneid*, III, 395, and X, 113 (*"invenient"*).

10 *One of Gardela's daughters:* Ursula Maria Gardela (1730–1793 or '94), daughter of the gondolier Antonio Gardela; appeared as a dancer in Strassburg, Stuttgart, and Munich. She married the ballet master Michele dall'Agata (1722–1794), who later became a theater manager in Venice (from 1792 or 1793 at the Teatro La Fenice) and who committed suicide, probably because of his lack of success.

11 *Duke of Württemberg:* Karl Eugen, reigning Duke of Württemberg from 1737 to 1793.

12 *Razzetta:* Antonio Lucio Razzetta, confidential agent of the Abate Grimani.

13 *Avogadore: Gli avogadori del comun*, three magistrates elected by the Senate and confirmed in their powers by the Grand Council for sixteen months and given supreme authority in legal matters and administration.

14 *La Tintoretta:* Stage name of the dancer Margherita Giovanna Grisellini (1724–1791). The appellation came from her father's trade of dyer (Ital. *tintore*).

15 *Waldeck:* Prince Karl August Friedrich von Waldeck (1704–1763) served Austria in the Seven Years' War.

CHAPTER VII

1 *The Bishop had arrived:* The reference is to Bernardo da Bernardis. (Cf. Chap. VI, n. 2.)

2 *Minimite monastery:* The monastery was named after the founder of the Minimite order, Francesco di Paola (cf. note 2 to Chap. VI). The building was secularized in 1806 and demolished in 1883.

3 *Thirty-four years:* C. is in error: born in 1699, Bernardo da Bernardis was then forty-four.

4 *Cavaliere da Lezze:* Andrea da Lezze (1710–1780), Venetian Senator, Ambassador of the Republic in Paris (1739–1742), in Rome (1743–1744), and in Constantinople (1748–1751). The title Cavaliere was conferred only on Venetian patricians who had distinguished themselves in public office. They wore a golden stole, whence the designation *cavaliere della stola d'oro*.

5   *Signor Joli:* Antonio Joli (1700–1777), Italian painter.

6   *Peota* (also *peotte*): A kind of covered gondola sufficiently sturdy for traffic on the Lagoon. The port of Chioggia is at the southern end of the Lagoon.

7   *Quarantine:* The isolation of persons suspected of being carriers of an infectious disease had been rigorously enforced by the Venetian Republic from the 15th century. All travelers had to conform to this regulation. Originally for a period of 40 days, the duration of quarantine was later often shortened.

CHAPTER VIII

1   *Lingua franca:* The corrupted Italian used in the Levant in commercial dealings between Occidentals and the natives.

2   *Lesser Bairam:* Mohammedan festival celebrated seventy days after the Greater Bairam, which follows the Ramadan fast.

3   *Piasters:* Here the Turkish piaster, a silver coin originally introduced into Turkey by Spanish merchants and soon minted at a lesser weight.

4   *Milo of Crotona:* The most famous athlete of Greek Antiquity; beginning in 540 B.C. he won at Olympia six times in succession.

5   *Carlini:* Silver coins minted at Naples from 1458 to 1859; their value was the tenth part of the ducato.

6   *Two hundred miles:* Roman miles, about 180 English miles.

7   *Royal palace:* Built in 1738; now the Agricultural Institute.

8   *Zantiote:* Native of Zante (Zakynthos), one of the Ionian Islands, which was a possession of the Venetian Republic from the 14th century (until 1797).

9   *The Levant:* Il Levante was the official Venetian designation for the Ionian Islands.

10 *Cephalonia:* An Ionian island which produced a famous wine.

11 *Magistery:* "The magistery of the philosophers" (= mages, alchemists), an alchemical term.

12   *Kerdaleophron:* From the Greek for "sly."

13   *I am after:* Original, *après à*, one of C.'s Italianisms.

14   *Once:* The oncia (plural, once) was a silver coin of the Kingdom of Naples (= 30 carlini).

15   *Torre del Greco:* The famous manufactory of arms was not at Torre del Greco but farther south, at Torre Annunziata.

16   *Mare Ausonium:* In Roman times the southern part of the Tyrrhenian Sea was called the Ausonian Sea, after the Ausonians (*Ausones*), who chiefly inhabited the Campagna and southern Latium.

17   *Magna Graecia:* Southeastern portion of the Italian peninsula, so named from the 6th century B.C. because of its numerous Greek colonies.

18   *Pythagoras:* 6th century B.C., native of Samos. He emigrated to Crotona in southern Italy, where he founded the Pythagorean school.

19   *Terra di Lavoro:* Former name of the province of Caserta in the Campagna, an outstandingly fertile area. C. erroneously applies it to Calabria.

20   *Bruttii:* Inhabitants of Brutium or Bruttium, the Roman name for what is now Calabria. *Brutus* means "brutish, clumsy."

21   *Chersydrus:* A snake which lives in the water and on land (Lucan, 9, 711; Verg., *Georg.*, 3, 405).

22   *Georgics:* In Vergil's didactic poem on farming, the *Georgics*, a passage in Book III (ll. 414 ff.) treats of the danger from poisonous snakes, especially in Calabria.

23   *Ducati del regno:* Gold coin of the Kingdom of Naples (= 10 carlini).

24   *In the prime of life:* Bernardo da Bernardis did not die until 1758.

25   *The Archbishop of Cosenza:* Francesco Antonio Cavalcanti, died 1748.

26   *Not uncultivated:* Original, *infarinés*, from Italian *infarinati*, men of wide but superficial education. (*Farina* = flour, hence with a thin coating of knowledge.)

27 *The celebrated Genovesi:* Antonio Genovesi (1712–1769), philosopher and economist, professor at the Universities of Naples and Milan. The first European scholar to teach political economy.

CHAPTER IX

 1 *Hippocrates:* 460–370 B.C., the founder of scientific medicine; in the 18th century he was still considered a medical authority.

 2 *Li flati:* Intestinal winds. It was believed that these could rise and invade the brain, causing morbidity and melancholy.

 3 *Hypochondrium:* Either lateral half of the epigastric region, under the costal cartilages.

 4 *Duchess of Bovino:* Eleonora Guevara, wife of Duke Innico Guevara.

 5 *Guidi:* Carlo Alessandro Guidi (1650–1712), well-known neo-classical poet of the period.

 6 *Vitruvius:* Vitruvius Pollio (82–26 B.C.), Roman architect, author of the treatise *De architectura*. The Marchese Bernardo Galiani (1724–1772 or '74) made a translation of it into Italian, which was published at Naples in 1758. He was the elder brother of the famous Abbé Galiani.

 7 *Cantillana:* José Maria Carmelin Enrique Baeza y Vicentello, Count of Cantillana (1714–1770), Spanish grandee and his country's ambassador in Venice, Turin, and Paris.

 8 *Apostolo Zeno:* 1668–1750, Venetian historian and dramatic poet.

 9 *Conti:* Antonio Conti (1677–1749), well-known translator and tragic dramatist.

10 *Raccolta:* Collection.

11 *Duchess of Matalona:* Vittoria Guevara married Carlo Caraffa, Duke of Matalona (Maddaloni), in 1755.

12 *Caraffa:* Lelio Caraffa, Marchese d'Arienzo (died 1761), Spanish grandee and field marshal of the Neapolitan army.

13 *Acquaviva:* Troyano Francisco Acquaviva d'Aragona (1696–1747), Cardinal from 1732, ambassador of Spain and the Kingdom of Naples in Rome from 1737.

14 *Churchman:* C. writes "Padrasse," after Italian *papasso*, a disrespectful augmentative. Antonio Agostino Georgi (1711–1797) was head of the Augustinian order and director of the Biblioteca Angelica in Rome.

15 *Vivaldi:* The Marchese Gaspare Vivaldi (1699–1767).

16 *Strada di Toledo:* Constructed in the 16th century as a main thoroughfare through the old city. (Now Via Roma, and still one of the busiest streets in Naples.)

17 *Become a Capuchin:* Capuchins wore beards.

18 *The Minerva:* Santa Maria sopra Minerva, called "la Minerva," church built on the ruins of the ancient temple of Minerva, near the Pantheon.

19 *Bank:* Banco dello Spirito Santo, still a well-known Italian banking house.

20 *The same* lazzi: *Lazzi* were traditional jokes and pieces of comic business in the *commedia dell'arte*, appropriate to the various characters. The word is plural, but C. uses it as a singular.

21 *De Amicis:* The reference can only be to Castruccio Bonamici (1710–1761), who described the battles at Velletri in 1744 in his commentary *De rebus ad Velitras gestis* (1746). He was compared by contemporaries to the Roman historian Gaius Sallustius Crispus (first century B.C.).

22 *The Tower:* Tor di mezza via, inn and first posthouse on the road from Rome to Naples, seven Roman miles from the Porta di San Giovanni.

23 *Piazza di Spagna:* Famous square in Rome; the name dates from the 17th century, when the Spanish Embassy was transferred there.

24 *Infarinato:* See note 26 to Chap. VIII.

25 *Campo di Fiore:* Once the site of Pompey's theater, it was still a place for executions and the site of the earlier great inns of the city.

26 *Ordini santissimi:* Papal ordinances.

27 *Lettres de cachet:* Originally, secret royal letters in general; in the decades before the French Revolution the term was used only to designate secret orders for imprisonment.

28 *Villa Negroni:* Built at the end of the 16th century, between the Viminal and the Esquiline, by Cardinal Montalto, later Pope Sixtus V; still famous in the 18th century for the beauty of its gardens; it no longer exists.

29 *His palace:* The Palazzo di Spagna, on the Piazza di Spagna; it belonged to the King of Spain and was used to house his ambassadors.

30 *Abate Gama:* Giovanni Patrizio da Gama de Silveira (1704 or 1705–1774), of Portuguese birth, was granted Roman citizenship ca. 1735, was secretary to cardinals and ambassadors; from 1743 to 1747 secretary to Cardinal Acquaviva.

31 *Roman scudi:* The "scudo papale d'argento," also called "scudo d'argento di Roma," or "scudo romano," silver coin minted from 1588. Value: 10 paoli or 100 baiocchi.

32 *Across from the Palazzo di Spagna:* In the Palazzetto Belloni, no. 31 Piazza di Spagna.

33 After Seneca, *Epist.*, CVII, 11: *Ducunt volentem fata, nolentem trahunt.*

34 Horace, *Epist.*, I, 2, 62: *animum rege, qui, nisi paret, imperat* ("control your heart which, unless it obeys, commands").

35 "Bind it in chains," *ibid.*, 63.

36 *Villa Medici:* Villa situated on Monte Pincio; built in 1544 and famed for its garden. Since 1803 it has been the seat of the Académie de France.

37 *Due romanelle:* Two Roman girls.

38 *Quartino:* Quartino d'oro, coin minted by Clement XII (1730) and Benedict XIV (1748–1758). The quartino d'oro, one

fourth of a zecchino, was worth half a scudo or 5 paoli or 50 baiocchi.

39   *Beppino della Mammana:* Giuseppe Ricciarelli (died 1776), castrato and singer, lived in Rome 1738–1743, performed in many European capitals; a Freemason from 1774.

40   *Middle course . . . Horace:* The reference is to Horace, *Carm.*, II, 10, 5: *aurea mediocritas.*

41   *Salicetti:* Natale Salicetti (1714–1789), of Corsican birth, physician and professor at the University of Rome.

42   *Voglie:* The irrational longings of pregnant women.

43   *The Marchesa G.:* Probably the Marchesa Caterina Gabrielli, née Trotti, of Ferrara.

44   *Cardinal S. C.:* Prospero Sciarra Colonna (1707–1765), Cardinal from 1743.

45   *The only pyramid in Rome:* The pyramid of Gaius Cestius, at the foot of Monte Testaccio (so called from the shards of earthenware pottery, or *testes*, which were deposited there).

46   *Roland:* Carlo Roland (died 1785), of Avignon, kept a livery stable and served as a guide; he later became an innkeeper.

47   *Barbaruccia:* Pet name, from Barbara.

48   *Ripetta:* The Via Ripetta led to the small port of Ripetta on the Tiber near the Mausoleum of Augustus, where ships coming from Sabina and Umbria unloaded.

49   *Vis-à-vis:* A light carriage for two persons sitting face to face.

50   *Villa Ludovisi:* One of the celebrated patrician villas at Frascati, with splendid gardens.

51   Ariosto, *Orlando furioso*, XIX, stz. 34.

52   *Spanish tobacco:* A snuff, also called Spaniol, made from Havana leaves pulverized and colored with red ocher.

53   *Aldobrandini:* The Villa Aldobrandini, also called Belvedere, near Frascati, with a formal garden, palace, and theater, built ca. 1600 for Cardinal Aldobrandini, nephew of Clement VII.

CHAPTER X

1 *Monte Cavallo:* Part of the Quirinal; its name was derived from two colossal late Roman statues of Castor and Pollux with horses, set up by Sixtus V in front of the papal palace. The palace was begun about 1540 by Paul III and was enlarged by his successors. As the highest point in Rome, it was the summer residence of the Popes, since the air of the Vatican was considered unhealthy. From 1870 it was the residence of the Kings of Italy; today it is the seat of the President of the Republic.

2 *Bolognese:* Benedict XIV was a native of Bologna and had been its Archbishop from 1731 to 1740. C.'s account shows how greatly the Italian dialects differed (as they still do). From the 16th century Tuscan served as the common literary language.

3 *Annibale Albani:* 1682–1751, Cardinal from 1711.

4 *From Herod to Pilate:* C. literally translates *rimandere da Erodo a Pilato*, an expression which has survived in this old form in Italy, whereas in French, German, and English it has become "send from Pontius to Pilate."

5 *Caduceus:* A rod with two snakes twined around it.

6 *Campagnani:* The reference is probably to Giuseppe Compagnoni (1754–1833), one of the earliest Italian journalists.

7 *Anaideia:* Personification of immodesty at Athens (Xenophon, *Conv.*, 8, 35).

8 *Zephyrus:* In Greek mythology the southwest wind.

9 *Surprise attack:* Frederick the Great had invaded Silesia in December 1740. It was ceded to him by Austria by the Peace of Breslau on June 11, 1742.

10 *Silesia is a woman:* In French and Italian the name of the province is feminine.

11 Altered from *Orlando furioso*, VII, stz. 15.

12 *Negrillo from Havana:* A Cuban tobacco.

13 Altered from Martial, XII, *praep.*—Already quoted in the author's Preface, p. 9.

14   *Belvedere:* Terrace.

15   *Bargello:* Chief constable. In this case, the papal chief constable.

16   *Jurisdiction:* The quarter of the Piazza di Spagna (in which almost 14,000 people lived at the time, hence one tenth of the population of Rome) was under the jurisdiction not of the Vicar General but of the Spanish Ambassador (to 1808). The whole territory was marked out by white stones bearing the inscription "R.C.D.S." (Regia Corte di Spagna).

17   *Auditore santissimo:* Derived from the Latin title *Auditor Sanctissimi Domini Nostri Papae,* one of the four prelates who served the Pope in the Vatican as privy councilors in legal matters. The office was formerly a most important one.

18   *Sbirri:* Police (cf. Chap. III, n. 15).

19   *A carriage:* C. writes *"une biroche,"* perhaps from the Italian *biroccino* or *barroccino,* a light two-wheeled carriage.

20   *Scala di Trinità dei Monti:* The so-called "Scala di Spagna," the stairway which leads from the Piazza di Spagna to the Church of Trinità dei Monti.

21   Ariosto, *Orlando furioso,* XXIII, stz. 112.

22   *Teatro Aliberti:* This theater, near the Piazza di Spagna, was then one of the largest in Rome, and was chiefly used for the performance of operas during the Carnival. It was demolished in the 19th century.

23   *Indifferent:* At the time there were frequent disputes between the papal Vicarate General and the Spanish Embassy; Cardinal Acquaviva, no doubt to pacify the Vicar General, sacrificed C.

24   *Tomando el sol:* Spanish, "taking the sun."

25   *Constantinople:* The Venetian Ambassador in Rome, Francesco Venier, had just turned over the business of his office to his successor, Andrea da Lezze. It is possible that Venier was already selected for the post of Venetian Ambassador in Constantinople, which he assumed in August 1745, and that C. had made his acquaintance in Rome and knew of his new post.

26 *Ispahan:* Until 1797, the capital of Persia.

27 *Two armies in winter quarters:* During the War of the Austrian
    Succession, a Spanish and an Austrian army faced each other in
    Italy. In October 1743 the Austrians advanced to Rimini and
    then went into winter quarters in Romagna, while the Span-
    iards remained farther south. The fighting began again in
    March 1744. (Cf. C.'s adventure between the two armies,
    Vol. 2, Chap. II.)

28 *Osman Bonneval:* Count Claude Alexandre Bonneval (1675–
    1747), French and later Austrian general, entered the service
    of the Turks about 1730, became a Mohammedan under the
    name of Ahmed Pasha, and Governor of the Provinces
    of Karamania and Rumelia. C.'s "Osman" is an error.

29 *Doblones de a ocho:* Spanish gold coins of the weight and value of
    8 gold escudos.

Volume Two

CHAPTER I

1 *Count de Gages:* J. B. Thierry du Mont, Comte de Gages (1682–
   1753), had been appointed commander of the Spanish armies
   in Italy, replacing Montemar, on August 21, 1743. In 1749 he
   was appointed Viceroy of Navarra.—*His Catholic Majesty:*
   Here, Philip V of Spain (reigned 1702–1746); the title was
   conferred on the Kings of Spain by Pope Alexander VI in 1497.

2 *Duke of Modena:* Francesco III Maria d'Este, Duke of Modena
   from 1737 to 1780, was appointed Generalissimo of the Spanish
   and Neapolitan troops in March 1743, after allying himself
   with the house of Bourbon.

3 *The theater in Ancona:* In the Papal States (to which Ancona
   belonged from 1532 to 1860, with a few interruptions caused
   by the Napoleonic Wars), feminine roles were played by castrati, since women were not permitted to appear on the stage.

4 *Sinigaglia:* City in the legateship of Urbino-Pesaro in the Papal
   States.

5 *Giton:* A character in the *Satyricon* of Petronius (Petronius
   Arbiter, died A.D. 66); the prototype of the male prostitute.

6   *Spolaitis:* Modern Greek σπολλάττη = εις πολλά έτη = many thanks.

7   *Felucca:* A long, narrow vessel, with a sail and oars.

8   *Seguidilla:* An Andalusian song and dance tune.

9   *Pessimists:* "Pessimism" and "pessimist" were then neologisms, which C. still considered very daring. "Pessimist" was not admitted into the dictionary of the French Academy until 1835.

10 *Valgame Dios!:* Spanish, "God help me!"

11 *Peralta ... Pedro Ximenes:* Spanish wines: the former from the Pamplona district, the latter from southern Spain.

12 *Dio provvederà:* Italian, "God will provide."

13 Horace, *Epist.*, I, 16, 60–62. Laverna is the goddess of gain, including illicit gain.

14 *Justo sanctoque:* Several Horatian manuscripts read *justum sanctumque*, which must be the reading the Jesuit knew.

15 *Anadyomene:* Greek epithet for Aphrodite risen from the sea. C. may be thinking of the Greek relief of the birth of the goddess on the so-called "Ludovisi Throne," or of one of the famous statues of Venus.

CHAPTER II

1   *Institute at Bologna:* The Istituto delle Scienze, successor to an Accademia degli Inquieti founded in 1690. In 1802 the Institute was annexed to the University.

2   *Salimbeni:* Felice Salimbeni (1712–1751), well-known Italian singer and musician.

3   *The Elector of Saxony, the King of Poland:* Friedrich August II (1696–1763), King of Poland as Augustus III from 1733 to 1763. Salimbeni did not perform in Dresden until 1750, having been in the service of Frederick the Great from 1743 to April 1750.

4   *The Queen:* Elisabeth Maria Josepha (1669–1757), Queen of Poland, wife of Augustus III.

5   *Died ... last year:* Actually, Salimbeni died in September 1751, at Laibach.

6   *At Pesaro:* The following story is comprehensible only in the light of the historical circumstances. During the War of the Austrian Succession (1740–1748), England, Austria, Saxony, and Sardinia had formed an alliance in 1743 against France, Spain, and Bavaria. The battles between Austrian and Spanish troops took place on Italian soil. In March 1744 Prince Lobkowitz left his winter quarters near Rimini to march on Rome, so that the troops Casanova came upon in Pesaro at this time could be first Spanish and then Austrian. (Cf. Vol. 1, Chap. X, note 27.)

7   *The principal guardpost . . . Santa Maria:* This guardpost took its name from the ruined church of Santa Maria di Monte Granaro, near Pesaro.

8   *Stockfish:* German *Stockfisch* (dried cod), sobriquet applied to a stupid, indolent man; much in use in the 16th century and down to the 19th.

9   Horace, *Epist.*, I, 1, 108. (Phlegm: one of the four bodily humors.)

10   *Piquet:* A card game for two players, or exceptionally three, played with 32 cards.

11   *Faro:* Another card game, the rage in the 18th century (from Pharaoh, old name for a king card).

12   *Greek:* Cheat, especially a cardsharper. The word is probably derived from the celebrated Greek swindler Theodoros Apoulos, who achieved notoriety at Versailles about the middle of the 17th century. The spread of the term increased enormously after the publication of the anonymous *Histoire des Grecs, ou de ceux qui corrigent la fortune au jeu* (3 vols., London, 1758).

13   *Don Bepe il cadetto:* Giuseppe Afflisio, also Affligio, often called Don Bepe il cadetto or Don Giuseppe Marcati (died 1787), adventurer, gambler, officer in the Austrian service, impresario of the Austrian court theater 1767–1779, sentenced to the galleys at Leghorn in 1779.

14   *Cagliostro:* Count Alessandro Cagliostro (1743–1795), by his right name Giuseppe Balsamo, of Ballaro near Palermo, famous adventurer of the period, who won fame and fortune in the highest society of several European countries by secret elixirs, alchemy, and spiritualism, but whose frauds kept him moving from city to city. When he attempted to found a Masonic lodge in Rome in 1787, the Pope sentenced him to death for heresy but then commuted the sentence to life imprisonment in the fortress of San Leo. Casanova tells more of him in Vol. 11.

15   Adapted from Seneca, *Epist.,* CVII.

16   *Lobkowitz:* Prince Georg Christian Lobkowitz (1686–1755) became Governor of Sicily in 1732, was given the rank of field marshal in the Austrian army in 1733, and during the War of the Austrian Succession commanded an army in Italy from 1743 to 1746.

17   *Weiss:* C. writes "Vais." Probably Gottlieb von Weiss (died 1757), an Austrian officer in the Esterhazy regiment.

18   *Legateship:* Rimini belonged to the Ecclesiastical Province of Ravenna. The Cardinal-Legates who governed these provinces of the Ecclesiastical State could obviously act in accordance with their own judgment in particular cases.

CHAPTER III

1   *Morte:* Italian, "death."

2   *Al Pellegrino:* In the street now named the Via Ugo Bassi; the inn no longer exists.

3   *The finest of the arcades:* There were numerous arcades in Bologna, among which the ones leading to the Church of La Madonna di San Lucca had been completed a few years earlier (1739), and the most frequented at the time were those of the Archiginnasio (popularly known as Il Pavaglione).

4   *La Montagnola:* A small hill, the public promenade of Bologna, very fashionable in the 18th century.

5   *Cornaro:* Giovanni Cornaro (1720–1789), a Venetian patrician, Vice-Legate at Bologna 1743, made a cardinal in 1778.

6   *Pyrrhonist:* Skeptic of the school of Pyrrho, Greek philosopher of the 4th century B.C.

7   *Duke of Castropiñano:* Francisco Eboli (1688–1758), of Spanish descent, Neapolitan general and diplomat.

8   *Teatro San Carlo:* Opened in 1737 and thereafter one of the leading theaters of the period.

9   *Doblones:* Here probably the ordinary doblón, a Spanish gold coin (until 1868), also called pistole (value: 4 piasters).

10 *Two governments:* That of the Ecclesiastical State and that of the Venetian Republic.

11 *Rialto:* The principal group of islands, the "heart" of Venice, to which the seat of the Doge was transferred and where the great Venetian families took up residence at the beginning of the 9th century.

12 *Zane:* Name of a patrician family of Venice; but this Captain Zane has not been identified.

13 *Red cockade:* Red was the national color of Spain and the Two Sicilies; black was that of Austria.

14 *Bailo:* Official title of Venetian ambassadors to Constantinople (from Latin *baiulus*, originally meaning "carrier," extended to mean "messenger" and "ambassador").

15 *Savio for War:* The Savio alla Scrittura, who was elected by the Senate for six months and could be re-elected.

16 *Procuratie:* The two palaces, with porticoes, situated on either side of the Piazza San Marco; previously used to house the nine Procuratori, the highest administrative officers of the Republic.

17 *Contumacia:* The term used for a quarantine imposed on a district in which there was an epidemic.

18 *Proveditor for Health:* The Provveditori alla Sanità had charge of quarantine, the activities of physicians and charlatans, the cleanliness of the public streets, and the unloading of ships.

19   *To sell his commission:* The practice of buying governmental posts was well established in France from the 16th century and was early extended to officers' commissions in the army. From France the practice spread to Italy.

20   *Bala:* Venetian dialect for Palla. This is probably a confusion of names. The "Galli" regiment was stationed in Corfu in 1745.

21   *Venier:* Francesco Venier (also Veniero), Venetian patrician and diplomat, ambassador in Rome 1740–1743, in Constantinople 1745–1749; awarded the title of Cavaliere della Stola d'Oro.

22   *Zante:* The southernmost large island of the Ionian Islands; from 1481 a Venetian possession. Greek: Zakynthos.

23   *Dolfin:* Giovanni (Zuan) Antonio Dolfin (1710–1753), called Bucintoro, Venetian patrician and high official of the Republic, Governor of Zante from 1744. He married Donata, née Salamon, and was the father of Caterina Dolfin-Tron (cf. n. 25 to this chapter).

24   *Bucintoro:* Il Bucintoro, state galley of the Republic, which at an annual festival celebrated on Ascension Day conveyed the Doge out into the Adriatic, where he threw a gold ring to symbolize the marriage of Venice and the sea. The festival commemorated the joint visit of Pope Alexander III and the Emperor Barbarossa in 1177.

25   *Charming young daughter:* The celebrated Caterina Dolfin Tron (1736–1793), one of the Venetian women of letters of the latter 18th century whose drawing rooms were the gathering places of men of letters and fashionable society. She married Andrea Tron in 1772.

26   *The Leads:* I Piombi, notorious Venetian prison under the lead roof (*piombi*) of the Doges' Palace; abolished in 1797.

27   *The Great Council:* Il Gran Consiglio (Maggior Consiglio), the assembly of all Venetian noblemen more than twenty-five years of age.

28   *Malamocco:* The port of Venice, near the southwestern end of the Lido.

29 *Orsara:* Otherwise Orsera (Yugoslavian Vrsar), small fishing port on the west coast of Istria.

30 *Savorna (savorra, zavorra):* Ballast.

CHAPTER VII

1 *Campo Sant'Angelo:* This marble table is not mentioned in any contemporary descriptions of the city.

2 *League of Cambrai:* Alliance concluded in 1508 against the Venetians among Pope Julius II, the Emperor Maximilian, Louis XII of France, and Ferdinand of Aragon.

3 *Magazzeno:* The *magazzeni* were shops where at most two grades of very cheap wine were sold. They also took articles in pawn; two thirds of the value was paid in cash; the other third in wine of poor quality.

4 *Santa Croce:* The parish of Santa Croce was in the northwestern part of the city, near the present railway station. The church and the conventual establishment of the same name were demolished at the end of the 19th century.

5 *Heads of the Council of Ten:* The "Capi del Consiglio dei Dieci" were chosen each month from among the members of the Council of Ten; they opened and considered all proposals and summoned the Council to meet at their good pleasure.

6 *San Giorgio:* San Giorgio Maggiore is an island with a church of the same name, opposite San Marco.

7 *San Geremia:* Parish church built in the 11th century; near the present railway station.

8 *San Marcuola:* District taking its name from the parish church of San Marcuola, on the Grand Canal. The Campiello del Remer is a small square in the same quarter.

9 *"Two Swords":* The hostelry named "Alle Spade," in the Rialto district.

10 *San Giobbe:* Parish church built in the 15th century, in Cannaregio, north of the present railway station.

11 *Cornaro della Regina:* A branch of the ancient patrician family of Cornaro which had adopted this surname because an ancestor, Caterina Cornaro (1454–1510), had been Queen of Cyprus.

12 *Palazzo Soranzo:* On the Campo San Polo; it is decorated with frescoes by Giorgione.

13 *Red robe:* The official costume of patricians, whether as functionaries or in the street, was the *toga*; Senators wore red.

14 *Santa Marina:* The Palazzo Bragadin, probably built in the 14th century, was restored ca. 1530. Senator Matteo Giovanni Bragadin (1689–1767) became C.'s protector.

15 *Of the same name:* Daniele Bragadin (1683–1755), Procuratore di San Marco from 1735.

16 *Key of Solomon:* After an anonymous book of magic which teaches the art of acquiring power over the spirits of hell and of the elements. It was first printed in Hebrew, then in Latin as *Clavicula Solomonis.* In the Middle Ages Solomon was held to be the first necromancer.

17 *Monte Carpegna:* A steep, isolated mountain in the northern Apennines (southwest of San Marino).

18 *Pyramid:* The possibility of expressing figures by letters and vice versa was a favorite theme of the cabalists. Since the 22 letters of the Hebrew alphabet express both letters and figures, it was possible to arrange two different *arcana* (from Latin *arcanum*, "secret") in the form of pyramids, the so-called "great arcanum" with the 22 letters and the "lesser arcanum" with the figures from 1 to 9. From the Orient these *arcana* passed to the medieval magicians and alchemists, and from them to the writings of the Rosicrucians. Agrippa von Nettesheim (1486–1535), from whom C. drew the greater part of his cabalistic knowledge, treated this subject at length in his *De occulta philosophia* (1510).

19 *Ten o'clock:* About 4 A.M. Cf. note 33 to Vol. 1, Chap. IV. Since the incident described occurred in March, the first hour would be 7 P.M., the sixth hour midnight, and the tenth hour 4 A.M.

20   *Hierophant:* Properly, the priest who presided over the Eleusinian mysteries. It was his office to display the sacred symbols.

21   *Universal medicine:* The panacea (from Panakeia, daughter of Aesculapius, who was credited with the ability to cure all diseases), the *aurum potabile* (potable gold) of the alchemists, which prolongs life and cures diseases.

22   *Elemental spirits:* According to the cabalists, spirits of an extremely subtle nature which preside over the elements: gnomes (over earth), undines (over water), sylphs (over air), salamanders (over fire).

23   *In magic:* White magic, or high magic, which was addressed to the celestial powers and taught secrets for avoiding misfortunes, obtaining cures, and performing supernatural acts. Black magic, or low magic, was addressed to evil spirits.

24   *Great Work:* The philosopher's stone, *Lapis philosophorum*, alchemical term for the substance which would transmute base metals into gold and cure all diseases. (cf. n. 21 to this chapter.)

CHAPTER VIII

1   *Casino:* The *casini* were pleasure houses, much in fashion in the 18th century, among both the nobility and the citizenry of Venice, who rented or owned them. Plain on the outside, their interiors were often furnished with every refinement of luxury. The patricians frequented them in an attempt to escape from the inflexible code which regulated their public life.

2   *Signora Avogadro:* Angela Avogadro, née Vezzi (born 1680), of a Venetian patrician family; she married Marin Avogadro in 1717.

3   *Zawoiski:* Count Gaetan Zawoiski (1725–1788), from 1765 court marshal to the Elector of Trier; from ca. 1772, his envoy to Dresden.

4   *Elector of Trier:* Clemens Wenzeslaus (1739–1812), son of Augustus III, King of Poland and Elector of Saxony. Elector of Trier from 1768 to 1802 (secularization of the electorate).

5 *Angelo Querini:* Freemason and a celebrated wit in Venice.

6 *Lunardo Venier:* Venetian patrician (born 1716); Senator, 1751; notorious for his dissolute life.

7 *La Giudecca:* Island south of the city. It contained a large number of gardens and vineyards, frequented in summer by the Venetians, who enjoyed going on outings there.

8 *Castelletto:* A group of houses in the parish of San Matteo in the Rialto quarter; in the 14th century prostitutes were confined to them and shut up there every night and during holidays. Later this custom was abolished and prostitutes spread throughout the city. Doubtless the name of the inn mentioned by C. preserved the name of the former establishment.

CHAPTER XI

1 *Sesostris:* Greek form of Sen-Usret, patronymic of three Egyptian pharaohs of the Twelfth Dynasty (1991–1778 B.C.). Sesostris III (1878–1843 B.C.) is the best known.

2 *Semiramis:* Legendary Queen of Assyria, to whom the founding of Babylon is ascribed.

3 *Knife:* C. writes *couteau* ("knife"), which is not in accordance with the Biblical tradition referred to later.

4 *Three kingdoms:* Reference to the old division of the realm of nature into the animal, vegetable, and mineral kingdoms.

5 *Malek:* Servant of the Jewish High Priest (John XVIII, 10, where Malek appears as "Malchus"); C. writes "Malck."

6 *This knife:* Among the relics in the treasury of San Marco, Venice, there was a sword believed to be the one with which St. Peter cut off Malchus' ear.

7 *Mitte,* etc.: John XVIII, 11.

8 *Mean king:* In Semitic, *malek, melek,* means king.

9 *Raffaello:* The reference to the great Italian Renaissance painter is probably meant ironically, to point up the commissary's ridiculous boastfulness.

10 *Rubicon:* The small river now called the Rubicon rises in the Apennines near Savignano, about 19 miles east of Cesena. The river which flows past Cesena is the Savio.

11 *Public library:* Probably the library of Don Gaspare Albarghi, which was open to the public. The Biblioteca Communale of Mantua dates from 1780.

12 *Godfrey of Bouillon:* 1061–1100, leader of the First Crusade, first King of Jerusalem.

13 *Matilda:* Countess of Tuscany (1046–1115), allied to the popes in the dispute over investitures.

14 *Henry IV:* 1050–1106, German Emperor from 1084.

15 *Gregory VII:* 1020–1085, Pope from 1073. C. has no authority for calling him a magician.

16 *Over hidden treasures:* According to ancient magical doctrine there were several genii who had command over hidden treasures: Aciel (gold), Marbuel (silver), Ariel (water).

17 *Great Circle: Circulus maximus*, mathematical and astronomical term, but here used for "magic circle."

18 *Count Palatine: Conte palatino*, title of the Knights of the Order of the Golden Spur, conferred by the Pope (earlier also the title of an ecclesiastical magistrate).

19 *Reigning Pope:* Benedict XIV (1740–1758).

20 *The Inquisition:* C., who did not fear the Inquisition at Venice, where it was practically independent of Rome, had good reason to fear the much more rigorous Inquisition in the Papal States, to which Cesena belonged.

21 *Sangiovese:* C. writes *Saint-Jevese*; San Giovese wine, from La Romagna, is still well known in Cesena.

22 *I needed:* C. follows to the letter the directions given by Agrippa von Nettesheim in his *De occulta philosophia*.

23 *Evening:* The events of two days seem to be telescoped in this paragraph. After supper on the first day, Francia falls asleep and does not wake until the morning of the second, when his wife

brings C. his breakfast chocolate. The "evening" of Genoveffa's arrival is that of the second day.

24 *Spirito folletto:* Will-o'-the-wisp, hobgoblin. The Italian for
will-o'-the-wisp is *fuoco fatuo*. C. seems to derive *folletto* from
the *follet* in French *feu-follet*.

25 *At night . . . :* In the manuscript the chapter ends with these
words, followed by an erasure. The rest of the incident is
recounted in the next chapter (Vol. 3, Chap. I).

Volume Three

CHAPTER I

1 *1748:* C. had not left Venice until December 1748. Various
considerations lead to the conclusion that the following events
took place in the summer of 1749.

2 *Great Circle:* Mathematical and astronomical concept, but here
meaning a magician's circle.

3 *Inquisition:* Cf. Vol. Two, Ch. XI, n, 20.

4 *Godfrey . . . princess:* Allusions to events in the course of the
dispute over investitures between the Emperor and the Pope.
Matilda of Tuscany, widow of Godfrey of Lorraine, was allied
with Pope Gregory VII and the Emperor Henry IV. Henry's
penance at Canossa (1077) only interrupted the struggle for a
time.

5 *Gregory VII:* Pope from 1073 to 1085, educated at Cluny, the
great reforming Pope of the medieval Church; he sought to
subordinate secular to ecclesiastical power. He was canonized
in 1606. From what source Casanova drew the allegation that
Gregory was a great magician is unknown.

6 *Lugo:* A small city in the valley of the Po, between Ravenna
and Bologna; at the period it belonged to the Ecclesiastical
State.

7 *Scudi:* The Roman scudo was a silver coin which was minted
at Rome from the time of Pope Sixtus V (1585–1590) to that
of Pope Pius IX (1846–1878); its value was 10 paoli or 100
baiocchi.

8   *Zecchini:* The zecchino was a gold coin minted at Venice from the 15th century. Its value was 22 Venetian lire.

9   *Sbirri:* Policemen.

10   *Paolo:* A coin whose value was 11 soldi, minted from the time of Pope Paul III.

11   *Innkeeper:* In the 18th century officers were not required to register at inns.

12   *Albani:* At the time there were three Cardinals named Albani: Annibale Albani, Cardinal from 1711, his brother Alessandro, Cardinal from 1721, and their nephew Gian Francesco, Cardinal from 1747. Cardinal Alessandro Albani (1692–1779) was the "Protector Hungariae"; hence the Hungarian officer's connection with him.

13   *Dutillot:* Guillaume Léon Dutillot (or Du Tillot) (1711–1774), major-domo to the ducal house of Parma from 1749, Minister from 1756 to 1771.

14   *Vetturino:* Hire coachman.

15   *Not measuring my words:* Original, *parlant hors des dents*, one of C.'s more extreme Italianisms.

16   Horace, *Sat.*, I, 6, 57.

17   *Twenty years later:* C. was in Spain in 1767–1768, hence eighteen years after the events here narrated.

CHAPTER II

1   *Carriage of his own:* In addition to travel by mailcoach, it was possible at the period to travel in one's own carriage, horses and driver being furnished by the post.

2   *Henriette:* Obviously a fictitious name. According to recent research the woman whom C. so designates was probably Jeanne Marie d'Albert de Saint-Hippolyte (1718–1795), who married Jean Baptiste Laurent Boyer de Fonscolombe (died 1788) in 1744. She had separated from her husband, probably in 1749.

3   *Caffè della Nobiltà:* The name given to coffeehouses which principally catered to members of the nobility.

4   *Count Dandini:* Son of Count Ercole Francesco Dandini (1691–1747) of Cesena, from 1736 Professor of Jurisprudence at the University of Padua.

5   *Spanish links:* Chains composed of interlocking links of gold wire.

6   *Philosopher:* In accordance with 18th-century Italian usage, the word here means "alchemist."

7   *Terence, etc.:* Publius Terentius Afer (ca. 201–159 B.C.), born in Carthage, and Titus Maccius Plautus (ca. 250–184 B.C.), born in Umbria, the greatest Roman comic dramatists; Marcus Valerius Martialis (ca. 40–102), born in Spain, celebrated Roman epigrammatist.

8   *Forlì:* Town between Bologna and Rimini on the Via Emilia.

9   *Centum cellae:* In Roman times Civitavecchia was called "Centum cellae," after the many small basins for ships there; under the Emperor Trajan it received the name "Portus Traiani." The present name goes back only to the 9th century, when the inhabitants, after the town was destroyed by the Saracens, returned to the "old city."

10   *Tartan:* A small vessel used in the Mediterranean and carrying a mast with a lateen sail and two jibs.

11   *Ponte Molle:* The route from Rome northward was by the Via Flaminia, which left the city by the Porta del Popolo and then crossed the Tiber by the Ponte Molle (later Ponte Milvio).

12   *Institute:* The reference is to the Istituto delle Scienze (Accademia Benedettina) in Bologna.

CHAPTER III

1   *Reggio:* Town at the foot of the Apennines, between Bologna and Piacenza.

2   *D'Andremont:* No innkeeper of this name in Parma is documented in contemporary sources.

3   *New government:* By the Treaty of Aix-la-Chapelle (1748), which marked the end of the War of the Austrian Succession, the Infante Philip of Spain, second son of the Bourbon King Philip V of Spain and Elisabetta Farnese, received the duchies of Parma, Piacenza, and Guastalla. He entered Parma on March 7, 1749.

4   *Madame de France:* In France the King's eldest daughter was called "Madame"; "Mesdames de France" was the designation for the French Princesses. The reference here is to Louise Elisabeth, eldest daughter of King Louis XV, who married Duke Philip (Don Filippo) and entered Parma on Nov. 23, 1749.

5   *Bornisa's:* An Osteria Bornisa still existed in Parma in the 19th century; it was in the section of the city across the River Parma.

6   *Lire:* The Parmesan lira was a silver coin whose value was 20 soldi.

7   *Caudagna:* Nowhere else in his memoirs does C. say that a sister of his father's had married a Caudagna.

8   *Copernican system:* The famous work by Nicolaus Copernicus (1473–1543) on the revolutions of the heavenly bodies (*De revolutionibus orbium coelestium libri VI*, Nuremberg, 1543) was on the Index of Forbidden Books from 1616 to 1757 because it replaced the geocentric by the heliocentric system.

9   *Tartuffe:* A hypocrite; from the name of the leading character in Molière's comedy *Tartuffe*.

10   *Sous:* The French sou was a copper coin first minted under Louis XV; its value was the twentieth part of a franc (which was also called "livre").

11   *Farnese:* The house of Farnese came to an end with Antonio Francesco, who died in 1731 leaving no male descendant.

12   *The theater:* The Teatro Ducale (built 1689) in Parma was open to the public. It was replaced by the Teatro Regio in 1829.

13 *Arlecchino:* One of the principal characters ("masks") of the *commedia dell'arte.*

14 *His mother:* Elisabetta Farnese, from 1714 second wife of King Philip V of Spain.

15 *Duke Antonio:* Antonio Francesco Farnese (1679–1731); became Duke of Parma in 1727.

16 *What time of day it is:* In Italy the hours of the day were reckoned from the first hour at the ringing of the Angelus (hence a half hour after sunset) and continuing to the twenty-third hour. The actual time of any given hour of course changed with the seasons. The decree abolishing the system was not issued until 1755; however, the French doubtless introduced the French system of reckoning into the Duchy of Parma in 1749.

17 *De La Haye:* According to C., Valentin de La Haye (ca. 1699–1772) was a Jesuit; however, his name does not appear as such in contemporary sources.

18 *Madame Dacier:* Anne Dacier, née Lefèvre (1654–1720), was married to the French philologist André Dacier (1651–1722); she was considered one of the most learned women of her time and was known especially for her translations from ancient writers.

19 *Dubois-Chatellerault:* Baron Michel Dubois-Chatellerault (1711–1776 or '77), ennobled by Frederick the Great, was an engraver in the service of the Duke of Parma; he reformed the Venetian coinage in 1755, became a member of the Reale Accademia di Belle Arti at Parma in 1757, and was appointed Director General of the Parmesan mint in 1766.

CHAPTER IV

1 *Opera buffa:* The reference is probably to the comic opera *L'Arcadia in Brenta*, with a libretto by Carlo Goldoni.

2 *Buranello:* Byname of the composer Baldassare Galuppi (1706–1785), who came from the island of Burano, near Venice.

3 *Spartito:* Score in parts.

4   *Tusculans:* Cicero wrote his *Tusculanae Disputationes* in 45–44
    B.C. after the death of his daughter; it is a moral and philo-
    sophical discussion on death, suffering, and passion.

5   *Closing of the opera:* The reference is probably to the nine-day
    suspension on account of the Christmas season.

6   *Virtuosi:* Musicians.

7   *Laschi:* Filippo Laschi, Italian singer, who appeared in opera in
    Italy, England, and Austria from 1743 to 1775.

8   *La Baglioni:* Presumably Giovanna Baglioni, Italian singer,
    whose four sisters, however, were also well-known singers.
    Giovanna is documented as appearing in Italy and in Vienna
    until 1772.

9   *Symphony:* Composition for orchestra (not a "symphony" in
    the modern sense).

10 *Vandini:* Antonio Vandini (died 1770), celebrated Italian
    violoncellist, performed in Prague in 1723 but later resided
    principally in Padua.

11 *De La Combe:* Louis de La Combe (died 1757), intimate friend
    of Duke Philip of Parma.

12 After Vergil, *Aeneid*, III, 395 and X, 113.

13 *Porta di Colorno:* Later called Porta di San Barnabà, in the
    northern part of Parma, near the present railway station. Col-
    orno, some nine miles north of Parma, was the spring and
    summer residence of the Dukes.

14 *Dutillot:* See note 13 to Chap. I of this volume.

15 *Entertainment:* The events described took place in December
    1749; it is improbable that a night garden-party was given at
    that time of year.

16 *Order of St. Louis:* Established by Louis XIV in 1693; in the 18th
    century it had about 16,000 members.

17 *D'Antoine:* Count François d'Antoine-Placas, Gentleman
    of the Bedchamber to the Duke of Parma and Chief Equerry to

the Duchess Louise Elisabeth; he must have been an old man in 1749.

CHAPTER V

1 *Mont Cenis:* The Col du Mont Cenis, at an altitude of 6800 feet, had long served as a pass over the Alps for travelers from the Piedmont to Savoy.

2 *Sledge:* In the winter months the descent from the top of the pass was made in sledges. Casanova is in error regarding the name "La Novalaise." The modern Novalesa is south of the pass; the first community to the north is Lanslebourg.

3 *"Scales":* This inn ("À la Balance") was still considered the best hotel in Geneva in the 19th century. Goethe, Schopenhauer, and Stendhal lodged there. It no longer exists.

4 *Tronchin:* The reference appears to be only to the Genevan representative of the well-known banker Jean Robert Tronchin (1702–1788) of Lyons, possibly to his brother François Tronchin (1704–1798) or to their cousin Jacob Tronchin (1717–1801), both of whom long resided in Geneva.

5 *Louis:* French gold coin first minted under Louis XIII in the 17th century; value, 24 francs.

6 *Châtillon:* First post station on the road from Geneva to Lyons (some 28 miles from Geneva).

7 *Fifteen years later:* C. met Henriette again in 1763, but did not speak to her; he saw her once more in 1769, but did not recognize her.

8 *The Leads:* In 1755 (cf. Vol. 4).

9 *Buen Retiro:* Name of a royal palace in Madrid, with an extensive garden, built in the 17th century under Philip IV.

10 *Service of France:* Corsica, which had belonged to the Republic of Genoa since 1299, began to struggle for its independence early in the 18th century and was supported by France, which, however, bought the island in 1768. Hence in the War of the Austrian Succession Corsican officers were fighting in Italy on the side of France.

11 *Frémont:* Jacques Frémont was court surgeon and dentist to the Duke of Parma.

12 *Great cure:* Treatment with mercury.

13 *1749:* C. is mistaken in the date; the events he relates occurred in January 1750.

14 *The pox:* Here, as often in the memoirs, C. writes *v...*, for *vérole* ("the pox," "syphilis").

15 *Mercury:* A deliberate pun; Mercury both means the metal and is the Latin name for Hermes as guide of souls.

16 *Botta:* Jacopo Botta-Adorno (1729–1803), Austrian diplomat and Field Marshal.

17 *Bavois:* Louis de Saussure, Baron de Bavois (1729–1772), served the King of Naples until 1748, entered the service of the Venetian Republic in 1752. He was of Swiss extraction.

18 *Duke of Modena:* Francesco III Maria d'Este (1698–1780), from 1737 Duke of Modena, Reggio, and Mirandola.

19 *Too much talk:* The father of Louis de Saussure was Georges de Saussure, Baron de Bercher et Bavois (1704–ca. 1752), Commander of the Swiss regiment of the Duke of Modena; he was demoted in 1748 for serious derelictions.

20 *Bragadin:* Matteo Giovanni Bragadin (1689–1767), Venetian Senator and one of C.'s patrons (cf. especially Vol. 2).

21 *Ambassador:* The reference is either to Alvise Mocenigo, Venetian Ambassador in Rome until Feb. 28, 1750, or to his successor Pietro Andrea Capella, who was in Rome from Jan. 20, 1750.

22 *Aquileia:* The disputes between Venice and Austria over Aquileia were already long-standing, since the jurisdiction of the Patriarch, who was always chosen from among the Venetian patricians, extended into Austrian territory. In 1751 Pope Benedict XIV abolished the Patriarchate of Aquileia and created two archdioceses (Udine in Venetian territory, Görz in Austria).

23 *Jus eligendi:* The right to choose the Patriarch of Aquileia.

CHAPTER VI

1   *Cases against me:* The two accusations which had been the cause of C.'s leaving Venice.

2   *Savio di Settimana:* Title of the ranking administrative official of the Venetian Republic, appointed for a term of one week.

3   *Fusina:* A small port on the mainland, south of Mestre.

4   *Foreigner:* As a patrician and a Senator of the Republic, Bragadin was forbidden to lodge foreigners in his house.

5   *Forty hours:* The Forty-hour Prayer, "Oratio quadraginta horarum" (commemorating the forty hours during which Christ lay in the tomb), at which the Holy Sacrament is exhibited, originated in 1527; in 1623 it was made obligatory in all churches, and was finally confirmed by Pope Clement XI in 1705.

6   *Barca corriere:* Packet boat.

7   *Signor Dandolo:* Marco Dandolo (1704–1779), younger brother of the Venetian patrician Enrico Dandolo and friend of Senator Giovanni Bragadin.

8   *Savio for War:* The Venetian Minister for War was officially entitled *Savio alla Scrittura*; he was one of the five "Savi di Terra Firma," members of the "Collegio," elected (from 1430) every six months by the senate to handle the affairs of the Republic's possessions on the mainland.

9   *Rosicrucian:* Member of a secret brotherhood with mystical and reformatory tendencies, founded by Johannes V. Andreae, who wrote a book on the legendary Christian Rosy Cross of the 15th century in 1605. Rosicrucian Brotherhoods existed in Germany, England, and France. In the 18th century an alchemistically oriented secret society appears to have sprung up under the same name. At the same period Masonic Lodges adopted many Rosicrucian concepts.

10   *Carpegna:* Monte Carpegna, a mountain in the Apennines, southwest of Rimini. Casanova had asserted that he was initiated into the occult sciences by a hermit who lived there (cf. Vol. 2, Chap. VII, n. 17).

11   Paralis: Name of the spirit from whom C. claimed to receive

commands. C. later adopted it as his own Rosicrucian name, and even received letters addressed to "Mr. Paralis." In all likelihood C. modeled the name after the title of a book on the occult sciences which was famous at the period: *Le Comte de Gabalis, ou Entretiens sur les sciences secrètes*, by the Abbé Monfaucon de Villars (Paris, 1670). The most recent reprint in C.'s time appeared in 1742.

12 *French Ambassador:* The reference is probably to the Envoy Extraordinary Paul François Galucci, Sieur de l'Hôpital, Marquis de Châteauneuf-sur-Cher, who was temporarily conducting his negotiations with Venice from Naples.

13 *Foreign envoys:* A law originally promulgated in 1481 and reenacted on several occasions, most recently in 1717, forbade patricians to talk with foreign diplomats; conversations were permitted only on purely official business.

CHAPTER VIII

1 *Flaminia:* Elena Virginia Riccoboni, née Balletti (1686–1771), sister of Mario, actress with the Comédie Italienne at Paris. She played the role of the *prima amorosa* Flaminia; hence her byname. As a writer and translator she was a member of several academies, among them the Arcadian Academy of Rome. She married the Italian actor and author Lodovico Andrea Riccoboni (see note 8, below).

2 *Republic of Letters:* As used in 18th-century France, the term included both writers and scholars.

3 *Sojourn:* The "three famous men" (see the three following notes) were said to have come to Paris only to compete for the favor of Elena Virginia Riccoboni. Their rivalry must already have begun in Italy, before the Italian troupe, including Flaminia, was summoned back to Paris in 1716.

4 *Maffei:* Marchese Scipione Maffei (1675–1755), Italian writer and literary critic; he composed his tragedy *Merope* for Flaminia in 1712.

5 *Conti:* Antonio Conti, known as the Abate Conti (1677–1749), Italian philosopher and poet, chiefly celebrated for his tragedies.

6   *Martelli:* Pier Giacomo Martelli (1665–1727), Italian poet; composed a virulent satire on Maffei in 1724.

7   *V:* The argument appears to be without foundation, since the question is at most one of orthography, not of pronunciation.

8   *Eighty years old:* Lodovico Riccoboni, known as Lelio (1677–1753), Italian actor, playwright, and writer on the theater, was 74 years old at the time.

9   *Duke-Regent:* After the death of Louis XIV (1715), Duke Philip of Orléans (1674–1723) assumed the Regency during the minority of Louis XV. Louis XIV had banished the Italian actors from Paris, at the instigation of Madame de Maintenon, in 1697; the Regent brought them back in 1716.

10   *Marivaux:* Pierre Carlet de Chamblain de Marivaux (1688–1763), celebrated author of plays and novels.

11   *Marivaux's comedy:* The reference is to his *Le Jeu de l'amour et du hasard* (1730).

12   *Saint-Sauveur:* Parish church, built in the 13th century, in the 2nd Arrondissement.

13   *Profession:* In France in the 18th century the Church still denied Christian marriage and burial in consecrated ground to actors. Voltaire protested hotly against this severity.

14   *Palais-Royal:* Built by Cardinal Richelieu from 1629 to 1634; he left it to the King after his death, hence Palais-Royal. Its garden, which was open to the public, was a favorite spot for walks and assignations.

15   *Bavaroise:* A beverage supposed to have been brought to Paris by Bavarian princes in the 18th century. It was made of strong tea sweetened with cane sugar, to which were added the yolk of an egg, milk, and kirsch.

16   *Orgeat:* A decoction of barley or almonds.

17   *Gentleman of the robe:* An advocate. Here Claude Pierre Patu (1729–1758), advocate at the Parlement (High Judicial Court) of Paris, and writer. He and C. soon became close friends.

HISTORY OF MY LIFE

18   *Civet cat:* La Civette, a well-known 18th-century tobacco shop;
     at the time it was located opposite the Café de la Régence, near
     the Palais-Royal.

19   *Duchess of Chartres:* Louise Henriette (1726–1759), from 1752
     Duchess of Orléans.

20   *Neuilly:* Earlier a small fishing port on the Seine, with a ferry;
     the first bridge there was built in 1606. The present Pont de
     Neuilly was built from 1768 to 1772.

21   *Ratafia:* A very sweet fruit liqueur, esteemed in the 18th cen-
     tury as a cure for stomach disorders.

22   *Great Chamber:* The Grande Chambre was the principal cham-
     ber of the Parlement (High Judicial Court).

23   *States-General:* Body created in 1302 to represent the three
     "estates" (clergy, nobility, third estate); it was supposed to be
     summoned by the King to discuss all important political ques-
     tions with him. During the Age of Absolutism it was not once
     convoked (from 1614). The present National Assembly
     evolved from it during the French Revolution.

24   *St. Louis:* Louis IX (1215–1270), King of France from 1226, was
     canonized in 1297.

25   *Louis XII:* 1462–1515, King from 1498; he was called "the
     Father of the People."

26   *Henri IV:* 1553–1610, King of France from 1589; brought peace
     to the country after the Wars of Religion by enforcing
     tolerance through the Edict of Nantes (1598); wished every
     Frenchman to have "a chicken in the pot" on Sundays.

27   *Madame la M.:* The Marquise de Pompadour.

28   *Bordello:* The original has *b..d.l.*.

29   *Is not the case:* In the States-General the third estate (the people)
     had the same number of representatives as the clergy and the
     nobility; hence the two privileged estates together had twice as
     many votes.

30   *Patu:* See note 17 to this chapter.

31   *Crébillon:* Prosper Jolyot de Crébillon (1674–1762), dramatist
      and royal censor. Famous in his time, he was soon eclipsed by
      his son Claude, the novelist and short-story writer.

32   *Zénobie et Rhadamiste:* Correctly, *Rhadamiste et Zénobie*, a
      tragedy by the elder Crébillon (1711).

33   *Marais:* The Marais was then an aristocratic quarter, on the right
      bank of the Seine.

34   *Royal censor:* Censorship, which from the Middle Ages had
      been exercised by the theological faculty of the Sorbonne,
      began to be regularly practiced by the State from the time of
      Richelieu. But it was not until 1741 that permanent royal
      censors were appointed; of these, there were 79 in all, of
      whom 35 had jurisdiction over belles-lettres.

35   *Livy:* Titus Livius (59 B.C.–A.D. 17), famous Roman historian;
      he was a native of Padua and was criticized for using provincial
      expressions in his writings.

36   Original: le *je ne sais quoi*.

37   *Louis XIV:* Though he had died in 1715, he was much talked of
      at the time because of Voltaire's *Le Siècle de Louis XIV*, which
      was published in 1751.

38   *Siamese Ambassadors:* The King of Siam had sent ambassadors to
      the French court in 1682, 1684, and 1686, because he feared
      Dutch colonial policy; but there is nothing to substantiate C.'s
      allegation that Madame de Maintenon had a role in the missions.

39   *Cromwell:* Crébillon later used material from his forbidden *Crom-
      well* in his tragedy *Le Triumvirat* (1754).

40   *Catilina:* Tragedy by Crébillon, first performed in 1748.

41   *Medea:* In Greek legend, Medea was the daughter of the King
      of Colchis and married Jason; to punish her unfaithful husband
      she killed her children (tragedy by Euripides).

42   *The Senate scene:* Voltaire wrote his tragedy *Catilina* in 1752.

43   *Man in the Iron Mask:* In Chapter 24 of *Le Siècle de Louis XIV*,
      Voltaire states that the Man in the Iron Mask was a brother of

the King. There is no doubt that he existed; he was Count Ercole Mattioli, Secretary of State to the Duke of Mantua.

44 *Cénie:* The play was performed June 25, 1750, but at the Théâtre Français, not at the Comédie Italienne.

45 *Madame de Graffigny:* Françoise de Graffigny (1695–1758), woman of letters, aunt of Helvétius.

46 *Amphitheater:* Accommodations for spectators in the French theaters of the period were: *théâtre* (on the stage itself), *parterre* (standing room on the floor of the house), *loges* (first-tier boxes), *amphithéâtre* ("dress circle"), *loges hautes* (second-tier boxes), *loges du troisième rang* (third-tier boxes).

47 *Beauchamp:* A fictitious name; no Receiver-General of this name is documented at the period.

CHAPTER IX

1 *Fontainebleau:* A favorite residence of the French Kings from the time of Louis XIII. In 1750 Louis XV stayed there from October 7 to November 17.

2 *There:* I.e., to Fontainebleau.

3 *Morosini:* Francesco II Lorenzo Morosini (1714–1793), Venetian patrician, Ambassador of the Republic in Paris 1748–1751, from 1755 Procuratore di San Marco.

4 *Lully:* Jean Baptiste Lully (1632–1687), French composer of Italian origin; director of the Paris Opéra (Académie Royale de Musique).

5 *Madame de Pompadour:* Jeanne Antoinette Poisson (1721–1764), married to Charles Guillaume Le Normand d'Étioles 1741; mistress of Louis XV, who created her Marquise de Pompadour in 1745 and a Duchess in 1752.

6 *Lemaure:* Catherine Nicole Lemaure or Le Maure (1703–1786), French opera singer.

7 *Blue Ribbon:* Knight of the Order of the Holy Ghost. The order was established in 1578 by Henri III in honor of his accession to the throne of France and his election as King of Poland.

Both events took place on Whitsunday (the feast of the descent of the Holy Spirit), which accounts for the name of the order. The emblem of the order was worn on a blue ribbon. The Knight of the order to whom C. refers is the Duke of Richelieu. (See the following note.)

8 *Maréchal de Richelieu:* Louis François Armand, Duke of Richelieu and Fronsac (1696–1788), Marshal of France from 1747.

9 *Calfeutrées:* "Stopped up." C.'s mispronunciation involves the vulgarism *foutre* ("to have sexual intercourse").

10 *Put apart:* Original, *écarter,* which means both "to spread apart" and "to set aside."

11 *He:* I.e., Richelieu.

12 *Lord Keith:* George Keith, 10th Earl Marischal of Scotland (1693–1778), exiled as a Jacobite in 1716, lived in Berlin from 1745, was Prussian Ambassador in Paris 1751–1754. In Vol. 2, Chap. IV, C. says that he met him in Constantinople in 1745.

13 *Madame de Brionne:* Louise Julie Constance, Countess of Brionne (1734–1815), married to the Count of Brionne in 1748.

14 *Monsieur d'Argenson:* Marc Pierre de Voyer de Paulmy, Count of Weil-d'Argenson (1696–1764), from 1720 Lieutenant-General of Police, from 1742 Minister of War.

15 *The face of Louis XV:* The many portraits of Louis XV show him to have been, in fact, a very handsome man.

16 *The Queen of France:* Maria Leszczyńska, daughter of the dethroned King of Poland, Stanislaus Leszczyński, married to Louis XV in 1725.

17 *Monsieur de Lowendal:* Ulrik Frederik Volmar, Freiherr von Lowendal (1700–1755), Russian Count from 1738, Marshal of France from 1747.

18 *Bergen-op-Zoom:* The famous fortress of Bergen-op-Zoom in Brabant was captured by Lowendal in 1747 during the War of the Austrian Succession.

19 *Mesdames de France:* Title of the daughters of the reigning King of France. Here the daughters of Louis XV: Elisabeth (born

1727, married to the Duke of Parma in 1739, lived in Parma from 1749), Henriette (1727–1752), Adélaïde (born 1732), Victoire (born 1733), Sophie (born 1734), Louise (born 1737).

20   *Giulietta:* Giulia Ursula Preato, known as La Cavamacchie (1724–1790), Venetian singer and courtesan (cf. Chap. I of this volume).

21   *Marquis de Saint-Simon:* Maximilien Henri, Marquis de Saint-Simon-Sandricourt (1720–1799), Adjutant-General to the Prince of Conti.

22   *Prince de Conti:* Louis François, Prince of Bourbon-Conti (1717–1776), Marshal of France and diplomat.

23   *Queen Elizabeth:* Elizabeth I of England (1533–1603).

24   Ovid, *Fasti*, I, 218. Giulietta refers to a well-known epigram addressed to Queen Elizabeth; but her memory of it is inaccurate, for the speaker is not the Queen but the poet: *In thalamis, Regina, tuis hac nocte iacerem / Si foret hoc verum, pauper ubique iacet* ("I should sleep in your bed tonight, O Queen, if it were true that the poor man makes his bed everywhere").

25   *Marry a Grimani:* The marriage did not take place until 1757.

26   *Monsieur de Saint-Quentin:* Nothing is known of this Gentleman of the Bedchamber to the King.

27   *Beginning of these memoirs:* See Vol. 1, Chap. IV.

28   *Countess Preati:* Giulietta, whose name was Preato, assumed the name of the noble Veronese family of Preati.

29   *Count Kaunitz:* Wenzel Anton, Count Kaunitz, from 1764 Prince of Kaunitz-Rietberg (1711–1794), was Austrian Ambassador in Paris from 1750 to 1753.

30   *Count Zinzendorf:* Ludwig Friedrich Julius, Count Zinzendorf (1721–1780), first served the Elector of Saxony, then entered the service of Austria; he was in Paris 1750–1752.

31   *Abbé Guasco:* Octavien de Guasco, Count of Clavières (1712–1780), of Piedmontese origin; Canon of Tours, member of the Academy of Inscriptions.

32 *Signor Uccelli:* Francesco Antonio Uccelli (born 1728), Venetian notary, later secretary to the Venetian Embassy in Vienna, married Giulietta Preato in 1752 (cf. Vol. 1, Chap. IV).

33 *Madame Préaudeau:* Catherine Étiennette Charlotte Préaudeau, née Gaulard, married Claude Jean Baptiste Préaudeau (died 1762) in 1751.

34 *Déchargé:* "Discharged, unloaded," but incorrectly used in C.'s context.

35 *Savoyards:* In Italian *savoiardo* is the name of a biscuit which originated in Savoy. In French *Savoyard* means a native of Savoy.

36 *Whom you call Savoyards:* In Paris porters, chimney sweeps, bootblacks, and the like, who offered their services in the streets, were called "Savoyards," since many of them came from Savoy.

37 *Derrière:* C. not only commits an error in French, as Crébillon explains to him in the next paragraph, but also perpetrates an obscenity, since Italian *vi* ("you") sounds exactly like French *vis* (slang for "penis").

38 *Charon:* C. added the name in his revision. The reference may be to the wife of the Councilor Élie Bochart de Saron.

39 *Lady Lambert:* Lady Mary Lambert (ca. 1717–1762) was married to the English baron and banker John Francis Lambert (died 1755).

40 *Fair at Saint-Germain:* The fair, which originated in the 12th century, was held yearly from Feb. 3 to Palm Sunday in front of the Church of Saint-Germain-des-Prés.

41 *Borghese:* Marcantonio Niccolò, Prince Borghese (1730–1800), and Giovanni Battista Francesco, Prince Borghese (born 1733).

42 *Knez:* "Prince" in Slavonic languages.

43 *Being a woman:* C. is mistaken; he was a man. Charles Chevalier d'Éon de Beaumont (1728–1810), French diplomat, from 1755 secret agent of Louis XV, lived in Paris as a woman from 1777 to 1785, and died in England.

44 *Gave birth to a son:* Erica, Princess of Ardore (1708–1766), bore a son named Luigi Maria at Paris in 1743; her husband was Neapolitan Ambassador in Paris from 1741 to 1753.

45 *Duchess of Fulvy:* C. probably refers to Hélène Louise Henriette Orry de Fulvy (died 1768), who was not a Duchess but the wife of an Intendant of Finances.

46 *Gaussin:* C. confuses La Gaussin with Louise Gaucher, called Lolotte (died 1765), actress and mistress of Lord Albemarle.

47 *Lord Albemarle:* William Anne Keppel, 2nd Earl of Albemarle (1702–1754), appointed English Ambassador in Paris in 1749.

48 *Canada:* France lost Canada to England by the French and Indian War, which ended in 1759 when the English took Quebec.

49 *Venetian lady:* Lady Anna Wynne, née Gazini (1713–1780), was married in 1739 to Sir Richard Wynne, whose mistress she had been and who died in 1751.

50 *Her eldest daughter:* Giustiniana Franca Antonia Wynne (1736 or '37–1791); in 1761 she married Philipp Joseph, Count Orsini-Rosenberg (1691–1765), who was Austrian Ambassador in Venice from 1754 to 1764.

CHAPTER XI

1 *Morphy:* Victoire Morphy (born ca. 1734), actress in comic opera. She was the daughter of an Irishman, Daniel Morphy, but had acted in Flanders.

2 *Half écu:* Petit écu, coin worth 3 francs or livres; the *grand écu,* or *écu de six francs*, was worth twice as much.

3 *Twenty-five louis:* = six hundred francs.

4 *Helen:* C. calls her Helen because of her beauty. She was Marie Louise Morphy, known as Louison (1737 or '38–1815). Mistress of Louis XV from 1752 to 1755.

5 *A Greek:* Slang for "sharper."

6   *A German painter:* Probably the Swedish painter Gustaf Lundberg (1695–1786); but perhaps Johann Anton Peters (1725–1795), who lived in Paris from 1746 to after 1787, was ennobled by Louis XV in 1763, and who chiefly copied paintings by Boucher.

7   *O-Morphi:* Modern Greek ὄμορφη = "beautiful" (feminine).

8   *Monsieur de Saint-Quentin:* See note 26 to Chap. IX.

9   *Six-franc piece: Écu de six francs* (see note 2, above). It bore a portrait of Louis XV.

10 *Double louis:* Gold coin worth 48 francs.

11 *Parc aux Cerfs:* Originally a game preserve created by Louis XIII in Versailles. It later became a residential section of the city and, as such, kept its old name.

12 *At the end of a year:* The boy was probably born in the summer of 1753.

13 *Staff officer:* Jacques de Beaufranchet, Count of Ayat (died 1757), from the Auvergne.

14 *Tablets:* A portable set of leaves or sheets, used for writing, especially for memoranda; in the 18th century, often made of ivory.

15 *Madame de Valentinois:* Marie Christine Chrétienne de Rouvroi de Saint-Simon de Ruffec (1728–1774), married Charles Maurice Grimaldi-Goyon de Malignon (1727–1790), Count of Valentinois, Chevalier of Monaco, in 1749.

16 *Old wife:* See note 16 to Chap. IX.

17 Altered from Horace, *Epistles*, II, 1, 176.

18 *Sanson:* Possibly a descendant of the cartographer Nicolas Sanson, of Abbeville (1600–1667), and his son Adrien (died 1718).

19 *Garnier:* His father, Jean Garnier, long in the service of the Count of Argenson, made a fortune supplying the army; he became Major-Domo to the Queen in 1749.

20 *Duchess of Chartres:* Louise Henrietta, née Princess of Bourbon-Conti (1726–1759), married Louis Philippe, Duke of Chartres

(later Duke of Orléans) in 1743. She was president of the women's Masonic Lodges in France.

21 *Madame de Polignac:* Marie, Marquise de Polignac, née Rioult de Courzay (died 1784).

22 *Plantain water:* In the 18th century plantain in various forms was much employed in medicine. The likelihood is that the Duchess's pimples were the result of a venereal disease.

23 *Abbé de Brosses:* Probably the Abbé Marcel de Brosses, for whose arrest the Parlement de Paris issued a warrant in 1761.

24 *Duke of Montpensier:* Louis Philippe II, from 1785 Duke of Orléans, best known as the "Citizen King" under the name of Philippe Égalité (1747–1793).

25 *Madame La Pouplinière:* Mimi Le Riche de La Pouplinière, née Boutinon des Hayes, earlier an actress under the name of Mimi Dancourt (ca. 1713–1756), married the tax farmer Alexandre Jean Joseph Le Riche de La Pouplinière in 1737.

26 *Hole:* Richelieu had rented an apartment in the house next door, from which he had access to Madame de La Pouplinière's bedroom through an opening in the fireplace. Her husband discovered it and left his wife. She died of cancer.

CHAPTER XII

1 *Migliavacca:* Giovanni Ambrogio Migliavacca (born ca. 1718 at Milan), Italian poet, pupil of Metastasio; from 1752 court poet to the King of Poland at Dresden.

2 *Metastasio:* Pietro Antonio Metastasio (real name Trapasso; 1698–1782), celebrated Italian poet, best known for his opera librettos; from 1730 court poet at Vienna.

3 *Gravina:* Gian Vincenzo Gravina (1664–1718), professor of law at the University of Rome and well-known literary critic, founder of the Arcadian Academy, adoptive father of Metastasio.

4 *Attilio Regolo:* Tragedy with music (1740), first performed at Dresden in 1750.

5   *French prose:* The first French prose translation of Metastasio's
    works was published in 12 volumes by J. Richelet from 1751 to
    1756.

6   *Ariosto:* Metastasio was presumably referring to the translation
    by F. de Rousset, published in 1615.

7   *Imperial Library:* The library, later the National Library, was
    founded by Maximilian I and enlarged by his successors. The
    splendid building which houses it on the Josefsplatz was built in
    1721 by order of Karl VI, the father of Maria Theresa.

8   *A young Venetian:* Probably Felice Calvi, whose education De La
    Haye undertook in Paris, subsequently taking him to Poland.

9   *Border commissioner:* As the result of a long series of boundary
    disputes between Austria and the Republic of Venice, a com-
    mission of plenipotentiaries from either side was set up in the
    18th century: Francesco II Lorenzo Morosini (1714–1793) was
    a commissioner for Venice from 1752 to 1754.

10 *Kremnitz ducats:* Austrian gold coin, value four gulden; it was
    minted at Kremnitz, in Slovakia.

11 *Archduchesses:* Maria Anna (born 1738); Maria (born 1742);
    Elisabeth (1743); Maria Amalia (1746); Johanna (1750); Josepha
    (1751); Karoline (1752). Marie Antoinette, later married to
    Louis XVI of France, had not been born at the time of
    which C. writes.

12 *Eldest son:* Joseph II (1741–1790), Emperor from 1765, ruined
    his health by unremitting work, though he knew that his
    constitution was not equal to the strain.

13 *Laxenburg:* Summer palace near Vienna, favorite resort of
    Joseph II.

14 *Brambilla:* Gian Alessandro Brambilla (1728–1800), born in
    Pavia, physician-in-ordinary to Joseph II. Anton von Störck
    (1741–1803), physician-in-ordinary to Maria Theresa, was also
    in the service of Joseph II after the death of the Empress and
    did not conceal his serious condition from him. Presumably C.
    refers to him here.

15 Ovid, *Remedia amoris*, 91.

16 *His brother:* Leopold II (1747–1792), Emperor from 1790. Hence C. wrote this account after 1790 and before 1792 (accession of Franz II).

17 *The intelligent physician:* The reference is either to von Störck (cf. note 14) or to Joseph Quarin (1734–1814), from 1758 professor at the University of Vienna.

18 *His niece:* Elisabeth, Princess of Württemberg (1767–1790), married the Archduke Franz of Austria in 1788, died in child-bed in 1790.

CHAPTER XIV

1 *Twenty o'clock:* Old Italian reckoning, about 5:00 P.M.

2 *To engage a box:* There were already several shops in Venice at which theater tickets could be purchased.

3 *Giudecca:* Venetian, Zuecca. In the 18th century this island, to the south of the city proper, had many gardens and country houses; it was a favorite place for excursions.

4 *San Biagio:* The eastern part of the island, so called after the church of the same name (built in 1222, demolished in 1860).

5 Altered from Ariosto in Domenico Batacchi's *La Rete di Vulcano.*

6 *Montealegre:* José Joaquín, Duke of Montealegre, was Spanish Ambassador in Venice from 1748 to 1771.

7 *Brows not given to anger:* I.e., narrow eyebrows, according to the doctrine of Lavater (1741–1801), whose *Physiognomical Fragments* C. knew in the French translation by the author (published 1781–1785).

8 Old Italian reckoning: about midnight.

9 *Campo di Santa Sofia:* On the Grand Canal, a short distance north of the Rialto bridge.

CHAPTER XV

1 *Season of masks:* In 1753 the fair, and with it the time during which masks might be worn, lasted from May 30 to June 12.

Many of the dates given later in this chapter are erroneous, as is often the case with C.

2   *Morosini:* Francesco Morosini (born 1751), nephew of Francesco Lorenzo Morosini (1714–1793); for the latter, who was a hereditary Cavaliere della Stola d'Oro, see note 3 to Chap. IX of this volume.

3   *Cristiani:* Beltrame, Count Cristiani (also Christiani, 1702–1758), Austrian privy councilor, Grand Chancellor of Austrian Lombardy.

4   *Ch.:* I.e., Christoforo, Christian name of Caterina Capretta's father.

5   *Patriarch:* The Bishop of Venice bore this title from 1451. The office of Patriarch of Venice was held by Alvise Foscari from 1741 to 1758.

6   *June 13th:* The Fiera del Santo, in honor of the saint whose feast it was, began in Padua on this day. There is another error in dates here (cf. note 1).

7   *XXX:* Recent research has led to the supposition that the convent was that of Santa Maria degli Angeli in Murano.

8   *Burchiello:* A vessel carrying passengers and freight, which made a daily round trip between Venice and Padua.

9   *Palazzo Bragadin:* Senator Bragadin owned a palace in the Santa Sofia quarter of Padua, in which he usually spent the summer and autumn with his friends.

10   *Signora Tiepolo:* Cornelia Tiepolo, née Mocenigo, married to the Venetian patrician Francesco Tiepolo (1697–1750) in 1722.

11   *Croce:* Antonio Croce, alias Della Croce, De La Croix, Santa Croce, Castelfranco, Crozin (died 1796), son of Giovanni Battista Croce, of Milan, adventurer; in Italy the title "Don" was given to priests, Roman noblemen, and noblemen of the provinces which had been under Spanish rule.

12   *Gillenspetz:* Swedish army officer, sentenced to death *in absentia* for fomenting rebellion, moved to Venice and became the lover of Marina Pisani, the wife of a patrician.

CHAPTER XVI

1   *Prato della Valle:* A large square in Padua; its present aspect dates only from 1775. Croce appears to have lived in a house on the square.

2   *Rosenberg:* Philipp Joseph, Count Orsini-Rosenberg (1691–1765), did not enter on his office as Austrian Ambassador in Venice until July 1754. C. doubtless refers to the Chargé d'Affaires Stephan von Engel, later secretary to the Ambassador, who represented his country's interests until Rosenberg arrived.

3   *Mendex:* Probably an English Jew named Joshua Mendes da Costa, who settled in Venice in 1750.

4   *Doblones de a ocho:* Spanish gold coin, value 8 gold scudi.

5   *Venetian ducati:* Originally a gold coin minted in Venice from 1284, and which in the 16th century came to be called a zecchino. In the 17th century a new ducato was minted, with a value of 14 lire.

6   *Podestà:* In general the mayor of an Italian town; in the towns of the Venetian mainland possessions the podestà, as a high judicial officer, was almost always a Venetian patrician.

7   *In Venice:* According to contemporary sources, Croce had been banished from the territories of the Venetian Republic as early as November 7, 1753. However, this is contradicted by the birth of his child in Venice (cf. note 18).

8   *Venetian noblemen:* In the 18th century Venetian patricians were permitted to make bank for games of chance, but not to play themselves.

9   *Dolo:* On the post road from Padua to Venice, on the Brenta, some ten miles east of Padua.

10 *P. S.:* Perhaps for "Pères Somasques" (monks of the Somaschian Order; cf. Vol. 1, Chap. V, n. 7); if so, then the reference is to the Church of Santa Maria della Salute.

11 *Bollettone:* A sort of ticket which could be paid for in advance and which gave the holder priority at post stations.

12 *Fiesso:* Post station some eight miles east of Padua.

13 *Gondoin:* A professional gambler of this name, of Greek origin, was banished from Padua in July 1756.

14 *Catherine:* C. here gives away C. C.'s Christian name (Caterina).

15 *The "Sign of the Hat":* Al Cappello rosso; it was known as the best inn in Vicenza from the 15th century. Goethe lodged there in 1786.

16 *Her mother was fond of me:* Signora C. (Maria Colonda) was the daughter of Carlo Ottaviani of Padua. His wife Elisabetta, née Marcolini, had welcomed the nine-year-old C. most affectionately at Padua in 1734 (cf. Vol. 1, Chap. I).

17 *Counts:* In the 18th century there were some twelve families with a legitimate claim to the title of Count in Vicenza; there were also some 300 noble families which currently used the title.

18 *A boy:* Actually the child, which was born and baptized on March 15, 1754, was a girl, Barbara Giacoma Croce; C.'s name as one of her two godfathers appears in the register of the Church of Santa Maria Formosa in Venice.

Volume Four

CHAPTER I

1 *Aventurine:* A brownish colored glass flecked with gold, first manufactured at Murano; also, a variety of quartz of the same color.

2 *San Canziano:* Church northeast of the Rialto Bridge, near the Church of Santa Maria dei Miracoli.

3 *Countess S.:* C. wrote Seguro, but crossed it out and substituted the initial. Countess F. or T. Seguro, wife of Count Seguro, probably came, like the whole Seguro (Sigouros) family, from the island of Zante in the Ionian Sea.

4 *Riva del Rio Marin:* Original, *quai du Romarin* ("Rosemary Quay"). C. undoubtedly means one of the streets on either side of the Rio Marin (directly opposite the present railway station, south of the Grand Canal).

5 *Convent of the XXX:* Presumably the convent of Santa Maria degli Angeli, on the island of Murano.

6   *M. M.:* It has not yet been possible to identify M. M. with certainty. Earlier Casanova scholars (Gugitz) believed she was a certain Maria Lorenza Pasini, whose name in religion was Maria Maddalena; as she was of the citizen class and nothing has yet been discovered which would indicate that she enjoyed any celebrity, the possibility must be excluded. Further on in the manuscript C. several times first wrote "Mathilde," then substituted "M. M." Probably she is Maria Eleonora Michiel (or Micheli), of a Venetian patrician family, who had become a nun in the convent of Santa Maria degli Angeli in Murano in 1752. Her mother was born a Bragadin. This fact would explain not only M. M.'s acquaintance with Countess S. and her references to her high birth but also her turning to C., of whom she had presumably heard from the Bragadin family.

CHAPTER II

1   *Countess Coronini:* Maria Theresia, née Countess Salburg (died 1761), married to Johann Anton, Count Coronini-Cronberg, in 1700, lady in waiting at the Bavarian court and later at the Imperial Court of Charles VII.

2   *Santa Giustina:* A very old Venetian church, property of the nuns of the Augustinian Order from 1448; it no longer exists.

3   *Nun of the Celsi family:* This nun has not yet been identified beyond doubt; she may have been the abbess of the convent of San Sepolcro, whose name was Celsi and who died in 1785 at the age of sixty-nine.

4   *Nun of the Micheli family:* This reference to a nun bearing this family name speaks against the assumption that she is the mysterious M. M. (cf. note 6 to Chapter I of this volume). Yet C. may here have been deliberately trying to mislead.

5   Horace, *Satires*, II, 2, 79.

6   Horace, *Epistles*, I, 2, 54.

7   *Friulian:* Friuli (the name is derived from the Roman settlement Forum Julii) is a district south of the Carnic Alps; it belonged to the Venetian Republic from 1420. Friulians often served as

porters, lantern-carriers, and messengers in Venice, and had a reputation for reliability.

8   *Savoyards:* Many inhabitants of Savoy, which was a part of Italy in the 18th century, emigrated to Paris and had a similar reputation for reliability in their more or less menial occupations.

9   *Zecchini:* 1 soldo = 1/20 of a Venetian lira; 1 lira = 1/22 of a zecchino.

10 *Honor:* The Brockhaus-Plon edition reads *honneur.* Laforgue gives *bonheur* ("happiness," "good fortune"), which is more probably right.

11 *Montealegre:* José Joaquín, Duke of Montealegre (died 1771), was Spanish Ambassador in Naples from 1740 to 1746 and in Venice from 1748. C. probably met him in Naples rather than in Parma.

12 *Rosenberg:* Philipp Joseph, Count Orsini-Rosenberg (1691–1765), was Austrian Ambassador in Venice from 1754 to 1764.

13 *French Ambassador:* François Joachim de Pierre de Bernis (1715–1794) was French Ambassador in Venice from 1752 to 1755. See note 10 to the following chapter.

14 *Vestal:* Vesta, the Roman goddess of the hearth fire, had a circular temple in the Forum in which the perpetually burning hearth of the State was tended by six vestals. These priestesses lived a cloistered life near the temple; they had to take a vow of chastity, the penalty for breaking which was death.

15 *Augustine:* Aurelius Augustinus (354–430), saint and celebrated Father of the Latin Church. Casanova here refers to his *De civitate Dei*, Book XXII, Chap. 24.

16 Slightly altered from Horace, *Epistles,* I, 2, 62–63.

CHAPTER III

1   *Julius Florus:* Roman historian who accompanied the Emperor Tiberius (A.D. 14–37) to the Near East.

2   Horace, *Epistles,* II, 2, 191–192.

3   *Casino:* The exact location of the Abbé de Bernis's pleasure house (according to C. he was M. M.'s lover) is not known. (Cf. note 10 to this chapter and Chaps. IV, V).

4   *Half past the first hour of night:* According to the Italian reckoning the first hour of the day of twenty-four hours began at the Angelus, a half hour after sunset. As the season was winter the time mentioned would be about 8:00 P.M.

5   *Four o'clock:* I.e., about 11:00 P.M.

6   *Sèvres porcelain:* The famous manufactory, which was originally in Vincennes, was moved to Sèvres in 1753.

7   *Cook:* The cook employed by the Abbé de Bernis from 1753 to 1755 was named Durosier.

8   *"Oeil de perdrix" champagne:* A pink champagne from Villes-Allerand. Its color resembles that of a partridge's eye; hence the name.

9   *Signor Mocenigo:* Alvise II Zuan Mocenigo (1710–1756), Venetian patrician; he was Venetian Ambassador in Paris from 1751 to 1756.

10 *The A. de B.:* Here the Abbé de Bernis is first referred to by his initials. His full name does not appear until Chapter VI. François Joachim de Pierre de Bernis (1715–1794), abbé from 1727, writer, member of the French Academy and the Arcadian Academy. French Ambassador in Turin 1752, in Venice from Oct. 1752 to Oct. 1755, made a cardinal in 1758; later held other high diplomatic posts. Some of C.'s biographers consider his account of De Bernis slanderous, especially since the Cardinal's own memoirs mention no such adventures. However, contemporary sources tend to show that C.'s portrait is accurate on the whole.

11 *Count of Lyons:* Members of the Cathedral Chapter of Lyons bore this title. To be received into the chapter candidates had to show descent from sixteen noble ancestors. De Bernis received the title in 1748.

12 *Belle-Babet:* After a Parisian flower vendress whose beauty was greatly admired. Voltaire called De Bernis "the flower girl of Parnassus."

13   *His poems: Poésies de M.L.D.B.*, Paris, 1744.

14   *St. Catherine's Day:* The feast of St. Catherine of Alexandria was celebrated on November 25th.

15   *Palazzo Morosini del Giardino:* This palace of the Morosini family near the Church of the Santi Apostoli took its name from an especially beautiful and elaborate garden, which disappeared at the beginning of the present century.

16   *Flanders post:* The imperial post, operated by the Thurn und Taxis family.

17   *Here:* C. appears to have forgotten that the conversation is taking place not at M. M.'s casino but in the convent visiting room.

18   *Bartolomeo da Bergamo:* Bartolomeo Colleoni (1400–1475), from 1455 Captain-General of the Venetian Republic. The famous equestrian statue of him by Verrocchio (1436–1488) stands in the square in front of the Church of SS. Giovanni e Paolo.

19   *Lord Holderness:* Robert d'Arcy, fourth Earl of Holderness (1718–1778), was English Ambassador in Venice from 1744 to 1746.

20   *Second hour:* Cf. note 4 to this chapter.

21   *Alençon point:* A kind of lace. Laces played a great part in 18th-century fashion. After Venetian laces, those from Alençon, in northern France, were most highly esteemed.

22   *Saxon porcelain:* From the manufactory at Meissen, founded in 1710.

23   *First hour:* Cf. note 4 to this chapter.

24   *Bautta:* A sort of mantle worn by maskers.

25   *Henriette:* Cf. Vol. III, Chaps. 1–5.

26   *L'Étorière:* Marquis de l'Étorière (died 1774), French general staff officer, was considered one of the handsomest men in Paris.

27   *Antinoüs:* A beautiful Bithynian youth, favorite of the Emperor Hadrian; he accompanied him to Egypt and was drowned in the Nile in A.D. 130. Hadrian paid him divine honors after his

death. He is represented in countless antique statues and bas-reliefs.

28 *Third Heaven:* According to the Ptolemaic system, the Heaven of Venus.

29 *The Mother and the Son:* Venus and Love.

CHAPTER IV

1 *No masking:* Going masked was forbidden in Venice from December 16th to December 25th because of the novena (see note 5) before Christmas.

2 *Lord Bolingbroke:* Henry St. John, Viscount Bolingbroke (1678–1751), English statesman and writer. His collected works (*On Authority in Matters of Religion, Concerning the Nature, Extent and reality of Human Knowledge, On the Rise and Progress of Monotheism*, etc.) were published in 1754.

3 *Charron:* Pierre Charron (1541–1603), French moralist and disciple of Montaigne. His *Traité de la sagesse* was published at Bordeaux in 1601. Charron's advocacy of the Stoic philosophy and his skepticism made it a handbook for the freethinkers of the 18th century.

4 *Bishop Diedo:* Vincenzo Maria Diedo (died 1753), Carmelite monk and Bishop of Altino-Torcello; the nuns of Murano were under his jurisdiction.

5 *Novena:* In the Roman Catholic Church, nine days of devotion for any religious object. C. here refers to the novena preceding Christmas.

6 *Portier des Chartreux: Histoire de Dom Bougre, portier des Chartreux, écrite par lui-même* ("History of Dom Bugger, Porter of the Carthusians, written by himself") by J. C. Gervaise de Latouche; it was first published at Rome in 1745.

7 *Meursius:* Johannes Meursius (Jean de Meurs, the Younger, 1613–1654), Dutch antiquary; he wrote his essays in Latin. The obscene book *Joannis Meursii Elegantiae latini sermonis, seu Aloisiae Sigeae Toletanae Satyra Sotadica de Arcanis Amoris et Veneris* (first published in Holland in 1680) at first passed as a Latin

translation by Meursius from a Spanish text by Luisa Sigea of Toledo. Its real author was Nicolas Chorier (1609–1692).

8   *Opera:* The feast of St. Stephen is celebrated on December 26th. The theaters in Venice reopened on that date.

9   *Ridotto:* Gambling casino in the San Moisè quarter. All its patrons had to be masked unless they were patricians. It was closed in 1774.

10   *Robe:* The obligatory dress for Venetian patricians was a black robe. Senators wore red.

11   *Corrector:* The Correttori delle Leggi e del Palazzo were the members of a magistracy made up of five patricians and established in 1553; their chief duty was to amend laws.

12   *Lucca oil:* Olive oil from the Lucca district in Tuscany was considered especially good.

13   *Four Thieves vinegar:* Acetum quattuor latronum, a vinegar with herbs.

14   *Frustratoires:* From Latin *frustratio*, "frustration," but in slang use (see note 16 to this chapter) apparently meaning "stimulant."

15   *Muff:* In the 18th century men also carried muffs in winter.

16   *À gogo, etc.:* À gogo, slang "going to it hard"; *frustratoire*, see note 14; *dorloter*, "to coddle." The last is a perfectly ordinary word but apparently M. M. had not heard it until C. used it, like the others, in an obscene sense.

17   *Madame de Boufflers:* Marie Louise, Marquise de Boufflers-Rouverel.

18   *Con rond:* In French it has the obscene meaning "round cunt," but what letters of the Italian alphabet Madame de Boufflers had in mind remains a mystery. Cf. Count Lamberg writing to C. in 1792: "I do not understand how Mme. de Boufflers can have asked you why one says *con rond* in the Italian alphabet. What are the letters which are thus pronounced?" (*Casanova und Graf Lamberg, Briefe*, ed. G. Gugitz, Vienna and Leipzig, 1935, p. 234).

19   *Condoms:* Contraceptive sheaths, then made of fine linen.

20 *Masulipatam:* An Indian cotton cloth, so named from the city in which it was woven.

21 *St. Andrew's cross:* A cross in the shape of the letter X.

22 *Straight tree:* One of the thirty-five erotic positions described by Pietro Aretino (1492–1556) in his *Sonetti lussuriosi* composed for engravings by Raimondi after drawings by Giulio Romano (1492–1546).

CHAPTER V

1 *Sappho:* The Greek poetess Sappho (ca. 600 B.C.) lived on the island of Lesbos and gathered girls about her as votaries of Aphrodite and the Muses. The community was later misunderstood, so that Sappho came to be regarded as the most celebrated representative of Lesbian love.

2 *Correggio's Magdalen:* Antonio Allegri da Correggio (1494–1534), Italian Renaissance painter; C. probably saw his Mary Magdalen (painted ca. 1520) in Dresden (according to some experts, the painting at Dresden is a copy of the original).

3 *Poisoned:* There is no historical support for C.'s allegation that Bartolomeo Colleoni (see note 18 to Chapter III of this volume) was poisoned. In fact C. himself refutes it in the third volume of his *Confutazione della Storia del Governo Veneto d'Amelot de La Houssaie* (1769).

4 The saying is attributed to the Emperor Caracalla (188–217) after the murder of his brother Geta.

5 *Two o'clock:* About two and a half hours after sunset.

6 *Mocenigo:* Alvise II Girolamo (called Momolo) Mocenigo (born 1721), Venetian patrician.

7 *Signora Marina Pisani:* Marina Pisani, née Sagredo, married to the patrician Almorò II Andrea Pisani in 1741; passionately addicted to gambling, in 1751 she was forbidden to enter the Ridotto. The prohibition was later withdrawn.

8 *Marcello:* Piero Marcello di San Polo (1719–1790), of a Venetian patrician family, sentenced to six years of imprisonment under the Leads in 1755 and later banished to Corfu. However, it is

possible that the reference is to a Piero Marcello di San Caterina (born 1720).

9   *Signora Venier:* Elisabetta Venier, née Mocenigo, married to the patrician Sebastiano Venier in 1741.

10 *Pierrot:* Pierrot wore white and powdered his face with flour. The masks named later on are from the *commedia dell'arte* or its French derivatives.

11 *Furlanas:* The furlana was a lively dance from Friuli; it was always danced by a couple.

CHAPTER XII

1   *Key of Solomon: Clavicula Salomonis,* a book of magic lore; first printed in Hebrew, then in Latin, and finally translated into the modern languages. King Solomon was regarded in the East and in the Christian Middle Ages as a great magician.

2   *Zecor-ben:* Otherwise *Zohar,* also known in earlier literature as *Midrasch-Na-Zohar,* it professed to contain the divine revelation of a certain Rabbi Ben Yohai to his pupils. The book is composed partly in Hebrew and partly in Aramaic; first published in Spain in the 13th century by Moses de León; printed in Italy in 1558. It is considered a key work of cabalism.

3   *Picatrix:* A medieval treatise on conjuring up the devil; the original manuscript is in the Bibliothèque de l'Arsenal, Paris. It was mentioned by Rabelais in his *Pantagruel,* Book 3, Chapter 23.

4   *Treatise on the planetary hours:* It is impossible to determine to which of the many books on the subject current in the 18th century C. here refers.

5   *Philosophe militaire:* "The Philosophical Soldier"; the manuscript was published at London in 1768 by Jacques André Naigeon under the title *Le Militaire philosophe ou difficultés sur la Religion proposées au R. P. Malebranche prêtre de l'Oratoire par un ancien officier.* The book is outspokenly antireligious.

6   *Mathilde:* This name appears here for the first time. It is possible that it is M. M.'s real name; more probably, however, C. was

still concealing her real name here. In any case, the reading represents words which C. crossed out in his manuscript.

7 *Opeska:* Antonio Niccolò Manuzzi was created a count by Stanislas Poniatowski when he married the latter's mistress Countess Opeska.

8 *C. D.:* Perhaps Clotilda Cornelia Dal Pozzo, daughter of the widow in whose house C. was then lodging and younger sister of the "beautiful patient"; she married Giovanni G. Gabrieli in 1768.

9 Greek proverb, based on Hercules' fight with the Hydra; quoted by Plato in his *Phaedo.*

10 *Flight from the Leads:* C.'s account was printed at Prague in 1788 under the title *Histoire de ma fuite des prisons de la République de Venise qu'on appelle les Plombs écrite à Dux en Bohême l'année 1787,* and published at Leipzig.

11 *Terza:* Name of a bell in the campanile of San Marco; it was rung only to summon the members of the magistracy to their regular afternoon sessions. According to the season, the hour varied from noon to 5:00 P.M.

12 *Under the Leads:* The prison was installed under the lead roof of the Doge's Palace in 1561. According to C.'s account it contained 7 cells, according to other sources only 4. The cells disappeared sometime in the 19th century.

13 *Quay of the Prisons:* C. writes *quai des prisons,* which might correspond to the Fondamenta delle Prigioni, which was on the Rialto in front of the prisons on the ground floor of the Palazzo dei Camerlenghi. But he can here only refer to the quayside on the Rio delle Prigioni, officially the Rio del Palazzo, next to the Doge's Palace.

14 *Enclosed bridge:* The famous Ponte dei Sospiri ("Bridge of Sighs") which connected the Doge's Palace with the Prigioni Nuove (see note 7 to Chap. XIII); the bridge and the Prigioni Nuove were built in 1589.

15 *Rio del Palazzo:* Also called Rio delle Prigioni (cf. n. 13).

16 *Circospetto:* Title of the Secretary to the Senate and the Council of Ten.

17 *Twenty-one o'clock:* 2½ hours before sunset.

18 *Eight o'clock:* 8½ hours after sunset; about 5:30 A.M. in July.

19 *Lorenzo:* Lorenzo Basadonna, warden from 1755. After C.'s escape he was imprisoned and in 1757 was sentenced to ten years in jail for murder.

20 *La Cité mystique . . . : La mística ciudad de Dios* ("The Mystical City of God") was written by the nun María de Agreda, by her civil name María Coronel (died 1665) and first published at Madrid in 1670. A French translation appeared in 1729 at Brussels. The work, which was in three volumes, was heavily attacked in the 17th and 18th centuries and until 1748 was on the Index. It enjoyed a sort of renaissance in the 20th century.

21 *Forgotten:* C. later added the name Caravita in the margin. However, Vincenzo Caravita (1681–1734), a learned Neapolitan Jesuit, did not write a book on this subject. C. perhaps refers to *La Dévotion au Sacré Coeur,* by the Jesuit Jean Croiset (1656–1738), which was first published in 1689 and instituted the adoration of the Sacred Heart.

22 *Franciscan nuns:* The name of the convent was La Inmaculada Concepción.

23 *Agreda:* A small town some sixty miles east of Soria.

24 *Palafox:* Juan de Palafox y Mendoza (1600–1659) was made Bishop of Puebla de Los Angeles in America, served as Vice-Regent of Mexico from 1640 to 1642, and was made Bishop of Osma (Spain) in 1653. Proceedings to canonize him were begun in 1726 but were definitively abandoned in 1777.

25 *Mystical city:* Original, *cette cité mystique.* This is probably a reference to Agreda; but as C. is more than careless about capitals and underlinings he may have been referring to the title of the book.

26 *Malagrida:* Gabriele Malagrida (1689–1761), Italian Jesuit and missionary in Brazil, later confessor to a convent in Lisbon. He wrote his *La vida de gloriosa Santa Anna* in prison from 1759 to 1761. The book was put on the Index and in 1761 Malagrida was strangled and burned by order of the Inquisition. But the real reason for his condemnation would appear to have been

that in 1758 he urged the assassination of the King of Portugal and prophesied his death.

27 *Ancient splendor:* In the course of the 18th century the Society of Jesus was outlawed in several European countries (Portugal 1759, France 1764, Spain and the Kingdom of Naples 1767) and was finally suppressed by Pope Clement XIV in 1773. It was restored in 1814 by Pope Pius VII.

28 *Fifty soldi:* Contemporary sources confirm that Basadonna was authorized to expend 48 soldi a day for C. The amount was later reduced to 30 soldi.

29 *Gazette de Leyde:* So named from its place of publication (Leiden, Holland), it bore the subtitle *Nouvelles extraordinaires de divers endroits.* It had been published regularly from 1680.

30 *Physician:* The archives of the Venetian Inquisition show that his name was Bellotto or Bellotti.

31 *Boethius:* Anicius Manlius Severinus Boethius (480–524), minister to Theodoric the Great, wrote his famous treatise *De consolatione philosophiae* in prison.

32 *New Inquisitors:* The three Inquisitors who sentenced C. were Andrea Diedo, Antonio Condulmer, and Antonio da Mula. On October 1, 1755, they were succeeded by Alvise Barbarigo, Lorenzo Grimani, and Francesco Sagredo (the latter pardoned C. in 1774).

33 *Sentence:* C. was actually sentenced to five years' imprisonment under the Leads for atheism on September 12, 1755.

34 At this point C. crossed out nearly a whole page of his manuscript so heavily that what he wrote cannot be deciphered.

35 Horace, *Odes*, I, 37, 29.

36 *The same time:* The great Lisbon earthquake occurred on November 1, 1755.

CHAPTER XIII

1 *Line:* One-twelfth of an inch.

2   *Bussola:* Name of the anteroom of the Council of Ten and the State Inquisitors.

3   *Businello:* Pietro Businello, also Busenello, was the Venetian Resident in London from 1748 to 1751, then became Secretary to the Council of Ten. The Venetian Republic appointed ambassadors, who were always patricians, only to Constantinople, Rome, Paris, Vienna, and Madrid. To all other countries it sent residents appointed from among the secretaries to the Senate and the Council of Ten; they belonged to the class of *cittadini.* C. presumably met Businello in Paris in 1751, when Businello was on his way from London to Venice.

4   *Maggiorin:* C. is either mistaken or is purposely concealing his companion's name. The man was Lorenzo Mazzetta, of Milan; he was valet to Count Giorgio Marchesini, of Vicenza.

5   *Poggiana:* A patrician family of Vicenza.

6   *"The Four":* I Quattro, four prison cells in the Doge's Palace which were at the disposition of the State Inquisitors. The same name was also applied to cells in the so-called "New Prisons" (see the following note) which were connected with the Doge's Palace by the Bridge of Sighs.

7   *Prison building:* Built by Antonio da Ponte, separated from the Doge's Palace by the Rio del Palazzo.

8   *Cerigo:* Mazzetta escaped from prison in January 1762. It is not known if he was recaptured. There is no record of his having been exiled to Cerigo.

9   *Lire:* One Venetian lira was worth 20 soldi.

10   *Diedo:* Andrea Diedo (born 1691), Senator, State Inquisitor from October 1754 to October 1755.

11   *Ration biscuits:* Venetian ration biscuit was famous for its keeping qualities; it was prepared for soldiers and prisoners.

12   *Nobili:* According to the documents in the case his name was Carlo (not Sgualdo) Nobili.

13   *Charron's* Wisdom: See note 3 to Chap. IV of this volume. The first Italian translation of *De la sagesse* appeared in 1698 and a second in 1768.

14 *Montaigne:* Michel de Montaigne (1533–1592), author of the world-famous *Essais*.

15 *Seriman:* Roberto, Count Seriman, of Persian descent, diamond dealer in Venice, known in his day as a great gambler.

16 *Extrajudiciary:* A document drawn up by a notary for the purpose of settling a suit without going to court, that is, "extrajudicially," whence the name.

17 *Montealegre:* See note 11 to Chap. II of this volume.

18 *Lista:* The zone around and belonging to a foreign embassy; the embassy's right of asylum usually extended to it. For reasons of surveillance the foreign embassies were all in one part of the city (near the present railway station). The street now named the Lista di Spagna points back to this circumstance.

19 Adapted from Horace, *Epistles*, I, 2, 58–59.

20 *Twenty inches:* Earlier in this chapter C. gave its length as two feet.

21 *Young wigmaker:* Probably a certain Giacomo Gobbato, who died on November 25, 1755, at the age of twenty-one.

22 *Is expedient:* C. uses the Latin verb *expedit*.

23 *Schalon:* Gabriel Schalon, also Schalom, Salom, of Padua. According to the documents in the case he became C.'s cellmate as early as December 19, 1755.

24 *Five Savi:* The Cinque Savi alla Mercanzia constituted a sort of ministry of commerce (established in 1506).

25 *Eight or nine weeks:* C. first wrote "nearly three months," then canceled it.

26 *Micheli:* Domenico Micheli (1732–1782), Venetian patrician, Senator from 1745; he may have been M. M.'s brother.

27 *Corner:* Flaminio Corner, also Cornaro (1692–1779), Venetian patrician, Senator, and author.

28 *In Latin:* His principal work was a history of the Church in Venice and Torcello, *Ecclesiae venetae et torcellanae antiquis monumentis*, etc., Venice, 1749.

29 *St. James of Compostela:* Italian, Giacomo. He was revered in the West as the "first martyr." His tomb in Santiago de Compostela in northern Spain was and still is a famous place of pilgrimage. His feast is celebrated on July 25th.

30 *St. George:* His feast is celebrated on April 23rd.

31 *The other St. James:* His feast is celebrated on May 1st, with that of St. Philip.

32 *St. Anthony:* His feast is celebrated on June 13th.

33 *Diameter:* C. must mean "radius"; he could not get through a hole only ten inches across.

34 *Terrazzo marmorin:* A flooring made of small pieces of marble held together by lime.

35 *Livy:* Book XXI, Chap. 37.

36 *Asceta . . . ascia:* C.'s hypothesis is completely unfounded. Livy wrote *infuso aceto* ("after vinegar had been poured in").

37 *St. Theodore:* St. Theodore of Euchaita, martyred during the reign of the Emperor Diocletian, was the first patron saint of Venice. Since tension between Venice and the Patriarchate of Aquileia, whose patron saint was St. Hermagoras, a pupil of St. Mark the Evangelist, had already begun in the early Middle Ages, the Venetians sought an opportunity to outdo the neighboring State. In 828 the relics of St. Mark were secretly brought from Alexandria to Venice, and installed in a chapel which was later replaced by the church of San Marco. Thereafter the winged lion, St. Mark's emblem, became the emblem of the Venetian Republic.

38 *Eusebius:* Eusebius, Bishop of Caesarea (died 339), court theologian to the Emperor Constantine the Great, wrote the first history of the Church. He describes St. Mark as St. Peter's companion in Book II, Chap. 15 of his history.

39 *Fenaroli:* Count Tommaso Fenaroli, known in his day as a great gambler, was imprisoned under the Leads July 22–30, 1755.

40 *Origo:* Father Origo, earlier a Jesuit, was in the service of the Abbé de Bernis during his term as ambassador in Venice.

41   *Twenty o'clock:* About three and a half hours before sunset.

42   *Signora Alessandri:* Margherita Alessandri, Italian singer, born in Bologna.

43   *Martinengo:* Paolo Emilio, Count of Martinengo da Barco (1704 –after 1795), Venetian patrician.

44   *Signora Ruzzini:* Arpalice Ruzzini, née Manin, married to Giovanni Antonio Ruzzini (1713–after 1766) in 1746; he was a Venetian patrician and diplomat, ambassador in Madrid 1750–1754, in Vienna 1755–1761, in Constantinople 1766.

45   *Proved to be the case:* Count Fenaroli had broken the strict Venetian law which forbade any conversation between patricians and foreign ambassadors except in connection with official business.

46   *Canary wine:* Wine from the Canary Islands, especially from Tenerife, had long been esteemed.

47   *St. Augustine's Day:* His feast is celebrated on August 28th.

48   *Zeno:* Greek philosopher (late 4th–early 3rd century B.C.), founder of the Stoic school.

49   *Pyrrhonists:* Disciples of the Greek philosopher Pyrrho (360– 271[?] B.C.), founder of the Skeptic school. The Greek word *ataraxia* means complete tranquillity of soul; according to the doctrine of Epicurus and the Pyrrhonists, achieving it is the highest moral duty of man.

50   *Abstine . . . sustine:* From a maxim of Epictetus, quoted in Aulus Gellius, *Noctes atticae*, XVII, 19.

CHAPTER XIV

1   *"Wells":* I Pozzi; the prison cells so named were eighteen in number, located in the Doge's Palace under the offices of the State Inquisitors and the Council of Ten, and could be reached only from there by a secret stairway. It is possible that the nine lower cells were occasionally flooded; but the condition was certainly not constant.

2 *Beguelin:* Probably Domenico Lodovico Beghelin, also Bighelin (ca. 1696–after 1775), of Mantua, captain in the service of the Venetian Republic; he was first sentenced to the "pozzi" and later to the "camerotti" (cells without windows).

3 *Count Schulenburg:* Johann Mathias, Count von der Schulenburg (1661–1747), first in the service of Poland, from ca. 1715 Venetian Field Marshal; he distinguished himself by his defense of Corfu against the Turks.

4 Seneca, *Epistles*, CI, where the saying is attributed to Maecenas.

5 *Spielberg:* The citadel of Spielberg in Brünn (now Brno) was the state prison of the Austro-Hungarian monarchy; it was destroyed by the French in 1809.

6 After Horace, *Epistles*, I, 2, 58.

7 *Maffei:* See Vol. 3, Chap. VIII, n. 4. His collected works were not published until 1790; so it was a matter of buying various books of his, some of them in several volumes.

8 *Rationarium:* The *Rationarium temporum*, a work on chronology by Denys Pétau, called Petavius (1583–1652); it was published at Paris in 1633–1634.

9 *Wolff:* Baron Christian von Wolff, also Wolf (1679–1754), German philosopher of the Age of Reason. Since there was no edition of his collected works, it is not possible to determine to which of his writings C. refers; possibly to his latest book at the time, *Philosophia moralis sive ethica*, 5 vols., Halle, 1750–1753.

10 Seneca, *Epistles*, XCVIII.

11 *Latet:* C. first wrote *quaere* ("seek"), then crossed it out and substituted *latet*.

12 *Balbi:* Marin Balbi (1719–1783), Venetian patrician and monk of the Somaschian Order (founded in 1532 and confirmed by Pope Paul IV in 1540; it exists only in Italy).

13 *Asquin:* Count Andrea Asquin, also Asquini (died after 1762), of Udine.

14 *Four years:* According to the Venetian judicial archives Balbi
    was not arrested until November 5, 1754.

15 *Father Superior:* Either Girolamo Barbarigo (1723–1782),
    Somaschian monk and professor at the University of Padua, or
    his brother Luigi Barbarigo, who was Superior of the
    Somaschian monastery of Santa Maria della Salute.

16 *Priuli Gran Can:* Alvise Priuli (1718–after 1763), Venetian
    patrician; sentenced to the Leads in August 1755. His sobriquet
    may have been derived from the famous representative of the
    Veronese family of Scaliger, Can Grande della Scala (1291–
    1329).

17 *Five years:* Count Asquin was sentenced to life imprisonment
    on September 20, 1753, but in 1762 he managed to escape with
    sixteen other prisoners.

18 *Two gentlemen:* They were the brothers Bernardo and Dom-
    enico Marcolongo. The Sette Comuni is a German-language
    enclave in upper Italy, between the Astico and the Brenta
    Rivers.

19 *Two notaries:* They were Giovanni Boldrin and Pietro Zuccoli,
    sentenced to the Leads on April 2, 1756.

20 *Veronese Marchese:* Count (not Marchese) Desiderato Pinde-
    monte, of Verona, sentenced to the Leads in 1756.

21 *Vulgate:* The official Latin text of the Bible approved by the
    Roman Catholic Church, in large part translated by St. Jerome.
    A Venetian printer did bring out an edition of the Bible
    in an unusually large format about this time; it is nearly 18
    inches high.

22 *Septuagint:* A Greek translation of the Old Testament made,
    according to tradition, by order of Ptolemy Philadelphus II
    (284–247 B.C.) by 72 Egyptian Jewish scholars (*septuaginta*
    means seventy, hence the name).

23 *St. Michael's Day:* The feast of St. Michael is celebrated on
    September 29th.

24 *Macaroni:* The name did not mean the form of pasta to which it
    is applied today but what are now known as "gnocchi."

25 *Twice the width of the Bible:* The Bible was a folio, so its width was some 13 inches.

26 *Eighteen o'clock:* About 1:00 P.M.

27 *Monday:* Reckoning from the last date given by C.—October 16th—Soradaci became his cell-mate on October 18th; but in 1756 October 18th was a Saturday.

28 *Office of the Holy Virgin:* The *Officium parvum*, a book of prayers in honor of the Virgin Mary, used in the Roman Catholic Church from the 11th century.

29 *Isola:* Town on the north coast of the Istrian peninsula (now Izola); it is an island connected with the mainland, hence the name.

30 *First Chaplain:* Probably the priest Pietro Madecich, who was born in Mantua and hence was a subject of the Empress Maria Theresa.

31 *Ambassador:* See Vol. 3, Chap. IX, n. 50.

32 *Refosco:* A well-known wine from the vicinity of Udine.

33 *Soradaci:* Francesco Soradaci, barber and wigmaker, of Isola in Istria.

CHAPTER XV

1 *Brought back to my cell:* According to the extant documents in his case, Francesco Soradaci had already been arrested on September 1, 1756, but was probably kept in another prison until October 18th and was set free on December 31, 1756. The account given in the documents does not correspond with the story C. puts in his mouth.

2 *Nineteen o'clock:* About 2:00 P.M.

3 *First three days of November:* The first days of November were official holidays in Venice; many patricians spent them in their country houses in the Terra Ferma (the parts of the mainland ruled by the Republic), especially in the celebrated villas along the Brenta between Venice and Padua.

4   *Sortes virgilianae:* A form of divination in which an inquirer opened the works of Vergil at random and read a meaning applicable to his situation in the first verse that met his eye.

5   Ariosto, *Orlando furioso*, IX, 7, 1.

6   In his first account of his escape (published in 1788), C. added *dit le Tasse* ("says Tasso") after this quotation. However, the line is not found in Tasso. It occurs in Metastasio's *Didone abbandonata*, Act I, Scene 4.

7   *Braccia:* A Venetian measure of length, equivalent to about 26 inches.

8   *Tartuffe:* Type of the pious hypocrite, from the famous comedy by Molière (1622–1673).

9   *Two o'clock:* About 8:00 P.M.

10 *Aeneas ... Anchises:* According to Vergil, *Aeneid*, II, 707 ff., Aeneas carried his father Anchises out of burning Troy on his shoulders.

11 *Arsenalotti:* Workers in the Arsenal, the military port of Venice. They also formed the guard of the Great Council; their weapons were a sword and a red stick.

12 *Sant'Apollonia:* District of the city taking its name from a confraternity dedicated to St. Apollonia. It is in the Sestiere di San Marco, near the Ponte della Canonica.

13 *Scudi:* The scudo was a gold coin which had been minted in Venice from the 16th century; its value was 8 lire or 160 soldi. One hundred scudi were worth about 46 zecchini.

14 Vulgate, Psalm 117, verse 17.

15 Vulgate, Psalm 117, verse 18.

16 Dante, *Divina commedia*, "Inferno," XXXIV, 139. It is the last line of the "Inferno."

CHAPTER XVI

1   *San Giorgio Maggiore:* This island, on which is the domed church of the same name (begun by Palladio in 1565 but not

completed until 1610, by V. Scamozzi), lies south of the Piazzetta, some 1500 feet from the Doge's Palace.

2   *La Canonica:* Street immediately north of San Marco. The
canons of the church lived there, hence its name.

3   *Rio del Palazzo:* C. provides a French translation of the name in
the margin.

4   *Doge's family:* The Doge in office lived in the palace with his
family; the Doge at the time was Francesco Loredan.

5   *Pyramidal summit:* So C. (*sommet pyramidal*), though his previous description—to say nothing of the existing monument—
shows that the roof was not a pyramid.

6   *Twelve o'clock:* About 6:00 A.M.

7   *Ducal chancellery:* The Cancelleria ducale chiefly served the
purpose of an archive; laws, decrees, and ordinances were
preserved there.

8   *Lead seals:* At the time only the Republic of Venice, the Roman
Curia, and the Grand Master of the Teutonic Order had the
privilege of sealing with lead; in general wax was used.

9   *Provveditor-General:* The Provveditor General di Mar was to all
intents and purposes supreme commander of the Venetian
naval forces; he resided in Corfu.

10 *Royal Stairs:* This stairway, commonly called the Scala dei
Giganti, took its name from large statues of Mars and Neptune
by J. Sansovino (1554). The Doges were crowned on the
highest landing. The stairs lead from the north side of the
inner courtyard to the lobby on the second floor of the palace.

11 *Savio alla Scrittura:* The closest counterpart to this official in
other countries is the Minister of War.

12 *Hall of the Four Doors:* The Sala delle Quattro Porte is on the
third floor and takes its name from four symmetrically placed
doors. C.'s topography is not entirely accurate.

13 Perhaps after Psalm 147, 14, in the Vulgate version.

14 Ariosto, *Orlando furioso*, XXII, 57, 3–4.

15 *Thirteen o'clock:* About 7:00 A.M.

16 *A man alone:* His name was Andreoli. At the inquiry he testified that the two fugitives knocked him down.

17 *Most Serene Republic:* Venice had assumed the sobriquet of La Serenissima, as her great rival Genoa had assumed that of La Superba.

18 *Porta della Carta:* The official entrance to the Doge's Palace from the Piazzetta (directly beside the Church of San Marco). Built from 1438 to 1443, it took its name from the fact that the government posted all laws and ordinances on it.

19 *Customs House:* The Dogana da Mare, the Venetian customs office, is situated on the point in the southern part of the city formed by the confluence of the Grand Canal and the Giudecca Canal, near the Church of Santa Maria della Salute.

20 *Osteria della Campana:* So called in the 18th century; in the 19th it was known as the Albergo della Campana ("The Bell") and was a much frequented hotel (in 1825 the Austrian Emperor Franz I stayed there with his family). It was in the center of the city.

21 *Seventeen o'clock:* About 11:00 A.M.

22 *San Tomasso:* C. seems to have used the wrong name. The reference should be to the Porta San Teonisto (now Porta Cavour).

23 *Twenty-four miles:* It appears from what follows that C. was really only about half that distance northwest of Treviso.

24 *Borgo di Valsugana:* The principal town of the Val Sugana, between Trento and Bassano del Grappa, some seventy miles from Mestre (Venice). It belonged to the Bishopric of Trento and so was not under the rule of the Venetian Republic.

25 *Forest of Mantello:* Bosco del Mantello, an oak forest north of Treviso belonging to the Republic, which harvested timber there for shipbuilding.

Volume Five

CHAPTER II

1   *Écu:* Silver coin of two denominations; the *gros écu* was worth six francs, the *petit écu* three.

2   *She:* C. first wrote "Mathilde," then crossed it out and substituted the pronoun (cf. Vol. 4, Chap. XII, n. 6).

3   *Louis:* Gold coin, first minted ca. 1640. Value: 24 francs.

4   *Erizzo:* Niccolò Erizzo (1722–1806), Venetian patrician, Ambassador of the Republic in Paris from 1754 to 1760, later in Vienna; Procurator from 1761.

5   *Madame la Marquise:* The Marquise de Pompadour (cf. Vol. 3, Chap. IX, n. 5).

6   *Choiseul:* Étienne François, Count of Stainville (1719–1785), from 1758 Duke of Choiseul, French Ambassador in Rome from 1753 to 1757, in Vienna from 1757 to 1758, Minister of Foreign Affairs from 1758 to 1761 and from 1766 to 1770; Minister of Marine from 1761 to 1766, Minister of War from 1761 to 1770.

7   *Boulogne:* Jean de Boulogne, also Boullogne, Count of Nogent (1690–1769), Comptroller-General from 1757 to 1759. The office of Comptroller-General (Contrôleur général) had existed from 1547; but it was not made a ministerial post until 1661. From then on the Comptroller-General was at the head of the entire administration in the departments of agriculture, commerce, finance, and domestic affairs.

8   *My first visit:* Choiseul later asserted that he had never met C. personally. Perhaps he did not remember him or thought it best to disavow his acquaintance; in any case he provided C. with a letter of recommendation.

9   *Under the Leads: I Piombi,* prison so named from its situation under the lead roof of the Doge's Palace. For C.'s confinement there and his escape, see Vol. 4, Chaps. XII ff.

10 *Chancellery:* The Cancelleria Ducale (Doge's Chancellery), through which C. passed when he made his escape from the Leads (see Vol. 4, Chap. XVI).

11 *Pâris-Duverney:* Joseph de Pâris-Duverney (1684–1770); son of a tavernkeeper, he made a fortune from provisioning the army, was ennobled ca. 1720, from 1751 First Intendant of the École Militaire; intimate friend of De Bernis.

12 *Military School:* The École Militaire Royale, on the Champ de Mars, was founded in 1751; it was open to sons of the nobility between the ages of eight and eleven, who were educated there for four years. Upon completing their studies they were commissioned second lieutenant (*sous-lieutenant*) or cornet (*cornette*).

13 *Plaisance:* Name of the château which Pâris-Duverney had built at Neuilly-Plaisance, east of Paris.

14 *Pâris de Montmartel:* Jean Pâris de Montmartel, Count of Sampigny (1690–1760), Councilor of State, banker to the Court, and Comptroller-General.

15 *Le Normand:* Charles François Paul Le Normand de Tournehem, Farmer-General; about 1720 he was the lover of Louise Madeleine Poisson, the mother of Jeanne Antoinette Poisson, later Marquise de Pompadour.

16 *Law:* John Law of Lauriston (1671–1729), Scottish financier; in 1715 he was granted a patent to establish an issuing bank in France. His "system" was based on issuing notes secured by the French colonial possessions in North America. Under his direction the Compagnie d'Occident, which he founded in 1717 (later the Compagnie des Indes), issued stock which soon became the object of frenzied speculation. His excessive issuing of stock and bank notes brought on an inflation in 1720 and then a desperate economic crisis in France. Law had to leave the country and died in poverty in Venice.

17 *Minister of Foreign Affairs:* C. first wrote "de l'abbé de Bernis," then canceled it and substituted "M. de R. S.," which he finally replaced by "ministre des Affaires étrangères." This indicates that, when he was writing this chapter, C. was at pains to conceal De Bernis's name. It further indicates that the existing version of his relationship with M. M. and De Bernis, in which the name of the latter is given in full, did not receive its final form until after De Bernis's death in 1794.

18   *Intendant of Finances:* In 18th-century France there were usually six Intendants des Finances; they divided the various aspects of the financial administration among them, under the direction of the Finance Minister.

19   *Harpocrates:* Greek form of the name of an Egyptian god, the son of Isis and the dying Osiris; his images show him holding one finger to his mouth, so he was (probably erroneously) later taken to be the God of Silence.

20   *Fontenelle:* Bernard Le Bovier de Fontenelle (1657–1757), celebrated French writer, a forerunner of the Enlightenment.

21   *Soubise:* Charles de Rohan, Prince of Soubise (1715–1787), Marshal of France. The Franco-Austrian army under his command was defeated by Frederick the Great at Rossbach, Thuringia, in 1757, early in the Seven Years' War (1756–1763). A protégé of the Marquise de Pompadour, he was appointed to the supreme command of the French army on Feb. 5, 1758.

22   *Calzabigi:* Giovanni Antonio Calzabigi (born ca. 1714), Secretary to the Ambassador from the Kingdom of the Two Sicilies in Paris from 1750; co-organizer of the Loterie de l'École Militaire (C.'s lottery) in 1757, financial adviser in Berlin ca. 1760.

23   *Lottery:* C. refers to a "lottery." Lotteries in various forms had long been known in France. But C. applies the term to the so-called *lotto genovese,* the basic conception of which is very similar to that of the modern "numbers game." This form of lottery goes back to the election of the Great Council in the Republic of Genoa; ninety names were written on slips and placed in an urn, from which five were drawn; the citizens bet on the results. The *lotto* with ninety numbers was officially instituted in Genoa in 1620. Players could stake on one, two, three, four, or five numbers. A combination of two numbers was termed an *ambo,* of three a *terno,* of four a *quaterna,* of five a *cinquina.*

24   *Insurance companies:* There were already insurance companies in the 18th century, but they only covered marine risks.

25   *Castelletto:* Schedule of the players' ventures in public lotteries.

26 *Council:* The Council (Conseil) of the École Militaire then consisted of the Minister of War, the First Intendant, the Commander-in-Chief of the army, and the Intendant Pâris-Duverney.

27 *Quaterna ... cinquina:* Combinations of four or five numbers staked on in a lottery and coming out in the same drawing (cf. note 23, above). The winner of a *quaterna* received 60,000 times his stake, the winner of a *cinquina* received an astronomical sum. According to A. Zottoli (*G. Casanova*, Rome, 1945, I, 57 ff.) C.'s calculations here contain many errors.

28 *Terno:* Combination of three numbers staked on in a lottery and coming out at the same drawing (cf. note 23, above). The winner of a *terno* received 4800 times his stake.

29 *Courteuil:* Jacques Dominique de Barberie, Marquis de Courteuil (1697–1768), statesman, Intendant of Finances from 1752.

30 *My brother:* Ranieri Calzabigi (1714–1795), co-organizer of the École Militaire lottery in 1757, later held a government financial post in Vienna; he was also a writer and composed the libretti for his friend Gluck's *Orfeo ed Euridice* (1762) and *Alceste* (1767).

31 *L'Hôpital:* Paul François de Galucci, Sieur de l'Hôpital (1697–1776), French Ambassador Extraordinary in Naples from 1740 to 1750 and in St. Petersburg from 1756 to 1761.

32 *Till the Greek Kalends:* I.e., "indefinitely," "for ever and ever." (Unlike the Romans, the Greeks did not reckon by kalends.)

33 *La Générale La Mothe:* Calzabigi's wife Simone was the widow of General Antoine Duru de La Mothe (died 1735). She had inherited from him the privilege of being the sole distributor of "gouttes d'or," a medicine highly esteemed at the time.

34 *Baroness Blanche:* Baroness Anne Pétronille Thérèse Blanche (ca. 1714–1763).

35 *De Vaux:* Louis Basile de Bernage, Sieur de Vaux, Baroness Blanche's lover from 1746.

36   *La Présidente:* Since many French ladies of some distinction used this title at the period, it is impossible to determine to which of them C. here refers.

37   *Madame Razzetti:* Wife of A. Razzetti, musical director of the Royal Theater in Turin (1743–1751), later violinist at the Paris Opéra.

38   *Fondpertuis:* Papillon de Fondpertuis, Intendant and Farmer-General from 1762. C. confuses him with his relative Denis Pierre Jean, Marquis de Papillon de la Ferté (1727–1794), also a Master of the Revels, who was Madame Razzetti's lover.

39   *Master of the Revels: Intendant des Menus Plaisirs du Roi.* This official disbursed the funds set aside for concerts, balls, entertainments, theatrical performances, and the like.

40   *Private apartments:* The *petits appartements* in the Palace of Versailles were the living quarters of the royal family. Louis XV's suite of rooms was connected by a staircase with the suite occupied by the Marquise de Pompadour.

41   *Laville:* Jean Ignace de Laville (ca. 1690–1774), abbé and diplomat; Secretary for Foreign Affairs.

42   *Up there:* The Marquise alludes to the exchange between herself and C. at their first meeting (cf. Vol. 3, Chap. IX). "Those gentlemen" are the Venetian State Inquisitors.

43   *D'Alembert:* Jean Le Rond d'Alembert (1717–1783), famous mathematician and philosopher and a co-editor of the *Encyclopédie*. Natural son of Madame de Tencin and the Chevalier Destouches, he was found on the steps of the Church of Saint-Jean-le-Rond in Paris, and taken to the Foundlings' Home. According to custom, he was given a family name and Christian name which suggested the circumstances under which he had been found ("Jean le Rond"). He later changed his name to D'Alembert.

44   *Franc:* Silver coin first minted in 1575; later, money of account which, by the 18th century, had become a synonym for the livre; value, 20 sous.

45   *I opened the sixth:* C.'s name does not appear in the extant list of lottery collectors for 1758, presumably because he used the title

of Director; he is listed late in 1758 and in 1759 as the manager of an office in the Rue Saint-Martin.

46   *La Cattolica:* Giuseppe Agostino Bonanno Filingeri e del Bosco, Principe di Roccafiorita e della Cattolica (died 1779), Spanish Grandee, Neapolitan Ambassador Extraordinary in Madrid from 1761 to 1770.

47   *First drawing:* It did not take place until April 18, 1758; C. is here anticipating events.

48   *Ambi:* The player of an *ambo* staked on two numbers. If he won he received 240 times his stake (cf. note 23 to this chapter).

49   *Madame Silvestre:* Antonia de Silvestre (1683–after 1757), wife of the painter Louis de Silvestre (1675–1760), who was Director of the Dresden Academy from 1727 to 1748 and from 1752 Director of the Académie Royale de Peinture, Sculpture et Gravure in Paris.

50   *The celebrated gallery:* The Dresden Gallery, founded in 1722.

51   *He was received:* Francesco Casanova was admitted to the Académie in Aug. 1761 but was not made a full member until May 1763.

CHAPTER IV

1   *At The Hague:* The Abbé de Laville had worked closely with the French Ambassador in The Hague, the Marquis de Fénelon, at various times between 1735 and 1745 and had represented him during his absences. In 1746 he was appointed Secretary to the Minister of Foreign Affairs. He was made a bishop four days before his death (1774).

2   *Garnier:* Jean Garnier was in D'Argenson's service for many years, he made a fortune in army provisions, and in 1749 was appointed Major-domo to the Queen. C. had met his son during his first stay in Paris (cf. Vol. 3, Chap. XI).

3   *D'Argenson:* Marc Pierre de Voyer de Paulmy, Count of Weild'Argenson (1696–1764), from 1720 Lieutenant-General of Police, from 1742 Minister of War; he was exiled in 1757.

4 *Galiani:* Fernando Galiani (1728–1787), of Naples, served as his country's Embassy Secretary in Paris from 1759 to 1769; writer and political economist, a leading figure in the Enlightenment; his correspondence (written in French), especially his letters to Madame d'Épinay, constitutes a notable contribution to French literature. Since Galiani did not arrive in Paris until June 1759, C. could not have met him before his journey to Dunkirk in 1757.

5 *Henriade:* Epic poem by Voltaire, in which he celebrates Henri IV as a champion of religious freedom (first published at Rouen in 1723; second, enlarged edition, London 1728). In his treatise on the Neapolitan dialect (*Sul dialetto napoletano*) the Abbé Galiani mentions a translation of the *Iliad* into Neapolitan by Niccolò Capasso; no copy of it is extant.

6 *May:* Contemporary sources show that C.'s journey to Dunkirk did not take place until Aug. 1757.

7 *First Gentleman of the Bedchamber:* The office of Gentilhomme de la Chambre du Roi was created by François I in 1545. From the reign of Louis XIV four such officers were appointed at once and served in succession. They worked in close collaboration with the Intendant des Menus Plaisirs (cf. note 39 to Chap. II of this volume).

8 Cf. Horace, *Satires*, I, 9, 57: *muneribus servos corrumpam* ("I will corrupt the servants with gifts").

9 *Gesvres:* François Jacques Potier, Duke of Gesvres (1692–1757), was Intendant des Menus Plaisirs from 1743 to 1746 and later a Gentleman of the Bedchamber and Governor of Paris.

10 *Île de France:* One of the former French provinces, with Paris as its capital; divided among several of the modern Départements in the reorganization of 1791.

11 *Saint-Ouen:* Then a village, now one of the northern suburbs of Paris.

12 *Conciergerie:* A *conciergerie* was properly the residence of a bailiff; here doubtless some official building part of which was used as an inn.

13 *Du Bareil:* Jacques Charles Prévot, Marquis du Bareil (died 1762), Field Marshal 1748, Vice-Admiral 1753.

CHAPTER V

1   *Camilla:* Giacoma Antonia Veronese, called Camilla (1735–1768), Italian actress and dancer; she first appeared at the Comédie Italienne in 1744 (cf. Vol. 3, Chap. XI).

2   *Barrière Blanche:* One of the sixty customs barriers at which duties were levied on certain goods entering Paris. The Barrière Blanche ("White Barrier"), on the right bank of the Seine, took its name from the white cross on an inn sign.

3   *Égreville:* Nicolas Rouault, Count of Égreville (born 1731).

4   *Gamaches:* Charles Joachim Rouault, Marquis de Gamaches (1729–1773).

5   *Countess du Rumain:* Constance Simone du Rumain, née Rouault de Gamaches (1725–1781).

6   *La Tour d'Auvergne:* Nicolas François Julie La Tour d'Apchier, Count of La Tour d'Auvergne (born 1720).

7   *Rue Taranne:* Originally Rue de la Courtille, later Rue Taranne, near the Church of Saint-Germain-des-Prés (6th Arrondissement); it no longer exists.

8   *Princess of Anhalt:* Johanna Elisabeth, Princess of Anhalt-Zerbst (1712–1760), lived in Paris from July 1758 under the name of Countess of Oldenbourg. C. again anticipates events here.

9   *Line:* One-twelfth of an inch.

10 *Talisman of Solomon:* More usually "Seal of Solomon," was the five-pointed star, which in Western cabalism was held to protect against evil demons.

11 *Marquise d'Urfé:* Jeanne, Marquise d'Urfé, née Camus de Pontcarré, married in 1724 to Louis Christophe de Larochefoucauld de Lascaris, Marquis d'Urfé et de Langeac, Count of Sommerive (1704–1734).

12 *Anne d'Urfé:* Anne de Lascaris d'Urfé (1555–1621), French poet; he divorced his wife about 1598 and became a priest. C., however, is probably thinking of his younger brother, Honoré de Lascaris d'Urfé (1568–1625), author of the pastoral novel *L'Astrée* (5 vols., 1607–1627), which was widely read both in France and abroad.

13   *Duchess of Lauraguais:* Diane Adélaïde, Duchess of Lauraguais (ca. 1713–1769).

14   *Duchess of Orléans:* Louise Henriette, née Princess of Bourbon-Conti (1726–1759), married in 1743 to Louis Philippe, Duke of Chartres, who became Duke of Orléans in 1752 (cf. Vol. 3, Chap. XI).

15   *Madame de Boufflers:* Marie Louise, Marquise de Boufflers-Rouverel, from 1749 lady-in-waiting to the Duchess of Chartres and Orléans.

16   *Madame du Blot:* Niece of Madame de Mauconseil, became a lady-in-waiting to the Duchess of Chartres and Orléans in 1749.

17   *Melfort:* André Louis Hector, Count of Drummond-Melfort (1722–1788), of Scottish extraction; officer in the French army and Freemason.

18   *Quai des Théatins:* Now the Quai Voltaire (renamed in 1791). The Hôtel de Bouillon is no. 17 on the present Quai Malaquais.

19   *Regency:* On the death of Louis XIV in 1715 the Duke of Orléans became Regent until Louis XV came of age in 1723. The period of the Regency brought a relaxation in the formality of court etiquette.

20   *Turenne:* Godefroy Charles Henri La Tour d'Auvergne, Prince de Turenne (1727–1791), from 1772 Duke of Bouillon; the Count of La Tour d'Auvergne's cousin.

21   *Great Work:* The *opus alchemicum* was the highest goal of alchemy, the transmutation of all metals into gold.

22   *Her library:* The d'Urfé library was famous for its richness; it was sold in 1770 and later came into the possession of the Bibliothèque Nationale and the Bibliothèque de l'Arsenal.

23   *The great D'Urfé:* Claude d'Urfé, Baron of Châteauneuf (1501–1558), Steward of the King's Household, French Envoy to the Council of Trent in 1547.

24   *Renée of Savoy:* She was married to Jacques I d'Urfé (not to Claude d'Urfé) in 1554.

25 *Paracelsus:* Philippus Aureolus Theophrastus Paracelsus (1493–1541), his real name Theophrastus Bombastus von Hohenheim, of Einsiedeln (Switzerland); famous physician and philosopher, founder of hermetic medicine.

26 *The universal medicine:* The "panacea" of the alchemists, from the mythical Panakeia, daughter of Aesculapius, who was credited with the ability to cure all diseases; also known as *aurum potabile.*

27 *Steganography:* Cryptography.

28 *Powder of projection:* According to alchemical doctrine, a powder which, scattered over molten metals, turned them into gold.

29 *Tree of Diana:* An artificial form of vegetation produced by the mixture of two metals with a solvent such as nitric acid. The most suitable metals are silver and lead.

30 *Talliamed:* Benoît Maillet (1656–1738), author of *Talliamed ou entretiens d'un philosophe indien avec un missionaire* ("Talliamed or conversations between an Indian philosopher and a missionary"), Amsterdam, 1748.

31 *Le Maserier:* Jean Baptiste Le Maserier (1697–1760), abbé and writer; edited *Talliamed* (cf. note 30), adding a biography of Maillet.

32 *Regent:* See note 19, above. The Regent was an ardent disciple of alchemy.

33 *Égérie:* Egeria, a fountain nymph; in Roman mythology she was credited with advising King Numa Pompilius, hence her name came to be applied to any woman who acted as an adviser.

34 *Raymond Lully:* Ramón Lull (1235–1316), Catalan mystic, writer, philosopher, and missionary. The authenticity of the alchemical works ascribed to him is doubtful.

35 *Arnold of Villanova:* Provençal or Catalan physician and alchemist (ca. 1235–1313). The authenticity of his alchemical writings has been questioned.

36 *Roger Bacon:* English Franciscan and scholar (ca. 1214–1294); composed numerous works in philosophy, theology, and natural history; known as "Doctor Mirabilis."

37   *Geber:* Europeanized name of the Arabian or Persian physician and natural historian Jabir ibn Hayyan (8th century); in the Middle Ages he was considered the foremost authority on alchemy.

38   *Platina del Pinto:* The Rio Pinto is a river in Peru. Platinum, which was brought to Europe in 1743 (see the next note), was at first supposed to be a kind of silver; its true nature was not ascertained until 1752.

39   *Wood:* Charles Wood found platinum in 1741 and brought the new metal to London for the first time in 1743.

40   *Aqua regia:* A mixture of nitric acid and hydrochloric acid.

41   *Burning glass:* Convex mirror used to concentrate the sun's rays on a particular point.

42   *Athanor:* A self-feeding furnace, made of bricks or clay, used by alchemists. Openings in its sides allowed the heat to be used for various purposes.

43   *"Lepers":* Alchemical term for the six baser metals: silver, mercury, lead, copper, iron, and zinc.

44   *Fixed salt:* According to the alchemical doctrine of Paracelsus, there were three basic substances: salt, sulphur, and mercury. Urine was often used as a salt.

45   *Pentacle:* A five- or six-pointed star. Here the five-pointed star (see note 10 to this chapter).

46   *Planetary Geniuses:* The cabala, which took over the Ptolemaic system of the universe, assigned a genius to each of the planets: Aratron to Saturn, Bethor to Jupiter, Phal to Mars, Och to the Sun, Hagith (or Hagioh) to Venus, Ophiel to Mercury, Phul to the Moon.

47   *Agrippa:* Cornelius Heinrich Agrippa von Nettesheim (1486–1535), German physician, philosopher, and astrologer; his works on magic, especially his *De occulta philosophia*, were considered authoritative by the alchemists.

48   *Count of Trèves:* Presumably Abraham B. Gershon, French cabalist of Jewish descent, born in Trèves, and known in the

second half of the 18th century as the author of several occult treatises. He was not a count.

49 *Polyphilus:* Francesco Colonna's allegorical romance, the *Hypnerotomachia Polyphili*, written ca. 1467, was published at Venice in 1499 in an illustrated edition which is considered one of the masterpieces of Renaissance printing.

50 *Ineffable names:* The names of the angels of the seven planetary heavens.

51 *The planetary hours:* In astrology each hour has a cabalistic name and is governed by a particular planet and its angel.

52 *Anael:* The angel Anael governs Friday under the rule of the planet Venus, whose Genius is Hagith (or Hagioh).

53 *Zoroaster:* The reformer of the ancient Persian religion was later held to be the inventor of magic.

54 *Artephius:* Latinized name of a Jewish or Arabian philosopher who lived ca. 1130. His treatise on the philosopher's stone was translated into French by Pierre Arnauld in 1612.

55 *Sandivonius:* Latinized name of a 17th-century German physician.

56 *Brothers of the Rosy Cross:* Secret associations which began to spring up in Europe in the 17th century and in the 18th were identified especially with alchemy (cf. Vol. 3, Chap. VI, n. 9).

57 Cf. Genesis 24, 9: "And the servant put his hand under the thigh of Abraham his master and sware to him. . . . " (The Vulgate text is more specific: *sub femere* ["under his upper thigh"].)

58 *Word:* The meaning is "male semen" (cf. Vol. 8, Chap. IV).

59 *Electrum:* Alchemical term for an alloy composed of three parts of gold and one part of silver.

60 *Gerin:* Neither this person nor the Macartney (C. writes "Macartnei") named in the next sentence has been identified.

61   *Esprit des Lois:* By Charles de Secondat, Baron de Montesquieu (1689–1755), first printed in 1748; one of the most important works of political philosophy produced in the 18th century.

62   *D'Arzigny:* Probably Joseph Charles Luc Costin Camus, Count of Arginy (died 1779), high-ranking cavalry officer.

63   *Charon:* No councilor of this name has been identified. C. may be referring to Élie Bochart de Saron, who was a councilor.

64   *Great Chamber:* The Grand' Chambre was the highest chamber in each Parlement; it dealt with judicial cases involving great noblemen, cases of lèse-majesté, and the like.

65   *Madame du Châtelet:* The Marquise Adélaïde Marie Thérèse du Châtelet-Fresnières, née d'Urfé (1717–after 1776); she accused her mother, Madame d'Urfé, of unlawfully withholding large sums of money from her; her mother succeeded in having her placed under guardianship and disinherited her.

66   *Had bought it:* High offices, including judgeships, were freely bought and sold at the period. C.'s play here on "*faire* raison" ("do justice"), where the second *faire* becomes "fabricate," seems impossible to translate.

67   *Viarmes:* Nicolas Élie Pierre Camus de Viarmes, Councilor in the Rouen Parlement from 1752.

68   *Remonstrances au Roi:* The French Parlements had gained the right to refuse to regard the King's edicts as law until after they were registered by the Paris Parlement; the same was true of the provincial Parlements in respect to the edicts of provincial governors. Registration could be refused; in such cases the King made his appearance and held a so-called *lit de justice* (from the throne under a baldachin) to compel registration. Not content with merely refusing, the Parlements also set forth their objections in the so-called "remonstrances." The King could also reject these in a *lit de justice*; however, the possibility of making remonstrances gave the Parlements considerable influence on public opinion.

69   *Madame de Gergy:* Anne Languet, Countess of Gergy, widow of the Count of Gergy (died 1734), who had been French Ambassador in Venice from 1723 to 1731.

70 *Saint-Germain:* Also Count Tzarogy, Prince Racoczy, General Soltikoff, Marquis of Montferrat, etc. (ca. 1696–1784), adventurer extraordinary, whose real origin is unknown. In his *Soliloque d'un penseur* (Prague, 1784) C. maintains that Saint-Germain was none other than an Italian fiddler named Catalani.

71 *"Elemental spirits":* The doctrine of the cabala assigns particular spirits to each of the four elements: gnomes to earth, undines to water, sylphs to air, salamanders to fire.

72 *Paralis:* This name first appears in Vol. 2, Chap. VIII, where it designates the guardian angel of C. and his three patrician friends, Bragadin, Dandolo, and Barbaro; he later makes it the name of his own Genius.

CHAPTER VI

1   *Pontcarré . . . Viarmes:* Geoffroy Macé Camus de Pontcarré, Councilor from 1753, and Jean Baptiste Élie Camus de Viarmes (1702–after 1764).

2   *Provost of the Merchants:* The merchants of Paris had a provostal court of their own made up of the Provost of the Merchants, four municipal magistrates, a royal advocate, a city advocate, and a substitute. Monsieur de Viarmes held the office of Provost from 1758 to 1764.

3   *I have mentioned:* Cf. Chap. V, n. 67.

4   *Was never present:* Cf. Chap. V, n. 65.

5   *We:* I.e., C. and Madame d'Urfé.

6   *An estate:* Madame d'Urfé owned estates in Forez in the upper Loire Valley and the château of Pontcarré near Paris.

7   *Livre:* Livre is synonymous with franc.

8   *Hypostasis:* Union of the divine and human natures in one person.

9   *Salamander:* One of the four kinds of elemental spirits of the cabala, associated with fire.

10 *Word:* See note 58 to the preceding chapter.

11 *Academy:* The Académie Royale de Peinture, de Sculpture et de Gravure. For C.'s brother's admission to it, see Chap. II, n. 51.

12 *Married a dancer:* Francesco Casanova's marriage to Jeanne Jolivet, who had danced in the ballet of the Comédie Italienne under the name of Mademoiselle d'Alancour from 1759, did not take place until June 1762.

13 *Bursar...benefices:* Louis Pierre Sébastien Marchal de Saincy was "écdnome général du clergé" from 1750 to 1762.

14 *Holland:* The name was applied to the seven United Provinces of the Netherlands from the 17th century.

15 *Duke of Choiseul:* Étienne François, Count of Stainville (1719–1785), was made Duke of Choiseul in 1758 (cf. Chap. II, n. 6).

16 *D'Affry:* Louis Auguste, Count d'Affry (1710–1793), of Swiss extraction, from 1755 French Envoy, from 1759 French Ambassador, in The Hague.

17 *Invalides:* The Hôtel Royal des Invalides (7th Arrondissement) was built as a home for retired and invalid soldiers under Louis XIV from 1670 to 1674.

18 *About to be made:* The peace treaty which ended the Seven Years' War was not signed until 1763.

19 *Berkenrode:* Mattheus (Matthys) Lestevenon, Heer van Berkenrode en Strijen (1715–1797), was Ambassador of the United Netherlands in Paris from 1749 to 1792.

20 *Landelle:* He was the proprietor of a then well-known restaurant, the Hôtel de Buci, in the street of the same name (6th Arrondissement).

21 *Ex-Jansenist:* Madame XXX. "Jansenist" was applied in the 18th century to persons of rigorous morals.

22 *Quai de Gesvres:* Street along the Seine opposite the Île de la Cité near the Hôtel de Ville (4th Arrondissement).

23 *Gothenburg:* The Swedish East India Company, founded in 1731, had its main office at Gothenburg until 1814.

24   *Tourton & Baur:* The banking firm of Tourton & Baur, founded
by the Swiss Christophe Jean Baur in 1740, had its office from
1754 in a building on the Place des Victoires (on the boundary
between the 1st and 2nd Arrondissements).

25   *Florin:* The guilder (or florin) had been minted in the United
Netherlands from 1679 and remained current until 1838. One
guilder (florin) = 20 stuivers.

26   *Boas:* Tobias Boas, banker at The Hague.

27   *Jacht:* Dutch, "light sailing vessel."

28   *"English Parliament":* The famous inn "Het Parlament van
Engeland" was closed in 1795 and reopened in 1814 under
the name "Wapen van Engeland"; it was near the "Korte
Poten," in the center of the city.

29   *Kauderbach:* Johann Heinrich Kauderbach (1707–1785), Saxon
diplomat and writer, lived in The Hague from 1730; after
serving as Corresponding Minister, then as Resident, he was
appointed Ambassador from the Elector of Saxony in 1750.

30   *Feast of the Maccabees:* The Jewish festival of Hanukkah, celebrated for a week beginning on Dec. 25th.

31   *Ducats:* The ducat of the Netherlands was a gold coin which had
been minted from 1586. For its value, see the following note.

32   *Stuivers:* A ducat was worth 3 guilders, 9 stuivers; it was roughly
equivalent to 10 francs. C.'s figures are inaccurate (cf. note 34).

33   *Bank of Amsterdam:* Founded in 1609, it was the oldest bank in
northern Europe.

34   *Livres tournois:* The French franc (or livre) was minted from the
13th century in the city of Tours (whence the name), and later
by the royal mint in Paris; from 1667 it became a standard coin
throughout France. C.'s figures (400,000 Netherlands ducats
= 4 million livres tournois or francs) show that he was correctly
informed as to the value of the ducat (cf. note 32).

35   *Pels:* The banking firm of Andries Pels & Zoonen in Amsterdam, founded by Andries Pels (1655–1731). In 1758 the
director of the firm was Henrick Bicker (1722–1783), whom
C. erroneously calls "Pels."

36 *Swedish Ambassador:* Joachim Frederik Preis (1666–1759), Swedish Resident from 1719, Swedish Ambassador in The Hague from 1725.

37 *D. O.:* Together with canceled versions such as "Op" or "O. p.," C.'s "D. O." undoubtedly designates the Hope family. The reference is probably to Thomas Hope (1704–1779), of Scottish descent but born at Amsterdam, who founded a bank there ca. 1726. C. at first writes "Mr. D. O.," but soon gives it up for the usual French "M." (for Monsieur). Perhaps Hope, though born in Holland, was thought of as an Englishman. Cf. C.'s use of "Miss" for Giustiniana Wynne, whose father was English, in Chap. VIII of this volume.

38 *St. John's Day:* St. John the Baptist was the original patron saint of Freemasonry; his feast was celebrated on June 24th. Later the Apostle John was also made a patron of the lodges; his feast day was Dec. 27th. The anniversary of the founding of the Grand Lodge of Holland was celebrated on the same day.

39 *Count de Tott:* Baron (not Count) de Tott, of Hungarian descent but born in France; officer in the French army; brother of François, Baron de Tott (1733–1793), who in 1755 went to Constantinople in the suite of the French Ambassador Vergennes and was made French Consul in the Crimea in 1763.

40 *Mother:* The Regent Anne, daughter of King George II of England and widow of the Stathouder William IV of Orange, who died in 1751. She ruled for her son William V (1748–1806). She died on Jan. 12, 1759, after a long illness.

41 *Stathouder:* The Republic of the United Provinces (from 1581) declared its independence in the Peace of Westphalia (1648). Sovereignty resided in the Estates (Staaten) of the provinces and the Estates General; executive power in the Stathouder, of the House of Orange.

42 *Sinzendorf:* Philipp Joseph, Count Sinzendorf (1726–1788), Austrian diplomat; he spent two weeks in The Hague at the end of Dec. 1758.

43 *The Porte:* The official designation of the government of the Turkish Empire was "the Sublime Porte," from the gate of the Sultan's palace. There was no accredited representative

of Turkey in The Hague at the time; perhaps C. met some high Turkish dignitary who was there unofficially.

44   *Bonneval:* Count Claude Alexandre Bonneval (1675–1747), commander in the French and Austrian armies; about 1730 he entered the service of Turkey and became a Mohammedan.

45   *Iphigenia:* The reference is to *Iphigénie en Aulide*, by Racine (1639–1699).

46   *"Prince of Orange":* No inn by this name is documented in The Hague; however, there was an inn named "De Prins van Oranje" in the Keizerstraat in Scheveningen, to which C. probably refers.

47   *Greek philosopher:* Diogenes Laërtius (VII, 185) relates concerning the Greek philosopher Chrysippus (282–209 B.C.) that he gave his donkey, which had eaten some figs which belonged to him, undiluted wine and died laughing at the spectacle of the drunken donkey.

48   *Special rights:* In the 18th century in most European countries there were strict regulations intended to assure post coaches of precedence under all circumstances.

49   *"Star of the East":* In Dutch, "De Ster van Osten"; a letter from Manon Balletti to C. dated Dec. 9, 1758, is addressed to him at the "Rondeel," which was one of the oldest and best hostelries in Amsterdam. C. may have changed his lodging or may have confused the names.

50   *Cape wine:* Wine was already brought to Europe from South Africa in the 18th century, especially from the Cape of Good Hope.

51   *Esther:* Fictitious name, probably Lucia Hope (1741–1765), possibly the daughter of Zachary Hope (1711–1770), brother of Thomas Hope (cf. note 37 to this chapter). If this is so, she was not Thomas Hope's daughter but his niece; in 1764 she married Adolf Jan Heshuysen (born 1736), partner in a banking firm in Haarlem and Amsterdam.

52   *Teresa Imer:* Italian singer (1723–1797), married to the dancer Angelo Pompeati before 1744 (cf. Vol. 1, Chap. VI).

53   *The Margrave:* Friedrich von Bayreuth (1711–1763), Margrave from 1735.

54   *M. M.:* Here again "M. M." replaces a canceled "Mathilde." (For C. C. cf. Vol. 3, Chaps. XIV–XVI; for M. M., Vol. 4, Chaps. I–V.)

55   This recitative has not been identified. A possible alternative translation is: "You have come to your end..."

56   *A widow:* Teresa Imer had separated from her husband in 1754, but he was still alive.

57   *Eau de Luz:* There was an "eau de Luz," a mineral water from the spring of Saint-Sauveur, near Luz in the Pyrenees. However, C. probably means "eau de Luce," a kind of smelling salts.

58   *Sophie:* Teresa Imer had three children: a son Joseph (born 1746), a daughter Wilhelmine Friederike (born 1753), and a third child the date of whose birth is not known. Possibly the last is the Sophie to whom C. here refers.

59   *Montperny:* Théodore Camille, Marquis de Montperny (died 1753), from 1746 Gentleman of the Bedchamber at the Margrave's Court in Bayreuth.

60   *Prince Charles of Lorraine:* Karl Alexander, Prinz von Lothringen (1712–1780), brother of Emperor Franz I; Austrian Field Marshal, 1746; Governor of the Austrian Netherlands (Flanders, Brabant, Hennegau, Namur, and Luxemburg), 1748–1756.

61   *In Vienna:* Angelo Francesco Pompeati did not commit suicide in Vienna until 1768.

62   *Exchange:* The splendid building of the Amsterdam Exchange (De Beurs), dedicated in 1611, housed the most important institution of the kind in 18th-century Europe; the great hall could hold 6000 people.

63   *Daler:* The Swedish daler was a silver coin minted from the beginning of the 16th century. 1 daler = 4 marks = 32 oere.

64   *Five percent:* C. writes "cinq pour cent" though he has previously spoken of fifteen percent and calculates with the latter figure.

65   *Zaandam:* C. writes "Cerdam" and "Serdam." Town some six miles northwest of Amsterdam, formerly a favorite residence of rich Netherlanders.

CHAPTER VII

1   *Medea:* Medea appears with her two children, whom she is about to kill, in the climactic scene of Euripides' tragedy of the same name.

2   *V. D. R.:* Perhaps Pieter Meermann, son of Jan Meermann, who was Burgomaster of Rotterdam in 1758.

3   *Princess Galitzin:* Ekaterina, Princess Galitzin, also Golitsyn (1719–1761), daughter of Antioch Dmitrovich, Prince Kantemir; married to Dmitri Mikhailovich Galitzin, who was Russian Ambassador in Paris in 1761.

4   *Louis:* A louis was worth 24 francs.

5   *Agio:* Premium.

6   *"Second Bible":* There were three inns in Amsterdam all named "Byble" and all in the same street (Warmaesstraat); they were distinguished from one another as "First," "Second," and "Third."

7   *Rigerboos:* Jan Cornelis Rigerboos, obviously a close friend of Teresa Imer. It is possible that his name was really Jan Rigerboos Cornelis, and that Teresa Imer took the name "Cornelys" when she went to London (cf. Vol. 9, Chaps. VII and VIII).

8   *States-General:* The parliament of the seven United Provinces was called "De Staten Generaal"; it was made up of sixty members and met in The Hague.

9   *Musicau:* Apparently C.'s attempt to spell Dutch *musiekhuis*, a tavern where there was music and dancing. They were plentiful in Amsterdam in the 18th century.

10   *Contrada:* The six *sestieri* (municipal districts) of Venice were divided into *contrade*.

11 *Lucia:* Daughter of the caretaker on the Count of Montereale's estate at Pasiano (cf. Vol. 1, Chaps. IV and V).

12 *Reischach:* Judas Thaddaeus, Freiherr von Reischach (1696–1782), Austrian diplomat.

13 *Pesselier:* Charles Étienne Pesselier (1712–1763), French financier.

14 *Pounds sterling:* According to C.'s later figures, the pound sterling was then worth 11 guilders.

15 *French East India Company:* The Compagnie des Indes Orientales, founded by Richelieu in 1642, was merged in 1719 with Law's newly created Compagnie des Indes, but continued to exist under its original name after Law's bankruptcy. The Dutch East India Company, founded in 1602, was very powerful in the 17th century, but then lost ground to the competition of English influence in India and was dissolved in 1795.

16 *Texel:* Dutch island in the North Sea, at the entrance to the former Zuider Zee.

17 *Carnival:* In all probability C. was not in Holland during the Carnival either in 1758 or 1759, but had already returned to Paris in January. But it is possible that in Amsterdam Carnival was considered to begin as early as January.

18 *One hundred thousand florins:* This and the following amount add up to the ten percent which O. D. had promised C. as his share of the profit from the supposedly lost ship.

19 *Pâris de Montmartel:* Jean Pâris de Montmartel (1690–1760), Comptroller-General and banker to the French Court, brother of Joseph de Pâris-Duverney, Intendant of the École Militaire (cf. this volume, Chap. II).

20 *Masulipatam:* A fine cotton fabric, from the State of Masulipatam in southern India.

21 Seneca, *Epistles,* CVII.

22 *10th of February:* C.'s dates for his stay in Holland are not reliable; he probably means Jan. 10, 1759.

23 *Rue Montorgueil:* These streets are in the 1st and 2nd Arrondissements.

CHAPTER VIII

1   *My patron*: In Dec. 1758 De Bernis was disgraced and from then
    on lived at his château of Vic-sur-Aisne, near Soissons. Hence
    C. cannot have visited him at his official quarters in the Hôtel
    de Bourbon in Jan. 1759.

2   *Venetian Ambassador:* Niccolò Erizzo (1722–1806) was the Ven-
    etian Ambassador in Paris from 1754 to 1760 (cf. note 4 to
    Chap. II of this volume).

3   *Gentleman-in-ordinary:* Appointment to this office was accom-
    panied by the issuance of a patent of nobility. The document
    which made Voltaire "Monsieur de Voltaire" is dated June 8,
    1758.

4   *Viar:* Probably a certain Viard who appears in contemporary
    documents as a *permissionnaire*, that is, a teacher who was
    licensed to board up to twenty pupils and who also taught
    them.

5   *Was playing:* Rosa Giovanna Balletti, called Silvia, died on Sept.
    18, 1758, hence before C.'s first journey to Holland.

6   *Madame* XCV: Lady Anna Wynne, née Gazzini (1713–after
    1780); born on the island of Leukas in the Ionian Sea, she
    married Sir Richard Wynne, whose mistress she had been, in
    1739, and after his death in 1751 made several journeys be-
    tween Venice and London in order to have her children
    brought up as Roman Catholics but at the same time to assure
    them of receiving their inheritance in England.

7   *Four girls:* Of her four daughters, Anna Amalia had already died
    (1748–1750); C. presumably counts in Toinon, a French girl
    who lived in the household as the friend and confidante of the
    eldest daughter.

8   *Attended to all that:* In England Lady Wynne and her children
    had been obliged to renounce Roman Catholicism in order to
    obtain possession of the inheritance.

9   *1758:* Perhaps an error on C.'s part, since the events he relates
    took place at the beginning of 1759. Or perhaps he is reckon-
    ing in the Venetian manner, *more Veneto*, as he often does in the

memoirs. In Venice the new year began on March 1, so that January and February still belonged to the previous year.

10 *Eldest daughter:* Giustiniana Franca Antonia Wynne (1737–1791) was married in 1761 to Philip Joseph, Count Orsini-Rosenberg, the Austrian Ambassador in Venice. C. has already mentioned her and her mother at the end of Chapter IX, Volume 3, where he gives their right names. The events which follow obviously decided him to conceal the name; what led him to choose the letters *XCV* remains a mystery.

11 *Fifteen:* Giustiniana was already sixteen in 1753.

12 *Algarotti:* Francesco, Count Algarotti (1712–1764), a prominent figure of the Enlightenment both in his poetry and in his prose works, was made an honorary member of the Berlin Academy of Sciences and a Gentleman of the Bedchamber to Frederick the Great in 1747.

13 *Memmo di San Marcuola:* Probably Andrea Memmo (1729–1793), Venetian patrician, diplomat, and Senator, who married Elisabetta Piovene in 1769 and became Procurator in 1785. Different branches of a Venetian patrician family added to their names a determinative drawn from the name of the parish in which they lived. The Church of San Marcuola is on the Grand Canal near the Palazzo Vendramin.

14 *Miss* XCV: According to English usage, Giustiniana Wynne, as the eldest daughter, was addressed or referred to simply as Miss Wynne, her younger sisters by their Christian names, as Miss Mary, and so on. C.'s later use of "Miss" standing alone, like French "Mademoiselle," is of course completely unidiomatic.

15 *Hôtel de Bretagne:* This was a very modest hostelry in the Rue Saint-André-des-Arts (6th Arrondissement). In the extant letters of Giustiniana Wynne there is mention only of the Hôtel de Hollande, which was in the same street and of a better class.

16 *Pouplinière:* Alexandre Jean Joseph Le Riche de la Pouplinière, also Popelinière (1692–1762), Farmer-General from 1718.

17 *Passy:* Le Riche de la Pouplinière's château was in what was then the village of Passy, now the Rue Raynouard (16th Arrondissement).

18   *East India Company:* Cf. note 15 to the preceding chapter.

19   *The mother:* Since Silvia had died in Sept. 1758, C. may be
     confusing the events of his return from Holland with those
     of his earlier return from Dunkirk in 1757. His asking if he
     was rich enough to give such presents points to the same
     supposition, for he was certainly rich enough on his return
     from Holland.

20   *Two sons:* Silvia had three sons; however, her second son, Luigi
     Giuseppe, had been a ballet master in Stuttgart from Sept.
     1757, and her youngest son, Guglielmo Luigi (born 1736),
     died before 1757.

21   *Calencar:* A colored fabric from India.

22   *My friend:* Antonio Stefano Balletti (1724–1789), dancer and
     actor, C.'s intimate friend.

23   *The Cadet:* Luigi Giuseppe Balletti (born 1730), from 1751 dancer
     at the Comédie Italienne, from 1757 ballet master in Stuttgart
     (cf. note 20), whose nickname in the family was "the Cadet."

24   *"Down there":* Allusion to the Venetian State Inquisitors (cf.
     note 42 to Chap. II of this volume).

25   *Council of Trent:* This Council, which ushered in the Counter-
     Reformation, was held from 1545 to 1563.

26   *Armed magnet:* To conserve its magnetism the poles of a magnet
     were connected by a piece of soft iron.

27   *Chambord:* Magnificent Renaissance château, built by order of
     François I from 1523 to 1533. It is in Touraine, south of the
     Loire and not far from Blois.

28   *Zweibrücken:* Christian IV, Duke of Zweibrücken (1722–1775).

29   *Magisterium:* Term for the higher secrets of alchemy; probably
     goes back to the hermetic philosopher Artephius (12th cen-
     tury) and his treatise on the philosopher's stone.

30   *Maréchal de Saxe:* Moritz (French, Maurice), Count of Saxony
     (1696–1750); entered the French service in 1720, made Marshal
     of France in 1744, became a French citizen in 1746.

31   *Lewenhaupt:* Adam, Count of Lewenhaupt (died 1775) (C. writes "Levenhoop"), of Swedish origin, entered the French service in 1713, made a Field Marshal in 1762.

32   *"King Dagobert" inn:* In the 18th century the Auberge du Roi Dagobert was a famous hostelry in the present Rue Tête d'Or; it was demolished early in the 19th century.

33   *Bayreuth:* Giuseppe Pompeati (1746–ca. 1797) was born in Vienna, not in Bayreuth.

CHAPTER X

1   *J. J. Rousseau:* Jean Jacques Rousseau (1712–1778).

2   *Montmorency:* From 1756 to 1762 Rousseau lived at Montmorency, north of Paris, from May to Aug. 1759 as the guest of the Maréchal de Luxembourg in the latter's château there.

3   *A woman:* Marie Thérèse Levasseur (1721–1801), of Orléans, housemaid; Rousseau's mistress, whom he married in 1768.

4   *Prince of Conti:* Louis François, Prince of Bourbon-Conti (1717–1776), French general and statesman.

5   *Count of La Marche:* Louis François Joseph, Prince of Bourbon-Conti, Count of La Marche (1734–1814).

6   *Good-by:* The historicity of this anecdote has been contested.

7   *Anagram:* Taking "u" and "v" as interchangeable, "Levasseur" contains all the letters of "Rousseau" except the "o."

Volume Six

CHAPTER V

1   *Post . . . in Soleure:* The then celebrated Auberge de la Couronne was also the post station in Soleure.

2   *"The Court":* In the 16th century part of the Franciscan monastery in Soleure was rebuilt as the residence of the French Ambassador and was thereafter known as "Maison de France" or "Cour des Ambassadeurs."

3 *Duchess of Gramont:* The Duchess Béatrix de Gramont (1730–1794) was the sister of the Duke of Choiseul.

4 *Thirty years:* C. is in error: the Marquis de Chavigny was French Ambassador in Venice from 1750 to 1751; however, he had traveled in Italy on diplomatic missions (Genoa, Modena, Naples, Florence) from 1719 to 1722, that is, some 40 years before C. made his acquaintance in Soleure.

5 *The Regency:* The Duke of Orléans was Regent from the death of Louis XIV in 1715 until the minority of the Dauphin (later Louis XV) ended in 1723.

6 *Stringhetta:* Name of a Venetian courtesan celebrated ca. 1730.

7 *Vis-à-vis:* A light carriage with two facing seats.

8 *Coppers:* Text: *liards.* The liard was a copper coin worth one fourth of a sou.

9 *Twenty sous:* 20 sous are equivalent to one franc or livre.

10 *The . . . joke:* The marks of elision presumably stand for some unprintable adjective.

11 *L'Écossaise:* Voltaire's comedy *Le Café ou l'Écossaise* was published in April 1760 as a translation from the English of a "M. Hume." Voltaire at first denied being the author of it. The first performance in Paris was given on July 26, 1760. The heroine of the play is the beautiful Scottish girl Lindane, who is beloved by Murray; Monrose is her father; and Lady Alton appears as an intriguing and jealous woman who tries to win Murray.

12 *She:* I.e., Madame F.

13 *Voltaire:* Voltaire was enamored of the theater, often produced plays in his house, and acted in them himself.

14 *L'Écossaise,* Act 5, Scene 3. C. misquotes slightly.

15 *Ibid.* C. again misquotes slightly.

16 *De Seingalt:* C. first wrote "de Casanova," crossed it out, and substituted "de Seingalt." This is the first time he gives himself this name in his memoirs.

17 *Sternutative:* A substance which provokes sneezing.

18 *Herrenschwandt:* Johann Friedrich von Herrenschwandt (1715–1798), physician to the Swiss Guards Regiment and to the Duke of Orléans in Paris, 1750–1755; physician in ordinary to King Stanislaus II Poniatowski, 1764–1773; medical Consultant of the City of Bern, 1779–1784. He invented the *Herrenschwandtsches Pulver* which he apparently prescribed for C.'s baths.

19 *Friend of mine:* Anton Gabriel Herrenschwandt (died 1785), of Swiss descent. He succeeded his brother Johann Friedrich (cf. note 18, above) as physician to the Swiss Guards Regiment in Paris, and as physician in ordinary to the Duke of Orléans and to King Stanislaus II Poniatowski.

20 *Monsieur F.:* Text: *M. F.* Probably a slip of C.'s for "Mme F." Madame F. was a widow.

21 *Swiss Guards:* A select corps which formed part of the King's household troops. It goes back to the Swiss mercenaries hired by Louis XI and his successors. The post of Colonel-général des Suisses et Grisons, created in 1571, was of great importance. Choiseul was not appointed to it until Feb. 24, 1762.

22 *A cousin:* François Joseph Roll von Emmenholtz, officer in the French service from 1759.

23 *La Muette:* Royal hunting lodge in Passy (now the 16th Arrondissement of Paris). The last traces of it vanished in 1926.

24 *The Duke her father:* Probably an error on C.'s part. The Duke of Choiseul, to whom as minister the appeal was made, was the Duchess of Gramont's brother, not her father.

25 *Chauvelin:* François Claude, Marquis de Chauvelin (1716–1773), French commander; Ambassador in Genoa (1747–1753) and Turin (1754–1765); friend of Louis XV and Voltaire.

26 *"Les Délices":* In 1755 Voltaire bought a property near Geneva, changing its name from "Saint Jean" to "Les Délices"; it is now within the Geneva city limits and is the seat of the Musée Voltaire. In the same year he rented a country house in Montrion, near Lausanne, but in 1757 also took a house in Lausanne itself. Finally, in 1758, he bought the small château of Ferney, north of Geneva, and from then on lived now at one of these

properties, now at another, but most frequently at "Les Délices." In 1760 he gave them all up except Ferney, which remained his permanent residence until his death.

CHAPTER VI

1 *Quadrille:* An old card game for four persons, played with the 40 cards remaining after the eights, nines, and tens are discarded.

2 *Fine house:* Until recently it was assumed that this was the château of Waldeck, built in the 16th century by Jean Victor de Besenval de Brunnstatt. But since that property served in the 18th century as the summer residence of the French Ambassador, the assumption must be abandoned. Presumably the house was the château of Rienberg, which belonged to the Roll family and was demolished in 1798; C.'s description of the building and grounds supports this assumption.

3 *In the service of the French Ambassador:* In Vol. 4, Chaps. III and IV, C. says that De Bernis had a French cook, but does not name him.

4 *Neuchâtel:* Town at the north end of the Lac de Neuchâtel (Neuenburger See), with many vineyards in the vicinity.

5 *"La Côte":* The shore of the Lac de Neuchâtel which lies in the canton of Vaud; it is still famous for its wines.

6 *Madame d'Hermenches:* Louise d'Hermenches, Baroness de Constant de Rebecque (died 1772); her husband, David Louis d'Hermenches, whom she married in 1754, was a friend of Voltaire's.

7 *Lady Montagu:* C. writes "Miladi Montaigu"; probably Elizabeth Montagu, née Robinson (1720–1800), English woman of letters, who, however, did not have a title; it is also possible that C. means Lady Mary Wortley Montagu (1689–1762), though she lived in Italy until 1761.

8 *Roxburghe:* C. writes "de Rosburi"; probably John Ker, Duke of Roxburghe (1740–1804).

9 *Lebel:* Obviously an invented name, as is "Madame Dubois"; the manuscript shows that C. started to write a different name

here, then decided on "Lebel" (which in other places he writes "Le-bel").

10 *Admirable conquest:* Ironically, of Madame F.

11 *Locke:* C. writes "Loke"; John Locke (1632–1704), English philosopher.

12 *L'Hospital:* Paul François Galucci de l'Hospital, Marquis de Châteauneuf-sur-Cher (1697–1776), from 1741 to 1762 French Envoy Extraordinary to the Court of the Czarina (see the next note).

13 *Elisabeth Petrovna:* Daughter (1709–1762) of Peter the Great, Czarina from 1741.

14 *The:* The text has *"du,"* which is either a typographical error or shows that C. changed his construction in the middle of the sentence.

15 *Nivernais:* Louis Jules Henri Barbon Mancini-Mazarini, Duke of Nivernais and Donziois (1716–1798), French diplomat; he was Envoy Extraordinary to the English Court during the negotiations for the peace treaty (Sept. 15, 1762–May 11, 1763) which ended the Seven Years' War.

16 *Court of St. James's:* A frequent designation for the English Court (from St. James's Palace).

17 *Whose acquaintance I had made . . . in Versailles:* C. probably met the Marquis de Chauvelin (cf. note 25 to Chap. V of this volume) on one of the latter's periodical trips from Turin when he was serving as Ambassador there.

18 *His charming wife:* Agnès Thérèse, née Mazade, Marquise de Chauvelin (born ca. 1741).

19 *Poem on the Seven Deadly Sins:* Published in 1758, and attributed to the Abbé Philippe de Chauvelin (ca. 1716–1770), brother of the Marquis. C.'s translation of it into the Venetian dialect (*I sette Capitali, canzone*) was preserved among his papers at Dux. According to other sources the Marquis himself was the author of the poem, which he composed at the Prince de Conti's estate of L'Isle-Adam when he was there alone with seven beautiful women.

20 *Égérie:* Cf. Vol. 5, Chap, V, n. 33.

21 *Megaera:* Name of one of the three Furies.

22 *Styx:* A river in Hades; its water was held to be poisonous.

23 *Eau des Carmes: Aqua carmelitarum,* melissa cordial, whose manufacture was formerly the secret of the Carmelite nuns. Highly reputed as a medicament in the 18th century.

CHAPTER VII

1 *Twentieth:* To this date (1760) in his memoirs C. has recorded eight such infections.

2 *Secrets:* Possibly a reference to C.'s being a Freemason or to his activities as a secret agent.

3 *Minerva . . . Telemachus:* In the *Odyssey* Pallas Athena (in Roman mythology, Minerva) frequently gives Odysseus' son Telemachus good advice. But rather than the *Odyssey,* C. very probably had in mind Fénelon's celebrated didactic novel *Les Aventures de Télémaque* (first published in 1690).

4 *Anacreon:* Greek poet from Teos in Ionia (5th century B.C.), whose principal subjects were wine and love.

5 *Smerdies, Cleobulus, . . . Bathyllus:* Three youths whose beauty Anacreon praises.

6 *A Platonist:* C. doubtless refers to the Renaissance interpreters of the Platonic dialogues, who made an oversimplified distinction between sensual and so-called "Platonic" love.

7 *The whites:* Leukorrhea.

8 *Nuncio:* Lucerne was the seat of the nunciature for the Catholic cantons; from Nov. 1759 to Aug. 1760 the office of *administratore* was held by Niccolò Cassoni. He was succeeded as Nuncio by Niccolò Oddi, who had previously held the same office in Cologne.

9 *Coronation:* Leopold II was crowned Emperor at Prague on Sept. 6, 1791.

10 Vergil, *Georgics,* III, 67.

11 *Eau de nitre:* A solution of saltpeter.

12 *Dine at my house with Madame ... and her husband:* The text has *dîner chez moi la ... et son mari*, which makes no sense; the "with" of the translation is a conjecture based on C.'s account of the incident earlier in this chapter.

CHAPTER X

1 *Algarotti:* Francesco Algarotti (1712–1764), given the title of Count by Frederick the Great in 1740; born in Venice, he was a well-known writer and critic of the Enlightenment (cf. note 3).

2 *Padua:* Algarotti left the Prussian Court in 1753 and thereafter lived in Mirabello, near Padua.

3 *Ladies:* Algarotti's best-known work was *Il Newtonianismo per le dame ovvero Dialoghi sopra la luce ed i colori* ("Newtonianism for ladies, or Dialogues on light and colors"); following the example of Fontenelle, to whom the book was dedicated, it attempted to make scientific knowledge accessible to non-specialists. It was first printed at Naples in 1737.

4 *Pluralité des mondes:* Fontenelle's *Entretiens sur la pluralité des mondes* ("Conversations on the Plurality of Worlds") (Paris, 1686) was the first attempt in modern times to put scientific material into literary form and so give it a general audience.

5 *His letters on Russia:* The reference is to Algarotti's *Viaggi in Russia* ("Travels in Russia"), which was published at Venice in 1760. The second edition (Paris, 1763) was entitled *Saggio di Lettere sulla Russia*. Voltaire was then composing his history of Russia in the time of Peter the Great (*Histoire de l'Empire de Russie sous Pierre-le-Grand*).

6 *Livy ... Patavinity:* Titus Livius (59 B.C.–A.D. 17), famous Roman historian; he came from Padua (Latin, Patavium), whence "Patavinity," the dialect of that city.

7 *Lazzarini:* Domenico Lazzarini (1668–1734), Professor of Greek and Latin at the University of Padua.

8 *Sallust:* Gaius Sallustius Crispus (86–ca. 35 B.C.), Roman historian.

9   *Ulisse il giovane:* "The Young Ulysses," written in 1720; C. was nine years old when he first went to Padua in April 1734; Lazzarini died in July of the same year.

10 *Conti:* Antonio Schinella Conti (1677–1749), Italian poet. He had met Newton in London in 1715; his four tragedies, *Giunio Bruto*, *Marco Bruto*, *Giulio Cesare*, and *Druso*, were posthumously published in one volume (Florence, 1751).

11 *Procrustes:* Legendary highwayman of Attica, who bound his victims on an iron bed and either stretched or cut off their legs to make them fit it; whence the metaphorical expression "the bed of Procrustes."

12 *Have not one:* This dictum of Voltaire's only shows that he was as little appreciative as most of his contemporaries of French Renaissance poetry.

13 *Your strictures on him:* In his *Essai sur la poésie épique* (1726) Voltaire had placed Tasso far above Ariosto.

14 *Astolpho . . . St. John the Apostle:* In Ariosto's *Orlando furioso* Astolpho makes a fantastic journey to the moon to recover the mad Orlando's wits. In the course of it he meets St. John the Apostle. C. refers to Canto XXXIV, 61 ff., and Canto XXXV, 3 ff., of the *Orlando furioso*.

15 *Orlando furioso*, XLIV, 2. Voltaire included his translation, with minor changes, in the article "Épopée" in his *Dictionnaire philosophique* (1764). There he also praises Ariosto in the highest terms (cf. note 13 to this chapter).

16 *Madame Denis:* Louise Denis, née Mignot (1712–1790), Voltaire's niece; after her husband's death in 1744 she lived with Voltaire, who made her his sole heir; her second marriage (1780) was to a Commissary of War named Duvivier.

17 *Went mad too:* Ariosto did not go mad; C. may be momentarily confusing him with Tasso, who did.

18 *Fifty-one:* The first edition of the *Orlando furioso* (1516) contains 40 cantos; the final edition (1532) contains 46. The edition of 1545, brought out by Ariosto's son Virgilio, added five cantos of an epic similar in form and theme, which Ariosto had begun late in his life. So C. is justified in his "fifty-one."

19   *Orlando furioso*, XXIII, 122, 1–4.

20   *Angelica . . . Medoro:* Characters in the *Orlando furioso*. Orlando, who is passionately in love with Angelica, the daughter of an Oriental king and magician, discovers that she had given her love to the simple shepherd Medoro.

21   *Leo X:* Giovanni de' Medici (1475–1521), as Pope Leo X (from 1513), the great patron of the poets and artists of the Italian Renaissance.

22   *Este . . . Medici:* The Medici family in Florence and the Este family in Ferrara were the greatest fosterers of the arts in the Italy of the 15th and 16th centuries. Ariosto lived at the Este Court, as did Tasso later.

23   *Donation of Rome:* The so-called Donation of Constantine, a forged document of the 8th century, declares that the Emperor Constantine the Great, under whose rule Christianity was made the state religion of the Roman Empire, had conferred imperial rank and temporal rule over Rome and Italy on Pope Sylvester I.

24   *Sylvester:* St. Sylvester, Pope from 314 to 355.

25   *Orlando furioso*, XXXIV, 80, 6, where the original reads: *or putia forte.* The fact that the "Donation of Constantine" was a forgery was discovered by the Italian humanist Lorenzo Valla (1406–1457); hence Ariosto's *or* ("now").

26   *The hermit . . . Zerbino:* Characters in the *Orlando furioso*. "The African" is Rodomonte. The death of the hermit is described in XXIX, 6–7, whereas the line C. proceeds to quote is from the episode of Orlando killing the shepherds (XXIV, 6, 4).

27   *Syndic:* Title of the four highest officers of the commune of Geneva. Here perhaps Michel Lullin de Châteauvieux (born 1695), who, as "Seigneur scolarque," controlled the publication of books and in that capacity frequently had dealings with Voltaire.

28   *Quinze:* A card game in which the player who ends with 15 points or the closest approximation to it is the winner.

29   *"Les Délices"*: Name of Voltaire's house near Geneva (cf. note 26 to Chap. V of this volume).

30   *Villars*: Honoré Armand, Duke of Villars (1702–1770), French general and Governor of Provence; from 1734 member of the Académie Française.

31   *Tronchin*: Théodore Tronchin (1709–1781), celebrated Swiss physician; connected with the well-known banking family of the same name.

32   *Dent Blanche*: Mont Blanc.

33   *Pupil*: Tronchin entered the University of Leiden in 1728 and obtained his doctorate there in 1730.

34   *Seventy*: Villars was 58 years of age in 1760.

35   *Regency*: The period of the Regency (1715–1723) was characterized by a relaxation in manners after the formal etiquette of the Court of Louis XIV.

36   *Summa*: The *Summa theologiae* of Thomas Aquinas (1226–1274), the great monument of Scholasticism.

37   *Tassoni*: Alessandro Tassoni (1565–1635), Italian poet, famous especially for his heroi-comic epic *La Secchia rapita*, which narrates the bitter struggle between the cities of Modena and Bologna over a stolen pail.

38   *Discorsi academici*: C. doubtless means Tassoni's *Dieci libri di pensieri diversi* (1620), in which he attacks the Copernican system.

39   *Criticized . . . Petrarch*: In his *Considerazioni sopra le rime del Petrarca* (1609) Tassoni launches his satiric barbs at Petrarch's innumerable imitators rather than at Petrarch himself.

40   *Muratori*: Lodovico Antonio Muratori (1672–1750), Italian historian and literary critic. He also attacked Petrarchism.

41   Horace, *Epistles*, II, 1, 63.

42   *Fifty thousand*: Voltaire's extant letters number 20,054.

43   *Macaronic . . . Merlin Cocai*: Macaronic poetry was a kind of burlesque poetry in which the words of a modern language

are Latinized and mixed with Latin words. Its chief Italian representative was Teofilo Folengo (1490–1544), who wrote under the pseudonym of Merlin Cocai.

44 *A famous poem: Il Baldus*, a comic epic in macaronic Latin, of which there were four revisions, published in 1517, 1521, 1540, and 1552, respectively.

45 *Cramers:* The brothers Gabriel Cramer (1723–1793) and Philibert Cramer (1727–1779), printers and publishers in Geneva. From 1756 to 1775 they published nearly all of Voltaire's writings. Voltaire released all his author's rights to them in exchange for an unlimited number of author's copies.

46 *La Princesse de Babylone:* It was first published in 1768; hence C.'s statement is erroneous.

47 *Three young ladies:* Perhaps Pernette Elisabeth de Fernex (born 1730), her sister Marie (born 1732), and their cousin Jeanne Christine (born 1735); they belonged to an impoverished noble family, whose name was derived from the estate of Fernex (Ferney), which Voltaire acquired in 1758.

48 *Grécourt:* Jean Baptiste Joseph Villaret de Grécourt (1683–1743), Canon of Tours and poet. His licentious *Y grec* ("The Letter Y") reads in part:

> *Marc une béquille avait*
> *Faite en fourche, et de manière*
> *Qu'à la fois elle trouvait*
> *L'oeillet et la boutonnière.*
> *D'une indulgence plénière*
> *Il crut devoir se munir,*
> *Et courut, pour l'obtenir,*
> *Conter le cas au Saint-Père*
> *Qui s'écria: "Vierge Mère*
> *Que ne suis-je ainsi bâti!*
> *Va, mon fils, baise, prospère,*
> *Gaudeant bene nati!"*

49 *Teofilo Folengo:* Real name of the author of *Il Baldus* (cf. notes 43 and 44 to this chapter).

50 *Doblones de a ocho:* Spanish gold coins of the weight and value of 8 gold scudi.

51 *Capacelli:* The Marchese Francesco Albergati Capacelli (1728–1804), Bolognese Senator, author of comedies.

52 *Paradisi:* Count Agostini Paradisi (1736–1783), Italian scholar and poet.

53 *"Forty":* The Senate of Bologna was called the "Quaranta" ("Forty"), despite the fact that it numbered 50; the name was also applied to its members.

54 *Goldoni:* Carlo Goldoni (1707–1793), famous Italian writer of comedies; friend of the Marchese Albergati Capacelli.

55 *Tancrède:* Voltaire's tragedy of this name was first produced in his house in 1759 and at the Comédie Française the next year.

56 *Theatromania:* Albergati had a private theater built in his villa at Zola Predosa, some 5 miles west of Bologna.

57 *Author:* In 1760 Albergati had only translated French comedies and tragedies. The first of his own comedies was not published until 1768.

58 *Noon . . . eleven o'clock:* Until 1791 the clocks of Basel were set an hour fast. All the various explanations of the fact appear to be apocryphal.

59 *Council of Ten . . . seventeen:* The Venetian Council of Ten included, in addition to its 10 official members, the Doge and his six councillors, making 17 in all.

60 *Poet to the Duke of Parma:* In 1756 the Duke of Parma commissioned Goldoni to write plays for the Court theater and gave him this title and a yearly pension of 700 francs.

61 *Advocate:* Goldoni had studied law in Pavia and Modena, became a Doctor utriusque iuris in 1731, and practiced as an advocate in Venice and Pisa (1733).

62 *Cuma:* Otherwise Cyme, an important port on the coast of Asia Minor; it was one of the seven cities which claimed in antiquity to be the birthplace of Homer. C., who writes "Cume," perhaps confuses it with Cumae in Italy.

63 *Macaronicon:* Alternative title of Teofilo Folengo's *Il Baldus.*

64 *A Jesuit:* Antoine Adam, S.J. (1705–after 1786); he was Voltaire's almoner from ca. 1764 to 1776.

65 *Clement of Alexandria:* Titus Flavius Clemens (2nd–3rd century), Father of the Church; he discusses modesty in Books II and III of his *Paidagogos.*

66 *The cousin:* C. first wrote *la cadette* ("the youngest"); the change substantiates the identifications proposed in note 47 to this chapter.

67 *Chapelain:* Jean Chapelain (1595–1674), French poet and literary critic, first Secretary of the Académie Française. His epic poem *La Pucelle* ("The Maid"—i.e., Joan of Arc) was begun in 1630; the first 12 cantos were published in 1656.

68 *He disavowed it:* Voltaire finished his burlesque epic on Joan of Arc, *La Pucelle,* in 1739, but did not then dare to publish it. Though manuscript copies circulated in both Paris and Geneva, Voltaire denied his authorship of it. The first unauthorized editions began to appear from 1755 in Frankfurt, Geneva, London, and Paris. The first authorized edition was published by Cramer at Geneva in 1762. The work was condemned to be publicly burned in Paris in 1757.

69 *Crébillon:* Prosper Jolyot de Crébillon (1674–1762), French dramatist, Royal Censor from 1735 (cf. Vol. 3, Chap. VIII).

70 *Rhadamiste:* Crébillon's tragedy *Rhadamiste et Zénobie* (cf. Vol. 3, Chap. VIII).

71 *Martelli:* Pier Jacopo Martelli (1665–1727), Italian poet; he was the first to introduce an approximation of the French Alexandrine verse into Italian (see note 73, below).

72 *Works:* Pier Jacopo Martelli, *Opere,* 7 vols., Bologna, 1729–1733.

73 *Fourteen syllables:* The French Alexandrine has 12 syllables (not counting the allowable unaccented syllable after the caesura and the obligatory unaccented syllable in the rhyme words of every second pair of lines). Martelli's equivalent contains, according to Italian metrical reckoning, 14 syllables—the so-called *verso martelliano.*

74   Horace, *Satires*, I, 10, 74.

75   *Addison:* Joseph Addison (1672–1719), part author of the cele-
      brated *Spectator* papers. He supported liberal ideas in his tragedy
      Cato (1713).

76   *Hobbes:* Thomas Hobbes (1588–1679), English philosopher. He
      defended absolute monarchy in his *Leviathan* (1651).

77   Altered from Horace, *Epistles*, II, 1, 63 (cf. note 41, above).
      Instead of *Est* the text here has *Et*, presumably a typographical
      error.

78   *Don Quixote:* The reference is to Miguel de Cervantes Saavedra
      (1547–1616), *El ingenioso Hidalgo Don Quijote de la Mancha*, Pt.
      I, Chap. XXII.

79   *Sumptuary laws:* The laws of the time forbade the inhabitants of
      Bern to wear gold or silver embroidery, precious stones, lace,
      or costly furs.

79   *Sumptuary laws:* The laws of the time forbade the inhabitants of
      Bern to wear gold or silver embroidery, precious stones, lace,
      or costly furs.

80   *What I published against him:* Principally in C.'s *Scrutinio del libro
      "Éloges de M. de Voltaire"* (Venice, 1779).

81   *Zoilus:* Greek rhetorician from Amphipolis in Macedonia,
      probably flourished in the 3rd century B.C.; he was famous
      for his carping and malicious criticism of Homer.

Volume Seven

CHAPTER VII

1   *Ponte alla Carraia:* Built in 1218 and then called Ponte Nuovo
      (in distinction from the earlier Ponte Vecchio), it was several
      times destroyed and finally rebuilt in 1559 from plans by the
      architect Bartolomeo Ammanati. Blown up in 1944 during the
      Second World War, it was rebuilt in its old form.

2   *Vannini's:* The hostelry of Attilio Vannini in the Borgo Ognis-
      santi, Florence, enjoyed an excellent reputation in the 18th
      century. He was a doctor of letters, not of medicine.

3   *Accademia della Crusca:* The Accademia Nazionale della Crusca, or Accademia Furfuratorum, took its name from its purpose, which was to guard the purity of the Italian language by separating the chaff (*crusca*) from the wheat. It was founded by Cosimo I de' Medici in 1540. In 1591 it began to compile a dictionary. This work, though it was never completed, acquired great authority. It is unlikely that Vannini was ever a member of the Academy.

4   *The theater:* The Teatro del Cocomero, in the street of the same name; it survived until 1930, when it became a cinema (Teatro Nicolini).

5   *Roffi:* Giovanni Roffi (died after 1780), Tuscan actor and theater director, famous for his interpretation of the role of Arlecchino.

6   *Pertici:* Pietro Pertici, who appeared first as a singer from 1731 to 1744, and, from 1748, as an actor; from 1751 to 1756 he played in Florence with a company of his own.

7   *The opera in the Via della Pergola:* At the Teatro della Pergola, built about the middle of the 17th century in the street of the same name, and still standing.

8   *Teresa:* For C.'s account of his meeting with Teresa, then masquerading as the castrato Bellino, his discovery of her true sex, and his subsequent affair with her, see Vol. 2, Chaps. I and II. There C. calls her only by her first name; in the present chapter he gives her son the surname Lanti and her husband's name as Palesi; it is not until Vol. X that he reveals her real name: Angela Calori (born 1732, died ca. 1790).

9   *"The same":* This would seem to indicate that C. did not use the name Chevalier de Seingalt during this visit to Florence. But a contemporary document shows that he registered at Vannini's hostelry as "Cavaliere Sangalli."

10   *Mandane:* None of the operas produced at the Teatro della Pergola in 1760 and 1761 contained such a role. C. is obviously trying to conceal the identity of Teresa, who was a famous singer.

11 *Cirillo Palesi:* Presumably a fictitious name for Angela Calori's husband.

12 *Sancho Pico:* See Vol. 2, Chap. I.

13 *Ducati del regno:* The ducato del regno was a gold coin of the Kingdom of Naples, minted from the 16th century.

14 *Redegonda:* C. met her again at Turin in 1762 and at Brunswick in 1764; she may have been a certain Signora Blizzi.

15 *Corticelli:* Maria Anna Corticelli (1747–1767 or '73), Italian dancer.

16 *Gama:* Giovanni Patrizio da Gama de Silveira (ca. 1704–1774), born in Lisbon, made a Roman citizen in 1735 (cf. Vol. 1, Chaps. IX and X).

17 *Acquaviva:* Troyano Francisco Acquaviva d'Aragona (1696–1747); Cardinal from 1732; Spanish Ambassador in Rome from 1737 (cf. Vol. 1, Chaps. IX and X).

18 *Barbaruccia . . . the Marchesa G. . . . Cardinal S. C.:* Barbara Dallacqua, the Marchesa Caterina Gabrieli, Cardinal Prospero Colonna di Sciarra; acquaintances of C. during his first stay in Rome (cf. Vol. 1, Chap. X).

19 *The same Duke:* Francisco Eboli, Duke of Castropiñano (1688–1758), of Spanish descent, Neapolitan General and diplomat.

20 *When the Duke died:* In 1758.

21 *Della Riccia:* Bartolomeo de Capua, became Prince della Riccia in 1732, and died, the last of his line, in 1792.

22 *La Sensa:* The Fiera della Sensa, the great fair held yearly in Venice at Ascensiontide, at which time the theaters were open.

23 *Matalona:* Carlo Caraffa, Duke of Matalona (Maddaloni) (1734–1765), married Vittoria Guevara in 1755 (cf. Vol. 1, Chap. IX).

24 *A son:* Marzio Domenico V (1758–1829); his marriage (1774) to Donna Maria Josefa de Cardenas, Countess of Acerra, was annulled by Pope Pius VI on the ground of impotence, the same infirmity which had been attributed to his father.

25 *Daughter of the Duke of Bovino:* Vittoria Guevara was the daughter of Innico Guevara, Duke of Bovino, and his wife Eleonora.

1   *Almada:* Francisco, Marquês de Almada (Almeida, Almeda) y Mendoça, Portuguese Ambassador in Rome from 1757 to 1760 and from 1769 to after 1799.

2   *Rezzonico:* Carlo Rezzonico (1693–1769), Cardinal at Padua from 1743, Pope, as Clement XIII, from 1758.

3   *His Most Faithful Majesty:* Title of the King of Portugal.

4   *Intended to kill him:* Allusion to the attempted assassination of King Joseph Emanuel I (1715–1777) on Sept. 3, 1758, which was generally ascribed to the Jesuits. The petition to the Pope to empower the King to punish the suspected Jesuits was dismissed by Clement XIII. Thereupon the all-powerful Minister, the Marquês de Pombal, banished the Papal Nuncio from Lisbon and the Jesuits from Portugal (1759). The Portuguese Ambassador in Rome left the city on July 7, 1760, and did not return to it until 1769; the Abate Gamma followed him back in 1770.

5   *Carvalho:* Sebastião José de Carvalho e Mello, Marquês de Pombal (1699–1782), Prime Minister of Portugal from 1757 to 1777.

6   *State Inquisitors:* The three State Inquisitors (Inquisitori di Stato) constituted the highest court in the Republic of Venice. In 1755 they sentenced C. to indefinite imprisonment under the Leads.

7   *Botta-Adorno:* Antonio Ottone, Marchese Botta-Adorno (1688–1774), Austrian diplomat, field marshal, and supreme commander of the Austrian troops in Italy; Governor of Tuscany from 1757 to 1766.

8   *Governor of Tuscany:* In accordance with a treaty concluded among Austria, France, and Spain in 1735, Duke Franz Stephan of Lorraine was declared the heir to Tuscany. The Duke having married the Empress Maria Theresa in 1736, on the death of the last Grand Duke of the Medici family the Grand Duchy of Tuscany became a possession of the Hapsburgs and was administered by a Governor.

9   *Francis I:* Franz Stephan of Lorraine (1708–1765), Emperor of Austria from 1745 (cf. the previous note).

10   *Signora Laura:* Laura Corticelli, née Citti (also Cilli or Cigli), married to Antonio Corticelli.

11   *Impresario:* According to information furnished by the Biblioteca Comunale of Florence, the Teatro della Pergola was under the direction of the impresario Compostov from 1760 to 1761.

12   *Chavigny:* Anne Théodore Chavignard, Chevalier de Chavigny (1689–1771), French Ambassador in Soleure (Solothurn) from 1753 to 1762 (cf. Vol. 6, Chaps. V ff.).

13   *Orihuela:* Village in southern Spain, between Alicante and Murcia.

14   *Camerino:* Dressing room.

15   *Testone:* Originally a French silver coin called "têton" because it displayed the King's head; it was minted in France from the reign of Louis XI (1461–1483), and until the introduction of the franc in 1567 was the most important French coin. It was imitated in Rome and Tuscany from the 16th century. Value: 40 soldi.

16   *The Genoese affair:* In the War of the Austrian Succession Genoa sided with Spain, France, and the Kingdom of Naples in 1745. In Sept. 1746 the city was taken by the Austrian forces under the command of the Marchese Botta-Adorno; but they were driven out as early as Dec. of the same year by a popular uprising and were unable to retake the town.

17   *So easily ascended the throne of her father:* Elisabeth Petrovna, daughter of Peter the Great, caused the Regent Anna Leopoldovna and her son Ivan VI to be poisoned in Dec. 1741, banished the Regent's supporters to Siberia, and had herself proclaimed Czarina.

18   *Giton:* Name of a boy catamite in the *Satyricon* of Petronius (died A.D. 66).

19   *The wristband game:* Text, *le manège de la manchette* = pederasty.

20   *Mann:* Sir Horatio (Horace) Mann (1701–1786); he came to Florence in 1738 as the English Chargé d'Affaires, was appointed Resident in 1740, Envoy Extraordinary in 1765, and Plenipotentiary in 1782. He does not mention C. in his

letters to Horace Walpole, but he was one of the subscribers to C.'s translation of the *Iliad* (1775–1776).

21   *The gallery:* The celebrated gallery in the Palazzo degli Uffizi (built by Vasari from 1560 to 1574) and containing, among other treasures, the rich collection of paintings and other works of art assembled by the Medicis.

22   *Augsburg:* In March 1761 France and her allies proposed a congress at Augsburg to end the Seven Years' War; the proposal came to nothing because of the conditions laid down by Frederick the Great. The war was not ended until 1763, by the Peace of Hubertusburg.

23   *Aleatico:* The name of a sweet red muscat wine of Tuscany, as well as the name of a grape which is also cultivated in other parts of Italy.

24   Since neither the anecdote nor the passage cited occurs in Cicero's letters, C.'s source remains unknown.

25   Vergil, *Aeneid*, X, 113; C. quotes it frequently (e.g., in a somewhat similar context, in Vol. 1, Chap. VI, p. 106).

26   *Merit . . . guilt:* C. uses exactly the same language in his "Preface" (see Vol. 1, p. 7).

27   *Playful pinches:* The word in the manuscript, which is said to be "almost illegible" at this point, is printed as "ciguenaudes," presumably for *chiquenaudes*.

CHAPTER X

1   *Martorano:* In central Calabria, near Cosenza (cf. Vol. 1, Chap. VIII).

2   *Antonio Casanova:* A relative of C.'s in Naples (cf. Vol. 1, Chap. IX).

3   *Palo:* Gennaro Palo, of Naples, to whom the Bishop of Martorano had given C. a letter of introduction (cf. Vol. 1, Chaps. VIII and IX).

4   *Castelli:* Husband of "Donna Lucrezia" (probably Anna Maria d'Antoni, who married the painter Alessio Vallati in 1734).

5   *Caraffa:* The Marchese Lelio Caraffa, Duke of Arienzo, of the
    ducal family of Matalona (Maddaloni), died 1761.

6   *Palazzo Matalona:* Or Maddaloni; it was on the Via Toledo (cf.
    Vol. 1, Chap. IX).

7   *Daughter of the Duke of Bovino:* Carlo Caraffa, Duke of Matalona
    (Maddaloni) (1734–1765), was married in 1755 to Vittoria
    Guevara, of the ducal house of Bovino.

8   *Casalnuovo:* Antonio Como, Duke of Casalnuovo.

9   *A son:* Marzio Domenico V, the last Duke of Matalona (Mad-
    daloni) (1758–1829), son of Duke Carlo Caraffa and Vittoria
    Guevara.

10 *Pretended antiquities:* Francesco Maria Alfani (died 1798) was
    often accused at the time of selling spurious antiquities.

11 *Scathing satire:* The Duke of Matalona was imprisoned in the
    fortress of Gaeta in 1756 for composing a satirical comedy; this
    may be the work to which C. refers.

12 *Teatro San Carlo:* One of the most celebrated theaters in Italy. It
    was built under King Charles Bourbon and dedicated in 1737;
    the present building was not constructed until 1817.

13 *The very young King:* King Ferdinand IV of Naples (1751–1825)
    had ascended the throne in 1759.

14 *An anniversary:* The reference is presumably to the gala per-
    formance of the opera *Attilio Regolo* (libretto by Metastasio,
    music by Jomelli) given Jan. 12, 1761, on the occasion of the
    King's birthday.

15 *Intelligence . . . education:* C. may here be unconsciously echoing
    Montesquieu's *Esprit des lois.*

16 *Boerhaave:* Hermann Boerhaave (1668–1738), celebrated phys-
    ician and professor at the University of Leiden.

17 *Januarius:* Patron saint of the city of Naples. Two vials contain-
    ing what is held to be his coagulated blood are kept under strict
    guard in the Cappella del Tesoro. The blood is believed to
    become liquid on the day of the saint's festival and whenever

the city is in danger. In the 18th century the vials were constantly guarded by a deputation of twelve noblemen.

18   *Madame:* As appears from the sequel, they are speaking French.

19   *In the first edition:* Contrary to C.'s statement, this epigram is not by La Fontaine and is not included in any edition of his works. It is doubtless by one of his many 18th-century imitators.

20   *Monteleone:* Fabrizio Mattia Pignatelli, Duke of Monteleone (1718–1763).

21   *Livret:* The 13 cards dealt to each player in faro.

22   *Chilblains:* From his letters it appears that King Ferdinand IV was still complaining of his chilblains in 1821.

23   *San Nicandro:* Domenico Cattaneo, Prince of San Nicandro, Duke of Termoli and Count of Aversa, appointed Grand Master of the Crown Prince Ferdinand's household in 1755 and President of the Council of Regency in 1759.

24   *Companion of his studies:* See Vol. 1, Chap. IX.

25   *Vicissitudes . . . Acquaviva:* See Vol. 1, Chaps. IX and X.

26   *The Fiorentini:* The Teatro dei Fiorentini or, more properly, Teatro di San Giovanni dei Fiorentini, named from the adjoining church and also known as the Commedia Nuova, was built in 1618 and still exists.

27   *You:* At this point Leonilda begins to address C. in the second person singular.

28   *Fontana Medina:* One of the most beautiful fountains in Naples, built in the second half of the 16th century by M. A. Naccher-ino and Pietro Bernini (father of the celebrated Giovanni Lorenzo), and several times relocated. In C.'s day it was in the Strada delle Corregge (now Via Medina, near the Piazza del Municipio).

29   *Crébillon the Younger:* Claude Prosper Jolyot de Crébillon (1707–1777), usually known as Crébillon fils to distinguish him from his father, the celebrated tragic dramatist Prosper

Jolyot de Crébillon; well known as a writer of sometimes licentious stories, among them *Le Sopha* (1745).

30   *Princess della Valle:* Margherita Piccolomini d'Aragona, Princess della Valle di Scafati, née Caracciolo.

31   *Don Marco Ottoboni:* Perhaps a younger brother of Alessandro Ottoboni-Buoncompagni-Ludovisi, Duke of Fiano (1734–1780).

32   *Cassaro:* Cesare Gaetani e Lanza, Prince del Cassaro.

33   *Posilipo:* Hilly district on the Gulf of Naples, a favorite site for residences even in Greek and Roman times because of its magnificent view; now practically a part of the city of Naples.

34   *Virtuosa:* Her name, it appears from the following chapter, was Signora Diana. Three singers or actresses (*virtuose*) by the same name are recorded in the annals of the Italian stage at this period; but little more is known of them than their names, and it is impossible to determine which, if any, of them was the Prince's mistress.

35   *Once:* The oncia (plural, once) was a silver coin of the Kingdom of Naples worth 3 ducati or 30 carlini; there were also gold once, which were worth twice as much.

36   *Caserta:* The city of Caserta, some 20 miles north of Naples, was and still is famous for its great royal palace in a park with impressive fountains. The Palazzo Reale, containing some 1200 rooms, is one of the largest buildings in Italy; it was begun in 1752 and completed in 1774 by L. Vanvitelli.

37   *Galiani:* The Marchese Bernardo Galiani (1724–1772 or '74), elder brother of the celebrated Abbé Galiani, owned an estate at Sant'Agata di Sessa.

38   *Your daughter:* Leonilda's authenticity has been questioned because, in a notation in C.'s hand found at Dux in which he acknowledged having been the father of a child by Donna Lucrezia, he first wrote *un fils de* ("a son by"), then crossed it out and substituted *une fille de* ("a daughter by"). It is, however, possible that he wrote *fils* as the equivalent of Italian *figlio*, which can be used in the sense of "child," without specification of sex.

39   *Phèdre:* The theme of Racine's famous tragedy (1677) is the incestuous love of Phaedra, wife of King Theseus of Athens, for Hippolytus, his son by a previous marriage.

40   *Tivoli:* C. had first spent a night with Donna Lucrezia in Tivoli (see note 42, below).

41   *Gunfire . . . dark:* Allusion to the circumstances which defeated C.'s first attempt to make love to Donna Lucrezia (cf. Vol. 1, Chap. IX).

42   *Testaccio . . . Tivoli:* The scenes of C.'s successful pursuit of Donna Lucrezia in Rome (cf. Vol. 1, Chaps. IX and X).

43   Petrarch, *Canzoniere*, Sonnet X, line 4.

Volume Eight

CHAPTER III

1   *Lascaris:* A Byzantine family, documented from the end of the 12th century. In 1554 Jacques I d'Urfé (1534–1574) married Renée of Savoy, granddaughter of René of Savoy and Anne de Lascaris, Countess of Tenda. From then on the d'Urfé family often used the name Lascaris d'Urfé. Madame d'Urfé had earlier been taken in by a swindler who called himself Jean Paul Lascaris.

2   *Pont-Carré:* Near Tournan (Seine-et-Marne); after the French Revolution it was sold to Fouché, Duke of Otranto, as "national property," but it is now demolished.

3   *Civil wars:* C. refers either to the religious wars in France during the second half of the 16th century or, less probably, to the troubles during the period of the Fronde (beginning of the 17th century).

4   *Lyons:* A letter from Louis de Muralt, dated July 3, 1763, yields the information that D'Aranda was a pupil of Professor Daniel, or of Jean Bernoulli, in Basel in 1762 and 1763. However, he might have spent some time in Lyons before his stay in Basel.

5   *Rochebaron:* François La Rochefoucauld, Marquis de Rochebaron (1677–1766), was Commandant of Lyons at the time.

6   *Brougnole:* C. spells the name differently in different places: Brongnole, Brougnole, Brognole; it appears to have been an

invention of his own. In her will Madame d'Urfé left a legacy to her favorite maid Marguerite Regnaud-Sainte-Brune; C. may refer to her. But the text at this point is ambiguous, leaving it in doubt whether the maid was Madame d'Urfé's favorite or La Corticelli's.

7 *At Aix:* The list of foreigners visiting Aix (Aachen) for May 21, 1762, contains the notation, "Monsieur le Chevalier de Seingalt avec sa femme," among the names of the guests registered at the "St. Corneille" inn.

8 *Two Princesses of Mecklenburg:* Probably Louisa Friederika, Duchess of Mecklenburg (1722–1791), née Princess of Württemberg, and Charlotte Sophia, Princess of Mecklenburg (1731–1810), née Princess of Saxe-Coburg-Saalfeld.

9 *Bayreuth:* Friedrich, Margrave of Bayreuth (1711–1763).

10 *The Duchess of Württemberg:* Elisabeth Friederike Sophie (1732–1780), daughter of the Margrave of Bayreuth; she married Duke Karl Eugen of Württemberg in 1748 but was separated from him in 1754.

11 *D'Aché:* A name obviously coined by C., to conceal the identity of the mother and daughter. The officer so denominated may be the Captain of the Imperial Piedmontese Regiment, Alexandre Théodore Lambertz, who was dismissed from the service in Aix on May 11, 1762.

12 *Schmit:* Nothing is known of this person.

13 *Pienne:* A Chevalier de Pienne (C. writes Pyène) is mentioned as a professional gambler in a police report of 1760.

14 *Pythia . . . Delphi:* The Pythia was the priestess of Apollo at Delphi; she delivered her oracles seated on a tripod over a crevice in the earth from which vapors arose which put her into ecstasy.

15 *Write to the moon:* The moon played an important role in cabalism and magic; it was credited with power to foresee the future and to answer questions concerning it. As a cabalist, Madame d'Urfé would see nothing absurd in her being ordered to write to the moon.

16 *Monsieur D. O.:* Probably the banker Thomas Hope (1704–1779), of Amsterdam (cf. especially Vol. 5, Chaps. VI and VII).

17 *Selenis:* Name doubtless coined by C., after Selene, the Greek goddess of the moon.

18 *An English club:* There was no "English Club" in Aix until 1785; however, there was such a club in Spa. C. very likely confuses the two places. There were two coffeehouses in Aix at the period where billiards were played and card games and dicing were allowed.

19 *Militerni:* A Neapolitan Marchese di Militerni (C. writes Maliterni) (died 1776), an officer in the French army, was promoted to the rank of Field Marshal in 1768, but later served in the Neapolitan army.

20 *D'Estrées:* Louis Charles César Le Tellier, Duke of Estrées (1697–1771), from 1757 Marshal of France.

21 *Married:* Militerni married a certain Marquise de Puissieux as his second wife in 1744. Nothing is known of a later marriage with a Neapolitan heiress.

22 *A garden outside the city:* Probably in Burtscheid, whose baths then had the reputation of making childbirth easier for stout women. The inns there permitted couples to bathe together.

23 *Malingan:* Flemish or French officer (died ca. 1764); he introduced C. to La Charpillon in London (cf. Vol. 9, Chaps. X–XII).

24 *Ardennes:* Wooded plateau region in northern France, western Luxembourg, and southeastern Belgium; Shakespeare's "Forest of Arden" (in Warwickshire, England) was named after it. It was the scene of many knightly adventures in the Old French epics and later in Ariosto's *Orlando furioso.*

25 *Bayard:* Rinaldo's steed, in Ariosto's *Orlando furioso.*

26 *Bouillon:* The small city, dominated by the ruins of its ancient castle, is picturesquely situated in the narrow valley of the River Semois; it is on the border between France and Belgium (some 12 miles from Sedan).

HISTORY OF MY LIFE

27 *Duke of Bouillon:* Charles Godefroy de la Tour d'Auvergne, Duke of Bouillon (1706–1772).

28 *Sulzbach:* The village of Sulzbach, now Soultzbach-les-Bains, near Colmar in Alsace, enjoyed a certain reputation as a watering place in the 18th century because of its mineral springs.

29 *Schaumbourg:* The Lotharingian family of Schaumbourg had several branches, so it is impossible to identify the person to whom C. refers.

CHAPTER IV

1 *Count B.:* Not identified.

2 *St. Lawrence:* According to tradition, St. Lawrence suffered martyrdom in Rome in 258 by being roasted to death on a hot griddle. The church in which he was buried, San Lorenzo fuori le mura, is one of the seven principal churches of Rome.

3 *D'Aranda:* See this volume, Chap. III, n. 4. D'Aranda was clearly not yet in Basel at this time. Madame d'Urfé owned a house on the Place Bellecour in Lyons.

4 *Franche-Comté:* One of the provinces of France under the Old Régime; its capital was Besançon.

5 *Vetturino:* In the 18th century, travel was cheaper than by post if one engaged the services of a *vetturino,* who supplied the coach and saw to the hiring of the horses, obtained food and lodging for the travelers, and so on. He was paid according to the terms of a contract made beforehand.

6 *Raiberti:* Cavaliere Carlo Adalberto Flaminio Raiberti-Nizzardi (1708–1771), from 1761 Turinese Secretary of State for Foreign Affairs.

7 *Syndic:* See Vol. 6, Chap. X.

8 *House . . . Ferney:* From 1760 Voltaire resided at Ferney, some 5 miles north of Geneva. He let the Duke of Villars have his house "Les Délices" in Geneva in the winter of 1762–63.

9 *I do not intend to visit him:* C. bore Voltaire a grudge because the latter had pronounced C.'s translation of his comedy *Le Café ou l'Écossaise* bad.

10 *The beautiful theologian:* Here C. gives her the obviously fictitious name Hedwig; she was probably Anne Marie May (born 1731), who later married a certain Gabriel von Wattenwyl.

11 *Agnes:* C. later gives her name as Helena; he uses Agnes here generically in allusion to St. Agnes, the martyred virgin the symbol of whose innocence is a lamb.

12 *My cousin, the pastor's niece:* I.e., Hedwig, "the beautiful theologian" (cf. n. 10, above).

13 *Helena:* The name is doubtless fictitious. She has not been identified.

14 *D'Harcourt:* Perhaps François Henri d'Harcourt (1726–1794).

15 *Ximénès:* The Marquis Augustin Louis de Ximénès (1726–1817), of Spanish descent but born in Paris; he was Voltaire's secretary for a time.

16 Cf. Matthew 24:36.

17 *Futurity:* Text, *"futurité,"* a word which does not exist in French.

18 Horace, *Satires,* I, 9, 70–71. Properly, "I am without scruples"; but D'Harcourt seems to quote it, and Hedwig to take it, as a reference to religion.

19 *Amphidromia:* Ancient Attic festival at which, on the 5th, 7th, or 10th day after its birth, the infant was adopted into its family by being carried around the hearth, and was commended to the care of the gods and named.

20 *Chavigny:* See Vol. 7, Chap. VIII, n. 12.

21 *Madame de . . . :* Probably the Baroness Marie Anne Louise Roll von Emmenholtz (died 1825) (cf. Vol. 6, Chaps. V–VII).

22 *Twenty-one years hence:* C. died before reaching that date in his memoirs.

23 *Tronchin's . . . house:* Probably a small château in Louis XV style on the Lake of Geneva, which in 1762 belonged to Tronchin's intimate friend J. L. Labat. Now named "Mon Repos," it is owned by the city of Geneva, which has turned it into a small museum.

24 *Naiads:* The water nymphs of Greek mythology.

25 *The word:* Allusion to the opening sentence of St. John's Gospel: "In the beginning was the word...." C. has previously used "word" in this sense in Vol. 5, Chap. V.

26 *The passage:* See Genesis 2:17 ff.

27 *Hobbes:* Thomas Hobbes (1588–1679), English philosopher.

28 *Neuchâtel:* Town in western Switzerland, on the lake of the same name, the shores of which produce excellent grapes.

29 *Rosa . . . Orio:* Marco Niccolò Rosa (born 1687), Venetian advocate, married the widow Caterina Orio, née Bianchi, at some date after 1741. C. refers to events recounted in Vol. 1, Chap. V.

30 *Signora Orio's nieces:* The Countesses Nanetta and Marta (Marton) Savorgnan (cf. Vol. 1, Chap. V).

31 *Clement of Alexandria:* Titus Flavius Clemens (2nd–3rd century), Father of the Church; his dictum on modesty, which he discusses in Books II and III of his *Paidagogos*, was cited once before by C. (cf. Vol. 6, Chap. X).

32 *Medicean Venus:* The statue is now in the Uffizi in Florence.

33 *The Aretine's postures:* Pietro Aretino (1492–1556), celebrated satirist of the Italian Renaissance. The by-name Aretino comes from his birthplace Arezzo. His 35 "Sonetti lussuriosi" were composed for engravings by Raimondi after drawings by Giulio Romano.

34 *They did not have to wait so long:* C. apparently did return to Geneva late in 1762, but he does not recount his stay there in the memoirs.

35 *Bresse:* District of France northeast of Lyons.

36 *Gualdo:* Federico Gualdo resided in Venice as a Rosicrucian about 1680; he is said to have vanished from that city in 1688 at the age of 90. He was probably of German origin and named Friedrich Walter.

37 *Madame Pernon:* Her husband was a prominent textile manufacturer in Lyons. Seven letters from him to C. were found at Dux.

38 *Bono:* Giuseppe Bono (died 1780), resided in Lyons from 1756 as a silk merchant and banker.

39 *Sacco:* Nothing further is known of him.

40 *The beginning of December:* There is documentary evidence that C. arrived in Turin by the middle of Sept. 1762, perhaps even earlier, and remained there until his expulsion in Nov. of that year.

41 *Rivoli:* A small town, then belonging to the Kingdom of Sardinia, a few miles north of Turin on the road to the Mont Cenis and France.

Volume Nine

CHAPTER VI

1 *Comédie Italienne:* The Comédie Italienne performed at the time in a house on the Rue Mauconseil (1st Arrondissement), next to the Church of Saint-Eustache.

2 *Madame du Rumain:* Constance Simone Flore Gabrielle, née Rouault de Gamaches (1725–1781), married in 1746 to Charles Yves Levicomte, Comte du Rumain; her second husband, whom she married in 1771, was Jean Jacques Gilbert, Marquis de Fraigne. For C.'s previous relations with her see Vol. 5.

3 *Balletti:* Antonio Stefano Balletti (1724–1789), Italian actor and dancer, friend of C.'s; he appeared at the Comédie Italienne in Paris from 1742 to 1769. He did not actually retire until the latter date; but an accident long kept him from performing.

4 *Brother's . . . Porte Saint-Denis:* In 1762 Francesco Casanova lived on the Carré de la Porte Saint-Denis (on the border between the 4th and 10th Arrondissements); he married on June 26th of that year and then lived with his wife on the Rue des Amandiers Popincourt in the so-called Faubourg Saint-Antoine, outside the city walls (near the present Place de la Bastille).

5 *The Abate:* C.'s and Francesco C.'s younger brother Gaetano Alvisio Casanova (1734–1783).

6 *Saincy:* Louis Pierre Sébastien Marchal de Saincy was "économe général du clergé" from 1750 to 1762.

7 *Saint-Sauveur:* The Church of Saint-Sauveur stood where the
   Rue Saint-Sauveur crosses the Rue Saint-Denis (2nd Arrondissement); it was demolished in 1793.

8 *Mind...business:* C. writes "de l'envoyer...se faire f...." (for
   foutre).

9 *Cecco:* Italian diminutive for Francesco.

10 *Monsieur du Rumain...alive:* Madame du Rumain's first husband (see note 2 to this chapter) did not die until 1770.

11 *Herrenschwandt:* Anton Gabriel Herrenschwandt (died 1785), of
   Swiss extraction, from 1755 physician in ordinary to the Duke
   of Orléans and the Swiss Guard Regiment in Paris. C. here
   writes (more or less phonetically) "Hereschouand."

12 *Twenty-nine:* Madame du Rumain, born in 1725, was already
   38 years of age in 1763.

13 *Daughter...Polignac:* Constance Gabrielle Bonne du Rumain
   (1747–1783) was married in 1767 to Marie Louis Alexandre,
   Marquis de Polignac (died 1768).

14 *Teresa:* Teresa Imer (1723–1797), Italian singer, married to
   Angelo Pompeati in 1745; under the name of Trenti, she
   directed a theater in the Austrian Netherlands from 1756 to
   1758 and from 1760 lived in London as "Mrs. Cornelys."

15 *Parchment:* Text, "placard," an official document on parchment,
   which was not folded but rolled.

16 *Calais:* In the 18th century Calais was already the port most
   used for the crossing to England, since the distance to Dover
   on the opposite side of the Channel was the shortest (about 22
   miles).

17 *Tourton & Baur:* Parisian banking house founded in 1755; its
   offices were on the Place des Victoires.

18 *La Corticelli:* Maria Anna Corticelli (1747–1767 or 1773), Italian
   dancer. For C.'s previous relations with her see Vol. 7, especially Chaps. VII and VIII, and Vol. 8, especially Chap. III. It
   would seem that here, as elsewhere, C. confuses events of his
   stays in Paris in 1763 and 1767, and that this interview with La

Corticelli did not take place until 1767. Cf. note 27 to this chapter.

19   *Rue de Grenelle Saint-Honoré:* The present Rue de Grenelle (7th Arrondissement) in the former Faubourg Saint-Germain is still the site of a number of mansions from the 18th century (now housing ministries and embassies). The addition "Saint-Honoré" suggests that in C.'s time there was a Rue de Grenelle in the Faubourg Saint-Honoré or near the Rue Saint-Honoré (1st Arrondissement). The fact that, according to his account, C. seems to have walked to La Corticelli's lodging from the office of Tourton & Baur on the Place des Victoires (2nd Arrondissement) supports this suggestion.

20   *Droghi:* Nothing more is known of him.

21   *La Piacenza:* Not identified; the name can be either a surname or a given name.

22   *Santini:* Nothing is known of a dancer named Santini who had been a tailor.

23   *D'Auberval:* Jean Bercher (1742–1806) used the names D'Auberval and Dauberval; he made his debut as a dancer in Turin in 1759, settled in Paris in 1761, where by 1770 he had won high esteem in his profession.

24   *The Haymarket:* The "King's Theatre in the Haymarket," London, was built in 1705; from 1708 it principally housed Italian opera.

25   *Guineas:* The guinea was a gold coin worth 21 shillings, minted from 1662 to 1813 and made of gold from the Guinea Coast of Africa, whence the name; it is now only money of account.

26   *Collalto:* Antonio Collalto-Matteucci (ca. 1717–1777), famous Italian actor of the period, from 1759 succeeded Carlo Veronese in the role of Pantalone at the Comédie Italienne in Paris.

27   *An engagement at the Comédie Italienne:* Documents show that La Corticelli (Maria Anna Corticelli) appeared in Turin in October 1763, danced in Venice in 1764, and first came to Paris in 1765, where she was a member of the corps de ballet at the

Comédie Italienne until 1767. Another dancer of the same name appeared at the same time in Paris, perhaps Rosa Corticelli, sister of Maria Anna. C. confuses events which occurred during his stays in Paris in 1763 and 1767.

28 *Faget:* Jean Faget (ca. 1700 to 1762), celebrated Parisian physician.

29 *Rue de Seine:* In C.'s time there were two streets of this name, one in the parish of Saint-Germain, the other in the parish of Saint-Victor, by which names they were distinguished. The present Rue de Seine is in the Faubourg Saint-Germain (6th Arrondissement).

30 *Faubourg Saint-Antoine:* It was situated beyond the present Place de la Bastille.

31 *Palais-Royal:* The reference is to the garden in the inner court of the Palais-Royal, then a favorite promenade and meeting place.

32 *Boncousin:* Either Silvestro or Lodovico Boncousin (also Beaucousin), proprietor of a hostelry in Venice.

33 *Hôtel de Bouillon:* The Hôtel de Bouillon, built as a private house by Mansart in the 17th century, is now No. 17, Quai Malaquais, and since 1892 has belonged to the École Nationale Supérieure des Beaux-Arts.

34 *The opera:* In the 18th century performances of opera were given in the theater of the Palais-Royal until 1763, when the auditorium was destroyed by fire. From 1764 to 1770 they were given in the Tuileries Palace.

35 *Six years:* Unmistakable evidence that C. confused events of his stays in Paris in 1763 and 1767. Francesco Casanova did not marry until June 1762.

36 *He married another woman:* Francesco Casanova's first wife, Marie Jeanne Jolivet, died before 1775; in that year he married Jeanne Catherine Delachaux (1748–1818).

37 *Twenty years hence:* One of several indications that C. originally planned to continue his memoirs beyond the year 1774.

38 *Trenti's:* C. here calls Teresa Imer's son by one of the names she used (cf. note 14 to this chapter). Giuseppe Pompeati had

himself assumed the name of Count d'Aranda (cf. Vol. 5, Chap. X).

39   *The Français:* Unofficial name of the theater in which the Comédie Française performed.

40   *A new play . . . failed:* Probably *La Manie des arts ou la matinée à la mode,* by Marc Antoine Jacques Rochon de Chabannes (1730–1800); it had its first performance at the Comédie Française on June 1, 1763.

41   *Rue Montmartre:* The Rue Montmartre, in the 2nd Arrondissement, runs from the Church of Saint-Eustache to the Boulevard Montmartre.

42   *B . . . . . . :* C. writes "b. . . . " (for *bordel*).

43   *Died . . . treatment:* Maria Anna Corticelli probably died in the Hôtel-Dieu (public hospital) in Paris in 1767, though it is possible that she did not die until 1773. C. again appears to confuse events of his stays in Paris in 1763 and 1767.

44   *Van Robais:* In the 17th century the Hollander Josse van Robais founded a manufactory for fine fabrics in Abbeville under the patronage of the Finance Minister, Colbert; in the 18th century it became one of the most celebrated establishments of the kind in France. Abbeville is still a center of the textile industry. C. writes "de Varobes."

45   *The "Golden Arm":* No inn of this name is known to have existed in Calais in the 18th century, but James Boswell, in his diaries, does mention "The Golden Arm" ("Le Bras d'Or").

CHAPTER VII

1   *Packet boat:* Properly, a vessel carrying passengers and mail. C., who writes "paq-bot," perhaps uses the term incorrectly.

2   *Guineas:* See note 25 to the preceding chapter.

3   *Bedford:* John Russell, Duke of Bedford (1710–1771), from 1744 First Lord of the Admiralty, from 1748 Secretary of State; from 1762 to 1763 he was in France as Envoy Extraordinary negotiating the Peace of Fontainebleau. Contemporary documents show that he arrived in Dover on the evening of

June 11, 1763. If C. really traveled with him, this establishes the date of C.'s arrival in England.

4   *More impertinent than:* C. writes "plus impertinent du," an Italianism.

5   *Ebb and flow of the tides:* C. had previously known only the Mediterranean, in which the tides are little perceptible.

6   *Canterbury...Rochester:* Towns on the road from Dover to London.

7   *Had killed himself:* Angelo Francesco Pompeati did not commit suicide until 1768. Cf. Vol. 5, Chap. VI, n. 56.

8   *My fourth volume:* C. uses his own numeration, which is neither preserved nor indicated in the Brockhaus-Plon edition. For the events referred to, see Vol. 5, Chap. VII.

9   *Her house on Soho Square:* Teresa Imer (see note 14 to the preceding chapter), now Mrs. Cornelys, had rented Carlisle House, on the east side of Soho Square, from the noble family of Howard in 1760; here she gave her suppers and balls for the nobility and for well-to-do commoners. The house of the Venetian Resident, Zuccato, was on the same square.

10 *Raucour:* She has not been identified.

11 *Mr. Cornelys:* Young Giuseppe Pompeati, known in Paris as Count d'Aranda, in London becomes Mr. (or Sir Joseph) Cornelys.

12 *Sophie:* Illegitimate daughter of Teresa Imer-Pompeati by C. (or, according to her mother, by the Marquis de Montperny). She was born between Dec. 1753 and March 1, 1754.

13 *She was ten:* According to C.'s account (cf. Vol. 5, Chap. VI), Sophie was born in Dec. 1753. If this is true, at the time of which he is writing she was 9 years old.

14 *Fermer:* Probably George Fermor, Earl Pomfret (1724–1785), who married Anna Maria Drayton in 1764. Giuseppe Pompeati was later tutor to his son. There is no record of a Sir Frederic Fermer or Fermor.

15 *The "Prince of Orange":* Located opposite the Haymarket Theater, this coffeehouse was a favorite resort of the artists who appeared there in opera.

16 *Boccaccio:* The first edition of Boccaccio's *Decamerone* (1353) uses both the earlier spelling, *anchora*, and the later, *ancora*. Martinelli's edition uses only the spelling *ancora*.

17 *Martinelli:* Vincenzo Martinelli (1702–1785), Italian writer, went to London in 1748 and did not return to Italy until 1772.

18 *Calzabigi:* Ranieri Calzabigi (or da'Calzabigi) (1714–1795), with his brother Giovanni Antonio and C., organized the Military School Lottery in Paris in 1757 (see especially Vol. 5, Chap. II).

19 *Your satires:* Probably Martinelli's *Lettere familiari e critiche* (London, 1758) or his *Istoria critica della vita civile* (London, 1752).

20 *Your edition of the Decamerone: Decamerone di Giovanni Boccaccio cognominata Principe Galeotto, Diligentemente corretto, ed accresciuto della Vita dell'Autore, ed altre Osservazioni Istoriche e Critiche, Da Vincenzio* [sic] *Martinelli*. Though it bears the date 1762 on its title page, it was probably not published until 1763 or 1764.

21 *Subscribers:* In the 18th century books were often published "by subscription," which in practice meant that they were not printed until a number of subscriptions sufficient to cover the cost had been obtained. C.'s translation of the *Iliad* and his *Icosameron* were published by subscription.

22 Juvenal, *Satires*, 10, 22: C. has already quoted it in Vol. 8, Chap. IX, but with the variant *cantat*.

23 *Spencer:* John, Baron Spencer of Althorp and Viscount Spencer, from 1765 1st Earl (1734–1783), owner of the celebrated "Althorp Library," patron of Martinelli.

24 *Literary work:* Among other works, Martinelli composed the first history of England to be written in Italian (*Istoria d'Inghilterra*, 3 vols., London, 1770–1773) and a history of the government of England and the English colonies (*Storia del Governo d'Inghilterra e delle sue colonie in India e nell'America settentrionale*, London, 1776), in which he prophesied the revolt of the

English colonies in North America. He may well have been working on these books at the time he first met C.

25 Altered from Horace, *Odes*, 2, 18, 11–12, where the text has "nihil" instead of "nec."

26 *Speaking Tuscan with the greatest purity:* The language of Tuscany and especially of Florence was considered the purest Italian.

27 *Advertiser:* By the middle of the 18th century London already had 53 newspapers. The one with the largest circulation was the *Public Advertiser*. There was also a *Daily Advertiser*.

28 *Pall Mall:* A fashionable street in the 18th century, and still so today. C. writes "Pale-male."

29 *Housekeeper:* C. writes "Ausekeper."

30 *The Hague:* Finding Teresa Imer-Pompeati on the verge of destitution in Holland late in 1758, C. had taken her son Giuseppe to Paris with him. They had parted not at The Hague but at Rotterdam. (See Vol. 5, Chap. VI and especially Chap. VII.)

31 *The last assembly of that year:* Contemporary sources show that Mrs. Cornelys's last assembly had already taken place on May 19th; it was followed by a ball for her exclusive benefit on May 26th. So C. must be confusing the first ball of the winter of 1763 (Dec. 2nd) with the last ball of the spring of the same year. He first wrote "which she gave that spring," then substituted "of that year" (doubtless in the sense of "that season").

32 *House ... built:* Since Carlisle House already existed, "built" is a misstatement; Teresa's expenditures on it can have been only for alterations and embellishments.

33 *Court of Equity:* One of the two chambers of the Exchequer Court, which decided cases involving the Crown and cases in civil law.

34 Legal phrase, of uncertain origin, alluding to the privilege by which a person in possession is not required to prove that he is rightfully so.

35 *Pounds sterling:* Money of account until 1816, but in the 18th century already the basis for the denominations in which bank notes were issued. 1 pound = 20 shillings of 12 pence each.

36 *Frac:* In the 18th century in France, a colored coat with full skirt and a high collar; the word now designates a different kind of garment.

37 *Zuccato:* Giovanni Girolamo Zuccato, Secretary of the Venetian Senate, from 1761 to 1764 Venetian Resident in London.

38 *Egremont:* Charles Wyndham (1710–1763), from 1751 Earl Egremont, English Secretary of State. Since he died on Aug. 21, 1763, C. could not lay his plans before him.

39 *Brühl:* Hans Moritz, Count Brühl, Lord of (Herr auf) Martins-kirchen (1736–1809), Saxon and Polish Ambassador in St. Petersburg, in Paris, and, from 1764 to 1795, in London; from 1765 member of the Royal Society; in 1767 he married Alicia, née Carpenter (died 1794), widow of Earl Egremont. C. writes "de Brühl Messekicken."

40 *The Elector of Saxony:* Friedrich August III, Elector from 1763; in 1806 he became the first King of Saxony (until 1827).

41 *Guerchy:* Claude Louis François Régnier, Comte de Guerchy (1715–1767), French Ambassador in London from 1763 to 1767. Since he did not arrive there until Oct. 17, 1763, and presented his credentials on Oct. 21st, C. cannot have called on him until the latter date.

42 *Chauvelin:* François Claude, Marquis de Chauvelin (1716–1773), French officer and statesman. C.'s friendship with him dates from their meetings in Turin, where Chauvelin was the French Ambassador from 1754 to 1765. At this point in the ms. C. crossed out a surprising phrase: "qui en vertu de ma natur-alisation m'annonçait pour Français" ("who in virtue of my naturalization announced me as French"). Since in the sequel C. crossed out a similar formula (cf. note 53 to this chapter), it may safely be assumed that he really became a French citizen. Presumably, after the events of the French Revolution, he ceased to attribute any value to his French citizenship; this would account for these suppressions. C. had already referred (Vol. 5, p. 779, of the present translation) to the possibility of his becoming a French citizen and being granted a patent of nobility. It is possible that his naturalization was accompanied by the grant of the title of Chevalier de Seingalt, in which case the name would not be a mere invention of C.'s. It is striking

that all of his French friends, including those who belonged to the high nobility, always addressed him as de Seingalt in their letters, and with no overtones of mockery or condescension.

43   *Court of St. James's:* That is, of St. James's Palace, which was built under Henry VIII from 1532 to 1533 and remained the royal residence until 1809, in which year it was largely destroyed by fire. "The Court of St. James's" is still the official designation of the British Court.

44   *Sunday after chapel:* At the period presentations at Court were made every Sunday after service in the Chapel Royal.

45   *D'Éon:* Charles Geneviève Louis Auguste André Timothée, Chevalier d'Éon de Beaumont (1728–1810), French diplomat, from 1755 secret agent for Louis XV, in 1762 secretary to the Duke of Nivernais during the latter's term as Envoy Extraordinary to conclude the peace negotiations in London, then secretary to the Count of Guerchy, with whom he immediately fell out. He was the author of a great many political and historical works (13 vols., Amsterdam, 1775). From 1777 to 1785 he lived in Paris as a woman, an imposture which excited intense curiosity at the time and to which C. refers.

46   *Covent Garden . . . theater:* The most celebrated theater in London at the time; built toward the end of the 17th century, it was destroyed by fire in 1808. The present Covent Garden Theater, also known as the Royal Opera House, was built in 1858.

47   *Drury Lane Theater:* Built in 1663 and destroyed by fire in 1672, it was rebuilt in 1674 by Wren in the street of that name. From 1705 it housed acting companies only, opera being given at the King's Theater. It was several times gutted by the London populace (cf. note 78 this chapter); in 1809 it was destroyed by fire. The present building dates from 1812.

48   *The Exchange:* The Royal Exchange, in the City of London. The original building, destroyed in the Great Fire of 1666, was replaced in 1670. Among other offices it contained those of the Lord Mayor of London and those of the Royal Exchange Insurance Office, one of whose directors was Samuel Bosanquet (see the following note).

49   *Bosanquet:* Samuel Bosanquet, probably of French Protestant origin; from 1755 a director of the Royal Exchange Insurance Office.

50   *Bagnios:* A brothel of a special kind, sufficiently described in the text (C. writes "Begno").

51   *George III:* From 1760 King of England; the third English monarch of the House of Hanover (1738–1820).

52   *The Queen:* Sophie Charlotte, Princess of Mecklenburg-Strelitz (died 1818), from 1761 consort of George III.

53   *I was a Venetian:* At this point in the original ms. C. crossed out: "n'était français que pour m'être naturalisé" ("was French only because I had been naturalized"). Cf. note 42 to this chapter.

54   *For what reason:* C. here crossed out: "je m'étais fait français" ("I had become French").

55   *Jarba:* Iarbas, King of Mauritania, unsuccessful suitor of Dido (Vergil, *Aeneid*, IV, 36, 196, 326), figures as Jarba in several dramatizations of the Aeneas–Dido story, among them Metastasio's *Didone abbandonata*.

56   *Sir Joseph Cornelys:* C. ironically uses young Pompeati's new name.

57   *Her mother:* Text, "elle," the grammatical antecedent of which is Sophie, but which seems rather to designate her mother.

58   *St. James's Park:* Adjacent to the royal palace and subject only to the royal jurisdiction.

59   *Lady Harrington:* Caroline Stanhope, Countess of Harrington, née Fitzroy (died 1784), married in 1746 to William Stanhope, Viscount Petersham, who became the second Earl Harrington in 1756.

60   *A letter for her:* Given to C. by Morosini in Lyons.

61   *No one dares to play or to give concerts:* There were extremely strict laws against breaking the Sabbath.

62   *The third: Sic,* but C. has just said that he met four of them. They were: Caroline (1747–1767), Isabella (1748–1819; C.

writes "Belle"); Amelia (1749–1780; C. writes "Émilie"), and Henrietta (1750–1781); they all bore the title Lady Stanhope.

63 *Whist:* The favorite card game in England at the period, played by four players with 52 cards.

64 *Duchess of Northumberland:* Elizabeth, Countess Percy (ca. 1716–1776); she did not become Duchess of Northumberland until 1766.

65 *Lady Coventry:* Lady Mary Coventry, née Gunning (1732–1760), sister of Elizabeth (1733–1790), who became Duchess of Hamilton in 1752 and Lady Campbell in 1759.

66 *Duchess of Hamilton:* See the preceding note. But since Lady Mary Coventry died in 1760, the person referred to must be either the Duchess of Hamilton herself or Lord Coventry's second wife, Barbara, daughter of Lord St. John. However, their marriage did not take place until Sept. 1764.

67 *Gains fifteen shillings:* C. had paid in gold pieces (guineas), each of which was worth 21 shillings; if he had paid in bank notes, he would have paid in pounds, each of which was worth 20 shillings. The difference came to 15 shillings.

68 *Hervey:* The Honorable (not "Sir," as C. later writes) Augustus John Hervey (1724–1779) did not become Earl of Bristol until 1775; hence in 1763 he was not yet a Lord. He distinguished himself as an Admiral in naval engagements in the West Indies.

69 *Miss Chudleigh:* Elizabeth Chudleigh (ca. 1720–1788), married secretly in 1744 to Augustus John Hervey, whom she left after their wedding night; the marriage was annulled in 1769. In the same year she was married to Evelyn Pierrepont, Duke of Kingston-upon-Hull. The legality of the marriage was contested, and she was sentenced for bigamy but fled to the Continent.

70 *Princess of Wales:* Augusta, Princess of Saxe-Gotha (1719–1772), married in 1736 to Frederick Louis, Prince of Wales, who died in 1751; mother of George III of England.

71 *Meat-eater:* C. uses (or coins ?) the term "criophage," from the Greek word κριοφάγος, "devourer of rams." "Ram-eater" being inapplicable in reference to English diet, one is left

with the more specific possibility "mutton-eater," and the less specific one "meat-eater."

72 *The Museum:* The British Museum. Founded in 1753, in C.'s day it was still housed in Montague House, Bloomsbury.

73 *Maty:* Matthew Maty (1718–1776), first a practicing physician, later Librarian of the British Museum and Secretary of the Royal Society.

74 Proverbial expression, of uncertain origin, but already established in the Middle Ages.

75 *Its Bank:* The Bank of England, founded in 1694.

76 *The three kingdoms:* England, Scotland, and Ireland.

77 *Real wealth:* In the ms. there follows a section about a page in length, which, though C. canceled it, is still legible enough to show that he went on to treat various financial and economic problems of the time.

78 *Garrick:* David Garrick (1717–1779), famous English actor; part owner and manager of the Drury Lane Theater. The gutting of a theater by the disappointed or offended audience was a not uncommon occurrence at the period. The most notable examples, the so-called Drury Lane Riots, took place on Jan. 25 and Feb. 24, 1763.

79 *Twenty years later:* Garrick was buried in the so-called Poets' Corner of Westminster Abbey in 1779.

80 *Roscius:* Quintus Roscius Gallus (126–62 B.C.), celebrated Roman actor.

81 *The Green Park:* Between St. James's Park and Hyde Park. C. writes "Grim-parc."

82 *Lord Ferrers:* Laurence Shirley, Earl Ferrers (C. writes "Ferex"), born 1720, was hanged at Tyburn on May 5, 1760, for the murder of his major-domo Johnson. The brother to whom C. refers is presumably Washington Shirley, who inherited the earldom after 1760.

83 C. used this proverb as the epigraph to his *Histoire de ma fuite* (1788), ascribing it to Horace; but it does not occur in Horace's

works. It appears on the title page of a work by Petronio Zecchini, whom C. attacked in his *Lana caprina* (1772).

84   *Thief . . . hanged in London:* John Rice, an exchange broker, who was hanged at Tyburn for forgery on May 4, 1763.

85   *Nivernais:* Louis Jules Henri Barbon Mancini-Mazarini, Duke of Nivernais (1716–1798), French diplomat, in Rome from 1749 to 1752, in Berlin and London from 1762 to 1763. He was a member of the French Academy.

86   *The Minister:* I.e., Lord Halifax (see the following note).

87   *Halifax:* George Montagu Dunk, Earl of Halifax (1716–1771), English Secretary of State from 1762.

88   *His wife:* The fact is, however, that Mrs. Rice was arrested; 4700 pounds sterling in bank notes were found in her corset.

89   *Havana . . . was given back:* During the Seven Years' War England took a number of places in the West Indies, among them Havana in 1762. After securing a booty of 30 million gulden, she returned the city to Spain on July 6, 1763.

90   *Piasters:* Another name for the peso, a Spanish silver coin which circulated in all the Spanish colonies from the 16th to the 19th century. The text at this point has: "comme j'ai mis, or division, quarante millions . . ." where "division" might suggest that the 40 million was Hervey's *share* of the booty but where the phrase makes no sense as it stands.

91   *Lady Rochefort:* Probably Lady Lucy Rochford, née Young (1723–1773), married in 1740 to William Henry Nassau de Zuylestein, Earl of Rochford, English diplomat.

92   *Husband . . . Ambassador to Spain:* The 4th Earl of Rochford (see note 91) was English Ambassador in Madrid from 1763 to 1766.

CHAPTER VIII

1   *"Star" Tavern:* C. first wrote "Staren-taverne dans le Pique-Dille" (for Piccadilly), then crossed out the last three words. There were several "Star" Taverns in London at the time.

2 *Pembroke:* Henry Herbert, Earl of Pembroke (1734–1794); he was married to Lady Elizabeth Spencer, daughter of the Duke of Marlborough, in 1756, though C. later makes him say that he is a bachelor. It is possible that he maintained a bachelor establishment in London. He was a notorious libertine.

3 *Waiter:* C. writes *"Weter."*

4 *Ranelagh House:* A then celebrated pleasure resort in Chelsea, with extensive gardens. Its principal feature was the Ranelagh Rotunda, built by Sir Thomas Robinson and opened to the public in 1742. In the center of the pavilion, which had a diameter of 150 feet, an orchestra played for dancing. Supper was served in the 50 boxes which lined its circular wall. The Rotunda was demolished in 1805. C. presumably saw an advertisement of the place displayed in St. James's Park.

5 *Whitehall:* Originally the name of a palace which became a royal residence under Henry VIII. All of it except the "banqueting house," which still stands, was destroyed by fire in 1698. C. writes "Wite-ale."

6 *Bath:* Well-known English watering place, with medicinal springs, already famous in Roman times.

7 *Lady Betty Germaine:* Lady Elizabeth Germaine (died 1769), daughter of Lord Berkeley, married to Sir John Germaine, of Drayton.

8 *Madame Binetti:* Anna Binetti, née Ramon (died 1784), Italian singer, married in 1751 to the French dancer and theater director Georges Binet. In 1760 she had helped C. escape from the Duke of Württemberg's officers in Stuttgart.

9 *Haymarket Theater:* In addition to the King's Theater in the Haymarket there was the Little Theater, in which not only comedies and pantomimes were given but also performances by dancers and acrobats. C. writes "Hai-marcket."

10 *Louis:* C.'s alternation between guineas and louis is natural, since both coins had very nearly the same gold content.

11 *Kennedy:* Probably the well-known courtesan Polly Kennedy. She lived on Great Russell Street and was for a time the mistress of Lord Bolingbroke.

12 *Him:* I.e., Lord Pembroke.

13 *Berlendis:* Giovanni Berlendis, Venetian Secretary of Embassy in London from 1762 to 1763, Venetian Resident in Turin from 1768.

14 *The Park:* St. James's Park.

15 *Vauxhall:* The oldest and most celebrated pleasure resort in London. It existed as Spring Garden from 1661, and was reopened in its later form, as Vauxhall Gardens, in 1732. It was open from nine o'clock in the evening to four in the morning; it had a pavilion, a semicircular arcade, and an orchestra. It ceased to exist in 1859. The present Vauxhall Park is not on the same site.

16 *Malingan . . . Aix-la-Chapelle:* See Vol. 8, Chap. III.

17 *Goudar:* Ange Goudar (1720–ca. 1791), adventurer and journalist, published *L'Espion chinois ou l'envoyé secret de la Cour de Pékin pour examiner l'état présent de l'Europe* ("The Chinese Spy, or the secret envoy from the Court of Peking to examine the present state of Europe") (1764, and many subsequent editions). See notes 6 and 15 to Chap. XI of this volume.

18 *Mr. Frederick:* More often known in C.'s day as Colonel Frederick; probably a Polish adventurer named Wigliariski who adopted the name Neuhoff in 1758 and claimed to be the son of Baron von Neuhoff (see the following note).

19 *Theodore:* Theodor Stephan, Baron von Neuhoff (ca. 1690–1756), became a page to the Duke of Orléans at Versailles in 1709, was later in the service of Bavaria; deeply in debt, he tried to better his fortunes in Spain, where about 1717 he married Lady Sarsfield (died 1720 or 1724), one of the Queen's Ladies-in-Waiting. With the support of the Bey of Tunis, he led an expedition to Corsica in 1736 and was proclaimed King of Corsica as Theodore I. He died in poverty in London in 1756.

20 *Only half:* According to contemporary sources the entrance fee at Vauxhall Gardens was 1 shilling, at Ranelagh House a half crown ($2\frac{1}{2}$ shillings).

21   *St. James's Chronicle:* Founded in 1761 and published thrice
      weekly. J. Rives Childs has found the announcement in the
      Gazetteer and London Daily Advertiser for July 5, 1763.

22   *Chapel of the Bavarian Minister:* Catholics were not granted
      freedom of worship in England until 1829; in C.'s time only
      0.8% of the population were avowed Catholics. Mass was
      celebrated only in the chapels of the Ambassadors of Catholic
      countries. The Bavarian Minister in London was then Baron
      (later Count) Joseph Franz Xaver von Haslang; the embassy
      chapel was on Warwick Street, Golden Square.

23   *Pauline:* Of this Pauline, only daughter of a Portuguese Count,
      nothing is known except what C. relates of her or makes her
      relate.

24   *Fall in love with him:* C. here added, then canceled, a passage of
      which only the first few words can still be read ("This was true,
      but I generalized the rule too much; and I was cruelly"), which
      may have been intended to be an anticipatory reference to his
      disappointment in La Charpillon.

25   *Crown:* Silver coin minted from 1551; value, 5 shillings.

26   *Bailiff:* C. here writes "belai" and later "bili," "bilai," in ac-
      cordance with the former pronunciation.

27   *King's Bench:* Prison for debtors and persons sentenced by the
      Court of King's Bench. It was built in 1758, later became a
      military prison, and was demolished in 1880.

28   *Guineas:* Here, and in a number of later instances, C. writes
      "pièces" instead of his more usual "guinées." (The other in-
      stances will not be noted.)

29   *Three years old then ... five:* Sophie must have been born be-
      tween Dec. 1753 and March 1754. It would follow that at the
      time of C.'s stay in Holland (from Oct. 1758 to early in 1759)
      she was in fact five years old. In the ms. C. first wrote "two"
      and "four," then corrected them to "three" and "five." (Cf.
      Vol. 5, Chap. VII.)

30   *Montperny:* Théodore Camille, Marquis de Montperny (died
      1753), was major-domo to the Margravine of Bayreuth from
      1746; he died in Paris in 1753. He may have been the father of

Teresa Pompeati's second daughter (who was born on Feb. 14, 1753, and seems to have died young), for her sponsors in baptism were the Margrave Friedrich von Ansbach-Bayreuth and his sister.

31 *La Bruyère's* Characters: *Les caractères de Théophraste, traduits du grec, avec les caractères ou moeurs de ce siècle* (1688).

32 *Camoëns:* Luiz Vaz de Camões (ca. 1524–1580), famous Portuguese poet, author of the epic poem *Os Lusíadas* ("The Lusiads").

CHAPTER X

1 *The Thinkers' Club:* Later in this chapter C. refers indifferently to a Thinkers' Club and a Bettors' Club. Neither of them has been identified.

2 *Attila:* King of the Huns (5th century).

3 *Decamerone:* For Martinelli's new edition of this work, see notes 16, 17, and 20 to Chap. VII of this volume.

4 *Rochester:* City on the Thames estuary on the old road from Dover to London.

5 *Buckingham House:* Originally built by John Sheffield, Duke of Buckingham, it was bought in 1762 by King George III, who made it his residence and in 1775 ceded it by parliamentary decree to his consort Queen Charlotte, after which it was known as "The Queen's House." After extensive alterations it became the new royal residence, as Buckingham Palace, in 1837. C. writes "Bukingan aus."

6 *Something strange:* According to the English Casanovist Bleackley, the same incident is recounted in a letter of Horace Walpole's to Sir Horace Mann written in 1750. It is possible that Martinelli told C. the story, and that the latter gave it a place in his memoirs as his own experience.

7 *"The Bettors":* Cf. note 1 to this chapter.

8 *Undoubtedly... distinction:* The text has "Sans doute il y a des gens" etc., literally, "No doubt there are men of intelligence and distinction in it."

9   *"Dangerous"*: As C. explains a few lines farther on, a manslayer's hand was branded.

10   *"O laws, O customs"*: In C.'s day instantly recognizable as a parody of Cicero's famous "O Tempora, O Mores" (*Catiline* I, 1, 2).

11   *Spencer:* See note 23 to Chap. VII of this volume.

12   *Chelsea:* Now a part of London; in the 18th century still a village on the Thames outside of the city.

13   *Castel-Bajac:* Louis, Marquis (not Count) de Castel-Bajac.

14   *A Gascon:* A native of Gascony, a district of southern France between the Garonne and the Pyrenees. Gascons were notorious for boasting.

15   *Saint Albans:* A small city with a celebrated cathedral, some 25 miles northwest of the center of London.

16   *Maltese Cross:* Symbol of the order of the Knights of Malta. Only persons who could prove 16 quarters of nobility were admitted to it.

17   *Schwerin:* Heinrich Bogislav Detlef Friedrich, Count von Schwerin (after 1738–ca. 1800), lost great sums at play, became an adventurer, and was arrested in Hamburg in 1767 at the instigation of his family; after he was freed (1786) he lived on his estate of Schwerinsburg.

18   *Field Marshal:* Kurt Christoph, Count von Schwerin (1684–1757), uncle of Heinrich Bogislav (see the preceding note); officer in the Prussian service, adviser to Frederick the Great during the First Silesian War; he was killed at the battle of Prague while serving as Field Marshal General.

19   *Beckw...:* John Beckwith (died 1787), English Brigadier-General during the Seven Years' War. There seems to have been no reason why C. should not have given his name in full here, as he does in Vol. 10.

20   *The Black Eagle:* Founded by Frederick I on the occasion of his coronation in 1701, it was considered the leading Prussian order; in the 18th century its membership was limited to 30; the limitation was removed in the 19th century. The order was abolished in 1918.

21   *His Majesty:* Here Frederick the Great.

22   *The two foreign Counts:* Castel-Bajac and Schwerin.

23   *The Bank:* Text, "la banque," presumably meaning the Bank of England.

24   *Bill:* C. writes "bil," perhaps for "bill of particulars."

25   *Alderman:* In the 18th century London had 25 aldermen, one for each district of the city.

26   *Harwich:* Important port in Essex. But its being some 70 miles from London, whereas C. later says that the journey there took only an hour and a quarter, makes it impossible that it was the site of the school. Bleackley has shown that there was a well-known Catholic girls' boarding school in Hammersmith, then a village on the outskirts of London. But its headmistress was a nun, which does not agree with C.'s account.

27   *Newgate:* The oldest prison in London, dating from the 12th century; thieves, murderers, and forgers were confined to it. The building was demolished in 1902.

28   *Costantini:* Probably an invented name. According to C. he was the husband of the Italian singer Angela Calori (see the following note).

29   *Calori:* Angela Calori (1732–ca. 1790), Italian singer. She was the Teresa whom C. so greatly loved and whom he first knew as Bellino, whom he later calls Teresa Lanti, and to whom he also refers as married to a Roman named Cirillo Palesi ca. 1760 (cf. especially Vol. 2, Chaps. I and II, and Vol. 7, Chaps. VII and VIII). That all these names designate the same person is revealed only by a passage in Vol. 10, Chap. IX, which C. canceled but which can still be read: "We stopped four days in Prague (where there was Italian opera) and we went to it. When I entered the box I had taken, the first person I see is the leading actress, singing an air. It was La Calori, who, seeing me, lost her composure. The same thing had happened to me in Florence with Teresa. How delighted I was to see La Calori, and sorry that I could not go to speak with her at once; I wrote her a note the next morning, in which I asked her if I might pay her a visit with my wife, and at what hour. She replied that she would come to dine with me the

next day, for on that day she was engaged, and that she would be most pleased to have me introduce her to my wife (. . .).

"The *virtuosa* gave us the greatest pleasure. We told each other all our adventures from the time we had parted. We spent six happy hours; La Castel-Bajac simply listened, sighing from time to time when what we told each other reminded her that she had spent three years in continual misfortune. La Calori could not return our dinner because she was in a boarding-house. So we took leave of each other after cordial embraces, and we left on the next day but one with a passport from the government.

"My companion had taken the name of Mademoiselle Blasin, lace-seller. I took this precaution as soon as I learned of the (. . .) to which pretty women whose ill luck made them pass through Vienna were subjected there."

30 *La Binetti:* See note 8 to Chap. VIII of this volume.

31 *De Amicis:* Anna Lucia de Amicis (ca. 1740–1816), famous Italian singer of the period, whose great triumphs were achieved in *opera seria.*

32 *Mattei:* An opera impresario named Mattei is documented in St. Petersburg in 1770; the reference here may be to the same person.

33 *Virtuose:* Italian: leading female theatrical performers, whether actresses, singers, or dancers; also, women of virtue. Here, as in Vol. 7, Chap. VIII, C. may be playing on the double meaning of the word.

34 *Giardini:* Felice di Giardini (1716–1796), celebrated Italian violinist of the period.

35 *King's Bench Prison:* See note 27 to Chap. VIII of this volume.

36 *A Flemish officer. . . Aix-la-Chapelle:* His name was Malingan. For C.'s earlier encounters with him see Vol. 8, Chap. III, and Chap. VIII of this volume.

37 *Charpillon:* Marie Anne Geneviève Augspurgher (Auspurgher), known as La Charpillon (ca. 1746–after 1777), celebrated courtesan in London.

38 *My mother:* Rose Elisabeth Augspurgher (ca. 1720–after 1764), native of Bern, from which she was banished for her dissolute life; she settled in Paris for a time, then in London.

39 *Palais Marchand:* Alternative name for the old Palais de Justice, in which there were many shops. It was in one of these that C. had first met La Charpillon (then known as Mademoiselle de Boulainvilliers) and had bought her a pair of shoe buckles.

40 *Denmark Street:* This street, in the Parish of St. Giles in the Fields, still exists. The name Decharpillon has been found in the tax lists of the parish for 1763 and 1764.

CHAPTER XI

1 *I can count on nearly four years of life:* C. was wrong in his reckoning for he died only seven months later, on June 4, 1798.

2 Galileo Galilei, *De Motu*, Chap. 19.

3 *Is still alive:* Nothing is known of La Charpillon after 1777. From 1773 to 1777 she was the mistress of the English politician John Wilkes (1727–1797) in London.

4 *Introduced . . . bagnio:* C. seems to have forgotten that he had already found his own way to a bagnio. See Chap. VII of this volume and *ibid.*, n. 50.

5 *Bolomay:* David Bolomay, watchmaker, originally of Lausanne. C. says nothing of this incident in his account of his stay in Geneva; in any case, he was not there in 1759 but in 1760.

6 *Goudar . . . Paris:* C. fails to mention that he had already encountered Goudar again in London (see Chap. VIII of this volume, and *ibid.*, n. 17).

7 *Rostaing:* Antoine Louis Alphonse Marie, Count Rostaing (died after 1793); according to Paris police records, he was a young man in 1753. Though he was a professional gambler, his title seems to have been genuine.

8 *Coumon:* Nothing is known of this person except that he came from the southern French province of Languedoc.

9 *Journey. . . an hour and a quarter:* See note 26 to the preceding chapter.

10 *Vestal:* In Roman antiquity, one of the six virgin priestesses devoted to the goddess Vesta under a vow of perpetual chastity. Used as a type of virginity.

11 *Ba..:* C. writes "maq . . . " (for *maquerelle,* "bawd").

12 *Coterie:* C. writes "avec toute son infâme" (omitting the necessary noun). This chapter shows an unusually large number of such slips, perhaps due to haste in copying (see the following notes 18, 24, 31, and 33).

13 *Baltimore:* Frederick Calvert, Earl Baltimore (1731–1771).

14 *Grosvenor:* Richard, Earl Grosvenor (1731–1802).

15 *Author of several works:* In addition to his *Chinese Spy* (see note 17 to Chap. VIII of this volume) Goudar wrote not only other satirical pieces but also works on economic and political subjects. The *Chinese Spy* was a series of letters from an imaginary Chinese visitor to Europe, in imitation of Montesquieu's celebrated *Lettres persanes* ("Persian Letters").

16 *Amused myself by writing a number of them:* There is no way of determining which, if any, of the letters of the *Chinese Spy* were contributed by C.

17 *Lorenzi:* Nothing is known of this person, whose name would indicate that she was Italian. The "Miss" is C.'s.

18 *Would have:* C. writes: "Je vous aussi repondu," where "aussi" is a slip for "aurais" or "aurais" is omitted.

19 Ascribed to Publilius Syrus (1st century A.D.). C. has quoted it earlier—oddly enough, just before his first meeting with La Charpillon (then Mademoiselle de Boulainvilliers).

20 Ariosto, *Orlando furioso,* I, 56.

21 *Night watchman:* C. here writes "crieur d'heures," but later "Wach." Since there was no street lighting in London in C.'s time, late walkers often engaged the service of a linkboy, or of a night watchman with his lantern. C. describes the organiza-

tion and the functions of the "night watch" in the following chapter.

22 *Penny post:* A postal service established in 1683 and confined to London. There were six offices in various parts of the city at which letters could be deposited. The charge was one penny. Londoners were very proud of the service, which was the only one of its kind in Europe.

23 *An armchair:* Not an invention of C.'s, for chairs of the kind are described in various English and French works treating of the period.

24 *It:* C. writes "les" instead of "le."

25 *Franche-Comté:* District of France west of the Swiss Jura, formerly the independent County of Burgundy.

26 *Boulainvilliers:* Anne Gabriel Henri Bernard de Rieux Boulainvilliers, Marquis de Saint-Soire (1724–1798), well-known libertine.

27 *Kitty Fisher:* Catherine Mary Fisher (1740–1767), well-known English courtesan, mistress of Augustus John Hervey, Earl of Bristol, in 1759; she later married a Mr. Norris. C. writes "Keti-ficher."

28 *Strong beer:* C. writes "Strombir."

29 *Sarah:* Nothing is known of her origins except that she was Irish. She married Goudar some time after March 1764, followed him to Naples in 1767, became the mistress of King Ferdinand IV of Naples and later of Count Buturlin; Goudar left her, and she died in Paris ca. 1800.

30 *Lettre de cachet:* Originally, a sealed letter, especially one emanating from the sovereign; in the period before the French Revolution, often used to convey arbitrary orders for imprisonment.

31 *At home:* C. writes "chez," without the necessary "elle."

32 *Calumny . . . imagine its nature:* Probably C. was to be accused of pederasty, which in England was then punishable by death.

33 *Them:* C. writes "le" (for "les").

CHAPTER XII

1   *Chapter XII:* At the beginning of this chapter in C.'s ms. is the
    marginal notation *"duobus omissis"* ("two [pages] omitted"). As
    before, the reference would seem to be to an earlier version,
    for there is no break in the narrative.

2   Horace, *Epistles*, I, 20, 25; already quoted by C. in Vols. 1 and 2.

3   Dante, *Commedia*, "Inferno," I, 1.

4   *Here:* At Dux in Bohemia, where C., serving as librarian to
    Count Waldstein, began to write his memoirs about the year
    1790 and where he died on June 4, 1798.

5   Ariosto, *Orlando furioso*, XXIV, 1 (where the text has "Chi
    mette il piè . . . ").

6   *Walsh:* Proprietress of a well-patronized bordello in Cleveland
    Row and generally known in her day as "Mother Walsh" (also
    Walch, Welch). There was also a "Mother Wells," who is
    documented in 1753 at Enfield Wash, 10 miles from London,
    and who is known to have moved to London about 1760; she
    may be the same person.

7   *Atkins:* Sir Richard Atkins, Bart. (ca. 1728–1756); his mistress
    was not Kitty Fisher but Fanny Murray. The gesture of eating a
    bank note on a slice of bread and butter was attributed to
    several well-known courtesans and actresses.

8   *Mrs. Pitt:* Penelope Pitt, neé Atkins (ca. 1725–1795), married
    the English diplomat George Pitt (later Baronet Rivers; 1722–
    1803) in 1746.

9   *Phryne:* Celebrated Greek hetaira of the Periclean period (4th
    century B.C.), here used generically for courtesan.

10 *Bank of London:* No doubt for "Bank of England."

11 *Berlendis:* See note 13 to Chap. VIII of this volume.

12 *Richmond:* Then a village on the Thames, west of London, now
    part of Greater London. There was a royal summer residence
    there, Richmond Lodge, with a fine garden.

13 *Wh . . . :* C. Writes "p. . . . . ." (for *putain*).

14 *Maze:* In Richmond Park there was a small Gothic building called "Merlin's Cave," around which Queen Caroline had a maze planted.

15 *Bowling green:* C. writes "boulingrin," perhaps meaning simply "lawn."

16 *"Beast with two backs":* *Othello*, Act I, scene 1, line 118.

17 *Night watch:* Cf. note 21 to the preceding chapter.

18 *G . d d . . n it:* C. writes "Sacr . . . " (for one of a number of blasphemous expressions).

19 *Bragadin:* Matteo Giovanni Bragadin (1689–1767), Venetian patrician and Senator, C.'s faithful friend and patron (see especially Vol. 2, Chap. VIII).

20 *Tower of London:* The only remaining portion of the old fortifications of London; the oldest part of it, the White Tower, was built by William the Conqueror in 1078. From the 16th century to 1820 it served as the State Prison.

21 *Westminster Bridge:* The second bridge over the Thames, built in 1750 (reconstructed 1856–1862); it crosses the river near the Houses of Parliament. C.'s route is puzzling, for he did not need to cross the Thames to go to the Tower of London from his house in Pall Mall, since they were both on the same side of the river.

22 *Agar:* Sir Wellbore Ellis Agar (1735–1805), son of the Member of Parliament Henry Agar. C., who had trouble with the titles of English baronets and knights, here calls him "le Chevalier Egard." Cf. note 26 to this chapter.

23 *The "Cannon":* The well-known Cannon Coffee House in Cockspur Street, at the southwest corner of the present Trafalgar Square. It was named after its proprietor, Patrick Cannon.

24 *Goddamme:* C. writes *"Dieudamne."*

25 Ariosto, *Orlando furioso*, XXIII, 112; already quoted by C. in Vol. 1, Chap. X.

26 *Agar, Esquire:* C. here writes "Esqr Egard."

27 *An invalid:* Text, "un cacochyme"; i.e., one suffering from caco-chymia, a vitiated state of the body fluids, especially the blood.

28 *Roast beef:* C. writes "Rochebif."

29 *Pudding:* C. writes "boudin," a normal French word meaning "sausage." However, it seems probable that it represents his attempt to transcribe English "pudding," which is more likely than sausage to have formed part of an English dinner at the time.

30 *Hornpipe:* C. writes "Rompaipe."

31 *Blind musicians:* C. writes "aveugles," which means "blind-men," but the context shows that the need was for blind musicians.

32 *Ranelagh House:* See note 4 to Chap. VIII of this volume.

33 Stoic maxim, which Cicero (*De finibus*, III, 22) attributes to one of the Seven Sages. It was a favorite maxim of C.'s, who seems first to have been impressed by it when it was interpreted for him by his early patron the Venetian patrician Alvise Gasparo Malipiero (cf. Vol. 1, Chap. VI).

34 *Attorney . . . Schwerin:* The attorney was a Mr. Whitehead. For C.'s dealings with Count Schwerin, see Chap. X of this volume.

35 *Holborn:* District of London, until the mid-1960s one of its metropolitan boroughs; most of the courts were situated there. C. writes "Haiborn."

36 *The powerful rod:* The London constables carried no arms but only a rod some three feet long tipped with the royal crown. Anyone whom they touched with it was bound to follow them without resisting; in case of resistance, it was the duty of any citizen present to help the constables do their duty.

37 *Pi . . s:* C. writes "maq . . . . . . " (for *maquereaux*).

38 *The impassive man:* C. writes "l'ataraxe," i.e., "the man in possession of ataraxia," from Greek ἀταραξία, "without dis-turbance."

39 *Two weeks:* In his *Mémoire justificatif*, found at Dux, C. writes that the amount in question was 4000 francs and that the Augspurghers were released on bail after two days in custody.

40 *King's Bench:* See note 27 to Chap. VIII of this volume.

41 *Brunswick:* Karl Wilhelm Ferdinand (1735–1806), Hereditary Prince of Brunswick, married Augusta, Princess of Saxe-Gotha (1737–1813), daughter of the Prince of Wales (Frederick Louis, 1707–1751), in 1764; he became the Duke of Brunswick-Wolfenbüttel in 1780.

42 *Common Council:* Established in the 13th century as the municipal council of the City of London, the Court of Common Council was, and still is, made up of the Lord Mayor, the Aldermen, and councilors elected from the wards.

43 *Goldsmiths' Company:* Properly, The Wardens and Commonalty of the Mystery of Goldsmiths of the City of London; it was one of the twelve great guilds, ranking fifth in importance. Established in the 12th century, in 1756 it had 198 members, who met in their magnificent Hall in Foster Lane, built about 1407 and surviving until 1829. (The present Goldsmiths' Hall dates from 1835.) The Prince was presented with a gold box containing a document conferring the freedom of the City on him, but not by the Goldsmiths' Company.

44 *Lord Mayor:* Title of the Mayor of London from the 13th century, made official in 1545. He was elected from among the Aldermen.

45 *Aldermen:* Text: "échevins." Strictly speaking, the presentation was made by the "Court of Common Council."

46 *A thousand persons:* The newspapers of the time put the number at 250.

47 *Lady Grafton:* Lady Anne Grafton, née Liddell (1736–1804), married in 1756 to Augustus Henry Fitzroy, Earl Euston and Duke of Grafton. The marriage ended in divorce in 1769; her second husband, whom she married in the same year, was John Fitzpatrick, Earl of Upper Ossory. She was a friend of the celebrated writer Horace Walpole.

48 *Cumberland:* William Augustus, Duke of Cumberland (1721–1765), was the third son of King George II.

49 Ariosto, *Orlando furioso*, IV, 32.

50 *To his quarters in the City:* The commentators suggest that C.'s
    "chez lui" (translated "to his quarters") refers to a "watchhouse"
    (guardhouse); if this is correct, it must have had a pothouse on
    the ground floor, for C. later speaks of it as "the pothouse where
    I was" ("[le] cabaret ou j'étais") and of the chief constable as the
    proprietor ("Maître") of it. "The City" was and still is the term
    applied to the oldest part of London, on the north bank of the
    Thames.

51 *Pothouse:* See the preceding note.

52 *Magistrate:* C. writes "Sergens-fils" (and later "sergens-fil" and
    "Sergents-fil"). What English judicial title he intended to rep-
    resent is unclear. The magistrate who heard the case was the
    Justice of the Peace for Westminster and Middlesex; he sat in
    the famous Bow Street Police Office and Magistrate's Court,
    near Covent Garden. Unfortunately, the records of the court
    for the period were destroyed at the beginning of this century.

53 *Fielding:* C. confuses the writer Henry Fielding (1707–1754),
    who was also a judge in the Westminster and Middlesex district
    until 1751, with his successor, his half-brother Sir John Fielding
    (1721–1780). He was blind in consequence of an accident he
    suffered at the age of 19 while serving in the army.

54 *Newgate:* See note 27 to Chap. X of this volume.

55 *The jailer:* The jailer of Newgate Prison from 1754 to 1792 was
    a Richard Akerman.

56 *Pagus:* John Pagus, tailor, of Church Street, St. Ann's.

57 *Maisonneuve:* C. was arraigned on Nov. 27, 1763; his sureties
    were John Pagus (see the preceding note) and Lewis Chateau-
    neu of Marylebone Lane. For Chateauneu C. substitutes a
    name of similar meaning (Maisonneuve). Chateauneu was
    C.'s vintner.

58 *Bottarelli:* Giovanni Gualberto Bottarelli, of Siena, writer,
    librettist, and adventurer; he lived from 1741 in Berlin and
    from ca. 1755 in London. As the author of an anti-Masonic
    book (*L'Ordre des francs-maçons trahi et le secret des Mopses dévoilé*,
    1745), he was perhaps an enemy of C.'s, since the latter was a
    Freemason.

CHAPTER XIII

1   *Pocchini:* Antonio Pocchini (1705–1783), Venetian adventurer, of patrician birth; he was arrested in 1741 and banished to the island of Cerigo (Cythera). It was there that C. met him for the first time. He appeared in Padua in 1746, and later in many European cities, almost always in the company of girls whom he passed off as his daughters but to whom his relation was really that of fancy man and pimp.

2   *My name . . . given in full:* No such account has been found in any of the London newspapers of the time.

3   *Didone: Didone abbandonata* (Dido Forsaken), tragedy by Metastasio (1724), was set to music by a number of composers in the 18th century. The first performance of it (music by Domenico Sarri) was given in Naples in 1724.

4   *Demetrio:* Heroic drama by Metastasio; first performance (music by Caldara), Vienna, 1731. Nothing is known of Bottarelli's versions of these two works; but he specialized in "arrangements" of operas.

5   *The Secret . . . Exposed:* See note 58 to the preceding chapter.

6   *"Parrot Market":* No doubt Parrot Yard, in East Smithfield in the eastern part of London.

7   *Wh . . . :* C. writes "p. . . . ." (for *putain*), though he has written the word in full a few lines earlier.

8   *Grosvenor:* See note 14 to Chap. XI of this volume.

Volume Ten

CHAPTER IV

1   *Earl Marischal . . . Keith:* George Keith, Earl Marischal of Scotland (ca. 1693–1778); as a Jacobin, he was exiled in 1716; he settled in Berlin about 1745, and was Prussian Ambassador in Paris from 1751 to 1754 and in Madrid from 1758 to 1760; he was pardoned in 1759 and returned to England and Scotland, but in 1764 he went back to Potsdam and remained there as an intimate friend of Frederick the Great until his death. His brother, James Francis Edward Keith, died in 1758.

2   *Sans Souci:* Palace near Potsdam, built from 1745 to 1747 by order of Frederick the Great and from his own plans.

3   *"Fédéric":* Frederick always signed his personal letters thus.

4   *Picture gallery:* The gallery was a separate building, east of the palace, constructed from 1756 to 1763.

5   *Catt:* Henri Alexandre de Catt (1725–1795), of Morgues on the Lake of Geneva, was from 1756 reader and private secretary to Frederick the Great; he fell into disfavor in 1780.

6   *Spent . . . in vain to bring water here for them:* The fountains and waterworks in the park in Sans Souci were a particular concern of Frederick's; the fountains especially failed to play because of lack of pressure. Not until 1842, when a steam engine was installed, did the waterworks finally function.

7   *Peristyle:* A peristyle, in the sense in which C. uses the word, is an open space enclosed by columns. Figuring in the Hellenistic period chiefly as the courtyard in a private house, in modern Europe it became an element in landscape gardening. After Frederick's death the peristyle at Sans Souci was demolished.

8   *Ephraim:* Veitel Heine Ephraim (died 1775), banker and jeweler in Berlin.

9   *Duchess of Brunswick:* Philippine Charlotte, Duchess of Brunswick, née Princess of Prussia (1716–1801), sister of Frederick the Great, married in 1733 to Karl I, Duke of Brunswick.

10   *Her daughter . . . next year:* Elisabeth Christine Ulrike, Princess of Brunswick (1740–1840), married to the Crown Prince of Prussia in 1765. The official betrothal took place on July 18, 1764.

11   *The small theater in Charlottenburg:* The Italian comic opera *I portentosi effetti della natura* was performed in the Orangery Theater of Charlottenburg Palace on July 19, 1764.

12   *The celebrated Denis:* Giovanna Denis, née Corrini (1728–after 1797), daughter of the actor Corrini who always played the role of Pantalone in *commedia dell'arte* performances; hence her nickname "la Pantaloncina." A celebrated dancer, she was married in 1748 to Jean Baptiste Denis, ballet master and composer; they were in Berlin from 1749 to 1765.

13   *Gozzi:* Antonio Maria Gozzi (1709–1783), priest, Doctor of Civil and Canon Law; C. lived in his house and studied under him from the age of 10 until he entered the University of Padua at 14. See especially Vol. 1, Chap. II.

14   *Pantalone:* One of the stock characters in the *commedia dell'arte*, an elderly man of substance, usually a Venetian merchant.

15   *Pantaloncina:* Feminine diminutive of Pantalone.

16   *Giovannina . . . my mother's godchild:* C.'s mother's name was Giovanna Maria Casanova. Giovannina is the diminutive of Giovanna.

17   *Bettina:* Nickname of Elisabetta Maria Gozzi (1718–1777), younger sister of Antonio Maria Gozzi (cf. especially Vol. 1, Chaps. II–III).

18   *Banished him:* The documents show only that Jean Baptiste Denis ceased to be ballet master in 1765, being replaced by Franz Salomon. If, as seems likely, this was because of his age, it explains his wife's interest in C.'s bearing witness that she was ten years younger than she really was. She was then probably living apart from her husband, perhaps at the insistence of her influential lover.

19   *Teplitz:* Now Teplice; well-known watering place in what was then Bohemia.

20   *Aubry:* Pierre Aubry, celebrated dancer; appeared in Venice in 1752 and 1758, in St. Petersburg from 1760 to 1764, in Berlin in 1764, and in Paris in 1765.

21   *La Santina:* Santina Zanuzzi (died after 1775), Italian dancer, born in Padua, documented as appearing in Vienna from 1756 and later in Parma, Venice, Milan, and St. Petersburg.

22   *Dall'Oglio:* Giuseppe B. dall'Oglio (died between 1791 and 1796), Italian musician from Padua or Venice; with his better-known brother Domenico, he was a violoncellist in the orchestra at the Imperial Court of St. Petersburg from 1735 to 1764.

23   *The service of the Empress of Russia:* Dall'Oglio came to St. Petersburg under the Empress Anna Ivanovna, remained

there during the reigns of Elizabeth and Peter III, played an important part in the liaison between Catherine and Ponia-towski, and did not leave the Court until two years after Catherine's accession.

24 *Madonis:* Luigi Madonis, also Madonnis (before 1700–1767), of Venice, celebrated violinist. His daughter was married to Giuseppe dall'Oglio.

25 *Your mother:* Giovanna Maria Casanova, née Farussi, called Zanetta, stage name La Buranella (1708–1776). She played at the Dresden Theater from 1737 and remained in Dresden after she retired from the stage in 1756.

26 *The conspiracy:* Princess Sophie Augusta of Anhalt-Zerbst (1729–1796) was married in 1745 to the heir to the Russian throne, who succeeded in 1762 as Peter III and in the same year was murdered as the result of a conspiracy. She had herself proclaimed Czarina as Catherine II by the Guards on July 11, 1762. Her Court became one of the most brilliant cultural centers in Europe.

27 *Odart:* Probably Jean Dominique Joseph, Chevalier d'Odart, Piedmontese adventurer who, coming to the Russian Court in 1762, was soon made administrator of Catherine's estates and was given the title of Court Councilor; when Catherine ascended the throne he was forced to leave Russia with nothing but 1000 rubles for traveling money.

28 *A hundred thousand rubles:* Not 100,000, but only 1000 (see the preceding note). The ruble was a silver coin first minted in the 17th century. From 1756 there were also gold rubles, whose value was higher.

29 *A husband:* In 1742 Karl Peter Ulrich, Duke of Holstein-Gottorp (1728–1762), was summoned to Russia as the heir to the throne by the Czarina Elizabeth because he was a son of the daughter of Peter the Great. His marriage in 1745 to the later Catherine II (cf. note 26) was unhappy from the beginning.

30 *Her son:* Paul Petrovich, the future Paul I (reigned 1796–1801).

31 *The General:* Probably a certain General von Grumbkow.

32   The reference is to Suetonius's account ("Divus Julius," 2
      and 49) of the homosexual relation between Julius Caesar
      and Nicomedes III Philopator, King of Bithynia, during Caesar's
      stay at his Court in 81 B.C., and more especially to a line from a
      mocking song of Caesar's soldiers which Suetonius quotes: *Cae-
      sar Gallias subegit, Nicomedes Caesarem* ("Caesar subjugated all the
      Gauls, Nicomedes subjugated Caesar"). It will be observed that
      C.'s "subjuguait" corresponds exactly to the "subegit" of the
      song; however, C. reverses subject and object.

33   *La Reggiana:* Santina Olivieri, called La Reggiana because she
      was a native of Reggio, Italian dancer, who had appeared in
      Berlin in 1752.

34   *La Barberina:* Barberina Campanini (1721–1799), Italian dancer,
      created a countess after her divorce from Charles Louis de
      Cocceji, son of the Grand Chancellor of Prussia, whom she
      married in 1749; she had not lived with him since 1759.
      She appeared in Berlin from 1744 to 1748. She was Frederick
      the Great's mistress until she fell into disgrace in 1748 upon his
      discovering that she was having an affair with De Cocceji. The
      portrait of her which C. mentions, painted by Pesne, hung in
      the King's bedroom at Potsdam, which visitors were allowed to
      see through a glass door.

35   *La Cochois:* Marianne Cochois (born ca. 1723), French dancer
      (Paris, 1741, Berlin, 1742), married to the ballet master
      Desplaces.

36   *D'Argens:* Jean Baptiste de Boyer, Marquis d'Argens (1704–
      1771), was from 1744 to 1769 Chamberlain to Frederick the
      Great and Director of the Prussian Academy of Sciences. He
      married Barbe Cochois (before 1722–after 1771), French
      actress, elder sister of Marianne, in 1749.

37   *Half-burned notebooks:* There was a fire in the King's study on
      Oct. 1, 1763.

38   *It was published:* The *Histoire de la guerre de Sept Ans* did not
      appear until it was included in the *Oeuvres posthumes* of 1788.

39   *New corps of noble Pomeranian cadets:* C.'s description is not en-
      tirely accurate. The new Cadet School was to be an aristocratic
      academy, in which the fifteen most gifted cadets were to be

instructed by renowned masters. Since the academy building was not to be ready until March 1, 1765, the pupils were provisionally accommodated on the upper floor of the Royal Stables. The German commentators are at pains to assert that in view of these facts, "there was nothing humiliating in the King's offer to Casanova." But it may be allowed that, after witnessing Frederick's treatment of one of the "renowned masters," C. was in a better position than they to judge whether the post was humiliating or not. The King's visit to this provisional installation took place on Aug. 19, 1764. After C. declined the post, it was conferred on a Swiss named De Meirolles.

40 *Q. Icilius:* Pseudonym of Carl Gottlieb Guichard, also Guischardt (1724–1775), of Magdeburg. He was the son of French Huguenots, he studied theology and oriental languages at Leiden; he entered the service of Frederick the Great in 1757 and became his adviser and friend.

41 *Cross . . . around my neck:* In Chap. II of this volume C. says that he sold his cross in London.

CHAPTER V

1 *Chapter V:* At the top of the ms. page on which this chapter begins is the marginal note "octo rejectis" ("eight [pages] excised").

2 *Schlafwagen:* An especially commodious and comfortable traveling carriage, in which there was room to lie down and sleep. The word is German; C. spells it successively "Schlafs-vagen," "Schlasfvagen" (*sic*), and "Schlaffswagen."

3 *Braun:* Count Yuri Yurievich Braun (1704–1792), son of an Irish emigrant named Brown; Russian General and Governor of Livonia.

4 *Verst:* Russian measure of distance, about two-thirds of a mile.

5 *Chernichev:* Count Zachar Grigorievich Chernichev (1722–1784), Russian General.

6 *Uchitel:* Russian "tutor," "major-domo"; in C.'s day such positions in Russian were usually held by Frenchmen.

7 *Narva:* City on the former border between Estonia and Russia, some 90 miles west of St. Petersburg.

8   *No Russian envoy in Venice:* Russia had a diplomatic represen-
     tative in Venice only until 1724.

9   *Caporya:* The last post station on the road from Riga to St.
     Petersburg.

10   *Ingria:* Also Ingermanland; region along the banks of the Neva
     River and the east shore of the Gulf of Finland, named after its
     original Finnish inhabitants, the Ingers. Peter the Great recon-
     quered it from Sweden in 1702 and founded St. Petersburg
     there the following year. Its inhabitants spoke a dialect of
     Finnish.

11   *Millionnaya:* Still a well-known street in St. Petersburg, leading
     from the Winter Palace.

12   *Channels:* C. writes "ruelles," whose meaning in this context is
     not clear.

13   *London:* C. first wrote "Paris," then crossed it out and substi-
     tuted "Londres."

14   *The Imperial Palace:* The so-called Winter Palace, residence of
     the Czars, built from 1753 to 1762 by the Italian architect
     Rastrelli in Baroque style.

15   *Orlov:* Grigori Grigorievich Orlov (1734–1783), Count from
     1762, Prince of the Empire from 1772; favorite of Catherine
     the Great from 1762 to 1777.

16   *Kopeck:* Russian coin of copper; 100 kopecks = 1 ruble.

17   *Bautta:* A close-fitting, short mantle with a hood made of black
     silk, and reaching the waist. Combined with the cloak (*tabarro*),
     which was usually black or gray (scarlet only for the nobility),
     the tricorne, and the black velvet half mask, it was called
     maschera nobile or *nazionale*, since wearing it was not restricted
     only to the Carnival season.

18   *Bernardi:* A Venetian jeweler named Bernardi (died ca. 1760),
     lived in St. Petersburg from 1749.

19   *Volpati:* Nothing is known of him except what C. relates.

20   *I cannot tell you here:* C. traveled in Russia under the name of
     Comte de Farussi (from his mother's maiden name) and as

Cazanov de Farussi. For the Venetian Count Volpati to recognize him, he had to give his real name, by which he was well known in Venice because of his escape from the Leads.

21 *Balls at the Opéra:* The Académie Royale de Musique (the Opéra) had the privilege of giving public balls.

22 *La Baret:* Madame Baret, daughter of the Comptroller Gilbert, lived in the Rue des Prouvaires (1st Arrondissement) after her marriage; she became the mistress of a Councilor of the Parlement whom C. calls Monsieur de Langlade and whose name she is said to have assumed later. C. had a liaison with her in Paris. She died in St. Petersburg in 1765. The names Gilbert and Baret are both doubtless fictitious.

23 *Hôtel d'Elbeuf:* Parisian residence of the Duke of Elbeuf, by whom Baret was employed.

24 *Comic opera impresario:* The French comic opera in St. Petersburg was under the direction of a certain Renauld in 1764 and 1765; one of the actresses in the company was called "la belle Langlade."

25 *Rzewuski:* Count Franciszek Rzewuski (died after 1775), Grand Notary to the Polish Crown from 1752; Polish Envoy in St. Petersburg from June 1766. He may have been in St. Petersburg earlier.

26 *Recollect monks:* A branch of the Franciscan Order which adheres strictly to the Rule as laid down by the founder.

27 *Day...I really lost:* Taken by Laforgue to be an allusion to a remark attributed by Suetonius ("Titus," 8) to the Emperor Titus, who, after a day during which he had conferred no boon on anyone, is supposed to have said, "Friends, I have lost a day." The later commentators follow Laforgue; but he may rather be thought to have inquired too ingeniously, for there is really no reason to suppose that C. had Suetonius' anecdote in mind.

28 *Dall'Oglio:* See note 22 to Chap. IV of this volume.

29 *Poisoned...to tell:* The jeweler Bernardi had been one of the devoted adherents and confidants of Catherine when, still a Grand Duchess, she was preparing to seize the throne. In 1758,

while Elizabeth still reigned, a certain General Apraksin fell into disgrace; papers confiscated on this occasion compromised the Grand Duchess and a number of her confidants, among them Bernardi. He was exiled to Kazan, where he died.

30   *Passport . . . was about to leave:* This regulation remained in force in Russia until the end of the 19th century.

31   *La Fusi:* C. first wrote a name beginning with "S" and ending with "i," then crossed it out and substituted Fusi. She may have been a Gioseffa Fusi, who appeared as a dancer in Venice in 1763.

32   *Melissino:* Pyotr Ivanovich Melissino (1726–1797 or 1803), a native of the island of Cephalonia. He was a General of Artillery in the Russian service.

33   *His elder brother:* Ivan Ivanovich Melissino (1718–1795), Russian Court Councilor, later Chancellor and Curator of the University of Moscow, and at the same time Procurator of the Holy Synod.

34   *The Synod:* The Holy Synod, instituted by Peter the Great in 1721 to replace the Patriarchate, was the supreme governing body of the Russian Church.

35   *The celebrated [Lefort]:* Jacques (= Franz Jakob) Lefort, also Le Fort, Leffort (1656–1699), of Geneva, confidant of Peter the Great. His only son died in 1703. The person to whom C. here refers is the son of Franz Jakob's nephew, Peter, Baron Lefort, who had been Master of Ceremonies to the Czarina Elizabeth.

36   *Matiushkin:* Dmitri Mikhailovich Matiushkin (1725–1800).

37   *Zinoviov:* Stepan Stepanovich Zinoviov, also Zinoviev (1740–1794), Russian officer and diplomat; he was appointed Russian Ambassador in Madrid in 1773.

38   *Macartney:* Sir George Macartney (1737–1806), English Envoy Extraordinary in St. Petersburg from 1764 to 1767.

39   *Mademoiselle Shitrov:* Anna Alekseevna Shitrov (died 1795), lady in waiting to Catherine the Great.

40   *Forgave:* According to contemporary sources she was forced to enter a convent.

41 *Brother... an officer:* The Shitrov family was very numerous; in C.'s time at least four Shitrovs were officers.

42 *Mademoiselle Sievers ... now Princess N. N.:* Elisabeth Karlovna Sievers (born after 1745), daughter of Karl Sievers (1710 or '16–1774 or '75), a manservant and favorite of the Czarina Elizabeth, who made him a Count in 1760 and Court Marshal in 1762. From her first marriage to Jacob Efimovich Sievers (1731–1808) she had three daughters. Her second marriage was to Prince Nikolai Putyatin (1747–1830).

43 *Putini:* Bartolomeo Putini, also Puttini (born ca. 1730, died after 1766), Italian castrato, appeared in St. Petersburg from 1756.

44 *Galuppi:* Baldassare Galuppi (1706–1785), Italian composer, chapelmaster in St. Petersburg from 1745 to 1748 and from 1765 to 1768. He was called "Il Buranello" from his birthplace, the Island of Burano, Venice.

45 *Olsuviev:* Adam Vasilievich Olsuviev (1721–1784), Russian Councilor of State and Senator.

46 *Uppsala to study:* The Swedish University of Uppsala, founded in 1476, was one of the most celebrated institutions of higher learning in Europe in the 18th century.

47 *Locatelli:* Giovanni Battista Locatelli (between 1713 and '15–1785), of Milan, man of letters and theatrical impresario; he was in St. Petersburg in 1759–1762 and again later. C. had met him in Prague in 1753.

48 *Ekaterinhof:* A small palace near St. Petersburg, built by Peter the Great for his consort Catherine I.

49 *Teplov:* Grigori Nikolaevich Teplov (1711–1779), one of the leaders in the conspiracy against Peter III; after 1762 he became Secretary to Catherine the Great.

50 *Yelagin:* Ivan Porfirievich Yelagin (1725–1796), personal friend of Catherine the Great before her ascent to the throne; banished in 1758; appointed Secretary of State in 1762; so he could not have been in Siberia for more than four years.

51 *Mécour:* Giovanna Mécour, née Campi, Italian dancer from Ferrara, appeared in Petersburg from 1759.

52 *La Santina:* See note 21 to the preceding chapter.

53 *Luini:* Domenico Luini, called Il Bonetto, Italian castrato, appeared in St. Petersburg from 1765.

54 *La Colonna:* Perhaps Teresa Colonna, called La Venezianella (born 1734), Italian dancer, who appeared in Venice in 1746–1747 and later in Moscow. The singer Teresa Colonna is documented in Venice in 1760–1761 and in St. Petersburg ca. 1763–1764. It is not known if they are the same person.

55 *Millico:* Giuseppe Millico (1739–1802), Neapolitan castrato, appeared in St. Petersburg ca. 1765.

56 *Naryshkin:* Semen Kirillovich Naryshkin (1701 or 1710–1775), Russian Envoy to London, 1742; Court Marshal and Master of the Hunt, 1757; Grand Chancellor, 1775.

57 *Maria Pavlovna:* Maria Pavlovna Naryshkin, wife of Semen Kirillovich Naryshkin, notorious for her love affairs.

58 *Kaloyer:* Russian, "monk."

59 *Platon:* Levshin Platon (1737–1812), Bishop of Tver, later of Moscow, from 1767 Archbishop of Novgorod.

60 *Princess Dashkov:* Ekaterina Romanovna Dashkov (1743–1810), wife of Prince Mikhail Dashkov (1736–1764). From 1782 to 1796 she was President of the Russian Academy of Sciences.

61 *Panin:* Nikita Ivanovich Panin (1718–1783), Count from 1767, President of the College of Foreign Affairs from 1762.

62 *A thing which I saw:* The same story is told in two contemporary sources, so it may be doubted if C. actually witnessed the incident.

63 *Bregonzi:* Caterina Bregonzi, or Brigonzi, Venetian singer, appeared in Venice in 1741 and in St. Petersburg ca. 1750.

64 *Signora Roccolino:* Vincenza Roccolino, née Montellato (died after 1775), known as "Signora Vincenza," had come to St. Petersburg with the French comic opera troupe (cf. note 24 to this chapter).

65 *Proté:* Nothing more is known of Proté and his wife.

66 *The Ridotto:* Name of the celebrated gambling casino in Venice; it was closed in 1774.

67 *Pun:* C.'s pun depends upon taking "Proté" as Latin *pro te* (= for thee) and turning it into Latin *pro me* (= for me).

68 *Bryus:* Yakov Aleksandrovich, Count Bryus (1729–1791), Russian General, from 1784 Governor of Moscow, from 1787 member of the Council of State; he was descended from a Scottish family named Bruce which had emigrated to Russia at the end of the 17th century.

69 *Zinoviov:* C. appears to have forgotten that he had already mentioned Zinoviov in this chapter (cf. note 37).

70 *St. Nicholas:* Patron saint of Russia; his feast celebrated on Dec. 6th.

71 *Zaïre:* Name of a Christian female slave of the Sultan of Jerusalem in Voltaire's tragedy *Zaïre.*

CHAPTER VI

1 *Görz:* Then in Austrian Friulia, now the Italian city of Gorizia, north of Trieste, on the Yugoslav border.

2 *Inconceivable:* The text has "inconvevable," which, not being annotated, may be presumed to be one of the numerous typographical errors which disfigure the Brockhaus-Plon edition.

3 *Russian baths:* A sweat bath, of the type of the Finnish sauna.

4 *The Villa Borghese:* Also known as Villa Pinciana, built in 1615 for Cardinal Scipione Borghese on Monte Pincio. In C.'s day it was outside the city proper. In 1902 it was given to the City of Rome. In the contemporary guidebooks which list the sculptures in the Villa Borghese collection there is no mention of a Psyche. However, there was a Psyche in the Capitoline collection. C. may have confused the two places.

5 *Crèvecoeur:* Nothing is known of him.

6 *La Rivière:* Doubtless an adventuress. However, she can be neither the dancer Marguerite Rivière, also la Rivière, nor

her sister Marie, whose acquaintance C. had made in Dec. 1756, for he would certainly have recognized her.

7   *Baumbach:* He is not mentioned in C.'s account of his stay in England. C. writes "Bombac"; since he was a native of Hamburg the name must have been Baumbach.

8   *Krasni-Kabak:* Literally, "the Red Tavern," some three miles south of St. Petersburg on the road to Peterhof; it was well known, for it had been there that Catherine the Great spent some hours of the night of June 28–29, 1762, on which the uprising made her Czarina.

9   *Quinze:* A card game in which the player who ends with 15 points or the closest approximation to it is the winner.

10 *Wh . . . :* C. writes "p. . . . ." (for *putain*).

11 *The two Lunin brothers:* Aleksandr Mikhailovich Lunin (1745–1816), Russian Major-General, and his brother Pyotr (died 1822), a Lieutenant-General.

12 *Teplov:* See note 49 to the preceding chapter.

13 *B . . . . . . :* C. writes b . . . . . . (for *bougres*). And see note 10 to this chapter.

14 *Papanelopulo:* Demetrio Papanelopulo was a banker in St. Petersburg ca. 1765.

15 *Peterhof:* Villa built for Peter the Great by the French architect Leblond in 1720, some 25 miles from St. Petersburg on the south shore of the Gulf of Finland. With its gardens, it somewhat resembled Versailles. C. spells it "Petrow."

16 *Muzhik:* Russian, "peasant." C. writes "mosik."

17 *Rastrelli:* Count Bartolomeo Rastrelli (1700–1771), celebrated architect and creator of the so-called "Russian rococo"; he retired in 1764, but then worked on the palace of the Dukes of Kurland in Mitau and probably died there.

18 *Rinaldi:* Antonio Rinaldi (ca. 1709–1794), Italian architect; he was summoned to the Russian Court in 1752 (not earlier, as C. asserts), remained there until 1785, and died in Rome.

19 *Impossible to hold the tournament:* It was in fact not held until June 16th of the following year, 1766.

20 *Izvozchik:* Russian, "coachman." C. writes "chevochik."

21 *Italian miles:* An Italian mile in the 18th century was 1.86 kilometers.

22 *To become French:* Here in C.'s ms. follows a sentence which he crossed out: "For I am sure that if the King of France were to give a caning to the National Assembly, the twelve hundred worthies would accept it, though they would not ask for more." Hence this chapter must have been written or copied between 1789 and 1792.

23 *Voeikov:* Fedor Matvoievich Voeikov, also Voiakov (1703–1776), Russian General and diplomat (in Mitau, 1744–1745; in Warsaw, 1759–1762).

24 *Before the birth of Petersburg:* Voeikov was born in 1703; St. Petersburg was first built as a fortress in 1703 and then rebuilt in 1712 as the capital city of the Czars.

25 Slightly altered from Erasmus, *Adagia*, II, 2, 35.

26 After a fable of Aesop's, in which the fox mocks the lioness because, according to a belief current in Antiquity, she bears only one cub (ed. Halm, No. 240; ed. Perry, No. 257).

27 *Betskoi:* Count Ivan Betskoi (1702–1795), illegitimate son of Field Marshal Ivan Yurgievich Trubetskoi (in Russia in such cases the son often received his father's name abbreviated or slightly changed). Count Betskoi was a Lieutenant-General and at the same time Director of the Chancellery of Public Buildings and Curator of the Academy of Arts.

28 *Delamotte:* Vallen Jean Baptiste Delamotte (1729–1800), French architect, summoned to Russia in 1759.

29 *Where the staircases were:* Here in the ms. there follow two sentences which C. crossed out. "The Empire of Russia will finally become flourishing when another Catherine, or a male Catherine, ascends the throne and creates sumptuary laws. The Russians need them, for luxury among them is a veritable frenzy."

30   *Built of stone . . . cross it:* Catherine the Great had 30 stone bridges built during her reign, all of the same design.

31   *Repnin:* Prince Nikolai Vasilievich Repnin (1734–1801), nephew of Count Panin, Russian Major-General and diplomat. He was Catherine the Great's favorite for a time.

32   *Torelli:* Stefano Torelli (1721–1784), of Bologna, Italian painter; he lived in Petersburg from 1762, became a professor at the Academy of Arts and, in 1771, its second Director.

33   *Protopapas, or bishop:* Text: "proto-papa évêque." C. is in error, the two designations being irreconcilable, for in the Eastern Church a protopapas (which incidentally is the Greek equivalent of the Russian *protopop*) ranks below a bishop.

34   *Olimpiade:* The *Olimpiade*, lyric drama by Metastasio, written in 1730, was set by more than 30 composers during the century. The reference here is probably to the setting by Manfredini or Galuppi, both of whose operas to this text were performed in Russia in 1762.

35   *Buranello:* I.e., Baldassare Galuppi (see note 44 to the preceding chapter).

36   *Is made up of four cities:* Moscow was in fact then made up of four cities: the Kremlin, Kitai-gorod, Beloi-gorod, and Semlijanoi-gorod; each was surrounded by walls and a moat.

37   *Demidov:* There were then two Demidovs, brothers, living in Moscow; C. very probably became acquainted with them both. The elder was Grigori Akinfevich (1710–1786), the younger Nikita Akinfevich (1724–1789). The latter was much interested in the arts and sciences and corresponded with Voltaire.

38   *The famous bell:* The "Anna Ivanovna," cast in 1735 by order of the Czarina Anna, was still the largest bell in the world in the 19th century, weighing more than two tons. As the result of a fire it fell in 1737 and was half buried in the ground. Napoleon tried in vain to have it conveyed to Paris. It was left at the foot of the bell tower as a curiosity.

39   *Gosti:* Russian, "guests."

40   *A delicious drink:* Perhaps kvass, or perhaps a favorite beverage in C.'s time made from raspberries flavored with various herbs.

41   *Sherbet:* Arabian drink, made from pomegranates.

42   *St. Nicholas:* See note 70 to the preceding chapter.

43   *Illyrian:* In antiquity Illyria was the name applied to the regions north of Greece bordering on the Adriatic and to its people, represented by the modern Albanians. C. probably uses it to mean "Slavic."

44   *Morskaya:* Street near the celebrated Millionnaya and the River Neva.

45   *Philosopher:* Text: "Ce philosophe," where it is not clear whether C. means "philosopher" in the general sense or in the sense of an adherent of the doctrines of the Enlightenment.

46   *Simolin:* Karl Matveevich, Edler von Simolin (1715–1777), from 1758 Russian Resident at the Court of the Duke of Kurland.

47   *Kamchatka:* Peninsula and province in Eastern Siberia. C. writes "Cams-Kacta."

48   *Bilioti:* The name Bilioti appears in a letter from the Duke of Kurland to C., written in 1765. Nothing more is known of him.

49   *Sinopaeus:* Damian Sinopaeus, clearly a Latinized name, entered the Russian service as a physician in 1730, became Municipal Physician in Moscow in 1736, then settled in St. Petersburg and became a State Councilor.

50   *The French Secretary of Embassy:* In 1765 the French Ambassador in St. Petersburg was replaced. Under Baron de Breteuil the Secretary was a Monsieur Bérenger; on April 29th the Marquis de Bausset arrived as the new Ambassador; his Secretary was the Abbé Guyot d'Ussières.

51   Horace, *Epistles*, I, 5, 19.

52   *Tartarian:* Cf. the proverb, "Scratch a Russian and you find a Tartar."

53 *Philosophy of History:* C. confuses two works by Voltaire, the *Essai sur l'histoire générale et sur les moeurs et l'esprit des nations,* which had been published in 1753 and included the "Philosophie de l'Histoire," and the *Dictionnaire philosophique portatif,* published in 1764 and dedicated to Catherine the Great.

54 *Stroganov:* Count Aleksandr Sergeevich Stroganov (1733 or '38–1811), Russian high official and diplomat, a great admirer of Voltaire and of France.

55 *Shuvalov:* Count Ivan Ivanovich Shuvalov (1727–1797 or '98), favorite of the Czarina Elisabeth, Chief Gentleman of the Bedchamber; founded the University of Moscow in 1756.

56 *Dithyramb:* Originally designating a lyric or choric hymn in honor of the Greek god Dionysus, the term gradually came to mean a poem in irregular verse and characterized by enthusiasm.

57 C. quotes this saying several times in his memoirs, for example in Vol. 4, Chap. XIII, and in Vol. 8, Chap. VI, where he calls it a proverb.

58 *Beloselski:* Prince Aleksandr Mikhailovich Beloselski-Belozerski (1752–1809), Russian writer and diplomat; he was Ambassador in Dresden until 1790 and in Turin until 1792.

59 *Paul Petrovich:* Pavel Petrovich (1754–1801), son of Catherine II and Peter III; he was Czar as Paul I from 1796 to 1801.

60 *Francis I:* Francis Stephen (1708–1765), Duke of Lorraine, married Maria Theresa of Austria in 1736 and was Emperor from 1745. He died on Aug. 18, 1765.

61 *Krasnoe-Selo:* Town with an imperial palace, south of St. Petersburg.

62 *Lobkowitz:* Prince Joseph Maria Lobkowitz (1725–1802), Austrian Lieutenant-General and from 1763 to 1777 Ambassador in St. Petersburg.

63 *Esterházy:* Count Nikolaus Esterházy von Galantha (1711–1764), Austrian diplomat.

64   *Countess Bryus:* Countess Praskovia Aleksandrovna Bryus (1729–1786), wife of Count Yakov Aleksandrovich Bryus (see note 68 to the preceding chapter).

65   *A great infantry review:* The review, with splendid fireworks, was held near Krasnoe-Selo on June 28, 1765.

66   *Rousseau . . . a dialect of Greek:* C. refers to Rousseau's *Essai sur l'origine des langues.*

67   *Tott:* Brother of the better-known Baron François de Tott (1733?–1793), born in Paris but of Hungarian descent (cf. Vol. 5, Chap. VI).

68   *Difficulties . . . at the Battle of Minden:* Minden, one of the battles of the Seven Years' War, was fought on Aug. 1, 1759; in it the English troops won the day over the French. C. explained the "difficulties" in his ms. but then crossed the passage out: "Count Tott, with inconceivable stupidity, decamped on the eve of the battle on I know not what pretext, for it was not a desertion, but it was enough to dishonor him. Nevertheless he was brave."

69   *Madame Soltikov:* Matryona Pavlovna Soltikov (died before 1790), married in 1750 to Sergei Vasilievich Soltikov (1726–after 1764), Catherine the Great's first lover, who was Russian Ambassador in Paris from 1762 to 1763.

70   *A handsome young man:* C. here added, then crossed out: "the only defect in his face being that his eyes were rheumy."

71   *The troubles in Poland:* Repnin, the Russian Ambassador in Warsaw, took advantage of the weakness of Stanislaus Poniatowski to rule Poland despotically. His measures aroused strong opposition, the leader of which was the Bishop of Cracow, in defense of the Roman Catholic faith against the pretensions of Russia. What amounted to a civil war broke out in 1768, during which the Russians conquered the opposing confederation and pursued its members across the Turkish border. The result was a declaration of war by Turkey on Oct. 30, 1768. The Russo-Turkish War was not ended until 1774, by the Peace of Kuchuk Kainarji.

72 *Maruzzi:* There were three brothers of this name at the period: Constantino, Lambro, and Tano Maruzzi. The reference is probably to Lambro, who was first a banker in Corfu and then went to St. Petersburg, where he rose to be a Councilor of State.

73 *Tsarskoye-Selo . . . Kronstadt:* All four places were in the vicinity of St. Petersburg and all were the sites of imperial residences.

CHAPTER VII

1 *Summer Garden:* Garden with magnificent walks, extending from the left bank of the Neva to the Mikhailov Palace.

2 *Democritus . . . Avicenna:* Democritus (born ca. 460 B.C.), Heraclitus (576–480 B.C.), Greek philosophers; the statues reverse their usual attributes, the former having been known as the laughing, the latter as the weeping philosopher; Sappho (fl. 600 B.C.), Greek poetess; Avicenna (A.D. 980–1037), Arabian physician and philosopher.

3 *My worthy aunt:* The Czarina Elizabeth, aunt of Peter III, had no interest in art.

4 *Courtag:* From German *Cour-Tag* ("Court day"). The *courtag*, or simply *cour*, held regularly from the reign of the Czarina Anna, differed from the solemnity of great Court occasions by its informality.

5 *On those which were given there:* C. writes "sur qu'on y donnait" (omitting *ceux*).

6 *Gregorian calendar:* The Julian calendar, introduced by Julius Caesar in 46 B.C., in which the year was made to consist of 365 days, each bissextile year, or leap year, having 366 days, remained in use throughout the Middle Ages. Since the average length of the year thus obtained (365.25 days) differs slightly from that of the true solar year (365.2422 days), by the 16th century the accumulated difference amounted to 10 days. For this reason Pope Gregory XIII in 1582 ordered a reform of the calendar which, by a new distribution of the leap years, arrived at an average year of 365.2425 days. By the Gregorian calendar, the calendar year differs by a day from the solar year

only after 3000 years. All the Roman Catholic countries adopted the reform immediately, whereas the Protestant countries did not introduce it until much later (England not until 1751). Countries of the Greek Orthodox religion did not introduce a new calendar similar to the Gregorian until 1923, when the difference had grown to be 13 days.

7 *Peter ... ordered ... first of January:* Peter the Great ordered this change made in 1700. In the pre-Julian calendar the year began on March 1st, as the names of our months from Sept. to Dec. testify.

8 *Year ... Gregorian reform ... not be bissextile:* The Gregorian reform prescribed that a year which began a new century should be a leap year (bissextile) only if it was exactly divisible by 400 (thus 1600 was a leap year, but not 1700, 1800, and 1900).

9 *The epact:* The number of days by which the last new moon has preceded the beginning of the year. It is one of the factors used in calculating the date of Easter.

10 *The tropical year:* The period in which the earth makes one complete revolution around the sun, reckoning from spring equinox to spring equinox.

11 *The law of the March moon:* According to the rules for calculating the date of Easter, it is always the first Sunday after the full moon that falls on or next after March 21st.

12 *Embolism:* Insertion of days, months, or years in an account of time, for regularity. To bring the lunar and solar years into agreement, the Jewish reckoning intercalated a lunar month in the third, fifth, and eighth years of an 18-year cycle.

13 *Council of Nicaea:* Held in A.D. 325; it promulgated the rules by which the date of Easter is still calculated.

14 *Catherine II died happy:* She died on Nov. 18, 1796, 37 hours after having an apoplectic stroke. She had long suffered from abnormal obesity. The text has "Catherine II mourut heureuse comme elle vécut," which could also be translated, "Catherine II was fortunate in her death as she had been in her life." The same double meaning of "heureux," for which there is no

satisfactory rendering in English, recurs throughout the rest of the passage, and should be borne in mind by the reader of the translation.

15 *Only one each day:* This is not true, for the Roman Catholic Church also has more saints' days than there are days in the year.

16 *Begins the year on the first of March:* Venice had retained the old reckoning, according to which the year began on that date.

17 *M. V.:* Abbreviation for *More Veneto* ("according to the Venetian reckoning").

18 *Amusing figure . . . five Latin words . . . a grammatical error:* The emblem of Venice is a winged lion holding in its claws an open book with the words: *Pax Tibi Marce Evangelista Meus* ("Peace be unto thee, my Evangelist Mark"). According to the rules of Latin grammar, *meus*, which is in the nominative case, being in apposition to a vocative, should also be in the vocative (*mi*).

19 *Begin counting them at the beginning of the night:* In Italy until the end of the 18th century the hours of the day were counted from the ringing of the Angelus, that is, from a half hour after sunset. (Cf. Vol. 1, Chap. IV, n. 33.)

20 *Valville:* A Mademoiselle Valville is mentioned in a letter to C. by a certain Bilistein, dated Petersburg 1766. Nothing more is known of her.

21 *Les Folies amoureuses:* Comedy by Jean François Regnard (1655–1709), written in 1704. It was one of his most popular plays, and is still performed.

22 *Clairval:* Jean Baptiste Clairval (ca. 1735–1795), French singer and actor.

23 *Recruit a troupe of players:* Peter III, who had an aversion to everything French, had dismissed the French company which was playing in Petersburg; immediately after ascending the throne, Catherine the Great had a new French company brought to Russia.

24 *Seventy years of age:* Rinaldi, born in 1709, was then only 56 years old.

25   *Yelagin:* See note 50 to Chap. V of this volume.

26   *The Polish Resident:* Jakub Pisarski, first Polish Chargé d'Affaires in St. Petersburg, then Resident from April 1765 to August 1766.

27   *Sulkowski:* Prince August Kazimierz Sulkowski (1729–1786), from 1764 Grand Notary to the Polish Crown. There were five Grand Notaries in all (cf. note 45 to this chapter).

28   *An Anglican clergyman:* Catherine the Great was a declared Anglophile and had several Englishmen among her trusted advisers. So it is understandable that an Anglican clergyman would have been in good standing with the pro-Russian faction in Warsaw.

29   *Czartoryski:* Prince Adam Kazimierz Czartoryski (1734–1823), Governor of the Province of Podolia.

30   *Caporya:* See note 9 to Chap. V of this volume.

31   *Countess Löwenwolde:* Nothing is known of her. (C. writes "Lowenvold.")

32   *Princess Dolgoruki:* Probably Princess Praskovia Vladimirovna Melissino, née Dolgorukaya, wife of the Court Councilor Ivan Ivanovich Melissino (1718–1795).

33   *Villiers':* Villiers was the name of the proprietor of a then well-known inn in Warsaw.

34   *D'Aragon:* According to C. he was a Neapolitan. Two Russian officers of the Czarina's bodyguard, Grigori and Ilya Darragan, the first of whom made a journey to Germany, are documented; but the identity of C.'s D'Aragon has not been discovered.

35   *Tomatis:* Carlo Tomatis (born in Turin, died after 1787), created a Count in 1765 by King Stanislaus Augustus, whom he served as "directeur de plaisir"; he married the Italian dancer Caterina Catai.

36   *Catai:* Also Gattai and Gattei, Italian dancer, appeared in Venice from 1760, in Warsaw from 1764; she was married to Count Carlo Tomatis in 1766.

37   *Giropoldi . . . Bachelier:* Nothing is known of either.

38   *Conservatorio dei Mendicanti:* One of four foundations in Venice devoted to the education of (chiefly orphan) girls. They were principally instructed in music.

39   *Saby:* Antoine Saby (ca. 1716–after 1778), French adventurer and professional gambler.

40   *Sainte-Hélène:* Probably the adventurer and professional gambler Sainte-Hélène, who assumed the title of Baron (died after 1768); he may have belonged to the family of Sainte-Hélène, Counts of Baschi.

41   *Countess Fleming:* Princess Izabela Czartoryska, née Countess Fleming, also Flemming (1746–1835), married to Prince Adam Czartoryski in 1761.

42   *Saint-Pierre:* The Abbé Charles Irénée Castel de Saint-Pierre (1658–1743), French writer, propagandist for the Enlightenment, well known for his *Projet pour rendre la paix perpétuelle en Europe* ("Project for Maintaining Perpetual Peace in Europe").

43   *Repnin:* See note 31 to Chap. VI of this volume. Prince Repnin was Catherine the Great's favorite for a time; she sent him to Warsaw as Russian Ambassador to prepare the election of Stanislaus Poniatowski to the Polish throne.

44   *Krasicky:* Ignacy Krasicky (1735–1801), of the same family as the Counts of Krasicky, Prince of the Church and poet.

45   *Rzewuski:* Count Franciszek Rzewuski (died after 1775), from 1752 Grand Notary to the Crown, from 1766 to 1767 Envoy Extraordinary in St. Petersburg.

46   *Oginski:* Michal Kazimierz, Prince Oginski (ca. 1731–1800), from 1762 Voivod of Vilna. C. gives him the title "Palatine." There were some 34 Voivodships in Poland at the period.

47   *Ronikier:* Michal Ronikier (died ca. 1778), Polish General, decorated with the order of Alexander Nevski.

48   *Palatine of Russia:* Prince August Aleksander Czartoryski (1697–1782), Voivod (Palatine) of what was then called Red Russia (eastern Galicia, Volhynia, and Podolia).

49   *Augustus III:* From 1733 King of Poland and, as Friedrich August II, Elector of Saxony (1696–1763).

74 *"Wardrobe":* It was the last antechamber before the King's bedroom.

75 *Outliving his country:* The existence of Poland as an independent nation was ended by the third partition of Poland in Oct. 1795. Stanislaus Augustus died in 1798.

76 *Kosciuszko:* Tadeusz Kosciuszko (1746–1817), of a noble Lithuanian family, took part in the American War of Independence from 1778 to 1783 as an Adjutant to George Washington and in 1789 was appointed a General in Poland. He fought valiantly against the Russians before the second and third partitions of Poland, and after the defeat at Maciejowice (Oct. 10, 1794) was taken prisoner just as a Cossack was about to kill him. He was not released until after Catherine's death, when he was allowed to go to America.

77 *Poninski:* Count Adam Antoni Poninski (1732–1798) became the Major-Domo to the Crown in 1762 and Royal Treasurer in 1772. In 1774 he obtained the title of Prince from the King and the Diet, in contravention of Polish law; in 1790 he was proscribed as a traitor.

78 *Pic:* Charles Pic, also Piq, Le Picq, and Lepicq (ca. 1743–after 1783), celebrated French dancer; he won applause on many European stages and appeared in Warsaw in 1765 and 1766.

79 *The King's brother:* Andrzej Poniatowski (1734–1773), Prince from 1764; General in the Austrian army.

80 *Went to see her at Villiers' inn:* Earlier in this chapter C. says that he went to lodge at Villiers' inn when he arrived in Warsaw. It would seem that he moved elsewhere later, perhaps for reasons of economy.

81 *Moczynski:* August Nalecz, Count of Mosna-Moczynski (ca. 1735–1786), from 1752 Equerry (Stolnik) to the Crown; among his other offices, he was Director of the Royal Theater from 1755; he was the lover of the dancer Anna Binetti.

82 *Branicki:* Franciszek Ksawery Branicki (died 1819), from 1765 Count, from 1764 Chamberlain (Podstoli); in March and April 1765 he was in Berlin as Envoy of the King of Poland to treat with Frederick the Great.

83 *Lubomirski:* Prince Stanislaus Lubomirski (1722–1783), made Field Marshal (Straznik) in 1752; married to Princess Izabela Czartoryska in 1753 (cf. note 51 to this chapter).

84 *Xavier:* Branicki's given names (see note 82) are the Polish equivalent of Francis Xavier.

85 *The White Eagle:* Polish order founded by Augustus II in 1713.

86 *Vis-à-vis:* Light carriage for two persons on two facing seats.

CHAPTER VIII

1 *The two spectacles:* In the previous chapter C. has said that, on La Binetti's arrival in Warsaw, the dancer Pic arranged a ballet for which Tomatis spared no expense in supplying the costumes, scenery, and so on. The other "spectacle" would seem to have been the ballet which Tomatis had already mounted for La Catai.

2 *He was ... Russian:* Together with the Czartoryskis, Branicki was opposed to King Stanislaus Poniatowski, though the King heaped honors on him. His activities in the Russian interest brought him the rank of Grand Marshal to the Crown; in addition, he married Aleksandra Vasilievna, Baroness Engelhardt, a niece of the well-known favorite and Minister of Catherine the Great, Potemkin.

3 *The dissidents:* The Polish Diet of 1764 had made Roman Catholicism the only State religion; from then on Protestants and members of the Greek Orthodox Church were persecuted as "dissidents." Protecting them gave both Prussia and Russia the excuse to interfere in Polish internal affairs. It was not until the new constitution of 1791 that all faiths were granted equal rights.

4 *Under personal obligations to him ... political reasons:* During the time Stanislaus Poniatowski was in St. Petersburg and was Catherine's lover, Branicki had helped to extricate him from a difficult situation. Politically, Poniatowski, King by the grace of Russia, was obliged to support the Russian faction.

5 *St. Casimir:* Born 1458, the patron saint of Poland and Lithuania. His feast was celebrated on March 4th: hence its eve was on March 3rd, not March 4th.

6   *The King's elder brother:* Kazimierz Poniatowski (1721–1780), Prince from 1764 and Grand Chamberlain.

7   *Casacci:* Teresa Casacci, also Casazzi and Casassi, Italian dancer from Turin, first appeared in Venice in 1762.

8   *Bisinski:* Perhaps an officer named Biszewski, who is mentioned in a contemporary Viennese document.

9   *Takes to his legs:* C. makes Branicki use the vulgar expression *fout le camp.*

10 *Sarmatians . . . Dacians:* The Sarmatians were a nomadic people who in Antiquity inhabited the southern Russian steppes and at the beginning of the Christian era advanced to the mouth of the Danube. The name was also extended to peoples north of that area. The Dacians inhabited the area north of the lower Danube and were brought under Roman rule by Trajan in 101–106; hence the name Dacia given to the new province, which, however, was evacuated by the Romans in the 3rd century and roughly corresponds to the present Romania.

11 *Partner:* C. writes *"pertener,"* presumably for the English word.

12 *Pernigotti:* Carlo Pernigotti, of Italian descent, Chamberlain to the King of Poland and naturalized a Pole in 1767.

13 *Lubomirski:* Prince Kaspar Lubomirski (1734–1779), son of Prince Teodor Lubomirski, Voivod of Cracow.

14 *Starosty:* District governed by a Starost; originally a fief conferred on a nobleman by the King, later an administrative unit.

15 *Casanova:* Together with later passages this shows that C. did not travel in Poland as either Seingalt or Farussi.

16 *C. P.:* Abbreviation for *Coronae Poloniae* ("to the Crown of Poland").

17 *Thirty-two:* Substituted for twenty-seven, which had been substituted for the original twenty-six, which shows that C. returned to this chapter over a considerable period of years.

18 *Mniszek:* Doubtless the Counts Vandalin-Mniszek, whom Winckelmann mentions on their departure from Rome for Venice in 1767. However, there were two noble families of

the name: the Counts Mniszek of Buzenin and the Counts Vandalin-Mniszek.

19 *Bertrand:* Élie (de) Bertrand (1713–1797), theologian and natural historian, from 1744 to 1765 pastor of the French church in Bern, from 1765 to 1768 in Poland, where he was ennobled.

20 *Berlin:* Large closed traveling carriage with four wheels.

21 *A beautiful garden:* Probably the duel, as C. himself says later, was fought in Wola in a garden belonging to Count Brühl. Wola, now a suburb of Warsaw, was then a village about half a mile from the capital and hence was still within the limits of the Starosty.

22 *Varsaw:* So C., to suggest the Polish pronunciation; elsewhere he Gallicizes the name to "Varsovie."

23 *Recollect:* See note 26 to Chap. V of this volume.

24 *Podlasie:* Polish province east of Warsaw; capital, Siedlce. The Voivod (C.'s "Palatine") from 1762 was Stanislaus Bernard Gozdzki.

25 *Kalisz:* Southwest of Warsaw, capital of a Voivodship; the Voivod from 1763 was Ignacy Twardowski.

26 *Jablonowski:* Jozef Aleksander Pruss Jablonowski (1712–1777), Prince from 1743, from 1755 Voivod of Nowogrodek; celebrated patron of the arts, scholar, and writer.

27 *Sanguszko:* Janusz Aleksander Sanguszko, son of the Prince and Grand Marshal Pawel Sanguszko.

28 *The Grand Marshal:* Count Franciszek Bielinski (1683–1766), from 1742 Polish Grand Marshal. His successor in 1766 was Prince Stanislaus Lubomirski.

29 *The Grand Chamberlain:* Prince Kazimierz Poniatowski (cf. note 6 to this chapter).

30 Medical maxim of unknown source.

31 *Clary:* Johann Nepomuk Franz Borgia, Count Clary-Aldringen (1728–ca. 1780), officer in the Imperial service.

32 *It was then that I:* In C.'s ms. there follows a canceled but still legible passage: "took the bit in my teeth and wrote a four-page

letter to the King, all in a jesting tone, but cruel, in which I called all the surgeons in Warsaw ignoramuses and butchers and all the people who gave them the lie admirable, and all the others who claimed to know better than I did whether I had gangrene or not [*sic*]. I ended my rather impertinent letter by saying ———"

33   *Became visible:* There follows another canceled passage: "to my eyes, which had better sight than those of the ignorant surgeons who wanted me to trust them blindly."

34   *Gourel:* He remained in the service of Prince August Aleksander Czartoryski until 1772.

35   *I kept my hand:* There follows a canceled passage, a page in length, from which it appears that he asked Prince Sulkowski to bring him his French physician; it was not until this Frenchman had declared that gangrene had not set in that C. dismissed the four Polish surgeons. The Frenchman, having found C.'s wound not infected with gangrene, met the Polish surgeons the next morning and prevented the operation.

36   *Bishop of Poznan:* From 1738 to 1768 this office was held by Prince Teodor Kazimierz Czartoryski. Warsaw first became a bishopric in 1798 and an archdiocese in 1817.

37   *A lady:* As appears from what follows, she was Branicki's sister, Elzbieta Sapieha.

38   *Nonagenarian . . . Bielinski:* Bielinski was only 82 years old in 1765 (cf. note 28 to this chapter).

39   *Countess Salmour:* Countess Isabella Salmour, née Lubienska (not, as C. says, Bielinska), married in 1752 to Giuseppe Gabaleone, Count Salmour (1710–1759).

40   *The Saxon faction:* Poland was then divided into two great camps: the pro-Russian faction, led by the Czartoryskis, and the patriotic, pro-Saxon faction, which consisted largely of Roman Catholics.

41   *The same day I went to dine:* Either C. went to dinner twice in one day (first at the Grand Marshal's, then at the Prince Palatine's), or he is out in his reckoning by a day.

42 *The Palatine of Kiowia:* Count Franciszek Salezy Potocki (1700–1772), from 1753 Voivod of Kiowia; opponent of the Czartoryskis.

43 *Brühl:* Aloys Friedrich, Count Brühl (1739–1793), son of the celebrated Prime Minister to King Augustus III (see note 53 to the preceding chapter), was Starost of Warsaw.

44 *A Starost Sniatinski:* Text: "un Staroste Sniatinski." No Starost by this name is known.

45 *Madame Geoffrin:* Marie Thérèse Geoffrin, née Rodet (1699–1777), whose literary salon was one of the most celebrated in Paris. Stanislaus Poniatowski became a close friend of hers during his stay in Paris. She came to Warsaw at his invitation on June 6, 1766, and remained there until Sept. 13th of that year.

46 *Leopol:* Polish, Lwow. At the first partition of Poland (1772), it became Austrian and its name was changed to Lemberg.

47 *Zamojski ... Zamosc:* Zamosc was a famous fortress between Warsaw and Leopol, founded in 1588 by Jan Zamojski. The fortress belonged to a so-called "ordynacja," a kind of fief of which there were only three in Poland at the period. In 1766 the Ordynat of Zamosc was Count Klemens Zamojski (died ca. 1767); he was married in 1763 to Countess Konstancja Zamojska, née Czartoryska (1742–1797).

CHAPTER XII

1 *Gages:* Juan Bonaventura Thierry du Mont, Comte de Gages (1682–1753), in the Spanish service from 1703, was Captain General and Viceroy of Navarra from 1749.

2 *Had had me arrested:* See Vol. 2, Chap. II.

3 *Old Castile:* Province of Spain; when it was an independent kingdom its capital was Valladolid.

4 *Only wretched inns:* The highroad to Madrid ran and still runs through Burgos. From Pamplona C. must have traveled to Madrid by way of Tudela, Agreda, Soria, Medinaceli, Guadalajara, and Alcalá de Henares, part of which journey would have been by secondary roads.

5   *"A small coin for the noise"*: So C. ironically translates the Spanish; but *ruido* in this context can also mean "disturbance."

6   *Cigarro:* This is C.'s only mention of the cigar, which about this time became fashionable in Spain, to which it was brought from South America. Cigar smoking was not taken up in the rest of Europe until the second half of the 18th century. The first cigar factory outside of Spain was established in Hamburg in 1778.

7   *Gabacho:* From *gave*, Pyrenean term for a mountain stream; literally, "uncouth person." The term was first applied to Pyrenean peasants and then extended to all Frenchmen.

8   *French dog:* C. writes "Frence-dogue."

9   *The visionary's dreams . . . lose my mind:* See Vol. 4, Chap. XII.

10 *Bilbao:* City in northern Spain near the Bay of Biscay, some 85 miles from the French border; today an important industrial center.

11 *Grandee:* In the kingdom of Castile "Grande" was the inheritable title of the highest nobility from the 13th century; under the Emperor Charles V (1520) it became the designation of a nobleman of the highest rank at Court.

12 *Squillace:* Leopoldo di Gregorio, Marchese di Squillace (died 1785 in Venice) came from southern Italy, was Spanish Minister of Finance from 1759 and Minister of War from 1763. The heavy taxes he imposed and his numerous edicts directed against national customs led to an uprising in Madrid in 1766, which forced the King to dismiss him. Squillace retired to Naples and in 1772 was appointed Ambassador to Venice.

13 *The Holy Inquisition:* The Inquisition, though not confined to Spain, had more power there than in other European countries. It pronounced its last death sentence in Spain as late as 1781 and was not abolished there until 1834.

14 *Señor Don Jaime:* Jaime is the Spanish form of Jacques and Giacomo.

15 *The two Castiles:* For Old Castile, see note 3 to this chapter. New Castile as an independent kingdom had Toledo as its capital.

16   *The language of the Moors . . . left a quantity of words there:* The
     Moors ruled the greater part of the Iberian Peninsula from 713
     and developed a flourishing culture there, especially in the
     south. The Christian reconquest began as early as the 8th
     century from the mountainous northern provinces, but gained
     ground slowly; Toledo was not conquered until 1085, followed
     by Saragossa in 1118, Valencia in 1238, Seville in 1248. Gib-
     raltar fell in 1462, and Granada not until 1492. Thus many
     Arabic elements entered the Spanish language, particularly its
     vocabulary. C. seems to have been struck by the large number
     of words containing the Arabic article *al.*

17   *Ala . . . Alcavala:* Since C. wrote words from foreign languages
     entirely by ear, it is impossible to identify all of his list of
     Spanish words, many of them proper names.

18   Horace, *Art of Poetry*, 323.

19   *Three guttural letters:* C. can only mean the Spanish pronunci-
     ation of *g* before *e* and *i*, and of *j* before all vowels, when those
     consonants have the sound of *ch* in Scottish "loch," though he
     may also be thinking of the Castilian lisped sound (th). He
     would have heard none of these in Italian.

20   Medieval hexameter (see *Proverbia Sententiaeque Latinitatis Medii
     Aevi*, ed. H. Walther, Vol. 4, No. 25, 531).

21   *Puerta de Alcalá:* The Puerta de Alcalá was one of the 15 old city
     gates of Madrid. The gate which bears the name today was not
     built until 1788, by the architect Sabatini.

22   *Street of the Cross:* The Calle de la Cruz is not far from the
     Puerta del Sol and still exists.

23   *The coffeehouse . . . lodge:* C. lodged in the "Hôtel garni du Café
     français."

24   *The late Queen:* Maria Amalia Walburga (1724–1760), daughter
     of King Augustus III of Poland, married in 1738 to King Carlo
     Borbone of Naples, who became King of Spain as Carlos III in
     1759.

25   *Della Cattolica:* Giuseppe Agostino Bonanno Filingeri e del
     Bosco, Prince of Roccafiorita and della Cattolica (died 1779),

Spanish grandee from 1748, and from 1761 to 1770 Envoy Extraordinary from the Kingdom of Naples to Madrid.

26 *The highest city:* The altitude of Madrid is some 2130 feet, and so, with the exception of the pygmy states of Andorra and San Marino, it is the highest European capital.

27 *A thousand toises:* The Parisian toise was equal to just under six feet. This would make the altitude of Madrid 6000 feet! In his ms. C. first wrote, more reasonably, "three or four hundred toises," then substituted "a thousand."

28 *The Gate of the Sun:* The square La Puerta del Sol is still one of the most frequented places in the inner city. There was originally a gate there, whence the name.

29 *Duenna:* C writes "duegna" (for Spanish *dueña*).

30 *Banished all the Jesuits in . . . Spain:* The expulsion of the Jesuits from Spain took place on the night of March 31 to April 1, 1767. Portugal had expelled the Jesuits in 1759 and France in 1764.

31 *Proscribe hats . . . cloaks . . . heel:* They were used by questionable elements to avoid recognition. Squillace had issued his prohibition in March 1766; the result was the so-called *motín*, an uprising which forced the King to dismiss him (cf. note 12, to this chapter). His successor, the Count of Aranda, immediately rescinded the prohibition, but soon promulgated it again in a more acceptable form by a decree stating that the King would recognize true Spaniards by their cocked hats. Thereupon both slouch hats and long cloaks soon vanished.

32 *President of the Council of Castile:* The President of the Royal and Supreme Council of Castile was the most powerful person in Spain after the King. The Council was made up of some 30 high-ranking magistrates, who not only drafted laws but made appointments to governmental positions and served as the highest court of appeal.

33 *The Ambassador of your Republic:* Alvise Sebastiano Mocenigo (1725–1780), Venetian Ambassador in Rome, and from 1762 to 1768 in Madrid; he was married and had two daughters.

34 *The Neapolitan Ambassador:* Prince della Cattolica (see note 25, above).

35 *Mora:* José María Pignatelli, Marqués de Mora (died 1774), friend of Mademoiselle de Lespinasse and of Voltaire.

36 *Dandolo:* Marco Dandolo (1704–1779), Venetian patrician, friend of Senator Bragadin and of C.

37 *Soderini:* Gasparo Soderini, Venetian Secretary of Embassy in Madrid and Milan; appointed to the Venetian State Secretariat in 1775.

38 *My sovereign:* The Doge of Venice.

39 *Manuzzi:* Son of Giovanni Battista Manuzzi, who, as a spy for the Venetian State Inquisition, had contributed to C.'s being imprisoned under the Leads. C. calls the son a Count. Nothing is known of him or of his title.

40 *Loredan:* The Loredans were an ancient Venetian patrician family.

41 *Alexis . . . Corydon:* In Vergil's second Eclogue the shepherd Corydon is in love with the beautiful youth Alexis.

42 *Calle Ancha:* The Calle Ancha de San Bernardo was in the northern part of the city. Ancha means "wide"; there was also a Calle Angosta ("narrow") de San Bernardo. The "palace" is the Venetian Ambassador's residence.

43 *Sentenced . . . Brescia:* Mocenigo was imprisoned in the fortress of Brescia in 1773; the city then belonged to the Republic of Venice.

44 *Another Ambassador:* Alvise Piero M. Contarini (1731–1786), Venetian patrician, appointed Venetian Ambassador in Vienna in 1773.

45 *Wristband clique:* Text: "de la manchette," slang for pederast.

46 *Mengs:* Anton Raphael Mengs (1728–1779), celebrated painter of the period, from Aussig (Bohemia); from 1754 Director of the Capitoline Academy in Rome, from 1761 to 1771 Court painter to King Carlos III of Spain. He was a close friend of C.'s.

47 *Sabatini:* Francesco Sabatini (Sabattino), Italian architect (1722–1797); he was summoned to Madrid by the King of Spain in 1760.

48 *Vanvitelli:* Luigi Vanvitelli, of Dutch descent (real name Lodewijk van Wittel), celebrated architect (1700–1773), worked on St. Peter's in Rome from 1726; his best-known work is the Palace of Caserta, near Naples.

49 C. indicates that this is a quotation. It is from a poem by an unknown author in reply to a poem of C.'s addressed to the Italian actress and dancer Giacoma Annetta Veronese, known as Camilla. Both poems were published in the April 1757 issue of the *Mercure de France*, the reply under the title "Sur le portrait de Mlle Camille, fait en vers italiens."

50 *Theater... Los Caños del Peral:* In addition to the Buen Retiro, which had been closed in 1759, Madrid from the 17th century had had the Teatro de la Cruz (rebuilt in 1737) and the Teatro del Principe (rebuilt in 1745). To these in 1708 was added the theater called Los Caños del Peral, opened by the Italian actor and impresario Bartoli, and at first used for performances of Italian opera; from 1745 it was used for concerts and masked balls. (C. writes "los scannos.")

51 *Autos sacramentales:* Dramas, usually in one act, on sacred subjects, descendants of the medieval mystery plays but later composed by such famous writers as Tirso de Molina, Lope de Vega, and Calderón. From the 16th century they were performed on great feast days of the ecclesiastical calendar, the *autos sacramentales* on Corpus Christi Day and the *autos al nacimiento* on Christmas. Their performance had already been forbidden in 1765 at the instigation of the Archbishop of Toledo, Count Teba; so C. can hardly have seen one of them. Perhaps, however, the prohibition was not strictly enforced at first.

52 *Puñete:* C. writes "pugnetta." The word properly means "blow with the fist," but is here used in some obscene sense.

53 *Pichona:* Maria Teresa Palomino (1728–1795), called La Pichona, famous Spanish actress from 1750, mistress of the Dukes of Medina Celi and of Medina Sidonia; celebrated for her beauty and, later, for her wealth.

54 *Fandango:* A lively dance in 3/8 or 6/8 time, brought to Spain from the West Indies.

55 *St. Anthony:* Ca. 250–350, the founder of Egyptian monasti-
cism. His feast is celebrated on Jan. 17th. He is the patron saint
of Spain, of tailors, and of swineherds.

56 *La Soledad:* There were two churches at the time named
Nuestra Señora de la Soledad. The one to which Doña Ignacia
went was probably the one in the Calle de Fuencarral, near the
Puerta del Sol. It still exists.

57 *Del Desengaño:* The Calle del Desengaño still exists near the
Puerta del Sol.

58 *Hidalgo:* Title denoting a Spanish nobleman of the lower class.

59 The parenthetical translation is C.'s. He writes "vieco."

60 *Peso duro:* Spanish silver coin minted from 1497 and worth 8
reales. It circulated, at least in the Spanish colonies, until 1868,
when the peseta, which was worth half a peso, became the
monetary unit.

61 *Doña Ignacia:* Nothing is known of her except what C. relates.

Volume Eleven

CHAPTER I

1 *La Pichona:* Maria Teresa Palomino (1728–1795), called La
Pichona, Spanish actress (see Vol. 10, Chap. XII, n. 53).

2 *Fandango:* Well-known Spanish dance, which C. had been
taught by a Spanish actor (see Vol. 10, Chap. XII).

3 *Pareja:* Spanish, "partner" (feminine). C. had picked up the
term when the disguised Duke of Medina Celi had encouraged
him to find a partner for the next ball (see Vol. 10, Chap. XII).

4 *Plazuela:* C. writes "la plaquella."

5 *Calle del Desengaño:* This street, in the vicinity of the Puerta del
Sol, still exists.

6 *Ramos:* Obviously a fictitious name, for C. first began to write a
name beginning with Q, then substituted Ramos.

7 *Doblones:* The doblón was a gold coin minted in Spain until
1772; value 4 pesos.

8   *The Mint:* In the 17th century the Mint (Real Casa de la Moneda) was in the Calle de Segovia; it later occupied a building at the corner of the Paseo de Recoletos and the Calle de Goya.

9   *Medina Celi:* Luis Antonio Fernandez de Córdoba, Duke of Medina Celi (died 1768), Grand Master of the Royal Horse.

10 *Pesos duros:* Spanish silver coin worth 8 reales. Four pesos made 1 doblón.

11 *The Duke . . . had died:* The Duke of Medina Celi died in Jan. 1768.

12 *A son:* Pedro de Alcántara Fernandez de Córdoba, Duke of Medina Celi (died 1790); his son was Luis Maria (died 1806).

13 *An intelligent author:* To what author C. refers remains unascertained.

14 *Thirty hats: Sombrero* ("hat") was the term for the right of certain Spanish Grandees not to uncover in the King's presence.

15 *Marazzani:* Antonio Luigi Marazzani (ca. 1740–after 1780), priest who became an adventurer, assuming the title of Count. He appeared in Venice ca. 1779 and was banished as the result of information supplied by C. in his role of *confidente* ("informer") to the State Inquisitors.

16 *His Majesty:* Carlos III (1716–1788), King of Spain from 1759.

17 *Mercury:* Roman equivalent of the Greek god Hermes, the messenger of the gods, often employed by Jupiter as a procurer.

18 Martial, *Epigrams,* 1, 57, 2.

19 *Zapatero de viejo:* C. writes "*viecco.*" The meaning is "cobbler" (in contradistinction to "shoemaker").

20 *Accord the "Don" . . . a hidalgo:* A hidalgo (cf. Vol. 10, Chap. XII, n. 58), as a nobleman of the lower class, had the right to be addressed as Don.

21 *Princess of Asturias:* Asturias is a province in northwestern Spain. The titles Prince and Princess of Asturias were borne by the Heir Apparent and his wife. The reference is to Maria Luisa Teresa (1751–1819), daughter of the Duke of Parma; she was

married in 1765 to the son of Carlos III, who became King of Spain in 1788 as Carlos IV.

22 *Ratafia:* A sweet fruit liqueur (cf. Vol. 3, Chap. VIII, n. 21).

23 *Doblón de a ocho:* Spanish gold coin worth 8 escudos. (In Vol. 1, Chap. X, n. 29, "gold scudi" should be corrected to "escudos.")

24 *La Soledad:* There were then two churches in Madrid named Nuestra Señora de la Soledad. C. probably refers to the one which still stands in the Calle de Fuencarral, near the Puerta del Sol.

25 *Charlotte:* Charlotte de Lamotte, of Brussels (died 1767), whose acquaintance C. had made in Spa, where she was the mistress of the adventurer Croce (Crosin).

26 *Obligation . . . Count of Aranda . . . done:* As President of the Council of Castile from 1766, the Count of Aranda had issued new regulations governing theatrical performances and had licensed masked balls.

27 *Los padres de la Compañía:* I.e., the Jesuits, whom Aranda expelled in 1767.

28 *Cloaks . . . sombreros gachos:* Long cloaks (*capas largas*) and slouch hats (*sombreros gachos*) had already been forbidden by Aranda's predecessor Squillace (cf. Vol. 10, Chap. XII, n. 31).

29 *Los Caños del Peral:* Theater in Madrid (cf. Vol. 10, Chap. XII, n. 50).

30 *La Mancha:* Old province of central Spain, south of Madrid, famous for its wines, especially that from Valdepeñas; birthplace of Don Quixote.

31 *Marina:* St. Marina (5th century), whose feast is celebrated on July 17, lived in a Bithynian hermitage in men's clothing, first with her father, then as a hermit. Accused of being the lover of a girl to whom she had given religious counsel and who was found to be pregnant, she was sentenced to death. Only after her death was it discovered that she was a woman.

32 Altered from Erasmus, *Adagia*, Chil. III, Centur. IV, Prov. LXXVII. (C. has quoted it several times before.)

33 *I was five inches taller than she:* As C. states several times (e.g., Vol. 3, Chap. VIII), he was 5 feet 9 inches tall.

34 *Alcalde Messa:* An alcalde (from Arabic *al-qadi*) was a Spanish administrative official with judicial and police powers. Aranda had divided Madrid into 64 districts, each of which elected its alcalde from among its inhabitants. Of an Alcalde Messa nothing is known.

35 *Presidios:* Penitentiaries in which persons convicted of serious crimes and sentenced to hard labor were confined. The four principal ones were in North Africa.

36 *He was innocent:* C. here added, then crossed out, two sentences in which he expressed his doubt of his page's innocence.

37 *À la maréchale: Poudre à la maréchale* was highly scented.

38 *The Cavaliere di Casanova:* Text: *"le Chevalier de Casanova."* It follows that C. did not call himself de Seingalt in Spain. As a Knight of the Golden Spur, he had a right to the title Cavaliere.

39 *Buen Retiro:* The palace of Buen Retiro was the residence of the Spanish Kings from the 17th century until the Palacio Real was built in 1737. Of the 17th-century building almost nothing remains, so the name now designates the fine gardens of the former palace.

40 *Philip V. . . the Queen:* Philip V was King of Spain from 1700 to 1746. His first wife was Maria Louisa of Savoy, after whose death in 1714 he married Elizabeth Farnese of Parma; C. refers to the latter.

41 *The Parmesan Ambassador:* Piacenza belonged to the Duchy of Parma, which, however, had no regular representative in Madrid.

42 *The Venetian Ambassador:* Alvise Sebastiano Mocenigo (1725–1780), Procurator of San Marco, from 1762 to 1768 Venetian Ambassador in Madrid.

43 *Manuzzi:* Son of Giovanni Battista Manuzzi, who, as a spy for the Venetian State Inquisition, had contributed to C.'s being imprisoned under the Leads. C. calls the son a Count. Nothing is known of him or of his title. See Vol. 10, Chap. XII.

44   *Signora Zorzi ... Condulmer:* Maria Teresa Zorzi, née Dolfin, married in 1748 to the Venetian patrician Marcantonio Zorzi; according to C.'s account, she was courted by the patrician Antonio Condulmer, who was a State Inquisitor in 1755 and who sent C. to prison under the Leads.

45   *Roda:* Manuel, Marqués de Roda y Arrieta (ca. 1707–after 1776), Minister of Justice from 1765.

46   *His Catholic Majesty:* Title conferred on the Kings of Spain by Pope Alexander VI in 1497.

47   *Rojas:* C. writes "Royas"; Rojas was so common a name in Spain at the time that no identification is possible.

48   *Dandolo:* Marco Dandolo (1704–1779), Venetian patrician, and C.'s faithful friend.

49   *One of the three Inquisitors:* C. followed this by "who had me imprisoned under the Leads," then crossed it out. The reference is to Antonio da Mula (1714–after 1782), who was a State Inquisitor in 1755, and whom C. names a few lines further on.

50   *Zulian:* Girolamo Giuliano, Venetian Zulian (1730–1795), Venetian patrician and diplomat; State Inquisitor in 1774.

51   *Aranjuez:* Then a village some 30 miles south of Madrid on the Tagus, with a famous royal palace, built in the 16th century by Juan de Herrera. King Carlos III regularly spent the months of April and May in Aranjuez.

CHAPTER II

1   *Princess Lubomirska:* According to Chap. XI of the previous volume, C. had come to Madrid with a letter of introduction to the Duke of Losada from Princess Lubomirska, née Czartoryska.

2   *Béliardi:* Agostino Bigliardi, of Sinigaglia (1723–1803), Italian abate, entered the French service in 1757, after which he spelled his name Béliardi; the Duke of Choiseul appointed him "general commercial and naval agent" on the staff of the French Ambassador in Madrid, the Marquis d'Ossun, where he remained until his patron Choiseul was disgraced in 1770. (C. writes "Bigliardi.")

3   *Campomanes:* Don Pedro Rodríguez, Count of Campomanes (1723–1803), held several important governmental posts; in 1765 he became Director of the Royal Historical Academy; he wrote numerous works on political and economic subjects.

4   *Olavides:* Pablo Antonio José Olavides, Count of Pilos (1725–1803), of Lima, Peru, Spanish statesman and economist, and until 1775 superintendent of the Swiss and German settlements in the Sierra Morena (cf. note 19 to this chapter); he was tried by the Inquisition in 1776 and exiled to a monastery, but was able to escape to France in 1778 and did not return to Spain until 1797.

5   *Strabismics:* C. writes "strabons," an Italianism, augmentative of *strabo*, "squinter."

6   *Mortmains:* Mortmain is the condition of lands or tenements held inalienably by ecclesiastical or other corporations. Many religious orders were the beneficiaries of such testamentary dispositions.

7   *Sarpi:* Fra Paolo Sarpi, called Paolo Veneto (1552–1623), was an adviser to the Venetian Republic and, as an opponent of Papal absolutism, the author of numerous political treatises, which, after being forgotten, were rediscovered in the latter half of the 18th century and found to bear on problems then current.

8   *Campomanes was imprisoned . . . four years later:* There is no record that Campomanes was ever imprisoned; he retired from political life voluntarily in 1791.

9   *Olavides . . . treated more harshly:* Cf. note 4 to this chapter. His condemnation was principally due to his correspondence with Voltaire and Rousseau, as well as to his possession of erotic pictures and pieces of sculpture.

10 *Appointed Ambassador to France:* Aranda was the Spanish Ambassador in Versailles from 1773 to 1786.

11 *Carlos III . . . died mad:* C. exaggerates. Of a melancholy temperament by nature, the King had lost his wife in 1760 and then, one after the other in rapid succession, his daughter-in-law the Infanta of Portugal, her children, and finally his own

son the Infante Don Gabriel. All this naturally had its effect on the King's innate melancholy; but there is no evidence that he died insane.

12 *The excesses committed by the Jesuits:* The allusion is to the attempted assassination of the King of Portugal, which took place in 1758, and to the financial crisis in France brought on by the speculations and bankruptcy of the Superior of the Jesuits in Martinique.

13 *The Jesuit confessor of Don Fernando VI:* Fernando VI (1713–1759), King of Spain from 1746, had as his confessor the Jesuit Francisco de Rávago (1685–1763).

14 *Ensenada:* Zenón de Somodevilla y Bengoechea, Marqués de la Ensenada (1702–1781), Spanish statesman, holder of numerous high offices from 1737 to 1750, in which year he was disgraced and banished to Granada at the instigation of the King's confessor Rávago; however, he was not removed from his last offices until 1754, when his support of the pro-French faction brought the English diplomat Richard Wall into action against him.

15 *Los Teatinos:* English, Theatines; name of an order of monks founded in Italy in 1524 by St. Cajetan (1480–1547) and Pietro Caraffa, then Archbishop of Chieti (in antiquity Teate, whence "Theatines"), later Pope as Paul IV (1555–1559). But in Spain in the 17th and 18th centuries the name was applied to the Jesuits. (C. writes *"los Theatinos."*)

16 *Cayetanos:* Alternative Spanish name for the Theatines, from their co-founder St. Cajetan. (C. writes "Gaetanos.")

17 Cf. *pia fraus*, Ovid, *Metamorphoses*, IX, 711.

18 *Was given a new confessor:* Until 1760 his confessor was Fray José Casado, called (from his birthplace) Bolanos; when he resigned because of age and illness, the King himself chose the Franciscan Fray Joaquín Eleta (died 1788) as his confessor.

19 *Las sierras de Morena:* Properly La Sierra Morena, a mountain range in southern Spain, running east and west north of the Guadalquivir. The plan for an intensive settlement of the region had originated in 1749. But it was not until 1766 that

a Bavarian officer, Johann Caspar Thürriegel, presented a thorough study of the project, which was approved by the Council of Castile in 1767. The settlers came not only from Switzerland but also from Germany, and some of them were Protestants. After great difficulties at the beginning, the colony flourished.

20 *The Bishop:* Probably the Bishop of Córdoba.

21 *Heimweh:* Homesickness. (C. writes "le Heimvèh.")

22 *What the Greeks called* nostalgia: The word *nostalgia* did not exist in classical Greek; it was coined from Greek roots in the 17th century to represent the German *Heimweh* in medical writings.

23 *Customs . . . in regard to making love:* Allusion to the Swiss *Kilt-gang* or Bavarian *Fensterln.*

24 *The Portuguese lady:* In all probability a reference to Pauline (cf. Vol. 9, Chap. VIII).

25 *Signora Sabatini:* Wife of the Italian architect Francesco Sabatini (1722–1797), who was summoned to Spain in 1760. (Cf. Vol. 10, Chap. XII).

26 *Medina Sidonia:* Pedro de Alcántara Pérez de Guzmán el Bueno, Duke of Medina Sidonia (died ca. 1777), from 1765 Master of the Horse to the Prince of Asturias, from 1768 to King Carlos III.

27 *Varnier:* Don Domingo Varnier, valet to King Carlos III; two letters from him to C. are extant.

28 *Amigoni:* Jacopo Amigoni (1675–1752), Italian painter and engraver, summoned to Madrid in 1747.

29 *Hospitality to heretics:* Mengs had turned Catholic in 1749 and as a convert was probably particularly strict in matters of religion.

30 *Long Spanish leagues:* In the 18th century the league represented four different distances in Spain. C. probably refers to the *legua nueva* ("new league") introduced in 1760, the length of which was just over 4 miles.

31 *Al sitio:* "At the country seat"; here specifically Aranjuez, one of the Sitios Reales ("royal country seats") which Carlos III

regularly frequented at different seasons. The others were El Pardo (February and March), La Granja (July), the Escorial (October). He spent April at Aranjuez.

32 Ovid, *Tristia*, 5, 6, 13.

33 *The coffeehouse where I was staying:* C. was staying at the Café français on the Calle de la Cruz (cf. Vol. 10, Chap. XII, n. 23).

34 *The Tower of Babylon:* The ziggurat Etemenanki, the remains of which, however, were not brought to light until the archeological excavations at Babylon conducted by Robert Koldewey from 1898 to 1917.

35 *His eldest son:* According to the registries of baptisms of the Roman churches, Mengs had at least 14 children; his eldest son, Domenico Raffaello, born in 1750, died in infancy. Another son, Giovanni Antonio, born in 1754, died ca. 1759–1760. Of his other sons only Alberico (the dates of his birth and death are not recorded) is known to have survived and had children.

36 *Cavaliere:* Mengs, like C., had received the order of the Golden Spur and hence had the title Cavaliere.

37 *Correggio:* Antonio Allegri da Correggio (1494–1534), famous painter of the Italian Renaissance.

38 *Raffaello d'Urbino:* Raffaello Santi (Raphael), of Urbino (1483–1520), famous Italian painter of the Renaissance.

39 *Died before . . . fifty years:* Mengs was 51 years of age when he died.

40 *His biography:* C. doubtless refers to the biography by José Nicolas de Azara, which appeared in *Obras de don Antonio Rafael Mengs, primer pintor de Camara del Rey* (Madrid, 1780).

41 *Naumachia:* In classical antiquity, orginally a mock naval battle, then an artificial basin, usually surrounded by tiers of seats, especially constructed for the exhibition of such battles. The ruins of a Roman amphitheater are still to be seen in Toledo; they must have been more extensive in the 18th century.

42 *Alcázar:* The Alcázar (from the Arabic *al qaṣr*, "castle") of Toledo was first the residence of the Visigothic rulers of

Spain, then of the Moorish, and, from the 11th to the 16th century, of the Kings of Castile.

43   *The cathedral:* The celebrated cathedral of Toledo was built from 1227 to 1493. In C.'s time the Archbishop of Toledo was Don Luis III Fernandez de Córdoba.

44   *Collections:* What collections C. can have seen is not known, for the first natural history collection of which records exist was established by the Cardinal-Archbishop of Toledo after 1772.

45   *Grimaldi:* Don Pablo Jerónimo Grimaldi (1720–1786), of the celebrated Genoese patrician family, early entered the Spanish diplomatic service; from 1763 to 1777 he was Minister of Foreign Affairs, and then Spanish Ambassador in Rome until 1783.

46   *My opera:* Nothing is known of this libretto by C. It was not found among his papers.

47   *Pelliccia:* Clementina Pelliccia, Roman singer; documented as appearing in Spain in 1768 and 1769. Her younger sister was Maria Teresa Pelliccia, who was still singing at the opera in Madrid in 1777.

48   *Marescalchi:* Luigi Marescalchi (born ca. 1740), Bolognese impresario and composer of operas; he opened a music shop in Venice in 1770 and in 1785 moved it to Naples.

49   *The Governor of Valencia:* Until 1766 the Count of Aranda was Governor (Spanish, "capitán general") of Valencia (then, of course, no longer a kingdom but a province).

50   *Arcos:* Antonio Ponce de León y Spínola (1726–1780), Duke of Baños, from 1763 Duke of Arcos and personal friend of Carlos III.

51   *Don Diego Valencia:* Don Diego Valencia was a banker in the city of Valencia.

52   *Who now reigns:* The then Prince of Asturias became King of Spain as Carlos IV in 1788.

53   *Every day. . .go hunting:* It is a fact that Carlos III went hunting every day, except on Good Friday and the major ecclesiastical feast days, often continuing to hunt by torchlight after dark.

54   *His brother:* The Infante Don Luis Antonio Jaime, called Don
      Luis (1727–1785), Archbishop of Seville and Toledo, was made
      a Cardinal in 1735; in 1754 he renounced all his ecclesiastical
      offices and in 1776 married Countess Maria Teresa Vallabriga y
      Rozas. However, it was not he but his brother the King who
      delighted in Mengs's paintings of the Virgin and saints.

55   *Carrera de San Gerónimo:* In this street, which still exists between
      the Prado and the Puerta del Sol, there was in the 18th century
      a small church adjacent to the Franciscan Monastery of Espíritu
      Santo; it was demolished in 1823.

56   Paraphrased from Luke 11:27.

57   *Pico:* Alessandro Pico (died 1787), cousin of Francesco Maria
      Pico, Duke of Mirandola, who, after he was deprived of all his
      estates in Italy, went to Spain with Alessandro. The latter was
      the friend and adviser of the Marchese Grimaldi and almoner to
      King Carlos III.

58   *Barbarigo:* Piero Barbarigo was one of the three Venetian State
      Inquisitors from 1769 to 1770.

59   *St. Luke . . . as a painter:* According to a legend first documented
      in the 5th century, St. Luke the Evangelist was also a painter;
      hence he was considered the patron of painters and of artists in
      general. Numerous portraits of Christ are attributed to him;
      among the best known is the one (probably of the 6th century)
      in the Capella Sancta Sanctorum in the Lateran, Rome; the
      predominant color in all of them is brown. C. had known
      from his boyhood the well-known painting of the Madonna
      Nicopeia, attributed to St. Luke, in San Marco, Venice; this may
      account for his assertion that St. Luke painted with only three
      colors.

60   *This altar:* C. writes "cet hôtel," obviously a slip for "cet autel."

61   *Origen:* Origen of Alexandria, Christian theologian and apolo-
      gist of the 2nd–3rd centuries.

62   Paraphrased from Matthew 19:12.

63   *De Ségur:* Probably a member of the old Poitevin noble family
      of De Ségur, but he has not been identified.

64 Antique maxim, differently expressed by various authors (e.g., Tibullus, 3, 6, 43–44).

65 *The Grand Inquisitor:* From 1761 to 1775 the Spanish Inquisitor General was Archbishop Don Manuel Quintano y Bonifaz (died 1775).

66 *Squillace:* Leopoldo de Gregorio, Marchese di Squillace (died 1785 in Venice), native of southern Italy; from 1759 Spanish Minister of Finance, from 1763 Minister of War; he was dismissed in 1766, but was made Spanish Ambassador in Venice in 1772. On the occasion of the uprising of 1766 in Madrid (cf. Vol. 10, Chap. XII, n. 12) numerous satires accusing him of being an overly uxorious husband were published.

67 *Madame Adélaïde of France:* Marie Adélaïde (1732–1800), daughter of Louis XV of France, whence her title Madame de France; she died unmarried.

68 *Marriage of conscience:* An Infante of Spain was forbidden to marry a woman of lower rank. In 1776 Carlos III made an exception to the rule in the case of his brother.

69 *Carlos III . . . the Queen of Portugal . . . mad:* It is a fact that Maria I Francisca Isabela of Portugal (1734–1816) became insane after the death of her eldest son and her daughter. On the alleged insanity of Carlos III see note 11 to this chapter.

70 *The King of England was mad:* George III of England (1738–1820), of the House of Hanover, became King in 1760; he began to show signs of insanity in 1789, but the fact was kept secret. He was not declared incurable until 1810; his son George Frederick Augustus assumed the regency, and became King as George IV in 1820.

71 *A Biscayan maidservant:* Maidservants from the northern Spanish province of Vizcaya, on the Bay of Biscay, were still the most numerous and sought after in Madrid in the 19th century; they were reputed to be especially capable and clean.

72 *Calle de Alcalá:* The Calle de Alcalá is still one of the most important streets in Madrid; it runs from the Puerta del Sol to the Prado.

73   *Aranjuez . . . Madrid . . . Fontainebleau . . . Paris:*   The   distance
     from Aranjuez to Madrid is about 30 miles, from Fontainebleau
     to Paris about 34 miles.

74   *Bilbao:* Near the northern coast of Spain in the province of
     Vizcaya, today an industrial city with a population of some
     300,000.

75   *Criadillas:* A kind of roll; also a kind of truffle.

CHAPTER III

1   *He had done:* C. writes "qu'il m'avait" (omitting *fait*, "done").

2   *St. Ignatius of Loyola:* Spanish, Iñigo López de Loyola (1491–
     1556), of the lesser Basque nobility, first an army officer, then
     converted to the spiritual life in 1521; he founded the Society of
     Jesus (the Jesuit order) in Rome and obtained papal recognition
     of it in 1540. He was and still is especially revered in Spain. He
     was canonized in 1622.

3   *Peso duro:* see note 10 to Chap. I of this volume.

4   *Buen Suceso:* The church of Nuestra Señora del Buen Suceso is a
     large parish church in the present Calle de la Princesa, near the
     Puerta del Sol.

5   *Atocha:* The basilica of Nuestra Señora de Atocha, built as
     a Dominican church in the 16th century, is in the Calle
     de Atocha near the present southern railway station (del Med-
     iodia).

6   *Don Jaime:* Jaime is the Spanish form of Giacomo and Jacques.

7   *La Soledad:* See Vol. 10, Chap. XII, n. 56.

8   *Duchess of Villadarias:* Dukes or Duchesses of this name are not
     documented; probably C. refers to the wife of Juan Bautista,
     Marqués de Villadarias (died 1773), who was made a Grandee
     in 1760, or perhaps to the wife of his successor Don Francisco
     (died 1798).

9   *Duchess of Benavente:* María Josefa Alfonsa Pimentel, Countess
     (not Duchess) of Benavente; she inherited the estates of the
     Duke of Béjar in 1777, conducted a celebrated literary salon in
     Madrid, and was a patroness of poets.

10   *Los Balbazes:* C. is in error. There was and is no public garden, promenade, or street of this name in Madrid.

11   *Homer . . . dispute on the subject:* The dispute on the subject between Jupiter and Juno is not in Homer but in Apollodoros's *Bibliotheca* (III, 67).

12   *Tiresias:* According to legend, the blind prophet Tiresias, when he was a young man, was changed into a woman. While a woman he married, and later was changed back into a man. Jupiter and Juno refer their dispute to him, and he decides it in Jupiter's favor, declaring that the woman receives ten times as much pleasure as the man (Apollodoros, *ibid.*).

13   *This creature the womb:* This entire discussion of the influence of the womb on the feminine psyche seems to echo a controversy which took place in Bologna in 1771–72 and into which C. entered with his *Lana Caprina.*

14   *Canine hunger:* Old medical term for a morbidly voracious appetite.

15   *St. Theresa:* St. Teresa de Jesús, of Ávila (1515–1582), with the support of Juan de la Cruz, reformed the Carmelites; she is considered one of the great mystics, and her writings are classics of Spanish literature.

16   *St. Agreda:* The nun María Coronel (died 1665), of Agreda, was the author of a mystical work *La mística ciudad de Dios* (1670); she was never canonized. C., much to his annoyance, had been given her book to read when he was imprisoned under the Leads (cf. Vol. 4, Chap. XII).

17   *Messalinas:* Valeria Messalina was the third wife of the Roman Emperor Claudius; notorious for her loose life, she was executed in A.D. 48 for having taken part in a conspiracy against the Emperor.

18   *St. Anthony of Padua:* Born at Lisbon in 1195, died at Padua in 1231; he was first an Augustinian, and became a Franciscan in 1220; a great preacher, he was canonized in 1232.

19   *St. Aloysius Gonzaga:* The Jesuit Luigi Gonzaga (1568–1591) was canonized in 1726 for the purity of his life.

20 *St. Ignatius:* See note 2 to this chapter.

21 This concept, which the Scholastic philosophy made common intellectual property, goes back to Aristotle (*Eudemian Ethics*, VII, 2).

22 *Great amphitheater:* The great bull ring was erected in 1749 under King Fernando VI outside the Puerta de Alcalá and was later enlarged. The present building dates from 1874. From March or April to Oct. 12 corridas were held there each year, many of them lasting all day.

23 *Picadero:* Now usually *picador*; the mounted *torero* in a bullfight.

24 *Prado San Jerónimo:* Now the southern end of the Paseo del Prado. The magnificent street was first laid out under King Carlos III and the Count of Aranda; so C. saw it when it was new.

25 *Lyons embroidery:* Embroidery from Lyons was considered especially choice in the 18th century.

26 *Of your nobility:* As a hidalgo, Don Diego could not give his daughter in marriage to anyone but a nobleman.

27 *Whence comes:* "D'où vient" is supplied by the editor in brackets. If the question mark too is his and not C.'s, the sentence would mean: "My angel, tell me that I am happy" (which seems more likely).

CHAPTER VI

1 *D'Argens:* Jean Baptiste de Boyer, Marquis d'Argens (1704–1771), Chamberlain to Frederick the Great and Director of the Academy of Sciences in Berlin from 1744 to 1769.

2 *D'Éguilles:* Alexandre Jean Baptiste de Boyer, Marquis d'Éguilles, Président au mortier ("Presiding Judge") of the Parlement at Aix (died 1785). His country house, Mon Repos, was in Éguilles, some 5 miles northwest of Aix.

3 *The late Frederick II:* Frederick the Great died in 1786.

4 *His writings:* The literary works of the Marquis d'Argens consist of novels, philosophic, aesthetic, and critical essays, and a number of fictitious memoirs and collections of letters;

his collected works were published at Berlin in 1768 in 24 volumes.

5   *The actress Cochois:* Barbe Cochois (before 1722–after 1771), French dancer; she appeared in Berlin in 1742 and married the Marquis d'Argens in 1749.

6   *Lord Marischal:* George Keith (ca. 1693–1778), from 1712 Earl Marischal of Scotland; exiled as a Jacobite, he spent many years at the Court of Frederick the Great and served as the Prussian Ambassador first to Paris and later to Madrid.

7   *Jesuit "of the short robe":* The Jesuit order accepted lay affiliates whose high position could make them useful to it; they were not obliged to wear the dress of the order.

8   *Gotzkowski:* Son of an art dealer and banker in Berlin, Johann Ernst Gotzkowski (1710–1775); his sister was married ca. 1764 to the Comte de Canorgue (died ca. 1767), who was a nephew of the Marquis d'Argens. C. writes, variously, "Schofskouski," "Chouskouski," "Choskoski," "Choskouski," "Chofskouski."

9   *Making a mock of eternal bliss: Béatilles,* which also means "small articles of religion," is derived from *béat* ("blissful").

10 *Ganganelli:* Giovanni Vincenzo Antonio Ganganelli (1705–1774), Franciscan friar under the name of Fra Lorenzo, became a Cardinal in 1759 and Pope, as Clement XIV, in 1769.

11 *Pinzi:* Giuseppe Antonio Pinzi (1713–1769), Professor of Eloquence in the Seminary at Ravenna, from 1759 Auditor to the Papal Nuncio Lucigni, first in Cologne, then in Madrid.

12 *Polyeucte:* Tragedy on a Christian subject by Pierre Corneille, first performed in 1643.

13 *Argenis:* Political allegory in the form of a romance, written in Latin and published at Paris in 1621. Its author was the Scotch Humanist John Barclay (1582–1621).

14 *His adopted daughter:* Born in 1754, at the time of C.'s visit to Aix in 1769 she was called Mina Giraud and was said to be the niece of the Marquise d'Argens, née Cochois. Some months after C. left Aix in December of that year, the Marquis d'Argens recognized her, in the presence of a notary and his

whole family, as his legitimate daughter by his wife. After that she was recognized by the family as Barbe d'Argens; in 1774 she married the Solicitor-General of the Aix Parlement, Monsieur de Magallon.

15 *Porphyry:* Greek philosopher and scholar of the 3rd century of our era; among his writings were scholia on the *Iliad* and the *Odyssey.*

16 *Buffoonery:* C. writes "un lazzi." *Lazzi* (which C. makes a singular though it is plural) were stereotyped bits of comic business used by the improvising actors of the *commedia dell'arte.*

17 *Santiago de Compostela:* City in the province of Galicia, north-western Spain, and site of the shrine which, according to tradition, contains the bones of St. James the Greater. It has been a place of pilgrimage since the early Middle Ages.

18 *Cockle shells:* Symbol of a pilgrim, and especially of one who had made the pilgrimage to the shrine of St. James.

19 *Balsamo:* Giuseppe Balsamo (1743–1795), Italian adventurer from Ballaro, near Palermo; he assumed the name Count Alessandro Cagliostro in 1776. He married Lorenza Feliciani, of Rome, in 1768; when he had changed his name she had changed hers to Serafina. He gained fame and wealth by practicing magic and alchemy, but in 1790 was sentenced to death in Rome as a Freemason, his sentence being commuted in 1791 to life imprisonment in the papal fortress of San Leo (near Rimini). There he died insane in 1795. Neither he nor his wife was ever in Santiago de Compostela.

20 *Our Lady of the Pillar:* Miracle-working statue of the Virgin Mary (*Nuestra Señora del Pilar*), which stands on a pillar in a chapel of its own in the cathedral church of Saragossa.

21 *The Most Holy Sudary:* The handkerchief (literally "sweat cloth") of the legendary St. Veronica, on which Christ is supposed to have wiped his face, leaving the imprint of it, on his way to be crucified. Several churches in Europe claim to possess it.

22 *Sweating:* Text, "grondant de sueur" (which, if it is not a misreading, makes no sense).

23   *Testone:* See Vol. 7, Chap. VIII, n. 15.

24   *Rembrandt:* Rembrandt van Rijn (1606–1669), famous Dutch painter and etcher. (C. writes "Reimbrand.")

25   *"St. Omer" inn:* The Hôtel de Saint-Omer still exists in the Rue du Limas in Avignon.

26   *I have heard that he is dead:* Cagliostro died in 1795 in the fortress of San Leo (cf. note 19 to this chapter). His wife, who is said also to have gone insane after betraying him to the Inquisition in 1789, was relegated to the Convent of Sant'Apollonia in Rome and died there in 1794.

27   *King of Sweden . . . assassinated:* Gustav III (1746–1792), nephew of Frederick the Great, King of Sweden from 1771, was assassinated on March 29, 1792.

28   *All his works:* See note 4 to this chapter.

29   *Account . . . written in his youth:* He had published his *Mémoires* in London as early as 1735.

30   *The scoundrels . . . Waldstein's castle:* The major-domo Feldkirchner, the courier Wiederholt, and the steward Stelzel leagued together to make life as unpleasant as possible for C. in Waldstein's castle, where C. was librarian; they even had him set upon and cudgeled in the streets of Dux (Dec. 1791). Waldstein, who was away from Dux most of the year, did not dismiss the three accomplices until July 1793. C. went to Dux in 1785 and died there in 1798.

31   *When the time comes:* This shows beyond doubt that C. intended to carry his memoirs down to the time of his residence at Dux.

32   *Corpus Christi:* In 1769 it fell on May 25.

33   *Saturnalia:* Roman festival in honor of the god Saturn and in celebration of the mythical Golden Age during his reign. It was held for a week in December; during it masters and slaves were considered equal.

34   *Saint-Marc:* Perhaps Louis Sauvage de Saint-Marc, Seigneur des Marches (documented in 1757 and 1789), of a family ennobled in the 18th century for distinguished judicial service.

35 *Henriette:* See Vol. 3, Chaps. I–V.

36 *Croix d'Or:* Name of a crossroads south of Aix-en-Provence.

37 *Nina:* Nina Bergonzi (died ca. 1782), Italian dancer; C. met her in Valencia.

38 *Count Ricla:* Ambrosio Funes de Villalpando (died 1780), from 1767 Captain-General of Catalonia, from 1772 Spanish Minister of War.

39 *He:* The text has "elle," which is either a slip of C.'s or a misreading. Laforgue gives "il" ("he").

40 *Pelandi:* Unknown charlatan who sold "wonder-working" drugs on the Piazza San Marco in Venice.

41 *Molinari:* Probably a certain Francesco Molinari, Italian singer, about whom nothing more is known.

42 *Proc . . . . ship:* C. writes "maq . . . . . . ge" (for *maquerellage,* from *maquereau,* "pimp").

43 *Twenty-two years:* According to C.'s account he parted from Henriette in Dec. 1749 or Jan. 1750, which would be at most 20 years before the time of her letter.

44 *Cesena:* It was at Cesena that C. first met Henriette (see Vol. 3, Chap. I).

45 *D'Antoine:* See Vol. 3, Chap. IV, n. 17.

46 *Marcolina:* Fictitious name of Venetian C. encountered in Genoa.

47 *Letters which I shall add:* Henriette's letters to C. have not been preserved.

48 *Colle di Tenda:* Pass on the road from Nice or Ventimiglia to Cuneo in Piedmont; with an altitude of some 6,200 feet, it was one of the highest passes over the Alps (but not the highest) in the 18th century.

49 *Raiberti:* Carlo Adalberto Flaminio Raiberti-Nizzardi (1708–1771); he held several important posts in the Piedmontese administration.

50   *La Pérouse:* Count Gian Giacomo Marcello Gamba della Per-
      osa, called Comte de la Pérouse (1738–1817).

51   *Sir XXX:* The English Envoy Extraordinary in Turin from 1768
      to 1779 was Sir William Lynch. Turin was then the capital of
      the Kingdom of Sardinia.

52   *Campioni:* Giustina Campioni-Bianchi (died after 1781), Italian
      dancer from Parma.

53   *Nani:* Giambattista Nani (1616–1678), Venetian patrician and
      Procurator; by order of the Venetian Senate he composed the
      Storia di Venezia dal 1613 al 1671 ("History of Venice from 1613
      to 1671") (2 vols., Venice, 1676–1679).

54   *Inn . . . Taglioretti:* The Albergo Svizzero, opened ca. 1760 and
      operated by Pietro and Tommaso Taglioretti.

55   *Agnelli:* Giovan-Battista Agnelli (1706–1788), of Milan, Abate;
      in 1746 he was granted permission to establish a press for the
      cantons of Zurich and Lucerne. The privilege was renewed for
      Lugano in 1765.

56   *Bargello:* Title of the Chief of Police in many Italian cities.

57   *Monsieur de =:* Urs Victor Joseph, Baron Roll von Emmenholtz
      (1711–1786), Swiss statesman. He was Bailiff of Lugano from
      1768 to 1770. C. had known him and his wife earlier (see Vol.
      6, Chaps. V–VII, where he refers to them as Monsieur and
      Madame . . .).

INDEX

CHINUA ACHEBE
Things Fall Apart

AESCHYLUS
The Oresteia

ISABEL ALLENDE
The House of the Spirits

THE ARABIAN NIGHTS
(in 2 vols, tr. Husain Haddawy)

MARGARET ATWOOD
The Handmaid's Tale

JOHN JAMES AUDUBON
The Audubon Reader

AUGUSTINE
The Confessions

JANE AUSTEN
Emma
Mansfield Park
Northanger Abbey
Persuasion
Pride and Prejudice
Sanditon and Other Stories
Sense and Sensibility

HONORÉ DE BALZAC
Cousin Bette
Eugénie Grandet
Old Goriot

GIORGIO BASSANI
The Garden of the Finzi-Continis

SIMONE DE BEAUVOIR
The Second Sex

SAMUEL BECKETT
Molloy, Malone Dies,
The Unnamable
(US only)

SAUL BELLOW
The Adventures of Augie March

HECTOR BERLIOZ
The Memoirs of Hector Berlioz

WILLIAM BLAKE
Poems and Prophecies

JORGE LUIS BORGES
Ficciones

JAMES BOSWELL
The Life of Samuel Johnson
The Journal of a Tour to
the Hebrides

CHARLOTTE BRONTË
Jane Eyre
Villette

EMILY BRONTË
Wuthering Heights

MIKHAIL BULGAKOV
The Master and Margarita

SAMUEL BUTLER
The Way of all Flesh

JAMES M. CAIN
The Postman Always Rings Twice
Double Indemnity
Mildred Pierce
Selected Stories
(in 1 vol. US only)

ITALO CALVINO
If on a winter's night a traveler

ALBERT CAMUS
The Outsider (UK)
The Stranger (US)
The Plague, The Fall,
Exile and the Kingdom,
and Selected Essays
(in 1 vol.)

GIACOMO CASANOVA
History of My Life

WILLA CATHER
Death Comes for the Archbishop
My Ántonia

MIGUEL DE CERVANTES
Don Quixote

RAYMOND CHANDLER
The novels (in 2 vols)
Collected Stories

GEOFFREY CHAUCER
Canterbury Tales

ANTON CHEKHOV
The Complete Short Novels
My Life and Other Stories
The Steppe and Other Stories

KATE CHOPIN
The Awakening

CARL VON CLAUSEWITZ
On War

S. T. COLERIDGE
Poems

WILKIE COLLINS
The Moonstone
The Woman in White

CONFUCIUS
The Analects

JOSEPH CONRAD
Heart of Darkness
Lord Jim
Nostromo
The Secret Agent
Typhoon and Other Stories
Under Western Eyes
Victory

THOMAS CRANMER
The Book of Common Prayer
(UK only)

ROALD DAHL
Collected Stories

DANTE ALIGHIERI
The Divine Comedy

CHARLES DARWIN
The Origin of Species
The Voyage of the Beagle
(in 1 vol.)

DANIEL DEFOE
Moll Flanders
Robinson Crusoe

CHARLES DICKENS
Barnaby Rudge
Bleak House
David Copperfield
Dombey and Son
Great Expectations
Hard Times
Little Dorrit
Martin Chuzzlewit
The Mystery of Edwin Drood
Nicholas Nickleby
The Old Curiosity Shop
Oliver Twist
Our Mutual Friend
The Pickwick Papers
A Tale of Two Cities

DENIS DIDEROT
Memoirs of a Nun

JOAN DIDION
We Tell Ourselves Stories in Order
to Live (US only)

JOHN DONNE
The Complete English Poems

FYODOR DOSTOEVSKY
The Adolescent
The Brothers Karamazov
Crime and Punishment
Demons
The Double and The Gambler
The Idiot
Notes from Underground

W. E. B. DU BOIS
The Souls of Black Folk
(US only)

UMBERTO ECO
The Name of the Rose

GEORGE ELIOT
Adam Bede
Daniel Deronda
Middlemarch
The Mill on the Floss
Silas Marner

JOHN EVELYN
The Diary of John Evelyn
(UK only)

WILLIAM FAULKNER
The Sound and the Fury
(UK only)

HENRY FIELDING
Joseph Andrews and Shamela
(UK only)
Tom Jones

F. SCOTT FITZGERALD
The Great Gatsby
This Side of Paradise
(UK only)

PENELOPE FITZGERALD
The Bookshop
The Gate of Angels
The Blue Flower
(in 1 vol.)
Offshore
Human Voices
The Beginning of Spring
(in 1 vol.)

GUSTAVE FLAUBERT
Madame Bovary

FORD MADOX FORD
The Good Soldier
Parade's End

THE OLD TESTAMENT
(King James Version)

GEORGE ORWELL
Animal Farm
Nineteen Eighty-Four
Essays

THOMAS PAINE
Rights of Man
and Common Sense

BORIS PASTERNAK
Doctor Zhivago

SYLVIA PLATH
The Bell Jar (US only)

PLATO
The Republic
Symposium and Phaedrus

EDGAR ALLAN POE
The Complete Stories

MARCEL PROUST
In Search of Lost Time
(in 4 vols, UK only)

ALEXANDER PUSHKIN
The Collected Stories

FRANÇOIS RABELAIS
Gargantua and Pantagruel

JOSEPH ROTH
The Radetzky March

JEAN-JACQUES
ROUSSEAU
Confessions
The Social Contract and
the Discourses

SALMAN RUSHDIE
Midnight's Children

JOHN RUSKIN
Praeterita and Dilecta

WALTER SCOTT
Rob Roy

WILLIAM SHAKESPEARE
Comedies Vols 1 and 2
Histories Vols 1 and 2
Romances
Sonnets and Narrative Poems
Tragedies Vols 1 and 2

MARY SHELLEY
Frankenstein

ADAM SMITH
The Wealth of Nations

ALEXANDER SOLZHENITSYN
One Day in the Life of
Ivan Denisovich

SOPHOCLES
The Theban Plays

MURIEL SPARK
The Prime of Miss Jean Brodie,
The Girls of Slender Means, The
Driver's Seat, The Only Problem
(in 1 vol.)

CHRISTINA STEAD
The Man Who Loved Children

JOHN STEINBECK
The Grapes of Wrath

STENDHAL
The Charterhouse of Parma
Scarlet and Black

LAURENCE STERNE
Tristram Shandy

ROBERT LOUIS STEVENSON
The Master of Ballantrae and
Weir of Hermiston
Dr Jekyll and Mr Hyde
and Other Stories

HARRIET BEECHER STOWE
Uncle Tom's Cabin

ITALO SVEVO
Zeno's Conscience

JONATHAN SWIFT
Gulliver's Travels

JUNICHIRŌ TANIZAKI
The Makioka Sisters

W. M. THACKERAY
Vanity Fair

HENRY DAVID THOREAU
Walden

ALEXIS DE TOCQUEVILLE
Democracy in America

LEO TOLSTOY
Collected Shorter Fiction (in 2 vols)
Anna Karenina
Childhood, Boyhood and Youth
The Cossacks
War and Peace

This book is set in BEMBO which was cut
by the punch-cutter Francesco Griffo
for the Venetian printer-publisher
Aldus Manutius in early 1495
and first used in a pamphlet
by a young scholar
named Pietro
Bembo.